THE SUPREME COURT AND THE POWERS OF THE AMERICAN GOVERNMENT

THE SUPREME COURT AND THE POWERS OF THE AMERICAN GOVERNMENT

Second Edition

David G. Savage

CQ PRESS

A Division of SAGE
Washington, D.C.

CQ Press
2300 N Street, NW, Suite 800
Washington, DC 20037

Phone: 202-729-1900; Toll-free, 1-866-4CQ-PRESS (1-866-427-7737)

Web: www.cqpress.com

Cover design: Cynthia Richardson, RICHdesign Studio
Cover photos: Clockwise from top, Landov, CORBIS, AP Images, AP Images
Composition: C&M Digitals (P) Ltd.

♾ The paper used in this publication exceeds the requirements of the American National Standard for Information Sciences—Permanence of Paper for Printed Library Materials, ANSI Z39.48-1992.

Printed and bound in the United States of America

13   12   11   10   09   1   2   3   4   5

LIBRARY OF CONGRESS CATALOGING-IN-PUBLICATION DATA

Savage, David G.,
  The Supreme Court and the powers of the American government / By David Savage. — 2nd ed.
    p. cm.
  Includes bibliographical references and indexes.
  ISBN 978-0-87289-425-9 (pbk. : alk. paper) 1. United States. Supreme Court. 2. United States. Congress—Powers and duties. 3. Executive power—United States. 4. Separation of powers—United States. 5. Political questions and judicial power—United States. I. Title.

  KF8742.S287 2009
  347.73′26—dc22

                                2009022136

★ TABLE OF CONTENTS

★ PREFACE

The Constitution, as ratified in 1789, sets out the structure for the government of the United States, and it does so in just 4,400 words. It is a beautifully simple document, but it has raised enough questions to keep the Supreme Court busy for more than two hundred years.

For example, Article I says "all legislative powers" are vested in Congress, and these include the power "to declare war, . . . and make rules concerning Captures on Land and Water." Article II says the "President shall be the Commander in Chief of the Army and Navy of the United States." Who, then, makes the rules when prisoners are captured? President George W. Bush was not the first chief executive to claim broad, wartime powers as commander in chief, even when Congress did not formally declare war. And on November 13, 2001, two months after the terrorist attacks on New York and Washington, he issued an executive order on the "detention, treatment and trial" of prisoners in the "war on terrorism."

"By the authority vested in me as President and as Commander in Chief of the Armed Forces of the United States," Bush said these accused terrorists would be held under rules he established, after consulting with the military. Congress would have no role, although the president noted that lawmakers had given him broad authority to attack terrorists in the Authorization for the Use of Military Force Joint Resolution adopted a week after the 9/11 attacks. The courts would have no role either, Bush said. The prisoners may not "seek any remedy or maintain any proceeding . . . in any court," his order said. With that, the president laid out the legal basis for the prison camp at Guantánamo Bay, Cuba—and set the stage for a showdown with the Supreme Court.

In four separate decisions from 2004 to 2008 the Court rebuked Bush's bold go-it-alone approach to the war on terror. Congress and the courts had roles to play, the justices said in rulings that reflected the Constitution's separation-of-powers principle. "A state of war is not a blank check for the president," wrote Justice Sandra Day O'Connor in *Hamdi v. Rumsfeld* (2004).

Bush was certainly not alone among presidents in being disappointed by the Supreme Court. In 1997 President Bill Clinton faced a sexual harassment lawsuit brought by a former Arkansas state employee. Because the suit had the potential to do great damage to him and his presidency, Clinton asked the justices to accord him a "temporary immunity" from responding to the suit until he left the White House. In a 9-0 decision the Court refused, reasoning that the chief executive is not shielded from civil actions that result from his private life. The ruling in *Clinton v. Jones* set in motion the chain of events that led to Clinton's impeachment by the House of Representatives.

These dramatic decisions are among the many recounted in *The Supreme Court and the Powers of the American Government*. For more than two centuries, the Court has seen defining the powers and limits of government as its chief role. The unique structure of the United States set the stage for legal conflict and, during the 1860s, military conflict as well. The nation began as a federation of independent states that came together to "form a more perfect Union." The Constitution, however, did not draw a precise line between federal and state authority. Which, for example, would control shipping and sailing on the rivers? In 1824 Chief Justice John Marshall answered it was the federal government, not the states. New York State had granted a monopoly license to Aaron Ogden to operate steamships on the Hudson River, but in *Gibbons v. Ogden* Marshall said the Constitution had given "the power over commerce, including navigation" to the federal government. This authority does not stop at the state's border, he said, but extends "into the interior" of the growing nation. Marshall's opinion established the principle that the Constitution protects the free flow of trade across state lines, and that the federal government holds the primary role in matters of commerce.

The legal battles over the commerce power helped to shape the nation. The late nineteenth-century disputes were dominated by the railroads and factories. In the early decades of the twentieth century, the Court struggled over whether government could regulate the workplace in such ways as setting minimum wages for workers. Until the Court-packing crisis of 1937 the Court had said no, but it gradually conceded that Congress's power to regulate commerce extended to workplace rules and unions. And in the mid-1960s, Congress and the Court agreed that this federal power over commerce extended to civil rights. The Civil Rights Act of 1964 made it illegal for employers and public businesses such as hotels and restaurants to discriminate based on race, color, gender, religion, or national origin.

Questions concerning Congress's constitutional powers still come to the Court. May the states forbid out-of-state wineries from shipping cases of wine directly to residents? No, the Court said in *Granholm v. Heald* (2005), because the state may not discriminate against interstate commerce. May federal authorities raid the homes of Californians who grow marijuana for their personal use when the state permits patients to use this drug? In *Gonzales v. Raich* (2005) the Court said yes, because the federal narcotics law gives U.S. agents the overriding power to control dangerous drugs. May a state give a tax break to the owners of municipal bonds, but only if the bonds are for projects within the state? Yes, the Court said in *Kentucky v. Davis* (2008), because a home-state tax preference does not restrict interstate commerce.

Through history, in disputes large and small, the Court has held on to its role as interpreter of the Constitution. As John Marshall put it in *Marbury v. Madison* (1803): "It is emphatically the province and duty of the judicial department to say what the law is." The chapters that follow recount the Court's work in four areas: the powers of the judiciary, Congress, and the president, and the federal power over the states.

chapter 1

The Court's Role in Shaping the Powers of Government

The Supreme Court's unique role in the American system of government has been to define the powers of government, including those of elected lawmakers. This function may seem an extraordinary one for judges, who, after all, are unelected and not accountable to the voters for their decisions. Yet from the beginning, an independent and nonpartisan judiciary was understood to be essential to a constitutional government and to the rule of law. The framers of the Constitution placed great faith in the notion that a written plan for government, ratified by the people's representatives, would stand as the law. No officer could make his will the law by dismissing the Constitution and its limits on his power. And no officer of the government could reach beyond his just powers and take away the legitimate authority of another officer in a separate branch of government. This separation of powers would protect the liberties of the people, or so the framers believed.

But for this grand plan to work, someone had to define the Constitution and enforce it as the fundamental law of the land. And it was not long before the Supreme Court stepped forward and assumed the duty. "It is emphatically the province of the judicial department to say what the law is," Chief Justice John Marshall declared in *Marbury v. Madison* in 1803. The "very essence of judicial duty" is to refuse to enforce a law that was "in opposition to the Constitution," he added.[1] Marshall's opinion in *Marbury* set forth three principles that formed the basis of American constitutional law. First, the Constitution itself stood above and overrode laws passed by Congress and signed by the president. Second, the Supreme Court would define the Constitution and say "what the law is." And third, the Court would review and invalidate laws that it believed conflicted with the Constitution. The declaration put the Court in the role of arbiter of the Constitution.

Although Marshall's declaration in 1803 is remembered as a legal landmark, the chief justice had not invented a new or unforeseen role for the Court. Marshall was a young lawyer in Richmond, Virginia, when the Constitution was drafted, and he led the fight there to ratify it. Two of its foremost proponents— James Madison and Alexander Hamilton—had stressed the importance of an independent judiciary. In their essays known as the Federalist Papers, they said the judiciary would enforce the Constitution as law. In Federalist No. 78, Hamilton laid out this view explicitly:

> The complete independence of the courts of justice is peculiarly essential in a limited Constitution. By a limited Constitution, I understand one which contains certain specified exceptions to the legislative authority; such, for instance, as it shall pass no bills of attainder, no *ex-post-facto* laws, and the like. Limitations of this kind can be preserved in practice no other way than through the medium of courts of justice, whose duty it must be declare all acts contrary to the manifest tenor of the Constitution void. Without this, all the reservations of particular rights and privileges would amount to nothing.[2]

Hamilton continued:

> No legislative act, therefore, contrary to the Constitution, can be valid. . . .
>
> [T]he courts were designed to be an intermediate body between the people and the legislature, in order, among other things, to keep the latter within the limits assigned to their authority. The interpretation of the laws is the proper and peculiar province of the courts.[3]

In 2005, shortly after he was nominated to be chief justice, John G. Roberts Jr. said he came to fully appreciate the role of the Supreme Court when he argued as private lawyer on behalf of a client who was battling the U.S. government. "Here was the United States, the most powerful entity in the world, aligned against my client. And yet, all I had to do was convince the court that I was right on the law and the government was wrong and all that power and might would recede in deference to the rule of law. That is a remarkable thing," he told the Senate Judiciary Committee on September 12. "It is what we mean when we say that we are a government of laws and not of men. It is that rule of law that protects the rights and liberties of all Americans. It is the envy of the world. Because without the rule of law, any rights are meaningless. President Ronald Reagan used to speak of the Soviet constitution, and he noted that it purported to grant wonderful rights of all sorts to the people. But those rights were empty promises, because that system did not have an independent judiciary to uphold the rule of law and enforce those rights. We do, because of the wisdom of our founders and the sacrifices of our heroes over the generations to make their vision a reality."[4]

As Roberts indicated, the notion of a strong and independent judiciary may have been born when the United States was founded, but it took several generations to become reality. During the nation's first twelve years, it had neither a federal system of courts nor a Supreme Court under the Articles of Confederation. The lack of a federal court system seemed to many a major factor contributing to the "national humiliation" that the young nation suffered during the early period of its government.[5] Article III of the Constitution of 1787 remedied that deficiency with two concise provisions. The first says, "The judicial Power of the United States, shall be vested in one supreme Court" and whatever inferior federal courts Congress "from time to time" sees fit to establish. The second provision sets out the types of cases and controversies that should be considered by a federal—rather than a state—tribunal.

Despite Hamilton's hopes for an independent national judiciary, he recognized that "the judiciary is beyond comparison the weakest of the three departments . . . it is in continual jeopardy of being overpowered, awed, or influenced by its coordinate branches."[6] Congress filled in the skeletal structure of national judicial power with the Judiciary Act of 1789 and subsequent statutes, but it was left chiefly to the Supreme Court to precisely define the jurisdiction of the federal courts—itself included—and to guide the use of the powers of the federal judiciary. With every decision it has issued since its initial term, the Court has shaped the power of the federal courts.

Because the federal judicial power is limited, extending only to certain types of cases and controversies, and its arsenal is small, its authority has necessarily been exercised with care and restraint. Federal judicial power grew slowly through the interaction of the courts, the president (who appoints members), and Congress (which exerts statutory control over much of the jurisdiction and most of the powers of the federal courts). Questions of jurisdiction, proper remedies, abstention, and comity seem technical matters to many—and are often overlooked by those who find more interest in the substantive issues resolved by the courts—but it is the resolution of these seemingly esoteric matters that governs the breadth of access and the scope of remedies that are available to those who seek redress in the federal courts.

These technical and jurisdictional issues often mask a far larger issue. The great debates in the Court's history often have turned on *whether* the justices should decide a question, rather than what they should decide. In 1857 the Court's aggressive intervention on behalf of slave owners sparked a fire that led to the Civil War. In the prior decades, Congress had adopted several great "compromises" between the slave-holding South and the free states of the North, including the Missouri

Compromise of 1820. It allowed slavery in some newly admitted states and prohibited it in others. Until then, the Court had avoided broad rulings on slavery on the grounds that it was a political question that must resolved by compromise. But when Dred Scott sued his owner in Missouri and sought his freedom, Chief Justice Roger B. Taney wrote a broad opinion saying that Negroes had no rights and that the Missouri Compromise was unconstitutional because it deprived slave owners of their rights to their property.[7] Several dissenters said the Court should have ruled narrowly on Scott's status under state law and avoided the broad pronouncement on the constitutional status of slavery.

In the late nineteenth century, the Court devised a doctrine known as the "liberty of contract" and used it to void state laws that protected workers from exploitation. In a famous example, the justices in *Lochner v. New York* (1905) struck down a state law that prohibited bakers from working more than ten hours a day or sixty hours a week.[8] Joseph Lochner, who owned a bakery in Utica, New York, sued, and won a 5-4 ruling that declared the law unconstitutional because it violated his "general right to make a contract in relation to his business." The dissenters, including Justice Oliver Wendell Holmes Jr., pointed out that the Constitution includes no such right, and therefore, state legislators were entitled to decide matters involving the health, safety, and welfare of workers. The Court did not bury the "Lochner era" until 1937, when the majority switched and the justices upheld New Deal's regulations of industry and labor.

The best known example of recent decades is *Roe v. Wade,* the 1973 opinion that struck down state laws restricting abortion on the grounds that they violated an implied privacy right in the Fourteenth Amendment.[9] The dissenters pointed out that nothing in the Constitution or the right to "due process of law"

implied a right to abortion. They said the Court should have avoided deciding such a question and instead left this controversy to be decided by state lawmakers. That criticism of "judicial activism" has only grown louder since then, and an entire political movement has developed around the notion that judges in general, and the Supreme Court in particular, must avoid deciding social controversies.

Chief Justice Roberts, who spoke during his confirmation hearings about the importance of the Court as the enforcer of the rule of law, also warned about the danger of going too far. "One threat to the rule of law," he said, "is a tendency on behalf of some judges to take that legitimacy and that authority and extend it to areas where they're going beyond interpretation of the Constitution, where they're making law." He continued:

> Judges have to recognize that their role is a limited one. That is the basis of their legitimacy. . . . The framers were not the sort of people, having fought a revolution to get the right of self-government, to sit down and say, "Let's take all the difficult issues before us and let's have judges decide them." That would have been the farthest thing from their mind.[10]

Roberts had neatly summed up both sides of the equation. On the one side, the Supreme Court has a duty to enforce the Constitution and to limit the powers of government—local, state, or federal—whenever they conflict with the fundamental law. On the other side, the Court has to restrain itself and not use its extraordinary authority to enforce its view on what is good law or good policy. Much of the Court's work in the area of judicial power has been in developing rules and doctrines to limit itself. Like red lights at an intersection and speed limits on a highway, these rules help ensure the justices proceed with caution and deliberation and avoid the kind of recklessness that leads to regret.

Federal Jurisdiction

Jurisdiction has been described as the vessel into which judicial power may be poured, the prerequisite to the exercise of judicial power.[1] Judicial power is of no use to a court that lacks jurisdiction, for unless a court has jurisdiction over the persons or issues in a dispute, its power cannot reach the matter. In 1869 Chief Justice Salmon P. Chase explained:

> Without jurisdiction the court cannot proceed at all in any cause. Jurisdiction is the power to declare the law, and when it ceases to exist, the only function remaining to the court is that of announcing the fact and dismissing the cause.[2]

All federal courts are courts of limited jurisdiction, in contrast to state courts, which are presumed to have jurisdiction over a case, unless jurisdiction is disproved. Most questions of federal jurisdiction affect the distribution of power between the states and the federal government. "Expansion of the jurisdiction of the federal courts," one scholar notes, "diminishes the power of the states."[3]

CONSTITUTIONAL POSSIBILITIES AND POLITICAL REALITIES

Article III, section 2, of the Constitution outlines a broad area for the exercise of federal judicial power:

> The Judicial Power shall extend to all Cases, in Law and Equity, arising under this Constitution, the Laws of the United States, and Treaties made, or which shall be made, under their Authority;—to all cases affecting Ambassadors, other public Ministers and Consuls;—to all Cases of admiralty and maritime Jurisdiction;—to Controversies to which the United States shall be a party;—to Controversies between two or more States;—between Citizens of different States;—between Citizens of the same State claiming Lands under Grants of different States, and between a State, or the Citizens thereof, and foreign States, Citizens, or Subjects.

This general grant of jurisdiction is divided into two categories: cases that merit federal consideration because of their subject matter—a claim or question arising under the Constitution, federal statutes or treaties, or admiralty or maritime law—and cases that merit federal attention because of the parties involved—the United States, a state, citizens of different states, and representatives of foreign countries. Article III gives the Supreme Court original jurisdiction over two cases of the latter category. (The Court may decline original jurisdiction, and in some cases jurisdiction may be concurrent, or shared, with other federal courts or with state courts depending upon relevant statutes.) The Court has the right to hear cases initially, before any other court, if they involve ambassadors or other foreign diplomats or if they involve states. With those exceptions, the Constitution grants Congress the power to determine how much of the broad area outlined in Article III actually falls within the jurisdiction of the federal courts.

The Supreme Court clearly has kept in mind the language of Article III giving Congress complete control over the existence and jurisdiction of all federal courts below the Supreme Court itself. "[T]he judicial power of the United States," stated the Court in 1845, is "dependent for its distribution and organization, and for the modes of its exercise, entirely upon the action of Congress," with some exceptions related to the Court itself.[4] Some years later the Court reiterated that point: "[T]wo things are necessary to create jurisdiction. . . . The Constitution must have given to the court the capacity to take it, and an Act of Congress must have supplied it."[5] Congress moved quickly to exercise this power.

The First Congress enacted the Judiciary Act of 1789, which established the system of lower federal courts (including district courts and circuit courts with limited jurisdiction), spelled out the appellate jurisdiction of the Supreme Court, and gave the Court the power to review state court rulings rejecting federal

MAJOR ACTS OF CONGRESS RELATING TO THE SUPREME COURT

Article III of the Constitution broadly outlines the exercise of the federal judicial power, but it was Congress's task to fill in the details of the new judicial system. The Judiciary Act of 1789 was Congress's first statutory measure to that effect. Much of the legislation concerning the Supreme Court passed since then spells out the number of justices and the scope of the Court's jurisdiction.

Judiciary Act of 1789	Provided basic appellate jurisdiction
	Created a three-tier judiciary staffed by Supreme Court justices and district court judges
	Required Supreme Court justices to ride circuit
	Mandated that the Court consist of a chief justice and five associate justices, any four of whom would be a quorum
Judiciary Act of 1807	Set the number of justices at seven
Judiciary Act of 1837	Divided the country into nine circuits
	Brought the number of justices to nine
	Expanded the Court's jurisdiction to include appeals from new states and territories
Judiciary Act of 1863	Added a tenth justice
Judiciary Act of 1866	Allowed the Court to fall to seven members
Judiciary Act of 1869	Increased the size of the Court to nine
	Allowed federal judges to retire at full pay at seventy (changed to sixty-five in 1954) if they had at least ten years of service
Act of 1873	Formally fixed October as the start of the Court's term
Judiciary Act of 1891	Established nine Circuit Courts of Appeals (renamed Courts of Appeals in 1948)
	Broadened Court review of criminal cases
	Provided for limited discretionary review via writs of certiorari
Judicial Code of 1911	Created general right of appeal from criminal convictions to the circuit court of appeals, with ultimate review lying with the Supreme Court
Judiciary Act of 1925	Greatly extended the Court's discretionary jurisdiction by replacing mandatory appeals with petitions for certiorari
Act to Improve the Administration of Justice (1988)	Eliminated virtually all of the Court's nondiscretionary jurisdiction, except for appeal in reapportionment cases and suits under the Civil Rights Act, the Voting Rights Act, antitrust laws, and the Presidential Election Campaign Act

SOURCE: Lee Epstein et al., *The Supreme Court Compendium: Data, Decisions, and Developments,* 4th ed. (Washington, D.C.: CQ Press, 2006); Robert L. Stern and Eugene Gressman, *Supreme Court Practice* (Washington, D.C.: Bureau of National Affairs, various years); David M. O'Brien, *Storm Center* (New York: Norton, 1999); U.S. Senate, *Creation of the Federal Judiciary,* Doc. 91, 75th Cong., 1st sess., July 22, 1937 (Washington, D.C.: Government Printing Office, 1938); U.S. Code.

claims.[6] The act made clear that most cases would be resolved in state courts. Federal district courts were to hear admiralty and maritime matters; circuit courts would hear cases involving disputes between residents of different states, the United States and aliens, and where more than $500 was at stake. Circuit courts also had some limited "federal question" jurisdiction concurrent with state courts, as well as some jurisdiction to hear appeals from district court rulings.

The Supreme Court acquiesced in this congressional limitation of federal jurisdiction. In a 1799 decision holding federal courts without jurisdiction over a particular case, Chief Justice Oliver Ellsworth—himself one of the authors of the Judiciary Act—declared that "[a] circuit court . . . is of limited jurisdiction and has cognizance, not of cases generally, but only of a few specially circumstanced."[7] Underscoring that point, Justice Samuel Chase added a footnote:

THE JURISDICTIONAL AMOUNT

To keep trivial matters out of the federal courts, Congress sets a "jurisdictional amount," that is, a dollar figure for the minimum amount that must be in controversy before most cases can enter the federal judicial system. In 1789 the amount was set at $500. In 1887 the figure was quadrupled to $2,000. The next increase, in 1911, was to $3,000, where it remained until 1958, when Congress raised it to $10,000. In 1988 it was increased to $50,000. In 1996 it was raised to $75,000.

From 1789 until 1925 there was also a jurisdictional amount (of varying levels) required for appeal to the Supreme Court in certain cases. Since 1925 there has been no such requirement. In the 1970s the main categories of cases affected by the jurisdictional amount requirement were diversity cases and some federal question cases.

In many modern statutes, Congress has granted federal courts jurisdiction over cases without regard to the amount of money involved. Among the areas in which this requirement for federal jurisdiction is waived by statute are admiralty and maritime cases, bankruptcy matters, and cases arising under acts of Congress regulating commerce; patent, trademark, and copyright cases; internal revenue, customs duty, and postal matters; most civil rights cases and elections disputes; and cases to which the United States is a party.

SOURCE: Charles Alan Wright, *Law of Federal Courts*, 4th ed. (St. Paul, Minn.: West Publishing, 1983), 176–208.

The notion has frequently been entertained that the federal courts derive their judicial power immediately from the constitution; but the political truth is, that the disposal of the judicial power (except in a few specified instances) belongs to Congress. If Congress has given the power to this court, we possess it, not otherwise; and if Congress has not given the power to us or to any other court, it still remains at the legislative disposal. Besides, Congress is not bound . . . to enlarge the jurisdiction of the federal courts, to every subject, in every form, which the constitution might warrant.[8]

A Matter of Subject

Although Article III clearly envisions that federal courts have the final word on cases raising claims under the Constitution, federal laws, and treaties, eighty years would pass before a congressional grant of such jurisdiction to those courts. Until then, most federal questions were resolved in state courts, subject to review—if the federal claim were denied—by the Supreme Court. The Judiciary Act of 1789 granted the Supreme Court the power to consider the constitutionality of state laws—when state courts rejected federally based challenges to them—but the act said nothing about any power of the Court to review acts of Congress for their constitutional validity. The Court simply assumed that power early in its history. *(See "Review of Acts of Congress," pp. 20–24.)*

Federal Questions

In the Jurisdiction and Removal Act of 1875, Congress granted lower federal courts virtually the entire federal question jurisdiction outlined in Article III. For the first time, all cases arising under the Constitution, federal laws, or treaties could be initiated in federal district courts. Professors Felix Frankfurter and James M. Landis, half a century later, described the 1875 act as revolutionary:

From 1789 down to the Civil War the lower federal courts were, in the main, designed as protection to citizens litigating outside of their own states and thereby exposed to the threatened prejudice of unfriendly tribunals. Barring admiralty jurisdiction, the federal courts were subsidiary courts. The Act of 1875 marks a revolution in their function. . . . These courts ceased to be restricted tribunals of fair dealing between citizens of different states and became the primary and powerful reliances for vindicating every right given by the Constitution, the laws and treaties of the United States. Thereafter, any suit asserting such a right could be begun in federal courts; any such action begun in state court could be removed to the federal courts for disposition.[9]

No subsequent jurisdictional statute has so greatly enlarged the jurisdiction of the federal courts, but as Congress has enacted laws reaching into areas previously left

Under the Judiciary Act of 1789, jurisdiction over admiralty and maritime matters was assigned to federal district courts. The Brooklyn Bridge can be seen in the background of this 1887 view of New York Harbor.

to state control, federal question jurisdiction has become a larger and larger category. The new statutes brought particular expansion of this category of federal cases to labor law and civil rights law.

Admiralty and Maritime Law

"Like the Constitution itself," wrote Frankfurter and Landis, the Judiciary Act of 1789 "was a response to the practical problems and controversies of our early history."[10] At that time, the admiralty and maritime jurisdiction of federal district courts did not appear the limited area it does to modern interpretation. Instead, it reflected a fact of life:

> Trade requires dependable laws and courts. Maritime commerce was then the jugular vein of the Thirteen States. The need for a body of law applicable throughout the nation was recognized by every shade of opinion in the Constitutional Convention.[11]

Therefore, to ensure that a uniform body of admiralty and maritime law would develop, Congress vested jurisdiction over all such cases in the federal district courts. Although the Supreme Court initially adopted a narrow definition of the waters covered by the grant, it eventually expanded its view to include virtually all navigable and potentially navigable waterways within the country.[12]

A Question of Party

To preserve national sovereignty, to provide a neutral forum, and to ensure federal control of foreign relations, the Constitution gives federal courts jurisdiction over cases in which the United States is a party, in cases between states and between citizens of different states, and in cases involving representatives of foreign governments.

United States versus . . .

Because of the protection of sovereign immunity, most cases involving the United States are initiated by the federal government. *(See The Sovereign's Immunity, p. 14.)* When the United States comes into the federal courts as a plaintiff, however, it must satisfy the same requirements as any other party seeking to file a federal suit. It must demonstrate a real interest that is seriously threatened in a manner susceptible of judicial resolution. The Supreme Court, however, has made clear that such an interest need not be simply one of property or of monetary concern: "The obligations which it [the United States] is under to promote the interest of all, and to prevent the wrongdoing of one resulting in injury to the general welfare, is often of itself sufficient to give it a standing in court."[13] *(See "Standing to Sue," pp. 54–59.)*

Cases brought by the United States against a state are adjudicated in federal court. The first such case before the Supreme Court arrived in 1890—with no challenge from the state to Supreme Court jurisdiction. Two years later, however, when the United States sued Texas in the Supreme Court, Texas argued that such federal jurisdiction was an infringement of its sovereignty. The Court quickly disposed of that argument: When Texas entered the Union, it had acquiesced in the provisions of Article III extending federal judicial power to all cases arising under the Constitution, federal laws, or treaties, without regard to the parties involved; and to all controversies in which the United States is a party, without regard to the subject of the dispute; and granting the Supreme Court original jurisdiction over cases in which states are parties.[14] The Court does not automatically take jurisdiction of all such cases. It has refused those in which it appeared that the matter at issue was only a difference of opinion and not an actual collision of interests between a state and the national government.[15]

State versus State

The Supreme Court has original and exclusive jurisdiction over cases between states. *(See "Interstate Relations," pp. 484–487.)* As in the case of suits brought by the United States, the Court does not necessarily agree to accept jurisdiction over all interstate cases. Refusing to consider a tax-based dispute between Massachusetts and Missouri in 1939 the Court explained,

> To constitute . . . a [justiciable] controversy, it must appear that the complaining State has suffered a

wrong through the action of the other State, furnishing ground for judicial redress, or is asserting a right against the other State which is susceptible of judicial enforcement according to the accepted principles of the common law or equity systems of jurisprudence. . . . In the exercise of our original jurisdiction so as truly to fulfill the constitutional purpose we not only must look to the nature of the interest of the complaining state—the essential quality of the right asserted—but we must also inquire whether recourse to that jurisdiction . . . is necessary for the State's protection.[16]

Citizen versus State

Taking the language of Article III literally, the Supreme Court—in *Chisholm v. Georgia* (1793), its first major decision—overrode claims of state immunity from suits brought without a state's consent and held that citizens of one state could sue another state in federal court, even over the state's objection.[17] Within five years, the decision in *Chisholm v. Georgia* was overruled by ratification of the Eleventh Amendment, which narrowed federal jurisdiction to cases initiated by a state against citizens of another state or initiated by those citizens against the state with its consent. *(See details of Chisholm v. Georgia, pp. 377–378.)* The Supreme Court has original, but not exclusive, jurisdiction over such cases. Only civil cases between states and nonresidents may come into federal court under the Eleventh Amendment; states may not use federal courts to enforce state criminal laws against nonresidents.[18] The Court has also held that a state's suit against its own citizens is outside the scope of federal judicial power and can be initiated only in state courts.[19] Furthermore, when the state is allowed to come into federal court to sue a nonresident—often a corporation—the Supreme Court has required that the state be defending its own interest or the general welfare of its population—not simply the private interest of some individual resident of the state.[20]

Citizen versus Citizen

"A . . . powerful influence behind the demand for federal courts was due to the friction between individual states which came to the surface after the danger of the common enemy had disappeared," wrote Frankfurter and Landis. "In one respect it gave rise to lively suspicions and hostilities by the citizens of one state toward those of another as well as toward aliens. This fear of parochial prejudice, dealing unjustly with litigants from other states and foreign countries, undermined the sense of security necessary for commercial intercourse."[21] To ensure a neutral forum for the resolution of disputes between citizens of different states, Congress concurred with the grant of jurisdiction in Article III, giving circuit courts authority to hear such "diversity" cases. The Supreme Court generally has required "complete diversity" of residence, ruling in 1806 that if diversity was the basis for federal jurisdiction over a case, no party on one side of a case could be a citizen of the same state as any party on the other side.[22] In certain types of cases, the Court has held that Congress can waive this strict interpretation of the diversity of residence requirement.[23]

A few years after the 1806 ruling, the Court applied a corollary to make it more difficult for persons challenging corporate actions to move their cases into federal courts by citing diversity of residence. In 1810 the Court held that such a case could come into federal court only if all a corporation's stockholders were citizens of a state other than that of the plaintiff.[24] As a result, there was very little corporate litigation in federal courts until 1844, when the Court overruled itself and decided that for purposes of determining diversity jurisdiction, a corporation would be assumed to be a citizen of the state in which it was chartered. This assumption was subsequently replaced by one that viewed all of a corporation's stockholders as citizens of the state of its incorporation.[25] This "developing doctrine of corporate citizenship," noted Frankfurter and Landis, "enormously extended" the reach of federal diversity jurisdiction.[26]

One primary limitation on diversity cases is the "jurisdictional amount" imposed by law for federal jurisdiction. Initially $500, this amount has been increased over time and in 2003 was $75,000.[27] Cases between residents of different states involving less than $75,000 are heard by state courts. Certain types of cases—such as divorce and custody cases—generally are left to state courts regardless of the amount of money involved.[28] *(See The Jurisdictional Amount, p. 6.)*

Since 1890 efforts have been made to abolish federal diversity jurisdiction as an anachronism that simply burdens the federal courts. These efforts have been consistently unsuccessful. The jurisdiction of federal courts over cases in which citizens of the same states claimed land under grants from different states quickly became obsolete.

Foreign Relations

To ensure that control of foreign relations remained unmistakably in the hands of national authorities, the Constitution grants the federal courts power to hear all cases between a state or American citizens and a foreign state or its citizens or subjects as well as all cases involving ambassadors, public ministers, or consuls. After the Supreme Court made clear that a foreign nation, like a state, could be sued in federal court only if it gave its consent to the suit, few such suits arose.[29] A century later the Court further narrowed this category of cases, ruling that a state could not be sued by a foreign nation without the state's consent.[30]

Since the late nineteenth century, it has been firmly established that a foreign nation may come into federal court with a civil claim, just as a citizen or domestic corporation may. In 1871 the Supreme Court had "not the slightest difficulty" in upholding the right of Emperor Napoleon III to sue in federal court for damages caused to a French ship that had collided with a U.S. vessel. "A foreign sovereign, as well as any other foreign person, who has a demand of a civil nature against any person here, may prosecute it in our courts. To deny him this privilege would manifest a want of comity and friendly feeling."[31] The privilege survives for all nations recognized by and at peace with the United States.[32]

Federal jurisdiction over cases involving ambassadors, public ministers, and consuls extends only to foreign officials in the United States, not to U.S.

THE RIGHT TO REMOVE CASES FROM STATE COURTS INTO FEDERAL COURTS

Along with enlarging federal jurisdiction, Congress has expanded the right of persons charged initially in state courts to "remove," or transfer, their cases into federal courts for trial and final resolution. The Judiciary Act of 1789, which left most matters to state courts, provided a limited right of removal from state to federal courts in civil suits involving aliens, diversity of residence or of land grant sources, and suits where more than $500 was at stake. In 1815 Congress provided a similar right of removal in all cases involving federal customs officials and, in 1833, involving federal revenue officials. The Civil War brought further expansion of this right to include all persons sued in state courts for actions under federal authority during the war. The Supreme Court upheld the validity of these removal statutes in 1868:

> It is the right and the duty of the National Government to have its constitution and laws interpreted and applied by its own judicial tribunals. In cases arising under them, properly brought before it, this court is the final arbiter.[1]

Without such a provision for removal, state courts could punish federal officials for carrying out federal law or policy. A government without the power to protect such an official, wrote the Court, "would be one of pitiable weakness, and would wholly fail to meet the ends which the framers of the Constitution had in view."[2] Twelve years later the Court upheld the right of a federal revenue officer, charged with murder for killing a man who was defending an illegal still, to have his trial take place in federal rather than state courts. Wrote Justice William Strong for the Court,

> If, whenever and wherever a case arises under the Constitution and laws or treaties of the United States, the National Government cannot take control of it, whether it be civil or criminal, in any stage

of its progress, [the national government's] judicial power is, at least, temporarily silenced, instead of being at all times supreme."[3]

The Court viewed the power of Congress to enact removal statutes as part of its power to enact all laws necessary and proper to carry into effect the enumerated powers granted it and the federal courts by the Constitution. As Congress enlarged the "federal question" jurisdiction of the federal courts after the Civil War, it also expanded the right of removal. That right remains firmly established: the defendant in any civil case that could have been initiated in federal court may transfer the case to a federal court; a federal official sued or prosecuted in state court for official acts may remove his case into federal court; a defendant in any case, civil or criminal, who can show that he is denied, or is unable to enforce, his constitutional civil rights in a state court may have his case transferred into federal court.

The first civil rights removal provision was part of the Civil Rights Act of 1866. Concerned about how the removal of civil rights cases might affect the federal-state relationship, the Court has allowed such cases to be removed only when a defendant presents convincing evidence that he will be denied his federally ensured rights if brought to trial in state courts. Two pairs of cases from 1880 and 1966 illustrate this caution on the part of the Court.

1880 RULINGS

Taylor Strauder, a black man charged with murder in West Virginia, was allowed to remove his trial from state to federal courts because he could point to a state law that excluded blacks from jury duty. The Court found this law persuasive

officials accredited to foreign governments.[33] Because diplomatic immunity protects most high-ranking figures from lawsuits, most cases involve consuls or suits brought by diplomatic personnel against U.S. citizens. The Supreme Court has granted state courts jurisdiction over some cases involving consular officials, particularly if the subject of the case, like domestic relations, is one normally left to the states. In so doing, however, the Court indicated that Congress could require that all such cases be heard in federal courts.[34]

SUPREME COURT JURISDICTION

The Constitution grants the Supreme Court original jurisdiction in "all cases affecting Ambassadors, other public Ministers and Consuls, and those in which a State shall be a Party." These cases may be heard initially by the Supreme Court. This original jurisdiction may be exclusive or concurrent, shared with other federal courts or with state courts. Cases brought under the Court's original jurisdiction comprise a very small portion of the modern Court's caseload, and most of those cases

evidence that he would, by state action, be denied his equal rights during a state trial.[4] Burwell and Lee Reynolds, two black brothers charged with murder in Virginia, were not so lucky. Their claim was similar to Strauder's, but they could cite no state law excluding blacks from the juries of the state. They could only point to the fact that there was no black on the jury that had indicted them or the one impaneled to try them. This was evidence, they argued, of strong community prejudice that would operate to deny them equal rights. Taking a narrow view of state action, the Court refused to allow removal of the Reynolds's trial to federal courts.[5] For the next eighty years the Supreme Court had no occasion to rule on the scope of this right because there was no law providing for appeal of a federal judge's refusal to allow removal of a case from state court.

1966 RULINGS

The Supreme Court renewed its insistence upon a careful application of the removal law in one of its first modern statements on the right of removal. Some civil rights demonstrators were charged with trespassing under Georgia law for attempting to exercise their right of equal access to public accommodations; such rights had been secured by the Civil Rights Act of 1964. The demonstrators sought to remove their trials to federal court, and the Supreme Court granted that request.[6] On the same day in 1966 that the Court issued this ruling, it refused to allow removal of a case in which civil rights demonstrators were charged under Mississippi law with obstructing the streets and otherwise disrupting the peace of the town of Greenwood.[7] The situations in Georgia and in Mississippi, in the Court's view, were different.

The Georgia demonstrators were exercising a right granted by federal law, but no federal law gave the Mississippi demonstrators the right

"to obstruct a public street, to contribute to the delinquency of a minor, to drive an automobile without a license, or to bite a policeman."[8] Justice Potter Stewart stated the Court's view of the authority granted under the Civil Rights Act of 1866. The law

> does not require and does not permit the judges of the federal courts to put their brethren of the state judiciary on trial. Under . . . [the law] the vindication of the defendant's federal rights is left to the state courts except in the rare situations where it can be clearly predicted by reason of the operation of a pervasive and explicit state or federal law that those rights will inevitably be denied by the very act of bringing the defendant to trial in the state court.[9]

Congress could enlarge the conditions under which civil rights cases could be transferred from state to federal courts, Stewart wrote, but "if changes are to be made in the long-settled interpretation of the provisions of this century-old removal statute, it is for Congress and not for this Court to make them."[10]

---

1. *Nashville v. Cooper, 6 Wall. (73 U.S.) 247 (1868).*
2. Id. at 253 (1868).
3. *Tennessee v. Davis,* 100 U.S. 257 at 266 (1880).
4. *Strauder v. West Virginia,* 100 U.S. 303 (1880).
5. *Virginia v. Rives,* 100 U.S. 313 (1880).
6. *Georgia v. Rachel,* 384 U.S. 780 (1966).
7. *City of Greenwood, Miss. v. Peacock,* 384 U.S. 808 (1966).
8. Id. at 826–827.
9. Id. at 828.
10. Id. at 833–834.

involve interstate controversies. Few original cases have been brought involving foreign diplomats.

Congress may not expand or curtail the Court's original jurisdiction, restrictions established by the Court in *Marbury v. Madison* (1803). In that landmark decision, the Court found unconstitutional the thirteenth section of the Judiciary Act of 1789 authorizing the Court to issue writs of mandamus to federal officials. The Court viewed this provision as an expansion of its original jurisdiction granted by the Constitution and therefore unconstitutional. Congress lacked the

power to amend that grant, reasoned Chief Justice John Marshall:

> It has been insisted . . . that as the original grant of jurisdiction to the Supreme and inferior courts, is general and the clause, assigning original jurisdiction to the Supreme Court, contains no negative or restrictive words, the power remains to the legislature, to assign original jurisdiction to that court in other cases than those specified in the article . . . provided those cases belong to the judicial power of the United States.

If it had been intended to leave it in the discretion of the legislature to apportion the judicial power between the supreme and inferior courts . . . it would certainly have been useless to have proceeded further than to have defined the judicial power, and the tribunals in which it should be vested. The subsequent part of the section [of Article III assigning original jurisdiction to the Supreme Court] is mere surplusage, is entirely without meaning, if such is to be the construction. . . . It cannot be presumed that any clause in the constitution is intended to be without effect; and, therefore, such a construction is inadmissible.[35]

Congress, however, has successfully asserted the power to decide whether the Court's original jurisdiction over certain matters is exclusive or concurrent with the jurisdiction of other courts. The Judiciary Act of 1789 gave the Court exclusive jurisdiction over all civil suits between a state and the United States or between two states; suits between a state and an individual might be heard in other courts and only later before the Supreme Court. In addition, the act gave the Court exclusive jurisdiction over all suits against ambassadors, public ministers, or their domestics, but not over all cases brought by ambassadors or public ministers, nor over all cases involving consuls. The reasoning behind this division of original jurisdiction was set out by the Supreme Court a century later. The purpose of the grant of original jurisdiction, explained Chief Justice Morrison Waite, was

to open and keep open the highest court of the Nation, for the determination, in the first instance, of suits involving a State or a diplomatic or commercial representative of a foreign government. So much was due to the rank and dignity of those for whom the provision was made; but to compel a State to resort to this one tribunal for the redress of all its grievances or to deprive an ambassador, public minister or consul of the privilege of suing in any court he chose having jurisdiction . . . would be, in many cases, to convert what was intended as a favor into a burden.[36]

Therefore, continued Waite, "Congress took care to provide that no suit should be brought against an ambassador or other public minister except in the Supreme Court, but that he might sue in any court he chose that was open to him." The same approach gave a state the right—any time it was sued by the United States or another state—to have its case heard originally by the Supreme Court. It could, however, bring its own cases against individuals in any court it chose.[37]

Exercise of the Court's original jurisdiction is not mandatory. Just before the Civil War, Kentucky came to the Court asking for an order directing the governor of Ohio to return a fugitive free black man indicted in Kentucky for helping a slave to escape. The Court reaffirmed its jurisdiction over such a case—and then declined to issue the requested order.[38] Several decades later the Court declared it would not exercise its original jurisdiction over criminal cases between states and citizens of other states. Wisconsin came to the Supreme Court in 1887 seeking assistance in enforcing penalties that state courts had assessed against an out-of-state corporation. The Court declined to take original jurisdiction over the case. Justice Horace Gray explained:

[T]he mere fact that a State is the plaintiff is not a conclusive test that the controversy is one in which this court is authorized to grant relief against another State or her citizens. . . . [T]his court has declined to take jurisdiction of suits between States to compel the performance of obligations which, if the States had been independent nations, could not have been enforced judicially, but only through the political departments of their governments.

The penal laws of a country do not reach beyond its own territory, except when extended by express treaty or statute to offenses committed abroad by its own citizens; and they must be administered in its own courts only, and cannot be enforced by the courts of another country. . . .

[T]he jurisdiction conferred by the Constitution upon this court, in cases to which a State is a party, is limited to controversies of a civil nature.[39]

Appellate Jurisdiction

Article III grants the Supreme Court appellate jurisdiction over cases falling within the scope of federal judicial power "both as to Law and Fact, with such Exceptions, and under such Regulations as the Congress shall make." Congress quickly accepted the invitation to make exceptions and regulations concerning the high court's jurisdiction over appeals from lower courts. The Judiciary Act of 1789 granted the Court jurisdiction over appeals from the decisions of the circuit courts in civil cases, so long as more than $2,000 was at stake. Not until 1889 did the Court have the jurisdiction to hear appeals in criminal cases. In addition, the famous Section 25 of the Judiciary Act granted the Supreme Court authority to take appeals from rulings of high state courts upholding state laws or state actions against challenges that they conflict with the U.S. Constitution, federal laws, or treaties. The Supreme Court has always concurred in the assertion of congressional power over its appellate jurisdiction.[40] In 1866 the Court declared,

> The original jurisdiction of this court, and its power to receive appellate jurisdiction, are created and defined by the Constitution; and the Legislative Department of the Government can enlarge neither one nor the other. But it is for Congress to determine how far, within the limits of the capacity of this court to take, appellate jurisdiction shall be given, and when conferred, it can be exercised only to the extent and in the manner prescribed by law. In these respects, it is wholly the creature of legislation.[41]

The full truth of this statement was brought home to the Court and the nation three years later. In 1867 Congress expanded the availability of the writ of habeas corpus to persons who felt they were illegally detained by state or federal authorities. The 1867 act allowed federal judges to issue such a writ in "all cases where any person may be restrained of his or her liberty, in violation of the Constitution, or of any treaty or law of the United States." The purpose of the post–Civil War law was to provide protection from state prosecution and detention for federal officials enforcing Reconstruction laws in the South.

Ironically, the first major test of the law resulted from its use by William McCardle, a southern editor who had been charged by a military tribunal with impeding Reconstruction through his newspaper articles. McCardle came to the Court seeking a writ of habeas corpus ordering the military authorities to release him. He contended that the military commission had no jurisdiction to try him because he was a civilian. It was widely believed, according to histories of the time, that the Court would avail itself of this opportunity to declare the Reconstruction Acts unconstitutional.[42] The first question under consideration in the McCardle case was whether the Supreme Court had jurisdiction to hear an appeal of a lower court's refusal to issue the writ. The unanimous Court held in *Ex parte McCardle* (1868) that it did. Describing the 1867 act, it said,

> This legislation is of the most comprehensive character. It brings within the habeas corpus jurisdiction of every court and of every judge every possible case of privation of liberty contrary to the National Constitution, treaties, or laws. It is impossible to widen this jurisdiction.
>
> And it is to this jurisdiction that the system of appeals is applied. From decisions of a judge or of a district court appeals lie to the Circuit Court, and from the judgment of the Circuit Court to this court. . . . Every question of substance which the Circuit Court could decide upon the return of the habeas corpus . . . may be revised here on appeal from its final judgment.[43]

March 1868 was an eventful month. From March 2 until March 9 the Supreme Court heard arguments on the merits of McCardle's appeal for a writ of habeas corpus. Three days into the arguments, Chief Justice Salmon P. Chase left the high court bench to preside over the Senate impeachment trial of President Andrew Johnson. On March 12 Congress acted to prevent the Court's possible use of the McCardle case to strike down the Reconstruction Acts. As a rider to a revenue bill, it added a provision repealing the portion of the 1867 Habeas Corpus Act extending the Supreme Court's appellate jurisdiction over cases arising under it. Despite his own difficult position, President Johnson vetoed the bill on March 25. Congress overrode his veto two days later.[44] A week later, on April 2, the Supreme Court agreed to hear further arguments in the McCardle case, now focusing on the impact of the repeal on the case already argued. The Court then delayed matters further by postponing these arguments until its next term, a move much protested by at least two of the justices.

THE SOVEREIGN'S IMMUNITY

The United States cannot be sued in federal court unless Congress expressly authorizes such lawsuits. This legal doctrine is a corollary of the theory that the king could do no wrong. It has been applied, wrote a Supreme Court justice, "by our courts as vigorously as it had been on behalf of the crown."[1] This immunity was recognized by the Court as early as 1834. In that year Chief Justice John Marshall stated that "the party who institutes such suit [against the United States] must bring his case within the authority of some act of Congress, or the Court cannot exercise jurisdiction over it."[2] Subsequently, the Court held the federal government immune even from suits seeking recompense for damages or injuries inflicted by its agents or employees.[3]

In 1940 the Supreme Court explained that "the reasons for this immunity partake somewhat of dignity and decorum, somewhat of practical administration, somewhat of the political desirability of an impregnable legal citadel where government as distinct from its functionaries may operate undisturbed by the demands of litigants." The Court continued, however, noting that "[a] sense of justice has brought a progressive relaxation by legislative enactments of the rigor of the immunity rule."[4] This relaxation through acts of Congress waiving immunity actually began with the Supreme Court decision in *United States v. Lee* (1882).[5] George Lee, a son of Robert E. Lee, had sued to recover his family home, Arlington, which had been seized by federal officials acting under presidential order and was being used as a cemetery and a fort. The government claimed that such a suit could not be brought because of sovereign immunity. The Supreme Court, in a 5-4 decision, disagreed and rejected the defense of sovereign immunity. When it was claimed that a federal officer was holding property illegally, a federal court could take jurisdiction to hear out the claim, held the Court.

The doctrine of sovereign immunity, wrote Justice Samuel F. Miller for the majority, was "not permitted to interfere with the judicial enforcement of the established rights of plaintiffs, when the United States is not a defendant or necessary party to the suit."[6] The use of the sovereign immunity defense in such a case, Miller said,

> seems to be opposed to all the principles upon which the rights of the citizen, when brought in collision with the acts of the Government, must be determined. In such cases there is no safety for the citizen, except in the protection of the judicial tribunals, for rights which have been invaded by the officers of the Government, professing to act in its name.[7]

Miller continued:

> No man in this country is so high that he is above the law. No officer of the law may set that law at defiance, with impunity. All the officers of the Government, from the highest to the lowest, are creatures of the law and are bound to obey it.
>
> It is the only supreme power in our system of government, and every man who, by accepting office, participates in its functions, is only the more strongly bound to submit to that supremacy, and to observe the limitations which it imposes upon the exercise of the authority which it gives.[8]

In May President Johnson was acquitted by one vote in the Senate. In March 1869 the Court heard the postponed arguments, after which, on April 12, 1869, it held that Congress had eliminated the Court's jurisdiction over the case. Chief Justice Chase spoke for the Court; there was no dissenting opinion:

> The provision of the Act of 1867, affirming the appellate jurisdiction of this court in cases of habeas corpus, is expressly repealed. It is hardly possible to imagine a plainer instance of positive exception.
>
> We are not at liberty to inquire into the motives of the Legislature. We can only examine into its power under the Constitution; and the power to make exceptions to the appellate jurisdiction of this court is given by express words.
>
> What, then, is the effect of the repealing Act upon the case before us? We cannot doubt as to this. Without jurisdiction the court cannot proceed at all in any cause. . . .
>
> It is quite clear, therefore, that this court cannot proceed to pronounce judgment in this case, for it has no longer jurisdiction of the appeal; and judicial duty is not less fitly performed by declining ungranted jurisdiction than in exercising firmly that which the Constitution and the laws confer.[45]

Five years later Congress passed the Tucker Act of 1887, specifically granting to the Court of Claims (now the U.S. Claims Court) and federal district courts jurisdiction over cases such as *United States v. Lee.*

In 1946 Congress approved the Federal Tort Claims Act, waiving the government's immunity from certain personal injury claims against government employees or contractors. "The United States shall be liable . . . in the same manner and to the same extent as a private individual under like circumstances," the act said. One exception concerned the armed forces. The government would not be liable for "any claim arising out of the combatant activities of the military and naval forces, or the Coast Guard, during time of war."

Despite the new law, the Court in 1950 ruled active-duty service members may not sue for compensation if they were injured or killed in noncombat duty because of negligence, including medical malpractice, by the government or its employees. This rule is known as the "Feres doctrine" because it arose in *Feres v. United States.*[9] Feres's widow sued after he died in a barracks fire.

A second plaintiff whose case was decided at the same time sued after he had undergone abdominal surgery in an army hospital. A few months later, he had removed from his abdomen "a towel 30 inches long by 18 inches wide, marked 'Medical Department U.S. Army.'" Although the words of the law appeared to allow such suits, the Court said this would be a "radical departure from established law," and it held "the Government is not liable under the Federal Tort Claims Act for injuries to servicemen where the injuries arise out of or are in the course of activity incident to service."

This rule was criticized as being unfair to service members and their families, and in 1987 the Court agreed to reconsider it in two cases. In *United States v. Johnson* the widow of a Coast Guard helicopter pilot sued, contending her husband death's was due to negligence by a civilian air traffic controller.[10] In the second case, James Stanley, a retired army sergeant, sued after he learned he had been given LSD without his knowledge in a secret army experiment. He blamed the LSD for altering his personality and ruining his marriage.[11] In a pair of 5-4 decisions, the Court upheld the Feres doctrine and rejected the lawsuits.

---

1. *Feres v. United States, 340 U.S. 135 at 139 (1950).*

2. *United States v. Clarke,* 8 Pet. (19 U.S.) 436 at 444 (1834).

3. *Gibbons v. United States,* 8 Wall. (75 U.S.) 269 (1869).

4. *United States v. Shaw,* 309 U.S. 495 at 500–501 (1940).

5. *United States v. Lee,* 106 U.S. 196 (1882).

6. Id. at 207–208.

7. Id. at 218–219.

8. Id. at 220.

9. *Feres v. United States,* 340 U.S. 135 (1950).

10. *United States v. Johnson,* 481 U.S. 681 (1987).

11. *United States v. Stanley,* 483 U.S. 669 (1987).

Later in the year Chase would comment, in another opinion, that such a repeal of jurisdiction was "unusual and hardly to be justified except upon some imperious public exigency."[46] Historian Carl Swisher has pointed out that passage of this legislation was, to date, "the only instance in American history in which Congress has rushed to withdraw the appellate jurisdiction of the Supreme Court for the purpose of preventing a decision on the constitutionality of a particular law."[47] (The Supreme Court's appellate jurisdiction in cases of habeas corpus was restored in 1885.) As Charles L. Black Jr. notes, however, the McCardle case "marks the extent of the vulnerability of the Judiciary to congressional control, and hence underlines the significance of Congress' never (except for this case and perhaps one or two other ambiguous and minor instances) having tried to employ this power to hamper judicial review even of its own acts."[48] *(See "Pressures on the Institution," pp. 516–528)*

The Modern System of Appeals

During the nation's first century the Supreme Court was virtually the only federal appeals court. The circuit and district courts functioned as trial courts. The Supreme Court therefore was obliged to rule on all appeals brought from the rulings of those lower courts

A FEDERAL COMMON LAW?

When federal judges, dealing with diversity cases, resolve matters normally dealt with by state courts and state law, what law do they apply? This question resulted in one of the most remarkable turnabouts in Supreme Court history. The Court not only overturned a century-old precedent, but also declared that precedent-setting ruling unconstitutional. The Judiciary Act of 1789 provided that "the laws of the several states" should in general "be regarded as the rules of decision in trials at common law" in applicable cases in federal courts. "No issue in the whole field of federal jurisprudence has been more difficult than determining the meaning of this statute," wrote one scholar. "The central question has been whether the decisions of state courts are 'laws of the several states' within the meaning of the statute, and thus of controlling effect in some situations at least in the federal courts."[1]

In *Swift v. Tyson* (1842) the Supreme Court stated that the "laws of the several states" applied in diversity cases by federal courts included only the written statutes of the states; the common law or interpretation of the statutes set out by the decisions of state courts were not to be considered.[2] The apparent basis for the ruling, Carl Swisher wrote, was the belief of the justices that state courts would follow the federal courts' interpretation of the common law, resulting in uniform application among the states. He also

notes, however, that "the strategy failed.... State courts continued to follow in their own interpretations, with the result that state courts and federal courts ... were handing down different interpretations" of the same law.[3]

In the 1930s the Supreme Court took the opportunity presented by a diversity case and overruled *Swift v. Tyson* declaring it unconstitutional. The Constitution, the Court said in *Erie Railroad Co. v. Tompkins* (1938), required that the law in diversity cases be the written laws and the decisions of the courts of the applicable state. The most essential uniformity was consistency of interpretation and application of a state's laws within its limits by federal as well as state courts.[4] "There is no federal general common law," stated the Court.[5]

---

1. Charles Alan Wright, *Law of Federal Courts,* 4th ed. (St. Paul, Minn.: West Publishing, 1983), 347.

2. *Swift v. Tyson,* 16 Pet. (41 U.S.) 1 (1842).

3. Carl B. Swisher, *American Constitutional Development,* 2nd ed. (Cambridge, Mass.: Houghton Mifflin, 1954), 980.

4. *Erie Railroad Co. v. Tompkins,* 304 U.S. 64 (1938).

5. Id. at 78.

---

as well as on those brought under the Judiciary Act of 1789 from state courts. Wrote Frankfurter and Landis,

> for a hundred years the range of Supreme Court litigation remained practically unchanged. The same types of cases which in 1789 the framers of the Judiciary Act had designated for review by the Supreme Court continued to come before it till 1891. Despite the vast transformation of thirteen seaboard colonies into a great nation, with all that this implied in the growth of judicial business and the emergence of new controversies of vast proportions, a heavy stream of petty litigation reached the Supreme Court.[49]

The number of cases flowing to the Supreme Court began to swell after the Civil War. First in 1891 and then most notably in 1925, Congress gave the Supreme Court the power to select the most important of these cases for review and to refuse to review others.

There are two primary routes to Supreme Court review of the decision of an inferior court. The first is through the "writs of right"—first the writ of error issued to state courts under the 1789 act and then the appeal still in use today. If the Court finds that it has jurisdiction over an appeal, it is obligated to decide the issue or issues it raises. The second is through the writ of certiorari—a discretionary writ issued by the Supreme Court to a lower court ordering it to forward the record of the case. In the twentieth century the overwhelming majority of the cases coming to the Court have been transferred from the appeals route to the discretionary certiorari route, giving the Court great control over its docket.

The Circuit Court of Appeals

This process of the Supreme Court gaining more control over its docket began in 1891 with the creation by

Congress of a new level of federal courts between the circuit and district courts on the one hand and the Supreme Court on the other. These new courts—circuit courts of appeals—were to hear all appeals from decisions of the district and circuit courts. Their word was to be final in almost all diversity, admiralty, patent, revenue, and noncapital criminal cases. The old circuit courts continued, however, for another twenty years. "Congressional traditionalists refused to abolish [them], and they retained original trial jurisdiction over capital cases, tax cases and certain diversity cases," notes legal historian Rayman L. Solomon.[50] By 1911 Congress, however, recognized that the old circuit courts were redundant and unnecessary and eliminated them by statute. Afterward, district courts handled trials, and the appeals were reserved for the circuit courts. The Supreme Court had already been empowered by the 1891 act to review the decisions of the appeals court.

A Broader Jurisdiction

Early in the twentieth century Congress twice found it necessary to enlarge the Court's appellate jurisdiction. In 1907 the Criminal Appeals Act granted the government the right to appeal directly to the Supreme Court a federal judge's ruling dismissing an indictment, so long as the defendant's trial had not begun before dismissal of the charges. This statute remedied an omission in the 1891 act, which, the Court had ruled in 1892, left the government without this right.[51] Therefore, if a federal judge dismissed an indictment, finding the law on which it was based unconstitutional, no appeal of that ruling was possible under the 1891 act. The prosecution was terminated. After a federal district judge blocked the Roosevelt administration's prosecution of the Beef Trust in this manner, Congress acted to remedy the deficiency in the law.[52]

In 1914 Congress broadened the power of the Supreme Court to review state court decisions. In 1911 the New York Court of Appeals had held that state's workmen's compensation law—the nation's first—unconstitutional under the state and federal constitutions. Because the Supreme Court could review only state court rulings in which the state court denied a

federal challenge to a state law or held a federal law invalid, this ruling was outside the scope of judicial review. Congress therefore authorized the Court to review—through issuing a writ of certiorari—rulings of a high state court upholding, as well as denying, a federal right or challenge.[53] Later Congress made review of state court rulings on federal questions subject to Supreme Court discretion with the exception of those where a state court held a federal treaty, law, or action invalid or upheld a state law or action against federal challenge.[54] Review in those categories of cases remained obligatory.

The "Judges Bill"

The cases coming to the Supreme Court continued to increase in such numbers that as early as 1909, President William Howard Taft urged Congress to confine the Court's appellate jurisdiction to statutory and constitutional questions. After he became chief justice in 1921, Taft shifted his campaign for Court reform into high gear. The result was passage of the Judiciary Act of 1925, which is often referred to as the "judges bill," because the original legislation was drafted by members of the Court.[55] Under the act, the Supreme Court retains a broad right of review over federal cases, which it exercises at it discretion. The act made the circuit courts of appeals, well established after three decades, the last word on most cases they decided. The only cases in which there would be an appeal of right from an appeals court ruling were those in which the appeals court held a state law invalid under the Constitution, federal laws, or treaties. In such cases, review by the Supreme Court would be limited to the federal question involved. In all other cases, Supreme Court review of appeals court decisions would be available only through the issuance of a writ of certiorari, over which the Court had complete discretion.[56]

Under the 1925 act—and for half a century after that—the right of direct appeal to the Supreme Court from district court decisions remained available in cases decided under antitrust or interstate commerce laws; appeals by the United States under the Criminal Appeals Act; suits to halt enforcement of state laws or other official state actions; and suits designed to halt

THE DUTY TO DECIDE

In 1821 Chief Justice John Marshall set out, in clear and certain terms, his view of the Supreme Court's duty to decide all cases that properly fall within its jurisdiction. The Court, however, would many times disagree on whether a matter was within its jurisdiction and thus appropriate for decision. Marshall wrote,

> It is most true that this Court will not take jurisdiction if it should not: but it is equally true, that it must take jurisdiction if it should.

The judiciary cannot, as the legislature may, avoid a measure because it approaches the confines of the constitution. We cannot pass it by because it is doubtful. With whatever doubts, with whatever difficulties, a case may be attended, we must decide it, if it be brought before us. We have no more right to decline the exercise of jurisdiction which is given, than to usurp that which is not given. The one or the other would be treason to the constitution.[1]

1. *Cohens v. Virginia,* 6 Wheat. (19 U.S.) 264 at 404 (1821).

---

enforcement of Interstate Commerce Commission orders. During the 1970s, however, these avenues of direct appeal were redirected by Congress through the courts of appeals. From state courts, only two types of cases retained a right of direct appeal to the Supreme Court (under the 1925 act)—those in which a state law is upheld against a federally based challenge and those in which a federal law or treaty is held invalid. The Court's power to review state court rulings, however, remained, as always, quite limited in contrast to its broad power to review federal court decisions. The Court could review only such cases in which substantial federal questions were raised and in which state courts had rendered final judgment.

In 1988, after years of urging from the Court, Congress eliminated virtually all of the Court's remaining mandatory jurisdiction for cases. The legislation removed obligatory review of decisions striking down acts of Congress, appeals court decisions striking down state laws as unconstitutional, and final judgments

of state supreme courts questioning the validity of a federal law or treaty. The Court retained mandatory review of decisions of three-judge district courts (for example, involving reapportionment and voting rights). At the end of the twentieth century, the Judiciary Act of 1925 stood with the acts of 1789 and 1891 as one of the great organizational statutes in the history of the federal judiciary. For the most part, Chief Justice Taft's hopes for the accomplishments of the new law seem to have been achieved. In late 1925 he wrote in the *Yale Law Journal,*

> The sound theory of the new Act is that litigants have their rights sufficiently protected by the courts of first instance, and by one review in an intermediate appellate federal court. The function of the Supreme Court is conceived to be, not the remedying of a particular litigant's wrong, but the consideration of those cases whose decision involves principles, the application of which are of wide public and governmental interest.[57]

Federal Judicial Power

Once it is decided that a court has jurisdiction over a case, the scope of judicial power determines what the court may do about the dispute before it. Late in the nineteenth century Justice Samuel Miller defined judicial power as "the power of a court to decide and pronounce a judgment and carry it into effect."[1] Federal judicial power includes the power of judicial review—the power to measure the acts of Congress, the actions of the executive, and the laws and practices of the states against the Constitution and to invalidate those that conflict with the requirements of the national charter. In addition, the courts have the power to enforce their judgments through the use of writs, to punish persons for contempt, and to make rules governing the judicial process and admission to the bar.

JUDICIAL REVIEW

"If men were angels, no government would be necessary," wrote James Madison in the *Federalist Papers*. He continued:

> If angels were to govern men, neither external nor internal controls on government would be necessary. In framing a government which is to be administered by men over men, the great difficulty lies in this: you must first enable the government to control the governed; and in the next place, oblige it to control itself.[2]

The power of judicial review is one of the major self-control mechanisms of the U.S. system of government. Judicial review—especially as exercised over acts of the national legislature—is a uniquely American concept. The Constitution makes no explicit mention of this power, but many of those who drafted its language made clear their belief that the "judicial power" must include the power to nullify statutes enacted by the states as well as by Congress that contravene the Constitution.[3] Within fifteen years of the framing of the Constitution, the Supreme Court assumed this power for itself, exercising it to establish its validity in practice. This power not only operates as a constant admonition to Congress—and the states, which first felt the full force of its workings—but also to the executive. One hundred and seventy-one years after the Supreme Court struck down the first act of Congress, it cited that ruling as it informed a president, Richard M. Nixon, that he too must comply with the law, even at the cost of disgrace and resignation from office.[4]

A long and scholarly debate has developed over the legitimacy of the power of judicial review as assumed and exercised by the Supreme Court. Some scholars have argued that the framers assumed the courts would exercise this power, but others consider its assumption a clear usurpation. Yet, as one legal scholar noted several decades ago, by the mid-twentieth century the debate had become irrelevant in light of the long tradition of national acquiescence in the exercise of this power.[5] The origins of judicial review are obscure. During the colonial period, the Privy Council in London had the power to review and nullify acts of the colonial assemblies. During the revolutionary period, state courts exercised the power to strike down laws found to violate state constitutions, although such rulings usually provoked considerable controversy.[6]

The delegates to the Constitutional Convention apparently did not discuss an express grant of judicial review to the Supreme Court, but, as noted above, there is some evidence that many delegates assumed that the judicial power included judicial nullification of unconstitutional legislation.[7] The framers considered and rejected a proposal set forth by James Madison that would have lodged the veto power in a council composed of members of the executive and judicial branches. In the debate on this proposal, some members of the convention expressed their belief that "the Judges in their proper official character . . . have a negative on the laws," and so should not be given the chance to impose "a double negative."[8]

Review of State Acts

Clearly granted to the Supreme Court, however, was the power to review and reverse certain state court decisions. From 1789 until the Civil War, this aspect of judicial review was the most vigorously exercised, debated, protested, and resisted. *(See "Judicial Review and the States," pp. 377–385.)* The Judiciary Act of 1789, of which future chief justice Oliver Ellsworth was the main sponsor, expressly granted the Supreme Court the power to review and reverse or affirm the final rulings of state courts upholding a state law against a challenge that it was in conflict with the U.S. Constitution, federal laws, or a treaty. This provision, Section 25 of the act, was viewed as implementing the Supremacy Clause—the portion of the Constitution stating that the Constitution, federal laws, and federal treaties are the supreme law of the land. Congress in 1914 expanded this aspect of judicial review further, allowing the Supreme Court to review state court decisions finding state laws invalid because they conflicted with the Constitution, federal laws, or federal treaties. *(See "A Broader Jurisdiction," p. 17.)*

Section 25 was highly controversial, especially after the Court, in 1810, began exercising this power to hold certain state laws unconstitutional. Twice the early Court firmly rejected state challenges to Section 25 as unconstitutional. First, Justice Joseph Story in *Martin v. Hunter's Lessee* (1816) and, second, Chief Justice John Marshall in *Cohens v. Virginia* (1821) defended the Court's power over such state rulings as essential for preserving national sovereignty.[9] *(See details of these two cases, pp. 380–384.)* Despite innumerable proposals that the legislative branch abolish or curtail this aspect of judicial review, Congress has not given its final approval to any such measure. Part of the reason this power has survived may lie in the restraint with which the Court has exercised it. *(See "Judicial Restraint," pp. 50–65.)*

After Section 25 was amended in 1867, it appeared that Congress, by omitting a restrictive sentence, had granted the Court—when reviewing state court decisions—the power to review all the issues in such cases, not simply the federal issue or issues that justified its review in the first place. The Court in 1875 refused, however, to interpret the 1867 amendment as expanding its power in that direction.[10] In 1945 Justice Robert H. Jackson described the traditional approach in reviewing state court rulings:

> This Court from the time of its foundation has adhered to the principle that it will not review judgments of state courts that rest on adequate and independent state grounds. . . . The reason is so obvious that it has rarely been thought to warrant statement. It is found in the partitioning of power between the state and federal judicial systems and in the limitations of our own jurisdiction. Our only power over state judgments is to correct them to the extent that they incorrectly adjudge federal rights.[11]

Review of Acts of Congress

The first case challenging the validity of an act of Congress came to the Supreme Court in 1796. Both sides in the matter—a tax question—simply assumed that the Supreme Court could strike down the act. The Court instead upheld it.[12] Five years later, just before the end of President John Adams's term in office, Adams named William Marbury a justice of the peace for the District of Columbia. Although Marbury was confirmed and his commission duly signed by Adams, Secretary of State John Marshall failed to deliver the commission before Adams left office. President Thomas Jefferson, Adams's successor, declined to deliver the commission. Marbury, with former attorney general Charles Lee as his attorney, asked the Supreme Court to issue a writ of mandamus ordering James Madison, Jefferson's secretary of state, to deliver the commission. (*Mandamus* means "we command.") In response, the Court directed Madison to show cause why they should not issue such an order. Arguments in the case were set for the Court term scheduled to begin in June 1802.

Congress, however, repealed the law providing for a June Court term and replaced it with one providing that the next term would begin in February. As a result, the Court did not meet for fourteen months, during which Marbury's request remained pending.[13]

The case was finally argued, and on February 24, 1803, the Court issued a unanimous decision. The justices refused to issue the order Marbury requested despite its finding, announced by Chief Justice John Marshall, that Marbury had a legal right to his commission, that failure to deliver the commission violated that right, and that a writ of mandamus was the proper remedy for such a situation. The Court refused to issue a writ of mandamus because, it said, it lacked the power to issue one: the law that purported to authorize it to issue such orders was unconstitutional. Section 13 of the Judiciary Act of 1789 specifically authorized the Supreme Court "to issue writs of *mandamus* in cases warranted by the principles and usages of law, to any courts appointed or persons holding office, under the authority of the United States." Citing this provision, Marbury had come directly to the Supreme Court with his request. With reasoning more notable for its conclusion than its clarity, Marshall found that this provision expanded the Court's original jurisdiction.

> It is the essential criterion of appellate jurisdiction, that it revises and corrects the proceedings in a cause already instituted, and does not create that cause. Although, therefore, a mandamus may be directed to courts, yet to issue such a writ to an officer for the delivery of a paper, is in effect the same as to sustain an original action for that paper, and, therefore, seems not to belong to appellate, but to original jurisdiction.[14]

Congress, continued the Court, had no power to modify its original jurisdiction, and so this grant of authority was unconstitutional. The Court then asserted its power:

> It is emphatically the province and duty of the judicial department to say what the law is. . . .
> . . . [I]f a law be in opposition to the constitution; if both the law and the constitution apply to a particular case, so that the court must either decide that case conformably to the law, disregarding the constitution; or conformably to the constitution, disregarding the law; the court must determine which of these conflicting rules governs the case. This is of the very essence of judicial duty.

If then, the courts are to regard the constitution, and the constitution is superior to any ordinary act of the legislature, the constitution, and not such ordinary act, must govern the case to which they both apply.[15]

To rule to the contrary, Chief Justice Marshall said,

> would subvert the very foundation of all written constitutions. It would declare that an act which, according to the principles and theory of our government, is entirely void, is yet, in practice, completely obligatory. It would declare that if the legislature shall do what is expressly forbidden, such act, notwithstanding . . . is in reality effectual. It would be giving to the legislature a practical and real omnipotence, with the same breath which professes to restrict their powers within narrow limits. It is prescribing limits, and declaring that those limits may be passed with pleasure.
> . . . [I]t thus reduces to nothing what we have deemed the greatest improvement on political institutions, a written constitution.[16]

Defining the Constitution

With that decision, and the firm establishment of the power of the Court to nullify unconstitutional acts of Congress, the Supreme Court changed the meaning of the word *constitution*. Prior to the founding of the United States, the word referred not to a written basic law but simply to the principles observed in the operation of the government. Every government had some constitution, but not every government was bound by its constitution as a supreme law.[17] With *Marbury v. Madison* (1803) the Supreme Court became the effective instrument for enforcing the supremacy of the U.S. Constitution.

Criticism of judicial review, led after *Marbury* by none other than President Jefferson, continued. As Charles Evans Hughes noted in 1928, however, "The reasoning of Chief Justice Marshall's opinion has never been answered. . . . The doctrine of judicial review . . . practically is as much a part of our system of government as the judicial office itself."[18] Adding another perspective, Charles P. Curtis wrote that John Marshall "snatched from the majority and offered to our courts,

JUDICIAL REVIEW: SUPREME COURT OR SUPERLEGISLATURE?

In its second century the Supreme Court often wielded its power of judicial review to overturn acts of Congress and state legislatures. Its critics repeatedly charged that the Court was acting as a superlegislature, engaging in "judicial legislation" and substituting its judgment for that of elected representatives. One of the justices most critical of this development was John Marshall Harlan, who dissented from the 1895 decision voiding the peacetime income tax:

> Is the judiciary to supervise the action of the legislative branch of the government upon questions of public policy? Are they to override the will of the people, as expressed by their chosen servants, because, in their judgment, the particular means employed by Congress in execution of the powers conferred by the Constitution are not the best that could have been devised, or are not absolutely necessary to accomplish the objects for which the government was established? ...
>
> The vast powers committed to the present government may be abused, and taxes may be imposed by Congress which the public necessities do not in fact require, or which may be forbidden by a wise policy. But the remedy for such abuses is to be found at the ballot-box, and in a wholesome public opinion which the representatives of the people will not long, if at all, disregard.[1]

Ten years later, in 1905, Justice Harlan was joined by Justice Oliver Wendell Holmes Jr. in dissent, as the Court struck down New York's law setting maximum hours for bakers. Harlan wrote, "Whether or not this be wise legislation, it is not the province of the court to inquire. Under our system of government, the courts are not concerned with the wisdom or policy of legislation."[2] Justice Holmes elaborated:

> This case is decided upon an economic theory which a large part of the country does not entertain. If it were a question whether I agreed with that theory, I should desire to study it further and long before making up my mind. But I do not conceive that to be my duty, because I strongly believe that my agreement or disagreement has nothing to do with the right of a majority to embody their opinions in law. It is settled by various decisions of this court that state constitutions and state laws may regulate life in many ways which we as legislators might think as injudicious, or, if you like as tyrannical as this....
>
> But a constitution is not intended to embody a particular economic theory, whether of paternalism ... or of laissez faire. It is made for people of fundamentally different views, and the accident of our finding certain opinions natural and familiar or novel and even shocking ought not to conclude our judgment upon the question whether statutes embodying them conflict with the Constitution of the United States.[3]

"THE PROPER ADMINISTRATION OF JUSTICE"

Chief Justice William Howard Taft led the Court in the 1920s, during which the Court invalidated more legislation than it had in the half century

preceding it. Taft easily accepted the idea that the Court did, in fact, "make" law. He dismissed the idea that judges should try to ascertain and apply "the exact intention of those who established the Constitution." People with that view did not understand "the proper administration of justice."[4] In 1913 he wrote,

> Frequently, new conditions arise which those who were responsible for the written law could not have had in view, and to which existing common law principles have never before been applied, and it becomes necessary for the Court to make applications of both.... [Such an application] is not the exercise of legislative power ... [but] the exercise of a sound judicial discretion in supplementing the provisions of constitutions and laws and custom, which are necessarily incomplete or lacking in detail essential to their proper application, especially to new facts and situations constantly arising.... Indeed it is one of the highest and most useful functions that courts have to perform in making a government of law practical and uniformly just.[5]

As might be expected, justices serving with Taft took issue with his view. Among them was Louis D. Brandeis. When the Court held invalid a state law setting standard sizes for loaves of bread, Justice Brandeis wrote,

> It is not our function to weigh evidence. Put at its highest, our function is to determine ... whether the measure enacted in the exercise of an unquestioned police power and of a character inherently unobjectionable, transcends the bounds of reason. That is, whether the provision as applied is so clearly arbitrary or capricious that legislators acting reasonably could not have believed it to be necessary or appropriate for the public welfare.
>
> To decide, as a fact, that the prohibition of excess weights "is not necessary for the protection of the purchasers" and that it "subjects bakers and sellers of bread" to heavy burdens, is in my opinion, an exercise of the powers of a super-legislature—not the performance of the constitutional function of judicial review.[6]

The Court majority that so consistently struck down New Deal legislation in the 1930s was not insensitive to charges that it was imposing its own will on Congress, the president, and the American people. In *United States v. Butler* (1936) Justice Owen J. Roberts, whose vote during this period often meant the difference between the Court's declaring a statute valid or invalid, sought to answer these charges by minimizing the Court's role:

> It is sometimes said that the court assumes a power to overrule or control the action of the people's representatives. This is a misconception.... When an act of Congress is appropriately challenged in the courts as not conforming to the constitutional mandate, the judicial branch of Government has only one duty—to lay the article of the Constitution which is invoked beside the statute which is challenged and to decide whether the latter squares with the former.... The only power [the judiciary] has, if such it may be called, is the power of judgment. This court neither approves nor condemns any legislative policy.[7]

Roberts's claim did not go unanswered. In a strong dissent, Justice Harlan Fiske Stone said that the majority in *Butler* had assumed the very power Roberts contended the Court did not have: the power to judge the wisdom of the statute and not its constitutionality. There were two guiding principles for the judiciary to follow, Stone said:

> One is that courts are concerned only with the power to enact statutes, not with their wisdom. The other is that while unconstitutional exercise of power by the executive and legislative branches ... is subject to judicial restraint, the only check upon our own exercise of power is our own sense of self-restraint. For the removal of unwise laws from the statute books appeal lies not to the courts but to the ballot and to the processes of democratic government.... The present levy is held invalid, not for any want of power in Congress to lay such a tax ... but because the use to which its proceeds are put is disapproved.[8]

Justice Benjamin N. Cardozo, another of Roberts's colleagues, had earlier written critically of judges who took the approach Roberts outlined:

> Their notion of their duty is to match the colors of the case at hand against the colors of many sample cases spread out upon their desk. The sample nearest the shade supplies the applicable rule. But, of course, no system of living law can be evolved by such a process, and no judge of a high court, worthy of his office, views the function of his place so narrowly. If that were all there was to our calling, there would be little of intellectual interest about it. The man who had the best card index would also be the wisest judge. It is when the colors do not match ... that the serious business of the judge begins.[9]

In the years following resolution of the New Deal crisis—political, economic, and judicial—the debate over "judicial legislation" intensified as the Court extended its scrutiny into the area of controversial state laws and practices affecting individual rights and freedoms.

"A GENERAL HAVEN FOR REFORM MOVEMENTS"

The Court in the early 1960s moved into legislative malapportionment, ordering states to redraw their legislative districts to make them more equal in population. Chief Justice Earl Warren defended the Court's involvement in a matter traditionally left entirely to legislative power:

> We are told that the matter of apportioning representation in a state legislature is a complex and many-faceted one. We are advised that States can rationally consider factors other than population in apportioning legislative representation. We are admonished not to restrict the power of the States to impose differing views as to political philosophy on their citizens. We are cautioned

about the dangers of entering into political thickets and mathematical quagmires. Our answer is this: a denial of constitutionally protected rights demands judicial protection; our oath and our office require no less of us.[10]

This assertion was vigorously rebutted in 1964 by the second justice named John Marshall Harlan:

> What is done today deepens my conviction that judicial entry into this realm is profoundly ill-advised and constitutionally impermissible.
> ... I believe that the vitality of our political system, on which in the last analysis all else depends, is weakened by reliance on the judiciary for political reform; in time a complacent body politic may result.
> These decisions also cut deeply into the fabric of our federalism....
> Finally, these decisions give support to a current mistaken view of the Constitution and the constitutional function of this Court. This view, in a nutshell, is that every major social ill in this country can find its cure in some constitutional "principle," and that this Court should "take the lead" in promoting reform when other branches of government fail to act.
> The Constitution is not a panacea for every blot upon the public welfare, nor should this Court, ordained as a judicial body, be thought of as a general haven for reform movements. The Constitution is an instrument of government, fundamental to which is the premise that in a diffusion of governmental authority lies the greatest promise that this Nation will realize liberty for all its citizens.
> This Court, limited in function in accordance with that premise, does not serve its high purpose when it exceeds its authority, even to satisfy justified impatience with the slow workings of the political process.[11]

1. *Pollock v. Farmers' Loan and Trust Co.,* 158 U.S. 601 at 679–680 (1895).

2. *Lochner v. New York,* 198 U.S. 45 at 69 (1905).

3. Id. at 75–76.

4. Alpheus T. Mason, *The Supreme Court from Taft to Warren* (Baton Rouge: Louisiana State University Press, 1958), 46, citing William Howard Taft, *Popular Government: Its Essence, Its Permanence, Its Perils* (New Haven: Yale University Press, 1913), 222–223.

5. Ibid.

6. *Burns Baking Company v. Bryan,* 264 U.S. 504 at 533–534 (1923).

7. *United States v. Butler,* 297 U.S. 1 at 62–63 (1936).

8. Id. at 78–79.

9. Benjamin N. Cardozo, "The Nature of the Judicial Process," in *Selected Writings,* ed. Margaret E. Hall (New York: Fallon, 1947), 113.

10. *Reynolds v. Sims,* 377 U.S. 533 at 566 (1964).

11. Id. at 624–625.

the function of rendering our political decencies and aspirations into immanent law. What we owe to Marshall is the opportunity he gave us of combining a reign of conscience with a republic."[19]

The Power Exercised

For the first century of the nation's history, the Supreme Court exercised the power of judicial review primarily to enhance national power by striking down state laws and upholding acts of Congress challenged as infringing upon states' rights. As one scholar wrote, the Marshall Court wielded the power of judicial review "to place its stamp of approval upon the idea of the Constitution as an instrument of expanding national power."[20] Not until 1857—fifty-four years after *Marbury*—was a second act of Congress declared unconstitutional by the Supreme Court. In the infamous *Scott v. Sandford* (1857) case, the Court held that the Missouri Compromise was unconstitutional because Congress lacked the power to exclude slavery from the territories. That decision contributed to intensification of the debate over slavery and its eventual explosion into civil war; it also inflicted severe damage upon the Court. Hughes later would describe the case as the first of three of the Court's "self-inflicted wounds . . . a public calamity."[21] *(See "Slavery in the Territories," pp. 179–185.)*

Fifteen years after *Scott,* the Court dealt itself the second such injury. In the *Legal Tender Cases,* it first struck down (and fifteen months later reversed itself to uphold) the acts of Congress making paper money legal tender in payment of debts incurred before the passage of the acts.[22] *(See "First Legal Tender Decision" and "Second Legal Tender Decision," pp. 158–160.)* In the following century—from 1870 through 1970—the pace of judicial invalidation of congressional acts quickened. By 2008, 162 acts of Congress had been struck down, in whole or in part, by the Supreme Court (excluding all the laws affected by the Court's ruling on the legislative veto in the *Immigration and Naturalization Service v. Chadha.*).

As the Court exercised its power of judicial review more frequently, it found itself more and more the center of controversy. Proposals to curb the power of judicial review proliferated, but as one legal scholar wrote in 1956, such proposals "have been directed mainly, if not always, not against the existence of the power but against the manner or the finality of its exercise."[23] The judicial consensus seemed to be the same as that set out in 1928 by Hughes, a man who had served on the Court, left it to run for president, and later returned to the Court as chief justice:

> The dual system of government implies the maintenance of the constitutional restrictions of the powers of Congress as well as of those of the States. The existence of the function of the Supreme Court is a constant monition to Congress. A judicial, as distinguished from a mere political, solution of the questions arising from time to time has its advantages.[24]

THE POWER TO ISSUE WRITS

The Judiciary Act of 1789 authorized all federal courts to issue all writs "which may be necessary for the exercise of their respective jurisdictions, and agreeable to the principles and usages of law." That provision, slightly reworded, remains the general statutory authority for federal courts to issue orders to carry out their decisions.[25] Most significant and most controversial of the writs generally employed by the federal courts is the "Great Writ"—the writ of habeas corpus. When issued, it requires government officials to justify their decision to hold a person in custody over his or her objection. This writ has been described with many superlatives as "the best and only sufficient defense of personal freedom."[26] Other writs used by the courts have included the writ of error, used until early in the twentieth century to notify a state court that the Supreme Court was to review one of its rulings; the writ of certiorari, now the most common notice, sent to a lower or state court informing it that the Supreme Court has granted review of its decision; and the writ of mandamus, the writ involved in *Marbury v. Madison.* A federal court, the Supreme Court has said, may use all these "auxiliary writs as aids in the performance of its duties, when the use of such historic aids is calculated in its sound judgment to achieve the ends of justice entrusted to it."[27]

Habeas Corpus

First in importance of the writs available to the federal courts is the writ of habeas corpus. An integral part of the nation's English common law heritage, this writ is used by a court to inquire into the reasons for a person's detention by government authority. Loosely translated from the Latin, it means "you have the body." A writ orders the government to produce the prisoner—the corpus—so that the prisoner may make his case to a court. Habeas corpus, the Court has noted, "has time and again played a central role in national crises, wherein the claims of order and of liberty clash most acutely." The Court continued:

> Although in form the Great Writ is simply a mode of procedure, its history is inextricably intertwined with the growth of fundamental rights of personal liberty because its function has been to provide a prompt and efficacious remedy for whatever society deems to be intolerable restraints. Its root principle is that in a civilized society, government must always be accountable to the judiciary for a person's imprisonment: if the imprisonment cannot be shown to conform with the fundamental requirements of law, the individual is entitled to immediate release.[28]

Since the nation's founding, the use of the writ of habeas corpus has changed in a fundamental way. In England, habeas corpus gave a prisoner a right to a hearing before a judge. That right to go before a judge was written into the Constitution. But over time, particularly since the mid-twentieth century, habeas corpus became a second-chance appeal system for persons who were tried and convicted. Most criminal defendants are prosecuted in state courts, and there, they are entitled to the protections of the rights set out in the U.S. Constitution. They may also appeal to higher state courts if they believe their rights were violated. If those state appeals are rejected, the defendant may try again in the federal system. Acting on a writ of habeas corpus, federal judges can review the entire case—from arrest to prosecution, conviction, and sentence—to ensure the state procedures comported with the Constitution. Over time, habeas corpus became a means to reform federal and state criminal procedures.[29] Federal courts have broad discretion in determining when the issuance of this writ is appropriate to order release of a prisoner, but the Supreme Court has emphasized that "[d]ischarge from conviction through habeas corpus is not an act of judicial clemency, but a protection against illegal custody."[30] It may be issued to military or civilian authorities.[31] In addition, "[m]ere convenience cannot justify use of the writ as a substitute for an appeal [after a conviction]," wrote Justice Felix Frankfurter in 1942. "But dry formalism should not sterilize procedural resources which Congress has made available to the federal courts."[32] The Supreme Court has declared that the power of federal courts to issue this writ must be given by written law—as it always has been.

Despite the antiquity of this last assertion, it is open to debate in light of the express statement in the Constitution forbidding suspension of the privilege of the writ except when the public safety demands it.[33] The Court also has maintained that proceedings begun by a petition for this writ are entirely separate from the question of a defendant's guilt or innocence and are no substitute for a direct appeal of a conviction. The writ has been used in modern times to challenge a lack of jurisdiction of the sentencing court or to charge constitutional error, which, if proved, makes the entire detention illegal, regardless of the guilt of the person detained.[34]

Restricted Use

For most of the nineteenth century, the use of the writ of habeas corpus by federal courts was strictly limited by two factors. First, the Supreme Court at the time viewed the writ as properly used only to challenge the jurisdiction of the sentencing court. In 1830 the Court declared that the inquiry sparked by a request for this writ began and ended with the question of jurisdiction. If a person was detained under the judgment of a court with jurisdiction over him and his case, his detention was lawful.[35] Second, the Court faithfully observed the statutory restriction of the federal use of the writ to question the detention of federal prisoners only. In 1845 the Court refused to issue such a writ to state officials, even though the state prisoner seeking the writ argued that his state jailers were blocking all his efforts to appeal to the Supreme Court.[36]

Exceptions to the latter limitation were approved by Congress in 1833 and 1842, when it extended the use of habeas corpus to order state officials to release federal officers imprisoned for enforcing federal laws and to order state officials to release foreign nationals detained by a state in violation of a treaty. Despite these restrictions, in the pre–Civil War period some individuals did use a request for a writ of habeas corpus, coupled with a writ of certiorari, as a clumsy method of invoking the appellate jurisdiction of the Supreme Court. A few prisoners using this device were successful in obtaining their release.[37]

The Beginning of Expansion

The great expansion of habeas corpus was a product of the Civil War and the Reconstruction that followed it. Northern Republicans who controlled Congress did not trust Southern judges to protect the rights of the newly freed slaves or Union sympathizers. In 1867 they adopted the Habeas Corpus Act so that federal judges would have the authority to hear appeals from persons held by state authorities. The new law empowered federal judges "to grant writs of habeas corpus in all cases where any person may be restrained of his or her liberty in violation of the Constitution, or of any treaty or law of the United States." The 1867 act also provided for appellate review by the Supreme Court of lower court rulings denying habeas corpus relief to persons seeking it under this law. Almost before the ink was dry on the statute, the case of *Ex parte McCardle* (1869) was argued before the Court, and Congress—fearful of a ruling that would invalidate the Reconstruction Acts—repealed this provision for the expansion of the Supreme Court's appellate jurisdiction.[38] *(See details of Ex parte McCardle, pp. 520–523.)*

Despite the repeal, the basic expansion of the federal use of the writ remained intact. Lower federal courts could now use the writ to release state prisoners detained in violation of their federal rights, and the Supreme Court soon made clear that the 1868 repeal

affected only the 1867 enlargement of its appellate jurisdiction. The Court's preexisting jurisdiction over questions of habeas corpus relief—although procedurally cumbersome—was still valid. The Court made this point in *Ex parte Yerger* (1869). Edward Yerger, a civilian, was held by military authorities in Mississippi after his conviction by a military commission for killing an army major. A lower federal court granted his petition for a writ of habeas corpus, reviewed the reasons for his detention, and found them proper. The Supreme Court agreed to review that decision and affirmed its jurisdiction to issue an "original" writ of habeas corpus under the Judiciary Act of 1789.[39]

In 1885 Congress restored the jurisdiction of the Supreme Court to consider direct appeals from circuit court rulings denying habeas corpus relief, but before the 1885 legislation, in a set of cases decided in 1880, the Court used the original writ to consider situations in which persons accused of violating civil rights laws sought release through habeas corpus, arguing that the laws under which they were convicted were not constitutional. In each case, the Court denied the writ and upheld the challenged law.[40] Returning to the jurisdictional view of the writ, the Supreme Court based its power to act upon the reasoning that if the law was in fact unconstitutional, then the court that convicted the prisoner lacked jurisdiction to detain him, so the writ should be issued to order his release. The Court explained that questions concerning the constitutionality of the law under which an indictment is brought or a conviction obtained affect the foundation of the entire proceeding:

> An unconstitutional law is void, and is as no law. An offense created by it is not a crime. A conviction under it is not merely erroneous, but is illegal and void, and cannot be a legal cause of imprisonment.[41]

Nine years later, after Congress had restored the Court's jurisdiction over lower court denials of habeas corpus relief to persons alleging that they were detained in violation of their federal rights, the justices found a logical link between the jurisdictional basis for such relief and the new rights-based grounds for the writ.

It is difficult to see why a conviction and punishment under an unconstitutional law is more violative of a person's constitutional rights, than an unconstitutional conviction and punishment under a valid law. In the first case, it is that the court has no authority to take cognizance of the case; but in the other it has no authority to render judgment against the defendant.[42]

The Modern Writ

Although Congress in its 1867 expansion of the right to habeas corpus clearly contemplated federal intervention in state matters, for half a century after the act there were few collisions of state and federal power in this area. This lack of conflict resulted from the narrow definition of federal rights, the Court's continuing limited view of the issues properly raised by a petition for habeas corpus relief, and the fact that most of the Bill of Rights was not applied to protect persons against state action. As the Court expanded the category of federally protected rights and applied the guarantees of the first eight amendments to the states, the use of the writ to challenge and overturn state convictions became more frequent and more controversial.

The modern federal use of the writ of habeas corpus to question the detention of state prisoners can be traced to the Court's decision in *Frank v. Mangum* (1915). This ruling signaled an end to the Court's traditional view that so long as a sentencing court had jurisdiction to impose the challenged sentence, the Supreme Court would not inquire further into the legality of a person's confinement. In *Frank v. Mangum* the Court refused to order the release of a man convicted of murder by a state court, although he alleged that he had been denied a fair trial because the court was dominated by a mob. In an opinion, written by Justice Mahlon Pitney, however, the Court enlarged its traditional view of the responsibility of a federal court to examine state convictions. First, the Court indicated its belief that a court with jurisdiction over a case could lose jurisdiction if it allowed events to deny a defendant his federal rights. Second, the Court held that the 1867 Habeas Corpus Act gave state prisoners the right to "a judicial inquiry in a court of the

United States into the very truth and substance of causes of his detention," even if that required the federal court "to look behind and beyond the record of his conviction."[43]

The Court denied habeas corpus relief in this case because the defendant's claim of mob domination had been reviewed fully—and rejected—by a state appeals court. Eight years later the Court granted a similar plea. In *Moore v. Dempsey* (1923) the Court, speaking through Justice Oliver Wendell Holmes Jr., declared that

> if the case is that the whole proceeding is a mask— that counsel, jury and judge were swept to the fatal end by an irresistible wave of public passion, and that the State Courts failed to correct the wrong, neither perfection in the machinery for correction nor the possibility that the trial court and counsel saw no other way of avoiding an immediate outbreak of the mob can prevent this Court from securing to the petitioners their constitutional rights.[44]

In 1942 the Court acknowledged that habeas corpus relief involved far more than jurisdictional issues.

> [T]he use of the writ in the federal courts to test the constitutional validity of a conviction for crime is not restricted to those cases where the judgment of conviction is void for want of jurisdiction of the trial court to render it. It extends also to those exceptional cases where the conviction has been in disregard of the constitutional rights of the accused and where the writ is the only effective means of preserving his rights.[45]

Subsequently, the Court has broadened the power of federal courts, when considering state prisoners' petitions for habeas corpus, to review matters already considered and resolved by state courts. In 1953 the Court held that federal courts could rehear such a prisoner's claims "on the merits, facts or law" to be certain that his federal rights had been protected.[46] Ten years later the Court in *Townsend v. Sain* (1963) ruled that although a federal judge might defer to a state court's reliable findings of fact, where the facts remained in dispute, the federal judge should rehear the relevant evidence if there was not a "full and fair evidentiary hearing" on the prisoner's claim in a state court either at the time of his trial or in subsequent proceedings. Furthermore, the Court made clear in that decision that a federal judge should not defer to a state judge's findings of law: "It is the district judge's duty," stated the Court, "to apply the applicable federal law . . . independently."[47]

Exhausting State Remedies

To prevent unnecessary collisions between state and federal authority through the exercise of this expanded power of habeas corpus, the Supreme Court adopted the general rule that federal courts should await completion of state proceedings before ordering release of a state prisoner on habeas corpus. In *Ex parte Royall* (1886) the Court refused to order the release, before trial, of a state prisoner who sought a writ of habeas corpus from federal court. In its decision, the Court affirmed the power of the federal courts to issue such a pretrial writ, but it urged discretion in the use of that power in the interest of comity and preservation of the balance between state and federal power.[48] This rule, slowly enlarged on a case-by-case basis, became the "exhaustion requirement" set out in a 1944 ruling:

> Ordinarily an application for habeas corpus by one detained under a state court judgment of conviction for crime will be entertained by a federal court only after all state remedies available, including all appellate remedies in the state courts and in this court by appeal or writ of certiorari, have been exhausted.[49]

Four years later, when the Judicial Code was revised, this requirement was included. In *Darr v. Burford* (1950) the Court reaffirmed that this rule meant that a direct challenge to a state conviction should be taken all the way to the Supreme Court before a prisoner could then begin a collateral attack on his conviction by seeking a writ of habeas corpus from federal district court:

> Since the states have the major responsibility for the maintenance of law and order within their borders, the dignity and importance of their role as guardians of the administration of criminal justice merits review of their acts by this Court before a prisoner, as a matter of routine, may seek release . . . in the district courts of the United States. It is this Court's conviction that orderly federal procedure under our dual system of government demands that the state's highest court should ordinarily be subject to reversal only by this Court and that a state's system for the administration of justice should be condemned as constitutionally inadequate only by this Court.[50]

Three years later the Court was more succinct: "A failure to use a state's available remedy, in the absence of some interference or incapacity . . . bars federal habeas corpus."[51]

Exceptions to the Rule

Although the Court had always left open the possibility that it would not enforce the exhaustion requirement in exceptional circumstances, federal courts until 1963 were quite consistent in requiring adherence to it.[52] In *Fay v. Noia* (1963), however, the Court ruled that a state prisoner's failure to appeal his conviction did not necessarily bar him forever from obtaining habeas corpus relief from a federal court.[53] Charles Noia and two other men were convicted in 1942 of killing a Brooklyn storekeeper. All three were sentenced to life imprisonment in Sing Sing. The other two men unsuccessfully appealed their convictions; Noia did not. The other two eventually won release on federal habeas corpus after a federal judge agreed that their detention was unconstitutional because they had been convicted on the basis of confessions coerced from them. Despite identical circumstances concerning his confession and conviction, Noia was denied release on habeas corpus because he had not exhausted state remedies by appealing his conviction. Noia could not rectify the situation, for his right to appeal had terminated when he did not file an appeal within thirty days after conviction.

By a 6-3 vote the Supreme Court ordered Noia's release, despite his failure to appeal. Writing for the majority, Justice William J. Brennan Jr. declared that it was just this sort of situation, which "affront[ed] . . . the conscience of a civilized society," for which habeas corpus

STATE COURTS AND HABEAS CORPUS

State courts have the power to issue writs of habeas corpus, but federal supremacy places one major restraint on their use of the "Great Writ." State judges may not use it to require release of persons held in federal custody.

In the years preceding the Civil War, considerable resistance arose in abolitionist states to federal enforcement of the Federal Fugitive Slave Act. In Wisconsin, after newspaper editor Sherman Booth was convicted for helping fugitive slaves escape, state courts ordered his federal jailers to release him, issuing a writ of habeas corpus to them for this purpose. After the war the Supreme Court made clear that such an order exceeded the bounds of state power in the federal system. Federal supremacy, the Court

held in *Ableman v. Booth* (1859), meant that state courts could not use the writ to order release of federal prisoners.[1] *(See box, A Clash of Courts: The Fugitive Slave Law, p. 480.)*

More than half a century later the Court slightly modified this ban. With the consent of the United States, state courts could use the writ to direct federal officials to present a federal prisoner to state court for trial on state charges.[2]

---

1. *Ableman v. Booth*, 21 How. (62 U.S.) 506 (1859).

2. *Ponzi v. Fessenden*, 258 U.S. 254 (1922); *Smith v. Hooey*, 393 U.S. 374 (1969).

---

relief was intended. "If the States withhold effective remedy, the federal courts have the power and the duty to provide it."[54] The exhaustion requirement meant, wrote Justice Brennan, only that a state prisoner could not obtain federal habeas corpus relief unless he had first tried all state remedies still available. Because Noia's right to appeal had expired, his failure to avail himself of it did not foreclose habeas corpus relief. When a federal court was applying this rule to deny relief to a state prisoner, wrote Brennan, it must be certain that a person who had failed to exhaust his state remedies had done so deliberately, that he "understandingly and knowingly forewent the privilege of seeking to vindicate his federal claims in the state courts, whether for strategic, tactical, or any other reasons that can fairly be described as the deliberate by-passing of state procedures."[55]

Noia's choice not to appeal in 1942, when appeal could have resulted in a new trial and death sentence, could not realistically be viewed as his "considered choice," wrote Brennan, and so should not be held to bar him from habeas corpus relief in federal courts.[56] The Court in *Fay v. Noia* also overruled its 1950 decision that required a person to appeal his or her conviction all the way to the Supreme Court before seeking federal habeas corpus relief. That requirement, held the Court in 1963, placed an unnecessary burden on the prisoner and the Court.[57]

Restricting the Writ of Habeas Corpus

In the 1970s the Supreme Court began to narrow the impact of *Fay v. Noia*. A prisoner's claim that illegally obtained evidence had been improperly used to convict him could not serve as a basis for federal habeas corpus relief so long as the state had provided him an opportunity for "full and fair litigation" of that claim at an earlier time.[58] The Court also narrowed availability of federal habeas corpus relief through a stricter application of the exhaustion requirement. The Court abandoned the "deliberate bypass" standard of *Fay v. Noia*, under which state prisoners who had not deliberately bypassed their right to assert their federal claim earlier could obtain federal habeas corpus review. In its place it adopted, first for federal prisoners and then for state prisoners seeking this relief, a new standard: an earlier failure to assert a federal claim would bar habeas corpus relief unless the prisoner could show good reason for the earlier omission *and* actual prejudice to his case as a result of the claimed violation of his federal right.[59]

In 1986 Justice William H. Rehnquist was elevated to become chief justice. He had long criticized the use—and in his view, the abuse—of habeas corpus. He believed that lawyers were delaying death penalty cases for decades by filing and litigating duplicative habeas appeals in federal court. Rehnquist persuaded his colleagues to limit an inmate's access to successive petitions and thereby bring finality to the process. One of the first and most important restrictions imposed by the Rehnquist Court on the "Great Writ" came in *Teague v. Lane* (1989).[60] Frank Dean Teague, a black man, was convicted of attempted murder in 1982 by an all-white jury. During his trial and on appeal, he objected to the prosecutor's use of peremptory strikes to eliminate black jurors. He said the prosecutor's action denied him the right to be tried by a jury that was representative of the community. Teague lost initial appeals, but while he was continuing to contest his case, the Supreme Court ruled in a separate dispute, *Batson v. Kentucky* (1986), that defendants may challenge race bias in peremptory strikes.

Teague argued that he should receive the benefit of the *Batson* decision. No, ruled the Supreme Court in February 1989: new constitutional rules of criminal procedure would not be applied retroactively unless the new rule affects the fundamental fairness of a trial. That very high standard was not met by a challenge to jury composition. Justice Sandra Day O'Connor wrote the opinion, joined by Chief Justice Rehnquist and Justices Antonin Scalia, Anthony M. Kennedy, and, for the most part, Byron R. White. Justices Brennan, Thurgood Marshall, Harry A. Blackmun, and John Paul Stevens dissented. Justice O'Connor said Teague's "conviction became final two and a half years prior to *Batson,* thus depriving petitioner of any benefit from the rule announced in that case."[61] The opinion drew a sharp dissenting statement from Brennan:

> Out of an exaggerated concern for treating similarly situated habeas petitioners the same, the [O'Connor opinion] would for the first time preclude the federal courts from considering on collateral review a vast range of important constitutional challenges; where those challenges have merit, it would bar the vindication of personal constitutional rights and deny society a check against further violations until the same claim is presented on direct review.[62]

In 1990 the Court refined *Teague* and continued to narrow avenues for prisoners' petitions. It ruled that a trial judge's good faith interpretation of legal principles at the time of a conviction could stand even when later rulings in other cases contradicted the judge's interpretation.[63] It held that a defendant could not challenge his conviction based on a new constitutional rule that a state court could not reasonably have predicted.[64] It also said that a defendant is not entitled to federal habeas corpus relief based on a new court ruling in another case unless the principle of the new case is "fundamental to the integrity of the criminal proceeding."[65]

In 1991 the Court further narrowed *Fay v. Noia* (1963) and said a death row inmate may not file a habeas corpus petition in federal court if he failed to abide by state court procedural rules.[66] The convicted murderer in this case, *Coleman v. Thompson* (1991), missed a deadline for filing an appeal at the state level by three days. O'Connor wrote the opinion. Justice Brennan had been succeeded in fall 1990 by David H. Souter, who voted with Rehnquist, White, O'Connor, Scalia, and Kennedy in the majority. Justices Blackmun, Marshall, and Stevens dissented. The same six-justice majority ruled in *McCleskey v. Zant* (1991) that death row prisoners should be allowed (barring extraordinary circumstances) only one round of federal court review through petitions for habeas corpus, after state court appeals are exhausted.[67] The Court in this case held that a prisoner may file a second habeas corpus petition only if good reason exists for not having raised the new constitutional error in the first round. The prisoner is also required to show that he suffered "actual prejudice" from the error he asserts. Under earlier Court rulings, second and subsequent habeas corpus petitions were dismissed out of hand only if a prisoner deliberately withheld grounds for appeal (possibly to raise the arguments in later petitions and prolong the process).

In 1992 the Court reversed *Townsend v. Sain* (1963) and ruled that federal courts no longer were required to hold a hearing to weigh evidence based on the claim that important facts had not been adequately presented in state court. Under the new standard of *Keeney v. Tamayo-Reyes* (1992), a federal judge must hold a hearing only when a prisoner asserts a credible claim of "factual innocence."[68] In the majority were Chief Justice Rehnquist and Justices White (who wrote the opinion), Scalia, Souter, and Clarence Thomas. Justices O'Connor, Blackmun, Stevens, and Kennedy dissented. The majority stressed that it is up to state courts, not federal courts, to resolve factual issues. It said that a prisoner is entitled to an evidentiary hearing in federal court only if he can show "cause" for his failure to develop the facts in state proceedings and actual "prejudice" resulting from the failure. The "cause and prejudice" standard is very difficult for a defendant to meet.

In 1996 Congress placed new obstacles in the way of state prisoners seeking review of their sentences in federal court. This legislation, the Antiterrorism and Effective Death Penalty Act, set a one-year time limit for state prisoners whose appeals were exhausted to file a writ of habeas corpus in federal court. It also ordered that federal judges not grant a writ of habeas corpus from a state inmate unless it could be shown that the state court's decision "involved an unreasonable application of clearly established federal law, as determined by the Supreme Court of the United States." This provision was immediately challenged as effectively suspending the writ of habeas corpus.[69] The provision at issue in *Felker v. Turpin* (1996), the first case testing the act, required prisoners filing second or successive petitions to first obtain permission from a court of appeals. The law set a tough standard for whether the petition would be heard, and it barred any appeal to the Supreme Court of the court of appeals' decision to hear or not to hear the case. The Court unanimously upheld the provision of the law, finding that it neither breached the Court's jurisdiction nor constituted an impermissible "suspension" of the writ. Writing for the Court, Chief Justice Rehnquist observed that although the law established new criteria for consideration of habeas corpus petitions, the statute did not affect the Court's authority to hear cases brought as original writs of habeas corpus.

The Court, in close cases, has invoked the stricter federal law to throw out constitutional claims. In 2003, for example, the Court by a 5-4 vote reversed the federal appeals court in California, which had declared unconstitutional a petty criminal's fifty-year sentence for shoplifting videotapes from two K-Marts. In *Lockyer v. Andrade* (2003) Justice O'Connor explained candidly that "our cases exhibit a lack of clarity" as to when a prison term is so long that it violates the Eighth Amendment's ban on cruel and unusual punishment. Therefore, the judges of the California state courts acted reasonably when they rejected the claim of career criminal Leandro Andrade that he did not deserve such a lengthy sentence for his most recent, rather minor crimes. Because it was "not an unreasonable application of our clearly established law," the federal appeals court should have denied him a writ of habeas corpus, O'Connor concluded.

War on Terror and the Return of Habeas

During the "war on terrorism" that followed the attacks of September 11, 2001, the Court was called upon once again to consider the reach of habeas corpus. The George W. Bush administration transported hundreds of foreign prisoners to the U.S. naval base at Guantánamo Bay, Cuba. They were labeled as "unlawful enemy combatants," and the administration insisted these men could be held indefinitely without charges and without a chance to contest the basis for holding them. Many of them had writs of habeas corpus filed on their behalf by family members.

In a pair of rulings, the Court concluded the right to habeas corpus extended to these prisoners. Congress had authorized federal judges to hear habeas claims from persons who say they are being held "in custody in violation of the Constitution or laws or treaties of the United States." In *Rasul v. Bush* the Court in 2004 concluded the "habeas statute confers a right to judicial review of the legality of Executive detention of aliens in territory over which the United States" exercises complete control.[70]

This ruling did not resolve the matter, however. Congress decided to change the habeas statute. The Detainee Treatment Act of 2005 and the Military Commissions Act of 2006 included provisions that denied the right to habeas corpus to any noncitizen who is held as "an enemy combatant" by the military. "No court, justice or judge shall have the jurisdiction to hear or consider an application for a writ of habeas

The Supreme Court determined that "unlawful enemy combatants" held in the detention facility at the U.S. naval base in Guantánamo Bay, Cuba, have the right to file habeas corpus petitions in U.S. federal court in *Boumediene v. Bush* (2008).

corpus filed by or on behalf of an alien detained by the United States" for engaging in hostile acts or for aiding terrorists, the MCA said.

In *Boumediene v. Bush* (2008) the Court struck down this provision as unconstitutional.[71] "The Framers considered the writ a vital instrument for the protection of liberty," Justice Kennedy wrote. They added a clause specifying, "The Privilege of the Writ of Habeas Corpus shall not be suspended, unless when in Cases of Rebellion or Invasion the public Safety may require it." And because Congress had not declared such a state of emergency, the "MCA thus effects an unconstitutional suspension of the writ." The ruling cleared the way for the longtime prisoners at Guantánamo to seek their freedom from federal judges, but it did not ensure that any of them would go free.

Writs of Mandamus

"The remedy of *mandamus* is a drastic one," the Supreme Court has written, "to be invoked only in extraordinary situations."[72] The writ of mandamus is a

court order to a government official requiring him or her to take some action related to his or her post. The writ may be peremptory—an absolute and unqualified command—or it may be an alternative command, giving the individual to whom it is addressed the opportunity to show cause to the court why compliance with its order is not warranted. Companion to the mandamus is the writ of prohibition, which bars a government official or lower court from taking certain action, instead of ordering action.

In modern times, the Supreme Court issues few writs of mandamus, even when it finds the person seeking them entitled to such an order. It customarily rules that the party is entitled to that remedy, but withholds the issuance of the writ assuming that the official or the lower court will act in conformity with its ruling.[73] In *Marbury v. Madison* (1803) the Supreme Court made clear that this writ was to be used only in cases over which the issuing court already had jurisdiction. The Court held that Marbury was entitled to his commission and that a writ of mandamus was the proper remedy for the situation, but it refused to issue that order to Secretary of State James Madison. The reason for the Court's refusal was its finding that it lacked original jurisdiction over the case, which involved neither a state nor a foreign minister.[74] *(See details of Marbury v. Madison, pp. 79–83 and pp. 336–337.)* Subsequent rulings reinforced this requirement, but as the jurisdiction of the federal courts has been expanded, so have the types of cases in which the writ of mandamus may be used.

The separation of powers has limited the issuance of these writs from federal courts to federal executive officials. Not until 1838 did the Supreme Court rule that any lower federal court could issue such a writ to a federal official in the executive branch.[75] In *Marbury* the Court distinguished between the types of action that a court might order an executive branch official to take and those in which the separation of powers forbids judicial interference. Only ministerial acts, wrote Chief Justice John Marshall, could be the subject of writs of mandamus:

> Where the head of a department acts in a case, in which executive discretion is to be exercised; in which he is the mere organ of executive will . . . any application to a court to control, in any respect, his conduct, would be rejected. . . .
>
> But where he is directed by law to do a certain act affecting the absolute rights of individuals, in the performance of which he is not placed under the particular direction of the President, and the performance of which the President cannot lawfully forbid . . . in such cases, it is not perceived on what ground the courts . . . are further excused from the duty of giving judgment that right be done to an injured individual.[76]

When the Court, in 1838, upheld the issuance of a writ of mandamus to the postmaster general, it made clear that it so ruled because the action ordered was "a precise, definite act, purely ministerial, and about which the Postmaster-General had no discretion whatever."[77]

The extraordinary nature of these writs in the federal system has been further underscored by the Court's insistence that such writs be issued only to persons who lack any other legal remedy. As early as 1803 the Court has reiterated this point:

As a means of implementing the rule that the writ will issue only in extraordinary circumstances, we have set forth various conditions for its issuance [including that] the party seeking issuance . . . of the writ have no other adequate means to attain the relief he desires . . . and that he satisfy "the burden of showing that [his] right to issuance of the writ is 'clear and indisputable.'"[78]

It is a general rule within the federal judicial system that only final judgments are eligible for review by a higher court; that is, intermediate rulings should not be reviewed until the trial or proceeding has concluded in a final judgment. In keeping with this policy, the Supreme Court has resisted most efforts by parties to obtain a writ of mandamus to review or undo an interim, or interlocutory, ruling of a lower court. The Court also has steadfastly insisted, since early in its history, that the writ of mandamus is not to be used as a substitute for a direct appeal from a ruling.[79] In 1943 the Court affirmed this last point with particular emphasis:

> Mandamus, prohibition and injunction against judges are drastic and extraordinary remedies. . . . These remedies should be resorted to only where appeal is a clearly inadequate remedy. We are unwilling to utilize them as a substitute for appeals. As extraordinary remedies, they are reserved for really extraordinary cases.[80]

The most frequent modern use of writs of mandamus is by an appellate court to confine a lower court "to a lawful exercise of its prescribed jurisdiction" or to compel it "to exercise its authority when it is its duty to do so."[81] These writs, the Court has made clear, are "meant to be used only in the exceptional case where there is clear abuse of discretion or 'usurpation of judicial power.'"[82] Most such orders are issued by the court immediately superior to the receiving court, but the Supreme Court possesses the power to issue a writ directly to a district court "where a question of public importance is involved or where the question is of such a nature that it is peculiarly appropriate that such action by this court should be taken."[83] The Supreme Court also has the power to issue the writ to a state court, so long as the case involved is within the appellate jurisdiction of the Supreme Court.[84]

"GOVERNMENT BY INJUNCTION"

In the early days of organized labor in the United States, federal courts were so receptive to the requests of employers to issue injunctions against boycotts, picketing, and other now-legitimate union activity that this unity of judiciary and management came to be termed "government by injunction."[1] *(See "Antitrust and Labor," pp. 114–115.)* In the Clayton Act of 1914 Congress attempted to restrict this use of federal injunctive power.

The Clayton Act included provisions forbidding the issuance of federal injunctions in labor disputes unless necessary to prevent irreparable injury to property and providing a limited right to a jury trial for persons charged with contempt for disobeying an injunction. In two cases in 1921, however, the Supreme Court interpreted the Clayton Act restriction into ineffectiveness. It upheld, as still appropriate, injunctions against a union—rather than against particular employees—and against a variety of "unlawful" labor activities.[2]

A more successful effort to limit government by injunction came in 1932 with the passage of the Norris-LaGuardia Act. That act prohibited issuance of injunctions by federal courts in labor disputes except after a hearing and findings that the order is necessary to prevent substantial and irreparable injury and that the injury inflicted by granting the injunction would be outweighed by the injury resulting if it is not granted.

Some questions were raised about the power of Congress to impose such a limit on the equity jurisdiction of the federal courts. In 1938 the Supreme Court upheld this restriction. Writing for the Court, Justice Owen J. Roberts stated that "[t]here can be no question of the power of Congress thus to define and limit the jurisdiction of the inferior courts of the United States."[3] The Supreme Court has held that this restriction does not foreclose federal injunctions to halt a strike by a union against mines being operated by the government.[4] The Court has also upheld the provision of the Taft-Hartley Act granting federal courts jurisdiction to issue such an injunction against a strike when the court finds that the strike affects an entire industry or a substantial part of it and, if allowed to continue, would potentially threaten the nation's health or safety.[5]

---

1. *Carl B. Swisher, American Constitutional Development,* 2nd ed. (Cambridge, Mass.: Houghton Mifflin, 1954), 806–812; *In re Debs,* 158 U.S. 564 (1895); *Gompers v. Buck's Stove & Range Co.,* 221 U.S. 417 (1911).

2. *Duplex Printing Press v. Deering,* 254 U.S. 443 (1921); *American Steel Foundries v. Tri-City Central Trades Council,* 257 U.S. 184 (1921).

3. *Lauf v. E. G. Shinner & Co.,* 303 U.S. 323 at 330 (1938).

4. *United States v. United Mine Workers,* 330 U.S. 258 (1947).

5. *United Steelworkers of America v. United States,* 361 U.S. 39 (1959).

Although the decision to issue or deny the request for such a writ is left to the discretion of the court to whom the request is addressed, the Supreme Court has not hesitated to overturn what it considers unnecessary use of this writ. The Court has held that the writ of mandamus should not be used to order a trial judge to reinstate certain pleas, because the judge's decision to dismiss them can be reviewed on appeal.[85] On the other hand, the Court has upheld the use of the writ to override trial judges' decisions to appoint a special master to hear a case, to deny a jury trial, and to reverse a federal judge's decision that in order to avoid delay in hearing a case, it should be tried in state, rather than federal, court.[86]

Injunctions

Complementing the affirmative function of the writ of mandamus is the negative function of the injunction—an order directing someone to halt a course of action

that will cause irreparable injury to another for which no adequate recompense can be made by a subsequent lawsuit. Injunctions are issued under the federal courts' equity power—their general responsibility to ensure fairness and justice—rather than under their more specific jurisdiction over matters arising from the Constitution and laws. Injunctions may be temporary, simply preserving the status quo pending final resolution of the issues in a dispute, or they may be permanent bans on certain courses of action. A federal judge may issue a preliminary or temporary injunction even before deciding whether he or she has jurisdiction over a case. The order must be obeyed until it is reversed or lifted.[87]

Some people consider the power to issue injunctions, as well as the other writs, to be inherent in the nature of the federal courts, but the Supreme Court traditionally has held that Congress must authorize the federal courts to issue such orders. Congress issued such statutory authority in 1789 and has steadily exercised its power to limit the circumstances in which federal courts may issue injunctions. The Judiciary Act of 1789 made clear that equity suits were to be brought only when no legal remedy existed to resolve a dispute. More specific limitations followed quickly. In 1793 Congress forbade the courts to use injunctions to stay state court proceedings. The Anti-Injunction Act, which set out the fundamental policy of federal noninterference with state judicial proceedings, remains in effect today. In 1867 Congress forbade federal courts to use injunctions to interfere with the assessment or collection of federal taxes. One result of this ban is the landmark *Pollock v. Farmers' Loan and Trust Co.* (1895), which challenged the constitutionality of the peacetime income tax. *Pollock* was a suit seeking an injunction directing a bank *not* to pay its federal income taxes.[88]

The extensive use of the injunction by federal courts sympathetic to the efforts of property owners and employers to curtail the activities of organized labor brought the enactment of laws in 1914 and 1932 limiting such "government by injunction." *(See box, "Government by Injunction," p. 34.)* In similar fashion, Congress in 1910 and 1937 required that injunctions halting enforcement of state laws or acts of Congress challenged as unconstitutional be granted only by panels of three federal judges, not by a single federal judge. Appeals from the decisions of these panels could be taken directly to the Supreme Court. These provisions were repealed in 1976. In the 1930s Congress had further restricted the use of federal injunctions to interfere with state affairs, forbidding their use to halt the collection or enforcement of public utility rates fixed by state order or the collection of state or local taxes. These bans were not effective in situations where no adequate state remedy was available to persons protesting the rates or the taxes. During World War II Congress again demonstrated its power to limit the use of this remedy by the courts, when it provided that only one court in the country could enjoin rules or orders issued by the Office of Price Administration. The Supreme Court upheld even this limitation on injunctive relief.[89]

The Executive and the Legislature

The question of the Supreme Court's power—or that of any other federal court—to use the injunction to halt the proceedings of either Congress or the executive branch arose soon after the Civil War and was quickly and decisively settled. When Mississippi came to the Court seeking an injunction ordering President Andrew Johnson, as an official or as an individual, to cease enforcing the allegedly unconstitutional Reconstruction Acts, the Court held that it lacked the power to issue such an order. The Court reasoned that this request fell under the same general principles set out in the mandamus cases of *Marbury v. Madison* and *Kendall v. United States ex rel. Stokes* (1838), which "forbid judicial interference with the exercise of executive discretion." Only purely ministerial duties of executive officials were subject to such orders.[90] In his opinion in *Mississippi v. Johnson* (1867), Chief Justice Salmon P. Chase provided a succinct statement of the Court's view of the impropriety of its enjoining the operations of either of the other coordinate branches:

> The Congress is the Legislative Department of the Government; the President is the Executive Department. Neither can be restrained in its action by the Judicial Department; though the acts of both, when performed, are, in proper cases, subject to its cognizance.[91]

This ruling, however, did not prevent federal courts from exercising the power to enjoin federal officials from enforcing an unconstitutional act of Congress, an action that falls into the ministerial category. The courts assumed this power long before any statutory authorization could be found for it, but an authorization was provided in the 1937 statute requiring that such injunctions be issued by three-judge panels.

Federal Courts and State Power

Few problems regarding the exercise of federal judicial power have been more persistent than those resulting from the power of federal judges to enjoin state officials and halt state proceedings. It was to that clearly evident point of friction that Congress spoke in 1793, when it passed the Anti-Injunction Act, which established a nearly complete ban on such federal interference in state affairs. In recent decades the Court has supplemented the statute with the judicial doctrine of abstention, that is, the rule that federal courts should normally deny requests to halt state enforcement of state laws. Although its rationale is lost in history, the language of the Anti-Injunction Act is clear: federal courts should not use injunctions to stay proceedings in state courts unless Congress approves such use of these writs. The modern version of the law, revised in 1948, states,

> A court of the United States may not grant an injunction to stay proceedings in a state court except as expressly authorized by Act of Congress, or where necessary in aid of its jurisdiction or to protect or effectuate its judgments.

Through the years the Court has found express exception to this ban in a number of federal laws, including removal statutes, those giving federal courts jurisdiction over farm mortgages, federal habeas corpus statutes, and federal price control laws.[92] Furthermore, the Court found implicit exceptions to this ban allowing it to permit federal courts to halt state court proceedings when necessary to protect jurisdiction of the federal court over a case or to prevent relitigation in state courts of issues already resolved in federal court.[93] (In 1941 the Court appeared to abandon this last exception, but seven years later, when the anti-injunction statute was rewritten, this exception was reinstated as proper.[94]) The Court has found additional exceptions to the ban in cases brought by the United States and in cases brought under civil rights law that authorizes individuals to sue for damages in federal court when they have been deprived of a constitutional right by someone acting under color of state law.[95]

The Anti-Injunction Act applies only when a federal court is asked to halt an ongoing state court proceeding. It does not affect the power of federal courts to order state officers to stop enforcing unconstitutional state laws. This latter aspect of federal judicial power was recognized by the Supreme Court as early as 1824, and the decision in *Ex parte Young* (1908) allowed that federal judges could issue such injunctions to state officials even before the challenged law is actually ruled invalid.[96] *(See the details of Ex parte Young, pp. 463–464.)* To curtail instances of clear federal intervention in state business, however, the Court had required that individuals exhaust their state legislative and administrative remedies before seeking a federal injunction of this sort.[97] As noted, in 1910 Congress limited the power to issue such injunctions to three-judge panels, denying it to a single federal judge acting alone. The exercise of this power has been tempered by concern for preserving the balance of the federal system. As Justice William J. Brennan Jr. wrote in 1965,

> [T]he Court has recognized that federal interference with a State's good-faith administration of its criminal laws is peculiarly inconsistent with our federal framework. It is generally to be assumed that state courts and prosecutors will observe constitutional limitations . . . and that the mere possibility of erroneous initial application of constitutional standards will usually not amount to the irreparable injury necessary to justify a disruption of orderly state proceedings.[98]

To win such an injunction, a defendant must show a threat of irreparable injury "both great and immediate," substantially more than simply that attendant upon any criminal prosecution or enforcement of the laws.[99] In a series of rulings in the 1940s, the Court reinforced this requirement with the new doctrine of abstention. Under this approach to federal injunctive power, federal judges were generally to refrain from enjoining state officials until state courts had full opportunity to consider the challenged law or practice and revise or interpret it to remove the constitutional problem.[100] The Court applied the doctrine to requests that federal judges halt ongoing state court proceedings and that they halt enforcement of challenged state laws by forbidding any future prosecutions under them. The civil rights revolution of the following decades strained this doctrine and resulted in several exceptions to its application.

In 1963 the Court ruled that when a civil rights case involved no question of state law sufficient to resolve the dispute, there was no need to require the people bringing the case to exhaust state remedies before seeking a federal injunction.[101] Two years later the Court held that there was no reason for federal courts to defer to state proceedings in a case where no possible reinterpretation of state law could bring the challenged provisions within constitutional bounds.[102]

INJUNCTIONS AND FREE SPEECH

Labor picketing and judicial injunctions often came before the Court in the first third of the twentieth century. In the last decades of the century, however, abortion protests and injunctions were far more common. The Court ruled that judges could restrain the protesters, so long as they remained free to speak their message—perhaps from a distance.

Madsen v. Women's Health Center (1994) involved a Florida state judge's injunction limiting demonstrations around a health clinic. In a 6-3 vote, the justices permitted judges to establish "buffer zones" to keep antiabortion protesters from blocking access to abortion clinics but warned judges that they could not restrict more speech than necessary to safeguard access. Chief Justice William H. Rehnquist was joined in the majority by Justices Harry A. Blackmun, John Paul Stevens, Sandra Day O'Connor, David H. Souter, and Ruth Bader Ginsburg. Dissenting were Justices Antonin Scalia, Anthony M. Kennedy, and Clarence Thomas.

Writing for the Court, Rehnquist rejected the protesters' argument that the injunction should be subject to the highest level of judicial review—"strict scrutiny"—because it singled out antiabortion views. Instead, Rehnquist wrote, the injunction was "content neutral" and could be upheld if it "burdens no more speech than necessary to serve a significant government interest."[1] Rehnquist listed "a woman's freedom to seek lawful medical counseling or counseling services in connection with her pregnancy" as one of the interests that would justify "an appropriately tailored injunction."[2] On that basis he upheld a thirty-six-foot buffer zone around most of the clinic and a broad noise ban during hours when abortions were performed.

1. *Madsen v. Women's Health Center,* 512 U.S. 753 (1994.)

2. Id.

Still another (and even more significant) exception to the abstention doctrine was the apparent result of the Court's decision in *Dombrowski v. Pfister* (1965), in which it held that abstention was inappropriate in cases in which state laws were "justifiably attacked on their face as abridging free expression or as applied for the purpose of discouraging protected activities."[103]

James A. Dombrowski, executive director of the Southern Conference Educational Fund, a civil rights group, and several of his associates had been arrested in 1963 by Louisiana officials and charged with violating that state's laws against subversive activities and communist propaganda. The charges were dropped, but state officials continued to threaten Dombrowski with prosecution. Charging that the threats were part of the state's campaign to discourage civil rights activity and that the state laws under which the charges had been brought against him violated his First Amendment rights, Dombrowski sought a federal injunction against the alleged harassment. The Anti-Injunction Act did not apply because there were no pending state court proceedings, but the three-judge panel hearing Dombrowski's request found this an appropriate case for abstention, to give state courts an opportunity to interpret the challenged

laws to bring them into line with the First Amendment. The Supreme Court, by a vote of 5-2, overturned that ruling. Abstention served no legitimate purpose in such a case, held the majority, especially in the face of the clear "chilling effect" that prosecution under the challenged laws would have on the First Amendment freedoms involved. Many observers, including a number of federal judges, saw this ruling as broadening the permissible use of federal injunctions to halt or forestall state criminal prosecutions. The decision seemed to allow such orders in cases in which a state law on its face was so vague or so broad as to collide with the First Amendment, even if the particular case involved no showing of bad faith or harassment on the part of state officials, or any other clear threat of irreparable injury.

This interpretation of *Dombrowski* was short-lived. Six years later, in a set of five cases handed down together, the Supreme Court reaffirmed the basic requirement that before an injunction is issued, there must be a showing of threatened irreparable injury. In cases involving ongoing prosecutions, "the normal thing to do when federal courts are asked to enjoin pending proceedings in state courts is not to issue such injunctions," said the Court in *Younger v. Harris* (1971), one of

The Court in *Pennzoil Company v. Texaco Inc.* (1987) ruled that federal judges should not have become involved in an ongoing state case between two oil companies.

the five cases.[104] Justice Hugo L. Black, who had not participated in the *Dombrowski* decision although a member of the Court at the time, wrote the Court's opinions. Only Justice William O. Douglas dissented in *Younger,* although several other justices took issue with the application of the abstention doctrine in one of the other cases decided that day. In each case the Court reversed a lower court's decision to enjoin state prosecution based on a law challenged as violating the First Amendment. "[T]he existence of a 'chilling effect,' even in the area of First Amendment rights," wrote Justice Black, "has never been considered a sufficient basis, in and of itself, for prohibiting state action."[105] In his view, *Dombrowski* permitted an injunction because of a clear threat of irreparable injury from a possible prosecution, not because the law at issue was alleged to violate the First Amendment. In the cases before it, the Court had found no such threat, no showing of bad faith or harassment sufficient to justify an immediate injunction.

In *Younger v. Harris* the Court did not base its ruling on the Anti-Injunction Act, but on the broader notion of the "comity" necessary to preserve the federal system. Comity, Black explained, was simply "a proper respect for state functions."[106] In a series of rulings following *Younger,* the Court, by narrowing margins, extended the doctrine of nonintervention to limit federal injunctions halting state criminal proceedings begun *after* the injunction is requested and to curtail their use to intervene in some state civil proceedings.[107] In each case the Court based the extensions of the *Younger* rule on the general principle of comity rather than on any statutory prohibition.

One of the Court's invocations of the *Younger v. Harris* doctrine came in *Pennzoil Company v. Texaco Inc.* (1987), in which the Court was unanimous in holding that federal judges were wrong to become involved in an ongoing state case between the two oil companies. The result of the ruling was to remove a shield that the federal courts had imposed to protect Texaco from having to post a bond of more than $10 billion in order to appeal a damage award that Pennzoil had won. Writing for the Court, Justice Lewis F. Powell Jr. reemphasized that in all but the most extreme cases, federal judges should refrain from interfering in ongoing state litigation. "Proper respect for the ability of state courts," Powell wrote, requires that federal courts stay their hands in such cases. Comity, he said, requires federal courts to abstain from becoming involved "not only when the pending state proceedings are criminal, but also when certain civil proceedings are pending, if the State's interests in the proceedings are so important that exercise of the federal judicial power would disregard the comity between the states and the federal government."[108]

Declaratory Judgments

A milder and less intrusive judicial remedy than the injunction is the declaratory judgment. In such a ruling a federal court simply declares conclusively the rights and obligations of the parties in dispute. No coercive or consequential order is necessarily attached to the declaration, although the judgment may be accompanied by or may serve as the basis for an injunction. Because neither the Supreme Court nor other federal courts may issue advisory opinions, the Court initially wavered in its view of the propriety of declaratory judgments. The Court faced the issue after a number of states adopted laws early in the twentieth century authorizing their courts to issue such judgments. When some cases decided in this way found their way to the Supreme Court, the question of the Court's jurisdiction over them arose. Were they actual "cases and controversies" as required by the Constitution? *(See "Cases and Controversies," pp. 50–54.)* In 1928 the answer seemed to be no, but five years later, in an apparent change of mind, the Court took jurisdiction over a case requesting a declaratory judgment.[109] Congress effectively resolved any remaining doubts with passage of the Federal Declaratory Judgment Act of 1934, specifically authorizing the issuance of such judgments by federal courts in "cases of actual controversy."

The Supreme Court upheld the constitutionality of the Declaratory Judgment Act three years later. By confining the use of declaratory judgments to actual controversies, wrote Chief Justice Charles Evans Hughes, the act simply provided a new procedural remedy for the courts to use in cases already within their jurisdiction.[110] Nevertheless, the line between declaratory judgments and advisory opinions is a thin one. In 1941 the Court wrote,

> The difference between an abstract question and a "controversy" contemplated by the Declaratory Judgment Act is necessarily one of degree, and it would be difficult, if it would be possible, to fashion a precise test for determining in every case whether there is such a controversy. Basically, the question in each case is whether the facts alleged, under all the circumstances, show that there is a substantial controversy, between parties having adverse legal interests, of sufficient immediacy and reality to warrant the issuance of a declaratory judgment.[111]

Although the Court has insisted that "case or controversy" requirements are applied just as strictly to cases seeking declaratory judgments as to other cases, it has hesitated to approve resolution of major constitutional questions through such judgments. In 1961 it refused a doctor's request for a declaratory judgment that Connecticut's law against all contraceptive devices was unconstitutional. Four years later the Court reversed the

doctor's conviction for violating that law and held the statute unconstitutional.[112] "The Declaratory Judgment Act was an authorization, not a command," the Court has stated. "It gave the federal courts competence to make a declaration of rights; it did not impose a duty to do so."[113] Federal courts therefore have broad discretion in deciding whether to grant requests for such judgments. The judgment is available as a remedy in all civil cases except those involving federal taxes, an area Congress excluded in 1935.

Unlike the injunction, a declaratory judgment may be issued even though another adequate remedy for the dispute exists and even though other pending state or federal suits concerning the same matter are pending; the latter circumstance may, however, bring stricter standards into play on the decision whether to grant the judgment. The Supreme Court has tended to limit the use of declaratory judgments, particularly when its use would leave a state law unenforceable. The law barring injunctions against state taxes makes no mention of declaratory judgments, but in 1943 the Court applied the abstention doctrine to preclude use of this remedy in such cases as well.[114] Is a showing of threatened irreparable injury necessary to justify a declaratory judgment against a law under which the person seeking the judgment is being prosecuted or threatened with prosecution? The Court has waffled on this point, but the answer appears to be that such a threat must be demonstrated only if the judgment would disrupt ongoing state proceedings. Otherwise, there is no need to prove such possible injury.

Following the Court's seeming relaxation of the abstention doctrine in cases where injunctions were sought against state laws challenged as violating the First Amendment, the justices appeared to adopt a broader view also of the power of federal judges to issue declaratory judgments against such laws. In a New York case, *Zwickler v. Koota* (1967), the Court ruled that federal judges had a duty to hear constitutional challenges to state laws. "[E]scape from that duty is not permissible," it said, "merely because state courts also have the solemn responsibility" of protecting constitutional rights. The Court held that the abstention doctrine allowed escape from this duty only in special circumstances. Injunctions and declaratory judgments were not twin remedies, ruled the Court: when a plaintiff in a single case

"MILDER MEDICINE"

Declaratory judgments, wrote Justice William J. Brennan Jr. in 1974, were plainly intended by Congress "as an alternative to the strong medicine of the injunction," particularly when the medicine is to be administered to state officials. Justice William H. Rehnquist chimed in, "A declaratory judgment is simply a statement of rights, not a binding order."[1] Earlier, in a 1971 dissenting opinion, Brennan, joined by Justices Byron R. White and Thurgood Marshall, had outlined the differences between these two forms of judicial relief:

> The effects of injunctive and declaratory relief in their impact on the administration of a State's criminal laws are very different.... An injunction barring enforcement of a criminal statute against particular conduct immunizes that conduct from prosecution under the statute. A broad injunction against all enforcement of a statute paralyzes the State's enforcement machinery: the statute is rendered a nullity. A declaratory judgment, on the other hand, is merely a declaration of legal status and rights; it neither mandates nor prohibits state action....
>
> What is clear ... is that even though a declaratory judgment has "the force and effect of a final judgment," ... it is a much milder form of relief than an injunction. Though it may be persuasive, it is not ultimately coercive; non-compliance with it may be inappropriate, but is not contempt.[2]

---

1. *Steffel v. Thompson,* 415 U.S. 452 at 466, 482 (1974).

2. *Perez v. Ledesma,* 401 U.S. 82 at 124, 125–126 (1971).

---

requested both, the factors in favor and against each remedy should be weighed separately by the judge.[115]

Injury Standard

In 1971 the Court made clear that when a declaratory judgment is sought to halt an ongoing state criminal prosecution, only a clear threat of immediate and irreparable injury justified its issuance. The same standard required for an injunction applied, explained Justice Black, because "ordinarily a declaratory judgment will result in precisely the same interference with and disruption of state proceedings that the long-standing policy limiting injunctions was designed to avoid."[116] The Court subsequently held, however, that if prosecution under the state law is not pending against the person seeking the judgment, there need be no demonstration of irreparable injury to justify a declaratory judgment against the law.[117] When there is no ongoing state proceeding that a judgment would disrupt, "considerations of equity, comity, and federalism have little vitality," the Court stated in 1974; therefore, the individual's right to have his federal claim considered in a federal court is paramount.[118] "Requiring the federal courts totally to step aside when no state criminal prosecution is pending against the federal plaintiff would turn federalism on its head," wrote Justice Brennan for a unanimous Court.[119]

The Court also has rejected the argument that for "case or controversy" to exist, there must be pending state prosecution under the challenged law against the person bringing the challenge. Rather, the Court held that so long as a genuine threat of enforcement of such a law exists, there is a case or controversy falling within federal jurisdiction.[120]

THE CONTEMPT POWER

To maintain decorum within the courtroom and to enforce obedience to its orders, courts possess the inherent power to punish persons for contempt. Contempt may be civil or criminal, depending upon the action involved and the purpose of the penalty imposed. A judge may punish individuals summarily for contempt committed in his or her presence. In recent years, however, the Supreme Court has used the due process guarantee to impose procedural restraints on the exercise of this judicial power. The contempt power was reinforced by the Judiciary Act of 1789, which authorized the new federal courts "to punish by fine or imprisonment, at the[ir] discretion ... all contempts of authority in any cause or hearing before the same."

As early as 1821, the Supreme Court urged restraint in the exercise of this power, cautioning courts to use "the least possible power adequate to the end proposed."[121] At least one judge, James H. Peck,

ENFORCEMENT POWERS

Beyond the power of contempt, federal courts have little equipment with which to enforce their rulings. This is particularly true of the Supreme Court. As Justice Samuel F. Miller wrote in 1890,

> [I]n the division of the powers of government between the three great departments, executive, legislative and judicial, the judicial is the weakest for the purposes of self-protection and for the enforcement of the powers which it exercises. The ministerial officers through whom its commands must be executed are marshals of the United States, and belong emphatically to the Executive Department of the government. They are appointed by the President, with the advice and consent of the Senate. They are removable from office at his pleasure. They are subjected by Act of Congress to the supervision and control of the Department of Justice, in the hands of one of the cabinet officers of the President, and their compensation is provided by Acts of Congress. The same may be said of the district attorneys of the United States, who prosecute and defend the claims of the government in the courts.[1]

"The court's only effective power is the power to persuade," wrote Henry J. Abraham, and at times that power has failed. Although the writ of mandamus is available to compel federal officials to carry out some duties, the Court has been reluctant to use it against lower federal court judges,

who have been among the most notable resisters to decisions of the higher court.[2]

Early in the twentieth century, one remarkable case arose in which the Supreme Court exercised the contempt power to punish a person who had deliberately disregarded its order, with tragic consequences. A man named Johnson, sentenced to death by a state court in Tennessee, convinced the Court to hear his challenge to his conviction. In granting his request for review, the Court issued an order staying his execution. Despite that order, Johnson was taken from jail and lynched. Sheriff John F. Shipp, who had custody over Johnson, was charged by the attorney general with conspiring in the death. Shipp was found guilty of contempt of the Supreme Court, a verdict that resulted in a brief imprisonment.[3] The Supreme Court acted in this case through a commissioner appointed to take testimony.[4]

1. *In re Neagle, 135* U.S. 1 at 63 (1890).

2. Henry J. Abraham, *The Judicial Process,* 2nd ed. (New York: Oxford University Press, 1968), 231, 225–231, 338–340; Abraham, *The Judicial Process,* 7th ed. (New York: Oxford University Press, 1998); and Stephen T. Early, *Constitutional Courts of the United States* (Totowa, N.J.: Littlefield, Adams, 1977), 64–69, 156–160.

3. *United States v. Shipp,* 203 U.S. 563 (1906).

4. Henry M. Hart Jr. and Herbert Wechsler, *The Federal Courts and the Federal System* (Brooklyn, N.Y.: Foundation Press, 1953), 421.

disregarded this advice, and in 1830 was impeached for using the contempt power to disbar and imprison a man who had published an article criticizing one of his opinions. Peck was acquitted, but the event resulted in an 1831 statute limiting the use of the contempt power to punishing, by fine or imprisonment, three types of offenses: "the misbehavior of any person in their presence, or so near thereto as to obstruct the administration of justice, the misbehavior of any of the officers of said courts in their official transactions, and the disobedience or resistance by any such officer, or by any party, juror, witness, or other person, to any lawful writ, process, order, rule, decree, or command of the said courts." With the decision in *Ex parte Robinson* (1874), the Court upheld the limitations imposed upon the use of the contempt power by the 1831 law. In doing so, it reversed the disbarment of an attorney

found to be guilty of contempt of court for actions outside the presence of the judge. The Court held that the 1831 law limited not only the types of misconduct punishable as contempt but also the penalties that might be imposed. Disbarment was not among them.[122]

Contumacious Conduct

The essential characteristic of contempt is obstructiveness, blocking the proper judicial functions of the court. Little question has been raised about judicial power to maintain peace within the courtroom through the use of the contempt power. As the Court declared in 1888,

> it is a settled doctrine . . . that for direct contempts committed in the face of the court . . . the offender may, in its discretion, be instantly apprehended and immediately imprisoned, without trial or issue, and without other proof than its actual knowledge of

what occurred; . . . such power, although arbitrary in its nature and liable to abuse, is absolutely essential to the protection of the courts in the discharge of their functions. Without it, judicial tribunals would be at the mercy of the disorderly and the violent, who respect neither the laws . . . nor the officers charged with the duty of administering them.[123]

In 1970 the Supreme Court affirmed the power of a judge to keep peace in his courtroom, even at the cost of having a defendant bound and gagged or physically removed from the room.[124] Direct disobedience of a court order is perhaps the most frequent conduct outside the courtroom penalized as contempt. Affirming the contempt conviction of labor leader Eugene V. Debs for such disobedience in 1895, the Court wrote,

The power of a court to make an order carries with it the equal power to punish for a disobedience of that order, and the inquiry as to the question of disobedience has been, from time immemorial, the special function of the court.[125]

Willful disregard of a court order may be both civil and criminal contempt, the Court has ruled.[126]

"The Vicinity of the Court"

The Supreme Court has generally viewed the 1831 act as allowing use of the contempt power only to punish conduct actually impeding a trial or other judicial proceeding. In the early 1900s, however, the Court strayed from its usual practice. In *Toledo Newspaper Co. v. United States* (1918) the Court, 5-2, upheld a contempt citation against a newspaper for publishing articles and cartoons about a railway rate dispute pending in court. The judge viewed the articles as an attempt to provoke public resistance to his eventual order and to intimidate him. For the first time, the Court approved the use of the contempt power to punish conduct simply intended to obstruct the courts in carrying out their duty.[127]

Two decades later the Court reversed this ruling and returned to the strict construction of the contempt power as defined by the 1831 law. In *Nye v. United States* (1941) the Court reversed the contempt convictions of persons who had successfully used liquor and other methods of persuasion—miles from the courtroom—to convince a

plaintiff to drop his case. These actions were reprehensible, stated the Court, but were punishable under other laws. The phrase used in the 1831 law—allowing courts to punish misconduct "in their presence or so near thereto as to obstruct the administration of justice"—meant that the conduct should be geographically near the courtroom or it should not be punished as contempt, held the Court. The conduct in this case, although it did obstruct justice, "was not misbehavior in the vicinity of the court disrupting to quiet and order or actually interrupting the court in the conduct of its business."[128]

The Obstinate Witness

The Fifth Amendment guarantees witnesses before courts or grand juries the right to refuse to incriminate themselves, but no other privilege allows persons simply to refuse to answer proper questions addressed to them in those forums. Furthermore, once a witness is granted immunity from prosecution for crimes revealed by his or her testimony, the privilege of silence ends altogether. False testimony is prosecutable as perjury, even if given by an immunized witness. In *Ex parte Hudgings* (1919) the Supreme Court held that a witness committing perjury should not be held in contempt as a penalty for his false testimony unless the perjury was clearly an obstructive tactic. "[I]n order to punish perjury as a contempt," wrote Chief Justice Edward D. White for the Court, "there must be added to the essential elements of perjury . . . under the general law the further element of obstruction to the court in the performance of its duty."[129]

The Court has, however, backed the use of the contempt power to punish obstinate witnesses who simply refused, for reasons other than self-incrimination, to respond to certain questions. In 1958 Justice Felix Frankfurter commented,

Whatever differences the potentially drastic power of courts to punish for contempt may have evoked, a doubt has never been uttered that stubborn disobedience of the duty to answer relevant inquiries in a judicial proceeding brings into force the power of the federal courts to punish for contempt.[130]

In *United States v. Wilson* (1975) the Court upheld the use of the summary contempt power to punish an immunized trial witness who persisted in his refusal to respond to questions. Such "intentional obstructions of court proceedings," held the Court, could destroy a prosecution. "In an ongoing trial with the judge, jurors, counsel, and witnesses all waiting," wrote Chief Justice Warren Burger, the summary contempt power is "an appropriate remedial tool to discourage witnesses from contumacious refusals to comply with lawful orders essential to prevent a breakdown of the proceedings."[131] Although grand jury witnesses who refuse to answer questions despite a grant of immunity may be cited for contempt, such punishment cannot be summary; it may be imposed only after a hearing at which the accused witness is allowed to defend himself against the charge. This holding, from *Harris v. United States* (1965), overruled the decision in *Brown v. United States* (1959) allowing summary punishment of grand jury witnesses in this situation.[132]

Attorneys and Fugitives

Lawyers—as officers of the court—have received their share of contempt citations. In 1952 the Supreme Court upheld the contempt citations and convictions of the defense attorneys for eleven Communist Party leaders convicted of violating the Smith Act. Lower court judges reviewing the attorneys' actions during the trial described their conduct as "wilfully obstructive," "abominable," and "outrageous, . . . conduct of a kind which no lawyer owes his client, which cannot ever be justified."[133] *(See details of Sacher v. United States, p. 47.)* The Court continues to insist, however, that the element of obstruction be clear before a contempt conviction can be properly imposed. In 1962 the Court reversed the contempt conviction of an attorney penalized simply for asserting his right to ask questions until he was stopped by a court official.[134] The Court also has upheld the use of the contempt power of federal judges to punish—by additional prison terms—persons convicted of a crime who have absconded and were fugitives from justice for a period of years before surrendering to serve the sentences for those crimes.[135]

Civil and Criminal Contempt

Contempt may be civil or criminal in nature. As the justices have had many occasions to acknowledge, it is

United Mine Workers of America and its president, John L. Lewis *(above)*, were convicted of contempt for disobeying a court order forbidding a strike. The Supreme Court upheld the conviction in *United States v. United Mine Workers* (1947).

sometimes difficult to distinguish between the two. The test developed by the Court—and used consistently since 1911—focuses upon the character and purpose of the penalty imposed. In *Gompers v. Buck's Stove and Range Co.* (1911) the Court declared that if the penalty "is for civil contempt the punishment is remedial, and for the benefit of the complainant [generally the other party to a case]. But if it is for criminal contempt the sentence is punitive, to vindicate the authority of the court."[136] Justice Joseph R. Lamar continued:

> [I]mprisonment for civil contempt is ordered where the defendant has refused to do an affirmative act required by the provisions of an order. . . . Imprisonment in such cases . . . is intended to be remedial by coercing the defendant to do what he had refused to do. . . .
>
> For example, if a defendant should refuse to pay alimony . . . he could be committed until he complied with

THE COURT: SUPERVISOR OF FEDERAL COURTS, THE FEDERAL BAR, AND FEDERAL PROCEDURE

By virtue of its position at the apex of the nation's judiciary, the Supreme Court exerts broad supervisory power over the administration of justice in the federal courts. This responsibility is multifaceted. Among its elements are the Court's power to review the functioning of the lower courts, to propose rules of procedure governing processes in the federal courts, and to oversee the admission, conduct, and expulsion of members of the federal bar.

All federal courts have an inherent power to supervise their officers, the conduct of litigants, witnesses, attorneys, and jurors, and to protect property within their custody.[1] To help them resolve certain issues, the Supreme Court and other federal courts are empowered to appoint persons of special skills. For example, the Supreme Court may appoint special masters to hear evidence and recommend judgment in original cases involving complex factual matters, such as boundary locations. The rationale for the use of special personnel was set out by Justice Louis D. Brandeis in 1920:

> Courts have (at least in the absence of legislation to the contrary) inherent power to provide themselves with appropriate instruments required for the performance of their duties … [including] authority to appoint persons unconnected with the court to aid judges in the performance of specific judicial duties, as they may arise.[2]

GENERAL SUPERVISION

The Court's general supervisory power over lower federal courts is exercised randomly and sporadically through its decisions reviewing their actions, approving some and rebuking others. The Court at times has taken the opportunity to go beyond the decision required to resolve a particular dispute and prescribed or clarified rules of procedure. An example of this mode of supervisory power is the Court's decision in *Cheff v. Schnackenberg* (1966).[3] While upholding the lower court's refusal of a jury trial to the plaintiff in that case, the Court ruled, in its supervisory role, that anyone sentenced by a federal judge to more than six months in prison for contempt should be given a jury trial.

Several years earlier, in 1958, the Court had exercised its supervisory power to reduce a contempt sentence, after the sentencing court had ignored the justices' recommendation that a reduction was necessary.[4] "The Supreme Court's review power," wrote one student of the judicial system, "is probably its most extensively used method for instructing the lower courts in the constitutional or statutory law and procedural niceties they are to apply. Processes of appeal and reversal are parts—most important parts—of the internal control mechanism of the constitutional court system."[5] "Judicial supervision of the administration of criminal justice in the federal courts," wrote Justice Felix Frankfurter in 1943, "implies the duty of establishing and maintaining civilized standards of procedure and evidence."[6] Frankfurter indicated his belief that such standards might be considerably stiffer than those required by the Constitution itself.

RULE-MAKING POWER

The Judiciary Act of 1789 authorized all federal courts to make rules for the orderly conduct of their business. In addition, Congress has enacted "process acts" to specify certain forms and procedures for use in the federal courts.[7] In 1825 the Supreme Court sustained the power of Congress to make procedural rules for the federal courts and to delegate considerable responsibility for drafting such rules to the courts themselves.[8] The Court in the ensuing century set out various rules applying to different types of lawsuits, but not until the 1930s was there a uniform set of rules governing procedures in all federal courts.[9]

In 1933 Congress authorized the Supreme Court to propose rules governing postverdict proceedings in all federal criminal cases. The following year it granted similar authority to the Court to propose rules of civil procedure, subject to veto by Congress. In 1940 Congress gave the Court authority to propose rules governing criminal case procedures prior to a verdict. Using advisory committees of distinguished attorneys and legal scholars and judges, the Supreme Court proposed, and Congress approved, the Federal Rules of Civil Procedure, which took effect in 1938, and the Federal Rules of Criminal Procedure, which took effect in 1946. Both have been subsequently amended through this same process of committee drafting, Supreme Court recommendation, and congressional examination and approval.[10]

the order. Unless there were special elements of contumacy, the refusal to pay . . . is treated as being rather in resistance to the opposite party than in contempt of the court.[137]

Citing the often-quoted statement that a person imprisoned for civil contempt carries the keys of the prison in his pocket, Justice Lamar pointed out that such a person "can end the sentence and discharge himself at any moment by doing what he had previously refused to do."[138] Criminal contempt, on the other hand, results when

> the defendant does that which he has been commanded not to do, the disobedience is a thing

OVERSEEING THE BAR

It is well settled, declared Chief Justice Roger B. Taney in 1857, "that it rests exclusively with the court to determine who is qualified to become one of its officers, as an attorney and a counselor, and for what cause he ought to be removed. That power, however, is not an arbitrary and despotic one, to be exercised at the pleasure of the court, or from passion, prejudice, or personal hostility; but it is the duty of the court to exercise and regulate it by a sound and just judicial discretion, whereby the rights and independence of the bar may be as scrupulously guarded and maintained by the court, as the rights and dignity of the court itself."[11]

Ten years later the Court invalidated an act of Congress imposing a test oath requirement upon all attorneys wishing to practice before federal courts. Congress may set statutory qualifications for admission to the bar, the Court held in *Ex parte Garland* (1867), but those qualifications are subject to judicial review and disallowance. Writing for the majority, Justice Stephen Field elaborated upon the federal courts' responsibility for admission to the bar:

> The order of admission is the judgment of the court that the parties possess the requisite qualifications as attorneys and counselors, and are entitled to appear as such and conduct causes therein. From its entry the parties become officers of the court, and are responsible to it for professional misconduct. They hold their office only during good behavior and can only be deprived of it for misconduct ascertained and declared by the judgment of the court after opportunity to be heard has been afforded.... Their admission or their exclusion is not the exercise of a mere ministerial power. It is the exercise of judicial power....
>
> The attorney and counselor being, by the solemn judicial act of the court, clothed with his office, does not hold it as a matter of grace and favor. The right which it confers upon him to appear for suitors, and to argue causes, is something more than a mere indulgence, revocable at the pleasure of the court, or at the command of the Legislature. It is a right of which he can only be deprived by the judgment of the court, for moral or professional delinquency.[12]

In modern times the Court has ruled on questions of state bar qualifications and disqualifications. It has held that alienage alone is insufficient reason to deny someone admission to a state bar, but has allowed state bar officials to exclude conscientious objectors and individuals refusing to answer questions concerning possible membership in the Communist Party.[13] Delving into First Amendment issues in recent years, the Court has held that lawyers may be prohibited from making extrajudicial statements to the press that present a "substantial likelihood of materially prejudicing a trial."[14] The Court also has upheld a bar rule preventing lawyers from sending letters of solicitation to accident victims and their relatives for thirty days after an incident.[15]

1. Congressional Research Service, *The Constitution of the United States of America: Analysis and Interpretation* (Washington, D.C.: U.S. Government Printing Office, 1973), 583–584.

2. *Ex parte Peterson*, 253 U.S. 300 at 312 (1920).

3. *Cheff v. Schnackenberg*, 384 U.S. 373 at 380 (1966).

4. *Yates v. United States*, 356 U.S. 363 at 366 (1958).

5. Stephen T. Early Jr., *Constitutional Courts of the United States* (Totowa, N.J.: Littlefield, Adams, 1977), 149; see also 149–156.

6. *McNabb v. United States*, 318 U.S. 332 at 340 (1943).

7. Julius Goebel Jr., *History of the Supreme Court of the United States*, vol. 1, *Antecedents and Beginnings to 1801* (New York: MacMillan Publishing, 1971), 509–551.

8. *Wayman v. Southard*, 10 Wheat. (23 U.S.) 1 (1825).

9. Henry M. Hart Jr. and Herbert Wechsler, *The Federal Courts and the Federal System* (Brooklyn, N.Y.: Foundation Press, 1953), 577–611.

10. Charles Alan Wright, *Law of Federal Courts*, 4th ed. (St. Paul, Minn.: West Publishing, 1983), 402–403.

11. *Ex parte Secombe*, 19 How. (60 U.S.) 9 at 13 (1857).

12. *Ex parte Garland*, 4 Wall. (71 U.S.) 333 at 378–379 (1867); see also *Ex parte Robinson*, 19 Wall. (86 U.S.) 505 (1874).

13. *In re Griffiths*, 413 U.S. 717 (1973); *Konigsberg v. California*, 366 U.S. 36 (1961) and 353 U.S. 252 (1957); *In re Summers*, 325 U.S. 561 (1945).

14. *Gentile v. State Bar of Nevada*, 501 U.S. 1030 (1991).

15. *Florida Bar v. Went for It Inc.*, 515 U.S. 618 (1995).

accomplished. Imprisonment cannot undo or remedy what has been done, nor afford any compensation for the pecuniary injury caused by the disobedience. If the sentence is limited to imprisonment for a definite period, the defendant . . . cannot shorten the term by promising not to repeat the offense. Such imprisonment operates . . . solely as punishment.[139]

Summarizing the test, one can say that civil contempt consists of the refusal to act as the court commands, a disobedience punished by imprisonment until the person obeys. Criminal contempt consists of doing the forbidden and being punished for a definite term.

"THE LEAST POSSIBLE POWER"

The Court has cautioned judges against using the power of contempt to threaten individual lawmakers with personal fines for failing to take action. In a long-running battle over housing segregation in Yonkers, N.Y., the justices drew a distinction in 1990 between fining the city for not acting and fining city council members for not voting for action.

In a 5-4 vote, the Court held that a federal district judge had abused his power when he imposed contempt fines on a city's elected officials who failed to put in place a court-ordered plan to desegregate housing in the city. The Court said that the fines levied against the individual officials were not a proper exercise of judicial power. Upholding the much larger fines against the city, totaling more than $800,000, the Court said that the lower court should have waited a reasonable time to see if

that fine was sufficient to win compliance with the judge's order before levying the fines against the individual officials.

Chief Justice William H. Rehnquist acknowledged that stiff monetary penalties were sometimes necessary to enforce court orders. Fining officials charged with making laws, however, is an extreme step because it "effects a much greater perversion of the normal legislative process than does the imposition of fines on the city." He continued, stating that fining legislators "is designed to cause them to vote, not with a view to the interest of their constituents or of the city, but with a view solely to their own personal interests."[1]

---

1. *Spallone v. United States, Chema v. United States, Longo v. United States,* 493 U.S. 265 at 279, 280 (1990).

In 1925 the Supreme Court reinforced the distinction between civil and criminal contempt, ruling that the president's power of pardon extended to allow pardons of persons convicted of criminal (but not of civil) contempt.[140] In 1947 the Court muddied somewhat the distinction between civil and criminal contempt by ruling that the same action could be both—and by upholding the conviction of the United Mine Workers of America and its president, John L. Lewis, on both types of contempt as a result of his and the union's disobedience of a court order forbidding a strike. "Common sense," wrote Chief Justice Fred M. Vinson, "would recognize that conduct can amount to both civil and criminal contempt. The same acts may justify a court in resorting to coercive and to punitive measures."[141] The distinction was, however, reiterated in a section of the decision.

Lewis and the union argued that the order they had disobeyed was invalid, a violation of statutory restrictions on the use of injunctions in labor disputes. *(See box, "Government by Injunction," p. 34.)* The Supreme Court found the injunction valid but declared that even if it had been illegally issued, it was to be obeyed—on pain of contempt—until it was reversed "by orderly and proper proceedings." If the injunction had been found invalid, Vinson explained, the civil

contempt citation would be set aside because any duty to obey the order had vanished. The criminal contempt conviction—punishment for disobedience to an outstanding and unreversed court order—would, however, remain in effect.[142]

The Court in 1966 ruled that individuals imprisoned for contempt, after refusing to answer grand jury questions despite a grant of immunity, were being penalized for civil contempt. Whether the contempt is civil or criminal depends on the character of the disobedience and the purpose of the penalty. Such disobedience, wrote Justice Tom Clark, would be in refusing to do what the court ordered, and the punishment would be "for the obvious purpose of compelling the witnesses to obey the orders to testify," and whenever they did so, they would be released.[143] In *United Mine Workers v. Bagwell* (1994) the Court unanimously rejected a $52 million contempt-of-court fine imposed on the union, ruling that the penalty was too serious to be applied without a jury trial.[144] A state judge in Virginia had imposed the fine after finding United Mine Workers in contempt of court for violating an injunction intended to prevent violence in a 1989 coal strike. The Virginia Supreme Court said the fine was a proper sanction for civil contempt because it was intended to force compliance with the injunction, not to punish the union. The U.S. Supreme Court disagreed, ruling that the fine could not be regarded as a civil penalty because it was not intended to compensate a private party, the alleged contempt did not occur in the judge's presence, and the conduct involved a broad range of activities instead of a single, discrete act.

A Summary Power

"A contempt proceeding," stated the Court in 1904, "is *sui generis*"—a unique type of judicial process.[145] One aspect of this uniqueness is the fact that contempt has traditionally been a summary power. That is, a judge could, on the spot, hold someone in contempt and impose punishment without a trial before a jury or many of the other procedural safeguards guaranteed by the Bill of Rights. The summary nature of this power is directly related to its original purpose—to enable a judge to maintain order in the courtroom. As the Supreme Court, quoting a lower court, wrote in an 1888 ruling:

> The judicial eye witnessed the act and the judicial mind comprehended all the circumstances of aggravation, provocation or mitigation; and the fact being thus judicially established, it only remained for the judicial arm to inflict proper punishment.[146]

A few years later, in 1895, in upholding the use of the contempt power to punish disobedience of a court order, the Court rejected the suggestion that a person charged with contempt of the orders of one court or one judge should be sentenced by another judge. "To submit the question of disobedience to another tribunal, be it a jury or another court, would operate to deprive the proceedings of half its efficiency," stated the Court.[147]

An Unbiased Judge

By the 1920s the Court had begun to apply some of the elements of the due process guarantee to contempt proceedings. The Court recommended that when a judge became so personally involved with an allegedly contemptuous course of behavior that he lacked the necessary neutrality to be fair in imposing a sentence, he should turn the matter over to a colleague. In *Cooke*

v. United States (1925) Chief Justice William Howard Taft wrote for the majority,

> [W]here conditions do not make it impracticable, or where the delay may not injure public or private right, a judge called upon to act in a case of contempt by personal attack upon him, may, without flinching from his duty properly ask that one of his fellow judges take his place.[148]

Nevertheless, the Court continued to defer to the discretion of the trial judge in most situations. The most notable example of this judicial deference came in *Sacher v. United States* (1952), when the Court upheld as proper the criminal contempt citations imposed by federal judge Harold Medina upon the attorneys who had, during a long and controversial trial before him, defended eleven men accused of violating the Smith Act in their roles as leaders of the U.S. Communist Party. Noting that Medina waited until after the trial to cite and sentence them for contempt, the attorneys challenged the summary nature of the contempt proceedings and argued that Medina should have referred the contempt charges to another judge for hearing and sentencing. Justice Robert H. Jackson set out the reasoning behind the decision to uphold Medina's actions:

> It is almost inevitable that any contempt of a court committed in the presence of the judge during a trial will be an offense against his dignity and authority. At a trial the court is so much the judge and the judge so much the court that the two terms are used interchangeably. . . . It cannot be that summary punishment is only for such minor contempts as leave the judge indifferent and may be evaded by adding hectoring, abusive and defiant conduct toward the judge as an individual. Such an interpretation would nullify, in practice, the power it purports to grant.[149]

Just two years later, in a less highly publicized case, *Offutt v. United States* (1954), the Court held that a judge who had become involved in a wrangle with a defense attorney presenting a case before him should have sent contempt charges against that attorney to another judge for resolution. Justice Felix Frankfurter, who had dissented from the ruling upholding Medina's actions, wrote for the Court:

The pith of this rather extraordinary power to punish without the formalities required by the Bill of Rights for the prosecution of federal crimes generally, is that the necessities of the administration of justice require such summary dealing with obstructions to it. It is a mode of vindicating the majesty of law, in its active manifestation, against obstruction and outrage. The power thus entrusted to a judge is wholly unrelated to his personal sensibilities, be they tender or rugged. But judges also are human, and may . . . quite unwittingly identify offense to self with obstruction to law. Accordingly, this Court has deemed it important that district judges guard against this easy confusion by not sitting themselves in judgment upon misconduct of counsel where the contempt charged is entangled with the judge's personal feeling against the lawyer.[150]

A unanimous Court reaffirmed this holding in 1971.[151]

The Right to Trial

As early as the nineteenth century, the Supreme Court had begun to place some limits on the summary nature of the contempt power, requiring the use of normal adversary procedures to deal with contempts occurring out of the presence of the court. In 1946 new rules of federal criminal procedure allowed summary punishment only of conduct seen or heard by the judge and "committed in the actual presence of the court." All other criminal contempt was to be prosecuted separately, after notice, with a hearing at which a defense to the charge could be presented and opportunity for release on bail. Furthermore, the rule stated that if the contempt involved "disrespect to or criticism of a judge, that judge is disqualified from presiding at the trial or hearing except with the defendant's consent."

This was not a sudden change. The Court had taken the opportunity in earlier cases to state that the presumption of innocence applied in criminal contempt cases, that guilt must be proven beyond a reasonable doubt, that a person charged with contempt could not be compelled to be a witness against himself, and that persons accused of contempt other than that occurring in open court should be advised of the charges and should have an opportunity to present a defense against them with the aid of counsel and to call witnesses.[152] In a long

and unbroken line of cases, however, the Court had insisted that persons charged with contempt did not generally have the right to a trial by jury (the exception being such cases as those in which Congress by law provided that right).[153] The Sixth Amendment states that "in all criminal prosecutions the accused shall enjoy the right to a speedy and public trial, by an impartial jury." The Court's position was simply that criminal contempt was not a crime in the sense of this amendment and its guarantee therefore did not apply. Citing a steady stream of precedents, the Court in 1958, 1960, and 1964 reaffirmed that there was no constitutional right to a jury trial for persons charged with contempt.[154] Then, almost in passing, the Court in 1966 announced that federal courts could not sentence persons to more than six months in prison for criminal contempt unless they had been tried by a jury or had waived their right to such a trial.[155]

The Court's turnabout came in the case of Paul Cheff, who did not benefit because his contempt sentence was for six months. The Court did not base its statement imposing the jury trial requirement upon a constitutional basis but upon its power to supervise the conduct of lower federal courts. (See box, The Court: Supervisor of Federal Courts, the Federal Bar, and Federal Procedure, pp. 44–45.) Two years later, however, the Court placed the requirement of a jury trial for serious criminal contempt charges upon a constitutional basis. On the same day that it extended the Sixth Amendment right to a jury trial to state proceedings in Duncan v. Louisiana (1968), the Court ruled that state courts, like federal ones, must accord the right to a jury trial to persons charged with serious criminal contempts.[156] Writing for the seven-justice majority in Bloom v. Illinois (1968), Justice Byron R. White explained:

> Our deliberations have convinced us . . . that serious criminal contempts are so nearly like other serious crimes that they are subject to the jury trial provisions of the Constitution, now binding on the states. . . .
>
> Criminal contempt is a crime in the ordinary sense; it is a violation of the law, a public wrong which is punishable by fine or imprisonment or both. . . .
>
> Indeed, in contempt cases an even more compelling argument can be made for providing a right to jury trial as a protection against the arbitrary

exercise of official power. Contemptuous conduct, though a public wrong, often strikes at the most vulnerable and human qualities of a judge's temperament. Even when the contempt is not a direct insult to the court or the judge, it frequently represents a rejection of judicial authority, or an interference with the judicial process or with the duties of officers of the court.[157]

White cited the Court's 1895 statement in *In re Debs* that contempt proceedings would be less efficient if they were conducted before a court other than that which was the object of the contempt. The modern Court, he wrote, disagreed:

> In our judgment, when serious punishment for contempt is contemplated, rejecting a demand for jury trial cannot be squared with the Constitution or justified by considerations of efficiency or the desirability of vindicating the authority of the court. . . . Perhaps to some extent we sacrifice efficiency, expedition, and

economy, but the choice in favor of jury trial has been made, and retained, in the Constitution.[158]

Six years later, in 1974, a more closely divided Court, 5-4, affirmed this extension of the right to a jury trial in contempt cases. Due process, the Court held in 1974, required that persons whose aggregate criminal contempt sentences were more than six months should have a jury trial on the contempt charges against them.[159]

In 1996, however, the Court ruled that no right exists to a jury trial when a defendant is prosecuted for multiple "petty" offenses, even if the aggregate sentence might exceed six months in prison. The Court distinguished the decision from its 1974 ruling, saying that in the earlier dispute it was not clear whether the legislature considered the offense—criminal contempt—petty or serious because it did not set a specific penalty. In the new case, however, Congress had established a six-month maximum penalty for the crime—obstructing the mail—placing the offense in the "petty" category.[160]

★

Judicial Restraint

The Supreme Court constantly faces a dilemma that is apparent in its very name. It is supreme in the field of law, standing at the pinnacle of the U.S. legal system, but it is also a court. Its members are not elected by the people and therefore cannot claim the ultimate decision-making power in a democracy. Nevertheless, nearly every governmental dispute can be characterized as a legal or constitutional matter: Does this particular government agency have the power to do what it is doing, or is it instead violating individual rights or those of another institution? Because the Court's legal power could in theory become boundless, the Court has seen the need to establish rules and doctrines that limit its authority. As one scholar notes, "[N]early all of the specific limitations which are said to govern the exercise of judicial review have been announced by the Supreme Court itself."[1]

The rules, principles, and doctrines that comprise this posture of restraint have evolved as the Court has said yes to accepting some cases but no to others. They usually develop from "threshold questions"—the seemingly technical issues that the Court must resolve before moving on to the merits, or the substance, of the controversy—and the elements of restraint are overlapping: evaluating the "case or controversy" requirement, determining whether to issue an advisory opinion, possible "mootness," deciding to accept "friendly" suits and test cases, determining "standing to sue," assessing precedent and *stare decisis,* determining whether an issue is a "political question," and comity.

Even during "activist" periods in Supreme Court history the rules have rarely changed. Only their application has varied. Justices often differ on whether a case is moot, whether a litigant has standing, or whether a question is "political," but few have advocated discarding any of those standards. Justice Louis D. Brandeis, in his concurring opinion in *Ashwander v. Tennessee Valley Authority* (1936), set out some of the rules in a classic exposition of judicial restraint. In deciding whether to take on cases involving constitutional questions, the Court would adhere to what became known as the "Brandeis rules":

- It would not consider the constitutionality of legislation in friendly, nonadversary cases.
- It would not decide any constitutional question before a decision on such matter was necessary.
- It would not set out any constitutional rule broader than warranted by the facts in the particular case before it.
- It would resolve a dispute on a nonconstitutional basis rather than a constitutional basis, if possible.
- It would not consider a challenge to a law's validity brought by someone who fails to demonstrate that he has been injured by the law or by someone who had benefited from the law.
- When an act of Congress was challenged as invalid, the Court would be certain there was no possible interpretation under which the law would be found constitutional before striking it down as unconstitutional.[2] *(See box, Justice Brandeis and Rules of Restraint, p. 52.)*

These rules, as Chief Justice Earl Warren and others have taken pains to point out, are neither absolute nor purely constitutional. In them, the Court has blended political reality, policy considerations, and constitutional elements into a posture of judicial restraint, which the Court applies as it wishes from case to case. Therefore, it is quite possible to find major decisions of the Court that count as exceptions to every one of Brandeis's rules as well as to other rules he did not mention.

CASES AND CONTROVERSIES

The single most basic restriction on the work of the federal courts is the requirement that they decide only cases or controversies. Article III, section 2, states that federal judicial power extends to certain types of "cases" and certain "controversies." As interpreted by the Supreme Court, those words limit the power of federal courts to resolving disputes between adversarial parties whose legal rights and interests are truly in collision, for which federal courts may have a remedy. A controversy, Chief Justice Charles Evans Hughes once explained,

> must be definite and concrete, touching the legal relations of parties having adverse legal interests. . . . It must be a real and substantial controversy admitting of specific relief through a decree of a conclusive character, as distinguished from an opinion advising what the law would be upon a hypothetical state of facts.[3]

In the words of Justice Felix Frankfurter, real cases and controversies have "that clear concreteness provided when a question emerges precisely framed and necessary for decision from a clash of adversary argument exploring every aspect of a multifaced situation embracing conflicting and demanding interests."[4] A more modern term to describe a case or controversy properly before the court is "justiciable." Chief Justice Warren in 1968 described this concept and its link to the "case or controversy" doctrine. *(See box, The Tip of an Iceberg, p. 53.)*

Advisory Opinions

One of the earliest corollaries developed by the Court from the Constitution's use of "case" and "controversy" was its firm decision that neither it nor lower federal courts would give advisory opinions. That is, it would not give advice on abstract issues or hypothetical situations. In 1793 the justices politely refused to answer a set of questions submitted to them by Secretary of State Thomas Jefferson (on behalf of President George Washington) concerning neutrality and the Court's interpretation of several major treaties with Britain and France.[5] The Court indicated in correspondence that it found the issuance of advisory opinions contrary to the basic separation of powers and functions in the federal government.

More than a century later, the Court reaffirmed this stance with its decision in *Muskrat v. United States* (1911).[6] Congress, desiring to determine the constitutionality of certain laws it had passed concerning Native American lands, authorized certain Indians to sue the United States to obtain a Supreme Court ruling on the question. When the case reached the Court in 1911, the justices dismissed it as outside the Court's power because no actual dispute existed: all parties to the case were in reality working together to ascertain the constitutionality of the law, not to resolve any actual conflict between legal rights or concrete interests. Justice William R. Day wrote for the Court that a judgment in such a case would be "no more than an expression of opinion upon the validity of the acts in question." That was not the function of the Supreme Court.[7] When the use of declaratory judgments by lower courts began a few years later, one of the main questions raised by this remedy was whether it was appropriate for use by federal courts, given the case or controversy requirement of federal jurisdiction. *(See "Declaratory Judgments," pp. 38–40.)*

Mootness

Another corollary of judicial restraint is the rule that the Court will not decide a case when circumstances are sufficiently altered by time or events to remove the dispute or conflict of interests. Such cases are then dead, or "moot." For purposes of federal jurisdiction, they no longer exist. There is nothing left for the Court to resolve; a judgment would have no effect beyond a mere expression of opinion. The Court has long defined its function as "to decide actual controversies by a judgment which can be carried into effect, and not to give opinions upon moot questions or abstract propositions, or to declare principles or rules of law which cannot affect the matter in issue in the case before it."[8]

In 1974 Marco DeFunis came to the Court charging that he had been denied admission to a state university law school in order that his place in the class might be given, under an affirmative action program,

JUSTICE BRANDEIS AND RULES OF RESTRAINT

In a concurring opinion in *Ashwander v. Tennessee Valley Authority* (1936), Justice Louis D. Brandeis delineated a set of Court-formulated rules useful in avoiding constitutional decisions. The portion of his opinion setting forth those rules follows:

The Court developed, for its own governance in the cases confessedly within its jurisdiction, a series of rules under which it has avoided passing upon a large part of all the constitutional questions pressed upon it for decision. They are:

1. The Court will not pass upon the constitutionality of legislation in a friendly, non-adversary, proceeding, declining because to decide such questions "is legitimate only in the last resort, and as a necessity in the determination of real, earnest and vital controversy between individuals. It never was the thought that, by means of a friendly suit, a party beaten in the legislature could transfer to the courts an inquiry as to the constitutionality of the legislative act." *Chicago & Grand Trunk Ry v. Wellman,* 143 U.S. 339, 345. Compare *Lord v. Veazie,* 8 How. 251; *Atherton Mills v. Johnston,* 259 U.S. 13, 15.

2. The Court will not "anticipate a question of constitutional law in advance of the necessity of deciding it." *Liverpool, N.Y. & P.S.S. Co. v. Emigration Commissioners,* 113 U.S. 33, 39;[1] *Abrams v. Van Schaick,* 293 U.S. 188; *Wilshire Oil Co. v. United States,* 295 U.S. 100. "It is not the habit of the Court to decide questions of a constitutional nature unless absolutely necessary to a decision of the case." *Burton v. United States,* 196 U.S. 283, 295.

3. The Court will not "formulate a rule of constitutional law broader than is required by the precise facts to which it is to be applied." *Liverpool, N.Y. & P.S.S. Co. v. Emigration Commissioners, supra.* Compare *Hammond v. Schappi Bus Line,* 275 U.S. 164, 169–172.

4. The Court will not pass upon a constitutional question although properly presented by the record, if there is also present some other ground upon which the case may be disposed of. This rule has found most varied application. Thus, if a case can be decided on either of two grounds, one involving a constitutional question, the other a question of statutory construction or general law, the Court will decide only the latter. *Siler v. Louisville & Nashville R. Co.,* 213 U.S. 175, 191; *Light v. United States,* 220 U.S. 523, 538. Appeals from the highest court of a state challenging its decision of a question under the Federal Constitution are frequently dismissed because the judgment can be sustained on an independent state ground. *Berea College v. Kentucky,* 211 U.S. 45, 53.

5. The Court will not pass upon the validity of a statute upon complaint of one who fails to show that he is injured by its operation.[2] *Tyler v. The Judges,* 179 U.S. 405; *Hendrick v. Maryland,* 235 U.S. 610, 621. Among the many applications of this rule, none is more striking than the denial of the right of challenge to one who lacks a personal or property right. Thus, the challenge by a public official interested only in the performance of his official duty will not be entertained. *Columbus & Greenville Ry. v. Miller,* 283 U.S. 96, 99–100. In *Fairchild v. Hughes,* 258 U.S. 126, the Court affirmed the dismissal of a suit brought by a citizen who sought to have the Nineteenth Amendment declared unconstitutional. In *Massachusetts v. Mellon,* 262 U.S. 447, the challenge of the federal Maternity Act was not entertained although made by the Commonwealth on behalf of all its citizens.

6. The Court will not pass upon the constitutionality of a statute at the instance of one who has availed himself of its benefits.[3] *Great Falls Mfg. Co. v. Attorney General,* 124 U.S. 581; *Wall v. Parrot Silver & Copper Co.,* 244 U.S. 407, 411–412; *St. Louis Malleable Casting Co. v. Prendergast Construction Co.,* 260 U.S. 469.

7. "When the validity of an act of the Congress is drawn in question, and even if a serious doubt of constitutionality is raised, it is a cardinal principle that this Court will first ascertain whether a construction of the statute is fairly possible by which the question may be avoided." *Crowell v. Benson,* 285 U.S. 22, 62.[4]

---

1. E.g., *Ex parte Randolph,* 20 Fed. Cas. No. 11,558, pp. 242, 254; *Charles River Bridge v. Warren Bridge,* 11 Pet. 420, 553; *Trademark Cases,* 100 U.S. 82, 96; *Arizona v. California,* 283 U.S. 423, 462–464.

2. E.g., *Hatch v. Reardon,* 204 U.S. 152, 160–161; *Corporation Commission v. Lowe,* 281 U.S. 431, 438; *Heald v. District of Columbia,* 259 U.S. 114, 123; *Sprout v. South Bend,* 277 U.S. 163, 167; *Concordia Fire Insurance Co. v. Illinois,* 292 U.S. 535, 547.

3. Compare *Electric Co. v. Dow,* 166 U.S. 489; *Pierce v. Somerset Ry.,* 171 U.S. 641, 648; *Leonard v. Vicksburg, S. & P. R. Co.,* 198 U.S. 416, 422.

4. E.g., *United States v. Delaware & Hudson Co.,* 213 U.S. 366, 407–408; *United States v. Jin Fuey Moy,* 241 U.S. 394, 401; *Baender v. Barnett,* 255 U.S. 224; *Texas v. Eastern Texas R. Co.,* 258 U.S. 204, 217; *Panama R. Co. v. Johnson,* 264 U.S. 375, 390; *Linder v. United States,* 268 U.S. 5, 17–18; *Missouri Pacific R. Co. v. Boone,* 270 U.S. 466, 471–472; *Richmond Screw Anchor Co. v. United States,* 275 U.S. 331, 346; *Blodgett v. Holden,* 275 U.S. 142, 148; *Lucas v. Alexander,* 279 U.S. 573, 577; *Interstate Commerce Comm'n v. Oregon-Washington R. & N. Co.,* 288 U.S. 14, 40.

THE TIP OF AN ICEBERG

The concept of justiciability—the characteristic that makes a case appropriate for review—was described by Chief Justice Earl Warren in 1968. He linked the concept to the Court's self-imposed rules implementing the "case and controversy" doctrine:

> The jurisdiction of federal courts is defined and limited by Article III of the Constitution. In terms relevant to the question for decision in this case, the judicial power of federal courts is constitutionally restricted to "cases" and "controversies." As is so often the situation in constitutional adjudication, those two words have an iceberg quality, containing beneath their surface simplicity submerged complexities which go to the very heart of our constitutional form of government. Embodied in the words "cases" and "controversies" are two complementary but somewhat different limitations. In part those words limit the business of the federal courts to questions presented in an adversary context and in a form historically viewed as capable of resolution through the judicial process. And in part those words define the role assigned to the judiciary in a tripartite allocation of power to assure that federal courts will not intrude into areas committed to the other branches of government. *Justiciability* is the term of art employed to give expression to this dual limitation placed upon federal courts by the case-and-controversy doctrine.

> Justiciability is itself a concept of uncertain meaning and scope. Its reach is illustrated by the various grounds upon which questions sought to be adjudicated in federal courts have been held not to be justiciable. Thus no justiciable controversy is presented when the parties seek adjudication of only a political question, when the parties are asking for an advisory opinion, when the question sought to be adjudicated has been mooted by subsequent developments, and when there is no standing to maintain the action.[1]

1. *Flast v. Cohen*, 392 U.S. 83 at 94–95 (1968).

to a less-qualified minority applicant. DeFunis, in the course of his lawsuit, had obtained a court order directing the school to admit him. By the time his case was argued before the Supreme Court, he was in his final year of law school. The Court—in the spring that he would graduate—held the case moot; whatever their decision, it would not have affected DeFunis, who was to graduate regardless.[9]

In a controversial application of this tenet of judicial restraint, the Court overturned a court order barring Los Angeles police from using choke holds on suspects except in unusual circumstances. The Court held in *City of Los Angeles v. Lyons* (1983) that the individual bringing the case—although he had been subjected to this potentially fatal type of hold after he was stopped by police for a traffic violation—could not obtain a court order without showing that the choke hold would be used against him in the future.[10]

The Court has, however, developed a number of exceptions to the rigid application of mootness. In criminal cases in which the defendant has served out his sentence, the Court still finds his case viable if there is the possibility he will continue to suffer adverse legal consequences as a result of the conviction being challenged.[11] A similar rule applies in civil cases if the challenged judgment or situation may continue to have an adverse effect on the plaintiff. Such an exception also exists for conduct and situations that are necessarily of short duration, "capable of repetition, yet evading review" if the mootness rule is strictly applied. Election law cases challenging the application of certain election requirements are an example where the actual dispute may end—after an election is held—yet the problem remains.[12]

Another case of the application of the "capable of repetition" exception is the 1973 abortion decision in *Roe v. Wade* and *Doe v. Bolton*. The plaintiffs in the cases challenging state laws against abortions included pregnant women. Given the predictable nine-month term of a pregnancy, and the less predictable and usually slower term of a constitutional case making its way to the Supreme Court, it was no surprise that the women were no longer pregnant when the case arrived before the Court. The Court, 7-2, rejected the argument that the end of these pregnancies made the case moot. This, wrote Justice Harry A. Blackmun for the Court, was a clear situation in which a condition "capable of repetition" might never win Supreme Court review if the standard of mootness were applied rigidly.[13]

"Friendly" Suits and Test Cases

Taken at face value, the Court's insistence on hearing only actual cases and disputes involving clearly colliding legal interests would preclude its ruling in "friendly" suits, those in which no real or substantial controversy exists but each side agrees to pursue the suit in order to attain a mutually desired judicial resolution. In 1850 Chief Justice Roger B. Taney minced no words when he spoke for the Court in dismissing such a case. He found such collusion "contempt of the court, and highly reprehensible."[14] The classic statement on friendly suits came in 1892, when the Court backed up a state court's refusal to declare unconstitutional a state law regulating railroad fares. Writing the Court's opinion, Justice David J. Brewer explained:

> The theory upon which, apparently, this suit was brought is that parties have an appeal from the Legislature to the courts; and that the latter are given an immediate and general supervision of the constitutionality of the acts of the former. Such is not true. Whenever, in pursuance of an honest and actual antagonistic assertion of rights by one individual against another, there is presented a question involving the validity of any Act of any Legislature, state or federal, and the decision necessarily rests on the competency of the Legislature to so enact, the court must, in the exercise of its solemn duties, determine whether the Act be constitutional or not; but such an exercise of power is the ultimate and supreme function of courts. It is legitimate only in the last resort, and as a necessity in the determination of real, earnest, and vital controversy between individuals. It never was the thought that, by means of a friendly suit, a party beaten in the Legislature could transfer to the courts an inquiry as to the constitutionality of the legislative Act.[15]

Yet some of the landmark decisions in the Court's history have come in friendly cases, arranged because both sides were interested in obtaining a final judicial determination of a question. Perhaps the first was the tax case *Hylton v. United States* (1796). The government paid the attorneys for both sides to get the case to the Supreme Court.[16] Among other major cases that could have been rejected as friendly suits are *Fletcher v. Peck* (1810), *Scott v. Sandford* (1857), and—only a few years after Justice Brewer's ringing statement—*Pollock v. Farmers' Loan and Trust Co.* (1895).[17] In the last case, brought by a stockholder in a bank seeking an order directing the bank not to pay certain federal income taxes—an action the bank would not disapprove of—the Court held the peacetime federal income tax unconstitutional. Justice Brewer made no comment on the "friendly" nature of the suit. *(See "Dred Scott," p. 180; details of Fletcher v. Peck, pp. 387–388 and Pollock v. Farmers' Loan and Trust Co., pp. 144–145.)*

Another example is *Carter v. Carter Coal Co.* (1936), in which the Court struck down a major New Deal statute. The case was brought by the president of the company against the company and the other officers, among whom was his own father.[18] *(See details of Carter v. Carter Coal Co., pp. 122–124.)* In the same vein, although the Court has refused to rule on some obviously concocted test cases, like *Muskrat,* it does not dismiss cases simply because they have been selected by the administration or some pressure group as the proper vehicle to test a law. The Court's decision to hear or dismiss a test case usually turns on whether it presents an actual conflict of legal rights susceptible of judicial resolution.

"STANDING TO SUE"

In addition to the need for an actual legal dispute to justify a federal case, the case must be brought only by persons directly involved in or affected by the dispute. The question of whether a person has a sufficient interest at stake in a dispute is described as a question of legal "standing." Such questions serve "on occasion, as a short-hand expression for all the various elements of justiciability," Chief Justice Warren once commented.[19] To bring a federal suit, a person must have "such a personal stake in the outcome of the controversy as to assure that concrete adverseness which sharpens the presentation of issues upon which the court so largely depends for illumination of difficult constitutional questions."[20] In most cases involving private disputes, the injury or interest asserted is clear beyond question. Issues of legal standing tend to generate more discussion and debate in cases in which laws or other government action are challenged as unconstitutional. In these cases the relationship between the plaintiff and the challenged action is more remote than it is in cases involving private disputes.

For example, senators and representatives who voted against a particular bill that became law do not have standing to challenge the measure as unconstitutional, the Court said in 1997.[21] Unlike private parties who suffer a physical injury or a financial setback, lawmakers have only a general interest in good legislation. They do not suffer a "concrete injury" if a bad bill becomes law, said Chief Justice Rehnquist. In the case before the Court, Sen. Robert Byrd, D-W.Va., and five other lawmakers sued to challenge the Line Item Veto Act, a measure they said violated the separation of powers and badly weakened Congress. It allowed the president to "cancel" certain spending items after they had been passed by Congress. Although the Court ruled that the lawmakers lacked standing, the legislators prevailed in the end. The following year, the Court took up a suit filed by city officials in New York who sued when their funding was cut after President Clinton canceled a spending measure. In *Clinton v. City of New York* (1998) the Court agreed they had standing, and it struck down the Line Item Veto Act as unconstitutional.[22]

Like the lawmakers, taxpayers usually have only a general interest in how their tax money is spent, and for that reason, they have been denied standing to challenge most government programs. The first major case on "taxpayer standing" was actually a pair of cases in 1923: *Massachusetts v. Mellon* and *Frothingham v. Mellon*. The state of Massachusetts and Mrs. Frothingham, a federal taxpayer, came to the Supreme Court challenging as unconstitutional the use of federal grants-in-aid to states for maternal and child health programs. Massachusetts argued that such federal aid invaded the powers reserved to the states by the Tenth Amendment; Mrs. Frothingham asserted in addition that such an improper use of her tax money effectively deprived her of her property without due process of law as guaranteed by the Fifth Amendment.

The Supreme Court refused to address those constitutional arguments, finding that neither the state nor the taxpayer had standing to bring the cases in the first place. Writing for the Court, Justice George Sutherland found the question posed by Massachusetts to be "political, and not judicial in character" and thus outside the Court's jurisdiction.[23] In addition, Mrs. Frothingham's interest in the use of federal revenues was "comparatively minute and indeterminable," and the effect of federal payments from those funds upon her future tax burden "so remote, fluctuating, and uncertain," that she lacked an adequate personal interest in the situation to bring the federal challenge.[24] (The Court did note, however, that local taxpayers often had sufficient interest at stake to bring justiciable cases challenging local expenditures.[25]) Sutherland explained the Court's reasoning concerning federal taxpayer suits:

> The administration of any statute, likely to produce additional taxation to be imposed upon a vast number of taxpayers, the extent of whose several liability is indefinite and constantly changing, is essentially a matter of public and not of individual concern. If one taxpayer may champion and litigate such a cause, then every other taxpayer may do the same . . . in respect of every other appropriation act and statute whose administration requires the outlay of public money, and whose validity may be questioned. The bare suggestion of such a result, with its attendant inconveniences, goes far to sustain the conclusion which we have reached, that a suit of this character cannot be maintained.[26]

In conclusion, Sutherland reiterated the Court's view that its power to review the validity of acts of Congress was not a general one, but was properly invoked "only when the justification for some direct injury suffered or threatened, presenting a justiciable issue, is made to rest upon such an act." The person invoking the exercise of this aspect of federal judicial power, declared the Court, "must be able to show not only that the statute is invalid, but that he has sustained or is immediately in danger of sustaining some direct injury as the result of

JUDICIAL IMMUNITY

One restraint to which judges are not vulnerable in their exercise of judicial power is the threat of civil damage suits. Judges may not be sued for their official actions, no matter how erroneous or injurious these acts may be. That rule has been the policy of the federal judicial system throughout its history, proclaimed most firmly by the Supreme Court in a decision involving the judge who presided over the trial of one of the men accused of the assassination of Abraham Lincoln. In *Bradley v. Fisher* (1872) Justice Stephen J. Field wrote:

> [I]t is a general principle of the highest importance to the proper administration of justice that a judicial officer, in exercising the authority vested in him, shall be free to act upon his own convictions, without apprehension of personal consequence to himself. Liability to answer to everyone who might feel himself aggrieved by the action of the judge, would be inconsistent with the possession of this freedom, and would destroy that independence without which no judiciary can be either respectable or useful.[1]

Furthermore, stated the Court, this immunity is not breached even if the judicial actions protested are taken in bad faith.

> The purity of their motives cannot in this way be the subject of judicial inquiry. . . . If civil actions could be maintained . . . against the judge, because the losing party should see fit to allege in his complaint that the acts of the judge were done with partiality, or maliciously, or corruptly, the protection essential to judicial independence would be entirely swept away. Few persons sufficiently irritated to institute an action against a judge for his judicial acts would hesitate to ascribe any character to the acts which would be essential to the maintenance of the action.[2]

A judge can, however, be impeached or removed for illegal actions undertaken in an official capacity, but cannot be sued personally for actions taken from the bench. Ruled the Court in 1872, "[F]or malice or corruption in their action whilst exercising their judicial functions within the general scope of their jurisdiction," the Court concluded, "judges can only be reached by public prosecution in the form of impeachment, or in such other form as may be specially prescribed."[3]

In a 1967 ruling the Court affirmed the complete protection of this immunity. The justices held it unaffected by the federal civil rights law that allows damage suits to be brought against anyone who deprives another person of his civil rights while acting under "color of law."[4] In a 1978 decision the Court held that the immunity protected a state judge from a damage suit resulting from his allowing a teenager to be sterilized without her knowledge or consent.[5]

Judges may be prosecuted if they commit a crime outside their judicial office, and they may be sued as an employer or administrator of their office. In 1988 the Court cleared the way for a female probation officer to sue an Illinois state judge for allegedly firing her because of her gender. Although judges may not be sued over "truly judicial acts," their immunity does not extend to the "administrative, legislative or executive functions" of their offices, the Court said.[6]

The Constitution stipulates that the compensation paid to judges shall not be reduced during their time in office. Using this provision as the basis for their holding, the Supreme Court in 1920 ruled that a federal judge appointed to his post before passage of the federal income tax law could not be forced to pay income taxes because to do so would unconstitutionally reduce his salary. Five years later the Court extended this immunity to judges appointed after the income tax law took effect.[7] This exemption was, however, short-lived. Congress in 1932 expressly applied the income tax to the salaries of judges taking office after mid-1932, and in 1939 the Court upheld the 1932 law, overruling its 1920 decision. The Court held in *O'Malley v. Woodrough* (1939) that to require judges to pay a nondiscriminatory federal income tax was "merely to recognize that judges are also citizens, and that their particular function in government does not generate an immunity from sharing with their fellow citizens the material burden of the government whose Constitution and laws they are charged with administering."[8]

---

1. *Bradley v. Fisher,* 13 Wall. (80 U.S.) 335 at 347 (1872).

2. Id. at 347, 348.

3. Id. at 354.

4. *Pierson v. Ray,* 386 U.S. 547 (1967).

5. *Stump v. Sparkman,* 435 U.S. 349 (1978).

6. *Forrester v. White,* 484 U.S. 219 (1988).

7. *Evans v. Gore,* 253 U.S. 245 (1920); *Miles v. Graham,* 268 U.S. 501 (1925).

8. *O'Malley v. Woodrough,* 307 U.S. 277 at 282 (1939).

A WRONG, BUT NO RIGHT

Unless a person can assert a federally protected right or interest that has been injured or threatened with injury, he or she lacks the essential element of a federal case. The Latin maxim *damnum absque injuria* describes the situation: there is loss, but no injury sufficient to provide a basis for judicial remedy. In 1938 such a situation came before the Court in *Alabama Power Company v. Ickes* (1938).[1] The privately owned company came into federal court seeking to halt within its service area federal grants to cities that would enable them to set up their own utility systems as competitors to private industry. The company argued that such grants were unlawful and asserted, as the necessary injury, the loss of business it would suffer from such competition.

The Supreme Court dismissed the case. The company had no protected legal or equitable right to operate free of competition, and so it had no standing to challenge the validity of the grants. The Court wrote that if the company's business was destroyed or curtailed, "it will be by lawful competition from which no legal wrong results." What the company sought to claim, continued the Court, was "damage to something it does not possess—namely, a right to be immune from lawful municipal competition."[2]

---

1. *Alabama Power Company v. Ickes,* 302 U.S. 464 (1938).

2. Id. at 480.

---

its enforcement, and not merely that he suffers in some indefinite way in common with people generally."[27]

Until 1968 the Court's ruling in *Frothingham v. Mellon* was interpreted to bar virtually all taxpayer efforts to challenge the constitutionality of a federal law, unless the taxpayer could show some additional personal stake in its enforcement. The Court, however, modified this rule with its decision in *Flast v. Cohen* (1968). Florence Flast, a federal taxpayer, sued Secretary of Health, Education, and Welfare Wilbur J. Cohen to halt the use of federal funds under the Elementary and Secondary Education Act of 1965 to aid pupils in parochial schools. This use of her tax monies, argued Flast, violated the First Amendment ban on establishment of religion and on government efforts to impede the free exercise of religion. A three-judge federal panel dismissed her case, citing *Frothingham v. Mellon,* but the Supreme Court reversed the decision, ruling that a federal taxpayer does have standing to bring constitutional challenges to federal spending and taxing programs when he alleges that they conflict with constitutional provisions restricting the taxing and spending power of Congress.

A federal taxpayer, wrote Chief Justice Warren, "may or may not have the requisite personal stake in the outcome, depending upon the circumstances of the

particular case. Therefore, we find no absolute bar in Article III to suits of federal taxpayers challenging allegedly unconstitutional federal taxing and spending programs."[28] To prove the "requisite personal stake," wrote Warren, a taxpayer must establish a logical connection, or nexus, between his taxpayer status and the claim he brought to the Court. Flast had established this nexus, so the lower federal court should go on to consider the substance of her challenge. The establishment of this connection assured that a taxpayer was not simply seeking "to employ a federal court as a forum in which to air his generalized grievances about the conduct of government or the allocation of power in the Federal System," Warren continued. That was still an impermissible use of the federal courts.[29]

This last portion of the *Flast* opinion was cited frequently by the Court in the 1970s, as it made clear that despite *Flast,* there was still a standing requirement for federal cases. In *United States v. Richardson* (1974) the Court held that a taxpayer did not have standing to challenge the secrecy of the Central Intelligence Agency's budget, a secrecy he alleged to be in direct conflict with the Constitution. Writing for the Court, Chief Justice Warren E. Burger explained that this was not a challenge to the power to tax or to spend—the only sort of taxpayer challenge that *Flast* had addressed—but rather to the laws concerning the CIA. Furthermore, he wrote, William Richardson did not allege that as a taxpayer he was suffering any particular concrete injury as a result of this secrecy.[30] A concurring opinion by Justice Lewis F. Powell Jr. noted the lowering of standing requirements over the three preceding decades through statutes granting standing to bring certain cases and through Court rulings such as *Flast v. Cohen* and *Baker v. Carr* (1962), which allowed voters to challenge state malapportionment.[31] Despite these developments, wrote Powell, "the Court has not broken with the traditional requirement that, in the absence of a specific statutory grant of the right of review, a plaintiff must allege some particularized injury that sets him apart from the man on the street."[32] This point was emphasized in a series of rulings in which the Court held that persons lacked standing to challenge military surveillance programs, the membership of some members of Congress in the armed forces reserves, municipal zoning ordinances, and the tax-exempt status of certain hospitals.[33]

It was not clear the Court would allow taxpayer suits to challenge how the executive branch spends money, even when the suit alleges a violation of the First Amendment's ban on an "establishment of religion." In 2007 the Court threw out a suit filed by several Wisconsin taxpayers who said President George W. Bush's Faith-based Initiative amounted to an unconstitutional promotion of religion by the government. An appeals court in Chicago, citing the *Flast* decision, cleared the suit to go forward. But in *Hein v. Freedom from Religion Foundation,* the Court said these taxpayers did not have standing to challenge Bush's program. Justice Samuel Alito pointed out that Congress had not appropriated special money to fund the White House project. Instead, Bush used general executive branch funds, and his appointees held several conferences to encourage religious groups to participate in government-funded social programs. Because no federal appropriation was being attacked as unconstitutional, these taxpayers lacked standing. "In short, this case falls outside 'the narrow exception' that *Flast* 'created to the general rule against taxpayer standing established in *Frothingham,*'" Alito wrote.[34] Justices Antonin Scalia

and Clarence Thomas said they would have gone further and overruled *Flast* entirely.

Even though taxpayer standing has been frowned upon, the Court cleared the way for citizens to sue over alleged violations of federal environmental laws. They could cite economic interests. Pollution in the water or air may harm their business. Or they could cite aesthetic or recreational interests. Pollution could make it unhealthy or dangerous to go boating or fishing in a river or bay. Still, their alleged injury must be personal, rather than general, although in certain voting rights and environmental cases that requirement, too, has been applied flexibly.[35] But the Rehnquist and Roberts Courts tightened the standing requirements somewhat. In the environmental case of *Lujan v. Defenders of Wildlife* (1992) the Court insisted that there be demonstrated injury to the parties bringing the lawsuit before standing is granted, and in the voting rights case *United States v. Hays* (1995) the Court said that white voters could not challenge the creation of a black-majority voting district unless they were resident in the district or could otherwise demonstrate a clear and direct interest.[36]

"Courts have no charter to review and revise legislative and executive action," wrote Justice Scalia in 2009 in rejecting on standing grounds a suit brought by environmentalists to challenge the timber-sale policies of the U.S. Forest Service. "The doctrine of standing . . . is founded in the concern about the proper—and properly limited—role of the courts in a democratic society."[37]

Although the Court generally has insisted that a plaintiff be arguing his own interest as the primary one—not that of a third party—there have been notable exceptions to that rule.[38] As early as 1915, the Court allowed alien *employees* to challenge a state law requiring *employers* to hire four times as many residents as aliens.[39] A decade later the Court allowed a religious organization that operated a parochial school to challenge a state law penalizing parents who did not send their children to public schools.[40] In situations where it appears unlikely that the people most directly affected by the challenged law will be able to bring their own legal protest to the Court, the justices generally have allowed others to make the challenge for them. Such was apparently the reasoning behind several cases in which white plaintiffs challenged laws restricting the rights of blacks to live or buy property in certain neighborhoods.[41] In some more recent cases, the Court has allowed doctors to challenge laws restricting the advice or treatment they may give their patients.[42]

Organizations whose members are injured by government action may assert the interest of their members in seeking judicial review, but the Court has made clear that there must be injury—as well as an interest—in such cases.[43] States, acting as a kind of legal guardian, are allowed to bring some federal suits in behalf of their citizens, challenging acts that are injurious to the health or welfare of the entire population. *Massachusetts v. Mellon,* however, made clear that such *parens patriae* suits may not be brought against the federal government.[44]

POLITICAL QUESTIONS

Chief Justice John Marshall declared in his classic discussion of judicial power in *Marbury v. Madison,*

> The province of the court, is, solely, to decide on the rights of individuals, not to inquire how the executive, or executive officers, perform duties in which they have a discretion. Questions in their nature political, or which are, by the constitution and laws, submitted to the executive, can never be made in this court.[45]

Since that time, the Court has employed the "political question" doctrine as a convenient device for avoiding head-on collisions with Congress, the president, or the states on matters ranging from foreign relations to malapportioned congressional districts. The attributes of this doctrine are quite variable. One modern justice has observed that they "in various settings, diverge, combine, appear and disappear in seeming disorderliness."[46] Several decades earlier a scholar suggested that expediency was indeed the chief determinant of "political questions."[47]

The Constitution provides that the United States shall guarantee to every state a republican form of government. When the question of enforcing that guarantee came to the Supreme Court, the justices made clear that this was indeed a political question.

Luther v. Borden (1849) involved two competing groups, each asserting that it was the lawful government of Rhode Island. In the Court's opinion Chief Justice Taney stated firmly that "it rests with Congress to decide what government is the established one in a state."[48] Taney continued:

> [W]hen the senators and representatives of a State are admitted into the councils of the Union, the authority of the government under which they are appointed, as well as its republican character, is recognized by the proper constitutional authority. And its decision is binding on every other department of the government, and could not be questioned in a judicial tribunal.[49]

In the same case the Court displayed a similar deference to the decision of the president, as authorized by law, to call out the militia of a state to suppress an insurrection there.[50] The Court has remained quite consistent in applying the political question doctrine to refuse cases in which individuals attempt to use this "guaranty" provision of the Constitution as a basis for challenging state government or state action.[51] Tennessee was unsuccessful, however, when it attempted to use this line of precedents to shield its state legislative apportionment statute from judicial review in *Baker v. Carr.*[52]

The Court generally has left questions of foreign policy and foreign affairs to the political branches. In 1829 the Court refused to settle an international border question, stating that it was not the role of the judiciary to assert national interests against foreign powers.[53] Throughout its history the Court has steadily reaffirmed that point, based firmly on its view that in foreign affairs the nation should speak with a single voice.[54] *(See "The States' Role," pp. 282–283.)*

In similar fashion, the Court has used the political question doctrine to refuse to intervene in questions of legislative process or procedure, including issues concerning constitutional amendments. It has left the resolution of those matters to Congress or the states.[55] The exceptions have been cases raising questions of basic constitutional standards—such as the power of Congress over certain subjects or the propriety of a chamber's excluding a member who meets the constitutional qualifications and has been duly elected—or in matters such as the *Pocket Veto Case,* where the political branches deadlock on an issue.[56] *(See "Qualifications," pp. 221–225; details of the Pocket Veto Case, pp. 312–313.)*

For most of the nation's history, the Court also viewed challenges to state decisions allocating population among electoral districts as a political question outside the realm of judicial consideration. In *Colegrove v. Green* (1946) Justice Felix Frankfurter reiterated this view, making clear that it was based on practical political considerations.

> Nothing is clearer than that this controversy [over malapportionment of Illinois congressional districts] concerns matters that bring courts into immediate and active relations with party contests. From the determination of such issues this Court has traditionally held aloof. It is hostile to a democratic system to involve the judiciary in the politics of the people.[57]

Twenty-six years later the Court overturned that ruling and held that its earlier refusal to intervene in apportionment matters was based on an overbroad view of the political question doctrine. The decision came in *Baker v. Carr* (1962), in which the Court held that challenges to malapportionment of state legislatures *were* justiciable questions. After reviewing the line of political question cases, Justice William J. Brennan Jr. stated for the majority that

> it is the relationship between the judiciary and the coordinate branches of the Federal Government, and not the federal judiciary's relationship to the States, which gives rise to the "political question." . . .

. . . The nonjusticiability of a political question is primarily a function of the separation of powers.[58] The basic question of fairness at the heart of the lawsuit that had begun *Baker v. Carr,* Brennan concluded for the Court, was constitutional, not political, and was well within the jurisdiction of the Court. Simply "the presence of a matter affecting state government does not [in and of itself] render the case nonjusticiable."[59]

Writing in 1936, C. Gordon Post described the political question doctrine as a judicial concession founded "in the inadequacy of the judiciary itself." He continued:

If the court found it better to limit its jurisdiction, to restrict its power of review, it was not because of the doctrine of the separation of powers or because of a lack of rules, but because of expediency. If the court left certain questions pertaining to foreign relations in the hands of the political departments, it was because in our foreign relations a unified front is sensible, practical and expedient. If the court placed the question of whether a state . . . possessed or did not possess a republican form of government within the jurisdiction of the political departments, it was because of very practical considerations. If the court was fully conscious that its mandate could not, or would not, be enforced in the particular case, obviously it was more expedient to leave the matter to the political departments exclusively. In general, judicial review or not, the court has found it more expedient to leave the decision of certain questions to governmental bodies more appropriately adapted to decide them.[60]

THE ROLE OF PRECEDENT

Supreme Court decisions are final, unless Congress overrules them by statute, Congress and the states amend the Constitution to reverse the Court, or the Court decides to overturn precedent. The doctrine of *stare decisis*—"let the decision stand"—binds the Court to adhere to the decisions of an earlier day. This rule of precedent, wrote one scholar, is linked to "the idea that our law and judicial decisions have a historical continuity—as opposed to a system by which courts might endeavor to render justice in each case anew, as though each case constituted a problem unto itself, in no way related to any previous problems which courts have disposed of."[61]

The doctrine has a practical basis: the need for stability in law. As Justice Brandeis once wrote, "in most matters it is more important that the applicable rule of law be settled than that it be settled right."[62] Justice William O. Douglas, no advocate of slavish adherence to precedent, wrote,

> *Stare decisis* provides some moorings so that men may trade and arrange their affairs with confidence. *Stare decisis* serves to take the capricious element out of law and to give stability to a society. It is a strong tie which the future has to the past.[63]

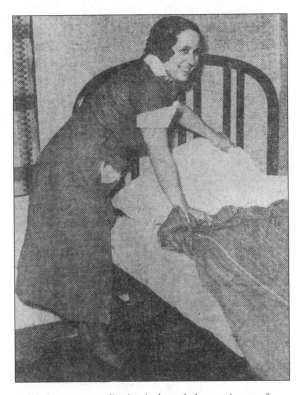

A faded newspaper clipping is the only known image of Elsie Parrish, a chambermaid and plaintiff in *West Coast Hotel Co. v. Parrish* (1937). This landmark decision upheld the right of states to impose minimum wage laws on private employers, thereby dramatically reversing the Court's ruling in *Adkins v. Children's Hospital* (1923). The Court occasionally departs from the doctrine of *stare decisis,* which means "let the decision stand," because of changing circumstances or a majority of the justices agree that a case was wrongly decided.

The application of precedent is not, however, as simple as it might appear. Robert K. Carr explains:

> In actual practice, two cases are rarely, if ever, exactly alike. . . . Thus a judge may have wide discretion in deciding in a given case to follow either precedent A or precedent B, both of which seem to have considerable bearing on the case but which, unfortunately, are completely contradictory to one another.[64]

From 1810 to 2003 the Court made more than 230 exceptions to the doctrine of *stare decisis* in more than 170 situations and expressly overruled an earlier decisions. Century-old precedents fell, as did some barely a year old. *(See box, Supreme Court Cases Expressly Overruling Precedents, 1789–2007, p. 62)* The Court in *Hudson and Smith v. Guestier* (1810) overruled an 1808 decision concerning the jurisdiction of a foreign power over vessels offshore. Chief Justice John Marshall disagreed with the Court's decision to overrule the earlier holding. Only two other decisions were overruled by the Court during Marshall's tenure as chief justice, but only *Hudson and Smith* was expressly overruled during the chief justiceship of his successor, Roger B. Taney.[65] After the Civil War, changing conditions and changing Court personnel placed increasing strain on the reverence for precedent. In 1870 the Court held the Legal Tender Acts unconstitutional; a year later, with two new members, it reversed itself and upheld the same laws.[66] *(See details of the Legal Tender Cases, Hepburn v. Griswold and Knox v. Lee, pp. 158–160.)* Twenty-five years later, in 1895, the Court found the statute authorizing a peacetime income tax unconstitutional. In doing so, it revised a century-old definition of "direct taxes" and ignored previous rulings that would seem to dictate that the Court should uphold the tax law.[67] This 1895 ruling was eventually reversed by adoption of the Sixteenth Amendment in 1913. *(See details of Pollock v. Farmers' Loan and Trust Co., pp. 144–145.)*

The Supreme Court of the twentieth century clearly has felt free to overrule previous decisions. Some three out of four of the Court's reversals have come since 1900. Its change in opinion on child labor, minimum wage and maximum hour laws, New Deal legislation, and state flag salute laws are among the major chapters in modern Supreme Court history. As the modern Court's actions have made clear, it views *stare decisis* as "a principle of policy and not a mechanical formula of adherence to the latest decision, however recent and questionable, when such adherence involves collision with a prior doctrine more embracing in its scope, intrinsically sounder, and verified by experience."[68] The modern Court also tends to apply the doctrine more faithfully to questions of statutory law than to constitutional issues. As Justice Stanley Reed explained for the Court in 1944,

SUPREME COURT CASES EXPRESSLY OVERRULING PRECEDENTS, 1789–2007

Although *stare decisis*—"let the decision stand"—is a guiding principle in the Supreme Court's decision making, justices are not always reluctant to overturn previous rulings. The norm of precedent is most vulnerable when questions of constitutional interpretation are involved. The following table includes only reversals stated in express terms by the Court or those agreed upon by the multiple sources cited below. It is not uncommon for a later Court to state that an earlier Court overruled a decision even though there may be no language to that effect in the prior decision. In addition, some decisions may overrule an indeterminable number of precedents. Decisions falling into these two categories are not tallied here.

	Years	Cases Overruling Precedent	Precedents Overruled
Marshall Court	1801–1836	1	1
Taney Court	1836–1864	2	3
Chase Court	1864–1874	1	1
Waite Court	1874–1888	9	11
Fuller Court	1888–1910	3	4
White Court	1910–1921	4	4
Taft Court	1921–1930	5	6
Hughes Court	1930–1941	15	22
Stone Court	1941–1946	8	11
Vinson Court	1946–1953	6	11
Warren Court	1953–1969	37	53
Burger Court	1969–1986	46	62
Rehnquist Court	1986–2005	40	46
Roberts Court	2005–2007	3	3
Total		180	238

NOTE: No precedents were overruled under Chief Justices John Jay (1789–1795), John Rutledge (1795), or Oliver Ellsworth (1796–1800).

SOURCES: For 1789–1990: Congressional Research Service, *The Constitution of the United States of America: Analysis and Interpretation* (Washington, D.C.: U.S. Government Printing Office, 1973), and supplements. For 1991–2000: U.S. Supreme Court Judicial Database, www.polisci.msu.edu/pljp/supremecourt.html; Lee Epstein et al., *The Supreme Court Compendium: Data, Decisions, and Developments,* 4th ed. (Washington, D.C.: CQ Press, 2006); Albert P. Blaustein and Andrew H. Field, "'Overruling' Opinions in the Supreme Court," *Michigan Law Review* 47 (December 1958): 151–194, reprinted in *The Courts: A Reader in the Judicial Process,* Robert Scigliano (Boston: Little, Brown, 1962), 393–408. In general, Kenneth Jost, "Reversals of Earlier Rulings," [various terms] CQ Press Electronic Library, Supreme Court Yearbook Online Edition (2009).

we are not unmindful of the desirability of continuity of decision in constitutional questions. However, when convinced of former error, this Court has never felt constrained to follow precedent. In constitutional questions, where correction depends upon amendment, and not upon legislative action this Court throughout its history has freely exercised its power to re-examine the basis of its constitutional decisions. This has long been accepted practice, and this practice has continued to this day.[69]

The rule of precedent is also made more flexible by the Court's practice of "distinguishing" a new case from a precedent that would seem to be controlling, pointing out factors that distinguish one case from the other and justifying a different result. A precedent can eventually be distinguished into complete uniqueness and utter uselessness. This sort of erosion took place during the late 1930s and 1940s with regard to *Plessy v. Ferguson* (1896), which endorsed "separate, but equal" facilities

PRECEDENT AND PUBLIC ACCEPTANCE

The importance of adhering to precedent and the Court's need for public acceptance of its decisions, in order for them to have real effect, were emphasized in 1992, when the Supreme Court reaffirmed the central holding of *Roe v. Wade* (1973), the landmark decision that made abortion legal. The Court must speak in a way that enables people to accept its decisions as grounded and shaped by principle, not the political winds of the day, said Justices Sandra Day O'Connor, Anthony M. Kennedy, and David H. Souter. Following is an excerpt from their opinion in *Planned Parenthood of Southeastern Pennsylvania v. Casey* (1992).

> Our analysis would not be complete . . . without explaining why overruling *Roe's* central holding would not only reach an unjustified result under principles of *stare decisis,* but would seriously weaken the Court's capacity to exercise the judicial power and to function as the Supreme Court of a Nation dedicated to the rule of law. To understand why this would be so it is necessary to understand the source of this Court's authority, the conditions necessary for its preservation, and its relationship to the country's understanding of itself as a constitutional Republic.
>
> The root of American governmental power is revealed most clearly in the instance of the power conferred by the Constitution upon the Judiciary of the United States and specifically upon this Court. As Americans of each succeeding generation are rightly told, the Court cannot buy support for its decisions by spending money and, except to a minor degree, it cannot independently coerce obedience to its decrees. The Court's power lies, rather, in its legitimacy, a product of substance and perception that shows itself in the people's acceptance of the Judiciary as fit to determine what the Nation's law means and to declare what it demands.
>
> The underlying substance of this legitimacy is of course the warrant for the Court's decisions in the Constitution and the lesser sources of legal principle on which the Court draws. That substance is expressed in the Court's opinions, and our contemporary understanding is such that a decision without principled justification would be no judicial act at all. But even when justification is furnished by apposite legal principle, something more is required. Because not every conscientious claim of principled justification will be accepted as such, the justification claimed must be beyond dispute. The Court must take care to speak and act in ways that allow people to accept its decisions on the terms the Court claims for them, as grounded truly in principle, not as compromises with social and political pressures having, as such, no bearing on the principled choices that the Court is obliged to make. Thus, the Court's legitimacy depends on making legally principled decisions under circumstances in which their principled character is sufficiently plausible to be accepted by the Nation.[1]

---

1. *Planned Parenthood of Southeastern Pennsylvania v. Casey,* 505 U.S. 833 (1992).

for blacks and whites. By the time the Court in 1954 officially overruled *Plessy,* the decision's value as a precedent had long been destroyed. In terms of social conditions, quite the opposite occurred in 1992, when the Court decided not to overturn *Roe v. Wade* (1973), the landmark ruling that made abortion legal nationwide. In the closely divided decision in *Planned Parenthood of Southeastern Pennsylvania v. Casey* (1992) a plurality of justices articulated their view of precedent.[70] *(See box, Precedent and Public Acceptance, above.)* According to the three controlling justices, Sandra Day O'Connor, Anthony M. Kennedy, and David H. Souter,

> The obligation to follow precedent begins with necessity, and a contrary necessity marks its outer limit. . . . Indeed, the very concept of the rule of law underlying our own Constitution requires such continuity over time that a respect for precedent is, by definition, indispensable. At the other extreme, a different necessity would make itself felt if a prior judicial ruling should come to be seen so clearly as error that its enforcement was for that very reason doomed.[71]

The rule of precedent preserves stability and continuity and creates a certain predictability in the law as proclaimed by the Supreme Court, but departure from the doctrine of *stare decisis* is one way by which the Court adapts the Constitution to new and changing circumstances.[72]

The debate over whether to overrule a shaky precedent, or merely to limit it, remains a lively one within the Court. Several justices have adopted different approaches. Justices Thomas and Scalia regularly call for overruling past decisions they believe were wrongly decided. Chief Justice John Roberts and Justice Samuel Alito have been more inclined to limit a past decision, rather than overrule it. During their Senate confirmation hearings, Roberts and Alito pledged to respect precedent, and they have been reluctant to reverse a past decision. One such example came in 2007 when several taxpayers sued to halt the White House's "Faith-based Initiative" launched by President Bush. The justices were forced to confront a controversial precedent, the 1968 ruling in *Flast v. Cohen.* Before the *Flast* decision, the Court had clearly said persons do not have standing as taxpayers to sue to challenge programs or policies of the government. But in *Flast* Chief Justice Earl Warren made an exception for suits that alleged federal funds were being spent to promote religion in violation of the First Amendment and the ban on "establishment of religion." The taxpayers are objecting to spending their tax money on religion, Warren said, and they should be permitted to make that claim in court.

When faced with the challenge to Bush's White House project, five justices, led by Roberts, voted to reject the taxpayers' claim of standing, but they disagreed on the reasons for doing so. Roberts, Alito, and Kennedy said *Flast* "recognized a narrow exception to the general rule against federal taxpayer standing," and they said it did not extend to "a purely discretionary Executive Branch expenditure." Bush's office was merely holding conferences, they noted. Congress had not appropriated money to subsidize religion.

Scalia and Thomas said this distinction made little sense. They said *Flast* should be overruled. "If this Court is to decide cases by rule of law rather than show of hands, we must surrender to logic and choose sides: Either *Flast v. Cohen* should be applied to (at a minimum) all challenges to the governmental expenditure of general tax revenues in a manner alleged to violate a constitutional provision that specifically limited the taxing and spending power, or *Flast* should be repudiated," wrote Scalia in a concurring opinion joined by Thomas. "For me, the choice is easy. . . . I can think of few cases less warranting of *stare decisis* respect. It is time—it is past time—to call an end. *Flast* should be overruled."[73]

The same divide was on display in another case in 2007 involving the First Amendment and the campaign spending laws. The same five justices—Roberts, Scalia, Kennedy, Thomas, and Alito—voted to shield a Wisconsin anti-abortion group's radio ad from the McCain-Feingold Act, but again, they did so for different reasons.[74] The act, whose official name was the Bipartisan Campaign Reform Act of 2002, made it illegal for groups to use corporate or union money to broadcast ads just prior to the election that mentioned a candidate for office. Corporations and unions were barred by law from funding campaigns or candidates, and the limited ban on broadcast ads was designed to enforce that rule. The Court in 2003 upheld the entire McCain-Feingold Act as constitutional in a 5-4 decision in *McConnell v. Federal Election Commission.*[75] Four years later, when the case of the Wisconsin anti-abortion group was to be decided, the Court had shifted. Justice O'Connor, a supporter of the campaign funding law, had retired, and Justice Alito, her replacement, believed the restrictions on political spending violated the First Amendment. But Alito, like Roberts, hesitated to overrule the four-year-old *McConnell* decision. Instead, Roberts and Alito joined together to shield the Wisconsin group's ad on the grounds that the radio spot did not urge voters to oust Wisconsin's Sen. Russ Feingold from office. The ad criticized Feingold for not supporting President Bush's judicial nominees.[76]

Scalia, Thomas, and Kennedy said they would have gone further and overturned the *McConnell* precedent entirely. "Overruling a constitutional case decided just a few years earlier is far from unprecedented," Scalia wrote. "*Stare decisis* considerations carry little weight when an erroneous governing decision has created an unworkable legal regime." In a footnote, he derided Chief Justice Roberts for his unwillingness to forthrightly overrule a precedent. His "opinion effectively overrules *McConnell* without saying so," Scalia said.[77] "This faux judicial restraint is judicial obfuscation."

THE DEMANDS OF COMITY

The existence of dual judicial systems in the United States—state courts and federal courts—imposes certain peculiar restraints upon the conduct of the federal judiciary. Law enforcement remains primarily the responsibility of state officials, yet the final word on questions of federal law and federal rights is left to the federal courts. The operation of this dual system requires continuing adjustment. As noted above, federal judges have several powerful instruments to wield against improper state action: the writ of habeas corpus, to order the release of a state prisoner detained in violation of his constitutional rights; the injunction, to halt improper state proceedings; and the declaratory judgment, to hold a state law unconstitutional, invalid, and unenforceable. When state action is challenged by persons who ask that a federal judge intervene in state matters, the Supreme Court often counsels restraint, citing the demands of comity, which Edward S. Corwin describes as "a self-imposed rule of judicial morality, whereby independent tribunals of concurrent or coordinate jurisdiction exercise a mutual restraint in order to prevent interference with each other and to avoid collisions of authority."[78]

More simply, Justice Hugo L. Black wrote in 1971, comity is "a proper respect for state functions, a recognition of the fact that the entire country is made up of a Union of separate state governments, and a continuance of the belief that the National Government will fare best if the States and their institutions are left free to perform their separate functions in their separate ways."[79] Black, years earlier a local police judge, continued:

> This, perhaps for lack of a better and clearer way to describe it, is referred to by many as "Our Federalism." . . . The concept does not mean blind deference to "States' Rights" any more than it means centralization of control over every important issue in our National Government and its courts. . . . What the concept does represent is a system in which there is sensitivity to the legitimate interest of both State and National Governments, and in which the National Government, anxious though it may be to vindicate and protect federal rights and federal interests, always endeavors to do so in ways that will not unduly interfere with the legitimate activities of the States.[80]

The demands of comity have produced at least two corollary rules: the requirement that individuals who challenge state actions in federal courts first "exhaust" all possible state remedies for their complaint, and the "abstention" doctrine, which requires federal judges to refrain from acting or asserting federal jurisdiction over a matter within state hands until the state courts have had a full opportunity to correct the situation at issue The application of these rules by the Supreme Court has led to much debate on and off the bench, particularly since the Court has applied most of the procedural guarantees of the Bill of Rights to state court proceedings. In the 1960s the Supreme Court tended to find or create new exceptions to these rules of restraint. Under more conservative leadership since, the Court has tended to narrow such exceptions. The process of adjustment continues.

★

NOTES

INTRODUCTION (PP. 1–3)

1. *Marbury v. Madison,* 1 Cr. (5 U.S.) 137 (1803).
2. James Madison, Alexander Hamilton, and John Jay, *The Federalist Papers,* ed. Clinton Rossiter (New York: New American Library, 1961), No. 78, 466.
3. Ibid., No. 78, 467.
4. Testimony of John G. Roberts Jr. before the Senate Judiciary Committee, September 12, 2005.
5. Madison, Hamilton, Jay, *The Federalist Papers,* No. 15, 106.
6. Ibid., No. 78, 465–466.
7. *Scott v. Sandford,* 19 How. (60 U.S.) 393 (1857).
8. *Lochner v. New York,* 198 U.S. 45 (1905).
9. *Roe v. Wade,* 410 U.S. 113 (1973).
10. Testimony of John G. Roberts Jr. before the Senate Judiciary Committee, September 13, 2005.

FEDERAL JURISDICTION (PP. 4–18)

1. *Michaelson v. United States,* 291 F. 940 (7th Cir. 1923), revised by *Michaelson v. United States,* 266 U.S. 42 (1924).
2. *Ex parte McCardle,* 7 Wall. (74 U.S.) 506 at 514 (1869).
3. Charles Alan Wright, *Handbook of the Law of Federal Courts,* 2nd ed. (St. Paul, Minn.: West Publishing, 1970), 2.
4. *Cary v. Curtis,* 3 How. (44 U.S.) 236 at 245 (1845).
5. *Nashville v. Cooper,* 6 Wall. (73 U.S.) 247 at 252 (1868).
6. See Felix Frankfurter and James M. Landis, *The Business of the Supreme Court: A Study in the Federal Judicial System*

(New York: Macmillan, 1928), 1–14; see also Julius Goebel Jr., *History of the Supreme Court of the United States,* vol. 1, *Antecedents and Beginnings to 1801* (New York: Macmillan, 1971), 457–508.

7. *Turner v. Bank of North America,* 4 Dall. (4 U.S.) 8 at 11 (1799).

8. Id. at 10.

9. Frankfurter and Landis, *Business of the Supreme Court,* 64–65.

10. Ibid., 6–7.

11. Ibid.

12. *The Thomas Jefferson,* 10 Wheat. (23 U.S.) 428 (1825); *The Genessee Chief,* 12 How. (53 U.S.) 443 (1851); *United States v. Appalachian Power Co.,* 311 U.S. 377 (1940).

13. *In re Debs,* 158 U.S. 564 at 584 (1895).

14. *United States v. Texas,* 143 U.S. 621 (1892).

15. *United States v. West Virginia,* 295 U.S. 463 (1935).

16. *Massachusetts v. Missouri,* 308 U.S. 1 at 15, 18 (1939).

17. *Chisholm v. Georgia,* 2 Dall. (2 U.S.) 419 (1793).

18. *Wisconsin v. Pelican Insurance Co.,* 127 U.S. 265 (1888).

19. *California v. Southern Pacific Railway Co.,* 157 U.S. 220 (1895).

20. *Georgia v. Tennessee Copper Co.,* 206 U.S. 230 (1907); *Georgia v. Pennsylvania Railroad Co.,* 324 U.S. 439 (1945).

21. Frankfurter and Landis, *Business of the Supreme Court,* 8–9.

22. *Strawbridge v. Curtiss,* 3 Cr. (7 U.S.) 267 (1806).

23. *State Farm, Fire & Casualty Co. v. Tashire,* 386 U.S. 523 (1967).

24. *Bank of the United States v. Deveaux,* 5 Cr. (9 U.S.) 61 (1809).

25. *Louisville RR v. Letson,* 2 How. (43 U.S.) 497 (1844); *Marshall v. Baltimore and Ohio R. Co.,* 16 How. (57 U.S.) 314 (1854); *Muller v. Dows,* 94 U.S. 444 (1877).

26. Frankfurter and Landis, *Business of the Supreme Court,* 65, 89; see also Wright, *Handbook,* 89.

27. 28 U.S.C. § 1332 (a).

28. Wright, *Handbook,* 84–85; *Ex parte Burrus,* 136 U.S. 586 (1890); *Barber v. Barber,* 21 How. (70 U.S.) 582 (1858).

29. *The Schooner Exchange v. McFadden,* 7 Cr. (11 U.S.) 116 at 145 (1812).

30. *Monaco v. Mississippi,* 292 U.S. 313 (1934).

31. *The Ship Sapphire v. Napoleon III,* 11 Wall. (78 U.S.) 164 at 167 (1871).

32. *Pfizer Inc. v. Government of India,* 434 U.S. 308 (1978).

33. *Ex parte Gruber,* 269 U.S. 302 (1925).

34. *Popovici v. Agler,* 280 U.S. 289 (1930).

35. *Marbury v. Madison,* 1 Cr. (5 U.S.) 137 at 174 (1803).

36. *Ames v. Kansas,* 111 U.S. 449 at 464 (1884).

37. Id. at 464–465.

38. *Kentucky v. Dennison,* 24 How. (65 U.S.) 66 (1861).

39. *Wisconsin v. Pelican Insurance Co.,* 127 U.S. 265 at 287, 288, 289–290, 297 (1888).

40. *Wiscart v. Dauchy,* 3 Dall. (3 U.S.) 321 at 327 (1796); *Durousseau v. United States,* 6 Cr. (10 U.S.) 307 at 314 (1810).

41. *Daniels v. Chicago & Rock Island Railroad Co.,* 3 Wall. (70 U.S.) 250 at 254 (1866).

42. Carl B. Swisher, *American Constitutional Development,* 2nd ed. (Cambridge, Mass.: Houghton Mifflin, 1954), 324.

43. *Ex parte McCardle,* 6 Wall. (73 U.S.) 318 at 325–326, 327 (1868).

44. Charles Warren, *The Supreme Court in United States History,* 2 vols. (Boston: Little, Brown, 1926), 2:474–485.

45. *Ex parte McCardle,* 7 Wall. (74 U.S.) 506 at 514, 515 (1869).

46. *Ex parte Yerger,* 8 Wall. (75 U.S.) 85 at 104 (1869).

47. Swisher, *American Constitutional Development,* 325.

48. Charles L. Black Jr., *Perspectives in Constitutional Law* (Englewood Cliffs, N.J.: Prentice-Hall, 1963), 13.

49. Frankfurter and Landis, *Business of the Supreme Court,* 299.

50. *The Oxford Companion to the Supreme Court,* ed. Kermit L. Hall (New York: Oxford University Press, 1992), 145.

51. *United States v. Sanges,* 144 U.S. 310 (1892).

52. Frankfurter and Landis, *Business of the Supreme Court,* 113–119.

53. Ibid., 193–198.

54. Ibid., 211.

55. Ibid., 255–286.

56. Wright, *Handbook,* 477.

57. William Howard Taft, "The Jurisdiction of the Supreme Court under the Act of February 13, 1925," *Yale Law Journal* (November 1925): 2, cited in Alpheus T. Mason, *The Supreme Court from Taft to Warren* (Baton Rouge: Louisiana State University Press, 1958), 222 n. 83.

FEDERAL JUDICIAL POWER (PP. 19–49)

1. Samuel F. Miller, *Lectures on the Constitution* (Albany, N.Y.: Banks and Brothers, 1891), 314.

2. James Madison, Alexander Hamilton, and John Jay, *The Federalist Papers,* ed. Clinton Rossiter (New York: New American Library, 1961), No. 51, 322.

3. Randy E. Barnett, *Restoring the Lost Constitution: The Presumption of Liberty* (Princeton, N.J.: Princeton University Press, 2004).

4. *United States v. Nixon,* 418 U.S. 683 at 705 (1974).

5. Thomas Reed Powell, *Vagaries and Varieties in Constitutional Interpretation* (New York: Columbia University Press, 1956; reprint, New York: AMS Press, 1967), 20.

6. Robert K. Carr, *The Supreme Court and Judicial Review* (New York: Farrar and Rinehart, 1942), 43. For a brief review of revolutionary-era legal precedents, see Scott Douglas Gerber, "The Myth of *Marbury v. Madison* and the Origins of Judicial Review," in *Marbury v. Madison: Documents and Commentary,* ed. Mark A. Graber and Michael Perhac (Washington, D.C.: CQ Press, 2002), 1–15.

7. Barnett, *Restoring the Lost Constitution,* citing James Madison, *Notes of Debates in the Federal Convention of 1787* (New York: Norton, 1987), 304–305, 336–337, 340, 351–353, 462–463, 511, 518.

8. Carr, *Supreme Court and Judicial Review,* 45, citing Max Farrand, *The Records of the Federal Convention of 1787* (New Haven, Conn.: Yale University Press, 1911), 2:73.

9. *Martin v. Hunter's Lessee,* 1 Wheat. (14 U.S.) 304 (1816); *Cohens v. Virginia,* 6 Wheat. (19 U.S.) 264 (1821).

10. *Murdock v. Memphis,* 20 Wall. (87 U.S.) 590 (1875).

11. *Herb v. Pitcairn,* 324 U.S. 117 at 125–126 (1945).

12. *United States v. Hylton,* 3 Dall. (3 U.S.) 171 (1796).

13. Charles Warren, *The Supreme Court in United States History,* 2 vols. (Boston: Little, Brown, 1926), 2:222–223.

14. *Marbury v. Madison,* 1 Cr. (5 U.S.) 137 at 175–176 (1803).

15. Id. at 177–178.

16. Id. at 178.

17. Carl B. Swisher, *American Constitutional Development,* 2nd ed. (Cambridge, Mass.: Houghton Mifflin, 1954), 10.

18. Charles G. Haines, *The American Doctrine of Judicial Supremacy* (Berkeley: University of California Press, 1932), 202–203; Charles Evans Hughes, *The Supreme Court of the United States* (New York: Columbia University Press, 1928), 87–89.

19. Charles P. Curtis, "Review and Majority Rule," in *Supreme Court and Supreme Law,* ed. Edmond Cahn (New York: Simon and Schuster, 1971), 198.

20. Carr, *Supreme Court and Judicial Review,* 71.

21. Hughes, *Supreme Court,* 50–51.

22. *Hepburn v. Griswold,* 8 Wall. (75 U.S.) 603 (1870); *Knox v. Lee,* 12 Wall. (79 U.S.) 457 (1871).

23. Powell, *Vagaries and Varieties,* 18.

24. Hughes, *Supreme Court,* 95–96.

25. The current version of that provision—referred to as the All Writs Act—grants federal courts power to issue "all writs necessary or appropriate in aid of their respective jurisdictions and agreeable to the usages and principles of law." 28 U.S.C. 1651(a).

26. *Ex parte Yerger,* 8 Wall. (75 U.S.) 85 at 95 (1869).

27. *Adams v. United States ex rel. McCann,* 317 U.S. 269 at 273 (1942).

28. *Fay v. Noia,* 372 U.S. 391 at 401–402 (1963).

29. Congressional Research Service, *The Constitution of the United States of America: Analysis and Interpretation* (Washington, D.C.: U.S. Government Printing Office, 1973), 617–618.

30. *Brown v. Allen,* 344 U.S. 443 at 465 (1953).

31. *Gusik v. Schilder,* 339 U.S. 977 (1950).

32. *Adams v. United States ex rel. McCann,* 317 U.S. 269 at 274 (1942).

33. Congressional Research Service, *Constitution,* 616–617.

34. *Ex parte Bollman,* 4 Cr. (8 U.S.) 75 at 101 (1807).

35. *Ex parte Watkins,* 3 Pet. (28 U.S.) 193 at 202 (1830).

36. *Ex parte Dorr,* 3 How. (44 U.S.) 103 at 105 (1845).

37. Charles Fairman, *History of the Supreme Court of the United States,* vol. 6, *Reconstruction and Reunion, 1864–1888,* part 1 (New York: MacMillan, 1971), 443–447.

38. Ibid., 451; *Ex parte McCardle,* 7 Wall. (74 U.S.) 506 (1869).

39. *Ex parte Yerger,* 8 Wall. (75 U.S.) 85 (1869).

40. *Ex parte Virginia,* 100 U.S. 339 (1880); *Ex parte Clarke,* 100 U.S. 399 (1880); *Ex parte Siebold,* 100 U.S. 371 (1880).

41. *Ex parte Siebold,* 100 U.S. 371 at 376–377 (1880).

42. *Ex parte Nielsen,* 131 U.S. 176 at 183–184 (1889).

43. *Frank v. Mangum,* 237 U.S. 309 at 327, 331 (1915).

44. *Moore v. Dempsey,* 261 U.S. 86 at 91 (1923); see also *Hawk v. Olson,* 326 U.S. 271 at 276 (1945).

45. *Waley v. Johnston,* 316 U.S. 101 at 104–105 (1942).

46. *Brown v. Allen,* 344 U.S. 443 at 464–465 (1953).

47. *Townsend v. Sain,* 372 U.S. 293 at 312, 318 (1963).

48. *Ex parte Royall,* 117 U.S. 241 (1886).

49. *Ex parte Hawk,* 321 U.S. 114 at 116–117 (1944); see also *Darr v. Burford,* 339 U.S. 200 at 217 (1950).

50. *Darr v. Burford,* 339 U.S. 200 at 217 (1950).

51. *Brown v. Allen,* 344 U.S. 443 at 487 (1953).

52. *Darr v. Burford,* 339 U.S. 200 at 210, 216 (1950).

53. *Fay v. Noia,* 372 U.S. 391 (1963).

54. Id. at 441.

55. Id. at 438–439.

56. Id. at 440.

57. Id. at 435–437.

58. *Stone v. Powell,* 428 U.S. 465 (1976).

59. *Davis v. United States,* 411 U.S. 233 (1973); *Francis v. Henderson,* 425 U.S. 536 (1976); *Wainwright v. Sykes,* 433 U.S. 72 (1977); *Rose v. Lundy,* 455 U.S. 509 (1982); *Engle v. Isaac,* 456 U.S. 107 (1982).

60. *Teague v. Lane,* 489 U.S. 255 (1989).

61. Id.

62. Id.

63. *Saffle v. Parks,* 494 U.S. 484 (1990).

64. *Butler v. McKellar,* 494 U.S. 407 (1990).

65. *Sawyer v. Smith,* 497 U.S. 227 (1990).

66. *Coleman v. Thompson,* 501 U.S. 722 (1991).

67. *McCleskey v. Zant,* 499 U.S. 467 (1991).

68. *Keeney v. Tamayo-Reyes,* 504 U.S. 1 (1992).

69. *Felker v. Turpin,* 518 U.S. 651 (1996).

70. *Rasul v. Bush,* 542 U.S. 466 (2004).

71. *Boumediene v. Bush,* 553 U.S. —- (2008).

72. *Kerr v. United States District Court,* 426 U.S. 394 at 402 (1976).

73. *United States v. Haley,* 371 U.S. 18 (1962); *Deen v. Hickman,* 358 U.S. 57 (1958).

74. *Marbury v. Madison,* 1 Cr. (5 U.S.) 137 (1803).

75. *McIntire v. Wood,* 7 Cr. (11 U.S.) 504 (1813); *McClung v. Silliman,* 6 Wheat. 598 (1821); *Kendall v. United States ex rel. Stokes,* 12 Pet. (37 U.S.) 524 at 624 (1838).

76. *Marbury v. Madison,* 1 Cr. (5 U.S.) 137 at 170–171 (1803).

77. *Kendall v. United States ex rel. Stokes,* 12 Pet. (37 U.S.) 524 at 613 (1838).

78. *Kerr v. United States District Court,* 426 U.S. 394 at 403 (1976); see also *Marbury v. Madison,* 1 Cr. (5 U.S.) 137 at 169 (1803); *United States v. Duell,* 172 U.S. 576 at 582 (1899); *Ex parte Republic of Peru,* 318 U.S. 578 at 584 (1943).

79. *The Bank of Columbia v. Sweeny,* 1 Pet. 26 U.S. 567 at 569 (1828).

80. *Roche v. Evaporated Milk Association,* 319 U.S. 21 at 26, 29 (1943); *Ex parte Fahey,* 332 U.S. 258 at 259–260 (1947); see also *Parr v. United States,* 351 U.S. 513 at 520 (1956).

81. *Ex parte Republic of Peru,* 318 U.S. 578 at 583 (1943).

82. *Bankers Life & Casualty v. Holland,* 346 U.S. 379 at 383 (1953).

83. *Ex parte United States,* 287 U.S. 241 at 248–249 (1932).

84. *Deen v. Hickman,* 358 U.S. 57 (1958).

85. *Roche v. Evaporated Milk Association,* 319 U.S. 21 (1943).

86. *La Buy v. Howes Leather,* 352 U.S. 249 (1957); *Beacon Theatres Inc. v. Westover,* 359 U.S. 500 (1959); *Thermtron Products v. Hermansdorfer,* 423 U.S. 336 (1976).

87. *United States v. United Mine Workers,* 330 U.S. 258 (1947).

88. *Pollock v. Farmers' Loan and Trust Co.,* 158 U.S. 601 (1895).

89. *Lockerty v. Phillips,* 319 U.S. 182 (1943).

90. *Mississippi v. Johnson,* 4 Wall. (71 U.S.) 475 at 498–499 (1867).

91. Id. at 500.

92. See *Mitchum v. Foster,* 407 U.S. 225 at 234–235 (1972).

93. Id. at 235–236.

94. *Toucey v. New York Life Insurance Co.,* 314 U.S. 118 at 139 (1941).

95. *Leiter Minerals v. United States,* 352 U.S. 220 (1957); *Mitchum v. Foster,* 407 U.S. 225 (1972).

96. *Osborn v. Bank of the United States,* 9 Wheat. (22 U.S.) 738 (1824); *Ex parte Young,* 209 U.S. 123 (1908).

97. *Prentis v. Atlantic Coast Line Co.,* 211 U.S. 210 (1908).

98. *Dombrowski v. Pfister,* 380 U.S. 479 at 484–485 (1965).

99. *Fenner v. Boykin,* 271 U.S. 240 at 244 (1926).

100. *Beal v. Missouri Pacific R.R. Co.,* 312 U.S. 45 (1941); *Railroad Commission of Texas v. Pullman Co.,* 312 U.S. 496 (1941); *Douglas v. City of Jeannette,* 319 U.S. 157 (1943).

101. *McNeese v. Board of Education for Community Unit School District,* 373 U.S. 668 (1963).

102. *Harman v. Forssenius,* 380 U.S. 528 at 534–535 (1965).

103. *Dombrowski v. Pfister,* 380 U.S. 479 at 489–490 (1965).

104. *Younger v. Harris,* 401 U.S. 37 at 45 (1971); *Samuels v. Mackell, Fernandez v. Mackell,* 401 U.S. 66 (1971); *Byrne v. Karalexis,* 401 U.S. 216 (1971); *Perez v. Ledesma,* 401 U.S. 82 (1971); *Dyson v. Stein,* 401 U.S. 200 (1971).

105. *Younger v. Harris,* 401 U.S. 37 at 51 (1971).

106. Id. at 44; *Imperial County v. Munoz,* 449 U.S. 54 (1980); *Deakins v. Monaghan,* 484 U.S. 193 (1988).

107. *Hicks v. Miranda,* 422 U.S. 332 (1975); *Huffman v. Pursue Ltd.,* 420 U.S. 592 (1975); *Trainor v. Hernandez,* 431 U.S. 434 (1976); *Juidice v. Vail,* 430 U.S. 327 (1976).

108. *Pennzoil Company v. Texaco Inc.,* 481 U.S. 1 at 14, 11 (1987).

109. *Willing v. Chicago Auditorium Association,* 277 U.S. 274 at 289 (1928); *Nashville, Chicago & St. Louis Railway Company v. Wallace,* 288 U.S. 249 at 264 (1933).

110. *Aetna Life Insurance Co. v. Haworth,* 300 U.S. 227 (1937).

111. *Maryland Casualty Co. v. Pacific Coal & Oil Co.,* 312 U.S. 270 at 273 (1941); *Alabama State Federation of Labor v. McAdory,* 325 U.S. 450 at 461 (1945).

112. *Poe v. Ullman,* 367 U.S. 497 (1961); *Griswold v. Connecticut,* 381 U.S. 479 (1965).

113. *Public Affairs Associates v. Rickover,* 369 U.S. 111 at 112 (1962); *Brillhart v. Excess Insurance Co.,* 316 U.S. 491 at 494 (1942).

114. *Great Lakes Dredge and Dock Co. v. Huffman,* 319 U.S. 293 (1943).

115. *Zwickler v. Koota,* 389 U.S. 241 at 254, 248 (1967).

116. *Samuels v. Mackell,* 401 U.S. 66 at 72 (1971).

117. *Steffel v. Thompson,* 415 U.S. 452 (1974); *Ellis v. Dyson,* 421 U.S. 426 (1975).

118. *Steffel v. Thompson,* 415 U.S. 452 at 462 (1974).

119. Id. at 472.

120. *Lake Carriers Association v. MacMullan,* 406 U.S. 498 (1972); *Steffel v. Thompson,* 415 U.S. 452 (1974); *Ellis v. Dyson,* 421 U.S. 426 (1975).

121. *Anderson v. Dunn,* 6 Wheat. (19 U.S.) 204 at 231 (1821).

122. *Ex parte Robinson,* 19 Wall. (86 U.S.) 505 (1874).

123. *Ex parte Terry,* 128 U.S. 289 at 313 (1888).

124. *Illinois v. Allen,* 397 U.S. 337 (1970).

125. *In re Debs,* 158 U.S. 564 at 594–595 (1895).

126. *United States v. United Mine Workers,* 330 U.S. 258 (1947).

127. *Toledo Newspaper Co. v. United States,* 247 U.S. 402 (1918).

128. *Nye v. United States,* 313 U.S. 33 at 52 (1941).

129. *Ex parte Hudgings,* 249 U.S. 378 at 383 (1919); see also *In re Michael,* 326 U.S. 224 (1945).

130. *Brown v. United States,* 356 U.S. 148 at 153 (1958).

131. *United States v. Wilson,* 421 U.S. 309 at 315–316, 319 (1975).

132. *Harris v. United States,* 382 U.S. 162 (1965), overruling *Brown v. United States,* 359 U.S. 41 (1959).

133. *Sacher v. United States,* 343 U.S. 1 at 3 (1952).

134. *In re McConnell,* 370 U.S. 230 (1962).

135. *Green v. United States,* 356 U.S. 165 (1958).

136. *Gompers v. Buck's Stove and Range Co.,* 221 U.S. 418 at 441 (1911).

137. Id. at 442.

138. Id.

139. Id. at 442–443.

140. *Ex parte Grossman*, 267 U.S. 87 (1925).

141. *United States v. United Mine Workers*, 330 U.S. 258 at 300 (1947).

142. Id. at 295.

143. *Shillitani v. United States, Pappadio v. United States*, 384 U.S. 364 at 368 (1966).

144. *United Mine Workers v. Bagwell*, 512 U.S. 821 (1994).

145. *Bessette v. W. B. Conkey*, 194 U.S. 324 at 326 (1904).

146. *Ex parte Terry*, 128 U.S. 289 at 312 (1888).

147. *In re Debs*, 158 U.S. 564 at 595 (1895).

148. *Cooke v. United States*, 267 U.S. 517 at 539 (1925).

149. *Sacher v. United States*, 343 U.S. 1 at 12 (1952).

150. *Offutt v. United States*, 348 U.S. 11 at 14 (1954).

151. *Mayberry v. Pennsylvania*, 400 U.S. 455 (1971).

152. *Michaelson v. United States*, 266 U.S. 42 at 66 (1924); *Cooke v. United States*, 267 U.S. 517 at 537 (1925).

153. The Clayton Act of 1914 provided a jury trial for persons charged with contempt for disobeying court orders when their disobedient conduct also constitutes a crime under other state or federal law. Some limited right to jury trial for contempt was provided by portions of the Civil Rights Acts of 1957 and 1964.

154. *Green v. United States*, 356 U.S. 165 (1958); *Levine v. United States*, 362 U.S. 610 (1960); *United States v. Barnett*, 376 U.S. 681 (1964).

155. *Cheff v. Schnackenberg*, 384 U.S. 373 (1966).

156. *Duncan v. Louisiana*, 391 U.S. 145 (1968); *Bloom v. Illinois*, 391 U.S. 194 (1968).

157. *Bloom v. Illinois*, 391 U.S. 194 at 198, 201, 202 (1968).

158. Id. at 208, 209.

159. *Codispoti v. Pennsylvania*, 418 U.S. 506 (1974).

160. *Lewis v. United States*, 518 U.S. 322 (1996).

JUDICIAL RESTRAINT (PP. 50–65)

1. Robert K. Carr, *The Supreme Court and Judicial Review* (New York: Farrar and Rinehart, 1942), 185.

2. *Ashwander v. Tennessee Valley Authority*, 297 U.S. 288 at 346–348 (1936).

3. *Aetna Life Insurance Co. v. Haworth*, 300 U.S. 227 at 240–241 (1937).

4. *United States v. Fruehauf*, 365 U.S. 146 at 157 (1961).

5. Alexander M. Bickel, *The Least Dangerous Branch* (Indianapolis: Bobbs-Merrill, 1962), 113–114; Charles Warren, *The Supreme Court in United States History*, 2 vols. (Boston: Little, Brown, 1926), 1:110–111.

6. *Muskrat v. United States*, 219 U.S. 346 (1911).

7. Id. at 362.

8. *Mills v. Green*, 159 U.S. 651 at 653 (1895); see also *California v. San Pablo & Tulare Railroad Company*, 149 U.S. 308 at 314 (1893).

9. *DeFunis v. Odegaard*, 416 U.S. 312 (1974).

10. *City of Los Angeles v. Lyons*, 461 U.S. 95 (1983).

11. *Sibron v. New York*, 392 U.S. 40 (1968); *Benton v. Maryland*, 395 U.S. 784 (1969).

12. *Moore v. Ogilvie*, 394 U.S. 814 (1969).

13. *Roe v. Wade, Doe v. Bolton*, 410 U.S. 113, 179 (1973); *Southern Pacific Terminal Co. v. Interstate Commerce Commission*, 219 U.S. 498 at 515 (1911).

14. *Lord v. Veazie*, 8 How. (49 U.S.) 251 at 255 (1850).

15. *Chicago & Grand Trunk Railway Co. v. Wellman*, 143 U.S. 339 at 344–345 (1892).

16. *Hylton v. United States*, 3 Dall. (3 U.S.) 171 (1796).

17. *Fletcher v. Peck*, 6 Cr. (10 U.S.) 87 (1810); *Scott v. Sandford*, 19 How. (60 U.S.) 393 (1857); *Pollock v. Farmers' Loan and Trust Co.* 157 U.S. 429, 158 U.S. 601 (1895).

18. *Carter v. Carter Coal Company*, 298 U.S. 238 (1936).

19. *Flast v. Cohen*, 392 U.S. 83 at 99 (1968).

20. *Baker v. Carr*, 369 U.S. 186 at 204 (1962).

21. *Raines v. Byrd*, 521 U.S. 811 (1997).

22. *Clinton v. City of New York*, 524 U.S. 417 (1998).

23. *Massachusetts v. Mellon, Frothingham v. Mellon*, 262 U.S. 447 at 483 (1923).

24. Id. at 487.

25. See *Everson v. Board of Education*, 330 U.S. 1 (1947); *Doremus v. Board of Education*, 342 U.S. 429 (1952); *Engel v. Vitale*, 370 U.S. 421 (1962).

26. *Frothingham v. Mellon*, 262 U.S. 447 at 487 (1923).

27. Id. at 488.

28. *Flast v. Cohen*, 392 U.S. 83 at 101 (1968).

29. Id. at 106.

30. *United States v. Richardson*, 418 U.S. 166 at 175, 177 (1974).

31. *Baker v. Carr*, 369 U.S. 186 (1962).

32. *United States v. Richardson*, 418 U.S. 166 at 193 (1974).

33. *Laird v. Tatum*, 408 U.S. 1 (1972); *Schlesinger v. Reservists Committee to Stop the War*, 418 U.S. 208 (1974); *Warth v. Seldin*, 422 U.S. 490 (1975); *Simon v. Eastern Kentucky Welfare Rights Organization*, 426 U.S. 26 (1976).

34. *Hein v. Freedom from Religion Foundation*, 551 U.S. —- (2007).

35. *Association of Data Processing Organizations v. Camp*, 397 U.S. 150 at 154 (1970); *Sierra Club v. Morton*, 405 U.S. 727 at 738–739 (1972); *United States v. Richardson*, 418 U.S. 166 at 193–194 (1974); *Baker v. Carr*, 369 U.S. 186 (1962); *United States v. SCRAP*, 412 U.S. 669 (1973).

36. *Lujan v. Defenders of Wildlife*, 504 U.S. 555 (1992); *United States v. Hays*, 515 U.S. 737 (1995).

37. *Summers v. Earth Island Institute*, 555 U.S. —- (2009).

38. *Tileston v. Ullman*, 318 U.S. 44 (1943); *United States v. Raines*, 362 U.S. 17 at 20–24 (1960).

39. *Truax v. Raich*, 239 U.S. 33 (1915).

40. *Pierce v. Society of Sisters*, 268 U.S. 510 (1925).

41. *Buchanan v. Warley,* 245 U.S. 60 (1917); *Barrows v. Jackson* 346 U.S. 249 (1953). Also see, however, *Allen v. Wright,* 468 U.S. 737 (1984).

42. *Griswold v. Connecticut,* 381 U.S. 479 (1965); *Doe v. Bolton,* 410 U.S. 179 (1973); *Singleton v. Wulff,* 428 U.S. 106 (1976).

43. *Joint Anti-Fascist Committee v. McGrath,* 341 U.S. 123 (1951); *NAACP v. Alabama ex rel. Patterson,* 357 U.S. 449 (1958); *NAACP v. Button,* 371 U.S. 415 (1963); *Sierra Club v. Morton,* 405 U.S. 727 at 739 (1972).

44. *Missouri v. Illinois,* 180 U.S. 208 (1901); *Georgia v. Tennessee Copper Company,* 206 U.S. 230 (1907); *Pennsylvania v. West Virginia,* 262 U.S. 553 (1923); *Georgia v. Pennsylvania R. Co.,* 324 U.S. 439 (1945); *Massachusetts v. Mellon,* 262 U.S. 447 (1923).

45. *Marbury v. Madison,* 1 Cr. (5 U.S.) 137 at 170 (1803).

46. *Baker v. Carr,* 369 U.S. 186 at 210 (1962).

47. C. Gordon Post, *Supreme Court and Political Questions* (Baltimore: Johns Hopkins University Press, 1936; reprint, New York: Da Capo Press, 1969), 130.

48. *Luther v. Borden,* 7 How. (48 U.S.) 1 at 42 (1849).

49. Id.

50. Id. at 43; see also *Martin v. Mott,* 12 Wheat. (25 U.S.) 19 (1827).

51. *Pacific States Telephone and Telegraph v. Oregon,* 223 U.S. 118 (1912).

52. *Baker v. Carr,* 369 U.S. 186 at 209–210 (1962).

53. *Foster v. Neilson,* 2 Pet. (27 U.S.) 253 at 307 (1829).

54. *Oetjen v. Central Leather Co.,* 246 U.S. 297 at 302 (1918); *United States v. Curtiss-Wright Export Corporation,* 299 U.S. 304 (1936).

55. *Hawke v. Smith,* 253 U.S. 221 (1920); *Coleman v. Miller,* 307 U.S. 433 (1939); *Powell v. McCormack,* 395 U.S. 486 (1969).

56. *Okanogan Indians et al. v. United States (Pocket Veto Case),* 279 U.S. 655 (1929).

57. *Colegrove v. Green,* 328 U.S. 549 at 553–554 (1946).

58. *Baker v. Carr,* 369 U.S. 186 at 210 (1962).

59. Id. at 232.

60. Post, *Supreme Court and Political Questions,* 129–130.

61. Carr, *Supreme Court and Judicial Review,* 18–19.

62. *Burnet v. Coronado Oil & Gas Company,* 285 U.S. 393 at 406 (1932).

63. William O. Douglas, "Stare Decisis," in Association of the Bar of the City of New York, *The Record* 4 (1949): 152–179, reprinted in *The Supreme Court: Views from Inside,* ed. Alan F. Westin (New York: W. W. Norton, 1961), 123.

64. Carr, *Supreme Court and Judicial Review,* 18–19.

65. *Hudson and Smith v. Guestier,* 6 Cr. (11 U.S.) 281 (1810), overruling *Rose v. Himely,* 4 Cr. (8 U.S.) 241 (1808).

66. *Knox v. Lee,* 12 Wall. (79 U.S.) 457 (1871), overruling *Hepburn v. Griswold,* 8 Wall. (75 U.S.) 603 (1870).

67. *Pollock v. Farmers' Loan and Trust Co.,* 157 U.S. 601 (1895).

68. *Helvering v. Hallock,* 309 U.S. 106 at 119 (1940).

69. *Smith v. Allwright,* 321 U.S. 649 at 665–666 (1944), overruling *Grovey v. Townsend,* 295 U.S. 45 (1935).

70. *Planned Parenthood of Southeastern Pennsylvania v. Casey,* 505 U.S. 833 (1992).

71. Id.

72. Loren P. Beth, *The Constitution, Politics and the Supreme Court* (New York: Harper and Row, 1962), 49.

73. *Hein v. Freedom from Religion Foundation,* 551 U.S. —- (2007), Justice Scalia concurring.

74. *FEC v. Wisconsin Right to Life,* 551 U.S. —- (2007).

75. *McConnell v. Federal Election Commission,* 540 U.S. 93 (2003).

76. *FEC v. Wisconsin Right to Life,* 551 U.S. —- (2007).

77. Id., Justice Scalia concurring, fn 7.

78. Edward S. Corwin, ed., *The Constitution of the United States of America: Analysis and Interpretation* (Washington, D.C.: U.S. Government Printing Office, 1953), 626.

79. *Younger v. Harris,* 401 U.S. 37 at 441 (1971).

80. Id.

The Court and the Powers of Congress

THE NEW GOVERNMENT created by the Constitution included an executive to carry out the laws and a judiciary to resolve conflicts, but the legislature—Congress—was the heart of the new democracy. The House of Representatives was the only part of the federal government originally elected by the people. Not unexpectedly then, it was to Congress that the people looked for a direct response to their needs and concerns. So it was that the framers entrusted to the legislature the lion's share of the power necessary to govern. The Constitution granted Congress the power to tax, to control commerce, to declare war, to approve treaties, and to raise and maintain armies. Congress also was granted some authority over its coequal branches. It had the power to establish whatever federal courts, other than the Supreme Court, became necessary, and it was empowered to impeach, convict, and remove from office the president, Supreme Court justices, and other federal officers for treason, bribery, or other high crimes and misdemeanors.

Specific constitutional limitations were, however, placed on Congress's exercise of power. Congress was forbidden to single out individuals for punishment through the passage of ex post facto laws or bills of attainder. It was denied the power to impose a direct tax that is unapportioned or an indirect tax that is not uniform. Perhaps the most significant limits were added by the First Amendment—which prohibits Congress from interfering with the free exercise of speech, the press, assembly, or religion—and the Fifth Amendment—which prohibits the taking of life, liberty, or property without due process of law. In addition, the Tenth Amendment reserves to the states and the people all powers not granted to Congress.

JUDICIAL REVIEW

Nothing was said in the Constitution about who would enforce the limitations on Congress. Was Congress to police itself, or would the judiciary—most particularly the Supreme Court—take on this role? Alexander Hamilton, writing as Publius in the *Federalist Papers,* asserted that enforcement belonged to the courts: "[T]he courts," Hamilton wrote, "were designed to be an intermediate body between the people and the legislature in order, among other things, to keep the latter within the limits assigned to their authority."[1] Most constitutional scholars agree that a majority of the framers expected the Supreme Court to assume this role, but the question of whether the Court could actually nullify an act of Congress as unconstitutional remained unanswered until 1803, when the Court issued its decision in *Marbury v. Madison.* When Chief Justice John Marshall stated that Congress had impermissibly enlarged the Court's original jurisdiction, he declared that "a law repugnant to the Constitution is void." In so doing, he firmly asserted the power of the Supreme Court to make such determinations: "It is, emphatically, the province and duty of the judicial department, to say what the law is."[2]

Although scholars have questioned the legal reasoning in *Marbury,* its significance has never been challenged. The nation might have survived if the Court had not claimed the power to review and declare invalid acts of Congress, but without the power of judicial review, a clear check on the exercise of legislative power, wrote historian Charles Warren,

> the Nation could never have remained a Federal Republic. Its government would have become a consolidated and centralized autocracy. Congress would have attained supreme, final and unlimited power over the Executive and the Judiciary branches and the States and the individual citizens could have possessed only such powers and rights as Congress chose to leave or grant to them. The hard-fought-for Bill of Rights and the reserved powers of the States guaranteed by the Constitution would have been subject to the unlimited control of the prejudice, whim or passion of the majority as represented in Congress at any given moment. Though such a government might possibly have operated in this country, it would not have been the form of government which the framers of the Constitution intended, but a government with unlimited powers over the States.[3]

Having claimed this power, the Marshall Court never again exercised it to nullify an act of Congress. Rather than confine the exercise of legislative powers, the Marshall Court consistently defined the power of Congress in broad terms. Perhaps most important of such instances was the Court's declaration that the clause giving Congress the power to make all laws "necessary and proper" to the exercise of its specific powers gave the legislature the authority to enact any measure that was an appropriate means to a constitutional end. Two decades after *Marbury,* the Court further broadened the scope of congressional power when it acknowledged the authority of Congress to delegate some legislative responsibility to other branches. In 1828 the Court acknowledged that Congress had, along with its enumerated powers, additional powers that were inherent in the fact of national sovereignty.

THE COMMERCE POWER

Even as the Marshall Court established the supremacy of the Constitution over acts of Congress, it was careful to protect congressional power from encroachment by the states. This point was made forcefully by the famous steamship monopoly decision, *Gibbons v. Ogden* (1824). The Court ruled that a federal permit overrode a state-granted monopoly. Navigation between two states was interstate commerce, Marshall wrote, and state action would not be permitted to limit Congress's power to regulate interstate commerce.[4] The congressional power over commerce, the Court emphasized in *Gibbons,* was not limited to transportation but extended to all commercial intercourse affecting two or more states. The only commerce Congress could not legislate, Marshall said, was that wholly within one state not affecting any other state.

The importance of this broad definition was not fully apparent until the late nineteenth century, when Congress exercised this power to regulate not only the railroads, but also the huge trusts that monopolized many of the nation's major industries. Although some of the railroads and many of the trusts operated within single states, Marshall's definition left room for Congress to regulate them, because they affected more than one state. The Court, sympathetic to business interests, temporarily narrowed Marshall's definition to hold that Congress could only regulate those intrastate matters that directly affected interstate commerce. Intrastate matters affecting interstate commerce indirectly were for the states to regulate. It was for the Court to determine which effects were direct and which indirect. From these two versions of Marshall's view, the Court developed two lines of precedent that it applied in unpredictable and conflicting fashion. Using the narrow view in 1895, for example, the Court held that a trust processing more than 90 percent of all refined sugar did not violate the antitrust law. Sugar refining was manufacturing, the Court held, and manufacture was not commerce and did not affect commerce directly.[5] Ten years later the Court, taking the broad view, ruled that an intrastate stockyard operation did violate the antitrust act. Even though it was an intrastate processing operation, the Court said the stockyard was an integral part of a stream of interstate commerce.

During this same period, Congress began to use its commerce and tax powers for social as well as economic purposes, developing a federal "police" power used to protect public health and morals. In 1903 the Supreme Court sustained a congressional prohibition on the interstate sale and shipment of lottery tickets.[6] In 1904 it upheld a tax placed on colored oleo to remove this competition to butter from the market.[7] In subsequent terms, the Court sanctioned other uses of this new federal power. Encouraged, Congress exercised this power to bar from interstate commerce goods made by child labor.[8]

In 1918, however, the Court returned to the narrow view of the commerce power and struck down the child labor law. Congress, the Court ruled, had attempted to regulate manufacturing, not commerce.[9] Although this assessment might be accurate, the child labor law was similar to the ban on lottery tickets. The Court distinguished the two cases by saying that lottery tickets were harmful in themselves while goods made by children were not. Congress responded by imposing a heavy tax on the profits of any company that employed children. The Court in 1922 struck down the tax as a penalty, not a revenue-raising device.[10] The Court distinguished the child labor tax from the oleo tax by refusing to acknowledge that the oleo tax had any other purpose than to raise revenue. For the next few years, the two child labor cases stood as anomalies while the Court upheld other uses of the federal police power, including some wider federal regulation of intrastate matters. Only against labor unions did the Court maintain a consistently conservative stance; it ruled repeatedly that many strikes and boycotts were illegal restraints of trade under the antitrust law and diluted the force of new laws designed to protect the rights of organized workers.[11] By 1930, however, the Court was rethinking its position on labor. It upheld a federal law guaranteeing collective bargaining rights to railway workers.

With the advent of the Great Depression, President Franklin D. Roosevelt proposed and Congress enacted recovery laws regulating business to an unprecedented degree. When these laws were challenged as unconstitutional, in almost every instance the Supreme Court struck them down, ruling that Congress did not have the broad power necessary to cope with the national crisis. The Court struck down a law encouraging wage and hour standards for coal miners on the grounds that mining was an intrastate operation with no direct effect on interstate commerce. It struck down fair competition codes because they affected some industries that did not directly affect interstate commerce. The Court invalidated a plan to tax food processors and use the revenue to pay benefits to farmers who curtailed production of certain crops as an unconstitutional scheme to regulate agricultural production, which was not, it held, interstate commerce. It declared that a federal pension plan for retired railroad workers was outside the reach of the interstate commerce power. In other words, a majority of the Court during the New Deal era refused to acknowledge that local economic conditions had any direct bearing on the health of the national economy or that Congress had the authority, through its commerce and tax powers, to try to ameliorate local conditions.

Apparently responding to FDR's landslide reelection, the Court in 1937 reassessed the scope of the commerce power and returned to Marshall's broad view. In quick succession, the Court upheld acts of Congress banning unfair labor practices and regulating wages and hours and agricultural production. It approved federal laws establishing the Social Security pension system[12] and the federal-state unemployment compensation system. The justices even upheld application of agricultural marketing regulations to a farmer who produced wheat solely for his own consumption.[13] (See "Agriculture and Commerce," pp. 128–129.) In the words of Justice Benjamin N. Cardozo, the Court finally "confronted…the indisputable truth that there were ills to be corrected, and ills that had a direct relation to the maintenance of commerce among the states without friction or diversion."[14] Congress, using its commerce power, could reach those problems.

At this point, the Court relinquished its effort to judge whether Congress had acted *wisely* in exercising its commerce power and returned to simply deciding whether Congress had acted *constitutionally.* According to the Court, unless Congress's choice was clearly arbitrary, it had the power to determine whether an intrastate matter affected interstate commerce to a sufficient degree to require federal regulation. For well more than half a century after 1937, that deferential view of the commerce power governed. Only twice did the Court declare an act of Congress an unconstitutional exercise of the commerce power. During the same period, it sustained the commerce power as a tool to reach and prohibit racial discrimination in public places and to guarantee the right to travel within the United States.

It seemed that Congress had virtually unlimited discretion to regulate commercial intercourse. Writing in 1963, constitutional scholars C. Herman Pritchett and Alan F. Westin articulated the prevailing view: "[I]f we moved into an era of novel economic measures or major nationalization programs, the Court might reassert its authority, but the decades since 1937 have been years of consolidation rather than innovation in economic regulation, and the Court's withdrawal from constitutional intervention is therefore not likely to change in the immediate future."[15] Three decades later, however, the period of deference appeared to be ending. In *United States v. Lopez* (1995) the Court struck down a 1990 act of Congress banning guns near schools, declaring that this law was impermissible and unjustified intervention in local affairs. The peculiarities of this particular law, the 1990 Gun-Free School Zones Act, made it vulnerable and left uncertain the reach of the Court on Commerce Clause questions. Congress had made no explicit findings of a connection between interstate commerce and the dangers of guns on school grounds nor had it distinguished the law from state gun-control statutes applicable to school grounds. To uphold this law in the face of those facts, wrote Chief Justice William H. Rehnquist for the Court, would convert Congress's commerce power to a general police power.[16]

Some scholars argued that the Court was not truly retreating from an approach that had ushered in the modern national economy, but others hailed this ruling as the signaling that there were indeed limits to Congress's power under the Commerce Clause. Among the latter, law professor Douglas W. Kmiec declared, "*Lopez* is the first step in nearly 60 years toward the restoration of a constitutional order premised upon a national government of enumerated and, therefore, limited powers. The legal riddle of what precisely falls within the national commerce power has not been solved," he acknowledged, but "*Lopez* supplies some useful clues."[17]

FISCAL AND MONETARY POWERS

The Court has sustained most congressional decisions concerning taxes, spending, and currency. In three instances, the Court declared such laws unconstitutional only to have the declarations overturned through legislation. Those three decisions occurred between 1870 and 1936, the period in which the Court was delivering its often contradictory opinions on the commerce and federal police powers. All three decisions favored business interests and states' rights at the expense of congressional authority.

In *Hepburn v. Griswold* (1870), the first of the *Legal Tender Cases,* the Court, by a vote of 4-3, declared that Congress had unconstitutionally exercised its war powers during the Civil War in substituting paper money for gold and silver as legal tender for the payment of debts.[18] As the decision was being announced, President Ulysses S. Grant was in the process of naming two new justices. Within fifteen months, the Court, in a 5-4 vote, overturned its 1870 decision. That quick reversal pleased debtors, the government, and many businesses, but engendered considerable public criticism of its speed, the narrow margin of the vote, and the role of the two new justices.

In 1895 the Court declared the first general peacetime income tax unconstitutional. A tax on income from real estate was a direct tax, it held. Because the Constitution requires that direct taxes be apportioned among the states on the basis of population, and this tax was not, it was unconstitutional. This flaw, the Court held, invalidated the entire tax statute.[19] To reach this conclusion, the Court overlooked its earlier declaration that the only direct taxes were head and property taxes and its earlier decision sustaining a wartime income tax. The Sixteenth Amendment overturned the decision in 1913, exempting income taxes from the apportionment requirement.

In 1936 the Court ruled for the first time on the scope of Congress's power to spend for the general welfare, striking down a New Deal effort to raise farm prices by taxing food processing companies and using the revenue to pay benefits to farmers who reduced their production of certain crops. The Court held that the tax-benefit scheme was unconstitutional because it was intended to regulate production, which was beyond the scope of congressional power. This decision was one of many during the New Deal that precipitated the "Court-packing" threat; although the decision was never specifically overruled, its value as a precedent largely vanished when the Court in 1937 approved similar tax-benefit plans contained in the federal Social Security Act. There has been no subsequent move by the Court to limit Congress's fiscal and monetary powers.

FOREIGN AFFAIRS

Though it played an active role in shaping the commerce and federal police powers, the Supreme Court has taken little part in defining congressional powers in the field of foreign affairs. Responsibility for exercising these powers, including the war powers, is shared by the executive and the legislature. The president, as commander in chief, conducts war, but Congress declares war and raises and maintains the army. The president negotiates treaties, and the Senate must ratify them. Although the president has great discretion in dealing with foreign nations on a wide range of issues, many presidential actions ultimately must be approved by Congress through the appropriation of funds.

In many instances, the Supreme Court has refused even to review a foreign affairs or war powers issue, describing it as a political question that the political branches of government must decide. The Court first adopted this stance in 1829 in a case involving an international dispute over title to part of the Louisiana Territory.[20] In cases the Court has agreed to hear, it generally has upheld exercise of the power in question, particularly the war powers. The Court has sustained establishment of the draft and large delegations of discretionary power to the executive branch to conduct war. In the rare instances in which the Court has felt compelled to declare a wartime statute unconstitutional, it has done so usually on a ground other than the war power and after combat has ceased. In short, the Court for the most part has refused to limit Congress's flexibility to exercise its powers over foreign affairs. It undoubtedly realizes that a decision contrary to the will of the political branches and the people might go unobeyed. "[F]or better or for worse," observes political scientist Robert G. McCloskey, "the fact remains that [the powers over foreign affairs] are now subject to constitutional limits only by legislative and executive self-restraint and by the force of public opinion."[21]

STATES AND CITIZENS

Congress is authorized by the Constitution to admit new states to the union, to govern territories, and to make rules for the naturalization of aliens.[22] The Supreme Court has been steadfast in its insistence that new states be admitted on an equal political footing with those already in the Union, a precept now clearly established. Questions of citizenship in the United States and its territories have, however, posed continuing problems.

In its most infamous opinion, the *Scott v. Sandford* (1857) decision, the Court declared that blacks were not and could not become citizens.[23] The Civil War overturned that decision, and ratification of the Fourteenth Amendment made citizens of all persons born or naturalized in the United States and subject to its jurisdiction. Residents of the territories of the continental United States generally enjoyed the guarantees and protections of the Constitution as those areas were prepared for statehood. In the 1890s and 1900s, when the nation acquired several new territories in the

KEEPING THE POWERS SEPARATE

Since the mid-1970s the Supreme Court has been unusually busy reviewing acts of Congress and presidential orders or claims that were challenged as infringing on the separation of powers among the three branches of the federal government. More often than not, the Court agreed. Among the Court's decisions in these cases are the following:

•*Buckley v. Valeo,* 424 U.S. 1 (1976) – The 1974 Federal Election Campaign Act Amendments infringed executive power by giving Congress the power to appoint four of the five members of the Federal Election Commission that would enforce the law.

•*Nixon v. General Services Administration,* 433 U.S. 425 (1977) – The Presidential Recordings and Materials Preservation Act of 1974, placing the tapes and papers of the Nixon administration in federal custody, did not violate the separation of powers.

•*Northern Pipeline Construction Co. v. Marathon Pipe Line Co., United States v. Marathon Pipe Line Co.,* 458 U.S. 50 (1982) – The 1978 Bankruptcy Reform Act infringed on the independence of the federal courts by creating a corps of bankruptcy judges with the authority, but not the independence—for example, life tenure and fixed compensation—of federal judges.

•*Immigration and Naturalization Service v. Chadha, United States House of Representatives v. Chadha, United States Senate v. Chadha,* 462 U.S. 919 (1983) – The one-house legislative veto—under which Congress claimed the power to review and veto executive branch decisions implementing laws—violated the separation of powers between the executive and legislative branches.

•*Bowsher v. Synar, United States Senate v. Synar, O'Neill v. Synar,* 478 U.S. 714 (1986) – Congress impinged on the prerogatives of the president when it included in the 1985 Balanced Budget and Emergency Deficit Control Act a provision giving the comptroller general, an officer removable from office only at the initiative of Congress, the power to tell the president where to cut federal spending.

•*Morrison v. Olson,* 487 U.S. 654 (1988) – The 1978 Ethics in Government Act did not usurp executive power when it authorized a panel of judges to appoint independent prosecutors to investigate charges of misconduct by officials who work for the president.

•*Mistretta v. United States, United States v. Mistretta,* 488 U.S. 361 (1989) – The Sentencing Reform Act of 1984—which created an independent commission in the judicial branch with power to set forth binding guidelines for sentencing—did not violate the separation of powers by delegating too much legislative power to judges.

•*Metropolitan Washington Airports Authority v. Citizens for the Abatement of Aircraft Noise,* 501 U.S. 252 (1991) – Congress violated the separation of powers by giving a congressional review board the power to veto the directors of the interstate airport authority created in the 1986 Metropolitan Airports Act as an independent entity.

•*Loving v. United States,* 517 U.S. 748 (1996) – The Court upheld the military death penalty, rejecting a separation of powers challenge to a 1984 presidential directive.

•*Clinton v. Jones,* 520 U.S. 681 (1997) – The Court ruled that a sitting president could be sued for private, unofficial conduct that occurred before or while in office. The separation of powers does not shield the chief executive from having his private conduct reviewed by a judge.

•*Clinton v. City of New York,* 524 U.S. 417 (1998) – Congress violated the separation of powers when it passed the Line Item Veto Act, giving the president the power to delete specific items in a budget bill without having to veto the entire bill.

•*Boumediene v. Bush,* 553 U.S. — (2008) – Congress violated the separation of powers doctrine in the Military Commissions Act when it took away from judges the authority to hear and rule on appeals from the foreign prisoners held at Guantánamo Bay, Cuba.

Caribbean and the Pacific, a debate ensued as to whether the Constitution automatically followed the flag there. In a series of decisions known as the *Insular Cases* (1901–1920), the Court adopted a rule still in use.[24] If Congress formally incorporated the territory into the United States, the rights, responsibilities, and protections of the Constitution would devolve on the inhabitants of the territory. If Congress did not incorporate the territory, its residents were not guaranteed those protections.

Congressional control over citizenship is extensive. In addition to setting conditions for naturalization, Congress, with the Court's approval, has prohibited several categories of people from entering the country or applying for citizenship. It was Congress that wrote the Fourteenth Amendment, the first definition of citizenship to appear in the Constitution. Following that language, the Court has sustained the citizenship of any person born in the United States, even if the child's parents were not and could not become citizens. Not fully resolved by the Court, however, is the question of whether Congress may revoke the citizenship of a native born or naturalized citizen against his or her will. The ruling case holds that Congress may not revoke citizenship.

AMENDING POWER

As with foreign policy, the Court views the adoption of constitutional amendments as political decisions in which it is reluctant to interfere. Most of its decisions in this area concern procedural questions of ratification, although it did rule that liquor was a proper subject matter for a constitutional amendment and that the amendment extending suffrage to women did not destroy the political autonomy of those few states that refused to ratify it. Several of the twenty-seven amendments to the Constitution confer political rights and give Congress specific power to enforce them. The most significant of these are the Thirteenth, Fourteenth, and Fifteenth Amendments—the Civil War Amendments—which extended citizenship and political rights to blacks. To enforce these newly won rights and freedoms, the Reconstruction Congress, 1865 to 1877, quickly enacted several civil rights statutes, but the Supreme Court, construing the enforcement power narrowly, struck down almost all of them. In general, the Court held that Congress could act only to correct, not to prevent, discriminatory action. It had no power, the Court said, to reach discriminatory actions by private individuals.

These restrictive rulings, coupled with a waning public concern, meant that blacks remained victims of political and social discrimination in many states of the Union for almost a century, until an activist Court began to reassess national authority to enforce the rights guaranteed by the Civil War Amendments. In the 1950s and 1960s the Court sustained congressional power to prevent state discrimination before it occurred and to reach certain private discrimination, particularly in public places and housing.

INVESTIGATIONS AND INTERNAL AFFAIRS

The Court has never questioned the right of Congress to investigate its own members for possible misconduct, nor has it denied the use of such power to examine issues so that Congress might legislate more effectively. In aid of both kinds of investigations, the Court has sustained the right of Congress to compel witnesses to testify and to punish those who refuse. The Court has even been reluctant to curb the exercise of the investigatory power in order to protect constitutionally guaranteed individual rights. To protect witness rights, the Court requires that the investigations serve a valid legislative purpose and that the questions asked of witnesses be pertinent to the investigation. At the same time, the Court, in the interest of national security, has upheld investigations that were clearly designed only to focus publicity upon witnesses holding unpopular political beliefs.

The Constitution gives Congress powers over its own internal affairs. By no means insignificant, these powers include judging the qualifications of members, punishing members it finds guilty of misconduct, regulating federal elections, and establishing rules of procedure. Congress has taken few of its internal problems to the Court. In only one major case has the Court clearly limited Congress's power over its own affairs. In 1969 it held that Congress did not have the authority to add to the Constitution's list of qualifications for membership in the House and Senate.[25] The Court in 1995 cited those specific criteria, relating to age, citizenship, and residency, when it ruled that neither Congress nor the states could impose term limits on members of Congress.[26] The Court has zealously guarded the institutional integrity of Congress. Nowhere has this been more apparent than in its interpretation of the Speech or Debate Clause. The Court has extended this constitutional grant of immunity for actions taken during the course of legislating to cover criminal acts and certain actions of employees.[27]

Judicial Review and Legislative Power

The Constitution does not expressly grant the Supreme Court the power of judicial review—the right to measure acts of Congress against constitutional standards and to nullify those that do not pass the test. The implicit justification for this judicial role lies in the Supremacy Clause (Article VI, section 2):

> This Constitution, and the Laws of the United States which shall be made in Pursuance thereof; and all Treaties made, or which shall be made, under the Authority of the United States, shall be the supreme Law of the Land; and the Judges in every State shall be bound thereby, any Thing in the Constitution or Laws of any State to the Contrary notwithstanding.

Few constitutional scholars believe that the omission of an express grant of power of judicial review from the Constitution meant that the framers intended to deny this power to the Court. The concept of judicial review was relatively well established in the colonies. The Privy Council in London had reviewed the acts of the colonies for compliance with English law prior to the revolution. Several state courts had struck down state laws that they had found inconsistent with their state constitutions.

The Constitutional Convention considered and rejected the proposal that the Supreme Court share the veto power over acts of Congress with the president. The major reason this idea was voted down seems to have been the feeling that the Court should not be involved in enacting a law that it might later be required to enforce, rather than any strong opposition to the concept of judicial review. According to the records of the Constitutional Convention compiled by Max Farrand, only two of the framers expressed reservations about judicial review, although other scholars feel that the number of opponents was larger.[1] During the ratification period, James Madison (who would later qualify his endorsement) and Alexander Hamilton supported the concept in the *Federalist Papers.* Future Supreme Court chief justices Oliver Ellsworth and John Marshall endorsed the principle at their state ratification conventions. *(See "The Proper and Peculiar Province," p. 81.)*

The First Congress, in Section 26 of the Judiciary Act of 1789, specifically granted the Supreme Court the right of judicial review over state court decisions

> where is drawn in question the validity of a treaty or statute of, or an authority exercised under, the United States and the decision is against their validity; or where is drawn in question the validity of a statute of, or an authority exercised under any State, on the ground of their being repugnant to the constitution, treaties, or laws of the United States, and the decision is in favor of their validity, or where is drawn in question the construction of any clause of the constitution, or of a treaty, or statute of, or commission held under the United States, and the decision is against the title, right, privilege, or exemption, specially set up or claimed by either party, under such clause of the said constitution, treaty, statute or commission.

Most of the early Supreme Court justices seemed to believe that they enjoyed a similar power of judicial review over federal statutes. Several of the justices, sitting as circuit court judges, refused to administer a 1792 federal pension law, arguing that the administrative duties it required of them were not judicial and so were in conflict with the constitutional separation of powers.[2] Sitting as the Supreme Court in 1796, the justices assumed that they had this power of judicial review when they held valid a federal tax on carriages.[3] Because

President John Adams signing judicial commissions, the so called midnight appointments, on his last night in office. Several appointees, including William Marbury, did not receive their commissions. The Jefferson administration's refusal to deliver them led to the famous case of *Marbury v. Madison* (1803) in which the Supreme Court clearly asserted its power of judicial review.

the Court upheld the law rather than nullified it, the ruling occasioned little comment. A few days later, the Court for the first time invalidated a state law because it conflicted with a federal treaty.[4] By the time John Marshall was appointed chief justice in 1801, the Court already had exercised the power of judicial review, but it had not tested the extent of that power by declaring an act of Congress unconstitutional.[5] When it did find the opportunity, the occasion arose as much from the politics of the day as from a clear-cut reading of the law.

MARBURY V. MADISON

The aftermath of the bitter presidential election of 1800 brought forth the Court's decision in *Marbury v. Madison,* which many believe is the single most important ruling in the Court's history.[6] In 1800 Republican

Thomas Jefferson defeated the incumbent, Federalist John Adams, for the presidency. The Federalists, unwilling to relinquish the power that they had held since the founding of the country, sought to entrench themselves in the only branch of government still open to them—the judiciary. One of Adams's first acts in the interim between his electoral defeat and his departure from office was to appoint Secretary of State John Marshall, a committed Federalist, as chief justice. Congress speedily confirmed Marshall, who continued to serve as secretary of state until Adams left office on March 4, 1801. Congress, at Adams's behest, also approved legislation creating sixteen new circuit court judgeships, authorizing Adams to appoint as many justices of the peace for the newly created District of Columbia as he deemed necessary, and reducing the number of Supreme Court justices from six to five with the next vacancy. This last measure was intended to deprive Jefferson of a quick appointment to the bench.

Adams named and Congress confirmed the sixteen new circuit court judges and forty-two justices of the peace. On the night of March 3, Adams's last day in office, he signed the commissions for the new justices of the peace and had them taken to Marshall, who was to attach the Great Seal of the United States and have the commissions delivered to the appointees. Marshall affixed the seal but somehow failed to see that all the commissions were actually delivered. William Marbury, an aide to the secretary of the navy, was one of the appointees who did not receive his commission. With three other men in the same position, he asked Jefferson's secretary of state, James Madison, to give him the commission. When Madison, at Jefferson's direction, refused, Marbury asked the Supreme Court to issue a writ of mandamus ordering Madison to give the four men their commissions. In December 1801 Chief Justice Marshall asked Madison to show cause at the next session of the Court why he should not comply with the order.

The Republicans were already talking of repealing the 1801 act creating the new circuit court judgeships, and in March 1802 Congress did so. To forestall a challenge to the repeal as invalid, Congress also delayed the next term of the Supreme Court for almost a year—until February 1803. Exacerbating the antagonism between the two political parties was the considerable personal animosity between Chief Justice Marshall and President Jefferson. Marshall did not relish the thought that Jefferson would best him in this contest. Under modern standards, Marshall, whose oversight had led to Marbury's suit in the first place, probably would have had to disqualify himself. There also would be some suggestion that the case would be moot by the time the Court heard it argued. Neither factor, however, deterred Marshall from taking it up.

His insistence created an apparent dilemma. If the Court ordered delivery of the commission, Madison might refuse to obey the order, and the Court's lack of a means to enforce compliance would be bared. It seemed likely that Madison would refuse; the government did not even argue its viewpoint before the Court. If the Court did not issue the writ, it would be surrendering to Jefferson's point of view. Either way, the Court would be conceding its lack of power. Marshall resolved his problem with a remarkable decision that has been called a "masterwork of indirection, a brilliant example of Marshall's capacity to sidestep danger while seeming to court it, to advance in one direction while his opponents are looking in another."[7]

Ignoring the question of jurisdiction, Marshall ruled that once the president had signed the commissions and the secretary of state had recorded them, the appointments were complete.[8] He also ruled that a writ of mandamus was the proper tool to use to require the secretary of state to deliver the commissions.

Having thus rebuked Jefferson, Marshall turned to the question of whether the Supreme Court had the authority to issue the writ, concluding that it did not. Congress, Marshall said, had added unconstitutionally to the Court's original jurisdiction when, under the Judiciary Act of 1789, it authorized the Court to issue such writs to officers of the federal government. To justify striking down a section of a federal statute, Marshall drew heavily on Hamilton's reasoning in the *Federalist Papers,* No. 78. The chief justice wrote,

> The powers of the legislature are defined and limited; and that those limits may not be mistaken or forgotten, the constitution is written. To what purpose are powers limited, and to what purpose is that limitation committed to writing, if these limits may, at any time, be passed by those intended to be restrained? The distinction between a government with limited and unlimited powers is abolished, if those limits do not confine the persons on whom they are imposed, and if acts prohibited and acts allowed, are of equal obligation. It is a proposition too plain to be contested, that the constitution controls any legislative act repugnant to it.[9]

Having established the Constitution's supremacy over legislative enactments, Marshall turned to the question of whether the judiciary had the authority to determine when acts of Congress conflicted with the Constitution:

> It is, emphatically, the province and duty of the judicial department to say what the law is. Those who apply the rule to particular cases, must of

"THE PROPER AND PECULIAR PROVINCE"

Writing in No. 78 of *The Federalist Papers,* Alexander Hamilton made a strong case for the principle of judicial review in the new government of the United States, reminding readers of the need to limit legislative authority:

> Limitations ... can be preserved in no other way than through the medium of courts of justice, whose duty it must be to declare all acts contrary to the manifest tenor of the Constitution void. Without this, all the reservations of particular rights or privileges would amount to nothing. ...
>
> ... There is no position which depends on clearer principles than that every act of a delegated authority, contrary to the tenor of the commission under which it is exercised, is void. No legislative act, therefore, contrary to the Constitution, can be valid. To deny this would be to affirm that the deputy is greater than his principal; that the servant is above his master; that the representatives of the people are superior to the people themselves; that men acting by virtue of powers may do not only what their powers do not authorize, but what they forbid.
>
> If it be said that the legislative body are themselves the constitutional judges of their own powers and that the construction they put upon them is conclusive upon the other departments it may be answered that this cannot be the natural presumption where it is not to be collected from any particular provisions in the Constitution. It is not otherwise to be supposed that the Constitution could intend to enable the representatives of the people to substitute their will to that of their constituents. It is far more rational to suppose that the courts were designed to be an intermediate body between the people and the legislature in order, among other things, to keep the latter within the limits assigned to their authority. The interpretation of the laws is the proper and peculiar province of the courts. A constitution is, in fact, and must be regarded by the judges as, a fundamental law. It therefore belongs to them to ascertain its meaning as well as the meaning of any particular act proceeding from the legislative body. If there should happen to be an irreconcilable variance between the two, that which has the superior obligation and validity ought, of course, to be preferred; or, in other words, the Constitution ought to be preferred to the statute, the intention of the people to the intention of their agents.
>
> Nor does this conclusion by any means suppose a superiority of the judicial to the legislative power. It only supposes that the power of the people is superior to both, and that where the will of the legislature, declared in its statutes, stands in opposition to that of the people, declared in the Constitution, the judges ought to be governed by the latter rather than the former.[1]

---

1. James Madison, Alexander Hamilton, and John Jay, *The Federalist Papers,* ed. Clinton Rossiter (New York: New American Library, 1961), No. 78, 466–468.

necessity expound and interpret that rule. If two laws conflict with each other, the courts must decide on the operations of each. So, if a law be in opposition to the constitution; if both the law and the constitution apply to a particular case, so that the court must either decide that case, conformable to the law, disregarding the constitution; or conformable to the constitution, disregarding the law; the court must determine which of these conflicting rules governs the case: this is of the very essence of judicial duty. If then the courts are to regard the constitution, and the constitution is superior to any ordinary act of the legislature, the constitution, and not such ordinary act, must govern the case to which they both apply.

. . . The judicial power of the United States is extended to all cases arising under the constitution.

Could it be the intention of those who gave this power, to say, that in using it, the constitution should not be looked into? That a case arising under the constitution should be decided, without examining the instrument under which it arises? This is too extravagant to be maintained.[10]

While refusing the power to issue writs of mandamus in such cases, Marshall claimed for the Court the far more significant power of judicial review. Marshall's claim of authority, however, was not generally viewed by his contemporaries with the same importance that future scholars would confer on it. In fact, Jefferson, who believed that the legislature was the only branch capable of determining the validity of its actions, apparently did not find Marshall's claim of power particularly significant. According to historian Charles

Warren, "Jefferson's antagonism to Marshall and the Court at that time was due more to his resentment at the alleged invasion of his Executive prerogative than to any so-called 'judicial usurpation' of the field of Congressional authority." [11]

Moreover, in the face of a later political threat from the Republicans it appears that Marshall himself may have been willing to sacrifice the Court's role as the final authority on the constitutional validity of federal statutes. Attempting to remove Federalist judges from office, the Republican Congress impeached and tried Justice Samuel Chase in 1805. Chase escaped conviction by the Senate, but not before Marshall, plainly concerned about the security of his own position, wrote in a letter to Chase,

> I think the modern doctrine of impeachment should yield to an appellate jurisdiction in the legislature. A reversal of those legal opinions deemed unsound by the legislature would certainly better comport with the mildness of our character than [would] removal of the Judge who has rendered them unknowing of his fault. [12]

The Power Exercised

The Court's next two major rulings striking down acts of Congress both had decidedly negative effects on the Court itself. The ill-conceived decision in *Scott v. Sandford* (1857) invalidating the already repealed Missouri Compromise of 1820 was followed in 1870 by the Court's holding in *Hepburn v. Griswold*, the first of the *Legal Tender Cases*, denying Congress power to make paper money legal tender for the payment of certain debts. [13] Considered two of three "self-inflicted wounds" by historian Charles Evans Hughes—the third was the 1896 invalidation of the federal income tax—these two opinions severely strained public confidence in the Court. Both were subsequently reversed—the Dred Scott case by the Fourteenth Amendment and the legal tender case by the Court itself. *(See "Dred Scott," pp. 180; "First Legal Tender Decision," pp. 158–160.)* More than half a century had elapsed between the *Marbury* and *Scott* decisions. During that time, the Court reviewed and upheld several federal statutes.

Each time, it reinforced the power it had claimed in *Marbury*, and each time that the government appeared in Court to argue for the federal statute, it conceded the Court's right of review.

As Congress began to exercise its powers more fully in the late nineteenth century, the number of federal laws the Court found unconstitutional increased. In several instances—such as the *Legal Tender Cases* [14] and the *Income Tax Cases* [15]—judicial opinion ran directly contrary to popular opinion and stirred bitter public animosity against the Court. Yet the power of judicial review, once firmly established under Chief Justice Marshall, survived despite several moves (though no direct assaults) by Congress to restrict the Court's authority. As two constitutional historians observed:

> It is interesting to note that at no time in our history has the power of judicial review been seriously endangered. Despite attacks on the Court's decisions, on its personnel, and even on the procedures by which review is exercised, no major political party has ever urged the complete abolition of the power of review itself. The resounding defeat in Congress of the so-called "Court Packing Plan," suggested by President Franklin D. Roosevelt at the height of his popularity, indicates that popular dissatisfaction with the use of the power of judicial review does not necessarily imply a feeling that the Court should be dominated by the political branches of the government. [16]

Rules of Restraint

The Supreme Court has forestalled successful challenge to its power of judicial review by its own recognition of the need for restraint in its exercise. *(See "Judicial Restraint," pp. 50–65.)* Over the years, the Court has developed several rules to guide its deliberations. The Court will not hear a case unless it involves a real controversy between real adversaries. It generally refuses to take "friendly" or collusive suits, although, as with most of these rules of restraint, the rule is often honored in the breach. Major exceptions to this rule were the 1895 *Income Tax Cases*, in which a stockholder in a bank sought to prevent the bank from paying the income tax. It was clear that neither party wanted to pay the tax and that both wanted to test the constitutionality of the tax law. *(See "The Income Tax Cases," pp. 144–147.)* The Court will not pass on the constitutionality of a federal statute if it can decide the issue without doing so. A major exception to this rule was *Scott*, in which the Court invalidated the already repealed Missouri Compromise in order to make a pronouncement on slavery in the territories when it might have decided the case on much narrower grounds. *(See "Dred Scott," p. 180.)*

If there are two reasonable interpretations of a statute, one upholding it and one striking it down, the Court will favor the one upholding it. By corollary, if the constitutionality of a statute must be considered, the Court will make every effort to find it valid. A major exception to these two rules was John Marshall's opinion in *Marbury v. Madison*. In this first case asserting the judiciary's right to strike down acts of Congress, Marshall held that in authorizing the Court to issue writs of mandamus to federal officials, Congress had added impermissibly to the Court's original jurisdiction. Most scholars agree that Marshall could have found the statute valid by viewing the power to issue this order to federal officials as incidental to the Court's original jurisdiction.

If a statute is valid on its face, the Court will not look beyond it to examine Congress's motives for enacting it. Two exceptions to this rule are the opinions striking down congressional attempts to eliminate child labor. In *Hammer v. Dagenhart* (1918) the Court said Congress did not design the Child Labor Act of 1916 as a regulation of interstate commerce but to discourage the use of child labor, an impermissible objective.[17] A subsequent attempt to tax goods manufactured by children was struck down in *Bailey v. Drexel Furniture Co.* (1922) based on identical reasoning: the tax was not intended to raise revenue, the Court said, but to penalize employers of children.[18]

If the rest of a statute can stand on its own when part of it has been invalidated, the Court will strike down only the unconstitutional portion. Major exceptions to this rule of separability were the *Income Tax Cases* and *Carter v. Carter Coal Co.* (1936), the case invalidating New Deal legislation regulating coal production.[19] In both cases the Court found one section of the law invalid, and then, without further examination, used that infirmity to strike down the rest of the statute. *(See, Severability: Divided It Stands, p. 150; "The Income Tax Cases," pp. 144–147; "Coal Codes," pp. 122–124.)*

The Court is reluctant to review cases that present so-called political questions—that is, those that involve matters regarded as within the discretion of the political branches of government. Intervention by the Courts in such questions has been considered a violation of the principle of separation of powers. A major exception to this rule was the Court's decision in *Baker v. Carr* (1962), in which it held that federal courts could review state apportionment plans for violations of federally guaranteed rights.[20] Until that landmark decision, the federal courts had consistently refused to review challenges to federal and state apportionment. The primary significance of these rules of judicial restraint, wrote constitutional scholar Robert K. Carr,

> probably lies in the conscious strategic use which the Court has made of them. They are often available as props to strengthen the particular decision which the Court has chosen to render and have frequently had no small value in enabling the Court to support the view that judicial review is subject to many limitations which have been self-imposed by the justices.[21]

Exceptions to the rules are probably inevitable. Carr continues:

> For the most part these rules are of such a character that they cannot always be followed in an absolutely consistent manner. At the same time they have been followed so often that it would be misleading to suggest that they have had no significance at all.[22]

IMPLIED POWERS

The first seventeen clauses of Article I, section 8, of the Constitution specifically enumerate the powers granted to Congress, but the eighteenth clause is a general grant to Congress of the power "To make all laws which shall be necessary and proper for carrying into Execution the Foregoing Powers, and all other Powers vested by this Constitution in the Government of the United States, or in any Department or Officer thereof." Does this "Elastic" Clause restrict or expand the enumerated

Despite the Supreme Court's decision in *McCulloch v. Maryland* (1819) the Bank of the United States remained under criticism. This cartoon depicts President Andrew Jackson attacking the bank with his veto stick. Vice President Martin Van Buren, center, helps kill the monster, whose heads represent Nicholas Biddle, bank president, and directors of the state banks.

powers of Congress? That was a major question before the Court early in its history.

Thomas Jefferson and Alexander Hamilton in 1791 argued opposing viewpoints on this question after Congress passed legislation establishing the first national bank. Before deciding whether to sign the bill, President George Washington solicited opinions on its constitutionality and then placed them before Hamilton, chief advocate of the bank, for rebuttal. Jefferson viewed the legislation as invalid: the Constitution did not specifically give Congress the power to incorporate a bank. He said that the phrase "necessary and proper" meant Congress could enact only those laws that were *indispensable* to carrying out one of the other enumerated powers. Hamilton, on the other side, contended that Congress had two sorts of implied powers—those derived from the fact of the national

government's sovereignty, such as its autonomous control over territories, and those derived from the Necessary and Proper Clause. The criterion for determining if an act of Congress is constitutional, Hamilton said,

> is the end, to which the measure relates as a mean. If the end be clearly comprehended within any of the specified powers, and if the measure have an obvious relation to that end and is not forbidden by any particular provision of the Constitution, it may safely be deemed to come within the compass of the national authority.[23]

The Marshall Court early on indicated that it would adopt Hamilton's broader view. In 1805 the Court upheld a federal statute that gave payment priority to the United States in cases of bankruptcies. It "would produce endless difficulties if the opinion should be maintained that no law was authorized which was not indispensably necessary to give effect to a specified power," Marshall said. "Congress must possess the choice of means and must be empowered to use any means which are in fact conducive to the exercise of a power granted by the Constitution." [24]

"Not a Splendid Bauble"

Marshall's view on this point would not be fully developed until 1819, when it emerged in *McCulloch v. Maryland* with the unanimous support of the Court. *McCulloch* involved the second national bank. [25] Chartered in 1816, the bank was extremely unpopular, particularly in the eastern and southern states, many of which tried to keep it from opening branches at all or, failing that, tried to tax branches out of existence. Maryland chose the latter strategy, imposing a hefty tax on the notes issued by the bank's Baltimore branch. James McCulloch, a bank cashier, refused to pay the tax. McCulloch claimed the state tax was an unconstitutional infringement on the federally chartered bank, while Maryland contended that Congress had exceeded its powers when it chartered the bank. The state also claimed that in any event it had the power to tax the bank within its borders.

For the Court, Marshall first upheld the power of Congress to incorporate the bank. He noted that the national government is "one of enumerated powers," but asserted that "though limited in its powers [it] is supreme within its sphere of action." [26] The Constitution said nothing about the power to establish a bank and create corporations, Marshall acknowledged, but, he wrote,

there is no phrase in the instrument which, like the articles of confederation, excludes incidental or implied powers; and which requires that everything granted shall be expressly and minutely described. Even the 10th amendment, which was framed for the purpose of quieting the excessive jealousies which had been excited, omits the word "expressly," and declares only that the powers "not delegated to the United States, nor prohibited to the states, are reserved to the states or to the people"; thus leaving the question, whether the particular power which may become the subject of contest has been delegated to the one government, or prohibited to the other, to depend on a fair construction of the whole instrument. [27]

Although the Constitution did not specifically authorize Congress to incorporate banks, Marshall said, it did grant it "great powers"—to tax, to regulate commerce, to declare war, and to support and maintain armies and navies. Therefore, he said,

it may with great reason be contended, that a government, entrusted with such ample powers, on the due execution of which the happiness and prosperity of the nation so vitally depends, must also be entrusted with ample means for their execution. [28]

Incorporation, Marshall said, was one of these means. "It is never the end for which other powers are exercised, but a means by which other objects are accomplished," he said. [29] Marshall then turned to the meaning of the word "necessary" as it is used in the Constitution. The attorneys for Maryland had used Jefferson's argument that the word limited Congress to those means indispensable for implementing a delegated power. "Is it true that this is the sense in which the word "necessary" is always used?" asked Marshall. He continued:

Does it always import an absolute physical necessity, so strong that one thing to which another may be termed necessary, cannot exist without the other? We think it does not....To employ the means necessary to an end, is generally understood as employing any means calculated to produce the end, and not as being confined to those single means, without which the end would be entirely unattainable....

... It must have been the intention of those who gave these powers, to insure, so far as human prudence could insure, their beneficial execution. This could not be done by confiding the choice of means to such narrow limits as not to leave it in the power of Congress to adopt any which might be appropriate, and which were conducive to the end. This provision is made in a constitution intended to endure for ages to come, and, consequently, to be adapted to the various crises of human affairs....To have declared that the best means shall not be used, but those alone without which the power given would be nugatory, would have been to deprive the legislature of the capacity to avail itself of experience, to exercise its reason, and to accommodate its legislation to circumstances. [30]

The central government had already relied on the concept of implied powers in exercising its delegated powers, Marshall pointed out. The Constitution specifically empowers Congress to punish only a few federal crimes, such as counterfeiting currency and crimes committed on the high seas, Marshall said. Yet, he added, no one has questioned the power of Congress to provide punishment for violations of other laws it passes. The Constitution, while it gives Congress authority to establish post roads and post offices, does not specify that the government has the authority to carry the mail, Marshall noted; yet the government assumed that authority. In conclusion, Marshall wrote:

> The result of the most careful and attentive consideration bestowed upon this clause is, that if it does not enlarge, it cannot be construed to restrain the powers of Congress, or to impair the right of the legislature to exercise its best judgment in the selection of measures to carry into execution the constitutional powers of the government. If no other motive for its insertion can be suggested, a sufficient one is found in the desire to remove all doubts respecting the right to legislate on that vast mass of incidental powers which must be involved in the constitution, if that instrument be not a splendid bauble.

> We admit, as all must admit, that the powers of the government are limited, and that its limits are not to be transcended. But we think the sound construction of the constitution must allow to the national legislature that discretion, with respect to the means by which the powers it confers are to be carried into execution, which will enable that body to perform the high duties assigned to it, in the manner most beneficial to the people. Let the end be legitimate, let it be within the scope of the constitution, and all means which are appropriate, which are plainly adapted to that end, which are not prohibited, but consist with the letter and spirit of the constitution, are constitutional.[31]

In the remainder of the opinion Marshall developed the now-famous doctrine that because "the power to tax involves the power to destroy," the state tax on the federal bank threatened the supremacy of the federal government: "[T]here is a plain repugnance, in conferring on one government a power to control the constitutional measures of another, which other, with respect to those very measures, is declared to be supreme," Marshall wrote.[32] (See "A Concurrent but Limited Power," pp. 418–419.)

In the eyes of constitutional scholar Robert G. McCloskey, McCulloch v. Maryland was "by almost any reckoning the greatest decision John Marshall ever handed down—the one most important to the future of America, most influential in the court's own doctrinal history, and most revealing of Marshall's unique talent for stately argument."[33] Holding the opposite opinion, the Jeffersonians were outraged over this decision. Virginians Spencer Roane and John Taylor of Caroline wrote lengthy attacks on it. Marshall responded anonymously as "A Friend of the Constitution" in the Alexandria Gazette.

McCulloch forcefully upheld the supremacy of federal law over conflicting state law, reaffirmed the Supreme Court's judicial review powers, and espoused a broad construction of the Necessary and Proper Clause in particular and congressional power in general that has been in use ever since. Hardly a bill passed by Congress does not rely to some extent on the Necessary and Proper Clause for its validity. It has been especially significant to congressional control over fiscal affairs and to the establishment of the vast network of regulatory agencies. As Marshall pointed out, it is the basis of the federal power to punish violations of the law. It is also the foundation for the doctrine of eminent domain. All these powers have in one way or another touched the life of every citizen of the United States. Marshall's contribution was summarized by R. Kent Newmyer:

> As in Marbury v. Madison, the genius of the McCulloch opinion lay not in its originality but in its timing, practicability, clarity and eloquence. Original it was not.... Marshall did not create these nationalist principles. What he did do was seize them at the moment when they were most relevant to American needs and congenial to the American mind, and (aided by the rhetoric of Alexander Hamilton) he translated them gracefully and logically into the law of the Constitution. Basing his interpretation of the law on the needs and spirit of the age, Marshall gave it permanence. Hamilton himself was unable to do as much.[34]

Inherent Powers

In addition to its implied powers, the Court has acknowledged that Congress has certain inherent powers derived from the fact of the nation's sovereignty. In *Commentaries on the Constitution of the United States*, Justice Joseph Story defined this authority as that which results "from the whole mass of the powers of the National Government, and from the nature of political society, [rather] than a consequence or incident of the powers specially enumerated."[35]

Chief Justice John Marshall relied on these inherent powers in 1828 to declare that the absolute authority conferred on the central government to make war and treaties gave it the power to acquire territory by either war or treaty.[36] The principle of inherent power has also been used to justify federal authority to acquire territory by discovery, to exclude and deport aliens, and to legislate for Indian tribes.[37] Inherent power has generally been invoked only to rationalize an exercise of power over external affairs. As Justice George Sutherland wrote in 1936,

> [S]ince the states severally never possessed international powers, such powers could not have been carved from the mass of state powers but obviously were transmitted to the United States from some other source....The powers to declare and wage war, to conclude peace, to make treaties, to maintain diplomatic relations with other sovereignties, if they had never been mentioned in the Constitution would have vested in the federal government as necessary concomitants of nationality.[38]

DELEGATION OF POWER

The Latin phrase *delegata potestas non potest delegari* summarizes an old legal doctrine—a power once delegated cannot be redelegated. Some have used this doctrine to contend that because Congress's powers have been delegated to it by the Constitution, Congress cannot in turn delegate them to any other body. Practically speaking, however, Congress does delegate its power and has done so almost from the beginning of its history. The Supreme Court occasionally pays lip service to the doctrine, but the justices acknowledge that it has little meaning for Congress. "Delegation by Congress has long been recognized as necessary in order that the exertion of legislative power does not become a futility," the Court has said.[39]

There are two types of legislative delegation. In the first, Congress sets an objective and authorizes an administrator to promulgate rules and regulations that will achieve the objective. The administrator may have only the broadest standards guiding regulation making, or the administrator may be required to incorporate a host of congressionally approved details into the regulations. This type of delegation was first upheld in 1825. Congress had granted authority to the federal courts to set rules of practice so long as they did not conflict with the laws of the United States. The Court approved this delegation:

> The difference between the departments undoubtedly is, that the legislature makes, the executive executes, and the judiciary construes the law; but the maker of the law may commit something to the discretion of the other departments, and the precise boundary of this power is a subject of delicate and difficult inquiry, into which a court will not enter unnecessarily.[40]

Nevertheless, Chief Justice John Marshall felt capable of distinguishing between "those important subjects, which must be entirely regulated by the legislature itself, from those of less interest, in which a general provision may be made, and power given to those who are to act under such general provisions to fill up the details."[41] Congress and the Court have found few subjects to require "entire regulation" by Congress, viewing most as amenable to delegation.

Congress enacted and the Court in 1904 sustained a law that gave the secretary of the Treasury authority to appoint a board of tea inspectors to set standards for grading tea. The statute also barred the import of any tea that did not meet the inspection standards. The act was challenged as an unconstitutional delegation of a policymaking function, that is, the establishment of the standards. The Court, however, said no, that Congress had set a "primary standard" that was sufficient.[42] Justice Edward D. White explained:

Congress legislated on the subject as far as was reasonably practicable, and from the necessities of the case was compelled to leave to executive officials the duty of bringing about the result pointed out by the statute. To deny the power of Congress to delegate such a duty would, in effect, amount but to declaring that the plenary power vested in Congress to regulate foreign commerce could not be efficaciously exerted.[43]

In another case, the Court upheld congressionally mandated penalties for violations of administrative regulations, while making clear in a subsequent case that the administrative agency could not impose additional punishments.[44] One major use by Congress of the delegation power has been the creation of agencies to regulate the nation's transportation and communications systems, trade practices, securities, and interstate power distribution and sales. The authority of Congress to make this delegation of power was first upheld in 1894, soon after the creation of the Interstate Commerce Commission.[45]

Authorizing Action

A second type of legislative delegation authorizes an administrator to take a certain course of action if and when he or she determines that certain conditions exist. This contingency delegation was first upheld by the Supreme Court in 1813, when it sustained the right of Congress to authorize the president to reinstate the Non-Intercourse Act of 1809 under certain conditions: "[W]e can see no sufficient reason, why the legislature should not exercise its discretion in reviving the act…either expressly or conditionally, as their judgment should direct," the Court declared.[46]

Expansion of this contingency delegation came in 1892, when the Court upheld congressional delegation of authority to the president to prohibit free entry of certain items when he determined that foreign governments were imposing unreasonable duties on U.S. imports. The Court held that the president was not making law but finding fact. The president, the Court said, was a "mere agent of the lawmaking department to ascertain and declare the event upon which its expressed will was to take effect."[47] In 1928 the Court

sustained a delegation of tariff authority to the president. Upholding the Fordney-McCumber Act, which authorized the president to raise or lower tariffs by as much as 60 percent to equalize production costs between the United States and competing countries, Chief Justice William Howard Taft offered an oft-quoted "common sense and inherent necessities" doctrine to govern the delegation of powers:

> The well-known maxim (Delegata potestas non potest delegari), applicable to the law of agency in the general and common law, is well understood and has had wider application in the construction of our Federal and State Constitutions than it has in private law. The Federal Constitution and the State Constitutions of this country divide the governmental power into three branches....[I]n carrying out that constitutional division…it is a breach of the national fundamental law if Congress gives up its legislative power and transfers it to the President, or to the Judicial branch, or if by law it attempts to invest itself or its members with either executive power or judicial power. This is not to say that the three branches are not co-ordinate parts of one government and that each in the field of its duties may not invoke the action of the other two in so far as the action invoked shall not be an assumption of the constitutional field of action of another branch. In determining what it may do in seeking assistance from another branch, the extent and character of that assistance must be fixed according to common sense and the inherent necessities of the governmental coordination.[48]

Congressional Standards

When the Court has examined a challenge to a particular legislative delegation, it has usually considered the guidelines and standards Congress set out for the delegated agency to follow. Most of the time, it has found them sufficient. Occasionally, it has upheld a delegation when the law provided no standards at all.[49] The Court whose conservatism clashed with the New Deal philosophy of President Franklin D. Roosevelt, however, found inadequate congressional standards ample reason to negate two major elements of the New Deal program.

"Hot Oil"

The first of these was a provision of the National Industrial Recovery Act (NIRA) that authorized the president to ban "hot oil"—oil produced in violation of state limits on production—from interstate commerce. In *Panama Refining Co. v. Ryan* (1935) this delegation of power was challenged from several angles, including the argument that this delegation to the president was too broad.[50] The Court had never before held an act of Congress invalid on the basis of being too broad a delegation of power, so the government gave only 13 pages of its 427-page brief to refuting that charge.[51] To the government's surprise, the Court struck down the provision on the ground that it transferred too much legislative power to the president. According to the Court,

> Among the numerous and diverse objectives broadly stated [in the act], the President was not required to choose. The President was not required to ascertain and proclaim the conditions prevailing in the industry which made the prohibition necessary. The Congress left the matter to the President without standard or rule, to be dealt with as he pleased. The effort by ingenious and diligent construction to supply a criterion still permits such a breadth of authorized action as essential to commit to the President the functions of a Legislature rather than those of an executive or administrative officer executing a declared legislative policy.[52]

The only dissenting justice, Benjamin N. Cardozo, found enough "definition of a standard" in the statute's declaration of intent to justify the delegation. "Discretion is not unconfined and vagrant," Cardozo wrote. "It is canalized within banks that keep it from overflowing."[53]

Sick Chickens

The next time the Court struck down a law on the delegation issue, Cardozo agreed that Congress had left the president "virtually unfettered" in his exercise of the delegated power.[54] The case of *A. L. A. Schechter Poultry Corp. v. United States* (1935), popularly known as the "sick chicken" case, involved a challenge to the fair competition codes set for various industries under the NIRA. The statute authorized the president to approve an industry code if he had been asked to do so by at least one association representing the industry. The Schechters had been charged with violating the poultry code, so they responded by challenging this delegation of power. *(See "Black Monday," pp. 119–122.)*

Cardozo conceded that the "banks" set up by the NIRA were not high enough, that discretion was "unconfined and vagrant," and that, in short, it was a case of "delegation running riot."[55] Congress quickly caught on to this test. When it passed the Fair Labor Standards Act in 1938, it added what two commentators referred to as "a rather detailed, though uninstructive, list of factors to guide the administrator's judgment."[56] The Court upheld this delegation.[57]

Delegations to Private Parties

In *Schechter* the Court also struck down the provisions of the NIRA that authorized trade associations to recommend fair competition codes to the president for approval. Writing for the Court, Chief Justice Charles Evans Hughes asked whether Congress had this power. "The answer is obvious," he wrote. "Such a delegation of legislative power is unknown to our law, and is utterly inconsistent with the constitutional duties and prerogatives of Congress."[58] Similar concern about delegating legislative power to private parties moved the Court to strike down the Guffey Coal Act of 1935, which authorized the coal industry to establish mandatory wage and hour regulations for the industry. In *Carter v. Carter Coal Co.* (1936), the Court explained its decision:

> The power conferred upon the majority [of the coal industry] is, in effect the power to regulate the affairs of an unwilling minority. This is legislative delegation in its most obnoxious form; for it is not even delegation to an official or an official body…but to private persons whose interests may be and often are adverse to the interests of others in the same business.[59]

The Court, however, later upheld a federal law that required two-thirds of tobacco growers to approve the markets to which the growers could sell in interstate commerce. The justices said this was not an attempt to delegate power, but simply a condition of the federal regulation.[60]

Prior to *Schechter* and *Carter*, the Court had sustained federal statutes giving the force of law to local

SPECIFIC CONSTITUTIONAL LIMITS ON CONGRESSIONAL POWERS

Article I, section 9, of the Constitution contains prohibitions on congressional action with regard to taxes, the writ of habeas corpus, bills of attainder, ex post facto laws, export duties, and several matters that, over time, have become less and less important.

TAXES

One prohibition of prime importance in the nation's first century forbids Congress to levy a direct tax unless it is apportioned among the several states on the basis of population. Until 1895 the Supreme Court had defined only capitation taxes and taxes on land as direct taxes. In that year, however, the Court struck down a general income tax, holding that a tax based on income from land was a direct tax and that the tax passed by Congress was invalid because it had not been apportioned.[1]

This decision was overturned by adoption of the Sixteenth Amendment, which exempts income taxes from the apportionment requirement. *(See box, The "Income Tax" Amendment, p. 146.)*

The second tax requirement stipulated that all indirect taxes be uniform throughout the country. That requirement has presented little difficulty because the Court in the early twentieth century defined it to mean only that indirect taxes must be applied uniformly to the group being taxed.[2] *(See "Uniformity," p. 147.)*

HABEAS CORPUS

Section 9 also forbids Congress to suspend the privilege of the writ of habeas corpus, "unless when in Cases of Rebellion or Invasion the public Safety may require it." Intended to protect citizens against illegal imprisonment, a writ of habeas corpus commands whoever is holding a prisoner to bring him before the court to justify his continued detention. The clause does not state who has the authority to suspend the writ in emergencies. During the early Civil War years, President Abraham Lincoln suspended the privilege. That action was challenged by Chief Justice Roger B. Taney's ruling in *Ex parte Merryman*.[3] Despite Taney's ruling, Lincoln continued to assert this power until March 1863, when Congress specifically authorized him to do so. In three instances, Congress has asserted its power to suspend the writ—in nine South Carolina counties during a conflict with the Ku Klux Klan in 1871, in the Philippines in 1905, and in Hawaii during World War II.

The Court in 2008 limited the power of Congress and the president to restrict habeas corpus in territory that is "under the complete and total control" of the U.S. government. In the Military Commissions Act of 2006, Congress stripped the prisoners at Guantánamo Bay, Cuba, from the right to file a writ of habeas corpus, but the Court declared this act unconstitutional. Its decision noted that Congress had not "suspended" habeas corpus by declaring a national emergency.[4]

BILLS OF ATTAINDER

The Constitution's third clause of prohibition forbids enactment of bills of attainder and ex post facto laws. The Court has defined a bill of attainder as "a legislative act which inflicts punishment without a judicial trial."[5] In 1867 the Court struck down, as a bill of attainder, an 1865 law that barred attorneys from practicing before federal courts unless they had sworn an oath that they had remained loyal to the Union throughout the Civil War. Persons taking the oath falsely could be charged with and convicted of perjury. A. H. Garland of Arkansas had been admitted to practice law before the federal courts during the 1860 Supreme Court term. When Arkansas subsequently seceded, Garland went with his state, becoming first a representative and then a senator in the Confederate Congress.

In 1865 Garland received a full pardon from the president for his service to the Confederacy, and his case, *Ex parte Garland*, came to the Court two years later, when he sought to practice in federal courts without taking the required loyalty oath.[6] *(See "The Effect of a Pardon," pp. 317–319.)* Justice Stephen J. Field, explaining the Court's position, said that lawyers who had served with the Confederacy could not take the oath without perjuring themselves. He continued, therefore,

> the act, as against them, operates as a legislative decree of perpetual exclusion. And exclusion from any of the professions or any of the ordinary avocations of life for past conduct can be regarded in no other light than as punishment for such conduct.[7]

Close to eighty years later, in 1946, the Court nullified as a bill of attainder an act of Congress barring appropriations to pay the salaries of customs regarding miners' claims on public lands and to the determination by the American Railway Association of the standard height of freight car draw bars.[61] The Court has never reconciled these seemingly conflicting rulings.

Wartime Delegations

Since 1827, when the Court first upheld an act of Congress delegating to the president the power to decide when to call out the militia, the Court has steadily affirmed all wartime delegations of legislative power.[62]

three government employees who had been declared to be affiliated with communist front organizations by Rep. Martin Dies, D-Texas, who was chairman of the House Committee on Un-American Activities.[8] The Court struck down this law, declaring: "Legislative acts, no matter what their form, that apply either to named individuals or to easily ascertainable members of a group in such a way as to inflict punishment on them without a judicial trial are bills of attainder."[9]

Twenty years later, in *United States v. Brown* (1965), the Court again found that Congress had enacted a bill of attainder when it approved a provision of the Labor Management and Reporting Act of 1959, which declared it a crime for a present or former member of the Communist Party to serve as an officer or employee of a labor union.[10] Designed to prevent politically motivated strikes, this provision replaced a section of the 1947 Taft-Hartley Act that had required labor unions to swear that none of their officers was affiliated with the Communist Party. That requirement had been upheld.[11] The Supreme Court, however, found the successor provision unconstitutional. Chief Justice Earl Warren explained that the former provision was permissible and the latter not, because one could be escaped simply by resigning from the Communist Party, while the offending act applied to persons who had been members of the party for the last five years.

EX POST FACTO LAWS

An ex post facto law makes illegal an act that has already taken place, or it makes the punishment greater than it was at the time of the act. In *Calder v. Bull* (1798), the earliest Supreme Court discussion of ex post facto laws, the Court held that the constitutional prohibition did not apply to civil statutes but only to criminal laws.[12] In *Ex parte Garland* (1867) the Court had also found the loyalty oath requirement an ex post facto law because to prohibit an attorney from practicing before federal courts without taking the oath was to punish him for past acts not defined as illegal at the time they were committed. In other instances, however, the Court has upheld, against charges they were ex post facto laws, statutes that denied to polygamists the right to vote in a territorial election, that deported aliens for criminal acts committed prior to the deportation law's enactment, and that revoked naturalization papers obtained fraudulently before passage of the law.[13]

EXPORT DUTIES AND OTHER LIMITS

The Constitution prohibits Congress from imposing duties on items exported from any state. Using this prohibition, the Court has declared invalid a stamp tax on foreign bills of lading and a tax on charter parties that operated from U.S. ports to foreign ports.[14] The Court, however, has said that the prohibition does not extend to a general property tax that affects goods intended for export so long as the tax is not levied only on goods for export and so long as the goods are not taxed in the course of exportation.[15] The Court also has held that a tax on corporate income, including income from exportation, is not forbidden by constitutional limitation.[16]

The remaining restrictions on congressional authority have required little interpretation. The first barred Congress from banning the importation of slaves for the first twenty years after the Constitution was ratified. Others stipulate that Congress shall give no preference to the ports of one state over those of another, that it cannot grant titles of nobility, and that it must appropriate all money before it can be drawn from the Treasury.

---

1. *Pollock v. Farmers' Loan and Trust Co.,* 157 U.S. 429 (1895), 158 U.S. 601 (1895).

2. *Knowlton v. Moore,* 178 U.S. 41 (1900).

3. *Ex parte Merryman,* 17 Fed. Cas. (C.C.D. Md. 1861).

4. *Boumediene v. Bush,* 553 U.S. —– (2008).

5. *Cummings v. Missouri,* 4 Wall. (71 U.S.) 277 (1867).

6. *Ex parte Garland,* 4 Wall. (71 U.S.) 333 (1867).

7. Id. at 377.

8. *United States v. Lovett,* 328 U.S. 303 (1946).

9. Id. at 315.

10. *United States v. Brown,* 381 U.S. 437 (1965).

11. *American Communications Association v. Douds,* 339 U.S. 382 (1950).

12. *Calder v. Bull,* 3 Dall. (3 U.S.) 386 (1798).

13. *Murphy v. Ramsey,* 114 U.S. 15 (1885); *Rahler v. Eby,* 264 U.S. 32 (1924); *Johannessen v. United States,* 225 U.S. 227 (1912).

14. *Fairbank v. United States,* 181 U.S. 283 (1901); *United States v. Hvoslef,* 237 U.S. 1 (1915).

15. *Cornell v. Coyne,* 192 U.S. 418 (1904); *Turpin v. Burgess,* 117 U.S. 504 (1886).

16. *Peck & Co. v. Lowe,* 247 U.S. 165 (1918); *National Paper Co. v. Bowers,* 266 U.S. 373 (1924)

This record is particularly striking because the discretion given by Congress to the president during times of war has far exceeded any peacetime delegation. The reason that wartime legislative delegations are viewed differently was explained in *United States v. Curtiss-Wright Export Corp.* (1936), in which the Court upheld a grant of authority to the president allowing him to bar the sale of arms to warring countries in South

Courts and Base Closing Decisions

The Supreme Court in 1994 ruled that once Congress has delegated to the president power to decide to close certain military bases, courts have no authority to review those decisions unless Congress explicitly provides for judicial review in the enacting legislation. Under the Defense Base Closure and Realignment Act of 1990, a commission developed a list of unneeded military and naval facilities and submitted its recommendations to the White House. The president could then accept or reject the package as a whole. If the president accepted the commission's decision, Congress similarly could disapprove the package only as a whole.

The law was designed to reduce political maneuvering over the issue, but several members of Congress from Pennsylvania brought a lawsuit seeking to prevent the recommended closure of the Philadelphia Naval Shipyard. They alleged that the base-closing commission and military personnel who had recommended various closings had violated several substantive and administrative requirements of the 1990 act. Republican senator Arlen Specter of Pennsylvania argued the case before the Court. The justices ruled unanimously that courts had no power to review decisions under the base-closing law. Chief Justice William H. Rehnquist wrote for the Court, "Where a statute . . . commits decisionmaking to the discretion of the President, judicial review of the President's decision is not available."[1]

---

1. *Dalton v. Specter*, 511 U.S. 462 (1994).

America if he thought the ban might help restore peace.[63] Justice George Sutherland wrote,

> It is important to bear in mind that we are here not dealing alone with an authority vested in the President by an exertion of legislative power, but with such an authority plus the very delicate, plenary and exclusive power of the President as the sole organ of the federal government in the field of international relations—a power which does not require as a basis for its exercise an act of Congress. . . . It is quite apparent that if, in the maintenance of our international relations, embarrassment . . . is to be avoided and success for our aims achieved, congressional legislation which is to be made effective through negotiation and inquiry within the international field must often accord to the President a degree of distinction and freedom from statutory restriction which would not be admissible were domestic affairs alone involved.[64]

(For details on specific cases involving wartime delegations, see "Wartime Legislation," pp. 170–172; "President Wilson and World War I," pp. 266–267; and "FDR and Total War," pp. 267–272.)

Delegations to States

Sometimes Congress delegates power to the states, a delegation that the Court has also upheld while generally refusing to call it a delegation. One leading case involved the Federal Assimilative Crimes Act of 1948, which made any crime committed on a federal enclave and not punishable under federal law punishable under state law. The Court reasoned that because Congress had the power to assimilate state laws on a daily or annual basis, it also had the power to do it on a permanent basis. The Court held, "Rather than being a delegation by Congress of its legislative authority to the States, it is a deliberate continuing adoption by Congress for federal enclaves of such unpreempted offenses and punishments as shall have been already put in effect by the respective States for their own government."[65] Earlier the Court had upheld a 1913 law that prohibited the shipment of liquor in interstate commerce into any state that was dry. Because the same law allowed states to ban liquor, the federal statute was challenged as an unconstitutional delegation of power. The Court disagreed, declaring that it was not a delegation because the act established the precise conditions under which it would take effect.[66] *(See "Public Health and Morals," pp. 410–413.)*

POWER AND PROCESS

Article I spells out the lawmaking process in clear and certain terms: for a measure to become law it must be approved by the House and the Senate and then be presented to the president for signature. Almost two hundred years of constitutional history had passed before the Court struck down an act of Congress because it deviated too far from that process. That occasion came in 1983, and the subject was the legislative veto.

The legislative veto, which enabled Congress to retain a measure of control over the implementation or execution of a law, originated during the Hoover administration. The first legislative veto was part of the fiscal 1933 legislative appropriations bill; it provided that either house of Congress could veto President Herbert Hoover's executive branch reorganization proposal by a vote of disapproval. This device, controversial from the start, was used the very next year to disapprove a reorganization plan. Over the next fifty years, legislative veto provisions were included, in one guise or another, in more than two hundred laws. Some permitted a veto by a single chamber or even a committee; others required action by both chambers. All legislative vetoes, however, were alike in that they permitted Congress to block executive action—with or without the president's approval.

Presidents from Hoover on protested the veto as an encroachment on their power, but it was not until the early 1980s, during President Ronald Reagan's first term, that a challenge to this device reached the Court. The case, *Immigration and Naturalization Service v. Chadha,* began in 1974, when Jagdish Rai Chadha, a Kenyan East Indian who had overstayed his student visa, persuaded the Immigration and Naturalization Service (INS) to suspend his deportation. Congress, however, had amended the Immigration and Nationality Act of 1952 to give either of its chambers the power to veto an INS decision to suspend an individual's deportation. In December 1975 the House exercised its power to veto Chadha's stay of deportation. Chadha contested the House veto, arguing that it was unconstitutional for the House to overrule the INS in this way. In 1980 the U.S. Court of Appeals for the Ninth Circuit agreed, holding the one-house veto unconstitutional.

The Supreme Court heard arguments to appeal that ruling in February 1982. On the last day of that term, the Court ordered a second round of arguments, which were held on the opening day of the October 1982 term. Chadha, in the meantime, had married an American, fathered a child, and settled down in the United States. It took the Court all term to reach a decision. On June 23, 1983, it held the legislative veto unconstitutional by a 7-2 vote.[67] The majority found the device an impermissible abrogation of "the Framers' decision that the legislative power of the Federal Government be exercised in accord with a single, finely wrought and exhaustively considered, procedure."[68] That procedure required that bills be passed by both houses and then presented to the president for signature. Chief Justice Warren E. Burger wrote for the majority, noting that only in four situations had the framers specifically authorized one chamber to act alone with the force of law, not subject to a presidential veto: in initiating an impeachment, in trying a person impeached, in approving presidential appointments, and in approving treaties. Legislative vetoes might indeed be useful and convenient, Burger acknowledged, but "convenience and efficiency are not the primary objectives—or the hallmarks—of democratic government and our inquiry is sharpened rather than blunted by the fact that congressional veto provisions are appearing with increasing frequency in statutes which delegate authority to executive and independent agencies."[69] Burger concluded:

> The choices...made in the Constitutional Convention impose burdens on governmental processes that often seem clumsy, inefficient, even unworkable, but those hard choices were consciously made by men who had lived under a form of government that permitted arbitrary governmental acts to go unchecked. There is no support in the Constitution or decisions of this Court for the proposition that the cumbersomeness and delays often encountered in complying with explicit Constitutional standards may be avoided, either by the Congress or by the President. With all the obvious flaws of delay, untidiness, and potential for abuse, we have not yet found a better way to preserve freedom than by making the exercise of power subject to the carefully crafted restraints spelled out in the Constitution.[70]

In dissent, Justice Byron R. White wrote one of the longest dissenting opinions of his career, equaling the majority's in length. The legislative veto, he said, was "an important if not indispensable political invention that allows the president and Congress to resolve major constitutional and policy differences, assures the accountability of independent regulatory agencies and preserves Congress' control over lawmaking."[71] To deny Congress the use of this device, he continued, the Court required Congress "either to refrain from delegating the necessary authority, leaving itself with a hopeless task of writing laws with the requisite specificity to cover endless special circumstances across the entire political landscape, or in the alternative, to abdicate its lawmaking function to the executive branch and independent agencies."[72] Describing the decision as destructive, he pointed out that "in one fell swoop," the Court had struck down provisions in more acts of Congress—about 200—than it had invalidated in its entire history to that point.

Among the laws containing legislative vetoes were the War Powers Resolution of 1973, the Congressional Budget and Impoundment Control Act of 1974, the Nuclear Non-Proliferation Act of 1978, the Airline Deregulation Act of 1978, and the Federal Election Campaign Act Amendments of 1979. In 1987, in a case concerning the legislative veto in the Airline Deregulation Act, the Court held unanimously that in most of these laws only the legislative veto provision itself was nullified by its ruling. The remainder of the law could stand, unless the inclusion of the veto was critical to the decision of Congress to pass the law in the first place. "The unconstitutional provision must be severed unless the statute created in its absence is legislation that Congress would not have enacted," said the Court in *Alaska Airlines v. Brock.*[73]

The limits of the Supreme Court's power to change the way Congress and the president relate to each other soon became apparent. Legislative veto provisions continued to appear in acts of Congress, and five years after *Chadha* scholar Louis Fisher of the Congressional Research Service wrote that "the practical effect was not nearly as sweeping as the Court's decision." Indeed, in *Constitutional Dialogues,* Fisher notes the following:

> The Court's decision simply drove underground a set of legislative and committee vetoes that used to operate in plain sight. No one should be misled if the number of legislative vetoes placed in statutes gradually declines over the years. Fading from view will not mean disappearance. In one form or another, legislative vetoes will remain an important method for reconciling legislative and executive interests.[74]

The Commerce Power

In Gibbons v. Ogden (1824) Chief Justice John Marshall wrote that the Constitution grants Congress the power to regulate interstate commerce, that is, all commercial intercourse that is not wholly within one state. This grant of power "is complete in itself, may be exercised to its utmost extent, and acknowledges no limitations other than those prescribed by the Constitution."[1] With that declaration, Marshall laid the basis for the Supreme Court's subsequent interpretations of the Commerce Clause. This broad view gives Congress virtually unfettered authority to regulate all interstate matters and any intrastate matter—production, business practices, labor relations—that in any way affects interstate commerce.

More than a century passed, however, until the Court gave full approval to Marshall's expansive interpretation. From the late nineteenth century until well into the twentieth century, the Court rulings described manufacture and labor relations as intrastate matters beyond the reach of Congress. For several decades after Gibbons v. Ogden, Congress found little need to regulate commerce. Most cases before the Supreme Court involved the question of state power to regulate commerce in the absence of federal controls. In 1851 the Court adopted the Cooley doctrine under which the federal government would regulate those matters of commerce that required a uniform national approach, such as immigration. Matters in interstate commerce but of primarily local concern, such as insurance, would be reserved for state regulation. It was up to the Court to determine which matters were national and which were local in scope.[2]

REGULATION AND CONCENTRATION

Only in the last decades of the nineteenth century did Congress begin actively to regulate interstate commerce.

With the Interstate Commerce Act of 1887 and the Sherman Antitrust Act of 1890, Congress responded to a changing economic scene in which post–Civil War industrial growth produced interstate railroads and large national corporations and trusts. Concentration meant less competition and higher prices. The laissez-faire doctrine of little or no government regulation of business became less acceptable to farmers, laborers, consumers, and owners of small businesses. With states foreclosed by the Constitution from regulating businesses that spread over more than one state, farmers and laborers sought relief from Congress.

Many of this era's Supreme Court justices were disinclined to favor government regulation of business. Some had been corporation and railroad company lawyers before joining the Court. Several were part of the majority that construed the Fourteenth Amendment to protect business from state regulation. The conservative Court did not, however, view all federal regulation as inherently bad. To uphold regulation that it approved while striking down that which it disapproved, the Court developed two lines of contradictory precedent. In 1895, the year that it declared a federal income tax unconstitutional[3] and sanctioned the use of federal troops to quell the Pullman strike,[4] the Supreme Court held that a sugar trust, which processed more than 90 percent of all refined sugar in the country, did not violate the antitrust law because processing was not a part of, and did not directly affect, interstate commerce.[5] In other words, the federal commerce power did not reach intrastate manufacture unless that manufacture directly affected interstate commerce. With this ruling the Court took a narrow view of Marshall's 1824 statement that Congress could regulate intrastate matters that "extended to or affected" other states. For the 1895 Court to allow regulation, that effect must be direct. The Court, in claiming for itself the power to determine direct effect, seemed to some to usurp the power to legislate. Such judicial legislation was sharply criticized by Justice Oliver Wendell Holmes Jr., an economic conservative and an advocate of judicial restraint. "It must be remembered," Holmes told his colleagues in 1904, "that legislators are the ultimate guardians of the liberties and welfare of the people in quite as great a degree as the courts."[6]

The Labor Exception

Labor law was the one area in which the Court consistently refused to heed Holmes's admonition. In 1908 the Court converted the antitrust law into an antiunion weapon, ruling that a union-organized secondary boycott was an illegal restraint of interstate trade. Congress subsequently exempted unions from the reach of antitrust law, but the Court in 1921 narrowed that exemption to normal union activities. Secondary boycotts still were a restraint of trade in violation of the antitrust act, the Court said.[7]

In a second 1908 case the Court ruled that Congress exceeded the scope of the commerce power when it outlawed "yellow dog" contracts that required employees to abstain from union membership. Union membership had no direct effect on interstate commerce, the majority declared.[8] While sustaining federal worker safety laws and even upholding an emergency and temporary minimum wage for railway workers to avert a nationwide strike in 1917, the Court generally viewed unions and labor relations as intrastate matters that Congress could not regulate. At the height of its pre–New Deal efforts to protect business from government-imposed labor regulations, the Court struck down the act of Congress that prohibited the transportation in interstate commerce of any goods made by child laborers. Congress was not regulating transportation, the Court said in *Hammer v. Dagenhart* (1918), but manufacture, which its power did not reach.[9]

Innovation

These restrictions on the exercise of the commerce power, however, were in large part exceptions to the Court's fundamentally broad view of that power. For during this same period, the Court endorsed innovative uses of the commerce power. Beginning with a 1903 decision upholding a federal ban on the interstate sale of lottery tickets,[10] the Court, with the notable exception of the child labor case, sanctioned the use of the commerce power as a federal police power to protect the public health and morals. Among the police power statutes sustained were those prohibiting transportation across state lines of impure food and drugs, women for immoral purposes, and stolen cars.

In 1905 the Court modified its sugar trust decision to hold unanimously that the federal antitrust act did reach a combine of stockyard operators even though the individual stockyards were wholly intrastate. Because the yards received shipments of cattle from out of state for slaughter and sale in other states, the Court found that they were part of a stream of interstate commerce subject to federal regulation. Although the Court still further modified its antitrust position in 1911, ruling that the antitrust act applied only to unreasonable combinations and restraints of trade, the "stream of commerce" doctrine was subsequently applied to other intrastate businesses that were part of a larger interstate enterprise and so held subject to federal regulation. Extending federal power over intrastate commerce in another direction, the Court in 1914 held that the Interstate Commerce Commission could regulate intrastate rail rates when necessary to achieve effective interstate regulation. To do otherwise, the Court said, would make the federal power to regulate subordinate to the state's power to regulate.[11]

The New Deal

By 1930 the Court had begun to retreat from its reluctance to protect organized labor, sustaining that year a law providing for collective bargaining in the railway industry. The Court had not specifically overturned any of its restrictive rulings on the federal commerce power, so it had both sets of precedents to draw on when it came to review New Deal legislation that called for unprecedented federal regulation of the economy. That regulation proved too pervasive for a majority of the Court, which struck down as unconstitutional eight of the first ten statutes enacted to reinvigorate the economy. Among these were three acts based on the Commerce Clause—a railway workers pension plan, the National Industrial Recovery Act, and the Bituminous Coal Conservation Act of 1935. In all three instances, the Court held that Congress had unconstitutionally intruded into intrastate matters.

Irate that the Court had blocked most of his economic recovery programs, President Franklin Roosevelt offered his famous Court-packing plan, and the initial likelihood of support by Congress apparently had an impact on the Court. By a 5-4 vote, the Court in 1937 abandoned its distinction between direct and indirect effects on interstate commerce. In upholding federal regulation of labor-management relations, the Court sustained the federal power to regulate intrastate matters, even if their effect on interstate commerce was only indirect. Four years later the Court upheld a federal minimum wage law, acceding to the congressional opinion that substandard labor conditions unconstitutionally burdened interstate commerce. These two decisions were capped in 1942 by the Court's ruling that even a farmer's production of goods for his own consumption—in this case, wheat—directly affected the demand for those goods in interstate commerce and was therefore subject to federal regulation.[12] One commentator summarized this series of decisions as follows:

> The Commerce Clause was now recognized as a grant of authority permitting Congress to allow interstate commerce to take place on whatever terms it may consider in the interest of the national well-being, subject only to other constitutional limitations, such as the Due Process Clause. The constitutional grant of power over commerce was now interpreted as enabling Congress to enact all appropriate laws for the protection and advancement of commerce among the states, whatever measures Congress might reasonably think adopted to that end, without regard for whether particular acts regulated in themselves were interstate or intrastate. No mechanical formula any longer excluded matters which might be called "local" from the application of these principles.[13]

This view accurately summed up the Court's view of the commerce power until the mid-1990s: Congress would decide what legislation was in the "national well-being," and the Court would defer to the judgment of the elected lawmakers. Only once between 1937 and 1995 did the justices declare that Congress had exceeded its lawmaking authority under the Commerce Clause, and that venture in judicial second-guessing proved to be short lived. In a 1976 opinion by Justice William H. Rehnquist, the Court struck down a law that extended the federal minimum wage and maximum hour standards to state and local employees.[14] Nine years later, that decision was reversed in a 5-4 ruling reasserting the view that Congress should set the boundaries of federal power.[15] By the mid-1990s, however, Rehnquist, who became chief justice in 1986, had a solid, if narrow, majority that was determined to set limits on congressional power. As a practical matter, the ruling in *United States v. Lopez* (1995) was insignificant: The 5-4 decision struck down the federal Gun-Free School Zones Act, but most state laws also made it illegal to have a firearm at or near a school.[16] More important, the decision signaled a shift in the direction of constitutional law, as it was the first in a series of rulings limiting congressional power. *(See box, The Court, Congress, and Commerce: A Chronology, p. 118.)*

Federal Control

The necessity for federal control over interstate and foreign commerce was one of the primary reasons for the Constitutional Convention in 1787. "Most of our political evils may be traced to our commercial ones," James Madison had written to Thomas Jefferson the previous year.[17] Under the Articles of Confederation, adopted in 1781 during the Revolutionary War, Congress had power to regulate trade only with the Indians. Control of interstate and foreign commerce was left to the individual states, and each state attempted to build its own prosperity at the expense of its neighbors. State legislatures imposed tariffs on goods entering from other states as well as from foreign countries. New York levied duties on firewood from Connecticut and cabbage from New Jersey.

Having different currencies in each of the thirteen states likewise hampered commercial intercourse. Even if a merchant were able to conduct interstate business despite tariff and currency difficulties, trouble would often arise in collecting on bills. Local courts and juries were less zealous

The lawsuit of onetime business partners Aaron Ogden (*left*) and Thomas Gibbons (*right*) led to a landmark Commerce Clause decision in 1824. John Marshall's opinion for the Court defined commerce and stated that Congress has the power to regulate interstate commerce.

in protecting the rights of distant creditors than those of their neighbors and friends. This condition was universally recognized as unacceptable. Even framers such as Samuel Adams and Patrick Henry, who feared that a federal executive would repeat the tyranny of the English monarch, favored regulation of commerce by Congress. As a result, at the Philadelphia conference comparatively little discussion surrounded the inclusion in Article 1 of the congressional power "to regulate Commerce with foreign Nations, and among the several States, and with the Indian Tribes." It is ironic, therefore, that the Commerce Clause should have generated more cases, if not more controversy, than any other power the framers granted to Congress.

GIBBONS V. OGDEN

Not until 1824 did the Supreme Court rule on the scope of the commerce power. The sort of commercial warfare at issue in *Gibbons v. Ogden* was precisely what had prompted the drafting of the Constitution in the first place.[18] New York in 1798 granted Robert R. Livingston, chancellor of the state, a monopoly over all steamboat operations in New York waters. Taking on the inventor Robert Fulton as a partner, Livingston turned the steamship monopoly into a viable transportation system. So successful were they that in 1811 the pair was granted similar exclusive rights to operate in the waters of the territory of New Orleans. The monopoly, therefore, controlled transportation on two of the nation's largest waterways and ports. Attempts to break the monopoly were frequent but unsuccessful. Connecticut, New Jersey, and Ohio enacted retaliatory measures closing their waters to ships licensed by the New York monopoly, and five other states granted steamship monopolies of their own. The ensuing navigational chaos brought the states to what one attorney would describe as "almost . . . the eve of war."[19]

Aaron Ogden, a former New Jersey governor, ran a steam-driven ferry between Elizabethtown, New Jersey, and New York City in uneasy partnership with Thomas Gibbons. In 1815 Ogden had acquired a license from the Livingston-Fulton monopoly, and Gibbons held a permit under the federal Coastal Licensing Act of 1793 for his two boats. Despite the partnership, Gibbons ran his boats to New York in defiance of the monopoly rights that Ogden held. In 1819 Ogden sued for an injunction to stop Gibbons's infringement of his rights to monopoly. New York courts sided with Ogden, ordering Gibbons to halt his ferry service. Gibbons appealed to the Supreme Court, arguing that his federal license took precedence over the state-granted monopoly license and that he should be allowed to continue his ferrying in New York waters.

Public interest in the case ran high during the four years between the time the Court said it would take the case and the time it heard arguments. The steamboat monopolies were unpopular with many, who were eager for the Court to prohibit them. In addition, the case fueled the public debate between the nationalist beliefs of the Federalists and the states' rights beliefs of the Republicans. As historian Charles Warren wrote, the New York monopoly "had been created by Republican legislators, owned by Republican statesmen and defended largely by Republican lawyers."[20] Those lawyers, some of the ablest in the land, argued their case before Chief Justice John Marshall, a leading exponent of a strong centralized government. It was widely assumed that Marshall would side with Gibbons, but whether the remainder of the Court would follow Marshall was uncertain.

Argument and Decision

The case presented several questions: Did Congress have power under the Commerce Clause to regulate navigation and, if so, was that power exclusive? Could federal regulation of commerce leave room for the states to act and still be supreme? In Gibbons's behalf, Daniel Webster argued "that the power of Congress to regulate commerce was complete and entire, and, to a certain extent, necessarily exclusive."[21] Navigation was one of the areas where federal power precluded all state action, Webster claimed. The attorneys for Ogden, however, construed the commerce power narrowly, contending that it applied only to "transportation and sale of commodities," not to navigation, a matter left to the states to regulate.[22] Delivering the Court's opinion on March 2, 1824, Chief Justice Marshall refused to construe the federal commerce power narrowly or to omit navigation from its scope:

> The subject to be regulated is commerce; and . . . to ascertain the extent of the power, it becomes necessary to settle the meaning of the word. . . . Commerce undoubtedly is traffic, but it is something more; it is intercourse. It describes the commercial intercourse between nations, and parts of nations, in all its branches, and is regulated by prescribing rules for carrying on that intercourse. The mind can scarcely conceive a system for regulating commerce between nations, which shall exclude all laws concerning navigation. . . . All America understands, and has uniformly understood, the word "commerce" to comprehend navigation. . . . The power over commerce, including navigation, was one of the primary objects for which the people . . . adopted their government, and must have been contemplated in forming it.[23]

To what commerce does the power apply? asked Marshall. The first type was commerce with foreign nations. The second, he said,

> is to commerce "among the several states." The word "among" means intermingled with. A thing which is among others, is intermingled with them. Commerce among the states cannot stop at the external boundary line of each state, but may be introduced into the interior.[24]

Marshall did not, however, find that the commerce power foreclosed all state regulation:

> It is not intended to say that these words comprehend that commerce which is completely internal, which is carried on between man and man in a state, or between different parts of the same state, and which does not extend to or affect other states. Such a power would be inconvenient or unnecessary.
> Comprehensive as the word "among" is, it may very properly be restricted to that commerce which concerns more states than one. . . . The completely internal commerce of a state, then, may be considered as reserved for the state itself.[25]

With regard to the supremacy of the federal power, Marshall said,

> This power, like all others vested in congress, is complete in itself, may be exercised to its utmost extent, and acknowledges no limitations, other than are prescribed in the constitution.... If, as has always been understood, the sovereignty of congress, though limited to specified objects, is plenary as to those objects, the power over commerce with foreign nations, and among the several states, is vested in congress as absolutely as it would be in a single government, having in its constitution the same restrictions on the exercise of the power as are found in the constitution of the United States.[26]

Marshall did not address whether states could regulate areas Congress has not regulated. Here, he said, Congress had acted when it passed the Coastal Licensing Act. He also did not answer the question of whether states could regulate commerce simultaneously with Congress. Marshall did say that in exercising its police powers a state might take actions similar to those Congress adopted in the exercise of its commerce power, but if the state law impeded or conflicted with the federal law, the federal law would take precedence. The chief justice then enumerated the ways in which the New York law interfered with the federal act and declared the state law invalid. Justice William Johnson's concurring opinion argued that the commerce power "must be exclusive . . . leaving nothing for the states to act upon."[27]

Reaction

The decision in *Gibbons v. Ogden* was politically popular, but staunch Republicans, including Thomas Jefferson, were appalled. In 1825 Jefferson wrote a friend that he viewed "with the deepest affliction, the rapid strides with which the federal branch of our government is advancing towards the usurpation of all the rights reserved to the states."[28] Also disturbed were slave owners who feared that Congress might exercise the commerce power to wrest control over slavery from the states and then abolish it.

Marshall's opinion settled only one point: where a state's exercise of its power conflicts with federal exercise of the commerce power, the state must give way. In reaching that pronouncement, however, Marshall laid the groundwork for extending the commerce power to forms of transportation and communications not yet contemplated. By leaving the power to regulate wholly internal commerce to the states only so long as that commerce did not "extend to or affect" other states, he planted the seeds that would eventually allow Congress to regulate the manufacture of goods and matters that themselves were not in commerce but were deemed to affect interstate commerce.

Scholars have wondered why Marshall, having gone so far, did not go on to claim exclusivity for the federal commerce power. To do so would have avoided many of the inconsistencies, confusions, and contortions that found their way into constitutional law as the Court sought to determine what was in or affected interstate commerce and how far Congress could reach to regulate that commerce. Also, why did the Marshall Court not adopt, as a later Court would, Daniel Webster's argument that congressional power over some areas of commerce was exclusive? Professor Felix Frankfurter provided perhaps the best answer when he noted the double-edged potential of Webster's argument: Marshall may have "ignored Webster's formula not because it would have failed to serve in his hands as an instrument for restricting state authority, but because its very flexibility was equally adaptable in hands bent on securing state immunity." Frankfurter also postulated that Marshall did not endorse Webster's theory because it would then be apparent what "large powers of discretion . . . judges must exercise" in determining over which subjects Congress had exclusive control.[29]

Commerce and the States

Congress did not use the power claimed for it by Marshall until later in the century. Between 1824, when *Gibbons v. Ogden* was decided, and the 1880s, when need for federal regulation of the interstate railroads and interstate corporations became apparent, the Court's rulings on the commerce power focused primarily on determining when state actions impinged unconstitutionally on the federal commerce power. Before Marshall's death in 1835, the Court handed down two more major decisions defining the range of

Congress created the Tennessee Valley Authority, which built dams and powerhouses on the Tennessee River to prevent floods and produce cheap electricity for the farmers who lived in the impoverished area. The constitutionality of the act establishing the TVA was challenged in *Ashwander v. Tennessee Valley Authority* (1936)

state power to affect commerce. In *Brown v. Maryland* (1827) it forbade states to tax imports as long as they remained unopened in their original packages.[30] In *Willson v. Blackbird Creek Marsh Co.* (1829) it held that a state could exercise its police power over matters affecting interstate commerce in the absence of conflicting federal legislation.[31]

The commerce power rulings by Marshall's successor, Roger B. Taney, reflected the Court's uncertainty as to the proper line between state regulation and federal power. At various times, different judges put forth various doctrines as a standard for determining that line. Taney, for instance, maintained that Congress and the states held the commerce power concurrently; Justice John McLean held it exclusive to Congress. Rarely did any one doctrine win a majority. If it did, the majority dissolved when the next case was heard.[32]

The conflict was temporarily resolved in *Cooley v. Port Wardens of Philadelphia* (1852), when the Court upheld state regulation of city harbor pilots and adopted the so-called selective exclusiveness doctrine first enunciated by Webster in 1824.[33] In the majority opinion, Justice Benjamin R. Curtis shifted the focus of judicial scrutiny from the power itself to the nature of the subject to be regulated. Some fields of commerce were of necessity national in nature and demanded a uniform regulation provided by Congress, he said. Others demanded local regulation to accommodate local circumstances and needs. This doctrine left it up to the Court to determine on a case-by-case basis what matters were reserved to Congress and which were local in nature. *(See "The Control of Commerce," pp. 395–407.)*

COMMERCE AND NAVIGATION

The opinion in the steamboat monopoly case also settled a second issue: navigation was commerce.

MARITIME LAW: A MATTER OF COMMERCE?

The Constitution gives Congress no express authority over admiralty and maritime matters. The only mention of the subject is in Article III, section 2, which states that the "judicial power shall extend . . . to all Cases of admiralty and maritime jurisdiction." This phrase implies the existence of a body of admiralty and maritime law, but the question remained whether Congress had any power to modify this law. In *The Lottawanna* (1875) the Court asserted that the framers of the Constitution could not have meant to leave changes in this law to the states. Justice Joseph P. Bradley wrote,

> One thing . . . is unquestionable; the Constitution must have referred to a system of law coextensive with, and operating uniformly in, the whole country. It certainly could not have been the intention to place the rules and limits of maritime law under the disposal and regulation of the several states, as that would have defeated the uniformity and consistency at which the Constitution aimed on all subjects of a commercial character affecting the intercourse of the States with each other or with foreign states.[1]

Bradley continued, nor can it be "supposed that the framers . . . contemplate that the law should forever remain unalterable. Congress undoubtedly has authority under the commercial power, if no other, to introduce such changes as are likely to be needed."[2] In two cases denying states authority in this field, however, Bradley declared for the Court that

Congress's power over maritime law was based not on the Commerce Clause but on Article III, section 2, supplemented by the Necessary and Proper Clause. In 1889 Bradley wrote,

> As the Constitution extends the judicial power of the United States to "all cases of admiralty and maritime jurisdiction," and as this jurisdiction is held to be exclusive, the power of legislation on the same subject must necessarily be in the national legislature and not in the state legislatures.[3]

Two years later, he wrote,

> It is unnecessary to invoke the power given to Congress to regulate commerce in order to find authority to pass the law in question. The act [being challenged in the case] was passed in amendment of the maritime law of the country, and the power to make such amendments is coextensive with that law. It is not confined to the boundaries or class of subjects which limit and characterize the power to regulate commerce; but, in maritime matters, it extends to all matters and places to which the maritime law extends.[4]

---

1. *The Lottawanna*, 21 Wall. (88 U.S.) 558 at 574 –575 (1875).

2. Id. at 577; see also, for example, *Providence and New York Steamship Co. v. Hill Manufacturing Co.*, 109 U.S. 578 (1883); *The Robert W. Parsons*, 191 U.S. 17 (1903).

3. *Butler v. Boston & S. Steamship Co.*, 130 U.S. 527 at 557 (1889).

4. *In re Garnett*, 141 U.S. 1 at 12 (1891).

The question then became one of state power: Was the federal power over navigation exclusive or were there some situations in which states could regulate traffic on the waterways? Five years after *Gibbons v. Ogden* the Marshall Court sustained Delaware's right to build a dam across a small but navigable tidal creek as an exercise of its police power in the absence of conflicting federal legislation.[34] The chief justice conveniently ignored the fact that the owner of the ship protesting the dam as an obstruction to interstate commerce was licensed under the same federal coastal licensing act that figured so prominently in Marshall's reasoning in the monopoly case. (See "Gibbons v. Ogden," pp. 98–101.)

In the next major navigation case, however, the Court held that Congress could use its commerce power to override state law and an 1852 Court decision in which the justices had ruled that a bridge on the Ohio River must either be raised so that ships could pass under it or be taken down altogether. The Court held that the bridge not only obstructed interstate commerce but also violated a congressionally sanctioned compact between Virginia and Kentucky agreeing to keep the river free of such obstructions.[35] Congress immediately overruled the Court by declaring that the bridge was not an obstruction and requiring instead that ships be refitted so they could pass under the bridge. In 1856 the Court upheld this act of Congress:

So far . . . as this bridge created an obstruction to the free navigation of the river, in view of the previous acts of Congress, they are regarded as modified by this subsequent legislation; and although it still may be an obstruction in fact, [the bridge] is not so in the contemplation of law. . . . [Congress] having in the exercise of this power, regulated the navigation consistent with its preservation and continuation, the authority to maintain it would seem to be complete.[36]

In the same period, the Court held that navigation on a river wholly in one state and involving commerce that was not connected to interstate or foreign commerce could not be regulated by Congress.[37] In 1866 the Court reaffirmed Congress's complete control over navigable waters "which are accessible from a State other than those in which they lie."[38] In 1871 congressional authority over navigation was further extended to permit federal regulation of a boat that transported goods in interstate commerce even though the boat operated solely on waters entirely within one state. The Court issued an opinion that was clearly a forerunner of the "stream of commerce" doctrine. *(See "The 'Stream of Commerce,'" p. 112.)* It stated,

So far as [the ship] was employed in transporting goods destined for other States, or goods brought from without the limits of Michigan and destined to places within that State, she was engaged in commerce between the States, and however limited that commerce may have been, she was, so far as it went, subject to the legislation of Congress. She was employed as an instrument of that commerce; for whenever a commodity has begun to move as an article of trade from one State to another, commerce in that commodity between the States has commenced.[39]

Control over the nation's waterways eventually led to disputes over who controlled the power generated by those waterways. In 1913 the Court sustained an act of Congress allowing the federal government to sell excess electricity generated as a result of a plan to improve the navigability of a stream. "If the primary purpose [of the legislation] is legitimate," the Court wrote, "we can see no sound objection to leasing any excess of power."[40]

The Court in 1931 ruled in *Arizona v. California* that it would not inquire into the motives behind congressional waterways projects—in this case the Boulder Canyon Project Act—so long as the waterway concerned was navigable and the project not unrelated to the control of navigation.

Whether the particular structures proposed are reasonably necessary is not for this Court to determine. . . . And the fact that purposes other than navigation will also be served could not invalidate the exercise of the authority conferred even if those other purposes would not alone have justified an exercise of congressional power.[41]

In 1933 Congress created the Tennessee Valley Authority (TVA), a three-member board authorized to set up a comprehensive development program for the Tennessee Valley that included flood control, power generation, and agricultural and industrial development. Although its establishment involved no extension of federal authority over navigation, the TVA represented a major source of government-sponsored competition for the private power companies in the area, and its constitutionality was immediately challenged.

In *Ashwander v. Tennessee Valley Authority* (1936) the stockholders of a power company challenged the validity of a contract between the company and the TVA for the sale of the excess energy generated by a TVA-operated dam.[42] The stockholders hoped that the Court would declare the act authorizing the TVA unconstitutional, but the Court restricted itself to the narrower issue before it and upheld the TVA's authority to make the contract. Direct challenges to the constitutionality of the TVA by the power companies failed in 1939, when the Court ruled that the companies did not have a right to be free from competition and therefore had no standing to bring the challenge.[43]

Congressional power over the nation's waterways was made virtually complete in 1940, when the Court held that federal authority even extended to some waters that were not at the time navigable. In *United States v. Appalachian Electric Power Co.* the Court ruled that the Federal Power Commission had the authority to regulate dam construction on a portion of Virginia's New River that might be made navigable by the dam. Wrote the Court, "A waterway, otherwise suitable for navigation, is not barred from that classification merely because artificial aids must make the highway suitable for use before commercial navigation may be undertaken."[44]

More recently, the Court was closely split over whether Congress's power over navigable waterways extends to wetlands that are far removed from a river or lake. In 2001 the Court said isolated ponds are beyond the reach of federal regulators. The Army Corps of Engineers had maintained that its authority extended to these inland ponds, including gravel pits near Chicago that periodically filled with water. Chief Justice Rehnquist and the Court disagreed, saying these isolated ponds had no link to navigable rivers. But in 2006 the Court in a splintered decision agreed that wetlands could be regulated if filling them or dumping pollution into them could affect the downstream navigable waters. In that case, John Rapanos, a Michigan developer, objected when the Environmental Protection Agency fined him for filling in wetlands on farm land that was miles from the nearest river.[45]

CONGRESS, COMMERCE, AND THE RAILROADS

Although the extension of Congress's commerce power over the nation's railroads came less directly than it did over navigation, ultimately it was just as complete. Like ships, railroads were clearly carriers in interstate commerce. Although privately owned, the rails were public in nature, a fact recognized by the Supreme Court. As it observed in 1897 that interstate railroads were public corporations organized for public reasons and supported by public grants and the use of public lands, the Court clearly viewed the railroads as owing "duties to the public of a higher nature even than that of earning large dividends for their shareholders. The business which the railroads do is of public nature, closely affecting almost all classes in the community."[46]

The first railway lines were strictly local ones, and most early regulation came from the states. As late as 1877, the Court upheld the authority of the states to set rates for hauling freight and passengers within their boundaries.[47] *(See "Railroad Rates," pp. 401–402.)* The business panics of the 1870s and 1880s and the nation's westward expansion led to the consolidation of railroads into vast interstate networks. As a result, state regulation became less effective even as the public was demanding tougher rules to prohibit rebate and price-fixing practices that resulted in high costs for shippers and passengers and favored certain companies and regions over others.

Two events shifted the responsibility of regulating the railroads from the states to the federal government. In 1886 the Court essentially ended state authority over interstate railroads by holding that the states could not set even intrastate freight rates for goods traveling interstate. Basing its decision in part on the selective exclusiveness doctrine accepted in the 1851 *Cooley* decision, the Court found that "this species of regulation is one which must be, if established at all, of a general and national character, and cannot be safely and wisely remitted to local rules and local regulations."[48]

Creation of the Interstate Commerce Commission

The Court's decision in *Wabash, St. Louis & Pacific Railway Co. v. Illinois* (1886) made it necessary for Congress to regulate interstate railroads. The Interstate Commerce Act of 1887 did just that, stipulating that all rates should be reasonable and just, and prohibiting rebate and price-fixing practices. To enforce the law, Congress set up the Interstate Commerce Commission (ICC), which could issue cease-and-desist orders to halt any railroad violating the act's provisions. The ICC was not given specific power to set rates or adjust those it found to be unreasonable—and it was unclear whether Congress intended the commission to have these powers although ultimately it attained them.

At the time the ICC was created and for several years thereafter, a majority of the members of the Supreme Court endorsed the principles of economic laissez-faire, opposing regulation that impinged on the free development of business and industry. Moreover, many of the justices came to the bench from careers in corporate law; three of them—Chief Justice Melville W. Fuller and Justices Henry B. Brown and George Shiras Jr.—numbered major interstate railroads among their clients. It was therefore not surprising that the Court viewed the ICC with little pleasure.

Nevertheless, in 1894 the Court upheld the ICC as an appropriate delegation of congressional power.[49] But three years later, it stripped the fledgling commission of its essential regulatory authority, holding that it had no rate-fixing powers. "There is nothing in the act fixing rates," said the Court, and so "no just rule of construction would tolerate a grant of such power by mere implication."[50] The Court majority also thought that the power to establish rates was a legislative function that could not constitutionally be delegated to an executive agency without violating the separation of powers. "The power given [by Congress to the ICC] is partly judicial, partly executive and administrative, but not legislative," the majority wrote.[51] In another 1897 decision, the Court rendered the commission's findings of fact subject to judicial review and reinterpretation.[52]

These cases left the ICC toothless, and the practices that it was created to control resumed with full force. Renewed demands from the public as well as some of the rail companies encouraged Congress to attempt to revive the ICC as an enforcement mechanism. In 1906 it passed the Hepburn Act, which among other things specifically authorized the commission to adjust rates that it judged to be unreasonable and unfair. The following year, the Court signaled that these new powers would pass constitutional muster when it curtailed the extent of review authority it claimed, saying that it would accept the commission's findings of fact as true, confining its review of the commission's decisions to constitutional questions.[53]

In 1910 the Court upheld the commission's authority to adjust interstate railroad rates. The case arose after the ICC substituted a lower rate schedule for that set by several western lines. The Court said the "commission is the tribunal entrusted with the execution of the interstate commerce laws, and has been given very comprehensive powers in the investigation and determination of the proportion which the rates charged shall bear to the service rendered."[54] With the agency's rate-adjusting power established, Congress then gave the ICC authority to set original rates. The railroads challenged the act as an unconstitutional delegation of legislative authority, but the Court in 1914 found the contention "without merit." How could it be, the Court asked, that the authority to set rates "was validly delegated so long as it was lodged in the carriers but ceased to be susceptible of delegation the instant it was taken from the carriers for the purpose of being lodged in a public administrative body?"[55]

The Court had now sanctioned what it had forbidden less than twenty years earlier. As one commentator noted, "The Court, which had long accepted the principle of rate regulation by the states, could find no constitutional reason to refuse to accept the same power when exercised unambiguously by the national government."[56] With federal control established over interstate rail rates, the next questions became when and whether the federal government could regulate intrastate rates. The Court addressed this question in the *Minnesota Rate Cases* (1913). Justice Charles Evans Hughes wrote,

> [T]he full control by Congress of the subjects committed to its regulation is not to be denied or thwarted by the commingling of interstate and intrastate operations. This is not to say that the nation may deal with the internal concerns of the State, as such, but that the execution by Congress of its constitutional power to regulate interstate commerce is not limited by the fact that intrastate transactions may have become so interwoven therewith that the effective government of the former incidentally controls the latter.[57]

This statement was extraneous to the case at hand and did not have the full force of law, but it was a harbinger of the Court's ruling the following year in the *Shreveport Rate Cases,* which concerned a railroad based in Shreveport, Louisiana, that carried freight and passengers into East Texas in competition with two Texas-based railroads. The rail rates set by Texas officials for the state lines were substantially lower than those set by the ICC for the interstate Shreveport line, giving the Texas railroads a decisive competitive edge. To equalize the competition, the ICC required the intrastate lines to charge the same rates as the interstate rail company. They protested, but the Court upheld the ICC order:

> Wherever the interstate and intrastate transactions of carriers are so related that the government of the one involves the control of the other, it is Congress, and not the State, that is entitled to prescribe the final and dominant rule, for otherwise Congress would be denied the exercise of its constitutional authority and the States, and not the Nation, would be supreme in the national field.[58]

In time, the Court expanded the so-called Shreveport doctrine beyond transportation to justify congressional intervention in other intrastate matters, such as manufacture, that touched on interstate commerce. The Court endorsed an even greater expansion of federal control over intrastate rail rates in 1922, when it upheld the section of the 1920 Transportation Act that authorized the ICC to set intrastate rates high enough to guarantee the railroads a fair income based on the value of their railway property. The 1920 law had been passed to return the railroads to private control after being run by the government during World War I. The Court held that a state burdened interstate commerce by lowering its intrastate rates to undercut interstate rates. Lower intrastate rates meant proportionately less income from intrastate companies, which in turn could force interstate rates higher in order to guarantee the congressionally mandated rate of return. Noting that intrastate systems used the same tracks and equipment as the interstate systems, Chief Justice William Howard Taft wrote, "Congress as the dominant controller of interstate commerce may, therefore, restrain undue limitation of the earning power of the interstate commerce system in doing state work."[59]

On the other hand, the Court in 1924 also upheld the profits recapture clause of the 1920 Transportation Act. That provision authorized the federal government to recover half of all railroad profits above 6 percent. The excess profits were put into a fund to compensate those rail lines earning less than a 4.5 percent profit.

Stressing the public nature of railroads, a unanimous Court declared that a railroad "was not entitled, as a constitutional right, to more than a fair operating income upon the value of its properties."[60] The recapture provisions proved ineffective, however, and were repealed in 1933.

Railway Labor

The Court's initial antipathy to organized labor was particularly evident in railway union cases. In 1895 the Court upheld contempt citations against Eugene V. Debs and other leaders of the Pullman strike and sanctioned the use of federal troops to control strike-related violence. In the early 1900s the Court handed down two major decisions adverse to labor and its unions. In *Loewe v. Lawlor* (1908) it held that certain labor practices, such as organized boycotts, were illegal restraints of trade under the Sherman Antitrust Act of 1890.[61] In *Adair v. United States* (1908) it struck down a federal law aimed at strengthening the organized railway labor movement.[62] *(See details of In re Debs, pp. 308–309; details of Loewe v. Lawlor, p. 114.)*

"Yellow-Dog Contracts"

To ensure collective bargaining rights for railway employees, an 1898 railway labor law contained a provision prohibiting employers from making contracts that required an employee to promise not to join a union as a condition of employment. These so-called yellow-dog contracts had been effective in management's fight against the railway brotherhoods, and the statute barring them was challenged as exceeding congressional power over interstate commerce and violating the Fifth Amendment "freedom of contract."

In *Adair* the Supreme Court sustained the challenge, striking down that portion of the law. "In our opinion," said Justice John Marshall Harlan, "the prohibition is an invasion of the personal liberty, as well as of the right of property, guaranteed by that [Fifth] Amendment." As to the Commerce Clause, Harlan said that there was not a sufficient "connection between interstate commerce and membership in a labor organization" to justify outlawing the yellow dog contracts.[63] Justice Oliver Wendell Holmes Jr. disagreed, saying that "it hardly would be denied" that labor relations in the railroad industry were closely enough related to commerce to rationalize federal regulation. He also chastised the majority for interfering with congressional policy: "Where there is, or generally is believed to be, an important ground of public policy for restraint [of the freedom of contract], the Constitution does not forbid it, whether this Court agrees or disagrees with the policy pursued."[64]

The same year, the Court, in a 5-4 decision, declared unconstitutional a second effort to regulate labor-management relations in the rail industry.[65] The 1906 Employers' Liability Act made every common carrier liable for the on-the-job deaths of employees. This act modified two common law practices that held the employer not liable if the employee died through negligence on his own part or on the part of fellow workers. Finding the law invalid, the Court said the statute infringed on states' rights because it covered railway employees not directly involved in interstate commerce as well as those who were. Congress shortly thereafter enacted a second liability act that covered only railway workers in interstate commerce. The Court upheld the modified law in 1912.[66]

As part of the Transportation Act of 1920, Congress created the Railway Labor Board to review and decide railway labor disputes, but in two subsequent cases, the Court held that the board had no power to enforce its decisions.[67] Congress then enacted the Railway Labor Act establishing new procedures for settling railway labor disputes. Among the provisions of the act was a prohibition against employer interference with the right of employees to select their bargaining representatives. In 1930 the Court upheld an injunction against railway employers who had violated this ban by interfering with the representative selection process. In so doing, it upheld the constitutionality of the Railway Labor Act as a valid means for Congress to avoid interruptions of interstate commerce by resolving disputes before they resulted in strikes. The Court also distinguished the case from the 1908 *Adair* ruling, rejecting the railroad company's claim that the statute infringed on the employers' Fifth Amendment freedom of contract:

The Railway Labor Act of 1926 does not interfere with the normal exercise of the right of the carrier to select its own employees or to discharge them. The statute is not aimed at this right of the employers but at the interference with the right of employees to have representatives of their own choosing. As the carriers subject to the act have no constitutional right to interfere with the freedom of the employees in making their selections, they cannot complain of the statute on constitutional grounds.[68]

Railway Safety

In 1911 the Court, which already had approved the use of the federal tax and commerce powers as police tools to regulate such matters as the color of oleo and the interstate shipment of lottery tickets, upheld the application of this same police power to encourage railway safety, even if that meant federal regulation of intrastate equipment and employees. In *Southern Railway Co. v. United States* (1911) the Court upheld the federal Safety Appliance Act, which required safety couplers on railroad cars used in interstate commerce. In an opinion that foreshadowed its reasoning in the Minnesota and Shreveport rate cases, the Court ruled that this law also applied to intrastate cars, because the cars used in interstate and intrastate traffic were so intermingled that to regulate one necessitated regulation of the other.[69] *(See Minnesota and Shreveport cases under "Creation of the Interstate Commerce Commission," p. 104.)*

In the same year the Court upheld as an appropriate use of the federal police power a federal safety measure setting maximum hours that interstate railway employees could work:

In its power suitably to provide for the safety of employees and travelers, Congress was not limited to the enactment of laws relating to mechanical appliances, but it was also competent to consider, and to endeavor to reduce, the dangers incident to the strain of excessive hours of duty on the part of engineers, conductors, train dispatchers, telegraphers, and other persons embraced within the class defined by the act.[70]

Minimum Wage

In 1917—just a year before the Court would hold that Congress did not have the power to set minimum wages and maximum hours for child laborers—the justices upheld congressional authority to set temporary wage and permanent hour standards for interstate railway employees. The case of *Wilson v. New* (1917) arose after unionized rail workers asked that they be permitted to work eight, not ten, hours, for the same wages they made for the longer day.[71] When their employers refused, the unions threatened a nationwide strike. To avoid such an economic calamity, President Woodrow Wilson urged Congress to establish an eight-hour workday for railway employees with no reduction in wages pending a six-to-nine-month commission study.

With U.S. entry into World War I imminent, the Court, in a 5-4 decision, ruled the emergency legislation constitutional. Congress's power to set an eight-hour workday was "not disputable," the Court said, although the question of wages was not so clear-cut. Acknowledging that wage agreements were "primarily private," but emphasizing the public nature of the railways and the failure of the unions and management to settle the dispute, the Court concluded that Congress had the authority

> to exert the legislative will for the purpose of settling the dispute, and bind both parties to the duty of acceptance and compliance, to the end that no individual dispute or difference might bring ruin to the vast interests concerned in the movement of interstate commerce.[72]

The four dissenters—Justices William R. Day, Willis Van Devanter, Mahlon Pitney, and James McReynolds—said the act went beyond the power granted by the Commerce Clause and furthermore was a violation of due process guaranteed by the Fifth Amendment because it took property (wages) from one party (employers) and gave it to another (employees) by legislative proclamation.

Pensions

The Railroad Retirement Pension Act, which set up a comprehensive pension system for railroad workers, was one of the major pieces of legislation struck down by the Court during its anti–New Deal period of the mid-1930s. A majority of the Court in 1935 found that several parts of the pension plan violated the guarantee of due process. It also held that the pension plan was unrelated to interstate commerce. Speaking for the Court, Justice Owen J. Roberts wrote,

> The theory [behind the legislation] is that one who has an assurance against future dependency will do his work more cheerfully, and therefore more efficiently. The question at once presents itself whether the fostering of a contented mind on the part of any employee by legislation of this type, is in any just sense a regulation of interstate commerce. If that question be answered in the affirmative, obviously there is no limit to the field of so-called regulation.[73]

For the minority, Chief Justice Hughes agreed that parts of the plan were unconstitutional, but he refused to hold that the plan itself was altogether outside the scope of congressional commerce powers. "The fundamental consideration which supports this type of legislation is that industry should take care of its human wastage, whether that is due to accident or age," said Hughes, adding that the "expression of that conviction in law is regulation."[74] Because railroads are interstate carriers, and their employees are engaged in interstate commerce, said Hughes, regulation of pension benefits falls under the interstate commerce power. Federal legislation passed in 1935, 1937, and 1938 set up a railroad employees' pension fund financed by a tax on employers and on employees. The constitutionality of the pension plan was not challenged during the ensuing forty years.

Other Common Carriers

Once it established that Congress had broad authority to regulate the railroads, the Court did not hesitate to permit Congress to regulate other common carriers. The *Pipe Line Cases* (1914) upheld inclusion of oil pipelines under the coverage of the Interstate Commerce Act. The Standard Oil Company, either through complete or almost complete stock ownership of several pipeline companies, had made itself, in the words of Justice Holmes, "master of the only practicable oil transportation between the oil fields east of California

THE NORTH AMERICAN

PHILADELPHIA, TUESDAY, MARCH 15, 1904

ONE CENT

SUPREME COURT DEALS DEATH BLOW TO TRUSTS
IN DISSOLVING THE NORTHERN SECURITIES MERGER

MAJORITY OF THE JUDGES
BROADLY ESTABLISHES THE
SHERMAN LAW'S VALIDITY

Melville W. Fuller presided over the Supreme Court when it decided a series of cases determining the strength of the Sherman Antitrust Act, which Congress had passed to break up monopolies. When President Theodore Roosevelt dissolved the Northern Securities Company, which held the stock of three major railroads and enjoyed a monopoly over transportation in the Northwest, the Court upheld his action. It ruled that stock transactions were within the realm of interstate commerce, which the federal government may regulate.

and the Atlantic Ocean." Standard Oil required that any oil transported through the pipelines it owned be sold to it. The Court, speaking through Holmes, rejected the oil company's contention that it was simply transporting its own oil from the well to the refinery. Holmes said that the "lines we are considering are common carriers now in everything but form" and that Congress has the power under the Commerce Clause to "require those who are common carriers in substance to become so in form."[75]

The Court subsequently held that the transmission of electric power from one state to another was interstate commerce and that rate regulation of that power by the original state was an interference with and a burden on interstate commerce. The Court also upheld the right of the Federal Power Commission to set the price for natural gas found in one state and sold wholesale to a distributor in another state.[76] The Court furthermore ruled that forms of communication crossing state borders, though intangible, were nonetheless interstate commerce. In 1878 the Court held that Florida's attempt to exclude out-of-state telegraph companies by granting a monopoly to a Florida company was a burden on interstate commerce.[77] In 1933 the Court upheld federal regulation of radio transmissions. "No state lines divide the radio waves, and national regulation is not only appropriate but essential to the efficient use of radio facilities," the Court said.[78]

CONGRESS AND THE TRUSTS

The development of the nation's railroads into interstate networks paralleled and facilitated the growth of "combinations," or "trusts," in many areas of business and industry. Designed to forestall the vicious competition that so often resulted in bankruptcy, the trusts frequently eliminated all competition of any significance and drove smaller entrepreneurs out of the market. By

1901 trusts dominated the steel, oil, sugar, meat packing, leather, electrical goods, and tobacco industries. The clear threat that this development posed to the traditional concept of the free enterprise system and the unsavory methods frequently used by trusts to gain control and enlarge their hold on an industry generated considerable public outcry. Congress responded in 1890 by passing the Sherman Antitrust Act, which made illegal "[e]very contract, combination in the form of trust or otherwise, or conspiracy, in restraint of trade or commerce among the several states, or with foreign nations."

Commerce and Manufacture

Like the Interstate Commerce Act, the Sherman Antitrust Act represented a major assumption of power by Congress. The trusts as well as economic conservatives in general warned of the day when laissez-faire principles would fall to congressional attempts to control all phases of commercial enterprise, including manufacture and production. The Court had already spoken to this issue. In *Veazie v. Moor* (1852) it had asserted that the federal power over commerce did not reach manufacturing or production, even of products to be sold in interstate or foreign commerce:

> A pretension as far reaching as this, would extend to contracts between citizen and citizens of the same state, would control the pursuits of the planter, the grazier, the manufacturer, the mechanic, the immense operations of the collieries and mines and furnaces of the country; for there is not one of these avocations, the results of which may not become the subject of foreign [interstate] commerce, and be borne either by turnpikes, canals or railroads, from point to point within the several States, towards an ultimate destination.[79]

This viewpoint became law with the decision in *Kidd v. Pearson* (1888) upholding a state prohibition on producing liquor for interstate shipment. In that case, the Court said,

> No distinction is more popular to the common mind, or more clearly expressed in economic and political literature, than that between manufactures and commerce. Manufacture is transformation— the fashioning of raw materials into a change of

form for use. The functions of commerce are different. The buying and selling and the transportation incident thereto constitute commerce.[80]

The full significance of *Kidd* became apparent seven years later, when the Court delivered its first antitrust ruling in *United States v. E. C. Knight Co.* (1895).[81] The defendants in the suit were American Sugar Refining Company and four smaller Philadelphia processors. Through stockholders' agreements, the larger company had purchased stock in the smaller ones, and the resulting trust controlled more than 90 percent of all the sugar processed in the United States. The federal government's case, prosecuted less than vigorously by Attorney General Richard Olney, who had opposed passage of the Sherman Antitrust Act and later worked for its repeal, challenged the sugar combination as an illegal restraint of trade in interstate commerce designed to raise sugar prices. Relying on the narrow interpretation of commerce expounded in *Veazie v. Moor* and *Kidd v. Pearson*, Chief Justice Melville W. Fuller declared, again, that manufacture was not part of interstate commerce:

> Doubtless, the power to control the manufacture of a given thing involves in a certain sense the control of its disposition, but this is a secondary and not the primary sense; and although the exercise of that power may result in bringing the operation of commerce into play, it does not control it, and affects it only incidentally and indirectly.[82]

The fact that the sugar was manufactured for eventual sale, possibly in another state, also had only an indirect effect on interstate commerce, Fuller said:

> The fact that an article is manufactured for export to another state does not of itself make it an article of interstate commerce, and the intent of the manufacture does not determine the time when the article or product passes from the control of the state and belongs to commerce.[83]

That view basically limited the definition of interstate commerce to transportation. "Slight reflection will show," said Fuller, that if the federal antitrust law covers all manufacturing combinations "whose ultimate result may affect external commerce, comparatively little of business operations and affairs would be left for state control."[84] The majority claimed that the combination in question related solely to the acquisition of refineries in Pennsylvania and to sugar processing in that state and was therefore not in interstate commerce and not touchable by the Sherman Act. The state had authority under its police power to relieve the situation if the monopoly burdened intrastate commerce, the Court said. Fuller's insistence that the states were the proper instruments to deal with manufacturing monopolies ignored the reality that states were incapable of regulating the gigantic trusts, which meant no effective mechanism for regulation existed at either the state or national level. As Justice John Marshall Harlan wrote in his vigorous dissent, the public was left "entirely at the mercy" of the trusts.[85]

Fuller's rather artificial distinction between the direct and indirect effects of manufacture on interstate commerce significantly qualified Chief Justice Marshall's opinion that sanctioned congressional regulation of intrastate matters that "affect" other states. It would provide a handy tool for future Courts that wished to thwart congressional regulation of intrastate matters. As Justice Wiley B. Rutledge wrote in 1948, "The *Knight* decision made the [antitrust] statute a dead letter for more than a decade and, had its full force remained unmodified, the Act today would be a weak instrument, as would also the power of Congress to reach evils in all the vast operations of our gigantic national industrial system antecedent to interstate sale and transportation of manufactured products."[86] Although the *Knight* ruling seriously limited the scope of the Sherman Act, it did not declare it unconstitutional, and the Court in 1897 readily applied the law to strike down a combination of railway companies joined together to set freight rates that all the companies would charge.[87]

In 1899 the Court sustained for the first time the use of the Sherman Antitrust Act against an industrial combine. It held that a regional marketing agreement drawn up by six corporations that made and sold iron pipe interstate was an illegal restraint of trade in violation of the act. Justice Rufus W. Peckham said the situation in this case was unlike that in the sugar trust case because the pipe combine "was clearly involved in selling as well as manufacturing."[88]

The Holding Company Case

In the early 1900s the Court moved farther away from the narrow view set out in the sugar ruling. The case of *Northern Securities Co. v. United States* (1904)—a result of President Theodore Roosevelt's trust-busting campaign—involved the government's challenge to a holding company set up by the major stockholders of two competing railroads to buy the controlling interest of the roads. By a 5-4 vote, the Court ruled that the holding company was clearly intended to eliminate competition between the two rail lines: "This combination is, within the meaning of the act, a 'trust;' but if not, it is a combination in restraint of interstate and international commerce and that is enough to bring it under the condemnation of the act," wrote Justice Harlan for the majority.[89]

In an important modification of its decision in the sugar trust case, Harlan declared that the holding company, unlike the sugar company, really was in commerce. The antitrust act, he maintained, applied to "every combination or conspiracy which would extinguish competition between otherwise competing railroads engaged in interstate trade or commerce, and which would in that way restrain such trade or commerce."[90] Harlan was unimpressed with the defendants' contention that because the holding company was incorporated by a state, the attempt to enforce the antitrust act was an undue interference with the internal commerce of the state:

> An act of Congress constitutionally passed under its power to regulate commerce among the States . . . is binding upon all. . . . Not even a State, still less one of its artificial creatures, can stand in the way of its enforcement. If it were otherwise, the Government and its laws might be prostrated at the feet of local authority.[91]

The four dissenters—Chief Justice Fuller and Justices Edward D. White, Peckham, and Holmes—adhered to the reasoning in the *Knight* case, contending that commerce did not extend to stock transactions or corporations even if they were indirectly involved with matters in interstate commerce.

The "Stream of Commerce"

In 1905, with the adoption of the "stream of com-merce" doctrine, the Court did away almost entirely with the distinction it had drawn between direct and indirect effects on commerce. *Swift & Co. v. United States* (1905) concerned the "beef trust"—meatpack-ing houses that had made extensive agreements among themselves to control livestock and meat prices in many of the nation's stockyards and slaughtering houses.[92] Swift claimed that its livestock was bought and sold locally and was therefore not in interstate commerce. Justice Holmes wrote the unanimous opinion rejecting that claim: "Although the combina-tion alleged embraces restraint and monopoly of trade within a single State, its effect upon commerce among the States is not accidental, secondary, remote or merely probable." Holmes then enunciated what became known as the "stream of commerce" doctrine:

> When cattle are sent for sale from a place in one state, with the expectation that they will end their transit, after purchase, in another, and when in effect they do so, with only the interruption neces-sary to find a purchaser at the stock yards, and when this is a typical constantly recurring course, the current thus existing is a current of commerce among the states, and the purchase of the cattle is a part and incident of such commerce.[93]

The stream of commerce doctrine eventually would be used to rationalize federal regulation of actual production, but the significance of the *Swift* case was acknowledged long before that. Chief Justice Taft wrote in 1923,

> [The Swift] case was a milestone in the interpreta-tion of the commerce clause of the Constitution. It recognized the great changes and development in the business of this vast country and drew again the dividing line between interstate and intrastate com-merce where the Constitution intended it to be. It refused to permit local incidents of great interstate movement, which, taken alone, were intrastate, to characterize the movement as such. The Swift case merely fitted the commerce clause to the real and practical essence of modern business growth.[94]

The stream of commerce doctrine was reinforced and applied to questions outside the realm of antitrust in 1922, when the Supreme Court upheld federal regu-lation of business practices that might contribute to an illegal interference with interstate commerce. *Stafford v. Wallace* (1922) concerned the validity of the Packers and Stockyards Act of 1921, which prohibited certain unfair and discriminatory practices believed to lead to restraint of trade. The Court backed federal regulation, ruling that packers and stockyards were part of the stream of interstate commerce. As Chief Justice Taft put it, the stockyards were "a throat through which the current flows, and the transactions which occur therein are only incidents to this current."[95]

The Court also used the stream of commerce doctrine to uphold the Grain Futures Act of 1922. The shipment of grain to market, its temporary storage, sale, and reshipment in large part to other states were all parts of the flow of interstate commerce, Taft wrote in *Board of Trade of Chicago v. Olsen* (1923). This opinion was somewhat ironic since it effectively overturned an earlier decision, also written by Taft, that held unconstitutional a congressional attempt to regulate boards of trade dealing in commodities futures.[96] The Court's adoption of this doctrine restric-ted state power to regulate commerce as illustrated in *Lemke v. Farmers Grain Co.* (1922), in which the Court held that wheat delivered and sold by farmers to North Dakota grain elevators and then resold mostly to buyers in Minnesota was in a stream of interstate commerce. Therefore, the Court said, a state statute regulating the price and profit of wheat sales interfered with the free flow of interstate commerce.[97]

The "Rule of Reason"

After the first decade of the twentieth century, the Court abandoned the literal interpretation of the language of the Sherman Antitrust Act set out by Justice Harlan in the *Northern Securities* case. A slim majority of the Court in *Standard Oil Co. v. United States* (1911) adopted the con-troversial "rule of reason," under which only unreason-able combinations and undue restraints of trade are considered illegal. The Court first discussed the rule in *United States v. Trans-Missouri Freight Association* (1897).

There the majority held that a combination of railroads that set freight rates was illegal even though the rates were reasonable. The majority flatly rejected the argument that the Sherman Antitrust Act applied only to unreasonable combinations. Justice Peckham wrote for the Court:

> When, therefore, the body of an act pronounces as illegal every contract or combination in restraint of trade or commerce among the several States . . . the plain and ordinary meaning of such language is not limited to that kind of contract alone which is unreasonable restraint of trade, but all contracts are included in such language.[98]

Disagreeing with this interpretation, Justice Edward D. White wrote a dissenting opinion:

> The theory upon which the contract is held to be illegal is that even though it be reasonable, and hence valid under the general principles of law, it is yet void, because it conflicts with the act of Congress already referred to. Now, at the outset, it is necessary to understand the full import of this conclusion. As it is conceded that the contract does not unreasonably restrain trade, and that if it does not so unreasonably restrain, it is valid under the general law, the decision, substantially, is that the act of Congress is a departure from the general principles of law, and by its terms destroys the right of individuals or corporations to enter into very many reasonable contracts. But this proposition, I submit, is tantamount to an assertion that the act of Congress is itself unreasonable.[99]

Over the next few years, the majority continued to apply the antitrust act to all combinations, not only those considered unreasonable. In 1911, however, in the case that broke up the Standard Oil complex, the advocates of the rule of reason became the majority. In an elaborate and lengthy opinion, White, now chief justice, traced the development of the rule of reason in English common law and its use in the United States at the time the antitrust act was enacted. He then declared that because the act did not enumerate the kinds of contracts and combines it embraced, the act "necessarily called for the exercise of judgment which required that some standard should be resorted to" for determining whether the act had been violated.[100] Clearly,

he said, Congress meant that standard to be the rule of reason. Although he concurred with the majority's conclusion that the Standard Oil combination violated the antitrust act, Justice Harlan criticized the majority for "usurpation . . . of the functions" of Congress. By endorsing the rule of reason, Harlan said,

> the Court has now read into the act of Congress words which are not to be found there, and has thereby done that which it adjudged . . . could not be done without violating the Constitution, namely, by interpretation of a statute, changed a public policy declared by the legislative department.[101]

Two weeks later the Court again endorsed the rule of reason when it decided that the tobacco trust must be dissolved. White wrote that the rule "was in accord with all the previous decisions of this Court, despite the fact that the contrary view was sometimes erroneously attributed to some of the expressions" in prior decisions.[102]

Harlan's fear, expressed in his *Standard Oil* dissent, that unreasonableness would prove a difficult standard to apply, was not unwarranted. In 1913 the Court found reasonable a combination of manufacturers of shoemaking equipment that controlled between 70 percent and 80 percent of the market. Because the three manufacturers involved individually controlled about the same percentage of the market before they joined forces, the Court found that their combination sought only greater efficiency.[103] Under this rule, the Court held in 1920 that U.S. Steel Corporation was not in violation of the antitrust act, despite the fact that the company had attempted to create a monopoly and failed. "It is against monopoly that the statute is directed, not against an expectation of it," the Court wrote.[104] Declaring in 1918 that "[e]very agreement concerning trade, every regulation of trade, restrains," the Court enunciated the procedure it still uses to determine whether a combination or trust is reasonable. Justice Louis D. Brandeis, for the Court in *Chicago Board of Trade v. United States* (1918), wrote,

> The true test of legality is whether the restraint imposed is such as merely regulates and perhaps thereby promotes competition or whether it is such as may suppress or even destroy competition. To determine that question the court must ordinarily

consider the facts peculiar to the business to which the restraint is applied; its condition before and after the restraint was imposed; the nature of the restraint and its effect, actual or probable. The history of the restraint, the evil believed to exist, the reasons for adopting the particular remedy, the purpose or end sought to be attained, are all relevant facts.[105]

More recently, the Court has retreated from strict enforcement of the antitrust laws. It overturned several earlier rulings that held certain business arrangements were automatically illegal under the Sherman Act. A notable example came in 2007 when the Court overruled a nearly century-old rule that barred manufacturers from fixing the retail prices for their products. Typically, automakers and others posted a "Manufacturers Suggested Retail Price," but dealers were permitted to sell the product for less. In *Dr. Miles Medical Co. v. John H. Park* (1911) the Court said that contracts or deals between manufacturers and retailers that fixed prices were "per se" or automatically illegal. But the justices in 2007 called that rule outdated and contrary to modern economics. Some manufacturers of brand-name goods required retailers to provide displays in their stores in exchange for a mark-up in the price. These deals should not be deemed illegal, the Court said, even if they fixed the retail price. The ruling overturned a price-fixing verdict against a California maker of women's handbags who was sued by a Dallas store that was cut off from further business with the manufacturer for selling the bags at a discount.[106]

Antitrust and Labor

Efforts to include a specific exemption for labor unions in the 1890 Sherman Antitrust Act were unsuccessful; as a result, the act was used almost from its passage against labor, justifying the issuance of orders halting strikes by labor unions. In 1894 a federal circuit court relied partially on the Sherman Act to uphold an injunction against Eugene V. Debs and other leaders of the Pullman strike on the grounds that the railroad workers had conspired to restrain trade. *(See details of In re Debs, pp. 308–309.)* The Supreme Court upheld the injunction against the strike and the resulting convictions for contempt of the order, resting its opinion

on the broad grounds that the federal government's responsibility for interstate commerce and the mails gave it the authority to interfere with the strike to prevent obstruction of those functions. Of its failure to look to the antitrust act for authority to issue the injunction, the Court said, "It must not be understood from this that we dissent from the conclusion of that [circuit] court in reference to the scope of the act."[107]

That the Court agreed in the application of the antitrust act against labor unions was made abundantly clear in its 1908 decision in *Loewe v. Lawlor*. A union attempting to organize workers at a hat factory in Danbury, Connecticut, was supported by the American Federation of Labor, which coordinated boycotts of stores selling the hats in several states. Speaking for the Court, Chief Justice Fuller asserted that because the antitrust act covered "any combination whatever" in restraint of trade, it extended to labor unions whose activities—as in this case—were "aimed at compelling third parties and strangers involuntarily not to engage in the course of trade except on conditions that the combination imposes."[108] Fuller also employed the stream of commerce doctrine to show that the boycotts, although intrastate, had a direct effect on interstate commerce: "If the purposes of the combinations were, as alleged, to prevent any interstate transportation [of the hats] at all, the fact that the means operated at one end before the physical transportation commenced and at the other end after the physical transportation ended was immaterial."[109]

As a result of that decision Congress inserted provisions in the Clayton Antitrust Act of 1914 exempting labor unions from antitrust actions. Section 6 of the act stipulated that labor was "not a commodity or article of commerce." Section 20 provided that "no restraining order or injunction shall be granted by any court of the United States . . . in any case between an employer and employees . . . unless necessary to prevent irreparable injury to property, or to a property right." The Court did not consider the validity of these sections until the 1920s, when it narrowed the Clayton Act labor exemption in *Duplex Printing Press Co. v. Deering* (1921). An interstate union wanted to organize workers at a press manufacturer in Michigan. Workers at the Michigan plant went on strike, and a secondary boycott of the press markets was organized, primarily in the New York City area. The question was whether the Clayton Act prohibited the issuance of an injunction against those persons engaged in the secondary boycott. With three dissenting votes, the Court ruled that it did not, holding that the Clayton Act exemptions pertained only to legal and normal operations of labor unions. There was nothing in the act, the Court said, "to exempt such an organization or its members from accountability where it or they depart from its normal and legitimate objects and engage in an actual combination or conspiracy in restraint of trade."[110] The secondary boycott was such a restraint, the justices held.

The *Duplex Printing Press* decision was the first in a series of cases in the 1920s in which the Court continued to use the antitrust laws against labor unions. In 1925 the Court held that an intrastate strike against a coal company directly affected commerce and violated the antitrust laws. In 1927 the Court overruled two lower federal courts to grant an injunction against a stonecutters union that had instituted a secondary boycott of stone cut by nonunion workers.[111] To force the Court to expand its interpretation of the labor exemption in the Clayton Act, Congress in 1932 passed the Norris-LaGuardia Act, which prohibited the issuance of injunctions by federal courts in labor disputes except where unlawful acts were threatened or committed.

The Court in *Lauf v. E. G. Shinner & Co.* (1938) upheld the act on the grounds that it was within congressional power to determine the jurisdiction of the federal courts.[112] The Court has maintained that ruling in the face of several subsequent challenges to the law.[113] In 1941 the Court gave additional vigor to the Clayton Act when it sustained a provision of Section 20 that stated that certain acts, such as strikes and secondary boycotts, would not be considered violations of any federal law.[114] In 1945 the Court ruled that a union that conspired with manufacturers to boycott a nonunion competitor was violating the Sherman Antitrust Act,[115] but a union's refusal to work for a trucking firm or to take as members any of the persons who worked for the firm did not violate the antitrust law but was a proper exercise of union rights under the Clayton and Norris-LaGuardia Acts.[116]

THE FEDERAL POLICE POWER

The Constitution does not authorize Congress to protect the health, welfare, or morals of the public. Those responsibilities are traditionally left to the states acting through the police power. Nevertheless, Congress in the late 1800s began to develop a federal police power to deal with a growing list of social and economic problems that were national in scope. Congress used its constitutional grant of authority over interstate commerce to justify much of this regulation, claiming power to regulate any matter that at any point was a part of interstate commerce. As scholar Robert K. Carr describes it, "Where the commerce power had previously been used primarily to regulate, foster or promote commerce for its own sake, . . . it now seemed that Congress might seek to regulate social and economic practices within the states, provided only that at some point they involved a crossing of state lines."[117]

Congress's initial attempts to exercise a police power were largely unsuccessful; the Court ruled that such regulations could apply only in areas of the United States outside of state boundaries, such as the District of Columbia. In 1870, for example, the Court vitiated most of a federal statute barring the sale of certain illuminating oils "except so far as the [prohibition] operates within the United States, but without the limits of any State."[118] The Court explained:

[The] grant of power to regulate commerce among the States has always been understood as limited by its terms; and as a virtual denial of any power to interfere with the internal trade and business of the separate states; except, indeed, as a necessary and proper means for carrying into execution some other power expressly granted or vested.[119]

The first sign of change in the Court's view on this matter came in 1902, when it upheld a federal statute prohibiting the transportation of diseased cattle in interstate commerce.[120] But it was a later controversial case that was of greater significance. The Court heard arguments three times in *Champion v. Ames* (1903), or the *Lottery Case*, a challenge to Congress's 1895 act making it illegal to transport lottery tickets from a state or foreign country into another state.[121]

The statute had been challenged on the grounds that lottery tickets were not commerce, that it was up to the states to regulate them, and that Congress could not prohibit commerce, in any case. The five-man majority, speaking through Justice John Marshall Harlan, declared that lottery tickets were indeed commerce subject to regulation by Congress. Federal regulation, Harlan said, did not interfere with intrastate commerce in lottery tickets and so did not infringe on states' right to regulate that traffic. In effect, he said, federal regulation supplemented state regulation:

> As a State may, for the purpose of guarding the morals of its own people, forbid all sales of lottery tickets within its limits, so Congress, for the purpose of guarding the people of the United States against the "wide-spread pestilence of lotteries" and to protect the commerce which concerns all the States, may prohibit the carrying of lottery tickets from one State to another.[122]

Recalling John Marshall's declaration that the commerce power is plenary and complete, Harlan said that the power to regulate included the power to prohibit. If Congress finds a subject of interstate commerce noxious, "can it be possible that it must tolerate the traffic, and simply regulate the manner in which it may be carried on?" Harlan asked.[123] On the contrary, he said, "we know of no authority in the Courts to hold that the means thus devised [prohibition of shipment] are not appropriate and necessary to protect the country against a species of interstate commerce which has become offensive to the entire people of the nation."[124] Harlan also noted that the Court had sustained the Sherman Antitrust Act, which prohibited contracts that restrained interstate commerce. (See "Congress and the Trusts," pp. 109–115.)

Justice Harlan anticipated the dissenters' predictions that the use of the commerce power as a police tool would "defeat the operation" of the Tenth Amendment, which reserved to the states powers not granted to the federal government. While plenary and complete, the power of Congress over interstate commerce is not arbitrary, Harlan said, and may not infringe rights protected by the Constitution. This

decision, as historian Charles Warren wrote, "disclosed the existence of a hitherto unsuspected field of national power":

> The practical result of the case was the creation of a federal police power—the right to regulate the manner of production, manufacture, sale and transportation of articles and the transportation of persons, through the medium of legislation professing to regulate commerce between the states. Congress took very swift advantage of the new field thus opened to it.[125]

The Court went on to sustain the Pure Food and Drug Act of 1906, the Mann Act, which penalized persons convicted of transporting women across state lines for immoral purposes, and two statutes regulating safety for railway workers.[126] (See box, Commerce and Prostitution, p. 120.) For a dozen years the federal police power appeared well entrenched, but in 1918 the Court rendered a decision that left further expansion of that power in doubt. The federal police power collided with states' rights and came out the loser.

Child Labor

In *Hammer v. Dagenhart* (1918) the Court struck down a 1916 act of Congress that sought to discourage employment of children by prohibiting the shipment in interstate commerce of any products made in factories or mines that employed children under age fourteen or allowed children aged fourteen to sixteen to work more than a limited number of hours per week.[127] The statute was contested by Roland Dagenhart, whose two teenage sons worked in a North Carolina cotton mill. Dagenhart sought an injunction against U.S. District Attorney W. C. Hammer to prevent him from enforcing the act and costing his sons their jobs. (See box, Doubtful Victory, p. 121.)

By a 5-4 vote the Court declared the 1916 law unconstitutional. Congress, Justice William R. Day said, had exceeded its authority when it prohibited goods made by children from interstate commerce. The power to regulate commerce is the authority "to control the means by which commerce is carried on," and not the "right to forbid commerce from moving,"

Day said.[128] This statement required Day to distinguish his holding in the child labor act from the cases in which the Court had sanctioned a congressional prohibition against the movement of items such as lottery tickets and adulterated food in interstate commerce. Day did so by declaring these latter articles harmful in themselves and asserting that their regulation "could only be accomplished by prohibiting the use of the facilities of interstate commerce to effect the evil intended." That "element is wanting in the present case," he said; the goods manufactured by children "are of themselves harmless."[129]

Day did not stop at this point, but went on to examine the reasons Congress enacted the law. "The act in its effect does not regulate transportation among the states," Day said, "but aims to standardize the ages at which children may be employed in mining and manufacturing within the states."[130] Retreating to the earlier distinction between commerce and manufacture, Day said mining and manufacture were subject only to state regulation. The fact that goods "were intended for interstate commerce transportation does not make their production subject to federal control under the commerce power," he maintained.[131] In conclusion, the justice stated that the act "not only transcends the authority delegated to Congress over commerce but also exerts a power as to a purely local matter to which the federal authority does not extend."[132]

Justice Holmes's dissenting opinion left little doubt that the minority believed the majority's ruling had been motivated by the five justices' personal opposition to the law. On its face, Holmes said, the act was indisputably within the federal commerce power. That being the case, he said, "it seems to me that it is not made any less constitutional because of the indirect effects that it may have (that is, the discouragement of child labor), however obvious it may be that it will have those effects."[133] In support of this proposition, Holmes cited a number of cases in which the Court had upheld a regulatory measure without considering the probable effect of the measure. It was also irrelevant that the evil was not itself in interstate transportation. "It does not matter whether the supposed evil precedes or follows

the transportation," Holmes declared. "It is enough that in the opinion of Congress that transportation encourages the evil."[134] Holmes also maintained that Congress and not the Court should determine when prohibition was necessary to effective regulation, adding that "if there is any matter upon which civilized countries have agreed it is the evil of premature and excessive child labor."[135] The federal law did not interfere with the state police power, asserted Holmes, and in any event the Court had made clear that the exercise of the federal commerce power could not be limited by its potential for interfering with intrastate regulation of commerce. States, he said,

> may regulate their internal affairs and their domestic commerce as they like. But when they seek to send their products across the State line they are no longer within their rights. Under the Constitution such commerce belongs not to the States but to Congress to regulate. It may carry out its views of public policy whatever indirect effect they may have upon the activities of the state.[136]

Congressional efforts to circumvent the ruling in *Hammer v. Dagenhart* proved unsuccessful. Congress in 1919 sought to use its tax power to discourage the use of child labor by placing a high tax on goods that had been manufactured in factories employing youngsters, but the Court declared the tax unconstitutional.[137] Congress then passed a constitutional amendment forbidding the employment of children, but the states had not ratified it by the time the Court itself in *United States v. Darby Lumber Co.* (1941) overturned its own ruling.[138] *(See "Wages and Hours," pp. 126–128.)*

Effect of *Dagenhart*

The Court did not much rely on *Dagenhart* as a precedent, the major exception being the invalidation of the child labor tax law. The justices continued to sanction use of the commerce power as a police tool when it was applied to universally recognized social evils. A few weeks after the child labor case decision, the Court unanimously upheld the constitutionality of the 1906 Meat Inspection Act, which called for

THE COURT, CONGRESS, AND COMMERCE: A CHRONOLOGY

The following are the major Supreme Court decisions on the power of Congress to tax and regulate commerce.

1824 *Gibbons v. Ogden* Defines the commerce power: Congress may regulate all commerce affecting more than one state.

1851 *Cooley v. Board of Port Wardens of Philadelphia* The *Cooley* doctrine gives Congress authority to regulate areas of commerce national in scope but allows states to regulate areas local in nature.

1871 *The Daniel Ball* Forerunner of the stream of commerce doctrine: Congress may regulate boats operating solely intrastate but transporting goods in interstate commerce.

1888 *Kidd v. Pearson* Manufacture is not commerce.

1895 *United States v. E. C. Knight Co.* Processing is manufacture, not commerce, and does not affect commerce directly; therefore a sugar processing trust is not a restraint of trade under federal antitrust law.

1903 *Champion v. Ames* Congress may use the commerce power as police power to outlaw the interstate sale and shipment of lottery tickets.

1904 *McCray v. United States* Congress may use the tax power as police power to impede the sale of yellow oleo.

1905 *Swift & Co. v. United States* Stream of commerce doctrine: Congress may regulate intrastate commerce that is a part of a stream of interstate commerce.

1908 *Adair v. United States* Labor relations do not directly affect interstate commerce; therefore, Congress may not use its commerce power to prohibit "yellow dog" contrasts.

Loewe v. Lawlor Union boycotts are restraints of trade and interstate commerce in violation of antitrust act.

1909 *First Employers' Liability Case* Congress lacks power to make employers liable for on-the-job deaths of railway employees not involved with interstate commerce.

1911 *Standard Oil of New Jersey v. United States* Adoption of the "rule of reason": only unreasonable trusts are violations of antitrust act.

1914 *Shreveport Rate Cases* Congress may regulate intrastate rail rates when such regulation is necessary to ensure effective regulation of interstate rates.

1917 *Wilson v. New* Congress may set emergency wage and hour standards for railway workers.

1918 *Hammer v. Dagenhart* Congress may not use the commerce power as police power to set hour standards for child laborers; such use is an unconstitutional attempt to regulate manufacturing, which is not commerce.

1921 *Duplex Printing Co. v. Deering* The Clayton Act does not exempt unions involved in boycotts from prosecution under antitrust act.

1922 *Stafford v. Wallace* Stream of commerce doctrine expanded: Congress may regulate unfair business practices in intrastate industries that are a part of the flow of interstate commerce.

Bailey v. Drexel Furniture Co. Congress may not use the tax power as police power to place high taxes on profits of companies employing child laborers; such a use of the tax power is an unconstitutional imposition of a penalty, not an effort to raise revenue.

---

local inspection of meat products and banned those rejected or not inspected from interstate commerce.[139] Subsequent decisions approved federal statutes prohibiting the interstate transportation of stolen cars, making transportation of kidnapped persons in interstate commerce a federal crime, and preventing the interstate shipment of prisoner-made goods to those states that prohibited them.[140] Like child labor, the goods involved in these three cases—cars, kidnapped persons, and horse collars—were not in and of themselves harmful. Yet the Court upheld the federal regulation in all three cases. It explained in the stolen cars case:

> Congress can certainly regulate interstate commerce to the extent of forbidding and punishing the use of such commerce as an agency to promote immorality, dishonesty or the spread of any evil or harm to the people of other states from the state of origin. In doing this, it is merely exercising the police power, for the benefit of the public, within the field of interstate commerce.[141]

The Court sanctioned use of the police power in 1971, when it sustained provisions of the 1968 Consumer Credit Protection Act prohibiting loan-sharking. Although individual loan-sharking activities might be wholly intrastate, the Court said that it was in a "class of activity" that affected interstate commerce and therefore could be regulated under the commerce power.[142]

1935 *A. L. A. Schechter Poultry Corp. v. United States* Stream of commerce doctrine does not allow Congress to regulate companies receiving goods from out of state but selling them locally.

Railroad Retirement Board v. Alton Railroad Co. Law establishing a pension system for railroad workers exceeds the commerce power.

1936 *Carter v. Carter Coal Co.* Mining is not commerce and does not affect commerce directly, so Congress may not regulate labor relations in the coal mining industry. A coal tax that is refundable if the producer complies with regulations is an unconstitutional penalty.

United States v. Butler Congress may not regulate agricultural production by taxing food processors in order to pay benefits to farmers who reduce production of certain crops.

1937 *NLRB v. Jones & Laughlin Steel Corp.* Congress may regulate labor relations in manufacturing to prevent possible interference with interstate commerce, overturning *Carter* and *Schechter.*

Helvering v. Davis, Steward Machine Co. v. Davis Congress may use its taxing and spending powers to enact benefit plans as part of Social Security and unemployment compensation statutes, overturning *Butler* and *Alton.*

1939 *Mulford v. Smith* Congress may set marketing quotas for agricultural production, regulating commerce at the beginning of the stream.

1941 *United States v. Darby Lumber Co.* Congress may use the commerce power to prohibit from interstate commerce goods made under substandard labor conditions, overturning *Dagenhart.*

1942 *Wickard v. Filburn* Congress may regulate agricultural production affecting interstate commerce even if the produce is not meant for sale.

1964 *Heart of Atlanta Motel v. United States* Congress may use the commerce power to prohibit racial discrimination by private individuals operating public accommodations that cater to interstate clientele or use goods made in interstate commerce.

1976 *National League of Cities v. Usery* Congress exceeds its commerce power when it establishes wage and hour standards for state employees, because such standards are unconstitutional infringements on state sovereignty.

1985 *Garcia v. San Antonio Metropolitan Transit Authority* Congress may apply federal minimum wage and hour standards for state employees; the Constitution does not limit this exercise of the commerce power to curtail the power of states. *Usery* overturned.

1995 *United States v. Lopez* Congress exceeded its commerce power with a law banning guns within 1,000 feet of a public school; the statute had "nothing to do with commerce" or an "economic enterprise."

2000 *United States v. Morrison* Congress overstepped the commerce power with part of the Violence Against Women Act of 1994, which allowed federal civil suits by victims of "gender-motivated" violence against their attackers, an issue traditionally within the states' police power.

2005 *Gonzales v. Raich* Congress may restrict the use of home-grown marijuana because this "purely local activity" could have an "substantial effect on interstate commerce"—in this instance, in the sale of illegal drugs.

NEW DEAL AND OLD POWER

In the decades between *Dagenhart* and the Great Depression, Congress made little use of the commerce power to regulate business. When, under President Franklin D. Roosevelt's guidance, Congress attempted to use federal regulation to stimulate economic recovery, the Supreme Court, still dominated by a small majority strongly disposed toward protection of private property rights—and states' rights—again resisted. The resulting collision—and the threat by Roosevelt to increase the size of the Court to ensure approval of his New Deal legislation—marked the birth of modern commerce power. In 1937 the Court accepted Justice Benjamin N. Cardozo's view that the power was equal to the nation's problems. In subsequent years, the Court would uphold the use of the commerce power to deal with problems ranging from civil rights violations to environmental pollution.

Black Monday

The centerpiece of Roosevelt's recovery program was the National Industrial Recovery Act (NIRA) of 1933. It declared a "national emergency productive of widespread unemployment and disorganization of industry, which burdens interstate and foreign commerce, affects the public welfare and undermines the standards of living of the American people." To speed industrial recovery, the NIRA authorized the president to approve codes of fair competition. Each of these codes, among other conditions, had to contain hour and wage standards for

COMMERCE AND PROSTITUTION

Initial congressional efforts to curb prostitution were thwarted by the Supreme Court. In 1907 Congress made it illegal for anyone to harbor an alien woman for purposes of prostitution within three years after her arrival in the country. Two years later, however, the Court held 6-3 that regulating houses of prostitution was a state affair beyond the reach of Congress.[1] In 1910, with continuing concern over reports of women held as virtual slaves and forced to engage in prostitution, Congress adopted the Mann Act, which punished any person found guilty of transporting women for "immoral purposes" in interstate or foreign commerce. The Court in *Hoke v. United States* (1913) unanimously upheld the act without referring to its decision in the earlier prostitution case. "Of course, it will be said that women are not articles of merchandise but this does not affect the analogy of the cases," wrote Justice Joseph McKenna. He continued,

[I]f the facility of interstate transportation can be taken away from the demoralization of lotteries, the debasement of obscene literature, the contagion of diseased cattle or persons, the impurity of food and drugs, the like facility can be taken away from the systematic enticement to and the enslavement in prostitution and debauchery of women, and, more insistently, of girls.[2]

In subsequent cases, the Court backed enforcement of the Mann Act against persons transporting women across state lines for immoral purposes, although there was no commercial gain involved, and against Mormon men who transported their multiple wives across state lines.[3]

1. *Keller v. United States,* 213 U.S. 138 (1909).

2. *Hoke v. United States,* 227 U.S. 308 at 322 (1913).

3. *Caminetti v. United States,* 242 U.S. 470 (1917); *Cleveland v. United States,* 329 U.S. 14 (1946).

workers in the particular industry. The first inkling of how the Supreme Court would treat the NIRA came in January 1935, when it declared the "hot" oil section of the law an unconstitutional delegation of legislative authority. The provisions permitted the president to prohibit the interstate transportation of oil produced in excess of amounts allowed by the states. The "hot oil" case—*Panama Refining Co. v. Ryan*—did not deal, however, with the codes of fair competition the NIRA authorized.[143] *(See "Hot Oil," p. 89.)*

Five months later, on what came to be known as Black Monday, the Court declared the entire NIRA invalid. *A. L. A. Schechter Poultry Corp. v. United States* (1935) was a test case brought by the government in the hope that a favorable response from the Court would encourage industry compliance, which had been flagging.[144] The circumstances involved, however, made it less than an ideal test. The Schechter brothers bought live poultry shipped into New York City largely from points outside of the state, slaughtered it, then sold it locally. They were accused of violating several provisions of the New York City live poultry industry code, including the wage and hour standards and the prohibition against "straight killing," or allowing a customer to select individual poultry for slaughter.

They were also charged with selling an "unfit chicken" to a local butcher. As a result, the suit was quickly dubbed the "sick chicken" case.

The Supreme Court unanimously held that the Schechters' operation was a local concern that did not directly affect interstate commerce. Federal regulation through the fair competition codes was, therefore, an unconstitutional abridgment of states' rights. The Court noted that the provisions of the code that the Schechters were charged with violating applied to the slaughtering operation and subsequent sale in local markets, activities that the Court said were not in interstate commerce. The Court also denied that these activities were part of the stream of commerce. Chief Justice Charles Evans Hughes wrote,

The mere fact that there may be a constant flow of commodities into a state does not mean that the flow continues after the property has arrived and has become commingled with the mass of property within the state and is there held solely for local disposition and use.[145]

The Court acknowledged that Congress had the power not only to regulate interstate commerce but also to protect interstate commerce from burden or injury

Doubtful victory

Five years after the Supreme Court's decision in *Hammer v. Dagenhart* (1918) striking down the child labor law, a journalist interviewed Reuben Dagenhart, whose father had sued to prevent Congress from interfering with his sons' jobs in a North Carolina cotton mill. Reuben was twenty when he was interviewed. The following is an excerpt of that interview.

"What benefit . . . did you get out of the suit which you won in the United States Supreme Court?"

"I don't see that I got any benefit. I guess I'd have been a lot better off if they hadn't won it.

"Look at me! A hundred and five pounds, a grown man and no education. I may be mistaken, but I think the years I've put in the cotton mills have stunted my growth. They kept me from getting any schooling. I had to stop school after the third grade and now I need the education I didn't get."

"Just what did you and John get out of that suit, then?" he was asked.

"Why, we got some automobile rides when them big lawyers from the North was down here. Oh yes, and they bought both of us a Coca-Cola! That's all we got out of it."

"What did you tell the judge when you were in court?"

"Oh, John and me never was in court. Just Paw was there. John and me was just little kids in short pants. I guess we wouldn't have looked like much in court. . . . We were working in the mill while the case was going on."

Reuben hasn't been to school in years, but his mind has not been idle.

"It would have been a good thing for all the kids in this state if that law they passed had been kept. Of course, they do better now than they used to. You don't see so many babies working in the factories, but you see a lot of them that ought to be going to school." [1]

---

1. *Labor,* November 17, 1923, 3, quoted in Leonard F. James, *The Supreme Court in American Life,* 2nd ed. (Glenview, Ill.: Scott, Foresman, 1971), 74

---

imposed by those engaged in intrastate activities. The effect of the burden must be direct, however, said the Court, recalling the Court's distinction between direct and indirect effects first discussed in the 1895 sugar trust case. Wrote Hughes,

> In determining how far the federal government may go in controlling intrastate transactions upon the ground that they "affect" interstate commerce, there is a necessary and well-established distinction between direct and indirect effects. The precise line can be drawn only as individual cases arise, but the distinction is clear in principle.[146]

That distinction, the Court said, was essential to maintenance of the federal system. Without it the federal government would have complete power over domestic affairs of the states and there would be a centralized government. "It is not the province of the Court," Hughes wrote, "to consider the economic advantages or disadvantages of such a centralized system. It is sufficient to say that the Federal Constitution does not provide for it."[147] The Court found no way in which the alleged violations by the Schechters directly affected interstate commerce. It also held that the delegation to the president by Congress of the authority to establish the codes of competition was excessive and therefore unconstitutional. On both these grounds, it declared the NIRA invalid. *(See "Delegations to Private Parties," "Wartime Delegations," and "Delegations to States," pp. 89–92.)*

Some scholars have argued that the Court could have upheld the NIRA so far as it was based on the federal power over interstate commerce. Robert Carr has suggested that the justices could have extended the stream of commerce doctrine to cover the Schechters' business even though it was at the end of the stream.[148] It should not be overlooked, however, that the Court was unanimous and that the justices considered to be more likely to approve the New Deal legislation found the NIRA, as presented in *Schechter*, unconstitutional. Justice Cardozo, in a concurring opinion for himself and Justice Harlan Fiske Stone, claimed that the distinction between direct and indirect effects on commerce was a matter of degree, but, he added, "[t]o find

The Court in *Schechter Poultry Corp. v. United States* (1935) declared unconstitutional portions of the National Industrial Recovery Act, a major piece of New Deal legislation. Here, the Schechter brothers celebrate with their attorney upon learning of the Supreme Court's decision.

immediacy or directness [in this case] is to find it almost everywhere."[149]

Coal Codes

No such unanimity marked the next New Deal decision. In *Carter v. Carter Coal Co.* (1936) the Court struck down the 1935 Bituminous Coal Conservation Act, which declared that the production and distribution of coal so closely affected interstate commerce that federal regulation was necessary to stabilize the industry.[150] Passed despite the adverse ruling in *Schechter,* the act authorized fixed prices for coal, provided for collective bargaining rights for coal miners, allowed a two-thirds majority of the industry to establish wage and hour standards for the entire industry, and established a tax scheme to ensure compliance with the regulations.

Divided 6-3, the Court in May 1936 declared the act unconstitutional. Justice George Sutherland, speaking for the majority, focused first on the labor relations provisions, declaring that mining was production, not commerce, and that the relation between a mine operator and mine workers was purely local in character. Because mining itself was not interstate commerce, Sutherland continued, it became necessary to determine if its effect on that commerce was direct. Here, Sutherland set forth a definition of a direct effect that turned not on the degree to which a thing affected interstate commerce but on the manner in which the effect occurred:

The word "direct" implies that the activity or condition invoked or blamed shall operate proximately—not mediately, remotely, or collaterally—to produce the effect. . . . And the extent of the effect bears no logical relation to its character. The distinction between a direct and an indirect effect turns, not upon the magnitude of either the cause or the effect, but entirely upon the manner in which the effect has been brought about.[151]

It made no difference, said Sutherland, whether one man mined coal for sale in interstate commerce or several men mined it. Labor problems were local controversies affecting local production. "Such effect as they have upon commerce, however extensive it may be, is secondary and indirect," Sutherland proclaimed.[152] Further, mining was not a part of the stream of commerce. Looking to *Schechter,* Sutherland noted,

> The only perceptible difference between that case and this is that in the Schechter case, the federal power was asserted with respect to commodities which had come to rest after their interstate transportation; while here, the case deals with commodities at rest before interstate commerce has begun. That difference is without significance.[153]

Having declared the labor provisions an invalid exercise of federal power under the Commerce Clause, Sutherland proceeded to hold the price-fixing provisions invalid on the grounds that they were so dependent on the labor provisions, they could not stand on their own. That he determined despite a severability clause in the legislation that said the price-fixing provisions could stand if other provisions were found unconstitutional. *(See box, Severability: Divided It Stands, p. 150.)* The majority also held the statute an unconstitutional delegation of legislative powers to the executive branch and to the coal industry. It further invalidated the taxes on the basis that the tax provisions were not for the purpose of raising revenue, but for coercing compliance with the regulations. Because the commerce power had been exercised unconstitutionally, the tax provisions were also invalid, the majority said.

In a concurring opinion, Chief Justice Hughes disagreed with the majority ruling that the price-fixing provisions were inseparable from the labor provisions, but he agreed that the distinction between direct and indirect effects on interstate commerce was a matter of kind and not degree. "The power to regulate interstate commerce embraces the power to protect that commerce from injury," Hughes said, and then added

> But Congress may not use this protective authority as a pretext to regulate activities and relations within the states which affect interstate commerce only indirectly. . . . If the people desire to give Congress the power to regulate industries within the State, and the relations of employers and employees in those industries, they are at liberty to declare their will in the appropriate manner, but it is not for the Court to amend the Constitution by judicial decision.[154]

As historians Alfred H. Kelly and Winfred A. Harbison note, "The most extraordinary thing about Sutherland's opinion was the absurdity of his contention that while the labor provisions of the act were only indirectly related to interstate commerce, they were nonetheless so intimately related to those portions of the law dealing with interstate commerce as to be inseparable from them."[155] In fact, Sutherland never discussed whether the price-fixing provisions were in interstate commerce or directly affected it. If he had, he would have had to reconcile his opinion with the *Shreveport Rate Cases* precedent permitting federal regulation of intrastate matters that are inextricably mingled with interstate commerce. *(See "Creation of the Interstate Commerce Commission," pp. 104–106.)*

Cardozo in dissent used this precedent to prove the validity of the price-fixing provisions. The provisions, he wrote, were valid as they applied to transactions in interstate commerce and to transactions in intrastate commerce if such local transactions "directly or intimately affected" interstate commerce. Joined by Justices Stone and Louis D. Brandeis, Cardozo then reiterated his *Schechter* opinion that the distinction between direct and indirect effects was one of degree, not kind. "At all events," wrote Cardozo, "'direct' and 'indirect' . . . must not be read too narrowly. The power is as broad as the need that evokes it."[156] In this instance, Cardozo said, that need was great:

> Congress was not condemned to inaction in the face of price wars and wage wars. . . . Commerce had been choked and burdened; its normal flow had been diverted from one state to another; there had

been bankruptcy and waste and ruin alike for capital and for labor. . . . After making every allowance for difference of opinion as to the most efficient cure, the student of the subject is confronted with the indisputable truth that there were ills to be corrected, and ills that had a direct relation to the maintenance of commerce among the states without friction or diversion. An evil existing, and also the power to correct it, the lawmakers were at liberty to use their own discretion in the selection of the means.[157]

Cardozo's opinion recognized what the majority failed to acknowledge—that the local but widespread economic problems of the depression were national in scope. In protecting state sovereignty and private property rights, the majority almost totally rejected the concept of national supremacy. The Court's rejection of the theory that Congress might act to protect what it perceived to be the general welfare is the attitude that led to Roosevelt's attempt to moderate the conservative voice of the Court through his Court-packing plan. (See "The Court Versus FDR, pp. 341–348.) Roosevelt, to use an apt cliché, lost the battle but won the war. Congress rejected his Court-packing scheme, but not before Justice Owen J. Roberts, who generally voted with the conservative majority, did an about-face, converting the more liberal minority into a majority. In April 1937 Cardozo's reasoning in the Carter dissent became the majority opinion in a case upholding the 1935 National Labor Relations Act (NLRA).[158]

A National Labor Law

Passed in 1935, the NLRA declared that denying the rights of workers to organize and bargain collectively caused strikes and other labor problems that directly burdened and obstructed interstate commerce. To eliminate the obstruction and to guarantee workers' rights, Congress prohibited employees and employers from engaging in specified unfair labor practices. The act also established the National Labor Relations Board (NLRB) to administer the law and hear charges of violations. In view of the precedents established in the Schechter and Carter cases, it seemed likely that the Supreme Court would also invalidate the NLRA's application to employers and employees engaged in

manufacturing and production. The question was put to the Court in 1937 in the midst of public and congressional debate over Roosevelt's Court-packing plan.

The case of NLRB v. Jones & Laughlin Steel Corp. (1937) arose after the steel company fired ten union employees from one of its Pennsylvania factories. The employees claimed that they had been let go solely because they were union members. The NLRB agreed and ordered the steel company to stop discriminating against its union workers. When the company failed to comply, the NLRB asked a court of appeals to enforce its order. Relying on the Carter decision, the court refused the petition, saying Congress did not have the power to regulate local labor relations. Arguing the case before the Supreme Court, attorneys for the NLRB contended that the Pennsylvania factory was in a stream of commerce, receiving raw materials from and transporting its products to other states through interstate commerce. The corporation argued that the NLRA was regulating labor relations, a local concern not subject to federal regulation.

The Supreme Court, in a 5-4 decision, reversed the lower court, sustaining the National Labor Relations Act. Joining Justices Cardozo, Brandeis, and Stone to make a majority were Chief Justice Hughes and Justice Roberts. Hughes wrote the majority opinion, relying to a great extent on the reasoning of Cardozo's dissent in the Carter Coal case. Reiterating that Congress has the authority to regulate intrastate matters that directly burdened or obstructed interstate commerce, Hughes said the fact that the employees were engaged in the local activity of manufacturing was not "determinative." The question was what effect a strike at the factory would have on interstate commerce:

> In view of respondent's far-flung activities, it is idle to say that the effect would be indirect or remote. It is obvious that it would be immediate and might be catastrophic. We are asked to shut our eyes to the plainest facts of our national life and to deal with the question of direct and indirect effects in an intellectual vacuum. . . . When industries organize themselves on a national scale, making their relation to interstate commerce the dominant factor in their activities, how can it be maintained that their

REGULATION OF FOREIGN COMMERCE

Chief Justice John Marshall wrote in *Gibbons v. Ogden* (1824) the classic interpretation of the Commerce Clause: The constitutional grant "comprehend[s] every species of commercial intercourse between the United States and foreign nations. No sort of trade can be carried on between this country and any other, to which this power does not extend."[1] Congress may set tariffs, regulate international shipping, aviation, and communications, and establish embargoes against unfriendly countries. In conjunction with its powers to coin money, regulate its value, and borrow it, Congress may authorize U.S. participation in international financing, banking, and monetary affairs. Exercise of the power has seldom been challenged in the courts; it was not until 1928 that protective tariffs, long a matter of controversy, came before the Supreme Court and then as a test of the taxing power.[2]

Congressional grants of discretionary authority to the president to adjust tariff schedules have been upheld against challenges that they were improper delegations of power.[3] *(See "Delegation of Power," pp. 306–307.)* Federal power over foreign commerce includes the power to prohibit that commerce. "The Congress may determine what articles may be imported into this country and the terms upon which importation is permitted. No one can be said to have a vested right to carry on foreign commerce with the United States," wrote the Court in 1933.[4] Under this principle, the Court upheld federal statutes prohibiting the importation of inferior and impure tea, prize fight films, and natural sponges from the Gulf of Mexico and the Florida straits.[5]

The federal authority over foreign commerce is exclusive. The Constitution expressly forbids the states to enter into treaties with foreign nations or to lay imposts and duties on foreign imports and exports. The "original package" doctrine first put forward by Chief Justice Marshall in 1827 undergirds the prohibition against state duties on imports, although that doctrine has been diluted in recent years, and some state taxing of imported goods is permitted.[6] *(See "Taxing Imports," pp. 419–421.)* In the absence of federal regulation, however, the Supreme Court has allowed state inspection and quarantine laws to stand, even though they might affect foreign commerce.[7]

1. *Gibbons v. Ogden,* 9 Wheat. (22 U.S.) 1 at 193–194 (1824).
2. *J. W. Hampton Jr & Co. v. United States,* 276 U.S. 394 (1928).
3. *Field v. Clark,* 143 U.S. 649 (1892); *Buttfield v. Stranahan,* 192 U.S. 470 (1904); *J. W. Hampton Jr. & Co. v. United States,* 276 U.S. 394 (1928).
4. *Board of Trustees v. United States,* 289 U.S. 48 at 57 (1933).
5. *Buttfield v. Stranahan,* 192 U.S. 470 (1904); *Weber v. Freed,* 239 U.S. 325 (1915); *The Abby Dodge,* 223 U.S. 166 (1912).
6. *Brown v. Maryland,* 12 Wheat. (25 U.S.) 419 (1827); *Michelin Tire Corp. v. Wages,* 423 U.S. 276 (1976); *R. J. Reynolds Tobacco Co. v. Durham County, N.C.,* 479 U.S. 130 (1986).
7. *Gibbons v. Ogden,* 9 Wheat. (22 U.S.) 1 (1824); *Compagnie Francaise de Navigation a Vapeur v. Louisiana State Board of Health,* 186 U.S. 380 at 385 (1902).

industrial labor relations constitute a forbidden field into which Congress may not enter when it is necessary to protect interstate commerce from the paralyzing consequences of industrial war? We have often said that interstate commerce itself is a practical conception. It is equally true that interferences with that commerce must be appraised by a judgment that does not ignore actual experience.[159]

Hughes's majority opinion did not specifically overturn the Court's holdings in *Schechter* and *Carter,* but it did do away with Justice Sutherland's artificial and unrealistic definition of what intrastate matters directly affected interstate commerce. Once again the Supreme Court held that the distinction was a matter of degree to be determined on a case-by-case basis, and not a matter of kind, which did not take into account the realities of the economic system and the nation's needs.

For the four dissenters, Justice James C. McReynolds said he found no material difference between the *Jones & Laughlin* case and those of *Schechter* and *Carter:* "Every consideration brought forward to uphold the Act before us was applicable to support the Acts held unconstitutional in causes decided within two years," he wrote.[160] The steel company was not in the middle of the stream of commerce but at the end of one stream when it received the raw materials and at the beginning of a second when it shipped its finished product, the minority justices wrote. As a result, the company was not in interstate commerce, and its labor relations were not regulative by the federal government but by the states, McReynolds argued. To uphold the NLRA was to give its board "power of control over purely local industry beyond anything heretofore deemed permissible."[161]

More Wins for Labor

The same day the Court announced *Jones & Laughlin,* it upheld the NLRB in four other cases. One involved a large trailer manufacturing company, and another a men's clothing manufacturer, both of which sold a large portion of their products interstate.[162] A labor strike in either of these businesses would not have the catastrophic effect on the national economy of a steel strike, so the effect of these decisions was to broaden the Court's holding in the steel case. The third case involved the Associated Press (AP).[163] Holding that interstate communication of any sort was interstate commerce, the Court rejected the AP's argument that the labor law violated the news association's First Amendment right to freedom of the press. The NLRA, the Court said, has "no relation whatever to the impartial distribution of news." In the fourth case, the Court held that a small company running buses between Virginia and the District of Columbia was an instrumentality of interstate commerce subject to the labor relations act.[164]

Three later NLRB cases also are noteworthy. In *Santa Cruz Fruit Packing Co. v. National Labor Relations Board* (1938) the Court upheld enforcement of the NLRA against a California fruit and vegetable packing company that sold less than 50 percent of its goods in interstate and foreign commerce. A company lockout of union employees resulted in a strike and refusal by warehouse workers, truckers, and stevedores to handle the packed food. "It would be difficult to find a case in which unfair labor practices had a more direct effect upon interstate . . . commerce," the Court wrote.[165] The *Santa Cruz* case is significant because the labor problem stopped the goods at the beginning of the stream of interstate commerce—unlike *Jones & Laughlin,* in which a strike would have stopped the goods in midstream.

In the second case, *Consolidated Edison v. National Labor Relations Board* (1938), a utility that was not in interstate commerce was nevertheless subject to the NLRA because of "the dependence of interstate and foreign commerce upon the continuity of the service."[166] The utility provided electricity, gas, and steam to three railroads, the Port of New York, several steamship piers, two telegraph companies, and a telephone company. In the third case, *National Labor Relations Board v. Fainblatt* (1939), the Court ruled that the NLRA covered unfair labor practices by a clothing manufacturer that resulted in a strike that reduced significantly the amount of goods normally available for shipment in interstate commerce. The manufacturer's contention that he only indirectly affected interstate commerce because only a small portion of his product was shipped interstate was to no avail. The Court said,

> The power of Congress to regulate interstate commerce is plenary and extends to all such commerce be it great or small. . . . The amount of the commerce regulated is of special significance only to the extent that Congress may be taken to have excluded commerce of small volume from the operation of its regulatory measure by express provision or fair implication.[167]

With these decisions, the Court drew the powers of the NLRB so broadly that few cases have since challenged its authority. Its declaration that labor problems in any industry at all dependent on interstate commerce could burden interstate commerce effectively demanded their regulation under the NLRA.

Wages and Hours

Given the newfound willingness of the Supreme Court to construe the commerce power broadly—as evidenced by the NLRB rulings—Congress decided to try once again to set federal minimum wage and maximum hours standards. After the Court in 1918 held that hours limitations for child workers were an unwarranted federal intrusion into intrastate matters, wage and hour reform attempts had been restricted to the individual states. For almost two decades, the Court had approved state maximum hour statutes, but not until 1937 did it abandon its opposition to state minimum wage laws with a decision upholding Washington State's minimum wage law.[168] *(See details of West Coast Hotel Co. v. Parrish, p. 417.)*

In 1938 Congress passed the Fair Labor Standards Act, which established a forty-hour work week and an eventual minimum wage of forty cents an hour with time and a half for overtime. The act covered most workers "engaged in commerce or in the production of goods for commerce." It barred production of goods by workers paid less or working more than the standards prescribed, and, in a provision almost identical to that struck down by the Court in the child labor case, *Hammer v. Dagenhart,* it barred the shipment in interstate commerce of any products made in violation of the standards.

A test of this statute came to the Court in 1941, after the government charged Fred W. Darby with violating it.[169] Darby ran a lumber company in Georgia, converting raw wood into finished lumber and selling a large part of it in other states. The Court unanimously upheld the federal minimum wage statute. Justice Stone, writing the opinion in *United States v. Darby Lumber Co.,* first considered the power of Congress to prohibit shipment of goods manufactured in violation of the standards:

> While manufacture is not of itself interstate commerce, the shipment of manufactured goods interstate is such commerce and the prohibition of such shipment by Congress is indubitably a regulation of the commerce. . . .
>
> The motive and purpose of the present regulation is plainly to make effective the Congressional conception of public policy that interstate commerce should not be made the instrument of competition in the distribution of goods produced under substandard labor conditions, which competition is injurious to the commerce and to the states from and to which the commerce flows. The motive and purpose of a regulation of interstate commerce are matters for the legislative judgment upon the exercise of which the Constitution places no restriction and over which the courts are given no control.[170]

Although based on different precedents, Stone acknowledged that this conclusion was directly contrary to the finding in *Hammer v. Dagenhart.* Of that case, Stone wrote,

> The distinction on which the decision was rested that Congressional power to prohibit interstate commerce is limited to articles which in themselves have some harmful or deleterious property—a distinction which

was novel when made and unsupported by any provision of the Constitution—has long since been abandoned. The thesis of the opinion that the motive of the prohibition or its effect to control in some measure the use or production within the states of the article thus excluded from commerce can operate to deprive the regulation of its constitutional authority has long since ceased to have force. . . .

> The conclusion is inescapable that *Hammer v. Dagenhart* was a departure from the principles which have prevailed in the interpretation of the commerce clause both before and since the decision and that such vitality, as a precedent, as it then had has long since been exhausted. It should be and now is overruled.[171]

The Court also held that the prohibition of the actual production of goods in violation of the standards was a proper means of protecting interstate commerce. This conclusion, said Stone, did not violate the Tenth Amendment reserving to the states those powers not delegated to the federal government:

> There is nothing in the history of its [the amendment's] adoption to suggest that it was more than declaratory of the relationship between the national and state governments as it had been established by the Constitution before the amendment, or that its purpose was other than to allay fears that the new national government might seek to exercise powers not granted, and that the states might not be able to exercise fully their reserved powers. . . .
>
> From the beginning and for many years the amendment has been construed as not depriving the national government of authority to resort to all means for the exercise of a granted power which are appropriate and plainly adapted to the permitted end.[172]

With this decision the Court reestablished a strong federal police power and further extended federal opportunities for regulation of production. The idea that the Tenth Amendment restricted the full exercise of federal power was dead. As several scholars have noted, Stone's opinion brought back to prominence the nationalistic interpretation of the Commerce Clause first outlined by John Marshall, and the Court has not swerved significantly from it since. A year later, the Court went beyond *Darby* to uphold wage and hour standards applied to employees who maintained a building in which tenants produced goods for sale in interstate commerce.[173] In subsequent cases, the Court held that the standards applied to operators of oil well drilling rigs, night watchmen, and elevator operators.[174] A few employees were not covered, however. In 1943 the Court said the minimum wage did not apply to workers for a wholesaler who bought goods outside the state but sold them locally.[175] Nor did the standards apply to maintenance workers in an office building in which some tenants were executives and sales personnel for manufacturing goods sold in interstate commerce but where no actual manufacturing occurred.[176]

Writing in 1942 Robert Carr said that after the *Darby* decision, "about the only further step the Court might take in its general reasoning concerning the commerce power would be to cease denying that manufacture is not of itself commerce and conclude that where goods are produced for, or affect, interstate trade, the act of production is a phase of the total process of commerce."[177] The Court took that step the same year.

Agriculture and Commerce

In 1938 Congress passed a law to replace the Agricultural Adjustment Act, which the Court in 1936 had declared an unconstitutional infringement on state power. Rather than paying farmers to produce less of certain commodities as the first act had, the second act established marketing quotas for the various commodities and penalized producers who exceeded them. *(See details of United States v. Butler, pp. 155–157.)* The following year the Court upheld the 1938 act against the challenge that it too infringed on the reserved powers of the states by attempting to regulate production. Ironically, the opinion was written by Justice Owen J. Roberts, who had written the Court's opinion in the 1936 case. The Court found that the 1938 act did not regulate production, but marketing, which was at the "throat" of interstate commerce.[178]

The same broad interpretation was given to the 1937 Agricultural Marketing Act, which established milk marketing agreements to control milk prices. The Court upheld the act twice, in 1939 and again in 1942,

rejecting in all three cases the argument that Congress lacked authority to regulate milk produced and sold within a single state.[179] In the 1942 case, *United States v. Wrightwood Dairy Co.*, Chief Justice Harlan Fiske Stone wrote for the Court:

> Congress plainly has power to regulate the price of milk distributed through the medium of interstate commerce . . . and it possesses every power needed to make that regulation effective. The commerce power is not confined in its exercise to the regulation of commerce among the States. It extends to those activities intrastate which so affect interstate commerce, or the exertion of the power of Congress over it, as to make regulation of them appropriate means to the attainment of a legitimate end, the effective execution of the granted power to regulate interstate commerce. The power of Congress over interstate commerce is plenary and complete in itself, may be exercised to its utmost extent, and acknowledges no limitations other than are prescribed in the Constitution. . . . It follows that no form of State activity can constitutionally thwart the regulatory power granted by the commerce clause to Congress. Hence the reach of that power extends to those intrastate activities which in a substantial way interfere with or obstruct the exercise of the granted power.[180]

Just how "substantial" that intrastate activity had to be was tested in *Wickard v. Filburn* (1942).[181] Under the 1938 Agricultural Adjustment Act, Claude R. Wickard had been allotted eleven acres of wheat. He planted twenty-three acres and harvested 269 bushels more than his quota permitted. He intended to sell what he was allowed, and use the excess for feed and for seed for future crops. Although he did not sell the excess in intrastate or interstate commerce, he still was penalized for raising more than his quota. Wickard challenged the penalty.

The Court's opinion was written by Justice Robert H. Jackson, who, after the case was first argued, professed bewilderment as to how Congress could regulate "activities that are neither interstate nor commerce."[182] Reargument apparently erased his doubts. Upholding Congress's authority to regulate Wickard's production, Jackson wrote,

Whether the subject of the regulation in question was "production," "consumption," or "marketing" is ... not material for purposes of deciding the question of federal power before us. ... But even if appellee's activity be local and though it may not be regarded as commerce, it may still, whatever its nature, be reached by Congress if it exerts a substantial economic effect on interstate commerce, and this irrespective of whether such effect is what might at some earlier time have been defined as "direct" or "indirect."[183]

Jackson then pointed out that by growing his own wheat, Wickard would not buy wheat and would reduce the market demand:

That appellee's own contribution to the demand for wheat may be trivial by itself is not enough to remove him from the scope of federal regulation where, as here, his contribution, taken together with that of many others similarly situated, is far from trivial. ... Homegrown wheat in this sense competes with wheat in commerce. The stimulation of commerce is a use of the regulatory function quite as definitely as prohibitions or restrictions thereon. This record leaves us in no doubt that Congress may properly have considered that wheat consumed on the farm where grown, if wholly outside the scheme of regulation, would have a substantial effect in defeating and obstructing its purpose to stimulate trade therein at increased prices.[184]

The Court had found a rationale to uphold regulation by Congress of production that was not in commerce. Constitutional historian C. Herman Pritchett calls this case the "high-water mark of commerce clause expansionism."[185]

THE MODERN COMMERCE POWER

The broad view of the commerce power adopted by the New Deal Court in the late 1930s gave Congress a free hand to regulate in the national interest. Congress became the engine for progressive national reform. In this capacity it mandated minimum wages for workers and extra pay for overtime hours; protected workers' right to organize unions; required equal pay for women and prohibited discrimination on account of pregnancy;

required private businesses to open their doors to all customers without regard to their race, color, religion, sex, national origin, or disabilities and prohibited employers from discriminating against workers or applicants based on these same criteria; and gave the federal government the lead role in combating pollution of the environment and protecting endangered species of plants and animals.

These federal initiatives often provoked controversy, but the points of contention almost never focused on whether Congress had the power to extend federal regulation nationwide. The source of its power—"to regulate Commerce among the several States"—was ignored, indeed almost forgotten until the mid-1990s, when the Rehnquist Court revived the notion that the federal authority was limited to "economic activity." That holding appeared to send the Court on a new path of skeptically scrutinizing acts of Congress and cast doubt on the fate of new social legislation.

Racial Discrimination

Early in the nation's history slaveholders realized that Congress might use its power over interstate commerce to prohibit slavery, but it was never wielded for that purpose. After the Civil War, however, Congress attacked racial discrimination in public accommodations through several different means, all with little success. An 1875 statute, based on the Fourteenth Amendment's guarantees of due process and equal protection of the laws, barred segregation in public accommodations. The Supreme Court in the 1883 *Civil Rights Cases* struck down that law, holding that the Fourteenth Amendment applied only to discriminatory actions by states, not by individuals.[186] The amendment could not therefore be used to reach discriminatory action on railroads and other privately owned public carriers and accommodations.

Opponents of segregation also tried to use the commerce power to reach discriminatory practices. The Interstate Commerce Commission (ICC), however, dismissed a challenge to segregated railroad facilities based on a section of the Interstate Commerce Act that prohibited "undue or unreasonable prejudice or disadvantage" in

THE RIGHT TO TRAVEL: FIRMLY ESTABLISHED ON SHIFTING BASE

The right of a citizen to travel freely in the United States has been acknowledged by the Supreme Court for almost a century and a half. As early as 1849, Chief Justice Roger B. Taney wrote in the *Passenger Cases,*

> For all great purposes for which the Federal government was formed we are one people, with one common country. We are all citizens of the United States; and, as members of the same community, must have the right to pass and repass through every part of it without interruption, as freely as in our own States.[1]

The Court has not, however, been consistent in locating the source of this right. The Court has struck down some restrictions on an individual's right to travel as impermissible burdens on interstate commerce and others as violations of the Fourteenth Amendment's Privileges and Immunities Clause. Both arguments were offered in *Edwards v. California* (1941). At issue was California's "anti-Okie" law, which penalized people who brought indigents into the state. Edwards was charged with bringing his penniless brother-in-law into California from Texas. The Court was unanimous in its decision that the California law must fall, but divided in its reasoning. A majority of five claimed that the state statute was a burden on interstate commerce. The purpose and effect of the law, the majority wrote,

> is to prohibit the transportation of indigent persons across the California border. The burden upon interstate commerce is intended and immediate; it is the plain and sole function of the statute. Moreover, the indigent nonresidents who are the real victims of the statute are deprived of the opportunity to exert political pressure upon the California legislature in order to obtain a change in policy. . . . We think this statute must fall under any known test of the validity of State interference with interstate commerce.[2]

The other four justices believed the state law invalid because it conflicted with the clause of the Fourteenth Amendment that states "No State shall make or enforce any law which shall abridge the privileges or immunities of citizens of the United States." "This Court," wrote Justice Robert H. Jackson, "should . . . hold squarely that it is a privilege of citizenship of the United States, protected from state abridgement, to enter any state of the Union, either for temporary sojourn or for the establishment of permanent residence therein and for gaining resultant citizenship thereof. If national citizenship means less than this, it means nothing."[3]

The Court has never made a choice between these two lines of reasoning. In cases upholding the Civil Rights Act of 1964, it said that refusal of public accommodations to blacks traveling interstate was an unconstitutional burden on interstate commerce.[4] *(See "Civil Rights and Commerce," p. 131.)* In another case, the Court struck down state laws requiring persons to live in a state for a certain period before becoming eligible for welfare payments. Such laws violated the right to travel, the majority said, adding that it felt no need to "ascribe the source of this right . . . to a particular constitutional provision."[5] Justice Potter Stewart referred to the right to travel as a "virtually unconditional personal right, guaranteed by the Constitution to us all."[6]

"The word 'travel' is not found in the text of the Constitution. Yet the 'constitutional right to travel from one state to another' is firmly embedded in our jurisprudence," Justice John Paul Stevens wrote in a 1999 decision that struck down a California welfare law. The right consists of at least three components, he said. "It protects the right of a citizen of one state to enter and to leave another state, the right to be treated as a welcome visitor rather than an unfriendly alien when temporarily present in the second state, and, for those travelers who elect to become permanent residents, the right to be treated like other citizens of that state." The California law violated the third part of this right because it paid lower benefits for one year to new residents, the Court said. "Citizens of the United States, whether rich or poor, have the right to choose to be citizens of the state wherein they reside. The States, however, do not have any right to select their citizens," Stevens wrote.[7]

---

1. *Passenger Cases,* 7 How. (48 U.S.) 283 at 492 (1849).

2. *Edwards v. California,* 314 U.S. 160 at 174 (1941).

3. Id. at 183.

4. *Heart of Atlanta Motel v. United States,* 379 U.S. 241 (1964); *Katzenbach v. McClung,* 379 U.S. 294 (1964).

5. *Shapiro v. Thompson,* 394 U.S. 618 at 630 (1969).

6. Id. at 643

7. *Saenz v. Rose,* 526 U.S. 489 (1999).

---

such facilities. "The disposition of a delicate and important question of this character, weighted with embarrassments arising from antecedent legal and social conditions, should aim at a result most likely to conduce to peace and order," said the commission, in effect ruling that it would not enforce the prohibition.[187] An attempt to reach racial segregation on public carriers was successful in *Hall v. DeCuir* (1878) but produced the opposite result; the decision voided the Louisiana law that prohibited segregation.[188] Using the *Cooley* rule, the Court said prohibition of segregation was a matter on which there should be national uniformity and only Congress could act on the matter. Congress had acted in passing the Civil Rights Act of 1875, but the Court struck it down.

A state statute that required segregation on public carriers was challenged with the hope that the Court would apply the reasoning of *Hall v. DeCuir*, but instead the Court in 1890 ruled that the law affected only intrastate traffic and imposed no burden on interstate commerce.[189] This case was cited in *Plessy v. Ferguson* (1896) as precedent for denying the claim that separate but equal facilities for blacks and whites in railway cars unduly burdened interstate commerce.[190]

Despite subsequent sporadic attempts at ending segregation through the Commerce Clause, congressional and public interest in addressing the issue waned in the first decades of the twentieth century.

Civil Rights and Commerce

The tide began to turn in the late 1940s, when the Court ruled that segregation on a public carrier burdened interstate commerce. The case of *Morgan v. Virginia* (1946) arose when Irene Morgan, a black woman traveling from Virginia to Maryland, refused to move to the back of the bus to make her seat available to a white person.[191] The Court upheld Morgan's refusal. In 1950 the Court ruled that separate dining facilities on interstate trains were a violation of the long-unenforced provision of the Interstate Commerce Act.[192] In 1955 the ICC announced that it was prohibiting racial discrimination in all trains and buses that crossed state lines, but it was not until the 1964 Civil Rights Act that Congress attempted again to prohibit racial discrimination in all public accommodations. Title II of the 1964 act barred discrimination on the grounds of race, color, religion, or national origin in public accommodations if the discrimination was supported by state law or official action, if lodgings were provided to transient guests or if interstate travelers were served, or if a substantial portion of the goods sold or entertainment provided moved in interstate commerce.

This portion of the act was immediately challenged as unconstitutional. Six months after the statute was enacted, the Supreme Court upheld Title II. *Heart of Atlanta Motel v. United States* (1964) involved a motel in downtown Atlanta that served out-of-state travelers.[193] The motel challenged the validity of the act on the grounds that Congress had exceeded its power to regulate interstate commerce and had violated Fifth Amendment guarantees by depriving businesses of the right to choose their own customers. Despite the motel's contention that its business was purely local in character, the Court upheld the application of Title II to it. Justice Tom C. Clark explained that Congress's power to regulate interstate commerce gave it the authority to regulate local enterprise that "might have a substantial and harmful effect" on that commerce.[194] The fact that Congress intended to correct what it considered a moral and social evil in no way undercut the law's constitutionality, Clark continued. The moral implications of the discrimination did "not detract from the overwhelming evidence of the disruptive effect" that discrimination had on interstate commerce, he said.[195]

In *Katzenbach v. McClung* (1964), a companion case decided the same day, the Court upheld Title II as it applied to a restaurant in Birmingham, Alabama.[196] Ollie's Barbeque did not cater to an interstate clientele, but 46 percent of the food it served was meat supplied through interstate commerce. Five years later, the Court in *Daniel v. Paul* (1969) upheld the application of Title II to a small rural recreation area that attracted few interstate travelers and that offered few food products sold in interstate commerce.[197] Justice Hugo L. Black dissented, saying he would have supported the majority if it had used the Fourteenth Amendment to reach the discriminatory practices at the recreational facility but that he objected to the lengths to which the majority went to find a nexus between that discrimination and interstate commerce.

Insurance

The Court used the Commerce Clause to give Congress control of a field of trade that the legislature did not want (and quickly gave away). Since its 1869 decision in *Paul v. Virginia,* the Supreme Court had held consistently that such purely financial or contractual transactions as insurance were not commerce, even if the transactions involved parties in different states.[198] The ruling left the states full authority to regulate the insurance business. In

1944 the Justice Department sought to use the Sherman Antitrust Act to break up a conspiracy of insurance companies that sought to monopolize fire insurance sales in six southern states. Using the precedent established by *Paul v. Virginia,* the companies, all members of the South-Eastern Underwriters Association, defended themselves with the argument that they were not reachable in this way because they were not engaged in commerce.

Overturning *Paul,* the Court, 4-3, rejected that argument. "No commercial enterprise of any kind which conducts its activities across state lines has been held to be wholly beyond the regulatory power of Congress under the Commerce Clause," wrote Justice Hugo L. Black. "We cannot make an exception for the business of insurance."[199] Congress, not the Court, must make the exceptions to the antitrust act, Black concluded. This ruling called into question the validity of all state insurance regulations. In response, Congress in 1945 passed the McCarran Act, which stated that "no Act of Congress shall be construed to invalidate, impair or supersede" a state law regulating or taxing insurance unless the federal act specifically related to insurance. In 1946 the Court upheld the McCarran Act.[200]

Environmental Law

Congress's police power, derived mainly from the commerce power, has become the constitutional basis for federal legislation regulating air and water pollution. The Water Quality Improvement Act of 1970, the primary vehicle for water pollution prevention and control, states in its declaration of policy that it is enacted in "connection with the exercise of jurisdiction over the waterways of the Nation and in consequence of the benefits resulting to the public health and welfare by the prevention and control of water pollution." Likewise, the primary purpose given for passage of the Air Quality Act of 1967 is "to promote health and welfare and the productive capacity of [the nation's] population." Although various regulations promulgated under these statutes have been challenged in the courts, the Supreme Court has not sustained any direct challenge

to the authority of Congress to exercise its commerce power in these areas.

State Sovereignty

For nearly sixty years, from the late 1930s to the mid-1990s, Congress had an essentially unchecked authority to legislate in the national interest. Because virtually any human activity—for example, such as crime, education, and the environment—could be said to have an "effect" on commerce, Congress could pass national laws governing these activities under the guise of regulating commerce. Moreover, the Supreme Court's earlier missteps in this area, such as striking down child labor laws and upholding the sugar trust, had convinced a generation of lawyers that the justices were wise to stand back and let the elected lawmakers decide on the appropriate reach of federal authority.

This posture of "judicial restraint" was, however, challenged in the 1990s by legal conservatives, who argued that the Court had a duty to maintain the limits on power set out in the Constitution. If Congress were free to regulate any activity, what was left of the notion of a federal government of "enumerated powers"? they asked. Chief Justice William H. Rehnquist and four of his colleagues—Justices Anthony M. Kennedy, Sandra Day O'Connor, Antonin Scalia, and Clarence Thomas—were determined to restore the limits on Congress's lawmaking power. They took their first step toward that goal in *United States v. Lopez* (1995).[201]

The Gun-Free School Zones Act

At first glance, Alfonso Lopez Jr. looked to be an unlikely candidate for favorable attention from the conservative Rehnquist Court. A senior at Edison High School in San Antonio, he was arrested for carrying a concealed .38 caliber handgun with five bullets on March 10, 1992. He was charged initially with violating a Texas law against having a gun at school, but the local authorities turned him over to federal prosecutors to be charged with violating the Gun-Free School Zones Act of 1990. Members of Congress, alarmed by reports of shootings on school campuses, had made it a federal crime "for any individual knowingly to possess a firearm [in] a school zone."

BANKRUPTCY LAWS

The Constitution authorizes Congress to make "uniform Laws on the subject of Bankruptcies." Federal laws were enacted in 1800, 1841, and 1867 to meet specific economic crises, but each survived public criticism and political pressure only a few years before being repealed. In the intervals between passage of federal laws, state bankruptcy laws were controlling. When Congress chose to act in the field, however, it broadly interpreted its powers, an approach the Supreme Court usually sanctioned.

Rather than restrict the coverage of bankruptcy laws to tradesmen, as was the English practice, Congress in its first bankruptcy law extended coverage to bankers, brokers, commodities agents, and insurance underwriters. The belief that the grant of power was broad enough to cover such categories of bankruptcies was sanctioned by the Court in 1902, and the Court has since given its implicit approval to laws extending bankruptcy coverage to almost every class of person and corporation.[1] The Court also has approved federal laws to rehabilitate the debtor as well as to provide appropriate relief to creditors.[2]

Despite its liberal interpretation of this clause, the Supreme Court in the 1930s recognized some limitations on the power. Congress must be mindful of the creditor's due process rights as guaranteed by the Fifth Amendment. Because of the states' power of incorporation, a corporation dissolved by a state court decree may not file a petition for reorganization under the federal bankruptcy laws. Congress may not place the fiscal affairs of a city, county, or other state political unit under the control of a federal bankruptcy court.[3]

In 1982 the Court for the first time struck down a federal bankruptcy law because it violated the constitutional standard of uniformity. A 1980 law passed to protect the employees of the Rock Island Railroad was held invalid by a unanimous Court because it gave the employees protection not available to people who worked for other bankrupt railroads.[4] The same year the Court sent Congress back to the drawing board in its effort to reform the nation's bankruptcy laws. The Court held that a comprehensive reform law passed in 1978 violated Article III—which provides that federal judicial power be exercised only by federal judges whose independence is assured—by creating a new corps of bankruptcy judges with broad powers but without the guarantees of life tenure and fixed compensation.[5]

---

1. *Hanover National Bank v. Moyses,* 186 U.S. 181 (1902); *Continental Bank v. Chicago, Rock Island & Pacific Railway Co.,* 294 U.S. 648 (1935); *United States v. Bekins,* 304 U.S. 27 (1938).

2. *Continental Bank v. Chicago, Rock Island & Pacific Railway Co.,* 294 U.S. 648 (1935); *Wright v. Vinton Branch,* 300 U.S. 440 (1937); *Adair v. Bank of America Association,* 303 U.S. 350 (1938).

3. *Louisville Bank v. Radford,* 295 U.S. 555 (1935); *Chicago Title & Trust Co. v. Wilcox Building Corp.,* 302 U.S. 120 (1937); *Ashton v. Cameron County District,* 298 U.S. 513 (1936).

4. *Railway Labor Executives' Association v. Gibbons,* 455 U.S. 457 (1982).

5. *Northern Pipeline Construction Co. v. Marathon Pipe Line Co., United States v. Marathon Pipe Line Co.,* 458 U.S. 50 (1982).

Lopez was assigned a federal public defender, James Carter, who moved to dismiss the indictment on the grounds that it is unconstitutional for Congress "to legislate control over our public schools." A federal judge rejected that argument, found Lopez guilty, and sentenced him to six months in prison. Lopez appealed, and the Supreme Court took the case to consider this challenge to congressional power. The matter came before the justices in November 1994, the same month that Republicans won a historic victory at the polls, giving them control of the House and the Senate for the first time in forty years. The new GOP leadership promised to pursue a bold conservative agenda. That same conservative tide seemed to sweep over the Supreme Court.

In cases involving crime, the justices tend to be deferential to the government's lawyer and skeptical of a defense advocate arguing that a criminal law should be removed from the books. In *Lopez,* however, the Clinton administration's solicitor general, Drew Days III, ran into a barrage of sharp questions. If this gun law is constitutional, "what's left that Congress cannot do?" asked Justice O'Connor. Others repeated the inquiry: What is the limit on Congress's power? What is an example of a law that would fail the test? Days was unable to offer an example. The Court answered on April 26, 1995, by coincidence just one week after Timothy McVeigh blew up the Federal Building in Oklahoma City, apparently to express his rage at an overly powerful federal government. "We start with first principles. The Constitution creates a Federal government of enumerated powers," said Chief Justice Rehnquist for the 5-4 majority. "As James Madison wrote, '[t]he powers delegated to the proposed Constitution to the federal government are few and defined. Those which are to remain in the State governments are numerous and indefinite.' This constitutionally mandated division of authority was adopted by the Framers to ensure protection of our fundamental liberties."[202]

The chief justice reviewed the Court's early struggle to define the commerce power in cases involving steamboat monopolies. He also conceded that twentieth-century precedents had broadly expanded this power to uphold federal laws regulating loan-sharking, hotels, and even the production of homegrown wheat. Rehnquist added, however, that even these cases "confirm that this power is subject to outer limits," because all dealt with "economic activity." But Lopez was not charged with selling a gun or transporting firearms. He was charged with possessing a weapon. "A gun in a local school zone is in no sense economic activity," Rehnquist wrote, and Lopez's offense did not "affect any sort of interstate commerce. [Lopez] was a local student at a local school; there is no indication that he had recently moved in interstate commerce, and there is no requirement that his possession of the firearm have any concrete tie to interstate commerce." "To uphold the Government's contentions here, we would have to pile inference upon inference in a manner that would bid fair to convert congressional authority under the Commerce Clause to a general police power of the sort retained by the States. . . . To do so would require us to conclude the Constitution's enumeration of powers does not presuppose something not enumerated . . . and that there will never be a distinction between what is truly national and what is truly local. This we are unwilling to do."[203]

Two concurring opinions offered differing clues about the future. In the first, Justices Kennedy and O'Connor described the Lopez decision as narrow. Past rulings allowing for broad federal power over the economy and civil rights "are not called in question by our decision today," Kennedy wrote. It is, however, he added, "our duty to recognize meaningful limits on the commerce power of Congress," and "our intervention is required" when lawmakers stray beyond regulating commercial matters.[204] Justice Thomas in the second opinion called for a return to the pre-1930s view of Congress's power: "In a future case, we ought to temper our Commerce Clause jurisprudence in a manner that . . . is more faithful to the original understanding," he wrote.[205] In the late eighteenth century, "'commerce' consist[ed] of selling, buying and bartering, as well as transporting for those purposes," he said. It did not encompass farming, manufacturing, or mining. According to Thomas, "Agriculture and manufacturing involve the production of goods; commerce encompasses traffic in such articles." Thomas did not say that he was ready to strike down the federal laws that regulate cars made in Detroit or coal mines in West Virginia, but he concluded by saying "we must modify our Commerce Clause jurisprudence. . . . The wrong turn was the Court's dramatic departure in the 1930s from a century and a half of precedent."[206] Justice Scalia joined the Rehnquist opinion and did not comment further. The four dissenters faulted the majority for second-guessing Congress's decision that guns near schools are dangerous and require special regulation. "Guns are both articles of commerce and articles that can be used to restrain commerce," said Justice John Paul Stevens. He also derided "the radical character of the Court's holding and its kinship with the discredited, pre-Depression version" of the law.[207]

The Violence Against Women Act

The Lopez ruling signaled the beginning of a new era of federalism at the Supreme Court. With Rehnquist leading a narrow but determined majority, the justices cut back Congress's power and shielded the states from what they considered overly intrusive federal laws. Five years after Lopez, the chief justice spoke for the Court in striking down part of the Violence Against Women Act of 1994. This measure, enacted by a Democrat-controlled Congress and signed into law by President Bill Clinton, gave victims of sexual assault a right to sue their attackers in federal court. Women's rights groups had pressed for the new law, arguing that rapists and spousal abusers were not always punished in state courts. At the time, the nation was

POSTAL POWERS

Article I, section 8, clause 7, gives Congress the power "To establish Post Offices and post Roads." Whether this phrase meant that Congress had the power actually to construct post offices and post roads or simply to designate those that would be used as postal facilities was settled in 1876, when the Supreme Court upheld federal appropriation of land on which to build a post office.[1] The postal power has been interpreted to include the authority to ensure the speedy delivery and protection of the mail.[2] This principle was the basis for the federal government's winning an injunction against leaders of the 1894 Pullman strike, which had halted mail delivery along with the trains. At the same time, federal troops were sent to Illinois to quell the violence that had erupted. Eugene V. Debs and other labor leaders were convicted of contempt for violating the injunction. The Supreme Court upheld the convictions and the use of federal troops in 1895, declaring that "[t]he strong arm of the national Government may be put forth to brush away all obstructions to the freedom of interstate commerce or the transportation of the mails."[3]

The postal power also has been interpreted to allow Congress to bar items from the mails that it believes might defraud the public or injure its morals. The first such case was *Ex parte Jackson* (1878), in which the Supreme Court sustained congressional action barring from the mails certain circulars relating to lotteries.[4] In more recent cases, the Court has said that the federal power to exclude matter from the mails is limited by other constitutional guarantees. In 1965, for example, the Court struck down a federal law authorizing the post office not to forward mail it regarded as communist propaganda unless the addressee specifically said he wanted to receive it.[5] Declaring the statute a violation of the First Amendment, the Court said the law impinged on the right of a person to receive whatever information he or she wanted to receive. The Congressional Research Service of the Library of Congress notes that this case was the first in which the Court had invalidated a federal statute because it conflicted with the First Amendment.[6]

Congress frequently has invoked its postal power to aid it in the exercise of other express powers. In 1910 the Court held that correspondence schools were in interstate commerce and therefore susceptible to federal regulation because of their reliance on the mails.[7] In 1938 the Court upheld provisions of the Public Utility Holding Company Act requiring gas and electric utilities to register with the Securities and Exchange Commission partially on the grounds that such holding companies conducted a large and continuous portion of their business through the mails.[8]

---

1. *Kohl v. United States,* 91 U.S. 367 (1876).
2. *Ex parte Jackson,* 96 U.S. 727 (1878).
3. *In re Debs,* 158 U.S. 564 at 582 (1895).
4. *Ex parte Jackson,* 96 U.S. 727 (1878).
5. *Lamont v. Postmaster General,* 381 U.S. 301 (1965).
6. Congressional Research Service, *The Constitution of the United States of America: Analysis and Interpretation* (Washington, D.C.: U.S. Government Printing Office, 1973), 310 n. 10.
7. *International Textbook Co. v. Pigg,* 217 U.S. 91 (1910).
8. *Electric Bond & Share Co. v. Securities and Exchange Commission,* 303 U.S. 419 (1938).

---

focused on what looked to be just such a case—the acquittal of former football star O. J. Simpson in the stabbing death of his ex-wife Nicole. The new federal law, they said, would give victims of sexual assaults their day in court.

A first test of the new measure came in 1995, when Christy Brzonkala, a freshmen at Virginia Polytechnic Institute, sued a college football player, Antonio J. Morrison, for allegedly raping her in his dormitory room. She waited weeks before reporting the assault to a crisis center on campus. The university held a hearing on her complaint, after which Morrison was found guilty of sexual assault and suspended from school. Morrison appealed and succeeded in having his suspension reversed in time for the football season.

Local prosecutors looked into the complaint, but brought no charges. Brzonkala then sued Morrison under the terms of the new federal law, but she never quite got her day in court. A federal judge dismissed her suit on the grounds that the law was unconstitutional. The U.S. Court of Appeals for the Fourth Circuit agreed. The Clinton administration appealed on Brzonkala's behalf in *United States v. Morrison* (2000).[208]

Before passing the law, Congress had held hearings and compiled information on violence against women. "Three of four American women will be victims of violent crimes sometime during their life," a House committee report said, citing a Justice Department report.[209] "Violence is the leading cause of injuries to women age 15 to 44,"

Surgeon General Antonia Novello testified.[210] "Estimates suggest that we spend $5 to $10 billion a year on health care, criminal justice and other social costs of domestic violence," said Sen. Joseph Biden, D-Del., a sponsor of the law.[211] The lawmakers argued that Congress had authority under its commerce power and its civil rights power to enact the Violence Against Women Act.

Chief Justice Rehnquist and the Court were unswayed. "Gender-motivated crimes of violence are not, in any sense of the phrase, economic activity," he wrote for the 5-4 majority that invalidated the law. "A fair reading of *Lopez* shows that the non-economic, criminal nature of the conduct at issue was central to our decision in that case." Moreover, Congress cannot rely on "the nationwide, aggregated impact" of these crimes, because doing so would allow the federal authorities to set up a national police force, Rehnquist said. "The Founders denied the National government and reposed in the States" the power to suppress violent crime. He concluded, "We accordingly reject the argument that Congress may regulate non-economic, violent criminal conduct based solely on that conduct's aggregate effect on interstate commerce."[212]

The second half of the opinion dealt a blow to Congress's power to enforce civil rights. The Fourteenth Amendment states, "No state shall…deny to any person within its jurisdiction the equal protection of the laws." Section 5 sets forth that "The Congress shall have the power to enforce, by appropriate legislation, the provisions of this article." In the late nineteenth century, the Supreme Court in *United States v. Harris* (1883) had interpreted this clause to mean that Congress's authority to enact civil rights laws was limited to official state discrimination, not private acts of violence committed by the Ku Klux Klan.[213] In the 1960s the liberal court read this provision more broadly as authorizing federal laws that combated discrimination, even when it was not directly perpetrated by the state. In *United States v. Morrison* Rehnquist returned to the Court's older view of the law, citing cases from the 1880s that limited federal action against the Klan. Reviving *Harris,* he contended that Congress could not use its power under the

Fourteenth Amendment to pass laws "directed exclusively against the action of private persons." The Violence Against Women Act "is directed not at any State or state actor, but at individuals who have committed criminal acts motivated by gender bias," he said.[214] Congress had therefore exceeded its power when it relied on Section 5 to empower a victim of private violence to take her claim into federal court. The 5-4 lineup among the justices was identical to the one in *Lopez.*

Rehnquist's opinion cast doubt on whether Congress had the constitutional power to enact a national hate crimes act, which was being considered on Capitol Hill. The *Morrison* decision put "non-economic, criminal conduct" perpetrated by private individuals and occurring within one state beyond Congress's power over interstate commerce and civil rights. The strict emphasis on the "economic nature of the regulated activity" also raised questions about the Endangered Species Act: How can the federal government protect an endangered insect or bird that lives within one state given that protecting an insect or a lizard is not an economic activity? A coalition of developers and property rights advocates raised this issue in several appeals to the Court. One asked the Court to invalidate a federal wildlife regulation that protected the Delhi Sands flower-loving fly, an insect that spends most of its life buried in the sands of the California desert. To protect it, federal officials had blocked some building projects. Only Chief Justice Rehnquist and Justices Scalia and Thomas voted to take up the appeal, which signaled that the Court as a whole was not ready to consider restricting federal authority over environmental protection. Rehnquist's opinion, however, laid the groundwork for a possible future challenge to the federal environmental laws.

States' Rights Revival

The Rehnquist Court also limited Congress's commerce power in matters involving the states, including state agencies and public hospitals, prisons, and colleges and universities. Since the New Deal era, Congress had given workers certain rights, including a minimum wage and extra pay for overtime. In the 1960s these rights were expanded to include employee protections against discrimination based on race, sex, religion, national origin, and later, age or disability. Workers who believed that their rights had been violated were entitled to sue their employers to obtain the money they were owed. Congress enacted these workers rights laws as regulations of commerce. In *Seminole Tribe v. Florida* (1996), however, Rehnquist, speaking for the 5-4 majority, proffered that "sovereign immunity" shielded states from being sued, even by persons whose rights were violated under federal law.[215] The case involved an obscure federal law, and the ruling relied on a constitutional amendment that was unfamiliar to many constitutional lawyers The impact of the decision, like the *Lopez* ruling a year earlier, triggered a series of rulings in its wake.

In the Indian Gaming Regulatory Act of 1988, Congress had tried to force states and tribal leaders to agree on rules for governing gambling on reservations. In Florida, Gov. Lawton Chiles refused to negotiate a tribal-state compact with the Seminoles for submission to Washington. The Seminoles sued and asked a federal judge to force the state to comply. The Supreme Court took up the case not because of an interest in resolving a gambling dispute, but to rein in Congress's power to impose such duties on the states. "We hold that notwithstanding Congress's clear intent to abrogate the States' sovereign immunity," Rehnquist wrote, "the Commerce Clause does not grant Congress that power, and therefore [the law at issue] cannot grant jurisdiction over a State that does not consent to be sued."[216] Justices Kennedy, O'Connor, Scalia, and Thomas agreed.

The ruling relied on the rarely cited Eleventh Amendment. In 1793 two South Carolina men had sued the state of Georgia in a federal court seeking repayment of a debt from the Revolutionary War. Georgia's lawyers maintained that the state could not be sued outside of its own courts. In one of the Court's first significant rulings, *Chisholm v. Georgia* (1793), the justices upheld the Court's federal jurisdiction, but the states reacted angrily and insisted on a change in the Constitution.[217] *(See box, Judicial Review and State Courts, p. 378.)* The Eleventh Amendment, ratified in 1798, states, "The Judicial Power of the United States

shall not be construed to extend to any suit in law or equity, commenced or prosecuted against one of the United States, by Citizens of another State, or by Citizens or Subjects of any Foreign State." The amendment effectively overturned *Chisholm,* because the South Carolinians were suing Georgia.

At first glace, the Eleventh Amendment would not appear to control the Seminoles' case, because they were residents of Florida. Undeterred, Rehnquist argued that the Eleventh Amendment meant more than just what it literally stated; he pointed to the underlying principle it furthered: "Although the text of the Amendment would appear to restrict only the Article III diversity jurisdiction [referring to interstate suits], we have understood the Eleventh Amendment to stand not so much for what is says, but for the presupposition which it confirms." That presupposition is "that each State is a sovereign entity in our federal system, and that it is inherent in the nature of sovereignty not to be amenable to the suit of an individual without its consent."[218] His opinion went on to describe state sovereign immunity as a "fundamental principle" embedded in the Constitution that Congress cannot alter. "Even when the Constitution vests in Congress complete law-making authority over a particular area, the 11th Amendment prevents congressional authorization of suits by private parties against unconsenting States," Rehnquist concluded.[219]

The impact of this ruling became clearer three years later, when state probation officers in Maine sued to obtain the extra wages they were due for working overtime. The Fair Labor Standards Act of 1938 had given private sector workers a right to a minimum wage and overtime pay, and Congress had later extended the law to cover state and local employees as well. John Alden and his fellow state probation workers, however, had their claims thrown out of federal court in Maine after the *Seminole* ruling. They filed the same claim in a state court, and U.S. solicitor general Seth Waxman took up their cause when their case reached the Supreme Court. During oral arguments in March 1999, he pointed out the constitutional principle that federal laws trump state laws and that state judges must enforce these laws. He quoted Article VI: "The laws of the United

States . . . shall be the supreme Law of the Land, and the Judges in every State shall be bound thereby, any Thing in the Constitution or Laws of any State to the Contrary notwithstanding." Regardless, the Rehnquist Court found a "Thing" to the contrary—the principle of state sovereign immunity as understood even before the Constitution was drafted: "The States' immunity from suit is a fundamental aspect of the sovereignty which the States enjoyed before the ratification of the Constitution, and which they retain today," said Justice Kennedy in *Alden v. Maine* (1999).[220] The 5-4 ruling tossed out the claim brought by the Maine workers.

Most of the opinion in *Alden v. Maine* was devoted to constitutional history and theory. "Congress has vast power but not all power," Kennedy wrote. "When Congress legislates in matters affecting the States, it may not treat these sovereign entities as mere prefectures or corporations. Congress must accord the States the esteem due to them as joint participants in a federal system."[221] He conceded that neither the Constitution nor its authors directly said the states were shielded from federal lawsuits. "We believe, however, that the founders' silence is best explained by the simple fact that no one, not even the Constitution's most ardent opponents, suggested the document might strip the States of the immunity," he wrote. In a concluding comment, Kennedy noted that the Labor Department could sue a state agency on behalf of workers whose rights were violated, but the principle of sovereign immunity bars the workers from suing on their own behalf.[222]

Justice David Souter, speaking for the four dissenters, described Kennedy's opinion as "clearly wrong" in its history and legal theory. "The Court abandons a principle . . . much closer to the hearts of the Framers: that where there is a right, there must be a remedy," he said. "Some 4.7 million employees of the 50 States of the Union" now find themselves unable to enforce their rights under federal law, he wrote.[223] Justice Stephen Breyer, voicing his dissent from the bench, described sovereign immunity as a legal doctrine "more akin to the thought of James I than James Madison."

For Rehnquist, the "state sovereignty" decisions marked a triumph that was nearly a quarter century in the making. He had suffered through an earlier false start, when in 1976, as an associate justice, he spoke for a 5-4 majority in a ruling that shielded the state and local agencies from having to pay minimum wages or overtime required by the federal labor law. "One undoubted attribute of state sovereignty is the state's power to determine the wages which shall be paid to those whom they employ," he wrote in *National League of Cities v. Usery* (1976).[224] He said the federal law went too far and violated the Tenth Amendment tenet that "powers not delegated to the United States . . . are reserved to the States." Rehnquist's opinion sent a shock through the world of constitutional law, because it came after forty years of Congress asserting authority over workers' rights. That Tenth Amendment ruling did not, however, last. Nine years after *Usery,* the Court, by another 5-4 vote, reversed itself and upheld federal authority over state and local employees. The switch was attributable to Justice Harry A. Blackmun, who had voted with Rehnquist in 1976 but later changed his mind and spoke for the liberal contingent in *Garcia v. San Antonio Metropolitan Transit Authority* (1985).[225] Blackmun had become convinced that the elected representatives of Congress were better suited than judges to decide the proper boundaries between federal government and the states: "In sum, . . . the Court tried to repair what did not need repair," he said.[226]

Blackmum retired in 1994, and by the end of the decade, Chief Justice Rehnquist had revived the principle of state sovereignty as a check on federal power. As if to highlight the issue, the Court handed down three rulings on June 23, 1999, that relied on the doctrine of state sovereign immunity to crimp the enforcement of federal law. All were decided by a 5-4 vote. The first was the abovementioned *Alden v. Maine.* The second ruling determined that states could not be sued for false advertising and trademark infringement under the Trademark Act, and the third ruled that states could not be sued for infringing a patent. These last two cases arose from a single lawsuit in which a New Jersey bank sued a Florida agency for

PATENTS, TRADEMARKS, AND COPYRIGHTS

Congressional authority over patents, copyrights, and trademarks comes from Article I, section 8, clause 8, which empowers Congress "To promote the Progress of Science and useful Arts, by securing for limited Times to Authors and Inventors the exclusive Right to their respective Writings and Discoveries." By giving authors and inventors a temporary monopoly on their works, the framers intended that these creators would profit and be encouraged to produce more. The public would profit as well from their books and inventions. It fell to Congress to set the terms of these monopolies in the copyright and patent laws. It has repeatedly extended the terms of copyright over the years. The Court has regularly turned away challenges to congressional decisions on copyright. In 1987, for example, the Court upheld Congress's decision to give the U.S. Olympic Committee the exclusive right to use the trademarked word *Olympic* for commercial or promotion purposes. The justices rejected a free speech claim from a group that had sponsored the "Gay Olympics" before running afoul of the officially designated organization.[1]

The Copyright Act of 1790, the first copyright law, gave authors the exclusive right to their works for fourteen years, which could be extended by a living author for fourteen more years. In the twentieth century, however, Congress greatly extended the length of copyrights, bowing to the wishes of Hollywood studios, which sought to protect their early films. In the Sonny Bono Copyright Term Extension Act of 1998, Congress added twenty more years to all new and existing copyrights. Corporate works, such as films, were protected for ninety-five years after their release, while the works of authors and composers would be protected for seventy years after

their creator's deaths. The Court took up a challenge to this law from Internet archivists who sought to scan old books, poems, and magazine articles for posting on free Web sites. They argued that Congress had ignored the phrase "for limited Times" in the Constitution and had made copyrights into a nearly unlimited monopoly. The challengers called on the Court to rein in Congress, but after considering the matter, the justices upheld the 1998 law, stating that they would continue to defer to lawmakers in such matters: "We are not at liberty to second-guess congressional determinations and policy judgments of this order, however debatable or arguably unwise they may be," said Justice Ruth Bader Ginsburg for the 7-2 majority.[2] Justices John Paul Stevens and Stephen G. Breyer dissented, contending that extending to dead authors "monopoly privileges" over their works would do nothing to spur creativity and would harm the public's interest in having these works freely available to a new generation of readers.

The exception to the Court's policy of deference to Congress came about when state agencies were sued for violating patents and trademarks. In a pair of decisions in 1999, the Court ruled that the principle of state sovereign immunity bars holders of a patent or trademark from suing a state for infringement. The 5-4 decisions struck down laws in which Congress specified that state violators could be sued.[3]

---

1. *San Francisco Arts & Athletics Inc. v. U.S. Olympic Committee,* 483 U.S. 522 (1987).

2. *Eldred v. Ashcroft,* 537 U.S. 186 (2003).

3. *College Savings Bank v. Florida,* 527 U.S. 666 (1999); *Florida Prepaid Postsecondary Education Expense Board v. College Savings Bank,* 527 U.S. 628 (1999).

---

essentially stealing its patented idea of financing college through prepaid tuition. The Constitution "does not give Congress the power to enact such legislation," Rehnquist said.[227] *(See also box, Patents, Trademarks, and Copyrights, above.)* The doctrine of state sovereignty also shielded state agencies from being sued by employees who allege that they are victims of discrimination based on their age or disability.[228]

In 2002 the Court extended the shield of sovereign immunity to protect state agencies from being hauled before federal administrative hearings. The earlier rulings had concerned lawsuits in a court, but "[w]e see no reason why a different principle should apply in the realm of administrative law," said Justice Thomas in

Federal Maritime Commission v. South Carolina Ports Authority (2002).[229] In the Shipping Act of 1916, Congress had barred ports from discriminating in favor of some ships and against others and empowered the Federal Maritime Commission (FMC) to enforce the law. The state port authority at Charleston, South Carolina, refused berthing space to a cruise ship, *M/V Tropic Sea,* because it offered gambling at sea. Its owners then complained that state officials had granted berths to two Carnival Cruise ships that had casinos on board. When the FMC called a hearing to take testimony from both sides, the state refused to participate. Once again, the Supreme Court sided with the state, determining that federal authorities could not regulate commerce in this

Angel Raich addresses the press after the Supreme Court decision prohibiting the use of marijuana for medical purposes.

manner. It would be "an affront to the State's dignity" to force its officials to appear before a federal administrative hearing, Justice Thomas declared. "By guarding against encroachments by the Federal Government on fundamental aspects of state sovereignty," he wrote, "we strive to maintain the balance of power in our Constitution and thus to reduce the risk of tyranny and abuse from either front."[230]

Reassertion of Congressional Power

In the last years of the Rehnquist Court, the so-called "federalism revolution" appeared to have run out of steam. The justices were unwilling to press the doctrine of state sovereign immunity to void some popular federal measures, nor were some of its conservative justices eager to limit Congress's power in areas such as narcotics.

In 2003 the Court upheld the Family and Medical Leave Act of 1993 against a state's claim of sovereign immunity. William Hibbs, a state welfare worker in Nevada, sought an unpaid leave to care for his wife, who had been injured in an auto accident. When he failed to return to work on schedule, he was

fired. Hibbs sued, alleging the state had violated the terms of the federal law. In something of a surprise, Rehnquist spoke for the 6-3 majority in upholding Hibbs's right to sue. The Fourteenth Amendment forbids states from denying any person the "equal protection of the laws," Rehnquist explained, and Congress has the power under this amendment to enact laws against "gender motivated" discrimination by the states. The Family and Medical Leave Act is such a law, the chief justice said.[231] Scalia, Kennedy, and Thomas dissented.

The next year, the Court upheld the right of two individuals who use wheelchairs to sue the state of Tennessee for violating the Americans with Disabilities Act. George Lane, an accident victim, and Georgia Jones, a court reporter, had humiliating experiences when they sought to enter county courthouses that had no ramps or elevators. Lane had crawled up the steps to a second-floor courtroom. On a second occasion, he refused to be carried up the steps and was arrested for failure to appear in court. Jones claimed she was denied work because she could not reach every courtroom. They

THE DORMANT COMMERCE CLAUSE

The Constitution says "The Congress shall have Power … To regulate Commerce with foreign Nations and among the several States." The Supreme Court, for much of its history, has read these words to say the justices may strike down state laws that interfere with the free flow of interstate commerce. In 1978, for example, the Court struck down a New Jersey law that prohibited trash haulers from moving garbage from Philadelphia into New Jersey for disposal. Even garbage can be an item of commerce, and states may not enact "protectionist" laws that discriminate against out-of-state products.[1]

The opinion made no mention of the fact that Congress had not sought to regulate shipments of garbage. Instead, the justices relied on a principle that is said to "lie dormant" within the Commerce Clause. It holds that the Constitution gives the federal government and federal judges the power to protect the flow of commerce among the states.

As Chief Justice John G. Roberts Jr. put it in 2007, "Although the Constitution does not in terms limit the power of States to regulate commerce, we have long interpreted the Commerce Clause as an implicit restraint on state authority, even in the absence of a conflicting federal statute. To determine whether a law violates this so-called 'dormant' aspect of the Commerce Clause, we first ask whether it discriminates on its face against interstate commerce."[2]

Justices Antonin Scalia and Clarence Thomas reject this approach. They say the Court has usurped a role that the Constitution, by its own words, leaves to Congress. Scalia has said he favors a retreat by the Court and to "leave essentially legislative judgments to the Congress."[3] Thomas has been even more insistent. Because this doctrine "'has no basis in the Constitution and has proved unworkable in practice,' I would entirely 'discard the Court's negative Commerce Clause jurisprudence.' …[T]he text of the Constitution makes clear that the Legislature—not the Judiciary—bears the responsibility of curbing what it perceives as state regulatory burdens on interstate commerce."[4]

---

1. *Philadelphia v. New Jersey,* 437 U.S. 617 (1978).

2. *United Haulers Assn. v. Oneida-Herkimer Solid Waste Management Authority,* 550 U.S. — (2007).

3. *Bendix Autolite Corp. v. Midwesco Enterprises, Inc.,* 486 U.S. 888 at 897 (1988).

4. *Department of Revenue of Kentucky v. Davis,* 553 U.S. —- (2008).

---

sued the state under the ADA, and the Court rejected the state's claim of "sovereign immunity." Lane and Jones were denied the "fundamental right of access to the courts," Stevens said for a 5-4 majority. Rehnquist, Scalia, Kennedy, and Thomas dissented.[232]

Perhaps the most telling decision came in the final month of the Rehnquist Court. In a 6-3 decision, the justices ruled that Congress's power under the Commerce Clause extended to home-grown marijuana. They did so by relying on *Wickard v. Filburn* (1942), the famous case of the Depression-era farmer who wanted to grow, but not sell, more than his allotted amount of wheat. California voters had approved an initiative that exempted sick persons from the laws forbidding the use of marijuana. Under this measure, the Compassionate Use Act, these Californians were permitted to grow and use marijuana to relief pain or nausea. Federal officials, however, insisted the possession of marijuana was illegal under the federal Controlled Substances Act, and, therefore, federal agents had the authority to raid homes and seize home-grown marijuana.

Angel Raich of Oakland suffered from a debilitating disease, and she and her doctor testified that marijuana was uniquely effective in relieving her suffering. She sued, contending the federal government had no authority over her home-grown marijuana because she neither sold nor bought it. Her suit relied heavily on *Lopez v. United States* (1995). If gun possession in a school zone is not commercial activity, how can marijuana possession at home be considered commercial activity? she asked. She won before the U.S. Court of Appeals for the Ninth Circuit, but lost at the Supreme Court. In *Gonzales v. Raich* (2005) the Court said the federal government had the authority to regulate the market in dangerous drugs, including marijuana, and that included the power to forbid even possession of these drugs. Justices Scalia and Kennedy joined the majority opinion citing *Wickard* as having made clear that Congress and the federal government had broad power to regulate commodities that reached even into backyards.[233]

O'Connor, Rehnquist, and Thomas dissented and wondered what had become of the principles of state rights and the limits on federal power. O'Connor said this case was "materially indistinguishable from *Lopez*." In a separate dissent, Thomas said, "If Congress can regulate this, it can regulate virtually anything—and the Federal government is no longer one of limited and enumerated powers."

The decision in the case of the home-grown marijuana, the last of the Rehnquist era, spoke more to the limits of the Court's role rather than limits of Congress's power. Over the previous decade, Rehnquist had revived the view that the regulatory power of Washington had limits under the Constitution, and that the Court would police those limits. But in the end, the relationship between Congress and the states may be better described as one of balances that rise and fall with the times, rather than one of clear legal rules. Under Rehnquist, the Court had shifted the balance somewhat toward the states and made clear the claims of federal power will not always win out. The Constitution does indeed impose checks and balances on the power of Congress, even if the checks are rare.

★

Fiscal and Monetary Powers

Recognizing that an effective national government must have unquestioned power to raise and spend money, the framers gave Congress clear authority to lay and collect taxes, pay the national debt, and spend for the common defense and general welfare. That power is the first enumerated in Article I, section 8. To make congressional control over fiscal and monetary matters complete, the framers then gave Congress the power to coin money and regulate its value. The Constitution places one prohibition on the federal tax power—Congress may not tax exports—and three limitations, only two of which have had any lasting significance—that all duties, imposts, and excises be levied uniformly throughout the country and that all direct taxes be apportioned among the states on the basis of their relative populations. The third limitation set a federal tax on the importation of slaves at $10 per person. One important implied limitation restricted federal power to tax state government.

Both Congress and the Supreme Court have interpreted the taxing and spending power liberally. C. Herman Pritchett notes in *The American Constitution* that because adequate revenue and broad power to spend were absolutely necessary to the conduct of an effective central government, "the first rule for judicial review of tax statutes is that the heavy burden of proof lies on anyone who would challenge any congressional exercise of fiscal power. In almost every decision touching the constitutionality of federal taxation, the Supreme Court has stressed the breadth of congressional power and the limits of its own reviewing powers."[1]

Only three times has the Court disapproved a major act of Congress involving its fiscal and monetary powers. These rulings had only a negligible effect on the power of Congress, but they caused the Court considerable embarrassment. In each case, the Court's decision was eventually negated. The Court ruled in 1870 that paper money could not be substituted for gold as legal tender; fifteen months

This 1895 editorial cartoon, published after the Supreme Court's decision in *Pollock v. Farmers' Loan and Trust Co.* illustrates the Court's invalidation of the federal income tax law. In 1913, however, the situation was reversed when the states ratified the Sixteenth Amendment, which gave the federal government the power to tax incomes regardless of source.

later it reversed that decision. The Court's 1895 decisions barring a federal income tax were nullified by adoption of the Sixteenth Amendment in 1913.[2] Forty years later the Court attempted to limit the power of Congress to spend for the general welfare, striking down the Agricultural Adjustment Act of 1933, but that decision too was soon disavowed by a Court faced with President Franklin D. Roosevelt's Court-packing plan.

DIRECT TAXES

The Supreme Court wrestled for a century with the definition of direct taxes. The Constitution is of little assistance, referring only to "capitation, or other direct taxes." The history of the Constitutional Convention is equally unhelpful. The apportionment limitation was inserted at the urging of southern states to prevent heavy taxation of their lands and slaves, but the convention did not discuss what sorts of levies were direct. As early as 1796 the government asked the Court to define "capitation, or other direct taxes" in a test case concerning a federal tax on carriages.[3] That the government paid the attorneys on both sides of the case demonstrates its intense interest in clarifying the issue.[4] The Court found the carriage tax an indirect use tax and only head taxes and taxes on land to be direct taxes and therefore necessarily apportioned by population. This definition remained in place until the Court in 1895 struck down an income tax as unconstitutional on the grounds that it was a direct tax not levied proportionately among the states.[5]

The Income Tax Cases

In the first half of the nineteenth century the federal government's need for revenue was modest and easily met by excise taxes and duties on imports. A federal tax on personal income was first imposed during the Civil War to meet the need for additional revenue. The statute, enacted in 1862, levied a tax on individual incomes in excess of $600; the exemption rose to $2,000 in 1870. The law expired in 1872. The tax was upheld unanimously by the Court in 1881 as an indirect tax. The justices once more agreed: the only direct taxes were head taxes and taxes on land.[6] During the 1870s and 1880s there was little interest in a second income tax law, but with the nation's economic base shifting from wealth based on land to wealth based on earnings, the 1890s brought increasing pressure for an income tax. After the depression of 1893 reduced federal revenues, Congress yielded and in 1894 levied a tax of 2 percent on personal and corporate incomes in excess of $4,000. Only about 2 percent of the population earned more than this amount.[7] The tax was immediately challenged.

The First Case

Charles Pollock, a stockholder in the Farmers' Loan and Trust Company, sought to enjoin that New York bank from paying the new tax. He claimed the tax was direct and therefore invalid because it was not apportioned on the basis of state populations. It was clear that Pollock and the bank both wanted the law struck down and that the case had been deliberately arranged to evade the federal ban on suits seeking to stop the collection of taxes. Although the Court generally refuses to hear cases in which the opposing parties have agreed to bring the suit, the Court set aside its rule in this instance. Because so much was at stake, Pollock and the bank hired the best available attorneys, and the Court allowed the U.S. attorney general to appear in behalf of the law even though the government was not a party to the suit.

Attorneys for Pollock argued two basic points: first, a tax on the income from land was indistinguishable from a tax on the land itself and therefore was an unconstitutional direct tax because it had not been apportioned; second, even if the tax was indirect, it was still unconstitutional, because as a tax applied only to incomes over a certain amount it did not meet the uniformity test. Most historians agree that these arguments were weak at best, but the plaintiff's attorneys also portrayed the income tax as a weapon that could be used by a populist government to destroy private property rights, a political argument calculated to appeal to the more economically conservative justices on the bench: "I believe there are private rights of property here to be protected," prominent attorney Joseph H. Choate declaimed. The income tax law "is communistic in its purposes and tendencies, and is defended here upon principles as communistic, socialist—what should I call them—populistic as ever have been addressed to any political assembly in the world."[8]

Only eight justices heard the arguments in *Pollock v. Farmers' Loan and Trust Co.* (1895); Justice Howell E. Jackson, ill with tuberculosis, was absent. Six of the eight agreed that the tax on the income from land was identical to a tax on the land and was therefore unconstitutional, but the eight divided evenly on the issue of whether a tax on income from personal property was also a direct tax and whether the law failed to meet the uniformity test.[9]

The Second Case

Pollock's attorneys asked for reargument so that the Court might settle these crucial points. The Court agreed, and the Court, with Justice Jackson participating, rendered its second decision on May 20, 1895, only six weeks after the first. By a 5-4 vote, the Court struck down the entire income tax law as unconstitutional.[10] (Justice Jackson voted with the minority, which meant that one justice who voted to uphold the law in the first case reversed his opinion in the second. Because there was no opinion written and no breakdown given in the earlier 4-4 decision, who the justice was has been the subject of great speculation.)

Chief Justice Melville W. Fuller, speaking for the majority, reaffirmed the point settled in the first case: "Taxes on real estate being indisputable direct taxes, taxes on the rents or income of real estate are equally direct taxes." He next declared that the majority was "of the opinion that taxes on personal property, or on the income from personal property, are likewise direct taxes." Finally, Fuller held that the remainder of the law was invalid on the principle that the parts of the legislation were so inseparable that if any of them were voided, all of them must fall. Because "it is obvious that by far the largest part of the anticipated revenue" was to come from the tax on income from real estate and personal property, Fuller said, it was equally obvious that the Court's decision to strike down those taxes "would leave the burden of the tax to be borne by professions, trades, employments, or vocations; and in that way what was intended as a tax on capital would remain in substance a tax on occupations and labor."[11] The majority still avoided the question of what constituted uniformity for indirect taxes.

To reach its conclusions the Court found it necessary to gloss over the precedents. Fuller said that the Court's statement in the carriage tax case—that the only direct taxes were head taxes and those on land itself—was only a comment that did not have the force of law. The decision upholding the Civil War income tax involved a tax on earned income, Fuller rationalized, not on income from land. In the second opinion, Fuller did not even mention the earlier *Income Tax* case. The extralegal argument in defense of private property rights had its intended effect: Justice Stephen J. Field's concurring opinion in the first *Pollock* case warned, "The present assault upon capital is but the beginning…the stepping stone to others…till our political contests will become a war of the poor against the rich."[12]

The four dissenters—Justices Jackson, John Marshall Harlan, Henry B. Brown, and Edward D. White—submitted separate opinions, sharply reproving the majority for disregarding a century of precedent and even more sharply criticizing it for the political implications of its ruling. Justice Harlan was most forceful:

> The practical effect of the decision today is to give certain kinds of property a position of favoritism and advantage inconsistent with the fundamental principles of our social organization, and to invest them with power and influence that may be perilous to that portion of the American people upon whom rests the larger part of the burden of the government, and who ought not to be subjected to the dominion of aggregated wealth any more than the property of the country should be at the mercy of the lawless.[13]

Criticism of the Court's decision was widespread and blunt. The editor of the generally conservative *American Law Review* wrote,

> [I]t appears, at least from one of the opinions which was rendered, that the Justice [Field] who rendered it proceeded with an imagination inflamed by the socialistic tendencies of the law, as involving an attack upon private property; a consideration which lay totally outside the scope of his office as a judge interpreting the Constitution. It is speaking truthfully, and therefore not disrespectfully, to say that some of the judges of the Court seem to have no adequate idea of the dividing line between judicial and legislative power, and seem to be incapable of restraining themselves to the mere office of judge.[14]

Dissatisfaction with the decision resulted eighteen years later in enactment of the Sixteenth Amendment. It also cost the Court prestige. Along with its refusal to apply the Sherman Antitrust Act to sugar manufacturers

THE "INCOME TAX" AMENDMENT

Despite the Supreme Court's holding in *Pollock v. Farmers' Loan and Trust Co.* (1895) that a tax on personal income was unconstitutional, agitation for an income tax continued.[1] Laborers and farmers overburdened by regressive federal taxes, such as tariffs, and incensed at the accumulation of greater and greater wealth by fewer and fewer people, kept the issue alive, electing to Congress a steadily increasing number of Democrats and progressive Republicans who favored such a tax. Proposals for an income tax followed one of three strategies. The first was that Congress simply reenact an income tax statute and hope that the Supreme Court—with several new justices since 1895—would overturn *Pollock.* The second called for adoption of a constitutional amendment to eliminate the requirement that direct taxes be apportioned among the states. The third alternative was to fashion an income tax as an indirect excise tax and in that way avoid the apportionment problem. Little action was taken on any of these proposals until 1909, the first year of William Howard Taft's presidency.

When Taft took office, a two-year-long depression had depleted government revenues. At the same time, the Republicans had promised during the 1908 campaign to do something about the high tariffs. When a tariff bill was introduced in the Senate, the Democrats offered an income tax rider almost identical to the law declared unconstitutional. According to Sen. Joseph W. Bailey, D-Texas, its chief sponsor, "Instead of trying to conform the amendment to the decision of the Court, the amendment distinctly challenges that decision. I do not believe that that opinion is a correct interpretation of the Constitution and I feel confident that an overwhelming majority of the best legal minds in the Republic believe it was erroneous."[2]

Fearful that the Democrats and insurgent Republicans had enough strength to pass the Bailey proposal, the conservative Senate Republican leadership countered with a proposed constitutional amendment that would permit an income tax without apportionment. Even if the amendment were approved by Congress, the conservatives did not believe enough state legislatures could be persuaded to ratify it. Taft supported the constitutional amendment because he believed that passage of a simple income tax statute would injure the Supreme Court by forcing it to choose between

loss of prestige (if it overturned its earlier decision) or loss of popularity (if it found a new income tax law unconstitutional). Democrats and progressive Republicans—despite their fears that the conservative Republicans were correct and that the states would not ratify an income tax amendment—nevertheless favored the amendment in principle and felt bound to vote for it. The measure passed the Senate, 77-0, in July 1909. The House approved it, 318-14, a week later. Contrary to expectation, state legislatures did approve the amendment. It became the Sixteenth Amendment to the Constitution on February 23, 1913.

In November 1912 the Democrats won majorities in both houses of Congress and quickly passed a law reducing tariffs on a number of imports and made up the consequent deficit in revenue by enacting an income tax law. The statute levied a 1 percent tax on all net income above $3,000 for individuals and above $4,000 for married couples living together. An additional graduated tax was levied on incomes above $20,000. According to the Internal Revenue Service, 437,036 income tax returns were filed for 1916, the first tax year.[3] The Court upheld the income tax law in 1916.

The Sixteenth Amendment was the third constitutional amendment ratified especially to overturn a decision of the Supreme Court. The Eleventh Amendment had been passed to nullify the decision in *Chisholm v. Georgia* (1793) that allowed a citizen of another state or a foreign citizen to sue a state in federal court.[4] The Fourteenth Amendment was passed in part to overturn the decision in *Scott v. Sandford* (1857), which held that blacks could not be citizens of the United States.[5] *(See details of Chisholm v. Georgia, pp. 377–378; details of Scott v. Sandford, pp. 179–180.)*

---

1. *Pollock v. Farmers' Loan and Trust Co.,* 157 U.S. 429 (1895).

2. Alpheus T. Mason and William M. Beaney, *The Supreme Court in a Free Society* (Englewood Cliffs, N.J.: Prentice-Hall, 1959), 133. Other sources include Alfred H. Kelly and Winfred A. Harbison, *The American Constitution: Its Origins and Development,* 5th ed. (New York: Norton, 1976); and Sidney Ratner, *American Taxation: Its History as a Social Force in Democracy* (New York: Norton, 1942).

3. Interview with the Statistics of Income Branch, Statistics Division, Internal Revenue Service, September 19, 1978.

4. *Chisholm v. Georgia,* 2 Dall. (2 U.S.) 419 (1793).

5. *Scott v. Sandford,* 19 How. (60 U.S.) 393 (1857).

and its affirmance of Eugene V. Debs's conviction for his involvement in the Pullman strike, the *Pollock* decision, Pritchett wrote, "earned the Court a popular reputation as a tool of special privilege which was not dispelled for forty years."[15]

Retreat

Not deaf to the outcry, the Fuller Court did not apply the *Pollock* precedent to succeeding tax cases. Instead the Court found the taxes on certain kinds of incomes "incidents of ownership" and therefore excise or indirect taxes rather than direct taxes. This reasoning was applied to uphold taxes on commodity exchange sales, inheritances, tobacco, and stock sales.[16] The Fuller Court also considered indirect a tax on the business of refining sugar based on gross receipts from the sale of refined sugar.[17] These modifications allowed the Court in 1911 to call a tax on corporate income an excise tax "measured by income" on the privilege of doing business.[18]

Ratification of the Sixteenth Amendment in 1913 gave Congress the power to impose taxes on income "from whatever source derived, without apportionment among the several States, and without regard to any census or enumerations." *(See box, The "Income Tax" Amendment, p. 146.)* Congress later that year enacted an income tax law that the Court upheld in 1916.[19] Implicitly criticizing its 1895 position, the Court said that the Sixteenth Amendment gave Congress no new powers of taxation but simply guaranteed that the income tax would never again be "taken out of the category of direct taxation to which it inherently" belongs.[20] After 1916 the Court's concern shifted from whether a tax was direct or indirect to a determination of what was properly considered income. A major case on this point was *Eisner v. Macomber* (1920), in which the Court invalidated part of an income tax law providing that "a stock dividend shall be considered income, to the amount of its cash value." The Court held that stock dividends (as opposed to cash dividends) could not be treated as income. Instead they were capital, and taxes on them were direct and had to be apportioned. Only when the dividends were converted or sold did they become taxable as income. This holding has been modified, but its basic premise remains operative.[21]

Uniformity

In 1884 the Court held that a tax met the Constitution's requirement of uniformity if it operated in the same way on all subjects being taxed. A tax, the Court held in the *Head Money Cases*, did not necessarily fail the uniformity test simply because the subject being taxed was not distributed uniformly throughout the United States.[22] The question of whether the tax rate had to be uniform—left unanswered in the *Income Tax Cases*—was finally settled in 1900.

During the Spanish-American War Congress had imposed an inheritance tax on legacies of more than $10,000; the tax rate varied with the amount of the bequest and the relationship of the heir to the deceased. The law was challenged on the grounds that if it was a direct tax, it was not apportioned, and that if it was an indirect tax, it was not uniform. The Court ruled that the tax was not direct, but was uniform so long as it applied in the same manner to the class throughout the United States.[23]

In 1927 the Court held that geographic uniformity was not violated by the fact that Florida residents were not able to take advantage of a federal tax deduction for state inheritance taxes because that state did not impose such a tax. Fifty-six years later, the Court upheld a windfall profits tax on domestic oil production against a challenge that it violated this requirement by exempting new oil produced on Alaska's North Slope. Such a geographic exemption did not violate the uniformity requirement, the Court unanimously held.[24]

TAXING AS POLICE POWER

Congress has always used the taxing power as a regulatory tool as well as a revenue source. The protective tariff was an early example of a regulatory tax. The second statute passed by the First Congress provided that "it is necessary for the support of government, for the discharge of the debts of the United States and the encouragement and protection of manufacturers, that duties be laid on goods, wares and merchandise imported." The validity of such tariffs was much debated and not conclusively settled until 1928. Writing for the Court, Chief Justice William Howard Taft stated,

> Whatever we may think of the wisdom of a protection policy, we cannot hold it unconstitutional. So long as the motive of Congress and the effect of its legislative action are to secure revenue for the benefit of the general government, the existence of other motives in the selection of the subject of taxes cannot invalidate Congressional action.[25]

When the tax power has been used as a regulatory tool to support or enforce another constitutional power, the Court has generally sustained it, even if the tax was designed to eliminate the matter taxed. A landmark decision illustrating this point is *Veazie Bank v. Fenno* (1869), involving a 10 percent tax that Congress put on

Fruit or Vegetable?

The Supreme Court has declared that the tomato is a vegetable, not a fruit. The question arose in a nineteenth-century tariff case because fruits could be imported duty free under an 1883 tariff act, but vegetables required a duty equal to 10 percent of their value. Maintaining that tomatoes were fruits, an importer sued the New York port collector to recover back duties. The Court in *Nix v. Hedden* (1893) held that tomatoes were vegetables. Delivering the opinion of the Court, Justice Horace Gray wrote,

> Botanically speaking, tomatoes are the fruit of a vine, just as are cucumbers, squashes, beans and peas. But in the common language

of the people, whether sellers or consumers of provisions, all these are vegetables, which are grown in kitchen gardens, and which, whether eaten cooked or raw, are, like potatoes, carrots, parsnips, turnips, beets, cauliflower, cabbage, celery and lettuce, usually served at dinner in, with, or after the soup, fish or meats which constitute the principal part of the repast, and not, like fruits generally, as dessert.[1]

---

1. *Nix v. Hedden,* 149 U.S. 305 (1893).

---

the circulation of state bank notes in order to give the untaxed national bank notes the competitive edge and drive the state notes out of the market.[26] The Court upheld the statute on the ground that it was a legitimate means through which Congress could exercise its constitutional authority to regulate the currency.

The taxing power has also been upheld as an auxiliary to the commerce power. In the *Head Money Cases* (1884) the Court held that a fifty cent tax levied on ship owners for each immigrant landed and used to support indigent immigrants was not a use of the tax power as such, but rather the exercise of the foreign commerce power.[27] *(See box, Regulation of Foreign Commerce, p. 125.)*

In 1940 the Court upheld the Bituminous Coal Act of 1937, which imposed a stiff tax on sales of coal in interstate commerce but exempted those producers who agreed to abide by industry price and competition regulations. The Court acknowledged that the exemption was intended to force compliance with the code, but added that Congress "may impose penalties in aid of the exercise of any of its enumerated powers," in this case, the Commerce Clause.[28] That ruling effectively overturned the Court's decision in *Carter v. Carter Coal Co.* (1936), which held a similar tax in the 1935 Bituminous Coal Conservation Act to be an unconstitutional penalty for noncompliance with the industry regulations rather than a tax designed to raise revenues.[29] *(See "Coal Codes," pp. 122–124.)*

Colored Oleo

Where Congress used the taxing power on its own to achieve a desired social or economic goal, the Court developed two distinct lines of precedents on this matter, just as it had in its early review of the use of the commerce power as a policing mechanism. The first line essentially held that so long as the tax produced some revenue, the Court would not examine the motives behind its imposition. The Court sustained use of the commerce power as a police tool in the *Lottery Case.*[30] One year later it upheld use of the taxing power to attain similar objectives. *McCray v. United States* (1904) involved a federal statute that placed a tax of ten cents per pound on oleo colored yellow to resemble butter, but taxed uncolored oleo only one-fourth of a cent per pound. The tax was clearly intended to remove the competition to butter by making it too expensive to manufacture colored oleo. It was challenged as an invasion of state police powers and as a violation of due process.[31]

The Court disagreed, holding that the tax was an excise tax and therefore was permissible. "The decisions of this Court," wrote Chief Justice Edward D. White, "lend no support whatever to the assumption that the judiciary may restrain the exercise of a lawful power on the assumption that a wrongful purpose or motive has caused the power to be exerted."[32] Similar reasoning was used by the Court to uphold the Harrison Anti-Narcotics Act of 1914. This statute required people dealing in narcotics, such as pharmacists, to pay a small annual registration fee and to keep certain records. It also made the manufacture, sale, and shipment of narcotics illegal, unless they were prescribed by a physician. A five-justice majority in *United States v. Doremus* (1919) upheld the narcotics registration tax. "The Act may not be declared unconstitutional because its effect may be to accomplish another purpose as well as the raising of revenue," wrote Justice William R. Day.[33] The four dissenters—Chief Justice White and Justices Joseph McKenna, James C. McReynolds, and Willis Van Devanter—contended that the tax was an exercise of the police power that they believed was reserved to the states.

Child Labor

Three years later, the dissenting view in *Doremus* became the majority position, beginning the second line of precedents. In the next major tax regulation case, the Court decided that a tax was unconstitutional if its primary purpose was to punish a certain action, not to raise revenue. *Bailey v. Drexel Furniture Co.* (1922) focused on Congress's second attempt to end child labor.[34] After the Court ruled in 1918 that the commerce power could not be used to reach what many considered a despicable practice, Congress turned to its taxing power, imposing a 10 percent tax on the net profits of any company that employed children under a certain age. Although similar to statutory tax schemes the Court had approved before, the Court nevertheless declared the tax unconstitutional. *(See "Child Labor," pp. 406–407.)*

Chief Justice William Howard Taft, for the eight-justice majority, argued that the child labor tax was a penalty intended to coerce employers to end their use of child labor.

> Taxes are occasionally imposed…on proper subjects with the primary motive of obtaining revenue from them and with the incidental motive of discouraging them by making their continuation onerous. They do not lose their character as taxes because of the incidental motive. But there comes a time in the extension of the penalizing features of the so-called tax when it loses its character as such and becomes a mere penalty with the characteristics

of regulation and punishment. Such is the case in the law before us.[35]

Linking that ruling with its holding in *Hammer v. Dagenhart* (1918), Taft said that just as use of the commerce power to regulate wholly internal matters of the state was invalid, so was use of the taxing power to achieve the same purpose.[36] The consequences of validating such a law were grave, Taft continued. "To give such magic to the word 'tax,'" he said, "would be to break down all constitutional limitation of the powers of Congress and completely wipe out the sovereignty of the States."[37]

Taft distinguished the ruling in the child labor tax case from the holdings in *McCray* and *Doremus* by asserting that the primary purpose of the taxes in the latter case was to raise revenue. He further distinguished the *Doremus* case by claiming that the regulations outlined in the narcotics control statute were necessary to the collection of the tax "and not solely to achievement of some other purpose plainly within state power."[38] Commentators have questioned the logic of Taft's reasoning. If it was clear that Congress wanted to stop child labor, it was just as clear that Congress intended to terminate the colored oleo industry and closely regulate the manufacture and sale of narcotics. The significant factor, however, was Taft's implicit claim that the Court would determine when a tax became a penalty; the Court would be the final authority in determining the primary motive of Congress in imposing a tax.

Taft reinforced the reasoning laid out in the child labor decision by applying it to a second case decided the same day. In an attempt to stop some unethical practices by some commodity exchanges, the Futures Trading Act of 1921 imposed a tax of twenty cents per bushel on all contracts for sales of grain for future delivery, but it exempted those sales arranged through boards of trade that met certain requirements set out in the act. The Court struck down the statute. When the stated purpose of the statute is to regulate the boards of trade, wrote Taft, and when the purpose "is so clear from the effect of the provisions of the bill itself, it leaves no ground upon which the provisions…can be sustained as

SEVERABILITY: DIVIDED IT STANDS

Severability refers to the ability of part of a law to survive even after another part of the same statute has been held invalid. Without this capability, an entire statute would become void because of a single flawed provision. As one authority wrote,

> Whether or not the judicial determination of partial validity will so disembowel the legislation that it must fall as a whole, or whether the valid portion will be enforced separately is a question of importance second only to the initial determination of validity. That parts of a statute may be enforced separately provided certain conditions are met has become a fundamental legal concept.[1]

Severability, or separability as it is also called, grows out of the concept that the judiciary should uphold the constitutionality of legislative acts where possible. For a court to find a statute separable, that finding must coincide with legislative intent and the design of the law. To determine intent, the court may examine the act's history, its object, context, title, and preamble. Legislative intent was one of the reasons the Court gave for striking down the general income tax in 1895. Having declared that the tax on income from property was unconstitutional, the Court said that would leave only taxes on occupations and labor, adding, "We cannot believe that such was the intention of Congress."[2] (See "The Income Tax Cases," pp. 144–147.)

Despite a severability clause in the Bituminous Coal Conservation Act of 1935, the Supreme Court in 1936 ruled that the price-fixing provisions of the act were inseparable from the labor regulations provisions it had declared unconstitutional: "The statutory mandate for a [coal industry] code upheld by two legs at once suggests the improbability that Congress would have assented to a code supported by only one," asserted the Court.[3] (See "Coal Codes," pp. 122–124.) To be severed, the valid portion of the law must be independent and complete in itself. If eliminating part of the law would defeat or change its purpose, the entire act should be declared void. The Court applied this principle in 1935, when it declared the Railroad Retirement Pension Act of 1934 unconstitutional. Finding certain portions of the act invalid, the Court said that those portions "so affect the dominant aim of the whole statute as to carry it down with them."[4] (See "Pensions," p. 108.)

Congress commonly includes a severability or saving clause in legislation, declaring that if one part of the statute is found unconstitutional, the rest of the act may stand. The clause is of relatively modern usage and is not critical to a court determination as to separability. Justice Louis D. Brandeis wrote that the saving clause was sometimes an aid in determining legislative intent, "but it is an aid merely, not an inexorable command."[5] The general rule followed by the Court on separability clauses was enunciated in 1929. When a separability clause is included, wrote Justice George Sutherland, the Court begins

> with the presumption that the legislature intended the act to be divisible; and this presumption must be overcome by considerations

a valid exercise of the taxing power."[39] The Court in 1923 approved a second attempt to regulate commodity exchanges when it upheld the Grain Futures Act of 1922 as a valid exercise of the commerce power.[40]

The *Bailey* precedent was applied again in 1935 to invalidate a provision of the 1926 Revenue Act that imposed a $1,000 excise tax on liquor dealers doing business in violation of state or local prohibition laws. The Court held that the tax was actually a penalty and was valid only so long as Congress had the authority under the Eighteenth Amendment to enforce Prohibition nationwide. When the amendment was repealed (by adoption of the Twenty-first Amendment in 1933), the $1,000 penalty also fell.[41] This line of precedent culminated in two 1936 New Deal cases involving the taxing power. In *Carter v. Carter Coal Co.* the Court struck down the Bituminous Coal Conservation Act of 1935 partly because of its provision reducing a coal tax for coal producers who complied with labor regulations set out in the statute. The Court found this provision a penalty on producers who refused to comply.[42] In *United States v. Butler* (1936) the Court invalidated a tax on certain food processors, the revenue from which was used to pay farmers to cut their production of certain foods. The Court said the tax was part of an unconstitutional regulatory scheme.[43] (See "Coal Codes," pp. 122–124; details of *United States v. Butler*, pp. 155–157.)

Regulatory Tax Upheld

A few months later, following Roosevelt's "Court-packing" plan, the Court abandoned this line of precedent

which make evident the inseparability of its provisions or the clear probability that the invalid part being eliminated the legislature would not have been satisfied with what remains.[6]

Riders to appropriations or revenue bills are the most typical examples of severability. For example, the sections of the 1919 Revenue Act imposing a tax on articles made by child labor were ruled unconstitutional in 1922, but the rest of the statute was unaffected.[7] Robert E. Cushman observes that the Court has never invalidated an appropriations or revenue bill just because one rider was found invalid.[8] The Court reiterated its severability doctrine in 1992, when it reviewed an innovative federal law making states responsible for the disposal of low-level radioactive waste generated within their borders and severed a provision that violated the Tenth Amendment guarantee of state sovereignty.[9] The section deemed unconstitutional declared that states that failed to provide for disposal of low-level radioactive waste became the legal owners of the waste and assumed liability for any injuries caused by it. The Court went on to uphold the Low-Level Radioactive Waste Policy Amendments Act of 1985, saying that severance of the unconstitutional clause would not prevent enforcement of the rest of the act or defeat its purpose of encouraging the states to be responsible for the disposal of radioactive waste.

Justice Sandra Day O'Connor wrote for the Court, citing precedent: "The standard for determining the severability of an unconstitutional provision is well established: Unless it is evident that the Legislature would not have enacted those provisions which are within its power, independently of that which is not, the invalid part may be dropped if what is left is fully operative as a law." Although the act contained no severability clause, she continued, "Common sense suggests that where Congress has enacted a statutory scheme for an obvious purpose, and where Congress has included a series of provisions operating as incentives to achieve that purpose, the invalidation of one of the incentives should not ordinarily cause Congress' overall intent to be frustrated."[10]

1. C. Dallas Sands, *Statutes and Statutory Construction,* 4th ed. (Chicago: Callaghan, 1973), 2:335.

2. *Pollock v. Farmers' Loan and Trust Co.,* 1 U.S. 601 at 637 (1895).

3. *Carter v. Carter Coal Co.,* 298 U.S. 238 at 314 (1936).

4. *Railroad Retirement Board v. Alton Railway Co.,* 295 U.S. 330 at 362 (1935).

5. *Dorchy v. Kansas,* 264 U.S. 286 at 290 (1924).

6. *Williams v. Standard Oil Co. of Louisiana,* 278 U.S. 235 at 242 (1929).

7. *Bailey v. Drexel Furniture Co.,* 259 U.S. 20 (1922).

8. Robert E. Cushman and Robert F. Cushman, *Cases in Constitutional Law,* 3rd ed. (New York: Appleton-Century-Crofts, 1968), 70.

9. *New York v. United States,* 505 U.S. 144 (1992).

10. Id.

and retreated to the reasoning in the oleo case. It upheld the National Firearms Act of 1934, which imposed an annual license tax on manufacturers of and dealers in certain classes of firearms, such as sawed-off shotguns and machine guns, likely to be used by criminals. The act, which also required identification of purchasers, clearly was intended to discourage sales of such weapons. Upholding the validity of the tax, the Court directly criticized Taft's opinion in the *Bailey* child labor tax case. Noting that the license tax produced some revenue, the Court added,

> Every tax is in some measure regulatory....But a tax is not any the less a tax because it has a regulatory effect,...and it has long been established that an Act of Congress which on its face purports to be an exercise of the taxing power is not any the less so because the tax is burdensome or tends to restrict or suppress the thing taxed.
>
> Inquiry into the hidden motive which may move Congress to exercise a power constitutionally conferred upon it is beyond the competency of the courts....They will not undertake...to ascribe to Congress an attempt, under the guise of taxation, to exercise another power denied by the Federal Constitution.[44]

Taxes on marijuana and on gamblers were subsequently upheld with similar reasoning.[45] The statute authorizing a tax on persons in the business of accepting wagers also, however, required them to register with the Internal Revenue Service. The Court refused to find the registration requirement a violation of the Fifth Amendment's Self-Incrimination Clause, even

CRIME PAYS . . . TAXES

The Internal Revenue Service does not believe the old saying "crime doesn't pay," and the Supreme Court has consistently held that income from illegal activities is taxable. "We see no reason . . . why the fact that a business is unlawful should exempt it from paying the taxes that if lawful it would have to pay," wrote Justice Oliver Wendell Holmes Jr. in 1927.[1] The Court has held taxable the income from illegal sales of liquor, extortion, and embezzlement.[2]

If taxes are due on illegal incomes, are illegal expenses, such as bribery, deductible? "This by no means follows," said Holmes, "but it will be time enough to consider the question when a taxpayer has the temerity to raise it."[3] A taxpayer finally did. In 1958 the Court was asked to determine

if a bookmaking operation could deduct as ordinary and necessary business expenses the salaries of its bookies and the rent it paid. Both paying employees and renting space to conduct illegal activities were against the law in Illinois, where the case arose. Writing for the Court, Justice William O. Douglas held that the expenses fit the meaning of the Treasury regulations regarding taxable income and were therefore deductible.[4]

---

1. *United States v. Sullivan*, 274 U.S. 259 (1927).
2. Id.; *Rutkin v. United States*, 343 U.S. 130 (1952); *James v. United States*, 366 U.S. 213 (1961).
3. *United States v. Sullivan*, 274 U.S. 259 at 264 (1927).
4. *Commissioner of Internal Revenue v. Sullivan*, 356 U.S. 27 (1958).

---

where the gambler was doing business in a state that prohibited gambling. In 1968 and 1969 the Court reversed this part of the decision, holding that registration requirements of regulatory tax laws did in fact compel self-incrimination where the activity taxed was unlawful. These decisions in no way diminished the ability of Congress to use the tax power as a regulatory or penalty mechanism, however.[46]

Federal-State Tax Immunities

"The power to tax involves the power to destroy," declared Chief Justice John Marshall in 1819, setting out the basis for the major implied limitation on the federal government's taxing power.[47] Marshall announced this maxim as the Court ruled that a state could not tax the national bank, intending by this holding to prevent the states from taxing the new and still fragile central government out of existence. In 1842 federal immunity from state taxation was expanded further when the Court ruled that states could not tax the incomes of federal officers.[48]

The immunity conferred by these holdings, however, cut two ways. In 1871 the Court held that the federal government could not tax the income of state officials. If the states could not threaten the sovereignty of the federal

government by taxing its officers, instrumentalities, and property, then neither could the national government use the taxing power to threaten the sovereignty of the states, the Court declared.[49] The Court had applied this doctrine even before the 1871 decision and continued its use until the late 1930s. In 1829 it held that a state could not tax federally owned real estate.[50] In 1895 the Court ruled, as part of the *Income Tax Cases*, that the national government could not impose a tax on state or municipal bonds.[51] At various times the most tangential of relationships with one or the other level of government conferred immunity upon the taxpayer. For example, in 1931 a federal tax on the sales of motorcycles to a city police department was held invalid.[52]

Gradually, however, the Court began to limit immunities granted to the federal and state governments. State immunity from federal taxation was restricted to activities of a "strictly governmental nature." States generally were no longer immune from federal taxes on activities that, if performed by a private corporation, would be taxable. Federal contractors were much less often granted immunity from state taxation, and income tax immunity for state and federal officials was overturned in 1938 and 1939.[53] As the doctrine of immunity stood in the late 1970s, the federal

JUDGES AND TAXES

Would the salaries of federal judges—including Supreme Court justices—be immune from the federal income tax? That question was offered by Justice Howell E. Jackson in 1895 during the Court's consideration of the 1890 income tax law. In a letter to Chief Justice Melville W. Fuller, Jackson asked if the income tax conflicted with the constitutional prohibition against reducing a judge's salary during his term of office. "Does that [1890] Act include our salary as members of the Supreme Court?" Jackson queried. "It seems to me that it cannot. That Congress cannot do indirectly what it is prohibited from doing directly."[1] The question was put aside after the Court declared the income tax unconstitutional, but it came up again shortly after the federal income tax law implementing the Sixteenth Amendment was enacted. In 1920 the Court agreed with Jackson's assessment and ruled that the salaries of sitting federal judges were immune from the federal income tax.[2] *(See "Direct Taxes," pp. 144–147.)*

Joined by Justice Louis D. Brandeis, Justice Oliver Wendell Holmes Jr. dissented: "[T]he exemption of salaries from diminution is intended to secure the independence of judges on the ground, as it was put by Hamilton in the *Federalist* (No. 79), that 'a power over a man's subsistence amounts to a power over his will....' That ... seems to me no reason for exonerating [a judge] from the ordinary duties of a citizen, which he shares with all others."[3]

In 1925 the Court expanded this immunity to include judges who were appointed after the income tax law was enacted.[4] Congress subsequently passed a law providing that salaries of judges appointed after its passage would be subject to the income tax. The Court upheld this statute in 1939, specifically overruling the earlier cases.[5] To impose a nondiscriminatory income tax on judges' salaries "is merely to recognize that judges are also citizens, and that their particular function in government does not generate an immunity from sharing with their fellow citizens the material burden of the government whose Constitution and laws they are charged with administering," the Court wrote.[6] Holmes until his retirement in 1932 and Brandeis until his retirement in 1939 voluntarily paid federal income tax.

In 2001 the Court reaffirmed the principle that judges are not exempt from a nondiscriminatory tax that applies generally to the public, even if it had the effect of reducing their compensation. The justices, however, voided part of extra, "catch-up" assessments for Social Security that were imposed on judges who bought into the retirement system after 1983.[7]

---

1. Quoted in Leo Pfeffer, *This Honorable Court* (Boston: Beacon Press, 1965), 223; see also Carl Swisher, *American Constitutional Development*, 2nd ed. (Cambridge, Mass.: Houghton Mifflin, 1954), 437.

2. *Evans v. Gore*, 253 U.S. 245 (1920).

3. Id. at 265.

4. *Miles v. Graham*, 268 U.S. 501 (1925).

5. *O'Malley v. Woodrough*, 307 U.S. 277 (1939).

6. Id. at 282.

7. *United States v. Hatter*, 532 U.S. 557 (2001).

government was prohibited from taxing state government property and instrumentalities. The most significant of the prohibitions continued to bar federal taxation of state and municipal bonds, but this limit was nullified with the Supreme Court's decision in *South Carolina v. Baker* (1988). Effectively burying the doctrine of intergovernmental tax immunity, the Supreme Court declared that nothing in the Constitution restrained Congress from taxing the interest paid on state and municipal bonds. States and cities wishing to preserve that immunity must do so by working through the political process to convince their representatives in Congress to refrain from taxing the funds, the Court held.[54]

Federally owned property remains generally immune from state taxation.[55] States may not tax congressionally chartered fiscal institutions without the consent of Congress, although they may assess property taxes on other federally chartered corporations.[56] Income from federal securities and tax-exempt bonds may not be taxed by the states, but the Court has ruled that a state may tax the interest accrued on government bonds and estates that include U.S. bonds.[57] Government contractors are generally subject to state taxes, even if the taxes increase the cost of the contract to the federal government. States generally, however, cannot levy a property tax on government property used by a private person in the fulfillment of a government contract, although a privilege tax measured by the value of the government property held is permissible.[58] *(See "Intergovernmental Immunity," p. 469.)*

THE POWER TO SPEND

The authority of Congress to appropriate and spend money under the Necessary and Proper Clause to carry out any of its enumerated powers has been broadly interpreted by the Court. From the early days of the Union, the power to spend money for internal improvements has been justified by the authority given Congress over war, interstate commerce, territories, and the mails. Use of the spending power rarely has been challenged, partly because the Court, by finding that neither a taxpayer nor a state has standing to sue the federal government, has made it extremely difficult to bring a challenge.

In a pair of cases considered together in 1923, a taxpayer, Harriet Frothingham, and a state, Massachusetts, questioned the validity of a federal grant-in-aid program, a mechanism whereby the federal government gives a certain amount of money, generally for a certain purpose and usually with the requirement that the states meet certain conditions, such as matching the grant. Such programs were just coming into use and were considered by many an infringement of states' rights. The first challenge came in the two 1923 cases and concerned the Sheppard-Towner Act, which subsidized state maternity and infant welfare programs. The plaintiffs claimed that the grant-in-aid was a subtle form of federal invasion of state sovereignty and that if a state refused the grant, it was a burden on the state's citizens, whose federal taxes supported the grants in participating states.

In the majority opinion, Justice George Sutherland implied that the Court would uphold grants-in-aid as constitutional. Because Frothingham's "interest in the moneys of the Treasury...is comparatively minute and indeterminate" and because "the effect upon future taxation, of any payment out of the funds...[is] remote, fluctuating and uncertain," the Court held that the taxpayer did not have sufficient

injury to sue.[59] This holding was modified subsequently to permit some taxpayer challenges. *(See "'Standing to Sue,'" pp. 54–59.)* The Court also ruled that the state, which had sought to sue in behalf of its citizens, had no standing. "It cannot be conceded that a state...may institute judicial proceedings to protect citizens of the United States from the operation of the statutes thereof," the Court said.[60] In addition, "Probably," Sutherland wrote, "it would be sufficient to point out that the powers of the state are not invaded, since the statute imposes no obligation, but simply extends an option which the state is free to accept or reject."[61]

Challenges to spending for internal improvements or public works projects also were rebuffed by the Court. In 1938 the Court upheld federal loans to municipalities for power projects, ruling that the state-chartered power companies that had questioned the loans had no right to be free from competition and had not suffered sufficient damages to have standing to bring the case as federal taxpayers.[62] The Court also had refused to limit congressional use of grants-in-aid programs. With the passage of time, Justice Sutherland's dicta gained the force of law. In 1947 Oklahoma challenged a provision of the Hatch Act under which its federal highway funds would be reduced if it did not remove a state highway commission officer who had actively participated in partisan politics in violation of the act. The state challenged this requirement as improper federal control over its internal political matters. The Court rejected the claim, noting, "While the United States is not concerned with, and has no power to regulate local political activities as such of State officials, it does have power to fix the terms upon which its money allotments to States shall be disbursed."[63] This point was reaffirmed in *South Dakota v. Dole* (1987). The Court held that Congress may condition a state's receipt of the full allocation of federal highway funds upon the state's decision to raise the drinking age to twenty-one. South Dakota had challenged this condition as barred by the Twenty-first Amendment's grant to states of the authority to control the sale and consumption of liquor within their boundaries.[64]

SPENDING FOR THE GENERAL WELFARE

Article I, section 8, clause 1, gives Congress the power "to provide for the common defense and general welfare." From the start, differences arose over what that clause meant. The strict interpretation, associated with James Madison, limited it to spending for purposes connected with the powers specifically enumerated in the Constitution. "Nothing is more natural nor common," Madison wrote in No. 41 of the *Federalist Papers*, "than first to use a general phrase, and then to explain and qualify it by recital of particulars."[65] The other view, associated with Alexander Hamilton, argued that the General Welfare Clause conferred upon the government a power independent from those enumerated. This broad construction eventually came to be the accepted view, but not for quite a while. It would take almost 150 years for the Court to find it necessary to interpret the clause at all.

The first time the Court addressed the interpretation of the General Welfare Clause, it gave lip service to Hamilton's stance, but then limited the interpretation by claiming that the power to spend had been combined in this instance with the power to tax in pursuit of regulating a matter outside the scope of the federal government's powers—agricultural production. In other words, the Court said Congress had combined the two powers in an improper exercise of the federal police power. The question before the Court was the constitutionality of the Agricultural Adjustment Act of 1933 (AAA), the New Deal measure passed during the first hundred days of Roosevelt's presidency to boost farm prices and farmers' purchasing power. The statute provided that an excise tax would be levied on the processors of seven food commodities and the proceeds of the tax would be used to pay benefits to farmers who reduced their production of those commodities. The case of *United States v. Butler* (1936) arose when William M. Butler, a receiver for a bankrupt cotton mill, refused to pay the processing tax.[66]

In addition to determining whether the benefit payment scheme was a valid exercise of the power to spend for the general welfare, the Court also was required to choose between two lines of precedent to determine the validity of the tax portion of the statute. Under one set of cases, the Court could find the tax valid; under the other, it could declare it invalid because in reality it was a penalty designed to regulate a wholly intrastate matter. As in earlier New Deal cases, the Court chose the more restrictive interpretation. Writing for the six-justice majority, Justice Owen J. Roberts said the tax was not a tax in the normal sense of the word, but "an expropriation of money from one group for the benefit of another" as part of a regulatory device. The tax was unconstitutional under the taxing power, although, Roberts said, it might be valid if it were enacted as "an expedient regulation" of another enumerated power.[67] This was not the case here either, Roberts continued. Clearly, the enumerated power could not be the power over interstate commerce because agricultural production was an intrastate matter, he said, noting that the government had not argued the validity of the act on the basis of the commerce power.

Roberts then turned to the benefit payments and the General Welfare Clause. Reviewing the interpretations of the clause by Madison and Hamilton, Roberts concluded that Hamilton's was correct. "[T]he power of Congress to authorize is not limited by the first grants of legislative power found in the Constitution," Roberts declared.[68] This point notwithstanding, Roberts next declared the crop benefit payments an unconstitutional invasion of rights reserved to the states. The AAA, he said,

> is a statutory plan to regulate and control agricultural production, a matter beyond the powers delegated to the federal government. The tax, the appropriation of funds raised, and the direction of their disbursement, are but parts of the plan. They are but means to an unconstitutional end.[69]

In contrast to Justice Sutherland's dicta in the 1923 grant-in-aid cases, Roberts rejected the argument that compliance with the federal statute was voluntary. "The power to confer or withhold unlimited benefits is the power to coerce or destroy," Roberts said.[70] He also rejected the contention that the national economic emergency empowered Congress to regulate agricultural production:

It does not help to declare that local conditions throughout the nation have created a situation of national concern; for this is but to say that whenever there is a widespread similarity of local conditions, Congress may ignore constitutional limitations upon its own powers and usurp those reserved to the states....If the act before us is a proper exercise of the federal taxing power, evidently the regulation of all industry throughout the United States may be accomplished by similar exercises of the same power.[71]

For the minority, Justice Harlan Fiske Stone argued that regulation contemplated under the AAA was not accomplished by the tax, but by the way the proceeds were used. The same regulation could be achieved by spending any Treasury funds, no matter what their source, he said, adding that the processing tax simply defrayed the public expense of the benefit payments. Stone also castigated the majority's weakening of the spending power and invalidation of the benefit payments. "It is a contradiction in terms to say that there is a power to spend for the national welfare, while rejecting any power to impose conditions reasonably adopted to the attainment of the end which alone would justify the expenditure," he said.[72] Stone's dissent presaged the stand the Court, chastened by Roosevelt's Court-packing plan, would take a year and a half later in upholding portions of the 1935 Social Security Act in two separate cases. Although the Court did not formally overturn its decision in *Butler,* it effectively left it a dead letter.

The first case, *Steward Machine Co. v. Davis* (1937), was a test of the unemployment compensation provisions of a statute that taxed employers; employers could earn a tax credit if they contributed to a federally approved state unemployment compensation insurance system.[73] The law was challenged on the grounds that the tax was not intended to raise revenue but to regulate employment, which was an internal matter for the states, and that the states had been coerced into yielding a portion of their sovereignty to the federal government. The challenges were rejected, 5-4. Justice Roberts, who had written the opinion in *Butler,* now joined the majority in minimizing its impact. Justice Benjamin N. Cardozo for the majority first explained

its view that Congress had the power to tax employment: "Employment is a business relation...without which business could seldom be carried on effectively," he said, adding that the power to tax business extended to the power to tax any of its parts.[74]

The Court found the statute no invasion of states' rights or sovereignty but rather an example of cooperation between the national government and the state to overcome the common evil of unemployment. The statute represented a national means to solve what had become a national problem insoluble by the states acting independently of each other. "It is too late today for the argument to be heard with tolerance that in a crisis so extreme the use of the moneys of the nation to relieve the unemployed and their dependents is a use for any purpose narrower than the promotion of the general welfare," Cardozo wrote.[75] He acknowledged that the tax credit granted on the basis of the fulfillment of certain conditions was "in some measure a temptation. But to hold that motive or temptation is equivalent to coercion is to plunge the law into endless difficulties." In any event, Cardozo added, the point of coercion had not been reached in the case at hand,[76] nor were the conditions themselves coercive. The states were given a wide range of choice in enacting laws to fulfill the requirements, and they could withdraw at any time from the state-federal cooperative arrangement. Cardozo distinguished the unemployment compensation case from *Butler* on two other points. First, unlike the agricultural production case, the proceeds from the employment tax were not earmarked for a specific group of people, but instead went into the general revenues of the country. Second, the states specifically had to approve the tax credit by passing a law allowing it, unlike the AAA, which attempted to regulate without permission from the states.

In the second case, *Helvering v. Davis* (1937), decided the same day by a 7-2 vote, the Court upheld the constitutionality of federal old-age benefits.[77] In this opinion, Cardozo acknowledged that in spending for the general welfare, a

line must still be drawn between one welfare and another, between particular and general. Where this shall be placed cannot be known through a formula in advance of the event. There is a middle ground...in which discretion is at large. The

An 1862 greenback. No national currency existed until the Civil War, when Congress authorized the printing of paper money, called "greenbacks," and made it legal tender for the payment of debts. In 1870, in the first of the *Legal Tender Cases*, the Court ruled against the constitutionality of using paper money to pay debts contracted before passage of the greenback legislation in1862. Amid great political controversy, the Court reversed itself on the issue just fifteen months later.

discretion, however, is not confided to the courts. The discretion belongs to Congress, unless the choice is clearly wrong, a display of arbitrary power, not an exercise of judgment.[78]

Cardozo then showed that Congress had not been arbitrary in this case, but that the statute was warranted by a need to solve a national problem that the states could not cure individually. He added that the states could not oppose what Congress determined to be the national welfare: "[T]he concept of welfare or the opposite is shaped by Congress, not the states. So [long as] the concept be not arbitrary, the locality must yield."[79]

THE CURRENCY POWERS

The power "[to] coin Money, regulate the Value thereof, and of foreign Coin, and fix the Standard of Weights and Measures" has been construed, with one brief but significant exception, to give Congress complete control over the nation's currency. As the Court upheld creation of the national bank, established largely to give some stability to the various state and foreign currencies in use during the Union's early history, Chief Justice John Marshall gave his classic definition of the Necessary and Proper Clause.[80] *(See "Implied Powers," pp. 83–87.)*

A national currency did not exist until the Civil War, when Congress authorized the printing of paper money, or "greenbacks," and made them legal tender for the payment of debts. In 1869 the Court upheld a federal tax that was intended to drive state bank notes out of circulation and leave a single uniform national currency.[81] *(See details of Veazie Bank v. Fenno, pp. 147–148.)* Also in 1869 the Court ruled that greenbacks could not be substituted as payment in cases where the contract specifically stipulated payment in gold, which was then the preferred medium of exchange.[82] Left unanswered was whether a creditor could refuse payment in greenbacks if the contract did not specify gold. This question was raised in *Roosevelt v. Meyer* (1863), but the Court refused to take the case, claiming that it did not have jurisdiction.[83] Constitutional scholar Robert G. McCloskey finds this claim contrived: "We must assume," McCloskey wrote, "either that the judges were unfamiliar with the law that furnishes their very

THE BORROWING POWER

The federal government's power to borrow money is not only expressly conferred in the Constitution, but also it is one of the very few federal powers "entirely unencumbered by restrictions—with the result that Congress may borrow from any lenders, for any purposes, in any amounts, or on any terms, and with or without provision for the repayment of loans, with or without interest."[1] The power to borrow is so broad that it has been rarely challenged.

The Supreme Court cases dealing with this power have produced decisions that give the widest possible latitude to the government in exercising it. For example, the Court has struck down state taxes on federal bonds and securities because such taxes would impair the central government's ability to borrow money.[2] *(See "The Taxing Power," pp. 468–469.)* The only restriction the Court has placed on the power to borrow came in one of the three *Gold Clause Cases* 1935, which held that Congress may not change the terms of a loan.[3] *(See "The Currency Powers," pp. 157–164.)*

---

1. Frederick A. Ogg and P. Orman Ray, *Introduction to American Government* (New York: Appleton-Century-Crofts, 1951), 527.

2. *Weston v. City Council of Charleston*, 2 Pet. (27 U.S.) 449 (1829).

3. *Perry v. United States*, 294 U.S. 330 (1935).

---

basis for being, or that they deliberately chose a Pickwickian interpretation in order to avoid deciding, in wartime, a question so central to the conduct of war."[84] The government had issued the paper money to finance its war debts, including the salaries of its fighting men. It could not have afforded to pay them in gold. When the war ended, the Court no longer avoided deciding the issue, at least so far as it pertained to contracts entered into prior to 1862, when the paper currency was first issued.

First Legal Tender Decision

President Ulysses S. Grant was accused of packing the Court after his first two appointees, William Strong and Joseph Bradley, voted to overturn the ruling in the first Legal Tender case.

The case of *Hepburn v. Griswold* (1870) came to the Court in 1865.[85] It was argued in 1867 and reargued in 1868. In the words of historian Charles Warren,

> The probable action of the Court had been the subject of long and excited debate in the community. On the one side, were the National and the State banks, the mortgagees and creditors who demanded payment in gold; lined up with these interests were those men who, on principle, denied the right of the Federal Government to make paper currency legal tender, and opposed legalized cheating through the enforced payment of debts in depreciated currency. On the other side, were the railroads, the municipal corporations, the mortgagors of land and other debtors who now sought to pay, with a depreciated legal tender currency, debts contracted on a gold basis before the war; and with these interests, there were associated all those men who felt strongly that the Government ought not to be deprived of a power which they considered so necessary to its existence in time of war.[86]

The Court was not ready to deliver its opinion until February 7, 1870. At the time the Court had only seven justices, because Congress in 1866 had reduced its size to deprive President Andrew Johnson of an appointment. When Ulysses S. Grant succeeded to the presidency, Congress returned the number of justices to nine but then refused to confirm Grant's first nominee, Attorney General Ebenezer R. Hoar. A week before the Court announced the *Hepburn* decision, Justice Robert C. Grier retired. Therefore, it was by a 4-3 split that the Court invalidated the law. It was the third major act of Congress that the Court had found unconstitutional. *(See box, Significant Acts of Congress Struck Down as Unconstitutional, pp. 162–163.)*

President Ulysses S. Grant was accused of packing the Court after his first two appointees, William Strong and Joseph Bradley, voted to overturn the ruling in the first Legal Tender case.

Rejecting the government's claim that the legal tender laws were a valid means of exercising the war power, the Court ruled against the constitutionality of using paper money to pay debts contracted prior to 1862. The opinion was delivered by Chief Justice Salmon P. Chase, who, ironically, as President Abraham Lincoln's secretary of the Treasury, had advocated enactment of the legal tender statutes. Lincoln in fact had nominated Chase to the Court because, he said, "we wish for a Chief Justice who will sustain what has been done in regard to emancipation and the legal tenders."[87]

For the Court, Chase acknowledged that Congress in the exercise of its express powers had the unrestricted right to choose "among means appropriate, plainly adapted, really calculated."[88] But, he said, it was up to the Court, not Congress, to decide whether the means chosen were appropriate. Chase denied that the express power to issue currency implied a power to make that currency legal

tender in the payment of debts. Furthermore, Chase said, whatever benefit might come from allowing paper money to be used as legal tender was "far more than outweighed by the losses of property, the derangement of business, the fluctuations of currency and values, and the increase of prices to the people and the government and the long train of evils which flow from the use of irredeemable paper money." Given that, Chase continued, "[W]e are unable to persuade ourselves that an expedient of this sort is an appropriate and plainly adapted means for the execution of the power to declare and carry on war."[89] Chase concluded that the statutes were not an appropriate use of Congress's implied powers under the Necessary and Proper Clause.

Chase then noted that the statute could be viewed as impairing the obligations of contracts. He acknowledged that Congress under its express power to establish national bankruptcy laws incidentally had the right to impair contract obligations, but, Chase said, "we cannot doubt that a law not made in pursuance of an express power, which necessarily and in its direct operation impairs the obligation of contracts, is inconsistent with the spirit of the Constitution."[90] The legal tender acts were also a similar spiritual violation of the Fifth Amendment's prohibition against taking private property for public use without due process of law, Chase added. Although the decision applied only to contracts made before the paper currency was issued, Chase's reasoning brought into serious question the validity of using paper money to pay debts incurred after 1862. The consequences, if this were found to be the case, would be grave. The next year the Court, in *Knox v. Lee* (1871), described them:

It is also clear that if we hold the acts invalid as applicable to debts incurred…which have taken place since their enactment, our decision must cause, throughout the country, great business derangement, widespread distress, and the rankest injustice. The debts which have been contracted since…1862…constitute, doubtless, by far the greatest portion of the existing indebtedness of the country….Men have bought and sold, borrowed and lent, and assumed every variety of obligations contemplating that payment might be made with such notes….If now…it be established that these debts and obligations can be discharged only by gold coin;…the government has become an instrument of the grossest injustice; all debtors are loaded with an obligation it was never contemplated they should assume; a large percentage is added to every debt, and such must become the demand for gold to satisfy contracts, that ruinous sacrifices, general distress and bankruptcy may be expected.[91]

The narrow margin of the vote, and public perception of such horrors as the Court eventually described, intensified criticism of the Court, which was still suffering the loss of prestige resulting from its ill-fated decision in the Dred Scott case thirteen years earlier. *(See box, Dred Scott Reversed: The Fourteenth Amendment, p. 183.)* As Chase was delivering the Court's opinion striking down the Legal Tender Act, President Grant sent to the Senate for confirmation the names of his nominees to fill the Court's two vacancies: William Strong and Joseph P. Bradley. In light of subsequent events, Grant was charged with "packing" the Court with these appointments.

Second Legal Tender Decision

Strong was confirmed on February 18,1870, and Bradley on March 21. On April 1, 1870, the Court announced that it would hear two more pending legal tender cases—*Knox v. Lee* and *Parker v. Davis*—and in so doing would review its decision in *Hepburn.* On May 1, 1871, by another slim majority, 5-4, the Court overruled *Hepburn,* giving that decision the distinction of having the shortest life—fifteen months—of any major decision of the Court in the nineteenth century. Strong wrote the Court's opinion in the *Second Legal Tender Cases,* rebutting, point by point, the arguments that Chief Justice Chase had made in the first decision. With regard to the weakest point of Chase's opinion, his claim that it was the Court's duty to determine if Congress had used an appropriate means to implement an express power, Strong responded,

> Is it our province to decide that the means selected were beyond the constitutional power of Congress, because we may think other means to the same ends would have been more appropriate and equally efficient?…The degree of the necessity for any congressional enactment, or the relative degree of its appropriateness,…is for consideration in Congress, not here.[92]

No matter where one stood on the merits of the legal tender issue, the Court's quick reversal was almost universally deplored. A later chief justice, Charles Evans Hughes, was to call the reversal one of the Court's "self-inflicted wounds" and a serious mistake with respect to its effect on public opinion.[93] That effect was summarized in the well-respected *Nation:*

> The present action of the Court is to be deplored, first, because this sudden reversal of a former judgment which had been maturely considered after full argument, will weaken popular respect for all decisions of the Court including this one; second, because the value of a judgment does not depend on the number of Judges who concur in it—Judges being weighed, not counted, and because of the rehearing of a cause, in consequence of the number of Judges having been increased, is peculiarly, and for obvious reasons, objectionable, where the number is dependent on the will of the very body whose acts the Court has to review, and which in this very case it is reviewing; and third, because the Judges who have been added to the Bench since the former decision are men who were at the Bar when that decision was rendered, and were interested professionally and personally in having a different decision. We do not mean to insinuate that this has affected their judgment, but we do say that it is not enough for a Judge to be pure; he must be likewise above suspicion; that is, he must not only be honest, but must give no man any reason for thinking him otherwise than honest.[94]

The decision in the *Second Legal Tender Cases* was reaffirmed in 1884, when the Court upheld the use of legal tender notes in peacetime.[95] The Court in 1872 also reaffirmed its 1869 decision that creditors holding contracts specifically calling for payment in gold did not have to accept paper money in repayment.[96] As a consequence, more and more creditors insisted on gold clauses, and they were eventually contained in almost every private and public bond.

Gold Clause Cases

In 1933, to counter gold hoarding and exporting and speculation in foreign exchange, Congress required all holders to surrender their gold and gold certificates to the Treasury in return for an equivalent amount of

A FISCAL MISSTEP

Although the Court has found that Congress can do almost no wrong in regulating fiscal matters, in 1986 it decided that Congress had chosen the wrong way to go about trying to reduce the national deficit. In 1985 Congress passed the Balanced Budget and Deficit Reduction Act, which gave considerable power to the comptroller general, the head of the General Accounting Office. Among those duties was the power to tell the president how much spending must be reduced in various areas in order to meet the deficit reduction targets for the year. The president was obliged to follow the comptroller's suggestions.

This arrangement was quickly challenged by members of Congress who had opposed the act, and within six months the Court had ruled that this portion of the act, commonly referred to as Gramm-Rudman-Hollings for its three Senate sponsors, was an unconstitutional violation of the separation of powers because it would "permit Congress to execute the laws."[1] Congress had foreseen this possibility and had already written into the law a "fallback" process to replace the one found unconstitutional. The Court "severed" the unconstitutional provisions and left the remaining structure of the Gramm-Rudman-Hollings mechanism intact.

---

1. *Bowsher v. Synar*, 478 U.S. 714 (1986).

---

paper currency. In an effort to raise prices, Congress next devalued the dollar by lowering its gold content. With a third law, Congress then nullified all gold clauses in contracts. The clauses could not be enforced because gold was no longer in circulation, and the statute also prevented creditors from enforcing collection in enough of the devalued currency to equal the value of the gold stipulated in the contract.

The nullification statute was challenged on several grounds—taking private property without compensation, violating the Fifth Amendment's Due Process Clause, and invading the powers of the states—but in a series of four cases, the *Gold Clause Cases,* the Court handed Congress and the president one of their few victories of the early New Deal period. In the first two cases—*Norman v. Baltimore & Ohio Railroad Co.* and *United States v. Bankers Trust Co.* (1935)—the Court upheld the power of Congress to regulate the value of currency. Chief Justice Charles Evans Hughes, who wrote the 5-4 majority opinions in all four cases, noted,

> We are not concerned with consequences, in the sense that consequences, however serious, may excuse an invasion of constitutional right. We are concerned with the constitutional power of the Congress over the monetary system of the country and its attempted frustration. Exercising that power, the Congress has undertaken to establish a

uniform currency, and parity between kinds of currency, and to make that currency, dollar for dollar, legal tender for the payment of debts. In the light of abundant experience, the Congress was entitled to choose such a uniform monetary system, and to reject a dual system, with respect to all obligations within the range of the exercise of its constitutional authority. The contention that these gold clauses are valid contracts and cannot be struck down proceeds upon the assumption that private parties, and States and municipalities, may make and enforce contracts which may limit that authority. Dismissing that tenable assumption, the facts must be faced. We think that it is clearly shown that these clauses interfere with the exertion of the power granted to the Congress and certainly it is not established that the Congress arbitrarily or capriciously decided that such interferences existed.[97]

In the third case, *Nortz v. United States* (1935), the plaintiff sought to recover the difference between the gold content of $10,000 in gold certificates and the gold content of the currency he had been issued in replacement for the certificates. Chief Justice Hughes explained that the certificates were a form of currency, rather than a receipt for gold, the implication being that Congress could replace the certificates with another form of currency. The Court also held that the plaintiff had not sustained sufficient damage to sue in

SIGNIFICANT ACTS OF CONGRESS STRUCK DOWN AS UNCONSTITUTIONAL

Since the first declaration that an act of Congress was unconstitutional—in *Marbury v. Madison* (1803)—the Supreme Court has found 162 particular federal laws to be in violation of the Constitution. (This number does not take into account the hundreds of laws containing legislative veto provisions that were indirectly held unconstitutional when the Court invalidated that device in 1983.) Only a handful of the laws struck down have been of major significance for the Court and the country. Following is a brief explanation of those statutes and the Court's decisions.

MISSOURI COMPROMISE OF 1820

In *Scott v. Sandford* (1857) the Supreme Court declared unconstitutional the recently repealed Missouri Compromise of 1820, which prohibited slavery in the Louisiana territories lying north of 36° 30´. Chief Justice Roger B. Taney wrote that slaves were property and that Congress had no authority to regulate local property rights. Taney also held that even free blacks were not citizens of the United States and could not become citizens. The opinion seriously damaged the Court's prestige, and, rather than settling the slavery issue, the decision probably hastened the onset of the Civil War. The *Scott* decision was overturned by the Thirteenth Amendment, ratified in 1865, prohibiting slavery, and by the Fourteenth Amendment, ratified in 1868, making citizens of all persons born in the United States.

TEST OATH LAW OF 1865

The Court in 1867 declared invalid an 1865 act that required attorneys, as a condition for practicing in federal courts, to swear that they had never engaged in or supported the Southern rebellion against the Union. In *Ex parte Garland* (1867) the Court said that the statute was an unconstitutional bill of attainder because it punished persons by prohibiting them from practicing their professions. The Court also held the statute to be an ex post facto law because it was enacted after the commission of the offense. The Court's opinion in this case and other cases originating in the states indicated that it would not review other federal Reconstruction legislation favorably. To avoid this possibility, Congress removed from the Court's jurisdiction cases arising under certain of those laws. It is the only time in the Court's history that Congress specified a group of laws the Court could not review.

LEGAL TENDER ACTS OF 1862 AND 1863

The Legal Tender Acts, passed in 1862 and 1863, made paper money a substitute for gold as legal tender in the payment of public and private debts. In *Hepburn v. Griswold* (1870) the Supreme Court ruled that Congress had exceeded its authority by making paper money legal tender for the payment of debts incurred before passage of the laws. The outcry from debtors and the potential economic repercussions from this decision were so great that within fifteen months the Court—with two new members—reconsidered, and in *Knox v. Lee* (1871) overturned its earlier decision, thereby establishing paper money as legal currency.

CIVIL RIGHTS ACT OF 1875

The Civil Rights Act of 1875—one of several federal statutes enacted in the first decade after the Civil War to end discrimination against blacks—barred discrimination in privately owned public accommodations, such as hotels, theaters, and railway cars. The Court held that neither the Thirteenth Amendment nor the Fourteenth Amendment gave Congress the power to act to bar private discrimination of this type. The decision was one in a series that vitiated Congress's power to enforce effectively the guarantees given to blacks by the two amendments. It would be almost a century before Congress and the Court effectively overturned this series of rulings.

FEDERAL INCOME TAX

The Court's decision in *Pollock v. Farmers' Loan and Trust Co.* (1895) struck down the first general peacetime income tax enacted by Congress. The Court held that the section of the statute taxing income from real estate was a direct tax and violated the Constitution's requirement that direct taxes be apportioned among the states. This defect, the Court held, was inseparable from the rest of the tax provisions, so all were struck down. The ruling was overturned in 1913 with the ratification of the Sixteenth Amendment specifically exempting income taxes from the apportionment requirement.

"YELLOW-DOG" CONTRACTS

Exhibiting antipathy toward organized labor, the Court in *Adair v. United States* (1908) declared unconstitutional a section of the 1898 Erdman Act making it unlawful for any railway employer to require as a condition of employment that employees not join a labor union. The act was an infringement on property rights guaranteed by the Fifth Amendment, the Court said. Congress had exceeded its authority under the Commerce Clause, the Court added, because labor relations were not part of interstate commerce and did not directly affect it. It was not until 1930 that the Court sanctioned a federal law guaranteeing railway employees collective bargaining rights and not until 1937 that the Court acknowledged that labor relations affected interstate commerce.

CHILD LABOR LAWS

The Court in *Hammer v. Dagenhart* (1918) struck down a 1916 law that sought to end child labor by prohibiting the shipment via interstate commerce of any goods made by children under a certain age who had worked more than a specified number of hours. The majority said that Congress was not regulating commerce but manufacture, an authority it did not possess. Congress then passed a second statute placing a heavy tax on any goods made by children. In *Bailey v. Drexel Furniture Co.* (1922) the Court struck down this statute as well, declaring that the tax was not intended to raise revenue but to penalize employers of children. *Hammer v. Dagenhart* was finally reversed in *United States v. Darby* (1941), in which the Court upheld a federal minimum wage and maximum hour law that applied to children and adults.

AGRICULTURAL ADJUSTMENT ACT OF 1933

Designed to restore farm prices and farmers' purchasing power, the Agricultural Adjustment Act of 1933 levied an excise tax on seven basic food commodities and used the revenue to pay benefits to farmers who reduced their production of the commodities. Striking down the act in *United States v. Butler* (1936), the majority held that Congress had no constitutional authority to regulate agricultural production. The following year, after President Franklin D. Roosevelt's Court-packing threat, the majority approved similar tax benefit schemes when it upheld federal Social Security and unemployment compensation legislation in *Helvering v. Davis* (1937) and *Steward Machine Co. v. Davis* (1937). In 1938 Congress passed a second agricultural adjustment act, which substituted marketing quotas for the processing tax and production quotas of the first act. This second act was upheld in *Mulford v. Smith* (1939).

NATIONAL INDUSTRIAL RECOVERY ACT OF 1933

The centerpiece of President Franklin D. Roosevelt's economic recovery program, the National Industrial Recovery Act (NIRA) authorized the president to approve industry-wide fair competition codes containing wage and hour regulations. In *Panama Refining Co. v. Ryan* (1935) the Court struck down as an unconstitutional delegation of legislative power a section that authorized the president to prohibit from interstate commerce so-called hot oil, produced in violation of state regulations controlling production. The Court held that Congress had not drawn specific enough standards to guide the president in exercising such discretionary authority. *Panama* was followed quickly by the sick chicken case—*A. L. A. Schechter Poultry Corp. v. United States* (1935)—in which a unanimous Court struck down the entire NIRA, because it gave the president too much discretion in establishing and approving fair competition codes and because it exceeded congressional power by applying to intrastate as well as interstate commerce.

COAL CONSERVATION ACT OF 1935

The Coal Conservation Act of 1935 authorized fixed prices for coal, provided collective bargaining rights for miners, allowed two-thirds of the industry to establish mandatory wage and hour regulations for the whole industry, and set up a tax system to ensure compliance. Divided 6-3, the Court in *Carter v. Carter Coal Co.* declared the act an invalid delegation of powers to private industry and an unconstitutional extension of the interstate commerce power. Although not directly overruled, this case and the ruling in *A. L. A. Schechter Poultry Corp. v. United States* (1935) were effectively nullified in *National Labor Relations Board v. Jones & Laughlin Co.* (1937), in which the Court accepted congressional assertion of its power to regulate intrastate production.

GUN FREE SCHOOL ZONES ACT OF 1990

Congress made it a federal crime to have a gun within a school zone, but the Court said mere gun possession was not economic activity and, therefore, was outside Congress's power under the Commerce Clause. The decision in *Lopez v. United States* (1995) signaled the Court's renewed willingness to limit Congress's authority to regulate matters in the guise of interstate commerce.

LINE ITEM VETO ACT OF 1996

The Line Item Veto Act gave the president the authority to "cancel" certain spending items that were contained in large appropriations bills. Presidents of both parties had sought this authority, which they said would help them control wasteful spending. But the Court struck down the law in *Clinton v. City of New York* (1998) on the grounds that the Constitution gives presidents only two choices when presented with a bill passed by Congress: sign it or veto it. The justices said Congress may not alter this basic structure.

MILITARY COMMISSIONS ACT OF 2006

Congress passed this measure at the behest of the George W. Bush administration to overcome two Court rulings related to the "war on terror" and the prisoners held at Guantánamo Bay, Cuba. The law established rules for military trials of prisoners at Guantánamo, a response to the Court's decision in *Hamdan v. Rumsfeld* (2006), which struck down rules set by Bush and the Defense Department. In addition, the law said "no court, justice or judge" may hear an appeal from a prisoner through a writ of habeas corpus. In *Boumediene v. Bush* (2008) the Court struck down that provision as unconstitutional and said Congress may not deprive long-term prisoners held on U.S.-controlled territory of the right to seek their freedom through a writ of habeas corpus.

the Court of Claims, where the case had originated, thereby avoiding a decision on whether the gold certificates were actually contracts with the federal government and whether their required surrender was a violation of due process.[98]

In the last case, *Perry v. United States* (1935), the holder of a government bond sued for the difference between its gold value and the amount he had received for it in devalued dollars. In this instance, the Court ruled against the government, declaring that although Congress had the right to abrogate the gold clauses in private contracts, it had no power to do so with regard to contracts to which the government itself was a party. Wrote Hughes,

> By virtue of the power to borrow money "on the credit of the United States," the Congress is authorized to pledge that credit as an assurance of payment as stipulated,—as the highest assurance the Government can give, its plighted faith. To say that the Congress may withdraw or ignore that pledge, is to assume that the Constitution contemplates a vain promise, a pledge having no other sanction than the pleasure and convenience of the pledgor. This Court has given no sanction to such a conception of the obligations of our Government.[99]

Hughes, however, softened the blow to the government by holding that the plaintiff, as in the previous case, had not sustained sufficient damages to be entitled to standing in the Court of Claims. Speaking for the four dissenters in all four cases, Justice James C. McReynolds wrote what has been called "one of the bitterest minority opinions ever recorded."[100] "Just men regard repudiation and spoliation of citizens by their sovereign with abhorrence; but we are asked to affirm that the Constitution has granted power to accomplish both," McReynolds lamented.[101]

The Power over Foreign Affairs

To the framers of the Constitution, foreign policy was the making of treaties and the waging of war. Wary of entrusting all authority for the conduct of foreign relations to the president, they divided these responsibilities. Congress would declare war, and the president would conduct war with armies raised and maintained by Congress. The president would negotiate treaties; Congress would approve treaties. Congressional influence over foreign policy has, however, ranged far beyond these shared and somewhat limited powers. Congress's power to regulate foreign commerce and its other express powers have played a role, in conjunction with the Necessary and Proper Clause, in shaping numerous facets of the nation's foreign policy. Despite the widely recognized prerogatives of the president in foreign relations, Congress has significant power to support or undercut presidential foreign policy decisions. The Supreme Court's role in this arena has been minor. Challenges to the foreign policy decisions of Congress and the president come to the Court infrequently, and the Court rarely has found fault with the actions Congress has taken in the exercise of its foreign affairs powers.[1]

THE WAR POWER

As noted, the Constitution divides responsibility for waging war between the president and Congress. The president is commander in chief of the army and navy when they are called into actual service, and Congress is expressly granted power to declare war, raise and support armies, provide and maintain a navy, and make rules and regulations to govern the armed forces. Congress also may organize, arm, and discipline the state militias, but the states have express authority to train them. (See "The Commander in Chief," pp. 259–280.)

The war powers of the federal government have never been seriously questioned, although their source has been disputed. Chief Justice John Marshall implied in *McCulloch v. Maryland* (1819) that the power to declare war carried with it the power to conduct war.[2] Others have contended, as did Justice George Sutherland in *United States v. Curtiss-Wright Export Corp.* (1936), that the power to wage war is inherent in the fact of the nation's sovereignty and is not dependent on the enumerated powers of the Constitution.[3] Still others, among them Alexander Hamilton, contended that the power to wage war comes from the enumerated powers amplified by the Necessary and Proper Clause.[4]

Whatever the source of the power, the Supreme Court has been extremely reluctant to place any limits on it as exercised by either Congress or the president. Rarely has it heard cases challenging the exercise of the war power during an ongoing conflict. When it did, however, by the time a decision was rendered, there was usually little chance that an adverse decision could impede the war effort. The Court has sanctioned substantial congressional delegation of power to the executive—a wartime delegation of power has never been held unconstitutional—and has supported large-scale intrusions into state sovereignty and the rights of private citizens and corporations. In those cases where it has declared a statute drawn in wartime unconstitutional, it has almost always done so on the grounds that the law abused a power other than the war power. (See "Wartime Legislation," pp. 170–172.) "In short," constitutional scholar Robert E. Cushman states, "what is necessary to win the war Congress may do, and the Supreme Court has shown no inclination to hold void new and drastic war measures."[5] Some of the justices have acknowledged the dangers inherent in such an unchecked power. "No one will question that this power is the most dangerous one to free government in the whole catalogue of powers," wrote Justice Robert H. Jackson in 1948. "It usually is invoked in haste and excitement when calm legislative consideration of the constitutional limitation is difficult. It is executed in a time of patriotic fervor that makes moderation unpopular. And, worst of all, it is interpreted by the Judges under the influence of the same passions and pressures."[6]

Declaration of War and Congressional Resolutions Authorizing Military Force

The president as commander in chief has the primary responsibility to conduct war, but Congress has the express power to declare it, which it has formally done in only five of the nation's conflicts: the War of 1812, the Mexican War, the Spanish-American War, World War I, and World War II. No formal declaration was made in the Naval War with France (1798–1800), the First Barbary War (1801–1805), the Second Barbary War (1815), the Civil War, the various Mexican-American clashes of 1914–1917, the Korean War, or the Vietnam War.

Since the Vietnam era, Congress on several occasions has voted to authorize the president to use military force, but without formally declaring war. In January 1991 Congress authorized the use of force against Iraq, which had invaded Kuwait. The authorization allowed the president to use U.S. military personnel to enforce an ultimatum against Iraq set by the United Nations. Although far more limited than earlier declarations of war, that congressional resolution marked the first time since World War II that lawmakers had confronted the issue of sending large numbers of American forces into combat. Passage of the resolution put the political and constitutional weight of the legislative branch behind President George H. W. Bush as he prepared the nation for battle. (The administration's most immediate concern—and the public's—was the threat to oil supplies in the Middle East and to stable oil prices.) The fighting lasted six weeks, and the multinational coalition organized against Iraq swept to victory.

On September 18, 2001, just one week after the terrorist attacks in New York and Washington, Congress passed the Authorization for the Use of Military Force to go after those who were behind the attacks. Told that he could "use all necessary and appropriate force" against those who harbored terrorists, President

George W. Bush ordered the U.S. forces into a war in Afghanistan to topple the Taliban regime. A similar scenario was repeated in 2002, when President Bush decided to take action against Iraq ostensibly in his administration's so-called war on terrorism. Congress did not declare war, but approved a resolution authorizing the president "to use the Armed Forces of the United States as he determines to be necessary and appropriate in order to defend the national security of the United States against the continuing threat from Iraq." Bush ordered U.S. troops to invade in March 2003, and they drove Iraqi president Saddam Hussein from power in about three weeks.

From time to time the absence of a formal declaration of war has been challenged before the Supreme Court. In 1800 the Court held that Congress need not declare full-scale war but could provide for a limited conflict. "Congress is empowered to declare a general war, or Congress may wage a limited war; limited in place, in objects and in time," wrote Justice Samuel Chase in reference to the Naval War with France.[7] With Congress in recess when the Civil War broke out, President Abraham Lincoln declared a blockade of Confederate ports in April 1861. In May 1861 he issued a proclamation increasing the size of the army and the navy and calling for eighty thousand volunteers. He also ordered nineteen new vessels for the navy and requested $2 million from the Treasury to cover military requisitions.

In July 1861 Congress passed a measure acknowledging that a state of war existed and authorizing the closing of southern ports. On August 6, 1861, Congress adopted a resolution stating "All the acts, proclamations, and orders of the President respecting the Army and Navy…and calling out or relating to the militias or volunteers…are hereby approved and in all respects made valid…as if they had been issued and done under the previous express authority and direction of the Congress of the United States." The Supreme Court upheld this retroactive ratification in a group of rulings known as the *Prize Cases* (1863).[8] The cases were brought by owners of vessels that had attempted to run the blockade of the southern ports before Congress acted to ratify the blockade but had been seized and condemned as "prizes." The owners sued for redress on the ground that no war had been declared between the North and the South. Observing that "civil war is never solemnly declared," the Court said that although a president does not initiate war, he is "bound to accept the challenge without waiting for any special legislative authority."[9] Justice Robert C. Grier for the 5-4 majority continued,

> If it were necessary to the technical existence of a war, that it should have a legislative sanction, we will find it in almost every Act passed at the extraordinary session of the Legislature of 1861, which was wholly employed in enacting laws to enable the Government to prosecute the war with vigor and efficiency.…Without admitting that such [a ratification] Act was necessary under the circumstances, it is plain that, if the President had in any manner assumed powers which it was necessary should have the authority or sanction of Congress,…this ratification has operated to perfectly cure the defect.[10]

The Court has ruled in several cases that the subsequent ratification of an executive action or appropriation of money to carry out that action is equivalent to a prior authorization of that action.[11] None of these cases involved declarations of war, but one involved a challenge to the president's authority to create war agencies under the First War Powers Act of 1941. The Court in 1947 ruled that "the appropriation by Congress of funds for the use of such agencies stands as confirmation and ratification of the action of the Chief Executive."[12]

Modern Undeclared Wars

Debate surrounding the Vietnam War included the contention that declarations of war were outmoded given the existence of nuclear weapons and the need to commit troops overseas in emergencies on a limited war basis. Testifying before the Senate Foreign Relations Committee in 1971, Prof. Alpheus T. Mason of Princeton University commented,

> The Framers, with deliberate care, made war-making a joint enterprise. Congress is authorized to "declare war"; the President is designated "commander in chief." Technology has expanded the President's role and correspondingly curtailed the

power of Congress. Unchanged are the joint responsibilities of the President and Congress. The fact that a congressional declaration of war is no longer practical does not deprive Congress of constitutionally imposed authority in war-making. On the contrary, it is under obligation to readjust its power position.[13]

The Supreme Court refused to inject itself in the argument over whether the war in Vietnam should have been formally declared. Lower federal courts in several instances ruled that challenges to the war as undeclared by Congress raised political questions not resolvable in the courts. The Supreme Court refused all appeals that it review the lower court rulings.[14] *(See box, Court, Congress, and Cambodia, p. 168.)* The Court, however, was not unanimous in its denials. In *Mora v. McNamara* (1967), brought by three enlisted men seeking to stop their transfer to Vietnam, Justices Potter Stewart and William O. Douglas dissented from the Court's refusal to hear the case. Whether a president can commit troops to combat in an undeclared war and whether Congress had in effect declared war by appropriating funds, Stewart wrote, were "large and deeply troubling questions. Whether the Court would ultimately reach them depends, of course, upon the resolution of serious preliminary issues of justiciability. We cannot make these problems go away simply by refusing to hear the cases."[15] Douglas quoted from the majority opinion in another "political question" case, *Nixon v. Herndon* (1927):

> The objection that the subject matter of the suit is political is little more than a play upon words. Of course the petition concerns political action but it alleges and seeks to recover for private damage. That private damage may be caused by such political action and may be recovered for in a suit at law hardly has been doubted for over two hundred years…and has been recognized by this Court.[16]

The Constitution makes no provision for terminating a state of war. The Supreme Court has indicated that there must be some sort of formal termination, but it has left the appropriate means to the two political branches. In 1948 the Court wrote,

COURT, CONGRESS, AND CAMBODIA

The Supreme Court's reluctance to become involved in disagreements between the president and Congress over the war power is clearly demonstrated in a series of events in 1973. Rep. Elizabeth Holtzman, D-N.Y., and several Air Force officers challenged as unconstitutional the continued bombing of Cambodia after the United States had signed cease-fire agreements concerning the war in Vietnam. Later that year, Congress voted to cut off funds, effective as of August 15, for further bombing operations.

Late in July, federal district judge Orrin G. Judd, ruling in the Holtzman suit, issued a permanent injunction halting all military operations in Cambodia after July 27. Judd stated that he found no congressional authority for U.S. fighting in Cambodia.[1] He rejected the government's argument that congressional acceptance of the August 15 cutoff amounted to legislative approval of Cambodian military activities until that time. "It cannot be the rule," Judd said, "that the President needs a vote of only one-third plus one of either House in order to conduct a war, but this would be the consequence of holding that Congress must override a Presidential veto in order to terminate hostilities which it has not authorized."[2]

On July 27, at the request of the government, the U.S. Court of Appeals for the Second Circuit delayed the Judd injunction and agreed to hear the government's appeal. Holtzman then appealed to Supreme Court justice Thurgood Marshall, who reviewed the appeal but refused to reinstate the injunction. Acknowledging that he might well find continued combat in Cambodia unconstitutional, Marshall said he could not make such a momentous decision alone:

> It must be recognized that we are writing on an almost entirely clean slate in this area. The stark fact is that although there have been numerous lower court decisions concerning the legality of the war in Southeast Asia, this Court has never considered the problem, and it cannot be doubted that the issues posed are immensely important and complex.
>
> Lurking in this suit are questions of standing, judicial competence, and substantive constitutional law which go to the roots of the division of power in a constitutional democracy. These are the sort of issues which should not be decided precipitously or without the benefit of proper consultation.[3]

Holtzman next appealed to Justice William O. Douglas, who was at his home in Goose Prairie, Washington. Her attorney flew to Seattle, drove five hours toward Goose Prairie, and walked the last mile through the woods to deliver the appeal to Douglas's cabin. On August 4 Douglas reinstated the injunction against bombing Cambodia. The government immediately asked Chief Justice Warren E. Burger to call the full Court into session to reverse Douglas's order. Under the Court's rules, this request went to Marshall, who reversed Douglas's action on August 4. That same day, the Court of Appeals for the Second Circuit reversed the district court's original ruling halting military operations in Cambodia. The Supreme Court on August 9 refused to review that decision. Although the bombing of Cambodia did indeed cease as of August 15, it is interesting to note that the Defense Department had refused to comply with Douglas's reinstatement of the injunction halting the bombing even for the few hours it was in effect.

---

1. *Holtzman v. Schlesinger*, 361 F. Supp. 553 (1973).

2. Id. at 565.

3. *Holtzman v. Schlesinger*, 414 U.S. 1304 at 1313–1314 (1973).

"The state of war" may be terminated by treaty or legislation or Presidential proclamation. Whatever the mode, its termination is a political act.... Whether and when it would be open to this Court to find that a war though merely formally kept alive had in fact ended, is a question too fraught with gravity even to be adequately formulated when not compelled.[17]

Raising Armies, Administering Justice

Although the federal government conscripted men into the army during the Civil War, its authority to raise armies through a compulsory draft was not tested in the federal courts until after Congress adopted the Selective Service Act of 1917. The law was challenged on several grounds, including the charge that it violated the Thirteenth Amendment's prohibition against involuntary servitude. In 1918 the Supreme Court unanimously upheld the law in a series of cases known collectively as the *Selective Service Draft Law Cases*. The authority to institute the compulsory draft, said Chief Justice Edward D. White, was derived from the express war powers and the Necessary and Proper Clause, strengthened by historical practice. It also derived from the nature of a "just government" whose "duty to the citizen includes the reciprocal obligation of the citizen to render military service in case of need and the right to compel it."[18] Conscription was not involuntary servitude, said White, reaffirming a 1916 decision in which the Court held that the Thirteenth Amendment was intended to cover the kinds of compulsory labor similar to slavery and not those "duties which individuals owe to the States, such as service in the army, militia, on the jury, etc. . . ."[19]

The Court has never ruled on whether a "peacetime" draft is constitutional. Lower federal courts, however, have upheld the draft in the absence of declared war.[20] Even so, the draft continues to be a fertile source of legal questions. In 1981 the Court upheld the power of Congress—without violating the Constitution—to exclude women from the military draft. In *Rostker v. Goldberg* (1981) the Court held, 6-3, that because women were barred by law and policy from combat, they were not "similarly situated" with men for the purposes of draft registration. Three years later the Court held that Congress did not violate the ban on bills of attainder when it denied federal student aid to male college students who had failed to register for the military draft.[21] *(See box, Specific Constitutional Limits on Congressional Powers, pp. 90–91.)*

In the exercise of its power to govern and regulate the armed services, Congress has established a military justice system complete with its own laws, courts, and appeals. The Supreme Court has held that it has no jurisdiction to review courts-martial through writs of certiorari but may do so through writs of habeas corpus.[22] The Court has traditionally reviewed only those cases challenging the jurisdiction of military courts over the person tried and the crimes committed. The Fifth Amendment guarantee of indictment by a grand jury in any capital case specifically exempts cases involving "land or naval forces, or . . . the Militia, when in actual service in time of War or public danger." The Court also has indicated that such cases might be exempted from the Sixth Amendment guarantee of trial by jury.[23] This exemption has left in question whether someone serving in the military is entitled to a civilian trial for a capital offense when he or she is not in actual service and it is not wartime. In deciding this question the Court generally has restricted the instances in which courts-martial are appropriate. In 1955, for example, the Court ruled that once discharged, a soldier may not be court-martialed for an offense committed when he was in the service.[24]

At the end of the 1960s a serviceman challenged the jurisdiction of a court-martial to try him for a nonmilitary offense, attempted rape, committed off post while he was on leave. In *O'Callahan v. Parker* (1969) the Court said that courts-martial could try only "service-connected" crimes. The justices did not explain what they meant by service-connected crimes, but in holding that the serviceman had been improperly court-martialed, the majority pointed out that his offense was committed during peacetime in a territory held by the United States, that it did not relate to his military duties and that the victim was not engaged in any military duties, that the crime was traditionally cognizable by civilian courts, which were available to try the offense, and that the commission of the crime did not directly flout military authority or violate military property.[25] In 1971 another serviceman was court-martialed for the rape and kidnapping on a military post of two women; one woman worked on the base, and the other was visiting her brother, a serviceman. Although several of the conditions present in *O'Callahan* applied in this case, the Court held that a crime by a serviceman on a military post violating the security of persons on the post was service-connected and was punishable by a court-martial.[26]

That narrowing of rights grew in importance for the military after the Court overturned *O'Callahan v. Parker* by ruling in *Solorio v. United States* (1987) that courts-martial had jurisdiction to try any member of the armed forces for any crime. Jurisdiction no longer depended upon the "service-connected" nature of the crime, but upon the status of the defendant as a member of the armed forces.[27] Although the Uniform Code of Military Justice provides many due process rights to military personnel comparable to those that civilians enjoy under the Constitution, the Court in 1976 held that persons undergoing summary courts-martial did not have a constitutional right to legal counsel.[28]

The Court in the 1990s rejected a constitutional challenge to the method of appointing military judges. By a unanimous vote, it refused to require that officers be given a separate presidential appointment before serving as military judges or that military judges have fixed terms of office. The decision in *Weiss v. United States* (1994) upheld procedures by which any commissioned military officer who was also a lawyer could be appointed a judge by the judge advocate general of his or her branch of service.[29]

WARTIME LEGISLATION

During wartime Congress often adopts legislation placing extraordinary controls and regulations on all phases of the economy, including matters over which the federal government has doubtful authority in peacetime. Relatively few of these statutes have been challenged before the Supreme Court; almost always the Court has upheld the extraordinary exercise of power.

Civil War

With the federal government desperately in need of money to pay the armed forces and to finance the Union war effort, Congress in 1862 and 1863 passed laws making Treasury notes legal tender, meaning that creditors had to accept paper money, rather than gold or silver, in the payment of debts. Challenged in Court, the statutes were defended by the government as necessary and proper means of exercising the federal powers over war, commerce, and the borrowing of money. Five years after the war had ended, the Supreme Court in 1870 disagreed, striking down the Legal Tender Acts on the ground that they carried "the doctrine of implied powers very far beyond any extent hitherto given to it."[30] Little more than a year later, the Court reversed itself and upheld the acts. That the acts were appropriate to an exercise of the war powers, that they achieved the desired effect was "not to be doubted," the Court said in 1871. "[W]hen a statute has proved effective in the

execution of powers confessedly existing, it is not too much to say that it must have some appropriateness to the execution of those powers," the majority wrote.[31] *(See details of Legal Tender Cases, pp. 158–160.)*

World War I

War measures enacted during World War I authorized the federal government to force compliance with war contracts, to operate factories producing war goods, and to regulate the foreign-language press. In conjunction with other express powers, the federal government also ran the nation's railroads, censored mail, and controlled radio and cable communication. Among the more important war measures—and the one that most significantly impinged on traditional state authorities—was the Lever Act of 1917, which authorized the federal government to regulate all phases of food and fuel production, including importation, manufacturing, and distribution.

In 1921 the Court held unconstitutional the section of the Lever Act that provided penalties for anyone who sold necessary food items at an unreasonable price. According to the Court, the section was so vague as to violate the right of the accused to due process under the Fifth Amendment and the right to be informed of the nature and cause of the accusation guaranteed by the Sixth Amendment. The justices added that "the mere existence of a state of war could not suspend or change the operation upon the power of Congress of the guarantees and limitations" of the two amendments.[32] The decision was of relatively little significance to the war effort, as it came three years after the war had ended and involved language that Congress could have easily corrected. In a 1924 case involving a price-fixing provision of the Lever Act, the Court, by deciding the case on other grounds, carefully avoided discussing the constitutional issue of whether the government could set coal prices that resulted in uncompensated losses to the sellers. As one commentator wrote, "It is to be noted that the Court avoided an adverse action on the war measure, in a decision handed down more than five years after the cessation of hostilities."[33]

The Court firmly upheld the federal takeover of the railroads against a challenge that it violated states' rights. The specific challenge was to the authority of the Interstate Commerce Commission to set intrastate rail rates. In *Northern Pacific Railway Co. v. North Dakota ex rel Langer* (1919) the Court wrote that if a conflict occurs in a sphere that both the federal government and the states have authority to regulate, federal power is paramount.[34]

World War II

Mobilization of private industry and delegation of authority to the president to conduct war were even more extensive during World War II than they had been in World War I. Among the more important measures passed by Congress were the Selective Service Act of 1940; the Lend-Lease Act of 1941, which allowed the president to ship supplies to U.S. allies; the First War Powers Act of 1941, which gave the president the power to reorganize executive and independent agencies when necessary for more effective prosecution of the war; the Second War Powers Act of 1942, which gave the president authority to requisition plants and to control overseas communications, alien property, and defense contracts; the Emergency Price Control Act of 1942, which established the Office of Price Administration (OPA) to control the prices of rent and commodities; the War Labor Disputes Act of 1943, which authorized seizure of factories threatened by strike or other labor dispute; and the Renegotiation Act, which gave the executive branch authority to require compulsory renegotiation to recapture excessive profits made on war contracts.

During the war itself, the Supreme Court agreed to hear only one major case involving these enormous grants of power. *Yakus v. United States* (1944) challenged the Emergency Price Control Act as an unconstitutional delegation of legislative power to the executive branch.[35] The Court upheld Congress's power to delegate to the OPA the authority to set maximum prices and to decide when they should be imposed. The Constitution, the Court said,

> does not require that Congress find for itself every fact upon which it desires to base legislative action or that it make for itself detailed determinations

which it has declared to be prerequisite to the application of the legislative policy to particular facts and circumstances impossible for Congress itself properly to investigate. The essentials of the legislative function are the determination of the legislative policy and its formulation and promulgation as a defined and binding rule of conduct—here the rule, with penal sanctions, that prices shall not be greater than those fixed by maximum price regulations which conform to standards and will tend to further the policy which Congress has established. These essentials are preserved when Congress has specified the basic conditions of fact upon whose existence or occurrence, ascertained from relevant data by a designated administrative agency, it directs that its statutory command shall be effective.[36]

Only if there were an absence of standards for judging whether the OPA administrator had obeyed the will of Congress in administering the law would this price-fixing statute be unconstitutional, the Court said. In this case, the Court continued, the standards, "with the aid of the 'statement of the considerations' required to be made by the Administrator, are sufficiently definite…to enable Congress, the courts and the public to ascertain whether the Administrator…has conformed to those standards."[37] As in World War I, the Court avoided answering the question of whether Congress had the authority under its war powers to empower the executive branch to fix prices. In a postwar case, *Lichter v. United States* (1948), the Court gave some indication of how extensive it believed congressional powers during wartime to be:

> Congress, in time of war, unquestionably has the fundamental power…to conscript men and to requisition the properties necessary and proper to enable it to raise and support its Armies. Congress furthermore has a primary obligation to bring about whatever production of war equipment and supplies shall be necessary to win a war.[38]

In *Lichter* the Court upheld the Renegotiation Act, which authorized the executive branch to recover excessive profits from war industries, against a challenge of unconstitutional delegation of powers. "A constitutional power implies a power of delegation of authority under it sufficient to effect its purposes," the majority wrote. In no less sweeping terms, the majority continued,

> This power is especially significant in connection with constitutional war powers under which the exercise of broad discretion as to methods to be employed may be essential to an effective use of its war powers by Congress. The degree to which Congress must specify its policies and standards in order that the administrative authority granted may not be an unconstitutional delegation of its own legislative power is not capable of precise definition. In peace or in war it is essential that the Constitution be scrupulously obeyed, and particularly that the respective branches of the Government keep within the powers assigned to each by the Constitution. On the other hand, it is of the highest importance that the fundamental purposes of the Constitution be kept in mind and given effect in order that, through the Constitution, the people of the United States may in time of war as in peace bring to the support of those purposes the full force of their united action. In time of crisis nothing could be more tragic and less expressive of the intent of the people than so to construe their Constitution that by its own terms it would substantially hinder rather than help them in defending their national safety.[39]

POSTWAR LEGISLATION

In the wake of the Civil War, the Supreme Court stated that "the [war] power is not limited to victories in the field....It carries with it inherently the power to guard against the immediate renewal of the conflict and to remedy the evils which have arisen from its use and progress."[40] This reasoning has allowed the Court to sanction enforcement of measures based on the war powers long after the actual hostilities have ended. For example, the Court in 1921 upheld a federal statute continuing rent control in the District of Columbia first imposed during World War I, when a housing shortage occurred in the nation's capital.[41] The Court said the statute's extension was made necessary by the continuing housing shortage resulting from the war

emergency. In 1924, however, the Court denied another extension of the law.[42] "A law depending upon the existence of an emergency or other certain state of facts to uphold it may cease to operate if the emergency eases or the facts change even though valid when passed," the Court said.[43] In this case, the facts had changed—the government was hiring fewer people, and more new housing was available in the District. If an increased cost of living persisted after the war, the Court said, that was no justification for a continuation of the rent control measure.

The Court has also sanctioned a measure based on the war powers but not enacted until after hostilities had ended. Ten days after the World War I armistice was signed, Congress passed a law prohibiting the production, sale, and transportation of liquor for the duration of the war emergency. Finding that it was within congressional power to require prohibition in order to conserve manpower and increase efficiency during the demobilization period, the Court upheld the law in 1919 and 1920.[44] A similar issue was addressed following World War II in *Woods v. Miller Co.* (1948), which questioned the validity of a 1947 statute continuing the rent control program established under the Emergency Price Control Act.[45] The Court upheld the statute on the basis of the World War I precedents, but Justice William O. Douglas, writing for the majority, added a note of caution:

> We recognize the force of the argument that the effects of war under modern conditions may be felt in the economy for years and years, and that if the war power can be used in days of peace to treat all the wounds which war inflicts on our society, it may not only swallow up all other powers of Congress but largely obliterate the Ninth and Tenth Amendments [reserving rights and powers to the people of the states] as well.[46]

In a separate concurring opinion, Justice Robert H. Jackson also voiced his misgivings: "I cannot accept the argument that war powers last as long as the effects and consequences of war for if so they are permanent—as permanent as the war debts."[47]

After terrorists in 2001 hijacked airplanes and crashed them into the World Trade Center in New York and the Pentagon near Washington, President Bush denounced the attacks as acts of war. A week later, Congress adopted a resolution—the Authorization for Use of Military Force (AUMF)—that empowered the president to "use all necessary and appropriate force" against "nations, organizations or persons" that he believes "planned, authorized, committed or aided" the attacks of September 11, 2001. Congress then stood aside and allowed the president to make policy for this new kind of war.

Bush ordered the U.S. military into action in Afghanistan with the goal of toppling the Taliban regime and capturing Osama bin Laden, the leader of the al Qaeda network. U.S. troops quickly succeeded in driving the Taliban from power, but bin Laden escaped.

During this operation, U.S. troops captured hundreds of men who were believed to be Taliban fighters or allies of bin Laden. Many of them were shipped to the U.S. naval base at Guantánamo Bay, Cuba, and held as "unlawful enemy combatants." One of them, Yaser Hamdi, was discovered to be an American citizen. He was born in Louisiana, but grew up in Saudi Arabia.

Hamdi challenged Bush's decision to hold him indefinitely as an "unlawful enemy combatant," but the Court pointed to the AUMF as authorizing the president to hold war prisoners. Justice Sandra Day O'Connor noted that Congress had said the president could use "all necessary and appropriate force." Holding prisoners during hostilities is "an incident of war" and hardly unusual, she said. "There can be no doubt that individuals who fought against the United States in Afghanistan as part of the Taliban, an organization known to have supported the al Qaeda network responsible for the attacks, are individuals Congress sought to target in passing the AUMF," O'Connor wrote.[48]

But the decision was mixed because the Court also said the military must give a citizen such as Hamdi a fair hearing before a "neutral decisionmaker." Shortly after the ruling, the administration released Hamdi and sent him home to Saudi Arabia.

After a long period on the sidelines, Congress in 2006 passed the Military Commission Act (MCA) to authorize military trials at Guantánamo and to prevent judges from interfering. The law itself was a direct response to two Supreme Court setbacks for the administration. One ruling, *Hamdan v. Rumsfeld* (2006), struck down Bush's proposed rules for the military trials, and the other, *Rasul v. Bush* (2004), said the detainees could file writs of habeas corpus and seek their release before judges. In an attempt to close the courthouse door, the MCA said "no court, justice or judge" may act on a writ of habeas corpus filed by an "alien" who is held as "enemy combatant."

The Court struck down that provision as unconstitutional in 2008. The justices said the Constitution enshrined the "Privilege of the Writ of Habeas Corpus" as a fundamental protection for liberty, and this right may not be taken away, except when it is "suspended" during times of "rebellion or invasion." Because Congress had no cause to suspend habeas corpus, the Court said, the detainees at Guantánamo had a right to challenge in a federal court the government's basis for holding them.[49]

TREATY POWERS

The 1787 Constitutional Convention considered giving the Senate sole authority to make treaties with foreign countries. Ultimately, that power was to be shared with the president, who had the "Power, by and with the Advice and Consent of the Senate, to make Treaties." How equal a partner this phrasing made the Senate in the actual negotiation of treaties was debated for several decades. Some senators advocated that the Senate actually direct treaty making by proposing negotiations. Such initiative, they said, was the right and duty of the Senate under the Constitution and showed the United States was united in its demands. This debate was laid to rest in 1936, when the Supreme Court declared, "The President alone negotiates. Into the field of negotiation the Senate cannot intrude, and Congress itself is powerless to invade it."[50] *(See "The 'Sole Negotiator,'" pp. 283–285.)* Although the president holds the primary treaty powers, Congress plays a crucial role through Senate ratification, congressional implementation, and repeal.

Approval

The Constitution is silent on the subject, but the Senate since 1795 has claimed the right to amend and modify treaties once they have been submitted for approval. Twice this power has been reviewed and sanctioned by the Supreme Court. Speaking in 1869, the Court stated,

> In this country, a treaty is something more than a contract, for the Federal Constitution declares it to be the law of the land. If so, before it can become a law, the Senate, in whom rests the authority to ratify it, must agree to it. But the Senate are [sic] not required to adopt or reject as a whole, but may modify or amend it.[51]

In 1901 the Court reiterated that the Senate might make approval conditional upon adoption of amendments to the treaty.[52]

Congressional Implementation

Some treaties are self-executing and when ratified become the law of the land, equivalent to legislative acts. Others once ratified still require Congress to pass enabling legislation to carry out the terms and conditions of the treaty. Chief Justice John Marshall in 1829 described the kinds of treaties needing additional implementation as those where "the terms of the stipulation import a contract—when either of the parties engages to perform a particular act—the treaty addresses itself to the political…department; and the legislature must execute the contract, before it can become a rule for the Court."[53]

If the treaty deals with a subject outside the coverage of its enumerated powers, Congress may use its authority under the Necessary and Proper Clause to justify enactment of implementing legislation. It is under this authority that Congress has, for example, conferred judicial power upon American consuls abroad to be exercised over American citizens and has provided for foreign extradition of fugitives from justice. Without a treaty on these subjects, Congress would have no power to act. An extreme example of the use of the Necessary and Proper Clause in conjunction with treaty making is found in *Missouri v. Holland* (1920).[54]

Congress wished to protect certain migratory birds from hunters. When lower federal courts ruled an act of Congress to this effect unconstitutional as an invasion of state sovereignty, the executive branch negotiated a treaty with Canada for the protection of the birds. The Senate ratified it, and Congress again passed legislation barring hunting of the birds and providing other protections. Because this legislation was to implement the treaty, the Supreme Court upheld it:

> We do not mean to imply that there are no qualifications to the treaty-making power; but they must be ascertained in a different way. It is obvious that there may be matters of the sharpest exigency for the national well-being that an act of Congress could not deal with but that a treaty followed by such an act could, and it is not lightly to be assumed, that in matters requiring national action, "a power which must belong to and somewhere reside in every civilized government" is not to be found.[55]

Several commentators have noted that this opinion "is one of the most far-reaching assertions of national power in [U.S.] constitutional history."[56] Historians Alfred Kelly and Winfred Harbison found the implications of the case "astounding." They wrote, "If a treaty could accomplish anything of a national character so long as its subject matter were plausibly related to the general welfare, what limits were there to federal authority, if exercised in pursuance of the treaty-making power?"[57]

Repeal

The Court has ruled that a treaty may supersede a prior act of Congress and that an act of Congress may in effect repeal prior treaties or parts of them.[58] In the *Head Money Cases* (1884) the Court wrote that there was nothing in a treaty that made it

> irrepealable or unchangeable. The Constitution gives it no superiority over an act of Congress in this respect, which may be repealed or modified by an act of Congress of a later date. Nor is there anything in its essential character, or in the branches of the government by which the treaty is made, which gives it this superior sanctity.…In short, we are of opinion that, so far as a treaty made by the United

States with any foreign nation can become the subject of judicial cognizance in the courts of this country, it is subject to such acts as Congress may pass for its enforcement, modification or repeal.[59]

GENERAL POWERS

In addition to Congress's war and treaty powers, the legislature, as Louis Henkin points out, has general powers that

enable it to reach virtually where it will in foreign as in domestic affairs, subject only to constitutional prohibitions protecting human rights. The power to tax (Article I, Section 8, Clause 1) has long been a power to regulate through taxation....Major programs depend wholly on the "spending power"...—to "provide for the common Defence and general Welfare of the United States"—and it has been used in our day for billions of dollars in foreign aid.

Other, specialized powers also have their international uses: Congress has authorized a network of international agreements under its postal power (Article I, Section 8, Clause 7), and there are international elements in the regulation of patents and copyrights. The express power to govern territory (Article IV, Section 3) may imply authority to acquire territory, and Congress determines whether territory acquired shall be incorporated into the United States. Congress can exercise "exclusive legislation" in the nation's capital, its diplomatic headquarters (Article I, Section 8, Clause 17). The power to acquire and dispose of property has supported lend-lease and other arms programs and sales or gifts of nuclear reactors or fissionable materials ....By implication in the Constitution's grant of maritime jurisdiction to the federal judiciary (Article III, Section 2), Congress can legislate maritime law.[60] *(See box, Maritime Law: A Matter of Commerce? p. 102.)*

In addition, that the appointment of ambassadors, public ministers, and other diplomatic officers requires the advice and consent of the Senate gives that body a degree of control over foreign relations. The power to appropriate funds for defense, war, and the general execution of foreign policy rests solely with Congress.

In those cases where it has reviewed these powers, the Supreme Court has supported their exercise; for example, regulation of foreign imports through tariffs was upheld in 1928.[61] As early as 1828 the Court endorsed the power to acquire territory through conquest or treaty, and in 1883 it supported the power to acquire territory through discovery.[62] In a series of cases in the early 1900s, the Court left it up to Congress to determine whether to incorporate a territory into the United States.[63] The power of Congress to dispose of federal property was deemed absolute in 1840.[64] *(See "Taxing as Police Power," pp. 147– 154; "The Insular Cases," pp. 185–187; box, Power over Federal Property, p. 186.)* The Court has never invalidated a spending program or appropriation passed for the common defense.

The Power to Admit States, Govern Territories, and Grant Citizenship

The Constitution gives Congress the authority to admit new states, govern territories, and establish uniform rules for naturalization of foreign-born persons as citizens. These three seemingly straightforward grants of power have raised some of the most difficult questions the Supreme Court has ever been asked to answer: Did Congress have the power to prohibit slavery in the territories? Do the residents of territories automatically enjoy the rights and privileges guaranteed by the Constitution? Who qualifies for citizenship in the United States? Can Congress revoke a person's citizenship against his or her will?

NEW STATES

Article IV, section 3, of the Constitution gives Congress the power to admit new states to the Union so long as it does not form a new state by dividing an existing one or by joining parts or all of two or more states without their consent. Five states were formed from land that was originally part of the first thirteen states. In the first four instances—Vermont, Maine, Kentucky, and Tennessee—the ceding states agreed to the division. The fifth state, West Virginia, was formed when the western counties of Virginia that wanted to remain in the Union split away from the rest of the state, which had joined the Confederacy. Residents from the western counties convened a special legislature to approve the split, but Virginia did not formally agree to it until after the Civil War ended. Texas was an independent nation before its admission to the Union in 1845, and California was carved from a region ceded by Mexico in 1848. The remaining thirty states were all territories before being granted statehood.[1]

When the Confederation Congress adopted the Northwest Ordinance of 1787 providing for the eventual transition of the Northwest Territory into states, it was stipulated that these new states would enter the Union on equal footing in all respects with the original states. Later the Constitutional Convention formally rejected insertion of a similar phrase into Article IV, section 3, but the "equal footing" principle, at least as it concerns political standing and sovereignty, remained a valid guide for Congress and the courts. In *Pollard v. Hagan* (1845) the Court declared that the "right of…every…new state to exercise all the powers of government, which belong to and may be exercised by the original states of the Union, must be admitted, and remain unquestioned."[2] "Equality of constitutional right and power is the condition of all the States of the Union, old and new," the Court declared again in 1883.[3] Relying on the equal footing doctrine, Oklahoma challenged a provision in the congressional resolution granting it statehood that required the state's capital to remain at Guthrie for at least seven years. The state legislature moved it to Oklahoma City after only four years. In *Coyle v. Smith* (1911) the Court held that Congress could not place in statehood resolutions restrictions on matters wholly under the state's control. Justice Horace H. Lurton wrote for the Court:

> The power is to admit "new States into this Union." "This Union" was and is a union of States, equal in power, dignity and authority, each competent to exert that residuum of sovereignty not delegated to the United States by the Constitution itself. To maintain otherwise would be to say that the Union, through the power of Congress to admit new States, might come to be a union of States unequal

THE TIDELANDS OIL CONTROVERSY

When oil was discovered off the coasts of California, Texas, and Louisiana, the question of who owned the submerged lands developed into a raging controversy. In the first case, California presumed that it owned the land, so it leased drilling rights to oil companies as early as 1921. The federal government also claimed ownership, so in 1945 it brought an original suit against California in the Supreme Court, asking the Court to prevent California from further exploiting the oil. California argued that the thirteen original coastal states held title to the three-mile strip of sea adjacent to their shores, and because California entered the Union on an equal footing with the original states, it too held title to the three-mile belt off its shore.[1] The federal government contended that it had the right to control the offshore lands because of its responsibility to protect and defend the nation. Moreover, in its exercise of its foreign relations, the federal government asserted that it had a right to make whatever agreements were necessary concerning offshore lands without interference from commitments made by the states.

The Supreme Court found in favor of the federal government in 1947. Writing for the majority, Justice Hugo L. Black denied that the thirteen original states had title to the three-mile ocean zone. On the contrary, he said,

> the idea of a definite three-mile belt in which an adjacent nation can, if it chooses, exercise broad, if not complete dominion, has apparently at last been generally accepted throughout the world.... That the political agencies of this nation both claim and exercise broad dominion and control over our three-mile marginal belt is now a settled fact.... And this assertion of national dominion over the three-mile belt is binding upon this Court.[2]

Even without this acquisition by assertion, Black said, the federal government would control the offshore lands as "a function of national external sovereignty":

The three-mile rule is but a recognition of the necessity that a government next to the sea must be able to protect itself from dangers incident to its location. It must have powers of dominion and regulation in the interest of its revenues, its health, and the security of its people from wars waged on or too near its coasts. And insofar as the nation asserts its rights under international law, whatever of value may be discovered in the seas next to its shores and within its protective belt, will most naturally be appropriated for its use.[3]

The Court in 1950 applied its ruling in the California case to assert federal control over Louisiana's coastal lands.[4] In another 1950 case, the Court denied Texas's claim that because it was an independent and sovereign nation prior to its admission as a state, it had in fact owned the three-mile strip along its shores.[5] The Court acknowledged that this was so, but then added that when Texas came into the Union it did so on an equal footing with the other states and therefore relinquished its claim to the coastal lands.

These rulings became an issue in the 1952 presidential campaign, with the Republicans promising to grant authority over the three-mile zone to the states. In 1953 the Republican-controlled Congress passed the Submerged Lands Act ceding to the states the mineral rights to lands lying offshore between the low tide mark and the states' historic boundaries, which stretched to between three and ten and one-half miles from the shore. Congress's authority to overturn the effect of the Court's 1947 ruling was upheld in 1954.[6]

---

1. *United States v. California,* 332 U.S. 19 (1947).

2. Id. at 33–34.

3. Id. at 35.

4. *United States v. Louisiana,* 339 U.S. 699 (1950).

5. *United States v. Texas,* 339 U.S. 707 (1950).

6. *Alabama v. Texas,* 347 U.S. 272 (1954); see also *United States v. Louisiana,* 363 U.S. 1 (1960).

---

in power, as including States whose powers were restricted only by the Constitution, with others whose powers had been further restricted by an act of Congress accepted as a condition of admission.[4]

In most instances, the equal footing theory has given new states constitutional rights and powers they did not possess as territories. Once, however, it required a new state to relinquish some of its sovereignty. In 1947 the Court held that the ocean bed beneath the three-mile coastal limit along the Atlantic Ocean did

not belong to the original states, but to the federal government, so states subsequently admitted to the Union did not own the ocean soil along their coasts either. *(See box, The Tidelands Oil Controversy, above.)* In 1950 Texas challenged that decision on the grounds that as an independent nation before its admission to the Union it had owned its coastal strip. The Court acknowledged Texas's original sovereignty but ruled that entry into the Union "entailed a relinquishment of some of her sovereignty," including the coastal strip, in

"An overseer doing his duty. Sketched from life near Fredericsburg," 1798, by Benjamin Latrobe. The Court ruled in 1857 that Congress did not have the authority to prohibit slavery in the territories. The decision in *Scott v. Sandford* has been seen over history as a great Court error, reflecting political rather than judicial motivations.

order that the new state be on an equal footing.[5] Justice William O. Douglas for the Court explained:

> The "equal footing" clause [in the statehood resolution] prevents extension of the sovereignty of a State into a domain of political and sovereign power of the United States from which the other States have been excluded, just as it prevents a contraction of sovereignty…which would produce inequality among the states.[6]

The doctrine has been held inapplicable to nonpolitical conditions imposed prior to admission. Before Minnesota became a state, it had agreed not to tax certain lands held by the federal government at the time of admission. Afterward, some of these lands were granted to a railroad that Minnesota sought to tax. The Court sustained the tax restriction agreement, saying that it was unaffected by the equal footing doctrine. "[A] mere agreement in reference to property involves no question of equality of status, but only of the power of a state to deal with the nation…in reference to such property," the Court ruled in 1900.[7]

THE POWER TO GOVERN THE TERRITORIES

There is no express constitutional authority for the federal government to acquire territory, but the authority is implied in some enumerated powers and is inherent in the nation's sovereignty. "The Constitution confers absolutely upon the government of the Union, the powers of making war and of making treaties; consequently, that government possesses the power of acquiring territory, either by conquest or treaty," declared Chief Justice John Marshall in a frequently cited 1828 case.[8] The Court also has held that the nation has an inherent power to acquire territory by discovery.[9] The only specific constitutional grant of power over territories conferred on Congress is contained in Article IV, section 3, clause 2, which authorizes the legislature "to dispose of and make all needful Rules and Regulations respecting the Territory or other Property belonging to the United States." With one important exception, the Court has consistently interpreted this power broadly and upheld its exercise.

Congress, the Court said in 1880, "has full and complete legislative authority over the people of the Territories and all the departments of the territorial governments. It may do for the Territories what the people, under the Constitution of the United States, may do for the States."[10] In 1899 the Court again ruled that Congress had the same full legislative powers over activities within the territories as state legislatures had in the states.[11] The Court also approved Congress's delegation of its legislative powers over local territorial affairs to a territorial legislature elected by citizens.[12]

Slavery in the Territories

The one exception to congressional control was the Court's ruling in *Scott v. Sandford* (1857) that Congress did not have the authority to prohibit slavery in the territories.[13] The decision, which also denied blacks citizenship in the United States, was possibly the Court's greatest strategic error. Instead of resolving the conflict that had divided the nation for decades, as many of the justices participating in the decision apparently had hoped, the ruling contributed to further division of North and South. Four years after the decision, the country plunged into civil war. The *Scott* decision was equally damaging to the Court itself—a "gross abuse of trust," as one eminent historian would describe it.[14] Rightly or wrongly, much of the public believed that the decision had been motivated by narrow political concerns and that the Court had not acted with the judicious dispassion that was expected of the men who were the final interpreters of the nation's laws.

Background

Slavery in the territories did not become an issue until 1819. With support from northern and southern delegates, the Confederation Congress had prohibited slavery in the Northwest Territory when it passed the Northwest Ordinance in 1787.[15] Slavery in the territories became a serious political and constitutional issue when the Missouri Territory applied for statehood in 1819. At the time the nation had eleven free states and eleven slave states. Northerners in the House of Representatives pushed through an amendment to the statehood resolution that would have prohibited slavery in the new state even though many Missourians were slaveholders. The Senate, dominated by southerners, objected to the amendment, claiming that Congress had no constitutional right to impose such a condition on a new state. Ironically, few southerners questioned Congress's right to prohibit slavery in the territories. The stalemate between the two chambers was not resolved until Maine applied for statehood the following year. The Missouri Compromise of 1820 provided for the entry of Maine as a free state and Missouri as a slave state, which maintained the numerical balance. The compromise also prohibited slavery in the remainder of the Louisiana Purchase that lay north of 36° 309′ north latitude, a line that was an extension of Missouri's southern boundary.

A second compromise became necessary when Missouri's constitution was presented to Congress for approval later in 1820. A section of the document barred the entry of free blacks into the new state. Representatives from several northern states that had given free blacks rights of citizenship objected to the provision, claiming it violated the Comity Clause (Article IV, section 2, clause 1) of the Constitution, which gave citizens of one state "all Privileges and Immunities of Citizens in the several States." Southerners, on the other hand, contended that free blacks did not have the same rights as whites—they could not vote in federal elections, for example—and therefore were not citizens under the Constitution. The Constitution, in fact, did not define federal or state citizenship or clearly stipulate whether those persons defined as citizens by one state retained that status when they moved to another state. In the immediate controversy, Congress reached a compromise that essentially barred Missouri from passing any law that would ban the entry of citizens of another state. Although the two Missouri compromises relieved sectional tensions at the time, they did not answer the greater questions of whether Congress had the authority to prohibit slavery in the territories and whether blacks, free or slave, were citizens with all the rights and privileges guaranteed by the Constitution.

With the formal acquisition of Texas in 1846 and the prospect of obtaining more land from Mexico, extension of slavery into the territories again became an issue. The extension of slavery was in reality a thin shield for the real issue of whether slavery could continue to exist at all. Once again, northern representatives proposed to bar slavery in the newly acquired territories. They contended that Congress, under the "Rules and Regulation" Clause of Article IV and under the treaty and war powers, had the power to prohibit slavery in the territories. They also noted that Congress had always exercised this authority. Southern opponents argued that slaves were property and that all the sovereign states owned the territories in common. The federal government, they continued, had no right to act against the interest of the sovereign states by barring their property in slaves from any of the territories. A corollary argument was that abolition of slavery was a violation of the Fifth Amendment's Due Process Clause because it took property without just compensation. The controversy over the western lands was settled in 1850, when Congress produced a three-part compromise. California would enter the Union as a free state, enforcement of the controversial Fugitive Slave Act (requiring citizens to assist in the capture of escaped slaves) would be turned over to the federal government, and the citizens of the newly organized Utah and New Mexico territories would determine whether they would allow slavery at the time those territories became states.

Dred Scott

It was at the beginning of this crisis in 1846 that the slave Dred Scott sought his freedom in the courts. Scott was owned originally by a family named Blow, who in 1833 sold him to an army surgeon, Dr. John Emerson of St. Louis. In 1834 Emerson was transferred to Rock Island, Illinois, and later to Fort Snelling in the Wisconsin Territory, returning to St. Louis near the end of 1838. Scott accompanied Emerson throughout this period. Some time later Emerson died, leaving Scott to his widow, Irene Emerson, who in the mid-1840s moved to New York, depositing Scott into the care of his original owners, the Blows. Opposed to the extension of slavery into the western territories, Henry Blow lent financial support to Scott to test in court whether his residence on free soil in Illinois and the Wisconsin

Territory made him a free man. A lower state court found in favor of Scott, but in 1852 the Missouri Supreme Court reversed the decision, holding that under Missouri law, Scott remained a slave.

The Strader v. Graham Precedent

The Missouri Supreme Court may have relied on an 1851 decision of the U.S. Supreme Court that dealt with the precise question of whether a slave's sojourn in free territory made him a free man if he returned to a slave state.[16] That case was brought by a Kentucky man, Christopher Graham, who owned three slaves. The three were traveling minstrels whom Graham had taken into Ohio to perform. In 1841 the slaves escaped by boat across the Ohio River to Cincinnati, and Graham sued Jacob Strader, the boat's captain. Strader argued that he had done no wrong, because the minstrels were free by virtue of their earlier travels. The Court unanimously dismissed the case for lack of jurisdiction. Wrote Chief Justice Roger B. Taney for the Court,

> Every state has an undoubted right to determine the status, or domestic or social condition, of the persons domiciled within its territory.... There is nothing in the Constitution of the United States that can control the law of Kentucky upon this subject. And the condition of the negroes, therefore, as to freedom or slavery, after their return depended altogether upon the laws of the State, and could not be influenced by the laws of Ohio. It was exclusively in the power of Kentucky to determine for itself whether their employment in another state should or should not make them free on their return. The Court of Appeals have determined, that by the laws of the state they continued to be slaves. And this judgment upon this point is...conclusive upon this court, and we have no jurisdiction over it.[17]

Repeal of the Missouri Compromise

In 1854 the issue of the extension of slavery into the territories flared up once more. Sen. Stephen A. Douglas of Illinois and his supporters wanted to organize the area known as Nebraska into a territory and encourage its settlement to improve the feasibility of building a railroad from Illinois to the Pacific Coast. Under the

Missouri Compromise, Congress had barred the introduction of slavery into the Nebraska area, but to secure southern support in Congress for his project, Douglas wrote a bill that repealed the 1820 compromise on slavery and substituted for it popular or squatters' sovereignty, which allowed newly organized territories to decide for themselves whether they would allow slavery. Antislavery members of Congress were outraged by the proposal, but with pressure from the executive branch, the bill was passed. It led to growing extremism on both sides and to a civil war in Kansas in 1856 between supporters of the proslavery government at Shawnee, which was regarded by the federal government as legitimate, and the antislavery government at Topeka.

A Matter for the Court

During these years more and more people began to look to the Supreme Court for a solution to the slavery question. Historian Carl B. Swisher wrote of the period that despite skepticism about entrusting a final decision to the courts,

> the belief was growing [that] there might be some point in turning to the judiciary in the hope that it could resolve a conflict which Congress was unable to settle. Many Southerners hoped and expected that the judiciary would decide their way and perhaps give a security which politics could not provide. Many Northerners hoped the courts could in some way find a pattern of rightness not too different from the pattern of their own beliefs.[18]

A court settlement of the issue was clearly what those around Dred Scott were seeking. In 1854 Irene Emerson arranged for the sale of Scott to her brother, John F. A. Sanford (misspelled in the court records as Sandford), and Scott's attorney brought suit for his freedom in the federal circuit court for Missouri. Suits may be brought in federal court by a citizen of one state against a citizen of another, so Scott's first task was to show that he was a citizen of Missouri. The circuit court held that Scott, as a black slave, was not a citizen of Missouri and therefore did not have the right to bring suit in federal court. Scott appealed to the Supreme Court. Faced with a civil war in Kansas over the precise issue of slavery in the territories, a Congress increasingly less able to find a political solution, and mounting demands for some final judicial solution, the Court agreed to accept the case. The Court first heard arguments in February 1856, but then decided to have the case reargued later in the year, because the justices disagreed on a number of the issues presented, and because they feared that their disagreement would be used for political ends in the upcoming presidential campaign, adding to the controversy rather than quieting it.

Although the circumstances of *Strader v. Graham* and *Scott* were not identical, most historians agree that the Court could have dismissed Scott's suit on the same reasoning that it employed in *Strader v. Graham*—that it was up to Missouri to determine whether Scott was a slave or free and the Court had no authority to interfere with that decision. After the case was reargued, seven of the nine justices were prepared to restrict themselves to this narrow judgment, and Justice Samuel Nelson was assigned to write the opinion. The two dissenters—Justices John McLean, a Republican from Ohio, and Benjamin R. Curtis, a Whig from Massachusetts—announced that their dissents would cover all the issues: whether Scott was a citizen, whether his stay on free soil made him a free man, and whether Congress had the authority to prohibit slavery in the territories. Unwilling to let the dissents go unanswered, each of the seven majority justices decided to write an opinion answering those issues he thought to be in question. Several were anxious to address the territorial question, partly out of personal belief, partly because they thought a decision might help resolve the dilemma, and partly because they thought the public expected the Court to address the issue. Several northern papers already had chided the Court for an opinion that they assumed would favor the South. Such an assumption was not unreasonable in those days of intense regional feeling because five of the nine justices were from the South.

James Buchanan, the newly elected president, also put some pressure on the Court to decide the territorial slavery issue. In letters to Justices John Catron and Robert C. Grier, Buchanan urged the Court to take up the issue so that at his inauguration he might say, as he finally did, that the issue was "a judicial question, which legitimately belongs to the Supreme Court…before whom it is now pending and will, it is understood, be speedily and finally settled. To their decision, in common with all good citizens, I shall cheerfully submit, whatever that may be."[19]

Taney's Opinion

The Court announced its decision on March 6, 1857, two days after Buchanan's inauguration. By a 7-2 vote, the Court ruled against Scott. Of the seven opinions written by members of the majority, Chief Justice Taney's is considered to present the formal view of the Court. Taney first dealt with the issue of whether Dred Scott, or any slave or descendant of slaves, could be a citizen under the Constitution. In Taney's words: "they are not, and that they are not included, and were not intended to be included, under the word 'citizens' in the Constitution, and can, therefore, claim none of the rights and privileges which that instrument provides for and secures to citizens of the United States."[20] Taney drew this conclusion from an examination of historical practices and the intent of the framers of the Constitution. Slaves, he said,

> had for more than a century before [the Constitution was ratified] been regarded as being of an inferior order, and altogether unfit to associate with the white race, either in social or political relations; and so far inferior, that they had no rights which the white man was bound to respect; and that the negro might justly and lawfully be reduced to slavery for his benefit.…This opinion was at that time fixed and universal in the civilized portion of the white race.[21]

Even the words "all men are created equal" in the Declaration of Independence did not encompass the black race. The authors of that declaration, Taney said,

> perfectly understood the meaning of the language they used, and how it would be understood by others; and they knew that it would not in any part of the civilized world, be supposed to embrace the negro race, which, by common consent, had been excluded from civilized Governments and the family of nations, and doomed to slavery.[22]

Taney also touched on the question of whether a person declared a citizen by one state was automatically a citizen of the United States, concluding that this was not so since the Constitution gave the federal government exclusive control over naturalization. With regard to whether other states were bound to recognize as citizens those granted citizenship by a single state, Taney wrote,

> Each state may still confer [citizenship rights] upon an alien, or anyone it thinks proper…; yet he would not be a citizen in the sense in which the word is used in the Constitution…nor entitled to sue as such in one of its courts, nor to the privileges and immunities of a citizen in the other States.[23]

Taney also used an examination of pre–Revolutionary War laws in the states to show that slaves, far from being citizens, were actually considered property:

> The unhappy black race were separated from the whites by indelible marks, and laws long before established, and were never thought of or spoken of except as property, and when the claims of the owner or the profit of the trader was supposed to need protection.[24]

That slaves were considered property was reflected in the only two provisions of the Constitution that specifically mentioned them, he continued. These provisions, Taney said, "treat them as property, and makes it the duty of the government to protect it; no other power, in relation to this race, is to be found in the Constitution."[25] Taney might have ended the matter there—declaring that because Scott was not a citizen under the meaning of the Constitution, he could not bring suit in federal court—but the chief justice felt it necessary to discuss whether Scott's residence in the Wisconsin Territory made him a free man. In this way he was able to reach the question of whether Congress had the constitutional authority to bar slavery in the states or territories.

Taney first declared that Congress did not have that power under Article IV, section 2, of the Constitution. This language, he said, allowed Congress to make rules and regulations only for the territories held at the time the Constitution was ratified. "It applied only to the property which the States held in common at that time and has no

DRED SCOTT REVERSED: THE FOURTEENTH AMENDMENT

It took a constitutional amendment to overturn the Supreme Court's ruling in *Scott v. Sandford* (1857) that blacks were not and could not be citizens under the Constitution.[1] Congress in early 1865 passed the Thirteenth Amendment abolishing slavery. It was ratified toward the end of the year, but hopes that its adoption would encourage the southern states to protect the civil rights of their former black slaves went unrealized. In fact, the southern states passed so-called black codes, which contained harsh vagrancy laws and sterner criminal penalties for blacks than for whites and established racially segregated schools and other public facilities. Fearing that these actions indicated that the southern states were unchastened by the war and that the Thirteenth Amendment would prove a hollow promise, Republicans, both radical and moderate, began to push for stronger guarantees of black rights. To secure political dominance in the South, the Radical Republicans also wanted to ensure that blacks had the right to vote and to keep former prominent Confederates out of state and federal office.

To these ends, the Republican-controlled Congress passed the Freedmen's Bureau Act and the Civil Rights Act of 1866. Both sought to protect basic rights, and the latter attempted to void by legislation the Supreme Court's denial of citizenship to blacks. The Civil Rights Act, however, was passed over President Andrew Johnson's veto, and its constitutionality was doubtful. Republicans therefore looked to the enactment of a constitutional amendment. In April of 1866 the Joint Committee on Reconstruction reported what would become the Fourteenth Amendment. With few changes, the five-part piece of legislation was submitted to the states for ratification in June 1866.

The third and fourth sections of the amendment were of only temporary significance. They barred from state or federal office anyone who had participated in rebellion after having previously taken an oath to support the U.S. Constitution—though dispensation by Congress was possible—and denied the responsibility of federal or state governments for debts incurred in aid of rebellion. The second section of the amendment in effect eliminated the clause of Article I, section 2, of the Constitution directing that only three-fifths of the slave population of a state be counted in apportioning the House of Representatives. This section also provided that if any state abridged the right of its citizens to vote for federal or state officers, the number of its representatives in the House would be reduced in proportion to the numbers denied the vote. In addition to ensuring blacks the right to vote, this language was intended to dilute the

strength of the southern states and Democrats in Congress. It did not, however, specifically give blacks the right to vote, because moderate Republicans feared that such an outright grant might jeopardize ratification of the amendment in those northern states that still restricted black voting rights. As a result, the southern states ignored this section of the amendment, and its inadequacy quickly led to adoption of the Fifteenth Amendment in 1870. *(See details of Fifteenth Amendment, p. 203.)*

The first section of the Fourteenth Amendment directly overruled the *Scott* decision by declaring that all persons born or naturalized in the United States and subject to its jurisdiction are citizens of the United States and the state in which they live. It also prohibited the states from making any law that abridged the privileges and immunities of citizens of the United States, deprived any person of life, liberty, or property without due process of law, or denied anyone equal protection of the laws.

The original sponsor of this section, Rep. John A. Bingham, R-Ohio, intended it not only to protect the civil rights of blacks, but also to override *Barron v. Baltimore* (1833), which held that the first eight amendments of the Bill of Rights protected individual rights only from infringement by the federal government, not by state governments.[2] Bingham intended that the Fourteenth Amendment protect these rights from infringement by the states. The final wording of the section, however, was a prohibition on the states and not a positive grant to Congress to protect civil rights against state encroachment, so the Court initially limited Congress's authority to enforce these protections against state infringement. Not until *Gitlow v. New York* (1925) would the Court begin to apply the Fourteenth Amendment to secure the guarantees of the Bill of Rights against state action.[3]

The Court was to frustrate the authors of the Fourteenth Amendment even further by applying the rights guarantees intended for persons to businesses instead. This interpretation of the Fourteenth Amendment's Due Process Clause was not abandoned until the New Deal era. After World War II the Court ruled that the Equal Protection Clause prohibited racial segregation in schools, and almost one hundred years after its ratification, the Court upheld federal civil rights legislation based in part on the Fourteenth Amendment.

---

1. *Scott v. Sandford,* 19 How. (60 U.S.) 393 (1857).

2. *Barron v. Baltimore,* 7 Pet. (32 U.S.) 243 (1833).

3. *Gitlow v. New York* 268 U.S. 652 (1925).

reference whatever to any territory or other property which the new sovereignty might afterwards itself acquire."[26] Taney acknowledged that the federal government had the power to acquire new territory for preparation for statehood and that Congress could in its discretion determine the form of government the territory would have. Congress must, however, exercise that power over territories within the confines prescribed by the Constitution. Congress, Taney said,

> has no power of any kind beyond [the Constitution]; and it cannot, when it enters a territory of the United States, put off its character, and assume discretionary or despotic powers which the Constitution has denied to it. It cannot create for itself a new character separated from the citizens of the United States, and the duties it owes them under the provisions of the Constitution.[27]

Among those duties was the obligation to protect property, Taney said. Noting that the Fifth Amendment provided that no persons should be deprived of life, liberty, or property without due process of law, Taney concluded that

> an Act of Congress, which deprives a citizen…of his liberty or property, merely because he came himself or brought his property into a particular Territory of the United States, and who had committed no offense against the laws, could hardly be dignified with the name of due process of law.[28]

Therefore, Taney contended, the portion of the Missouri Compromise that prohibited slavery in the northern portion of the Louisiana Purchase was void, and Dred Scott had not been freed by his residence there. Scott's residence in Illinois was also rejected as ground for a claim to freedom. Using the reasoning in *Strader v. Graham*, Taney said that because

> Scott was a slave when taken into the State of Illinois by his owner, and was there held as such, and brought back in that character, his status, as free or slave depended on the laws of Missouri, and not of Illinois.[29]

Justices Grier and James M. Wayne for the most part concurred with Taney's opinion. Justice Nelson submitted the original opinion he had written for the Court, dismissing the case on the basis of the ruling in *Strader v. Graham*. Justices Catron, Peter V. Daniel, and John A. Campbell, using different reasoning, all agreed that Congress had no authority to prohibit slavery in the territories. The dissenters, McLean and Curtis, also filed lengthy opinions, setting out their opposition to the majority. But it was Taney's opinion that, in historian Bruce Catton's words, "reverberated across the land like a thunderclap."[30]

Northern papers were quick to criticize the decision and the Court. For example, the Washington correspondent for the *New York Tribune* wrote on March 7, 1857, "If the action of the Court in this case has been atrocious, the manner of it has been no better. The Court has rushed into politics, voluntarily and without other purpose than to subserve the cause of slavery."[31] Northern abolitionists particularly excoriated Taney's statement that blacks were so inferior to whites "that they had no rights which the white man was bound to respect." Taney had said this, but in the context that this was the general belief at the time the Constitution was written and with the caveat that the accuracy or inaccuracy of the belief was not a question before the Court. As Taney biographer Carl B. Swisher has noted, the "phrase was torn from its context by critics of the decision and published as a statement by Taney that the Negro had no rights which the white man was bound to respect. The error found its way into the history of the period, was repeated in the classrooms of the country and persists to the present day."[32]

Legal scholars and constitutional historians generally agree that Taney's opinion was questionable in several respects. He made no mention either that Congress had been prohibiting slavery in territories for seventy years or that Missouri courts had accorded citizenship rights to several blacks considered citizens by other states. By the modern canons of judicial restraint, Taney erred grievously. He decided on the constitutionality of a federal law when it was not strictly necessary to do so. His opinion applied the law more broadly than was required by the facts of the case, and the Court could have observed the rule that no matter how grave the constitutional questions, the Court will try to put a construction on a federal law that will make it valid. *(See "Judicial Restraint," pp. 50–65.)* It also seems apparent that the justices allowed their political persuasions to influence their decisions. According to constitutional historian Edward S. Corwin, "When…the student finds six judges arriving at precisely the same result by three distinct processes of reasoning, he is naturally disposed to surmise that the result may possibly have induced the processes rather than that the processes compelled the result." [33]

What was the significance of *Scott?* Rather than dampening the controversy over slavery, the ruling fueled it, perhaps hastening the onset of civil war. The finding that blacks, both slave and free, were not and could not be citizens under the Constitution led to the adoption of the Fourteenth Amendment, which itself would play a complicated role in the development of constitutional law. *(See box, Dred Scott Reversed: The Fourteenth Amendment, p. 183.)* Certainly, one of the case's greatest impacts was on the Court's reputation. A contemporary editorial in the *North American Review* of October 1857 stated:

> The country will feel the consequences of the decision more deeply and more permanently in the loss of confidence in the sound judicial integrity and strictly legal character of their tribunals, than in anything beside; and this, perhaps, may well be accounted the greatest political calamity which this country, under our forms of government, could sustain. [34]

The Insular Cases

Because the territory acquired in the early decades of the nation's history was intended for eventual statehood, questions of imperialism and colonization over foreign peoples did not arise. With the acquisition of Hawaii, Puerto Rico, Guam, and the Philippines in 1898, the likelihood of statehood was not assumed, and the ensuing debate over U.S. imperialism raised a difficult question: Did the constitutional rights and guarantees afforded residents of the United States extend to residents of these new territories? In other words, did the Constitution follow the flag? The Court discussed the issue in a number of cases known as the *Insular Cases* in the early 1900s before reaching a final conclusion. [35]

Not a Foreign Country

In the first case, the collector for New York's port continued to collect duties on sugar imported from Puerto Rico after it was annexed, as if it were still a foreign nation. Contending that the island was no longer a foreign country, the sugar owners sued for return of the paid duties. The Court, by a 5-4 vote, held in *DeLima v. Bidwell* (1901) that Puerto Rico had ceased to be a foreign country so far as the tariff laws were concerned and that the duties had been illegally collected. [36] The controlling precedent, wrote Justice Henry B. Brown, was the decision in *Cross v. Harrison* (1853), in which the Court recognized that California had lost its status as a foreign country as soon as ratification of the annexation treaty was officially announced in the new territory. [37] Although that opinion did not directly involve the issue at hand in *DeLima*, Brown said, "it is impossible to escape the logical inference from that case that goods carried from San Francisco to New York after the ratification of the treaty would not be considered as imported from a foreign country." [38]

Not the United States

Although Puerto Rico was not a foreign country so far as tariffs were concerned, it was also not part of the United States, said a majority of the Court in a second case decided the same day as *DeLima*. *Downes v. Bidwell* (1901) upheld a provision of the Foraker Act of 1900 that established special import duties for Puerto Rican goods. [39] The New York port collector imposed the duty on a shipment of oranges, and the owners sued, citing the constitutional stricture that all duties must be uniform throughout the United States. In another 5-4 division, the Court ruled against the orange owners. The majority could not, however, agree on its reasons. In the official opinion of the Court, Justice Brown held that the Constitution applied only to the states and that it was up to Congress to decide if it wished to extend it to the territories. In passing the Foraker Act, Congress had clearly stated its decision not to extend the Constitution to Puerto Rico, Brown said. Thus the duties were not required to be uniform and were therefore legal.

POWER OVER FEDERAL PROPERTY

In addition to granting Congress power over territories, Article IV, section 3, clause 2, gives Congress the power "to dispose of and make all needful Rules and Regulations respecting . . . other Property belonging to the United States." The power to dispose of public property is considered absolute by the Supreme Court. In 1840 the Court rejected a contention that acknowledged Congress's authority to sell federal land but denied that it had the same authority to lease it. "The disposal must be left to the discretion of Congress," the Court asserted.[1]

The authority over disposal of federal property was expanded in 1913, when the Court held that the federal government could sell or lease any excess hydroelectric power it might generate in the process of improving the navigability of a stream.[2] In 1936 the Court held that because the construction of a federal dam created the energy from which electric power could be generated, the government had the authority to generate and sell the power.[3] Congressional authority to make rules and regulations for federally owned property is also absolute and may be delegated to the executive branch.[4] States may not tax federal lands within their boundaries nor may they take actions that interfere with the federal power to regulate federal lands.[5]

In the late 1970s, sixty members of the House of Representatives attempted to use this grant of power as the basis for which to carve out for themselves a role in the ratification of the treaty ceding the Panama Canal and the Canal Zone to Panama. They argued that because the land in question was owned by the United States, the consent of the House, as well as the Senate, was required for its disposal. Their efforts proved futile. The U.S. Court of Appeals for the District of Columbia ruled that the Senate's constitutional power to ratify treaties included the power to dispose of U.S. property.[6]

---

1. *United States v. Gratiot*, 14 Pet. (39 U.S.) 526 at 538 (1840).

2. *United States v. Chandler-Dunbar Water Co.*, 229 U.S. 53 (1913).

3. *Ashwander v. Tennessee Valley Authority*, 297 U.S. 288 (1936).

4. See, for example, *United States v. Fitzgerald*, 15 Pet. (40 U.S.) 407 at 421 (1841); *Sioux Tribe v. United States*, 316 U.S. 317 (1942).

5. *Van Brocklin v. Tennessee*, 117 U.S. 151 (1886); *Gibson v. Chouteau*, 13 Wall. (80 U.S.) 92 (1872); *Irvine v. Marshall*, 20 How. (61 U.S.) 558 (1858); *Emblem v. Lincoln Land Co.*, 184 U.S. 660 (1902).

6. *Edwards v. Carter*, 436 U.S. 907 (cert. denied, 1978).

In a concurring opinion, Justice Edward D. White, joined by Justices George Shiras Jr. and Joseph McKenna, put forth for the first time the theory that the Constitution fully applied only to residents in territories that had been formally "incorporated" into the United States either through ratified treaty or an act of Congress. In his opinion White envisioned a series of awful consequences that could ensue if the Constitution was automatically extended to acquired territory. He imagined discovery of an unknown island "peopled with an uncivilized race," yet desirable for commercial and strategic purposes. Automatic application of the Constitution could "inflict grave detriment on the United States from the immediate bestowal of citizenship on those absolutely unfit to receive it," White wrote.[40] He also imagined a war in which the United States would occupy enemy territory. "Would

not the war be fraught with danger if the effect of occupation was to necessarily incorporate an alien and hostile people into the United States?" he asked.[41] Once a treaty containing incorporation provisions is ratified by Congress, the full range of constitutional rights would be effective in the territory, White said. He added, however,

> where a treaty contains no conditions for incorporation, and, above all, where it expressly provides to the contrary, incorporation does not arise until in the wisdom of Congress it is deemed that the acquired territory has reached that state where it is proper that it should enter into and form a part of the American family.[42]

Dissenting, Justice John Marshall Harlan argued that the Constitution must follow the flag:

> In my opinion, Congress has no existence and can exercise no authority outside of the Constitution.

Still less is it true that Congress can deal with new territories just as other nations have done or may do with their new territories. This nation is under the control of a written constitution, the supreme law of the land and the only source of the powers which our Government, or any branch or officer of it, may exert at any time or at any place. The idea that this country may acquire territories anywhere upon the earth, by conquest or treaty, and hold them as mere colonies or provinces—the people inhabiting them to enjoy only such rights as Congress chooses to accord to them—is wholly inconsistent with the spirit and genius as well as the words of the Constitution.[43]

Two years later, White again offered his incorporation theory in a concurring opinion. A Hawaiian named Osaki Mankichi had been convicted of manslaughter by a nonunanimous jury during the period after the annexation of Hawaii in 1898 but before its incorporation into the United States in 1900. The annexation act had specified that Hawaiian laws not contrary to the Constitution would apply until such time as the islands were incorporated. Conviction by less than a unanimous jury, legal under Hawaiian law, was challenged as a violation of the Fifth and Sixth Amendments of the Constitution. The majority opinion, written by Brown, contended that although the annexation act said so, Congress had not really intended to provide the guarantees of the Fifth and Sixth Amendments to Hawaiians. To do so would have required the release of everyone convicted of crimes by nonunanimous juries after the annexation. "Surely such a result could not have been within the contemplation of Congress," Brown said.[44] White agreed with Brown's result but reasoned that because the islands were not incorporated at the time of Mankichi's trial, the guarantees of the Fifth and Sixth Amendments did not extend to him. For the four dissenters, Chief Justice Melville W. Fuller wrote, "The language [of the annexation act] is plain and unambiguous and to resort to construction or interpretation is absolutely uncalled for. To tamper with words is to eliminate them."[45]

Incorporation Theory Prevails

A few months later, a majority of the Court subscribed for the first time to White's incorporation doctrine. *Dorr v. United States* (1904) involved circumstances similar to the *Mankichi* case. The question was whether a criminal trial in the Philippines, held without indictment and heard by a jury of fewer than twelve persons, was a violation of the defendant's rights under the Constitution. It was not, held the Court. Justice William R. Day's majority opinion offered a succinct statement approving the incorporation doctrine:

> That the United States may have territory, which is not incorporated into the United States as a body politic, we think was recognized by the framers of the Constitution in enacting the Article [IV] already considered, giving power over the territories, and is sanctioned by the opinions of the Justices concurring in the judgment in *Downes v. Bidwell.*

> Until Congress shall see fit to incorporate territory ceded by treaty in the United States, we regard it as settled by that decision that the territory is to be governed under the power existing in Congress to make laws for such territories and subject to such constitutional restrictions upon the powers of the body as are applicable to the situation.[46]

The incorporation doctrine was reinforced when the Court in 1905 voided trial by six-person juries in Alaska on the grounds that Alaska had been largely incorporated into the United States.[47] In 1911 eight justices—Harlan continued to dissent—agreed that since Congress had not incorporated the Philippines, criminal trials did not require twelve-member juries.[48] The incorporation theory remained into the 1970s the rule for determining when constitutional rights and guarantees are extended to territorial residents.

CITIZENSHIP AND NATURALIZATION

"Citizenship," declared Chief Justice Earl Warren, "*is* man's basic right for it is nothing less than the right to have rights. Remove this priceless possession and there remains a stateless person, disgraced and

EMINENT DOMAIN: AN INHERENT POWER

"The right of eminent domain, that is, the right to take private property for public uses, appertains to every independent government," said the Supreme Court in 1879. "It requires no constitutional recognition; it is an attribute of sovereignty."[1] Evidence that the framers of the Constitution believed the federal government to possess this power is found in the clauses of the Fifth Amendment that prohibit the taking of private property without due process of law and payment of just compensation. An attempt to extend these Fifth Amendment guarantees to the taking of private land by the states failed when the Supreme Court in 1833 held that the first eight amendments to the Constitution protected rights only against infringement by the federal government, not by state governments.[2]

The Fourteenth Amendment, ratified in 1868, prohibits the states from depriving a person of property without due process of the law, but it makes no mention of just compensation. At first the Court interpreted this omission to mean that the states did not have to make compensation.[3] But in 1897 the Court reversed itself, holding that a state had not provided due process of law if it had not made just compensation: "The mere form of the proceeding instituted against the owner . . . cannot convert the process used into due process of law, if the necessary result be to deprive him of his property without compensation."[4]

PUBLIC USE

By virtue of their authority to review eminent domain cases, the courts are the final arbiters of what uses of private land may be considered public. The Supreme Court traditionally has given great weight to the federal legislature's designation of what constitutes a public use, even suggesting in 1946 that the Court might not have the authority to review a congressional determination of public use. "We think that it is the function of Congress to decide what type of taking is for a public use and that the agency authorized to do the taking may do so to the full extent of its statutory authority," the Court observed.[5]

Public uses include lands used for public buildings, highways, and parks and for preserving sites of historical interest, such as battlefields. In 1954 the Court upheld the right of Congress to use its power of eminent domain to facilitate slum clearance, urban renewal, and the construction of public housing, even though only a small portion of the public would be eligible to live in the housing.[6] In addition to exercising the eminent domain power itself, Congress may delegate it "to private corporations to be exercised by them in the execution of works in which the public is interested," such as railroad and utility companies.[7]

In 2005 the Court provoked outrage across the nation when it affirmed this broad view of the government's power to seize property for "public use." In this case, it was the houses of Susette Kelo and several of her neighbors in New London, Connecticut. They had steadfastly refused the city's offers to buy their property to make way for a riverside redevelopment project. City officials hoped to bring new jobs and additional tax revenue by luring a new pharmaceutical plant to the area, along with a hotel, restaurants, and a pedestrian "riverwalk." But Kelo wanted to stay in her house, and she went to court arguing that city-sponsored private development did not amount to "public use."

She lost when the Supreme Court, by a 5-4 vote, affirmed its "longstanding policy of deference to legislative judgment in this field."[8] The city's plan "unquestionably serves a public purpose," Justice John Paul Stevens said, and "we decline to second-guess the city's considered judgment" that it will succeed in revitalizing the downtown area. Stevens also said he saw "no principled way" of distinguishing this development project from past rulings that allowed the seizing of land for railroads, mines, and shopping districts. Justices Anthony Kennedy, David Souter, Ruth Bader Ginsburg, and Stephen Breyer joined him.

In dissent, Justice Sandra Day O'Connor warned that "all private property is now vulnerable to being taken" by the government and transferred to a private owner who can pay more in taxes for it. Chief Justice William H. Rehnquist and Justices Antonin Scalia and Clarence Thomas joined her. In the wake of the ruling, several states changed their

---

degraded in the eyes of his countrymen."[49] Although the Constitution refers to "citizens" in several instances, nowhere does the main body of the document define who is a citizen and how one acquires citizenship. The prevailing assumption was that a citizen was a person who was born in the country and who remained under its jurisdiction and protection. This definition, followed in England and known as *jus soli*, was in contrast to the common practice of *jus sanguines* in the rest of Europe, where citizenship was determined by parental nationality. In the 1857 *Scott* decision, the Supreme Court adopted an extremely

laws to limit the use of "eminent domain" by state agencies and local governments.

JUST COMPENSATION

The general standard set by the Court for determining whether the compensation paid is adequate is the amount a willing buyer would pay to a willing seller in the open market.[9] That amount may be adjusted to account for various contingencies. For example, the compensation may be reduced if the owner receives a benefit from the taking of the property greater than the benefit to the public at large.[10] In those instances in which the government has infringed on a person's property without actually taking it—for example, where noise from a nearby airport makes land unfit for the uses its owners intended—the Court has established another general rule: "Property is taken in the constitutional sense when inroads are made upon an owner's use of it to an extent that, as between private parties, a servitude [subjecting the property owned by one person to the use of another] has been acquired either by agreement or in the course of time."[11] In some cases, the Court has held that federal or state regulations prohibiting the use of property for certain purposes in order to protect the public welfare are exercises of the police power and not the taking of property under the eminent domain power, which would require compensation. In 1962 the Court wrote,

> A prohibition simply upon the use of property for purposes that are declared, by valid legislation, to be injurious to the health, morals or safety of the community, cannot, in any just sense, be deemed a taking or appropriation of property for the public benefit. Such legislation does not disturb the owner in the control or use of his property for lawful purposes, nor restrict his right to dispose of it, but is only a declaration by the State that its use by one, for certain forbidden purposes, is prejudicial to the public interests.[12]

In times of war or emergency, the Court has held that government actions destroying property or preventing its use for the purposes intended did not constitute a taking entitling the owners to compensation.[13] In the latter years of the twentieth century, the Court increased the level of scrutiny

it applies to cases based on this requirement of just compensation. It rejected a state plan that made a landowner's building permit contingent upon his allowing the public access across his private beachfront property.[14] Unless that permit requirement substantially advanced a legitimate state interest, the state must pay just compensation for the easement, said the Court. Several years later, the Court held that municipal governments must show a connection and a rough proportionality between conditions imposed on landowners with development permits and the claimed public harm from the development.[15] In 2002, however, the Court ruled that a development moratorium that prevents landowners from building on their property for months, or even a few years, does not deprive them of all use of the land and therefore does not entitle them to compensation.[16]

1. *Brown Co. v. Patterson,* 98 U.S. 403 at 405 (1879).

2. *Barron v. Baltimore,* 7 Pet. (32 U.S.) 243 (1833).

3. *Davidson v. City of New Orleans,* 96 U.S. 97 (1878).

4. *Chicago, Burlington & Quincy Railroad Co. v. City of Chicago,* 166 U.S. 226 at 236–237 (1897).

5. *U.S. ex rel. Tennessee Valley Authority v. Welch,* 327 U.S. 546 at 551–552 (1946).

6. *Berman v. Parker,* 348 U.S. 26 (1954).

7. *Boom Co. v. Patterson,* 98 U.S. 403 at 405 (1879); see also *Noble v. Oklahoma City,* 297 U.S. 481 (1936); *Luxton v. North River Bridge Co.,* 153 U.S. 525 (1894).

8. *Kelo v. New London,* 545 U.S. 469 (2005).

9. *United States v. Miller,* 317 U.S. 369 at 374 (1943); *United States ex rel. Tennessee Valley Authority v. Powelson,* 319 U.S. 266 at 275 (1943).

10. *Bauman v. Ross,* 167 U.S. 648 (1897).

11. *United States v. Dickinson,* 331 U.S. 745 at 748 (1947).

12. *Goldblatt v. Town of Hempstead,* 369 U.S. 590 at 593 (1962).

13. *United States v. Caltex,* 344 U.S. 149 (1952); *United States v. Central Eureka Mining Co.,* 357 U.S. 155 (1958); *National Board of YMCA v. United States,* 395 U.S. 85 (1969).

14. *Nollan v. California Coastal Commission,* 483 U.S. 825 (1987).

15. *Dolan v. City of Tigard,* 512 U.S. 374 (1994).

16. *Tahoe-Sierra Preservation Council v. Tahoe Regional Planning Agency,* 535 U.S. 302 (2002).

narrow definition of citizenship that stood for less than a dozen years. Not only did the Court exclude blacks, even native-born free blacks, from citizenship, it also held that national citizenship was dependent on and resulted from state citizenship. Chief Justice Roger B. Taney wrote,

> [E]very person, and every class and description of persons who were at the time of the adoption of the Constitution recognized as citizens in the several States, became also citizens of this new political body; but none other; it was formed by them, and for them and their posterity but for no one else.[50]

This ruling led ultimately to the post–Civil War Fourteenth Amendment, ratified in 1868. Its first sentence states, "All persons born or naturalized in the United States and subject to the jurisdiction thereof, are citizens of the United States and of the State wherein they reside." *(See details of Scott, p. 180; box, Dred Scott Reversed: The Fourteenth Amendment, p. 183.)* Designed primarily to confer citizenship on blacks, the Fourteenth Amendment made the concept of *jus soli* the law of the land. This concept was confirmed and further defined in the case of *United States v. Wong Kim Ark* (1898) in which the Supreme Court declared that—under the Fourteenth Amendment— children born in the United States to resident alien parents were citizens even if their parents were barred from becoming citizens. The Court wrote,

> The Fourteenth Amendment affirms the ancient and fundamental rule of citizenship by birth within the territory, in the allegiance and under the protection of the country, including all children here born of resident aliens, with the exceptions or qualifications…of children of foreign sovereigns or their ministers, or born on public ships, or of enemies within and during hostile occupation of part of our territory, and with the single additional exception of children of members of the Indian tribes owing direct allegiance to their several tribes.[51]

This last exception was eliminated in 1925, when Congress granted citizenship to Indians living in tribes.

Naturalization

Wong Kim Ark's parents could not become citizens because Congress, under its power "to establish a uniform rule of naturalization," in 1882 specifically prohibited citizenship by naturalization to Chinese. The Court has allowed Congress to establish whatever conditions it deems necessary for citizenship through naturalization. "Naturalization is a privilege, to be given, qualified or withheld as Congress may determine and which the alien may claim as of right only upon compliance with the terms which Congress imposes," the Court said in *United States v. Macintosh* (1931). In this case, the Court was upholding denial of naturalization to a pacifist who wanted to qualify his oath of allegiance by refusing to

support war unless he believed it morally justified.[52] The Court has held that Congress may exclude an entire class or race of people from eligibility for citizenship and may expel aliens from the country. Upholding a statute expelling Chinese laborers from the country if they did not obtain a required residence certificate within a specified time the Court wrote,

> The right of a nation to expel or deport foreigners, who have not been naturalized or taken any steps toward becoming citizens…is as absolute and unqualified as the right to prohibit and prevent their entrance into the country. . . .
>   . . . The power to exclude or expel aliens, being a power affecting international relations, is vested in the political departments of the government, and it is to be regulated by treaty or by act of Congress, and to be executed by the executive authority according to the regulations so established.[53]

Exclusions

After ratification of the Fourteenth Amendment, Congress enacted laws limiting naturalized citizenship to whites and to blacks of African descent. Citizenship was extended to the residents of some, but not all, of the U.S. territories. The residents of Hawaii became citizens in 1900, those of Puerto Rico in 1917, and those of the Virgin Islands in 1927. The residents of the Philippines were denied citizenship throughout the period that the United States held the islands as a trust territory. Other Asians did not fare any better in winning citizenship through naturalization. The final barriers were not removed until passage of the 1952 Immigration and Nationality Act, which barred the use of race as a reason for denying citizenship.

Other conditions set by Congress have excluded from naturalization anarchists, members of the Communist Party, and others who advocate the violent overthrow of the government. To qualify for naturalization, an alien must have been a resident of the country for five years and be of "good moral character." The latter phrase has been interpreted to exclude drunks, adulterers, polygamists, gamblers, convicted felons, and homosexuals. The Court has generally sustained these exclusions.[54] One exclusion that the Court disapproved was for conscientious objectors who refused to swear an oath of allegiance requiring them to bear arms. Initially, the Court agreed that this exclusion was valid. In one extreme case, the Court denied citizenship to a fifty-year-old female pacifist who would not have been required to bear arms in any event.[55] This ruling and two others like it were specifically overturned in *Girouard v. United States* (1946).

James Louis Girouard was a Seventh-day Adventist who refused to swear he would bear arms but said he would serve in a noncombatant position. In a ruling based entirely on its interpretation of the law, not the Constitution, the majority said it could not believe that Congress meant to deny citizenship in a country traditionally protective of religious freedom to those who objected to war on religious grounds.[56] Four years later, the Court ruled that citizenship could be granted to a pacifist who refused to serve in the army even as a noncombatant.[57] In 1952 Congress formally took notice of the 1946 and 1950 rulings by allowing naturalization of conscientious objectors so long as they agreed to perform approved alternative service.

Denaturalization

As early as 1824 the Supreme Court, speaking through Chief Justice John Marshall, declared that there was no difference between a naturalized citizen and one who was native born. A naturalized citizen, wrote Marshall,

> becomes a member of the society, possessing all rights of the native citizens, and standing, in the view of the constitution, on the footing of a native. The constitution does not authorize Congress to enlarge or abridge those rights. The simple power of the national Legislature is to prescribe a uniform rule of naturalization, and the exercise of its power exhausts it, so far as respects the individual.[58]

Aside from not being qualified to run for the presidency, naturalized citizens enjoy the same rights, privileges, and responsibilities as do native-born citizens. The exception is that naturalized citizens may be denaturalized.

Fraud. The Court has repeatedly held that a naturalized citizen may lose his or her citizenship if it was obtained fraudulently. "An alien has no moral or constitutional rights to retain the privileges of citizenship" won through fraud, the Court said in 1912.[59] The Court also has ruled that the lapse of time between naturalization and the time when the fraud is discovered is of no significance. In one case, the Court sustained deprivation of naturalization for a man who claimed to be in real estate when in fact he was a bootlegger. The fact that more than twenty-five years had lapsed between his naturalization and discovery of his fraud made no difference, although the Court subsequently barred his deportation.[60]

Bad Faith. Naturalization also may be lost if it was obtained in bad faith. In *Luria v. United States* (1913) the Court upheld denaturalization of a man who apparently never intended to become a permanent resident of the United States at the time he was naturalized. The decision upheld an act of Congress that made residence in a foreign country within five years of naturalization prima facie evidence of bad faith.[61] In the 1940s, however, the Court established a rule that a naturalized citizen could not be denaturalized unless the government could demonstrate by "clear, unequivocal and convincing" evidence that the citizenship had been fraudulently obtained. In *Schneiderman v. United States* (1943) the government sought William Schneiderman's denaturalization on the grounds that he had been a member of a communist organization five years prior to and at the time of his naturalization in 1927. The Court acknowledged the existence of a statute that foreclosed naturalization to those who advocated the violent overthrow of the government but said that the government had not proved sufficiently whether the organizations Schneiderman belonged to advocated such violence in a manner that was a clear and present public danger or merely in a doctrinal manner that put forward overthrow of the government simply for consideration and discussion.[62]

It was not until *Knauer v. United States* (1946) that the Court assented to the denaturalization of a person under the *Schneiderman* rule. Finding clear evidence that Paul Knauer, a naturalized citizen, was a Nazi before, at the time of, and after his naturalization, the Court said that "when an alien takes

THE CONSTITUTION ON CITIZENSHIP

The Constitution contains few specific references to citizens and citizenship. The body of the Constitution states only that the president, senators, and representatives must be citizens, that citizens of each state shall enjoy the privileges and immunities of all other states, and that citizens may bring certain suits in federal court. The latter was modified by the Eleventh Amendment. Not until ratification of the Fourteenth Amendment in 1868 was language added defining eligibility for citizenship. The Constitution does not specifically restrict the right to vote to citizens, but citizens are the only people whose right to vote is constitutionally protected. Following are the passages in the Constitution that refer to citizens:

Article I, Section 2. No Person shall be a Representative who shall not have … been seven Years a Citizen of the United States.

Article I, Section 3. No Person shall be a Senator who shall not have … been nine Years a Citizen of the United States.

Article II, Section 1. No Person except a natural born Citizen, or a Citizen of the United States, at the time of the Adoption of this Constitution, shall be eligible to the Office of President.

Article III, Section 2. The judicial Power shall extend to all Cases … between a State and Citizen of another State;*—between Citizens of different States;—between Citizens of the same State claiming Lands under Grants of different States, and between a State, or the Citizens thereof, and foreign States, Citizens or Subjects.*

Article IV, Section 2. The Citizens of each State shall be entitled to all Privileges and Immunities of Citizens in the several States.

Amendment XI. The Judicial power of the United States shall not be construed to extend to any suit in law or equity, commenced or prosecuted against one of the United States by Citizens of another State, or by Citizens or Subjects of any Foreign State.

Amendment XIV, Section 2. All persons born or naturalized in the United States and subject to the jurisdiction thereof, are citizens of the United States and of the State wherein they reside. No State shall make or enforce any law which shall abridge the privileges and immunities of citizens of the United States.

Amendment XIV, Section 2. Representatives shall be apportioned among the several States according to their respective numbers, counting the whole number of persons in each State, excluding Indians not taxed. But when the right to vote at any election for the choice of electors for President and Vice President of the United States, Representatives in Congress, the Executive and Judicial officers of a State, or the members of the Legislature thereof, is denied to any of the male inhabitants of such State, being twenty-one years of age, and citizens of the United States, or in any way abridged, except for participation in rebellion, or other crime, the basis of representation therein shall be reduced in the proportion which the number of such male citizens shall bear to the whole number of male citizens twenty-one years of age in such State.

Amendment XV, Section 1. The right of citizens of the United States to vote shall not be denied or abridged by the United States or by any State on account of race, color, or previous condition of servitude.

Amendment XIX. The right of citizens of the United States to vote shall not be denied or abridged by the United States or by any State on account of sex.

Amendment XXIV, Section 1. The right of citizens of the United States to vote in any primary or other election for President or Vice President, for electors for President or Vice President, or for Senators or Representative in Congress, shall not be denied or abridged by the United States or any State by reason of failure to pay any poll tax or other tax.

Amendment XXVI, Section 1. The right of citizens of the United States, who are eighteen years of age or older, to vote shall not be denied or abridged by the United States or by any State on account of age.

---

* These phrases were modified by the Eleventh Amendment.

the oath with reservation or does not in good faith forswear loyalty and allegiance to the old country, the decree of naturalization is obtained by deceit." [63] In a dissenting opinion that was eventually to gain the support of a slim majority of the Court, Justice Wiley B. Rutledge, joined by Justice Frank Murphy, said he did not believe that a naturalized citizen could be stripped of his citizenship in such a case. "My concern is not for Paul Knauer," Rutledge said.

"But if one man's citizenship can thus be taken away, so can that of any other.... [A]ny process which takes away their [naturalized] citizenship for causes or by procedures not applicable to native born citizens places them in a separate and an inferior class." [64] Rutledge said he did not believe such a difference was contemplated by the framers when they gave Congress the power to establish uniform naturalization rules.

Eighteen years after *Knauer v. United States,* Rutledge's dissent became the majority position in *Schneider v. Rusk* (1964).[65] The case tested the validity of a provision of the 1952 immigration law that revoked the citizenship of any naturalized citizen who subsequently resided in his or her native land for three continuous years. Angelika Schneider, born in Germany, came to the United States as a child and acquired derivative citizenship when her parents were naturalized. As an adult she returned to Germany, married a German national, and visited the United States only twice in eight years. Her case came to the Court after she was denied a U.S. passport on the grounds that she had lived in Germany for three continuous years. By a 5-3 vote the Court struck down the 1952 provision allowing revocation of Schneider's citizenship. Echoing Justices Rutledge and Murphy, and Chief Justice John Marshall before them, Justice William O. Douglas stated, "We start from the premise that the rights of citizenship of the native born and of the naturalized person are of the same dignity and are coextensive."[66] The 1952 provision, Douglas continued, "proceeds on the impermissible assumption that the naturalized citizens as a class are less reliable and bear less allegiance to this country than do the native born. This is an assumption that is impossible for us to make....The discrimination aimed at naturalized citizens drastically limits their rights to live and work abroad in a way that other citizens may."[67]

Expatriation

The *Knauer* and *Schneider* decisions set out the arguments in a continuing debate over whether Congress has the power to revoke the citizenship of any citizen, whether naturalized or native born. That citizens may voluntarily expatriate themselves has never been questioned. The Court also has held that Congress may stipulate the voluntary performance of certain acts as being the equivalent of voluntary expatriation. In 1915 the Court upheld a provision of the Citizenship Act of 1907 by which any female citizen who married an alien surrendered her citizenship in the United States.[68] That provision was repealed in 1922, but in 1950 the Court ruled that a woman who had voluntarily sworn allegiance to Italy in order to marry an Italian citizen had,

in essence, forsworn her allegiance to the United States and effectively renounced her citizenship in the United States.[69]

The Immigration and Nationality Act of 1952 contained a long list of circumstances under which a citizen would lose his or her citizenship. These included voting in a foreign election, being convicted for desertion during time of war and being discharged from the armed services, and leaving or remaining outside the country to avoid military service. The question was whether the performance of any of these actions amounted to voluntary renunciation of citizenship. If it did not, then their validity turned on whether Congress had the power to revoke citizenship.

Foreign Elections

In the first case to deal fully with this question—*Perez v. Brownell* (1958)—a divided Court upheld the provision revoking citizenship of a person who voted in a foreign election.[70] The majority held that Congress could revoke citizenship as a necessary and proper means of exercising its other powers. In this case the Court viewed this provision as enacted pursuant to Congress's implied power over foreign affairs. Justice Felix Frankfurter said the Court could not deny Congress the authority to regulate conduct of Americans—such as voting in foreign elections—that might prove embarrassing or even jeopardize the conduct of foreign relations. Frankfurter also rejected the argument that the Fourteenth Amendment denied Congress the power to revoke citizenship: "[T]here is nothing in the terms, the context, the history or the manifest purpose of the Fourteenth Amendment to warrant drawing from it a restriction upon the power otherwise possessed by Congress to withdraw citizenship."[71] Chief Justice Earl Warren dissented:

> The Government is without the power to take citizenship away from a native-born or lawfully naturalized American. The Fourteenth Amendment recognizes that this priceless right is immune from the exercise of governmental powers. If the Government determines that certain conduct by United States citizens should be prohibited because of anticipated injurious consequences to the conduct of foreign affairs or to

some other legitimate governmental interest, it may within the limits of the Constitution proscribe such activity and assess appropriate punishment. But every exercise of governmental power must find its source in the Constitution. The power to denationalize is not within the letter or the spirit of the powers with which our Government was endowed. The citizen may elect to renounce his citizenship, and under some circumstances he may be found to have abandoned his status by voluntarily performing acts that compromise his undivided allegiance to his country. The mere act of voting in a foreign election, however, without regard to the circumstances attending the participation, is not sufficient to show a voluntary abandonment of citizenship. The record in this case does not disclose any of the circumstances under which this petitioner voted. We know only the bare fact that he cast a ballot. The basic right of American citizenship has been too dearly won to be so lightly lost.[72]

Desertion

The same day the Court handed down its decision in *Perez,* it invalidated the provision of the immigration law that revoked citizenship for persons convicted for desertion and discharged from the armed services. In *Trop v. Dulles* (1958) five justices agreed that the provision was unconstitutional, but only four agreed on one line of reasoning. For them, Warren again stated the belief that Congress did not have the power to revoke citizenship. Moreover, he said, revocation of citizenship in this instance was a violation of the Eighth Amendment's proscription against cruel and unusual punishment. This punishment was more cruel than torture, Warren said, for it was "the total destruction of the individual's status in organized society."[73] Justice William J. Brennan Jr. agreed with the outcome but not with Warren's reasoning. He admitted that his support of the majority in the *Perez* case was paradoxical judged against his position in *Trop,* but, he said, revocation of citizenship for voting in a foreign election was within the authority of Congress under its powers to regulate foreign affairs. In the *Trop* case, revocation for desertion went beyond any legitimate means of regulation in exercise of the power to raise and maintain

armies, he said. The four dissenters maintained the position they had espoused in the majority opinion in *Perez.*

Draft Evasion

Five years after *Perez* and *Trop,* in *Kennedy v. Mendoza-Martinez* (1963), the Court struck down the provisions of the immigration act that revoked the citizenship of anyone who left or remained outside the country to evade military service. The sections were invalid, the Court said, "because in them Congress has plainly employed the sanction of deprivation of nationality as a punishment…without affording the procedural safeguards guaranteed by the Fifth and Sixth Amendments."[74] Deciding the case on these grounds made it unnecessary for the Court to choose between the powers of Congress and the rights of citizenship.

Foreign Elections Again

In 1967 the Court, again divided 5-4, made the choice between Congress's powers and the right to citizenship, declaring the government powerless to revoke citizenship. The case of *Afroyim v. Rusk* (1967) turned on the same issue involved in *Perez.*[75] Polish-born Beys Afroyim was a naturalized U.S. citizen who in 1951 voluntarily voted in an Israeli election. He was denied renewal of his passport for that reason. Urging the Court to review its decisions in *Perez,* Afroyim maintained that he could lose his U.S. citizenship only through voluntary renunciation. Following the *Perez* precedent, the lower courts ruled that Congress, through its implied power over foreign affairs, could revoke the citizenship of Americans voting in foreign elections. Overturning *Perez,* the majority rejected the idea

> that, aside from the Fourteenth Amendment, Congress has any general power, express or implied, to take away an American citizen's citizenship without his assent.…In our country the people are sovereign and the government cannot sever its relationship to the people by taking away their citizenship.[76]

Congress also did not have the power to revoke citizenship based on the Citizenship Clause of the Fourteenth Amendment. That clause, the majority said,

Control of Aliens

The congressional power over aliens is absolute and derives from the fact of the nation's sovereignty. This power was recognized by the Supreme Court in 1889 as it upheld an act of Congress barring entry of Chinese aliens into the country:

> That the government of the United States, through the action of the legislative department, can exclude aliens from its territory is a proposition which we do not think open to controversy. Jurisdiction over its own territory to that extent is an incident of every independent nation. It is a part of its independence. If it could not exclude aliens, it would be to that extent subject to the control of another power.... The United States, in their relation to foreign countries and their subjects or citizens, are one nation, invested with powers which belong to independent nations, the exercise of which can be invoked for the maintenance of its absolute independence and security throughout its entire territory.[1]

Under this authority, Congress has barred entry to convicts, prostitutes, epileptics, anarchists, and professional beggars. It has excluded people because of their race and established national origin quotas. The authority also empowers Congress to regulate to a large extent the conduct of aliens in the country and to provide that aliens convicted of certain crimes be deported. The Supreme Court has, however, held that aliens involved in deportation proceedings are entitled to certain constitutional rights, including bail and procedural due process protections and protection against self-incrimination, unreasonable searches and seizures, cruel and unusual punishment, and ex post facto laws and bills of attainder.[2] Nevertheless, the Court did uphold a provision of the Internal Security Act of 1950 that authorized the attorney general to jail without bail aliens who were members of the Communist Party pending decision on whether they would be deported.[3]

The Court in 2001 ruled that the Immigration and Naturalization Service (whose services and functions were transitioned into the Bureau of Citizenship and Immigration Services in 2003) cannot indefinitely detain an alien who has been ordered removed if it cannot find a country to which to send the individual. Instead, the alien is entitled, under normal circumstances, to release six months after a final removal order.[4] In 2003 the Court cited the cold war decision above as precedent for upholding part of a 1996 immigration reform act requiring federal officials to arrest and hold for deportation aliens who have a criminal record even if they are not dangerous or a flight risk. "In the exercise of its broad power over naturalization and immigration, Congress regularly makes rules [for aliens] that would be unacceptable if applied to citizens," wrote Chief Justice William H. Rehnquist.[5]

---

1. *Chae Chan Ping v. United States (Chinese Exclusion Case)*, 130 U.S. 581 at 603–604 (1889). See also *Fong Yue Ting v. United States,* 149 U.S. 698 (1893); *Lem Moon Sing v. United States,* 158 U.S. 538 (1895); *Harisiades v. Shaughnessy,* 342 U.S. 580 (1952); *Shaughnessy v. United States ex rel Mezei,* 345 U.S. 206 (1953).

2. *Kimm v. Rosenberg,* 363 U.S. 405 (1960); *Abel v. United States,* 362 U.S. 217 (1960); *Marcello v. Bonds,* 349 U.S. 302 (1955); *Carlson v. Landon,* 342 U.S. 524 (1952); *Wong Yang Sung v. McGrath,* 339 U.S. 33 (1950).

3. *Carlson v. Landon,* 342 U.S. 524 (1952).

4. *Zadvydas v. Davis,* 533 U.S. 678 (2001).

5. *Carlson v. Landon,* 342 U.S. 524 (1952); *Demore v. Kim,* 538 U.S. 510 (2003).

---

provides its own constitutional rule in language calculated completely to control the status of citizenship: "All persons born or naturalized in the United States...are citizens of the United States ...." There is no indication in these words of a fleeting citizenship, good at the moment it is acquired but subject to destruction by the government at any time.[77]

In a footnote the majority made an exception for those who obtained their naturalization through fraud. The four dissenters—Justices Harlan, Tom C. Clark, Potter Stewart, and Byron D. White—held to the reasoning of the majority in the *Perez* case. "The Citizenship Clause...neither denies nor provides to Congress any power of expatriation," wrote Justice Harlan. He continued:

> Once obtained, citizenship is of course protected from arbitrary withdrawal by the constraints placed around the Congress' powers by the Constitution; it is not proper to create from the Citizenship Clause an additional, and entirely unwarranted, restriction upon legislative authority. The construction now placed on the Citizenship Clause rests, in the last analysis, simply on the Court's *ipse dixit*, evincing little more, it is quite apparent, than the present majority's own distaste for the expatriation power.[78]

DISTRICT OF COLUMBIA

The power "to exercise exclusive Legislation in all Cases whatsoever, over the Seat of Government of the United States" has been interpreted to mean that Congress may make the laws and appoint the administrators of the District of Columbia or delegate the lawmaking powers to a locally elected government. The local government was partially elected from 1802, when the District was established, until 1874, when Congress, in the wake of financial scandals involving city officials, substituted a presidentially appointed commission to administer it under laws passed by Congress. In 1967 this form of government was changed to a presidentially appointed mayor and city council. In 1973 Congress once again turned over administration of the capital city to a locally elected government, although it retained a tight rein on the city's financial affairs and its judicial system and may enact laws for the District at any time. The reality of that power came home to residents of the District in 1995, when Congress responded to the District's precarious financial state by appointing a financial control board with broad powers to oversee the actions of the city's political leaders.

Residents of the District, although citizens of the United States entitled to all constitutional guarantees, were unable to vote for president until the Twenty-third Amendment was ratified in 1961. Congress in 1970 authorized the District to elect one nonvoting delegate to the House of Representatives. In 1978 Congress approved a proposed constitutional amendment to give District residents a voting representative in the House, but the proposal expired in 1985 after only sixteen states approved it. More recently, Congress has considered legislation to give District residents a voting representative in the House, but opponents have insisted this shortcut would be unconstitutional.

Nonresidence

Decided by such a narrow vote, the *Afroyim* decision was not considered a definitive answer to the question of congressional power to expatriate citizens. The case of *Rogers v. Bellei* (1971) clouded the issue of citizenship even further.[79] Aldo Mario Bellei was born overseas, in 1939, of one American parent and one alien parent. The 1953 immigration law stated that a person of such parentage would be considered a citizen of the United States so long as he or she lived in the United States for five continuous years between the ages of fourteen and twenty-eight. Bellei only visited the United States briefly on five occasions. Because he did not meet the residence requirement, his citizenship was revoked. He challenged the requirement, but by a 5-4 vote the Court upheld the provision.

Writing for the majority, Justice Harry A. Blackmun maintained that Bellei did not qualify for U.S. citizenship under the Fourteenth Amendment. Bellei "was not born in the United States. And he has not been subject to the jurisdiction of the United States," said Blackmun. "All this being so, it seems indisputable that the first sentence of the Fourteenth Amendment has no application to plaintiff Bellei. He simply is not a Fourteenth-Amendment-first-sentence citizen."[80] The decision in *Afroyim*, Blackmun continued, was based on the fact that Afroyim was a citizen by virtue of the Fourteenth Amendment, but Bellei was a citizen by an act of Congress, and if Congress may impose conditions that such a person must meet before he can become a citizen, Blackmun said, the majority could see no constitutional reason why it could not impose conditions that must be met after he became a citizen:

> Our National Legislature indulged the foreign-born child with presumptive citizenship subject to subsequent satisfaction of the reasonable residence requirement, rather than to deny him citizenship outright, as concededly it had the power to do, and relegate the child, if he desired American citizenship, to the more arduous requirements of the usual naturalization process. The plaintiff here would force the Congress to choose between unconditional conferment of United States citizenship at birth and deferment of citizenship until a condition precedent is fulfilled. We are not convinced that the Constitution requires so rigid a choice.[81]

The minority held that the *Afroyim* decision controlled this case and that Congress could not revoke Bellei's citizenship. In an unusually bitter dissent, Justice Hugo L. Black wrote,

Congress could not, until today, consistent with the Fourteenth Amendment enact a law stripping an American of his citizenship which he has never voluntarily renounced or given up. Now the Court, by a vote of five to four through a simple change in its composition, overturns the decision....This precious Fourteenth Amendment American citizenship should not be blown around by every passing political wind that changes the composition of this Court. I dissent.[82]

Congress repealed the residence requirement in 1978.

★

The Power to Amend the Constitution

Only a few times in U.S. history has the Supreme Court been asked to resolve questions concerning the power of Congress to propose amendments to the Constitution. More of the Court's rulings in this area have focused on the power of Congress to enforce the guarantees of new amendments. Several of the twenty-seven amendments to the Constitution, primarily those conferring a political right, such as voting, empower Congress to enforce them through legislation. The three Civil War Amendments, providing citizenship and political rights to blacks, were the first to include such enforcement provisions. The Court of the 1870s and 1880s, however, severely weakened Congress's power to execute these guarantees, ruling that Congress could regulate state discrimination only after it had occurred and could not reach private discrimination at all. It was almost one hundred years before the Court, playing a leading part in the civil rights revolution of the 1950s and 1960s, reversed this posture, sustaining a broad enforcement role for Congress.

THE AMENDING POWER

Article V of the Constitution states, "The Congress, whenever two thirds of both Houses shall deem it necessary, shall propose Amendments to this Constitution, or, on the Application of the Legislatures of two thirds of the several States, shall call a Convention for proposing Amendments, which, in either Case, shall be valid to all Intents and Purposes, as Part of this Constitution, when ratified by the Legislatures of three fourths of the several States, or by Conventions in three fourths thereof, as the one or the other Mode of Ratification may be proposed by the Congress." Since 1789, thousands of proposed amendments to the Constitution have been introduced in Congress.[1] Most of them are duplicate proposals, and some have been introduced repeatedly in successive Congresses. Only thirty-three amendments have been submitted to the states for ratification: twenty-seven have been ratified, four are still pending, and two were not ratified within the period Congress set for their approval.[2] The four pending amendments include one relating to apportionment of the House, which was originally introduced in 1789 by James Madison along with the ten that became the Bill of Rights. The two amendments that were not ratified and died were the equal rights amendment and a proposal to give the District of Columbia voting representation in Congress.

There has not yet been a constitutional convention called to propose an amendment. All of the thirty-three amendments submitted so far were approved by a two-thirds vote of Congress. By the mid-1990s thirty-two states had petitioned Congress for an amendment requiring that the federal budget be balanced, and nineteen had petitioned for an amendment outlawing abortion. Earlier, in the years immediately following the Supreme Court's ruling in *Reynolds v. Sims* (1964),[3] thirty-three states—one short of the necessary two-thirds required to call a convention—had petitioned Congress for an amendment allowing one chamber of a state legislature to be apportioned on the basis of geographic or political subdivisions, rather than strictly by population. The Supreme Court has tended to view constitutional amendments as political decisions and therefore has been reluctant to interfere in the process. Nevertheless, the Court has heard several cases challenging the constitutionality of ratified amendments and has handed down a number of decisions relating to amendment procedures.

Constitutional Challenges

The first challenge to a constitutional amendment came in 1798, after ratification of the Eleventh Amendment, which prohibited the citizens of one state from suing another state in federal court without the latter state's consent. The question before the Court was what effect did ratification of the amendment have on such suits pending at the time of ratification? To apply the amendment to pending suits, said petitioners, would give it the unconstitutional character of an ex post facto law. In *Hollingsworth v. Virginia* (1798) the Court ruled that once the amendment took effect upon ratification, the Court had no jurisdiction to hear any case of the type described by the amendment—including those still pending. The Court dismissed the case.[4]

The constitutional amendment prohibiting the manufacture, sale, and transportation of alcoholic beverages enjoyed only a brief life, but it engendered more Supreme Court cases testing a statute's validity than any other amendment. Most of these cases involved challenges to the way the Eighteenth Amendment was ratified, but in one case the Court was asked to decide whether liquor was a proper subject for a constitutional amendment. The Court in 1920 ruled that it was.[5] The Nineteenth Amendment, granting the vote to women, was challenged on the grounds that it made such a large addition to the electorate of the few states that had refused to ratify it that it undercut their political autonomy. The Supreme Court held that the Nineteenth Amendment affected the electorate no more than the Fifteenth Amendment did in forbidding voting discrimination on the basis of race, color, or previous condition of servitude.[6] The Court observed at the time that the latter amendment had been considered valid and enforced by the judiciary for a half-century.

Federal Ratification Procedures

The president is not required to sign and cannot block a congressional resolution proposing a constitutional amendment to the states. "The negative of the President applies only to the ordinary cases of legislation: He has nothing to do with the proposition, or adoption of amendments to the Constitution," wrote Justice Samuel

Chase in 1798.[7] The Court also has ruled that the two-thirds requirement for adoption of a proposed constitutional amendment applies to two-thirds of those members present and voting and not to two-thirds of the entire membership.[8] Whether a constitutional amendment has to be ratified within a certain time period is unclear. Congress first added a time limit in 1917, when it required that the prohibition amendment be ratified within seven years of its submission to the states. That requirement was contested in *Dillon v. Gloss* (1921).[9] The Court rejected the challenge, stating that "the fair inference or implication from Article V is that the ratification must be within some reasonable time after the proposal" and that Congress's power to set a time limit was "an incident of its power to designate the mode of ratification."[10] Only in the late 1930s did the Court hear a case on what constituted a reasonable time period for ratification. Such a determination, the Court said in *Coleman v. Miller* (1939), was a political question for Congress, not the Court, to decide.[11]

Four justices in a concurring opinion called into question the Court's finding in *Dillon v. Gloss* that ratification should occur within a reasonable time period. Because Congress has exclusive power over the amending process, they wrote, it "cannot be bound by and is under no duty to accept the pronouncements upon that exclusive power by this Court....Therefore any judicial expression...is a mere admonition to the Congress in the nature of an advisory opinion, given wholly without constitutional authority."[12] Although six amendments have been added to the Constitution since this 1939 decision, the Court has not since heard any cases concerning Article V. Time for ratification was an issue concerning the proposed equal rights amendment, but the matter was rendered moot before the Court could address it.

State Ratification Procedures

The Court has repeatedly held that ratification of constitutional amendments by a state must be accomplished either through the state legislature or by a state convention and that Congress has the sole authority to determine which method will be used for

EXTENSION AND RESCISSION

Does Congress have power to extend the deadline for ratification of a proposed constitutional amendment? Opponents of the equal rights amendment (ERA) posed that question in their challenge to a thirty-nine-month extension that was approved by Congress in October 1978. The proposed amendment, which would give men and women equal rights under the law, originally provided seven years for ratification, with an expiration date of March 22, 1979. The 1978 extension moved the deadline to June 29, 1982. At the time Congress passed the extension, thirty-five states had ratified the amendment, so three more states were needed for the ERA to become the Twenty-seventh Amendment.

Debate on the extension centered on its constitutionality, an issue that the Supreme Court had never considered. In *Dillon v. Gloss* (1921) the Court had ruled that Congress has the authority to set a reasonable time period in which the states must ratify a proposed constitutional amendment.[1] In *Coleman v. Miller* (1939) the Court had held that the question of what constitutes a reasonable time period was a nonjusticiable political matter for Congress to determine.[2] A corollary issue

concerning ERA ratification was whether states that had ratified the amendment could subsequently rescind ratification. As of July 1979, four states—Idaho, Nebraska, South Dakota, and Tennessee—had done just that. In *Coleman* the Court had written that the matter "should be regarded as a political question pertaining to the political departments, with the ultimate authority in the Congress in the exercise of its control over the promulgation of the adoption of the amendment."[3]

In 1981 a federal judge in Idaho ruled that Congress had exceeded its power in extending the ERA ratification deadline and that states could rescind their approval of the amendment if they acted during the ratification period. Early in 1982 the Supreme Court agreed to hear an appeal on these rulings, but after the ratification period expired on June 30, the Court dismissed the case as moot, leaving the issues unresolved.

---

1. *Dillon v. Gloss*, 256 U.S. 368 (1921).

2. *Coleman v. Miller*, 307 U.S. 433 (1939).

3. Id. at 450.

---

each amendment submitted to the states.[13] In 1920 the Court ruled that a provision of the Ohio Constitution requiring a popular referendum to approve its legislature's ratification of the Eighteenth Amendment was in violation of the U.S. Constitution.[14] In another case, the Court held that state-required procedures that barred two state legislatures from ratifying the Nineteenth Amendment were in conflict with the U.S. Constitution.[15] In both cases the Court held that "the function of a state legislature in ratifying a proposed Amendment to the Federal Constitution, like the function of Congress in proposing the Amendment, is a federal function, derived from the Federal Constitution; and it transcends any limitations sought to be imposed by the people of a state."[16]

The Court has indicated that whether a state may rescind its ratification of a constitutional amendment is a political question for Congress. Tennessee challenged the women's suffrage amendment on the grounds that it was counted as ratifying the

Nineteenth Amendment despite the fact that its legislature had subsequently rescinded the ratification. Basing its decision on narrow procedural grounds, the Court in 1922 held that official notice of the ratification to the secretary of state was conclusive upon him and that his certification of ratification was binding on the courts.[17] In a similar case, *Coleman v. Miller* (1939), when asked whether a state legislature that had first rejected an amendment could reverse itself and ratify it, the Court said the issue was one that only Congress could address.[18] *(See box, Extension and Rescission, above.)* The answers Congress has given to such questions have not been consistent. At the direction of Congress, the secretary of state counted the ratifications of the Fourteenth Amendment by Ohio, New Jersey, and Oregon despite votes by the three state legislatures to withdraw ratification. The secretary of state apparently, however, accepted North Dakota's rescission of its ratification of the Twenty-fifth Amendment.[19]

IT'S NEVER TOO LATE: THE RATIFICATION OF THE 27TH AMENDMENT

The Twenty-seventh Amendment took the modern Congress and many constitutional experts by surprise when it was ratified on May 7, 1992—that is, 203 years after it was first proposed. The Madison Amendment, named after its original sponsor, prohibits midterm pay raises for members of Congress. The new constitutional provision states: "No law varying the compensation for the services of the Senators and Representatives shall take effect, until an election of Representatives shall have intervened." This is the language that James Madison drafted in 1789, when this measure was first sent to the states as part of a package of twelve proposed amendments. Ten of them became the Bill of Rights, but the pay raise amendment was ratified by only six states between 1789 and 1792. It languished until 1873, when Ohio affirmed it. The other amendment in the original package related to apportionment of the House and was never ratified.

The Madison Amendment was again revived in the late 1970s, with thirty-three states approving it between 1978 and 1992, as the steady pace of congressional pay raises fueled public criticism. The final drive for ratification began in August 1991, when thirty-five members of the House of Representatives introduced a resolution calling on state legislatures to reexamine the amendment. The state of Michigan pushed it over the required three-quarters threshold on May 7, 1992. The Twenty-seventh Amendment was officially certified by the U.S. archivist on May 18, printed in the *Federal Register* on May 19, and at that time effectively became part of the Constitution.

Most modern proposed amendments are sent to the states with a deadline for ratification, but the Madison Amendment and the eleven others sent to the states in 1789 had no deadlines. Contemporary supporters of the amendment argued that the extensive gaps between state ratifications did not invalidate the proposal. In *Coleman v. Miller* (1939) the Court had concluded that questions of timeliness are political in nature, not within the jurisdiction of the courts. It therefore falls to Congress to determine whether the time span between introduction and ratification of a particular amendment is too long.[1]

---

1. *Coleman v. Miller,* 307 U.S. 433 (1939).

ENFORCING CIVIL RIGHTS

After the Civil War, the Reconstruction Congress established for itself a new constitutional power: the authority to enforce civil rights, including voting rights. Before 1861 the states alone decided who was a citizen and what rights were due such residents. Popular perception aside, the Bill of Rights put limits only on the power of Congress and the national government. It did not give persons in Georgia, New York, or Ohio, for example, the right to free speech or freedom of religion if state officials were determined to limit expression or worship. The Supreme Court had earlier confirmed that the Bill of Rights was intended only to limit Congress's power, and the *Scott v. Sandford* (1857) decision declared that Congress had no power to extend the rights of citizenship to free blacks.[20] *(See "Dred Scott," p. 180.)*

President Abraham Lincoln in his Gettysburg Address said that a Union victory in the war between the states would bring forth a "new birth of freedom." In 1866, after Lincoln's assassination, the northern Republicans in Congress took up Lincoln's torch. Responding to reports from the South that blacks were being subjected to violence and intimidation, they wrote the first national civil rights law to protect the newly freed slaves. Mississippi and several other Confederates states enacted "Black Codes" that denied the freedmen basic rights.

The Thirteenth Amendment, ratified in December 1865, abolished slavery and states that "Congress shall have the power to enforce this article by appropriate legislation." A few weeks later, Sen. Lyman Trumbull of Illinois introduced his civil rights bill to "give effect to that declaration [in the Thirteenth Amendment] that all persons in the United States should be free...and to secure to all persons practical freedom."[21] It further asserted that "all persons...of every race and color...shall have the same right...to make and enforce contracts, to sue...to inherit, purchase, leases and sell, hold and convey real and personal property and to full and equal benefit of all laws." A second provision gave federal judges the jurisdiction to enforce these rights.

In the House, Iowa representative James F. Wilson, the floor manager of the bill, noted the significance of this debate for Congress. "The possession of these rights by the citizen raises by necessary implication the power in Congress to protect them," he said.[22] That remained in some doubt, however, as critics of the bill questioned whether Congress indeed had authority over such traditional state law matters as work contracts or real estate sales. The Reconstruction era was a unique moment in U.S. history. Respect for the states and their rights—especially the rebellious states of the Confederacy—had reached a low ebb among the so-called Radical Republicans, who would draft the Fourteenth Amendment, the most important amendment to the Constitution: "All persons born or naturalized in the United States…are citizens of the United States and of the State wherein they reside," it began. "No State shall make or enforce any law which shall abridge the privileges or immunities of citizens of the United States; nor shall any State deprive any person of life, liberty or property, without due process of law; nor deny to any person within its jurisdiction the equal protection of the laws." Section 5, the final clause, states, "The Congress shall have the power to enforce by appropriate legislation, the provisions of this article." The Fourteenth Amendment was ratified in 1868 and was followed in short order by the Fifteenth Amendment, which was ratified in 1870 and provided that the right to vote "shall not be denied or abridged…on account of race, color or previous condition of servitude." It too allowed that Congress may enforce its provision by law.

Legal historian Robert J. Kaczorowski argues that the framers of the Reconstruction amendments saw them as "constitutionally revolutionary." The original Constitution and Bill of Rights had put many limits on Congress's power in the belief that the personal freedoms of Americans could be protected by limiting the reach of the national government. By contrast, the northern Republicans empowered the government in Washington in the belief that the nation must protect the freedom of U.S. citizens, particularly when the states could not be trusted with the task. "These amendments delegated to Congress the authority to render a radical change in the role of the national government in American life," Kaczorowski notes.[23]

Protecting "the fundamental rights of citizens" was now the duty of federal lawmakers and federal judges. "The Civil War experience provided powerful ideological, almost religious, reinforcement" for this shift in thinking, contends law professor Akhil Amar. "The war had taken a terrible toll in lives and limbs, and even victory tasted bittersweet. Republicans in 1866 need[ed] to convince their constituents that all had not been in vain, that the noble goals of the Union had been worth the fight and had been won."[24] The legal debate over the Reconstruction amendments began almost immediately. Clearly, the national government had new authority to protect the rights of its citizens, but what were those rights? Did Congress have the authority to define or shape the rights of Americans or was that power entirely with the states?

The Fourteenth Amendment was something of a compromise. Rep. John Bingham, R-Ohio, had drafted a version giving Congress the authority to write laws protecting individual rights and liberties. The final version, however, prohibits states from adopting laws that "deprive any person" of liberty, a change that would loom large. Nonetheless, the Republicans achieved their main goal in the Fourteenth Amendment, said historian Eric Foner: It "clothed with constitutional authority the principle Radicals had fought a lonely battle to vindicate: equality before the law, overseen by the national government."[25]

The Court and the Reach of the Fourteenth Amendment

The Supreme Court, which had stripped freed blacks of all rights before the Civil War, wasted little time after the war making the new civil rights power of Congress all but meaningless. The first blow came in the so-called *Slaughterhouse Cases* (1873). The dispute arose when butchers from New Orleans contested a state-created monopoly for a local slaughterhouse. Rather than deciding the issue narrowly, the Court took the occasion to pronounce that the Fourteenth Amendment did not enlarge the civil rights power of the federal government. The phrase "privileges and immunities of citizens of the United States" referred to those rights already protected by the federal government, such as the right to travel on the high seas, the Court said in its 5-4 decision. The amendment was not intended to add "any additional protection," such as the rights to freedom of speech or to a fair trial against state violations. If it were otherwise, the majority feared, federal courts would become "a perpetual censor upon all legislation of the states, on the civil rights of their own citizens."[26] With those few words, the Court went a long way in reversing the legal revolution wrought by the Civil War. The civil rights of blacks in the South were again under the control of the states.

The dismantling of the Fourteenth Amendment was completed with two decisions in 1883. The first involved a white mob led by a man named R. G. Harris that forced its way into a jail in Tennessee and beat four black men, one of whom died. The whites were indicted under a Reconstruction era law that made it a crime to deprive "any person or class of people of equal protection" of the laws. This enforcement measure gave federal authorities the power to protect blacks against white violence, including from the Ku Klux Klan, but in *United States v. Harris* (1883) the Court struck down the law.[27] According to its ruling, Congress's power to enforce civil rights did not extend to "the action of private persons," such as a white mob. The Court, 8-1, decided that the Fourteenth Amendment applied only to official state discrimination.

The second decision involved the Civil Rights Act of 1875—the last of the great Reconstruction statutes—intended to give all Americans the right to the "full and equal enjoyment of the accommodations…of inns, public conveyances on land or water, theaters or other places of public amusement," without regard to their race or previous condition of servitude. The Republican sponsors of the measure intended that the "privileges and immunities" of an American citizen include such basic freedoms as traveling on a steamboat, staying in an inn, or attending the theater. They relied on the enforcement power set out in the Thirteenth and Fourteenth Amendments, yet enforcement remained

in doubt. (*See "Privileges and Immunities," pp. 429–433.*) In deciding the issue, the Court combined five separate suits into one, and they became known collectively as the *Civil Rights Cases.*

Two of the cases involved black couples who had bought theater tickets in San Francisco and New York only to be denied seating. Two others concerned a hotel in Missouri and a restaurant in Kansas. The fifth involved a black woman who was excluded from the ladies' car on a Tennessee railroad. In an 8-1 decision, the Court struck down the Civil Rights Act and denied Congress the authority to "create a code of municipal law for the regulation of private rights." If blacks are unhappy with this type of discrimination, they should take their complaints to state lawmakers, the justices stated. "It would be running the slavery argument into the ground to make it apply to every act of discrimination which a person may see to make," wrote Justice Joseph Bradley.[28] Justice John Marshall Harlan was the lone dissenter in the civil rights and mob violence cases, and he accused his colleagues of turning their backs on the central purposes of the Reconstruction amendments. In Harlan's view, the amended Constitution empowered Congress to protect those "rights inhering in a state of freedom and belonging to American citizenship," rights to which blacks as well as whites were entitled.

The Fifteenth Amendment and Voting Rights

The Court generally recognized that Congress had an inherent power to protect a person's right to vote in federal elections, and once it was established that a person had the right to vote in state elections, the Court generally upheld Congress's power under the Fifteenth Amendment to enforce that right. In other rulings, however, the Court eased the way for the states to continue to discriminate against blacks. In *United States v. Reese* (1876) the Court ruled that the Fifteenth Amendment did not confer the right to vote on anyone but simply prohibited racial discrimination in voting.[29] As a result, southern states wrote statutes that prevented blacks from voting even though on their face the laws were not discriminatory.

Such statutes required voters to pass literacy tests or pay poll taxes. Occasionally, a state or locality would gerrymander voting districts to dilute the strength of the black vote. Some of the more obviously discriminatory of these state statutes were declared unconstitutional only to be replaced by other forms of discrimination.

As a result of this body of rulings, Congress was limited to enforcing the Civil War amendments against state infringements through remedial legislation alone. One common form of corrective legislation was to authorize persons denied their rights in state courts to bring their cases into federal court. Another method was to provide federal civil and criminal penalties for state officials who deprived persons of their rights. *(See box, The Right to Remove Cases from State Courts into Federal Courts, pp. 10–11.)*

Modern Enforcement

This situation prevailed until the civil rights movement of the 1950s and 1960s prompted passage of new legislation to enforce the guarantees of the Civil War Amendments. In reviewing this legislation, the Supreme Court interpreted the amendments' enforcement clauses expansively, sanctioning congressional authority to prohibit state action before it occurred and, in certain cases, prohibiting racial discrimination by private individuals.

Voting Rights

The Voting Rights Act of 1965 was upheld and given a broad reach in two cases. The statute abolished literacy tests for five years (the abolition was later made permanent) and required certain states and local political units to clear any changes in their election laws with the Justice Department before they took effect. Areas (primarily in southern states) covered by certain remedial provisions of the law were those that had invoked literacy tests or other practices that excluded black voters and where a substantial percentage of the voting-age population was not registered to vote. The bill also authorized dispatching federal examiners to supervise voter registration.

In *South Carolina v. Katzenbach* (1966) the Court upheld the law as a proper exercise of Congress's enforcement powers granted by the Fifteenth Amendment. South Carolina challenged the act as infringing on powers traditionally reserved to the states. "As against the reserved powers of the States, Congress may use any rational means to effectuate the constitutional prohibition of racial discrimination in voting," the Court wrote. Although the means used by Congress were described as "inventive," the Court found them appropriate for prohibiting voting discrimination.[30] The second case challenged a provision of the Voting Rights Act that prevented states from excluding persons who had completed a certain number of years in an accredited foreign-language school if they could not speak or write English. The question arose over a New York requirement that voters be able to speak and write English—a law that disenfranchised most of the state's large Puerto Rican population. The Court upheld the federal provision as a proper means of enforcing the Equal Protection Clause of the Fourteenth Amendment and the guarantee of the Fifteenth Amendment.[31]

In both instances, the Court said, the question was not whether the Court agreed with the provision barring such literacy requirements but whether "we perceive a basis upon which Congress might predicate a judgment that the application of New York's English literacy requirement constituted an invidious discrimination in violation of the Equal Protection Clause."[32] That the requirement violated the Equal Protection Clause was plain, the Court held. "Any contrary conclusion would require us to be blind to the realities familiar to the legislators."[33] In several important cases in the 1990s, the Court assessed the constitutionality not of the Voting Rights Act itself but of the way in which states and the federal government invoked it to increase the political participation of racial minorities.

Private Discrimination

The Court in the late 1960s broadened its interpretation of the enforcement power conferred by the Thirteenth Amendment. *Jones v. Alfred H. Mayer Co.* (1968) concerned the Civil Rights Act of 1866, enacted to ensure blacks the same right as whites to make and enforce contracts, sue, inherit, and buy, lease, sell, and occupy real estate. Persons who denied others these rights on the grounds of race or previous condition of servitude were guilty of a misdemeanor. The matter before the Court was whether this law was violated by the refusal of a private individual to sell a house to a black. Although the Court had never directly ruled on that issue, it had been assumed that the Thirteenth Amendment, like the Fourteenth and Fifteenth Amendments, reached only discrimination by state officials. The Court, 7-2, ruled that the statute did apply to private acts of discrimination. When Congress first enacted the statute granting blacks the right to buy and sell property, "it plainly meant to secure that right against interference from any source whatever, whether governmental or private," the majority wrote.[34] The issue then was whether the 1866 statute was a proper exercise of the Thirteenth Amendment's enforcement power. The Court held that it was.

> Surely, Congress has the power under the Thirteenth Amendment rationally to determine what are the badges and the incidents of slavery, and the authority to translate that determination into effective legislation. Nor can we say that the determination Congress has made is an irrational one.[35]

The Court extended the effect of this enforcement power when it held in 1971 that a section of the 1866 act prohibited private individuals, such as members of the Ku Klux Klan, from conspiring to prevent blacks from exercising their constitutional rights, such as freedom of speech and assembly.[36] In a 1976 decision the Court held that racially segregated private schools that refused to admit black students solely on account of their race violated the provision of the 1866 statute, which gives blacks "the same right to make and enforce contracts as is enjoyed by white citizens."[37]

Return to State Sovereignty

By the mid-1970s Congress at last had the broad power to enforce civil rights nationwide that the drafters of the Reconstruction amendments had envisioned. Racial discrimination in business, public accommodations, transportation, housing, and schools was prohibited by federal law. Some of these laws were enforced in a roundabout way. The Civil Rights Act of 1964, which barred discrimination in employment and public accommodations, was enforced as a regulation of interstate commerce, not a civil rights measure under Section 5 of the Fourteenth Amendment. Nevertheless, Congress's authority to combat discrimination was well accepted and nearly unchecked. In the late 1970s the Court confirmed that states could be sued for monetary damages if they discriminated against their employees on the basis of race or sex. If this ruling, in *Fitzpatrick v. Bitzer* (1976), held any surprise, it was that Justice William H. Rehnquist, the Court's leading advocate of states' rights, wrote the opinion.[38] He agreed that because the Fourteenth Amendment prohibited the states from denying persons the equal protection of the laws, states that discriminated against their workers because of their race or sex violated this clause and left themselves subject to lawsuits.

In the mid-1990s, however, as chief justice, Rehnquist led the effort to limit Congress's power to enforce civil rights in areas other than race and sex discrimination by the states. In a series of rulings, the Rehnquist Court stressed that Congress had the power to "enforce" only the rights set out in the Fourteenth Amendment, not the power to create or expand them. Who decides what rights are contained in the Fourteenth Amendment? The justices determined that they alone had this authority. Moreover, the states had a "sovereign immunity" that shielded them even from lawsuits that were intended to enforce federal civil rights. This doctrine of judicial supremacy and limited congressional power was spelled out in *City of Boerne v. Flores* (1997), a test of federal power in the most unlikely of contexts: a small-town Texas dispute over a church.[39]

St. Peter's Catholic Church had outgrown its old stone cathedral and intended to replace it with a larger, airy, and more modern facility. City officials in Boerne, near San Antonio, had other ideas. Since 1923 St. Peter's had stood as a prominent landmark on the main street, and city officials wanted it preserved to reflect the architectural heritage of the area. Because the cathedral was located in the city's historic preservation zone, the city board refused to give the church permission to tear it down and put up a new building.

This classic local zoning dispute reached the Supreme Court thanks to an earlier controversy involving the freedom of religion. In *Employment Division, Department of Human Resources of Oregon v. Smith* (1990) Justice Antonin Scalia, speaking for a 5-4 majority, said that religious claimants are not entitled to be exempted from a "neutral, generally applicable law" despite the First Amendment's protection for the free exercise of religion.[40] That ruling was sharply criticized by religious leaders and civil libertarians, conservatives and liberals. Congress took up the issue and with broad bipartisan support passed the Religious Freedom Restoration Act of 1993. "The framers of the Constitution, recognizing the free exercise of religion as an unalienable right, secured its protection in the First Amendment to the Constitution," lawmakers proclaimed. Therefore, the government—local, state, or federal—may "not substantially burden religious exercises without compelling justification." They took these words from earlier Supreme Court opinions holding that claims of religious freedom usually will prevail over a law or government policy. As an example, the law cited *Wisconsin v. Yoder* (1972), in which the Court ruled that Amish parents may not be compelled to send their children to high schools, despite a state law that required attendance.[41] Moreover, Congress added, section 5 of the Fourteenth Amendment gave it the "power to enforce, through appropriation legislation," the constitutional rights to freedom and religious liberty.

The archbishop of San Antonio, on behalf of St. Peter's, argued that the federal Religious Freedom Restoration Act confirmed that church leaders, not city officials, were entitled to decide the fate of their building. The Supreme Court disagreed and struck down the Religious Freedom Restoration Act on the ground that Congress had exceeded its power. "All must acknowledge that Section 5 is a positive grant of legislative power to Congress," wrote Justice Anthony Kennedy for the 6-3 majority; however, it "extends only to enforcing the provisions of the 14th Amendment....Legislation which alters the meaning of the

Free Exercise Clause cannot be said to be enforcing the clause. Congress does not enforce a constitutional right by changing what the right is."[42]

Kennedy went on to say that Congress can take action to "remedy or prevent" violations of constitutional rights, but it cannot change the "substantive nature" of these rights. "The distinction exists and must be preserved," he said. Because Congress had no evidence of a "widespread pattern of...religious bigotry" in the United States, it was not remedying a constitutional violation. The 1993 law, according to Kennedy, "appears, instead, to attempt a substantive change in constitutional protections." If Congress were free to write such laws, he concluded, "[S]hifting legislative majorities could change the Constitution and effectively circumvent the difficult and detailed process contained in Article V for amending the Constitution."[43] Left unnoted was the reality that shifting majorities on the Supreme Court can and do change the Constitution and its meaning. The dissenters— Justices Sandra Day O'Connor, David Souter, and Stephen Breyer—argued that the Court should have reconsidered Scalia's opinion narrowing the reach of the religious freedom protected by the First Amendment.

Limited Protection for State Employees

The Court also limited Congress's civil rights power in two cases involving discrimination against state employees. The Age Discrimination in Employment Act (ADEA) makes it illegal for employers to fire, refuse to hire, or otherwise discriminate against older workers because of their age. Victims can sue their employers for damages, but in *Kimel v. Florida Board of Regents* (2000) the Court decided that Congress did not have the power to extend this right to sue protection to state employees.[44] J. Daniel Kimel, a physics professor at Florida State University, led a group of faculty members who contended that the university's salary policies were biased against veteran professors. Without considering the merits of this claim, the Supreme Court ruled that this federal antidiscrimination law did not protect state employees. When the anti-age bias law came under challenge, Clinton administration lawyers defended it as a regulation of commerce and as a civil rights measure, but the 1996 ruling in *Seminole Tribe v. Florida* swept aside the first defense, because Congress cannot use its commerce power to pierce the state's shield of "sovereign immunity."[45] The case therefore focused instead on the Fourteenth Amendment and its mandate that states may not "deny to any person…the equal protection of the laws."

Justice O'Connor spoke for the 5-4 majority in January 2000: "We conclude that the ADEA is not appropriate legislation under Sec. 5 of the 14th Amendment." Age, unlike race, is not always an irrational way of judging workers, she said. For example, the Court had upheld state laws that set mandatory retirement ages for state troopers and judges. "States may discriminate on the basis of age without offending the 14th Amendment," O'Connor stated, and therefore, Congress may not "enforce" the Fourteenth Amendment by subjecting states to suits for discriminating against older workers.[46]

A year later, the Court applied the same logic to rule that Congress cannot give disabled state employees the right to sue if they are discriminated against because they are blind, deaf, wheelchair bound, or otherwise disabled.

Patricia Garrett, a nursing supervisor at the University of Alabama in Birmingham Hospital, was diagnosed with breast cancer in 1994 and underwent surgery, radiation treatment, and chemotherapy. When she returned to work a year later, she was demoted and given a lower salary. She sued the hospital, contending that she had been discriminated against because of her disability. The Americans with Disabilities Act of 1990 prohibited employers, including state agencies, from discriminating against qualified workers with a physical or mental disability. The Court took up Garrett's case to decide whether Congress could enforce the Fourteenth Amendment's guarantee of "equal protection of the laws" by prohibiting states from discriminating against persons with disabilities. "*City of Boerne* confirmed the long-settled principle that it is the responsibility of this Court, not Congress, to define the substance of constitutional guarantees," said Chief Justice Rehnquist in *Board of Trustees of the University of Alabama v. Garrett* (2001).[47] He then noted that the Court had not interpreted the "Equal Protection" Clause as forbidding all government discrimination against persons with disabilities.

"States are not required by the 14th Amendment to make special accommodations for the disabled, so long as their actions toward such individuals are rational. They could quite hard headedly—and perhaps hardheartedly—hold to job-qualification requirements which do not make allowance for the disabled," the chief justice said for the 5-4 majority in February 2001. He conceded that Congress had cited examples of state agencies refusing to hire persons who were blind or deaf or suffer epilepsy, but "these incidents taken together fall far short of even suggesting the pattern of unconstitutional discrimination" that would require a "remedial" law from Congress.[48] "Congress is the final authority as to desirable public policy," Rehnquist wrote, but "Section 5 does not so broadly enlarge congressional authority [so as to] allow Congress to rewrite the 14th Amendment law laid down by this Court."[49] Justices John Paul Stevens, Souter, Ruth Bader Ginsburg, and Breyer dissented, as they had in *Kimel*.

Rehnquist also drew a narrow interpretation of Congress's civil rights power in striking down the Violence Against Women Act in *United States v. Morrison* (2000). In doing so, he relied on the two post-Reconstruction rulings that drastically limited congressional authority over civil rights. In 1994, the year the nation's attention was focused on the murder of Nicole Brown Simpson, the ex-wife of football star O. J. Simpson, Congress had sought to give victims of sexual assault and spousal abuse new legal weapons against their attackers. The 1994 measure declared that "all persons within the United States shall have the right to be free from crimes of violence motivated by gender." Lawmakers contended that this "federal civil rights cause of action" could be sustained "pursuant to the affirmative power of Congress" under Section 5 of the Fourteenth Amendment. Chief Justice Rehnquist disagreed.

"The 14th Amendment, by its very terms, prohibits only state action," Rehnquist wrote. It "erects no shield against merely private conduct, however discriminatory or wrongful."[50] He cited as precedent "the enduring vitality of the *Civil Rights Cases* and *Harris*."[51] In the latter case, which involved a white mob that attacked and killed a black man, the Court construed the Fourteenth Amendment as covering "state action exclusively," Rehnquist said, and the *Civil Rights Cases* confirmed that the Fourteenth Amendment "adds nothing to rights of one citizen as against another," he noted, quoting the earlier ruling.[52] In the case before the Court, Christy Brzonkala, a Virginia Tech freshman, had sued Antonio Morrison, a Virginia Tech football star, alleging that he had raped her in a dormitory. If her allegation is true,

"she was the victim of a brutal assault," Rehnquist said, but one perpetrated by an individual, not by the state of Virginia. Congress cannot therefore use its power under the Fourteenth Amendment to make this a federal offense, the 5-4 majority ruled. Brzonkala's lawsuit was dismissed.

Undoubtedly, Congress retained strong authority to act against race or sex discrimination by states, because the Court agrees such discrimination is unconstitutional. The Supreme Court has, however, crimped Congress's authority to lead the way on civil rights or to expand federal protection in other areas.

The Power to Investigate

It is perhaps indicative of the history of congressional investigations that the development of this particular power of Congress began with a disaster. In 1791 some fifteen hundred soldiers commanded by Maj. Gen. Arthur St. Clair were on a road- and fort-building expedition in the Northwest Territory when they were attacked by Indians. Some six hundred men were killed, and another three hundred were wounded. The following year, the House of Representatives decided that rather than ask the president to investigate this tragedy, it would establish its own special committee to inquire into the circumstances surrounding it.

The special committee subpoenaed the War Department's papers concerning the expedition and witnesses, including St. Clair, Secretary of War Henry Knox, and Secretary of the Treasury Alexander Hamilton. The committee's report absolved St. Clair. Blame for the episode was placed on the War Department, particularly the quartermaster and supply contractors, who were accused of mismanagement, neglect, and delay in supplying necessary equipment, clothing, and munitions to the troops. The House took no action on the report, and the Federalists prevented its publication because of its reflections on Knox and Hamilton. So began congressional exercise of the right to investigate, one of Congress's most controversial powers.[1]

The power to investigate is an implied power based on the constitutional assignment in Article I, section 1, of "all legislative powers herein granted." The authority for legislative bodies to conduct inquiries had been established as early as the sixteenth century by the British House of Commons. The Commons first used this power in determining its membership. It then made increasing use of investigations to assist it in performing lawmaking functions and in overseeing officials responsible for executing the laws and spending funds made available by Parliament. Investigating committees of the House of Commons had authority to summon witnesses and examine documents, and the Commons could support its committees by punishing uncooperative witnesses for contempt. American colonial legislatures, the Continental Congress, and state legislatures relied on these parliamentary precedents in carrying out their own investigations. The power to investigate, to compel the attendance of witnesses, and to demand the production of documents was regarded by most members of the early Congresses as an intrinsic part of the power to legislate.

Writing as a graduate student in 1884, Woodrow Wilson asserted that "the informing function of Congress should be preferred even to its legislative function."[2] Serving as the eyes and ears of the two chambers of Congress, investigations have gathered information on the need for legislation, tested the effectiveness of already enacted legislation, inquired into the qualifications and performance of members and executive branch officials, and laid the groundwork for impeachment proceedings. The practices of some investigatory committees, however—particularly those looking into what were termed un-American activities—have been challenged in the courts. While generally giving Congress wide latitude in the exercise of its investigatory power, the Supreme Court has drawn some limits, primarily to protect the rights of witnesses and to maintain the separation of the legislative and judicial powers. The investigating power and its limits were described in 1957 by Chief Justice Earl Warren:

> The power of Congress to conduct investigations is inherent in the legislative process. That power is broad. It encompasses inquiries concerning the administration of existing laws as well as proposed or possibly needed statutes. It includes surveys of defects in our social, economic or political system for the purpose of enabling the Congress to remedy them. It comprehends probes into departments of

CONTEMPT OF CONGRESS

In 1857 Congress enacted a statute that allowed it to submit congressional contempt cases to the federal courts for indictment and trial. Under this statute, as it has been amended and interpreted, the courts are obligated to provide the defendant all the protections guaranteed defendants in other types of criminal cases. The language of the statute, known as Section 192, is as follows:

Every person who having been summoned as a witness by the authority of either House of Congress to give testimony or to produce

papers upon any matter under inquiry before either House, or any joint committee established by a joint or concurrent resolution of the two Houses of Congress, or any committee of either House of Congress, willfully makes default, or who having appeared, refuses to answer any question pertinent to the question under inquiry, shall be deemed guilty of a misdemeanor, punishable by a fine of not more than $1,000 nor less than $100 and imprisonment in a common jail for not less than one month nor more than twelve months. (U.S. Code 2 [1857], 192).

the Federal Government to expose corruption, inefficiency or waste. But broad as is this power of inquiry, it is not unlimited. There is no general authority to expose the private affairs of individuals without justification in terms of the functions of Congress....Nor is the Congress a law enforcement or trial agency. These are functions of the executive and judicial departments of government. No inquiry is an end in itself; it must be related to and in furtherance of a legitimate task of the Congress.[3]

THE CONTEMPT POWER

Like the investigative power it reinforces, the congressional power to punish for contempt has its source in parliamentary precedents dating from Elizabethan times. No express power to punish for contempt of Congress, except in the case of a member, was granted Congress in the Constitution, but Congress assumed that it had inherent power to jail nonmembers for contempt without a court order because such power was necessary to enforce its investigatory powers and to protect the integrity of its proceedings. The House issued its first contempt citation in 1795 against two men who had tried to bribe several members of Congress to support a grant of land to them. It was not until the early 1820s, however, that the Supreme Court was asked whether Congress has the power to punish nonmembers for actions it considers contempt. In

Anderson v. Dunn (1821) the Court upheld the constitutionality of the summary use of the contempt power of Congress. A denial of power to punish for contempt, the Court said, "leads to the total annihilation of the power of the House of Representatives to guard itself from contempts, and leaves it exposed to every indignity and interruption that rudeness, caprice, or even conspiracy, may meditate against it."[4]

The Court limited the contempt power, however, "to the least power adequate to the end proposed" and said that imprisonment for contempt of Congress could not extend beyond the adjournment of Congress.[5] Considering imprisonment only to the end of a legislative session inadequate, Congress in 1857 passed a law, still in effect in amended form, making it a criminal offense to refuse information demanded by either chamber of Congress. *(See box, Contempt of Congress, above.)* Even after passage of the 1857 law, Congress preferred to remain the agent of punishment for persons in contempt, reasoning that a few days of confinement might induce a witness to cooperate, while turning him over to a court might put him out of the reach of the investigating committee. As the press of legislative business mounted, however, and as court review of summary congressional punishment grew more frequent, Congress increasingly relied on criminal prosecution for contempt under the 1857 statute. The last time either house of Congress punished someone for contempt was in 1932. Since then, all contempt citations have been prosecuted under the criminal statute.[6]

The Supreme Court first asserted the right of federal courts to review congressional contempt citations in *Kilbourn v. Thompson* (1881).[7] The case originated with the refusal of a witness, Hallet Kilbourn, to produce papers demanded by a House committee investigating the failure of Jay Cooke and Company, a banking firm. The House ordered Kilbourn jailed for contempt. Released on a writ of habeas corpus, Kilbourn sued the Speaker, members of the investigating committee, and the sergeant-at-arms, John Thompson, for false arrest. In defense they contended that congressional exercise of the contempt power must be presumed legitimate and that the courts had no authority to review the exercise. Sustaining Kilbourn's claim, the Court held that the chambers of Congress do not have a general power to punish for contempt:

> If they are proceeding in a matter beyond their legitimate cognizance, we are of the opinion that this can be shown, and we cannot give our assent to the principle that, by the mere act of asserting a person to be guilty of contempt, they thereby establish their right to fine and imprison him, beyond the power of any court or any other tribunal whatever to inquire into the grounds on which the order was made.[8]

In 1897 the Court upheld the validity of the 1857 statute making contempt of Congress a criminal offense. The act was challenged as an illegal delegation of power from Congress to the courts. The Court wrote:

> We grant the Congress could not divest itself, or either of its Houses, of the essential and inherent power to punish for contempt, in cases to which the power of either House properly extended; but because Congress, by the Act of 1857, sought to aid each of the Houses in the discharge of its constitutional functions, it does not follow that any delegation of the power in each to punish for contempt was involved.[9]

The Court reiterated this position in 1935, when it ruled that the 1857 statute did not replace but supplemented Congress's authority to bring its own contempt citations. The case concerned a witness who had destroyed papers after a congressional investigating committee had issued a subpoena for them.[10] The Court in *Marshall v. Gordon* (1917) held that Congress may not use its contempt power as punishment for punishment's sake. That case arose out of a New York state grand jury investigation and indictment of a member of the House for violations of the Sherman Act.[11] The member, upon his indictment, asked a House judiciary subcommittee to investigate H. Snowden Marshall, the district attorney responsible for the member's prosecution. The subcommittee went to New York to make inquiries, whereupon Marshall wrote a letter accusing the subcommittee of interfering with the grand jury proceedings. In the letter, which was made public, Marshall used highly abusive language, and the House cited him for contempt. Ruling that the contempt power could be used only where there was actual interference with or resistance to the legislative process, the Court wrote,

> [W]e think from the very nature of that power it is clear that it does not embrace punishment for contempt as punishment, since it rests only upon the right of self-preservation, that is, the right to prevent acts which in and of themselves inherently obstruct or prevent the discharge of legislative duty or the refusal to do that which there is an inherent legislative power to compel in order that legislative functions may be performed.[12]

JUDICIAL REVIEW

With its assertion in *Kilbourn* of authority to review the validity of congressional contempt citations, the Court also assumed the power to review the legitimacy of congressional investigations. The Court held that the House could not punish Kilbourn for contempt because the investigation in which Kilbourn was required as a witness was beyond the authority of the House to conduct. The House investigation of a bankruptcy case that was still pending in the courts was a judicial exercise that infringed on the separation of powers, said the Court in *Kilbourn*. The Court ruled that Congress could not validly legislate in this area; in addition, Congress, in its resolution establishing the

Scandals plagued the Harding administration, including the revelation that Attorney General Harry M. Daugherty (*above*) had failed to prosecute those implicated in the Teapot Dome oil lease fraud. The congressional committee charged with the investigation subpoenaed Daugherty's brother, Mally. He refused to appear and challenged the Senate's power to compel him to testify. The Court in *McGrain v. Daugherty* (1927) broadly interpreted Congress's power to secure needed information by compelling private citizens to testify, even without an explicitly stated legislative purpose.

investigating committee, had shown no interest in developing legislation as a result of the investigation. The Court said that it was sure that

> no person can be punished for contumacy as a witness before either House, unless his testimony is required in a matter into which the House has jurisdiction to

inquire, and we feel equally sure that neither of these bodies possess the general power of making inquiry into the private affairs of the citizen.[13]

Having asserted the right to review congressional inquiries, the Court then ruled that congressional power to investigate had at least three limits: Investigations had to be confined to subject areas over which Congress had jurisdiction, their purpose had to be enactment of legislation, and they could not merely inquire into the private affairs of citizens. In the next test of the investigation power, however, the Court relaxed two of the limits it had established in *Kilbourn*. *In re Chapman* (1897) involved New York stockbroker Elverton R. Chapman, who was convicted of contempt after he refused to answer an investigating committee's questions about senators' trading in sugar stocks during action on a sugar tariff measure.[14] The Court held that in this instance the Senate had a legitimate interest in knowing whether any of its members had been involved in sugar speculations. As a result it could compel testimony from Chapman on matters he considered private:

> The [committee's] questions were not intrusions into the affairs of the citizen; they did not seek to ascertain any facts as to the conduct, methods, extent or details of the business of the firm in question, but only whether that firm, confessedly engaged in buying and selling stocks, and the particular stock named, was employed by any Senator or buy or sell for him any of that stock, whose market price might be affected by the Senate's action.[15]

Because the investigation was legitimate, the Court said that "it was certainly not necessary that the resolution should declare in advance what the Senate meditated doing when the investigation was concluded."[16] With this decision the Court removed its requirement that Congress must state the legislative purposes of its investigative committees, and it narrowed the category of situations in which witnesses might refuse to answer questions put to them by such committees.

SUBPOENA POWER

The Supreme Court has never questioned the power of the House and Senate and their authorized committees to issue subpoenas to ensure the attendance of witnesses or the production of documents for examination at congressional investigations. "Issuance of subpoenas ... has long been held to be a legitimate use by Congress of its power to investigate," the Court wrote in *McGrain v. Daugherty* (1927). "Experience has taught that mere requests for ... information often are unavailing."[1]

In 1975 use of the congressional subpoena power was challenged on First Amendment grounds. The 1975 case arose when the Senate Judiciary Subcommittee on Internal Security issued a subpoena for the bank records of the United States Servicemen's Fund (USSF), a group that protested U.S. involvement in the Vietnam War.[2] The records included lists of contributors to the organization. The USSF claimed that the subpoena was intended to impede the exercise of First Amendment rights, because contributors, fearing that their association with the organization might be made public, would withdraw their support.

The Supreme Court rejected the claim, holding that on its face the subpoena was issued to further a legitimate legislative inquiry. Because members of Congress are constitutionally protected from being questioned for legislative actions, the Court said it could not inquire into the motivations for issuing the subpoena. Concurring, Justices William J. Brennan, Thurgood Marshall, and Potter Stewart said they did not read the majority opinion to mean "that the constitutionality of a congressional subpoena is always shielded from more searching judicial inquiry."[3]

---

1. *McGrain v. Daugherty,* 273 U.S. 135 at 175 (1927).

2. *Eastland v. United States Servicemen's Fund,* 421 U.S. 491 (1975).

3. Id. at 515.

In 1927 the Court issued a landmark decision, *McGrain v. Daugherty,* in which it affirmed the *Chapman* decision and firmly established the power of Congress to conduct legislative and oversight investigations.[17] The case arose during a Senate investigation of Harry M. Daugherty's activities as attorney general under President Warren G. Harding from 1921 to 1924, particularly his failure to prosecute the primary instigators of the Teapot Dome oil lease scandal. The Senate subpoenaed the former attorney general's brother, Mally S. Daugherty, but he refused to appear. The Senate then had its sergeant-at-arms, John McGrain, take Daugherty into custody, but Daugherty won release on a writ of habeas corpus and challenged the Senate's power to compel him to testify. Upholding the Senate inquiry, the Court ruled that the Senate and the House had the power to compel private persons to appear before investigating committees and answer pertinent questions in aid of the legislative function. The "power of inquiry—with process to enforce it—is an essential and appropriate auxiliary to the legislative function," the Court said.[18] It continued,

A legislative body cannot legislate wisely or effectively in the absence of information respecting the conditions which the legislation is intended to affect or change, and where the legislative body does not itself possess the requisite information ... recourse must be had to others who possess it. Experience has taught that mere requests for such information are often unavailing, and also that information which is volunteered is not always accurate or complete, or some means of compulsion are essential to obtain what is needed.[19]

The Court denied Daugherty's contention that the inquiry was actually a trial of his actions, holding instead that it was an inquiry into the "administration of the Department of Justice—whether its functions were being properly discharged or were being neglected and misdirected," an area in which Congress was competent to legislate. "The only legitimate object the Senate could have in ordering the investigation was to aid it in legislating," the Court concluded, "and we think the subject-matter was such that this was the real object. An express avowal of the object would have been better; but ... was not indispensable."[20]

WITNESS RIGHTS

At the same time the Court gave Congress a broad field in which to conduct investigations, it also limited the investigatory power by reaffirming that witnesses in such investigations did have rights. Neither the House nor the Senate has authority to compel disclosures about private affairs, said the Court in *Daughterty*. "[A] witness rightfully may refuse to answer where the bounds of inquiry are exceeded or the questions are not pertinent to the matter under scrutiny."[21]

Pertinency

In the next case involving a congressional investigation, the Court confirmed the legislative branch's broad investigative power and witness rights set out in *Daugherty*. It upheld a Senate inquiry even though the matter under investigation was also pending in the courts. *Sinclair v. United States* (1929) was another case that grew out of the Teapot Dome scandal. Observing that Congress had authority over the naval petroleum reserves, the Court said it was legitimate for the Senate to conduct an inquiry into whether legislation to recover the leased oil lands was necessary or desirable, even though a suit for recovery of the lands had already begun. Congress may not compel testimony to aid the prosecution of court suits, the Court said, but its authority "to require pertinent disclosures in aid of its own constitutional power is not abridged because the information sought to be elicited may also be of use in such suits."[22]

The Court also used *Sinclair* to further spell out the rights of witnesses appearing before investigating committees. It reaffirmed the right of a witness to refuse to testify when the question was not pertinent to the matter at hand. If a witness who refused to answer a question was brought to trial under the 1857 contempt statute, the Court said, it was "incumbent upon the United States to plead and show that the question pertained to some matter under investigation."[23] Finally, the Court ruled that the pertinency of an inquiry is a question for determination by the courts as a matter of law. The Court added, however, that a witness who refused to answer questions could be punished for contempt, as in this case, if he were mistaken as to the law on which he based his refusal. It was no defense that the witness acted in good faith on the advice of counsel, the Court held.

Pertinency versus Balance

The post–World War II quest to uncover subversion in the United States produced a new style of congressional investigation and a host of lawsuits challenging it. Ostensibly seeking to discover the extent of communist infiltration of the government, the labor movement, and various other areas of American life, these investigations were used primarily to publicly expose persons suspected of belonging to or being affiliated with the Communist Party. This purpose was openly acknowledged by Rep. Martin Dies Jr., D-Texas, chairman of the House Special Committee to Investigate Un-American Activities: "I am not in a position to say whether we can legislate effectively in reference to this matter, but I do know that exposure in a democracy of subversive activities is the most effective weapon that we have in our possession."[24] As Chief Justice Warren put it in 1957,

> This new phase of investigative inquiry involved a broad-scale intrusion into the lives and affairs of private citizens. It brought before the courts novel questions of the appropriate limits of congressional inquiry....In the more recent cases, the emphasis shifted to problems of accommodating the interest of the Government with the rights and privileges of individuals.[25]

The first postwar Supreme Court case that pitted the right of a congressional committee to investigate against the right of a witness did not involve a member of the Communist Party; rather, it involved a publisher of politically conservative books. Publisher Edward A. Rumely refused to tell the House Select Committee on Lobbying Activities the names of individuals making bulk purchases of his company's books, which were distributed by the Committee for Constitutional Government, an archconservative organization. Rumely was convicted of contempt of Congress, but a court of appeals reversed the conviction. The Supreme Court upheld the appeals court ruling in *United States v. Rumely* (1953).[26]

A majority of the Court avoided the constitutional issue of whether the committee's questions violated Rumely's First Amendment rights by narrowly construing the authority granted by the resolution establishing the committee. The majority held that the mandate to investigate "lobbying activities" was limited to "representations made directly to the Congress, its members or its committees" and excluded attempts to influence Congress directly through public disseminations of literature.[27] Therefore, its interrogation of Rumely had been outside the committee's power. To interpret the resolution to cover indirect lobbying "raises doubts of constitutionality in view of the prohibition of the First Amendment," wrote Justice Felix Frankfurter for the majority.[28] It was this same narrow interpretation of the meaning of lobbying activities that allowed the Court in 1954 to uphold a federal lobby registration act. *(See "Regulation of Lobbying," pp. 237–239.)* Justices William O. Douglas and Hugo L. Black did not shy away from the First Amendment issues of the case. Claiming that the authorizing resolution in fact did intend the investigating committee to look into indirect lobbying activities, Douglas and Black said the demand for Rumely's book distribution list was a violation of the First Amendment guarantees of free speech and press. "If the present inquiry was sanctioned, the press would be subjected to harassment that in practical effect might be as serious as censorship," wrote Douglas.[29]

Watkins v. United States

The most severe limitations placed by the Supreme Court on the power of congressional investigating committees to inquire into the affairs of private citizens resulted from *Watkins v. United States* (1957).[30] John Watkins was a regional officer of the Farm Equipment Workers Union. Appearing before the House Special Committee to Investigate Un-American Activities in 1954, Watkins answered fully the questions pertaining to his association with the Communist Party. He also answered questions about individuals he knew to be current members of the party. Watkins refused, however, to answer questions about people who, to the best of his knowledge, had disassociated

themselves from the party: "I do not believe that such questions are relevant to the work of this committee nor do I believe that this committee has the right to undertake the public exposure of persons because of their past activities. I may be wrong and the committee may have this power, but until and unless a court of law so holds and directs me to answer, I most firmly refuse to discuss the political activities of my past associates," Watkins said.[31] Convicted of contempt of Congress under the amended 1857 statute, Watkins appealed.

Speaking for the majority, Chief Justice Warren held Watkins not guilty of contempt of Congress. The situation, Warren said, demanded that the Court balance the congressional need for particular information with the individual's interest in privacy. The critical element in this courtly juggling act, he said, "Is the existence of, and the weight to be ascribed to, the interest of the Congress in demanding disclosures from an unwilling witness." The majority, Warren said, had "no doubt that there is no congressional power to expose for the sake of exposure."[32] The only legitimate interest Congress could have in an investigation such as Watkins was subjected to was the furtherance of a legislative purpose. That required that the instructions authorizing the investigation fully spell out the investigating committee's purpose and jurisdiction. Claiming that it "would be difficult to imagine a less explicit authorizing resolution" than the one establishing the un-American activities committee, Warren said that such an "excessively broad" authorizing resolution

> places the courts in an untenable position if they are to strike a balance between the public need for a particular interrogation and the right of citizens to carry on their affairs free from unnecessary governmental interference. It is impossible in such a situation to ascertain whether any legislative purpose justified the disclosures sought and, if so, the importance of that information to the Congress in furtherance of its legislative function. The reason no court can make this critical judgment is that the House of Representatives itself has never made it.[33]

The majority also reaffirmed the holding in *Sinclair* that the questions asked must be pertinent to the matter under inquiry. A witness deciding whether to answer a question, Warren wrote, "is entitled to have knowledge of the subject to which the interrogation is deemed pertinent."[34] Such subject matter was not revealed by the authorizing resolution or by the resolution establishing the subcommittee. Although the matter under inquiry was communist infiltration of labor unions, that was not apparent to a majority of the Court, and if it was not apparent after trial and appeal, he said, it was doubtful the subject matter was apparent at the time of the interrogation. Warren then stated a rule for ascertaining pertinency of questions in the matter under inquiry:

> Unless the subject matter has been made to appear with indisputable clarity, it is the duty of the investigative body, upon objection of the witness on grounds of pertinency, to state for the record the subject under inquiry at that time and the manner in which the propounded questions are pertinent thereto. To be meaningful, the explanation must describe what the topic under inquiry is and connective reasoning whereby the precise questions relate to it.[35]

As the committee had not made its topic clear, Warren said, Watkins could not be held in contempt. Once again the Court had said that the congressional power to investigate was broad but not unlimited. One of the limits was that the investigation had to serve a legislative purpose; its purpose could not be solely to expose publicly people who held unpopular political beliefs or associations. The legislative purpose had to be spelled out in sufficient detail that a witness might know what the purpose was, and the investigating body was required to explain to the witness, if he or she asked, the relevance of its questions to that purpose. Most of these limitations already had been set out in previous decisions. The importance of the *Watkins* case was that the Court reaffirmed these individual rights in an era fraught with fear that the exercise of those rights could doom the existence of the nation itself.

Barenblatt v. United States

The Court cited the need for self-preservation two years later, when it retreated somewhat from its defense of the rights of witnesses. By a 5-4 vote, the Court ruled

that First Amendment rights may be limited where the public interest outweighs the private interest.[36] Justices Frankfurter and John Marshall Harlan deserted the majority in the *Watkins* case to join the only dissenter in that case, Justice Tom C. Clark. The other two justices in the majority in *Barenblatt v. United States* (1959) were Charles E. Whittaker, who did not participate in *Watkins,* and Potter Stewart, who had replaced Harold H. Burton on the Court. Burton had not participated in *Watkins.*

Lloyd Barenblatt refused to answer questions put by a House un-American activities subcommittee that was investigating communist infiltration into higher education. Barenblatt's challenge to his subsequent contempt conviction rested largely on the *Watkins* precedent. He claimed that the committee's authorizing resolution was too vague to determine whether the particular inquiry aimed at him was directed toward a legitimate legislative purpose. He also claimed that he was not adequately apprised of the relevance of the questions asked to the subject matter of the inquiry and that the questions he refused to answer were an encroachment on his First Amendment rights. Upholding Barenblatt's contempt conviction, the majority denied all three claims. First, Justice Harlan wrote, Watkins's conviction had been reversed only because he had not been informed fully of the pertinency to the subject under investigation of the questions he was asked. The vagueness of the mandate establishing the committee was only one facet that the Court examined in its search for the subject matter of the investigation, and it was not determinative. In the case at hand, the majority did not agree with Barenblatt's contention that the vagueness of the mandate deprived the subcommittee of its authority to compel his testimony:

> Granting the vagueness of the committee's charter, we may not read it in isolation from its long history in the House of Representatives. Just as legislation is often given meaning by the gloss of legislative reporters, administrative interpretations, and long usage, so the proper meaning of an authorization to a congressional committee is not to be derived alone from its abstract terms unrelated to the

definite content furnished them by the course of congressional actions.[37]

As to the pertinence of the questions asked to the subject of the investigation, the Court said the record showed that Barenblatt was well aware of their relevance. Therefore, Harlan continued, the only constitutional issue at stake was "whether the Subcommittee's inquiry into petitioner's past or present membership in the Communist Party transgressed the provisions of the First Amendment, which of course reach and limit congressional investigations." As the Court recognized in *Watkins,* an answer to that question, Harlan said, "involves a balancing by the courts of the competing private and public interests at stake in the particular circumstances shown."[38] On the public side, Harlan observed that Congress had the power to legislate in the field of communist activity in the United States:

> In the last analysis, this power rests on the right of self-preservation....To suggest that because the Communist Party may also sponsor peaceable political reforms the constitutional issues before us should now be judged as if that Party were just an ordinary political party from the standpoint of national security is to ask this Court to blind itself to policy since the close of World War II.[39]

In other words, Barenblatt's right to conduct theoretical classroom discussions on the nature of communism did not outweigh the committee's right to investigate those who might have advocated the overthrow of the government. "We conclude," Harlan said, "that the balance between the individual and the governmental interests here at stake must be struck in favor of the latter, and that therefore the provisions of the First Amendment have not been offended."[40]

Justice Black, speaking for himself, Chief Justice Warren, and Justice Douglas, charged that the majority had rewritten the First Amendment to read "Congress shall pass no law abridging freedom of speech, press, assembly and petition, unless Congress and the Supreme Court reach the joint conclusion that on balance the interests of the Government in stifling these freedoms is greater than the interest of the people in

having them exercised."[41] The majority's balancing test, Black continued,

> leaves out the real interest in Barenblatt's silence, the interest of the people in being able to join organizations, advocate causes, and make political "mistakes" without later being subject to governmental penalties for having dared to think for themselves....It is these interests of society, rather than Barenblatt's own right to silence, which I think the Court should put on the balance against the demands of the Government.[42]

In a separate dissent, Justice William J. Brennan Jr. argued that

> no purpose for the investigation of Barenblatt is revealed by the record except exposure purely for the sake of exposure. This is not a purpose to which Barenblatt's rights under the First Amendment can validly be subordinated. An investigation in which the process of law-making and law-evaluating are submerged entirely in exposure of individual behavior—in adjudication, of a sort, through the exposure process—is outside the constitutional pale of congressional inquiry.[43]

Succeeding Cases

In subsequent cases, the Court continued to employ a balanced approach to congressional investigations with mixed results, coming down at times for the witness but at other times for Congress. In *Wilkinson v. United States* (1961) and *Braden v. United States* (1961), both decided on the same day, the Court again found national interests to outweigh individual rights. These cases involved two men who had followed an un-American activities subcommittee to Atlanta, where the panel conducted an inquiry into the extent of communist propaganda in the South.[44] Both men actively and publicly protested the subcommittee proceedings and were subsequently subpoenaed to appear before it. Wilkinson and Braden refused to answer questions about their Communist Party affiliations and consequently were convicted of contempt. The two men complained that the subcommittee had intended to harass them rather than to elicit any information pertinent to its investigation. The Court upheld their convictions, ruling that the investigation was properly authorized and that the questions were pertinent to the subject matter on which legislation could be based.

Four months later, the balance tipped the other way. In *Deutsch v. United States* (1961) the Court overturned the contempt conviction of a man who, like Watkins, refused to answer questions on the possible "un-American activities" of some of his acquaintances.[45] The Court held that the government had not proved the pertinency of these questions to the inquiry at hand. Not only must the witness be aware of the relevance of the question at the time he refuses to answer, the relevance must be proved at the contempt trial, the majority said. The following year the Court reversed another contempt conviction, because the indictment for contempt failed to state the subject under investigation at the time of the interrogation. To omit this statement from the indictment violated the Fifth Amendment guarantee of due process and the Sixth Amendment right to be informed of the cause and nature of the accusation, the Court ruled in *Russell v. United States* (1962).[46]

In 1963 the Court overturned a contempt conviction on the grounds that the committee involved had violated its own rules when it refused a witness's request for a closed hearing.[47] In 1966 a unanimous Court held that a person could not be convicted of contempt in a criminal proceeding if the investigation at which he refused to answer questions was not authorized by the full committee, as required by congressional rules, and if the full committee had not made a "lawful delegation" to the subcommittee authorizing the inquiry. Justice Abe Fortas wrote that the "jurisdiction of the courts cannot be invoked to impose criminal sanctions in aid of a roving commission."[48] According to constitutional scholar C. Herman Pritchett, "These reversals were accomplished for the most part without challenging the scope of investigatory power or querying the motives of the investigators. They were achieved primarily by strict judicial enforcement of the rules on pertinency, authorization, and procedure, plus strict observance

of the constitutional standards governing criminal prosecutions."[49]

THE FIFTH AMENDMENT

Some witnesses in the early cold war years invoked the Fifth Amendment guarantee against self-incrimination when they refused to answer investigating committee questions. The relevant portion of the amendment states that no person "shall be compelled in any criminal case to be a witness against himself." The Court previously had interpreted this guarantee to mean that a person could not be required to divulge information that might make him liable to a criminal proceeding. In 1955 the Supreme Court considered its first contempt of Congress cases against witnesses who invoked the Self-Incrimination Clause

Prior to that first contempt case, the Court had handed down two important rulings dealing with grand jury investigations. In the first case, *Blau v. United States* (1950), the Court acknowledged that admission of communist activity might be incriminating.[50] In the second case, *Rogers v. United States* (1951), the Court ruled that a witness could not invoke the Fifth Amendment privilege after already having answered questions about materially incriminating facts. That case arose after Jane Rogers told a grand jury that she had been treasurer of the Communist Party in Denver. After making this admission she sought to end her testimony and refused to give the name of the person to whom she had turned over the party's books. A divided Supreme Court ruled that she had waived the right to silence by her initial testimony and that the further questions she had refused to answer did not involve a "reasonable danger of further incrimination."[51]

The validity of the Fifth Amendment as a defense against a contempt of Congress citation was considered by the Court in two cases decided on the same day. The circumstances in *Quinn v. United States* (1955) and *Emspak v. United States* (1955) were similar. Both men had refused to answer certain questions from congressional committees

THE COMPLICATIONS OF CONGRESSIONAL IMMUNITY

Congress has rarely exercised its power to grant immunity from prosecution to obtain testimony from individuals who would otherwise claim their Fifth Amendment right to remain silent. During the 1973 Senate Watergate hearings, however, more than two dozen witnesses were granted immunity. Special Prosecutor Archibald Cox had tried in vain to derail those grants, but in the end they did not impede his prosecutions. Most of the major figures pled guilty or were convicted in criminal trials. This was not the case after the 1987 Iran-contra hearings. The complications that arose in the 1980s from the grant of immunity to former White House aide Oliver L. North in the Iran-contra affair demonstrates how congressional immunity can cripple subsequent prosecutions.

The 1985–1986 Iran-contra operation was a triangular affair involving the sale of weapons by the United States to Iran in part to obtain the release of U.S. hostages. Some of the profit from the arms sales were then diverted and used to aid the contras in Nicaragua, in contravention of a congressional ban on aid to the rebels. This scheme was orchestrated secretly by the Reagan White House. North, a former Marine Corps officer and National Security Council aide, helped mastermind the operation and therefore became a central focus of the joint congressional hearings. He and some twenty other witnesses received grants of immunity to testify at the hearings. Committee members insisted at the time that the witnesses would not necessarily escape prosecution. The 1970 law governing such grants of immunity forbids the use of any compelled testimony against an immunized witness, but a witness can be prosecuted for crimes mentioned in his testimony if the evidence used to prosecute him was developed independently of his congressional testimony. This type of "use" immunity was challenged and upheld in *Kastigar v. United States* (1972).[1]

The criminal probe of the Iran-contra affair was led by Special Independent Counsel Lawrence E. Walsh. In May 1989, through Walsh's investigation and prosecution, North was convicted of three felonies: altering and destroying National Security Council documents, aiding and abetting the obstruction of a November 1986 congressional inquiry into the Iran-contra affair, and illegally accepting a home security system as a gift. On appeal, a three-judge panel of the U.S. Court of Appeals for the District of Columbia Circuit set aside the convictions, largely because the court found that trial witnesses had been tainted by their exposure to the immunized congressional testimony.[2]

According to the appeals panel, "A central problem in this case is that many grand jury and trial witnesses were thoroughly soaked in North's immunized testimony, but no effort was made to determine what effect, if any, this extensive exposure had on their testimony."[3] The appeals court asserted that the trial judge should not have focused on what Walsh and other prosecutors might have learned from North's congressional testimony, but on what the witnesses might have picked up from the televised hearings or how their memories might have been refreshed by hearing North. The full appeals court rejected Walsh's petition to rehear the case, as did the Supreme Court.[4] Former national security adviser John M. Poindexter, who was found guilty of lying to Congress about the Iran-contra affair, also won a reversal of his conviction based on similar grounds.

---

1. *Kastigar v. United States*, 406 U.S. 441 (1972).

2. *United States v. North*, 910 F. 2d 843 (1990).

3. Id. at 863.

4. *United States v. North*, 920 F. 2d 940 (1990); *United States v. North*, 500 U.S. 941 (1991).

---

pertaining to their affiliation with the Communist Party. Quinn did not expressly invoke the Self-Incrimination Clause, and Emspak's primary defense was that the questions infringed on his First Amendment rights. The Court held that the intent of each man to plead the Fifth Amendment was clear. There is not a "ritualistic formula" involved in invoking the protection, Chief Justice Warren said in Quinn's case. "If an objection to a question is made in any language that a committee may reasonably be expected to understand as an attempt to invoke the privilege, it must be respected," he added.[52] In the *Emspak* case, Warren wrote,

> [I]f it is true in these times a stigma may somehow result from a witness' reliance on the Self-Incrimination Clause, a committee should be all the more ready to recognize a veiled claim of the privilege. Otherwise, the great right which the Clause was intended to secure might be effectively frustrated by private pressures.[53]

To counter the frequent use of the Fifth Amendment by witnesses before congressional committees,

Congress in 1954 amended an immunity statute that had been on the books since 1857. The Immunity Act of 1954 permitted either chamber of Congress by majority vote or a congressional committee by a two-thirds vote to grant immunity to witnesses in national security investigations, provided an order was first obtained from a U.S. district court judge and the attorney general was notified in advance and given an opportunity to offer objections. The bill also permitted the U.S. district courts to grant immunity to witnesses before the court or grand juries. Witnesses thus immunized were faced with the choice of testifying or going to jail. The Fifth Amendment claim could not be raised.

The Supreme Court upheld the immunity act in *Ullmann v. United States* (1956). Affirming the conviction of William L. Ullmann, who had refused to testify before a grand jury despite a grant of immunity, the Court held that the Fifth Amendment Self-Incrimination Clause protected witnesses only against testimony that might lead to conviction on criminal charges. This possibility was ruled out by the grant of immunity. "Once the reason for the privilege ceases, the privilege ceases," Justice Felix Frankfurter wrote for the majority.[54] Observing that there was no indication that this immunity would protect a person forced to admit he was a communist from the loss of his job or other consequences, Justice Douglas entered a sharp dissent for himself and Justice Black: "My view is that the framers put it beyond the power of Congress to compel anyone to confess his crimes."[55]

INVESTIGATING ELECTIONS

Congress has investigative powers inherent in the constitutional right of each chamber to judge the elections, returns, and qualifications of its members. That point was settled in two cases involving the 1926 senatorial election in Pennsylvania in which Republican William S. Vare was declared the winner over Democrat William B. Wilson.

The first case, *Reed v. County Commissioners of Delaware County, Pa.* (1928), arose when the Senate established an investigating committee to look into reports of corruption in the election. Chairman James A. Reed, D-Mo., and his committee filed suit to compel local officials to produce the ballot boxes for inspection. Their right to do so was challenged. The Court upheld the right of each chamber "to secure information upon which to decide concerning elections," but held that the committee did not have the right to subpoena the ballot boxes because the resolution establishing the committee did not contain the proper authorization.[56]

The second case, *Barry v. United States ex rel. Cunningham* (1929), arose because Thomas W. Cunningham refused to answer certain questions concerning William S. Vare's campaign contributions. The Senate ordered Cunningham taken into custody. He petitioned for a writ of habeas corpus, charging that the Senate had exceeded its power when it arrested him. Justice George Sutherland, writing for the Court, disagreed:

> Exercise of power [to judge elections, returns and qualifications] necessarily involves the ascertainment of facts, the attendance of witnesses, the examination of such witnesses, with the power to compel them to answer pertinent questions, to determine the facts and apply the appropriate rules of law, and, finally, to render a judgment which is beyond the authority of any other tribunal to review.[57]

The Power over Internal Affairs

The first seven sections of Article I of the Constitution set out the duties of the House and the Senate and the powers each chamber has over its internal affairs. Among these are the authority of each house to judge the qualifications and elections of its members, to punish its members, to set the time, place, and manner of holding congressional elections, to establish its own rules for conducting official business, and to impeach, try, and convict or acquit federal civilian and judicial officers. Observing the doctrine of separation of powers, the Supreme Court has found little necessity to intervene in these internal prerogatives of Congress. The Court and Congress also have recognized a power that is not expressly mentioned in the Constitution—the power of self-preservation. This authority is implicit in the clause that grants senators and representatives immunity from being questioned by the executive or judicial branch for legislative actions they take. The necessity for Congress to be protected from intimidation and harassment by the other branches has led the Court to broadly interpret Article I, section 6, known as the Speech or Debate Clause, to the extent that immunity has been granted to members of Congress charged with criminal activity.

The power of self-protection also has been used as the authority for enacting laws regulating campaign financing and requiring registration to lobby. The Court sustained such laws against challenges that they conflicted with First Amendment rights. The Court has, however, held that some campaign financing regulations impermissibly conflict with First Amendment guarantees. Moreover, it has insisted that the law on registration for lobbyists be applied only to certain narrow categories of lobbyists and lobbying activity.

QUALIFICATIONS

Article I, section 5, clause 1, of the Constitution states, in part, "Each House shall be the judge of the…qualifications of its own members." The Constitution also requires that members meet certain age, citizenship, and residency requirements. *(See box, Constitutional Qualifications for Membership in Congress, p. 224.)* Whether Congress, or either house of Congress, had power to add qualifications for membership beyond those listed by the Constitution or power to overlook the absence of one of the constitutional requirements were questions answered sometimes in the affirmative and sometimes in the negative. Until the Supreme Court's decision in the 1969 case concerning Rep. Adam Clayton Powell Jr., D-N.Y., Congress had acted from time to time as if it were entitled to add qualifications as well as to wink at failures to fulfill certain constitutional requirements.

Alexander Hamilton initiated discussion of the question in the *Federalist Papers:* "The qualifications of the persons who may…be chosen are defined and fixed in the Constitution, and are unalterable by the legislature."[1] Later authorities, however, contended that the delegates at the Constitutional Convention intended to empower Congress to add to the listed qualifications. Of the three senators-elect that the Senate has excluded, only one was refused his seat because he did not meet a qualification added by the Senate—loyalty to the Union during the Civil War. (Loyalty was later made a constitutional requirement by the Fourteenth Amendment.) The other two failed to meet the citizenship requirement. Of the ten excluded representatives-elect, four were excluded for disloyalty during the Civil War. One was excluded because he did not live in the district he represented, another because he was a polygamist, one

Adam Clayton Powell walks through Los Angeles Airport on January 9, 1968. In 1967 the House of Representatives voted to exclude him from its chambers, even though he had been duly elected to office. In *Powell v. McCormack* (1969) the Court held that because Powell met the constitutional standards for membership, the House could not refuse to seat him.

for malfeasance, and yet another for misconduct. Two were excluded for seditious activities.

Exclusion

In 1967 the House voted to exclude Representative Powell. The exclusion ended one of the stormiest episodes in congressional history and precipitated a Supreme Court ruling that Congress could not add to the constitutional qualifications for membership in Congress. The pastor of Abyssinian Baptist Church in Harlem, one of the largest congregations in the country, Powell was elected to the Seventy-ninth Congress in 1944. He was reelected regularly, served as chairman of the House Committee on Education and Labor from 1961 to 1967, and was considered by many observers to be the most powerful black legislator in the United States. His downfall was brought about in part by his flamboyant personality and by his apparent disregard for the law. In 1958 Powell was indicted for income tax evasion, but the case was dismissed when the jury was unable to reach a verdict. In 1960 he was convicted of libel. Powell eventually paid the

libel judgment, but not before he had been held in contempt of court four times and had been found guilty of fraudulently transferring property to avoid paying the judgment.

Powell's real troubles, however, began when some of his questionable congressional activities came to light. In the 1950s and early 1960s Powell had enjoyed several costly pleasure trips at government expense. He was criticized for taking a female staff member along on numerous trips to Bimini Island in the Bahamas. Using government funds, he paid his wife almost $21,000 a year as a clerk although she lived in Puerto Rico. In addition, in the late 1960s Powell took long absences from Congress. His apparent misuse of public funds and continuing legal problems in New York created a furor among the public and members of the House, who felt he was discrediting the institution. Reelected in 1966, Powell arrived in Washington only to have the House Democratic Caucus strip him of his committee chairmanship. A day later, January 10, 1967, the House voted to deny Powell his seat, pending an investigation. The investigating committee recommended that Powell be

CONGRESS AND OFFICIAL CONDUCT

In addition to having authority over the conduct of representatives and senators, Congress as a body has also been the primary branch responsible for overseeing the conduct of executive branch employees below the level of presidential appointment. In 1882 the Court upheld a law forbidding officers and government employees from giving or receiving any money, property, or "other thing of value for political purposes." That law, the Court held in an opinion by Chief Justice Morrison R. Waite, was clearly an appropriate exercise of the legislative power "to promote efficiency and integrity in the discharge of official duties, and to maintain proper discipline in the public service."[1] Similar provisions appeared in the Civil Service Act of 1883 and the Hatch Act of 1939 and its later provisions and amendments.

The Court consistently has upheld the power of Congress to regulate such conduct, including severe restrictions on the political activities of civil servants.[2] In 1995, however, the Court ruled that Congress had gone too far in passing the Ethics Reform Act of 1989. That law, the Court held, had breached the First Amendment rights of executive branch employees by barring them from earning money from speeches or articles written on their own time and completely unrelated to their official positions.[3]

1. *Ex parte Curtiss,* 106 U.S. 371 at 373 (1882).

2. *United Public Workers v. Mitchell,* 330 U.S. 75 (1947).

3. *United States v. National Treasury Employees Union,* 513 U.S. 454 (1995).

censured for misconduct and fined to offset the public funds he had misspent. The full House rejected these recommendations, instead voting 307 to116 on March 1, 1967, to exclude Powell from Congress.

Powell ran successfully in the special election to fill his vacancy but did not try to claim his seat. He ran again in 1968, was elected, and was seated in Congress, subject to loss of seniority and a $25,000 fine. Meanwhile, Powell and several of his constituents had gone to the courts to challenge his 1967 exclusion. Powell sought a declaratory judgment that his exclusion was unconstitutional and a permanent order overriding House Speaker John W. McCormack's refusal to administer the oath of office to him, the House clerk's refusal to perform duties due a representative, the House sergeant at arms' refusal to pay Powell his salary, and the House doorkeeper's intent to refuse Powell admission to the House chamber.

Powell's suit focused on two main issues: Could the House add to the Constitution's qualifications for membership? Could the courts properly examine the actions of the House in such cases, order the House not to add to those qualifications, and enforce the order? The U.S. District Court for the District of Columbia dismissed the suit because it said it did not have jurisdiction over the subject matter. The Court of Appeals for the District of Columbia Circuit affirmed in February 1969 the action of the lower court in dismissing the suit. The court of appeals held that the lower court did have jurisdiction over the subject matter but that the case involved a political question, which, if decided, would constitute a violation of the separation of powers and produce an embarrassing confrontation between Congress and the courts. Judge Warren E. Burger wrote the court of appeals decision.

The Supreme Court nevertheless took up the case. In a 7-1 vote in *Powell v. McCormack* (1969), the justices held that the House had improperly excluded Powell.[2] For the Court, Chief Justice Earl Warren stated that because of Powell's claim for back salary, the case was not moot, as the dissent claimed. In addition, he stated, the Speech or Debate Clause did not protect from judicial review all those persons named by Powell in his suit; Warren dismissed the action against McCormack and the other members involved, but allowed Powell to maintain his suit against the House employees. Warren then dismissed the argument that the issue at hand was a political question the Court should not decide. Determination of Powell's right to his seat in the Ninetieth Congress, the Court held, required only

CONSTITUTIONAL QUALIFICATIONS FOR MEMBERSHIP IN CONGRESS

- A senator must be at least thirty years old and have been a citizen of the United States not less than nine years (Article I, section 3, clause 3).

- A representative must be at least twenty-five years old and have been a citizen not less than seven years (Article I, section 2, clause 2).

- Every member must be, when elected, an inhabitant of the state that he or she is to represent (Article I, section 2, clause 2, and section 3, clause 3).

- No one may be a member of Congress who holds any other "Office under the United States" (Article I, section 6, clause 2).

- No person may be a senator or a representative who, having previously taken an oath as a member of Congress to support the Constitution, has engaged in rebellion against the United States or given aid or comfort to its enemies, unless Congress has removed such disability by a two-thirds vote of both houses (Fourteenth Amendment, section 3).

interpretation of the Constitution, the traditional function of the Court.

Turning to that interpretation, Warren said, "Our examination of the relevant historical matters leads us to the conclusion that…the Constitution leaves the House without authority to exclude any person, duly elected by his constituents, who meets all the requirements for membership expressly prescribed in the Constitution."[3] Because Powell met these requirements, he could not be excluded. The Court did not deny the unquestionable interest of Congress in maintaining its integrity. In most cases, however, the Court felt that that interest could be properly safeguarded by the use of each chamber's power to punish or expel its members. The Court sent the case back to the court of appeals with instructions to enter a declaratory judgment stating that the House action was unconstitutional and to conduct further proceedings on the unresolved issues of seniority, back pay, and the $25,000 fine. Justice Potter Stewart dissented, holding that the end of the Ninetieth Congress and the seating of Powell in the Ninety-first Congress rendered the case moot.

Term Limits

Twenty-six years later, in 1995, the Supreme Court relied on its decision in *Powell v. McCormack* to strike down a state law limiting the number of terms members of Congress could serve. By a 5-4 vote in *U.S. Term Limits Inc. v. Thornton* (1995) the Court ruled that the three qualifications set out in the Constitution relating to age, citizenship, and residency are exclusive.[4] If individual states were allowed to adopt term limits, the Court argued, it would lead to a patchwork of state tenure qualifications, undermining the uniformity and national character of Congress. Although term limits had been debated since the nation's founding, the Arkansas law at issue in this case was the first of its kind to reach the Court.

Anti-incumbency fever swept the country in the 1990s, and at the time of the ruling in *Thornton* twenty-three states had approved limits on the tenure of their members of Congress. The Arkansas rule, adopted as an amendment to the state constitution in 1992, prohibited candidates from serving more than three terms in the House of Representatives and two terms in the Senate. To permit such state limits would effect a fundamental change in the Constitution, Justice John Paul Stevens wrote for the Court. "Any such change must come not by legislation adopted either by Congress or by any individual state, but rather…through amendment procedures."[5] Chief Justice William H. Rehnquist and Justices Sandra Day O'Connor, Antonin Scalia, and Clarence Thomas dissented. Writing for them, Thomas said it was "ironic" that the majority referred to the right of the people to choose who governs as the majority was voiding a "provision that won nearly 60 percent of the votes cast in a direct election and that carried every congressional district in the state."[6]

POWER TO PUNISH MEMBERS

Article I, section 5, clause 2, of the Constitution empowers each chamber of Congress to "punish its Members for disorderly Behavior, and with the Concurrence of two thirds, expel a Member." Expulsion has been a power little exercised. Fifteen senators have been expelled: one in 1797 for engaging in a conspiracy against a foreign country and fourteen during the Civil War for supporting a rebellion. In the House only five members have been expelled: three of them in 1861 for Civil War activities, one in 1980 for corruption, and another in 2002 for corruption. As of 1996 the Senate had used the milder punishment of censure to discipline nine of its members; the House has censured twenty-two of its members. From time to time, each chamber has employed other less severe forms of discipline to punish various kinds of misconduct.[7]

The Supreme Court has not been called upon to mediate directly in any of these cases. It is likely that the Court would view such a case as a political issue and therefore nonjusticiable. The Court has indicated that it considers the power to expel a broad one: "The right to expel extends to all cases where the offense is such as in the judgment of the Senate is inconsistent with the trust and duty of a member."[8] In a 1906 case touching on expulsion, the Court upheld a law providing that a member of Congress found guilty of accepting payment for services rendered in connection with a government proceeding "shall...be rendered forever thereafter incapable of holding any office...under the government of the United States."

Convicted under that statute, Sen. Joseph R. Burton, R-Kan., challenged the act's constitutionality on the grounds that it deprived the Senate of its right to decide on expulsion of its members. The Court disagreed, writing that the "final judgment of conviction did not operate *ipso facto,* to vacate the seat of the convicted Senator nor compel the Senate to expel him or to regard him as expelled by force alone of the judgment."[9] Although neither the House nor the Senate has ever found it necessary, the Supreme Court indicated that both chambers of Congress had the power to imprison members for misconduct. In *Kilbourn v. Thompson* (1881) the Court stated,

> [T]he Constitution expressly empowers each House to punish its own members for disorderly behavior. We see no reason to doubt that this punishment may in a proper case be imprisonment, and that it may be for refusal to obey some rule on that subject made by the House for the preservation of order.
>
> So, also, the penalty which each House is authorized to inflict in order to compel the attendance of absent members may be imprisonment, and this may be for a violation of some order or standing rule on the subject.[10]

As noted, in *Powell v. McCormack* the Court held that Congress could not exclude a member-elect for any reason other than failure to meet one of the constitutionally specified requirements for membership in Congress.[11] Powell met the requirements of age, residence, and citizenship, so in essence, the Court ruled that the House could not punish Powell for his indiscretions until after it had seated him. (*See details of Powell v. McCormack, pp. 223–224.*)

CONGRESSIONAL IMMUNITY

The concept of legislators' having some immunity from legal actions was well established in England and in the colonies by the time it became part of the U.S. Constitution. Article I, section 6, provides that "Senators and Representatives shall in all Cases, except Treason, Felony and Breach of the Peace, be privileged from Arrest during their Attendance at the Session of their respective Houses, and in going to and returning from the same; and for any Speech or Debate in either House, they shall not be questioned in any other Place."

The privilege from arrest clause has become practically obsolete, as various court decisions have narrowed its protection. As now interpreted, the clause applies only to arrests in civil suits, such as nonpayment of debts or breach of contract. Even this protection is of little significance, however, because most states do not arrest people in such actions. Civil arrests were more common at the time the Constitution was written. The Supreme Court has declared that the privilege from arrest clause does not apply to service of process—the delivery of writs or summons—in either civil or criminal cases,[12] nor to arrest in criminal cases. In 1908 the Court interpreted the phrase "treason, felony or breach of the peace" to exclude all criminal offenses from the privilege's coverage.[13]

Speech or Debate Clause

The Constitutional Convention adopted the Speech or Debate Clause without discussion or opposition. Its purpose was to protect the independence and integrity of Congress and to reinforce the separation of powers by preventing the executive and judicial branches from looking into congressional activities for evidence of criminality. The Supreme Court has stated repeatedly that the "immunities of the Speech or Debate Clause were not written into the Constitution simply for the personal or private benefit of Members of Congress, but to protect the integrity of the legislative process by insuring the independence of individual legislators."[14] To ensure that integrity, the Court has seen fit to apply the clause to a broader range of legislative activities than just speech and debate and even to protect legislative aides in certain instances. The Court has not, however, construed the clause so broadly as to grant complete immunity from all prosecution or to preclude all judicial review of the activities of individual legislation.

More Than Speech

In *Kilbourn v. Thompson,* the Supreme Court's first interpretation of the Speech or Debate Clause, the justices refused "to limit it to words spoken in debate."[15] The case involved a contempt of Congress citation against Hallet Kilbourn, manager of a District of Columbia real estate pool, for refusing to answer questions before a House committee investigating the bankrupt Jay Cooke and Company and its interest in the real estate pool. The House ordered Kilbourn jailed for contempt. He sued the Speaker of the House, members of the investigating committee, and Sergeant at Arms John G. Thompson for false arrest. The Supreme Court sustained Kilbourn's claim of false arrest on the ground that the investigation was not a legitimate one. *(See details of Kilbourn v. Thompson, p. 211.)* The Court concluded, however, that the Speaker and the members of the investigating committee could not be prosecuted for the false arrest because the report recommending contempt and the vote to direct Kilbourn's arrest were covered by the Speech or Debate Clause:

> The reason of the rule is as forcible in its application to written reports presented in that body [the House] by its committees, to resolutions offered which, though in writing, must be reproduced in speech, and to the act of voting, whether it is done vocally or by passing between the tellers. In short, to things generally done in a session of the House by one of its members in relation to the business before it.[16]

Extension to Aides

In *Kilbourn* the Court did not extend the protection of the Speech or Debate Clause to the sergeant at arms, who, as a result, was liable to prosecution for false arrest. A similar holding was made in *Dombrowski v. Eastland* (1967).[17] The petitioners charged that Sen. James O. Eastland, D-Miss., chairman of the Judiciary Committee's Internal Security Subcommittee, and the subcommittee counsel conspired with Louisiana officials to seize their property and records in violation of the Fourth Amendment. The Court, in a per curiam decision, held that Eastland was not liable to prosecution but that the subcommittee counsel was. Noting that the record contained no evidence of Eastland's involvement in any activity that he might be liable for, the Court said that "legislators engaged in the sphere of legislative activity should be protected not only from the consequences of litigation's results but also from the burden of defending themselves."[18] As to the subcommittee counsel, the Court said there was enough dispute over the facts involved in his alleged collaboration with the state officials to warrant prosecution. The Speech and Debate

Clause, though applicable to congressional employees, was not absolute, the Court said.

The Court later elaborated on this opinion. *Gravel v. United States* (1972) involved Sen. Mike Gravel, D-Alaska, and his actions in releasing portions of the then-classified Pentagon Papers detailing the history of U.S. involvement in the Vietnam War.[19] On June 29, 1971, during the controversy over publication of the Pentagon Papers by several newspapers, Gravel convened a special meeting of the Public Works Subcommittee on Public Buildings, of which he was chairman. With the press and public in attendance, Gravel read classified documents from the Pentagon Papers into the subcommittee record. Subsequently, the senator arranged for the verbatim publication of the subcommittee record by Beacon Press. In August 1971 a federal grand jury in Boston investigating the release of the Pentagon Papers ordered Gravel aide Leonard S. Rodberg to appear before it. Rodberg had been hired the night Gravel called the session of his subcommittee to read excerpts from the documents. He subsequently helped Gravel edit and make arrangements for publication of the papers. Rodberg moved to quash the subpoena on the grounds that he was protected from questioning by the Speech or Debate Clause.

In a 5-4 decision on June 29, 1972, the Supreme Court held that the constitutional immunity of a member of Congress from grand jury questioning extended to aides if the conduct in question fell within the category of a protected legislative act if performed by that member. "The day-to-day work of such aides is so critical to the Member's performance that they must be treated as [the member's] alter ego," wrote Justice Byron R. White for the majority.[20] The majority agreed, however, that such protection did not extend to arrangements that were made for the publication of the subcommittee report or to information about the source of the classified documents. Gravel, as well as Rodberg, could be required to testify to the grand jury about these nonlegislative matters:

> While the Speech or Debate Clause recognizes speech, voting and other legislative acts as exempt from liability that might attach, it does not privilege either senator or aide to violate an otherwise valid criminal law in preparing for or implementing legislative acts.[21]

Justice Potter Stewart dissented because the opinion held that a member of Congress could be forced to tell a grand jury about the sources of information used to prepare for legislative activity. Justices William O. Douglas, William J. Brennan Jr., and Thurgood Marshall argued in dissent that constitutional immunity protected Gravel, Rodberg, and Beacon Press even from questions concerning the publication of the papers read into the subcommittee record.

Immunity versus Individual Rights

The Speech or Debate Clause would appear to protect legislators and their aides from prosecution even in cases where their legislative activities have infringed on the constitutional rights of private individuals. One such case, *Tenney et al. v. Brandhove* (1951), involved the California state legislature, but the Court's ruling seems applicable to Congress.[22] William Brandhove sued members of a legislative committee investigating "un-American activities." Brandhove said their questioning of him was not for a legislative purpose but to harass and intimidate him and to prohibit him from exercising his right of free speech. The Court dismissed Brandhove's suit. "The claim of an unworthy purpose does not destroy the privilege" of congressional immunity, wrote Justice Felix Frankfurter. He continued:

> Legislators are immune from deterrents to the uninhibited discharge of their legislative duty, not for their private indulgence but for the public good. One must not expect uncommon courage even in legislators. In times of political passion, dishonest and vindictive motives are readily attributed to legislative conduct and as readily believed. Courts are not the place for such controversies. Self-discipline and the voters must be the ultimate reliance for discouraging or correcting such abuses. The Courts should not go beyond the narrow confines of determining that the committee's inquiry may fairly be deemed within its province.[23]

Justice Douglas dissented: "It is one thing to give great leeway to the legislative right of speech, debate, and investigation. But when a committee perverts its power, brings down on an individual the whole weight

"To support the right of the people"

The basic interpretation of the Speech or Debate Clause comes not from the Supreme Court of the United States but from the Supreme Court of Massachusetts, which included an immunity clause in its 1780 constitution. Charged with slander during a private conversation on the floor of the state legislature, three members of the lower chamber invoked the immunity clause. Speaking to the plea, Chief Justice Parsons of Massachusetts wrote in 1808,

> These privileges [of immunity] are thus secured, not with the intention of protecting the members against prosecutions for their own benefit, but to support the right of the People, by enabling their representatives to execute the functions of their office without fear of prosecutions, civil or criminal. I therefore think that the article ought not to be construed strictly, but liberally, that the full design of it may be answered. I will not confine it to delivering an opinion, but will extend it to the giving of a vote, to the making of a written report, and to every other act resulting from the nature and the execution of the office. And I would define the article as securing to every member exemption from prosecution for everything said or done by him as a representative, in the exercise of the functions of that office, without inquiring whether the exercise was regular, according to the rules of the House, or irregular and against those rules. I do not confine the member to his place in the House; and I am satisfied that there are cases in which he is entitled to this privilege when not within the walls of the Representatives' Chamber.[1]

---

1. *Coffin v. Coffin*, 4 Mass. 1, at 27 (1808).

of government for an illegal or corrupt purpose, the reason for the immunity ends."[24]

In *Doe v. McMillan* (1973) the Court held that members of Congress and their employees—in this case, John McMillan, D-S.C., chairman of the House District of Columbia Committee, the committee's members, and employees—were immune from charges that they violated the privacy rights of certain children by naming them as disciplinary and absentee problems in a committee report on the District of Columbia school system. Wrote Justice White,

> The business of Congress is to legislate; Congressmen and aides are absolutely immune when they are legislating. But when they act outside the "sphere of legitimate legislative activity"…they enjoy no special immunity from local laws protecting the good name or the reputation of the ordinary citizen.[25]

Because the committee members and employees had included the names of the children in a report that was a legitimate legislative activity, they were immune from prosecution. The Court held, however, that this immunity might not extend to the public printer and the superintendent of documents, also named in the suit. This protection did not cover persons, the Court said, "who publish and distribute otherwise actionable materials beyond the reasonable requirements of the legislative function."[26] It was left to the trial court to determine if these defendants had gone beyond those requirements.

In 1975 the Court held that a valid subpoena from a congressional committee falls within the protected sphere of legislative activity even if it is claimed that the subpoena was intended to impede the exercise of First Amendment rights. The case involved Sen. James O. Eastland, the Judiciary Subcommittee on Internal Security, and the subcommittee counsel. Eastland, chairman of the subcommittee, had issued a subpoena for the bank records of the United States Servicemen's Fund (USSF) as part of the subcommittee's inquiry into the enforcement of the Internal Security Act of 1950. The USSF set up coffeehouses and aided underground newspapers at military bases as vehicles for protest against U.S. involvement in Indochina. The courts could not investigate the propriety of the inquiry into the fund's activities beyond determining that such an inquiry was within the jurisdiction of the subcommittee, said the Court. If that is determined, "the speech or debate clause is an absolute bar to interference," the Court concluded.[27] In dissent, Justice Douglas claimed that "no official may invoke immunity for his actions for which wrongdoers normally suffer."[28]

In *Hutchinson v. Proxmire* (1979) the Court held that the Speech or Debate Clause did not immunize a member of Congress from libel suits for allegedly defamatory statements he made about a person in press releases and newsletters even though the statements had originally been made on the Senate floor. "Valuable and desirable as it may be" to inform the public of a member's activities, the Court said, transmittal of such information in press releases "is not part of the legislative function or the deliberations that make up the legislative process."[29]

Criminal Prosecutions

The Supreme Court in 1966 held, 7-0, that in prosecuting a former member of Congress the executive branch could not inquire into the member's motive for making a speech on the floor, even though the speech was allegedly made for a bribe and was part of an unlawful conspiracy. *United States v. Johnson* (1966) arose out of the June 1963 conviction of Rep. Thomas F. Johnson, D-Md., by a federal jury in Baltimore.[30] The government charged that Johnson, Rep. Frank W. Boykin, D-Ala., and two officers of a Maryland savings and loan company then under indictment entered into a conspiracy in which Johnson and Boykin would approach the Justice Department to urge a "review" of the indictment, and Johnson would make a speech on the floor of the House defending savings and loan institutions in general. Johnson made the speech in June 1960, and it was reprinted by the indicted company and distributed to the public. Johnson and Boykin allegedly received money in the form of "campaign contributions." Johnson's share was put at more than $20,000. The four men were convicted on seven counts of violating the federal conflict of interest law and one count of conspiring to defraud the United States. (President Lyndon B. Johnson, on December 17, 1965, granted Boykin a full pardon.)

The U.S. Court of Appeals for the Fourth Circuit in September 1964 set aside Johnson's conspiracy conviction and ordered a retrial on the other counts. The Supreme Court essentially affirmed the court of appeals ruling. Justice John Marshall Harlan wrote the opinion, which said that the precedents did not deal with a criminal prosecution based upon an allegation that a member of Congress abused his position by conspiring to give a particular speech in return for remuneration from private interests. However reprehensible such conduct may be, we believe the Speech or Debate Clause extends at least so far as to prevent it from being made the basis of a criminal charge against a member of Congress of conspiring to defraud the United States by impeding the due discharge of government functions. The essence of such a charge in this context is that the Congressman's conduct was improperly motivated, and…that is precisely what the Speech or Debate Clause generally forecloses from executive and judicial inquiry.[31]

Emphasizing the narrowness of its holding, the Court said the decision did not address whether congressional immunity would extend to a prosecution based on a specifically drawn statute passed by Congress to regulate the conduct of its own members. It also did not speak to a prosecution for a general criminal statute that did not rely for its proof on the member's motivation for performing his legislative activities. The Court said it would allow Johnson a new trial on the conspiracy charge only if the executive branch could purge all parts of its prosecution offensive to the Speech or Debate Clause. The government chose to drop the conspiracy charge. (On a retrial of the seven conflict of interest charges, Johnson was convicted a second time and sentenced to six months in prison.)

Brewster Case

The question of whether the government could—without violating congressional immunity under the Speech or Debate Clause—successfully prosecute a member of Congress for taking a bribe in return for casting a vote came before the Court in 1972. Former senator Daniel B. Brewster, D-Md., was indicted in 1969 on charges of accepting $24,000 in bribes between 1966 and 1968 from the Spiegel mail order firm while in office. During that time, Brewster was a member of the Senate Post Office and Civil Service Committee, which was considering proposed changes in postal rates. The indictment alleged that the bribes influenced

The Court in *United States v. Brewster* (1972) upheld the bribery conviction of former senator Daniel B. Brewster, D-Md. The Court held that the Speech or Debate Clause did not shield Brewster from prosecution for bribery related to the performance of legislative acts.

Brewster's legislative action on these proposals. In November 1970 a federal district judge in the District of Columbia dismissed the charges against Brewster, stating that the Speech or Debate Clause shielded him from prosecution for bribery related to the performance of legislative acts. The Justice Department immediately asked the Supreme Court to review this decision.

By a 6-3 vote the Court reversed the lower court ruling and held that Brewster could indeed be prosecuted on the bribery charge. Observing that a broad interpretation of the Speech or Debate Clause would immunize almost all legislators' activities, Chief Justice Warren E. Burger stated,

> In its narrowest scope, the Clause is a very large, albeit essential, grant of privilege. It has enabled reckless men to slander and even destroy others with impunity, but that was the conscious choice of the framers....[B]ut the shield does not extend

beyond what is necessary to preserve the integrity of the legislative process.[32]

The Court has never interpreted the clause "as protecting all conduct *relating* to the legislative process," said Burger. "In every case thus far before this Court, the Speech or Debate Clause has been limited to an act which was clearly part of the legislative process—the due functioning of the process."[33] Turning specifically to the *Brewster* case, Burger separated the act of taking a bribe from the act of casting a ballot:

> The illegal conduct is taking or agreeing to take money for a promise to act in a certain way. There is no need for the government to show that [Brewster] fulfilled the alleged illegal bargain; acceptance of the bribe is the violation of the statute, not performance of the illegal promise.

> Taking a bribe is, obviously, no part of the legislative process or function; it is not a legislative act.[34]

By this construction, the Court found that, unlike in *Johnson*, it would not be necessary for the government in prosecuting Brewster to inquire into the legislative acts or their motivations in order to provide a violation of the bribery statute.

In dissent, Justice Brennan argued that the majority had taken an artificial view of the charges. The indictment, Brennan said, was not for receipt of money, but for receipt of money in exchange for a promise to vote a certain way. To prove this crime, he continued, the government would have to inquire into Brewster's motives, and this it was prevented from doing by the immunity clause. The three dissenters also said that Congress, not the courts, was the proper forum for disciplining the misconduct of its members. "The speech or debate clause does not immunize corrupt congressmen," wrote Justice White. "It reserves the power to discipline [them] in the houses of Congress."[35]

Brewster stood trial and was convicted, but the conviction was reversed. Before a second trial could begin, Brewster pled no contest to a felony charge of accepting an illegal gratuity while he was a senator.

Dowdy Case

In 1973 the Court refused to review an appellate court ruling that had reversed the conviction of Rep. John Dowdy, D-Texas, on five of eight conspiracy, bribery, and perjury charges. The U.S. Court of Appeals for the Fourth Circuit held that the evidence used in Dowdy's trial directly related to the legislative process. The evidence "was an examination of defendant's actions as a Congressman, who was chairman of a subcommittee investigating a complaint, in gathering information in preparation for a possible subcommittee investigatory hearing," the appeals court said.[36] Although the alleged criminal act—bribery—was the same in *Dowdy, Johnson,* and *Brewster,* the major difference was the source of the evidence. In Brewster's case the Court found sufficient evidence available outside of Brewster's legislative activities to let the case go forward. In the *Dowdy* and *Johnson* cases, so much of the evidence was based on the representatives' legislative activities that introduction of that evidence violated their immunity and was therefore unconstitutional.

ELECTIONS REGULATION

The Constitution gives the states the authority to set the time, place, and manner of holding elections for Congress with the proviso that "Congress may at any time by law make or alter such Regulations, except as to the Places of chusing Senators," as stated in Article I, section 4, clause 1. The first law that Congress passed regulating the time, place, or manner of a federal election was an 1842 act requiring that representatives be elected by districts. Congress's first comprehensive regulation of elections was the Enforcement Act of 1870, adopted to enforce the right of blacks to vote granted under the Fifteenth Amendment. Together with two 1871 statutes, the Enforcement Act made it a federal offense to register falsely, bribe voters, interfere with election officials, and make false counts of ballots cast. Any election officer who failed to perform a duty required of him in a federal election under either federal or state law was also guilty of a federal offense.

In 1880 the act was challenged as an unconstitutional infringement on the states' right to conduct elections. The suit also questioned whether Congress had the authority to punish state election officers for violations of state election law affecting federal elections. In *Ex parte Siebold* the Court upheld the Enforcement Act:

> There is no declaration [in Article I, section 4] that the regulations shall be made wholly by the State legislature or wholly by Congress. If Congress does not interfere, of course they may be made wholly by the State, but if it chooses to interfere, there is nothing in the words to prevent its doing so, either wholly or partially. On the contrary, their necessary implication is that it may do either. It may either make the regulations, or it may alter them. If it only alters, leaving…the general organization of the polls to the State, there results a necessary cooperation of the two governments in regulating the subject. But no repugnance in the system of regulations can arise thence; for the power of Congress over the subject is paramount. It may be exercised as and when Congress sees fit to exercise it. When exercised, the action of Congress, so far as it extends and conflicts with the regulations of the State, necessarily supersedes them.[37]

It stood to reason that if Congress could regulate elections, it had the power to enforce its regulations, the Court continued. State election personnel officiating at a federal election have a responsibility to the federal government as well as to the state, and the fact that an official is a state official does not shield him from federal punishment for failure to perform his duty to the United States. To the argument that Congress cannot punish violations of state election law pertaining to federal elections, the Court said, "The State laws which Congress sees no occasion to alter, but which it allows to stand, are in effect adopted by Congress. It simply demands their fulfillment."[38] In subsequent cases, the Court has upheld Congress's authority under Article I, section 4, to protect against personal violence and intimidation at the polls and against failure to count all the votes cast.[39]

SERVICE IN CONGRESS

Twenty-seven of the 110 Supreme Court justices served in the Senate, the House, or both before appointment to the bench. Only one, David Davis, left the Court to serve in Congress, in 1877, when the Illinois legislature elected him to the Senate. Davis had served on the Court since 1862. He was a senator for only one term, serving as president pro tempore from 1881 to 1883, when he retired. The individuals who served in Congress as well as on the Supreme Court are listed below:

Justice	Congressional Service	Court Service
SENATE		
William Paterson	1789–November 13, 1790	1793–1806
Oliver Ellsworth	1789–March 8, 1796	1796–1799
Levi Woodbury	1825–1831; 1841–1845	1845–1851
David Davis	1877–1883	1862–1877
Salmon P. Chase*	1849–1855; March 4–6, 1861	1874–1873
Stanley Matthews	March 21, 1877–1879	1881–1889
Howell E. Jackson	1881–April 4, 1886	1894–1895
Edward D. White*	1891–March 12, 1894	1894–1921
Hugo L. Black	1927–August 19, 1937	1937–1971
Harold H. Burton	1941–September 30, 1945	1945–1958
Sherman Minton	1935–1941	1949–1956
HOUSE		
John Marshall*	1799–June 7, 1800	1801–1835
Joseph Story	May 23, 1808–1809	1811–1845
Gabriel Duvall	November 11, 1794– March 28, 1796	1812–1835
John McLean	1813–1816	1829–1861
Henry Baldwin	1817–May 8, 1822	1830–1844
James M. Wayne	1829–January 13, 1835	1835–1867
Philip B. Barbour	September 19, 1814–1825	1836–1841
Nathan Clifford	1839–1843	1858–1881
William Strong	1847–1851	1870–1880
Joseph McKenna	1885–1892	1898–1925
William H. Moody	November 5, 1895–May 1, 1902	1906–1910
Mahlon Pitney	1895–January 10, 1899	1912–1922
Fred M. Vinson*	January 12, 1924–1929; 1931–May 12, 1938	1946–1953
BOTH CHAMBERS		
John McKinley	S: November 27, 1826–1831; March 4–April 22, 1837 H: 1833–1835	1837–1852
Lucius Q. C. Lamar	H: 1857–1860; 1873–1877 S: 1877–March 6, 1885	1888–1893
George Sutherland	H: 1901–1903 S: 1905–1917	1922–1938
James F. Byrnes	H: 1911–1925 S: 1931–July 8, 1941	1941–1942

* Denotes a chief justice.

Primary Elections

Although the Court had ruled that congressional authority to regulate the time, manner, and place of holding elections was paramount to state authority, in 1921 it ruled that party primaries were not elections and that Congress consequently had no right to regulate them. *Newberry v. United States* (1921) arose when Truman H. Newberry, R-Mich., was convicted for having spent more money than he was allowed under the 1911 campaign expenditure law in his primary race against Henry Ford for the 1918 Republican Senate nomination in Michigan. Newberry's case was argued before the Supreme Court. On the constitutional question of whether Congress had the power to regulate primaries, the Court divided, 4-4. Justice Joseph McKenna, who voted to reverse the conviction, was unsure how ratification of the Seventeenth Amendment in 1913 affected Congress's power to act under the 1911 statute.

The four justices who claimed that Congress did not have authority to regulate primaries wrote that the word election "now has the same general significance as it did when the Constitution came into existence— final choice of an officer by duly qualified electors." Primaries, the four continued, "are in no sense elections for an office but merely methods by which party adherents agree upon candidates whom they intend to offer and support for ultimate choice by all qualified electors." The manner in which candidates are nominated for federal office "does not directly affect the manner of holding the election," they concluded.[40] This politically naive view of the role of the primary was assailed by Justice Mahlon Pitney, who observed that the primary had no reason to exist except as preparation for an election. Congressional authority to regulate the manner of holding an election "can mean nothing less," Pitney said, than the ability to regulate "the entire mode of procedure—the essence, not merely the form of conducting the elections."[41]

Pitney's dissent became the majority position twenty years later, when the Court reversed *Newberry* with its decision in *United States v. Classic* (1941). This case involved a government prosecution of

Louisiana election commissioners for altering and falsely counting votes in a primary election, a violation under the 1870 Enforcement Act. For the most part, winning the Democratic nomination to Congress in Louisiana was tantamount to winning the general election.[42] Writing for the 5-3 majority, Justice Harlan Fiske Stone stated, "[W]e think that the authority of Congress, given by [Article I, section 4], includes the authority to regulate primary elections when as in this case, they are a step in the exercise by the people of their choice of representatives in Congress."[43]

The three dissenting justices based their disagreement not on the ground that Congress did not have the authority to regulate primary elections, but on the ground that the statute making alteration and miscounting of ballots criminal offenses was not specific enough to encompass primaries.

Campaign Financing

Sensitive to charges that corporations were exerting undue influence on Congress through unrestrained spending on favored candidates, Congress in 1907 passed its first law regulating campaign financing. The Tillman Act prohibited corporations and national banks from making financial contributions to any candidate for federal office. A 1910 law required every political committee seeking to influence the election of House members in two or more states to file contribution and spending reports with the clerk of the House. A 1911 law provided similar regulation for Senate races. In 1925 Congress passed the Federal Corrupt Practices Act setting limits on the amounts candidates for the Senate and House could spend in general elections. Primary elections were omitted because of the Court's ruling in the *Newberry* case. The 1925 act also required political committees seeking to influence the election of presidential electors in two or more states to file contribution and spending reports that would be available to the public.

This last provision was challenged in *Burroughs and Cannon v. United States* (1934) as an infringement on the right of the states to appoint their presidential

Sen. James L. Buckley, C/R-N.Y., was among the plaintiffs challenging a 1974 campaign financing law in *Buckley v. Valeo* (1976). The Court ruled that key provisions of the law violated First Amendment rights.

electors in the manner they deemed appropriate (Article II, section 1, clause 2).[44] In upholding the federal disclosure provisions as they pertained to presidential electors, the Supreme Court implicitly sanctioned federal regulation of campaign financing in congressional elections. The provisions, observed Justice George Sutherland for the majority, applied to committees operating in two or more states. Such committees, "if not beyond the power of the state to deal with at all, are beyond its power to deal with adequately." Turning to the authority of Congress to supply adequate regulation, Sutherland said that the importance of the election of the president

> and the vital character of its relationship to and effect upon the welfare and safety of the whole people cannot be too strongly stated. To say that Congress is without the power to pass appropriate legislation to safeguard such an election from the improper use of money to influence the result is to deny to the nation in a vital particular the power of self-protection.[45]

In 1947 in the Labor Management Relations Act, or Taft-Hartley Act, Congress extended the ban on corporate funding of federal elections to unions.

First Amendment Conflict

In the early 1970s Congress, spurred in part by the Watergate scandal, further extended its campaign funding limits to include wealthy individuals. The Federal Election Campaign Act Amendments of 1974 barred individuals from giving a candidate for federal office more than $1,000 per election, and it established a $25,000 annual limit for all contributions by individuals. These restrictions were challenged on free speech grounds by several lawmakers, led by Sen. James L. Buckley, C/R-N.Y. They maintained that the limits on contributors and candidates curbed their freedom to express their political views, a core violation of the First Amendment.

In *Buckley v. Valeo* (1976) the Supreme Court handed down a compromise, split decision in an unsigned 137-page opinion. In five separate signed opinions, several justices concurred with and dissented from separate issues in the case. On the one hand, the justices in the unsigned opinion upheld the limits on donors' *contributions* to candidates, stating that they pose only "a marginal restriction upon the contributor's ability to engage in free communication." In addition, such limits would prevent the "appearance of corruption," because it is reasonable to assume that big donors will get special treatment in return for their money, the Burger Court asserted.[46] On the other hand, preventing individuals from spending their own money as they please to promote a candidate is a greater restriction on speech, so the justices struck down most of the *expenditure* limits as unconstitutional. The difference between a contribution and an expenditure, however, was not always clear. For example, if an individual spent large amounts of money for "communications that in express terms advocate the election" of a candidate, that funding would be considered a contribution to the candidate's campaign, not an independent expenditure, the Court held.[47]

The split result and the uncertainty over the definitions opened loopholes in the law that eventually led to a huge flow of unregulated money into federal campaigns. A "contribution" was defined as anything of value given "for the purpose of influencing any election for Federal office." When the Federal Election Commission, the agency established to oversee and enforce the campaign financing laws, was asked for its opinion in the 1980s, it advised officials of the Democratic and Republican national committees that they could solicit contributions to pay for drives to register new voters or to "get out the vote" on election day. These money gifts became known as "soft money," because they were not considered contributions to candidates that would be regulated by the law. In 1984 the parties took in and spent $21 million in soft money, a mere 5 percent of their total spending. By 2000 soft money contributions had soared to $498 million, nearly half of which the parties spent during the election year.[48]

Corporations, unions, and wealthy individuals also realized that they could evade the federal limits by funding broadcast ads that stopped short of advocating the election or defeat of a candidate "in express terms," as the Court had said in the *Buckley* opinion. This spawned a new wave of campaign ads that told the viewers they should "send a message" to a candidate, letting him know that they do not like his stand on a particular topic. These ads were deemed to be "issue ads," not campaign ads that were regulated by federal law. In 2000 an estimated $500 million was spent on theses unregulated ads.

A bipartisan group of campaign funding reformers led by Sens. John McCain, R-Ariz., and Russell Feingold, D-Wis., determined to close what a Senate report called "the twin loopholes of soft money and bogus issue advertising that have virtually destroyed our campaign finance laws."[49] They won passage of the Bipartisan Campaign Reform Act of 2002, which barred parties and politicians from seeking, accepting, or spending "soft money." It also coined a new term, *electioneering communication,* which was defined as a broadcast ad that appears within sixty days of a general election, or thirty days of a primary, that "refers to a clearly identified candidate for Federal office." Corporations, unions, and individuals were prohibited from funding such ads. Candidates and parties, however, remained free to run them, the law said, but they must do so with the money raised under the legal limits.

Once again, the entire law was challenged on free speech grounds by, among others, Sen. Mitch McConnell, R-Ky., the Republican National Committee, and advocacy groups, including the National Rifle Association and the American Civil Liberties Union. In *McConnell v. Federal Election Commission* (2003) the Court upheld the law virtually intact in a 5-4 ruling. "BCRA is the most recent federal enactment designed to purge national politics of what was conceived to be the pernicious influence of 'big money' campaign contributions," said Justices Stevens and O'Connor for the majority. Stopping the flow of big money contributions will "protect the integrity of the political process," and it will have "only a marginal impact on the ability of contributors, candidates, officeholders and parties to engage in effective political speech."[50]

They also stated that the justices had a special duty to defer to Congress on this issue, because its members knew as candidates and lawmakers the potentially corrupting influence of big contributions. "Congress has a fully legitimate interest in maintaining the integrity of federal office holders and preventing corruption of the federal electoral process," the Court said.[51] Justices David H. Souter, Ruth Bader Ginsburg, and Stephen G. Breyer joined their opinion in full. "This is a sad day for freedom of speech," said Justice Scalia in one of four dissents. According to him, the restrictions on political giving and broadcast ads "cut to the heart of what the First Amendment is meant to protect: the right to criticize the government."[52] Chief Justice Rehnquist and Justices Anthony M. Kennedy and Clarence Thomas also dissented. The majority stressed it was "under no illusion" that all the problems posed by the mix of money and politics were solved. "Money, like water, will always find an outlet," they said in closing.[53]

In 2007 the Court reversed course and gave corporate groups a new freedom to pay for broadcast ads just prior to the election. This ruling weakened, but did not strike down, the provision in the McCain-Feingold Act the Court had upheld just four years earlier. The change was possible because of the retirement of Justice O'Connor and the arrival of her replacement, Justice

Samuel A. Alito Jr. With O'Connor, the Court had a narrow majority to uphold campaign finance limits against free speech challenges. Alito, like Chief Justice John G. Roberts Jr., took the free speech view, and they helped form a new majority to strike down the restrictions on corporate groups and their political ads.

"The First Amendment requires us to err on the side of protecting political speech rather than suppressing it," Roberts wrote for a 5-4 majority in *Federal Election Commission v. Wisconsin Right to Life, Inc.* Corporate groups may broadcast preelection ads that mention a candidate's name so long as "the ad is susceptible of no reasonable interpretation other than an appeal to vote for or against a specific candidate," he said.[54]

Wisconsin Right to Life was incorporated as a nonprofit group to work against abortion. It accepted corporate donations, and in 2004 it proposed to buy radio ads that criticized Wisconsin senators Russell Feingold and Herb Kohl, both Democrats, for opposing the confirmation of several of President George W. Bush's conservative judges. "Contact Senators Feingold and Kohl and tell them to oppose the filibuster," one ad said.

The Federal Election Commission objected, saying these ads would violate the McCain-Feingold Act because Senator Feingold was up for reelection at the time the ads were to be run. The Court disagreed with the FEC. Although the act itself may be constitutional, the law may not be applied in ways that clearly abridge free speech rights. "These cases are about political speech," Roberts said, and "we give the benefit of the doubt to speech, not censorship." Alito agreed. Justices Scalia, Kennedy, and Thomas agreed as well, but they said they would have gone further and struck down the entire McCain-Feingold Act as unconstitutional.

Separation of Powers

The Court in *Buckley v. Valeo* also held unanimously that the Federal Election Commission, as originally designed, was unconstitutional. The Court said the method of appointment of commissioners violated the Constitution's Separation of Powers and Appointments Clauses because some members were named by congressional officials but exercised executive powers. According to the decision, the commission may exercise only those powers that Congress is allowed to delegate to congressional committees—investigating and information gathering. Only if the commission's members were appointed by the president, as required under the Constitution's Appointments Clause, could the commission carry out the administrative and enforcement responsibilities the law originally gave it, the Court ruled.

The justices stayed their ruling for thirty days to give the House and Senate time to "reconstitute the commission by law or adopt other valid enforcement mechanisms."[55] As events developed, Congress took more than three months to act, and instead of merely reconstituting the commission, it passed a considerably expanded campaign financing law.

ELECTION RETURNS

Because the Constitution makes each chamber of Congress the judge of the election returns of its members, the Court considers disputed elections political questions, which it will not review. Only once has the Court felt obliged to determine whether a state law interfered with this congressional right. *Roudebush v. Hartke* (1972) arose when Rep. Richard L. Roudebush, R-Ind., lost the 1970 Senate election to incumbent senator Vance Hartke, D-Ind., by a slim margin.[56] Roudebush asked for a recount by the state, and Hartke challenged it on the ground that the state's recount procedure would interfere with the Senate's right to judge the disputed election returns.

Denying Hartke's challenge, the Court said that the state "recount does not prevent the Senate from independently evaluating the election any more than the initial count does. The Senate is free to accept or reject the apparent winner in either count, and, if it chooses, to conduct its own recount."[57] Hartke was seated by the Senate pending the outcome of the recount, which did not change the election results. In an earlier case, however, the Senate had refused to seat the apparent victor of a disputed election until the investigation into alleged misdeeds in his campaign was

The enormous influence of the big business lobby on Congress is illustrated by this 1889 cartoon by Joseph Keppler.

completed. *Barry v. United States ex rel. Cunningham* (1929) involved the contested 1926 election of William S. Vare of Pennsylvania to the Senate. One of the issues involved was whether the Senate's refusal to seat Vare pending the outcome of the investigation deprived Pennsylvania of its equal representation. The Court concluded that it did not:

> The equal representation is found in Article V, which authorizes and regulates amendments to the Constitution, "provided,…that no state, without its consent, shall be deprived of its equal suffrage in the Senate." This constitutes a limitation upon the power of amendment and has nothing to do with a situation such as the one here presented. The temporary deprivation of equal representation which results from the refusal of the Senate to seat a member pending inquiry as to his election or qualifications is the necessary consequence of the exercise of a constitutional power, and no more deprives the state of its "equal suffrage" in the constitutional sense than would a vote of the Senate vacating the seat of a sitting member or a vote of expulsion.[58]

REGULATION OF LOBBYING

The right to lobby Congress—to assert rights or to win a special privilege or financial benefit for the group applying the pressure or to achieve an ideological goal—is guaranteed by the First Amendment to the Constitution. It provides that "Congress shall make no law…abridging the freedom of speech or of the press; or the right of the people peaceably to assemble and to petition the Government for redress of grievances." Pressure groups, whether operating through general campaigns designed to sway public opinion or through direct contact with members of Congress, help to inform Congress and the public about issues and make known to Congress the practical aspects of proposed legislation—whom it would help or hurt, who is for or against it, and so on. Against these benefits, there are liabilities. The most serious is that pressure groups, in pursuing their objectives, may lead Congress into decisions that benefit the groups but do not necessarily serve other parts of the public. Lobbyists resort occasionally to bribery or other unethical tactics in their efforts to influence legislation.

To guard against such activities, the House in 1876 passed a resolution requiring lobbyists to register with the clerk of the House. Congress subsequently passed a handful of specialized measures regulating certain kinds of lobbying activities, but it was not until 1946 that it enacted a general law to regulate lobbying. Because of the difficulty of imposing meaningful regulation on lobbying without infringing on the constitutional rights of free speech, press, assembly, and petition, the 1946 act did not actually "regulate." Rather, it simply required any person who was hired by someone else for the principal purpose of lobbying Congress to register with the secretary of the Senate and the clerk of the House and to file certain quarterly financial reports so that the lobbyist's activities would be known to Congress and the public. Organizations that solicited or received money for the principal purpose of lobbying Congress did not necessarily have to register, but they did have to file quarterly spending reports with the clerk detailing how much they spent to influence legislation.

The National Association of Manufacturers (NAM) brought a test suit in 1948 challenging the validity of the 1946 law. A federal court in the District of Columbia in 1952 held the act unconstitutional because its provisions were "too indefinite and vague to constitute an ascertainable standard of guilt."[59] Late in the same year, the Supreme Court reversed the lower court on a technicality, leaving the 1946 law in full force but open to future litigation.[60] The challenge came in *United States v. Harriss* (1954), which was actually begun at the time that the NAM case was being pursued.[61] In June 1948 the federal government had obtained indictments against several individuals and an organization for alleged violations of the registration and reporting sections of the 1946 lobbying law.

The government charged that without registering or reporting, New York cotton broker Robert M. Harriss had made payments to Ralph W. Moore, a Washington commodity trader and secretary of the National Farm Committee, for the purpose of pressuring Congress on legislation. In addition, Moore had made similar payments to James E. McDonald, the agriculture

commissioner of Texas, and Tom Linder, the agriculture commissioner of Georgia. A lower court in 1953 held the lobbying law unconstitutional on the grounds that it was too vague and indefinite to meet the requirements of due process and that the registration and reporting requirements violated the rights of free speech, free press, assembly, and petition.

In June 1954 the Supreme Court, in a 5-3 vote, reversed the lower court and upheld the constitutionality of the 1946 statute. In doing so, it narrowly interpreted the act. The statute, the majority said, applied only to lobbyists or organizations that solicited, collected, or received contributions in order to conduct their lobbying and at the same time whose main purpose was to influence legislation. Furthermore, the Court interpreted the act "to refer only to 'lobbying in its commonly accepted sense'—to direct communications with members of Congress on pending or proposed federal legislation."[62]

This limited interpretation omitted from coverage several categories of lobbying organizations, including those that spent money from their own funds to conduct lobbying activities rather than collecting funds specifically for the purpose of lobbying, those who could claim that their primary purpose was something other than attempting to influence legislation, and those whose lobbying activities were confined to influencing the public on legislation or issues, so-called grassroots lobbying. It was only under this limited construction that a majority of the Court would find the act constitutional. Sympathetic to the congressional dilemma, the majority observed that Congress was not trying to prohibit lobbying activities but merely wanted to find out

> who is being hired, who is putting up the money and how much. It acted in the same spirit and for a similar purpose in passing the Federal Corrupt Practices Act—to maintain the integrity of a basic governmental process.... Under these circumstances, we believe that Congress, at least within the bounds of the Act as we have construed it, is not constitutionally forbidden to require the disclosure of lobbying activities. To do so would be to deny Congress in large measure the power of self-protection.[63]

In dissent, Justices Douglas, Hugo L. Black, and Robert H. Jackson complained that to uphold the lobbying act, the Court had in essence rewritten it. The dissenters also contended that the majority's construction made the statute no less vague than it had been:

> The language of the Act is so broad that one who writes a letter or makes a speech or publishes an article or distributes literature or does many of the other things with which appellees are charged has no fair notice when he is close to the prohibited line. No construction we give it today will make clear retroactively the vague standards that confronted appellees when they did the acts now charged against them as criminal.[64]

RULES

The power of the House and Senate each to make its own rules for the conduct of its business was described by Justice David J. Brewer in 1892:

> The Constitution empowers each house to determine its rules of proceedings. It may not by its rules ignore constitutional restraints or violate fundamental rights, and there should be a reasonable relation between the mode or method of proceeding established by the rule and the result which is sought to be attained. But within these limitations all matters of method are open to the determination of the house, and it is no impeachment of the rule to say that some other way would be better, more accurate or even more just. It is no objection to the validity of the rule that a different one has been prescribed and in force for a length of time. The power to make rules is not one which once exercised is exhausted. It is a continuous power, always subject to be exercised by the house, and within the limitations suggested, absolute and beyond the challenge of any other body or tribunal.[65]

Twice the Court has ruled that where a rule of the House or Senate conflicts with the rights of a private person, the rule must give way. In *United States v. Smith* (1932) the Court held that the Senate rules on confirming nominees to executive agencies could not be construed to allow the Senate to reconsider its confirmation of a person already sworn into the office.[66] The Court was careful to say that the question before it was how the rule should be interpreted and not its constitutionality. In the second case, *Christoffel v. United States* (1949), a divided Court overturned the perjury conviction of a witness who claimed before a House committee that he was not affiliated with the Communist Party.[67] The majority held that although there was a quorum of the committee present at the time the hearing began, there was no proof that the quorum still existed at the time the alleged perjury occurred. Therefore, it was not proved that the committee was a "competent tribunal" before which an erroneous statement would amount to perjury. The four dissenters contended that, once established, a quorum was presumed to continue until a point of no quorum was raised. Article I, section 5, of the Constitution states that a majority of each house constitutes a quorum to do business.

In *United States v. Ballin* (1892) the Court held that in disputes over whether a majority was present, the *Congressional Record,* the official journal of the proceedings in each chamber, would be the unchallengeable proof of how many members were present.[68] This ruling upheld the most controversial of a new set of rules and procedures adopted by the House in 1890—the counting of present but nonvoting members to make a quorum. In a second case decided in 1892, the Court upheld a federal statute that had been authenticated by both houses and signed into law by the president despite a showing in the *Congressional Record* that the enacted statute omitted a section that had been passed by both chambers.[69]

In *McGrain v. Daugherty* (1927) the Court sustained the Senate's claim that it was a continuing body that did not need to reauthorize its committees with each new Congress. It may be true that the House must dissolve because its members "are all elected for the period of a single Congress," the Court said, "but it cannot well be the same with the Senate, which is a continuing body whose members are elected for a term of six years and so divided into classes that the seats of one-third only become vacant at the end of each Congress, two-thirds always continuing into the next Congress."[70]

The Court declared in *Nixon v. United States* (1993) that a Senate rule permitting evidence in impeachment proceedings to be heard by a fact-finding committee instead of the full Senate cannot be challenged in federal court. The unanimous decision upheld a procedural shortcut that the Senate had used in the impeachment process to remove three federal judges from office. Emphasizing the constitutional provision that the "Senate shall have the sole Power to try all Impeachments," Chief Justice Rehnquist stated that the issue was beyond the reach of the Court: "The common sense meaning of the word 'sole' is that the Senate alone shall have authority to determine whether an individual should be acquitted or convicted."[71] Rehnquist added that there was no evidence that the framers thought the courts should play a role in the impeachment process. The decision upheld the 1989 removal of Walter L. Nixon, formerly the chief judge in Mississippi, who was impeached and convicted following a criminal conviction for perjury. The same procedure had been used to remove Judge Harry T. Claiborne of Nevada in 1986 and Judge Alcee Hastings of Florida in 1989.

NOTES

INTRODUCTION (PP. 71–77)

1. James Madison, Alexander Hamilton, and John Jay, *The Federalist Papers,* ed. Clinton Rossiter (New York: New American Library, 1961), 467.

2. *Marbury v. Madison,* 1 Cr. (5 U.S.) 137 at 177 (1803).

3. Charles Warren, *The Supreme Court in United States History,* rev. ed., 2 vols. (Boston: Little, Brown, 1926), 1:16–17.

4. *Gibbons v. Ogden,* 9 Wheat. (22 U.S.) 1 (1824).

5. *United States v. E. C. Knight Co.,* 156 U.S. 1 (1895).

6. *Champion v. Ames,* 188 U.S. 321 (1903).

7. *McCray v. United States,* 195 U.S. 27 (1904).

8. For example, see the Child Labor Act of 1916.

9. *Hammer v. Dagenhart,* 247 U.S. 251 (1918).

10. *Bailey v. Drexel Furniture Co.,* 259 U.S. 20 (1922).

11. See, for example, *Coronado Coal Co. v. United Mine Workers,* 268 U.S. 295 (1925), and *Bedford Cut Stone Co. v. Journeymen Stone Cutters Association,* 274 U.S. 37 (1927).

12. *Helvering v. Davis,* 301 U.S. 619 (1937).

13. *Wickard v. Filburn,* 317 U.S. 111 (1942).

14. *Carter v. Carter Coal Co.,* 298 U.S. 238 at 332 (1936).

15. C. Herman Pritchett and Alan F. Westin, *The Third Branch of Government: Eight Cases in Constitutional Politics* (New York: Harcourt, Brace and World, 1963), 3.

16. *United States v. Lopez,* 514 U.S. 549 (1995).

17. Douglas W. Kmiec, "Supreme Court Restores the Constitutional Structure," *Chicago Tribune,* May 2, 1995.

18. *Hepburn v. Griswold,* 8 Wall. (75 U.S.) 603 (1870).

19. *Pollock v. Farmers' Loan and Trust Co.,* 157 U.S. 429 (1895), and *Pollock v. Farmers' Loan and Trust Co.,* 158 U.S. 601 (1895).

20. *Foster and Elam v. Neilson,* 27 U.S. 253 (1829).

21. Robert G. McCloskey, *The American Supreme Court,* ed. Sanford Levinson, 2nd ed. (Chicago: University of Chicago Press, 1994), 127.

22. Article IV, section 3, paragraph 1; Article IV, section 3, paragraph 2; Article I, section 8, respectively.

23. *Scott v. Sandford,* 19 How. (60 U.S.) 393 (1857).

24. *Neeley v. Henkel,* 180 U.S. 109 (1901); *DeLima v. Bidwell,* 182 U.S. 1 (1901); *Downes v. Bidwell,* 182 U.S. 244 (1901); *Dorr v. United States,* 195 U.S. 138 (1904); and *Dowdell v. United States,* 221 U.S. 325 (1911). See Paul Finkelman and Melvin I. Urofsky, *Landmark Decisions of the United States Supreme Court,* 2nd ed. (Washington, D.C.: CQ Press, 2008), 162–164.

25. *Powell v. McCormack,* 395 U.S. 486 (1969).

26. *U.S. Term Limits, Inc. v. Thornton,* 514 U.S. 779 (1995).

27. *Gravel v. United States,* 408 U.S. 606 (1972).

JUDICIAL REVIEW AND LEGISLATIVE POWER (PP. 78–94)

1. Max Farrand, *The Records of the Federal Convention of 1787,* rev. ed., vol. 1 (New Haven: Yale University Press, 1937), quoted in Library of Congress, Congressional Research Service, *The Constitution of the United States of America: Analysis and Interpretation,* 92nd Cong., 2nd sess., 1973, S. Doc. 92-82, 670 n. 5. For a summary of discussions on the topic, see Raoul Berger, *Congress v. The Supreme Court* (Cambridge: Harvard University Press, 1969), 37–143.

2. *Hayburn's Case,* 2 Dall. (2 U.S.) 409 (1792).

3. *Hylton v. United States,* 3 Dall. (3 U.S.) 171 (1796).

4. *Ware v. Hylton,* 3 Dall. (3 U.S.) 199 (1796).

5. See Scott Douglas Gerber, "The Myth of *Marbury v. Madison* and the Origins of Judicial Review," in *Marbury versus Madison: Documents and Commentary,* ed. Mark A. Graber and Michael Perhac (Washington, D.C.: CQ Press, 2002), 1–15.

6. *Marbury v. Madison,* 1 Cr. (5 U.S.) 137 (1803).

7. Robert G. McCloskey, *The American Supreme Court,* ed. Sanford Levinson, 2nd ed. (Chicago: University of Chicago Press, 1994), 25.

8. Political scientist Joel B. Grossman asks, if Marshall's conclusion has merit, then "[w]hy was the delivery of the commission even necessary? Why then didn't Marbury just assume his new role as a justice of the peace?" Joel B. Grossman, "The

200th Anniversary of *Marbury v. Madison*: The Reasons We Should Still Care about the Decision, and the Lingering Questions It Left Behind," *Writ: FindLaw's Legal Commentary,* February 24, 2003.

9. *Marbury v. Madison,* 1 Cr. (5 U.S.) 137 at 176–177 (1803).

10. Id. at 177–179.

11. Charles Warren, *The Supreme Court in United States History,* rev. ed., 2 vols. (Boston: Little, Brown, 1926), 1:232.

12. Albert J. Beveridge, *Life of Marshall,* 4 vols. (Boston: Houghton Mifflin, 1916–1919), 3:177, quoted by Robert H. Jackson, *The Struggle for Judicial Supremacy* (New York: Knopf, 1941), 28.

13. *Scott v. Sandford,* 19 How. (60 U.S.) 393 (1857); *Hepburn v. Griswold,* 8 Wall. (75 U.S.) 603 (1870).

14. *Hepburn v. Griswold,* 8 Wall. (75 U.S.) 603 (1870), *Knox v. Lee, and Parker v. Davis,* 12 Wall. (79 U.S.) 457 (1871).

15. *Pollock v. Farmers' Loan and Trust Co.,* 157 U.S. 429 (1895), and *Pollock v. Farmers' Loan and Trust Co.,* 158 U.S. 601 (1895).

16. Robert E. Cushman and Robert F. Cushman, *Cases in Constitutional Law,* 3rd ed. (New York: Appleton-Century-Crofts, 1968), 23.

17. *Hammer v. Dagenhart,* 247 U.S. 251 (1918).

18. *Bailey v. Drexel Furniture Co.,* 259 U.S. 20 (1922).

19. *Carter v. Carter Coal Co.,* 298 U.S. 238 (1936).

20. *Baker v. Carr,* 369 U.S. 186 (1962).

21. Robert K. Carr, *The Supreme Court and Judicial Review* (New York: Farrar and Rinehart, 1942), 20.

22. Ibid.

23. Alfred H. Kelly and Winfred A. Harbison, *The American Constitution: Its Origins and Development,* 5th ed. (New York: Norton, 1976), 169.

24. *United States v. Fisher,* 2 Cr. (6 U.S.) 358 at 396 (1805).

25. *McCulloch v. Maryland,* 4 Wheat. (17 U.S.) 316 (1819).

26. Id. at 405.

27. Id. at 406.

28. Id. at 408.

29. Id. at 411.

30. Id. at 413–415.

31. Id. at 421.

32. Id. at 431.

33. McCloskey, *American Supreme Court,* 43. Also see Gerald Gunther, ed., *John Marshall's Defense of* McCulloch v. Maryland (Stanford, Calif.: Stanford University Press, 1969).

34. R. Kent Newmyer, *The Supreme Court under Marshall and Taney* (New York: Crowell, 1968), 45–46.

35. Joseph Story, *Commentaries on the Constitution of the United States,* 3 vols. (1833; reprint, New York: Da Capo Press, 1970), 3:124, sec. 1251.

36. *American Insurance Company v. Canter,* 1 Pet. (26 U.S.) 511 (1828).

37. *United States v. Jones,* 109 U.S. 513 (1883); *Fong Yue Ting v. United States,* 149 U.S. 698 (1893); *United States v. Kamaga,* 118 U.S. 375 (1886).

38. *United States v. Curtiss-Wright Export Corp.,* 299 U.S. 304 at 316, 318, passim (1936).

39. *Sunshine Anthracite Coal Co. v. Adkins,* 310 U.S. 381 at 398 (1940), and *Mistretta v. United States,* 488 U.S. 361 (1989). See also Thomas O. Sargentich, "The Delegation of Lawmaking Power to the Executive Branch," in *Separation of Powers: Documents and Commentary,* ed. Katy J. Harriger (Washington, D.C.: CQ Press, 2003), 116–131.

40. *Wayman v. Southard,* 10 Wheat. (23 U.S.) 1 at 43 (1825).

41. Id.

42. *Buttfield v. Stranahan,* 192 U.S. 470 at 496 (1904).

43. Id.

44. *United States v. Grimaud,* 220 U.S. 506 (1911); *L. P. Steuart & Bro. v. Bowles,* 322 U.S. 398 (1944).

45. *Interstate Commerce Commission v. Brimson,* 154 U.S. 447 (1894).

46. *The Brig Aurora v. United States,* 7 Cr. (11 U.S.) 382 (1813).

47. *Field v. Clark,* 143 U.S. 649 (1892).

48. *J. W. Hampton Jr. & Co. v. United States,* 276 U.S. 394 at 405–406 (1928).

49. *Fahey v. Mallonee,* 332 U.S. 245 (1947); *Arizona v. California,* 373 U.S. 546 at 583 (1963).

50. *Panama Refining Co. v. Ryan,* 293 U.S. 388 (1935).

51. C. Herman Pritchett, *The American Constitution* (New York: McGraw-Hill, 1959), 176.

52. *Panama Refining Co. v. Ryan,* 293 U.S. 388 at 418 (1935).

53. Id. at 440.

54. *A. L. A. Schechter Poultry Corp. v. United States,* 295 U.S. 495 at 542 (1935).

55. Id. at 551, 533, passim.

56. Alpheus T. Mason and William M. Beaney, *The Supreme Court in a Free Society* (Englewood Cliffs, N.J.: Prentice-Hall, 1969), 33.

57. *Opp Cotton Mills v. Administrator of Wage and Hours Division,* 312 U.S. 126 (1941).

58. *A. L. A. Schechter Poultry Corp. v. United States,* 295 U.S. 495 at 537 (1935).

59. *Carter v. Carter Coal Co.,* 298 U.S. 238 at 311 (1936).

60. *Currin v. Wallace,* 306 U.S. 1 (1939).

61. *Jackson v. Roby,* 109 U.S. 440 (1883); *Erhardt v. Boaro,* 113 U.S. 527 (1885); *Butte City Water Co. v. Baker,* 196 U.S. 119 (1905); *St. Louis, Iron Mountain & Southern Railway Co. v. Taylor,* 210 U.S. 281 (1908).

62. *Martin v. Mott,* 12 Wheat. (25 U.S.) 19 (1827).

63. *United States v. Curtiss-Wright Export Corp.,* 299 U.S. 304 (1936).

64. Id. at 319–320.

65. *United States v. Sharpnack,* 355 U.S. 286 at 294 (1958).

66. *Clark Distilling Co. v. Western Maryland Railway Co.,* 242 U.S. 311 (1917).

67. *Immigration and Naturalization Service v. Chadha,* 462 U.S. 919 (1983). See also Barbara Hinkson Craig, *Chadha: The Story of an Epic Constitutional Struggle* (New York: Oxford University Press, 1988).

68. *Immigration and Naturalization Service v. Chadha,* 462 U.S. 919 at 951, 952 (1983).

69. Id. at 944.

70. Id. at 959.

71. Id. at 972.

72. Id. at 968.

73. *Alaska Airlines v. Brock,* 480 U.S. 678 at 685 (1987).

74. Louis Fisher, *Constitutional Dialogues* (Princeton, N.J.: Princeton University Press, 1988), 224–229.

THE COMMERCE POWER (PP. 95–142)

1. *Gibbons v. Ogden,* 9 Wheat. (22 U.S.) 1 at 196 (1824).

2. *Cooley v. Board of Port Wardens of Philadelphia,* 12 How. (53 U.S.) 299 (1851).

3. *Pollock v. Farmers' Loan and Trust Co.,* 157 U.S. 429 (1895), and *Pollock v. Farmers' Loan and Trust Co.,* 158 U.S. 601 (1895).

4. *In re Debs,* 158 U.S. 564 (1895).

5. *United States v. E. C. Knight Co.,* 156 U.S. 1 (1895).

6. *Missouri, Kansas & Texas Railway Co. of Texas v. May,* 194 U.S. 267 at 270 (1904).

7. *Duplex Printing Press Co. v. Deering,* 254 U.S. 443 (1921).

8. *Adair v. United States,* 208 U.S. 161 (1908).

9. *Hammer v. Dagenhart,* 247 U.S. 251 (1918).

10. *Champion v. Ames,* 188 U.S. 321 (1903).

11. *Shreveport Rate Cases,* 234 U.S. 342 (1914).

12. *Wickard v. Filburn,* 317 U.S. 111 (1942).

13. Robert L. Stern, "The Commerce Clause and the National Economy," *Harvard Law Review* 59 (May–July 1946): 946.

14. *National League of Cities v. Usery,* 426 U.S. 833 (1976).

15. *Garcia v. San Antonio Metropolitan Transit Authority,* 469 U.S. 528 (1985).

16. *United States v. Lopez,* 514 U.S. 549 (1995).

17. Charles Warren, *The Making of the Constitution* (Boston: Little, Brown, 1928), 16.

18. *Gibbons v. Ogden,* 9 Wheat. (22 U.S.) 1 (1824).

19. Id. at 184.

20. Charles Warren, *The Supreme Court in United States History,* rev. ed., 2 vols. (Boston: Little, Brown, 1926), 1:597.

21. *Gibbons v. Ogden,* 9 Wheat. (22 U.S.) 1 at 9 (1824).

22. Id. at 76.

23. Id. at 189–190.

24. Id. at 194.

25. Id. at 194–195.

26. Id. at 196–197.

27. Id. at 227.

28. Warren, *Supreme Court in United States History,* 1:620–621.

29. Felix Frankfurter, *The Commerce Clause under Marshall, Taney and Waite* (Chapel Hill: University of North Carolina Press, 1937), 25.

30. *Brown v. Maryland,* 12 Wheat. (25 U.S.) 419 (1827).

31. *Willson v. Blackbird Creek Marsh Co.,* 2 Pet. (27 U.S.) 245 (1829).

32. See, for example, *New York v. Miln,* 11 Pet. (36 U.S.) 102 (1837); *License Cases,* 5 How. (46 U.S.) 504 (1847); *Passenger Cases,* 7 How. (48 U.S.) 283 (1849).

33. *Cooley v. Port Wardens of Philadelphia,* 12 How. (53 U.S.) 299 (1852).

34. *Willson v. Blackbird Creek Marsh Co.,* 2 Pet. (27 U.S.) 245 (1829).

35. *Pennsylvania v. Wheeling and Belmont Bridge Co.,* 13 How. (54 U.S.) 518 (1852).

36. *Pennsylvania v. Wheeling and Belmont Bridge Co.,* 18 How. (59 U.S.) at 421 (1856).

37. *Veazie v. Moor,* 14 How. (55 U.S.) 568 (1852).

38. *Gilman v. City of Philadelphia,* 3 Wall. (70 U.S.) 713 (1866).

39. *The Daniel Ball,* 10 Wall. (77 U.S.) 557 at 565 (1871).

40. *United States v. Chandler-Dunbar Water Co.,* 229 U.S. 53 at 73 (1913).

41. *Arizona v. California,* 283 U.S. 423 at 455–456 (1931).

42. *Ashwander v. Tennessee Valley Authority,* 297 U.S. 288 (1936).

43. *Tennessee Electric Power Co. v. Tennessee Valley Authority,* 306 U.S. 118 (1939).

44. *United States v. Appalachian Electric Power Co.,* 311 U.S. 377 at 407 (1940).

45. *Solid Waste Agency of Northern Cook Co. v. Army Corps of Engineers,* 531 U.S. 159 (2001); *Rapanos v. United States,* 547 U.S. 715 (2007).

46. *United States v. Trans-Missouri Freight Assn.,* 166 U.S. 290 (1897).

47. *Munn v. Illinois,* 94 U.S. 113 (1877).

48. *Wabash, St. Louis & Pacific Railway Co. v. Illinois,* 118 U.S. 557 (1886).

49. *Interstate Commerce Commission v. Brimson,* 154 U.S. 447 (1894).

50. *Interstate Commerce Commission v. Cincinnati, New Orleans & Texas Pacific Railway Co.,* 167 U.S. 479 at 494–495, passim (1897).

51. Id. at 501.

52. *Interstate Commerce Commission v. Alabama-Midland Railway Co.,* 168 U.S. 144 (1897).

53. *Illinois Central Railroad Co. v. Interstate Commerce Commission,* 206 U.S. 41 (1907).

54. *Interstate Commerce Commission v. Chicago, Rock Island and Pacific Railway Co.,* 218 U.S. 88 at 108 (1910).

55. *United States v. Atchison, Topeka and Santa Fe Railroad Co.,* 234 U.S. 476 at 486 (1914).

56. Loren P. Beth, *The Development of the American Constitution, 1877–1917* (New York: Harper and Row, Harper Torchbooks, 1971), 151.

57. *Minnesota Rate Cases*, 230 U.S. 252 at 399 (1913).

58. *Shreveport Rate Cases*, 234 U.S. 342 at 351–352 (1914).

59. *Railroad Commissioner of Wisconsin v. Chicago, Burlington & Quincy Railroad Co.*, 257 U.S. 563 at 589–590 (1922).

60. *Dayton-Goose Creek Railway Co. v. United States*, 263 U.S. 456 (1924).

61. *Loewe v. Lawlor*, 208 U.S. 274 (1908).

62. *Adair v. United States*, 208 U.S. 161 (1908).

63. Id. at 172, 179.

64. Id. at 191.

65. *First Employers' Liability Cases*, 207 U.S. 463 (1908).

66. *Second Employers' Liability Cases*, 223 U.S. 1 (1912).

67. *Pennsylvania Railroad Company v. U.S. Railroad Labor Board*, 261 U.S. 72 (1923); *Pennsylvania Railroad System and Allied Lines Federation No. 90 v. Pennsylvania Railroad Company*, 267 U.S. 203 (1925).

68. *Texas & New Orleans Railroad Co. v. Brotherhood of Railway & Steamship Clerks*, 281 U.S. 548 at 571 (1930).

69. *Southern Railway Co. v. United States*, 222 U.S. 20 (1911).

70. *Baltimore & Ohio Railroad Co. v. Interstate Commerce Commission*, 221 U.S. 612 at 619 (1911).

71. *Wilson v. New*, 243 U.S. 332 (1917).

72. Id. at 350.

73. *Railroad Retirement Board v. Alton Railroad Co.*, 295 U.S. 330 at 368 (1935).

74. Id. at 384.

75. *Pipe Line Cases*, 234 U.S. 548 at 559, 561, passim (1914).

76. *Public Utilities Commission of Rhode Island v. Attleboro Steam & Electric Co.*, 273 U.S. 83 (1927); *Federal Power Commission v. Natural Gas Pipeline Co.*, 315 U.S. 575 (1942).

77. *Pensacola Telegraph Co. v. Western Union Telegraph Co.*, 96 U.S. 1 (1878).

78. *Federal Radio Commission v. Nelson Bros.*, 289 U.S. 266 at 279 (1933).

79. *Veazie v. Moor*, 14 How. (55 U.S.) 568 at 574 (1852).

80. *Kidd v. Pearson*, 128 U.S. 1 at 20 (1888).

81. *United States v. E. C. Knight Co.*, 156 U.S. 1 (1895).

82. Id. at 12.

83. Id. at 13.

84. Id. at 16.

85. Id. at 43.

86. *Mandeville Island Farms v. American Crystal Sugar Co.*, 334 U.S. 219 at 230 (1948).

87. *United States v. Trans-Missouri Freight Assn.*, 166 U.S. 290 (1897); *United States v. Joint Traffic Assn.*, 171 U.S. 506 (1898).

88. *Addystone Pipe & Steel Co. v. United States*, 175 U.S. 211 at 241 (1899).

89. *Northern Securities Company v. United States*, 193 U.S. 197 at 327 (1904).

90. Id. at 331.

91. Id. at 333.

92. *Swift & Co. v. United States*, 196 U.S. 375 (1905).

93. Id. at 396–399, passim.

94. *Board of Trade of Chicago v. Olsen*, 262 U.S. 1 at 35 (1923).

95. *Stafford v. Wallace*, 258 U.S. 495 at 518 (1922).

96. *Board of Trade of Chicago v. Olsen*, 262 U.S. 1 (1923), overturning *Hill v. Wallace*, 259 U.S. 44 (1922).

97. *Lemke v. Farmers Grain Co.*, 258 U.S. 50 (1922); see also *Eureka Pipeline Co. v. Hallanan*, 257 U.S. 265 (1921); *United Fuel Gas Co. v. Hallanan*, 257 U.S. 277 (1921); *Western Union Telegraph Co. v. Foster*, 247 U.S. 105 (1918).

98. *United States v. Trans-Missouri Freight Assn.*, 166 U.S. 290 at 328 (1897).

99. Id. at 344.

100. *Standard Oil Co. v. United States*, 221 U.S. 1 at 60 (1911).

101. Id. at 103, 104–105, passim.

102. *United States v. American Tobacco Co.*, 221 U.S. 106 at 179 (1911).

103. *United States v. Winslow*, 227 U.S. 202 (1913).

104. *United States v. United States Steel Corp.*, 251 U.S. 417 (1920).

105. *Chicago Board of Trade v. United States*, 246 U.S. 231 at 238 (1918).

106. *Dr. Miles Medical Co. v. John D. Park*, 220 U.S. 373 (1911), overruled by *Leegin Creative Leather Products v. PSKS*, 551 U.S. —-(2007).

107. *In re Debs*, 158 U.S. 564 at 600 (1895).

108. *Loewe v. Lawlor*, 208 U.S. 274 at 293–294 (1908).

109. Id. at 301.

110. *Duplex Printing Press Co. v. Deering*, 254 U.S. 443 at 469 (1921).

111. *Coronado Coal Co. v. United Mine Workers*, 268 U.S. 295 (1925); *Bedford Cut Stone Co. v. Journeymen Stone Cutters' Assn.*, 274 U.S. 37 (1927).

112. *Lauf v. E. G. Shinner & Co.*, 303 U.S. 315 (1938).

113. *New Negro Alliance v. Sanitary Grocery Co.*, 303 U.S. 552 (1938); *Brotherhood of Railroad Trainmen v. Chicago River and Indiana Railroad Co.*, 353 U.S. 30 (1957); *Boys Market v. Retail Clerks Union*, 398 U.S. 235 (1970).

114. *United States v. Hutcheson*, 312 U.S. 219 (1941).

115. *Allen Bradley Co. v. Local Union No. 3*, 325 U.S. 797 (1945).

116. *Hunt v. Crumboch*, 325 U.S. 821 (1945).

117. Robert K. Carr, *The Supreme Court and Judicial Review* (New York: Farrar and Rinehart, 1942), 108.

118. *United States v. DeWitt*, 9 Wall. (76 U.S.) 41 at 45 (1870).

119. Id. at 44.

120. *Reid v. Colorado*, 187 U.S. 137 (1902).

121. *Champion v. Ames,* 188 U.S. 321 (1903).

122. Id. at 357.

123. Id. at 355.

124. Id. at 358.

125. Warren, *Supreme Court in United States History,* 2:735–736.

126. *Hipolite Egg Co. v. United States,* 220 U.S. 45 (1911); *Hoke v. United States,* 227 U.S. 308 (1913); *Southern Railway Co. v. United States,* 222 U.S. 20 (1911); *Baltimore & Ohio Railroad Co. v. Interstate Commerce Commission,* 221 U.S. 612 (1911).

127. *Hammer v. Dagenhart,* 247 U.S. 251 (1918).

128. Id. at 268–269.

129. Id. at 271.

130. Id. at 271–272.

131. Id. at 272.

132. Id. at 276.

133. Id. at 277.

134. Id. at 279–280.

135. Id. at 280.

136. Id. at 281.

137. *Bailey v. Drexel Furniture Co.,* 259 U.S. 20 (1922).

138. *United States v. Darby Lumber Co.,* 312 U.S. 100 (1941).

139. *Pittsburgh Melting Co. v. Totten,* 248 U.S. 1 (1918).

140. *Brooks v. United States,* 267 U.S. 432 (1925); *Gooch v. United States,* 297 U.S. 124 (1936); *Kentucky Whip & Collar Co. v. Illinois Central Railroad Co.,* 299 U.S. 334 (1937).

141. *Brooks v. United States,* 267 U.S. 432 at 436–437 (1925).

142. *Perez v. United States,* 401 U.S. 146 (1971).

143. *Panama Refining Co. v. Ryan,* 293 U.S. 388 (1935).

144. *A. L. A. Schechter Poultry Corp. v. United States,* 295 U.S. 495 (1935).

145. Id. at 543.

146. Id. at 546.

147. Id. at 549.

148. Carr, *Supreme Court and Judicial Review,* 118–122.

149. *A. L. A. Schechter Poultry Corp. v. United States,* 554.

150. *Carter v. Carter Coal Co.,* 298 U.S. 238 (1936).

151. Id. at 307–308.

152. Id. at 309.

153. Id.

154. Id. at 317–318.

155. Alfred H. Kelly and Winfred A. Harbison, *The American Constitution: Its Origins and Development,* 5th ed. (New York: Norton, 1976), 707.

156. *Carter v. Carter Coal Co.,* 298 U.S. 238 at 328 (1936).

157. Id. at 331–332.

158. *National Labor Relations Board v. Jones & Laughlin Steel Corp.,* 301 U.S. 1 (1937).

159. Id. at 41–42.

160. Id. at 77.

161. Id. at 78.

162. *National Labor Relations Board v. Fruehauf Trailer Co.,* 301 U.S. 49 (1937); *National Labor Relations Board v. Friedman-Harry Marks Clothing Co.,* 301 U.S. 58 (1937).

163. *Associated Press v. National Labor Relations Board,* 301 U.S. 103 (1937).

164. *Washington, Virginia & Maryland Coach Co. v. National Labor Relations Board,* 301 U.S. 142 (1937).

165. *Santa Cruz Fruit Packing Co. v. National Labor Relations Board,* 303 U.S. 453 at 469 (1938).

166. *Consolidated Edison v. National Labor Relations Board,* 305 U.S. 197 at 220 (1938).

167. *National Labor Relations Board v. Fainblatt,* 306 U.S. 601 at 606 (1939).

168. *West Coast Hotel v. Parrish,* 300 U.S. 379 (1937); *Morehead v. New York ex rel. Tipaldo,* 298 U.S. 587 (1936); *Adkins v. Children's Hospital,* 261 U.S. 525 (1923); *Bunting v. Oregon,* 243 U.S. 426 (1917).

169. *United States v. Darby Lumber Co.,* 312 U.S. 100 (1941).

170. Id. at 113, 115, passim.

171. Id. at 116–117.

172. Id. at 124.

173. *A. B. Kirschbaum v. Walling,* 316 U.S. 517 (1942).

174. *Warren-Bradshaw Co. v. Hall,* 317 U.S. 88 (1942); *Walton v. Southern Package Corporation,* 320 U.S. 540 (1944); *Borden v. Borella,* 325 U.S. 679 (1945).

175. *Walling v. Jacksonville Paper Co.,* 317 U.S. 564 (1943).

176. *10 East 40th St. Bldg. v. Callus,* 325 U.S. 578 (1945).

177. Carr, *Supreme Court and Judicial Review,* 135.

178. *Mulford v. Smith,* 307 U.S. 38 at 47 (1939).

179. *United States v. Rock Royal Cooperative,* 307 U.S. 533 (1939); *H. P. Hood & Sons v. United States,* 307 U.S. 588 (1939); *United States v. Wrightwood Dairy Co.,* 315 U.S. 110 (1942).

180. *United States v. Wrightwood Dairy Co.,* 315 U.S. 110 at 118–119 (1942).

181. *Wickard v. Filburn,* 317 U.S. 111 (1942).

182. Quoted in Alpheus T. Mason and William M. Beaney, *The Supreme Court in a Free Society* (Englewood Cliffs, N.J.: Prentice-Hall, 1959), 98.

183. *Wickard v. Filburn,* 317 U.S. 111 at 124–125 (1942).

184. Id. at 128–129.

185. C. Herman Pritchett, *The American Constitution,* 3rd ed. (New York: McGraw-Hill, 1977), 198.

186. *Civil Rights Cases,* 109 U.S. 3 (1883).

187. Quoted in C. Herman Pritchett, *The American Constitution* (New York: McGraw-Hill, 1959), 604.

188. *Hall v. DeCuir,* 95 U.S. 485 (1878).

189. *Louisville, New Orleans & Texas Railway Co. v. Mississippi,* 133 U.S. 587 (1890).

190. *Plessy v. Ferguson,* 163 U.S. 537 (1896).

191. *Morgan v. Virginia,* 328 U.S. 373 (1946).

192. *Henderson v. United States,* 339 U.S. 816 (1950).

193. *Heart of Atlanta Motel v. United States,* 379 U.S. 241 (1964).

194. Id. at 258.

195. Id. at 257.

196. *Katzenbach v. McClung,* 379 U.S. 294 (1964).

197. *Daniel v. Paul,* 395 U.S. 298 (1969).

198. *Paul v. Virginia,* 8 Wall. (75 U.S.) 168 (1869).

199. *United States v. South-Eastern Underwriters Association,* 322 U.S. 533 at 553 (1944).

200. *Prudential Insurance Co. v. Benjamin,* 328 U.S. 408 (1946).

201. *United States v. Lopez,* 514 U.S. 549 (1995).

202. Id. at 552.

203. Id. at 567.

204. Id. at 574.

205. Id. at 587.

206. Id. at 599, 602.

207. Id. at 602.

208. *United States v. Morrison,* 529 U.S. 598 (2000).

209. Violence Against Women Act of 1993, H. Rept. 395, 103rd Cong., 1st sess., November 10, 1993, 25, citing Justice Department, *Report to the Nation on Crime and Justice,* 2nd ed. (1988), 29.

210. See "From the Surgeon General, U.S. Health Services," *JAMA* 267 (1992), 3132.

211. Violence Against Women Act of 1993, S. Rept. 138, 103rd Cong., 1st sess., September 10, 1993, 41.

212. *United States v. Morrison,* 529 U.S. 598 at 613, 617 (2000).

213. *United States v. Harris,* 106 U.S. 629 (1883).

214. *United States v. Morrison,* 529 U.S. 598 at 626, 639 (2000).

215. *Seminole Tribe v. Florida,* 517 U.S. 44 (1996).

216. Id. at 47.

217. *Chisholm v. Georgia,* 2 Dall. (2 U.S.) 419 (1793).

218. *Seminole Tribe v. Florida,* 517 U.S. 44 at 54 (1996).

219. Id. at 72.

220. *Alden v. Maine,* 527 U.S. 706 at 713 (1999).

221. Id. at 758.

222. Id. at 741, 759.

223. Id. at 811.

224. *National League of Cities v. Usery,* 426 U.S. 833 (1976).

225. *Garcia v. San Antonio Metropolitan Transit Authority,* 469 U.S. 528 (1985).

226. Id. at 556–557.

227. *Florida Prepaid Postsecondary Education Expense Board v. College Savings Bank,* 527 U.S. 627 at 648 (1999), and *College Savings Bank v. Florida,* 527 U.S. 666 (1999).

228. *Kimel v. Florida,* 528 U.S. 62 (2000), and *Board of Trustees of the University of Alabama v. Garrett,* 531 U.S. 356 (2001).

229. *Federal Maritime Commission v. South Carolina Ports Authority,* 535 U.S. 743 (2002).

230. Id.

231. *Nevada Department of Human Resources v. Hibbs,* 538 U.S. 721 (2003).

232. *Tennessee v. Lane,* 541 U.S. 509 (2004).

233. *Gonzales v. Raich,* 545 U.S. 1 (2005).

FISCAL AND MONETARY POWERS (PP. 143–164)

1. C. Herman Pritchett, *The American Constitution,* 3d ed. (New York: McGraw-Hill, 1977), 167.

2. *Hepburn v. Griswold,* 8 Wall. (75 U.S.) 603 (1870), and Knox v. Lee and Parker v. Davis, 12 Wall. (79 U.S.) 457 (1871); *Pollock v. Farmers' Loan and Trust Co.,* 157 U.S. 429 (1895), and *Pollock v. Farmers' Loan and Trust Co.,* 158 U.S. 601 (1895).

3. *Hylton v. United States,* 3 Dall. (3 U.S.) 171 (1796).

4. Alpheus T. Mason and William M. Beaney, *The Supreme Court in a Free Society* (Englewood Cliffs, N.J.: Prentice-Hall, 1959), 129.

5. See, for example, *Veazie Bank v. Fenno,* 8 Wall. (75 U.S.) 533 (1869); *Schley v. Rew,* 23 Wall. 331 (1875).

6. *Springer v. United States,* 102 U.S. 586 (1881).

7. Carl B. Swisher, *American Constitutional Development,* 2d ed. (Cambridge, Mass.: Riverside Press, 1954), 448.

8. Quoted by Mason and Beaney in *Supreme Court in a Free Society,* 131.

9. *Pollock v. Farmers' Loan and Trust Co.,* 157 U.S. 429 (1895).

10. *Pollock v. Farmers' Loan and Trust Co.,* 158 U.S. 601 (1895).

11. Id. at 637.

12. *Pollock v. Farmers' Loan and Trust Co.,* 157 U.S. 429 at 607 (1895).

13. *Pollock v. Farmers' Loan and Trust Co.,* 158 U.S. 601 at 685 (1895).

14. Editor's Notes, *American Law Review* (May–June 1895): 472, cited by Leo Pfeffer, *This Honorable Court, A History of the United States Supreme Court* (Boston: Beacon Press, 1965), 222.

15. *United States v. E. C. Knight Co.,* 156 U.S. 1 (1895); *In re Debs,* 158 U.S. 564 (1895); Pritchett, *American Constitution,* 169.

16. *Nicol v. Ames,* 173 U.S. 509 (1899); *Knowlton v. Moore,* 178 U.S. 41 (1900); *Patton v. Brady,* 184 U.S. 608 (1902); *Thomas v. United States,* 192 U.S. 363 (1904).

17. *Spreckles Sugar Refining Co. v. McClain,* 192 U.S. 397 (1904).

18. *Flint v. Stone Tracy Co.,* 220 U.S. 107 (1911).

19. *Brushaber v. Union Pacific Railroad Co.,* 240 U.S. 1 (1916); *Stanton v. Baltic Mining Co.,* 240 U.S. 103 (1916); *Tyee Realty Co. v. Anderson,* 240 U.S. 115 (1916).

20. *Stanton v. Baltic Mining Co.,* 240 U.S. 103 at 112 (1916).

21. *Eisner v. Macomber,* 252 U.S. 189 (1920).

22. *Head Money Cases,* 112 U.S. 580 (1884).

23. *Knowlton v. Moore,* 178 U.S. 41 (1900).

24. *Florida v. Mellon,* 273 U.S. 12 (1927); *United States v. Ptasynski,* 462 U.S. 74 (1983).

25. *J. W. Hampton Jr. & Co. v. United States*, 276 U.S. 394 at 412 (1928).

26. *Veazie Bank v. Fenno*, 8 Wall. (75 U.S.) 533 (1869).

27. *Head Money Cases*, 112 U.S. 580 (1884).

28. *Sunshine Anthracite Coal Co. v. Adkins*, 310 U.S. 381 at 393 (1940).

29. *Carter v. Carter Coal Co.*, 298 U.S. 238 (1936).

30. *Champion v. Ames*, 188 U.S. 321 (1903).

31. *McCray v. United States*, 195 U.S. 27 (1904).

32. Id. at 56.

33. *United States v. Doremus*, 249 U.S. 86 at 94 (1919).

34. *Bailey v. Drexel Furniture Co.*, 259 U.S. 20 (1922).

35. Id. at 38.

36. *Hammer v. Dagenhart*, 247 U.S. 251 (1918).

37. Id.

38. Id. at 43.

39. *Hill v. Wallace*, 259 U.S. 44 at 66–67 (1922).

40. *Board of Trade of Chicago v. Olsen*, 262 U.S. 1 (1923).

41. *United States v. Constantine*, 296 U.S. 287 (1935).

42. *Carter v. Carter Coal Co.*, 298 U.S. 238 (1936).

43. *United States v. Butler*, 297 U.S. 1 (1936).

44. *Sonzinsky v. United States*, 300 U.S. 506 at 513–514 (1937).

45. *United States v. Sanchez*, 340 U.S. 42 (1950); *United States v. Kahriger*, 345 U.S. 22 (1953).

46. *Marchetti v. United States*, 390 U.S. 39 (1968); *Grosso v. United States*, 390 U.S. 62 (1968); *Haynes v. United States*, 390 U.S. 85 (1968); *Leary v. United States*, 395 U.S. 6 (1969).

47. *McCulloch v. Maryland*, 4 Wheat. (17 U.S.) 316 at 431 (1819).

48. *Dobbins v. Erie County*, 16 Pet. (41 U.S.) 435 (1842).

49. *Collector v. Day*, 11 Wall. (78 U.S.) 113 (1871).

50. *Weston v. City Council of Charleston*, 2 Pet. (27 U.S.) 449 (1829); *Van Brocklin v. Tennessee*, 117 U.S. 151 (1886).

51. *Pollock v. Farmers' Loan and Trust Co.*, 157 U.S. 429 (1895).

52. *Indian Motorcycle Co. v. United States*, 283 U.S. 570 (1931).

53. *South Carolina v. United States*, 199 U.S. 437 (1905); *Helvering v. Gerhardt*, 304 U.S. 405 (1938); *Graves v. New York ex rel. O'Keefe*, 306 U.S. 466 (1939).

54. *South Carolina v. Baker*, 485 U.S. 505 (1988).

55. *Clallam County v. United States*, 263 U.S. 341 (1923).

56. *Maricopa County v. Valley Bank*, 318 U.S. 357 (1943); *Pittman v. Home Owners' Corporation*, 308 U.S. 21 (1939); *McCulloch v. Maryland*, 4 Wheat. (17 U.S.) 316 (1819); *Thomson v. Union Pacific Railroad Co.*, 9 Wall. (76 U.S.) 579 (1870); *Union Pacific Railroad Co. v. Peniston*, 18 Wall. (85 U.S.) 5 (1873).

57. *Northwestern Mutual Life Insurance Co. v. Wisconsin*, 275 U.S. 136 (1927); *Miller v. Milwaukee*, 272 U.S. 173 (1927); *Hibernia Savings Society v. San Francisco*, 200 U.S. 310 (1906); *Plummer v. Coler*, 178 U.S. 115 (1900); *Blodgett v. Silberman*, 277 U.S. 1 (1928); *Rockford Life Insurance Co. v. Illinois Department of Revenue*, 482 U.S. 182 (1987).

58. *Alabama v. King and Boozer*, 314 U.S. 1 (1941); *James v. Dravo Contracting Co.*, 302 U.S. 134 (1937); *United States v. Allegheny County*, 322 U.S. 174 (1944); *United States and Borg-Warner Corp. v. City of Detroit*, 355 U.S. 466 (1958); *United States v. Township of Muskegan*, 355 U.S. 484 (1958); *United States v. New Mexico*, 455 U.S. 720 (1982).

59. *Frothingham v. Mellon* and *Massachusetts v. Mellon*, 262 U.S. 447 at 487 (1923).

60. Id. at 485–486.

61. *Frothingham v. Mellon* and *Massachusetts v. Mellon*, 262 U.S. 447 (1923).

62. *Alabama Power Co. v. Ickes*, 302 U.S. 464 (1938); *Tennessee Electric Power Co. v. Tennessee Valley Authority*, 306 U.S. 118 (1939).

63. *Oklahoma v. Civil Service Commission*, 330 U.S. 127 at 143 (1947).

64. *South Dakota v. Dole*, 483 U.S. 203 (1987).

65. James Madison, Alexander Hamilton, and John Jay, *The Federalist Papers*, ed. Clinton Rossiter (New York: New American Library, 1961), No. 41, p. 263.

66. *United States v. Butler*, 297 U.S. 1 (1936).

67. Id. at 61.

68. Id. at 66.

69. Id. at 68.

70. Id. at 71.

71. Id. at 74–75.

72. Id. at 85.

73. *Steward Machine Co. v. Davis*, 301 U.S. 548 (1937).

74. Id. at 581.

75. Id. at 586–587.

76. Id. at 589–590.

77. *Helvering v. Davis*, 301 U.S. 619 (1937).

78. Id. at 640.

79. Id. at 645.

80. *McCulloch v. Maryland*, 4 Wheat. (17 U.S) 316 (1819).

81. *Veazie Bank v. Fenno*, 8 Wall. (75 U.S.) 533 (1869).

82. *Bronson v. Rodes*, 7 Wall. (74 U.S.) 229 (1869).

83. *Roosevelt v. Meyer*, 1 Wall. (68 U.S.) 512 (1863).

84. Robert G. McCloskey, *The American Supreme Court*, ed. Sanford Levinson, 2d ed. (Chicago: University of Chicago Press, 1994), 75.

85. *Hepburn v. Griswold*, 8 Wall. (75 U.S.) 603 (1870).

86. Charles Warren, *The Supreme Court in United States History*, rev. ed., 2 vols. (Boston: Little, Brown, 1926), 2:499.

87. Ibid., 401.

88. *Hepburn v. Griswold*, 8 Wall. (75 U.S.) 603 at 622 (1870).

89. Id. at 621.

90. Id. at 623.

91. *Knox v. Lee*, 12 Wall. (79 U.S.) 457 at 529–530 (1871).

92. Id. at 542.

93. Charles Evans Hughes, *The Supreme Court of the United States* (New York: Columbia University Press, 1928), 52–53.

94. *Nation,* April 27, 1871, quoted by Warren, in *Supreme Court in United States History,* 2:525–526.

95. *Julliard v. Greenman,* 110 U.S. 421 (1884).

96. *Trebilcock v. Wilson,* 12 Wall. (79 U.S.) 687 (1872).

97. *Norman v. Baltimore & Ohio Railroad Co.* and *United States v. Bankers Trust Co., (Gold Clause Cases),* 294 U.S. 240 at 316 (1935).

98. *Nortz v. United States (Gold Clause Cases),* 294 U.S. 317 (1935).

99. *Perry v. United States (Gold Clause Cases),* 294 U.S. 330 at 351 (1935).

100. Alfred H. Kelly and Winfred A. Harbison, *The American Constitution: Its Origins and Development,* 7th ed. (New York: Norton, 1991), 696.

101. *Gold Clause Cases,* 294 U.S. 240 at 362 (1935).

THE POWER OVER FOREIGN AFFAIRS (PP. 165–175)

1. See, generally, Nancy Kassop, "The Power to Make War," in *Separation of Powers: Documents and Commentary,* ed. Katy J. Harriger (Washington, D.C.: CQ Press, 2003), 64–79.

2. *McCulloch v. Maryland,* 4 Wheat. (17 U.S.) 316 (1819).

3. *United States v. Curtiss-Wright Export Corp.,* 299 U.S. 304 (1936).

4. James Madison, Alexander Hamilton, and John Jay, *The Federalist Papers,* ed. Clinton Rossiter (New York: New American Library, 1961), No. 23, p. 152.

5. Robert E. Cushman, *Leading Constitutional Decisions,* 12th ed. (New York: Appleton-Century-Crofts, 1963), 373.

6. *Woods v. Miller Co.,* 333 U.S. 138 at 147 (1948).

7. *Bas v. Tingy,* 4 Dall. (4 U.S.) 37 at 43 (1800).

8. *Prize Cases,* 2 Black (67 U.S.) 635 (1863).

9. Id. at 666.

10. Id. at 670–671.

11. See, for example, *Wilson v. Shaw,* 204 U.S. 24 (1907); *Brooks v. Dewar,* 313 U.S. 354 (1941); *Isbrandtsen-Moller Co. v. United States,* 300 U.S. 139 (1937).

12. *Fleming v. Mohawk Wrecking Co.,* 331 U.S. 111 at 116 (1947).

13. Senate Foreign Relations Committee, *Hearings on War Power Legislation,* 91st Cong., 1st sess., 1971 (Washington, D.C.: U.S. Government Printing Office, 1972), 254.

14. See, for example, *Luftig v. McNamara,* 373 F. 2d 664 (D.C. Cir.), cert. denied, 387 U.S. 945 (1967); *Mora v. McNamara,* 387 F. 2d 862 (D.C. Cir.), cert. denied, 389 U.S. 934 (1967). See additionally, *Massachusetts v. Laird,* 400 U.S. 886 (1970) and 451 F. 2d 26 (1st Cir. 1971); *Mitchell v. Laird,* 488 F. 2d 611 (D.C. Cir 1973); *Holtzman v. Schlesinger,* 361 F. Supp. 553 (EDNY 1973).

15. *Mora v. McNamara,* 389 U.S. 934 at 935 (1967).

16. Id. at 939, quoting from *Nixon v. Herndon,* 273 U.S. 536 at 540 (1927).

17. *Ludecke v. Watkins,* 335 U.S. 160 at 168–169 (1948).

18. *Selective Service Draft Law Cases,* 245 U.S. 366 at 378 (1918).

19. *Butler v. Perry,* 240 U.S. 328 at 333 (1916).

20. See, for example, *Hart v. United States,* 382 F. 2d 1020 (C.A. 3, 1967), cert. denied, 391 U.S. 956 (1968), 391 U.S. 936 (1968).

21. *Rostker v. Goldberg,* 453 U.S. 57 (1981).

22. *Ex parte Vallandigham,* 1 Wall. (68 U.S.) 243 (1864); *Ex parte Milligan,* 4 Wall. (71 U.S.) 2 (1866); *Ex parte Yerger,* 8 Wall. (75 U.S.) 85 (1869); *Ex parte Reed,* 100 U.S. 13 (1879).

23. *Ex parte Milligan,* 4 Wall. (71 U.S.) 2 (1866); *Ex parte Quirin,* 317 U.S. 1 (1942).

24. *United States ex rel Toth v. Quarles,* 350 U.S. 11 (1955).

25. *O'Callahan v. Parker,* 395 U.S. 258 (1969).

26. *Relford v. Commandant,* 401 U.S. 355 (1971).

27. *Solorio v. United States,* 483 U.S. 435 (1987).

28. *Middendorf v. Henry,* 425 U.S. 25 (1976).

29. *Weiss v. United States,* 510 U.S. 163 (1994).

30. *Hepburn v. Griswold,* 8 Wall. (75 U.S.) 603 at 617 (1870).

31. *Knox v. Lee,* 12 Wall. (79 U.S.) 457 at 543 (1871).

32. *United States v. L. Cohen Grocery Co.,* 255 U.S. 81 at 88 (1921).

33. *Matthew Addy Co. v. United States,* 264 U.S. 239 (1924); Carl B. Swisher, *American Constitutional Development,* 2nd ed. (Cambridge, Mass.: Houghton Mifflin, Riverside Press, 1954), 638 n. 51.

34. *Northern Pacific Railway Co. v. North Dakota ex rel Langer,* 250 U.S. 135 (1919).

35. *Yakus v. United States,* 321 U.S. 414 (1944).

36. Id. at 424.

37. Id. at 426.

38. *Lichter v. United States,* 334 U.S. 742 at 765–766 (1948).

39. Id. at 778–780.

40. *Stewart v. Kahn,* 11 Wall. (78 U.S.) 493 at 507 (1871).

41. *Block v. Hirsh,* 256 U.S. 135 (1921).

42. *Chastleton Corp. v. Sinclair,* 264 U.S. 543 (1924).

43. Id. at 547–548.

44. *Hamilton v. Kentucky Distilleries and Warehouse Co.,* 251 U.S. 146 (1919); *Ruppert v. Caffey,* 251 U.S. 264 (1920).

45. *Woods v. Miller Co.,* 333 U.S. 138 (1948).

46. Id. at 143–144.

47. Id. at 147.

48. *Hamdi v. Rumsfeld,* 542 U.S. 507 (2004).

49. *Boumediene v. Bush,* 553 U.S. — (2008).

50. *United States v. Curtiss-Wright Export Corp.,* 299 U.S. 304 at 319 (1936).

51. *Haver v. Yaker,* 9 Wall. (76 U.S.) 32 at 35 (1869).

52. *Fourteen Diamond Rings v. United States,* 183 U.S. 176 (1901). As to House of Representative efforts to assert some role in treaty ratification, note *Edwards v. Carter* (1978), decided by the U.S. Court of Appeals for the District of Columbia.

53. *Foster and Elam v. Neilson,* 2 Pet. (27 U.S.) 253 at 314 (1829).

54. *Missouri v. Holland,* 252 U.S. 416 (1920).

55. Id. at 433.

56. Henry Steele Commager, *Documents of American History,* 9th ed., 2 vols. (Englewood Cliffs, N.J.: Prentice-Hall, 1973), 2:163.

57. Alfred H. Kelly and Winfred A. Harbison, *The American Constitution: Its Origins and Development,* 7th ed. (New York: Norton, 1991), 644.

58. *Cherokee Tobacco,* 11 Wall. 616 (1871); *Foster v. Neilson,* 2 Pet. 253 (1829).

59. *Head Money Cases,* 112 U.S. 580 at 599 (1884).

60. Louis Henkin, *Foreign Affairs and the Constitution* (New York: Norton, Norton Library, 1975), 76–77.

61. *J. W. Hampton Jr. & Co. v. United States,* 276 U.S. 394 (1928).

62. *American Insurance Co. v. Canter,* 1 Pet. (26 U.S.) 511 (1828); *United States v. Jones,* 109 U.S. 513 (1883).

63. *Downes v. Bidwell,* 182 U.S. 244 (1901); *Darr v. United States,* 195 U.S. 138 (1904).

64. *United States v. Gratiot,* 14 Pet. (39 U.S.) 526 (1840).

THE POWER TO ADMIT STATES, GOVERN TERRITORIES, AND GRANT CITIZENSHIP (PP. 176–197)

1. C. Herman Pritchett, *The American Constitution,* 3rd ed. (New York: McGraw-Hill, 1977), 55.

2. *Pollard v. Hagan,* 3 How. (44 U.S.) 212 at 224 (1845).

3. *Escanaba Co. v. Chicago,* 107 U.S. 678 at 689 (1883).

4. *Coyle v. Smith,* 221 U.S. 559 at 567 (1911).

5. *United States v. Texas,* 339 U.S. 707 at 718 (1950).

6. Id. at 719–720.

7. *Stearns v. Minnesota,* 179 U.S. 223 at 245 (1900).

8. *American Insurance Co. v. Canter,* 1 Pet. (26 U.S.) 511 at 542 (1828).

9. *United States v. Jones,* 109 U.S. 513 (1883).

10. *First National Bank v. Yankton County,* 101 U.S. 129 at 133 (1880).

11. *Simms v. Simms,* 175 U.S. 162 (1899).

12. *Binns v. United States,* 194 U.S. 486 (1904).

13. *Scott v. Sandford,* 19 How. (60 U.S.) 393 (1857).

14. Edward S. Corwin, *The Doctrine of Judicial Review: Its Legal and Historical Basis and Other Essays* (Princeton, N.J.: Princeton University Press, 1914; reprint ed., Gloucester, Mass.: Peter Smith, 1963), 157.

15. General sources for historical background on the Dred Scott case include Alfred H. Kelly and Winfred A. Harbison, *The American Constitution: Its Origins and Development,* 7th ed. (New York: Norton, 1991), 234–256, 333–367; Carl B. Swisher, *History of the Supreme Court of the United States,* vol. 5, *The Taney Period, 1836–64* (New York: Macmillan, 1974), 528–652; Bruce Catton, "The Dred Scott Case," in *Quarrels That Have Shaped the Constitution,* ed. John A. Garraty and Don Fehrenbacher, rev. ed. (New York: Harper and Row, 1987), 87.

16. *Strader v. Graham,* 10 How. (51 U.S.) 82 (1851).

17. Id. at 93.

18. Carl B. Swisher, *American Constitutional Development,* 2nd ed. (Cambridge, Mass.: Houghton Mifflin, Riverside Press, 1954), 588–589.

19. James D. Richardson, ed., *A Compilation of the Messages and Papers of the Presidents* (New York: Bureau of National Literature, 1927), 7:2962.

20. *Scott v. Sandford,* 19 How. (60 U.S.) 393 at 404 (1857).

21. Id. at 407.

22. Id. at 410.

23. Id. at 405.

24. Id. at 410.

25. Id. at 425.

26. Id. at 436.

27. Id. at 449.

28. Id. at 450.

29. Id. at 452.

30. Catton, "Dred Scott," 85.

31. Quoted in Charles Warren, *The Supreme Court in United States History,* rev. ed., 2 vols. (Boston: Little, Brown, 1926), 2:304.

32. Swisher, *American Constitutional Development,* 248.

33. Corwin, *Doctrine of Judicial Review,* 156.

34. Quoted in Warren, *Supreme Court in United States History,* 2:316.

35. Generally see James Edward Kerr, *The Insular Cases: The Role of the Judiciary in American Expansionism* (Port Washington, N.Y.: Kennikat Press, 1982).

36. *DeLima v. Bidwell,* 182 U.S. 1 (1901).

37. *Cross v. Harrison,* 16 How. (57 U.S.) 164 (1853).

38. *DeLima v. Bidwell,* 182 U.S. 1 at 187 (1901).

39. *Downes v. Bidwell,* 182 U.S. 244 (1901).

40. Id. at 306.

41. Id. at 307–308.

42. Id. at 339.

43. Id. at 380.

44. *Hawaii v. Mankichi,* 190 U.S. 197 at 216 (1903).

45. Id. at 223.

46. *Dorr v. United States,* 195 U.S. 138 at 143 (1904).

47. *Rasmussen v. United States,* 197 U.S. 516 (1905).

48. *Dowdell v. United States,* 221 U.S. 325 (1911).

49. *Perez v. Brownell,* 356 U.S. 44 at 64–65 (1958), Chief Justice Earl Warren dissenting.

50. *Scott v. Sandford,* 19 How. (60 U.S.) 393 at 406 (1857).

51. *United States v. Wong Kim Ark,* 169 U.S. 649 at 693 (1898); see also *Perkins v. Elg,* 307 U.S. 325 (1939).

52. *United States v. Macintosh,* 283 U.S. 605 at 615 (1931).

53. *Fong Yue Ting v. United States,* 149 U.S. 698 at 707, 713, passim (1893).

54. On Communist Party membership, see *Galvan v. Press,* 347 U.S. 522 (1954); *Berenyi v. District Director,* 385 U.S. 630 (1967); on homosexuals, see *Boutilier v. Immigration and Naturalization Service,* 387 U.S. 118 (1967).

55. *United States v. Schwimmer,* 279 U.S. 644 (1929).

56. *Girouard v. United States,* 328 U.S. 61 (1946), overturning *United States v. Schwimmer,* 279 U.S. 644 (1929), *United States v. Macintosh,* 283 U.S. 605 (1931), and *United States v. Bland,* 283 U.S. 636 (1931).

57. *Cohnstaedt v. Immigration and Naturalization Service,* 339 U.S. 901 (1950).

58. *Osborn v. Bank of United States,* 9 Wheat. (22 U.S.) 738 at 827 (1824).

59. *Johannessen v. United States,* 225 U.S. 227 at 241 (1912).

60. *Costello v. United States,* 365 U.S. 265 (1961).

61. *Luria v. United States,* 231 U.S. 9 (1913).

62. *Schneiderman v. United States,* 320 U.S. 118 (1943).

63. *Knauer v. United States,* 328 U.S. 654 (1946).

64. Id. at 675–677.

65. *Schneider v. Rusk,* 377 U.S. 163 (1964).

66. Id. at 165.

67. Id. at 168–169.

68. *MacKenzie v. Hare,* 239 U.S. 299 (1915).

69. *Savorgnan v. United States,* 338 U.S. 491 (1950).

70. *Perez v. Brownell,* 356 U.S. 44 (1958).

71. Id. at 58, note.

72. Id. at 77–78.

73. *Trop v. Dulles,* 356 U.S. 86 at 101 (1958).

74. *Kennedy v. Mendoza-Martinez,* 372 U.S. 144 at 165–166 (1963).

75. *Afroyim v. Rusk,* 387 U.S. 253 (1967).

76. Id. at 257.

77. Id. at 262.

78. Id. at 292–293.

79. *Rogers v. Bellei,* 401 U.S. 815 (1971).

80. Id. at 827.

81. Id. at 835.

82. Id. at 836–837.

THE POWER TO AMEND THE CONSTITUTION (PP. 198–208)

1. See generally John R. Vile, *Encyclopedia of Constitutional Amendments, Proposed Amendments, and Amending Issues, 1789–2002,* 2nd ed. (Santa Barbara, Calif.: ABC-CLIO, 2003).

2. Ibid.

3. *Reynolds v. Sims,* 377 U.S. 533 (1964).

4. *Hollingsworth v. Virginia,* 3 Dall. (3 U.S.) 378 (1798).

5. *National Prohibition Cases,* 253 U.S. 350 (1920).

6. *Leser v. Garnett,* 258 U.S. 130 (1922).

7. *Hollingsworth v. Virginia,* 3 Dall. (3 U.S.) 378 at 381, note (1798).

8. *National Prohibition Cases,* 253 U.S. 350 (1920).

9. *Dillon v. Gloss,* 256 U.S. 368 (1921).

10. Id. at 375, 376.

11. *Coleman v. Miller,* 307 U.S. 433 (1939).

12. Id. at 459.

13. *United States v. Sprague,* 282 U.S. 716 (1931).

14. *Hawke v. Smith,* 253 U.S. 221 (1920).

15. *Leser v. Garnett,* 258 U.S. 130 (1922).

16. Id. at 137; see also *Hawke v. Smith,* 253 U.S. 221 at 230 (1920).

17. *Leser v. Garnett,* 258 U.S. 130 (1922).

18. *Coleman v. Miller,* 307 U.S. 433 at 450 (1939).

19. Robert E. Cushman and Robert F. Cushman, *Cases in Constitutional Law* (New York: Appleton-Century-Crofts, 1968), 8.

20. *Scott v. Sandford,* 19 How. (60 U.S.) 393 (1857).

21. Robert J. Kaczorowski, "The Enforcement Provisions of the Civil Rights Acts of 1866," *Yale Law Journal* 98 (January 1989): 570.

22. Robert J. Kaczorowski, "To Begin Anew: Congress, Citizenship and Civil Rights after the Civil War," *American Historical Review* 92 (February 1987): 48.

23. Ibid., 67.

24. Akhil Amar, *The Bill of Rights: Creation and Reconstruction* (New Haven: Yale University Press, 1998), 189–190.

25. Eric Foner, *Reconstruction* (New York: Harper and Row, 1998), 256.

26. *Slaughterhouse Cases,* 16 Wall. (83 U.S.) 36 at 78 (1873).

27. *United States v. Harris,* 106 U.S. 629 (1883).

28. *Civil Rights Cases,* 109 U.S. 3 (1883).

29. *United States v. Reese,* 92 U.S. 214 (1876).

30. *South Carolina v. Katzenbach,* 383 U.S. 301 at 324 (1966).

31. *Katzenbach v. Morgan,* 384 U.S. 641 (1966).

32. Id. at 656.

33. Id. at 653.

34. *Jones v. Alfred H. Mayer Co.,* 392 U.S. 409 at 424 (1968).

35. Id. at 653.

36. *Griffin v. Breckenridge,* 403 U.S. 88 (1971).

37. *Runyon v. McCrary,* 427 U.S. 160 (1976).

38. *Fitzpatrick v. Bitzer,* 427 U.S. 456 (1976).

39. *City of Boerne v. Flores,* 521 U.S. 507 (1997).

40. *Employment Division, Department of Human Resources of Oregon v. Smith,* 494 U.S. 872 (1990).

41. *Wisconsin v. Yoder,* 406 U.S. 205 (1972).

42. *City of Boerne v. Flores,* 521 U.S. 507 at 517, 519 (1997).

43. Id. at 520, 529.

44. *Kimel v. Florida Board of Regents,* 528 U.S. 62 (2000).

45. *Seminole Tribe v. Florida,* 517 U.S. 44 (1996).

46. *Kimel v. Florida Board of Regents,* 528 U.S. 62 at 83 (2000).

47. *Board of Trustees of the University of Alabama v. Garrett,* 531 U.S. 356 at 365 (2001).

48. Id. at 367.

49. Id. at 368, 374.

50. *United States v. Morrison,* 529 U.S. 598 at 621 (2000).

51. *United States v. Harris,* 106 U.S. 629 (1883), and *Civil Rights Cases,* 109 U.S. 3 (1883).

52. *United States v. Morrison,* 529 U.S. 598 at 622 (2000).

THE POWER TO INVESTIGATE
(PP. 209–220)

1. For general information on the St. Clair inquiry, see Marshall E. Dimock, *Congressional Investigating Committees* (Baltimore: Johns Hopkins University Press, 1929; reprint ed., New York: AMS Press Inc., 1971), 87–89; *Guide to Congress,* 6th ed. (Washington, D.C.: CQ Press, 2007), 289–327.

2. Woodrow Wilson, *Congressional Government* (Cleveland: World Publishing, Meridian Books, 1965), 198.

3. *Watkins v. United States,* 354 U.S. 178 at 187 (1957).

4. *Anderson v. Dunn,* 6 Wheat. (19 U.S.) 204 at 228 (1821).

5. Id. at 231.

6. Interviews with the offices of the parliamentarians of the Senate and the House, September 18–19, 1978.

7. *Kilbourn v. Thompson,* 103 U.S. 168 (1881).

8. Id. at 197.

9. *In re Chapman,* 166 U.S. 661 at 671–672 (1897).

10. *Jurney v. MacCracken,* 294 U.S. 125 (1935).

11. *Marshall v. Gordon,* 243 U.S. 521 (1917).

12. Id. at 542.

13. *Kilbourn v. Thompson,* 103 U.S. 168 at 190 (1881).

14. *In re Chapman,* 166 U.S. 661 (1897).

15. Id. at 669.

16. Id. at 670.

17. *McGrain v. Daugherty,* 273 U.S. 135 (1927).

18. Id. at 174.

19. Id. at 175.

20. Id. at 177–178.

21. Id. at 176.

22. *Sinclair v. United States,* 279 U.S. 263 at 295 (1929).

23. Id. at 296–297.

24. Quoted in August Raymond Ogden, *The Dies Committee* (Washington, D.C.: Catholic University Press, 1945), 44.

25. *Watkins v. United States,* 354 U.S. 178 at 195 (1957).

26. *United States v. Rumely,* 345 U.S. 41 (1953).

27. Id. at 47.

28. Id. at 46.

29. Id. at 57.

30. *Watkins v. United States,* 354 U.S. 178 (1957).

31. Quoted in Robert E. Cushman and Robert F. Cushman, *Cases in Constitutional Law,* 3rd ed. (New York: Appleton-Century-Crofts, 1968), 112.

32. *Watkins v. United States,* 354 U.S. 178 at 198, 200 (1957). See also David Caute, *The Great Fear: The Anti-Communist Purge under Truman and Eisenhower* (New York: Simon and Schuster, 1978).

33. *Watkins v. United States,* 354 U.S. 178 at 205–206 (1957).

34. Id. at 208–209.

35. Id. at 214–215.

36. *Barenblatt v. United States,* 360 U.S. 109 (1959). See also Stanley I. Kutler, *The American Inquisition: Justice and Injustice in the Cold War* (New York: Hill and Wang, 1982).

37. *Barenblatt v. United States,* 360 U.S. 109 at 117 (1959).

38. Id. at 126.

39. Id. at 127–129.

40. Id. at 134.

41. Id. at 143.

42. Id. at 144.

43. Id. at 166.

44. *Wilkinson v. United States,* 365 U.S. 399 (1961); *Braden v. United States,* 365 U.S. 431 (1961).

45. *Deutsch v. United States,* 367 U.S. 456 (1961).

46. *Russell v. United States,* 369 U.S. 749 (1962).

47. *Yellin v. United States,* 374 U.S. 109 (1963).

48. *Gojack v. United States,* 384 U.S. 702 at 715 (1966).

49. C. Herman Pritchett, *The American Constitution,* 3rd ed. (New York: McGraw-Hill, 1977), 161.

50. *Blau v. United States,* 340 U.S. 159 (1950).

51. *Rogers v. United States,* 340 U.S. 367 at 374 (1951).

52. *Quinn v. United States,* 349 U.S. 155 at 162–163 (1955).

53. *Emspak v. United States,* 349 U.S. 190 at 195 (1955).

54. *Ullmann v. United States,* 350 U.S. 422 at 439 (1956).

55. Id. at 445.

56. *Reed v. County Commissioners of Delaware County, Pa.,* 277 U.S. 376 at 380 (1928).

57. *Barry v. United States ex rel. Cunningham,* 279 U.S. 597 at 613 (1929).

THE POWER OVER INTERNAL AFFAIRS
(PP. 221–240)

1. James Madison, Alexander Hamilton, and John Jay, *The Federalist Papers,* ed. Clinton Rossiter (New York: New American Library, 1961), No. 60, 371.

2. *Powell v. McCormack,* 395 U.S. 486 (1969).

3. Id. at 522.

4. *U.S. Term Limits Inc. v. Thornton,* 514 U.S. 779 (1995).

5. Id.

6. Id.

7. See *Congress A to Z,* 5th ed. (Washington, D.C.: CQ Press, 2008), 529–532.

8. *In re Chapman,* 166 U.S. 661 at 669–670 (1897).

9. *Burton v. United States,* 202 U.S. 344 at 369 (1906).

10. *Kilbourn v. Thompson,* 103 U.S. 168 (1881).

11. *Powell v. McCormack,* 395 U.S. 486 (1969).

12. *Long v. Ansell,* 293 U.S. 76 (1934); *United States v. Cooper,* 4 Dall. 341 (C.C. Pa. 1800).

13. *Williamson v. United States,* 207 U.S. 425 (1908).

14. *United States v. Brewster,* 408 U.S. 501 at 507 (1972).

15. *Kilbourn v. Thompson,* 103 U.S. 168 at 204 (1881).

16. Id.

17. *Dombrowski v. Eastland,* 387 U.S. 82 (1967).

18. Id. at 85; also see *Powell v. McCormack,* 395 U.S. 486 at 505 (1969).

19. *Gravel v. United States,* 408 U.S. 606 (1972).

20. Id. at 616–617.

21. Id. at 626.

22. *Tenney et al. v. Brandhove,* 341 U.S. 367 (1951).

23. Id. at 377.

24. Id. at 383.

25. *Doe v. McMillan,* 412 U.S. 306 at 324 (1973).

26. Id. at 315–316.

27. *Eastland v. United States Servicemen's Fund,* 421 U.S. 491 at 503 (1975).

28. Id. at 518.

29. *Hutchinson v. Proxmire,* 443 U.S. 111 (1979).

30. *United States v. Johnson,* 383 U.S. 169 (1966).

31. Id. at 180.

32. *United States v. Brewster,* 408 U.S. 501 at 516–517 (1972); see also *United States v. Helstoski,* 442 U.S. 477 (1979).

33. *United States v. Brewster,* 408 U.S. 501 at 515–516 (1972).

34. Id. at 526.

35. Id. at 563.

36. *United States v. Dowdy,* 479 F. 2d 213 at 224 (1973); cert. denied, 414 U.S. 823 (1973).

37. *Ex parte Siebold,* 100 U.S. 371 at 383–384 (1880).

38. Id. at 388–389.

39. *Ex parte Yarbrough,* 110 U.S. 651 (1884); *United States v. Mosely,* 238 U.S. 383 (1915).

40. *Newberry v. United States,* 256 U.S. 232 at 250, 257 (1921).

41. Id. at 280.

42. See Louisiana House election results, 1920–1942, in *Guide to U.S. Elections,* 5th ed. (Washington, D.C.: CQ Press, 2005), 1066–1126.

43. *United States v. Classic,* 313 U.S. 299 at 317 (1941).

44. *Burroughs and Cannon v. United States,* 290 U.S. 534 (1934).

45. Id. at 544–545.

46. *Buckley v. Valeo,* 424 U.S. 1 at 20–21, 26 (1976).

47. Id. at 42.

48. *McConnell v. FEC,* 540 U.S. 93 at 124 (2003).

49. Id. at 129–130.

50. Id. at 187.

51. Id. at 124.

52. Id. at 248.

53. Id. at 224.

54. *Federal Election Commission v. Wisconsin Right to Life, Inc.,* 551 U.S. —- (2007).

55. *Buckley v. Valeo,* 424 U.S. 1 at 143 (1976).

56. *Roudebush v. Hartke,* 405 U.S. 15 (1972).

57. Id. at 25–26.

58. *Barry v. United States ex rel. Cunningham,* 279 U.S. 597 at 615–616 (1929).

59. *National Association of Manufacturers v. McGrath,* 103 F. Supp. 510 (D.C. 1952).

60. *McGrath v. National Association of Manufacturers,* 344 U.S. 804 (1952).

61. *United States v. Harriss,* 347 U.S. 612 (1954).

62. Id. at 620.

63. Id. at 625.

64. Id. at 632–633.

65. *United States v. Ballin,* 144 U.S. 1 (1892).

66. *United States v. Smith,* 286 U.S. 6 (1932).

67. *Christoffel v. United States,* 338 U.S. 84 (1949).

68. *United States v. Ballin,* 144 U.S. 1 (1892).

69. *Field v. Clark,* 143 U.S. 649 (1892).

70. *McGrain v. Daugherty,* 273 U.S. 135 at 181 (1927).

71. *Nixon v. United States,* 506 U.S. 224 (1993).

chapter 3

The Court and the Powers of the President

The Constitution created not only a new national government, but also a new type of national leader in the president of the United States. The framers of the Constitution knew all about the British monarchy and, from history, the Roman emperors. Having just broken free from England, they did not wish to recreate on the American continent an all-powerful sovereign. They also understood the British system, in which the prime minister is the leader of the majority party in Parliament and heads the government. The PM is a legislator, somewhat akin to the Speaker of the House of Representatives or the Senate majority leader. The framers wanted something different: a national leader who was the choice of the American people, who was independent of the legislature, but who would carry out the laws adopted by the people's representatives. "Nothing quite like this new office had existed before," wrote Yale law professor Akhil Reed Amar in *America's Constitution*. "Nevertheless, as Americans in 1787 tried to envision a republican head of state who could protect them against the old King George without becoming the new King George, they did have a particular George in mind."[1]

George Washington had come out of retirement at Mt. Vernon to preside in Philadelphia at the Constitutional Convention, where he was addressed as "Mr. President." General Washington had led the Continental army to victory in the Revolutionary War; he then resigned his commission and returned home. His act of giving up power—as much as his success at wielding it—won him the admiration and trust of those who gathered in Philadelphia. He was the model for the office of the president "precisely because he had already proved that he could protect Americans against a foreign tyrant without becoming a tyrant himself," Amar wrote.[2]

Washington did not disappoint on that score. After serving two four-year terms, he refused to run for election again, thereby setting a tradition of the two-term limit for presidents. In 1951 this two-term limit was added to the Constitution as the Twenty-second Amendment.

What are the powers of the president? Article II of the Constitution does not describe the office or its duties in great detail. Most of its words are devoted to describing how the president is to be chosen. "The executive Power shall be vested in a President of the United States," says section 1 in a one-sentence job description. The president's best known power is set out in section 2. "The President shall be Commander in Chief of the Army and Navy of the United States, and of the Militia of the several States, when called into the actual service of the United States." Note that the president is not the commander in chief of the nation, but the commander of its armed services when they are called into service. Article II also gives the president the "power to grant Reprieves and Pardons" for federal offenses, the power "to make Treaties," and the power to appoint "Officers of the United States" and "Judges of the supreme Court." The appointment power, like the treaty-making power, is not the president's alone. It must be exercised "with the Advice and Consent of the Senate." Similarly, the power to make laws is shared between Congress and the president. Article I says "all legislative power" is "vested" in Congress, but Article I says a bill becomes law only when it is presented to the president and he signs it. "If not, he shall return it," having exercised what is known now as a veto.

Article II closes with the President's primary duty, followed by a warning. The duty: "he shall take Care that the Laws be faithfully executed." The warning: "The President, Vice President and all civil Officers of the United States, shall be removed from Office on Impeachment for, and Conviction of, Treason, Bribery, or other high Crimes and Misdemeanors."

Much of the president's power simply comes with the office. The president is the one national leader, the head of the government, and the commander of the armed services. Particularly during a time of crisis, all eyes turn toward the president, whose words and decisions are the nation's words and decisions.

Throughout the nation's history, presidents have claimed expanded powers when faced with war and national emergency. In 1861 Abraham Lincoln took office as the southern states seceded from the Union. He called the army into service to put down the rebellion and suspended habeas corpus without seeking the advance approval of Congress. In 1933 Franklin D. Roosevelt took office amid the Great Depression and launched the federal government on a new course to revive and regulate the crippled economy. In 1940, as Britain stood alone against Nazi Germany, FDR negotiated a deal with Prime Minister Winston Churchill to send him a fleet of old destroyers, a move that some critics feared would entangle the nation in the European war. In 1950 Harry S. Truman was on vacation at his home in Independence, Missouri, when he learned that North Korean forces had launched a ferocious attack on South Korea. Acting on his own, Truman sent U.S. troops into a war in Korea. He claimed this was a "police action," not a war, and that

he was acting at the behest of the United Nations. In 1962 John F. Kennedy told the nation he had ordered a naval blockade of Cuba to halt shipments of Soviet missiles. And he warned the Russians that if a missile were fired from Cuba, the United States would launch a devastating nuclear attack on the Soviet Union. By then, hardly a voice was heard on Capitol Hill to say that JFK should have come to Congress before ordering a blockade and threatening war.

In 2001, when terrorists flew hijacked planes into the World Trade Center in New York City, George W. Bush announced he would take military action against any nation that had harbored or aided the terrorists. He also took a series of steps—some public, some in secret—to gather information about terrorists, their networks, and their plots. He secretly ordered the National Security Agency to intercept suspicious international calls and electronic messages, despite a federal law that said wiretapping within the United States requires a court order. He ordered the Central Intelligence Agency to harshly interrogate terrorists who were captured abroad. And he issued an executive order that called for "enemy combatants" to be imprisoned without any legal rights to challenge the evidence against them and without the privileges of "prisoner of war" status under the Geneva Conventions.

RARE CLASHES WITH THE COURT

Despite the steady expansion of presidential power, the Supreme Court has rarely intervened to check the chief executive, but the few contrary examples were memorable and dramatic. In the mid-1930s the conservative Court struck down many of Roosevelt's New Deal measures and questioned whether the federal government had any role to play in regulating the daily lives of workers, businesses, and the economy. This constitutional clash ended quickly in 1937 when the Court retreated and gave the reelected Roosevelt a nearly free hand to pass economic legislation. Truman, with his popularity sagging, was dealt a defeat in 1952 when he overplayed his hand and seized control of the steel mills to prevent interruption of steel production and supplies. Truman said he was acting as commander in chief during war, but the Court said he had no authority—and Congress had given him none—to use his military power on the home front.[3] Richard Nixon was in deep trouble over the Watergate scandal in 1974 when he cited "executive privilege" before the Court as a basis for shielding from prosecutors his Oval Office tape recordings. He lost in a unanimous ruling.[4]

Nixon was not the only president whose claim of immunity was rejected by the Court. The Iran-contra scandal bedeviled Ronald Reagan during his second term, and several of his aides were prosecuted by an independent counsel. Congress had authorized a panel of judges to appoint special counsels to investigate certain high officials. One of Reagan's lawyers, but not the president himself, challenged this arrangement as unconstitutional and argued it violates the notion that the president is entrusted as the chief prosecutor. The Court disagreed in a 7-1 ruling in 1988.[5] Bill Clinton was beset by sex scandals, and he went to the Court arguing that the chief executive should be immune from civil suits—in this instance, a lawsuit alleging sexual harassment—while he was in office. Clinton lost in a 9-0 ruling in 1997.[6]

George W. Bush's bold use of the commander in chief power in the "war on terror" led to three defeats in the Supreme Court. Twice, in 2004 and in 2008, the Court ruled that the foreign prisoners held at the U.S. naval base at Guantánamo Bay, Cuba, were entitled to plead their innocence before a federal judge.[7] And in 2006 the Court rejected Bush's proposed rules for military trials at Guantánamo, saying that Congress must adopt by law the rules for military commissions.[8]

Two factors contribute to the infrequency of Supreme Court rulings on the authority of the chief executive. The constitutional language outlining the powers of the president is phrased in very general terms: the president is vested with the executive power, is commander in chief, and is directed to take care that the laws are faithfully executed. Because of this language, the basis for constitutional challenges to presidential action is uncertain. Concurring in the Court's action in the steel seizure case, *Youngstown Sheet and Tube Co. v. Sawyer* (1952), Justice Robert H. Jackson commented on the imprecision of the language employed in the debate over the scope of the president's powers:

> Loose and irresponsible use of adjectives colors all non-legal and much legal discussion of presidential powers. "Inherent" powers, "plenary" powers, "war" powers and "emergency" powers are used, often interchangeably and without fixed or ascertainable meanings.

> The vagueness and generality of the clauses that set forth presidential powers afford a plausible basis for pressures within and without the administration for presidential action beyond that supported by those whose responsibility it is to defend his actions in court. The claim of inherent and unrestricted presidential powers has long been a persuasive dialectical weapon in political controversy.[9]

The aura that surrounds the office of the president and its occupant insulates somewhat from legal challenges. George Reedy, a former aide to Lyndon B. Johnson, noted the monarchic dimension of the modern presidency. Reedy observed that "the life of the White House is the life of a court," and the people who make up the court "serve the material needs and the desires of a single man."[10] Political scientist Louis Koenig remarked in this respect that even if the president "lags in donning monarchic trappings, others will put them on him."[11] The advantages the presidency therefore possesses over other branches of government in capturing the public eye and political support, Justice Jackson pointed out, make the task of curbing presidential power even more difficult:

> Executive power has the advantage of concentration in a single head in whose choice the whole Nation has a part, making him the focus of public hopes and expectations. . . . No other personality in public life can begin to compete with him in access to the public mind through modern methods of communications. By his prestige as head of state and his influence upon public opinion he exerts a leverage upon those who are supposed to check and balance his power which often cancels their effectiveness.[12]

In light of these characteristics, the Supreme Court has been cautious in locking constitutional horns with the chief executive on matters that juxtapose its authority and prestige against the president's will.

DIVERGENT VIEWS OF POWER

U.S. presidents have held strikingly divergent views on the limits of presidential power. William Howard Taft viewed executive power as limited to the specific powers granted in the Constitution:

> The true view of executive functions . . . is, as I conceive it, that the President can exercise no power which cannot be fairly and reasonably traced to some specific grant of power or justly implied and included within such grant as proper and necessary.[13]

Taft's constitutional view of executive authority prevailed throughout much of the nineteenth century. Theodore Roosevelt, however, viewed the presidential office differently. His "stewardship" theory of presidential leadership envisioned an active president acting responsibly on behalf of the public welfare. Roosevelt believed that

> every executive officer . . . was a steward of the people. . . . My belief was that it was not only his right but his duty to do anything that the needs of the nation demanded unless such action was forbidden by the Constitution or by the laws. . . . In other words, I acted for the public welfare . . . whenever and in whatever manner was necessary, unless prevented by direct constitutional or legislative provision.[14]

The broadest assertion of executive authority, however, was Franklin Roosevelt's, which was based on the concept of executive prerogative described by the seventeenth-century English political philosopher John Locke as "power to act according to discretion for the public good, without the prescription of the law, and sometimes even against it."[15] Acting on this theory, Roosevelt took steps to cope with the Great Depression and World War II, arguing, as the Court itself ultimately noted, that extraordinary times demanded extraordinary measures. The concept of executive prerogative carried over into the cold war, but the Court slowed its development when it rejected President Truman's claim of the authority to seize and operate the nation's steel mills.

The Shield of Joint Action

It is always possible in confrontations with the Court that the president will ignore or defy what the justices decide, as did Andrew Jackson and Abraham Lincoln, for example. Early in the nation's history, however, presidents realized that they held the strongest possible position against judicial challenge when they acted in conjunction with Congress. Joint action by the two political branches of government has consistently provided a high degree of insulation from Court challenge. As Justice Jackson wrote,

> Presidential powers are not fixed but fluctuate, depending upon their disjunction or conjunction with those of Congress. . . .
>
> When the President acts pursuant to an express or implied authorization of Congress, his authority is at its maximum, for it includes all that he possesses in his own right plus all that Congress can delegate. In these circumstances, and in these only, may he be said . . . to personify the federal sovereignty. If his act is held unconstitutional under these circumstances, it usually means that the Federal Government as an undivided whole lacks power.[16]

When presidents act without the backing of Congress, supported only by their claim of inherent power, they run the high risk of rejection by the Court.

Foreign and Domestic Powers

In foreign and military matters, the Court has upheld the presidential exercise of sweeping power. In the midst of its rulings denying FDR authority to cope with the economic crisis at home, the Court in 1936 upheld the president's inherent and virtually unlimited authority to conduct the nation's foreign affairs.[17] Justice George Sutherland's opinion in *United States v. Curtiss-Wright Export Corp.* (1936) claimed that the foreign affairs powers emanates from sources different from those bestowing other presidential powers. This reasoning provided the basis for Sutherland's view that the president could act entirely alone in matters of foreign relations. Although Sutherland's historical analysis has been criticized, the Court has not modified the broad grant of executive power sanctioned by this ruling.

The Court has, however, denied the president broad inherent power in domestic affairs. When President Truman seized the steel mills during the Korean War, the Court rejected his claim of the power to take such action, in part because Congress had, some years earlier, decided not to grant the president the power he sought to exercise in this case. The Court specifically recognized the need for a limited privilege to protect documents and information related to foreign affairs when it denied President Nixon an absolute executive privilege to withhold tapes made in the White House and sought for use as evidence in a trial. This decision came at a time when Congress—far from supporting the president's claim—was considering articles of impeachment against him.

PRESIDENTS AND JUSTICES

As Nixon learned, presidents can never be certain that the individuals they appoint to the Court will support their views when the Court is faced with a challenge to the exercise of presidential power. Thomas Jefferson made several appointments to the bench whom he hoped would counteract Chief Justice John Marshall's control over the Court's decisions, but Jefferson's effort to reduce Marshall's effectiveness failed. President Lincoln appointed Salmon P. Chase to the bench to deflect his presidential ambitions and to harness his legal talents for the administration. Chase, who had advocated passage of the Legal Tender Act as Treasury secretary, later opposed the Lincoln administration in the first of the *Legal Tender Cases, Hepburn v. Griswold* (1870), holding those acts unconstitutional.[18] Two of the four Truman appointments to the bench, Justices Tom C. Clark and Sherman Minton, named in October 1949, were close friends of the president. In the steel seizure decision, Clark joined with the majority, which included two other Truman appointees, and Minton dissented.

President Nixon appointed Warren E. Burger chief justice because—apart from his judicial qualifications—Burger had been outspoken in his criticism of the Warren Court's rulings limiting prosecutors' efforts to convict criminals. In an ironic turn of events, Burger wrote the Court opinion in *United States v. Nixon (1974)*, which left Nixon with the option of resigning or impeachment and a trial.[19]

"Although history teaches that Presidents are sometimes surprised by the Supreme Court, the surprise is almost always of their own making," wrote law professor Laurence Tribe. Examining "the myth of the surprised president," Tribe contends that "for the most part, and especially in areas of particular and known concern to a President, Justices have been loyal to the ideals and perspectives of the men who have nominated them."[20] Some presidents have ensured such loyalty by maintaining close ties with sitting justices. President James Buchanan sought and obtained information from Justice Robert C. Grier, a fellow Pennsylvanian, about how the Court would vote on the pending decision in *Scott v. Sandford* (1857).[21] Theodore Roosevelt continued his friendship with Justice William H. Moody after he appointed him to the bench in 1906. Perhaps the most famous friendship between a president and a justice was that of Franklin Roosevelt and Felix Frankfurter. Friends since undergraduate days at Harvard, the two maintained a lively correspondence throughout most of their respective careers. After Roosevelt appointed Frankfurter to the Supreme Court in 1939, they communicated freely, offering advice and criticism on politics and legal matters. Their correspondence ranged over every conceivable subject, from Washington society gossip to matters of administration patronage and political strategy.

President Johnson appointed his longtime friend and adviser Abe Fortas to the Supreme Court in 1965. After Fortas took his seat on the bench, he continued to advise Johnson on matters such as speeches on the Vietnam War. This came to light in 1968, when Johnson nominated Fortas to replace Earl Warren as chief justice. The controversy over this mixing of the role of justice and presidential adviser helped to kill Fortas's nomination. A year later, he resigned under a cloud after *Life* magazine reported that he had accepted a large amount of money from a foundation controlled by Louis Wolfson, who had gone to prison for stock manipulation. The era of presidents appointing friends and cronies as justices seemed to die with the Fortas controversy. President Nixon named six men to the Court—four of whom won confirmation—but he knew them mostly by reputation, not as friends or advisers. The closest of the nominees to the president was an assistant attorney general in his Justice Department whose name sometimes eluded the president. On the Watergate tapes, Nixon is heard referring to "Renchberg," but in October 1971, when Nixon had two seats on the Court to fill, a staff aide, Richard Moore, persuaded him that his young legal adviser was qualified because he had graduated first in his Stanford Law School class and had clerked for Justice Jackson, a favorite of Nixon's. The next day, the president announced the nomination of Assistant Attorney General William H. Rehnquist. At the same time he also nominated to the bench Lewis F. Powell Jr., a Democrat from Richmond, Virginia.[22]

Justice John Paul Stevens was recommended by Gerald R. Ford's attorney general, Edward Levi. On the day that President Reagan nominated Arizona judge Sandra Day O'Connor to be the first woman to serve on the Court, she recalled—but he did not—that they had met once before when he was the governor of California and she was an Arizona legislator. Justices Antonin Scalia and Anthony M. Kennedy were recommended by Reagan's legal advisers. Justices David H. Souter and Clarence Thomas were similarly recommended, primarily by George H. W. Bush's legal advisers. Bush met Souter for the first time on the day he nominated him. President Clinton and his wife, Hillary Rodham Clinton, were graduates of Yale Law School and had many friends and acquaintances who were lawyers, yet personal ties figured little in Clinton's choices of Ruth Bader Ginsburg and Stephen G. Breyer for the Court. Both were highly regarded federal appellate judges and emerged as the favorites of Clinton's legal advisers. George W. Bush followed the same pattern. He chose two highly regarded federal appellate judges, John G. Roberts Jr. and Samuel A. Alito Jr., who were the favorites of his legal advisers.

In the major tests of presidential power, however, the Clinton and Bush nominees diverged. In 1997, when Clinton sought a "temporary immunity" from responding to the civil suit lodged by Paula Jones, Ginsburg and Breyer joined a unanimous decision rejecting Clinton's claim. When Bush asserted his presidential power in the disputes over prisoners held at Guantánamo Bay, Roberts and Alito took Bush's side, but as dissenters.

The Commander in Chief

The president is the commander of the nation's military forces. The Constitution vests the executive with the role and title of "Commander in Chief of the Army and Navy of the United States, and of the Militia of the several States, when called into the actual service of the United States." "These cryptic words have given rise to some of the most persistent controversies in our constitutional history," wrote Justice Robert H. Jackson more than one hundred fifty years after the framers placed those phrases in the Constitution. Jackson, speaking from his experience as attorney general under President Franklin D. Roosevelt as well as a Supreme Court justice, continued, "Just what authority goes with the name has plagued Presidential advisors who . . . cannot say where it begins or ends."[1] In an earlier period, Alexander Hamilton had also noted the potentially vast scope of the executive role. Hamilton wrote that it "would amount to nothing more than the supreme command and direction of the military and naval forces, as first general and admiral of the Confederacy."[2] He soon amended his statement to acknowledge that "the direction of war most peculiarly demands those qualities which distinguish the exercise of power by a single hand."[3]

The framers of the Constitution divided the war power between the executive and the legislative branches of government, giving Congress the power to declare war and the president the power to conduct it. Mistrust of executive power vested in a single individual led to the creation of a unique divided institutional structure for making war.[4] *(See "The War Power," pp. 165–170.)* Subsequent experience, however, resulted in a blurring of the lines between the constitutionally distinct functions that has effectively insulated most exercises of the war power from judicial review.[5] Between 1789 and 1861 presidents regarded their role as commander in chief as purely military in nature.[6] Faced with a civil war, President Abraham Lincoln

began to expand the presidential war power beyond the original concept. He found constitutional justification for the exercise of broad discretionary powers by fusing the powers of the commander in chief with the executive's general constitutional responsibility to take care that the laws are faithfully executed.[7] The national emergency of secession and war, Lincoln said, required the swift and firm exercise of extraordinary powers by the chief executive.[8]

In World Wars I and II, Presidents Woodrow Wilson and Franklin Roosevelt took a similar view of presidential war powers as they further expanded them in wartime. Faced with war emergencies, Wilson and Roosevelt controlled the economy; fixed prices; set priority production targets; ran the transportation system, mines, and industrial plants; detained individuals and groups on the basis of their ethnic origin—many of whom were U.S. citizens not guilty of any crime—and threatened to ignore certain laws that did not comply with their objectives.[9] Moreover, this assertion of broad emergency power blurred the constitutional distinction between Congress's authority to declare war and the president's power to direct it. Congress delegated power and provided funds; the president directed policy. Fiscal and legislative support for the president was regarded as congressional approval of presidential decisions. In this way, the two political branches fused their war making powers, and the Court declined to challenge policies adopted and supported by them.[10] Political scientist Glendon Schubert describes the trend:

> One very interesting aspect which emerged from the World War II cases . . . was the consistency with which the courts came to conceptualize the fusion or merging of the power of the political branches of the national government so that either the President or the Congress might individually or cojointly exercise any power attributable to the

United States as a sovereign state at war. Under this theory, agreement between the President and Congress places any action in time of war beyond the pale of judicial review.[11]

Although the exercise of the war power in such a manner insulates the president's acts from judicial scrutiny, it does not prevent the Supreme Court from denying the president the right to use those war powers in time of peace. In *Youngstown Sheet and Tube Co. v. Sawyer* (1952) the Court rejected President Harry S. Truman's claim of authority to seize the nation's steel mills during the Korean War. The Court ruled that without congressional approval, the president lacked such authorization.

All in all, the Court has looked at only a small portion of presidential actions taken under the War Powers Clause. As Clinton Rossiter observes, the Court has examined only "a tiny fraction of [the president's] significant deeds and decisions as commander in chief, for most of these were by nature challengeable in no court but that of impeachment."[12] After two centuries, that judicial reluctance to review war powers, asserts Louis Fisher, has "created a climate in which Presidents have regularly breached constitutional principles and democratic values."[13] He goes on to observe that federal judges in the last quarter of the twentieth century readily sidestepped lawsuits brought by members of Congress challenging presidential war powers

> So great is the magnitude of executive power that President [George H. W.] Bush invaded Panama in 1989 without any involvement by Congress, and he threatened to take military action against Iraq in 1991 solely on the basis of resolutions adopted by the UN Security Council. Only at the eleventh hour did he obtain authority from Congress. . . .

> The best that can be argued in support of presidential war power after World War II is that the language of the Constitution, the intent of the framers, and the republican values operating at the time are no longer relevant, having been superseded by twentieth-century conditions and pressures.[14]

Early in its history the Supreme Court was careful to distinguish between the power of Congress to declare war and the power of the president to conduct it.[15] Congress granted part of its declaratory power to the president in 1795, when it authorized him to call out the militia of any state to quell resistance to the law. During the War of 1812 several New England states challenged that statute, claiming that neither Congress nor the president had the authority to determine when the state militia should be called out. The New Englanders opposed the war and had refused to place their state troops under federal control. In *Martin v. Mott* (1827) the Court upheld the delegation of that authority as a limited power, "confined to cases of actual invasion, or of imminent danger of invasion."[16] Justice Joseph Story, who wrote the Court's opinions, stated,

> [A]uthority to decide whether the exigency has arisen, belongs exclusively to the President, and . . . his decision is conclusive upon all other persons. We think that this construction necessarily results from the nature of the power itself, and from the manifest object contemplated by the act of Congress. . . .

> Whenever a statute gives a discretionary power to any person, to be exercised by him, upon his own opinion of certain facts, it is a sound rule of construction that the statute constitutes him the sole and exclusive judge of the existence of those facts.[17]

Conceding that the president possessed a limited discretionary power to declare that a crisis existed, the Court, nevertheless continued to regard the president's war power as primarily military in nature. As late as 1850 Chief Justice Roger B. Taney observed that under the War Powers Clause the president's

> duty and his power are purely military. As Commander in Chief, he is authorized to direct the movements of the naval and military forces placed by law at his command, and to employ them in the manner he may deem most effectual to harass and conquer and subdue the enemy. He may invade the hostile country, and subject it to the sovereignty and authority of the United States. But his conquests do not enlarge the boundaries of this Union, nor extend the operation of our institutions and laws beyond the limits before assigned them by legislative power.[18]

UNDECLARED WARS

The Constitution provides Congress with the power to declare war, but as of 2008 only five of the eleven major conflicts fought by the United States abroad were formally declared wars. The others were undeclared engagements commenced under presidential claims of authority as commander in chief, custodian of executive power, and, after World War II, under Article XLIII of the United Nations Charter. The effect of these undeclared wars has been to dim further the Constitution's separation of congressional and presidential war powers. The modern distinction might be that the president directs the war, while Congress funds it.

Congress acted in response to the president's acts or recommendations to declare the War of 1812, the Mexican War (1846–1848), the Spanish-American War (1898), and World Wars I and II (1917–1918, 1941–1945). Presidents engaged in hostilities without prior congressional sanction in an undeclared war with France (1798–1800), two Barbary wars (1801–1805, 1815), Mexican-American border clashes (1914–1917), the Korean War (1950–1953), and the Vietnam War (1964–1973). Two conflicts—the War of 1812 and the Spanish-American War—were clearly products of congressional policy.[1]

More recent examples of a president authorizing the use of armed force abroad without congressional assent include President Ronald Reagan's invasion of Grenada, bombing of Libya, and mining of Nicaraguan harbors; President George H. W. Bush's invasion of Panama in 1989; and President Bill Clinton's dispatching of peacekeeping troops to Haiti and Bosnia as well as use of the air force to bomb Serbian forces in Kosovo in the late 1990s.

In 1991 Bush obtained last-minute authority from Congress to use military force against Iraq, which had invaded Kuwait. The congressional vote on whether to approve U.S. military force in the Persian Gulf was taken in an atmosphere of almost mournful solemnity and marked the first time since World War II that Congress had publicly debated sending large numbers of U.S. forces into combat.

After the September 11, 2001, attacks on the World Trade Center and the Pentagon, President George W. Bush vowed to go after countries that harbored terrorists. He thereafter won congressional approval of a resolution that authorized him to send U.S. troops into Afghanistan to oust the Taliban government. In fall 2002 Bush sought congressional support for military action against Iraq, arguing that the government of Saddam Hussein posed a danger to the United States because it possessed chemical and biological weapons and was developing nuclear weapons. Congress did not pass a declaration of war, but in October 2002 it adopted Joint House Resolution 114-4 authorizing the president "to use the Armed Forces of the United States as he determines to be necessary and appropriate in order to defend the national security of the United States against the continuing threat posed by Iraq." Bush ordered an invasion of Iraq in March 2003.

1. Louis Koenig, *The Chief Executive,* 5th ed. (San Diego: Harcourt Brace Jovanovich, 1986), 207.

The Supreme Court has never opposed the president's deployment of forces abroad as commander in chief. Presidents assigned naval squadrons to cruise the Mediterranean (1815), the Pacific (1821), the Caribbean (1822), the South Atlantic (1826), the waters of the Far East (1835), and along the African coast (1842). These deployments showed the flag, encouraged trade, and protected shipping. No American bases were, however, established on foreign soil as a result of these actions.[19]

During the nineteenth century presidents controlled policy in time of war; in peacetime presidents generally deferred to Congress. Between 1836 and 1898, with the exception of the wartime administrations of James K. Polk, Abraham Lincoln, and Grover Cleveland, Congress provided the initiative in foreign policy. When the chief executive in peacetime advocated expansionist policies that threatened war—for example, Ulysses S. Grant concerning Santo Domingo—Congress blocked such projects.[20] Polk directed Gen. Zachary Taylor to occupy disputed territory claimed by Mexico; then, as a result of an alleged provocation by Mexican troops, Polk asked Congress to declare war in 1846.[21] Congressional opposition led a young Whig member of Congress named Abraham Lincoln to introduce resolutions demanding to know the exact spot where the armed forces clashed. The House censured the president for a war "unnecessarily and unconstitutionally begun," but Congress funded the war anyway.[22]

President William McKinley's decision to send the battleship *Maine* into Havana's harbor led to war with Spain over Cuban independence in 1898. Congress passed a joint resolution authorizing the use of armed force to obtain Cuba's separation from Spain and followed that with a declaration of war when Spain recalled its ambassador and refused to leave Cuba.[23] McKinley acted without congressional consultation, however, when he decided to insist on Spain's surrender of the Philippines. Later he deployed more than one hundred thousand troops to put down the insurrection led by Emilio Aguinaldo as part of the movement for Philippine independence. This deployment led to charges in Congress of unilateral war making by the president.[24] McKinley also sent several thousand U.S. troops to join an international brigade that rescued Americans trapped in Beijing by a Chinese nationalist uprising. Democrats criticized this action, but Congress was out of session, and calls for a special session in an election year were to no avail.[25] President Theodore Roosevelt engineered the 1903 revolution in Panama against Columbia to make the "dirt fly" on construction of the Panama Canal. Roosevelt's less-than-subtle sanction of the Panamanian revolution raised few objections from Congress or the public.[26]

Early in the twentieth century the Supreme Court considered and resolved questions of citizenship and constitutional rights for the inhabitants of newly acquired noncontiguous U.S. territories. The Court, however, never challenged the president's prerogative to conduct war or acquire the territories. *(See "The Insular Cases," pp. 185–187.)* Most of the instances of the presidential use of troops without congressional authorization between 1815 and 1912 involved small contingents of forces for limited purposes that had strong public support.

PRESIDENT LINCOLN AND THE CIVIL WAR

The first major Supreme Court pronouncement on the war powers of the president came as a result of the broad exercise of those powers by President Abraham Lincoln during the Civil War.[27] From the outbreak of hostilities at Fort Sumter on April 12, 1861, until Congress convened in special session on July 4, Lincoln prepared the nation for war without authority from Congress. He acted under his power as commander in chief and his presidential oath to maintain the Constitution and preserve the Union. Lincoln on his own authority declared the existence of a rebellion, called out the state militia to suppress it, and proclaimed a blockade of Southern ports—the legal equivalent to a declaration of war. In May he called for forty regiments of U.S. volunteers to serve for three years. He ordered increases made in the size of the army and navy, paid out $2 million from the federal Treasury without specific authorization, and indebted the government about $250,000 in pledged credit. Lincoln also ordered the suspension of habeas corpus in certain parts of the country and directed military commanders to arrest persons engaged in or likely to engage in "treasonable practices."[28]

When Congress convened, Lincoln's July 4, 1861, message to the special session explained the measures taken and recommended steps for the exercise of additional power. Bolstered by a corroborative opinion from Attorney General Edward Bates, Lincoln informed Congress that public necessity and the preservation of the Union required swift and bold action, "whether strictly legal or not." The president said he felt certain Congress would "readily ratify" his actions and noted that public safety required the "qualified suspension of the privilege of the writ [of habeas corpus] which was authorized to be made."[29] During the special session Congress intermittently debated a joint resolution sanctioning Lincoln's acts. Nagging doubts about the legality of the suspension of the writ of habeas corpus and the blockades prevented a vote on the approbatory resolution, but a rider attached to a pay bill for army privates, rushed through Congress at the close of the session, gave approval to the president's acts pertaining to the militia, the army, the navy, and the volunteers, stating that they were "in all respects legalized and made valid, to the same intent and with the same effect as if they had been issued and done under the previous express authority and direction of Congress."[30]

President Abraham Lincoln on the battlefield of Antietam in October 1862. Lincoln's assumption during the Civil War of broad wartime powers was challenged in *Ex parte Merryman* (1861), the *Prize Cases* (1863), and *Ex parte Milligan* (1866).

Congress made no challenge to Lincoln's management of the war until the December 1861 session. The Joint Committee on the Conduct of the War, established at first to investigate the Union disaster at the first battle of Bull Run, soon expanded the scope of its investigations. Headed by Radical Republican senator Benjamin F. Wade of Ohio, the committee tried unsuccessfully to wrest control of war policy from the president.[31]

Prize Cases

The Supreme Court was sharply divided on the issues raised by Lincoln's assumption of broad wartime powers. The *Prize Cases* arose when the owners of some captured ships challenged Lincoln's unilateral proclamation of the naval blockade.[32] Several neutral vessels were captured as they tried to pass the blockade; some ships were then brought to Union ports as prizes. Under international law, ships could legally be taken as

prizes only when a conflict had been recognized as a war between two belligerent powers. Lincoln had consistently refused to recognize the Confederate government as a sovereign—and belligerent— power, insisting that the conflict was an insurrection, not a war. This view effectively denied the South sovereign status or the possibility of recognition by neutral governments. If the Court adopted Lincoln's view that the South was not a belligerent, it would have to rule that under international law the blockade was illegal and the vessels improperly seized.

After twelve days of argument in February 1863, the Court announced its decision two weeks later in favor of Lincoln's power to impose the blockade. Lincoln's three appointees to the Court—Justices Noah H. Swayne, Samuel F. Miller, and David Davis—joined with Justices Robert C. Grier and James M. Wayne to form the 5-4 majority. Grier wrote the opinion, which accepted the president's definition of the conflict and his power to impose the blockade. The majority confirmed that Congress has the power to declare war but also ruled that the president had to meet the challenge in the emergency until Congress could act:

> By the Constitution, Congress alone has the power to declare a national or foreign war. It cannot declare war against a State or any number of States, by virtue of any clause in the Constitution. The Constitution confers on the President the whole executive power. He is bound to take care that the laws be faithfully executed. He is Commander-in-Chief of the Army and Navy of the United States, and of the militia of the several States when called into the actual service of the United States. He has no power to initiate or declare a war either against a foreign nation or a domestic State. But by the Acts of Congress of Feb. 28th, 1795 . . . and 3rd of March, 1807 . . . he is authorized to call out the militia and use the military and naval forces of the United States in case of invasion by foreign nations, and to suppress insurrection against the government of a State or of the United States.

> If a war be made by invasion of a foreign nation, the President is not only authorized but bound to resist force, by force. He does not initiate the war, but is bound to accept the challenge without waiting for any special legislative authority. And whether the hostile party be a foreign invader, or States organized in rebellion, it is none the less a war, although the declaration of it be "unilateral." . . .

> This greatest of civil wars was not gradually developed by popular commotion, tumultuous assemblies, or local unorganized insurrections. However long may have been its previous conception, it nevertheless sprung forth suddenly from the parent brain, a Minerva in the full panoply of war. The President was bound to meet it in the shape it presented itself, without waiting for Congress to baptize it with a name; and no name given to it by him or them could change the fact.

> It is not the less a civil war, with belligerent parties in hostile array, because it may be called an "insurrection" by one side, and the insurgents be considered as rebels or traitors. It is not necessary that the independence of the revolted province or State be acknowledged in order to constitute it a party

belligerent in a war according to the law of nations. Foreign nations acknowledge it as war by a declaration of neutrality. The condition of neutrality cannot exist unless there be two belligerent parties.[33]

Chief Justice Taney and Justices Samuel Nelson, John Catron, and Nathan Clifford found Grier's analysis inadequate. The dissenters argued that the war power belonged to Congress and that the blockade was illegal from the time of Lincoln's April proclamation until Congress approved it in July 1861. As to the matter of whether a war existed, Nelson wrote,

> [B]efore this insurrection against the established government can be dealt with on the footing of a civil war, within the meaning of the law of nations and the Constitution of the United States, and which will draw after it belligerent rights, it must be recognized or declared by the war making power of the government. No power short of this can change the legal status of the government or the relations of its citizens from that of peace to a state of war, or bring into existence all those duties and obligations of neutral third parties growing out of a state of war. The war power of the government must be exercised before this changed condition . . . can be admitted. . . .

> . . . [W]e find there that to constitute a civil war in the sense in which we are speaking, before it can exist, in contemplation of law, it must be recognized or declared by the sovereign power of the State, and which sovereign power by our Constitution is lodged in the Congress of the United States—civil war, therefore, under our system of government, can exist only by an Act of Congress which requires the assent of two of the great departments of the government, the Executive and Legislative. . . .

> The Acts of 1795 and 1807 did not, and could not, under the Constitution, confer on the President the power of declaring war against a State of this Union, or of deciding that war existed, and upon that ground authorize the capture and confiscation of the property of every citizen of the State whenever it was found on the waters. The laws of war . . . convert every citizen of the hostile State into a public enemy, and treat him accordingly, whatever may have been his previous conduct. This great power over the business and property of the citizen is

reserved to the Legislative Department by the express words of the Constitution. It cannot be delegated or surrendered to the Executive. Congress alone can determine whether war exists or should be declared. . . .

I am compelled to the conclusion that no civil war existed between this Government and the States in insurrection until recognized by the Act of Congress 13th July, 1861; that the President does not possess the power under the Constitution to declare war or recognize its existence within the meaning of the law of nations, which carries with it belligerent rights, and thus change the country and all its citizens from a state of peace to a state of war; that this power belongs exclusively to the Congress of the United States and consequently, that the President had no power to set on foot a blockade under the law of nations.[34]

The opinions of Grier and Nelson represented opposing constitutional theories about who might initiate war under the Constitution, but notwithstanding any constitutional shortcomings of his position, Lincoln continued to direct the war. He issued the Emancipation Proclamation of January 1, 1863, under his authority as commander in chief, and his authority to do so was never challenged before the Court.

Merryman and Milligan

Article I, section 9, of the Constitution states, "The Privilege of the Writ of Habeas Corpus shall not be suspended, unless when in Cases of Rebellion or Invasion the public Safety may require it." Under this clause Lincoln suspended the privilege of the writ in sections of the country where military forces were attempting to prevent Southern sympathizers from disrupting transportation and communications systems. The wartime suspension of habeas corpus was challenged as early as 1861 by none other than the chief justice of the United States. Lincoln, however, continued to suspend the writ during the war. In March 1863 Congress retroactively authorized the suspension of the privilege by the president at his discretion.

While holding circuit court in Baltimore in 1861 Chief Justice Taney ordered federal military officers to

The constitutionality of the arrest and trial of these five Southern sympathizers, charged with treason by military authorities, was settled by the Supreme Court in *Ex parte Milligan* (1866). *Clockwise from top:* William A. Bowles, Andrew Humphreys, Stephen Horsey, H. Heffren, and Lambdin P. Milligan.

justify their detention of John Merryman, a civilian Southern sympathizer detained in a military prison for his part in burning railroad bridges near Baltimore, and to show cause why Merryman should not be released for proceedings in a civilian court.[35] Citing Lincoln's suspension order, the military commander refused to respond. Taney regarded the officer's refusal as a violation of proper judicial procedure and proceeded to write an opinion lecturing the president on his duty to faithfully execute the laws. Failure to support the proceedings of the court, Taney remarked, amounted to usurpation of civilian authority and the substitution of military government.[36] Taney warned that "the people of the

United States are no longer living under a government of laws, but every citizen holds life, liberty and property at the will and pleasure of the army officer in whose military district he may happen to be found."[37] Merryman was eventually handed over to civilian authorities and indicted for treason, but to Southern sympathizers the *Merryman* case became a symbol of oppression.

It remained unresolved whether the president had the power to order that civilians be tried by military tribunals in regions outside the war zone, where civilian courts remained open. The administration argued that military trials were necessary because the civilian court and peacetime procedures were inadequate to deal with the problem of organized rebellion. In 1864 the Court refused to address the issue in the case of Clement L. Vallandigham, a "Copperhead"—a Northerner who sympathized with the Confederate cause—and a former Democratic representative from Ohio who denounced Lincoln's war policy in speeches. Vallandigham was arrested and tried by a military commission. The Supreme Court refused to hear the appeal of his conviction. Justice Wayne wrote that the Court "cannot without disregarding its frequent decisions and interpretation of the Constitution in respect to its judicial power . . . review or pronounce any opinion upon the proceedings of a military commission."[38] After the war, however, the Court took on that issue and resolved it—against the president.

In 1864 Lambdin P. Milligan was tried by a military commission in Indiana and convicted of conspiracy. He was sentenced to die for his part in a plot to release and arm rebel prisoners and march them into Missouri and Kentucky to join in an invasion of Indiana. President Andrew Johnson commuted Milligan's sentence to life in prison. Milligan, nevertheless, appealed to the Supreme Court, challenging his trial and conviction. In 1866 the Court unanimously ordered his release, holding that the president had no power to require that civilians be tried by military courts in areas where regular courts continued to function. Justice Davis, a Lincoln nominee to the Court, wrote the opinion, which was issued in December 1866, after the war emergency had passed and eight months after the decision itself was announced. The Court divided 5-4 on whether Congress had the power to authorize military trials under such circumstances, but the decision established that martial law must be confined to "the theater of active military operations":

> The Constitution of the United States is a law for rulers and people, equally in war and in peace, and covers with the shield of its protection all classes of men, at all times and under all circumstances. No doctrine, involving more pernicious consequences, was ever invented by the wit of man than that any of its provisions can be suspended during any of the great exigencies of government. . . . Martial law cannot arise from a threatened invasion. The necessity must be actual and present; the invasion real, such as effectually closes the courts. . . . Martial rule can never exist where the courts are open, and in the proper and unobstructed exercise of their jurisdiction. It is also confined to the locality of actual war.[39]

The assumption of broad presidential powers in a wartime emergency ended—temporarily—with Lincoln's death and the end of the war.

PRESIDENT WILSON AND WORLD WAR I

As a professor at Princeton University, Woodrow Wilson minimized the presidential role in the constitutional system.[40] Moreover, as Wilson's biographer has observed, Wilson did not concern himself with foreign affairs in the years prior to his election as president because "he did not think they were important enough to warrant any diversion from the mainstream of his thought."[41] President-elect Wilson changed his mind. A month before taking office, Wilson asserted that the chief executive "must be prime minister, and he is the spokesman of the nation in everything."[42] Wilson's terms as president represented the broadest assertion of presidential powers up to that time.

Even before World War I, Wilson had ordered U.S. troops to pursue Mexican bandits across the border into Mexico. American troops engaged Mexican regulars in a sporadic border war during Mexico's revolution and subsequent search for stable and democratic government.[43] As the war in Europe became of concern to the United States, and American troops entered the conflict in 1917, Wilson sought and obtained from Congress broad delegations of power to prepare for war and to mobilize the home front.[44] During the war, Wilson managed the nation's economy by delegating power to a series of war management and war production boards created to coordinate domestic production and supply. "It is not an army that we must shape and train for war," Wilson explained, "it is a nation."[45] Congress cooperated with Wilson and delegated vast authority to him for the conduct of the war. Legislative sanctioning of extraordinary presidential actions insulated Wilson's war policy—at home and abroad—from judicial review.

Wilson commandeered plants and mines, requisitioned supplies, fixed prices, seized and operated the nation's transportation and communications networks, and managed the production and distribution of food. The Council of National Defense, an umbrella agency created by Wilson, administered the economy during the war. Wall Street broker Bernard Baruch, appointed by Wilson to head the War Industries Board, became the nation's virtual economic dictator. The board had no statutory authority; Wilson simply created it under his authority as commander in chief.[46]

The delegation of legislative power by Congress to the president reached unprecedented heights during World War I. Many statutes simply stated their general objectives and left it to the president to interpret the goals and administer the measures he felt necessary to achieve them. When the Senate attempted to form a watchdog committee to oversee management of the war, Wilson opposed the measure as a check on his leadership. The House killed the proposal.[47] Issues that managed to raise constitutional questions reached the Court only after the armistice, when they were no longer urgent. All three branches of the government had seemed to assume that the broad powers exercised by Lincoln during the Civil War legitimately could be applied to foreign wars.

The closest the Court came to questioning executive war power during World War I was its 1921 decision declaring part of the Lever Food Control Act unconstitutional. The act provided for federal control of the distribution and production of food and the marketing of fuel. It also authorized the president to seize factories and mines to ensure continued production of defense-related commodities. In short, it subjected the nation's economy to

whatever regulations the president mandated to guarantee Allied victory. Section 4 of the act made it a criminal offense to charge excessive prices for commodities. The Court invalidated that section of the law because it set no ascertainable standard of guilt and failed to define unjust or unreasonable prices. The Court found that section 4 was, therefore, in conflict with the constitutional guarantees of due process of law and of adequate notice to persons accused of crimes of the nature and cause of the charge against them.[48]

FDR AND TOTAL WAR

The concept of expanded presidential powers in wartime, tested in the crisis of civil war and sanctioned by Congress in World War I, underwent further expansion during the twelve years of Franklin Roosevelt's tenure in the White House. In his March 4, 1933, inaugural address, Roosevelt said he would ask Congress "for the one remaining instrument to meet the crisis— broad Executive power to wage a war against the emergency as great as the power that would be given me if we were in fact invaded by a foreign foe."[49] The emergency was the Great Depression, and through the New

In his September 7, 1942, message to Congress, President Franklin D. Roosevelt claimed broad executive powers to "avert a disaster which would interfere with the winning of the war." The Supreme Court supported Roosevelt's exercise of unusual powers during the war crisis, recognizing the power of the president to conduct foreign affairs and upholding the constitutionality of laws and government agencies established for the war effort.

Wartime Seizure Power

Presidents since Woodrow Wilson have seized industrial plants to prevent interruption of production during wartime. The expression *government seizure* means that the government assumes temporary custody of the property. People responsible for management of the plant or industry continue to operate it. Seizures have been regarded as an effective way to break a stalemate in stalled labor-management contract negotiations to prevent production interruptions in vital industries during a national emergency.

President Franklin D. Roosevelt ordered some two thousand regular army troops to work at Los Angeles's North American Aviation Plant, whose workers went on strike June 5, 1941. The president's executive order said the action was necessary to ensure the continued production of aircraft while labor and management negotiated an end to the walkout over wages. The government retained control of the factory until July 2, 1941.

The strike was called less than ten days after Roosevelt had proclaimed an unlimited national emergency urging employers and employees to cooperate as war approached.[1] No specific statute authorized the president to seize plants during a labor dispute. The Selective Service Act provided for seizure of plants when they refused to obey government orders to manufacture necessary arms and supplies. Attorney General Robert H. Jackson's legal opinion justifying the seizure order derived the president's power from the "aggregate" of executive powers set out in the Constitution and federal statutes. Jackson said that the president had the inherent constitutional duty "to exert his civil and military as well as his moral authority to keep the defense effort of the United States a going concern."[2] In 1943 Congress enacted the War Labor Disputes Act, authorizing presidential seizures of plants involved in a labor dispute.

The single wartime court test of the seizure power proved inconclusive. After a three-year struggle between Montgomery Ward and Company and the War Labor Board, the president in 1944 ordered the company's property seized to prevent a work stoppage. A federal district court ruled that the company engaged in "distribution," not "production." The president therefore had no general war power to seize the property, the court said. An appeals court interpreted "production" in broader terms and reversed the lower court. The Supreme Court accepted the case, but then dismissed it as moot when the army returned the property to company control.[3]

---

1. Bennett M. Rich, *The Presidents and Civil Disorder* (Washington, D.C.: Brookings, 1941), 177–183.

2. Ibid., 184.

3. *Montgomery Ward & Co. v. United States*, 326 U.S. 690 (1944).

Deal legislative program Roosevelt sought to meet economic disaster with emergency measures similar to those Lincoln and Wilson had employed in wartime. The Supreme Court, however, was far more reluctant to sanction these measures than those taken in military crises. *(See "The Court versus FDR," pp. 341–348.)*

The rise of fascism in Germany and Italy and Japan's expansion into China and Southeast Asia changed the focus of the nation from economic recovery to foreign aggression abroad. Although the Neutrality Acts of 1935, 1936, and 1937 required that the president avoid negotiations that might involve the nation in another war, Roosevelt's personal diplomacy committed the United States to a "neutrality" weighted in favor of Anglo-American interests in Europe and the Far East against the plans of conquest pursued by Germany, Italy, and Japan.[50] Roosevelt in these years claimed broad executive powers as commander in chief to deal with belligerent nations. The Supreme Court supported Roosevelt's use of broad powers in the area of foreign policy, and after war came, of the war power. It recognized the "plenary and exclusive" power of the president in foreign affairs and sanctioned the president's use of the executive agreement, as well as treaties, to make binding foreign policy commitments on behalf of the United States.[51] *(See "The 'Sole Negotiator,'" pp. 283–285.)*

The president declared a limited national emergency in May 1939 and an unlimited emergency in May 1941. These declarations, though questioned by the Senate at the time, made available to Roosevelt statutory authority to wield extraordinary presidential powers. After the United States entered World War II, Roosevelt set out his own theory to justify the exercise of unusual power in a September 7, 1942, message to Congress:

> I ask the Congress to take this action by the first of October. Inaction on your part by that date will leave me with an inescapable responsibility to the people of this country to see to it that the war effort is no longer imperilled by threat of economic chaos.
>
> In the event that the Congress should fail to act, and act adequately, I shall accept the responsibility and I will act. . . .
>
> The President has the powers, under the Constitution and under Congressional acts, to take measures necessary to avert a disaster which would interfere with the winning of the war.
>
> . . . [T]he American people can be sure that I will use my powers with a full sense of my responsibility to the Constitution and to my country. The American people can also be sure that I shall not hesitate to use every power vested in me to accomplish the defeat of our enemies in any part of the world where our own safety demands such defeat.
>
> When the war is won, the powers under which I act automatically revert to the people—to whom they belong.[52]

In this speech, Roosevelt also demanded repeal of certain provisions of the Emergency Price Control Act of 1942, which Congress subsequently amended to assuage the president's objections.

Delegated Power

What prevented constitutional confrontation between Roosevelt and the legislative and judicial branches was the assumption that the war powers as exercised by Lincoln and Wilson carried over to the new emergency. During World War II, Congress and the president developed a working partnership, with the legislature again delegating vast federal powers to the president to prosecute war. Roosevelt created a large number of new administrative agencies responsible to him to deal with the war and war-related issues. By 1945 the Office of Emergency Management had oversight of twenty-nine separate agencies. The most significant Court challenge to the delegation of power during World War II involved the Emergency Price Control Act of January 30, 1942, which directed the Office of Price Administration (OPA) to set price ceilings on rents and consumer goods and to ration some products in short supply. Albert Yakus, Benjamin Rottenberg, and B. Rottenberg, Inc., were convicted of selling beef at wholesale prices above the maximum prescribed by the OPA. These wholesalers challenged their conviction, arguing that the Emergency Price Control Act was an unconstitutional delegation of legislative power by Congress to the executive.

The Supreme Court's ruling in *Yakus v. United States* (1944) upheld the price control act.[53] In contrast to the Court's rejection of earlier New Deal measures, in this case it declared this grant of power valid because it contained precise standards to guide executive regulations and orders. Moreover, the Court stated, judicial review offered sufficient remedy for transgression of the guidelines. In a dissenting opinion, Justice Owen J. Roberts registered his concern about Congress's delegation of power to the executive branch, raising the question of whether Congress could suspend any part of the Constitution in wartime:

> My view is that it may not suspend any of the provisions of the instrument. What any of the branches of government do in war must find warrant in the charter and not in its nullification, either directly or stealthily by evasion and equivocation. But if the court puts its decision on the war power I think it should say so. The citizens of this country will then know that in war the function of legislation may be surrendered to an autocrat whose "judgment" will constitute the law; and that his judgment will be enforced by federal officials pursuant to civil judgments, and criminal punishments will be imposed by courts as matters of routine.[54]

In an opinion delivered the same day as the *Yakus* decision, the Court upheld the rent control powers of the OPA.[55] Justice William O. Douglas's opinion justified this delegation of power to the OPA administrator as a necessary wartime measure:

> We need not determine what constitutional limits there are to price fixing legislation. Congress was dealing here with conditions created by activities resulting from a great war effort. . . . A nation which

can demand the lives of its men and women in the waging of that war is under no constitutional necessity of providing a system of price control on the domestic front which will assure each landlord a "fair return" on his property.[56]

In 1948 the Court upheld a similar rent control law as justified by the reduction in residential housing available to veterans demobilized at the end of the war. Again writing for the Court, Douglas observed, however, that the Court would not approve indefinite extension of wartime controls into peacetime "to treat all the wounds which war inflicts on our society."[57]

The Supreme Court did not uphold challenges to the authority of other wartime agencies or to the authority of the 101 government corporations created by the president that were engaged in production, insurance, transportation, banking, housing, and other lines of business related to the successful prosecution of the war effort. Furthermore, the Court upheld the power of the president to apply sanctions to individuals, labor unions, and industries that refused to comply with wartime guidelines. These sanctions had no statutory basis. A retail fuel distributor who admitted violating fuel-rationing orders challenged these sanctions; the Court ruled that where rationing supported the war effort, presidential sanctions forcing compliance with rationing guidelines were constitutional.[58]

Military Trials

In 1942 President Roosevelt established a military commission to try eight Nazi saboteurs captured after they had entered the United States clandestinely from a German submarine. The military commission tried the saboteurs for offenses against the laws of war. Although the president's proclamation creating the commission specifically denied the eight saboteurs access to U.S. courts, their lawyers obtained a writ of habeas corpus that contended that the president lacked statutory and constitutional authority to order trial by military commission, that they had been denied constitutional guarantees extended to persons charged with criminal offenses, and that they should have been tried in civilian courts. The Court convened a special term to hear the case, which was argued July 29–30, 1942.

On July 31 the Court ruled that the constitutional requirements did not apply to trials held by military commissions for people who entered U.S. territory as belligerents. It was not necessary for the commander in chief to set up military commissions, because Congress had authorized military commissions to try offenders against the laws of war. Therefore, the president's action was more broadly based than Lincoln's use of military commissions, struck down in 1866. *(See "Merryman and Milligan," pp. 265–266.)* This ruling, in *Ex parte Quirin,* also established the authority of civil courts to review a military commission's jurisdiction to try certain persons.[59]

Relocation Program

By Executive Order No. 9066, issued February 19, 1942, President Roosevelt placed Japanese Americans living on the West Coast under rigid curfew laws and restricted their movements. A congressional resolution of March 21, 1942, supported the president's action. Roosevelt subsequently ordered the removal of all Japanese from the coastal region for the duration of the war as a measure of protection against sabotage by persons of Japanese ancestry. Instituted under the powers of the commander in chief, the removal program made no distinction between citizens and aliens. Japanese Americans suffered great economic and psychological distress as the plan was hastily implemented. By spring 1942 more than 100,000 Japanese Americans had been relocated to internment camps by the War Relocation Authority. Seventy thousand U.S. citizens of Japanese ancestry were detained in camps for periods of up to four years, subjected to forcible confinement, and then resettled in areas away from the Pacific coast.[60] The constitutionality of the curfew, exclusion, and relocation programs came before the Supreme Court in three cases decided in 1943 and 1944. The effect of all three decisions was to uphold this extraordinary exercise of the war power by Congress and the president.

In *Hirabayashi v. United States* (1943) the Court unanimously upheld the curfew order as applied to U.S. citizens as "within the boundaries of the war power." The Court's opinion, written by Chief Justice Harlan Fiske Stone, made clear, however, that the

In 1944 the Supreme Court upheld the constitutionality of interning Japanese Americans in detention centers as a military necessity during World War II.

Court was not considering "whether the President, acting alone, could lawfully have made the curfew order."[61] Because Congress had ratified Roosevelt's executive order by statute, the issue became that of "the constitutional power of the national government through the joint action of Congress and the executive to impose this restriction as an emergency war measure." The Court held that the curfew order was within that jointly exercised power.[62] Eighteen months later in *Korematsu v. United States* (1944), the Court, 6-3, upheld the exclusion of Japanese Americans from their West Coast homes. The majority relied heavily upon the reasoning in *Hirabayashi* in concluding that it was not outside the power of Congress and the executive, acting together, to impose this exclusion.[63]

The same day, however, the Court granted a writ of habeas corpus to Mitsuye Endo, a Japanese American girl, freeing her from one of the detention centers.

These centers were intended as "interim places of residence" for persons whose loyalty was being ascertained. After one was determined to be loyal, the intent was that loyal persons be resettled outside the centers. Endo's loyalty had been determined, but she was still being held, so the Court ordered her release. Without ruling on the constitutionality of the relocation program, the Court held, "The authority to detain a citizen or grant him a conditional release as protection against espionage or sabotage is exhausted at least when his loyalty is conceded."[64]

The challenge of total war pointed up the tension between the idea of constitutional government and the demands of military policy and national security. The conduct of the war raised cries of executive dictatorship as it had in 1861 and 1917, but so long as the presidential war powers rested on the twin foundations of statutory authority *and* the prerogatives of the commander

COMMANDER IN THE FIELD, GOVERNOR AT HOME

Within the broad sweep of the power of the commander in chief to conduct war fall myriad related duties and powers.

FIELD DECISIONS

The president as commander in chief has the authority to make command decisions for field operations. Presidents generally have delegated that power to generals, although during the Civil War Abraham Lincoln ordered Gen. George McClellan to make a general advance in 1862 to bolster morale and to carry the war into the enemy's territory. President Woodrow Wilson settled a command controversy that erupted on the western front in 1918. Franklin D. Roosevelt personally participated in the decisions concerning strategies in World War II, the outcome of the war, and postwar territorial divisions. President Harry S. Truman ordered the atomic bombs dropped at Hiroshima and Nagasaki, and Presidents Lyndon B. Johnson and Richard M. Nixon selected or approved targets to be hit by air strikes during the Vietnam conflict. President George W. Bush consulted regularly with the generals who were fighting the war in Iraq, and he ordered an increase in the troop levels in 2007 to quell violence around Baghdad.

MILITARY JUSTICE

The commander in chief governs the creation of military commissions and tribunals in territories occupied by U.S. forces and fixes the limits of their jurisdiction absent congressional limits on this power. The president's authority also endures after hostilities have ceased.[1] The commander in chief is the ultimate arbiter of all matters involving the enforcement of rules and regulations related to courts martial.

The Court has also said there were limits on the commander in chief's power to hold and to put on trial prisoners in the undeclared and indefinite global "war on terror." After the attacks on the World Trade Center and the Pentagon on September 11, 2001, President George W. Bush said the U.S. military would pursue, capture, or kill those who were responsible. In November he issued a military order that gave the Defense Department the full authority to imprison terrorists and their allies and to try some of them before military tribunals. Early in 2002 the administration began transporting prisoners from Afghanistan to the U.S. naval base at Guantánamo Bay, Cuba. Bush said he could create these new military tribunals on his own authority and without approval by Congress. And he said none of the "enemy combatants" had a right to challenge the grounds for holding them before a judge.

The Court disagreed on both propositions. In 2006 the justices struck down Bush's proposed military tribunals because they had not been authorized by Congress.[2] The ultimate effect of this ruling remained unclear, however, because Congress only months later passed the Military Commissions Act to give legal authorization to such trials. In rulings in 2004 and 2008, the Court said the long-term prisoners at Guantánamo had a right to seek their freedom before a judge.[3]

CONDUCT OF WAR

In the conduct of war, the president may use secret agents to secure information,[4] authorize trade with the enemy if Congress approves,[5] and

in chief, they seemed safe from constitutional challenge. More than forty years later, however, the government's treatment of Japanese Americans during World War II would be revisited. In 1988 Congress passed and President Ronald Reagan signed legislation offering a formal apology on behalf of the nation to Japanese Americans held in U.S. camps during the war and promising the estimated sixty thousand surviving internees $20,000 each. The payments were to be spread over ten years, but estimates of the original number of claimants were about eighteen thousand too low and Congress did not appropriate enough money for the program. In 1992, after four years of continued controversy over the reparations, the federal fund was expanded to compensate all seventy-eight thousand estimated claimants.

COLD WAR POWERS

Between 1945 and 1947 postwar differences between the United States and the Soviet Union brought on the

compel the aid of citizens and friendly aliens in theaters of military operations. The chief executive can negotiate an armistice to end fighting and set conditions for the armistice that affect the terms of the subsequent peace agreement.[6] The president may authorize the occupation of a region or a nation and provide government administration for it.[7] To annex a region, the president needs the approval of Congress.[8]

CONTROL OF PROPERTY

In time of war, the commander in chief may requisition property for military use, an act that incurs the obligation of the United States to compensate the owner.[9] The Supreme Court has upheld broad presidential power to use or "take" private property for federal use in wartime, but the government is obligated by the Fifth Amendment to pay "just compensation" to the owners of private property converted or condemned for public use in wartime.[10] Property taken but not used also obligates the government to pay compensation.[11] The president has the power to declare someone an enemy and to order his property seized,[12] an authority that extends to the property of friendly aliens as well as to enemy aliens.[13] Although the concept of just compensation applies to citizens and friendly aliens, no such guarantee extends to alien enemies, nor is there an obligation on the part of the government to respond to suits by enemy aliens for return of seized properties.[14]

The president may, under the war power, fix prices, nullify private contracts,[15] and forbid, regulate, and control the use of foods and malt liquors.[16]

1. *Madsen v. Kinsella*, 343 U.S. 341 at 348 (1952); *Johnson v. Eisentrager*, 399 U.S. 763 at 789 (1950).

2. *Hamdan v. Rumsfeld*, 548 U.S. 557 (2006).

3. *Rasul v. Bush, 542 U.S. 466 (2004); and Boumediene v. Bush*, 533 U.S. —- (2008).

4. *Totten v. United States*, 92 U.S. 105 (1876).

5. *Hamilton v. Dillin*, 21 Wall. (88 U.S.) 73 (1875); *Haver v. Yaker*, 9 Wall. (76 U.S.) 32 (1869).

6. Protocol of August 12, 1898, in William McKinley's second annual address, in Fred L. Israel, ed., *The State of the Union Messages of the Presidents, 1790–1966*, 3 vols. (New York: Chelsea House, Robert Hector Publishers, 1966), 2:1848–96; Woodrow Wilson's address to Congress (Fourteen Points), in Henry S. Commager, ed., *Documents of American History*, 7th ed. (New York: Appleton-Century-Crofts, 1962), 137–144.

7. *Santiago v. Nogueras*, 214 U.S. 260 (1909); *Dooley v. United States*, 192 U.S. 222 at 230–231 (1901).

8. *Fleming v. Page*, 9 How. (50 U.S.) 603 at 615 (1850).

9. *Mitchell v. Harmony*, 13 How. (54 U.S.) 115 (1852); *United States v. Russell*, 13 Wall. (80 U.S.) 623 (1869).

10. *Davis v. Newton Coal Co.*, 267 U.S. 292 (1925).

11. *International Paper Co. v. United States*, 282 U.S. 399 at 406 (1931); *United States v. Caltex (Philippines) Inc.*, 344 U.S. 149 (1952).

12. *Central Union Trust v. Garvan*, 254 U.S. 554 (1921).

13. *Silesian American Corp. v. Clark*, 332 U.S. 469 (1947).

14. *Clark v. Uebersee-Finanz-Korp.*, 332 U.S. 480 at 484–486 (1947).

15. *Addy v. United States, Ford v. United States*, 264 U.S. 239 at 244–246 (1924).

16. *Starr v. Campbell*, 208 U.S. 527 (1908); *United States v. Standard Brewery Co.*, 251 U.S. 210 (1920).

cold war, a state of permanent international tension and crisis that shaped presidential policymaking for three decades. Superpower rivalries, and this permanent state of ideological war, permitted President Truman and his successors to retain control of policymaking in the postwar era. Congress placed few obstacles in the way of presidential formulation of cold war strategy. The Truman Doctrine, the Marshall Plan, and "containment" of communism met only token resistance in Congress.

When, six months after communists took control of mainland China, communist North Korea invaded South Korea, Truman acted decisively and unilaterally. On June 27, 1950, he announced that U.S. air and naval forces would help South Korea repel the invasion. Truman claimed authority for his actions from a United Nations Security Council vote that condemned North Korea's action and a June 27 resolution that urged UN members to assist South Korea.[65] The United States, however, had never signed an agreement to place U.S.

military forces at the disposal of the Security Council to participate in such "police actions." The decision to commit U.S. forces brought some criticism from the Senate as an abuse of the war power. The House, however, broke into applause when it received official news of the president's action.

The Steel Seizure Case

In *Youngstown Sheet and Tube Co. v. Sawyer* (1952) the Court administered a rebuff to presidential war powers. The idea of broad emergency powers in time of cold war as well as "hot" war met Court opposition when President Truman took over the nation's steel mills to prevent a strike and ensure continued steel production for the war in Korea. Six members of the Court held Truman's seizure an unconstitutional usurpation of powers and ordered the mills returned to private hands.[66] The president's directive stated simply that the action was taken under his powers as commander in chief and in accordance with the Constitution and the laws of the United States. It cited no statutory authority for the seizure.

Although a majority of the Court agreed that the president had by this action overstepped constitutional boundaries separating legislative and executive powers, they did not rule out the possibility that such seizures might be legal if done under statutory authority.[67] Justice Hugo L. Black's brief opinion for the Court rejected the proposition that either the president's powers as commander in chief or some inherent executive prerogative power authorized the seizure:

> Even though "theater of war" be an expanding concept, we cannot with faithfulness to our constitutional system hold that the Commander in Chief of the Armed Forces has the ultimate power as such to take possession of private property in order to keep labor disputes from stopping production. This is a job for the Nation's lawmakers, not for its military authorities.[68]

In a concurring opinion, Justice Robert H. Jackson wrote that the Commander in Chief Clause

> is sometimes advanced as support for any presidential action, internal or external, involving use of force, the idea being that it vests power to do anything, anywhere, that can be done with an army or navy. . . . But no doctrine that the court could promulgate would seem to me more sinister and alarming than that a President . . . can vastly enlarge his mastery over the internal affairs of the country by his own commitment of the nation's armed forces to some foreign venture. . . . There are indications that the Constitution did not contemplate that the title Commander-in-Chief of the Army and Navy will constitute him also Commander-in-Chief of the country, its industries and its inhabitants. He has no monopoly of "war powers," whatever they are. While Congress cannot deprive the President of the command of the army and navy, only Congress can provide him an army and navy to command. . . .

> That military powers of the Commander-in-Chief were not to supersede representative government of internal affairs seems obvious from the Constitution and from elementary American history. . . . Congress, not the Executive, should control utilization of the war power as an instrument of domestic policy.[69]

Three members of the Court dissented, arguing that the president possessed broad executive powers to take such action in the state of emergency created by the Korean War.[70] Chief Justice Fred M. Vinson's dissenting opinion, joined by Justices Stanley F. Reed and Sherman Minton, was a pragmatic argument in support of the president's action, drawing upon historical precedents and emphasizing the gravity of the threat presented by a steel strike during the conflict. The dissenters relied primarily on the general executive power, not the Commander in Chief Clause:

> Those who suggest that this is a case involving extraordinary powers should be mindful that these are extraordinary times. . . .

> The broad executive power granted by Article II to an officer on duty 365 days a year cannot, it is said, be invoked to avert disaster. Instead, the President must confine himself to sending a message to Congress recommending action. Under this messenger-boy concept of the Office, the President cannot even act to preserve legislative programs from

destruction so that Congress will have something left to act upon. There is no judicial finding that the executive action was unwarranted because there was in fact no basis for the President's finding of the existence of an emergency, for, under this view, the gravity of the emergency and the immediacy of the threatened disaster are considered irrelevant as a matter of law. . . . Presidents have been in the past, and any man worthy of the Office should be in the future, free to take at least interim action necessary to execute legislative programs essential to survival of the Nation.[71]

Congress and Intervention

As noted, Congress extended to Truman's successors carte blanche in foreign policy decision making as the cold war continued into the 1950s and 1960s. Congress in January 1955 authorized President Dwight D. Eisenhower to use force if necessary to defend Chiang Kai-shek's government on Taiwan against the threat of attack from China. In March 1956 Eisenhower sought and received congressional authorization to act to block communist aggression in the Middle East. Sixteen months later, he sent Marines to Lebanon to prevent an outbreak of fighting between warring factions there.[72] President John F. Kennedy obtained a joint congressional resolution on October 3, 1962, authorizing him to use force if necessary to prevent the spread of communism in the Western Hemisphere. The resolution followed discovery of a Soviet-supported missile capability in Cuba, ninety miles from the Florida coast. Kennedy's decision to "quarantine" Cuba to prevent the landing of Soviet ships laden with missiles and equipment brought the world to the brink of nuclear war.[73] As in the cases of Lincoln and Wilson, it seems likely that Presidents Eisenhower and Kennedy would have taken the actions they chose even without authorizing resolutions. The same is true for President Lyndon B. Johnson and his policies concerning Vietnam.

Vietnam and the War Powers Debate

As the United States increased its involvement in the ongoing war in Southeast Asia, President Johnson in 1964 sought and received from Congress passage of the Gulf of Tonkin Resolution that read, in part, "the United States . . . is prepared, as the President determines, to take all necessary steps, including the use of armed force, to assist any member or protocol state of the Southeast Asia Collective Defense Treaty requesting defense of its freedom."[74] Johnson asked Congress to pass the resolution after North Vietnamese patrol boats reportedly attacked U.S. destroyers on patrol in the Gulf of Tonkin. The vote in support of the resolution was 88-2 in the Senate and 416-0 in the House. Johnson relied on that expression of congressional support, and the broad language of the document, to justify U.S. intervention in Vietnam.[75] Thus began the escalation toward what would become the longest undeclared war in U.S. history. It would draw to a close on January 23, 1973, with the signing of a cease-fire agreement in Paris, after a cost of well over $100 billion and 360,000 American dead and wounded.

State Department adviser Leonard Meeker provided the fullest expression of the legal justification for the Vietnam War in a memorandum submitted March 11, 1966, to the Senate Committee on Foreign Relations.[76] Meeker argued that the framers of the Constitution had intended the president to be free to repel sudden attacks without congressional sanction, and in the modern era such an attack might occur halfway around the globe. Meeker's memorandum identified 125 historical precedents of congressionally unauthorized executive uses of military force.[77] The precedents, however, were mostly minor skirmishes that involved a minimum amount of force or actual fighting: landings to protect citizens, enforcement of laws against piracy, Indian skirmishes, and the occupation of Caribbean states (usually to prevent political instability, economic collapse, or European intervention). Meeker further contended that the Gulf of Tonkin Resolution and the SEATO Treaty authorized Johnson to act to defend Southeast Asia against communism. In a particularly intriguing point, Meeker noted the large majorities by which Congress had approved the Gulf of Tonkin Resolution and Congress's continuing support of the war through its appropriation of funds to prosecute the conflict.[78] Federal courts were asked repeatedly during the late 1960s and early 1970s to hold that U.S. involvement in the war in Southeast Asia was

THE PRESIDENT, THE GOVERNORS, AND THE NATIONAL GUARD

The Supreme Court in 1990 affirmed the sweep of federal power over the states' National Guard units, upholding a 1986 law in which Congress had expressly eliminated the requirement that governors consent before their states' units were called up and sent out of the country. The law—called the Montgomery Amendment after its sponsor, Rep. G. V. "Sonny" Montgomery, D-Miss.—amended the Armed Forces Reserve Act of 1952, which had required a governor's consent before a National Guard unit could be called to active duty. The provision was added to a defense authorization bill after several governors objected on political grounds to units going to Pentagon-sponsored training exercises in Central America. The new law barred a governor from blocking the participation of a state National Guard unit in a training exercise because of the location or purpose of the exercise.

The case that tested this issue was brought by Minnesota governor Rudy Perpich, who had objected to members of the Minnesota National Guard being put on active duty and sent to Honduras for joint exercises with that country's military. The call-up and subsequent activity of the National Guard had been authorized by the 1986 law. Perpich contended that the law intruded on states' control over the National Guard under the Constitution's militia clauses. Under Article I, section 8, Congress has the power to "provide for calling forth the Militia to execute the Laws of the Union, suppress Insurrections and repel Invasions." A second clause gives Congress power to govern the militia while "employed in the Service of the United States, reserving to the States respectively, the Appointment of the Officers, and the Authority of training the Militia according to the discipline prescribed by Congress."

Making quite clear that federal power is supreme in the area of military affairs, the Supreme Court ruled unanimously that the president, by statute, indeed has the power to order National Guard units to training missions outside the United States without the approval of governors. Writing for the Court in *Perpich v. Department of Defense* (1990), Justice John Paul Stevens said the 1986 law did not infringe on state powers and was valid. Wrote Stevens,

> [T]he members of the National Guard of Minnesota who are ordered into federal service with the National Guard of the United States lose their status as members of the state militia during their period of active duty.... If the discipline required for effective service in the Armed Forces of a global power requires training in distant lands, or distant skies, Congress has the authority to provide it.[1]

---

1. *Perpich v. Department of Defense,* 496 U.S. 334 at 347, 350–351 (1990).

unconstitutional because Congress had never declared the war. The Supreme Court steadily declined to hear such cases on the ground that war was a political question, not one to be settled by the judiciary.[79] *(See box, Court, Congress, and Cambodia, p. 168.)*

Nixon and War Powers

Even after President Richard Nixon signed a measure repealing the Gulf of Tonkin Resolution on January 12, 1971, he continued to prosecute the war in Vietnam under the aegis of the powers of the commander in chief. His administration emphasized the point made by Meeker that Congress was ratifying its policy by approving appropriations for the war and the Supreme Court's assertion that the conflict presented political questions beyond the purviews of judicial scrutiny.[80] Administration officials also put forth the "merger" theory of war powers, noting the progressive blurring of the constitutional distinction between Congress's war power and the president's role as commander in chief. Distinctions between the power to declare wars and the power to conduct them were invidious, proponents of the theory argued; the nation was in the strongest position when the president and Congress acted in unison. Therefore, Congress should support the president's policies through appropriations with a minimum of dissent so long as the president, in turn, informed Congress of the administration's political and military decisions on a regular basis.[81] The obvious result of this theory would be a virtual monopoly of the war power by the president.

Acting on the merger theory, Nixon, beginning in 1969, authorized secret U.S. air raids on neutral Cambodia without informing Congress. The following year

President George W. Bush speaks to soldiers during a controversial visit to the USS *Abraham Lincoln* off the California coast six weeks after the United States invaded Iraq. According to some press accounts, no president—even ones who have fought in wars—has worn military garb as commander in chief because it is a civilian position.

he ordered U.S. forces into Cambodia to destroy supply centers and staging areas used by the North Vietnamese for operations into the south. In 1972 Nixon directed that the ports of North Vietnam be mined to forestall the flow of arms to guerrilla and regular forces into South Vietnam, a decision that risked collisions with Russian and Chinese supply vessels. In 1973, in an attempt to force North Vietnam to agree to a truce, Nixon ordered the carpet bombing of Hanoi and Haiphong. Nixon neither sought nor obtained explicit congressional approval for any of his policies with respect to Vietnam. The 1973 Paris Accords were negotiated by the president's men, without congressional participation.[82]

War Powers Act of 1973

In response to the disregard shown by Nixon and his predecessors for congressional prerogatives involving the declaration of war, Congress passed the War Powers Act on November 7, 1973, over Nixon's veto.[83] The act authorized the president to undertake limited military action in the absence of a declaration of war, but within forty-eight hours of such action, the president would be required to submit a written report to Congress. Military action and deployment were limited to sixty days, but renewable for an additional thirty days to effect the safe removal of troops. At any time during the sixty-day period, Congress could order the immediate removal of forces by concurrent resolution, not subject to presidential veto.[84] The legislative veto provision was effectively nullified by the Court's decision in *Immigration and Naturalization Service v. Chadha* (1983), but Congress has not modified it.[85]

Although the War Powers Act appeared to limit presidential discretion, critics pointed out that it could be interpreted as expanding the president's war making ability. A blank check to commit troops anywhere, at any time, subject only to a sixty-day to ninety-day limit, indefinitely renewable, appeared to critics as an invitation to havoc or holocaust. Moreover, it was never spelled out how exactly Congress could reverse a presidential commitment of troops once deployed.[86] In the early 1980s a group of representatives sued President Reagan for violating the War Powers Act by sending military personnel to El Salvador. A federal district judge dismissed the suit in 1982, stating that it was up to Congress, not the courts, to decide whether Reagan's action violated the law. The Supreme Court refused to review the decision.[87] In a similar action, in late 1990, as the administration of George H. W. Bush and Congress braced for a possible war in the Persian Gulf, a group of representatives filed a lawsuit seeking a preliminary injunction to prevent Bush from ordering U.S. troops into offensive combat without prior authorization from Congress. Before a federal district court, the members of Congress argued that the Constitution's War Powers Clause dictated that Congress debate and vote in favor of a formal declaration of war before U.S. troops could be used to drive Iraqi forces from Kuwait. In response, the Justice Department contended that Article II gave the president the ultimate authority in foreign affairs as commander in chief. A federal judge refused to issue an injunction, stating that the case was not ripe because only 10 percent of Congress was seeking relief rather than a majority.[88] According to the judge, it would have been premature and presumptuous to issue a decision on the question.

On the same day, another federal judge issued a decision more in keeping with the courts' traditional reluctance to become embroiled in war making disputes.[89] That judge held that the courts could not decide whether the president needed congressional permission to go to war because it was a political question beyond the judicial realm. In doing so, the judge dismissed a complaint by a member of the National Guard protesting service in the gulf until Bush received congressional authorization. In January 1991 the legal issue became moot when Bush decided to request—and Congress approved—a resolution authorizing the use of U.S. military to force Iraq out of Kuwait.

THE WAR ON TERROR AND PRESIDENTIAL POWER

A new kind of war—a U.S.-led global war on terror—was triggered by the terrorist attacks of September 11, 2001. The al Qaeda network had infiltrated nineteen airline hijackers into the United States, and they took control of four early morning flights leaving from Boston, Newark, and Washington. Two of the planes crashed into the towers of the World Trade Center in New York, the third hit the Pentagon across the river from Washington, and a fourth was crashed in Pennsylvania when passengers broke into the cockpit. Nearly three thousand people were killed in the attacks.

One week later, Congress passed a resolution authorizing President George W. Bush to "use all necessary and appropriate force against those nations, organizations, or persons he determines planned, authorized, committed, or aided the terrorist attacks" or "harbored such organizations or persons, in order to prevent future acts of international terrorism against the United States." Saudi-born financier Osama bin Laden was the leader of al Qaeda, and he was believed to be hiding in Afghanistan, where he was protected by the radical Islamic Taliban regime.

Bush ordered U.S. troops to invade Afghanistan, and with the help of the Afghani Northern Alliance, the Taliban were driven from power. Bin Laden escaped, but U.S. forces continued to fight remnants of the regime and take prisoners. Some of those arrested were believed to be al Qaeda operatives. Others were fighters for the Taliban. Without consulting Congress, the president signed an executive order saying that persons captured in the war on terror were not prisoners of war subject to the Geneva Conventions, nor would they be treated as criminal suspects subject to U.S. law. Instead, they were designated as "unlawful enemy combatants," and as such, they were prisoners of the U.S. military with no rights.

Beginning early in 2002 several hundred of these military detainees were sent to the U.S. naval base at Guantánamo Bay, Cuba. Secretary of Defense Donald

Rumsfeld described them as "the worst of the worst," but it soon became clear that most had not been captured on the battlefield and few of them had direct ties to al Qaeda. Many of them were citizens of friendly nations, including Britain, Australia, and Kuwait. Their relatives, working with lawyers, sought their release through the courts, but Bush administration lawyers insisted that the detainees had no legal rights and that judges had no authority to intervene on their behalf. The president, acting as the commander in chief, had the power to set the rules for the captives in this new war, they said.

To complicate matters, the administration also designated two U.S. citizens as "enemy combatants." One of them, Yaser Hamdi, was born in Louisiana in 1980, but moved with his family to Saudi Arabia when he was child. He was captured in Afghanistan by Northern Alliance forces and said to be fighting with the Taliban. When U.S. troops realized he was an American citizen by birth, he was transferred from Guantánamo to a naval brig in Norfolk, Virginia. The second man, Jose Padilla, was born in New York City and converted to Islam. He was arrested at Chicago's O'Hare Airport in 2002 on suspicion of plotting to detonate a radioactive bomb. He too was imprisoned in a Navy brig.

The cases of the enemy combatants raised difficult questions. What is the reach of the president's power to hold prisoners in an undeclared war? And what power do judges have to intervene when the military is holding foreigners and U.S. citizens? A bedrock principle of American law—and of English common law from the Middle Ages—is the right to habeas corpus: an imprisoned person can ask to come before a judge and plead his innocence. The writ of habeas corpus is both a restraint on the power of the executive and a protection of liberty. It is also one of the few rights incorporated into the Constitution as it was originally written. Article 1, section 9, says: "The Privilege of the Writ of Habeas Corpus shall not be suspended, unless when in Cases of Rebellion or Invasion the public Safety may require it." Congress by law had given judges the authority to hear habeas claims from persons who say they were being held "in custody in violation of the Constitution or law or treaties of the United States."

In spring 2004 the Court took up three cases to decide this question: May the imprisoned men in the war on terror have their claims heard by a judge? The justices said yes, but their decision was neither sweeping nor final.

In *Rasul v. Bush* the Court in a 6–3 decision held that the "habeas statute [adopted by Congress] confers a right to judicial review of the legality of Executive detention of aliens in a territory over which the United States exercises plenary and exclusive jurisdiction, but not ultimate sovereignty."[90] Guantánamo Bay was in Cuban territory, but the United States had a legal treaty right to exercise total control.

Justice John Paul Stevens, speaking for the Court, said wartime did not strip judges of their power to hear claims from imprisoned men. He cited a well-known case following the Civil War and the Nazi saboteur case during World War II.[91] "Consistent with the historic purpose of the writ, this Court has recognized the federal courts' power to review applications for habeas relief in a wide variety of cases involving Executive detention, in wartime as well as in times of peace," he wrote. But he acknowledged the decision answered only a "narrow" question, because the justices did not spell out the rights of the Guantánamo detainees. Chief Justice William H. Rehnquist and Justices Antonin Scalia and Clarence Thomas dissented, saying habeas corpus should not extend to foreign prisoners during wartime.

In a second case decided the same day, June 28, 2004, the Court said enemy combatants are entitled to a hearing before a neutral judge, but this holding came in the case of Yaser Hamdi, a U.S. citizen.[92] This fractured decision amounted to a partial victory for both the Bush administration and the civil libertarians who had challenged the government. On one hand, five justices agreed that enemy combatants, even citizens, could be held indefinitely as military prisoners. A second group of six justices said these detainees deserve a fair hearing as well as a lawyer to challenge the government's basis for holding them. "We have long since made clear that a state of war is not a blank check for the President when it comes to the rights of the Nation's citizens," said Justice Sandra Day O'Connor for the Court. Two justices—Scalia and Stevens—would have gone further to rule that the military may not hold a citizen. The government may try someone for treason, Scalia said, but the Constitution makes clear no person may "be deprived of liberty without due process of law."

The Padilla case was turned away on a technicality.[93] The Court said Padilla's lawyers should have filed a writ of habeas corpus in South Carolina where he was imprisoned, not in New York City where he was first held. This ruling forced his lawyers to start over, but before the case could get back to the Supreme Court, the administration relented and brought criminal charges against Padilla in Florida. He was convicted of aiding terrorists and sentenced to prison.

The Bush administration wanted to do more than hold hundreds of men at Guantánamo Bay. It also wanted to try anyone connected with the 9/11 plot and put them to death. But the rules for these military trials were challenged and reached the Court in spring 2006. Salim Hamdan, a native of Yemen, was captured in Afghanistan and was said to be a driver for bin Laden. U.S. authorities charged him with being part of the conspiracy that led to the 9/11 attacks.

But in *Hamdan v. Rumsfeld* the Court, 5-3, struck down the special military tribunals because they had not been authorized by Congress and because the Geneva Conventions prohibited trying captives in hastily convened courts.[94] Justices Stevens, Anthony Kennedy, David Souter, Ruth Bader Ginsburg, and Stephen Breyer formed the majority. Justices Scalia and Thomas dissented, as did the Court's newest member, Justice Samuel A. Alito Jr. Chief Justice John G. Roberts Jr. took no part because he had ruled in favor of the administration when the case was before the U.S. court of appeals.

Although the *Hamdan* ruling was seen as a strong blow against administration policies, its holding again was narrow. The Court did not declare such military trials unconstitutional. Instead, the justices invited Congress to set rules for the military trials, and lawmakers did so a few months later in the Military Commissions Act of 2006. That law also stated clearly that no judge or justice had the authority to hear a writ of habeas corpus from an alien who was designated an enemy combatant. The law set the stage for yet another round of litigation on whether the Guantánamo detainees could go to court to challenge their imprisonment.

In 2008 the Court ruled again that the Guantánamo prisoners had a right to seek their freedom before a federal court. In a 5-4 decision, the justices struck down as unconstitutional the part of the Military Commissions Act that took away the prisoners' right to habeas corpus. Justice Kennedy described habeas corpus as an essential principle of liberty. "Protection for the privilege of habeas corpus was one of the few safeguards of liberty specified in a Constitution that, at the outset, had no Bill of Rights," he wrote in *Boumediene v. Bush*.[95] "The Framers viewed freedom from unlawful restraint as a fundamental precept of liberty, and they understood the writ of habeas corpus as a vital instrument to secure that freedom." The Court did not draw a clear line as to how far habeas corpus extended, or who could take advantage of it. It was understood that habeas corpus did not extend to battlefields or foreign lands. "Practical considerations and exigent circumstances inform the definition and reach of the law's writs, including habeas corpus," Kennedy said. At Guantánamo, prisoners had been held for up to six years, he said. This was far removed from a battlefield, and they were held on a base under the exclusive control of U.S. authorities. Under such circumstances, "[T]he detainees in these cases are entitled to a prompt habeas hearing," Kennedy said. Justices Stevens, Souter, Ginsburg, and Breyer joined Kennedy's opinion. "Our opinion does not undermine the Executive's powers as Commander in Chief," Kennedy concluded. "On the contrary, the exercise of these powers is vindicated, not eroded, when confirmed by the Judicial Branch."

The Architect of Foreign Policy

The Constitution grants the president the power to make treaties and to receive and appoint ambassadors. In addition to the foreign policy powers asserted by the president as commander in chief, these specific grants of power are the source of the president's authority to conduct the nation's foreign relations and shape its foreign policy. The treaty making power has proved to be the more significant grant, and it has been interpreted by the Supreme Court as a broad base for the president's power over foreign policy. The Court's traditional view on this matter was foreshadowed by Virginia representative John Marshall's speech on the floor of the House in 1800, when he defended President John Adams's unilateral decision to return a British fugitive to British authorities: "The President is the sole organ of the nation in its external relations, and its sole representative with foreign nations. Of consequence, the demand of a foreign nation can only be made on him. He possesses the whole executive power."[1]

As with the grant of war powers, the Constitution divides the power over foreign affairs and provides a check on the president. For example, the framers desired a strong executive but not another English monarch, so they brought Congress into the treaty making process; the president has the power to initiate policy and make treaties with other nations but must obtain the consent of two-thirds of the Senate for ratification of a treaty. Alexander Hamilton noted the reciprocal nature of the treaty making power when he observed: "The power of making treaties . . . seems therefore to form a distinct department and to belong, properly neither to the legislative nor to the executive."[2] Congress holds other powers related to foreign relations, notably, the appropriations power; the authority to raise, maintain, and regulate the armed forces; and the power "to declare War, grant Letters of Marque and Reprisal, and make rules concerning Captures on Land and Water."

The debate over control of foreign policy began at the Constitutional Convention when the framers pondered the merits of lodging the foreign relations power almost exclusively in the hands of the chief executive.[3] In 1793 Hamilton and James Madison engaged in an exchange of views over the executive prerogative in foreign affairs prompted by the debate over U.S. neutrality in the wars of the French Revolution. Hamilton, writing as "Pacificus," defended President George Washington's Neutrality Proclamation and his unilateral promulgation of it. Foreign policy was an executive function, Hamilton declared. Congress had the power to declare war, but the president had the power to make treaties and preserve peace until Congress declared war. Hamilton noted, "it belongs to the 'executive power' to do whatever else the law of nations, co-operating with the treaties of the country, enjoin in the intercourse of the United States with foreign powers."[4] Hamilton conceded that executive policy might influence the decision of Congress, but he insisted that each branch of government was free to perform its assigned duties according to its view of the matter.

At Thomas Jefferson's instigation, Madison responded to Hamilton's championing of executive prerogative. Under the pseudonym Helvidius, Madison defended the congressional initiative in foreign affairs, comparing Hamilton's assertions of presidential independence to the royal prerogative of British monarchs and arguing that Congress, too, could decide when matters of national policy should lead to war. Deliberations over grave matters of war and peace could not be foreclosed by the president's decisions, Madison said. What would be the result if Congress declared war and the president proclaimed neutrality?[5] Hamilton never formally replied, but in 1794 Congress passed its first neutrality act, superseding the presidential proclamation, establishing a congressional role in declarations of neutrality. By this time, however, even Jefferson had conceded that the role of Congress in the negotiation of treaties and in the conduct of diplomacy was limited. In 1790 he observed that "[t]he transaction of business with foreign nations is Executive altogether."[6]

The Supreme Court has sustained the "sole organ" principle upholding the president's preeminence in the conduct of foreign relations, and it has checked challenges to the president's exclusive treaty making power by the states and by the Senate. The Court has refused to hear some cases challenging the president's conduct of foreign affairs on the grounds that the issue was political in nature and therefore beyond the realm of judicial determination.

"A DIVIDED POWER"

The Supreme Court has extended to the president broad discretionary powers in foreign affairs even while limiting or denying such latitude in the exercise of power related to domestic affairs. As Edward Corwin has observed, in the field of foreign affairs "[t]he power to determine the substantive content of American policy is a divided power, with the lion's share falling, usually, though by no means always, to the president."[7] Other government actors in the policy process are the states, the Court, and Congress.

The States' Role

One of the first foreign policy matters settled by the Supreme Court was the question of the states' role in foreign affairs. The source of the foreign affairs power was debated in 1795 by Justices William Paterson and James Iredell. According to Iredell, that sovereignty belonged to the states in foreign affairs prior to ratification of the Constitution, but with ratification, it passed to the national government.[8] Paterson disagreed. From his perspective, sovereignty never belonged to the separate states; rather, the power to conduct foreign relations passed to the national government as an inheritance of power from the Continental Congress.[9] The outcome of the Court's argument in 1795 was, therefore, a flat denial to the states of any

control over or role in foreign policy matters. The treaty making power was not affected by the doctrine of "dual federalism" reserving undelegated powers to the states. Paterson's view of an inherent foreign affairs power was later expanded in *United States v. Curtiss-Wright Export Corp.* (1936).[10]

Ware v. Hylton (1796) involved a war law passed by Virginia during the Revolution that provided for British-owned property to be sequestered and individual debts owed to British citizens to be paid to a designated state official. The 1783 peace treaty between Britain and the United States permitted British subjects to sue in state courts to collect debts owed them prior to the Revolution. The year after the Iredell-Paterson debate, the Supreme Court ruled that the treaty provision nullified the state law. Powers reserved to the states by the Tenth Amendment did not include any powers in the field of foreign relations. Justice Samuel Chase observed,

> A treaty cannot be the Supreme law of the land, that is of all the United States, if any act of a State Legislature can stand in its way. . . . It is the declared will of the people of the United States that every treaty made, by the authority of the United States shall be superior to the Constitution and laws of any individual state.[11]

Exclusive federal control over foreign relations and the treaty making power was again asserted by the Court in an 1840 case concerning the state of Vermont's decision to comply with a Canadian request to extradite a fugitive Canadian murderer. Writing for the Court, Chief Justice Roger B. Taney denied the state authorities power to return the prisoner, because the U.S. government had the sole power to deal with foreign governments, and it had no extradition treaty with Great Britain. Taney wrote,

> It was one of the main objects of our Constitution to make us, so far as regarded our foreign relations, one people and one nation; and to cut off all communications between foreign governments and the several State authorities.[12]

Justice William O. Douglas reiterated this view in a 1942 opinion:

Power over external affairs is not shared by the States; it is vested in the national government exclusively.... And the policies of the States become wholly irrelevant to judicial inquiry when the United States, acting within its constitutional sphere, seeks enforcement of its foreign policy in the courts.[13]

The Supreme Court's Role

In the field of foreign policy, the Supreme Court often has invoked the "political question doctrine" to avoid head-on collisions with the president. The doctrine rests on the separation of powers theory: the Supreme Court exercises the judicial power and leaves political, or policy, questions to Congress and the president. Chief Justice John Marshall in 1829 explained the doctrine in one of the first cases in which it was applied, when the Court refused to rule on a boundary dispute between Spain and the United States.

> In a controversy between two nations concerning national boundary, it is scarcely possible that the courts of either should refuse to abide by the measures adopted by its own government. There being no common tribunal to decide between them, each determines for itself on its own rights, and if they cannot adjust their differences peaceably, the right remains with the strongest. The judiciary is not that department of the government to which the assertion of its interests against foreign powers is confided. ... A question like this respecting the boundaries of nations, is ... more a political than a legal question.[14]

Subsequent Court rulings increased the list of political questions, with the justices either supporting the decision of the political departments or refusing to judge them. These political questions include presidential decisions about the status of belligerents under international law;[15] the determination of when negotiated treaties have been ratified by another signatory nation;[16] decisions as to the recognition and treatment of de jure and de facto governments;[17] judgments about accredited diplomatic representatives to the United States;[18] the length of military occupations under treaty terms;[19] the effective date of treaties;[20] and when tacit consent renewal of lapsed treaties is permissible.[21]

In the landmark *Baker v. Carr* (1962), Justice William J. Brennan Jr. provided a concise statement of the Court's criteria for considering matters that concern foreign relations:

> There are sweeping statements to the effect that all questions touching foreign relations are political questions. . . . Yet it is error to suppose that every case or controversy which touches foreign relations lies beyond judicial cognizance. Our cases in this field show a discriminating analysis of the particular question posed, in terms of the history of its management by the political branches, of its susceptibility to judicial handling in the light of its nature and posture in the specific case, and of the possible consequences of judicial action.[22]

The Senate's Role

Although the Constitution divides the war powers fairly evenly between Congress and the executive, the only explicit foreign policy power it grants to Congress is the Senate's power to approve treaties that the president has negotiated. The Constitution does not give the Senate the right to amend and modify treaties submitted for its approval, but the Senate traditionally has claimed it, and the Supreme Court has upheld it. *(See "Treaty Powers," pp. 173–175.)* In 1901 the Court defined a valid treaty and the Senate's role in making it:

> Obviously the treaty must contain the whole contract between the parties, and the power of the Senate is limited to a ratification of such terms as have already been agreed upon between the President, acting for the United States, and the commissioners of the other contracting power. The Senate has no right to ratify the treaty and introduce new terms into it, which shall be obligatory upon the other power, although it may refuse its ratification, or make such ratification conditional upon the adoption of amendments to the treaty.[23]

The "Sole Negotiator"

The logical result of the Court's restrictive view of the roles left for the states, for the Court itself, and for the Senate in foreign affairs was its decision in *United States v. Curtiss-Wright Export Corp.* (1936) that the president is the "sole negotiator" of foreign policy. Improbable as it may seem, a war between Paraguay and Bolivia in 1932 was the catalyst for that broad ruling undergirding the president's primary role in foreign affairs.[24] Both sides in the war depended upon outside military suppliers, and U.S. arms manufacturers, facing a depressed economy at home, exported weapons to the belligerents. Revulsion against the war, isolationist sentiments, and pressure from Great Britain and the League of Nations caused the United States to move to end the arms sales.

On May 24, 1934, Congress approved a joint resolution that authorized President Franklin D. Roosevelt to embargo the arms shipments if, in his judgment, an embargo would contribute to ending the war.[25] The resolution provided for fines and imprisonment, or both, for those who violated the embargo. Roosevelt signed the resolution into law on May 28, 1934.[26] The resolution in no way restricted or directed his discretion in instituting the embargo. Curtiss-Wright Export Corporation and two other companies subsequently were convicted of selling aircraft machine guns to Bolivia in violation of the embargo. They challenged the constitutionality of the resolution, arguing that it was an improper delegation of congressional power to the president. The Court already had evinced sympathy for such challenges, striking down several major New Deal initiatives in 1935 on that basis.[27] (See "The Court Versus FDR," pp. 341–348.)

The Court upheld the embargo resolution by a vote of 7-1. Justice Harlan Fiske Stone took no part in the case, and Justice James C. McReynolds was the lone dissenter. Justice George Sutherland's majority opinion upheld sweeping executive powers in foreign affairs. In it, Sutherland distinguished between "external" and "internal" powers of the federal government, or foreign policy and domestic policy. Based on his reading of the historical evidence and on his studies of the foreign affairs power, Sutherland concluded that the source of national authority in foreign relations was the British crown, not the separate states. This source placed the foreign affairs power on an extraconstitutional footing, one different from that of the internal powers, which passed from the states to the federal government.[28] Sutherland's opinion elaborated on the theory of external sovereignty argued in 1795 by Justice Paterson:

The broad statement that the federal government can exercise no powers except those specifically enumerated in the Constitution, and such implied powers as are necessary and proper to carry into effect the enumerated powers, is categorically true only in respect of our internal affairs. In that field, the primary purpose of the Constitution was to carve from the general mass of legislative powers then possessed by the states such positions as it was thought desirable to vest in the federal government, leaving those not included in the enumeration still in the states. . . . That this doctrine applies only to powers which the state had is self-evident. And since the states severally never possessed international powers, such powers could not have been carved from the mass of state powers but obviously were transmitted to the United States from some other source. . . .

As a result of separation from Great Britain by the colonies, acting as a unit, the powers of external sovereignty passed from the Crown not to the colonies severally, but to the colonies in their collective and corporate capacity as the United States of America. . . . Rulers come and go; governments and forms of government change; but sovereignty survives. A political society cannot endure without a supreme will somewhere. Sovereignty is never held in suspense. When, therefore, the external sovereignty of Great Britain in respect of the colonies ceased, it passed to the Union. . . . It results that the investment of the federal government with the powers of external sovereignty did not depend upon the affirmative grants of the Constitution. The powers to declare and wage war, to conclude peace, to make treaties, to maintain diplomatic relations with other sovereignties, if they had never been mentioned in the Constitution, would have vested in the federal government as necessary concomitants of nationality.[29]

Echoing John Marshall, Sutherland then asserted that the president has the primary role in foreign affairs:

The President alone has the power to speak as a representative of the nation. He makes treaties with the advice and consent of the Senate; but he alone negotiates. Into the field of negotiation the Senate cannot intrude; and Congress is powerless to invade it. . . .

It is important to bear in mind that we are here dealing not alone with an authority vested in the President by an exertion of legislative power, but with such an authority plus the very delicate, plenary and exclusive power of the President as the sole organ of the federal government in the field of international relations—a power which does not require as a basis for its exercise an act of Congress, but which . . . must be exercised in subordination to the applicable provisions of the Constitution.[30]

Delegation of power to the president in the foreign affairs field, therefore, was not to be judged by the same standards as delegation of power over domestic matters.

When the President is to be authorized by legislation to act in respect of a matter intended to affect a situation in foreign territory, the legislator properly bears in mind the important consideration . . . that the form of the President's action—or, indeed whether he shall act at all—may well depend, among other things, upon the nature . . . of confidential information which he has or may thereafter receive. . . . This consideration discloses the unwisdom of requiring Congress in this field of governmental power to lay down narrowly definite standards by which the President is to be governed.[31]

THE TREATY POWER: ITS EFFECTS AND ITS LIMITS

Treaties—their effect and their relationship to conflicting laws, to the Constitution, and to the allocation of power between the states and the federal government— have been the subject of numerous Supreme Court rulings. In 1829 Chief Justice John Marshall discussed the nature and the force of a treaty:

A treaty is in its nature a contract between two nations, not a Legislative Act. It does not generally effect, of itself, the object to be accomplished, especially so far as its operation is infraterritorial; but is carried into execution by the sovereign power of the respective parties to the instrument.

In the United States a different principle is established. Our Constitution declares a treaty to be the law of the land. It is, consequently, to be regarded in courts of justice as equivalent to an Act of the Legislature, whenever it operates of itself without the aid

of any legislative provision. But when the terms of the stipulation import a contract—when either of the parties engages to perform a particular act—the treaty addresses itself to the political, not the judicial department; and the Legislature must execute the contract before it can become a rule for the court.[32]

The distinction that Marshall set out—between a self-executing treaty and a non-self-executing treaty, which requires legislative action—survives to the present. A self-executing treaty requires no legislation to put it into effect. For example, treaties that defined the rights of aliens in the United States would be self-implementing once approved by the Senate and would bind the courts to enforce their terms. A non-self-executing treaty, on the other hand, does not take effect until implemented through legislation approved by the political departments of the government and would not be enforced by the courts until then.

Neither a treaty nor a statute has intrinsic superiority, and the more recent will prevail. In the case of a non-self-executing treaty, however, congressional acts take precedence. Justice Samuel F. Miller stated the rule in the *Head Money Cases* (1884): "A treaty made by the United States with any foreign nation is subject to such acts as Congress may pass for its enforcement, modification, or repeal."[33] Despite treaties with several nations that guaranteed free admission of immigrants to the United States, in the *Head Money Cases* the Court upheld a law that imposed a tax on immigrants. The majority opinion defined a valid treaty and its relationship to acts of Congress:

A treaty is primarily a compact between independent nations. It depends for the enforcement of its provisions on the interest and the honor of the governments which are parties to it. If these fail, its infraction becomes the subject of international negotiations and reclamations, so far as the injured party chooses to seek redress, which may in the end be enforced by actual war. It is obvious that with all this the judicial courts have nothing to do and can give no redress. But a treaty may also contain provisions which confer certain rights upon citizens or subjects of one of the nations residing in the territorial limits of the other, which partake of the nature of municipal law, and which are capable of

The Constitution grants the president the authority to make treaties. In 1981 the Supreme Court upheld the agreement that President Jimmy Carter negotiated to secure the release of fifty-two Americans who had been held hostage inside the U.S. embassy in Iran for 444 days. Here Carter and former hostage Bruce Laingen wave to the crowd from the balcony of the U.S. Air Force hospital in Wiesbaden, West Germany.

enforcement as between private parties in the courts of the country. . . .

A treaty, then, is a law of the land as an act of Congress is, whenever its provisions prescribe a rule by which the rights of the private citizen or subject may be determined. And when such rights are of a nature to be enforced in a court of justice, that court resorts to the treaty for a rule of decision for the case as it would to a statute.[34]

A treaty, the Court has held, may shift regulation of a matter from state to federal control, thereby giving Congress new powers it would not possess without the treaty. In 1916 the United States, Britain, and Canada signed a treaty to protect migratory birds by limiting hunting seasons and by other measures. The treaty stipulated that the United States and Canada would seek domestic legislation to implement the law. The first two acts of Congress regulating migratory bird hunting were struck down by lower federal courts, which found them an unconstitutional extension of federal power into an area reserved to the states by the Tenth Amendment. The 1916 treaty was eventually implemented by a 1918 law that regulated the hunting of migratory birds and authorized the secretary of agriculture to administer the rules.[35] Missouri challenged the law, but the Court upheld it as necessary to carry treaty provisions into effect. The plenary nature of the federal treaty making power, said the Court, was sufficient to grant Congress control over matters otherwise ascribed to the states. The effect of the ruling in *Missouri v. Holland* (1920) was that ratification of a treaty could give Congress powers it would not otherwise have. Justice Oliver Wendell Holmes Jr.'s opinion viewed the treaty power broadly:

> To answer this question it is not enough to refer to the Tenth Amendment, reserving the powers not delegated to the United States, because by Article II, § 2, the power to make treaties is delegated expressly, and by Article VI treaties made under authority of the United States, along with the Constitution and the laws of the United States made in pursuance thereof, are declared the supreme law of the land. If the treaty is valid there can be no dispute about the validity of the statute under Article I, § 8, as a necessary and proper means to execute the powers of the Government. . . .

> It is said that a treaty cannot be valid if it infringes the Constitution, that there are limits, therefore, to the treaty making power, and that one such limit is that what an act of Congress could not do unaided, in derogation of the powers reserved to the States, a treaty cannot do. An earlier act of Congress that attempted by itself and not in pursuance of a treaty to regulate the killing of migratory birds within the States had been held bad in the District Court. . . . Those decisions were supported by arguments that migratory birds were owned by the States in their sovereign capacity for the benefit of their people, and that . . . this control was one that Congress had no power to displace. The same argument is supposed to apply now with equal force.

> Whether the two cases were decided rightly or not they cannot be accepted as a test of the treaty power. Acts of Congress are the supreme law of the land only when made in pursuance of the Constitution, while treaties are declared to be so when made under the authority of the United States. . . . We do not mean to imply that there are no qualifications to the treaty making power; but they must be ascertained in a different way. It is obvious that there may be matters of the sharpest exigency for the national

well-being that an act of Congress could not deal with but that a treaty followed by such an act could and it is not lightly to be assumed that, in matters requiring national action, "a power which must belong to and somewhere reside in every civilized government" is not to be found. . . . The treaty in question does not contravene any prohibitory words to be found in the Constitution. The only question is whether it is forbidden by some invisible radiation from the general terms of the Tenth Amendment. . . .

> Here a national interest of very nearly the first magnitude is involved. It can be protected only by national action in concert with that of another power. The subject-matter is only transitorily within the state and has no permanent habitat therein. But for the treaty and the statute there soon might be no birds for any power to deal with. We see nothing in the Constitution that compels the government to sit by while a food supply is cut off and the protectors of our forests and our crops are destroyed. It is not sufficient to rely upon the States.[36]

Termination of Treaties

The Court has held that the termination of treaties, even those terminable on notice, requires an act of Congress. The Court affirmed its support of congressional power to repeal treaties in 1899 when it held that "Congress by legislation and so far as the people and authorities of the United States are concerned, could abrogate a treaty made between this country and another country which had been negotiated by the President and approved by the Senate."[37] Also, an act of Congress has been held to have superseded a conflicting provision of an existing treaty. The Court has never declared a treaty unconstitutional, but it did void an executive agreement with Canada that conflicted with extant legislation.[38]

Legislative practice and executive opinion generally support the view that terminating international pacts belongs, as a prerogative of sovereignty, to Congress. The president, however, with the power to interpret treaties prior to their enforcement, may find that an agreement has been breached and may decide that a treaty is no longer binding on the United States. The

INTERPRETING A TREATY LITERALLY

In 1990 Humberto Alvarez-Machain, a Mexican citizen, was abducted from his home in Guadalajara and flown by private plane to Texas, where U.S. federal agents arrested him. He was indicted for participating in the kidnapping and murder of Enrique Camarena-Salazar, a special agent wit the Drug Enforcement Administration, and Alfredo Zavala-Avelar, a Mexican pilot working with Camarena. Alvarez-Machain, a medical doctor, was accused of participating in the agent's murder by prolonging his life with drugs so that others could torture and interrogate him. Widely reported in the United States, the crime came to represent part of the abomination of illegal drug trafficking.

Lower courts dismissed the indictment against Alvarez-Machain on the ground that his abduction violated the 1978 Extradition Treaty between the United States and Mexico. In June 1992 the Supreme Court, in a 6-3 vote, reversed those decisions, ruling that Alvarez-Machain could be tried in the United States. Reading the treaty literally, the Court stated, "The Treaty says nothing about the obligations of the United States and Mexico to refrain from forcible abductions of people from the territory of the other nation, or the consequence under the Treaty if such an abduction occurs."[1]

Writing for the majority, Chief Justice William H. Rehnquist asserted, "Mexico has protested the abduction of respondent through diplomatic notes, and the decision of whether respondent should be returned to Mexico, as a matter outside of the Treaty, is a matter for the Executive Branch."[2] In *United States v. Alvarez-Machain* (1992) the Court relied on a pair of 1886 cases: *United States v. Rauscher,* in which the Court held that an individual brought to the United States under an extradition treaty must be tried according to the provisions of the treaty, and *Ker v. Illinois,* in which the Court upheld the larceny conviction of a man who had been abducted in Lima, Peru, to face his charges in an Illinois court.[3]

The Court said the Alvarez-Machain case more aptly compared to *Ker,* because the defendant's seizure was not according to the terms of a treaty. The majority downplayed the fact that in *Ker* the U.S. government did not participate in the abduction and Peru did not object to the man's prosecution. Although the U.S.-Mexico treaty gives the two countries the

option of either extraditing the individuals in question or keeping them in their own country for prosecution, Rehnquist said the treaty

> does not purport to specify the only way in which one country may gain custody of a national of the other country for the purposes of prosecution. . . . The history of negotiation and practice under the Treaty also fails to show that abductions outside of the Treaty constitute a violation of the Treaty. As the Solicitor General notes, the Mexican government was made aware, as early as 1906, of the Ker doctrine, and the United States' position that it applied to forcible abductions made outside of the terms of the United States-Mexico extradition treaty.[4]

Rehnquist was joined by Justices Anthony M. Kennedy, Antonin Scalia, David H. Souter, Clarence Thomas, and Byron R. White. Dissenting were Justices Harry A. Blackmun, Sandra Day O'Connor, and John Paul Stevens. In a statement written by Stevens, the dissenters said the treaty with Mexico was a comprehensive document containing twenty-three articles and designed to cover the entire subject of extradition. Stevens said the Court's opinion

> fails to differentiate between the conduct of private citizens, which does not violate any treaty obligation, and conduct expressly authorized by the Executive Branch of the Government, which unquestionably constitutes a flagrant violation of international law, and in my opinion, also constitutes a breach of our treaty obligations. . . . [T]he desire for revenge exerts a kind of hydraulic pressure before which even well settled principles of law will bend, but it is precisely at such moments that we should remember and be guided by our duty to render judgment evenly and dispassionately according to law.[5]

---

1. *United States v. Alvarez-Machain,* 504 U.S. 655 (1992).

2. Id.

3. *United States v. Rauscher,* 119 U.S. 407 (1886), *Ker v. Illinois,* 119 U.S. 436 (1886).

4. *United States v. Alvarez-Machain,* 504 U.S. 655 (1992).

5. Id.

Court has stipulated that treaties may be abrogated by agreement between the contracting parties, by the treaty provisions, by the president, by congressional repeal, and by the president and the Senate acting jointly.[39] In 1979 the Court sidestepped a challenge to

President Jimmy Carter's unilateral abrogation of a mutual defense treaty with Taiwan, a consequence of Carter's recognition of the Chinese government in Beijing. As a result, political—if not legal—precedent exists for this type of action by a president.[40]

Constitutional Limits

In 1889 the Court discussed the unlimited nature of the treaty power but made clear that a treaty could be found unconstitutional:

> That the treaty power of the United States extends to all proper subjects of negotiation between our government and the governments of other nations, is clear. . . . The treaty power, as expressed in the Constitution, is in terms unlimited except by those restraints which are found in that instrument against the action of the government or of its departments, and those arising from the nature of the government itself and of that of the States. It would not be contended that it extends so far as to authorize what the Constitution forbids, or a change in the character of the government or in that of one of the States, or a cession of any portion of the territory of the latter, without its consent.[41]

The Court has never held a treaty unconstitutional, but it has made clear the continuing validity of the view that the treaty power is subject to the limits set by the Constitution. Writing for the Court in *Reid v. Covert* (1957), Justice Hugo L. Black stated,

> no agreement with a foreign nation can confer power of the Congress, or on any other branch of government, which is free from the restraints of the Constitution. . . . It would be manifestly contrary to the objectives of those who created the Constitution . . . let alone alien to our entire constitutional history and tradition—to construe Article VI [the Supremacy Clause] as permitting the United States to exercise power under an international agreement without observing constitutional prohibitions. . . .
>
> The prohibitions of the Constitution were designed to apply to all branches of the National Government and they cannot be nullified by the Executive and the Senate combined.
>
> There is nothing new or unique about what we say here. This Court has regularly and uniformly recognized the supremacy of the Constitution over a treaty. . . . This Court has also repeatedly taken the position that an Act of Congress, which must comply with the Constitution, is on a full parity with a treaty, and that when a statute which is subsequent in time is inconsistent with a treaty, the statute to the extent of conflict renders the treaty null. It would be completely anomalous to say that a treaty need not comply with the Constitution when such an agreement can be overridden by a statute that must conform to that instrument.
>
> There is nothing in *State of Missouri v. Holland* . . . which is contrary to the position taken here. There the Court carefully noted that the treaty involved was not inconsistent with any specific provision of the Constitution. The Court was concerned with the Tenth Amendment which reserves to the States or the people all power not delegated to the National Government. To the extent that the United States can validly make treaties, the people and the States have delegated their power to the National Government and the Tenth Amendment is no barrier.[42]

No "Unilateral" Presidential Power to Enforce Treaties

A treaty may well be part of "the supreme Law of the Land," but that does not mean the president, acting alone, may enforce the rulings of an international court with the authority to resolve treaty disputes. President George W. Bush was rebuked by the Supreme Court in 2008 when he tried to force Texas to reopen the death penalty case of a Mexican national at the behest of the International Court of Justice (ICJ) in The Hague. "Our Constitution does not contemplate vesting such power in the Executive alone," wrote Chief Justice John G. Roberts Jr. in *Medellin v. Texas* (2008).[43]

This unusual dispute began in 2004 when Mexico sued the United States in the ICJ, the judicial arm of the United Nations. Mexico claimed that the United States had violated the Vienna Convention by failing to notify its consulate when its nationals were arrested and prosecuted for serious crimes. The suit named fifty-one Mexican nationals who were sentenced to death in Texas, California, and several other states. One of those named was José Ernesto Medellín, who in 1993 had confessed to his role in the gang rape and murder of two young women in Houston.

The Vienna Convention on Consular Relations was agreed to in 1963 and was ratified by the Senate in

RECOGNITION AND NONRECOGNITION

The power of recognition of foreign governments or the reverse—nonrecognition—has been an important tool in the president's conduct of foreign relations. This power derives from the Constitution's acknowledgment that the executive "shall receive ambassadors and other public ministers." Although the president occasionally has sought the cooperation of Congress in recognizing nations, the act of recognition is a presidential function.

Presidential power to determine whether the United States recognizes one nation's sovereign jurisdiction over a region was sustained by the Court in the early nineteenth century. In *Williams v. Suffolk Ins. Co.* (1839) the Court refused to consider a challenge to President Martin Van Buren's decision not to recognize Argentina's claim of sovereignty over the Falkland Islands. The opinion defined the narrow purview of the Court's scrutiny where executive or "political" questions were involved:

> When the executive branch of the government, which is charged with our foreign relations, shall . . . assume a fact in regard to the sovereignty of any island or country, it is conclusive on the judicial department. . . . And in this view, it is not material to inquire, nor is it the province of the court to determine, whether the executive be right or wrong. It is enough to know, that in the exercise of his constitutional functions, he had decided the question. Having done this . . . it is obligatory on the people and government of the Union.[1]

An 1897 Senate Foreign Relations Committee report on the subject of recognition concluded that "the executive branch is the sole mouthpiece of the nation in communication with foreign sovereignties."[2]

The practice of refusing to recognize governments has been largely a political decision vested in the executive branch and unchallenged by the courts. President Woodrow Wilson decided not to recognize the de facto government of Mexico's provisional president Huerta in 1913, an act that hastened Huerta's downfall a year later.[3] Wilson used nonrecognition with considerable discretion, as did his successors.

Every president between Wilson and Franklin D. Roosevelt refused to recognize the Union of Soviet Socialist Republics, until Roosevelt's policy reversal in 1933.[4] President Herbert Hoover followed the nonrecognition principle with respect to the Japanese puppet government (Manchukuo) in Manchuria in 1932.[5] Every president from Harry S. Truman to Lyndon B. Johnson refused to recognize the communist government of mainland China until President Richard Nixon's de facto recognition in 1972.

In 1995 President Bill Clinton recognized Vietnam, urged in part by U.S. business interests that saw great potential in its oil reserves and economic development. A year earlier Clinton, with the legally unnecessary but politically important endorsement of the Senate, had formally ended eighteen years of trade sanctions against Vietnam imposed at the conclusion of the U.S. war in Southeast Asia.

---

1. *Williams v. Suffolk Ins. Co.*, 13 Pet. (38 U.S.) 415 at 419–420 (1839).

2. Senate Doc. 56, 54th Cong., 2nd sess., 1897, 20–22.

3. Samuel E. Morison, Henry Steele Commager, and William E. Leuchtenburg, *The Growth of the American Republic*, 2 vols. (New York: Oxford University Press, 1969), 2:354.

4. *Constitution of the United States of America: Analysis and Interpretation* (Washington, D.C.: U.S. Government Printing Office, 1973), 544.

5. Ibid.

1969. Congress did not, however, pass legislation to enforce its obligations.

The International Court ruled for Mexico on March 31, 2004, in what was known as the *Avena* decision, and it held the United States had violated the treaty. The remedy was left somewhat unclear. The ICJ said the fifty-one men were entitled to have their cases reviewed and reconsidered.[44]

The ICJ ruling gave new hope to foreign nationals who were in U.S. prisons. Many of them, and their lawyers, filed appeals in state and federal courts. They asserted they were entitled to have their convictions overturned, or at least reconsidered, because their rights had been violated. In addition, lawyers for Medellín, a named plaintiff, said the Texas state courts must reconsider his conviction and death sentence. While his case was pending, President Bush issued an extraordinary order on February 28, 2005, calling upon the Texas courts to give Medellín a new hearing:

> I have determined, pursuant to the authority vested in me as President by the Constitution and the laws of the United States of America, that the United States will discharge its international obligations under the decision of the International Court of

Justice in [*Avena*], by having the State courts give effect to the decision in accordance with the general principles of comity in case filed by the 51 Mexican nationals addressed in that decision.

Bush reasoned that because treaties are contracts between nations, and he was the leader of the United States in foreign affairs, he had a duty to enforce the terms of the treaty. Moreover, the United States had agreed prior to the *Avena* ruling to abide by the decisions of the ICJ. But Texas prosecutors refused to reopen Medellín's case. They said the prisoner had been given all the rights he was due, including Miranda warnings prior to his confession. The Texas Court of Criminal Appeals agreed with the state's lawyers concerning Medellín's rights and held that neither the ICJ ruling nor Bush's order "was binding federal law" in Texas.

The Supreme Court disposed of the issues raised by the ICJ ruling in two separate decisions. In 2006 the Court ruled that foreign nationals whose Vienna Convention rights were violated do not have a right to reopen their cases and to suppress their confessions. This issue arose in a case from Oregon. Moises Sanchez-Llamas, a native of Mexico, shot a police officer in a gun battle in 1999, made incriminating statements, and was convicted and sentenced to twenty years in prison. He said his confession should have been suppressed because he was not given the right to consult a Mexican lawyer. In *Sanchez-Llamas v. Oregon* Chief Justice Roberts said the ICJ decisions have "no binding force" in the cases of the thousands of foreign nationals who are jailed in the United States.[45]

Roberts also rejected the notion that the courts must exclude the confession as evidence. "It would be startling if the Convention were read to require suppression," the chief justice wrote. "The exclusionary rule as we know it is an entirely American legal creation. . . . There is no reason to suppose that Sanchez-Llamas would be afforded the relief he seeks here in any of the other 169 countries party to the Vienna Convention." Justices Antonin Scalia, Anthony Kennedy, Clarence Thomas, and Samuel Alito joined with Roberts to form the majority.

Two years later, the Court rejected Bush's intervention on behalf of José Medellín. "The President's authority to act, as with the exercise of any government power, must stem from an act of Congress or from the Constitution," Roberts said, and Congress has not passed a law to enforce the terms of the Vienna Convention. "The President has an array of political and diplomatic means available to enforce international obligations, but unilaterally converting a non-self-executing treaty into a self-executing treaty is not one of them," he said. Although the president has the "foreign affairs authority" to settle international disputes, that power "cannot stretch so far as to support" Bush's order to the Texas courts, Roberts added. "The Government has not identified a single instance in which the President has attempted (or Congress has acquiesced in) a Presidential directive issued to state courts, much less one that reaches deeply into the heart of the State's police powers and compels state courts to reopen final criminal judgments and set aside neutrally applicable state laws."[46]

Once again, Justices Scalia, Kennedy, Thomas, and Alito joined the chief justice in the majority. Stevens concurred in the judgment, saying the ICJ's ruling is not binding law within the United States. On August 5, 2008, Medellín was executed by Texas authorities.

EXECUTIVE AGREEMENTS

Secretary of State John Foster Dulles facetiously told a Senate subcommittee in 1953, "Every time we open a new privy, we have to have an executive agreement."[47] Dulles exaggerated, but he effectively underscored the growing preference by presidents to negotiate executive agreements to avoid the delays and debates that can occur when treaties are submitted for Senate approval. Dulles estimated that the United States had entered into roughly ten thousand executive agreements in connection with the North Atlantic Treaty Organization (NATO) alone.[48] Of the large number of executive agreements, however, only a small percentage rest solely upon the president's powers in foreign relations or as commander in chief. Many of such agreements, authorized in advance by Congress, rest in addition upon congressional statutes or Senate-ratified treaty provisions.[49] Therefore, executive agreements can be divided into two types: those authorized by Congress and those made on presidential initiative.

Authorized Agreements

Authorized agreements have been made on a wide variety of matters. Congress authorized the executive branch to enter into negotiations when the United States needed to borrow money from foreign countries early in its history and when it appropriated money to pay tribute to the Barbary pirates to prevent attacks on American shipping.[50] Texas, Hawaii, and Samoa became U.S. possessions by executive agreements approved by congressional resolution.[51] Similar broad grants of authority through congressional approval of executive agreements have allowed presidents to exercise their power in lowering tariff barriers and easing restrictions on international trade.

The Lend-Lease Act of March 11, 1941, granted President Franklin D. Roosevelt the power to enter into executive agreements to manufacture defense articles in government arsenals or "otherwise procure" them "to sell, transfer, exchange, lease, and lend . . . to the governments of any country deemed vital to the defense of the United States."[52] Another form of congressional authorization of presidential agreements was the United Nations Participation Act of December 20, 1945, which permitted the president to negotiate a series of agreements with the UN Security Council providing for the number and types of armed forces to be made available to the council for the purpose of maintaining peace and international security.[53] Presidents also have negotiated agreements with other nations about the status of forces stationed on foreign soil. These usually afforded American military personnel and their dependents a qualified privilege of trial by U.S. courts martial while within the jurisdiction of another country.

Presidential Initiatives

In 1817 President James Monroe agreed with Great Britain to limit arms on the Great Lakes. Executive treaty making, accomplished by an exchange of notes approved by the Senate, took place without an exchange of ratifications.[54] Native American raids along the border between Mexico and the United States led to a series of agreements between 1882 and 1896 that permitted troops of both nations to cross the international border in pursuit of marauding Indians. The Court in 1902 found "probable" justification for the agreements:

> While no act of Congress authorizes the department to permit the introduction of foreign troops, the power to give such permission without legislative assent was probably assumed to exist from the authority of the President as commander in chief.[55]

Four dissenting justices—Chief Justice Melvin W. Fuller and Justices Horace Gray, John Marshall Harlan, and Edward D. White—said that such acts by the president required treaty or statutory sanction.

President William McKinley ended the Spanish-American War by such an agreement, sent troops to China in the face of the Boxer Rebellion, and signed a Boxer Indemnity Protocol, along with other European powers without Senate approval.[56] Secretary of State John Hay agreed to the substance of the "open door" notes that guaranteed Chinese sovereignty and called a halt to the establishment of spheres of influence in China.[57] President Theodore Roosevelt initialed what amounted to a secret treaty between Japan and the United States that recognized Japan's military protectorate in Korea as well as agreements that dealt with Japanese immigration and the balance of power in the Pacific.[58] Woodrow Wilson's secretary of state, Robert Lansing, exchanged letters with Japan that recognized that nation's "special interests" in China in return for Japanese recognition of the open door policy.[59]

Franklin D. Roosevelt made executive agreements a primary instrument for attaining his foreign policy objectives to the extent that they nearly replaced the treaty making power in effect. He recognized the Soviet Union by an exchange of notes in 1933, and in the fall of 1940 an executive agreement that provided for hemispheric defense in the event of an attack changed U.S. policy from neutrality to a state of quasi belligerency with the Axis powers. The Hull-Lothian agreement of September 2, 1940, authorized the exchange of destroyers for bases.[60] A 1941 agreement with

Banning the Boat People

The relatively unfettered power of the president to use the Coast Guard to stop and return unwanted visitors beyond the territorial waters of the United States was underscored by a Supreme Court ruling in the early 1990s. In *Sale v. Haitian Centers Council Inc.* (1993) the Court was asked to invalidate the "interdiction policy" toward Haitian refugees attempting to reach the United States by boat.[1] This policy had been adopted by President George H. W. Bush and continued by President Bill Clinton.

To deter Haitians from making the dangerous journey from their homeland to the United States in small, unseaworthy boats, Bush and Clinton ordered the Coast Guard to intercept such boats on the high seas and return them to Haiti, without a hearing or other opportunity for the Haitians to argue their case for asylum. This policy was challenged as violating refugee protection provisions of U.S. immigration law and the 1951 United Nations Convention on the Status of Refugees. Two federal appeals courts heard the challenge and divided on the issue. When the Supreme Court reviewed the matter, it voted 8-1 to uphold the policy, ruling that neither the law nor the treaty applied outside U.S. borders. Only Justice Harry A. Blackmun dissented.

---

1. *Sale v. Haitian Centers Council Inc.,* 509 U.S. 155 (1993).

---

the Danish foreign minister, entered into after Nazi Germany occupied Denmark, permitted the United States to occupy Greenland for defense purposes.[61] Agreements at Cairo, Tehran, Yalta, and Potsdam outlined the contours of the postwar peace.[62]

Cold War Agreements

Treaty making reemerged for a time in the cold war era in the form of multinational defense pacts, such as the Southeast Asia Treaty Organization (SEATO), the Central Treaty Organization (CENTO), NATO, and the United Nations Charter. Executive agreements, however, remained a primary instrument of foreign policy. In 1956 congressional concern about the proliferation of commitments by executive agreement emerged in a Senate bill that would have required the president to submit all such agreements for Senate perusal within sixty days. The House took no action on the measure.[63]

A 1969-1970 study of executive agreements by the Senate Foreign Relations Subcommittee on Security Agreements and Commitments Abroad uncovered secret agreements made during the 1960s with a number of countries, including Ethiopia, Laos, South Korea, Spain, and Thailand. A 1971 agreement made by the Nixon administration with Portugal for the use of an air base in the Azores and an agreement with Bahrain for naval base facilities on the Persian Gulf stirred the Senate to pass a "sense of the Senate" resolution to the effect that both agreements should have been submitted to the Senate for approval as treaties.[64] In 1972 the Senate voted to cut off funding for these bases, but the House failed to act on the matter.

The Court and Executive Agreements

During the administration of FDR, the Supreme Court upheld the executive agreement as a valid exercise of presidential power. In *United States v. Belmont* (1936) the Court held that the presidential decision to recognize the Soviet Union in 1933 and the executive agreement that gave effect to that policy constituted a valid international compact. Moreover, the Court noted, such agreement, without Senate approval, had the effect of a treaty and superseded conflicting state laws. Justice Sutherland, author of the *Curtiss-Wright* opinion, delivered the Court's opinion:

> The recognition, establishment of diplomatic relations, the assignment, and agreements with respect thereto, were all parts of one transaction, resulting in an international compact between the two governments. That the negotiations, acceptance of the assignment and agreements and understandings in respect thereof were within the competence of the

President may not be doubted. Governmental power over external affairs is not distributed, but is vested exclusively in the national government. And in respect of what was done here, the Executive had authority to speak as the sole organ of that government. . . .

. . . [A]n international compact as this was, is not always a treaty which requires the participation of the Senate. There are many such compacts, of which a protocol, a modus vivendi, a postal convention, and agreements like that now under consideration are illustrations.[65]

In *United States v. Pink* (1942)—a decision reminiscent of the 1796 decision in *Ware v. Hylton* affirming the supremacy of a federal treaty over state law—the Court reaffirmed the force and validity of executive arguments: The 1933 executive agreement that extended diplomatic recognition to the Soviet Union provided that after settlement of U.S. claims against Russian-owned companies, the assets that remained would be returned to the Soviet Union. The state of New York, however, went to court to prevent the return of the remaining assets of an insurance company with New York offices. The Court upheld the terms of the executive agreement against the state's claims. The majority held that the terms of the agreement bound the state just as if they were treaty provisions, because the president possessed the power to remove obstacles to diplomatic recognition. It was, Justice Douglas said,

a modest implied power of the President who is the "sole organ of the Federal Government in the field of international relations." . . . It was the judgment of the political department that full recognition of the Soviet Government required the settlement of outstanding problems including the claims of our nationals. . . . We would usurp the executive function if we held that the decision was not final and conclusive in the courts.[66]

With respect to state power in the field of foreign affairs or the conflict of state laws with international agreements, Douglas affirmed the long-standing rule that

state law must yield when it is inconsistent with, or impairs the policy or provisions of, a treaty or of an international compact or agreement. . . . The power of a State to refuse enforcement of rights based on foreign law which runs counter to the public policy of the forum . . . must give way before the superior Federal policy evidenced by a treaty or international compact or agreement.[67]

No state had the power to modify an international agreement or to reject part of a policy that underpinned the broader diplomatic policy of recognition of a foreign government, in this case the Soviet Union, wrote Douglas. Such an exercise of state power would be a "dangerous invasion of Federal authority" that "would tend to disturb that equilibrium in our foreign relations which the political departments of our national government had diligently endeavoured to establish."[68]

Pink was cited by the Court almost forty years later when it upheld, in a lengthy opinion, President Carter's executive agreement resulting in freedom for fifty-two American hostages held by Iran for more than fourteen months. In *Dames & Moore v. Regan* (1981) the Court unanimously upheld Carter's multiple actions and agreements that constituted the financial arrangement necessary to free the hostages.[69] Central to the opinion, written by Justice William H. Rehnquist, was evidence, presented in a variety of ways, that Congress had approved fully of the use of executive agreements to settle individual claims. "We do not decide that the President possesses plenary power to settle claims, even as against foreign governmental entities," he wrote. "But where, as here, the settlement of claims had been determined to be a necessary incident to the resolution of a major foreign policy dispute between our country and another, and where, as here, we can conclude that Congress acquiesced in the President's action, we are not prepared to say that the President lacks the power to settle such claims."[70]

The President as Executive

"The executive Power shall be vested in a President of the United States of America," begins Article II, but the Constitution quickly follows this sweeping statement of power with a correspondingly broad responsibility: the president is obligated to "take Care that the Laws be faithfully executed." Presidents, justices, and scholars have disagreed over the import of the executive power provision.[1] Is this a broad grant of inherent executive authority, adding to the enumerated powers that follow, or is it simply a designation of office, adding nothing in substantive power? In practice, the provision has been interpreted as granting presidents virtually all power necessary for management of the executive branch in the public interest. Not only has pragmatic necessity bolstered the broad view of executive power, but those who have adopted it also have found support for it in the "decision of 1789," the discussion by the First Congress of the specific powers of the executive. *(See box, The "Decision of 1789," p. 299.)*

The Take Care Clause blended the founders' distrust of concentrated power with the practical necessity of vesting administrative and enforcement authority in the president. This provision clearly rendered the president subordinate to the laws to be administered. Through precedent and practice the Faithful Execution Clause has come to incorporate a broad series of powers that range from the administrative interpretation of acts of Congress to the declaration of martial law in times of civil disorder or national emergency. The Court generally has granted the president broad discretion to act under this clause. The Court also has viewed this clause as an acknowledgment of the executive's need to carry out many duties through subordinates. The clause does not direct the executive to faithfully *execute* the laws, but only to *take care* that the laws are faithfully executed, a clearly supervisory function.

In the early nineteenth century the Court set out the general rule that the duties and obligations placed on the president by law could be carried out by subordinates.

Under an 1823 law, public money could not be disbursed by officers of the United States except at the president's discretion. In *Wilcox v. McConnel* (1839) the Court ruled that the chief executive "speaks and acts through the heads of the several departments in relation to subjects which appertain to their respective duties."[2] Four years later the Court wrote,

> The President's duty in general requires his superintendence of the administration; yet this duty cannot require of him to become the administrative officer of every department and bureau, or to perform in person the numerous details incident to services which, nevertheless, he is, in a correct sense, by the Constitution and laws required and expected to perform. This cannot be, 1st. Because, if it were practicable, it would be to absorb the duties and responsibilities of the various departments of the government in the personal action of the one chief executive officer. It cannot be, for the stronger reason, that it is impracticable—nay, impossible.[3]

THE APPOINTMENT POWER

The president's power to appoint and remove subordinate officials is a necessary complement to the power to manage the executive branch. Members of the president's administration are responsible for carrying out the duties of the office they have been selected to fill and to serve the president who appointed them. Article II, section 2, provides that the president

> shall nominate, and by and with the advice and consent of the Senate, shall appoint Ambassadors, other public Ministers and Consuls, Judges of the supreme Court, and all other Officers of the United States, whose Appointments are not herein otherwise provided for, and which shall be established by Law: but the Congress may by Law vest the Appointment of such inferior Officers, as they think proper, in the President alone, in the Courts of Law, or in the Heads of Departments.

"Midnight appointee" William Marbury, whose suit against James Madison led to a landmark Supreme Court case in 1803. John Marshall's opinion in *Marbury v. Madison* established the Court's authority to review the constitutionality of acts of Congress.

The clause provides four methods of appointment: presidential appointments with Senate confirmation, presidential appointments without Senate confirmation, appointments by courts of law, and appointments by heads of departments. Congress exercises no power to appoint executive officers, although it may set qualifications for offices established by statute. Congressional requirements usually have pertained to citizenship, grade, residence, age, political affiliation, and professional competence. The appointment power of the president has been exercised in conformance with a blend of historical precedents, custom, constitutional requirements, and statutory provisions established by Congress. Congress has narrowed the range of officers over whom the president has the discretionary appointment power: The creation of the Civil Service Commission (now the Office of Personnel Management) and the steady addition of positions to the professional civil service have reduced the scope of the president's exercise of the appointment power. Moreover, the establishment of a professional foreign service and the enumeration of the list of diplomatic posts available for presidential appointments also narrowed the president's range of appointments.

The Supreme Court has ruled on relatively few cases concerning the appointment power, and the decisions that have been made, from *Marbury v. Madison* on, have restrained the president's power to appoint and limited the chief executive's discretionary power to remove officials.[4] *Marbury*, the most famous decision written by Chief Justice John Marshall, and perhaps the best known in the Court's history, began as a relatively unimportant controversy over a presidential appointment. William Marbury sought delivery of his commission of appointment as a justice of the peace. In addition to having political significance in constitutional history as the means by which the Marshall Court established the principle of judicial review, *Marbury v. Madison* also had something to say about the appointment process.[5] On the one hand, the Court held that Marbury should have received his commission, which had been duly signed and sealed, but not delivered. On the other, Marshall held that the Court lacked the power to issue an order commanding Secretary of State James Madison to deliver it. The effect of *Marbury* was that in making appointments, the president is under no enforceable obligation to deliver a commission, even after the nominee has been confirmed by the Senate.

Confirmation and Courtesy

Senate consent to executive appointments was a unique innovation incorporated into the Constitution. The original idea of Senate participation in the selection as well as confirmation of nominees never materialized, however. President George Washington collided with the Senate over approval of an Indian treaty and subsequently refused to consult it on appointment matters except to send up nominations for approval. Senate consent to an executive appointment came to mean simply that a

Diplomatic Appointments

With the establishment of the Foreign Service, Congress reduced the discretionary appointment power of the executive with respect to diplomatic posts. During the first sixty-five years of the nation's history, the president completely controlled the appointment and removal of diplomatic ministers. All matters of grade, rank, and compensation were left to presidential discretion during this period.

One example of the breadth of this power occurred in 1814. President James Madison, with the Senate in recess, appointed three commissioners to negotiate with the British to end the War of 1812. Opponents in Congress argued that the offices had not been created by statute; hence no vacancies existed to allow the president to appoint peace commissioners. Madison responded that there were two classes of offices under the Constitution. One included the range of posts created by law to manage the government, and the other related to foreign affairs

and included diplomatic posts, completely under presidential control and beyond congressional scrutiny. Congress protested, but took no action. The peace made by these commissioners ended the war.[1]

In 1955 Congress created an official list of envoys and ministers in the public service and specified salary and rank for each post. Today, Foreign Service appointments are nominally made by the president, but they are governed by the Foreign Service Act of 1946. The president retains the right and power to appoint ambassadors-at-large as personal emissaries for foreign missions without Senate consultation or approval. Such positions are not regarded as regular ambassadorial or ministerial appointments by Congress or the Supreme Court.[2]

1. *Constitution of the United States of America: Analysis and Interpretation* (Washington, D.C.: U.S. Government Printing Office, 1973), 520.
2. Ibid.

majority of the Senate approves the president's nomination. Presidents customarily have consulted individual senators of their own political party on matters of appointments related to their home states. Policy and political considerations, however, often take precedence over the practice of senatorial courtesy, and failure of the president to extend this courtesy to the appropriate senators usually has not alone resulted in a nominee's rejection.

Once the Senate has approved a nominee, it cannot reverse its decision, although earlier Senate rules permitted a move for reconsideration and recall of a confirmation resolution within two days after its passage. In December 1930 President Herbert Hoover nominated George O. Smith as chairman of the Federal Power Commission. The Senate, in executive session on December 20, confirmed Smith and ordered the resolution of confirmation sent to the president. Later that same day, the Senate adjourned until January. The president, notified of Smith's confirmation, delivered the commission of appointment, and Smith took office. On January 5, 1931, when the Senate was next in session, it voted to reconsider Smith's nomination. A month later it voted not to confirm him. Hoover refused to return the confirmation resolution as

requested by the Senate, describing this effort as a congressional attempt to exercise the power of removal. The Senate then took the matter to court to test Smith's right to continue in office. When the case came before the Supreme Court, it upheld Smith's right to the post on the ground that Senate precedent did not support the reconsideration of a confirmation action, after a nominee has assumed the duties of the office.[6]

Recess Appointments

The Constitution authorizes the president to fill vacant offices during a Senate recess. Recess is held to mean periods longer than a holiday observance or a brief and temporary adjournment. The Constitution states,

> The President shall have Power to fill up all Vacancies that may happen during the Recess of the Senate, by granting Commissions which shall expire at the End of their next Session.

If the vacancy occurs with the Senate in session, the president may fill the office with an ad interim appointment, if such an appointment is provided for by the statute creating the position. A recess appointee, however, may not receive the salary of the office until confirmed by the Senate. This practice has prevented the president from using recess appointments to keep people in office whom the Senate would refuse to confirm.[7]

THE REMOVAL POWER

The Constitution says nothing about the president's power to remove from office the officials he has appointed with the advice and consent of the Senate, but Article II provides for congressional impeachment and removal of some of those officers. The subsequent acknowledgment of the president's removal power derives from the power to appoint and from the discussions concerning the machinery of government in the First Congress in 1789. *(See box, The "Decision of 1789," p. 299.)* Much debate preceded the resolution of this aspect of the executive power.

In the nineteenth century President Andrew Jackson asserted the executive's right to remove officials as an essential element of his power to control the personnel within the executive branch. When he removed his secretary of the Treasury for failure to comply with a directive to remove government deposits from the Bank of the United States, the Senate condemned the action as an assumption of power "not conferred by the Constitution and laws, but in derogation of both." Jackson responded with a protest message to the Senate in which he asserted that the executive's removal power was a direct corollary of his responsibility to oversee the faithful execution of the laws:

> The whole executive power being invested in the President, who is responsible for its exercise, it is a necessary consequence that he should have a right to employ agents of his own choice to aid him in the performance of his duties, and to discharge them when he is no longer willing to be responsible for their acts.[8]

In 1839 the Court acknowledged that, as a practical matter, the president alone exercised the removal power. Although it was clear that the president and the Senate together had the power to remove officers appointed and

William Howard Taft, the only president to serve on the Supreme Court, wrote the opinion in *Myers v. United States* (1926) establishing that the president has the sole power to remove executive branch officers.

confirmed by them, "it was very early adopted as the practical construction of the Constitution that this power was vested in the President alone," wrote the Court.[9] The first major challenge by Congress to this executive power arose from the Tenure of Office Act of March 2, 1867, which was enacted amid the conflict between Congress and President Andrew Johnson over Reconstruction. The measure provided that any civil officer appointed by the president with the advice and consent of the Senate could be removed only with Senate approval. The law was intended to strip Johnson and future presidents of the discretionary removal power. Johnson protested the law and removed his secretary of war, Edwin M. Stanton, without complying with its consent provisions. That action became one of the factors in the unsuccessful attempt to remove him from office. Modified during the administration of Ulysses S. Grant, the law was repealed in 1887 without a judicial challenge to its constitutionality.

THE "DECISION OF 1789"

One of the major tasks facing the First Congress in 1789 was setting up the machinery needed to run the government. The Constitution provided the framework, but the legislative measures adopted by Congress were to determine the structure and organization of each of the branches. Chief Justice William Howard Taft explained in *Myers v. United States* (1926) why the Court gave such weight to the "decision of 1789" concerning the president's removal power:

> We have devoted much space to this discussion and decision of the question of the presidential power of removal in the First Congress, not because a congressional conclusion on a constitutional issue is conclusive, but first because of our agreement with the reasons upon which it was avowedly based, second because this was the decision of the First Congress on a question of primary importance in the organization of the government made within two years after the Constitutional Convention and within a much shorter time after its ratification, and third because that Congress numbered among its leaders those who had been members of the convention. It must necessarily constitute a precedent upon which many future laws supplying the machinery of the new government would be based and, if erroneous, would be likely to evoke dissent and departure in future Congresses. It would come at once before the executive branch of the government for compliance and might well be brought before the judicial branch for a test of its validity. As we shall see, it was soon accepted as a final decision of the question by all branches of the government.[1]

The decision of 1789 related to a bill proposed by James Madison to establish an executive department of foreign affairs. It provided that the principal officer was "to be removed from office by the President of the United States." Debate over the removal clause led to a change in wording so that the bill finally read, "whenever the principal officer shall be removed by the President of the United States." Taft's exhaustive analysis of the decision of 1789 in *Myers* led to the majority's conclusion that this change reflected the understanding of the First Congress that the president had the sole power to remove executive branch officers.

---

1. *Myers v. United States,* 272 U.S. 52 at 136–137 (1926).

Few presidents were as conscious of the prerogatives of the executive as Woodrow Wilson. A 1919 act of Congress created an executive budget bureau under the president's direction with an office of comptroller general and an assistant comptroller, who were to head an independent accounting department. The two officers were to be appointed by the president and confirmed by the Senate to serve during "good behavior." They were to be removed from office only by concurrent resolution of Congress on the grounds of inefficiency, neglect of duty, or malfeasance in office. Wilson favored the idea of a budget bureau but vetoed the measure, because the removal procedure violated the Constitution by denying the president the power to remove officials he had appointed to office. He explained that he regarded "the power of removal from office as an essential incident to the appointing power" and so could not "escape the conclusion that the vesting of this power of removal in the Congress is unconstitutional."[10]

The Recalcitrant Postmaster

An 1876 law made removal of postmasters subject to Senate consent. Nevertheless, President Wilson fired Frank S. Myers from his postmaster position without Senate consent, bringing about the first major Supreme Court decision on the removal power. The ruling in *Myers v. United States* (1926), handed down after Wilson and Myers had died, upheld the dismissal, determining that Congress could not properly limit the executive's removal power in this way and seeming to grant the president an unlimited power to remove all officers he appointed except judges. Chief Justice William Howard Taft traced the origins of the removal power back to the 1789 debates in the First Congress concerning the creation of a department of foreign affairs. Taft concluded that the removal power was understood in the "decision of 1789" to exist as a complement of the president's power to appoint:

It is very clear from this history that the exact question which the House voted upon was whether it should recognize and declare the power of the President under the Constitution to remove the Secretary of Foreign Affairs without the advice and consent of the Senate. That was what the vote was taken for . . . there is not the slightest doubt, after an examination of the record, that the vote was, and was intended to be, a legislative declaration that the power to remove officers appointed by the President and the Senate vested in the President alone.[11]

Those early decisions, Taft noted, "have always been regarded . . . as of the greatest weight in the interpretation of the fundamental instrument."[12] Taft discussed the removal power as it was considered early in the nation's history:

Mr. Madison and his associates in the discussion in the House dwelt at length upon the necessity there was for construing article 2 to give the President the sole power of removal in his responsibility for the conduct of the executive branch, and enforced this by emphasizing his duty expressly declared in the third section of the article to "take care that the laws be faithfully executed." . . .

The vesting of the executive power in the President was essentially a grant of the power to execute the laws. But the President alone and unaided could not execute the laws. He must execute them by the assistance of subordinates. This view has since been repeatedly affirmed by this court. . . . As he is charged specifically to take care that they be faithfully executed, the reasonable implication, even in the absence of express words, was that as part of his executive power he should select those who were to act for him under his direction in the execution of the laws. The further implication must be, in the absence of any express limitation respecting removals, that as his selection of administrative officers is essential to the execution of the laws by him, so must be his power of removing those for whom he cannot continue to be responsible. . . .

. . . A veto by the Senate—a part of the legislative branch of the government—upon removals is a much greater limitation upon the executive branch, and a much more serious blending of the legislative with the executive, than a rejection of a proposed appointment. It is not to be implied. The rejection of a nominee of the President for a particular office does not greatly embarrass him in the conscientious discharge of his high duties in the selection of those who are to aid him, because the President usually has an ample field from which to select for office, according to his preference, competent and capable men. The Senate has full power to reject newly proposed appointees whenever the President shall remove the incumbents. Such a check enables the Senate to prevent the filling of offices with bad or incompetent men, or with those against whom there is tenable objection.

The power to prevent the removal of an officer who has served under the President is different from the authority to consent to or reject his appointment. When a nomination is made, it may be presumed that the Senate is, or may become, as well advised as to the fitness of the nominee as the President, but in the nature of things the defects in ability or intelligence or loyalty in the administration of the laws of one who has served as an officer under the President are facts as to which the President, or his trusted subordinates, must be better informed than the Senate, and the power to remove him may therefore be regarded as confined for very sound and practical reasons, to the governmental authority which has administrative control. . . .

. . . Mr. Madison and his associates pointed out with great force the unreasonable character of the view that the convention intended, without express provision, to give to Congress or the Senate, in case of political or other differences, the means of thwarting the executive in the exercise of his great powers and, in the bearing of his great responsibility by fastening upon him, as subordinate executive officers, men who by their inefficient service under him, by their lack of loyalty to the service, or by their different views of policy might make his taking care that the laws be faithfully executed most difficult or impossible.

Made responsible under the Constitution for the effective enforcement of the law, the President needs as an indispensable aid to meet it the disciplinary influence upon those who act under him of a reserve power of removal. . . . Each head of a department is and must be the President's alter ego in the matters of that department where the President is required by law to exercise authority.

In all such cases, the discretion to be exercised is that of the President in determining the national public interest and in directing the action to be taken by his executive subordinates to protect it. In this field his cabinet officers must do his will. He must place in each member of his official family, and his chief executive subordinates, implicit faith. The moment that he loses confidence in the intelligence, ability, judgment, or loyalty of any one of them, he must have the power to remove him without delay. To require him to file charges and submit them to the consideration of the Senate might make impossible that unity and coordination in executive administration essential to effective action.[13]

The Court saw no reason why Congress should be allowed to limit the president's removal of postmasters:

There is nothing in the Constitution which permits a distinction between the removal of a head of a department or a bureau, when he discharges a political duty of the President or exercises his discretion, and the removal of executive officers engaged in the discharge of their other normal duties. The imperative reason requiring an unrestricted power to remove the most important of his subordinates in their most important duties must therefore control the interpretation of the Constitution as to all appointed by him.[14]

Taft's opinion seemed to extend the president's removal power even to officers appointed to independent regulatory commissions:

[T]here may be duties of a quasi-judicial character imposed on executive officers and members of executive tribunals whose decisions after hearing affect interests of individuals, the discharge of which the President cannot in a particular case properly influence or control. But even in such a case he may consider the decision after its rendition as a reason for removing the officer, on the ground that the discretion regularly entrusted to that officer by statute has not been on the whole intelligently or wisely exercised. Otherwise he does not discharge his own constitutional duty of seeing that the laws be faithfully executed.[15]

Justices James C. McReynolds, Louis D. Brandeis, and Oliver Wendell Holmes Jr. dissented, viewing the 1876 law as a legitimate exercise of congressional authority to impose statutory limits on grants of power. In a separate opinion, McReynolds emphasized that the office in question was that of a postmaster—an inferior and civil position created by Congress.

The Constitution empowers the President to appoint ambassadors, other public ministers, consuls, judges of the Supreme Court and superior officers, and no statute can interfere therein. But Congress may authorize both appointment and removal of all inferior officers without regard to the President's wishes—even in direct opposition to them. This important distinction must not be overlooked. And consideration of the complete control which Congress may exercise over inferior officers is enough to show the hollowness of the suggestion that a right to remove them may be inferred from the President's duty to "take care that the laws be faithfully executed." He cannot appoint any inferior officer, however humble, without legislative authorization; but such officers are essential to execution of the laws. Congress may provide as many or as few of them as it likes. It may place all of them beyond the President's control; but this would not suspend his duty concerning faithful execution of the laws. Removals, however important, are not so necessary as appointments.[16]

Brandeis wrote, "Power to remove . . . a high political officer might conceivably be deemed indispensable to democratic government and, hence, inherent in the President. But power to remove an inferior administrative officer . . . cannot conceivably be deemed an essential of government."[17] Holmes called the majority's arguments "a spider's web inadequate to control the dominant facts." He noted that the postmaster's position was

an office that owes its existence to Congress and that Congress may abolish tomorrow. Its duration and the pay attached to it while it lasts depend on Congress alone. Congress alone confers on the President the power to appoint to it and at any time may transfer the power to other hands. . . . The duty of the President to see that the laws be executed is a duty that does not go beyond the law or require him to achieve more than Congress sees fit to leave within his power.[18]

A few years later the Court would adopt the dissenters' focus to limit the removal power asserted in *Myers*.

The Federal Trade Commissioner

Nine years after the *Myers* ruling, the Court in *Humphrey's Executor v. United States* (1935) narrowed the scope of the president's removal power to include only "all purely executive offices." The Court explicitly rejected the president's claim to inherent power to remove members of regulatory agencies. William E. Humphrey had been appointed to the Federal Trade Commission (FTC) by President Calvin Coolidge and reappointed by President Hoover. When Franklin D. Roosevelt became president, he wanted to replace the conservative Humphrey with a moderate Republican. Roosevelt sought Humphrey's resignation, denied him a personal interview to discuss the matter, and then decided to view a subsequent communication from Humphrey as a letter of resignation, which Roosevelt made effective October 7, 1933.

Humphrey challenged Roosevelt's action, denying any intention to resign and claiming that the president had violated the Constitution and the terms of the act that created the FTC, an independent quasi-judicial body protected from political removal by the terms of its enabling statute. The act had designated seven-year terms for FTC members, with removal from office by the president limited to cause, such as inefficiency, neglect of duty, or malfeasance in office. Roosevelt never claimed any wrongdoing on Humphrey's part. Humphrey sued for his salary, but died during the court proceedings. His executor pursued the litigation, *Humphrey's Executor v. United States*.[19]

On May 27, 1935, "Black Monday" during the Court's battle with President Roosevelt over New Deal legislation, the Court ruled unanimously for Humphrey's executor. Justice George Sutherland stated for the Court that because the FTC was a quasi-judicial and a quasi-legislative body, it was not subject to the unlimited and absolute executive power of removal. The Court not only denied the president power to remove

members of independent regulatory agencies but also implied that other officers who performed functions not wholly executive in character might not be subject to executive removal. Sutherland's opinion distinguished between the duties of a postmaster, such as Myers, and the responsibilities of a member of the FTC:

> The office of a postmaster is so essentially unlike the office now involved that the decision in the *Myers* case cannot be accepted as controlling our decision here. A postmaster is an executive officer restricted to the performance of executive functions. He is charged with no duty at all related to either the legislative or judicial power. The actual decision in the *Myers* case finds support in the theory that such an officer is merely one of the units in the executive department, and, hence, inherently subject to the exclusive and illimitable power of removal by the Chief Executive, whose subordinate and aide he is.[20]

The Court discarded Taft's *dicta* in *Myers,* stating that

> the necessary reach of the decision goes far enough to include all purely executive officers. It goes no farther. . . . Much less does it include an officer who occupies no place in the executive department and who exercises no part of the executive power vested by the Constitution in the President.[21]

Sutherland then explained that the absolute executive removal power extended only to those officers whose functions are purely executive and that "illimitable power of removal is not possessed by the President" over FTC commissioners:

> The authority of Congress, in creating quasi-legislative or quasi-judicial agencies, to require them to act independently of executive control cannot well be doubted; and that authority includes . . . power to fix the period during which they shall continue in office, and to forbid their removal except for cause in the meantime. For it is quite evident that one who holds his office only during the pleasure of another cannot be depended upon to maintain an attitude of independence against the latter's will.[22]

The Court claimed for Congress the power to set the terms of office and conditions of removal for those offices whose functions were an amalgam of executive, legislative, and judicial functions. The decision limited the executive removal power, saying that the extent of that power depended upon the "nature of the office" involved:

> The fundamental necessity of maintaining each of the three general departments of government entirely free from the control or coercive influence, direct or indirect, of either of the others, has often been stressed and is hardly open to serious question. ... The sound application of a principle that makes one master in his own house precludes him from imposing his control in the house of another. ...

> The power of removal here claimed for the President falls within this principle, since its coercive influence threatens the independence of a commission, which is not only wholly disconnected from the executive department, but which, as already fully appears, was created by Congress as a means of carrying into operation legislative and judicial powers, and as an agency of the legislative and judicial departments. ... Whether the power of the president to remove an officer shall prevail over the authority of Congress to condition the power by fixing a definite term and precluding a removal except for cause, will depend upon the character of the office; the *Myers* decision, affirming the power of the President alone to make the removal, is confined to purely executive officers; and as to officers of the kind here under consideration, we hold that no removal can be made during the prescribed term for which the officer is appointed, except for one or more of the causes named in the applicable statute.[23]

Concerning *Humphrey's Executor,* Justice Felix Frankfurter would write more than twenty years later, the Court

> drew a sharp line of cleavage between officials who were part of the Executive establishment and were thus removable by virtue of the President's constitutional powers, and those who are members of a body "to exercise its judgment without the leave or hindrance of any other official or any department of the government," ... as to whom a power of removal exists only if Congress may fairly be said to have conferred it. This sharp differentiation derives from the difference in functions between those

who are part of the Executive establishment and those whose tasks require absolute freedom from executive interference.[24]

The *Humphrey's Executor* decision did not, however, prevent President Roosevelt from removing someone from an office for which Congress had not set terms of removal. In 1941 E. A. Morgan, chairman of the Tennessee Valley Authority (TVA), relied on the *Humphrey* ruling to challenge his removal by the president. A federal appeals court ruled that the TVA act did not limit the president's exercise of the removal power. Because Roosevelt's action promoted the smooth functioning of the TVA, the court viewed the removal as within the president's duty to see that the laws were faithfully executed. The Supreme Court declined to review that decision.[25]

The War Claims Commissioner

In *Humphrey's Executor* the Court seemed to rule that Congress must specify the terms and conditions of removal before courts would limit the executive power of removal. A case decided twenty-three years later extended this doctrine to limit the president's power to remove quasi-judicial officers even where no specific statutory language set out the terms of their removal. The Court reinforced the "nature of the office" approach to this question. The seeds of the case were planted when President Harry S. Truman appointed three Democrats to the War Claims Commission, which was established to settle certain types of claims resulting from World War II. The commission was to disband after it had settled all claims, and the law made no provision for removal of commissioners. When President Dwight D. Eisenhower took office in 1953, he wanted to name three Republicans to the commission and so requested the resignations of the three Democratic members. They refused, and Eisenhower removed them.

One of the commissioners, Myron Wiener, sued for his salary in the U.S. Court of Claims, arguing that his removal was illegal. The court agreed that his duties had been quasi-judicial, but denied his claim, relying on the fact that the statute creating the commission had not limited the executive's power to remove its members.[26] *Humphrey's Executor* did not apply, the court decided, because there was no explicit statutory explication of the removal procedure for a claims commissioner.[27] The Supreme Court, with Justice Frankfurter writing the opinion, ruled unanimously for Wiener. The Court noted the similarity of facts in this case with the facts in *Humphrey's Executor:*

> We start with one certainty. The problem of the President's power to remove members of agencies entrusted with duties of the kind with which the War Claims Commission was charged was within the lively knowledge of Congress. Few contests between Congress and the President have so recurringly had the attention of Congress as that pertaining to the power of removal. . . .
>
> . . . The ground of President Eisenhower's removal of petitioner was precisely the same as President Roosevelt's removal of Humphrey. Both Presidents desired to have Commissioners, one on the Federal Trade Commission, the other on the War Claims Commission, "of my own selection." They wanted these Commissioners to be their men. The terms of removal in the two cases are identic and express the assumption that the agencies of which the two Commissioners were members were subject in the discharge of their duties to the control of the Executive. An analysis of the Federal Trade Commission Act left this Court in no doubt that such was not the conception of Congress in creating the Federal Trade Commission. The terms of the War Claims Act of 1948 leave no doubt that such was not the conception of Congress regarding the War Claims Commission.[28]

Frankfurter, after analyzing the law, concluded that Congress did not intend that the commissioners be subject to the threat of presidential removal:

> If, as one must take for granted, the War Claims Act precluded the President from influencing the Commission in passing on a particular claim, *a fortiori* must it be inferred that Congress did not wish to have hang over the Commission the Damocles' sword of removal by the President for no reason other than that he preferred to have on that Commission men of his own choosing.
>
> For such is this case. . . . Judging the matter in all the nakedness in which it is presented, namely, the claim that the President could remove a member of

an adjudicatory body like the War Claims Commission merely because he wanted his own appointees on such a Commission, we are compelled to conclude that no such power is given to the President directly by the Constitution, and none is impliedly conferred upon him by statute simply because Congress said nothing about it. The philosophy of *Humphrey's Executor,* in its explicit language as well as its implication, precludes such a claim.[29]

The Comptroller and the Prosecutor

When the Supreme Court in 1986 held unconstitutional major provisions of the Balanced Budget and Emergency Deficit Control Act of 1985, much of its reasoning turned on the question of who could remove the nation's comptroller general. Two years later another question of separation of powers turned on the power to appoint an independent counsel to investigate charges of wrongdoing by top executive branch officials.

The deficit control act, popularly known as Gramm-Rudman-Hollings for its Senate sponsors, gave the comptroller general authority to dictate to the president where the executive branch must reduce its spending. That provision was its flaw, the Court held. The comptroller general, who heads the General Accountability Office (previously the General Accounting Office), the investigatory and auditing arm of Congress, is appointed by the president but is subject to removal only by Congress, not the president. The lower court that first heard the case of *Bowsher v. Synar* (1986) found that Congress, by retaining the power to remove the comptroller, placed the office firmly in the legislative branch, not the executive. The Supreme Court agreed, 7-2. Citing *Myers, Humphrey's Executor,* and the decision of 1789, Chief Justice Warren E. Burger wrote,

> Congress cannot reserve for itself the power of removal of an officer charged with the execution of the laws except by impeachment. To permit the execution of the laws to be vested in an officer answerable only to Congress would, in practical terms, reserve in Congress control over the execution of the laws. . . . The structure of the Constitution does not permit Congress to execute the laws; it follows that Congress cannot grant to an officer under its control what it does not possess.[30]

Burger continued, linking this reasoning with the decision in *Immigration and Naturalization Service v. Chadha* (1983):[31]

> To permit an officer controlled by Congress to execute the laws would be, in essence, to permit a congressional veto. Congress could simply remove, or threaten to remove, an officer for executing the laws in any fashion found to be unsatisfactory to Congress. This kind of congressional control over the execution of the laws, *Chadha* makes clear, is constitutionally impermissible.[32]

The executive branch won the day on the Gramm-Rudman-Hollings issue, but it lost a major separation of powers case two years later when the Court upheld the unusual arrangement that Congress had devised for the appointment of an independent prosecutor when charges of high-level wrongdoing warranted it. The independent counsel provision of the Ethics in Government Act of 1978 established a complex process for appointing such a counsel: judges, rather than a member of the executive branch, would appoint this official. The counsel was, however, subject to removal by the attorney general for good cause. Three high-ranking officers in the Justice Department who were under investigation by an independent counsel challenged this arrangement as a violation of the separation of powers. They argued that the way the counsel was appointed unduly interfered with the functions of the chief executive. They lost the first round, won the second, but lost again, 7-1, in the Supreme Court.[33]

Writing for the Court in *Morrison v. Olson* (1988), Chief Justice William H. Rehnquist explained that the majority found the independent counsel an "inferior" officer within the language of the Constitution that permits Congress to decide who can appoint someone to that post. "We do not mean to say that Congress' power to provide for interbranch appointments of 'inferior officers' is unlimited," he wrote, but in this situation

> Congress, of course, was concerned when it created the office of independent counsel with the conflicts of interest that could arise in situations when the Executive Branch is called upon to investigate its own high-ranking officers. If it were to remove the

appointing authority from the Executive Branch, the most logical place to put it was in the Judicial Branch.[34]

Citing *Bowsher, Myers, Humphrey's Executor,* and *Wiener,* Rehnquist addressed the issue of whether the Independent Counsel Act impermissibly interfered with the president's exercise of his constitutional functions. The Court decided it did not. By requiring that there be good cause before an attorney general could remove a special prosecutor, the law guaranteed the counsel a necessary measure of independence, the Court held. At the same time, this requirement did not interfere with the president's ability to ensure the faithful execution of the laws.

EXECUTIVE DISCRETION

Is the president's power to see that the laws are faithfully executed limited simply to carrying out the letter of the laws enacted by Congress or does the president have power to act, beyond or in conflict with those laws, if the public interest demands it? In general, the modern Court's decisions have tended to adopt the more expansive view, which is enhanced by the increasing practice of Congress to delegate power to the executive branch.

To Protect a Justice

One of the Court's first rulings on this overall question of executive power occurred in 1890 in one of the more bizarre cases ever to come before it. Despite the absence of any authorizing statute, the Court upheld the power of the president to provide federal protection for a Supreme Court justice whose life was threatened in the course of his judicial duties. Sarah Althea Terry and her husband, David, angry over a decision against their claim to an estate, threatened to kill Justice Stephen J. Field, who had led the panel of judges ruling against them. In response to these threats, the attorney general ordered federal marshals to protect Field. While he was in California on judicial business, Field was attacked by David Terry. Deputy Marshal David Neagle, who was protecting Field, shot Terry and killed him. California tried to hold Neagle and charge him with murder under state law.

The Supreme Court ruled that California could not try Neagle, because the killing had occurred in the course of his duties under federal law, even though there was no federal law authorizing the executive to protect the justice. The Court ordered Neagle released from state custody. Writing for the Court, Justice Samuel F. Miller asked,

> Is this duty [to take care that the laws be faithfully executed] limited to the enforcement of Acts of Congress or of treaties of the United States according to their express terms, or does it include the rights, duties and obligations growing out of the Constitution itself, our international relations, and all the protection implied by the nature of the government under the Constitution?[35]

The Court's answer implicitly adopted the latter view:

> In the view we take of the Constitution of the United States, any obligation fairly and properly inferable from that instrument, or any duty of the marshal to be derived from the general scope of his duties under the laws of the United States, is "a law." . . . It would be a great reproach to the system of government of the United States, declared to be within its sphere sovereign and supreme, if there is found within the domain of its powers no means of protecting the judges, in the conscientious and faithful discharge of their duties, from the malice and hatred of those upon whom their judgments may operate unfavorably.[36]

To Protect the Public Interest

The Court's broad view of presidential power was reaffirmed in 1915, with the decision in *United States v. Midwest Oil Co.* By law, all public lands containing minerals were declared open to occupation, exploration, and purchase by citizens. In 1909, however, President William Howard Taft withdrew from further public use some 3 million acres in public lands containing oil deposits in order to preserve oil supplies for the navy. This withdrawal was challenged by citizens who had subsequently explored and discovered oil on these lands; they cited the law declaring all such lands open to citizen exploration. The Court upheld the president's prerogative to withdraw the lands from private acquisition. Justice Joseph R. Lamar cited historical precedent:

> [The president] . . . has, during the past eighty years, without express statutory—but under the claim of power to do so—made a multitude of Executive orders which operated to withdraw public land that would otherwise have been open to private acquisition. They affected every kind of land—mineral and nonmineral. . . .

> The President was in a position to know when the public interest required particular portions of the people's lands to be withdrawn from entry or relocation; his action inflicted no wrong upon any private citizen, and being subject to disaffirmance by Congress, could occasion no harm to the interest of the public at large. Congress did not repudiate the power claimed or the withdrawal orders made. On the contrary, it uniformly and repeatedly acquiesced in the practice. . . .

> . . . Government is a practical affair, intended for practical men. Both officers, lawmakers and citizens naturally adjust themselves to any long-continued action of the Executive Department, on the presumptions that unauthorized acts would not have been allowed to be so often repealed as to crystallize into a regular practice.[37]

DELEGATION OF POWER

Congress vastly expanded the president's discretionary power in the twentieth century by delegating greater authority to the office.[38] The process had begun at the end of the nineteenth century. In 1890 Congress provided for the duty-free admission of certain imported items, but gave the president the authority to impose duties on these items if the country of origin began to impose unreasonable duties on U.S.-made goods. In *Field v. Clark* (1892) the Court upheld this congressional delegation of power: Congress furnished a remedy and authorized the president to decide when it should be applied. The Court held that this delegation did not violate the separation of powers or result in executive lawmaking.[39]

In 1891 Congress authorized the president to set aside public lands in any state or territory as forest reservations. A subsequent statute authorized the secretary of agriculture to administer these lands and to make rules governing their use and occupancy.

Violations of the rules were punishable by fines or imprisonment or both. This delegated power was challenged as unconstitutional. The Court upheld the president's authority, stating that

> the authority to make administrative rules is not a delegation of legislative power, nor are such rules raised from an administrative level to a legislative character because the violation thereof is punishable as a public offense.[40]

Not until 1935 did the Court invalidate a statute on the grounds that it constituted an improper delegation of power from Congress to the president. The ruling was followed with several in that term and the next that found New Deal legislation unconstitutional for this reason. *(See "The Court Versus FDR," pp. 341– 348.)* After the Court's turnabout on the New Deal in 1937, the justices also returned to their generally approving view of congressional delegation, a view that has prevailed since then.

If *Neagle* and *Midwest Oil* and the Court's general inclination to back congressional delegation of power to the executive, however, seemed to imply that there were no limits on the scope of the inherent powers a president could claim, that impression was dramatically corrected in 1952. A divided Court flatly rejected President Harry S. Truman's claim of inherent power to seize the nation's steel mills in order to avoid disruption of steel production and possibly of supplies to military forces in Korea. The executive order directing the seizure of the mills explained that a work stoppage would jeopardize national defense. *(See "The Steel Seizure Case," pp. 274–275.)* Congress had decided against giving the president such power in the Taft-Hartley Act, passed in 1947, and Truman chose to ignore other provisions of that law that might have been useful in the circumstances, relying instead on a broad view of inherent presidential power. For the majority, Justice Hugo L. Black wrote that the president was improperly "making" the law he wished to execute:

> In the framework of our Constitution, the President's power to see that the laws are faithfully executed refutes the idea that he is to be a lawmaker. The Constitution limits his function in the lawmaking process to the recommending of laws he thinks wise and the vetoing of laws he thinks bad.[41]

In a concurring opinion, Justice Robert H. Jackson commented,

> Loose and irresponsible use of adjectives colors all non-legal and much legal discussion of presidential powers. "Inherent" powers, "implied" powers, "incidental" powers, "plenary" powers, "war" powers and "emergency" powers are used, often interchangeably and without fixed or ascertainable meanings.
>
> The vagueness and generality of the clauses that set forth presidential powers afford a plausible basis for pressures within and without an administration for action beyond that supported by those whose responsibility it is to defend his actions in court.[42]

EXECUTIVES AND EMERGENCIES

The preservation of peace and order in the community is a requirement for the successful execution of the laws. Disregard or disobedience of the laws may require the president to act to preserve the peace and restore order in the community.[43] Since 1792 presidents have possessed statutory authority to use troops to quell disorder when, in their judgment, the disorder hinders the execution of the laws. Since *Martin v. Mott* (1827) the Supreme Court has steadily backed the president's authority to decide when and if an emergency exists that requires the use of federal troops. Justice Joseph Story's opinion in that case limited the exercise of the power to times of actual invasion or imminent danger thereof, but affirmed the president's authority "to decide whether the exigency has arisen." Moreover, Story wrote, the decision "belongs exclusively to the president, and . . . his decision is conclusive upon all other persons."[44]

Chief Justice Roger B. Taney reaffirmed the president's authority in such matters in *Luther v. Borden* (1849). Explaining that the president's decision to use troops to keep order was beyond the authority of judges to question, he wrote,

DEPUTIES TRYING TO MOVE AN ENGINE AND CAR ON THE CHICAGO, ROCK ISLAND, AND PACIFIC RAILROAD AT BLUE ISLAND, JULY 2, 1894.

THE GREAT RAILWAY STRIKES—SCENES IN AND ABOUT CHICAGO.—FROM SKETCHES BY G. A. COFFIN.—[SEE PAGE 655.]

656

President Grover Cleveland issued an injunction against a strike by Pullman railroad car workers in 1894 and sent federal troops into Chicago to protect U.S. property and keep the mail moving. During the strike, one of the most divisive labor disputes in U.S. history, the troops clashed with strikers, and Eugene V. Debs, president of the American Railway Union, which was involved in a secondary strike, was arrested for contempt. The Supreme Court upheld the injunction and Debs's six-month prison sentence, affirming broad executive power to deal with emergencies.

Judicial power presupposes an established government capable of enacting laws and enforcing their execution. . . . The acceptance of the judicial office is a recognition of the authority of the government from which it is derived.[45]

In emergencies, the president may employ several means short of calling out federal troops. President Thomas Jefferson used the *posse comitatus,* a body of persons summoned to assist in the preservation of public peace, to enforce the embargo imposed during the conflict with Britain. President Franklin Pierce's attorney general ruled that federal marshals could command citizens' aid to enforce the Fugitive Slave Act of 1850. During the "bleeding Kansas" episode in the pre–Civil War strife over slavery in the territories, Pierce placed military forces in a posse to prevent further bloodshed. The most extraordinary posse was the group of seventy-five thousand volunteers summoned by Lincoln to suppress the "civil disorder" in 1861. President Dwight D. Eisenhower invoked the same provision when he dispatched troops to Little Rock, Arkansas, to enforce court-ordered school desegregation. Eisenhower's actions set a modern precedent for executive support of judicial decisions, in contrast to President Andrew Jackson's stance in the Cherokee cases, 125 years earlier, of leaving the Court to fend for itself when a state ignored a Court decision.[46]

Presidents also have used troops to quell labor strikes and attendant civil disorders that threatened the public safety or disrupted services and functions under federal jurisdiction. One of the most hotly contested assertions of presidential power arose after a strike against the Pullman railroad car company in 1894 paralyzed rail traffic west of Chicago. Pullman workers went on strike because of a wage reduction order. Members of the American Railway Union, with the support of its president, Eugene V. Debs, carried out a secondary boycott against the Pullman company by refusing to service Pullman sleeping cars attached to trains. When violence threatened, President Grover

Cleveland dispatched federal troops to Chicago to preserve the peace. He ordered the U.S. attorney in the city to seek an order halting the Debs boycott on the basis that the strike crippled interstate commerce and interfered with the delivery of the mail. Debs and his associates ignored the court order and were arrested, convicted of contempt, and sentenced to prison. Debs then petitioned the Supreme Court for a writ of habeas corpus, challenging his detention as illegal.

Affirming broad executive power to deal with such emergencies the Court refused to issue the writ, thereby upholding Debs's conviction. For the Court, Justice David J. Brewer wrote,

> The entire strength of the nation may be used to enforce in any part of the land the full and free exercise of all national powers and the security of all rights entrusted by the Constitution to its care. The strong arm of the national government may be put forth to brush away all obstructions to the freedom of interstate commerce or the transportation of the mails. If the emergency arises, the army of the nation, and all its militia, are at the service of the nation to compel obedience to its laws. . . .

> . . . [W]henever the wrongs complained of are such as affect the public at large, and are in respect of matters which by the Constitution are entrusted to the care of the nation, and concerning which the nation owes the duty to all the citizens of securing to them their common rights, then the mere fact that the government has no pecuniary interest in the controversy is not sufficient to exclude it from the courts.[47]

Even after Congress restricted the use of injunctions against unions, the restrictions were not held to forbid government-sought orders to seize and operate mines in the face of a strike, nor did it forbid mine operators from obtaining court orders preventing government seizures.[48]

The Power to Veto and to Pardon

The Constitution equips the president with two means of nullifying actions of the other branches of the government: the veto and the pardon. The veto power allows the president to kill a measure that Congress has approved. From an infrequently used tool wielded only against laws the chief executive thinks unconstitutional or defective, this quasi-legislative device has developed into a policy weapon used often in political struggles between the White House and Congress over the proper shape of legislation.

The pardon power permits the president to reduce sentences, remit penalties, or exempt individuals and classes of persons from sentences imposed by the courts. The only express limitation on this power is that persons impeached may not be pardoned. This power has been sparingly exercised, and generally, with perhaps the exception of pardons issued at the end of presidential terms, occasions of its use draw little public notice.

THE VETO POWER

President Franklin D. Roosevelt, who vetoed more bills than any other president, is said to have told his aides on more than one occasion, "Give me a bill that I can veto." Roosevelt wanted to remind Congress of the executive power to reject every bill that it passed.[1] Article I of the Constitution provides that the president may veto a bill by returning it to the house of its origin unsigned and accompanied by a statement of objections to the measure. The veto kills the bill unless it is overridden by a two-thirds majority vote of the members of each house. Perhaps because Congress and the White House generally accept the politically determined outcome of veto battles, the Supreme Court has never been called upon to judge the validity of a direct veto.

Article I also provides the following:

If any Bill shall not be returned by the President within ten Days (Sundays excepted) after it shall have been presented to him, the Same shall be a Law, in like Manner as if he had signed it, unless the Congress by their Adjournment prevent its Return, in which Case it shall not be a Law.

In short, this section permits a bill to become a law without the president's signature, presumably a measure the president disapproves of but finds it impolitic to veto. With Congress adjourned, however, the president's failure to sign a bill constitutes a "pocket" veto, because Congress has no opportunity to override it. The Supreme Court's only significant decisions on the veto power have attempted to clarify the conditions under which a pocket veto can be used.

Alexander Hamilton considered the "qualified negative" of the veto a shield against encroachment on executive power by the legislative branch and a barrier to hasty enactment of "improper laws."[2] Hamilton viewed the veto power as a means of improving the spirit of cooperation between the president and Congress, producing further reflection on measures. He argued that the qualified veto was less harsh than an absolute veto. Hamilton declared that the framers,

have pursued a mean in this business [the veto power], which will both facilitate the exercise of the power vested in this respect in the executive magistrate, and make its efficacy to depend on the sense of a considerable part of the legislative body. . . . A direct and categorical negative has something in the appearance of it more harsh, and more apt to irritate, than the mere suggestion of argumentative objections to be approved or disapproved by those to whom they are addressed.[3]

THE POWER TO SIGN BILLS

For 150 years presidents went to Capitol Hill on the last day of the legislative session to sign all bills approved that session. The custom was based in part on the belief that all legislative power, including the president's power to sign legislation, expired with the end of a session. It meant, however, that certain bills received only hasty consideration by the president.[1]

Near the conclusion of the June 1920 congressional session President Woodrow Wilson asked the attorney general to determine if bills might be constitutionally approved within the ten days following adjournment. The attorney general reported affirmatively, and Wilson accordingly signed bills into law during this period after an interim adjournment.[2]

At the end of the final 1931 congressional session, President Herbert Hoover, on the advice of his attorney general, began the practice of signing measures after final adjournment.[3] On March 5, 1931, the day after Congress adjourned, Hoover signed a private bill. The question of its validity resulted in a Supreme Court decision upholding the president's action. The Court cited

> the fundamental purpose of the constitutional provision to provide appropriate opportunity for the President to consider the bills presented to him. The importance of maintaining that opportunity unimpaired increases as bills multiply.[4]

The Court noted that in the week prior to adjournment 269 bills were sent to the president, of which 184 reached his desk on the last day of the session.[5] The Court found no reason why the time for the president's consideration of bills should be cut short because Congress had adjourned.

> No public interest would be conserved by the requirement of hurried and inconsiderate examination of bills in the closing hours of a session, with the result that bills may be approved which on further consideration would be disapproved.[6]

The Court has not decided, however, whether bills passed less than ten days before the end of a president's term may be approved or vetoed by an incoming president. *Dicta* in the 1932 case suggested that the incoming president could not approve such a bill because it was not submitted to him, but to the previous president. President Harry S. Truman, however, signed bills sent to the White House before President Franklin D. Roosevelt's death. His authority to do so was not challenged.

---

1. Carl B. Swisher, *American Constitutional Development,* 2nd ed. (Cambridge, Mass.: Houghton Mifflin, 1954), 785.

2. Ibid., 786.

3. Ibid.

4. *Edwards v. United States,* 286 U.S. 482 at 493 (1932).

5. Id.

6. Id.

Employing the Veto

Use of the veto power has varied greatly from president to president. The first six presidents vetoed only ten measures in their entire administrations, usually on constitutional grounds or because of technical flaws in the legislation. Andrew Jackson, however, began to use the veto as a political device to defeat measures he opposed as a matter of political principle; he vetoed twelve measures in eight years. During the entire period up to the Civil War, only fifty-two bills were vetoed, and no presidential veto was overridden until 1866.

President Andrew Johnson used the veto in his battle with Radical Republicans in Congress over control of Reconstruction. His vetoes were overridden fifteen times. Eight presidents never cast a veto, the most recent being President James A. Garfield. During the late nineteenth century, numerous presidential vetoes were cast to block private bills and "pork barrel" legislation. Presidents Grover Cleveland and Franklin D. Roosevelt cast the most vetoes. Roosevelt cast 631 negatives, and Cleveland 584. Many of Cleveland's vetoes pertained to private bills that awarded individuals pensions or other government benefits. The New Deal and World War II broadened the scope of legislative activity and brought greater complexity to legislation, which resulted in a greater number of vetoes cast on substantive measures. Until Roosevelt vetoed a revenue bill, it had been assumed that tax measures were exempt from the presidential veto. Between 1789 and 2008 presidents vetoed 2,558 measures, with all but 58 of these cast after 1860. The direct veto was used 1,492 times and the pocket veto 1,066 times. Congress overrode only 109 vetoes.[4]

Pocket Veto Case

The Supreme Court's major ruling on the veto power resulted from an attempt to clarify the Constitution's intent with respect to the president's use of the pocket veto. In *Okanogan Indians et al. v. United States* (1929), also known as the *Pocket Veto Case,* the Court ruled that a bill must be returned to a sitting chamber of Congress and cannot be returned to an officer of the chamber during a recess. Therefore, the pocket veto could be used any time the chamber of a bill's origin was not in session on the tenth day following submission of the bill to the chief executive. Subsequent rulings, however, have undercut both points. The executive branch and Congress still remain at odds over what constitutes a congressional adjournment and permits the use of this veto.

The first time the Court considered the pocket veto, it upheld it, finding that it was appropriate for President Calvin Coolidge to use the pocket veto to kill a bill passed just before a four-month congressional recess. The bill, which gave certain Indian tribes the right to file claims in the U.S. Court of Claims, was sent to Coolidge for his signature on June 24, 1926. When the first session of the Sixty-ninth Congress adjourned nine days later, on July 3, Coolidge had neither signed nor returned the bill to Congress. He subsequently took no action on the measure and assumed he had pocket vetoed it. Congress did not reconvene until December, when the second session began.

Certain Indian tribes in Washington State sought to file claims under the measure, arguing that it had become law without the president's signature because Coolidge had not vetoed it. They contended that a pocket veto could be used only between Congresses, when there was no Congress. The word *adjournment* they read to mean only the final adjournment of a Congress, not simply an adjournment between sessions. Furthermore, they argued, the ten days allowed the president to consider and sign or return legislation

meant ten legislative, not calendar, days. Under this interpretation, the ten-day period for this particular bill would have run from June 24 until December 1926.

The Supreme Court rejected their arguments, holding that a pocket veto could properly be used between sessions of Congress and that adjournment included interim adjournments. Justice Edward T. Sanford wrote the Court's opinion, in which he described the president's exercise of the pocket veto power.

> The Constitution in giving the President a qualified negative over legislation—commonly called a veto—entrusts him with an authority and imposes upon him an obligation that are of the highest importance, in the execution of which it is made his duty not only to sign bills that he approves in order that they may become law, but to return bills that he disapproves, with his objections, in order that they may be reconsidered by Congress. The faithful and effective exercise of this momentous duty necessarily requires time in which the President may carefully examine and consider a bill and determine, after due deliberation, whether he should approve or disapprove it, and if he disapproves it, formulate his objections for the consideration of Congress. To that end a specified time is given, after the bill has been presented to him, in which he may examine its provisions and either approve it or return it, not approved, for reconsideration. . . . The power thus conferred upon the President cannot be narrowed or cut down by Congress, nor the time within which it is to be exercised lessened, directly or indirectly. And it is just as essential a part of the constitutional provisions, guarding against ill-considered and unwise legislation, that the President, on his part, should have the full time allowed him for determining whether he should approve or disapprove a bill, and if disapproved, for adequately formulating the objections that should be considered by Congress, as it is that Congress, on its part, should have an opportunity to repass the bill over his objections.[5]

Justice Sanford noted that the failure of the bill in question to become law could not "properly be ascribed to the disapproval of the President—who presumably would have returned it before the adjournment if there had been sufficient time in which to complete his consideration and take such action but is attributable solely to the action of Congress in adjourning before the time allowed the President for returning the bill that expired."[6] Moreover, Sanford wrote,

> The word "days," when not qualified, means in ordinary and common usage calendar days. This is obviously the meaning in which it is used in the constitutional provision, and is emphasized by the fact that "Sundays" are excepted.[7]

On the question of "adjournment," Sanford wrote,

> We think under the constitutional provision the determinative question in reference to an "adjournment" is not whether it is a final adjournment of Congress or an interim adjournment, such as the adjournment of the first session, but whether it is one that "prevents" the President from returning the bill to the House in which it originated within the time allowed. It is clear, we understand, it is not questioned, that since the President may return a bill at any time within the allotted period, he is prevented from returning it, within the meaning of the constitutional provision if by reason of the adjournment it is impossible for him to return it to the House in which it originated on the last day of that period. . . .
>
> We find no substantial basis for the suggestion that although the House in which the bill originated is not in session the bill may nevertheless be returned, consistently with the constitutional mandate, by delivering it, with the President's objections, to an officer or agent of the House, for subsequent delivery to the House when it resumes its sittings at the next session, with the same force and effect as if the bill had been returned to the House on the day it was delivered to such officer or agent. Aside from the fact that Congress has never enacted any statute authorizing any officer or agent of either House to receive for it bills returned by the President during its adjournment, and that there is no rule to that effect in either House, the delivery of the bill to such office or agent, even if authorized by Congress itself, would not comply with the constitutional mandate. . . . In short it was plainly the object of the constitutional provision that there should be a timely return of the bill, which should not only be a matter of official record . . . but should enable

Congress to proceed immediately with its reconsideration; and that the return of the bill should be an actual and public return to the House itself, and not a fictitious return by a delivery of the bill to some individual which could be given a retroactive effect at a later date when the time for the return of the bill to the House had expired.[8]

Wright and More Pocket Vetoes

Within a decade, the broad sweep of the Court's ruling in the *Pocket Veto Case* was limited by another Court decision. In *Wright v. United States* (1938) the Court held that during a short recess of one chamber—the one to which a vetoed bill must be returned—an official of that chamber could receive a veto message to deliver to the chamber after the recess. Therefore, a pocket veto could not be used in those circumstances.[9] The Court said that the statement in the *Pocket Veto Case* that a bill must be returned to a sitting chamber "should not be construed so narrowly as to demand that the President must select a precise moment when the House is within the walls of its chambers and that a return is absolutely impossible during a recess however temporary."[10] It has now become a routine practice for the House and Senate to appoint their clerk or secretary to receive messages from the president during a recess.

After a period of peace in the pocket veto arena, President Richard Nixon revived the controversy by using the pocket veto during the six-day Christmas recess in 1970. In a challenge brought by Sen. Edward M. Kennedy, D-Mass., a federal court of appeals held the veto invalid because the recess was not long enough to prevent Nixon from returning the bill to Congress with a direct veto message. Two years later, in 1972, another Nixon pocket veto was held invalid by a federal appeals court, which pointed out that Congress had appointed officials to receive veto messages during the time that the two chambers were not in session. Kennedy went to court again after President Gerald R. Ford pocket vetoed a bill passed before a break between sessions. Once again an appeals court held that pocket vetoes could not be used except after adjournment sine die—that is, unless Congress recesses without leaving agents appointed to receive presidential messages.[11]

President Ronald Reagan sparked a new round in this debate by declaring that the pocket veto was usable any time Congress recessed for longer than three days. During a brief recess, he pocket vetoed a bill barring aid to El Salvador. Thirty-three House members challenged the veto and won an appeals court ruling reaffirming the limit on pocket vetoes to periods following the final adjournment of a Congress. The administration appealed the case of *Burke v. Barnes* (1987) to the Supreme Court, which raised hopes that it would finally issue a definitive ruling on the matter. Such hopes were dashed when the Court found the dispute moot, leaving the lower court decision in place.[12]

The Line Item Veto

Throughout U.S. history, the president has had an all-or-nothing option when presented with a bill passed by Congress: either sign it into law or veto it. Many presidents, however, have wanted to veto part of a bill rather than the bill in its entirety. President Reagan wanted a "line item veto" so he could strike what he considered wasteful spending items from bills. Many state governors had this power, Reagan noted. His successor, President George H. W. Bush, also favored the idea. Republican legislators took up the case and in 1996 won passage of the Line Item Veto Act, which President Bill Clinton, a Democrat, signed into law. The act authorized the president to "cancel" certain spending items and tax benefits contained in bills presented for signing.

With the constitutionality of this scheme in doubt, its sponsors authorized a speedy appeal to the Supreme Court. The litigation got off to a false start, however. Six lawmakers who had opposed the Line Item Veto Act, including Sen. Robert Byrd, D-W. Va., filed a lawsuit to challenge it.[13] In *Raines v. Byrd* (1997) the Court rejected their claim, saying that members of Congress had no standing to sue. Rather, the justices asserted, plaintiffs must have suffered a personal injury to have standing, and dissenting members of a legislature could not be said to have suffered a "sufficiently concrete injury" to qualify as plaintiffs in a lawsuit challenging the act they opposed.[14]

Legitimate plaintiffs arose soon enough when Clinton used the line item veto to cancel spending and tax breaks for two special interests. The first would have saved New York City and New York State as much as $2.6 billion for having violated federal rules concerning their financing of the Medicaid program. Rather than repaying the Treasury, New York got approval of an item in the Balanced Budget Act of 1997 to spare it. Clinton eliminated this provision because, he said, "preferential treatment" for one state could not be justified. He also canceled a special tax exemption for farm cooperatives that was included in the Tax Relief Act of 1997. New York City and the Snake River Potato Growers of Idaho sued to challenge the constitutionality of the veto.

The Supreme Court took up the case of *Clinton v. City of New York* (1998) and struck down the Line Item Veto Act.[15] The Court reaffirmed that regardless of the wisdom of the line item as a means of controlling wasteful spending, the Constitution provides the president only two options when presented with a bill passed by Congress: to sign it or to veto it. The justices relied on a strict, or literal, reading of Article I, section 7, also know as the Presentment Clause: "Every Bill which shall have passed the House of Representatives and the Senate shall, before it become a Law, be presented to the President of the United States; If he approve he shall sign it, but if not he shall return it." The first president, George Washington, believed this meant he must either "approve all the parts of a Bill or reject it in toto," a line quoted by Justice John Paul Stevens in his opinion for the 6-3 majority.

"In both legal and practical effects, the President has amended two Acts of Congress by repealing a portion of each," Stevens wrote. He continued,

> There is no provision in the Constitution that authorizes the President to enact, to amend or to repeal statutes. . . . This [Line Item Veto] Act gives the President the unilateral power to change the text of duly enacted statutes. . . . If there is to be a new procedure in which the President will play a different role in determining the final text of what may "become a law," such change must come not by legislation but through the amendment procedures set forth in Article V of the Constitution.[16]

Chief Justice William Rehnquist and Justices Anthony Kennedy, David Souter, Clarence Thomas, and Ruth Bader Ginsburg agreed. In a concurring opinion, Kennedy wrote that the president's power to selectively cancel spending provisions could have been used to

> reward one group and punish another, to help one set of taxpayers and hurt another, to favor one State and ignore another. [It] enhances the President's powers beyond what the Framers would have endorsed.[17]

The dissenters—Justices Sandra Day O'Connor, Antonin Scalia, and Stephen Breyer—faulted the majority for what they said was an overly strict and literal reading of one passage of the Constitution. Scalia pointed out that in the early years of the nation, Congress had passed a lump-sum appropriation to run the government and permitted the president to spend or not spend, as he saw fit. In 1803 Congress appropriated $50,000 for the purpose of building fifteen gunboats to patrol the Mississippi River, but President Thomas Jefferson later reported back that because of a "favorable and peaceable turns of affairs on the Mississippi," the money appropriated for the boats "remains unexpended."[18] No one thought he had violated the Constitution, Scalia observed. "There is not a dime's worth of difference between Congress's authorizing the President to cancel a spending item, and Congress's authorizing money to be spent on a particular item at the President's discretion," Scalia argued.[19] He also offered a suggestion to Congress should it be interested in trying again: "The short of the matter is this: Had the Line Item Veto Act authorized the President to 'decline to spend' any item of spending contained in the Balanced Budget Act of 1997, there is not the slightest doubt that authorization would have been constitutional."[20]

THE POWER TO GRANT PARDONS AND REPRIEVES

The Constitution gives the president the power "to grant Reprieves and Pardons for Offenses against the United States" to all persons excepting those who have been impeached. A pardon is an exemption from a sentence and guilt; a reprieve is the suspension of a sentence or other legally imposed penalties for a temporary period. The Supreme Court has supported the president's discretion to exercise the pardon power against all challenges. A pardon may be full or partial, absolute or conditional, or general. The president may attach conditions to a pardon, the Court has held, so long as they are not contrary to the Constitution or federal laws.[21] Although acceptance of a pardon is generally considered a necessary act, conditional pardons (and commutations) have been upheld against challenges by the persons pardoned. The effect of a full pardon, the Court has held, is to end the punishment and blot out the guilt as if the offense had never occurred.[22]

The early view of the pardon power was set out by Chief Justice John Marshall, who defined a pardon as an act of grace. A century later, however, the individual act of mercy had become, as well, in the words of Justice Oliver Wendell Holmes Jr., "part of the Constitutional scheme."[23] Presidents have issued pardons and granted amnesty—a general pardon to groups or communities—since President Washington issued a general amnesty to the western Pennsylvania "whiskey rebels" in 1795. The most famous pardon in U.S. history to date is that granted by President Ford on September 8, 1974, to his predecessor, former president Nixon, who had resigned the presidency amid allegations of his involvement in crimes related to the Watergate cover-up. Nixon's pardon was "full, free and absolute . . . for all offenses against the United States which he . . . has committed or may have committed" as president.[24] Nixon accepted the pardon with a statement describing it as a "compassionate act." *(See box, Nixon Pardon Proclamation, p. 316.)*

The framers of the Constitution had granted the president of the United States a pardon power similar to that exercised by British monarchs.[25] Alexander Hamilton, writing in the *Federalist Papers,* advocated that the use of this power be unfettered.

> Humanity and good policy conspire to dictate that the benign prerogative of pardoning should be as little as possible fettered or embarrassed. The criminal code of every country partakes so much of necessary

NIXON PARDON PROCLAMATION

Following is the text of the proclamation by which President Gerald R. Ford pardoned former president Richard M. Nixon on September 8, 1974:

Richard Nixon became the thirty-seventh President of the United States on January 20, 1969, and was re-elected in 1972 for a second term by the electors of forty-nine of the fifty states. His term in office continued until his resignation on August 9, 1974.

Pursuant to resolutions of the House of Representatives, its Committee on the Judiciary conducted an inquiry and investigation on the impeachment of the President extending over more than eight months. The hearings of the committee and its deliberations, which received wide national publicity over television, radio, and in printed media, resulted in votes adverse to Richard Nixon on recommended articles of impeachment.

As a result of certain acts or omissions occurring before his resignation from the office of President, Richard Nixon has become liable to possible indictment and trial for offenses against the United States. Whether or not he shall be so prosecuted depends on findings of the appropriate grand jury and on the discretion of the authorized prosecutor. Should an indictment ensue, the accused shall then be entitled to a fair trial by an impartial jury, as guaranteed to every individual by the Constitution.

It is believed that a trial of Richard Nixon, if it became necessary, could not fairly begin until a year or more has elapsed. In the meantime, the tranquility to which this nation has been restored by the events of recent weeks could be irreparably lost by the prospects of bringing to trial a former President of the United States. The prospects of such trial will cause prolonged and divisive debate over the propriety of exposing to further punishment and degradation a man who has already paid the unprecedented penalty of relinquishing the highest elective office in the United States.

Now, therefore, I, Gerald R. Ford, President of the United States, pursuant to the pardon power conferred upon me by Article II, Section 2, of the Constitution, have granted and by these presents do grant a full, free, and absolute pardon unto Richard Nixon for all offenses against the United States which he, Richard Nixon, has committed or may have committed or taken part in during the period from January 20, 1969, through August 9, 1974.

In witness whereof, I have hereunto set my hand this 8th day of September in the year of Our Lord Nineteen Hundred Seventy-Four, and of the Independence of the United States of America the 199th.

---

severity, that without an easy access to exceptions in favor of unfortunate guilt, justice would wear a countenance too sanguinary and cruel.[26]

President Clinton, on his last day in office, issued a long list of pardons, including an infamous one for a fugitive financier, Marc Rich, who had fled to Switzerland after being indicted. Despite the controversy and media storm surrounding the Rich pardon, Clinton's action went unchallenged in court, as it is acknowledged that presidential pardons are final and irrevocable.

Acceptance

In one of the Court's first rulings on the pardon power, Chief Justice Marshall stated that acceptance of a pardon by the recipient was a necessary condition of its taking effect. In the case of *United States v. Wilson* (1833), Marshall wrote,

A pardon is an act of grace, proceeding from the power entrusted with the execution of the laws, which exempts the individual, on whom it is bestowed, from the punishment the law inflicts for a crime he has committed. It is the private, though official act of the executive magistrate, delivered to the individual for whose benefit it is intended, and not communicated officially to the court. . . . A pardon is a deed, to the validity of which delivery is essential, and delivery is not complete without acceptance. It may then be rejected by the person to whom it is tendered; and if it be rejected, we have discovered no power in a court to force it on him. A pardon may be conditional, and the condition may be more objectionable than the punishment inflicted by the judgment.[27]

This opinion reflected the common law tradition, which viewed the sovereign's pardon as an act of grace, and the common English practice that a pardon or commutation was often granted on the condition that the convicted felon move to another place. In *Burdick v. United States* (1915) the Court reaffirmed Marshall's view of the need for acceptance of a pardon.[28]

George Burdick, city editor of the *New York Tribune*, refused to testify before a federal grand jury investigating customs fraud, arguing that his testimony would incriminate him. President Woodrow Wilson then offered Burdick a full and unconditional pardon in connection with any matters he might be questioned about. Burdick refused the pardon and refused again to testify. He was imprisoned for contempt, but a unanimous Supreme Court upheld his right to reject the pardon, citing Marshall's 1833 opinion. Justice Joseph McKenna, writing for the Court, explained the risk of implied guilt in the granting of pardons to individuals who, although not convicted of a crime, nevertheless accepted a pardon:

> [T]he grace of a pardon . . . may be only in pretense or seeming . . . involving consequences of even greater disgrace than those from which it purports to relieve. Circumstances may be made to bring innocence under the penalties of the law. If so brought, escape by confession of guilt implied in the acceptance of a pardon may be rejected.[29]

The Effect of a Pardon

Ex parte Garland (1866) is the leading case defining the effect of a presidential pardon. The case involved one of the nation's leading attorneys, southerner Augustus H. Garland, and an 1865 act of Congress that required all attorneys who wished to practice in the Supreme Court and other federal courts to take an oath that they had not aided the Confederate cause by word or deed.[30] Garland had practiced before the Supreme Court prior to the Civil War. When Arkansas, his home state, joined the Confederacy, he served in the Confederate congress. Under the "test oath" requirement imposed by the 1865 law, Garland was forever disqualified from resuming his legal practice before the federal courts.

In July 1865, however, Garland received a full pardon from President Andrew Johnson for all offenses committed, direct or implied, in the Civil War. Garland cited the pardon and asked for permission to practice in federal court, although he was still unable, due to his

service to the Confederacy, to take the test oath. Garland argued that the disqualifying act of Congress, so far as it affected him, was unconstitutional and void as a bill of attainder prohibited by the Constitution. Beyond that, he argued that even if the act was constitutional, the pardon released him from compliance with its provisions.[31]

"The Benign Prerogative of Mercy"

The Supreme Court ruled for Garland on both points. For the first time, the Court struck down an act of Congress by the narrow margin of 5-4, finding the test oath law unconstitutional as a bill of attainder and an ex post facto law. *(See box, Specific Constitutional Limits on Congressional Powers, pp. 90–91.)* Even if the law were valid, wrote Justice Stephen J. Field for the majority, the pardon placed Garland "beyond the reach of punishment of any kind" for his Civil War role. "It is not within the constitutional power of Congress thus to inflict punishment beyond the reach of executive clemency," Field wrote.[32] Field then examined the presidential pardon power and its effect on the recipient and on Congress:

> The power thus conferred is unlimited, with the exception stated [impeachment]. It extends to every offence known to the law, and may be exercised at any time after its commission, either before legal proceedings are taken, or during their pendency, or after conviction and judgement. This power of the President is not subject to legislative control. Congress can neither limit the effect of his pardon, nor exclude from its exercise any class of offenders. The benign prerogative of mercy reposed in him cannot be fettered by any legislative restrictions.[33]

Having established the unlimited nature of the president's pardoning power, Field discussed the effect of a presidential pardon on the recipient:

> A pardon reaches both the punishment prescribed for the offense and the guilt of the offender; and when the pardon is full, it releases the punishment and blots out of existence the guilt, so that in the eye of the law the offender is as innocent as if he had never committed the offence. If granted

before conviction, it prevents any of the penalties and disabilities consequent upon conviction from attaching; if granted after conviction, it removes the penalties and disabilities, and restores him to all his civil rights; it makes him, as it were, a new man, and gives him a new credit and capacity.[34]

The dissenters, in an opinion written by Justice Samuel F. Miller, focused on the initial question of the constitutionality of the disqualifying law: whether it was an ex post facto law and whether Congress could pass laws to ensure the character and loyalty of the nation's lawyers. They found the law a proper exercise of congressional power, and disagreed that the pardon put Garland beyond its reach:

> The right to practice law in the courts . . . is a privilege granted by the law . . . not an absolute right . . . the presidential pardon relieves the party from all the penalties, or in other words, from all the punishment, which the law inflicted for his offence. But it relieves him from nothing more. If the oath required as a condition to practising law is not a punishment, as I think I have shown it is not, then the pardon of the President has no effect in releasing him from the requirement to take it. If it is a qualification which Congress had a right to prescribe as necessary to an attorney, then the President, cannot, by pardon or otherwise, dispense with the law requiring such qualification.

> This is not only the plain rule as between the legislative and executive departments of the government, but it is the declaration of common sense. The man who, by counterfeiting, by theft, by murder, or by treason, is rendered unfit to exercise the functions of an attorney or counselor-at-law, may be saved by the executive pardon from the penitentiary or the gallows, but is not thereby restored to the qualifications which are essential to admission to the bar. No doubt it will be found that very many persons among those who cannot take this oath, deserved to be relieved from the prohibition of the law; but this in no wise depends upon the act of the President in giving or refusing a pardon. It remains to the legislative power alone to prescribe under what circumstances this relief shall be extended.[35]

The Court thus allowed former Confederates to resume the practice of law in the nation's federal courts. The decision produced a furor in the North and led to legislative efforts to reform the Court. Congress even considered barring all ex-Confederates from the practice of law, but the bill was not approved. Garland later became attorney general of the United States, during the administration of President Grover Cleveland.

Broad, but Not Perpetual

Despite the broad effect of a pardon on a person convicted of or under investigation for a crime, the Court has held that a pardon cannot protect an individual who is convicted of a second, postpardon crime. A New York court tried and convicted a person whose first federal offense had been pardoned. The court nevertheless took the fact of a prior conviction into consideration in determining the penalty for the second offense. The convicted individual challenged consideration of that factor, but the Supreme Court warned that it was incorrect to think

> that a pardon would operate to limit the power of the United States in punishing crimes against its authority to provide for taking into consideration past offenses committed by the accused as a circumstance of aggravation even though for such past offenses there had been a pardon granted.[36]

The Court has held that a pardon restores a convict's competency as a witness in a court of law. The justices found that the disability resulted from the conviction and that the pardon obliterated the effect of the conviction, therefore restoring the competency to testify.[37]

Undoing the Past

A pardon, however, cannot make amends for the past. It cannot afford compensation for time spent in prison, nor can it restore property rights that have been legally vested in others. *Knote v. United States* (1877), the leading case on this aspect of the effects of a presidential pardon, arose, like *Ex parte Garland,* out of the Civil War. The property of a man who had served with the Confederacy was condemned and sold for his "treason." After the general pardon issued to ex-Confederates in 1868 by President Andrew Johnson, the former owner of the property sued for the proceeds of the sale. The Court denied his claim and declared that a pardon cannot

> make amends for the past. It affords no relief for what has been suffered by the offender in his person by imprisonment, forced labor, or otherwise; it does not give compensation for what has been done or suffered, nor does it impose upon the government any obligation to give it. The offense being established by judicial proceedings, that which has been done or suffered when they were in force is presumed to have been rightly done and justly suffered, and no satisfaction for it can be required. . . . Neither does the pardon affect any rights which have vested in others directly by the execution of the judgment for the offense, or which have been acquired by others whilst that judgment was in force. If, for example, by the judgment a sale of the offender's property has been had, the purchaser will hold the property notwithstanding the subsequent pardon. . . . The rights of the parties have become vested, and are as complete as if they were acquired in any other legal way. So, also, if the proceeds have been paid into the treasury, the right to them has so far become vested in the United States that they can only be secured to the former owner of the property through an act of Congress. Moneys once in the treasury can only be withdrawn by an appropriation by law. However large, therefore, may be the power of pardon possessed by the President, and however extended may be its application, there is this limit to it, as there is to all his powers, it cannot touch moneys in the Treasury of the United States, except expressly authorized by Act of Congress.[38]

Conditions and Commutations

The questions posed by conditional pardons came before the Court after President Abraham Lincoln, on December 8, 1863, offered pardons to all Confederates who swore allegiance to the Constitution and the Union. Lincoln's offer, if accepted, would have granted former Confederates the right to restoration of their property taken during the war. In *United States v. Klein* (1872) the Court upheld the president's right to offer the pardon and property restoration in exchange for allegiance.

> It was competent for the President to annex to his offer of pardon any conditions or qualifications he should see fit; but after those conditions and qualifications had been satisfied, the pardon and its connected promises took full effect.[39]

Congress had tried, through legislation, to block the property restoration effect of this pardon. The Court rejected that effort:

> To the Executive alone is intrusted the power of pardon; and it is granted without limit. Pardon includes amnesty. It blots out the offense pardoned and removes all its penal consequences. It may be granted on conditions. In these particular pardons, that no doubt might exist as to their character, restoration of property was expressly pledged; and the pardon was granted on condition that the person who availed himself of it should take and keep a prescribed oath.

> Now, it is clear that the Legislature cannot change the effect of such a pardon any more than the Executive can change a law.[40]

Challenges to Commutation

In a series of cases involving the president's use of the pardon to commute, or reduce, sentences, the Court has held that this aspect of the power may be exercised without the recipient's consent. William Wells, convicted of murder, was to be hanged on April 23, 1852. On the day of execution, President Millard Fillmore granted him a conditional pardon, commuting his sentence to life in prison. Wells accepted the pardon, but challenged the condition as illegal, seeking his release from prison through a writ of habeas corpus. In *Ex parte Wells* (1856) his attorneys argued to the Supreme Court that

> a President granting such a pardon assumes a power not conferred by the Constitution—that he legislates a new punishment into existence, and sentences the convict to suffer it; in this way violating the legislative and judicial power of the government, it being the power of the first to enact laws

for the punishment of offences . . . and that of the judiciary, to sentence . . . according to them.[41]

The Court rejected this argument, upheld the president's power to commute a sentence without the recipient's consent, and concluded that

> it may be said, [that] . . . the condition, when accepted, becomes a substitute for the sentence of the court . . . [and] is substantially the exercise of a new power. But this is not so, for the power to offer a condition, without ability to enforce its acceptance, when accepted by the convict, is the substitution, by himself, of a lesser punishment than the law has imposed upon him, and he cannot complain if the law executes the choice he has made.[42]

In subsequent cases, the Court declared that the president's prerogative includes the power to remit fines, penalties, and forfeitures and to pardon contempt of court.[43]

Biddle v. Perovich

Seventy years later, the Court reaffirmed its holding in the *Wells* case, ruling that a president could commute a death sentence entirely without the recipient's consent. Vuco Perovich, convicted of murder in Alaska in 1905 and sentenced to be hanged, received a commuted sentence of life imprisonment from President Taft in 1909. Authorities moved Perovich to a state penitentiary and then, some years later, to the federal prison at Leavenworth, Kansas. Perovich twice applied unsuccessfully for a pardon. He then applied for release through a writ of habeas corpus, arguing that his removal from an Alaskan jail to a federal penitentiary and the president's commutation of his death sentence were effected without his consent and without legal authority.

Perovich's attorney urged the Supreme Court to hold that a sentence could not be commuted without consent. The Court rejected that argument, ruling that consent was not required for commutation of a sentence: "When we come to the commutation of death to imprisonment for life," wrote Justice Holmes, "it is hard to see how consent has much to do with the effect of the president's action. Supposing that Perovich did

not accept the change, he could not have got himself hanged against the Executive order."[44] Holmes then set out the modern Court's view of the presidential pardon power:

> A pardon in our days is not a private act of grace from an individual happening to possess power. It is part of the Constitutional scheme. When granted it is the determination of the ultimate authority that the public welfare will be better served by inflicting less than what the judgment fixed. . . . Just as the original punishment would be imposed without regard to the prisoner's consent and in the teeth of his will, whether he liked it or not, the public welfare, not his consent, determines what shall be done. So far as a pardon legitimately cuts down a penalty, it affects the judgment imposing it.[45]

Schick v. Reed

In 1974 the Court for the third time rejected a challenge to the power of commutation. President Dwight D. Eisenhower commuted the death sentence of a child murderer to life in prison without possibility of parole, a sentence not at that time authorized by law for the crime of murder. After serving twenty years, the prisoner sued to require the parole board to consider him eligible for parole on the basis that he had served the equivalent to a "life" sentence, and, furthermore, that the death penalty had in the interim been outlawed by a Supreme Court decision of 1972.[46] Maurice Schick, the prisoner, argued that he had made a "bad bargain" in exchanging a death sentence for life in prison without opportunity for parole. The Supreme Court held that the conditional commutation of his sentence was lawful and that intervening events had not undermined its validity.[47] Writing for the Court, Chief Justice Warren E. Burger explained,

> A fair reading of the history of the English pardoning power, from which our Art. II, § 2, derives, of the language of that section itself, and of the unbroken practice since 1790 compels the conclusion that the power flows from the Constitution alone, and not from any legislative enactments, and that it cannot be modified, abridged, or diminished by the Congress. Additionally, considerations of

public policy and humanitarian impulses support an interpretation of that power so as to permit the attachment of any condition which does not otherwise offend the Constitution. The plain purpose of the broad power conferred . . . was to allow plenary authority in the President to "forgive" the convicted person in part or entirely, to reduce a penalty in terms of a specified number of years, or to alter it with conditions which are in themselves constitutionally unobjectionable. . . . We therefore hold that the pardoning power is an enumerated power of the Constitution and its limitations, if any, must be found in the Constitution itself.[48]

Three justices, however, questioned the "extralegal nature of the Executive action." Justice Thurgood Marshall, writing for Justices William O. Douglas and William J. Brennan Jr., argued that "in commuting a sentence the Chief Executive is not imbued with the constitutional power to create unauthorized punishments."[49]

Privilege and Immunity

The Constitution makes no mention of executive immunity or executive privilege, yet they are important aspects of presidential power. These two concepts, both of which are invoked to protect the presidency from undue interference by other branches, have evolved from the system of separated powers, the constitutional design of three coordinate branches, each protected from coercion by the others.[1] Executive immunity shields the chief executive against judicial interference with presidential policymaking. Once effected, a policy may be reviewed by a court concerning its results, but a court cannot order the president to take, or refrain from taking, any particular policy action. Yet the chief executive is not immune from all challenge to presidential actions. Article II, section 4, provides that the other political branch—Congress—may impeach and remove a president from office if it finds him guilty of "Treason, Bribery or other high Crimes and Misdemeanors." It is unresolved whether a sitting president can be charged and prosecuted for crimes of an unofficial nature in any court other than a court of impeachment. Once impeached, however, the Constitution is explicit in making the point that an official is then "liable and subject to Indictment, Trial, Judgment and Punishment, according to Law."

Executive privilege, on the other hand, generally has been asserted as the president's prerogative to withhold information, documents, and the testimony of his aides from public or congressional scrutiny. Congress has never fully accepted this principle, although it has been asserted and practiced by presidents since George Washington. Presidents find the basis for this claim in the separation of powers principle, vaguely stated at the beginning of Article II—"The executive power shall be vested in a President of the United States of America"—and their responsibility to "take Care that the Laws be faithfully executed." The Supreme Court's rulings on executive privilege have acknowledged the existence of a limited privilege as necessary to protect the national security and the conduct of diplomatic negotiations. The Court, however, has denied emphatically any absolute privilege to withhold information under all circumstances.

EXECUTIVE IMMUNITY

The turmoil of Reconstruction and the troubled presidency of Andrew Johnson provided the backdrop for the leading Supreme Court decision on the immunity of the president, as an official and an individual, from judicial interference in the conduct of the office. In *Ex parte Milligan* (1866) the Court had declared that President Abraham Lincoln had exceeded his authority in establishing military courts outside the war zone during the Civil War.[2] This ruling gave southerners reason to hope that the Court would also strike down the congressional program of Reconstruction outlined in the Reconstruction Act of 1867. *(See "Merryman and Milligan," pp. 265–266.)*

Mississippi came to the Court asking that the justices order the president to halt the Reconstruction program. The state challenged the constitutionality of the laws upon which it was based and the president's authority to carry it out.[3] In *Marbury v. Madison* (1803) the Court held that a court with jurisdiction could issue a writ to order the president to perform a ministerial duty, a duty as to which he had little discretion.[4] Here, however, Mississippi was asking the Court to exercise its authority to restrain the president's enforcement of an act of Congress. The Court rejected Mississippi's request. Chief Justice Salmon P. Chase wrote the Court's opinion, which distinguished between the ministerial duties of a president and the general responsibility for seeing that the laws are faithfully executed. Ministerial acts, wrote Chase, could be subject to court orders, but acts involving political discretion are beyond judicial reach. When a court issued an injunction against a political act, it interfered with the operation of the political branches and risked a collision between the judicial and political departments. There are practical reasons for avoiding such collisions, explained Chief Justice Chase in *Mississippi v. Johnson* (1867):

> If the President refuse obedience, it is needless to observe that the Court is without power to enforce its process. If, on the other hand, the President complies and refuses to execute the acts of Congress, is it not clear that a collision may occur between the executive and legislative departments . . . ? May not the House of Representatives impeach the President for such refusal? And in that case could this Court interfere in behalf of the President, thus endangered by compliance with its mandate . . . ?

> A ministerial duty . . . is one in respect to which nothing is left to discretion. It is a simple, definite duty, arising under conditions admitted or proved to exist, and imposed by law. . . .

> Very different is the duty of the President in the exercise of the power to see that the laws are faithfully executed. . . . The duty thus imposed on the President is in no just sense ministerial. It is purely executive and political.

> An attempt on the part of the Judicial Department of the Government to enforce the performance of such duties by the President might be justly characterized, in the language of Chief Justice Marshall, as "an absurd and excessive extravagance."

> It is true that in the instance before us the interposition of the court is not sought to enforce action by the Executive under constitutional legislation, but to restrain such action under legislation alleged to be unconstitutional. But we are unable to perceive that this circumstance takes the case out of the general principles which forbid judicial interference with the exercise of executive discretion. . . .

> The Congress is the Legislative Department of the Government; the President is the Executive Department. Neither can be restrained in its action by the Judicial Department; though the acts of both, when performed, are, in proper cases, subject to its cognizance.[5]

Mississippi suggested that the injunctive relief sought might be issued against Johnson as a private citizen if the office of the president were beyond the reach of such an order, but Chase declared that no such distinction could be entertained:

> [I]t is plain that relief as against the execution of an Act of Congress by Andrew Johnson, is relief against its execution by the President. A bill praying an injunction against the execution of an act of Congress by the incumbent of the presidential office cannot be received, whether it describes him as President or as citizen of a State.[6]

The Court dismissed Georgia's subsequent effort to prevent enforcement of the Reconstruction acts by Secretary of War Edwin M. Stanton and Gen. Ulysses S. Grant.[7] In *Georgia v. Stanton* (1868) the Court refused to issue to these presidential subordinates the order it would not issue to the president. The suit involved political questions and political rights, the Court reiterated, and the issue lay beyond the Court's jurisdiction. The rights involved were not personal or property rights, but "the rights of sovereignty, of political jurisdiction, of government, of corporate existence as a State, with all its constitutional powers and privileges."[8]

Therefore, held the Court, once the president moves into the realm of policy and politics, the Court cannot compel or prevent the chief executive from acting. Once an action is completed, however, the Court may consider a challenge to the results of the president's policies and at that point may review and disallow those policies. In such an instance, the president's subordinates may be ordered by a court not to carry out a threatened illegal act that would lead to irreparable damage. Those subordinates also may be commanded by a court to carry out some ministerial duty required by law. In *Kendall v. United States* (1838) the Court held that the postmaster general, William Berry, could be ordered by a court to pay an account due without breaching the powers and prerogatives of the president. Justice Smith Thompson's majority opinion discussed the president's discretionary powers and their derivation and exercise:

> The theory of the constitution undoubtedly is, that the great powers of the government are divided into separate departments; and so far as these powers derived from the constitution, the departments may be regarded as independent of each other. But beyond that, all are subject to regulations by law, touching the discharge of the duties required to be performed. The executive power is vested in a president; and so far as his powers are derived from the constitution, he is beyond the reach of any other department. . . . But it by no means follows, that every officer in every branch of that department is under the exclusive direction of the president. Such a principle, we apprehend, is not, and certainly cannot be claimed by the president. There are certain political duties imposed upon many officers in the executive department, the discharge of which is under direction of the president. But it would be an alarming doctrine, that congress cannot impose upon any executive officer any duty they may think proper, which is not repugnant to any rights secured and protected by the constitution; and in such cases, the duty and responsibility grow out of and are subject to the control of the law, and not to the direction of the president.[9]

The Court rejected the argument that the postmaster general, a presidential cabinet officer, was under the sole direction of the president. That principle, wrote the Court,

> if carried out in its results to all cases falling within it, would [result in] . . . clothing the President with a power entirely to control legislation of Congress, and paralyze the administration of justice.

> To contend that the obligation imposed on the President to see the laws faithfully executed implies a power to forbid their execution, is a novel construction of the Constitution, and entirely inadmissible.[10]

Subsequent rulings by the Court have held that subordinate executive officers may be held personally liable for damages wrought by acts in excess of their authority.[11] But some executive immunity protects them from liability for reasonable actions taken in good faith in the performance of their duties.[12] (See box, The Sovereign's Immunity, p. 14.) In the early 1980s the Court granted the president absolute immunity from personal liability as a result of injuries or losses caused by official actions. A. Ernest Fitzgerald lost his air force job during the Nixon administration, as reprisal, he contended, for revealing to Congress cost overruns on air force contracts. He sued President Richard Nixon and other top executive branch officers for causing him to lose his job. When the case came to the Supreme Court, Fitzgerald lost, 5-4. By that time, Nixon was no longer president, but the immunity for his actions as president remained. This absolute immunity, wrote Justice Lewis F. Powell Jr., is "a functionally mandated incident of the president's unique office, rooted in the constitutional tradition of the separation of powers and supported by our history."[13]

"Because of the singular importance of the President's duties, diversion of his energies by concern with private lawsuits would raise unique risks to the effective functioning of government," Powell continued in *Nixon v. Fitzgerald* (1982). If a president were vulnerable personally to lawsuits, it "could distract a President from his public duties, to the detriment not only of the President and his office, but also the Nation that the Presidency was designed to serve."[14] Although this immunity encompassed actions within the "outer perimeter" of the president's official responsibility, it "will not leave the Nation without sufficient protection against misconduct on the part of the chief executive," Powell concluded, mentioning the constitutional remedy of impeachment, constant scrutiny by the press, vigilant oversight by Congress, as well as the desire to earn reelection, to maintain prestige, and to preserve a proper historical reputation.[15] Justices Harry A. Blackmun, William J. Brennan Jr., Thurgood Marshall, and Byron R. White dissented.

In a companion case decided the same day, *Harlow v. Fitzgerald* (1982), the Court held that the president's close aides did not enjoy such absolute liability from these suits. Instead, Powell wrote, they had a qualified immunity that protected them unless their actions, upon which the claims against them are based, violated clearly established statutory or constitutional rights of which a reasonable person would have been aware.[16]

"Unofficial Acts" of the President

President Bill Clinton, like Richard Nixon, was the subject of private lawsuits and congressional impeachment resolutions. In Clinton's case, a sexual harassment lawsuit filed by Paula Corbin Jones, a former Arkansas state employee, triggered a chain of events that ultimately led to his impeachment. Along the way, it resulted in a Supreme Court ruling that shrank the legal buffer surrounding the presidency. Although the president cannot be sued for official acts taken while in office, the Court ruled unanimously in 1997 that the "current occupant" of the White House remains subject to the laws for his private behavior.[17]

The alleged incident that led to Jones's lawsuit took place in 1991 when Clinton was governor of Arkansas, but her suit was filed in 1994 while Clinton was president. The timing of the suit led Clinton's supporters to charge that it was a politically motivated attempt to harass and humiliate the chief executive. Jones's allegations, if true, told the story of a supervisor trying to take advantage of a subordinate. Jones was a twenty-four-year-old clerk working at the registration desk for a state conference held at the Excelsior Hotel in Little Rock in May 1991. Governor Clinton gave a speech to the group and returned to a suite on the upper floors. Jones said a state police officer asked her to go upstairs to the governor's room. There, she said, the governor dropped his pants and made a crude proposition. Jones said she rejected his advances, hurriedly left the room, and returned to the registration desk. She said little afterward about the incident. Three years later, she was shown an article in *American Spectator*, a conservative weekly, in which a state trooper referred to a woman named "Paula" who had been the governor's girlfriend. Offended again, Jones said she decided to sue for sexual harassment and defamation of character. The suit was filed in May 1994, two days before the three-year statute of limitation was to expire. She sought $75,000 in damages and $100,000 in punitive damages for each of four counts cited in the lawsuit. The president issued a statement through an aide denying that the incident took place.

At first, the case looked to be a classic "he said, she said" affair, because only Clinton and Jones were in the hotel room. Plaintiffs, however, have a right to "discovery," which in this case meant that lawyers for Jones could seek out other women who may have had similar encounters with Clinton. Reluctant witnesses could be forced, under court order, to submit a sworn statement or provide testimony under oath. Jones was simply exercising her rights as an ordinary plaintiff, but Clinton was no ordinary defendant. Statements from other women were almost certain to become public and thereby embarrass and damage the president, who was also a husband and father. Because the political stakes were so high, Clinton and his personal lawyers sought to block the lawsuit from going forward, at least until Clinton left office.

Clinton's attorneys filed a motion with U.S. district court judge Susan Webber Wright in Little Rock asking that Jones's suit be deferred until Clinton left the presidency. They cited *Nixon v. Fitzgerald* (1982), in particular, Justice Powell's comment about the "singular importance of the President's duties" and the concern that fighting a lawsuit could "distract a President from his public duties."[18] After all, Nixon was retired when A. Ernest Fitzgerald sued him, and Clinton was merely asking to defer Jones's suit until his retirement. Judge Wright agreed in large part and ordered that a trial in the Jones case be delayed until Clinton left office. A deferment would spare the president from distraction, she said, but to be fair to Jones, the judge said her lawyers could take discovery because the memories of witnesses would be fresher. Both parties appealed.

Jones wanted a trial and a verdict as soon as possible. Clinton's lawyers were as worried about discovery as they were about the trial. In a 2-1 vote, the U.S. Court of Appeals for the Eighth Circuit sided with Jones, ruling that the discovery and a trial should go forward. Clinton's private attorneys and the U.S. solicitor general asked the Supreme Court to hear Clinton's appeal and decide whether "a private civil damages action against an incumbent President" can take place while he is in office. They argued that such lawsuits could distract the chief executive and subject him to expensive harassment by his political enemies.

Moreover, they said, it would violate the separation of powers to place the president's fate in the hands of a judge. In June 1996 the justices announced that they would hear Clinton's appeal, a victory of sorts for the president and his supporters because the Court's intervention would delay matters until after the presidential election of November 1996.

Chief Justice William H. Rehnquist called the attorneys forward to argue *Clinton v. Jones* in January 1997, a week before he was to administer the oath of office to Clinton at his second inauguration. Robert S. Bennett, Clinton's lawyer, and Acting Solicitor General Walter Dellinger argued that a president was too busy to take time out to deal with a meddlesome lawsuit. The justices were unswayed. Justice Antonin Scalia commented that because presidents are seen regularly on vacation, doing such things as riding horses or playing golf, it is hard to argue that the chief executive does not have an hour to spare to answer questions in a deposition. Justice Sandra Day O'Connor asked about other possibilities. Suppose a president and his wife divorced, and there was a dispute over the custody of their child. Could the president say he was too busy and block court action for four years until he left office? Suppose he owned land and an environmental emergency threatened his neighbors. Could the president argue that he was immune from responding to a legal challenge in that situation? By the end of arguments, it was clear that the justices believed the president as a private citizen was asking for special immunity from ordinary laws.

In May 1997 the Court dealt Clinton a unanimous defeat, rejecting his claim that the president should have a "temporary immunity" from civil suits while in office. Justice John Paul Stevens, reading his majority opinion from the bench, began by referring not to "Clinton" or "the president" but to the "current occupant" of the office of the president. He stressed that the Court's past rulings that gave immunity to certain officials, such as prosecutors, legislators, judges and presidents, had always turned on their need to carry out their public duties, not to shield them from their private wrongdoing. "We have never suggested that the President, or any other official, has an immunity that extends beyond the scope of any action taken in an official capacity," he said, and "it is perfectly clear that the alleged misconduct of petitioner [Clinton] was unrelated to any of his official duties as President of the United States and, indeed, occurred before he was elected to that office."[19]

Stevens also brushed aside the argument that a trial would violate the separation of powers: "Whatever the outcome of this case, there is no possibility that the decision will curtail the scope of the official powers of the Executive Branch," because it concerns only "questions that relate entirely to the unofficial conduct of the individual who happens to be the President." On the issue of the lawsuit being distracting and time-consuming, Stevens offered a few comments that would prove to be spectacularly inaccurate: "As we have noted, in the more than 200 year history of the Republic, only three sitting Presidents have been subject to suits for private actions," he wrote. "We assume that the testimony of the President, both for discovery and for use at trial, may be taken at the White House at a time that will accommodate his busy schedule, and that, if a trial is held, there would be no necessity for the President to attend in person, although he could elect to do so," Stevens continued. "If the past is any indicator, it seems unlikely that a deluge of such litigation will ever engulf the Presidency. As for the case at hand, if properly managed by the District Court, it appears to us unlikely to occupy any substantial amount of petitioner's time."[20]

Eight justices, including Justice Ruth Bader Ginsburg, a Clinton appointee, signed on to Stevens's opinion. Justice Stephen Breyer, another Clinton appointee, concurred in the result but wrote separately to say that the Court had downplayed the danger that a lawsuit might distract the president from his duties. Unlike Congress or the courts, "the President never adjourns," Breyer wrote.[21] Contrary to the Court's prediction, the Jones lawsuit occupied a great amount of Clinton's time, engulfed his presidency in scandal, and nearly forced him from office. None of this was obvious in spring 1997, however, because the justices, like the rest of the world, knew nothing of the president's relationship with a White House intern named Monica Lewinsky. The Court's ruling cleared the way for Clinton to be questioned under oath by Jones's lawyers, and the president found himself trapped between an embarrassing revelation about his personal life and perjury.

In the few months following the Court's decision, Clinton tried to settle the Jones lawsuit. His attorney offered as much as $700,000, all that Jones had asked for, and her lawyers urged her to accept the deal. Jones rejected it and demanded a full apology from Clinton. He refused, so the deal died. Jones's lawyers then quit the case, and the attorneys hired to replace them set out aggressively to find other evidence to be used against Clinton. In a civil suit, the plaintiff's representation is entitled to question the defendant not only about the circumstances of the alleged incident, but also about other potential evidence that has been discovered. Because of the unusual nature of this case, Judge Wright flew to Washington to supervise Clinton's deposition, which was held under oath in his lawyer's office in January 1998. Clinton expected to be quizzed about what happened at the Excelsior Hotel in May 1991, but instead Jones's lawyers focused on Lewinsky, who had worked at the White House in 1995 and 1996 and, as it was revealed, had had sexual encounters with Clinton.

The president thought the affair remained a secret, but Lewinsky had confided in her friend Linda Tripp. Unbeknownst to Lewinsky, Tripp taped their phone conversations and turned them over to the office of Kenneth W. Starr, the independent counsel charged with investigating whether Clinton and his wife, Hillary Rodham Clinton, or some of their associates had violated laws regarding the Whitewater land development in Arkansas. Jones's lawyers were also briefed by Tripp. They had the president snared in a trap: If he admitted the affair with Lewinsky, it would eventually become public, but if he denied the affair under oath, he could be prosecuted for perjury. Clinton admitted to nothing other than knowing Lewinsky, and at one point he said he could not even recall whether the two of them had ever been alone together. The lawyers for Jones unwittingly aided Clinton in a sense by preparing a statement that defined sexual relations and by asking Clinton to respond to questions about the definition. They did not ask him direct questions about sexual acts that may have taken place.

The scandal broke within days, when Starr's office announced that it had expanded its investigation into alleged witness tampering in the Jones case. Initially, Starr's lawyers claimed that they needed to investigate whether Lewinsky had obstructed justice by trying to persuade Tripp to testify falsely in the Jones case. In reality, however, they were trying to build a case against Clinton, and they needed Lewinsky as their principal witness. After Lewinsky was threatened with prosecution, she agreed to cooperate with Starr in exchange for immunity. By then, Paula Jones and her lawsuit were almost forgotten, pushed into the background by the mushrooming sex scandal and Starr's drive to impeach Clinton.

Clinton v. Jones has two odd footnotes. In April 1998, as Starr was building his perjury case, Judge Wright dismissed Jones's lawsuit on the grounds that the former clerk had no claim of sexual harassment. Under federal law, sexual harassment is a type of illegal job discrimination. The Civil Rights Act of 1964 makes it illegal for employers to discriminate against workers because of their sex, but Wright concluded that Jones had not presented any evidence that she had suffered job discrimination; Jones's employment status was unaffected by her rebuff of the governor's alleged advances. The court of appeals, which had already handed Clinton several stinging defeats, announced that it would hear an appeal of Judge Wright's ruling. Clinton then offered to settle the case by paying Jones $850,000. It is not only unusual for a defendant in a civil suit to offer more than the plaintiff seeks, but it is also unheard of for a defendant to offer to pay to settle a suit that has been thrown out of court. So the landmark case establishing that a president can be sued in office and triggering the nation's first impeachment of an elected president ended quietly when a check for $850,000 was sent to Paula Jones.

EXECUTIVE PRIVILEGE

Although they acknowledge that Congress has the right to inquire into executive branch matters, presidents have from time to time claimed executive privilege to withhold information from the legislature. Until the mid-twentieth century, these claims were exceptions to the general rule of presidential compliance with such congressional requests: in "virtually every incident prior to the Civil War, presidents complied substantially with congressional requests, withholding information only if specifically authorized to do so by Congress."[22] Since 1954 the incidence of claims of privilege has risen sharply, resulting in a number of Supreme Court pronouncements on the subject. Until 1974 the legal basis for the privilege was much debated. Attorneys general and others seeking to justify a claim of privilege relied heavily on historical precedents of presidential refusals to provide requested information.[23] The precedents, however, often provided at best ambiguous support for the privilege. One writer, after investigating the precedents cited, concluded that contrary to presidential claims, "Congress prevailed, and got precisely what it sought to get" in most cases.[24] Raoul Berger, author of a book on the question, called executive privilege a "constitutional myth."[25]

In *United States v. Nixon* (1974) the Supreme Court for the first time placed a constitutional foundation under the privilege.[26] Upholding a limited privilege, the assertion of which the executive must justify in each case, the Court rejected President Nixon's particular claim of absolute privilege to withhold information. Yet in so doing, the Court provided a fortified basis for future presidential claims of executive privilege.

Presidents and Privilege

The phrase *executive privilege* did not come into use until 1958, when Justice Stanley F. Reed used it in an opinion,[27] but the practice it describes had begun much earlier. President Washington only once denied Congress access to information, refusing to allow the House of Representatives to see papers related to the negotiation of Jay's Treaty, which settled disputes with Britain concerning commerce and navigation. Washington acknowledged the right of Senate access to the papers, because of its role in the treaty making process, but denied the House access on the ground that it lacked power under the Constitution to demand treaty-related documents.[28]

Chief Justice John Marshall, writing for the Court in *Marbury v. Madison,* implicitly acknowledged a basis for some executive privilege:

> By the Constitution of the United States, the President is invested with certain important political powers, in the exercise of which he is to use his own discretion, and is accountable only to his country in his political character and to his own conscience.[29]

Marshall, however, saw limits to the president's prerogative of secrecy:

> Questions in their nature political, or which are, by the Constitution and the laws, submitted to the executive, can never be made in this court.
>
> But, if this be not such a question; if, so far from being an intrusion into the secrets of the cabinet . . . if it be no intermeddling with a subject over which the executive can be considered as having exercised any control; what is there in the exalted station of the officer, which shall bar a citizen from asserting, in a court of justice, his legal rights, or shall forbid a court to listen to the claim, or to issue a mandamus directing the performance of a duty, not depending on executive discretion, but on particular acts of congress, and the general principles of law?[30]

President Thomas Jefferson complied partially when the House requested information from him about the Aaron Burr conspiracy. Jefferson provided the information but withheld the names of individuals mentioned in parts of a letter requested because, he claimed, the names were not pertinent to the House inquiry. During Burr's 1807 treason trial, Jefferson was subpoenaed to appear, but declined to do so, instead producing the letter sought by Burr's counsel. The presiding judge, John Marshall (fulfilling circuit court duty), again recognized a limited privilege protecting state secrets, but said that the court would weigh the need for secrecy against the need of the accused for the document sought in order that he might have a fair trial.[31]

In 1835 President Andrew Jackson rejected a Senate request for a list of charges against Surveyor-General Gideon Fitz in connection with fraudulent land sales.[32] Presidents John Tyler, James K. Polk, and Franklin Pierce all withheld information demanded by Congress.

The Court and the Privilege

Early in the twentieth century the Court acknowledged that heads of executive departments could raise claims of executive privilege with respect to court-ordered demands for records of their department or the testimony of department employees.[33] In the late 1920s the Court held that executive privilege did not, however, protect the executive branch from legitimate legislative investigation. In *McGrain v. Daugherty* (1927) the Court upheld the right of the Senate to inquire into the failure of President Warren G. Harding's attorney general to prosecute major figures in the Teapot Dome scandal.[34] *(See details of the case, p. 213.)*

In 1948 the Court acknowledged that there were areas of executive power—military and national security matters, in particular—about which the president might properly refuse to disclose all facts relative to a decision. The case involved a challenge to the president's decision to award certain foreign air travel routes to one company while denying them to a competitor.[35] Justice Robert H. Jackson wrote,

> The President, both as Commander-in-Chief and as the Nation's organ for foreign affairs, has available intelligence services whose reports neither are nor ought to be published to the world. It would be intolerable that courts, without the relevant information, should review and perhaps nullify actions of the Executive taken on information properly held secret. … But even if courts could require full disclosure, the very nature of executive decisions as to foreign policy is political, not judicial. Such decisions are wholly confided by our Constitution to the political departments of the government, Executive and Legislative. They are delicate, complex, and involve large elements of prophecy. They are and should be undertaken only by those directly responsible to the people, whose welfare they advance or imperil. They are decisions of a kind for which the Judiciary has neither aptitude, facilities nor responsibility and have long been held to belong to the domain of political power not subject to judicial intrusion or inquiry.[36]

The State Secrets Privilege

Five years later the Court asserted a judicial role in assessing claims of executive privilege asserted to protect military or national security secrets. The decision in *United States v. Reynolds* (1953) set out guidelines for judging such claims. The case developed when the widows of three civilians sought copies of investigative reports concerning the accident in which their husbands, who were observing a test of secret military equipment, died when the plane crashed. The secretary of the air force rejected their request, claiming that the reports were privileged documents. The Supreme Court accepted his claim, but in doing so declared that in each case of this sort "the court itself must determine whether the circumstances are appropriate for the claim of privilege."[37] Chief Justice Fred M. Vinson continued,

> In each case, the showing of necessity which is made will determine how far the court should probe in satisfying itself that the occasion for invoking the privilege is appropriate. Where there is a strong showing of necessity, the claim of privilege should not be lightly accepted, but even the most compelling necessity cannot overcome the claim of privilege if the court is ultimately satisfied that military secrets are at stake.[38]

Despite Vinson's claim to have adopted a balanced approach, he and the Court majority accepted on faith the government's contention that the accident report involved military secrets. They did not see it for themselves, and they may have been deceived by the government. In 2000 the accident report was declassified, and it revealed the plane crashed due to a fire in one engine. It also suggested the craft had been poorly maintained. Although the report might have helped the widows in their suit, it did not reveal any military secrets. But the Court's decision in *United States v. Reynolds* stood for the proposition that the government could squelch a lawsuit by contending that it could expose "state secrets."

The George W. Bush administration relied on the "state secrets privilege" to block several lawsuits from persons who said they were wrongly detained or brutally treated. A German citizen, Khaled el-Masri, said he was taken from a tourist bus in Lebanon and tortured by the CIA, apparently because agents believed he was a wanted German-based terrorist with a similar name, Khaled al-Masri. When he sued CIA director

George Tenet, his case was thrown out based on the claim it could reveal state secrets. The Court turned away his appeal without comment on October 9, 2007.

In *Tenet v. Doe* (2005) the Court went further and said the government has an "absolute protection" for suits brought by secret agents and former spies.[39] A married couple who said they had been spies for the United States sued, claiming the CIA had reneged on a promise to support them when they left Russia and settled in the United States. In a unanimous decision, the justices threw out their suit and said secret deals involving espionage may not proceed in court.

THE MODERN PRIVILEGE

As noted above, after 1954 executive claims of an absolute privilege to withhold information accelerated.[40] In 1954 President Dwight D. Eisenhower wrote Defense Secretary Charles Wilson advising him to direct his subordinates not to testify about certain matters during the much publicized army-McCarthy hearings. In the course of that investigation by the Senate Permanent Subcommittee on Investigations, Chairman Joseph R. McCarthy, R-Wis., insisted that John Adams, counsel for the army, tell the subcommittee about a meeting held in the attorney general's office with high-level White House staff members.[41] In response, Adams submitted to the subcommittee copies of a letter from Eisenhower to Wilson invoking executive privilege with respect to testimony by executive department officials. The letter included copies of a memorandum that listed historical precedents of prior successful claims of executive privilege. Eisenhower's letter "became the major authority cited for exercise of 'executive privilege' to refuse information to the Congress for the next seven years," reported the Library of Congress.[42]

President John F. Kennedy refused a special Senate subcommittee's request for the identity of individuals assigned to edit speeches of military leaders. Kennedy directed Secretary of Defense Robert S. McNamara and all personnel under his jurisdiction not to comply with the committee's request. Such refusals of information, Kennedy said, would not be automatic. "Each case must be judged on its own merits," the

president maintained.[43] Kennedy reaffirmed that position in an exchange of correspondence with Rep. John E. Moss, D-Calif.: "Executive privilege can be invoked only by the President and will not be used without specific Presidential approval."[44]

President Lyndon B. Johnson assured Moss that "the claim of 'executive privilege' will continue to be made only by the President."[45] Moss later received a similar declaration from President Nixon, who issued a memorandum to the heads of all executive departments and agencies stating the policy that "executive privilege will not be used without specific Presidential approval."[46] The memorandum required that requests to invoke executive privilege in answer to an inquiry from Congress go to the attorney general. If he and the department head agreed the privilege should not be invoked, Congress would receive the information. If either or both wished, the issue would be submitted to the president. Despite such declarations, some executive branch officials during the Nixon administration did claim executive privilege without presidential approval.[47]

The Supreme Court denied the president's claim of executive privilege in the 1971 *Pentagon Papers* decision in which it held that President Nixon had not satisfied the heavy burden of proof required to enjoin publication of classified material allegedly injurious to national security.[48] The Court in 1973 ruled that federal courts lacked power to review executive branch classification decisions that exempted materials from disclosure under the 1966 Freedom of Information Act. Congress subsequently amended the law to allow courts to review classification decisions.[49]

United States v. Nixon

The most significant Supreme Court decision concerning claims of executive privilege resulted in the resignation of President Nixon. In *United States v. Nixon* (1974) the Court rebuffed the president's claim of an absolute privilege to reject judicial demands for information, holding that Nixon must surrender to the Watergate special prosecutor subpoenaed tapes of White House conversations between the president and his aides. The tapes were required as evidence in the criminal trial of former White House aides charged

The Supreme Court's decision in *United States v. Nixon* (1974) cost President Richard Nixon his job but provided a lot of work for editorial cartoonists across the country.

with attempting to obstruct justice by covering up White House involvement in the 1972 break-in at the Democratic National Committee headquarters in the Watergate office building.

In April 1974 special prosecutor Leon Jaworski obtained a subpoena ordering delivery of certain tapes, memoranda, and papers related to specific meetings of the president with particular White House aides. The president's counsel moved to quash the subpoena, formally claiming executive privilege as a defense against compliance. The district court denied all motions and ordered the president to deliver the requested materials. Nixon appealed to the Supreme Court, which heard arguments July 8 in the cases of *United States v. Nixon, Nixon v. United States.* On July 24, with Chief Justice Warren E. Burger speaking for a unanimous Court, the justices rejected Nixon's claim of privilege. Burger explained the derivation of executive privilege:

Whatever the nature of the privilege of confidentiality of presidential communications in the exercise of Art. II powers the privilege can be said to derive from the supremacy of each branch within its own assigned area of constitutional duties. Certain powers and privileges flow from the nature of the enumerated powers; the protection of the confidentiality of presidential communications has similar constitutional underpinnings.[50]

The Court then observed that

neither the doctrine of separation of powers, nor the need for confidentiality of high level communications, without more, can sustain an absolute, unqualified presidential privilege of immunity from judicial process under all circumstances. The President's need for complete candor and objectivity from advisers calls for great deference from the courts. However, when the privilege depends solely on the broad undifferentiated claim of public interest in the confidentiality of such conversations, a confrontation with other values arises. Absent a claim of need to protect military, diplomatic or sensitive national security secrets, we find it difficult to accept the argument that even the very important interest in confidentiality of presidential communications is significantly diminished by protection of such material for in camera inspection with all the protection that a district court will be obliged to provide.

The impediment that an absolute, unqualified privilege would place in the way of the primary constitutional duty of the Judicial Branch to do justice in criminal prosecutions would plainly conflict with the function of the courts under Art. III. In designing the structure of our Government and dividing and allocating the sovereign power among three coequal branches, the Framers of the Constitution sought to provide a comprehensive system, but the separate powers were not intended to operate with absolute independence. . . .

To read the Art. II powers of the President as providing an absolute privilege as against a subpoena essential to enforcement of criminal statutes on no more than a generalized claim of the public interest in confidentiality of nonmilitary and nondiplomatic discussions would upset the constitutional balance of "a workable government" and gravely impair the role of the courts under Art. III.[51]

In rejecting this particular claim of privilege, however, the Court for the first time acknowledged a constitutional basis for executive privilege:

> A President and those who assist him must be free to explore alternatives in the process of shaping policies and making decisions and to do so in a way many would be unwilling to express except privately. These are the considerations justifying a presumptive privilege for presidential communications. The privilege is fundamental to the operation of government and inextricably rooted in the separation of powers under the Constitution. . . .

> Nowhere in the Constitution . . . is there any explicit reference to a privilege of confidentiality, yet to the extent this interest relates to the effective discharge of a President's powers, it is constitutionally based.[52]

In this case the claim of an absolute privilege failed when weighed against the requirements of evidence in a criminal proceeding. Burger observed,

> No case of the Court . . . has extended this high degree of deference to a President's generalized interest in confidentiality. . . .

> In this case we must weigh the importance of the general privilege of confidentiality of presidential communications in performance of his responsibilities against the inroads of such a privilege on the fair administration of criminal justice. The interest in preserving confidentiality is weighty indeed and entitled to great respect. However we cannot conclude that advisers will be moved to temper the candor of their remarks by the infrequent occasions of disclosure because of the possibility that such conversations will be called for in the context of a criminal prosecution. . . .

> A President's acknowledged need for confidentiality in the communications of his office is general in nature, whereas the constitutional need for production of relevant evidence in a criminal proceeding is specific and central to the fair adjudication of a particular criminal case in the administration of justice. Without access to specific facts a criminal prosecution may be totally frustrated. The President's broad interest in confidentiality of communications will not be vitiated by disclosure of a limited number of conversations preliminarily

shown to have some bearing on the pending criminal cases.

> We conclude that when the ground for asserting privilege as to subpoenaed materials sought for use in a criminal trial is based only on the generalized interest in confidentiality, it cannot prevail over the fundamental demands of due process of law in the fair administration of criminal justice. The generalized assertion of privilege must yield to the demonstrated, specific need for evidence in a pending criminal trial.[53]

The Nixon Papers

In 1977 the Supreme Court rejected a second Nixon claim of executive privilege to restrict access to the records of his administration. Against such a claim, the Court upheld a 1974 act of Congress that placed the records, tapes, and papers of the Nixon administration in federal custody.[54] Presidents historically have retained control of their papers and have governed their use as well as public access to them. The unusual circumstances surrounding Nixon's departure from office, however, moved Congress to depart from that custom.[55] Nixon's attorneys argued that by removing control of the papers from the former president, Congress had infringed upon presidential prerogative and had opened the way for wide disclosure of privileged matters. The Supreme Court majority rejected that argument.

Justice Brennan wrote for the Court that the president's challenge to the act on these grounds rested on "an archaic view of the separation of powers as requiring three airtight departments of government."[56] Executive privilege would not be violated by government archivists' screening the papers any more than it had been when federal judge John Sirica privately reviewed the White House tapes used as evidence in the Watergate cover-up trials, Brennan said. The archivists'

> screening constitutes a very limited intrusion by personnel in the Executive Branch sensitive to executive concerns. These very personnel have performed the identical task in each of the presidential libraries without any suggestion that such activity

has in any way interfered with executive confidentiality. Nor should the American people's ability to reconstruct and come to terms with their history be truncated by an analysis of Presidential privilege that focuses only on the needs of the present.[57]

Chief Justice Burger and Justice William H. Rehnquist dissented. Burger argued that the law would severely affect the conduct of executive branch business. The law, Burger stated, would be "a 'ghost' at future White House conferences with conferees choosing their words more cautiously because of the enlarged prospect of compelled disclosure to others."[58] Justice Rehnquist warned that the Court's decision "will daily stand as a veritable sword of Damocles over every succeeding President and his advisers."[59]

The Supreme Court weighed Nixon's claim of privilege against the need to preserve intact the records of his administration. The majority as well as the dissenters recognized the existence of a limited privilege but in this instance found that the countervailing necessity of the public's right to know outweighed Nixon's claim.

Bush, Cheney, and the "Confidentiality of Communications"

President George W. Bush and Vice President Richard Cheney came to the White House determined to reassert the powers of the Executive Office, which they felt had been eroded during the Nixon era. Bush's father, President George H. W. Bush, had worked under Nixon, including a stint as the Republican Party chairman during the Watergate era. Cheney had been the chief of staff to Nixon's successor, President Gerald R. Ford. Beginning in 2001 Bush and Cheney made clear they planned to work behind closed doors with trusted aides, and they saw no need to respond to requests for information from Congress, the press, or public interest groups. For most of their eight years in office, they were able to fend off such requests. The Supreme Court took up only one case involving a claim for White House information, and the justices did so when Cheney and Bush claimed they should not be forced to disclose the members of the President's National Energy Policy Development Group (NEPDG).

Cheney was the chairman of this short-lived group, and its members included other federal officials. But environmental activists complained that energy industry officials and lobbyists were permitted to join the closed-door meetings. They argued not only that such participation skewed the administration's policy toward the views of the oil and gas industry but also that it might be illegal. An open-government measure known as the Federal Advisory Committee Act requires various federal task forces and commissions to meet in public and to allow outsiders to submit their views, but this law did not apply to committees whose members consisted only of federal employees. Did Cheney's energy policy team include outside lobbyists? If it did, its meetings should have been open, environmentalists maintained.

Sierra Club and Judicial Watch filed a suit against Cheney, seeking information on who met with his energy task force. The administration refused to comply, and its lawyers argued the request for information threatened "substantial intrusions on the process by which those in closest operational proximity to the President advise the President." Bush and his lawyers did not, however, invoke "executive privilege," a term that had been tainted by the Nixon scandals.

A federal judge and the U.S. Court of Appeals for the District of Columbia Circuit refused to dismiss the lawsuit. These judges cited *United States v. Nixon* and noted that the Court had rejected the president's broad claim of immunity. But rather than comply, Bush's lawyers took their appeal to the Supreme Court in a case known as *Cheney v. United States District Court for D.C.* In December 2003 the Court agreed to hear the case.[60]

An intervening incident heightened interest in the case. In the first week of January 2004, shortly after the Court had voted to hear Cheney's appeal, Justice Antonin Scalia joined Cheney to go duck hunting at a private camp in Louisiana. They flew from Washington in Cheney's government jet. When news of their trip was revealed, Sierra Club filed a motion with the Court on February 23, suggesting Scalia remove himself from deciding the case. A federal law says a judge or justice "shall disqualify himself in any proceeding in which his impartiality might reasonably be questioned." But

Scalia refused to step down, and the Court left it to him to decide whether his impartiality might "reasonably be questioned." On March 18 he issued a twenty-one-page memorandum to explain his reasons for not stepping aside. "As it turned out, I never hunted in the same blind with the vice president. Nor was I alone with him at any time during the trip, except, perhaps, for instances so brief and unintentional that I would not recall them—walking to or from a boat, perhaps, or going to or from dinner." Scalia also said the case before the Court concerned the office of the vice president. It was not about Dick Cheney as a person, he said, because he did not face a fine or jail time. "A rule that required members of this Court to remove themselves from cases in which the official actions of friends were at issue would be utterly disabling," Scalia said.

On June 24 the Court handed down a 7-2 decision in favor of Cheney that set aside the appeals court ruling. Scalia voted with the majority. "This is not a routine discovery dispute," wrote Justice Kennedy. "The discovery requests are directed to the Vice President and other senior government officials who served on the NEPDG to give advice and make recommendations to the President. The Executive Branch, at its highest level, is seeking the aid of the court to protect its constitutional prerogatives. . . . Special considerations control when the Executive Branch's interests in maintaining the autonomy of its office and safeguarding the confidentiality of its communications are implicated."[61] The Court did not say precisely whether the president or vice president can ever be required to turn over documents in response to a civil suit, but Kennedy's opinion stressed that President Nixon lost his bid to keep his tapes secret because he faced a criminal prosecution. "The need for information for use in civil cases, while far from negligible, does not share the urgency or significance of the criminal subpoena requests in *Nixon*," he wrote.[62] The ruling left the judge and appeals court with little choice but to withdraw the request for documents and to end the lawsuit. Without citing the words "executive privilege," the Court's decision gave the White House a strong shield against legal claims for internal information.

The President versus the Court

Among the most dramatic chapters in U.S. history are those that relate the collision between a president and the Supreme Court. Infrequent though they are, these confrontations span the nation's history. Some of these clashes have been personal as well as political, as in the case of fellow Virginians Thomas Jefferson and John Marshall. Others have resulted from the efforts of presidents—Abraham Lincoln, Franklin D. Roosevelt, and Harry S. Truman—to use extraordinary powers in extraordinary times. In some of these episodes the president has emerged the victor; in others the Court prevails in the constitutional battle, but in all of them the shape of the system has been altered, as have the powers of the Court and the executive to deal with future crises.

JEFFERSON VERSUS MARSHALL

The long conflict between the administration of President Thomas Jefferson and the Federalist-dominated Supreme Court led by John Marshall had its roots in the politics of Virginia and in the national debate between Democratic-Republicans (hereafter Republicans) and Federalists over the proper stance for the United States during the European wars following the French Revolution.[1] President George Washington's 1793 proclamation of neutrality had effectively terminated the French-American alliance of 1778.[2] Opponents of the policy saw it as evidence of the partiality of the Washington administration toward Great Britain. The Jeffersonians feared that this Federalist stance would enmesh the United States in Britain's imperial enterprises.[3]

This political conflict was heightened further by the actions of the Federalists, during the quasi-war with France (1798–1800), to put the nation on a war footing. During that undeclared maritime conflict, Congress passed the controversial Alien and Sedition Acts, which were intended to silence editors and pamphleteers who

opposed and attacked Federalist president John Adams's administration and the defense measures he supported. During the crisis, some twenty-five persons were arrested for seditious libel under the terms of the Sedition Act.[4] Most of them were Republican editors. Ten were convicted for violations of the act. One response to the Alien and Sedition Acts came in the form of resolutions drafted by Jefferson and James Madison and adopted by the legislatures of Kentucky and Virginia protesting what they perceived to be a dangerous usurpation of power by the central government.[5]

The "Revolution" of 1800

Jefferson saw his defeat of Adams for the presidency in 1800 and the transfer of power from one political group to another as a revolution. The revolution, however, was incomplete, as Federalist judges were firmly in control of the fledgling federal courts. Perhaps the most enduring legacy the Federalists left President Jefferson was the new chief justice of the United States—John Marshall.[6] President Adams had nominated Marshall, then secretary of state, on January 20, 1801, six weeks before the end of his term. The post had been vacant since September 1800, when Oliver Ellsworth resigned.

Adams had first nominated, and the Senate had approved, John Jay, who had been the nation's first chief justice, but he declined the post, grumbling about ill health and the rigors of circuit court duties. Adams also had considered Justice William Cushing for the position, but Cushing was sixty-eight years old and had declined appointment as chief justice in 1796. Justice William Paterson, another promising and younger candidate, was considered but dropped because Alexander Hamilton, the president's rival within Federalist ranks, supported Paterson's candidacy. Moreover, as Cushing was Paterson's senior on the high court, it would appear that Adams was slighting Cushing in appointing Paterson.[7] Marshall's appointment was opposed in the Senate by members who were unhappy that Paterson was not nominated; nevertheless, the Senate confirmed Marshall on January 27, 1801, in the waning days of the Adams administration. Marshall received his commission as chief justice on February 4. He would preside over the Supreme Court for thirty-four years.[8]

Marshall's legal and judicial experience was meager. He had been a successful lawyer in Richmond after only a few months' education at William and Mary College.[9] His mission to France as one of the three U.S. ministers in the abortive XYZ mission had won him a reputation in international law. Marshall had served as a Federalist in the House of Representatives from Virginia's Richmond district, staunchly supporting President Adams's policies before becoming Adams's secretary of state.[10]

Marshall's appointment rankled Jefferson. The two Virginians had been on opposite sides of the political fence since the revolution. Although third cousins, the two men had a mutual antagonism that probably dated to Jefferson's term as governor of Virginia in 1780, when he had been forced to flee the capital by the approach of the British army. Marshall had served in the revolutionary army, and his war experiences undoubtedly bred contempt for Jefferson's failure to stay and face the enemy.[11] One of Marshall's first official acts as chief justice was to administer the presidential oath of office to Jefferson. Jefferson's inaugural speech was conciliatory, but he moved within the year to repeal the newly enacted Judiciary Act of 1801, which the lame duck Federalist Congress had passed as a judicial reform measure.

The Judiciary Act of 1801

The Judiciary Act of 1801 was an admirable piece of legislation, but its passage was ill-timed. The House passed the law on January 20, 1801—the day of Marshall's nomination—without a single Republican vote. The Senate approved it on February 7, and Adams signed the bill on February 13. The law added new circuit judgeships, removed the requirement that Supreme Court justices ride circuit, and reduced the number of justices from six to five by stating that the

next vacancy would not be filled. Adams, also a lame duck, appointed sixteen new circuit court justices to fill the new posts, as well as a number of marshals and justices of the peace, whose posts were also created by the 1801 act. In his last full month in office, Adams appointed 217 individuals to public office, 93 of whom were legal or judicial officers.[12] The Judiciary Act of 1801 was repealed on March 31, 1802, and an act passed in April restored the number of seats on the Supreme Court to six, fixed one annual term for the Court instead of two, and established six circuits, each presided over by a Supreme Court justice.[13]

Marbury v. Madison

In the rush of business at the end of the Adams administration, Secretary of State Marshall failed to see to the delivery of several commissions of appointment. William Marbury, one of Adams's "midnight appointments," as justice of the peace for the District of Columbia, was among those who did not receive their commission, which Adams had signed and Marshall had sealed. Secretary of State James Madison, acting under President Jefferson's orders, refused to deliver the commission at Marbury's request.[14] Marbury then asked the Supreme Court to issue a writ of mandamus ordering Madison to deliver the commission. At its February 1803 session, the Court ruled on Marbury's application for the order. In a historic opinion written by Marshall, the Court held that Marbury had a vested right to the commission (but that the Court was powerless to issue such an order), declared part of the Judiciary Act of 1789 unconstitutional, and lectured Jefferson on the proper performance of his duties, reminding the president that he was not above the law.[15] Marshall's opinion was a bold and politically astute attack on Jefferson and his administration:

> The commission being signed, the subsequent duty of the secretary of state is prescribed by law, and to be guided by the will of the president. He is to affix the seal of the United States to the commission, and is to record it.
>
> This is not a proceeding which may be varied, if the judgment of the executive shall suggest one more eligible; but is a precise course accurately marked

out by law, and is to be strictly pursued. It is the duty of the secretary of state to conform to the law, and in this he is an officer of the United States, bound to obey the laws. He acts, in this respect, . . . under the authority of law and not by the instruction of the president. It is a ministerial act which the law enjoins on a particular officer for a particular purpose.[16]

Marshall protected the Court against the charge that it sought to aggrandize power by finding that the Court lacked jurisdiction to issue the writ. By so doing, the Court for the first time exercised the power to strike down an act of Congress as unconstitutional. That aspect of *Marbury* did not receive as much attention at the time as the Court's lecture to Jefferson.[17] Judicial review had been regarded by many as a necessary adjunct of the constitutional system. The Court had earlier assumed that it had this power.[18] *(See "Marbury v. Madison," pp. 79–83.) Marbury* was as close as the Court and the Jefferson administration came to an institutional collision, but neither Jefferson nor Marshall ceased his efforts to undercut the prestige and power of the other or of the branches the other headed.

Impeachment: A Political Weapon

Jefferson, convinced by *Marbury* that stronger measures were needed to blunt the Court's influence under Marshall, turned to the only way provided by the Constitution to remove judges from office: impeachment for high crimes and misdemeanors. Conviction after impeachment and trial in the Senate required removal from office. The Jeffersonians interpreted "high crimes and misdemeanors" broadly to allow impeachment for political acts and to consider as "crimes" such acts as ethical lapses and irresponsible political statements.

The House impeached New Hampshire district court judge John Pickering in proceedings begun in February 1803. Jefferson had sent a message to the House accompanied by evidence that Pickering was a hopelessly insane drunkard. For the previous three years his behavior on the bench had been irrational and irresponsible. In March 1804 the Senate tried and convicted him, in a 19-7 vote strictly along party lines, and removed him from office. Pickering's impeachment, however, settled

nothing with respect to the nature of impeachments brought against rational judges whose major "crime" was political opposition to Jeffersonian principles. Flawed precedent aside, with Pickering impeached and removed, Republicans went after bigger game.[19]

Republican leaders agreed that Justice Samuel Chase was an excellent target for impeachment.[20] He had campaigned for Adams while on the Supreme Court, tried and convicted a group of rebels of treason in Pennsylvania for their part in opposing a new tax law (1799–1800), made political harangues from the bench to grand juries, and conducted the trial of Republican editor James Thomson Callender under the Sedition Act.[21] Chase left no doubts about his staunch Federalism. In Republican minds he forfeited any claim to judicial impartiality on the bench. Moreover, the time was ripe for a counterattack against the judiciary. Republicans were still seething over the lecture that Marshall had given Jefferson in *Marbury v. Madison*. With John Randolph of Virginia guiding Republican forces, in January 1804 the House appointed a committee to inquire into Chase's conduct. On a strict party-line vote of 73 to 32, the House voted on March 12 to impeach Chase.[22]

The first seven articles of impeachment recounted Chase's "oppressive" conduct in the trials under the Sedition Act. The last article referred to an address by Chase characterized as an inflammatory diatribe designed to excite unrest against the government of the United States. The charges also referenced Chase's outspoken criticism of Republican policies at the state and national levels.[23] Vice President Aaron Burr, fresh from his duel with Alexander Hamilton, presided over the Senate trial that began in February 1805. Chase's attorneys maintained that an impeachable offense must be one indictable under law. It was clear to observers and participants alike that the independence of the federal judiciary was on trial. Removal of Chase would spur further Republican assaults on the bench.[24] The vote in the Senate fell short of the necessary two-thirds majority for each article of impeachment, and Chase remained on the bench.

Chase's impeachment and trial set a precedent of strict construction of the Impeachment Clause and bolstered the judiciary's claim of independence from political tampering. The failure of the Chase impeachment was a source of political embarrassment to Jefferson, so the Jeffersonians thereafter abandoned the idea of removing Federalist judges through impeachment. As a result of the trial, for a time federal judges exhibited greater restraint in their conduct and refrained from political lectures while on the bench.

The Burr Trial

In August 1807 former vice president Burr was tried for treason in a dramatic trial that pitted, once again, Chief Justice Marshall against President Jefferson. Marshall heard the case as judge of the U.S. circuit court for Virginia, but the antagonism between Jefferson and Marshall, and the tenacity with which Jefferson attempted to orchestrate Burr's conviction produced a trial with unmistakable political and personal overtones.[25] Burr had lost his political power base in New York when he refused to step aside and let Jefferson assume the presidency in the disputed election of 1800. Jefferson won the office after a compromise among the electors assured Jefferson enough electoral votes to win. Burr's failure to acknowledge Jefferson as the legitimate winner earned him Jefferson's everlasting animosity.

Burr's attempts to recoup his political fortunes led him into a protracted political struggle with Hamilton that ended with the duel that cost Hamilton his life and Burr all chances of regaining legitimate political power.[26] Burr went west to revive his political fortunes and assembled a small force of men at Blennerhassett Island on the upper Ohio River. The men and equipment moved down the Mississippi River to New Orleans.[27] Burr's plans for the band of adventurers have remained obscure, but rumors circulated that he intended to separate the Southwest from the Union. At first unconcerned, Jefferson in 1806 issued an order for Burr's arrest. Burr fled but was captured and returned to Richmond for trial.[28]

Marshall's rulings as presiding judge thwarted Jefferson's hopes that Burr would be convicted. The chief justice had no affection for Burr, but he refused to permit the court to be stampeded into a conviction simply because Burr was an unpopular and unscrupulous individual.[29] Marshall ruled first on Burr's request to obtain from Jefferson, by subpoena, certain letters Burr claimed he needed to provide an adequate defense.[30] Marshall ruled that the evidence sought was germane to the case and issued a subpoena seeking delivery of the letters to the court in Richmond. Jefferson declined to make an appearance at court or to furnish the documents without certain portions deleted.[31] He offered to provide transcripts of portions of the letters if the material was required.

The case turned on other issues, however, and the subpoena and confrontation over it faded away. The exchanges between Jefferson and Marshall were outwardly polite and solicitous of cooperation, but they masked the inner tension of the two adversaries. The main issue in the case was Marshall's definition of treason. Burr's attorneys maintained that treason consisted of an actual "levying of war" against the United States; they drew a distinction between the act of war and the advising of it.[32] The prosecution relied on a broader definition of treason found in English common law, which viewed all who contemplated treason as engaging in the act itself. They argued that Burr was guilty because he advised assembling an armed force and moving it down river to New Orleans.[33] Marshall ruled that because the prosecution failed to produce two witnesses to the act of treason or to the procurement of men and arms for the expedition, it had not met the burden of proving the charge of treason.[34] Following Marshall's ruling, the jury found "that Aaron Burr is not proved to be guilty under this indictment by any evidence submitted to us. We therefore find him not guilty."[35]

Neither Jefferson nor Marshall "won" the series of confrontations between them. Both men maintained the integrity of their departments. Jefferson managed to chastise the judiciary through the threat of impeachment, and Marshall raised the prestige of the Court and maintained the independence of the judiciary. Antagonism between Marshall and the executive branch subsided when Jefferson retired in 1809. The election of Madison, the appointment of several Republicans to the Court, the changing nature of national issues, and the demise of Federalism reduced the grounds of antagonism between the Court and the president.

JACKSON, THE COURT, AND THE INDIANS

President Andrew Jackson—whose determination to play a strong executive role laid the foundations for the modern concept of presidential power—clashed indirectly with the Supreme Court and claimed for the executive an independent role in constitutional interpretation. In vetoing the bill to charter the Second Bank of the United States in 1832, Jackson denied that the Supreme Court alone was the ultimate arbiter of constitutional questions. Jackson asserted that the president too might exercise an independent judgment separate from the Court and Congress in matters of policy:

> The Congress, the Executive, and the Court must each for itself be guided by its own opinion of the Constitution. Each public officer who takes an oath to support the Constitution swears that he will support it as he understands it, and not as it is understood by others. . . . The opinion of the judges has no more authority over Congress than the opinion of Congress has over the judges, and on that point the President is independent of both. The authority of the Supreme Court must not, therefore, be permitted to control the Congress or the Executive when acting in their legislative capacities, but to have only such influence as the force of their reasoning may deserve.[36]

Jackson's theory had its impractical side. If there was no final decision about the constitutionality of a statute, how would serious controversies be resolved? Jackson was vague in his response and frequently settled matters by sheer force of will, bolstered by his general popularity.[37]

Constitutional conflict between the president and the Court threatened to break into open warfare in the early 1830s, when the Supreme Court steadfastly rejected the efforts of Georgia to assert its jurisdiction over Cherokee Indians living on Indian land within its boundaries. The Cherokee had settled as farmers on the land, adopted a constitution, developed an alphabet, and proclaimed themselves an independent nation, but Georgia, anxious to expel the Native Americans and open their land for settlement, extended state authority over the region in 1829, declared Indian law nullified by state law, and passed measures designed to permit seizure of the Indians' lands.[38]

Asserting its newly claimed sovereignty over the region, the Georgia courts convicted a Cherokee named Corn Tassel of murder.[39] The Supreme Court granted Corn Tassel permission to contest his conviction. The basis for his challenge was that Georgia had no jurisdiction over Indians and their territory. The state ignored the Court's action and executed Corn Tassel on December 24, 1830, before the Court could hear his case.[40] Faced with such defiance, the Court could do nothing to enforce its authority; President Jackson, sympathetic to the state, did nothing. The Cherokee subsequently asked the Supreme Court to restrain Georgia from enforcing its laws over them. Acting as an independent nation, the Cherokee filed their request as an original case before the Court. The Court dismissed the suit, *Cherokee Nation v. Georgia* (1831), ruling that Indian tribes were not foreign nations, but "domestic dependent nations" under the sovereignty and dominion of the United States.[41]

In *Worcester v. Georgia* (1832), however, the Court ruled against Georgia's claim to jurisdiction over the Cherokee.[42] A missionary among the Indians had refused to pay a state license fee required of white persons living in Indian territory. Challenging the fee as unconstitutional state interference in Indian matters, the missionary took his case to the Court, which agreed with him, denying the state power to enforce the fee requirement and ordering him released from prison. The state declared it would resist enforcement of the Court's ruling.[43] President Jackson again refused to act. He is alleged to have said, "Well, John Marshall has made his decision, now let him enforce it." *(See box, Did Jackson Really Say That? p. 340.)*

For a few months, the stalemate held, until South Carolina followed Georgia's precedent and declared that it had the power to nullify—through nonenforcement—the controversial tariff act of 1832.[44] That threat prompted Jackson to issue a vigorous rebuttal,

DID JACKSON REALLY SAY THAT?

Historical research indicates that Andrew Jackson probably never made the remark attributed to him after the crisis between Georgia and the Supreme Court over the Cherokee Indians in 1832.[1] When the Court, led by Chief Justice John Marshall, ruled that Georgia had no jurisdiction over the Cherokees and their lands that lay within the state, Jackson allegedly commented: "Well, John Marshall has made his decision, now let him enforce it." The words reflected Jackson's views, but, like the story of George Washington and the cherry tree, Jackson's remarks probably were invented by folklorists to enhance the reputation of a famous man.

The remark was attributed by American journalist and newspaperman Horace Greeley in 1864 to Jackson's reported conversation with Rep. George N. Briggs of Massachusetts.[2] No writer before Greeley had reported

it. The remark reappeared in William G. Sumner's *Life of Andrew Jackson* (1899) and was reprinted by others. John S. Bassett, Jackson's biographer, wrote in 1910 that the remark was "a popular tradition. It is not sure that the words were actually uttered, but it is certain, from Jackson's view and temperament, that they might have been spoken."[3]

---

1. Joseph C. Burke, "The Cherokee Cases: A Study in Law, Politics and Morality," *Stanford Law Review* 21 (1968–1969): 500–531.

2. Horace Greeley, *American Conflict: A History of the Great Rebellion in the United States of America, 1860–1865,* 2 vols. (1894; reprint Westport, Conn.: Greenwood Press, 1969), 1:106.

3. John S. Bassett, *Life of Andrew Jackson,* 2 vols. in 1 (1931; reprint Hamden, Conn.: Shoe String Press, 1967), 2:688–692.

---

asserting federal authority against a state challenge to the enforcement of federal law.[45] Jackson's strong stand against nullification cooled the conflict between Georgia and the Court. Georgia realized that Jackson could not continue to support its defiance while condemning South Carolina for a similar action. *(See "Repeal and Resistance," pp. 384–385.)*

LINCOLN VERSUS TANEY

Chief Justice Roger B. Taney helped elect Abraham Lincoln to the presidency in 1860. The Supreme Court's decision in the controversial case *Scott v. Sandford* (1857)—for which Taney wrote the lead opinion—split the Democratic Party into northern and southern wings over the issue of slavery.[46] That schism gave Lincoln, a Republican, the victory over the northern Democrat Stephen A. Douglas and two southern candidates, John C. Breckinridge and John Bell. In *Scott* the Court held that Congress lacked the power to ban the expansion of slavery into the territories. Lincoln's opposition to this ruling had brought him to national prominence in 1858, when, running against Douglas for an Illinois Senate seat, Lincoln made public his opposition to the decision in a series of seven

head-to-head debates on slavery.[47] *(See "Slavery in the Territories," pp. 179–185.)* Lincoln promised to do all that he could to have the ruling overturned, and as president, he asserted the chief executive's right to render a solution as equal to that of the Court. In his first inaugural address, Lincoln declared,

> [I]f the policy of the Government upon vital questions affecting the whole people, is to be irrevocably fixed by decisions of the Supreme Court, the instant they are made in ordinary litigation between parties in personal actions, the people will have ceased to be their own rulers, having to that extent practically resigned their government into the hands of that imminent tribunal.[48]

Against this backdrop of confrontation, Taney, a Jacksonian Democrat, and the new Republican president locked horns over Lincoln's suspension of the privilege of the writ of habeas corpus during the Civil War. Their antagonism intensified along with the conflict. Six weeks after the outbreak of the war at Fort Sumter, Taney challenged Lincoln's decision to suspend the privilege of the writ.

Southern sympathizer John Merryman was arrested by Union soldiers in Maryland and charged with aiding Baltimore secessionists. Imprisoned by the military at Fort McHenry, Merryman obtained a writ of habeas corpus challenging his detention. Prison officials refused to comply with the writ, which ordered Merryman's release, citing Lincoln's proclamation suspending the writ when public safety was threatened.[49] Chief Justice Taney, acting as a circuit judge, issued a contempt citation against the fort commander and demanded the appearance of Merryman at circuit court proceedings in Baltimore. The military commander prevented the writ from being served and refused to surrender Merryman. Taney then wrote an opinion holding suspension of the writ unconstitutional.[50] Taney lectured Lincoln on his duty to enforce the law:

> I can see no ground whatever for supposing that the President in any emergency or in any state of things can authorize the suspension of the privilege of the writ of habeas corpus, or arrest a citizen except in aid of the judicial power. He certainly does not faithfully execute the laws if he takes upon himself legislative power by suspending the writ of habeas corpus—and the judicial power, also, by arresting and imprisoning a person without the process of law.[51]

Lincoln responded to the Taney opinion in a July 4, 1861, message to Congress, in which he maintained his theory that wartime emergency measures superseded constitutional niceties.[52] During the next two years, Lincoln, through Secretary of War Edwin M. Stanton, instituted censorship and military arrest and trial and continued to suspend or ignore habeas corpus requirements in the cases of individuals suspected of aiding the Confederate cause.[53] The State Department also directed arrests through an elaborate network of secret servicemen, federal marshals, and military authorities. Hundreds of people were arrested without being told why, because the suspension of habeas corpus enabled authorities to hold them while waiving standard rules of evidence and legal action until the emergency that led to the arrest passed. Military officers simply disregarded judicial orders to release such prisoners. Legal clashes between civil and military authorities were frequent during the war, but the military—backed by the president—held the upper hand.[54]

Lincoln declared that all persons resisting the draft or discouraging military enlistments were subject to court martial. Thousands of citizens suspected of disloyalty were arrested, imprisoned, and then released without trial after the particular emergency had passed.[55] Lincoln elaborated his theory of presidential leadership in an 1863 letter:

> Thoroughly imbued with a reverence for the guaranteed rights of individuals, I was slow to adopt the strong measures which by degrees I have been forced to regard as being within the exceptions of the Constitution and as indispensable to the public safety. . . . I concede that the class of arrests complained of can be constitutional only when in cases of rebellion or invasion the public safety may require them; and I insist that in such cases they are constitutional wherever the public safety does require them, as well as in places in which they may prevent the rebellion extending as in those where it may already be prevailing.[56]

Beneath the legal arguments, the clash between Taney and Lincoln rested on differences of opinion about the importance of preserving the Union. Lincoln believed it paramount. The federal government in such an emergency could exercise powers that required the temporary sacrifice of civil liberties and civil procedures. Taney considered the bloodshed and the extraconstitutional actions necessary to preserve the Union a greater disaster than dissolution.[57] Taney died on October 12, 1864. Two years later, in *Ex parte Milligan,* the Court vindicated his stance in *Merryman* by ruling in *Milligan* that the president's use of military tribunals outside the war zone was unconstitutional.[58] Lincoln appointed his secretary of the Treasury, Salmon P. Chase, to replace Taney as chief justice. In 1870 Chase would write the Court's opinion in the first of the *Legal Tender Cases,* declaring the Lincoln administration's Legal Tender Acts, which authorized the use of paper money during the war, unconstitutional.[59]

THE COURT VERSUS FDR

The stock market crash of 1929 and the ensuing Great Depression were economic crises of proportions unprecedented in U.S. history, but President Herbert Hoover was philosophically unable to view the Depression as anything more than an economic "adjustment period." He continued optimistically to predict that the economy would correct itself. Many business leaders believed Hoover, preaching confidently that prosperity was just around the corner, but the dream of recovery ultimately became a nightmare: unemployment reached 12 million, industrial production toppled to less than half of 1929 levels, and by 1933 the entire banking network was on the verge of collapse.[60] Economic crisis precipitated social crisis, and social discontent found its expression in a major political upheaval.

Hoover did not believe in broad governmental relief or social reform programs. His abiding faith in "rugged individualism" and limited government prevented his espousal of any full-scale economic recovery measures. His constitutional conservatism rejected any suggestion that federal power might be expanded to deal with the crisis. It was not surprising that Hoover was repudiated at the polls in 1932, with Democratic candidate Franklin D. Roosevelt, a former governor of New York, being elected president by an impressive margin.

The Hundred Days

Roosevelt took office in March 1933. Large Democratic majorities controlled both houses of Congress. Roosevelt made clear in his inaugural address his view of the economic crisis as a national emergency in which he would exercise "broad executive power to wage a war against the emergency as great as the power that would be given me if we were in fact invaded by a foreign foe."[61] The new president called a special session of Congress that convened March 9, 1933. In the next hundred days, Congress, led by Roosevelt and his so-called Brain Trust, attacked the Great Depression on all fronts through the New Deal.

The Emergency Banking Act of March 9, 1933, retroactively sanctioned a "bank holiday." Roosevelt had earlier closed all the nation's banks and suspended all gold exports and foreign exchange operations. The bill also called for surrender of all gold and gold certificates to the Treasury to be exchanged for an equal amount of other currency. The purpose of the act was to halt the hoarding of currency and to set the stage for a mild inflationary devaluation of the money supply. Those banking measures, the Gold Reserve Act of 1934, and a congressional resolution of June 5, 1933, took gold out of circulation, reduced the gold content of the dollar, and canceled the "gold clause" in private contracts that stipulated that a fixed amount of a debt be paid in gold.[62]

The most important agricultural relief measure of the New Deal was the Agricultural Adjustment Act (AAA) of May 12, 1933. The purpose of the act was to restore agricultural prices to prewar (1914) levels—reducing farm production by retiring acreage from use. The AAA provided for an agreement between farmers and the federal government that the farmers would plant fewer acres and in return for their goods would receive better prices, bolstered by a government subsidy.[63] The whole program was financed through a tax on processors of each affected commodity. An act of May 18, 1933, created the Tennessee Valley Authority (TVA), a government corporation authorized to construct dams and reservoirs as part of a development project for the Tennessee Valley region. The entire project included flood control, reforestation, and agricultural and industrial projects. TVA also produced fertilizer, explosives, and, eventually, electric power.

New Deal efforts to restore industrial production and reduce unemployment operated on a theory of limited industrial self-government. The program attempted to bring about cooperation between large and small manufacturing concerns and their employees. The National Industrial Recovery Act (NIRA) of June 16, 1933, established "codes of fair competition" for wages, prices, and trade practices. The codes, drafted by representatives of business and trade groups, were submitted for approval to the president, who was empowered to prescribe the codes. Once approved, the codes became the standard of commercial practice in a particular industry, with violations punishable as violations of the Federal Trade Commission Act. In addition, the NIRA stipulated that labor had the right to organize workers for collective bargaining.[64]

Roosevelt's relief and recovery program had its constitutional basis in emergency executive powers and the power of Congress to provide for the general welfare and to regulate interstate commerce. It was the most far-reaching assertion to date of national leadership. The need for immediate action eliminated the usual procedures of lengthy debate and deliberation. Roosevelt's Brain Trust hammered out the legislation in conference with the president and representatives of affected interest groups. Once drafted, the bills were presented to Congress as "must" legislation, and Congress generally responded with alacrity.

The New Deal and Old Court

The extraordinary exercise of legislative and executive power reflected and authorized by New Deal legislation was certain to be tested in the Supreme Court. Several of the major cases that came to the Court during the next three years were, in fact, test cases, brought by the administration itself. The Supreme Court of 1933, however, was not a body readily receptive to revolutionary uses of federal power. Six of the justices had been on the bench since the pre-Depression 1920s or earlier. Four of them were staunch conservatives known collectively as the Four Horsemen: William Howard Taft nominee Willis Van Devanter; Woodrow Wilson's choice, James C. McReynolds; and two Warren Harding nominees, George Sutherland and Pierce Butler.

Two justices—Louis D. Brandeis and Harlan Fiske Stone—had been appointed by Wilson and Calvin Coolidge, respectively, and tended to take more liberal views on questions of federal power. The three newest members of the Court were all Hoover nominees—Chief Justice Charles Evans Hughes and Justices Benjamin N. Cardozo and Owen J. Roberts. Hughes, a former associate justice, governor of New York, presidential nominee, and secretary of state, was considered a liberal earlier in his career, but he acquired a more conservative reputation as his fame and fortune increased. He succeeded William Howard Taft as chief justice in 1930. Cardozo, a liberal and well-regarded legal scholar and judge, had been appointed by Hoover in 1932. Roberts, a successful Republican attorney

from Pennsylvania, had been named to the Court in 1930. Hoover, noting Roberts's progressive reputation, considered him a liberal appointment.[65]

In 1934 the Court seemed to hint that it would take a favorable attitude toward the "emergency" exercise of extraordinary power in the New Deal statutes. In January of that year, the Court upheld against constitutional challenge a state law that gave homeowners a two-year extension before foreclosure.[66] Chief Justice Hughes explained that although emergencies did not create power, they did empower government to act in ways that might be considered unconstitutional in normal circumstances. The vote in the case was 5-4, with Sutherland, Van Devanter, McReynolds, and Butler dissenting. Two months later, by an identical vote, the Court upheld a state law creating a board empowered to fix minimum and maximum prices for milk.[67] In the majority opinion, Roberts wrote that the states possessed the power to decide and adopt whatever reasonable economic policy toward business promoted the public welfare. The hopes raised by these rulings were shattered by decisions announced in the next two Court terms.

Hot Oil and Black Monday

Between January 1935 and June 1936 the Supreme Court ruled against the administration in eight out of ten major cases involving New Deal statutes. The Court upheld only the emergency monetary legislation of 1933 and the creation of the Tennessee Valley Authority.[68] The first blow came in *Panama Refining Co. v. Ryan* (1935), the so-called hot oil case, in which the Court held unconstitutional the portion of the NIRA that provided for a code to govern the production of oil and petroleum products. With only Cardozo dissenting, the Court ruled that the contested portion unlawfully delegated legislative power to the president.[69]

Four months later, the Railroad Retirement Act was struck down in *Railroad Retirement Board v. Alton* (1935). The Court ruled that Congress had exceeded the scope of its power to regulate interstate commerce when it approved the creation of an industry-wide pension system. The vote was 5-4; Roberts sided with the conservatives. Chief Justice Hughes, dissenting with Brandeis, Cardozo, and Stone, scolded the majority for placing such "an unwarranted limitation upon the commerce clause of the Constitution."[70]

The most devastating single day of this period, however, came on "Black Monday," May 27, 1935. In unanimous decisions the Court overruled the heart of President Roosevelt's concept of presidential power. The Court struck down a federal farm mortgage relief act, finding it unfair to creditors.[71] In *A. L. A. Schechter Poultry Corp. v. United States* it held the main portion of the NIRA unconstitutional.[72] It ruled in *Humphrey's Executor v. United States* that the president lacked any inherent power to remove members of the Federal Trade Commission from their posts.[73] *(See "The Federal Trade Commissioner," pp. 302–303.)*

The most crushing was the ruling in *Schechter.* Rejection of that recovery plan threatened to nullify the entire New Deal program. The NIRA had encouraged the creation of industry-wide, presidentially approved codes of competition that were eventually adopted to govern almost every service trade and industry. Its critics saw the NIRA as government interference in matters that should be left to private enterprise. Even before the Court heard arguments in *Schechter,* difficulties with implementing the act had convinced the administration that a major overhaul of the program was needed.[74] Despite its shortcomings, however, the NIRA had provided needed action in time of crisis. It had worked psychologically to restore confidence among the American people—in themselves and in the economy—even though by 1935 there was also clear evidence that the codes were sometimes used by businesses to promote their interests at the expense of the public.

The Schechter brothers of Brooklyn had been convicted of violating the fair trade and the labor provisions of the poultry industry's code. *Schechter* was chosen as a test case by the administration although it readily acknowledged that it was not the best vehicle for ascertaining the validity of the NIRA program.[75] When the Supreme Court ruled on the matter, it found unanimously that the NIRA was an unconstitutional delegation of legislative power to the president,

allowing him to approve industry codes, which then had the force of law. Furthermore, wrote Chief Justice Hughes, allowing trade and industry groups to make the codes, as had been the case here, amounted to delegation of the legislative authority to private citizens.[76] Roosevelt assessed the implications of the Black Monday decisions in a press conference on May 31:

> Is the United States going to decide . . . that their Federal Government shall in the future have no right under any implied or any court-approved power to enter into a solution of a national economic problem, but that national economic problems must be decided only by the States? . . . We thought we were solving it, and now it has been thrown right straight in our faces. We have been relegated to the horse-and-buggy definition of interstate commerce.[77]

States' Rights Rulings

The year 1936 began with another blow to the New Deal. On January 6, the Court struck down the Agricultural Adjustment Act as an unconstitutional invasion of states' rights. The Court divided 6-3 on the question, and the divisions were bitter.[78] Justice Roberts and Chief Justice Hughes voted with the conservatives; Justices Stone, Brandeis, and Cardozo dissented. Writing for the majority in *United States v. Butler* (1936), Roberts set out the view that agriculture was a matter reserved to state, not federal, regulation. Therefore the AAA program was an improper use of congressional authority to regulate agriculture. The processing tax it imposed was a penalty to force compliance with the AAA acreage reduction program—an impermissible objective and an impermissible use of the taxing power.

In May the Court struck again, this time in *Carter v. Carter Coal Co.* (1936). The Bituminous Coal Conservation Act was held an unconstitutional invasion of states' rights. The law, also called the Guffey Act, set up a commission to adopt codes to regulate production in various regions and levied a tax on coal that was partially refunded to operators abiding by the code. It also guaranteed collective bargaining rights in the industry. According to the Court, mining, like agriculture, was a matter for states to regulate. The tax in this case, as in *Butler,* was a means to an impermissible end and therefore must not stand. Congress had overreached its proper power.[79]

A week later, the Court struck down the Municipal Bankruptcy Act, again citing an invasion of states' rights. The vote in *Ashton v. Cameron County District* (1936) was 5-4. Hughes, Cardozo, Brandeis, and Stone dissented. Writing for the majority, Justice McReynolds held that the law permitting subdivisions of the states to file for bankruptcy to readjust their debt obligations was an impermissible extension of federal power and therefore unconstitutional.[80] The dissenters responded that the voluntary municipal bankruptcy petitions to which the state consented were not an invasion of state sovereignty.[81]

The Roosevelt recovery and reform programs launched in the first hundred days extended federal authority over matters left previously to state authority. The shift in the balance between state and federal power seemed to many to threaten the structure of the Union. Such critics supported the Court's strict construction and dual federalism doctrines to counterbalance the New Deal's challenge to the traditional arrangements of power.

Counterattack

If the justices of the Supreme Court read the election results in November 1936, they received a clear message that Roosevelt had overwhelming popular support in his attempt to combat the Depression and its effects. In the 1936 presidential election a moderate economic recovery blended with a sense of pragmatic purpose, Roosevelt's personal charm, and his expressed concern for the "little man" defeated the mildly reform-minded Alfred E. Landon, the Republican standard-bearer. Landon's only issue was Roosevelt; even the Republicans had to admit the necessity of many New Deal reforms.[82] Landon carried Maine and Vermont. Roosevelt carried all the other states.

The Court's opposition to a program and a president with such an overwhelming mandate began to produce a public view of the Court as an obstacle to reform. Members of Congress recommended that

Justices James C. McReynolds, Willis Van Devanter, George Sutherland, and Pierce Butler were nicknamed the "Four Horsemen," a double allusion to the Four Horsemen of the Apocalypse and Notre Dame's defensive team, because of their persistent opposition to Franklin D. Roosevelt's New Deal legislation. This 1937 cartoon presents one view of Roosevelt's attempt to weaken the conservative bloc's power by trying to persuade Congress to allow him to appoint up to six new justices to the Supreme Court.

Congress curtail the Court's jurisdiction. Sen. Joseph O'Mahoney, D-Wyo., proposed that a two-thirds majority vote be required for the Court to declare an act of Congress unconstitutional. Sen. Burton K. Wheeler, D-Mont., proposed a constitutional amendment to permit Congress to override a Court decision by a two-thirds vote of both houses.[83] The thrust of the counterattack came, however, from Roosevelt, who in his second inaugural speech urged all agencies of the government to cooperate in advancing the common good.[84]

The Plan

On February 5, 1937, Roosevelt sent Congress a message proposing a judicial "reorganization." The measure would increase the number of Supreme Court justices to as many as fifteen, creating one new seat for each justice who, upon reaching the age of seventy, declined to retire.[85] In other words, for every justice age seventy or above, the president could appoint another one, up to a maximum of six. The measure also called for other changes: the addition of a total of fifty new judges to the federal courts; a rule that appeals on constitutional matters move directly to the Supreme Court; a requirement that government attorneys be heard before any court granted an injunction against enforcement of an act of Congress in cases where the act's constitutional status was questioned; and assignment of district judges to congested areas to relieve the backlog and expedite business.[86]

Roosevelt presented the plan as a bill to relieve the justices' workload. In his message he explained that the Court's work was "handicapped by insufficient personnel" and by the presence of old judges unable to perform their duties. As Roosevelt put it, "little by little, new facts became blurred through old glasses fitted, as it were, for the needs of another generation."[87] It was not a characteristic Roosevelt message. It lacked simplicity and clarity. The proposals were too technical and too confusing for easy public comprehension, and the president's purpose was only slightly concealed. It was a "Court-packing" scheme to get liberal, Roosevelt-appointed justices on the bench to reverse its anti–New Deal stance.

Public Reaction

Roosevelt miscalculated public reaction to such a proposal. He had not prepared the public or obtained the advice of Senate leaders before introducing the measure.[88] The message, and the remedy suggested, reflected the president's sense of desperate frustration with the Court's performance. With a number of important measures pending before the Court, the president felt compelled to make certain the justices would not further obstruct the New Deal. As Robert Jackson later wrote, "The Court seemed to have declared the mortality table unconstitutional and a nation was waiting for the President to move."[89]

The plan touched off a widespread and bitter debate in Congress and in the nation. Harold Ickes, Roosevelt's secretary of the interior, noted that no other single measure "has caused the spilling of so much

printer's ink or led to so many fervent discussions. The President has a first class fight on his hands. Practically all of the newspapers are against him. But the worst of it is that some of the progressives in Congress and outside are lining up with the reactionaries."[90] At a Democratic victory dinner March 4, 1937, Roosevelt assailed the Court for rendering the nation powerless to deal with the problems of economic recovery.[91] In a radio "fireside chat" broadcast a few days later, Roosevelt told the American people that the Court had

> cast doubts on the ability of the elected Congress to protect us against catastrophe by meeting squarely our modern social and economic conditions. . . . This plan will save our National Constitution from hardening of the judicial arteries.[92]

But the idea of tampering with the Supreme Court met vigorous public opposition. The public still regarded the nine-member Court as the guardian of the Constitution, properly aloof from politics. The proposal to increase the Court's membership was criticized as perverting the Constitution and destroying judicial integrity and independence.[93] The Court-packing plan split the Democrats in Congress. By early March, Senator Wheeler, a New Dealer, was leading the fight against the bill, whose supporters in the Senate were led by Carter Glass, D-Va., Joseph Robinson, D-Ark., and Edward Burk, D-Neb.[94] The Republican minority, content to let Democrats fight among themselves over the merits of the plan, remained in the background.

During hearings on the bill by the Senate Judiciary Committee, Senator Wheeler made public a letter from Chief Justice Hughes that denied every assertion the president had made with respect to the Court's workload and performance. An increase in the number of justices, wrote Hughes, would actually delay the Court's work by prolonging deliberation on each case. Justice Brandeis, convinced that Roosevelt's plan threatened the constitutional separation of powers, added his signature to the letter. Hughes had told Wheeler that in the interest of saving time he had not obtained the signatures of the other justices to the letter. Hughes's remark left Wheeler with the impression that the letter reflected the unanimous opinion of the Court. Later research revealed, however, that Justice Stone would not have supported Hughes or signed the letter.[95] Publication of the Hughes-Brandeis letter damaged the reorganization plan's chances for passage.

A Court Reversal

The justices dealt the death blow to the Court-packing plan with a series of decisions announced between late March and late May 1937 upholding New Deal measures. On March 29, by a 5-4 vote in *West Coast Hotel Co. v. Parrish,* the Court upheld Washington State's minimum wage law for women, which was nearly identical to another state law struck down ten months earlier, also by a 5-4 vote.[96] The same day, the Court unanimously upheld a revised farm mortgage moratorium act that had been passed by Congress after its predecessor was unanimously voided by the justices in 1935.[97] On April 12, again by a 5-4 vote, the Court upheld the National Labor Relations Act.[98] And on May 24, by votes of 5 to 4 and 7 to 2, the Court upheld the unemployment compensation and the old-age benefits of the Social Security Act.[99] In each 5-4 decision, Justice Roberts—now in favor of New Deal statutes—cast the deciding vote, abandoning the four conservatives with whom he had voted in previous terms to join Chief Justice Hughes and the three more liberal justices.

Justice Roberts's "switch in time" was long assumed to be a direct response to the Court-packing threat, but it had actually occurred before Roosevelt presented his plan. The first case indicating Roberts's shift to the left was *West Coast Hotel Co. v. Parrish.* When the Court in June 1936 struck down New York State's minimum wage law—citing a 1923 precedent— Roberts voted with the conservatives to form the five-man majority against the law. They found it an unconstitutional infringement on the freedom of contract.[100] In December 1936 *West Coast Hotel Co. v. Parrish* was argued before the Court.[101] On December 19 the justices voted in conference on that case. Justice Harlan Fiske Stone was absent. The Court divided 4-4, with Roberts this time voting to uphold the law. The justices decided to await Stone's return and his vote. On February 6, the day after Roosevelt sent his judicial

reorganization message to Congress, Stone voted, as he had done in the New York case, to uphold the minimum wage law. The decision, however, was not announced until March 29, after the Court-packing battle was under way. That Roberts's switch preceded the Court-packing threat publicly emerged later, after Felix Frankfurter obtained from Roberts a memorandum outlining these events.[102]

Other developments also spelled defeat for the plan. The Supreme Court Retirement Act, which Roosevelt signed in March 1937, permitted justices to retire rather than resign at age seventy and have pensions and other benefits. Justice Willis Van Devanter, a New Deal foe, announced on May 18 that he would retire at the end of the term, giving Roosevelt his first opportunity to appoint someone to the Court. Sen. "Joe" Robinson, the majority leader in the Senate floor fight on behalf of the Roosevelt plan, died of a heart attack on July 14. The Senate recommitted the Court-packing bill to the Judiciary Committee on July 22.[103] The administration later accepted a watered-down reorganization measure that reformed lower court procedure but included no provision for additional justices on the Supreme Court. Roosevelt signed the bill on August 26.[104] Roosevelt's victory was not without its costs. His proposal and the battle that ensued opened a breach in Democratic Party ranks that took years to close. After 1938 a conservative congressional coalition composed of southern Democrats and Republicans blocked New Deal measures with repeated regularity.[105]

Roosevelt made four appointments to the Court between 1937 and 1940. Sen. Hugo L. Black replaced Van Devanter in 1937. Stanley F. Reed replaced George Sutherland in 1938. Roosevelt's longtime friend Felix Frankfurter took Cardozo's seat in 1939, and Justice William O. Douglas was appointed when Brandeis retired in 1939. After 1937 the Supreme Court launched a revolution of its own, repudiating the dual federalism concept that federal power was limited by states' rights. In cases involving labor relations, manufacturing, agriculture, and the spending power, the Court espoused a broad concept of the federal power. The Court gradually repudiated the earlier limits it had imposed on the commerce power. In *United States v. Darby* (1941) the

Court approved federal wage and hour standards prescribed in the Fair Labor Standards Act. In *Mulford v. Smith* (1939) it had upheld the second Agricultural Adjustment Act, and soon thereafter the limitation on federal spending imposed in *Butler* also was swept away.[106] *(See "Wages and Hours," pp. 126–128; see also details of Steward Machine Co. v. Davis and Helvering v. Davis, p. 156.)*

TRUMAN VERSUS THE COURT

Late in his second term, President Harry S. Truman collided with the Supreme Court over his decision to seize and operate the nation's steel mills to avoid a strike that would disrupt production and, Truman felt, jeopardize the U.S. war effort in Korea. The result was a ruling in which the Court declared a halt to the steady expansion of "emergency" executive power that had begun in the days of World War I and accelerated during World War II. The 6-3 decision was announced in June 1953. Of the four justices named to the Court by Truman, two voted to uphold the president's action and two opposed it.

The Steel Seizure Order

The United Steel Workers of America announced an industry-wide strike to begin April 9, 1952. Bargaining sessions to avert the strike through negotiation, encouraged by the efforts of the Wage Stabilization Board (WSB), ended in failure when the plant operators rejected a WSB wage-settlement formula.[107] On April 8 Truman issued an executive order to Secretary of Commerce Charles Sawyer directing him to seize and operate the nation's steel mills. The order cited the state of national emergency proclaimed December 16, 1950—after the Chinese invasion of Korea—and the necessity to maintain uninterrupted steel production during the war. Truman explained his action as a proper exercise of the general executive authority granted by Article II, as well as his more specific power as commander in chief.[108]

Truman's advisers calculated that a halt in steel production would endanger the lives of soldiers on the battlefield by reducing supplies of guns and ammunition.

One cartoonist's view of the Court's decision in *Youngstown Sheet and Tube Co. v. Sawyer* (1952).

They forecast that shortages in steel would limit aircraft production, power plant construction, shipbuilding, and atomic weapons research. The steel companies attacked the order as unconstitutional and went to court, obtaining an injunction in the District of Columbia restraining Sawyer from carrying out the seizure order.[109] The court of appeals then stayed the district court injunction, and the case moved to the Supreme Court for consideration of the constitutional challenge to the president's seizure power.

Youngstown Sheet and Tube Co. v. Sawyer

The case of *Youngstown Sheet and Tube Co. v. Sawyer* was argued May 12 and 13, 1952. Three weeks later, on June 2, the Court ruled 6-3 against Truman. In an opinion written by Justice Black, the majority held that Truman's seizure of the steel mills was an unconstitutional exercise of power. The Court rejected the theory of executive prerogative implicit in the seizure order. The president lacked statutory authority for such an action, Black wrote; neither the commander in chief power nor any inherent executive prerogative provided authority for it. The executive order was invalid, the

Court held, because it attempted to make law although the Constitution limited the president "to the recommending of laws he thinks wise and the vetoing of laws he thinks bad." Black relied on the legislative history of the 1947 Labor-Management Relations (Taft-Hartley) Act, in which Congress had decided against authorizing the president to seize strikebound industrial plants. *(See "The Steel Seizure Case," pp. 274–275.)*

All of the five other members of the majority wrote concurring opinions. Justices Harold H. Burton and Frankfurter thought the president should have invoked the Taft-Hartley Act provisions for a cooling-off period. They declared that in light of Congress's rejection of such a seizure authority in that act, Truman's order contradicted "the clear will of Congress."[110] Justice Tom C. Clark agreed that the president had, in this instance, violated procedures set out by Congress for the settlement of strikes.[111] Justice Douglas wrote that Court sanction of Truman's seizure would have expanded Article II of the Constitution to "suit the political conveniences of the present emergency."[112]

Chief Justice Fred M. Vinson, joined by Justices Reed and Sherman Minton, dissented, emphasizing the nature of the national emergency and the discretionary power of the president in times of crisis. Vinson found the president's action supportive of congressional intention in that the seizure was for the purpose of ensuring steel for weapons to conduct a congressionally supported war in Korea. Vinson's dissent was a pragmatic argument that accepted the view of an expanded executive prerogative as a fact of constitutional life in the twentieth century.[113] Truman later wrote,

> [T]he Supreme Court's decision . . . was a deep disappointment to me. I think Chief Justice Vinson's dissenting opinion hit the nail right on the head, and I am sure that someday his view will come to be recognized as the correct one.[114]

The administration decided not to attempt a settlement. The following week Truman sought legislative authorization for the seizure. Congress refused. The strike lasted fifty-three days, ending on July 24; 600,000 steel workers and 25,000 iron-ore workers were idle for seven weeks. Losses in wages and production were estimated at \$2 billion. Truman claimed that the strike and the Court's refusal to sanction his handling of it occasioned military shortages in certain types of ammunition in the summer and fall of 1952.[115] According to Truman,:

> It is not very realistic for the justices to say that comprehensive powers shall be available to the President only when a war has been declared or when the country has been invaded. We live in an age when hostilities begin without polite exchanges of diplomatic notes. There are no longer sharp distinctions between combatants and noncombatants. . . . Nor can we separate the economic facts from the problems of defense and security. . . . The President, who is Commander-in-Chief and who represents the interests of all the people, must [be] able to act at all times to meet any sudden threat to the nation's security. A wise President will always work with Congress, but when Congress fails to act or is unable to act in a crisis, the President, under the Constitution, must use his powers to safeguard the nation.[116]

NIXON, WATERGATE, AND THE COURT

Richard Nixon campaigned for the presidency in 1968 as an anti-Court candidate, promising that, if elected, he would by his appointments change the Court from one that "coddled" criminals to one that was more responsive to the problems and needs of law enforcement officers. Nixon was able in his first term to place four new members on the Court: Chief Justice Warren E. Burger and Justices Harry A. Blackmun, Lewis F. Powell Jr., and William H. Rehnquist, all chosen for their conservative views on questions of law and order. In the most ironic of circumstances, however, Nixon in 1974 found himself before the Court arguing that he had the right to withhold evidence sought by a prosecutor for use in a criminal trial. The Court responded in the negative. After an initial silence, Nixon accepted the Court's decision. Two weeks later—realizing the significance of that evidence for his own reputation and his fate in an ongoing impeachment inquiry—Nixon resigned the presidency.

Nixon's resignation mooted the impeachment proceedings, which had begun as a result of Nixon's

JUSTICES FROM THE CABINET

Thirty-three justices of the Supreme Court—including ten chief justices—served as executive branch officials either before or after their appointment to the Court. Eighteen held cabinet-level posts—nine of them were attorneys general—and another eight served in other posts in the Justice Department.

Four men—Roger B. Taney, Levi Woodbury, William H. Moody, and William Howard Taft—held more than one cabinet post. Taft held more high executive branch posts than any other justice. He is also the only man to serve as president and as chief justice of the United States.

The following table lists the justices, the major executive branch positions they held, and their years of service.

Justice	Position	Court Service
John Jay*	Secretary for foreign affairs under the Articles of Confederation, 1784–1789; U.S. diplomat, 1794–1795	1789–1795
John Marshall*	Envoy to France, 1797–1798; secretary of state, 1818–1823	1801–1835
Smith Thompson	Secretary of the Navy, 1818–1823	1823–1843
Gabriel Duvall	Comptroller of the Treasury, 1802–1811	1812–1835
John McLean	Postmaster general, 1823–1829	1829–1861
Roger B. Taney*	Attorney general, 1831–1833; secretary of the Treasury, 1833–1834	1836–1864
Levi Woodbury	Secretary of the Navy, 1831–1834; secretary of the Treasury, 1834–1841	1845–1851
Nathan Clifford	Attorney general, 1846–1848	1858–1881
Salmon P. Chase*	Secretary of the Treasury, 1861–1864	1864–1873
Lucius Q. C. Lamar	Secretary of the interior, 1885–1888	1888–1893
Joseph McKenna	Attorney general, 1897–1898	1898–1925
William H. Moody	Secretary of the Navy, 1902–1904; attorney general, 1904–1906	1906–1910
Charles E. Hughes*	Secretary of state, 1921–1925	1910–1926; 1930–1941
Willis Van Devanter	Counsel, Interior Department, 1897–1903	1910–1937
James McReynolds	Attorney general, 1913–1914	1914–1941

response to the investigation of the Watergate scandal. The burglary of Democratic National Committee's headquarters in the Washington, D.C., Watergate complex in mid-1972 and the attempted cover-up of White House involvement in the affair were the immediate sources of Nixon's troubles. They were not, however, the only matters that set him on a collision course with the Supreme Court.[117] During his years in office, Nixon also argued before the Court for broad executive prerogative to act in the interests of national security, to refuse to spend congressionally provided funds, and to withhold information. In five of six cases, the Court ruled against him.

Pentagon Papers

In June 1971 the *New York Times* and the *Washington Post* began publication of articles based on a top-secret Defense Department analysis of the U.S. role in the war in Southeast Asia. Both newspapers had obtained copies of the classified documents. The Nixon administration, criticized for its conduct of the war, attempted to block publication of the documents. Administration attorneys argued that publication would result in a diplomatic imbroglio and would damage the nation's security.[118] Attorney General John N. Mitchell first asked the newspapers to halt publication. Both refused. Mitchell then obtained an injunction from a federal

William H. Taft*	U.S. solicitor general, 1890–1892; secretary of war, 1904–1908; president, 1908–1912	1921–1930
Edward T. Sanford	Assistant attorney general, 1907–1908	1923–1930
Harlan F. Stone*	Attorney general, 1924–1925	1925–1946
Owen J. Roberts	Prosecuting attorney, Teapot Dome scandal, 1924	1930–1945
Stanley Reed	Solicitor general, 1935–1938	1938–1957
William O. Douglas	Chairman, Securities and Exchange Commission, 1937–1939	1939–1975
Frank Murphy	Attorney general, 1938–1940	1940–1949
James F. Byrnes	Secretary of state, 1945–1947	1941–1942
Robert H. Jackson	Solicitor general, 1938–1939; attorney general, 1940–1941	1941–1954
Fred M. Vinson*	Secretary of the Treasury, 1945–1946	1946–1953
Tom C. Clark	Attorney general, 1945–1949	1949–1967
Byron R. White	Deputy attorney general, 1961–1962	1962–1993
Arthur J. Goldberg	Secretary of labor, 1961–1962	1962–1963
Abe Fortas	Under secretary of the interior, 1942–1946	1965–1969
Thurgood Marshall	Solicitor general, 1964–1967	1967–1991
Warren E. Burger*	Assistant attorney general, 1953–1955	1969–1986
William H. Rehnquist*	Assistant attorney general, 1969–1971	1971–
Clarence Thomas	Assistant secretary of education, 1981–1982; chairman, Equal Employment Opportunity Commission, 1982–1990	1991–

* Denotes chief justice.

SOURCES: Leon Friedman, Fred L. Israel, eds., *The Justices of the United States Supreme Court 1789–1969, Their Lives and Major Opinions*, 5 vols. (New York and London: Chelsea House, 1969, 1978); William F. Swindler, *Court and Constitution in the Twentieth Century*, 2 vols. (Indianapolis and New York: Bobbs-Merrill, 1969, 1970); *American Political Leaders, 1789–2005* (Washington, D.C.: CQ Press, 2005).

court in New York ordering the *Times* to halt publication of the articles, but a federal court in the District of Columbia refused to grant a similar order against the *Post*. Both cases were appealed to the Supreme Court.

The Nixon administration argued that national security interests justified such "prior restraint" of publication; the *Times* and the *Post* responded that such a curb on the freedom of the press violated the First Amendment. On June 30, 1971, the Court ruled 6-3 against the administration. The majority held that the government had failed to meet the heavy burden of justifying prior restraint based on the claim that publication would damage national security. The Court allowed publication of the articles to continue. The Court did not, however, deny that there might be circumstances in which such a restraint might be justified.[119]

Wiretapping

A year later, the Nixon administration again lost a national security argument in the Court. Only since 1968 had Congress provided statutory authority for the use of wiretaps or electronic surveillance by law enforcement officers. To minimize the invasion of individual rights that could result, Congress required that every wiretap or electronic surveillance be approved by a federal judge. This provision was part of the Omnibus Crime Control and Safe Streets Act of 1968.[120]

The Nixon administration claimed, however, that the court approval and warrant requirement did not apply to its use of wiretaps to keep track of the activities of domestic groups suspected of subversive activities. These wiretaps were legal, administration lawyers argued, as "a reasonable exercise of the President's power to protect the national security."[121] By a 6-2 vote the Supreme Court in 1972 rejected that claim of inherent power. In domestic security matters, wrote Justice Powell, the "convergence of First and Fourth Amendment values" requires strict observance of constitutional safeguards. "[U]nreviewed executive discretion," he warned, "may yield too readily to pressure to obtain incriminating evidence and overlook potential invasions of privacy and protected speech."[122]

Impoundment

When Congress earmarked funds for programs that Nixon wished to curtail, the president simply refused to spend the money. This assertion of the power to impound funds gave Nixon the equivalent of a line item veto over congressional appropriations bills, a seemingly unchallengeable mechanism to block any program involving federal expenditures.

Nixon was not the first chief executive to try to use this tool. Presidents Thomas Jefferson, Ulysses S. Grant, and Franklin D. Roosevelt had impounded funds, and the procedure had been used as an instrument of fiscal policy by Presidents Truman, Dwight Eisenhower, and John F. Kennedy.[123] Legislative authority for impoundment, however, could be derived from the language of the authorizing statute in most previous impoundment incidents. Furthermore, if the money impounded was for defense projects, the president could also argue that, as commander in chief, he had authority to withhold spending for such programs. Nixon used impoundment more frequently than his predecessors. Between 1969 and 1973 he impounded more than $15 billion in funds intended for more than one hundred programs. Those concerns affected included pollution control, housing, public education,

and other social programs. In January 1973 Nixon asserted the president's "constitutional right . . . to impound funds and that is, not to spend money, when the spending of money would mean either increasing prices or increasing taxes for all the people, that right is absolutely clear."[124]

On February 19, 1975, six months after Nixon had left office, the Court held unanimously that Nixon had exceeded his authority when he refused to allocate billions of dollars of water pollution funds to the states as required by the Water Pollution Control Act of 1972. The wording of the 1972 act, wrote Justice Byron R. White, left the president no power to withhold the funds. The decision did not set limits for the president's impoundment power generally, but its implication was that Nixon's claim of such a power was a shaky one.[125]

Watergate and the White House Tapes

The most dramatic of confrontations between the courts and chief executive were between the Supreme Court and Nixon in July 1974. The decision cost Nixon his office. In July 1973 a witness before the Senate

This subpoena *duces tecum*—a writ to produce documents or other evidence—was issued by the first Watergate special prosecutor on July 23, 1973. It ordered President Richard Nixon or his subordinates to appear before the grand jury and to bring tapes relevant to the Watergate investigation.

Select Committee on Presidential Campaign Activities revealed that many of President Nixon's conversations with his staff had been secretly recorded on tape. At the time of the revelation, the Watergate affair and alleged White House involvement in it were under investigation by the select committee, a federal grand jury, and a Watergate special prosecution team led by Archibald Cox. The disclosure of the taping system set off a year-long battle for certain White House tapes. The tug-of-war eventually brought Nixon's lawyers to the Supreme Court, defending his right to withhold the tapes as evidence.

Special prosecutor Cox quickly obtained a subpoena for certain tapes that he wished to present as evidence to the grand jury. Nixon refused to comply, setting off a legal battle that culminated in the "Saturday Night Massacre" of late October 1973. The "massacre," resulting from Cox's refusal to stop his efforts to obtain the tapes, included Cox's firing by Nixon and the resignations of Attorney General Elliot Richardson and his deputy, William Ruckelshaus, both of whom chose to resign rather than follow Nixon's order to fire Cox. Solicitor General Robert Bork eventually fired Cox.

The public outcry over Nixon's actions forced him to turn over some of the subpoenaed tapes and led to the initiation of a House impeachment inquiry into the president's conduct.[126] In March 1974, as the House Judiciary Committee's impeachment investigation was getting under way, former attorney general John N. Mitchell, former presidential assistants John D. Ehrlichman and H. R. (Bob) Haldeman, and four other former Nixon aides were indicted for conspiracy to defraud the United States and to obstruct justice. The charges related to their efforts to cover up White House involvement in the Watergate affair. In mid-April the new special prosecutor, Leon Jaworski, obtained a subpoena ordering Nixon to hand over additional taped conversations for use as evidence in the trial of Mitchell and the others. Nixon's lawyers moved to quash that subpoena. Judge John J. Sirica of the U.S. District Court for the District of Columbia refused and denied the motion. Late in the Supreme Court term, the case

moved onto its docket, and the Court decided to review the matter promptly.[127]

In an extraordinary summer session, the cases of *United States v. Nixon, Nixon v. United States* were argued on July 8, 1974. *(See details of the cases, pp. 330–332.)* The Court ruled unanimously on July 24 to reject Nixon's claim of an absolute executive privilege to withhold the evidence sought by the special prosecutor. Chief Justice Burger, Nixon's choice to head the Court, wrote the opinion. Justice Rehnquist, who had served in the Justice Department under Mitchell before moving to the Court, did not participate in the case. Nixon, the Court said, must surrender the tapes. That evening the House Judiciary Committee began nationally televised debates on the charges against Nixon. Within the week, it had approved three articles of impeachment. Two weeks later, on August 9, Nixon resigned.[128]

Presidential Records

Resignation did not end Nixon's battles before the Supreme Court. Soon thereafter, he and the head of the General Services Administration reached an agreement concerning control of and access to the tapes and papers of the Nixon administration. As had been the case with other former presidents, Nixon was to have control of such materials. Congress, however, sensitive to the unusual circumstances surrounding Nixon's departure from office, passed a law—the Presidential Recordings and Materials Preservation Act—placing the materials in federal custody.[129] Nixon immediately went to court, challenging the law as violating a long list of rights and privileges, including the separation of powers, executive privilege, right of privacy, First Amendment freedom of expression, Fourth Amendment protection against unreasonable search and seizure, equal protection under the law, and the constitutional ban on bills of attainder (that is, laws passed to punish individuals).[130] On June 28, 1977, the Court upheld the law by a 7-2 vote. The majority opinion, written by Justice William J. Brennan Jr., acknowledged that the law might infringe on some of Nixon's rights, but the Court then weighed the damage done to the former president as an individual against the public interest in preserving presidential materials intact. The justices concluded that the public interest outweighed Nixon's personal claim.

In 1978 the Supreme Court decided the last of the Nixon tapes cases, which the former president actually won. On April 18, 1978, by a 5-4 vote, the Court granted Nixon's request that lower courts not be allowed to permit broadcasters to copy and commercially market the White House tapes used as evidence in the trials of Mitchell, Haldeman, and Ehrlichman. The Court ruled that such access need not be granted immediately, especially because the 1974 act concerning the tapes and other Nixon materials had established procedures for public access to those items at some future date.[131]

The presidents who followed Nixon did not fare much better before the Court. Several of President Ronald Reagan's aides and advisers came under investigation by independent counsels. The Ethics in Government Act of 1978 authorized special prosecutors to investigate allegations involving top officials in the executive branch. Unlike ordinary U.S. attorneys, these prosecutors were chosen by a panel of three judges who were appointed by the chief justice of the United States. In 1988 three government employees challenged this scheme as unconstitutional. Among them was Theodore Olson, a Reagan administration lawyer who had come under suspicion for allegedly misleading a congressional committee investigating political wrongdoing at the Environmental Protection Agency. Though Olson was not ultimately charged with a crime, he argued that the independent investigation of him violated the separation of powers doctrine. Olson maintained that only the president has the executive power to prosecute. The Court rejected this challenge in *Morrison v. Olson* (1988) and upheld the law on a 7-1 vote.[132] The opinion was written by Chief Justice Rehnquist, who owed his appointment as chief justice to President Reagan.

In Article II, section 2, the Constitution allows Congress to "vest the appointment of such inferior officers, as they think proper, . . . in the courts of law," Rehnquist noted, and an independent counsel can be deemed an "inferior" officer. Although not under the day-to-day control of the president's appointees, a counsel may be dismissed for cause under the law, he added. Only Justice Antonin Scalia dissented. Reagan's last appointee to the Court, Justice Anthony M. Kennedy, who arrived shortly before the case was heard, recused himself. The ruling preserved the independent counsel investigations of the Iran-contra affair, which continued into the administration of Reagan's successor, George H. W. Bush. In a footnote to the 1988 ruling, the unsuccessful plaintiff, Theodore Olson, went on to have a prominent career as an advocate before the Supreme Court. He represented Republican presidential candidate George W. Bush in the Florida recount controversy that led to *Bush v. Gore* (2000). In 2001 he became U.S. solicitor general, the government's chief advocate before the Supreme Court.

The independent counsel provision lapsed in 1993, but when President Bill Clinton took office that year, repeated questions were raised about his dealings with the Madison Guaranty Savings and Loan in Arkansas. His attorney general, Janet Reno, chose a well-regarded New York Republican, Robert B. Fiske Jr., as an outside investigator to look into the matter. A few months later, Congress renewed the independent counsel statute, and Clinton signed it into law. In August the three-judge panel named by Rehnquist dismissed Fiske and replaced him with Kenneth W. Starr, a former Reagan and Bush administration lawyer. Starr pursued Clinton for the rest of his term in office and brought impeachment charges against him to the House of Representatives in 1998 for his actions revolving around his relationships with White House intern Monica Lewinsky and former Arkansas state employee Paula Jones.

The Court had dealt Clinton a setback in 1997 when it rejected his claim of "temporary immunity" from the civil lawsuit brought by Jones. *(See " 'Unofficial Acts' of the President," pp. 325–327.)* In a unanimous decision, the Court ruled that the "current occupant" of the White House has no general immunity from private suits stemming from "unofficial acts." That ruling set the stage for Clinton's impeachment, because it allowed Jones's lawyers—and ultimately

Starr's investigators—to question the president under oath about his relationship with Lewinsky. The scandals that beset Clinton, like those that drove Nixon from office, left the office of the presidency in a weakened position and demonstrated that the Court would not automatically shield the chief executive from legal attacks.

GEORGE W. BUSH, THE COURT, AND GUANTÁNAMO BAY

George W. Bush took the oath of office from Chief Justice Rehnquist on January 20, 2001, just six weeks after the Rehnquist-led Court had halted the ballot recount in Florida and secured Bush's narrow victory. As seven of the nine justices were Republican appointees—including two named by President George H. W. Bush—the new president might well have expected good relations with the Court. But Bush's bold use of his presidential authority following the attacks of September 11, 2001, led to a confrontation with the Court. The dispute did not concern whether Bush could deploy troops in Afghanistan or Iraq—Congress approved resolutions that authorized those military actions. The president was empowered to "use all necessary and appropriate force" against those he determines "planned, authorized, committed or aided" the terrorists, Congress said in a resolution adopted on September 18, 2001, a week after the attacks. Military operations overseas were under the full control of the president as commander in chief.

But civil libertarians objected when Bush asserted he had the unilateral authority to imprison "enemy combatants" at the U.S. naval base at Guantánamo Bay, Cuba, and to try some of them as war criminals before a newly devised system of military trials. Bush and his lawyers envisioned a form of martial law for suspected terrorists who were aliens. They would be held by the U.S. military under rules set by the Defense Department, and they would have no rights to see a lawyer, communicate with family or friends, or appeal to an independent judge. The Geneva Conventions and the protections for prisoners of war did not apply to these captives, Bush and his lawyers said, because terrorists

are not soldiers in uniform fighting under the rules of war. The administration labeled these new fighters "unlawful enemy combatants." At the same time, because they were not charged as criminals, they were not entitled to the legal protections of American law and the U.S. Constitution. On November 13, 2001, Bush issued a military order entitled "Detention, Treatment and Trial of Certain Non-Citizens in the War against Terrorism."[133] Its terms put the Defense Department in charge of these prisoners and their trials. The administration did not seek to have these rules approved by Congress, even though Article I, section 8, says: "Congress shall have Power To . . . make Rules concerning Captures on Land and Water." Bush's order also said none of these individuals may "seek any remedy or maintain any proceeding . . . in any court of the United States." This last provision set the stage for several years of litigation, and three defeats for the president in the Supreme Court.

By 2003 more than 640 men were imprisoned at Guantánamo, a forty-five-square-mile area held by the United States under a permanent lease. Administration lawyers chose this location because it was outside U.S. territory, and, they believed, federal judges would not have jurisdiction there. The lawyers also relied on a post–World War II decision of the Supreme Court that had turned away writs of habeas corpus from twenty-one German prisoners who had been convicted of war crimes and were held at Landsberg Prison in Germany.[134]

Rasul v. Bush

Nevertheless, lawyers for the families of the Guantánamo detainees filed writs of habeas corpus in federal court in Washington. Historically, these writs gave an imprisoned person an opportunity to have his case heard by a judge. The lawyers for the detained men said they were being wrongly held. One of them, Shafiq Rasul, was born and raised in the West Midlands area of England. His family said he had gone to Pakistan in October 2001 as a tourist, but apparently was caught up in the fighting between the Taliban regime and the U.S. military. He was captured there and sent to Guantánamo. In November 2003, over the strong opposition of the Bush administration, the Court agreed to hear a combined case involving Rasul, two Australians, and a dozen Kuwaitis. The justices did not seek to decide, or even consider, whether these men were or were not allied with al Qaeda or the Taliban. The sole issue was whether these men—foreigners who were held as military prisoners—could file a writ of habeas corpus in federal court. In a 6-3 decision in *Rasul v. Bush,* the Court said they could.[135]

The opinion by Justice John Paul Stevens was cryptic. "This Court has recognized the federal courts' power to review applications for habeas relief in a wide variety of cases involving Executive detention, in wartime as well as in times of peace," he wrote.

Stevens said the outcome was not controlled by the Court's decision in the case of the Germans held after World War II because they were at war with the United States and convicted of war crimes. In contrast, Rasul and the others said they were not at war with America, and they had not been tried or convicted on any charges. "What is presently at stake is only whether the federal courts have jurisdiction to determine the legality of the Executive's potentially indefinite detention of individuals who claim to be wholly innocent of wrongdoing," and he said the Court "answer[ed] that question in the affirmative."[136] Justices Sandra Day O'Connor, Anthony Kennedy, David Souter, Ruth Bader Ginsburg, and Stephen Breyer agreed. Stevens said the decision was based on "the habeas statute," and his opinion did not say what rights, if any, the detainees had when they came before a federal court.

Captive American Citizens

The decision in favor of the Guantánamo detainees was overshadowed by another, more broadly written opinion handed down the same day. Yaser Hamdi had grown up in Saudi Arabia, and he was in Afghanistan in 2001 when the Northern Alliance captured him and turned him over to U.S. troops. He was said to be a fighter for the Taliban, and he was sent to Guantánamo. There, officials learned he had been born in Louisiana in 1980 and, therefore, was a U.S. citizen. In April 2002 he was transferred to a navy brig in Norfolk, Virginia. The Bush administration determined that

Hamdi was an enemy combatant and could be held indefinitely without charges being filed. His father, Esam Fouad Hamdi, filed a writ of habeas corpus on his son's behalf, contending that Yaser Hamdi was being held unlawfully and in violation of the U.S. Constitution. He said his son, then age twenty, had gone to Afghanistan to do "relief work," and he did not have military training.

Hamdi's case, along with that of José Padilla, had attracted extra attention because of the extraordinary claims put forth by the administration. Bush and his lawyers asserted that the president as commander in chief had the power to arrest and to hold in military custody any person whom he determined was a so-called enemy combatant, including an American citizen. And once designated, these persons would have no right to speak to a lawyer, to hear the evidence against them, or to contest the charges. Bush's lawyers also said the congressional authorization adopted after the September 11 attacks made clear the president was empowered to hold alleged terrorists without charges.

José Padilla was born in 1970 in Brooklyn and grew up in Chicago, where he was a member of a street gang. He later moved to Florida and converted to Islam. On May 8, 2002, he was arrested at Chicago's O'Hare International Airport after arriving on a flight from Pakistan. U.S. intelligence agents said Padilla was allied with al Qaeda and that he was planning to detonate a radioactive "dirty bomb" somewhere in the United States. But these allegations and the evidence behind them were never introduced at a trial. Instead, administration officials decided to hold Padilla in solitary confinement and to question him intensely in hopes of penetrating the al Qaeda network.

For a time, the administration appeared unsure of what do with Padilla. He was moved to New York City and held as a "material witness" in a pending terrorism investigation. Donna Newman, a New York lawyer, was assigned to represent him and met briefly with him. Shortly afterward, the administration removed Padilla from the civil court system and put him in the custody of the military. He was jailed at the U.S. navy brig in Charleston, South Carolina. Newman then filed a writ of habeas corpus on his behalf, asserting it was illegal and unconstitutional to put an American citizen in military jail without giving him due process of law. In spring 2004 the Court heard the Hamdi and Padilla cases, and the decisions were announced June 28.

In *Hamdi v. Rumsfeld* the Court handed down a mixed decision. "We hold that although Congress authorized the detention of combatants in the narrow circumstances alleged here, due process demands that a citizen held in the United States as an enemy combatant be given a meaningful opportunity to contest the factual basis for that detention before a neutral decision-maker," wrote Justice O'Connor for the Court.[137]

The first part of her opinion amounted to a victory for the administration, although not necessarily for the president's commander in chief power. O'Connor said the congressional Authorization for the Use of Military Force (AUMF) gave Bush the authority to capture and hold enemy fighters such as Hamdi. "There can be no doubt that individuals who fought against the United States in Afghanistan as part of the Taliban, an organization known to have supported the al Qaeda network responsible for those attacks, are individuals Congress sought to target in passing the AUMF. We conclude that detention of [such] individuals . . . for the duration of the particular conflict in which they were captured is so fundamental and accepted an incident of war as to be the exercise of the 'necessary and appropriate force' Congress has authorized the President to use."[138] Chief Justice Rehnquist and Justices Kennedy, Breyer, and Clarence Thomas agreed on this point.

"There is no bar to this Nation's holding one of its own citizens as an enemy combatant," O'Connor added.[139] During World War II, one of the German saboteurs who was tried in a military court and executed in 1942 was a naturalized citizen, she noted. Although *Hamdi* dealt with a U.S. citizen, the Court's holding made clear that the hundreds of foreigners held at Guantánamo could be imprisoned for the "duration" of the conflict, assuming they were indeed "enemy combatants."

The second half of the opinion dealt with "what process is constitutionally due to a citizen who disputes

his enemy-combatant status." The two sides to the dispute proposed polar opposite positions. The Bush administration said Hamdi was entitled to no hearing and no rights, and the courts should defer to the military. Hamdi's lawyers said their client, a citizen, was entitled to a full due process of law, including a trial in a federal court. O'Connor fashioned a compromise, one that called for a fair hearing, but not a full trial.

"We hold that a citizen-detainee seeking to challenge his classification as an enemy combatant must receive notice of the factual basis for his classification, and a fair opportunity to rebut the Government's factual assertion before a neutral decision-maker," she wrote.[140] Chief Justice Rehnquist and Justices Kennedy, Breyer, Souter, and Ginsburg agreed with O'Connor on this point. In a partial dissent, Souter and Ginsburg said the government did not have the legal authority to hold a citizen in military custody, but they agreed that he should at least have a hearing to challenge the basis for holding him.

O'Connor's opinion closed with a strong rejection of Bush's contention that war gives the commander in chief the full power to decide alone on who can be imprisoned. "We have long since made clear that a state of war is not a blank check for the President when it comes to the rights of the Nation's citizens. Whatever power the United States Constitution envisions for the Executive in its exchanges with other nations or with enemy organizations in time of conflict, it most assuredly envisions a role for all three branches when individual liberties are at stake," she wrote. "Likewise, we have made clear that, unless Congress acts to suspend it, the Great Writ of habeas corpus allows the Judicial Branch to play a necessary role in maintaining this delicate balance of governance, serving as an important check on the Executive's discretion in the realm of detentions."[141]

These words were quoted often in the news reports and commentary on the decision, and they spoke loudly of the Court's determination to check presidential power and to protect individual liberty. They carried extra weight because Chief Justice Rehnquist joined O'Connor's opinion. Justice Scalia said he would have gone further and mandated a full trial for Hamdi. "The very core of the liberty secured by our Anglo-Saxon system of separated powers has been the freedom from indefinite imprisonment at the will of the Executive," Scalia wrote in a dissent joined by Justice Stevens. Scalia's view turned on the fact that Hamdi was a U.S. citizen. "Where the government accuses a citizen of waging war against it, our constitutional tradition has been to prosecute him in federal court for treason and some other crime," he said.[142]

Only Justice Thomas agreed entirely with the administration's position. "This detention falls squarely within the Federal government's war powers, and we lack the expertise and capacity to second-guess that decision," he wrote.[143]

Padilla's case was dismissed on a technicality. Rehnquist said Padilla's lawyer should have filed a writ of habeas corpus in South Carolina, where he was being held, not in New York. Habeas corpus is a suit against the jailer, the chief justice explained, and this suit should be filed where the jail is located.[144] Justices Stevens, Souter, Ginsburg, and Breyer dissented.

Civil libertarians hailed the Court's decisions. "Today's historic rulings are a strong repudiation of the administration's argument that its actions in the war on terrorism are beyond the rule of law and unreviewable by American courts," said Steven R. Shapiro, legal director of the American Civil Liberties Union, in a press release.

The White House saw the ruling as endorsing its position on holding enemy combatants. "The president's most solemn obligation is to defend the American people, and we're pleased that the Supreme Court upheld the president's authority to detain enemy combatants, including citizens, for the duration of the conflict," said Bush's spokeswoman Claire Buchan.

Two weeks after the ruling, the Defense Department initiated a new screening process of the detainees at Guantánamo. A panel of three military officers would review the basis for holding each of the prisoners. These brief hearings were known as Combatant Status Review Tribunals (CSRTs). Also in July 2004 Salim Hamdan, a driver for Osama bin Laden, was charged with conspiracy to commit crimes of terrorism, and he was slated to be tried before a military commission. That same week, Lakhdar Boumediene filed a writ of habeas corpus in the wake of the Rasul ruling. A native of Algeria who lived in Bosnia, Boumediene had been arrested in 2001 on the suspicion he was working with al Qaeda, but the supreme court of Bosnia ordered him released. U.S. troops were waiting for him, took him into custody, and sent him to Guantánamo. His case, like Hamdan's, would set the stage for the next battles in the Supreme Court. As for Hamdi, the Court's decision led to his freedom. Three months after the ruling, the administration announced it was deporting Hamdi to Saudi Arabia.

Hamdan v. Rumsfeld

The Court's attention turned next to the pending military trials. Hamdan, a native of Yemen, had been captured in Afghanistan in November 2001. He was not considered a "high value" detainee or an important figure in the al Qaeda network, even though he had worked directly for bin Laden. But the Defense Department wanted to establish the military commissions as an accepted system for trying terrorists who were then held in secret CIA prisons. Among these prisoners was Khalid Sheikh Mohammed, the self-professed "mastermind" of the 9/11 attacks. If convicted, he would face the death penalty. Hamdan was charged with a conspiracy, but he was not alleged to have had any command responsibilities nor was he said to have participated in the planning of any operation.

Lawyers for Hamdan filed a writ of habeas corpus and challenged the administration's authority for trying him before a military commission. They agreed he could be court-martialed under the Uniform Code of Military Justice, but they said Congress had not authorized the military commissions by law. The Geneva Conventions also frown upon specially created courts. Common Article 3, which appears in all four Conventions, says persons who are caught up in a "conflict not of an international character" shall be treated humanely and may not be punished criminally except "by a regularly constituted court affording all the judicial guarantees . . . recognized as indispensable by civilized peoples." A federal judge in Washington agreed with Hamdan's claim and barred his trial by military commission, but in July 2005 a three-judge panel of the U.S. Court of Appeals for the District of Columbia Circuit reversed that ruling and upheld the commissions. The panel noted that the Nazi saboteurs had been tried by a military commission in 1942 and the Supreme Court had affirmed their convictions.[145] The panel included Judge John G. Roberts Jr. The same week the decision was handed down, President Bush announced he was nominating Roberts to the Supreme Court.

In November, Roberts was chief justice when the Court announced it would hear *Hamdan v. Rumsfeld,* and Roberts said he would not participate because he had ruled on the matter in the lower court. Anxious about the outcome, the Bush administration and Congress made a last-minute move to bar the Court from deciding *Hamdan.* A provision saying "no court, justice, or judge shall have jurisdiction to hear or consider an application for a writ of habeas corpus filed by or on behalf of an alien detained by the Department of Defense at Guantánamo Bay, Cuba" was added to the pending Detainee Treatment Act. The act was signed into law by the president on December 30, 2005.

But the Court, undeterred, ruled the military commissions illegal in *Hamdan v. Rumsfeld* on June 29, 2006. For the 5-3 majority, Justice Stevens said Bush's proposed military trials had not been approved by Congress, nor did they qualify as a "regularly constituted court" as required by the Geneva Conventions.[146] The Court also dodged the jurisdictional provision in the Detainee Treatment Act by concluding this new provision of law did not apply to pending cases, such as Hamdan's. Justices Souter, Ginsburg, and Breyer joined Stevens's opinion, and Kennedy agreed on the main points. In a short concurring opinion, Breyer said the military commissions were flawed because they had not been approved by Congress. "Nothing prevents the President from returning to Congress to seek the authority he believes necessary," he said in a statement joined by Kennedy, Souter, and Ginsburg.

The three dissenters each wrote opinions. Justice Scalia said the Court had no jurisdiction to hear the case because of the Detainee Treatment Act. Justice Thomas said the military commissions were a military matter under the president's control as commander in chief. He said the Court's decision will "sorely hamper the President's ability to confront and defeat a new and deadly enemy." The Court's newest member, Justice Samuel Alito, said the military commissions qualify as a "regularly constituted court" that could administer justice fairly, and they should have been upheld on that basis.

Reactions to the ruling varied widely. Duke law professor Walter Dellinger, who served as U.S. solicitor general during the Clinton administration, called it "simply the most important decision on presidential power and the rule of law ever." He said the decision was profoundly important because the Court had rejected Bush's claim that the president on his own authority could determine the judge, the jury, and the prosecutor as well as the legal rules for a military trial. Some said extending the Geneva Conventions to suspects in the "war on terrorism" could have the most far-reaching impact. Still others disagreed, observing that the decision would not have a long-lasting impact because Congress could override it. "We believe the problems cited by the court can and should be fixed," said Sen. Lindsey Graham, R-S.C., and Sen. Jon Kyl, R-Ariz. "Working together, Congress and the administration can draft a fair, suitable and constitutionally permissible tribunal statute."

Boumediene v. Bush

The senators were true to their word. By October, Congress had passed and the president had signed into law the Military Commissions Act (MCA). It authorized military trials of "unlawful enemy combatants" who have engaged in or supported hostile actions against the United States. The law said again that no judge or justice "shall have jurisdiction to hear or consider an application for a writ of habeas corpus filed by or on behalf of an alien detained by the United States . . . as an enemy combatant." The passage of this act shifted the legal terrain. The Court was no longer confronting a president claiming broad powers as commander in chief, but instead a president acting under the authority explicitly given him by Congress.

But the MCA also raised an important constitutional question: May Congress take away the right to habeas corpus for some prisoners? Article I, section 9, says, "The Privilege of the Writ of Habeas Corpus shall not be suspended, unless when in cases of Rebellion or Invasion the Public Safety may require it." But rarely had the Court been called upon to rule on the reach of habeas corpus. In February 2007 the U.S. Court of Appeals for the District of Columbia Circuit dismissed habeas petitions filed on behalf of Boumediene and several other Guantánamo detainees, citing the MCA.

Lawyers for Boumediene petitioned the Supreme Court to hear his case, but on April 2 the petition was turned down, over dissents by Justices Breyer, Souter, and Ginsburg. In a separate statement, Justices Stevens and Kennedy said it was wise to wait to see how the new law would work. One provision said the detainees could appeal the decision of the CSRTs, the Pentagon's review panels at Guantánamo. Civil libertarians had denounced the CSRTs as a sham because only the military's evidence was considered. Several military lawyers, including one who had served at Guantánamo, agreed with that assessment and said the reviews were one-sided and unfair.

In a highly unusual move, the Court announced on June 29, 2007, that it had decided to hear Boumediene's case after all. The divisions on the Court were now clear on this issue, and the outcome in *Boumediene v. Bush* came as no surprise. In a 5-4 decision, the Court ruled on June 12, 2008, that the Guantánamo detainees had a constitutional right to habeas corpus, in part because they had been held for up to six years with no chance to plead their innocence.[147]

Justice Kennedy said that in medieval England, the right to go before a judge was seen as crucial to liberty, and this concept was brought to the American colonies. The "privilege of habeas corpus was one of the few safeguards of liberty specified in a Constitution that, at the outset, had no Bill of Rights," he wrote. "The Framers viewed freedom from unlawful restraint as a fundamental precept of liberty."

With that point as a backdrop, Kennedy explored the history of habeas corpus in England and in the United States. He acknowledged that no clear or simple rule could be gleaned. In England, Spanish sailors and African slaves had brought habeas claims before a judge, suggesting that the right was not limited to

Englishmen. In this country, the Court had extended the writ to persons in custody who had no other means to obtain a just hearing. "Practical considerations and exigent circumstances inform the definition and reach of the law's writs, including habeas corpus," Kennedy wrote. In this case, the detainees had been held at Guantánamo for years. This was not a battlefield or an emergency detention, he explained. In the light of these circumstances, Congress's action amounts to "an unconstitutional suspension of the writ. . . . The detainees in these cases are entitled to a prompt habeas hearing," Kennedy wrote.

"Our opinion does not undermine the Executive's powers as Commander in Chief. On the contrary, the exercise of these powers is vindicated, not eroded, when confirmed by the Judicial Branch. Within the Constitution's separation-of-powers structure, few exercises of judicial power are as legitimate or as necessary as the responsibility to hear challenges to the authority of the Executive to imprison a person," Kennedy said in closing. Justices Stevens, Souter, Ginsburg, and Breyer signed on to Kennedy's opinion.

In a concurring opinion, Souter objected to the dissenters' complaint that the Court had rushed in to take control of the Guantánamo detainees. "It is enough to repeat that some of these petitioners have spent six years behind bars. . . . Today's decision is no judicial victory, but an act of perseverance in trying to make habeas review, and the obligation of the courts to provide it, mean something of value both to prisoners and to the Nation," Souter wrote.

Chief Justice Roberts and Justice Scalia filed dissents. "Today the Court strikes down as inadequate the most generous set of procedural protections ever afforded aliens detained by this country as enemy combatants," Roberts wrote. "And to what effect? The majority merely replaces a review system designed by the people's representatives with a set of shapeless procedures to be defined by the federal courts at some point. One cannot help but think, after surveying the modest practical results of the majority's ambitious opinion, that this decision is not really about the detainees at all, but about control of federal policy regarded enemy combatants."

"So who has won? Not the detainees," Roberts continued. "The Court's analysis leaves them with only the prospect of further litigation. . . . Not Congress, whose attempt to determine—through democratic means—how best to balance security of the American people with the detainees' liberty interests, has been unceremoniously brushed aside. Not the Great Writ, whose majesty is hardly enhanced by its extension to a jurisdictionally quirky outpost, with no tangible benefit to anyone. Not the rule of law, unless by that is meant the rule of lawyers. . . . And certainly not the American people, who today lose a bit more control over the conduct of this Nation's foreign policy to unelected, politically unaccountable judges," Roberts wrote. Justices Scalia, Thomas, and Alito joined his dissent.

Scalia called the ruling a grave blunder. "Today, for the first time in our Nation's history, the Court confers a constitutional right to habeas corpus on aliens detained abroad by our military forces in the course of an ongoing war. . . . The writ of habeas corpus does not, and never has, run in favor of aliens abroad," he wrote in dissent. "The game of bait-and-switch that today's opinion plays upon the Nation's Commander in Chief will make the war harder on us. It will almost certainly cause more Americans to be killed." Roberts, Thomas, and Alito joined Scalia's dissent.

Reactions to the ruling were as sharply divided as was the Court. "We will abide by the decision. It was a deeply divided court, and I strongly agree with those who dissented," said President Bush.

"Today, the Supreme Court affirmed what almost everyone but the administration and their defenders in Congress always knew. The Constitution and the rule of law bind all of us even in extraordinary times of war. No one is above the Constitution," said Sen. John Kerry, D-Mass., Bush's opponent in the 2004 presidential election.

Despite his three defeats in the Guantánamo detainee cases, Bush did not always fare badly in the Supreme Court. In 2004 the Court shielded Bush and the White House from turning over documents in a civil suit involving the vice president's energy policy task force, and the decision spoke of "safeguarding the confidentiality of communications" in the White

House.[148] *(See also "Bush, Cheney, and the 'Confidentiality of Communications,'" pp. 333–334.)* The Court refused to hear legal challenges to other Bush policies, including alleged wiretapping without warrant and the use of the "state secrets privilege" to quash lawsuits involving overseas abductions.[149]

But the Court was determined that independent judges would have a role in overseeing imprisonments and trials, even in the war on terrorism. As Kennedy said in *Boumediene,* "The laws and Constitution are designed to survive, and remain in force, in extraordinary times. Liberty and security can be reconciled; and in our system they are reconciled within the framework of the law."

NOTES

INTRODUCTION (PP. 253–258)

1. Akhil Reed Amar, *America's Constitution: A Biography* (New York: Random House, 2005), 131.

2. Ibid., 141

3. *Youngstown Sheet and Tube Co. v. Sawyer,* 343 U.S. 579 (1952).

4. *United States v. Nixon,* 418 U.S. 683 (1974).

5. *Morrison v. Olson,* 487 U.S. 654 (1988).

6. *Clinton v. Jones,* 520 U.S. 681 (1997).

7. *Rasul v. Bush,* 542 U.S. 466 (2004); *Boumediene v. Bush,* 533 U.S. —- (2008).

8. *Hamdan v. Rumsfeld,* 548 U.S. 557 (2006).

9. *Youngstown Sheet and Tube Co. v. Sawyer,* 343 U.S. 579 at 646–647 (1952).

10. George E. Reedy, *The Twilight of the Presidency* (New York: New American Library, 1970), 4.

11. Louis Koenig, *The Chief Executive,* 5th ed. (San Diego: Harcourt Brace Jovanovich, 1986), 12–13.

12. *Youngstown Sheet and Tube Co. v. Sawyer,* 343 U.S. 579 at 653–654 (1952).

13. William Howard Taft, *Our Chief Magistrate and His Powers* (New York: Columbia University Press, 1916), 144.

14. Theodore Roosevelt, *An Autobiography* (New York: Macmillan, 1920), 406.

15. John Locke, *Treatise of Civil Government and a Letter concerning Toleration,* ed. Charles L. Sherman (New York: D. Appleton-Century-Crofts, 1937), 109.

16. *Youngstown Sheet and Tube Co. v. Sawyer,* 343 U.S. 579 at 635–636 (1952).

17. *United States v. Curtiss-Wright Export Corp.,* 299 U.S. 304 (1936).

18. *Hepburn v. Griswold,* 8 Wall. (75 U.S.) 603 (1870), and *Knox v. Lee,* 12 Wall. (79 U.S.) 457 (1871).

19. *United States v. Nixon,* 418 U.S. 683 (1974).

20. Laurence H. Tribe, *God Save This Honorable Court* (New York: Random House, 1985), 50, 74–75.

21. *Scott v. Sandford,* 19 How. (60 U.S.) 393 (1857).

22. John W. Dean, *The Rehnquist Choice: The Untold Story of the Nixon Appointment that Redefined the Supreme Court* (New York: Free Press, 2001).

Sarah: note 83 needs updated pg. numbers.

THE COMMANDER IN CHIEF (PP. 259–280)

1. *Youngstown Sheet and Tube Co. v. Sawyer,* 343 U.S. 579 at 641 (1952).

2. James Madison, Alexander Hamilton, and John Jay, *The Federalist Papers,* ed. Clinton Rossiter (New York: New American Library, 1961), No. 61, 417–418.

3. Ibid., No. 74, 447.

4. Louis Koenig, *The Chief Executive,* 5th ed. (San Diego: Harcourt Brace Jovanovich, 1986), 23–31. See also Katy J. Harriger, ed., *Separation of Powers: Documents and Commentary* (Washington, D.C.: CQ Press, 2003).

5. Nancy Kassop, "The Power to Make War," in *Separation of Powers: Documents and Commentary,* ed. Katy J. Harriger (Washington, D.C.: CQ Press, 2003), 64–79.

6. C. Herman Pritchett, *The American Constitution* (New York: McGraw-Hill, 1959), 344.

7. Arthur M. Schlesinger Jr., *The Imperial Presidency* (New York: Popular Library, 1973), 68–69.

8. James D. Richardson, ed., *Messages and Papers of the Presidents,* 20 vols. (New York: Bureau of National Literature, 1897), 7:3225–26.

9. Edward S. Corwin, *The President: Office and Powers, 1787–1984. History and Analysis of Practice and Opinion,* 5th rev. ed., ed. Randall W. Bland, Theodore T. Hindson, and Jack W. Peltason (New York: New York University Press, 1984), 270–278.

10. Glendon A. Schubert, *The Presidency in the Courts* (Minneapolis: University of Minnesota Press, 1957), 286–290.

11. Ibid., 287

12. Clinton Rossiter, *The Supreme Court and the Commander in Chief* (Ithaca, N.Y.: Cornell University Press, 1951), 126.

13. Louis Fisher, *Presidential War Power* (Lawrence: University Press of Kansas, 1995), xi.

14. Ibid., xii–xiii.

15. *Talbot v. Seeman,* 1 Cr. (5 U.S.) 1 (1801); *Bas v. Tingy,* 4 Dall. (4 U.S.) 37 (1800).

16. *Martin v. Mott,* 12 Wheat. (25 U.S.) 19 at 29 (1827).

17. Id. at 31–32.

18. *Fleming v. Page,* 9 How. (50 U.S.) 603 at 615 (1850).

19. Richard W. Leopold, *The Growth of American Foreign Policy* (New York: Knopf, 1962), 96–98.

20. W. Taylor Reveley III, "Presidential War-Making: Constitutional Prerogative or Usurpation?" *Virginia Law Review 55* (November 1969): 1258n–59n.

21. Samuel Eliot Morison, Henry Steele Commager, and William E. Leuchtenburg, *The Growth of the American Republic,* 2 vols. (New York: Oxford University Press, 1969), 1:550–551.

22. *Congressional Globe,* 30th Cong., 1st sess., 1848, 95.

23. Leopold, *Growth of American Foreign Policy,* 150–152, 180–188, 212.

24. Ibid.

25. Ibid., 215–218.

26. Ibid., 316–321.

27. See generally Matthew Pinsker, *Abraham Lincoln* (Washington, D.C.: CQ Press, 2002).

28. Corwin, *The President,* 264–265.

29. Richardson, *Messages and Papers of the Presidents,* 7:3225–26.

30. Carl B. Swisher, *American Constitutional Development,* 2nd ed. (Cambridge, Mass.: Houghton Mifflin, 1954), 29.

31. Elisabeth Joan Doyle, "The Conduct of the War, 1861," in *Congress Investigates: A Documented History, 1792–1974,* ed. Arthur M. Schlesinger Jr. and Roger Bruns (New York: Chelsea House, 1975), 72.

32. *Prize Cases,* 2 Black (67 U.S.) 635 (1863).

33. Id. at 668–669.

34. Id. at 688–689, 690, 693, 698.

35. Carl B. Swisher, *History of the Supreme Court of the United States,* vol. 5, *The Taney Period, 1836–1864* (New York: Macmillan, 1974), 844–846.

36. Ibid., 847–850.

37. *Ex parte Merryman,* 17 Fed. Cas. 144 (C.C.D. Md. 1861), quoted in *Documents of American History,* 7th ed., ed. Henry Steele Commager (New York: Appleton-Century-Crofts, 1963), 402.

38. *Ex parte Vallandigham,* 1 Wall. (68 U.S.) 243 (1864).

39. *Ex parte Milligan,* 4 Wall. (71 U.S.) 2 at 120–121, 126–127 (1866).

40. Woodrow Wilson, *Congressional Government* (Boston: Houghton Mifflin, 1885).

41. Arthur Link, *Wilson, the Diplomatist: A Look at His Major Foreign Policies* (New York: Watts, Franklin, 1965), 5–11. See also Kendrick A. Clements and Eric A. Cheezum, *Woodrow Wilson* (Washington, D.C.: CQ Press, 2003).

42. Morison, Commager, Leuchtenburg, *Growth of the American Republic,* 2:337.

43. Ibid., 2:349, 353–357.

44. Alfred H. Kelly and Winfred A. Harbison, *The American Constitution: Its Origin and Development,* 7th ed. (New York: Norton, 1991), 626.

45. Morison, Commager, Leuchtenburg, *Growth of the American Republic,* 2:337.

46. Corwin, *The President*, 272, 502.

47. Ibid., 235.

48. *United States v. L. Cohen Grocery Co.*, 255 U.S. 81 at 81–82 (1921).

49. *The Public Papers and Addresses of Franklin D. Roosevelt*, 5 vols. (New York: Random House, 1938), 2:15. See also generally Robert S. McElvaine, *Franklin Delano Roosevelt* (Washington, D.C.: CQ Press, 2002).

50. Morison, Commager, Leuchtenburg, *Growth of the American Republic*, 2:538–539.

51. *United States v. Curtiss-Wright Export Corp.*, 299 U.S. 304 (1936); *United States v. Belmont*, 310 U.S. 324 (1937); *United States v. Pink*, 315 U.S. 203 (1942).

52. *Congressional Record*, 77th Cong., 2nd sess., 1942, 88:7044.

53. *Yakus v. United States*, 321 U.S. 414 (1944).

54. Id. at 459–460.

55. *Bowles v. Willingham*, 321 U.S. 504 (1944).

56. Id. at 519.

57. *Woods v. Cloyd W. Miller Co.*, 333 U.S. 138 (1948).

58. *Steuart & Bros. Inc. v. Bowles*, 322 U.S. 398 at 405–406 (1944).

59. *Ex parte Quirin*, 317 U.S. 1 at 46, 48 (1942). See also Michal R. Belknap, "The Supreme Court Goes to War: The Meaning and Implications of the Nazi Saboteur Case," *Military Law Review* 89 (1980): 59.

60. James M. Burns, *Roosevelt: The Soldier of Freedom* (New York: Harcourt Brace Jovanovich, 1970), 214–217, 266–268. See also *United States v. Hohri*, 482 U.S. 64 (1987).

61. *Hirabayashi v. United States*, 320 U.S. 81 at 103 (1943). See also Page Smith, *Democracy on Trial: The Japanese-American Evacuation and Relocation in World War II* (New York: Simon and Schuster, 1995).

62. *Hirabayashi v. United States*, 320 U.S. 81 at 92 (1943).

63. *Korematsu v. United States*, 323 U.S. 214 (1944).

64. *Ex parte Endo*, 323 U.S. 283 at 302 (1944).

65. "Authority of the President to Repel the Attack in Korea," *State Department Bulletin* 23 (1950): 173.

66. *Youngstown Sheet and Tube Co. v. Sawyer*, 343 U.S. 579 at 641 (1952).

67. Id. at 585- 587.

68. Id. at 587.

69. Id. at 641–644.

70. Id. at 667–668.

71. Id. at 668, 708–709.

72. Dwight D. Eisenhower, *Waging Peace, 1956–1961* (Garden City, N.Y.: Doubleday, 1965), 272–273.

73. *Public Papers of the Presidents, John F. Kennedy, 1962* (Washington, D.C.: U. S. Government Printing Office, 1963), 806–815.

74. PL 408, 88th Cong., 2nd sess. (August 10, 1964); *U.S. Statutes at Large* 78 (1964), 384; *Public Papers of the Presidents, Lyndon B. Johnson, 1963–1964*, 2 vols. (Washington,

D.C.: U.S. Government Printing Office, 1965), 1:926–932, 946–947.

75. Lyndon B. Johnson, *The Vantage Point: Perspectives on the Presidency, 1963–1969* (New York: Holt, Rinehart, and Winston, 1971), 112–119.

76. Leonard Meeker, "The Legality of United States' Participation in the Defense of Vietnam," *State Department Bulletin* 54 (1966): 474.

77. Ibid., 484–489.

78. Ibid., 485–486.

79. *Mora v. McNamara*, 387 F. 2d 862 (D.C. Cir.), cert. denied, 389 U.S. 934 (1967); *Luftig v. McNamara*, 373 F. 2d 664 (D.C. Cir.), cert. denied, 387 U.S. 945 (1967); *United States v. Mitchell*, 369 F. 2d 323 (2d Cir. 1966), cert. denied, 386 U.S. 972 (1967); *Velvel v. Johnson*, 287 F. Supp. 846 (D. Kan. 1968).

80. Francis D. Wormuth, "The Nixon Theory of the War Power: A Critique," *California Law Review* 60 (May 1972): 624.

81. Senate Committee on Foreign Relations, *Hearings on U.S. Commitments to Foreign Powers before the Senate Committee on Foreign Relations*, 90th Cong., 1st sess., 1967, 108, 140–154.

82. Kelly and Harbison, *American Constitution*, 1016.

83. *Guide to Congress*, 6th ed. (Washington, D.C.: CQ Press, 2007), 1:267–270.

84. Ibid.

85. *Immigration and Naturalization Service v. Chadha*, 462 U.S. 919 (1983).

86. Koenig, *Chief Executive*, 210.

87. *Crockett v. Reagan*, 558 F. Supp 893 (D.D.C., 1982), cert. denied, 467 U.S. 1251 (1984); see Louis Fisher, *Constitutional Dialogues* (Princeton, N.J.: Princeton University Press, 1988), 32–33.

88. *CQ Almanac, 1990* (Washington, D.C.: Congressional Quarterly, 1991), 739; *Dellums v. Bush*, 752 F. Supp. 1141 (1990).

89. *Ange v. Bush*, 752 F. Supp. 509 (1990).

90. *Rasul v. Bush*, 542 U.S. 466 (2004).

91. *Ex parte Milligan*, 4 Wall. 2 (1866); *Ex parte Quirin*, 317 U.S. 1 (1942).

92. *Hamdi v. Rumsfeld*, 542 U.S. 507 (2004).

93. *Rumsfeld v. Padilla*, 542 U.S. 426 (2004).

94. *Hamdan v. Rumsfeld*, 548 U.S. 577 (2006).

95. *Boumediene v. Bush*, 553 U.S. —- (2008).

THE ARCHITECT OF FOREIGN POLICY (PP. 281–294)

1. *Annals of Congress* 10 (1800): 596, 613–614.

2. James Madison, Alexander Hamilton, and John Jay, *The Federalist Papers*, ed. Clinton Rossiter (New York: New American Library, Mentor Books, 1961), No. 75, 450–451.

3. Max Farrand, ed., *The Records of the Federal Convention of 1787*, rev. ed. (New Haven, Conn.: Yale University Press, 1937), 2:183.

4. John C. Hamilton, ed., *Works of Alexander Hamilton,* 7 vols. (New York: John F. Trow, 1851), 7:76, 82–83.

5. Gailiard Hunt, ed., *The Writings of James Madison,* 9 vols. (New York: Putnam's, 1900–1910), 6:128–188.

6. Paul L. Ford, ed., *The Writings of Thomas Jefferson,* 10 vols. (New York: Putnam's, 1892–1899), 5:161–162.

7. Edward S. Corwin, *The Constitution and What It Means Today* (Princeton, N.J.: Princeton University Press, 1958), 171.

8. See *Crosby v. National Foreign Trade Council,* 530 U.S. 363 (2000).

9. *Penhallow v. Doane's Administrators,* 3 Dall. (3 U.S.) 54 at 80–83 (1795).

10. *United States v. Curtiss-Wright Export Corp.,* 299 U.S. 304 (1936).

11. *Ware v. Hylton,* 3 Dall. (3 U.S.) 199 at 236–237 (1796).

12. *Holmes v. Jennison,* 14 Pet. (39 U.S.) 540 at 575 (1840).

13. *United States v. Pink,* 315 U.S. 203 at 233–234 (1942).

14. *Foster and Elam v. Neilson,* 2 Pet. (27 U.S.) 253 at 307, 309 (1829).

15. *United States v. Palmer,* 3 Wheat. (16 U.S.) 610 (1818).

16. *Doe v. Braden,* 16 How. (57 U.S.) 635 at 657 (1853).

17. *Jones v. United States,* 137 U.S. 202 (1890); *Oetjen v. Central Leather Co.,* 246 U.S. 297 (1918).

18. *In re Baiz,* 135 U.S. 403 (1890).

19. *Neely v. Henkel,* 180 U.S. 109 (1901).

20. *Terlinden v. Ames,* 184 U.S. 270 (1902).

21. *Charlton v. Kelly,* 229 U.S. 447 (1913).

22. *Baker v. Carr,* 369 U.S. 186 at 212 (1962).

23. *Fourteen Diamond Rings v. United States,* 183 U.S. 176 at 183 (1901).

24. *United States v. Curtiss-Wright Export Corp.,* 299 U.S. 304 (1936).

25. Charles A. Lofgren, "United States v. Curtiss-Wright: An Historical Assessment," *Yale Law Journal* 83 (November 1973): 1–13.

26. 48 Stat. 1744 (1934).

27. See *Schechter Poultry Corp. v. United States,* 295 U.S. 495 (1935); *Carter v. Carter Coal Co.,* 298 U.S. 238 (1936); *Panama Refining Co. v. Ryan,* 293 U.S. 288 (1935).

28. George Sutherland, *Constitutional Power and World Affairs* (New York: Columbia University Press, 1919), 25–47, 116–126.

29. *United States v. Curtiss-Wright Export Corp.,* 299 U.S. 304 at 315–318 (1936).

30. Id. at 319–320.

31. Id. at 321–322.

32. *Foster and Elam v. Neilson,* 2 Pet. (27 U.S.) 253 at 314 (1829).

33. *Head Money Cases,* 112 U.S. 580 at 598 (1884).

34. Id. at 598–599.

35. Migratory Bird Treaty Act, July 3, 1918, c. 183; 40 Stat. 755.

36. *Missouri v. Holland,* 252 U.S. 416 at 432–435 (1920).

37. *La Abra Silver Mining Co. v. United States,* 175 U.S. 423 at 460 (1899).

38. *Whitney v. Robertson,* 124 U.S. 190 (1888); *United States v. Guy W. Capps Inc.,* 348 U.S. 296 (1955).

39. *Charlton v. Kelly,* 229 U.S. 447 (1913); *Bas v. Tingy,* 4 Dall. (4 U.S.) 37 (1800); *Head Money Cases,* 112 U.S. 580 (1884).

40. *Goldwater v. Carter,* 444 U.S. 996 (1979).

41. *Geofroy v. Riggs,* 133 U.S. 258 at 266–267 (1889).

42. *Reid v. Covert,* 354 U.S. 1 at 16–18 (1957).

43. *Medellín v. Texas,* 552 U.S. —- (2008).

44. *Case Concerning Avena and Other Mexican Nationals,* Mex. vs. U.S. 2004, I.C.J. 12.

45. *Sanchez-Llamas v. Oregon,* 548 U.S. 331 (2006).

46. *Medellin v. Texas,* 552 U.S. —- (2008).

47. Senate Judiciary Committee, *Hearings on S.J. Res. 1 and S.J. Res. 43 before a Subcommittee of the Senate Judiciary Committee,* 83rd Cong., 1st sess., 1953, 877.

48. Ibid.

49. *The Constitution of the United States of America: Analysis and Interpretation* (Washington, D.C.: U.S. Government Printing Office, 1973), 506.

50. Wallace McClure, *International Executive Agreements: Democratic Procedure under the Constitution of the United States* (New York: AMS Press, 1941), 41.

51. Ibid., 62–70.

52. Henry S. Commager, ed., *Documents of American History,* 7th ed. (New York: Appleton-Century-Crofts, 1962), 449–450.

53. *A Decade of American Foreign Policy: Basic Documents, 1941–1949,* 81st Cong., 1st sess., 1950, S. Doc. 123, 126.

54. *The Constitution of the United States: Analysis and Interpretation,* 512.

55. *Tucker v. Alexandroff,* 183 U.S. 424 at 435, 467 (1902).

56. Samuel B. Crandall, *Treaties: Their Making and Enforcement,* 2nd ed. (New York: Columbia University Press, 1916), 103–104.

57. Samuel E. Morison, Henry S. Commager, and William E. Leuchtenburg, *The Growth of the American Republic,* 2 vols. (New York: Oxford University Press, 1969), 2:261–264.

58. McClure, *International Executive Agreements,* 96–97.

59. Commager, *Documents of American History,* 45, 52–53, 133–134.

60. McClure, *International Executive Agreements,* 391–393.

61. *State Department Bulletin* 4 (1941): 443.

62. *A Decade of American Foreign Policy,* pt. 1.

63. Arthur M. Schlesinger Jr., *The Imperial Presidency* (New York: Popular Library, 1973, 1974), 299–300.

64. *CQ Almanac, 1972* (Washington, D.C.: Congressional Quarterly, 1972), 279–280, 435.

65. *United States v. Belmont,* 310 U.S. 324 at 330–331 (1936).

66. *United States v. Pink,* 315 U.S. 203 at 229–230 (1942).

67. Id. at 230–231.

68. Id. at 233.

69. *Dames & Moore v. Regan,* 453 U.S. 654 (1981).

70. Id. at 688.

THE PRESIDENT AS EXECUTIVE (PP. 295–309)

1. See William E. Leuchtenburg, "The Evolution of Presidential Power," in *Separation of Powers: Documents and Commentary,* ed. Katy J. Harriger (Washington, D.C.: CQ Press, 2003), 39–48.

2. *Wilcox v. McConnel,* 13 Pet. (38 U.S.) 498 at 513 (1839).

3. *Williams v. United States,* 1 How. (42 U.S.) 290 at 197 (1843).

4. Two major modern rulings concerning the separation of powers, *Bowsher v. Synar* (1986) and *Morrison v. Olson* (1988), turned in large part on the power to appoint and remove officials.

5. *Marbury v. Madison,* 1 Cr. (5 U.S.) 137 (1803).

6. *United States v. Smith,* 286 U.S. 6 (1932).

7. C. Herman Pritchett, *The American Constitution* (New York: McGraw-Hill, 1959), 319.

8. James D. Richardson, ed., *Messages and Papers of the Presidents,* 20 vols. (New York: Bureau of National Literature, 1897), 3:1304.

9. *Ex parte Hennen,* 13 Pet. (38 U.S.) 230 at 257–259 (1839).

10. Carl B. Swisher, *American Constitutional Development,* 2nd ed. (Cambridge, Mass.: Houghton Mifflin, 1954), 742. President Warren G. Harding subsequently signed a similar bill, the Budget and Accounting Act, on June 10, 1921. Ibid., 743.

11. *Myers v. United States,* 272 U.S. 52 at 114 (1926).

12. Id. at 174–175 (1926).

13. Id. at 117, 121–122, 130–134.

14. Id. at 134.

15. Id. at 135.

16. Id. at 192–193.

17. Id. at 247.

18. Id. at 177.

19. *Humphrey's Executor v. United States,* 295 U.S. 602 at 618–619 (1935).

20. Id. at 627.

21. Id. at 627–628.

22. Id. at 629.

23. Id. at 629–632.

24. *Wiener v. United States,* 357 U.S. 349 at 353 (1958).

25. *Morgan v. TVA,* 312 U.S. 701 (1941), cert. denied; C. Herman Pritchett, *The Tennessee Valley Authority: A Study in Public Administration* (Chapel Hill: University of North Carolina Press, 1943), 203–216.

26. *Wiener v. United States,* 357 U.S. 349 (1958).

27. Id. at 352.

28. Id. at 353, 354.

29. Id. at 356.

30. *Bowsher v. Synar,* 478 U.S. 714 at 726 (1986).

31. *Immigration and Naturalization Service v. Chadha,* 462 U.S. 919 (1983).

32. Id. at 726–727.

33. *Morrison v. Olson,* 487 U.S. 654 (1988). See also Charles A. Johnson and Danette Brickman, *Independent Counsel: The Law and the Investigations* (Washington, D.C.: CQ Press, 2001).

34. Id. at 675–676, 677.

35. *In re Neagle,* 135 U.S. 1 at 64 (1890).

36. Id. at 59.

37. *United States v. Midwest Oil Co.,* 236 U.S. 459 at 469, 472–473 (1915).

38. See Thomas O. Sargentich, "The Delegation of Lawmaking Power to the Executive Branch," in *Separation of Powers: Documents and Commentary,* 116–131.

39. *Field v. Clark,* 143 U.S. 649 (1892).

40. *United States v. Grimaud,* 220 U.S. 506 at 521 (1911).

41. *Youngstown Sheet and Tube Co. v. Sawyer,* 343 U.S. 579 at 587 (1952).

42. Id. at 646–647.

43. See Harold C. Relyea, "Emergency Powers," in *Separation of Powers: Documents and Commentary,* 80–97.

44. *Martin v. Mott,* 12 Wheat. (25 U.S.) 19 at 28 (1827).

45. *Luther v. Borden,* 7 How. (48 U.S.) 1 at 40 (1849).

46. *Cherokee Nation v. Georgia,* 5 Pet. (30 U.S.) 1 (1831).

47. *In re Debs,* 158 U.S. 564 at 582, 584, 586 (1895).

48. *Youngstown Sheet and Tube Co. v. Sawyer,* 343 U.S. 579 (1952); *United States v. United Mine Workers,* 330 U.S. 258 (1947).

THE POWER TO VETO AND TO PARDON (PP. 310–321)

1. Louis Koenig, *The Chief Executive,* 5th. ed. (San Diego: Harcourt Brace Jovanovich, 1986), 162.

2. James Madison, Alexander Hamilton, and John Jay, *The Federalist Papers,* ed. Clinton Rossiter (New York: New American Library, 1961), No. 73, 442.

3. Ibid., 445.

4. Office of the Clerk, House of Representatives, http://clerk.house.gov.

5. *Okanogan Indians et al. v. United States (Pocket Veto Case),* 279 U.S. 655 at 677–679 (1929).

6. Id. at 678–679.

7. Id. at 679–680.

8. Id. at 680–681, 683–685.

9. *Wright v. United States,* 302 U.S. 583 (1938).

10. Id. at 594.

11. *CQ Almanac, 1970* (Washington, D.C.: Congressional Quarterly, 1971), 592–593.

12. *Burke v. Barnes,* 479 U.S. 361 (1987).

13. See *Congressional Record,* 103rd Cong., 1st sess., October 18, 1993, S13561–13565.

14. *Raines v. Byrd,* 521 U.S. 811 at 839 (1997). See also David J. Weiner, "The New Law of Legislative Standing," *Stanford Law Review* 54 (October 2001): 205–234.

15. *Clinton v. City of New York,* 524 U.S. 417 (1998).

16. Id. at 438, 447–449.

17. Id. at 451.

18. Id. at 467.

19. Id. at 466.

20. Id. at 469.

21. *United States v. Klein,* 13 Wall. (80 U.S.) 128 (1872).

22. *Ex parte Garland,* 4 Wall. (71 U.S.) 333 (1867).

23. *United States v. Wilson,* 7 Pet. (32 U.S.) 150 (1833); *Biddle v. Perovich,* 274 U.S. 480 at 486 (1927).

24. *Historic Documents of 1974* (Washington, D.C.: Congressional Quarterly, 1975), 816–817.

25. Edward S. Corwin, *The President: Office and Powers, 1787–1984. History and Analysis of Practice and Opinion,* 5th rev. ed., ed. Randall W. Bland, Theodore T. Hindson, and Jack W. Peltason (New York: New York University Press, 1984), 180–181.

26. Madison, Hamilton, Jay, *Federalist Papers,* No. 74, 447.

27. *United States v. Wilson,* 7 Pet. (32 U.S.) 150 at 160–161 (1833).

28. *Burdick v. United States,* 236 U.S. 79 (1915).

29. Id. at 90–91.

30. Charles Warren, *The Supreme Court in United States History,* rev. ed., 2 vols. (Boston: Little, Brown, 1926), 2:450–451.

31. *Ex parte Garland,* 4 Wall. (71 U.S.) 333 at 374–376 (1866).

32. Id. at 381.

33. Id. at 380.

34. Id. at 380–381.

35. Id. at 396–397.

36. *Carlesi v. New York,* 233 U.S. 51 at 59 (1914).

37. *Boyd v. United States,* 142 U.S. 450 (1892).

38. *Knote v. United States,* 95 U.S. 149 at 153–154 (1877).

39. *United States v. Klein,* 13 Wall. (80 U.S.) 128 at 142 (1872).

40. Id. at 147–148.

41. *Ex parte Wells,* 18 How. (59 U.S.) 307 at 307–309 (1856).

42. Id. at 314–315.

43. *The Laura,* 114 U.S. 411 (1885); *Illinois Central R.R. v. Bosworth,* 133 U.S. 92 (1890); *Ex parte Grossman,* 267 U.S. 87 (1925).

44. *Biddle v. Perovich,* 274 U.S. 480 at 487 (1927).

45. Id. at 485–486.

46. *Furman v. Georgia, Jackson v. Georgia, Branch v. Texas,* 408 U.S. 238 (1972).

47. *Schick v. Reed,* 419 U.S. 256 (1974).

48. Id. at 266–267.

49. Id. at 274.

PRIVILEGE AND IMMUNITY (PP. 322–334)

1. See Neal Devins, "Executive Privilege and Congressional and Independent Investigations," in *Separation of Powers: Documents and Commentary,* ed. Katy J. Harriger (Washington, D.C.: CQ Press, 2003), 149–162.

2. *Ex parte Milligan,* 4 Wall. (71 U.S.) 2 (1866).

3. *Mississippi v. Johnson,* 4 Wall. (71 U.S.) 475 (1867).

4. *Marbury v. Madison,* 1 Cr. (5 U.S.) 137 (1803).

5. *Mississippi v. Johnson,* 4 Wall. (71 U.S.) 475 at 500–501, 498–499 (1867).

6. Id. at 501.

7. *Georgia v. Stanton,* 6 Wall. (73 U.S.) 50 (1868).

8. Id. at 77.

9. *Kendall v. United States ex. rel. Stokes,* 12 Pet. (37 U.S.) 524 at 609–610, 613 (1838).

10. Id. at 613.

11. *Little v. Bareme,* 2 Cr. (6 U.S.) 170 (1804); *United States v. Lee,* 106 U.S. 196 (1882); *Bivens v. Six Unknown Named Agents of the Federal Bureau of Narcotics,* 403 U.S. 388 (1971).

12. *Barr v. Mateo,* 360 U.S. 564 (1959); *Butz v. Economou,* 438 U.S. 478 (1978).

13. *Nixon v. Fitzgerald,* 457 U.S. 731 at 749 (1982).

14. Id. at 751–753.

15. Id. at 757–758.

16. *Harlow v. Fitzgerald,* 457 U.S. 800 (1982).

17. *Clinton v. Jones,* 520 U.S. 681 (1997).

18. *Nixon v. Fitzgerald,* 457 U.S. 731 (1982).

19. *Clinton v. Jones,* 520 U.S. 681 at 694 (1997).

20. Id. at 701–702.

21. Id. at 713.

22. Norman Dorson and Richard Shattuck, "Executive Privilege, the Congress and the Court," *Ohio State Law Journal* 35 (1974): 13.

23. Herman Wollkinson, "Demand of Congressional Committees for Executive Papers," *Federal Bar Journal* 10 (1948–49): 103–150; Robert Kramer and Herman Marcuse, "Executive Privilege—A Study of the Period 1953–1960," *George Washington Law Review* 29 (1961): 623–718, 827–916; Irving Younger, "Congressional Investigations and Executive Secrecy: A Study in Separation of Powers," *University of Pittsburgh Law Review* 20 (1958–59): 757, 773.

24. J. Russell Wiggins, "Government Operations and the Public's Right to Know," *Federal Bar Journal* 19 (1959): 76.

25. Raoul Berger, *Executive Privilege: A Constitutional Myth* (Cambridge: Harvard University Press, 1974), 1.

26. *United States v. Nixon,* 418 U.S. 683 (1974).

27. *Kaiser Aluminum & Chem. Co. v. United States,* 157 F. Supp. 937, 943 (Ct. Cl. 1958).

28. Berger, *Executive Privilege,* 178–179, 232–233. For Washington's message to the House on this matter, see *A Compilation*

of the Messages and Papers of the Presidents (New York: Bureau of National Literature, 1897), or the Avalon Project at Yale Law School, "George Washington: Message to the House Regarding Documents Relative to the Jay Treaty March 30, 1796," http://avalon.law.yale.edu/default.asp.

29. *Marbury v. Madison,* 1 Cr. (5 U.S.) 137 at 165–166 (1803).

30. Id. at 170.

31. Berger, *Executive Privilege,* 179–181, 187–194.

32. Ibid., 181.

33. *Boske v. Comingore,* 177 U.S. 459 (1900); *United States ex rel. Touhy v. Ragan, Warden, et al.,* 340 U.S. 462 (1951).

34. *McGrain v. Daugherty,* 273 U.S. 135 (1927).

35. *Chicago & Southern Airlines v. Waterman S.S. Co.,* 333 U.S. 103, 105 (1948).

36. Id. at 111.

37. *United States v. Reynolds,* 345 U.S. 1 at 11 (1953).

38. Id.

39. *Tenet v. Doe,* 544 U.S. 1 (2005).

40. Government and General Research Division, Library of Congress, "The Present Limits of Executive Privilege," *Congressional Record,* 93rd Cong., 1st sess., March 28, 1973, H2243–2246.

41. Ibid.

42. President Eisenhower to the Secretary of Defense, May 17, 1954, *Public Papers of the Presidents, Dwight D. Eisenhower, 1954* (Washington, D.C.: U.S. Government Printing Office, 1960), 483–485.

43. Senate Committee on Armed Services, Special Preparedness Subcommittee, *Military Cold War and Speech Review Policies, Hearings,* 87th Cong., 2nd sess., 1962, 508–509.

44. Ibid.

45. President Johnson to the Hon. John E. Moss, April 2, 1965. *Public Papers of the Presidents, Lyndon B. Johnson, 1965,* 2 vols. (Washington, D.C.: U.S. Government Printing Office, 1966), 2:376.

46. Senate Committee on the Judiciary, Subcommittee on the Separation of Powers, *Executive Privilege: The Withholding of Information by the Executive, Hearings,* 92nd Cong., 1st sess., 1971, 2.

47. "Limits of Executive Privilege," H2243–2246.

48. *New York Times Co. v. United States, United States v. Washington Post,* 403 U.S. 713 (1971).

49. *Environmental Protection Agency v. Mink,* 410 U.S. 73 (1973); *Congress and the Nation,* vol. 4 (Washington, D.C.: Congressional Quarterly, 1977), 805–806.

50. *United States v. Nixon, Nixon v. United States,* 418 U.S. 683 at 705–706 (1974). See also *Watergate: Chronology of a Crisis* (Washington, D.C.: Congressional Quarterly, 1975, 1999).

51. *United States v. Nixon, Nixon v. United States,* 418 U.S. 683 at 706–707 (1974).

52. Id. at 708, 711.

53. Id. at 711–713.

54. *Nixon v. Administrator, General Services Administration,* 433 U.S. 425 (1977).

55. Id. at 433–435.

56. Id. at 443.

57. Id. at 451–452.

58. Id. at 520.

59. Id. at 545.

60. *Cheney v. United States Dist. Court for D.C.,* 542 U.S. 367 (2004).

61. Id. at 385.

62. Id. at 384.

THE PRESIDENT VERSUS THE COURT (PP. 335–360)

1. See generally James F. Simon, *What Kind of Nation: Thomas Jefferson, John Marshall, and the Epic Struggle to Create a United States* (New York: Simon and Schuster, 2002).

2. Samuel F. Bemis, *A Diplomatic History of the United States* (New York: Holt, 1936), 95–100.

3. Samuel E. Morison, Henry S. Commager, and William E. Leuchtenburg, *The Growth of the American Republic,* 2 vols. (New York: Oxford University Press, 1969), 1:218–319.

4. James M. Smith, *Freedom's Fetters: The Alien and Sedition Laws and American Civil Liberties* (Ithaca, N.Y.: Cornell University Press, 1956).

5. Frank M. Anderson, "Contemporary Opinion of the Virginia and Kentucky Resolutions," *American Historical Review* 5 (1899): 45–63, 225–252; Adrienne Koch, *Jefferson and Madison, The Great Collaboration* (New York: Knopf, 1950).

6. Eugene P. Link, *Democratic-Republican Societies* (New York: Octagon Books, 1965); Noble E. Cunningham Jr., *The Jeffersonian Republicans: The Formation of Party Organization, 1789–1801* (Chapel Hill: University of North Carolina Press, 1957); Alexander DeConde, *The Quasi-War: The Politics and Diplomacy of the Undeclared War with France, 1797–1801* (New York: Scribner's, 1966).

7. Donald O. Dewey, *Marshall versus Jefferson: The Political Background of* Marbury v. Madison (New York: Knopf, 1970), 3–4.

8. Ibid., 5–8.

9. Leonard Baker, *John Marshall: A Life in Law* (New York: Macmillan, 1974), 61.

10. William Stinchcombe, "The Diplomacy of the WXYZ Affair," *William and Mary Quarterly,* Vol. 3.34, Issue 4 (October 1977): 590–617.

11. Dewey, *Marshall versus Jefferson,* 31.

12. Erwin C. Surrency, "The Judiciary Act of 1801," *American Journal of Legal History* 2 (1958): 53–65; Kathryn Turner, "Federalist Policy and the Judiciary Act of 1801," *William and*

Mary Quarterly 22 (1965): 3–32; Dewey, *Marshall versus Jefferson*, 55, 58–59.

13. Dewey, *Marshall versus Jefferson*, 68–69; Richard E. Ellis, *The Jeffersonian Crisis: Courts and Politics in the Young Republic* (New York: Oxford University Press, 1971), 45, 50–51.

14. *Marbury v. Madison*, 1 Cr. (5 U.S.) 137 at 138–139 (1803). See generally Mark A. Graber and Michael Perhac, eds., *Marbury versus Madison: Documents and Commentary* (Washington, D.C.: CQ Press, 2002).

15. *Marbury v. Madison*, 1 Cr. (5 U.S.) 137 at 173 (1803).

16. Id. at 158.

17. Dewey, *Marshall versus Jefferson*, 135–141.

18. See *Holmes v. Walton* (New Jersey, 1780); *Trevett v. Weeden* (Rhode Island, 1786); *Bayard v. Singleton* 1 N.C. 5 (1787); *Ware v. Hylton*, 3 Dall. (3 U.S.) 199 (1796).

19. Dewey, *Marshall versus Jefferson*, 141; Ellis, *Jeffersonian Crisis*, 72–73, 76.

20. Baker, *John Marshall*, 148; Richard B. Lillich, "The Chase Impeachment," *American Journal of Legal History* 4 (1960): 49–72.

21. Baker, *John Marshall*, 418–419; Dewey, *Marshall versus Jefferson*, 148–149.

22. Ellis, *Jeffersonian Crisis*, 81.

23. Charles Warren, *The Supreme Court in United States History*, 2 vols. (Boston: Little, Brown, 1922), 1:236–237.

24. Ibid. See also Luther Martin's speech at the impeachment trial. *Annals of Congress*, 14:429–436.

25. Leonard Levy, *Jefferson and Civil Liberties: The Darker Side* (New York: Quadrangle, 1973).

26. Baker, *John Marshall*, 452–453.

27. Thomas P. Abernathy, *The Burr Conspiracy* (New York: Oxford University Press, 1954).

28. "The Deposition of William Eaton, Esq.," in *Ex parte Bollman*, 4 Cr. (8 U.S.) 75 Appendix A at 463–466 (1807).

29. Baker, *John Marshall*, 452–453.

30. Dewey, *Marshall versus Jefferson*, 162–163.

31. *United States v. Burr*, 25 Fed. Cas. 187 (No. 14,694) (1807).

32. Raoul Berger, *Executive Privilege: A Constitutional Myth* (Cambridge: Harvard University Press, 1974), 193.

33. Bradley Chapin, *The American Law of Treason: Revolutionary and Early National Origins* (Seattle: University of Washington Press, 1964).

34. Baker, *John Marshall*, 464–465, 513.

35. Ibid., 514–515. See also *A Compilation of the Messages and Papers of the Presidents* (New York: Bureau of National Literature, 1897), 2:576–591.

36. James D. Richardson, ed., *Messages and Papers of the Presidents*, 20 vols. (New York: Bureau of National Literature, 1897), 3:1145.

37. Morison, Commager, and Leuchtenburg, *Growth of the American Republic*, 1:419–423; John W. Ward, *Andrew Jackson:*

Symbol for an Age (New York: Oxford University Press, 1962); Richard E. Ellis, *Andrew Jackson* (Washington, D.C.: CQ Press, 2003).

38. Warren, *Supreme Court in United States History*, 1:730–731.

39. *Johnson and Graham's Lessee v. McIntosh*, 8 Wheat. (21 U.S.) 543 (1823); Warren, *Supreme Court in United States History*, 1:732–733.

40. Warren, *Supreme Court in United States History*, 1:1733–734.

41. *Cherokee Nation v. Georgia*, 5 Pet. (30 U.S.) 1 (1831).

42. *Worcester v. Georgia*, 6 Pet. (31 U.S.) 515 (1832).

43. Warren, *Supreme Court in United States History*, 1:754.

44. Morison, Commager, and Leuchtenburg, *Growth of the American Republic*, 1:438–442.

45. Richardson, *Messages and Papers of the Presidents*, 3:1203–1204.

46. *Scott v. Sandford*, 19 How. (60 U.S.) 393 (1857).

47. Lincoln called *Scott* a wrong interpretation of history and a violation of the Declaration of Independence. See Roy P. Basler, ed., *The Collected Works of Abraham Lincoln* (New Brunswick, N.J.: Rutgers University Press, 1953), 2:398–410. Lincoln's comments are also accessible at "The Collected Works of Abraham Lincoln," http://www.hti.umich.edu/l/lincoln.

48. Basler, *Collected Works of Abraham Lincoln* 7:3210.

49. *Ex parte Merryman*, 17 Fed. Cas. 144 (1861); Carl B. Swisher, *American Constitutional Development*, 2nd ed. (Cambridge, Mass.: Houghton Mifflin, 1954), 279.

50. Swisher, *American Constitutional Development*, 280–281.

51. *Ex parte Merryman* in Henry S. Commager, ed., *Documents of American History*, 7th ed. (New York: Appleton-Century-Crofts, 1963), 398–401.

52. Richardson, *Messages and Papers of the Presidents*, 7:3225–3226.

53. Carl B. Swisher, *History of the Supreme Court of the United States*, vol. 5, *The Taney Period, 1836–64* (New York: Macmillan, 1971), 852–853.

54. Warren, *Supreme Court in United States History*, 2:372–373.

55. Richardson, *Messages and Papers of the Presidents*, 7:3303–3305.

56. Lincoln to Erastus Corning, June 12, 1863, in *The Complete Works of Abraham Lincoln*, ed. John C. Nicolay and John Hay, 12 vols. (New York: Francis D. Tandy, 1905–1934), 8:298–314.

57. Alfred H. Kelly and Winfred A. Harbison, *The American Constitution*, 7th ed. (New York: Norton, 1991), 413.

58. *Ex parte Milligan*, 4 Wall. (71 U.S.) 2 (1866).

59. *Hepburn v. Griswold*, 8 Wall. (75 U.S.) 603 (1870).

60. Morison, Commager, and Leuchtenburg, *Growth of the American Republic,* 2:485–487, 502–503.

61. Samuel I. Rosenman, ed., *The Public Papers and Addresses of Franklin D. Roosevelt,* 5 vols. (New York: Random House, 1938), 2:15.

62. William F. Swindler, *Court and Constitution in the Twentieth Century,* 2 vols. (Indianapolis and New York: Bobbs-Merrill, 1970), 2:20–21; Morison, Commager, and Leuchtenburg, *Growth of the American Republic,* 2:484–489.

63. Swisher, *American Constitutional Development,* 848–859; Commager, *Documents of American History,* 242–246.

64. Swindler, *Court and Constitution in the Twentieth Century,* 2:23–24; *U.S. Statutes at Large* 48 (1934):195.

65. Robert H. Jackson, *The Struggle for Judicial Supremacy: A Study of a Crisis in American Power Politics* (New York: Random House, 1941), 83–84; Swisher, *American Constitutional Development,* 920–921.

66. *Home Building and Loan Association v. Blaisdell,* 290 U.S. 398 (1934).

67. *Nebbia v. New York,* 291 U.S. 502 (1934).

68. *Norman v. The Baltimore and Ohio Railroad Co.,* 294 U.S. 240 (1935); *John N. Perry v. United States,* 294 U.S. 330 (1935); *Ashwander v. Tennessee Valley Authority,* 297 U.S. 288 (1936).

69. *Panama Refining Co. v. Ryan,* 293 U.S. 388 (1935); *Amazon Petroleum Corp. v. Ryan,* 293 U.S. 389 (1935).

70. *Railroad Retirement Board v. Alton,* 295 U.S. 330 (1935).

71. *Louisville Bank v. Radford,* 295 U.S. 555 (1935).

72. *A. L. A. Schechter Poultry Corp. v. United States,* 295 U.S. 495 (1935).

73. *Humphrey's Executor v. United States,* 295 U.S. 602 (1935).

74. Jackson, *Struggle for Judicial Supremacy,* 12.

75. Ibid., 113.

76. *A. L. A. Schechter Poultry Corp. v. United States,* 295 U.S. 495 at 536–539, 541–542 (1935).

77. Rosenman, *Public Papers and Addresses of Franklin D. Roosevelt,* 4:215, 221.

78. *United States v. Butler,* 297 U.S. 1 (1936).

79. *Carter v. Carter Coal Co.,* 298 U.S. 238 at 288–289, 303 (1936).

80. *Ashton v. Cameron County District,* 298 U.S. 513 (1936).

81. Id. at 542–543.

82. Swindler, *Court and Constitution in the Twentieth Century,* 2:56.

83. Kelly and Harbison, *American Constitution,* 714.

84. Rosenman, *Public Papers and Addresses of Franklin D. Roosevelt,* 5:635–636, 638–639, 641–642.

85. *Reform of the Federal Judiciary,* 75th Cong., 1st sess., 1937, S. Rept. 711.

86. Commager, *Documents of American History,* 382–383.

87. U.S. Congress. *Recommendation to Reorganize Judicial Branch,* 75th Cong., 1st sess., H.R. Doc. 142. See also *Public Papers and Addresses of Franklin D. Roosevelt, 1937* (New York: McMillan, 1941), 122–133.

88. Harold L. Ickes, *The Secret Diary of Harold L. Ickes,* 3 vols. (New York: Simon and Schuster, 1954), 2:7.

89. Jackson, *Struggle for Judicial Supremacy,* 187.

90. Ickes, *Diary,* 2:74–75.

91. Ibid., 88–89.

92. "Address by the President of the United States, March 9, 1937," in Commager, *Documents of American History,* 383–387.

93. Ickes, *Diary,* 2:74–75, 93, 104, 109, 115, 251; Swindler, *Court and Constitution in the Twentieth Century,* 68–71.

94. Ickes, *Diary,* 2:70, 98, 100, 103, 105–106, 251, 424. See *Congressional Record,* 75th Cong., 1st sess., July 9, 1937, 6966–6981.

95. Swindler, *Court and Constitution in the Twentieth Century,* 71–73.

96. *West Coast Hotel Co. v. Parrish,* 300 U.S. 379 at 390 (1937).

97. *Wright v. Vinton Branch,* 300 U.S. 440 (1937), overturning *Louisville Joint Stock Land Bank v. Radford,* 295 U.S. 555 (1935).

98. *NLRB v. Jones & Laughlin Steel Corp.,* 301 U.S. 1 (1937).

99. *Steward Machine Co. v. Davis,* 301 U.S. 548 (1937); *Helvering v. Davis,* 307 U.S. 619 (1937).

100. *Morehead v. New York ex rel. Tipaldo,* 298 U.S. 587 (1936).

101. *West Coast Hotel v. Parrish,* 300 U.S. 379 (1937).

102. Max Freedman, ed., *Roosevelt and Frankfurter: Their Correspondence, 1928–1945* (Boston: Little, Brown, 1967), 392–395.

103. "Judiciary Reform Act of 1937, August 24, 1937," in Commager, *Documents of American History,* 391–393; Jackson, *Struggle for Judicial Supremacy,* 192–193; Ickes, *Diary,* 2:144, 152–153, 170–172.

104. Kelly and Harbison, *American Constitution,* 718.

105. James T. Patterson, *Congressional Conservatism and the New Deal: The Growth of the Conservative Coalition in Congress, 1933–1939* (Lexington: University of Kentucky Press, 1967).

106. *United States v. Darby,* 312 U.S. 100 (1941); *Mulford v. Smith,* 307 U.S. 38 (1939).

107. Harry S. Truman, *Memoirs,* 2 vols. (Garden City, N.Y.: Doubleday, 1956), 2:465–467, 468.

108. Ibid., 471–472.

109. Ibid., 469–470.

110. *Youngstown Sheet and Tube Co. v. Sawyer,* 343 U.S. 579 at 609 (1952).

111. Id. at 662.

112. Id. at 632.

113. Id.

114. Truman, *Memoirs,* 2:428.

115. Ibid., 477.

116. Ibid., 478.

117. See *Watergate: Chronology of a Crisis* (Washington, D.C.: Congressional Quarterly, 1975, 1999).

118. *New York Times Co. v. United States, United States v. The Washington Post,* 403 U.S. 713 (1971).

119. Id. at 714–715, 724–725.

120. *U.S. Statutes at Large* 82 (1968): 198 ff., PL 90–351.

121. *United States v. United States District Court,* 407 U.S. 297 at 301 (1972).

122. Id. at 317.

123. Kelly and Harbison, *American Constitution,* 1020–1021.

124. *Nixon: The Fifth Year of His Presidency* (Washington, D.C.: Congressional Quarterly, 1974), 153-A.

125. *Train v. City of New York,* 420 U.S. 35 (1975); *Train v. Campaign Clean Water,* 420 U.S. 136 (1975).

126. See *Watergate: Chronology of a Crisis,* 191–194, 220, 224–225, 293–294, 297, 341–345, 353–362.

127. Ibid., 535–537, 600–648.

128. Ibid., 689–692, 711–723, 734–742, 754–756.

129. PL 93-526 (1974); *Congress and the Nation,* vol. 4 (Washington, D.C.: Congressional Quarterly, 1977), 952.

130. *Nixon v. Administrator, General Services Administration,* 433 U.S. 425 (1977).

131. *Nixon v. Warner Communications Inc.,* 453 U.S. 589 (1978).

132. *Morrison v. Olson,* 487 U.S. 654 (1988).

133. "Detention, Treatment and Trial of Certain Non-Citizens in the War against Terrorism," *Federal Register,* November 13, 2001, 57833.

134. *Johnson v. Eisentrager,* 339 U.S. 763 (1950).

135. *Rasul v. Bush,* 542 U.S. 466 (2004).

136. Id. at 485.

137. *Hamdi v. Rumsfeld,* 542 U.S. 507 at 509 (2004).

138. Id. at 518.

139. Id. at 519.

140. Id. at 533.

141. Id. at 536.

142. Id. at 554.

143. Id. at 579.

144. *Padilla v. Rumsfeld,* 542 U.S. 426 (2004).

145. *Ex parte Quirin,* 317 U.S. 1 (1942).

146. *Hamdan v. Rumsfeld,* 548 U.S. 557 (2006).

147. *Boumediene v. Bush,* 553 U.S. —- (2008).

148. *Cheney v. United States Dist. Court for D.C.,* 542 U.S. 367 (2004).

149. *ACLU v NSA,* cert. denied Feb. 19, 2008; *El-Masri v. Tenet,* cert. denied, Oct. 9, 2007.

chapter 4

The Court and the States

WHEN DELEGATES FROM TWELVE STATES met in Philadelphia in 1787 to draft a constitution for the United States (Rhode Islanders stayed away) they designed a federal government whose laws would be the "supreme Law of the Land." They began the text of the Constitution with "We the People of the United States, in Order to form a more perfect Union." They set broad purposes for the federal government: providing a "common defence," establishing justice, and promoting "the general Welfare." What role then, one might ask, was left for the states? Were they independent and sovereign states with the full power to act on their own, rather like France and Germany in the European Union? Were they mere "subdivisions" of the federal government, subject to command from Washington? Were they something in between, semi-independent and sovereign in some ways but not in others? The framers left unresolved the conflict between federal authority and states' rights, somewhat like their treatment of the inherent conflict between slavery and liberty.

The role of the states in the federal Union has been at the center of a constitutional debate that has preoccupied the Supreme Court since 1787. Having two sovereign entities—the states and the federal government—seeking to occupy the same political turf could be a formula for war (and not only in the metaphorical sense). The Civil War was fundamentally a dispute over whether the ultimate source of sovereignty rested with the states or with the federal government. The Union's victory over the Confederacy settled one matter: the states are not free to secede or to break their ties to the federal government. Beyond that, nearly every other imaginable issue pitting the states against the federal government has come before the Court for resolution.

In 1869, just four years after the end of the Civil War, the Court referred to the states as "indestructible" and possessed of the "right of self-government."[1] It was a brave assertion, particularly during a time when the Reconstruction Congress was asserting federal control over the rebellious states of the defeated Confederacy. Throughout its history, the Supreme Court has often been out of step with the political tune of the times when dealing with states. It has acted as a brake on federal power, even when, as in the 1870s and the 1930s, elected leaders favored a more robust role for the national authority. At these moments, the Court has been more attuned to the Constitution and its original vision of a system of a divided government, with each branch having separate and distinct powers. Also from this perspective, the states play the role of equal partners in the system, not secondary players to the national government.

In the 1990s the Court again took stock of states' power, after a long period in which the reach of federal power had gone unchecked: "States are not mere political subdivisions of the United States. State governments are neither regional offices nor administrative agencies of the Federal Government," Justice Sandra Day O'Connor wrote in a 1992 opinion that trumpeted the revival of states' rights. "The positions occupied by state

JIM CROW LAW.

UPHELD BY THE UNITED STATES SUPREME COURT.

Statute Within the Competency of the Louisiana Legislature and Railroads—Must Furnish Separate Cars for Whites and Blacks.

Washington, May 18.—The Supreme Court today in an opinion read by Justice Brown, sustained the constitutionality of the law in Louisiana requiring the railroads of that State to provide separate cars for white and colored passengers. There was no interstate commerce feature in the case for the railroad upon which the incident occurred giving rise to case—Plessey vs. Ferguson—East Louisiana railroad, was and is operated wholly within the State, to the laws of Congress of many of the States. The opinion states that by the analogy of the laws of Congress, and of many of states requiring establishment of separate schools for children of two races and other similar laws, the statute in question was within competency of Louisiana Legislature, exercising the police power of the State. The judgment of the Supreme Court of State upholding law was therefore upheld.

Mr. Justice Harlan announced a very vigorous dissent saying that he saw nothing but mischief in all such laws. In his view of the case, no power in the land had right to regulate the enjoyment of civil rights upon the basis of race. It would be just as reasonable and proper, he said, for states to pass laws requiring separate cars to be furnished for Catholic and Protestants, or for descendants of those of Teutonic race and those of Latin race.

The Court in *Plessy v. Ferguson* (1892) upheld Louisiana's Jim Crow laws requiring separate railroad cars for white and black passengers. *Plessy v. Ferguson* established the "separate but equal" doctrine permitting legal segregation to flourish for the next sixty years. The Warren Court unanimously abandoned the doctrine in *Brown v. Board of Education* (1954), declaring racial segregation unconstitutional and setting off a reaction in the southern states comparable in intensity only to the hostility of the previous century's debate over slavery.

officials appear nowhere on the Federal Government's most detailed organizational chart. The Constitution instead 'leaves to the several States a residuary and inviolable sovereignty,'" she said, quoting *Federalist* No. 39.[2]

O'Connor's proclamation was more than a statement of the obvious. It was intended to counter the growing imbalance of power in the twentieth century in favor of Washington over the states. This balance has shifted back and forth over the years. In the nineteenth century, the Court under Chief Justice John Marshall leaned in favor of a national power. His successor, Roger B. Taney, tilted in favor of the states. Although the Civil War obviously dealt a defeat to states' rights, the Court in the years afterward repeatedly undercut the new constitutional power of the federal government to shape and enforce national civil rights. The reemergence of states' rights culminated in *Plessy v. Ferguson* (1896), in which the Court gave its blessing to southern segregation laws, ruling "separate but equal" treatment as constitutional. After World War II the Court reasserted the view that the states must bend to the will of federal authority on matters such as school segregation, civil rights, and equal voting rights. In the last decade of the twentieth century, the pendulum swung back, as Justice O'Connor and the Rehnquist Court reasserted the role of the states as central players within a federal system. Still, there remains no simple or clear formula for defining a state's authority versus federal power. The scales used by the Court to weigh their respective powers have risen and fallen often in the past, and surely will do so again.

THE NATIONAL PERIOD

"The general government, though limited as to its objects, is supreme with respect to those objects," wrote Chief Justice Marshall in 1821:

> With the ample powers confided to this supreme government are connected many express and important limitations on the sovereignty of the states. The powers of the Union, on the great subjects of war, peace, and commerce…are in themselves limitations of the sovereignty of the states.[3]

The success of the Union was by no means a certainty. The confederation that preceded it was a failure: the

THE NATURE OF THE UNION

Four years after the Civil War ended, the Supreme Court considered and discussed the meaning of a "state" and the nature of the Union in *Texas v. White* (1869). During the war, the Confederate government of Texas had sold some of the U.S. bonds in its possession to one George W. White and other purchasers in return for supplies. After the war, the new government of Texas sued White and the other purchasers to recover title to the bonds. The case was argued before the Supreme Court in February 1869 and was decided on April 12. The Court ruled that Texas could recover title to the bonds, because the actions of the Confederate government were not binding.[1]

Because this case was brought to the Court by Texas under the Constitution's grant of original jurisdiction over a case brought by a state, the Court first considered the status of the state of Texas. Had it, by its secession and participation in the rebellion against national authority, rendered itself ineligible to bring such suits? The answer was no. In the process of reaching that answer, Chief Justice Salmon P. Chase analyzed "the correct idea of a State" and its relationship to the Union:

> The word "state" ... describes sometimes a people or community of individuals united more or less closely in political relations, inhabiting temporarily or permanently the same country; often it denotes only the country or territorial region, inhabited by such a community; not unfrequently it is applied to the government under which the people live; at other times it represents the combined idea of people, territory, and government.
>
> It is not difficult to see that in all these senses the primary conception is that of a people or community. The people, in whatever territory dwelling, either temporarily or permanently, and whether organized under a regular government, or united by looser or less definite relations, constitute the State.
>
> This is undoubtedly the fundamental idea upon which the republican institutions of our own country are established....
>
> In the Constitution the term "state" most frequently expresses the combined idea just noticed of people, territory and government. A State, in the ordinary sense of the Constitution, is a political community of free citizens, occupying a territory of defined boundaries, and organized under a government sanctioned and limited by a written constitution, and established by the consent of the governed. It is the union of such States, under a common constitution, which forms the distinct and greater political unit, which that Constitution designates as the United States, and makes of the people and States which compose it one people and one country.[2]

Chase then recited the steps Texas took upon seceding:

> In all respects, so far as the object could be accomplished by ordinances of the Convention, by Acts of the Legislature, and by votes of the citizens, the relations of Texas to the Union were broken up. ... Did Texas, in consequence of these Acts, cease to be a State? Or, if not, did the State cease to be a member of the Union? ...
>
> The Union of the States never was a purely artificial and arbitrary relation. It began among the Colonies, and grew out of common origin, mutual sympathies, kindred principles, similar interests and geographical relations. It was confirmed and strengthened by the necessities of war, and received definite form, and character, and sanction from the Articles of Confederation. By these the Union was solemnly declared to "be perpetual." And when these articles were found to be inadequate ... the Constitution was ordained "to form a more perfect Union." It is difficult to convey the idea of indissoluble unity more clearly.... What can be indissoluble if a perpetual Union, made more perfect, is not?
>
> But the perpetuity and indissolubility of the Union by no means implies the loss of distinct and individual existence, or of the right of self-government by the States.... [W]e have already had occasion to remark ... that "without the States in union, there could be no such political body as the United States." ... [I]t may be not unreasonably said that the preservation of the States, and the maintenance of their governments are as much within the design and care of the Constitution as the preservation of the Union and the maintenance of the National Government. The Constitution, in all its provisions, looks to an indestructible Union, composed of indestructible States.
>
> When, therefore, Texas became one of the United States, she entered into a [sic] indissoluble relation. All the obligations of perpetual union, and all the guaranties of republican government in the Union, attached at once to the State. The Act which consummated her admission into the Union was something more than a compact; it was the incorporation of a new member into the political body. And it was final.[3]

---

1. *Texas v. White, 7 Wall.* (74 U.S.) 700 (1869).

2. Id. at 720–721.

3. Id. at 724, 725, 726.

central government was too weak; the states were too strong. During the nation's first century, the overriding question was a simple one: Would the nation survive? The threat was not from outside, but from within. Would centrifugal force—the states' insistence on retaining power that should belong to the national government—splinter the Union?

On the eve of the Civil War, Chief Justice Taney wrote, "The Constitution was not formed merely to guard the States against danger from foreign nations, but mainly to secure union and harmony at home; for if this object could be attained, there would be but little danger from abroad."[4] Until the conflict between states' rights and national power moved onto the battlefields of the Civil War, much of it was focused in the small courtrooms that served as early homes to the U.S. Supreme Court. As Charles Warren, historian of the Court's first century, explains,

> The success of the new government depended on the existence of a supreme tribunal, free from local political bias or prejudice, vested with power to give an interpretation to federal laws and treaties which should be uniform throughout the land, to confine the federal authority to its legitimate field of operation, and to control state aggression on the federal domain.[5]

Two of the nation's greatest statesmen, both Virginians, led the national debate of the early decades over the respective rights and powers of the states and the national government. Speaking for the states was Thomas Jefferson, the third president of the United States. Speaking for national supremacy was John Marshall, its fourth chief justice. Three years before Jefferson and Marshall moved into the White House and the Supreme Court chambers, respectively, Jefferson set out his view of the relationship of state to federal power in the Kentucky Resolutions, written to protest congressional enactment of the Alien and Sedition Acts.

Jefferson's view of this relationship contrasted sharply with the "supreme government" view set out by Marshall in 1821. The states, wrote Jefferson, "constituted a general government for special purposes, delegated to that government certain definite powers, reserving, each state to itself, the residuary mass of right to their own self-government....Whensoever the general government assumed undelegated powers, its acts are unauthoritative, void and of no force."[6] By Jefferson's death, in 1826, it was clear that Marshall's views, not his, had prevailed. The states were operating under clear and definite constitutional restraints applied firmly by the Supreme Court. The laws of ten states had been struck down by the Court because they were in conflict with federal treaties, impaired the obligation of contracts, or interfered too much with the broadly construed powers of Congress. Jefferson conceded defeat six months before his death, as he wrote to a friend,

I see, as you do...the rapid strides with which the Federal branch of our Government is advancing towards the usurpation of all the rights reserved to the States, and the consolidation in itself of all powers, foreign and domestic; and that too by constructions which, if legitimate, leave no limits to their power....

Under the power to regulate commerce, they assume indefinitely that also over agriculture and manufactures....Under the authority to establish postroads, they claim that of cutting down mountains for the construction of roads, of digging canals, and, aided by a little sophistry on the words "general welfare," a right to do, not only the acts to effect that which are sufficiently enumerated and permitted, but whatsoever they shall think or pretend will be for the general welfare.[7]

The process of subordination of state power to national power that Jefferson deplored slowed in the decades following his death and that of Marshall in 1835. Chief Justice Taney, Marshall's successor, held views much more congenial to Jefferson's. During Taney's tenure, the Court left undisturbed the basic principles of national supremacy set out by the seminal rulings of the Marshall Court. Within that framework, however, the Taney Court found room for broad state powers—the power to govern its land, its people, and its resources, to ensure the public health, and to preserve the public welfare. The rulings recognizing this "police power" survived as good law and strong precedent long after the Taney Court's decision in *Scott v. Sandford* (1857) was overturned, first by war and then by the Fourteenth Amendment.

JUDICIAL REVIEW AND THE STATES

In the Reconstruction era, the Supreme Court protected the southern states from "reforms" in the status of blacks desired by some members of Congress, and in so doing, the Court delayed for a century the movement of blacks toward equality. The first such ruling came in the *Slaughterhouse Cases* (1873). From that moment on, the Court steadily limited the list of rights protected by the Fourteenth Amendment against state infringement. Much of post–Civil War civil rights legislation was narrowly construed or invalidated altogether as unconstitutional. Half a century later, a scholar wrote that had this set of cases been decided otherwise, the States would have largely lost their autonomy and become, as political entities, only of historical interest. If every civil right possessed by a citizen of a State was to receive the protection of the National Judiciary, and if every case involving such a right was to be subject to its review, the States would be placed in a hopelessly subordinate position.... The boundary lines between the States and the National Government would be practically abolished.[8]

Yet even as this was written, the Supreme Court was beginning to extend national protection to the rights of individuals threatened by state action.

THE STATE AND THE ECONOMY: PROTECTING PROPERTY

In contrast to the Court's post–Civil War reluctance to extend federal control over states' treatment of the individual, the justices did not hesitate to extend federal protection over property threatened by overly vigorous assertion of state police powers. After a brief fling with state regulation in the 1870s and 1880s, the Court settled into a laissez-faire posture from which it wielded the Fourteenth Amendment's due process guarantee to control state regulatory efforts. As the Contract Clause faded from use in this fashion, the due process guarantee was wielded more often. Using the Tenth Amendment's concept of powers reserved to the states—and therefore, the Court reasoned, denied to the national government—the Court struck down federal regulatory laws as intruding upon the rights of the states. The result was a twilight zone or no-man's-land where regulation could not be effectively imposed by either state or national authority.

The Great Depression and the New Deal—and the new social and economic realities they created—brought a dramatic end to this period. The Court widened the field for state regulation, even as it upheld the extension of federal power deeper than ever into the domain of the states. Since 1937, explains one scholar, "the Court's function [has been] more like that of a traffic cop—to see that our multiple legislatures, in their many activities, do not collide, to make sure that the road is kept free for

national power, which, under the rules laid down in 1789, has the right of way."[9]

THE STATE AND INDIVIDUALS

As the Court relinquished as no longer necessary its role as guardian of property and commerce against state interference, it began to assert the role of protector of individuals against state action. The Bill of Rights, the first ten amendments, protects people only against action by the federal government. Early in the nation's history, the Court refused to extend those protections to anyone threatened by state action. In the mid-1920s, however, the Court began using the Fourteenth Amendment's guarantee of due process to protect certain of those individual rights against infringement by the state. The First Amendment freedoms of expression were the first to win such protection, followed by due process rights of fair trial and fair treatment for persons suspected or accused of crimes. Then, at mid-century, the Fourteenth Amendment's equal protection guarantee came into use as the effective guarantor of individual rights that its authors had intended it to be.

Using the Equal Protection Clause as a measure, the Court struck down state laws requiring racial segregation in public schools, public transportation, and public accommodations, setting off a civil rights revolution that continues today. Black citizens were not the only beneficiaries of equal protection rulings; during the second half of the twentieth century, the Court found a similar rationale useful for discarding laws that discriminated against women and aliens as well. Just as the Court's landmark rulings of the Marshall era establishing national supremacy over state rights were met with resistance from the states, so too were the Court's rulings under Chief Justice Earl Warren. The Court's decision decreeing an end to public school segregation set off a reaction in the southern states comparable in intensity only to the hostility of the previous century's debate over slavery. The antagonism was further inflamed by the Supreme Court's interference in matters previously left entirely to the states, such as the drawing of electoral district lines and the treatment of criminal suspects. An "Impeach Earl Warren" movement developed, motivated by a variety of grievances.

TOWARD A HEALTHY BALANCE

Just as Chief Justice Marshall's nationalism was moderated by Taney's sensitivity to state concerns, so Warren's tenure was followed by that of two chief justices—Warren E. Burger and William H. Rehnquist—who gave more weight to a state's right and need to operate with flexibility within the federal system. Justice Hugo L. Black—who came to the Court in 1937 as a liberal southern senator and Franklin D. Roosevelt's first appointment to the bench—sounded this theme for the Court of the 1970s as he described what he called "Our Federalism":

> a proper respect for state functions, a recognition of the fact that the entire country is made up of a Union of separate state governments, and a continuance of the belief that the National Government will fare best if the States and their institutions are left free to perform their separate functions in their separate ways.[10]

Throughout the 1970s the Court was sensitive to the needs of the states. No decision raised the hopes of state officials higher than the ruling in *National League of Cities v. Usery* (1976), in which the Court, 5-4, struck down an act of Congress imposing federal minimum wage and overtime rules on state employees. The majority—Chief Justice Burger and Justices Rehnquist, Potter Stewart, Harry A. Blackmun, and Lewis F. Powell Jr.—seemed to breathe new life into the constitutional language reserving power to the states. In Rehnquist's words, it declared that "there are attributes of sovereignty attaching to every state government which may not be impaired by Congress not because Congress may lack an affirmative grant of legislative authority to reach the matter, but because the Constitution prohibits it from exercising the authority in that manner."[11]

The Court, however, soon reneged on the promise of greater state autonomy implicit in this decision, overruling it nine years later by a single vote. Justice Blackmun wrote the Court's opinion in *Garcia v. San Antonio Metropolitan Transit Authority* (1985), acknowledging that he had changed his mind since *National League of Cities*.[12] Joined by the 1976 dissenters—Justices William J. Brennan Jr., Byron R. White, Thurgood Marshall, and John Paul Stevens—Blackmun declared that states must rely on the political process, not the Constitution, to protect them from such intrusions on internal affairs.

> Of course we continue to recognize that the States occupy a special and specific position in our constitutional system....But the principal and basic limit on the federal commerce power is that inherent in all congressional action—the built-in restraints that our system provides through state participation in federal government action. The political process ensures that laws that unduly burden the States will not be promulgated.[13]

A year after *Garcia*, Rehnquist succeeded Burger as chief justice. The guiding principle of Rehnquist's decisions, wrote University of Delaware political science professor Sue Davis, is federalism: "Protecting the states from what he perceives to be undesirable federal intrusion is so central to Rehnquist's decision making that he has adopted those tools of constitutional interpretation which are most useful in accomplishing his goal."[14] With the strength of his own convictions on this point, Rehnquist began to have some success in persuading his colleagues of the need to protect state prerogatives more vigorously. He won a significant victory when in *United States v. Lopez* (1995) the Court struck down a federal law banning guns at local schools, arguing that it reached too far into local affairs. For the first time in sixty years, the Court found that Congress, in passing a law regulating personal conduct, had overreached the powers provided it by the Commerce Clause.[15] Rehnquist wrote, "Just as the separation and independence of the coordinate branches of the Federal Government serves to prevent the accumulation of excessive power in any one branch, a healthy balance of power between the States and the Federal Government will reduce the risk of tyranny and abuse from either front."[16]

Also in 1995 the Court, with Rehnquist in dissent, struck down state limits on the number of terms their representatives could serve in Congress.[17] The only justice in the majority in both of these cases, Anthony M. Kennedy, seemed to agree with Rehnquist that the goal was a healthy balance between state and federal power: "That the states may not invade the sphere of federal sovereignty is as incontestable, in my view, as the corollary proposition that the federal government must be held within the boundaries of its own power when it intrudes upon matters reserved to the states."[18]

Judicial Review and the States

"I do not think that the United States would come to an end if we lost our power to declare an Act of Congress void," said Justice Oliver Wendell Holmes Jr. "I do think the Union would be imperilled if we could not make that declaration as to the laws of the several states."[1] Although the landmark assertion of judicial review over acts of Congress in *Marbury v. Madison* (1803) was left unused, uncontested, and undisturbed for more than half a century after its announcement, the history of the Court from its first term to the Civil War is a narrative of continuing controversy over the assertion of its statutory power to review state laws and the decisions of state courts. During that time, "the chief conflicts arose over the court's decisions restricting the limits of state authority and not over those restricting the limits of congressional power. Discontent with its actions on the latter subject arose, *not* because the court held an Act of Congress unconstitutional, but rather because it refused to do so."[2]

SOURCES OF POWER

Article III of the Constitution grants the federal courts jurisdiction over all controversies between states, those in which the United States is a party, controversies between a state and the citizens of another state, and between a state and foreign states, their citizens, or subjects. The Judiciary Act of 1789 expressly gave the Court the power to review state court rulings involving federal issues or claims. *(See box, Judicial Review and State Courts, p. 378.)*

Resistance: *Chisholm v. Georgia* (1793)

No sooner had the Court handed down its first major decision—*Chisholm v. Georgia* (1793)—than the states made clear their resistance to the assertion of federal judicial power. Within five years a new amendment overruling the Court's decision had become part of the Constitution. *Chisholm* arose when two South Carolinians sued Georgia in the Supreme Court, invoking the jurisdiction granted to the Court by Article III concerning a state and citizens of another state. As executors of the estate of a man to whom money was owed by persons whose property the state of Georgia had confiscated during the war of independence, the South Carolinians asked Georgia to pay the debt. Georgia refused even to appear before the Supreme Court, denying its authority to hear cases in which a state was the defendant. Finding clear authority for such suits in Article III, the Court on February 18, 1793, upheld the right of citizens of one state to bring a suit against another state in the Court. Chief Justice John Jay delivered the majority opinion. Only Justice James Iredell dissented.[3] Jay took note of the fact that Georgia was at that very time "prosecuting an action in this court against two citizens of South Carolina," while disclaiming the correlative right. Jay commented:

> That rule is said to be a bad one, which does not work both ways; the citizens of Georgia are content with a right of suing citizens of other states; but are not content that citizens of other states should have a right to sue them.[4]

To buttress his ruling in support of the Court's jurisdiction, Jay stated that he had no precedents to which he could refer, but he explained,

> The extension of the judiciary power of the United States to such controversies appears to me to be wise, because it is honest, and because it is useful…because it leaves not even the most obscure an [*sic*] friendless citizen without means of obtaining justice from a neighboring state; because it obviates occasions of quarrels between states on account of the claims of their respective citizens; because it recognizes and strongly rests on this great moral truth, that justice is the same whether

JUDICIAL REVIEW AND STATE COURTS

Unlike the power of the Supreme Court to review acts of Congress to measure their constitutionality, the authority of the Court to review acts of state courts is explicitly granted by law--by Section 25 of the Judiciary Act of 1789. That act provided

> That a final judgment or decree in any suit, in the highest court of law or equity of a State in which a decision in the suit could be had, where is drawn in question the validity of a treaty or statute of, or an authority exercised under the United States, and the decision is against their validity;

> or where is drawn in question the validity of a statute of, or an authority exercised under any State, on the ground of their being repugnant to the constitutions, treaties or laws of the United States, and the decision is in favour of such their validity.

> or where is drawn in question the construction of any clause of the constitution, or of a treaty, or statute of, or commission held under the United States, and the decision is against the title, right, privilege or exemption specifically set up or claimed by either party under such clause of the said Constitution, treaty, statute or commission, may be re-examined and reversed or affirmed in the Supreme Court of the United States.

due from one man or a million, or from a million to one man.[5]

This decision, reports historian Charles Warren, "fell upon the country with a profound shock....The vesting of any such jurisdiction over sovereign states had been expressly disclaimed...by the great defenders of the constitution, during the days of the contest over its adoption."[6] The day after the *Chisholm* ruling, a proposed constitutional amendment to override the decision was introduced in the House of Representatives. State pride was injured, but more than that was at issue. Already in delicate financial condition after the Revolution, the states feared fiscal disaster if suits such as that upheld in *Chisholm* were brought to recover property confiscated during the war. Georgia therefore reacted dramatically. The Georgia House approved a measure declaring that whoever carried out the Supreme Court's decision would be "guilty of felony and shall suffer death, with benefit of clergy, by being hanged." The bill did not become law.[7]

The following year, on January 8, 1798, the U.S. House, by a vote of 23 to 2, and the Senate, by a vote of 81 to 9, approved legislation that would become the Eleventh Amendment.[8] It states,

> The Judicial power of the United States shall not be construed to extend to any suit of equity, commenced or prosecuted against one of the United States by Citizens of another State, or by Citizens or Subjects of any Foreign State.

With *Chisholm* overruled, the states had won the first battle. The Court acquiesced. Within a month of the amendment's ratification, the Court dismissed a suit against the state of Virginia by citizens of another state, citing the Eleventh Amendment in support of its statement that it had no jurisdiction over the matter.[9] *(For further discussion of the Eleventh Amendment, see pp. 455–458.)*

Supremacy: *Ware v. Hylton* (1796)

A similar situation—but with more far-reaching consequences—characterized the Court's next major decision, which again involved a clear question of state rights. Article VI of the Constitution asserts federal supremacy, stating that the Constitution, federal laws, and treaties are the supreme law of the land and all conflicting state laws or constitutions are invalid. The peace treaty with Britain, which ended the Revolutionary War, provided that neither nation would raise legal obstacles to the recovery of debts due from its citizens to those of the other nation. This provision involved large sums of money. One scholar estimates that in Virginia alone as much as $2 million was owed to British subjects.[10] Like many other states, Virginia had confiscated the property of British loyalists during the Revolution, and state law had provided that people owing money to British subjects could satisfy their obligation by making payments to the state. After the treaty was signed, British creditors went to federal court to sue Virginia debtors for payment of their obligations. Defending the debtors and the state was John Marshall. He argued only this one case before the Supreme Court, and he lost.[11]

The Court ruled in *Ware v. Hylton* (1796) in favor of the British creditors and against the debtors and the state. The debts had to be paid.[12] The state had a moral obligation to return the payments made during the war, but regardless of whether it did so, the debtors remained liable. Federal supremacy was affirmed. "Here is a treaty," wrote Justice William Cushing, "the supreme law, which overrules all state laws upon the subject to all intents and purposes; and that makes the difference."[13]

Resistance: *United States v. Judge Peters* (1809)

For almost fifteen years after *Ware v. Hylton*, the Court—by a cautious approach to the use of its authority to review state court actions—avoided collisions with state power, but it eventually went head to head with the state of Pennsylvania. The controversy that culminated in 1809 had begun during the Revolutionary War, when Gideon Olmstead and his companions seized a British ship as a prize of war. The ship was sold as a prize vessel, and the proceeds became the object of a tug-of-war between Olmstead and the state of Pennsylvania. In 1803 a federal judge—Richard Peters—ordered that the money be paid to Olmstead. Instead of complying, the state legislature ordered the money placed in the state treasury. Until that time, it had been in the personal custody of the state treasurer, a man named David Rittenhouse. Apparently deterred by the legislature's action, Judge Peters did not actually issue the order directing payment to Olmstead. In 1808 the eighty-two-year-old Olmstead finally asked the Supreme Court to direct Peters to issue the order. The state of Pennsylvania responded that such a suit could not be brought in federal court because of the Eleventh Amendment denial of federal jurisdiction over suits brought by citizens against a state.

The Supreme Court on February 20, 1809, issued Olmstead's requested order. The Court found it necessary to grant his request, explained Chief Justice John Marshall, to preserve national supremacy:

> If the legislatures of the several states may, at will, annul the judgments of the courts of the United States, and destroy the rights acquired under those judgments, the constitution itself becomes a solemn mockery, and the nation is deprived of the means of enforcing its laws by the instrumentality of its own tribunals.[14]

On the Eleventh Amendment defense raised by the state, the Court found that it did not apply to this situation simply because the state was not the defendant. The Supreme Court decision did not, however, settle the matter. The governor of Pennsylvania declared that he would use the militia to prevent enforcement of its order, which Judge Peters issued on March 24. When the federal marshal attempted to deliver the order to the two women who were executors of the now-deceased Rittenhouse's estate, he was met by the state militia. The marshal called out a posse of two thousand men. A federal grand jury indicted the militia commander and ordered his arrest for resisting federal law. The governor asked President James Madison to intervene. Madison declined. The legislature then capitulated, removed the militia, appropriated the money due Olmstead, and made the payment, which ended the long-running quarrel.[15]

CHALLENGE TO POWER

The Judiciary Act of 1789 left to the state courts all cases arising within the states, even if they involved a federal question. To ensure that constitutional principles and federal law were uniformly applied, however, in such cases the act granted the right of appeal to the Supreme Court under the much-debated Section 25. *(See box, Judicial Review and State Courts, p. 378.)* Section 25 authorized the Supreme Court to reexamine and reverse or affirm the final judgment of the highest court in a state when the state court decided against the federal claim in cases involving the Constitution, federal laws, or federal treaties. In 1914 Congress expanded the scope of this power of review by allowing the Court to review state court decisions upholding—as well as

SUPREMACY: WHEN FEDERAL LAW TRUMPS STATE LAW

Under state laws, consumers who are hurt by a defective product can sue its maker for damages. States also enact laws or regulations to protect the health and safety of their residents. Congress and federal agencies enforce laws that regulate the same products and services. The two sets of laws often overlap, and sometimes may conflict. The Court has tended to rule that the federal law "preempts" or trumps the state's law, including the consumer's right to sue.

On February 20, 2008, two such decisions were handed down on the same day. In *Riegel v. Medtronic* the Court ruled that the makers of federally approved medical devices, such as a heart pacemaker, cannot be sued by patients who allege the device was defective and dangerous.[1] The 8-1 ruling threw out a suit by the widow of a New York man who died not long after a balloon catheter ruptured in his chest. The Court pointed to the Medical Device Amendments Act of 1976, which gave the Food and Drug Administration the authority to regulate devices and barred states from enforcing "any requirement" that conflicted with the federal law. The lone dissenter, Justice Ruth Bader Ginsburg, said Congress did not intend to prohibit lawsuits that, she said, protect consumers from dangerous products. In *Rowe v. New Hampshire Motor Transport Association* the Court rejected a Maine law that sought to prevent cartons of cigarettes from being delivered to minors.[2] The state wanted to require delivery services, such as United Parcel Service, to check to see that an adult had purchased the cigarettes. But the Court said this state law conflicted with a federal law deregulating the airline and trucking industries.

These decisions rest on Article VI of the Constitution, which says the laws of the United States "shall be the supreme Law of the Land; ... any Thing in the Constitution or Laws of any State to the Contrary notwithstanding." As Justice John Paul Stevens wrote in 1992, "[S]ince our decision in *McCulloch v. Maryland* (1819), it has been settled that state law that conflicts with federal law is 'without effect.'"[3]

Case by case, the clarity of that concept began to blur. The Court struck down state laws where valid federal statutes dominate the field or explicitly bar the state action. Closer cases arose, however, when federal law did not specifically detail its effect on state law or when federal legislation addressed only part of a field with regulation that did not make clear that it leaves no room for the states to act. Today's preemption standard has evolved over the last half century.[4] Stevens summarized it in *Cipollone v. Liggett Group* (1992):

> Consideration of issues arising under the Supremacy Clause starts with the assumption that the historic police powers of the States are not to be superseded by ... Federal Act unless that is the clear and manifest purpose of Congress. Accordingly, the purpose of Congress is the ultimate touchstone of pre-emption analysis. Congress' intent may be explicitly stated in the statute's language or implicitly contained in its structure and purpose. In the absence of an express congressional command, state law is pre-empted if that law actually conflicts with federal law, or if federal law so thoroughly occupies a legislative field as to make reasonable the inference that Congress left no room for the States to supplement it.[5]

In *Cipollone* Stevens and the Court ruled that the cigarette makers could not be sued for failing to warn smokers of the dangers of tobacco

those denying—a federal claim. (*See "A Broader Jurisdiction," p. 17.*) "In view of the extreme jealousy shown by the States from the outset towards the Federal government, it is a singular fact in our history that this Section was in force 24 years before any State resented its existence or attempted to controvert the right of Congress to enact it," wrote Charles Warren.[16]

Martin v. Hunter's Lessee (1816)

When the challenge to the Court's authority over state courts arose, in 1816, it came from Virginia, Marshall's

home state. The state court that denied the power of the Supreme Court to review its decisions was led by Judge Spencer Roane, a close friend of Thomas Jefferson and, it is said, the man who would have been chief justice instead of Marshall had Oliver Ellsworth resigned the post a few months later and had Jefferson, not John Adams, been president.[17]

Like *Chisholm* and *Ware*, this case involved land belonging to British subjects, which Virginia had confiscated and then granted to new owners. Lord Fairfax owned land in Virginia, which he willed at his death in

because Congress had specified the warning label.[6] The Court, however, also said the federal law did not preempt lawsuits making other claims, such as that tobacco companies had conspired to deceive the public and hide the true dangers of smoking.

This mixed message was typical of many of the Court's rulings in the area of preemption. In *Morales v. Trans World Airlines* (1992) the Court ruled that the federal Airline Deregulation Act of 1978 precluded states from regulating advertising of airline fares.[7] Three years later the Court allowed travelers to sue in state court for breach of contract over changes in frequent flier benefits.[8] In 1995 the Court held that the National Traffic and Motor Vehicle Safety Act did not shield truck companies from being sued for failing to install antilock brakes.[9] Five years later the justices in a 5-4 ruling shielded auto companies from being sued for not installing automatic seatbelts in cars built before 1988. In that case, *Geier v. American Honda Motor Co.* (2000), the Court concluded that because federal regulators decided against requiring automatic seat belts then, the federal standards must preempt contrary actions by states and their juries.[10] In the second major test of the cigarette labeling act, the Court in 2001 voided state regulations in Massachusetts that barred billboard advertisements for tobacco and ruled that these extra state measures were preempted by the federal law setting forth the warning on cigarette packs.[11]

The Court has also shielded health care providers from being sued by employees and their families. Congress in 1974 brought pension plans and employee benefits under federal regulation through the Employee Retirement Income Security Act. In 1987 the Court said this law preempted suits for damages from employees who complained of a loss of benefits.[12] This decision in turn barred suits by persons whose employer-provided health care plan refused to pay for certain treatments or care. Angry patients were left with no legal remedy in such cases. In reaction, many states established independent medical review boards to weigh claims when patients were denied surgery or treatment by their health care plan, and in 2002 the Court upheld this popular state reform in a 5-4 decision.[13] But two years later, the Court unanimously confirmed that employees could not sue their health care plans for damages on the grounds that these state claims were preempted by the federal employee-benefits law.[14]

---

1. *Riegel v. Medtronic, 552* U.S. — (2008).

2. *Rowe v. New Hampshire Motor Transport Association,* (552 U.S. — (2008).

3. *Cipollone v. Liggett Group,* 505 U.S. 504 (1992), *quoting from McCulloch v. Maryland,* 4 Wheat. (17 U.S.) 316 (1819).

4. *Rice v. Santa Fe Elevator Corp.,* 331 U.S. 218 (1947).

5. *Cipollone v. Liggett Group,* 505 U.S. 504 (1992).

6. *Id.*

7. *Morales v. Trans World Airlines,* 504 U.S. 374 (1992).

8. *American Airlines v. Wolens,* 513 U.S. 219 (1995).

9. *Freightliner Corp. v. Myrick,* 514 U.S. 280 (1995); *see also Medtronic Inc. v. Lohr,* 518 U.S. 420 (1996).

10. *Geier v. American Honda Motor Co.,* 529 U.S. 861 (2000).

11. *Lorillard Tobacco Co. v. Reilly,* 533 U.S. 525 (2001).

12. *Pilot Life Insurance Co. v. Dedeaux,* 481 U.S. 41 (1987).

13. *Rush Prudential HMO v. Moran,* 536 U.S. 355 (2002).

14. *Aetna Health Inc. v. Davila,* 542 U.S. 200 (2004).

1781 to his nephew, Denny Martin, a British subject. Virginia not only denied the right of aliens to inherit land within its boundaries, but it also claimed that it had confiscated the estate during the Revolution and subsequently granted portions to other owners, including one David Hunter. Eventually, some of this contested land was purchased by John Marshall's brother and perhaps the chief justice himself. At any rate, Marshall did not take part in the Court's considerations of this case. First titled *Hunter v. Fairfax's Devisee,* the case came to court in 1796, but it was postponed due to the death of Hunter's attorney.[18] Almost fifteen years passed before a Virginia court upheld Hunter's claim, and the Fairfax heirs moved the matter back to the Supreme Court, where it was argued in 1812 as *Fairfax's Devisee v. Hunter's Lessee.*

In 1813 the Court ruled for the British heirs in a 3-1 vote, with Justice William Johnson dissenting and two justices—Marshall being one—not taking part in the case. Justice Joseph Story wrote a forceful opinion, holding that aliens could inherit land in Virginia, state law to the contrary. Martin therefore held title to the disputed lands, and the state could not grant title to them to anyone else. The Court ordered the Virginia court to issue an order to this effect, settling the case in Martin's favor.[19] Resentful of the ruling and of the damage inflicted by Story's opinion upon the state's confiscation and inheritance laws, the state court refused to follow the Supreme Court's directive. Instead, it decided to consider the question of the constitutionality of the Supreme Court's claimed power to consider the case at all: Was Section 25 of the Judiciary Act constitutional? Late in 1815 the state court held the section invalid, declaring that the Supreme Court could not constitutionally review state court rulings. It would not therefore obey the Court's order:

> The appellate power of the Supreme Court of the United States does not extend to this Court, under a sound construction of the Constitution....So much of the Twenty-fifth Section of the Act...to establish the Judicial Courts of the United States as extends the appellate jurisdiction of the Supreme Court to this court, is not in pursuance of the Constitution.

Back went the matter to the Supreme Court. Again Marshall did not consider the case, now cited as *Martin v. Hunter's Lessee.* Within three months of the state court challenge, the Supreme Court responded, issuing a sweeping affirmation of the validity of Section 25 on March 29, 1816:

> [T]he appellate power of the United States does extend to cases pending in the state courts; and...the 25th section of the judiciary act, which authorizes the exercise of this jurisdiction in the specified cases, by a writ of error, is supported by the letter and spirit of the constitution. We find no clause in that instrument which limits this power; and we dare not interpose a limitation where the people have not been disposed to create one.[20]

Justice Story, author of the Court's opinion, also took the opportunity to deliver a ringing defense of federal supremacy:

> The constitution of the United States was ordained and established, not by the states in their sovereign capacities, but emphatically, as the preamble of the Constitution declares, by "the people of the United States." There can be no doubt that it was competent to the people to invest the general government with all the powers which they might deem proper and necessary; to extend or restrain these powers according to their own good pleasure, and to give them a paramount and supreme authority. As little doubt can there be that the people had a right to prohibit to the states the exercise of any powers which were, in their judgment, incompatible with the objects of the general compact; to make the powers of the state governments, in given cases, subordinate to those of the nation.[21]

Examining Article III, "creating and defining the judicial power of the United States," Story pointed out:

> It is the case, then, and not the court, that gives the jurisdiction [to federal courts]. If the judicial power extends to the case, it will be in vain to search in the letter of the Constitution for any qualification as to the tribunal where it depends.[22]

The Constitution, he continued,

> is crowded with provisions which restrain or annul the sovereignty of the states....When, therefore, the states are stripped of some of the highest attributes of sovereignty, and the same are given to the United States; when the legislatures of the states are, in some respects, under the control of Congress, and in every case are, under the constitution, bound by the paramount authority of the United States; it is certainly difficult to support the argument that the appellate power over the decisions of state courts is contrary to the genius of our institutions. The courts of the United States can, without question, revise the proceedings of the executive and legislative authorities of the states, and if they are found to be contrary to the constitution, may declare them to be of no legal validity. Surely the exercise of the same right over judicial tribunals is not a higher or more dangerous act of sovereign power.[23]

Further, wrote Story:

> A motive of another kind, perfectly compatible with the most sincere respect for state tribunals, might induce the grant of appellate power over the decisions. That motive is the importance, and even the necessity of uniformity of decisions throughout the whole United States, upon all subjects within the purview of the constitution. Judges of equal learning and integrity, in different states, might differently

interpret a statute, or a treaty of the United States, or even the constitution itself. If there were no revising authority to control these jarring and discordant judgments, and harmonize them into uniformity, the laws, the treaties, and the constitution of the United States would be different in different states, and might, perhaps, never have precisely the same construction, obligation, or efficacy, in any two states. The public mischiefs that would attend such a state of things would be truly deplorable…the [Supreme Court's] appellate jurisdiction must continue to be the only adequate remedy for such evils.[24]

Cohens v. Virginia (1821)

Despite the firmness of the Court's decision in *Martin v. Hunter's Lessee,* the Virginia Court of Appeals, led by Judge Roane, continued to resist the Supreme Court's authority to review its rulings. A second collision between the two judicial bodies came just five years after the first one in *Cohens v. Virginia* (1821). Although state law forbade the sale of out-of-state lottery tickets in Virginia, P. J. Cohen and M. J. Cohen sold tickets in Virginia to a congressionally authorized lottery in the District of Columbia. They were convicted of violating the Virginia law, after which they appealed to the Supreme Court, arguing that the Virginia law must fall before the conflicting (and overriding) federal law authorizing the D.C. lottery and the sale of tickets. Virginia argued that the case should be dismissed because the Supreme Court lacked jurisdiction over it. Arguing the state's case was Philip P. Barbour, who would later become a Supreme Court justice.

On March 3, 1821, the Court again rejected this argument, holding that it was founded upon a mistaken view of the relationship of the state and federal judicial systems. Writing for the Court, Chief Justice Marshall rejected the idea that these systems were totally separate and independent, like those of different sovereign nations.

That the United States form, for many, and for most important purposes, a single nation, has not yet been denied. In war, we are one people. In making peace, we are one people. In all commercial regulations, we are one and the same people. In many other respects, the American people are one; and the government which is alone capable of controlling and managing their interests in all these respects, is the government of the Union. It is their government, and in that character they have no other. America has chosen to be, in many respects, and to many purposes, a nation; and for all these purposes, her government is complete; to all these objects, it is competent. The people have declared, that in the exercise of all powers given for these objects it is supreme. It can, then, in effecting these objects, legitimately control all individuals or governments within the American territory. The constitution and laws of a state, so far as they are repugnant to the constitution and laws of the United States, are absolutely void. These states are constituent parts of the United States. They are members of one great empire—for some purposes sovereign, for some purposes subordinate.

In a government so constituted, is it unreasonable that the judicial power should be competent to give efficacy to the constitutional laws of the legislature? That department can decide on the validity of the constitution or law of a state, if it be repugnant to the constitution or to a law of the United States. Is it unreasonable that it should also be empowered to decide on the judgment of a state tribunal enforcing such unconstitutional law?…We think it is not.[25]

To hold that the Supreme Court lacked jurisdiction over this and similar cases, Marshall wrote, would have "mischievous consequences."

It would prostrate, it has been said, the government and its laws at the feet of every state in the Union. And would not this be its effect? What power of the government could be executed by its own means, in any state disposed to resist its execution? Each member will possess a veto on the will of the whole. . . .[26]

No government ought to be so defective in its organization as not to contain within itself the means of securing the execution of its own laws against other dangers than those which occur every day. Courts of justice are the means most usually employed; and it is reasonable to expect that a government should repose on its own courts, rather than on others. There is certainly nothing in the circumstances under which our constitution was formed; nothing in the history of the times, which would justify the opinion that the confidence reposed in the states was so implicit as to leave in them and their tribunals the power of resisting, or defeating, in the form of law, the legitimate measures of the Union.[27]

The Eleventh Amendment had no application here, the Court held, because this case was initiated by the state, not the Cohens. After this resounding decision on the question of jurisdiction, the Court's ruling on the merits of the case—against the Cohens and in favor of the state—was merely a postscript. In approving the District of Columbia lottery, the Court held, Congress had not intended to authorize the sale of tickets in a state forbidding such a transaction.[28]

Repeal and Resistance

During the decade after the Court's decision in *Cohens v. Virginia,* the states' battle against judicial review shifted to forums other than the Supreme Court. In Congress efforts were made to repeal Section 25 or otherwise terminate the Court's jurisdiction over state court rulings. It was proposed that the Senate become the court of appeals for all cases involving the states—or that a certain number of the justices, above a simple majority, be required to agree in any decision on the validity of a state law. None of these efforts succeeded. Perhaps the most celebrated clash of the Court and state power followed the decisions affirming judicial review. During Andrew Jackson's first term in the White House, the Court collided with the state of Georgia, but Jackson—unlike Madison in the Olmstead case—was on the side of the state.

The Cherokee Indians occupied land within Georgia's borders. In the 1820s the state attempted to assert control over the Indians and these lands through a number of stringent laws passed during the 1820s. Finally, the Cherokee—acting as an independent nation—filed a request with the Supreme Court, under its original jurisdiction, for an order directing Georgia to stop enforcing these laws. Not only did the state of Georgia fail to appear to defend against this request, but even before it was ruled upon, the governor and legislature executed an Indian convicted of murder under the contested laws. The execution was carried out in direct defiance of a Supreme Court notice to the

state that it was going to review the murder conviction in light of the challenge to the laws.[29]

The Court denied the Cherokee request in *Cherokee Nation v. Georgia* (1831), holding that its original jurisdiction did not extend to such a suit because the Cherokee nation was not a foreign state. "If it be true that wrongs have been inflicted, and that still greater are to be apprehended," wrote Chief Justice Marshall, "this is not the tribunal which can redress the past or prevent the future."[30] A second challenge to these laws quickly arrived before the Court. Georgia law required white persons living in Indian Territory to obtain a state license. Two missionaries, Samuel Worcester and Elizur Butler, refused, and were convicted of violating the law. They were sentenced to four years at hard labor. Butler and Worcester appealed to the Supreme Court, which issued a writ of error to the state court, notifying it to send the record of the case to Washington for review. The order was ignored. The case was argued February 20, 1832, without the appearance of counsel for the state. On March 3 the Court ruled in *Worcester v. Georgia* (1832) that federal jurisdiction over the Cherokee was exclusive and that the state therefore had no power to pass laws affecting them.[31] The missionaries' convictions were reversed because the laws under which they were charged were void. Worcester and Butler should be released, the Court ruled, but it did not actually issue the order directing their release before it adjourned its term two weeks later, leaving the matter suspended until its new term, in 1833.

There was reason for the Court to delay. President Jackson was known to side with the state. Often-repeated but unsubstantiated reports quote him as saying, "Well, John Marshall has made his decision, now let him enforce it." Whether Jackson made such a statement, his failure to act bore out the sentiment. Justice Story wrote a friend the week of the ruling:

Georgia is full of anger and violence. What she will do it is difficult to say. Probably she will resist the execution of our judgment, and if she does, I do not believe the President will interfere.... The rumor is, that he has told the Georgians he will do nothing.... The Court has done its duty. Let the Nation now do theirs. If we have a Government, let its command be obeyed; if we have not, it is as well to know it at once, and to look to consequences.[32]

As the year wore on, Marshall became increasingly pessimistic about the standoff. He wrote to Story:

> I yield slowly and reluctantly to the conviction that our Constitution cannot last. I had supposed that North of the Potomack [sic] a firm and solid government competent to the security of rational liberty might be preserved. Even that now seems doubtful. The case of the South seems to me to be desperate. Our opinions are incompatible with a united government even among ourselves. The Union has been prolonged thus far by miracles. I fear they cannot continue.[33]

Contrary to Marshall's suspicions, more miracles were to come, as events made it politically impossible for Jackson to continue to give even tacit support to Georgia's defiance of the Court. Late in 1832 South Carolina, protesting a new tariff law and other intrusions upon state's rights, approved the Nullification Ordinance, asserting the right of a state to disregard and thereby nullify federal laws it viewed as unconstitutional. The ordinance forbade any appeal to the Supreme Court from state courts in cases involving the ordinance or any federal law. President Jackson responded by describing the nullification theory as treason. Firmly planted on the side of federal power, he could hardly continue to sanction Georgia's disobedience to the Court's ruling in the missionary case. Realizing that political fact of life, the governor of Georgia pardoned Worcester and Butler in 1833. They subsequently dropped their case.

Judicial Review Entrenched

State resistance to federal judicial power did not, however, end with the Cherokee controversy. Ohio courts refused for a number of years in the 1850s to carry out a Supreme Court ruling on a tax matter. Also in the 1850s the California Supreme Court held Section 25 of the Judiciary Act invalid, but its legislature ordered the judges to comply with the federal law. In the years just before the Civil War, a great struggle between state and federal judicial power took place in Wisconsin over the trial of an abolitionist accused of violating the Federal Fugitive Slave Act.[34] *(See box, A Clash of Courts: The Federal Fugitive Slave Law, p. 480.)*

The Civil War, Justice Robert H. Jackson wrote years later, practically ended state resistance to the Supreme Court's power to review state laws and state court decisions. Yet after the Civil War the pace of that use of judicial review accelerated. From 1789 to 1863 only thirty-eight state or local laws had been held unconstitutional by the Supreme Court. In the two dozen years from 1864 to 1888 the Court struck down ninety-nine laws, but in the two dozen years between 1914 and 1938 the pace tripled, as the Court invalidated more than three hundred laws. As Jackson wrote,

> It is now an accepted part of our constitutional doctrine that conflicts between state legislation and the federal Constitution are to be resolved by the Supreme Court and, had it not been, it is difficult to see how the Union could have survived.[35]

Strong state and public reaction against some of the modern Court's rulings—on questions of civil rights, criminal law, individual rights, and state prerogatives—would continue. Yet even as the Court struck down hundreds of state and local laws between 1964 and 2009, the fierce opposition of some states to some of these rulings did not produce anything approaching a successful drive against the institution of judicial review.

The States and the Economy

For the first 150 years of its history, the Supreme Court exerted its greatest influence on the states of the Union through its decisions on matters of economic interest. In case after case—as the justices construed Article I's Contract Clause and Commerce Clause and defined the state's power of taxation—the Court defined the relationship between state and federal power. "Certainly," wrote Thomas Reed Powell in the mid-twentieth century, "the commerce powers of the nation and the state raise the most perennial and persistent problems of constitutional federalism."[1] The Commerce Clause, wrote Felix Frankfurter in 1937, "has throughout the Court's history been the chief source of its adjudications regarding federalism."[2] Anticipating the creation of a national economy, the framers of the Constitution granted the federal government the power to regulate interstate and foreign commerce. Supplementing that grant, states cannot tax imports or exports or impose tonnage duties on incoming ships without congressional consent. To guarantee the stability of commercial transactions and to protect property against legislative encroachment, the framers included a prohibition on the passage of state laws impairing the obligation of contracts. Further, they added language forbidding states to coin money, issue bills of credit, or make changes in the legal tender.

Each of these constitutional restrictions on state powers over interstate commerce received its initial interpretation during the tenure of John Marshall as chief justice of the United States from 1801 to 1835. The net effect of these rulings, particularly those interpreting the Commerce Clause, was to establish the Court's power to limit state authority. As Frankfurter wrote, "Marshall's use of the commerce clause…gave momentum to the doctrine that state authority must be subject to such limitations as the Court finds it necessary to apply for the protection of the national community."[3] During Marshall's tenure New York saw its steamboat monopoly fall before the Court's broad interpretation of the federal power over commerce. Georgia became the first state to have a law declared unconstitutional, when its effort to repeal a corruptly obtained land grant collided with the Contract Clause. Maryland was rebuked by the Court for taxing vendors of foreign goods, and Missouri was told firmly that it could not issue state loan certificates without violating the Constitution's ban on state issuance of bills of credit.

Once these limits were well established, the Court seemed willing to acknowledge that, within the structure of federal supremacy, states continued to retain certain basic powers with which to regulate commerce within their borders and protect their residents. This broad reserved power, most often called the police power, received the stamp of judicial approval in the 1830s and today still serves as a firm basis for a wide variety of state actions to protect citizens, public health and morals, and natural resources. "Because the 'police power' is a response to the dynamic aspects of society," wrote Frankfurter, "it has eluded attempts at definition. But precisely because it is such a response, it is one of the most fertile doctrinal sources for striking an accommodation between local interests and the demands of the commerce clause."[4]

During the Court's laissez-faire period of the late nineteenth and early twentieth centuries, the justices viewed many of the state laws enacted in exercise of this police power as too vigorous, particularly in their impact on the use of private property. In the Due Process Clause of the Fourteenth Amendment, the conservative Court found a useful instrument to counter such laws, many of which fell before the Court's finding that they deprived businessmen of their property without due process of law.

Dartmouth College's trustees, who had lost control of the renamed Dartmouth University, sued William H. Woodward, the college secretary, pictured here. The Supreme Court decided that the school's original charter was a contract that the Constitution forbade the state legislature to arbitrarily change.

The New Deal—and the traumatic economic depression that precipitated it—brought a conclusion to that period in the Court's history. Since 1937 the Court has been more tolerant of state regulation of business even as it has upheld the extension of federal power into areas of the economy formerly left entirely to state control. As Powell wrote, the modern Court tends to sanction state actions when they interfere with the national economy only so far as is necessary to protect community interests.[5]

THE OBLIGATION OF CONTRACTS

From the nation's founding to the Civil War, the Contract Clause served as one of the most effective instruments for establishing federal control over state actions. According to one scholar,

> The cases of *Fletcher v. Peck* and *Dartmouth College v. Woodward* formed the beginning of an extensive series of restrictions upon state legislation, made possible through the fact that many laws may be attacked on the ground of infringement of property rights....The [Court's early] decisions aligned on the side of nationalism the economic interests of corporate organizations.[6]

Land Grants

In *Fletcher v. Peck* (1810) the Court for the first time struck down a state law as unconstitutional, ruling that grants made by a state legislature cannot be repealed without violating the constitutional prohibition on impairment of contract obligations. In 1795 the Georgia legislature granted some 35 million acres of land along the Yazoo River to four land speculation companies. The price— for what is now most of the states of Alabama and Mississippi—was $500,000. Approval of the grant was facilitated by the promise of the speculators to many legislators that they would share in the land thus granted. Chagrined by the obvious bribery, a new legislature revoked the grant in 1796 and declared all claims resulting from it void. The land companies, however, had already resold much of the land to innocent purchasers, who now held questionable titles. Thus, a long debate began.

Pointing to the corruption that attended the 1795 land grant, Georgia argued that the titles held under it were worthless. The purchasers argued that the state legislature did not have the power to nullify their rights. Because many of the purchasers lived in New England, the case quickly became a federal problem. After several years of discussion in Congress, the matter moved into the federal courts. One of the attorneys arguing the case before the Supreme Court was Joseph Story, a thirty-year-old Massachusetts attorney who within two years would sit on the Supreme Court bench as the youngest nominee in its history. On March 16, 1810, the Court ruled. The original land grant was a valid contract; Georgia could not annul the titles granted under it, because such an attempt ran counter to the ban on state action impairing the obligation of contracts. The Court would not inquire into the motives behind approval of the 1795 land grant. Marshall wrote,

> That corruption should find its way into the governments of our infant republics, and contaminate the very source of legislation, or that impure motives should contribute to the passage of law, or the formation of a legislative contract, are circumstances most deeply to be deplored.
>
> [But if] the title be plainly deduced from a legislative act, which the legislature might constitutionally pass, if the act be clothed with all the requisite forms of a law, a court…cannot sustain a suit…founded on the allegation that the act is a nullity, in consequence of the impure motives which influenced certain members of the legislature which passed the law.[7]

Exploring the implications of upholding Georgia's right to repeal the grant, Marshall said,

> [S]uch powerful objections to a legislative grant…may not again exist, yet the principle, on which alone this rescinding act is to be supported, may be applied to every case in which it shall be the will of any legislature to apply it. The principle is this: that a legislature may, by its own act, devest [sic] the vested estate of any man whatever, for reasons which shall, by itself, be deemed sufficient.[8]

The Court rejected that principle. The Court agreed that one legislature could repeal any general legislation passed by a former legislature, but the new legislature could not undo an action taken under the repealed law: "The past cannot be recalled by the most absolute power." "When, then, a law is in its nature a contract, when absolute rights have vested under that contract, a repeal of the law cannot devest those rights."[9]

Tax Exemptions

Two years later the Court extended its interpretation of the Contract Clause as a restraint on the tendency of state legislators to change their minds. In the case of *New Jersey v. Wilson* (1812) the Court refused to allow the state to modify or revoke a clear contractual grant of exemption from taxes.[10] The colonial legislature of New Jersey had granted certain lands to the Delaware Indians. Included in the grant was an exemption from taxation for the lands held by the Indians. After the Indians sold the land, the state tried to tax it. The new owners challenged the tax as a violation of the contract in the original grant, and they won. As the Supreme Court noted, the state could have limited the tax exemption to the period when the land belonged to the Indians, but it had placed no such condition upon the exemption. Therefore, the exemption passed with title to the land, and efforts to repeal or ignore it impaired the original obligation.

Eighteen years later the Court made clear that tax exemption could never be assumed to be a part of a contract, grant, or charter. In *The Providence Bank v. Billings* (1830) the Court held that "[a]ny privileges which may exempt it [a corporation] from the burthens [sic] common to individuals do not flow necessarily from the charter, but must be expressed in it, or they do not exist."[11] The power to tax could indeed be used as a means of destroying a business—and thereby impairing a contract—Chief Justice Marshall conceded:

> but the Constitution of the United States was not intended to furnish the corrective for every abuse of power which may be committed by the State governments. The interest, wisdom and justice of the representative body, and its relations with its constituents, furnish the only security where there is no express contract against unjust and excessive taxation, as well as against unwise legislation generally.…[A]n incorporated bank, unless its charter shall express the exemption, is no more exempted from taxation than an unincorporated company would be, carrying on the same business.[12]

In 1854 the state of Ohio brought this issue back to the justices, leading to the first Supreme Court ruling finding a portion of a state's constitution unconstitutional. The state bank of Ohio was chartered under a law that provided that the bank would pay a certain percentage of its profits to the state in lieu of taxes. Subsequently, the state legislature passed a law providing for a tax on banks and assessed one branch of the state bank $1,266.63 as its share of the new tax. The bank refused to pay, arguing that the state's effort to impose this new tax on it impaired the contract of the original charter.[13] The Court upheld the bank's exemption from taxes. Justice John McLean wrote the majority opinion. The charter was perfectly clear, he wrote:

> Nothing is left to inference....The payment was to be in lieu of all taxes to which the Company or stockholders would otherwise be subject. This is the full measure of taxation on the Bank. It is in the place of any other tax which, had it not been for this stipulation, might have been imposed on the Company or stockholders. . . .
>
> Every valuable privilege given by the charter...is a contract which cannot be changed by the Legislature, where the power to do so is not reserved in the charter....A municipal corporation...may be changed at the will of the Legislature. Such is a public corporation, used for public purposes. But a bank, where the stock is owned by individuals, is a private corporation. . . .
>
> A state, in granting privileges to a bank...exercises its sovereignty, and for a public purpose, of which it is the exclusive judge. Under such circumstances, a contract made for a specific tax, as in the case before us, is binding....Having the power to make the contract, and rights becoming vested under it, it can no more be disregarded nor set aside by a subsequent Legislature, than a grant for land.[14]

Still determined to tax the bank, Ohio amended its constitution to provide for such a tax. Back the issue went to the Supreme Court, where once again, in 1856, the Court reiterated its holding that the effort to tax the bank impermissibly impaired the obligation of the original agreement with the bank. Justice James M. Wayne wrote for the Court:

> A change of constitution cannot release a state from contracts made under a constitution which permits them to be made....The moral obligations never die. If broken by states and nations, though the terms of reproach are not the same with which we are accustomed to designate the faithlessness of individuals, the violation of justice is not the less.[15]

Private Corporate Charters

Fletcher v. Peck extended to agreements involving the state the protection of a clause many had thought protected only agreements between two private parties. Nine years after the case, in the landmark *Dartmouth College v. Woodward* (1819) the Court further extended that protection to shield private corporate charters against alteration or repeal. Dartmouth College, in New Hampshire, was established by a royal charter. After the formation of the Union, the agreement with the king became an agreement with the state. In 1816 the state legislature passed several laws amending the college's charter to convert it into a university, to enlarge the number of its trustees, and otherwise to revise the means and purpose of its operations. The trustees of the college resisted, charging that these amendments impaired the obligation of the contract implicit in the original charter.

In 1818 the case came to the Supreme Court, with the famous advocate Daniel Webster arguing the college's case. The state defended the changes in the charter by contending that the school was a public corporation subject to such legislative action. Webster, however, was more convincing. In 1819 the Court ruled for the college, finding the amendments an unconstitutional impairment of the contract obligation. Chief Justice Marshall wrote the Court's opinion. Assuming a much-debated point, Marshall stated that the charter incorporating the private college was a contract within the protection of the Constitution:

> It is a contract made on a valuable consideration. It is a contract for the security and disposition of property. It is a contract, on faith of which real and personal estate has been conveyed to the corporation. It is then a contract within the letter of the constitution, and within its spirit also.[16]

Marshall conceded that this application of the Contract Clause probably never occurred to the men who wrote it into the Constitution: "It is more than possible that the preservation of rights of this description was not particularly in the view of the framers of the constitution when the clause under consideration was introduced into that instrument."[17] Regardless, the chief justice found no good reason to except these contracts from constitutional protection:

It is probable that no man ever was, and that no man ever will be, the founder of a college, believing at the time that an act of incorporation constitutes no security for the institution; believing that it is immediately to be deemed a public institution, whose funds are to be governed and applied, not by the will of the donor, but by the will of the legislature. All such gifts are made in the…hope, that the charity will flow forever in the channel which the givers have marked out for it. If every man finds in his own bosom strong evidence of the universality of this sentiment, there can be but little reason to imagine that the framers of our constitution were strangers to it, and that, feeling the necessity and policy of giving permanence and security to contracts, of withdrawing them from the influence of legislative bodies, whose fluctuating policy, and repeated interferences, produced the most perplexing and injurious embarrassments, they still deemed it necessary to leave these contracts subject to those interferences.[18]

In his concurring opinion, Justice Joseph Story made clear the avenue by which states could retain the power to make modifications in such charters without violating the Constitution. "If the legislature mean to claim such an authority, it must be reserved in the grant," Story wrote.[19] Most charters granted by the states since that time have contained language reserving to the state the power to repeal or modify them.

For the half-century following the *Dartmouth College* decision, the Contract Clause produced more litigation than any other part of the Constitution. Charles Warren, historian of the Court during this period, wrote that this ruling came at a "peculiarly opportune" time:

> [B]usiness corporations were for the first time becoming a factor in the commerce of the country, and railroad and insurance corporations were, within the next fifteen years, about to become a prominent field for capital. The assurance to investors that rights granted by state legislatures were henceforth to be secure against popular or partisan vacillation, and capricious, political or fraudulent change of legislative policy, greatly encouraged the development of corporate business.[20]

BANKRUPTCY LAWS

Using the Contract Clause to strike down state insolvency laws, the Supreme Court threw much of the nation into chaos during the 1820s. Two weeks after *Dartmouth College,* the Court held New York's insolvency law invalid as impairing the obligation of contracts. The law freed debtors and discharged them from liability for all previous debts once they surrendered their remaining property to the state. Although it was unclear at the time and contributed to the impression that all state insolvency laws would be held unconstitutional, the decision of the Court was based on the fact that the New York law freed a debtor from liability for debts contracted *before* the law was passed, and thus impaired the obligation of those existing "contracts." In the opinion Chief Justice Marshall stated that the constitutional power of Congress to pass a uniform bankruptcy law did not, by its mere existence, deny states the power to pass such laws. Until Congress exercised that power, he wrote, states could pass bankruptcy and insolvency laws so long as they did not violate the Contract Clause.[21]

Eight years later, in 1827, the Court cleared up the confusion on this matter, ruling that state laws discharging debts contracted *after* the laws' passage did not violate the Contract Clause. Argued in 1824 and reargued in 1827, *Ogden v. Saunders* (1827) divided the justices, 4–3, and for the only time in Marshall's long career as chief justice, he was on the losing side in a constitutional case.[22] The Court upheld a new version of the New York insolvency law, with Justice Bushrod Washington setting out his often-quoted opinion on how the Supreme Court should approach cases challenging a state law:

> It is but a decent respect due to the wisdom, the integrity, and the patriotism of the legislative body, by which any law is passed, to presume in favor of its validity, until its violation of the constitution is proved beyond all reasonable doubt.[23]

Marshall, joined in dissent by Justices Story and Gabriel Duvall, argued that the Contract Clause forbade any legislative impairment of future as well as existing contracts. The majority's view, Marshall warned, could be used to construe that clause "into an inanimate, inoperative, unmeaning" provision.[24] With its rejection of this viewpoint, the Court for the first time placed a limit on the protection of the Contract Clause. This decision concluded the Court's expansion of the Contract Clause as a curb on the powers of state legislatures.

During the same term the Court upheld the decision of the Rhode Island legislature to abolish imprisonment as a punishment for debtors. This modification of the remedy for defaulting on contracts did not impair the obligation imposed by the contract, held the Court, even though it applied to debtors already in default at the time of its passage.[25] In the first state bankruptcy case, *Sturges v. Crowninshield* (1819), Chief Justice Marshall had written that "without imparing [*sic*] the obligation of the contract, the remedy may certainly be modified....Imprisonment is no part of the contract, and simply to release the prisoner does not impair its obligation."[26] The Court made clear, however, that a state could go too far in modifying the remedy provided for enforcing debt obligations when in 1843 it held invalid—under the Contract Clause—an Illinois law that so altered the remedies for default on mortgages that it effectively impaired the obligation involved.[27]

The Court in 2005 refused to limit the state's eminent domain power to obtain land for economic development. In *Kelo v. City of New London* the Court upheld a Connecticut city's plan to buy up 90 acres near its riverfront to make way for private development. Susette Kelo refused to sell her house and sued to block the seizure as unconstitutional. She said private development was not a "public use" of the land, and therefore went beyond the eminent domain power. The Court disagreed in a 5-4 decision and said it would defer to city officials and the state legislators to set the boundaries on what is a public use. "For more than a century, our public use jurisprudence has wisely eschewed rigid formulas and intrusive scrutiny in favor of affording legislatures broad latitude in determining what public needs justify the use of the takings power," Justice John Paul Stevens wrote.[28] *(See also box, Eminent Domain: An Inherent Power, p. 188.)*

The Public Interest

Having made clear its insistence upon state respect of contract obligations, the Court in the 1830s began to open loopholes in the protection that the Contract Clause provided to property rights. Certain state powers were inalienable, the Court held; they could not be simply contracted away, even if the state wished to do so. Primary among them were a state's power of eminent domain and its police power. The relationship of these powers to contract obligations was set out by the Court in three nineteenth-century cases.

The Power of Eminent Domain

The case that began this narrowing of the Contract Clause protection was argued in Marshall's last years but was then set for reargument. It was finally decided during the first term of Chief Justice Roger B. Taney. For some, the decision in *Charles River Bridge v. Warren Bridge* (1837) marks the ideological shift from the Marshall Court to the Taney Court. In 1785 the Massachusetts legislature chartered a company to build a bridge across the Charles River to Boston, to operate it, and to collect tolls from passengers. The Charles River Bridge quickly became profitable; tolls were collected long after its costs were recovered. Decades later, in 1828, the legislature chartered another company to build a second bridge across the Charles. Located near the first bridge, the Warren Bridge would be a toll way only until its costs were paid—or for six years, whichever was shorter—and then it would be a toll-free bridge. The Charles River Bridge Company, realizing that its business would disappear once it was in competition with a free bridge, challenged the law authorizing the second bridge. This law, the company said, impaired the contract in its charter and destroyed the value of its franchise by preventing it from earning the tolls it was authorized to collect. By the time the case was decided, the Warren Bridge had not only been built, but it was paid for and operating on a toll-free basis.

The Charles River Bridge Company lost its case before the Court in a 4-3 vote. "[I]n grants by the public nothing passes by implication," wrote Chief Justice Taney for the Court. Without an explicit grant of exclusive

The monopoly of this chartered toll bridge, built in the 1780s to link Boston with Cambridge, Massachusetts, was later challenged by builders of a rival bridge. The result was the landmark Supreme Court decision in *Charles River Bridge v. Warren Bridge* (1837). The owners of the Charles River Bridge claimed that their state charter gave them exclusive right to traffic across the river, but the Court ruled that the state had the authority to approve construction of a second bridge because it was in the public interest.

privilege in the original bridge company charter, none was assumed to exist to limit the state's power to authorize construction of another bridge.[29] Taney said that the same rule applied in this case that Marshall had cited in *Providence Bank v. Billings* (1830): the Court would not read into a bank charter an implied grant of privilege against the state. *(See details of Providence Bank v. Billings, p. 388.)* The state power in question in the case of the bridge was no less vital than the taxing power, wrote Taney:

> The object and end of all government is to promote the happiness and prosperity of the community by which it is established, and it can never be assumed that the government intended to diminish its power of accomplishing the end for which it was created.
>
> And in a country like ours, free, active and enterprising, continually advancing in numbers and wealth; new channels of communication are daily found necessary, both for travel and trade, and are essential to the comfort, convenience and prosperity of the people. A State ought never to be presumed to surrender this power, because, like the taxing power, the whole community have an interest in preserving it undiminished.

> And when a corporation alleges that a State has surrendered for seventy years its power of improvement and public accommodation, in a great and important line of travel, along which a vast number of its citizens must daily pass; the community have a right to insist…"that its abandonment ought not to be presumed, in a case in which the deliberate purpose of the State to abandon it does not appear."
>
> The continued existence of a government would be of no great value, if by implications and presumptions, it was disarmed of the powers necessary to accomplish the ends of its creation, and the functions it was designed to perform, transferred to the hands of privileged corporations. . . .
>
> While the rights of private property are sacredly guarded, we must not forget that the community also have rights, and that the happiness and well being of every citizen depends on their faithful preservation. . . .
>
> The whole community are interested in this inquiry, and they have a right to require that the power of promoting their comfort and convenience, and of advancing the public prosperity, by providing safe, convenient, and cheap ways for the transportation of produce, and the purposes of travel, shall not be construed to have been surrendered or

diminished by the State, unless it shall appear by plain words that it was intended to be done.[30]

Considering the implications of the Charles River Bridge claim, Taney noted that turnpikes—like the toll bridge—had in many areas been rendered useless by the coming of the railroad. If the Court approved the Charles River Bridge claim, he warned,

> [Y]ou will soon find the old turnpike corporations awakening from their sleep, and calling upon this court to put down the improvements which have taken their place....We shall be thrown back to the improvements of the last century, and obliged to stand still until the claims of the old turnpike corporations shall be satisfied, and they shall consent to permit these States to avail themselves of the lights of modern science.[31]

The broad power of eminent domain gained further recognition a few years after *Charles River Bridge* as a result of the Court's resolution of a quarrel between the owners of a toll bridge and the town of Brattleboro, Vermont. The owners of the toll bridge had been granted a century-long franchise to build and operate the bridge, but after the state authorized the building of highways, the town of Brattleboro ran a free highway right across the toll bridge, converting it into a free bridge. Although compensated by the state, the bridge owners protested that this impaired their charter and the contract obligation it contained. In 1848 the Supreme Court rejected this claim, upholding a broad state power of eminent domain paramount to contract rights. Justice Peter V. Daniel wrote the Court's opinion:

> [I]n every political sovereign community there inheres necessarily the right and the duty of guarding its own existence, and of protecting and promoting the interests and welfare of the community at large....This power, denominated "eminent domain" of the State, is, as its name imports, paramount to all private rights vested under the government, and these last are, by necessary implication, held in subordination to this power, and must yield in every instance to its proper exercise.
>
> The Constitution of the United States...can, by no rational interpretation, be brought to conflict

with this attribute in the States; there is no express delegation of it by the Constitution; and it would imply an incredible fatuity in the States, to ascribe to them the intention to relinquish the power of self-government and self-preservation.[32]

The validity of this ruling was reemphasized sixty-nine years later, when the Court ruled that a state retained the power of eminent domain even in the face of its express agreement to surrender it and could thus exercise it properly in a way in which it had contracted to forgo.[33]

The Police Power

With the Court's decision in *Stone v. Mississippi* (1880) the police power joined eminent domain on the list of inalienable powers that a state could not surrender permanently. The "carpetbagger" legislature of Mississippi had chartered a state lottery corporation, the Mississippi Agricultural, Educational and Manufacturing Aid Society. As soon as a new legislature was in power, it amended the Mississippi constitution to ban lotteries from the state. The state then sued the society for existing in violation of this prohibition. The society responded with the argument that the state ban was invalid because it impaired the contract obligation of the society's charter. The Court ruled against the lottery. In a brief but weighty opinion, Chief Justice Morrison R. Waite announced the decision of the unanimous Court:

> All agree that the Legislature cannot bargain away the police power of a State....Many attempts have been made in this court and elsewhere to define the police power, but never with entire success. No one denies, however, that it extends to all matters affecting the public health or the public morals. No Legislature can bargain away the public health or the public morals....The supervision of both these subjects of governmental power is continuing in its nature, and they are to be dealt with as the special exigencies of the moment may require. Government is organized with a view to their preservation, and cannot devest [*sic*] itself of the power to provide for them. . . .
>
> Anyone, therefore, who accepts a lottery charter, does so with the implied understanding that the

People, in their sovereign capacity…may resume it at any time when the public good shall require.[34]

Remedies and Obligations

The climax in the use of the Contract Clause as a curb on state legislation came just after the Civil War. From 1865 to 1873 there were twenty cases in which state laws or actions were held invalid as in conflict with the clause. After this point, the combined effect of eminent domain and police power exceptions to the clause's protection for property began to reduce its restraining force.[35] The Due Process Clause, for a time, took the place of the Contract Clause as a shield for property rights. In *Allgeyer v. Louisiana* (1897) the Court linked the two with its statement—that the right to make contracts was an element of the liberty guarantee by the Due Process Clause.[36] This "freedom of contract" would be used for several decades by the Court to curtail state efforts to regulate wages, hours, and working conditions. *(See "Wages and Hours," pp. 414–417.)* The last major Contract Clause ruling came during the Great Depression. Since that time, the clause has become no more than "a tail to the due process of law kite…a fifth wheel to the Constitutional law coach."[37]

In 1933 the Minnesota legislature responded to the plight of the many people unable to meet mortgage payments during the depression by passing a mortgage moratorium act. The law allowed postponement of foreclosure sales and extension of the period during which the property might be retained and redeemed by the defaulting mortgagor. The law was clearly temporary, set to expire May 1, 1935. One mortgage holder, Home Building & Loan Association, challenged the law as impairing the obligation of contract contained in the mortgage. By a vote of 5-4, the Supreme Court upheld the law, emphasizing the emergency conditions that justified its passage. Chief Justice Charles Evans Hughes wrote the opinion in *Home Building & Loan Association v. Blaisdell* (1934):

> Emergency does not create power. Emergency does not increase granted power or remove or diminish the restrictions imposed upon power.…But while emergency does not create power, emergency may furnish the occasion for the exercise of power.[38]

The prohibition in the Contract Clause "is not an absolute one," Hughes continued, "and is not to be read with literal exactness like a mathematical formula."[39] The majority, in Hughes's words, declared that

> the state…continues to possess authority to safeguard the vital interests of its people. It does not matter that legislation appropriate to that end "has the result of modifying or abrogating contracts already in effect."…Not only are existing laws read into contracts in order to fix obligations as between the parties, but the reservation of essential attributes of sovereign power is also read into contracts as a postulate of the legal order. The policy of protecting contracts against impairment presupposes the maintenance of a government by virtue of which contractual relations are worthwhile,—a government which retains adequate authority to secure the peace and good order of society. This principle of harmonizing the constitutional prohibition with the necessary residuum of state power has had progressive recognition in the decisions of this court.[40]

In light of the rulings in *Charles River Bridge v. Warren Bridge, West River Bridge v. Dix, Stone v. Mississippi,* and their progeny, Hughes found it untenable to argue that the Contract Clause prevented "limited and temporary interpositions with respect to the enforcement of contracts if made necessary by a great public calamity":

> The reservation of state power appropriate to such extraordinary conditions may be deemed to be as much a part of all contracts as is the reservation of state power to protect the public interest in the other situations to which we have referred. And if state power exists to give temporary relief from the enforcement of contracts in the presence of disasters due to physical causes such as fire, flood, or earthquake, that power cannot be said to be nonexistent when the urgent public need demanding such relief is produced by other and economic causes.…
>
> Where, in earlier days, it was thought that only the concerns of individuals…were involved, and that those of the state itself were touched only remotely, it has later been found that the fundamental interests of the state are directly affected; and that the question is no longer merely that of one party to a contract as against another, but of the use of reasonable means to safeguard the

economic structure upon which the good of all depends.[41]

Making clear the significance of the emergency and temporary nature of the legislation upheld in *Blaisdell,* the Court struck down similar but more sweeping laws from other states.[42] This seemed to end the long line of Contract Clause cases decided by the Court. Edward S. Corwin explains: "Until after the Civil War the 'obligation of contracts' clause was the principal source of cases challenging the validity of state legislation. Today the clause is much less important. But," he adds, "it would be premature to issue the clause's death certificate."[43] Sounding a similar note, Justice Potter Stewart in 1978 wrote that "the Contract Clause remains part of the Constitution. It is not a dead letter."[44] Stewart wrote the Court's opinion striking down part of a state pension law as it was applied to increase the liability and obligations of employers who had pension agreements with their employees in force when the law was passed. The previous term the Court had applied the Contract Clause to hold that the legislatures of New Jersey and New York had acted unconstitutionally when they changed the terms under which bonds were issued by the Port Authority of New York and New Jersey.[45]

THE CONTROL OF COMMERCE

"The spirit of enterprise, which characterizes the commercial part of America, has left no occasion of displaying itself unimproved," wrote Alexander Hamilton in the *Federalist Papers.* "It is not at all probable that this unbridled spirit would pay much respect to those regulations of trade by which particular states might endeavor to secure exclusive benefits to their own citizens. The infractions of these regulations on one side, the efforts to prevent and repeal them, on the other, would naturally lead to outrages, and these to reprisals and war." Later Hamilton would carry his warning further, predicting that without a strong federal power to regulate interstate and foreign commerce, the United States might soon become like the German Empire "in continual trammels from the multiplicity of the duties which the several princes and states exact upon the merchandises passing through their territories."[46]

Hamilton would not have been surprised to hear Justice Felix Frankfurter say, some 175 years later, that "with us, the commerce clause is perhaps the most fruitful and important means for asserting authority against the particularism of State policy."[47] Unlike the Contract Clause, which is clearly a restriction on state action, the Commerce Clause in Article I, section 8, makes no mention of state powers. It simply gives Congress the power "to regulate commerce with foreign nations, and among the several states, and with the Indian tribes." Even as the twentieth century was coming to a close, Congress's reliance on its commerce power for ever-deepening involvement in state affairs continued to be a source of controversy in the nation. The justices themselves were sharply divided. A five-justice majority warned in *United States v. Lopez* (1995) that the dual system of government necessarily limits the interstate commerce power lest that power be used to destroy the distinction between what is national and what is local.[48]

The Steamboat Monopoly

From the states' perspective, the restrictive force of the Commerce Clause was driven home by the Court's decision in *Gibbons v. Ogden* (1824), the case of the New York steamboat monopoly and first ruling involving the grant of commerce power to Congress. In 1798 the New York legislature granted Robert R. Livingston and Robert Fulton the exclusive right to run steamboats in the state's waters. In 1811 Livingston and Fulton secured a similar monopoly for steamship transportation near New Orleans, the young nation's other great port. The monopoly was a source of aggravation to other states, which passed laws excluding the Livingston-Fulton boats from their waters while granting monopolies to other companies. Instead of unifying the states, steamboat transportation appeared to be dividing them further. Arguing this case before the Court, Attorney General William Wirt described the situation as one in which New York was almost at war with Ohio, Connecticut, and New Jersey.[49]

Aaron Ogden, a former New Jersey governor, operated steamboats in New York under license from the monopoly, but Thomas Gibbons, his former partner, was competing with Ogden—and the monopoly—by

In 1807 inventor Robert Fulton put a steam engine in the *Clermont*, pictured here, and proved that boats could be powered by something other than wind and manpower. New York state granted Fulton and his partner, Robert Livingston, a monopoly to operate steamboats on the Hudson River. The monopoly was contested, and the resulting case, *Gibbons v. Ogden* (1824), became an important test of Congress's right to regulate interstate commerce.

running steamboats between New York and New Jersey. Although Gibbons was not licensed by the monopoly, his ships were licensed under the federal law governing the coasting trade. Ogden obtained an order from the New York courts directing Gibbons to stop his operation. Gibbons took the case to the Supreme Court. For five days in February 1824 the case was argued before the justices. Daniel Webster argued along with Wirt for Gibbons.

On March 2 the Court announced its decision, rejecting a narrow definition of commerce and striking down the monopoly because it was in conflict with the broad federal power to regulate interstate commerce. Speaking for the Court, Chief Justice Marshall defined commerce as intercourse—not simply traffic or buying and selling alone. Commerce also included navigation, the particular subject at hand. Marshall explained, "The power over commerce, including navigation, was one of the primary objects for which the people of America adopted their government, and

must have been contemplated in forming it." [50] Furthermore, Marshall wrote,

> Commerce among the states cannot stop at the external boundary line of each state, but may be introduced into the interior.... The power of Congress, then, comprehends navigation within the limits of every state in the Union; so far as that navigation may be, in any manner, connected with "commerce with foreign nations, or among the several states, or with the Indian tribes." [51]

New York's effort to confine the use of its waters to the monopoly's ships and deny use to vessels such as Gibbons's, which were licensed under the federal coasting law, collided with federal regulation of commerce and so must fall:

> The nullity of any act, inconsistent with the constitution, is produced by the declaration that the constitution is the supreme law. The appropriate application of that part of the clause...is to such acts of the state legislature as do not transcend their

powers, but though enacted in the execution of acknowledged state powers, interfere with, or are contrary to the laws of Congress, made in pursuance of the constitution….In every such case, the act of Congress…is supreme; and the law of the state, though enacted in the exercise of powers not controverted, must yield to it.[52]

Much has been written about the significance of this decision. Felix Frankfurter, later to sit on the Supreme Court, wrote that the theme Marshall first sounded in *Gibbons v. Ogden* became the focal point of the constitutional system—"the doctrine that the commerce clause, by its own force, and without national legislation, puts it into the power of the Court to place limits upon state authority." "Marshall's use of the commerce clause," he continued, "gave momentum to the doctrine that state authority must be subject to such limitations as the Court finds it necessary to apply for the protection of the national community."[53]

In addition to the case's importance in the constitutional development of the United States, the ruling had a considerable effect on its economic development, as two historians observe:

Steamboat navigation, freed from the restraint of state-created monopolies…increased at an astonishing rate. Within a few years steam railroads, encouraged by the freedom of interstate commerce from state restraints, were to begin a practical revolution of internal transportation. The importance of national control of commerce in the rapid economic development is almost incalculable. For many years after 1824 Congress enacted but few important regulatory measures, and commerce was thus free to develop without serious monopolistic or governmental restraint.[54]

Another scholar, emphasizing the latter point, notes,

Like most of the important cases decided by Chief Justice Marshall, [*Gibbons v. Ogden*] involved, not the assertion of the power of the federal government over interstate commerce, but acted rather as a prohibition against state activity. Apart from granting coasting licenses, the federal government was not interested in the commerce involved. The decision was an act in

defense of laissez-faire, rather than of positive federal control.[55]

An Exclusive Power?

For thirty years after the *Gibbons* ruling, the nation would be preoccupied with the debate over whether the power of Congress to regulate commerce was exclusive or whether the states retained some concurrent authority in that area. Underlying this debate was the simmering issue of slavery. Charles Warren wrote:

Throughout the long years when the question of the extent of the Federal power over commerce was being tested in numerous cases in the Court, that question was, in the minds of Southerners, simply coincident with the question of the extent of the Federal power over slavery. So the long-continued controversy as to whether Congress had exclusive or concurrent jurisdiction over commerce was not a conflict between theories of government, or between Nationalism and State-Rights, or between differing legal construction of the Constitution, but was simply the naked issue of State or Federal control of slavery. It was little wonder, therefore, that the Judges of the Court prior to the Civil War displayed great hesitation in deciding this momentous controversy.[56]

The particular question left hanging by *Gibbons* was whether the existence of federal power to regulate navigation left the states entirely powerless in that area. In *Willson v. Blackbird Creek Marsh Co.* (1829) the Court held that the states did retain some power over navigation within their borders, so long as Congress had not acted to regulate it. As allowed under state law, the Blackbird Creek Marsh Company had built a dam on the creek of that name in Delaware. The operators of a federally licensed sloop, irritated by the obstruction, rammed and broke the dam. The dam company won a damage judgment in state court against the shipowners, who then appealed to the Supreme Court, arguing that the dam and the authorizing state law were impermissible infringements upon the federal power over navigation.

The mere existence of federal power to regulate navigation on such creeks—if not exercised—did not foreclose state action to regulate such matters, held the Court, particularly if the objectives of state action were, as in this case, to preserve the value of property and to enhance the public health. "Measures calculated to produce these objects, provided they do not come into collision with the powers of the general government, are undoubtedly within those which are reserved to the States," wrote Chief Justice Marshall.[57] The *Willson* decision paved the way for formulation of the concept of the state police power during the era of Chief Justice Taney. That concept served as a useful implement for carving out an area within which state regulation of commerce was permissible. *(See "The Police Power," pp. 407–417.)* For two decades after *Willson,* however, neither the Court nor the country found it easy to ascertain the line between permissible and impermissible state regulation affecting commerce. The Court's decisions grew more and more unpredictable.

In *Mayor of New York v. Miln* (1837) the Court upheld a New York law that required reports to be filed on all passengers arriving on ships in the city's port. Although the law was challenged as an invasion of the federal power over foreign commerce, the Court found no such intrusion. Instead, the justices viewed the law, which intended to minimize the possibility of the foreign passengers becoming public charges, as a proper exercise of the state police power not in conflict with federal authority.[58] Four years later, when the question of a state's power to forbid the importation of slaves came before the Court, the justices sidestepped a decision. All the justices, however, expressed their personal opinions, revealing "almost complete chaos of interpretation."[59]

In 1847 the Court decided the *License Cases,* in which it upheld the right of states to require that all sales of alcohol within the state be licensed, including the sales of imported alcohol. Again the Court held such a requirement a valid exercise of the police power, but the six justices wrote nine opinions, none of which could be characterized as a majority view. The decision provided little guidance for future state action.[60] Two years later, with a similar multiplicity of opinions, the Court,

divided 5-4, struck down New York and Massachusetts laws taxing all alien passengers arriving in their ports. Once again there was no opinion that could be identified as having the support of a majority of the justices.[61] The *Passenger Cases* (1849) were argued three times before the Court issued its ruling, with each justice reading his opinion in a process that took seven hours.[62] The numerical majority, led by Justice John McLean, found the taxes a direct infringement of the exclusive federal power over interstate and foreign commerce. The dissenters, led by Chief Justice Taney, viewed the states as having a concurrent power with Congress and saw the tax laws as a proper use of state police power.

"Yes, and No"

At last, in 1852, almost three decades after *Gibbons v. Ogden,* the Court managed to formulate its divergent opinions into some sort of rule for determining whether states could exercise any regulatory authority over matters of interstate and foreign commerce. *Cooley v. Board of Wardens of the Port of Philadelphia* (1852) turned on the question of whether the state of Pennsylvania could require vessels entering the port of Philadelphia to take on a pilot to enter it, or if they refused, to pay a certain fee. Aaron B. Cooley had refused to take on a pilot or to pay the fee, challenging the requirement as an infringement by the state on exclusive federal power over matters of commerce, such as pilotage. In 1789 Congress had enacted a law requiring that pilots continue to be regulated by state law until such time as Congress acted to impose a uniform system of regulation on them.

The Court upheld Pennsylvania's position. Writing the opinion was the most junior justice, Benjamin R. Curtis, a forty-one-year-old Boston attorney in his first term on the Court. Curtis explained that the Court found the state law permissible because Congress clearly had intended state regulation of this matter to continue, because Congress had not passed any superseding legislation concerning pilotage and because the subject was in fact one better dealt with by local regulation. In explaining this last point, Curtis set out what came to be known as the "Cooley rule," used to distinguish matters of exclusive federal control under the commerce power from

Speed Limits, Mud Flaps, and Brakes

Although the Supreme Court removed the subject of railroad rates from state control before the end of the nineteenth century, it left the states some authority to regulate interstate traffic to protect the public safety. In a series of cases, the Court upheld as permissible such regulation so long as it does not unduly burden interstate commerce. After World War II, however, the Court became less tolerant of such state regulation. In judging the validity of these state laws, the Court usually weighed the benefits produced by the regulation against the burden it imposes on the regulated vehicles.

In 1910 the Court had upheld Georgia's speed limit for interstate trains, but seven years later it struck down Georgia's requirement that trains slow down at all grade crossings. The effect of the latter requirement was to double the travel time of some trains that passed one crossing per minute.[1] In the Motor Carrier Act of 1935, Congress left to the states the regulation of the size and weight of interstate motor vehicles traveling through their territory. The Court subsequently upheld South Carolina's limits on the size of trucks and trailers, even though they were substantially stricter than those of adjoining states.[2] In 1945 the Court struck down Arizona's law restricting the length of railroad trains operating within the state. Although Congress had not regulated that subject, the Court held that the limits conflicted so much with the railroad industry's usual train length that they burdened commerce and did not sufficiently benefit the public safety to be justified.[3]

In general, the Court has held that states have more control over the highways than over the railroads within their boundaries. In 1959 the Court said Illinois burdened commerce by requiring that trucks passing through the state have a certain kind of rear-fender mudguard different from the usual mudflap, which Illinois declared illegal.[4] In 1978 the Court struck down Wisconsin's ban on double-trailer trucks. The justices held that the state did not provide any proof that the ban enhanced the safety of highway traffic, so its law must fall as an undue burden on interstate commerce. Three years later the Court similarly struck down an Iowa statute prohibiting the use of certain large trucks.[5] In 1983 Congress passed legislation requiring states to allow twin-trailer trucks to use interstate highways. In later legislation it allowed exceptions if a state could justify them as required for safety.

---

1. *Southern Railway Co. v. King,* 217 U.S. 524 (1910); *Seaboard Air Line R. Co. v. Blackwell,* 244 U.S. 310 (1917).

2. *South Carolina Highway Department v. Barnwell Brothers* 303 U.S. 177 (1938).

3. *Southern Pacific Co. v. Arizona,* 325 U.S. 761 (1945).

4. *Bibb v. Navajo Freight Lines,* 359 U.S. 520 (1959).

5. *Raymond Motor Transportation Inc. v. Rice,* 434 U.S. 429 (1978); *Kassel v. Consolidated Freightways Corp.,* 450 U.S. 662 (1981).

---

those for which a concurrent federal and state power existed:

> The grant of commercial power to Congress does not contain any terms which expressly exclude the States from exercising an authority over its subject matter. If they are excluded, it must be because the nature of the power, thus granted to Congress, requires that a similar authority should not exist in the States. . . .
>
> Now, the power to regulate commerce embraces a vast field, containing not only many, but exceedingly various subjects, quite unlike in their nature; some imperatively demanding a single uniform rule, operating equally on the commerce of the United States in every port; and some, like the subject now in question, as imperatively demanding that diversity, which alone can meet the local necessities of navigation.

> Either absolutely to affirm, or deny, that the nature of this power requires exclusive legislation by Congress, is to lose sight of the nature of the subjects of this power, and to assert concerning all of them, what is really applicable but to a part. Whatever subjects of this power are in their nature national, or admit only of one uniform system, or plan of regulation, may justly be said to be of such a nature as to require exclusive legislation by Congress. That this cannot be affirmed of laws for the regulation of pilots and pilotage is plain. . . . [A]lthough Congress has legislated on this subject, its legislation manifests an intention not to regulate this subject, but to leave its regulation to the several States.[63]

A century later one constitutional scholar would describe the *Cooley* decision this way:

To the question whether the power of Congress is exclusive, Mr. Justice Curtis took a great step forward by answering, "Yes, and no." This is the wisest initial answer to give to many questions that embrace such a variety and diversity of issues that no single answer can possibly be suitable for all.[64]

The line-drawing that the *Cooley* rule demanded was a difficult one. During the term the rule was announced, the Court held that Virginia had impermissibly built a bridge across the Ohio River, infringing on the federal power to regulate interstate commerce because the bridge was too low for some boats to pass under. Although the facts of the case seemed similar, except in scale, to those of the Blackbird Creek decision, the Court decided against the state. By licensing ships under the coasting law to navigate the Ohio River, held the Court, Congress clearly had asserted its authority over traffic there. In the earlier case, it was doubtful whether federal power had been extended over small creeks. "No state law can hinder or obstruct the free use of a license granted under an Act of Congress," wrote Justice McLean for the Court.[65]

Congress overrode this decision. By passing a law authorizing the already-built bridge, it removed any objection to its existence as in conflict with congressional power. This was the first time that Congress directly blocked the effect of a Court decision. In 1856 the Court reviewed and upheld this act as within the power of Congress to regulate navigation.[66]

National Concerns

Railroad rates and immigration were two subjects to which the Court applied the *Cooley* rule and found them to fall within the category of issues requiring exclusive federal regulation.

Immigration

Immigration had been an issue in the *Miln* case of 1837 and again in the *Passenger Cases* of 1849. In the former, the Court had upheld a state requirement of filing reports on all incoming alien passengers; in the latter, it had struck down state taxes on all incoming aliens. By the 1870s immigration clearly had become a matter of national concern. In 1876 the Court voided New York, Louisiana, and California laws that attempted to regulate immigration—and reduce the burden it might place on state finances—by requiring the owners of every ship bringing immigrants into their ports to give bond for each alien. In the New York case the bond was $300 a passenger; payment could be waived by payment of a tax of $1.50 per person within twenty-four hours of landing. The states defended these laws as "a suitable regulation" to protect their cities and towns "from the expense of supporting persons who are paupers or diseased, or helpless women and children, coming from foreign countries."

The Supreme Court, however, viewed these laws as merely imposing a tax on the privilege of landing passengers in the state, an impermissible interference with federal power over foreign commerce. Writing for the Court, Justice Samuel Miller explained that the transportation of persons from foreign lands to this country had become foreign commerce, the regulation of which was exclusively reserved to Congress. Over such a subject, the state could not exercise its police power:

> [T]he matter of these statutes may be and ought to be the subject of a uniform system or plan. The laws which govern the right to land passengers in the United States from other countries ought to be the same in New York, Boston, New Orleans and San Francisco.... [T]his whole subject has been confided to Congress by the Constitution.[67]

Emphasizing this point in the companion California case, Justice Miller wrote,

> The passage of laws which concern the admission of citizens and subjects of foreign nations to our shore belongs to Congress, and not to the states.... If it be otherwise, a single state can, at her pleasure, embroil us in disastrous quarrels with other nations.[68]

One result of these decisions was the passage by Congress, in 1882, of the nation's first general law governing immigration.

In the *Granger Cases* (1877) the Supreme Court endorsed state regulation of railroads. Less than a decade later, in 1886, the Court held that if a railroad was part of an interstate network, states could not regulate its rates, even for the intrastate portion of a trip.

Railroad Rates

By the Civil War, commerce was moving cross-country by rail as well as water. Reflecting this shift, many of the Court's postwar Commerce Clause rulings focused on the efforts of states to regulate the railroads. For a time the Court flirted with state regulation of railroad rates, but as the rail networks expanded across the nation, it became clear that the intrastate operations of an interstate railroad were hardly the subject for local regulation. In 1886 the Court issued a decision to that effect, and the following year Congress created the Interstate Commerce Commission. In many states it was pressure from farmers that resulted in the passage of state laws regulating railroad rates. A secret order called the National Grange won passage of a number of laws regulating how much railroads could charge farmers to carry their produce to market. In like fashion, some states passed laws to regulate rates that grain elevator companies could charge to store the farmers' grain.

In 1877 the Supreme Court appeared to sanction state regulation of these businesses with its decision in a set of cases involving railroad and grain elevator rate regulation. These decisions are referred to as the *Granger Cases* or by the title of the grain elevator case, *Munn v. Illinois*.[69] Acknowledging that these matters fell within the purview of federal power, the Court nevertheless upheld the state laws. Writing in the Wisconsin railroad rate case, Chief Justice Morrison R. Waite stated,

> Until Congress acts in reference to the relations of this Company to interstate commerce, it is certainly within the power of Wisconsin to regulate its fares, etc., so far as they are of domestic concern. With the people of Wisconsin, this Company has domestic relations. Incidentally, these may reach beyond the State. But certainly, until Congress undertakes to

legislate for those who are without the State, Wisconsin may provide for those within, even though it may indirectly affect those without.[70]

To limit the implications of the grant of this power to the states, the Court devised the criteria of "public interest" with which to distinguish those businesses that might be subject to state regulation from those that could not be. Chief Justice Waite outlined the rationale:

> Property does become clothed with a public interest when used in a manner to make it of public consequence and affect the community at large. When, therefore, one devotes his property to a use in which the public has an interest, he, in effect, grants to the public an interest in that use, and must submit to be controlled by the public for the common good, to the extent of the interest he has thus created.[71]

State regulation of grain elevators survived for several decades, upheld by the Court again in 1892.[72] State power to regulate railroad rates, however, was soon sharply curtailed. In 1886—less than a decade after the *Granger Cases*—the Supreme Court held that if a railroad was part of an interstate network, states could not regulate its rates, even for the intrastate portion of a trip.[73] Speaking for the Court, Justice Miller wrote,

> It cannot be too strongly insisted upon, that the right of continuous transportation from one end of the country to the other is essential in modern times to that freedom of commerce from the restraints which the States might choose to impose upon it, that the commerce clause was intended to secure. This clause...was among the most important of the subjects which prompted the formation of the Constitution....And it would be a very feeble and almost useless provision, but poorly adapted to secure the entire freedom of commerce among the States which was deemed essential to a more perfect union by the framers if, at every stage of the transportation of goods and chattels through the country, the State within whose limits a part of this transportation must be done could impose regulations concerning the price, compensation, or taxation, or any other restrictive regulation interfering with and seriously embarrassing this commerce....[74]

[I]t is not, and never has been, the deliberate opinion of a majority of this Court that a statute of a State which attempts to regulate the fares and charges by railroad companies within its limits, for a transportation which constitutes a part of commerce among the States, is a valid law....[75]

As restricted to a transportation which begins and ends within the limits of the State, it may be very just and equitable, and it certainly is the province of the State Legislature to determine that question. But when it is attempted to apply to transportation through an entire series of States a principle of this kind, and each one...shall attempt to establish its own rates of transportation...the deleterious influence upon the freedom of commerce among the States and upon the transit of goods through those States cannot be overestimated. That this species of regulation is one which must be, if established at all, of a general and national character, and cannot be safely and wisely remitted to local rules and local regulations, we think it is clear.[76]

The next year Congress enacted the long-pending Interstate Commerce Act of 1887, which included creation of the Interstate Commerce Commission, the primary mission of which was the regulation of interstate railroad systems. States were still able to regulate purely intrastate railroad rates and to exercise their police power to regulate other aspects of railroad operations, under judicial supervision to ensure that the states did not burden interstate commerce or deny the railroad due process of law. With passage of the Interstate Commerce Act, Congress began to extend affirmative federal control over commerce. The period in which most of the Supreme Court's Commerce Clause rulings viewed the clause chiefly as a limit on state power thus came to an end. The exercise of federal power in this area brought a whole new set of Commerce Clause issues to the Court, phrased in terms of national, not state, authority. (*See "Congress, Commerce, and the Railroads," pp. 104–109.*)

Local Concerns

Although the Court felt it necessary to remove the issues of immigration and railroad regulation from state control, it by no means left the states bereft of power over economic matters. Between the Civil War and the New Deal, the Court held that insurance, liquor, manufacturing, segregation, agriculture, and child labor were all matters of strictly local concern. After the first years of the New Deal, the line between local and national matters—preserved chiefly through the doctrine of dual federalism—became indistinct and of relatively little importance. *(See "The State as Sovereign," pp. 451–483.)*

Insurance

In the late 1860s the Court held that the business of insurance regulation should be left to the states. The justices upheld a Virginia law requiring out-of-state insurance companies to obtain a state license and post bond with the state before doing business there. This was a proper local law governing local transactions, held the Court in the case of *Paul v. Virginia* (1869), which remained the law for seventy-five years.[77] During World War II, several fire insurance companies were indicted under federal antitrust law. Insurance, they argued in their defense, was outside the category of "commerce," the subject of the Sherman Antitrust Act under which the charges were brought. The government contested this claim, and the Supreme Court rejected the insurers' argument. The Court upheld the indictment in 1944 and in so doing brought insurance within the definition of commerce subject to federal regulation. Writing for the Court, Justice Hugo L. Black said,

> No commercial enterprise of any kind which conducts its activities across state lines has been held to be wholly beyond the regulatory power of Congress under the Commerce Clause. We cannot make an exception of the business of insurance. . . .[78]
>
> In all cases in which the Court has relied upon the proposition that "the business of insurance is not commerce," its attention was focused on the validity of state statutes—the extent to which the Commerce Clause automatically deprived states of the power to regulate the insurance business. Since Congress had at no time attempted to control the insurance business, invalidation of the state statutes would practically have been equivalent to granting insurance companies

engaged in interstate activities a blanket license to operate without legal restraint.[79]

Congress, however, quickly handed this subject back to the state legislatures. In 1945 it passed the McCarran-Ferguson Act exempting the insurance business from the reach of all but a few major federal antitrust and labor laws. In 1946 the Supreme Court upheld this action.[80] The 1945 law would remain controversial for the next fifty years. Although proposals continually were introduced in Congress for the statute's repeal, none succeeded.

Manufacturing

By defining commerce to exclude manufacturing or production, the Supreme Court effectively placed a number of issues beyond federal reach and within state control. In 1888 the Court upheld an Iowa law that forbade the manufacture of liquor in Iowa for sale outside the state as well as in the state. Writing for the Court, Justice Lucius Q. C. Lamar proclaimed this distinction between production and commerce:

> No distinction is more popular to the common mind, or more clearly expressed in economic and political literature, than that between manufactures and commerce. Manufacture is transformation the fashioning of raw materials into a change of form for use. The functions of commerce are different. The buying and selling and the transportation incidental thereto constitute commerce; and the regulation of commerce in the constitutional sense embraces the regulation at least of such transportation. . . .
>
> If it be held that the term includes the regulation of all such manufactures as are intended to be the subject of commercial transactions in the future, it is impossible to deny that it would also include all productive industries that contemplate the same thing. The result would be that Congress would be invested, to the exclusion of the States, with the power to regulate, not only manufacture, but also agriculture, horticulture, stock raising, domestic fisheries, mining—in short, every branch of human industry. . . .
>
> The power being vested in Congress and denied to the States, it would follow as an inevitable result

GARBAGE AND COMMERCE

Garbage is a valued commodity for some, but for others, it is just unwanted waste. Viewing it as a commodity rather than waste, the Supreme Court has rejected most state laws that forbid private trash haulers from crossing the state line and bringing garbage to landfills.

"All objects of interstate trade merit Commerce Clause protection; none is excluded by definition at the outset," the Court said in 1978.[1] By a 7-2 vote, the justices struck down a New Jersey law forbidding the importation of solid or liquid waste originated or collected out of state. The court held this state law discriminated against interstate commerce. New Jersey, whose landfills had for years been used by the cities of Philadelphia and New York as depositories for their garbage, sought to preserve the remaining landfill space within its boundaries for dumping its own garbage. The Court, however, found that the state had chosen a constitutionally impermissible means of achieving that end. Wrote Justice Potter Stewart,

> [This law] falls squarely within the area that the Commerce Clause puts off-limits to state regulation. On its face, it imposes on out-of-state commercial interests the full burden of conserving the State's remaining landfill space.... What is crucial is the attempt by one State to isolate itself from a problem common to many by erecting a barrier against the movement of interstate trade.[2]

The Court has continued to view garbage as part of commerce. In 1992 it struck down a Michigan law that allowed county officials to stop private landfill operators from accepting solid waste from outside the county.[3] The Court also rejected surcharges imposed by some states on out-of-state waste.[4]

But states, counties, and cities may regulate the flow of trash, the Court said in 2007, so long as they do not discriminate between private companies. In a 6-3 decision, the Court upheld an ordinance in Oneida County, New York, that required all trash to be hauled to a central, publicly owned processing facility. Private haulers objected. They said they could have trash processed for less elsewhere. In 1994 the Court had struck down another New York "flow control" ordinance that directed trash to a private facility.[5] In upholding Oneida's ordinance, Chief Justice John Roberts said that government regulation is not protectionism. "Disposing of trash has been a traditional government activity for years, and laws that favor the government in such areas ... do not discriminate against interstate commerce for purposes of the Commerce Clause," he wrote.[6]

---

1. *Philadelphia v. New Jersey,* 437 U.S. 617 (1978).

2. Id. at 626–627, 628.

3. *Fort Gratiot Landfill Inc. v. Michigan Department of Natural Resources,* 504 U.S. 353 (1992).

4. *Chemical Waste Management Inc. v. Hunt,* 504 U.S. 334 (1992); *Oregon Waste Systems Inc. v. Department of Environmental Quality,* 511 U.S. 93 (1994).

5. *C & A Carbone Inc. v. Town of Clarkstown,* 511 U.S. 383 (1994).

6. *United Haulers Association Inc. v. Oneida-Herkimer Solid Waste Management Authority,* 550 U.S. — (2007).

---

that the duty would devolve on Congress to regulate all of these delicate, multiform, and vital interests—interests which in their nature are, and must be, local in all the details of their successful management....

It does not follow that, because the products of a domestic manufacture may ultimately become the subjects of interstate commerce,...the legislation of the State respecting such manufacture is an attempted exercise of the power of commerce exclusively conferred upon Congress.[81]

Seven years later the distinction used in the liquor case to uphold state regulation was exercised again—this time to preclude federal regulation. In *United States v. E. C. Knight Co.* (1895), the *Sugar Trust Case,* the Court held that the Sherman Antitrust Act, enacted under the federal commerce power, could not be used as a basis for prosecuting sugar manufacturers. Wrote Chief Justice Melville W. Fuller:

The relief of the citizens of each state from the burden of monopoly was left with the states to deal with, and this court has recognized their possession of that power even to the extent of holding that an employment or business carried on by private individuals, when it becomes a matter of such public interest and importance as to create a common charge or burden upon the citizen; in other words, when it becomes a practical monopoly, to which the citizen is compelled to resort...is subject to regulation by state legislative power....

... Commerce succeeds to manufacture, and is not a part of it. The power to regulate commerce is the power to prescribe the rule by which commerce shall be governed, and is a power independent of the power to suppress monopoly...It is vital that the independence of the commercial power and of the police power, and the delimitation between them, however sometimes perplexing, should always be recognized and observed, for while the one furnishes the strongest bond of union, the other is essential to the preservation of the autonomy of the states as required by our dual form of government.[82]

In subsequent similar decisions, the Court held mining, lumbering, fishing, farming, the production of oil, and the generation of electric power to be outside the scope of the federal commerce power and hence within the scope of state regulation.[83]

Although the Court did not directly overrule these particular decisions separating manufacture and commerce, in the late 1930s it simply abandoned the distinction, upholding federal laws that regulated manufacturing, such as the National Labor Relations Act.[84] Similarly, it upheld the Agricultural Adjustment Act of 1938, setting marketing quotas for farm products. This, the Court reasoned, regulated farm production at the point where it entered interstate commerce, the marketing warehouse. The justices dismissed the argument that not all products regulated were sold in interstate commerce.[85] Three years later, in 1942, the Court upheld the application of these quotas to a farmer who grew wheat in excess of his quota but only for use on his own farm. Despite the lack of any clear connection between the excess wheat on this farm and interstate commerce, the Court sustained the reach of federal power. Justice Robert H. Jackson explained the Court's rationale: if the price of wheat rose high enough, the farmer would be induced to put his wheat into interstate commerce—and if he did not, he would use it for his own purposes and therefore not buy wheat in interstate commerce that he otherwise would need to buy. "Homegrown wheat in this sense competes with wheat in commerce," Jackson said.[86]

At the same time, the Court continued to sanction state regulation of production. A few months after the farmer's wheat decision, the Court upheld California's detailed system for regulating raisin production and marketing, even to the point of controlling the flow of raisins into interstate commerce to maintain a certain price level.[87]

Segregation

Late in the nineteenth century the Court used the *Cooley* rule to deny Louisiana the power to prohibit racial discrimination while granting Mississippi the authority to enforce it. When Josephine DeCuir, "a person of color," boarded *The Governor Allen*, a Mississippi River steamboat, to travel from New Orleans to another point in Louisiana, she attempted to sit in the cabin set aside for white persons. Denied entrance, she subsequently sued the steamboat owners for violating an 1869 state law forbidding racial discrimination on common carriers. The state courts found that this law affected interstate commerce and thus was invalid. On appeal, the Supreme Court in 1878 declared itself bound by this finding of the state courts and ruled against DeCuir and against the law. Under the *Cooley* rule, the justices held that equal access to steamboat accommodations was a matter for national regulation. State regulation of such matters, if it affected interstate commerce, burdened interstate commerce. Chief Justice Waite explained:

If each State was at liberty to regulate the conduct of carriers while within its jurisdiction, the confusion likely to follow could not but be productive of great inconvenience and unnecessary hardship. Each State could provide for its own passengers and regulate the transportation of its own freight, regardless of the interests of others. Nay more, it could prescribe the rules by which the carrier must be governed within the State in respect to passengers and property brought from without. On one side of the river...he might be required to observe one set of rules, and on the other another. Commerce cannot flourish in the midst of such embarrassments. . . .

If the public good requires such legislation [decreeing equal access], it must come from Congress and not from the States.[88]

Just twelve years later, however, the Court upheld a Mississippi law requiring railroads doing business in the state to provide separate accommodations for black and white passengers. In this case, in *DeCuir,* the state court held that this law applied solely to intrastate railroad operations, and in accord with that finding the Supreme Court in 1890 held it no burden on interstate commerce.[89] In dissent, Justice John Marshall Harlan found Chief Justice Waite's comments in the earlier case "entirely pertinent to the case before us....It is difficult to understand how a state enactment, requiring the separation of the white and black races on interstate carriers of passengers, is a regulation of commerce among the States, while a similar enactment forbidding such separation is not."[90] Later, in the famous *Plessy v. Ferguson* (1896) decision, the Court upheld "separate but equal" accommodations on common carriers again, this time against the challenge of a violation of the Fourteenth Amendment. Harlan dissented.[91]

It would take fifty-six years for the Court to reverse its 1890 ruling allowing Mississippi to require railroads to segregate passengers. In *Morgan v. Virginia* (1946) the Court declared that "seating arrangements for the different races in interstate motor travel require a single uniform rule to promote and protect national travel." Hence the justices struck down a Virginia law requiring black passengers to ride in the rear of interstate buses, and it reversed the conviction of Irene Morgan who had refused to move to comply with the law.[92] The end to tolerance of local segregation of any segment of interstate transportation came in the mid-1950s with an Interstate Commerce Commission rule terminating racial segregation on all interstate trains and buses and in all public waiting rooms in railway and bus stations. In 1956 the Supreme Court affirmed a lower court's ruling striking down such segregation in intrastate transportation as a violation of the Fourteenth Amendment.[93]

Child Labor

Perhaps the most extreme of the Court's cases reserving areas of the economy for strictly state or local supervision were its child labor rulings of 1918 and 1922 in which the Court overturned the efforts of

Congress to prohibit child labor. The justices based these rulings on two principles—on the dichotomy between manufacturing and commerce and on the Tenth Amendment reservation of powers to the states with its accompanying doctrine of dual federalism, the idea that the state governments and the national government operate within neatly defined and separated domains within which each is supreme. The first child labor case was that of *Hammer v. Dagenhart* (1918), a challenge to Congress's attempt to forbid factories, quarries, or mines employing children under fourteen years of age from using the channels of interstate commerce for their products. The act, held the Court, intruded too far upon state concerns. Justice William R. Day wrote for the majority:

> Over interstate transportation...the regulatory power of Congress is ample, but the production of articles, intended for interstate commerce, is a matter of local regulation. . . .
>
> There is no power vested in Congress to require the states to exercise their police power to prevent possible unfair competition. . . .
>
> The grant of power to Congress...was to enable it to regulate such commerce, and not to give it authority to control the states in their exercise of the police power over local trade and manufacture.
>
> The grant of authority over a purely federal matter was not intended to destroy the local power always existing and carefully reserved to the states in the Tenth Amendment to the Constitution.
>
> . . . [I]f Congress can thus regulate matters entrusted to local authority by prohibition of the movement of commodities in interstate commerce, all freedom of commerce will be at an end, and the power of the states over local matters may be eliminated, and thus our system of government practically destroyed.[94]

In candid dissent, Justice Oliver Wendell Holmes Jr. declared,

> The Act does not meddle with anything belonging to the states. They may regulate their internal affairs and their domestic commerce as they like. But when they seek to send their products across the State line they are no longer within their rights. If there were no Constitution and no Congress

their power to cross the line would depend upon their neighbors. Under the Constitution such commerce belongs not to the States but to Congress to regulate. It may carry out its views of public policy whatever indirect effect they may have on the activities of the States.[95]

Four years later the Court struck down a second congressional effort to discourage child labor—this time through the use of the taxing power. Chief Justice William Howard Taft, speaking for the majority in *Bailey v. Drexel Furniture Co.* (1922), set out the same objections that Day had voiced:

> Grant the validity of this law, and all that Congress would need to do hereafter, in seeking to take over to its control any one of the great number of subjects of public interest, jurisdiction of which the states have never parted with, and which are reserved to them by the 10th Amendment, would be to enact a detailed measure of complete regulation of the subject and enforce it by a so-called tax....To give such magic to the word "tax" would be to break down all constitutional limitation of Congress and completely wipe out the sovereignty of the states.[96]

These two rulings stood until 1941, when the Court overruled *Hammer v. Dagenhart* and discarded the doctrine of dual federalism. In doing so, the Court upheld the Fair Labor Standards Act, which, among other provisions, prohibited child labor. The case bringing this landmark opinion was *United States v. Darby* (1941). Writing for the Court, Justice Harlan Fiske Stone declared that

> [s]uch regulation is not a forbidden invasion of state power merely because either its motive or its consequence is to restrict the use of articles of commerce within the states of destination....Whatever their motive and purpose, regulations of commerce which do not infringe some institutional prohibition are within the plenary power conferred on Congress by the Commerce Clause. . . .
>
> The power of Congress over interstate commerce...extends to the activities intrastate which so affect interstate commerce or the exercise of the power of Congress over it as to make regulation of them appropriate means to the attainment of a

legitimate end, the exercise of the granted power of Congress to regulate interstate commerce.[97]

A Changing Answer

A century after Justice Curtis formulated the *Cooley* rule to bring some clarity into the confusion of the exclusive and concurrent commerce power debate, the answer to the questions that debate posed still seemed to be "Yes, and No." As Thomas Reed Powell wrote in the mid-1960s,

> Once it was thought that the test of what states may do is what the nation may not do, or that the test of what the states may not do is what the nation may do, but the criteria are no longer so clear cut as that. The involutions of state power must be considered with a greater particularity than can be compressed into a formula.[98]

THE POLICE POWER

Early in the nation's history, the Court began to recognize a state police power, which is the power to govern its people and to regulate the use of its land to ensure the public welfare. The police power, in effect, grants the states some power to affect interstate commerce. Legal scholar Thomas Reed Powell wrote:

> By this judicial invention there is no constitutional division between concurrent and exclusive power over commerce. The power of Congress is concurrent with that of the states; the power of the states is concurrent with that of Congress. The exercise of state power, however, is subject to several restrictions. It must not impose regulation in conflict with regulations of Congress. It must not, even in the absence of conflict, impose regulations if Congress, by what it has done, is deemed to have "occupied the entire field."[99]

Oddly enough, the first recognition by the Court of this power came even as Chief Justice Marshall was asserting the sweeping federal power over commerce. In the opinion resolving the case of *Gibbons v. Ogden* (1824), Marshall acknowledged the power of a state "to regulate its police, its domestic trade, and to govern its

THE "PERILS" OF COLORED OLEO

To the modern view, one of the oddest sets of police power laws and accompanying Supreme Court decisions involved the efforts of states to protect their citizens from the "perils" of colored oleo (margarine). Ostensibly to protect the public health and to prevent fraud—the selling of oleo as butter—Pennsylvania banned the sale of colored oleo within the state. In 1888 the Supreme Court held the ban a reasonable exercise of the state police power.[1]

Six years later the Court upheld a Massachusetts law that forbade the sale of imported margarine, even in the original package, if the margarine was colored to resemble butter.[2] The Court found this a different question from that resolved in *Leisy v. Hardin* (1890) due to the risk of fraud.[3] In *Leisy* the Court had ruled against a state ban on the sale of imported liquor in the original package. *(See details of Leisy v. Hardin, p. 411.)* Subsequent rulings modified the scope of state power over colored margarine, but in 1902 Congress passed a law providing that oleomargarine was subject to state regulation upon arrival within the limits of the state.

---

1. *Powell v. Pennsylvania,* 127 U.S. 678 (1888).

2. *Plumley v. Massachusetts,* 155 U.S. 461 (1894).

3. *Leisy v. Hardin,* 135 U.S. 100 (1890).

---

own citizens." This power, he continued, might even enable the state to legislate—concurrently with Congress—on the subject of navigation. Earlier in the opinion, he had mentioned the state's power to require inspection of items departing the state before they entered into the stream of interstate or foreign commerce. Inspection laws, Marshall wrote, "form a portion of that immense mass of legislation which embraces everything within the territory of a state not surrendered to the general government....Inspection laws, quarantine laws, health laws of every description, as well as laws for regulating the internal commerce of a state, and those which respect turnpike-roads, ferries, etc. are component parts of this mass." [100]

Five years later in *Willson v. Blackbird Creek Marsh Co.* (1829), Marshall appeared to base the Court's approval of a state-built dam across a small creek upon the power of the state to act to preserve property values and enhance the public health.[101] It was during the tenure of Chief Justice Roger B. Taney, however, that the Court first fully enunciated the concept of police power. In the opinion of the Court in *Charles River Bridge v. Warren Bridge* (1837), Taney spoke of the importance of protecting the states' "power over their own internal police and improvement, which is so necessary to their well being and prosperity." [102]

In the same month as the *Charles River Bridge* decision, the Court in *Mayor of New York v. Miln* (1837) delivered its first extended exposition of the police power. In an effort to lighten the burden immigration placed upon its port city, New York law required the master of any ship arriving in New York harbor from outside the state to report to the mayor the birthplace, previous residence, age, and occupation of every passenger. George Miln, owner of the ship *Emily,* did not comply and was sued by the state for the penalties he incurred. In his defense, Miln argued that the state law was invalid in that it regulated foreign commerce and navigation in conflict with federal power over those areas. The Supreme Court rejected that defense. Writing for the majority, Justice Philip Barbour stated that

> the [challenged] act is not a regulation of commerce, but of police, and...being thus considered, it was passed in the exercise of a power which rightfully belonged to the States....It is apparent...that the object of the Legislature was to prevent New York from being burdened by an influx of persons brought thither in ships...and for that purpose a report was required...that the necessary steps might be taken by the city authorities to prevent them from becoming chargeable as paupers.[103]

Gibbons v. Ogden did not control the decision because this case concerned regulation of state territory, not of navigation, wrote Justice Barbour. In addition, here there was no colliding federal law, he continued. Thus, even under the reasoning of *Gibbons v. Ogden,* the New York law could stand. Barbour wrote for the majority:

> But we do not place our opinion on this ground. We choose rather to plant ourselves on what we consider impregnable positions. They are these: That a State has the same undeniable and unlimited jurisdiction over all persons and things within its territorial limits, as any foreign nation, where that jurisdiction is not surrendered or restrained by the Constitution of the United States. That, by virtue of this, it is not only the right, but the burden and solemn duty of a State, to advance the safety, happiness and prosperity of its people, and to provide for its general welfare, by any and every act of legislation which it may deem to be conducive to these ends; where the power over the particular subject, or the manner of its exercise is not surrendered or restrained, in the manner just stated. That all those powers which relate to merely municipal legislation, or what may, perhaps, more properly be called internal police, are not thus surrendered or restrained; and that, consequently, in relation to these, the authority of a State is complete, unqualified and exclusive.

In regard to the particular subject of this case, the Court held that the power exercised was encompassed in the recognized power of a state to pass and enforce inspection and quarantine laws, which operated directly upon items in interstate and foreign commerce, delaying and sometimes even destroying them.

> We think it as competent and as necessary for a State to provide precautionary measures against the moral pestilence of paupers, vagabonds, and possibly convicts, as it is to guard against the physical pestilence which may arise from unsound and infectious articles imported, or from a ship, the crew of which may be laboring under an infectious disease.[104]

The significance of the development of this concept by the Supreme Court under Chief Justice Taney—and of the underlying doctrine of dual federalism as a limit on federal power—has been described by Alpheus T. Mason and William M. Beaney:

> [I]n the context of his times, state police power was the only available weapon with which government could face the pressing problems of the day. In a period in which the national government was not yet prepared to deal realistically with economic and social problems, national supremacy had the effect of posing the unexercised commerce power of Congress, or the contract clause, as barriers to any governmental action. Taney's dual federalism…enabled the state to deal experimentally with problems that the national government would not face until another half-century had elapsed. Thus Marshall and Taney left as legacies two official conceptions of federalism [national supremacy and duel federalism] that succeeding justices were free to apply as their inclinations or the needs of the time dictated.[105]

The police power has been employed for a variety of ends: to control entry to the state, to protect the public health and public morals, to ensure public safety, to regulate business, and to regulate working conditions. The Court has by no means approved all of the uses to which the states have put the police power. A number were struck down as interfering with the federal power to regulate commerce; others fell as interfering with the freedom of contract or the liberty of property. The police power has, nonetheless, served as a broad basis for state efforts to control economic and business matters for the public good.

Control of Entry

After *Miln* recognized some state power to control the entry of individuals, the Court indicated that states possessed a correlative power to exclude out-of-state corporations from doing business within their boundaries. In that ruling, however, in *Bank of Augusta v. Earle* (1839), the Court held that it would be assumed—absent clear evidence to the contrary—that a state gave its consent to the conduct of business by an out-of-state corporation.[106] Although the right to exclude a foreign corporation obviously included the right to place conditions on such an entity's conduct of business within the state, the Court some four decades later made clear that a state could not exercise this power to place an undue burden on an out-of-state corporation wishing to engage in interstate commerce within the state. The decision in *Pensacola Telegraph Co. v. Western Union* (1877) made clear, notes one commentator,

With the enactment of the Twenty-first Amendment repealing Prohibition, the states were granted power to regulate all aspects of alcohol control. The Supreme Court has broadly construed the power granted by the amendment.

that the state's power to exclude foreign corporations was subject to "the overriding force of a congressional license to carry on interstate commerce," in this case, communication by telegraphic messages.[107]

In the *Passenger Cases* (1849) the Court held, by a narrow margin, that the federal commerce power clearly limited the state's power to control the entry of people. Striking down state laws taxing entering aliens, the Court, in the words of Justice John McLean, held that

> the police power of the State cannot draw within its jurisdiction objects which lie beyond it. It meets the commercial power of the Union in dealing with subjects under the protection of that power, yet it can only be exercised under peculiar emergencies and to a limited extent. In guarding the safety, the health, and morals of its citizens, a State is restricted to appropriate and constitutional means.

In dissent, Chief Justice Taney and his colleagues argued that "the several States have a right to remove from among their people, and to prevent from entering the State, any person, or class or description of persons, whom it may deem dangerous or injurious to the interests and welfare of its citizens.[108] The majority's view in the *Passenger Cases,* however, has prevailed to modern times. In 1876 the Court held that control of immigration from abroad was a matter exempt from state regulation and entrusted exclusively to Congress. In 1941 it struck down—as an obstruction of interstate commerce—a California law that penalized persons bringing poor people into the state to live.[109]

Public Health and Morals

Perhaps the acknowledged objective of the police power is the protection of the public health, the focus of the quarantine and inspection laws about which

Chief Justice Marshall commented in 1824 in *Gibbons v. Ogden*. When the Court in 1847 upheld state laws licensing the sale of alcohol, one of the few points upon which the justices could agree was the paramount responsibility of the state to use the police power to protect its public health and to preserve public morals. Justice McLean set forth his views:

The acknowledged police power of a State extends often to the destruction of property. A nuisance may be abated....Merchandise from a port where a contagious disease prevails, being liable to communicate the disease, may be excluded; and in extreme cases, it may be thrown into the sea. This comes in direct conflict with the regulation of commerce; and yet no one doubts the local power. It is a power essential to self-preservation....It is, indeed, the law of nature, and is possessed by man in his individual capacity. He may resist that which does him harm, whether he be assailed by an assassin, or approached by poison. And it is the settled construction of every regulation of commerce, that, under the sanction of its general laws, no person can introduce into a community malignant diseases, or anything which contaminates its morals, or endangers its safety....From the explosive nature of gunpowder, a city may exclude it. Now this is an article of commerce, and is not known to carry infectious disease; yet to guard against a contingent injury, a city may prohibit its introduction.

When in the appropriate exercise of these federal and State powers, contingently and incidentally the lines of action run into each other; if the State power be necessary to the preservation of the morals, the health, or safety of the community, it must be maintained.[110]

No better illustration of the complexities of applying the police power for the purpose of safeguarding public health and morals can be provided than the *License Cases*. Begun in 1847 and extending well into the twentieth century, these rulings concerned state power to regulate all aspects of intoxicating liquors. In 1874 the Court upheld Iowa's prohibition of the sale of liquor, even that owned at the time of the law's passage.[111] In 1887 the Court upheld a Kansas law that forbade the manufacture and sale of intoxicating liquor. Justice John Marshall Harlan, writing for the Court, made clear, however, that the police power was not without limits:

If...a statute purporting to have been enacted to protect the public health, the public morals, or the public safety, has no real or substantial relation to those objects, or is a palpable invasion of rights secured by the fundamental law, it is the duty of the courts to so adjudge....

[But in this case, we] cannot shut out of view the fact, within the knowledge of all, that the public health, the public morals, and the public safety, may be endangered by the general use of intoxicating drinks; nor the fact, established by statistics accessible to everyone, that the idleness, disorder, pauperism, and crime existing in the country are, in some degree at least, traceable to this evil. If, therefore, a State deems the absolute prohibition of the manufacture and sale, within her limits, of intoxicating liquors for other than medical, scientific and manufacturing purposes, to be necessary to the peace and security of society, the courts cannot, without usurping legislative functions, override the will of the people as thus expressed by their chosen representatives.[112]

The following year, 1888, the Court upheld a state's ban on the manufacture of liquor in the state for export but struck down a ban on the importation of liquor into that state. The ban on importation, the Court held, interfered with interstate commerce.[113] Two years later the Court further weakened state power over the importation of liquor by holding that a state could not forbid the first sale of such liquor in its original package. This ruling was based on the doctrine—first announced by Chief Justice John Marshall in *Brown v. Maryland* (1827)—that as long as an imported product remained in the package in which it had entered the state, it was beyond state regulation or taxation.[114] Iowa had banned the sale of imported liquor in any package. The firm of Gus. Leisy & Co., a Peoria, Illinois, brewer, challenged Iowa's ban on the first sale of imported liquor as infringing upon the federally protected flow of interstate commerce. The Court agreed with Leisy and struck down that portion of the law. Writing for the Court, Chief Justice Melville W. Fuller stated,

Up to that point of time [after the first sale in the original package], we hold that, in the absence of congressional permission to do so, the State had no power to interfere by seizure, or any other action, in prohibition of importation and sale by the foreign nonresident importer. Whatever our individual

SHIPPING WINE AND THE TWENTY-FIRST AMENDMENT

States may not erect trade barriers to protect their own products from out-of-state competitors, the Court has said repeatedly. Doing so violates the Commerce Clause. But the Twenty-first Amendment, which repealed Prohibition, gave the states special powers to regulate the sale of alcohol. The states adopted a three-tier system for selling beer, wine, and liquor. Producers, such as brewers or distillers, sold to licensed wholesalers (or distributors), who in turn sold to retailers.

But two trends in the wine industry undercut this system. Thousands of small wineries came of age, and the Internet gave wine sellers a way to market directly to consumers. When these wineries sought to ship bottles directly to consumers, they ran afoul of state laws that prohibited such direct sales to customers, creating a clash between the principles of free trade and state control of alcohol.

In *Granholm v. Heald* (2005) the Court in a 5-4 decision struck down laws in Michigan, New York, and several other states that prohibited direct shipments of wine from out-of-state vintners to customers.[1] One plaintiff, Eleanor Heald, a wine critic from Troy, Michigan, had sought to buy wine from a vintner in San Luis Obispo, California. Michigan and New York allowed in-state wineries to sell directly to customers, but they prohibited imports from out-of-state producers. They relied in section 2 of the Twenty-first Amendment, which says: "The transportation or importation into any State . . . of intoxicating liquors, in violation of the laws thereof, is hereby prohibited."

But the Court said this provision does not trump the principle of free and fair trade across state lines. "The differential treatment between in-state and out-of-state wineries constitutes explicit discrimination against interstate commerce," said Justice Anthony Kennedy. "The Twenty-first Amendment does not supersede other provisions of the Constitution, and in particular, does not displace the rule that States may not give a discriminatory preference to their own producers."[2] Justices Antonin Scalia, David Souter, Ruth Bader Ginsburg, and Stephen Breyer agreed.

In dissent, Justice Clarence Thomas said the Twenty-first Amendment and the Webb-Kenyon Act clearly gave the states the authority to forbid imports of alcohol. "Whatever the wisdom of that choice, the Court does this Nation no service by ignoring the textual commands of the Constitution and Acts of Congress," he said. Chief Justice William H. Rehnquist and Justices John Paul Stevens and Sandra Day O'Connor agreed.

Stevens was the only member of the Court who had lived through the Prohibition era, and he recalled America's public support for strict controls on alcohol. "Today many Americans, particularly those members of the younger generation who make policy decisions, regard alcohol as an ordinary article of commerce," he wrote in a separate dissent. "That was definitely not the view of the generations that made policy in 1919 when the Eighteenth Amendment was ratified or in 1933 when it was repealed by the Twenty-first Amendment. . . . The notion that discriminatory state laws violated the unwritten prohibition against balkanizing the American economy . . . would have seemed strange indeed to the millions of Americans who condemned the use of the 'demon rum' in the 1920's and 1930's. Indeed, they expressly authorized the 'balkanization' that today's decision condemns."[3]

---

1. *Granholm v. Heald*, 544 U. S. 460 (2005).

2. Id. at 486.

3. Id. at 496.

---

views may be, as to the deleterious or dangerous qualities of particular articles, we cannot hold that any articles which Congress recognizes as subjects of interstate commerce are not such, or . . . can be controlled by state laws amounting to regulations, while they retain that character.[115]

Fuller's opinion invited Congress to act. In 1890, the year of the decision, Congress approved the Wilson Act, stripping imported liquor of the protection of interstate commerce, or the original package. The law stated that upon arrival in a state, intoxicating liquors were subject to whatever police power laws the state wished to pass, just as if the liquor had been produced in the state and not imported. In 1891 the Supreme Court approved the act.[116]

Congress subsequently acted to place alcohol control even more completely under state authority. The Webb-Kenyon Act of 1913 forbade the shipment of liquor into any state where its use or sale would violate state law. In 1917 the Court upheld state power under this law to forbid the entry of intoxicating liquor.[117] The addition to the Constitution in 1933 of the Twenty-first Amendment (repeal of Prohibition) placed the matter

To help stabilize the milk market, the New York Milk Control Board fixed the price of a quart of milk at nine cents. When Leo Nebbia, pictured here, the owner of a grocery store, sold two quarts of milk and a loaf of bread for eighteen cents, the state convicted him of violating the board's order. In 1934 the Supreme Court rejected Nebbia's claim that the order violated his constitutional rights, ruling that it was a valid exercise of state power.

entirely under state control. Section 2 states that "the transportation or importation into any State, Territory, or possession of the United States for delivery or use therein of intoxicating liquors, in violation of the laws thereof, is hereby prohibited." The Court has construed the power granted by this amendment broadly, but it also held that states may not forbid the sale of liquor on federal property, that Congress may continue to regulate the importation of liquor from abroad, and that a state may only place reasonable restrictions on the passage of liquor through its territory.[118]

"Public Interest" Regulation

From 1877 until 1934, the Supreme Court used the doctrine of the "public interest" as its standard for determining the types of businesses that states might properly regulate. Businesses that appeared to the justices to be "clothed with a public interest" might be regulated; those that lacked this characteristic were to remain free of state control. Explaining the logic of this standard, Chief Justice Morrison R. Waite wrote in *Munn v. Illinois* (1877) that under the police power "the government regulates the conduct of its citizens one towards another, and the manner in which each shall use his own property, when such regulation becomes necessary for the public good....Property does become clothed with a public interest when used in a manner to make it of public consequence, and affect the community at large."[119]

Although the "public interest" doctrine survived for half a century, as a standard for decisions by courts or state legislatures, it never acquired any clear meaning. The Court held that bakeries, meatpackers, ticket-scalpers, employment agencies, gas stations, and ice vendors were not businesses "clothed with a public interest" but railroads, public utilities, grain elevators, stockyards, fire insurance companies, and tobacco warehouses were.[120] The Court abandoned this rationale for state regulation with its decision in *Nebbia v. New York*

When Oregon imposed a sixty-hour maximum work week for women, laundry owner Curt Muller (with arms folded) argued that the law violated his rights. In 1908 a unanimous Supreme Court upheld the validity of state maximum working hour laws, accepting sociological arguments about the negative effects of long hours on women's health.

(1934). New York, it said, could set the acceptable range of prices to be charged for milk within the state. States could regulate virtually any business for the public good, held the Court, so long as the regulation was reasonable and effected through appropriate means. Discarding the *Munn* approach, Justice Owen J. Roberts wrote for the majority:

It is clear there is no closed class or category of businesses affected with a public interest.... The function of courts...is to determine in each case whether circumstances vindicate the challenged regulation as a reasonable exertion of governmental authority or condemn it as arbitrary or discriminatory.... The phrase "affected with a public interest" can, in the nature of things, mean no more than that an industry, for adequate reason, is subject to control for the public good.... [T]here can be no doubt that upon proper occasion and by appropriate measures the state may regulate a business in any of its aspects. . . .

The Constitution does not secure to any one liberty to conduct his business in such fashion as to inflict injury upon the public at large, or upon any substantial group of the people. Price control, like any other form of regulation, is unconstitutional only if arbitrary, discriminatory, or demonstrably irrelevant to the policy the legislature is free to adopt, and hence an unnecessary and unwarranted interference with individual liberty.[121]

Wages and Hours

As the Court found the Contract Clause a less and less useful instrument for countering the increasingly vigorous assertions of the police power to regulate property or business, it began to use the Fourteenth Amendment's Due Process Clause instead. The Supreme Court moved into a period of laissez-faire rulings, finding that there were some areas of business that neither federal nor state power could reach. As a companion to this philosophy, the Court began espousing the freedom of contract doctrine, a part of the liberty protected by the Fourteenth Amendment. Thus armed, the Court for decades dealt unkindly with the efforts of states to control the hours, and later the wages, of workers within their jurisdiction.

The first of these laws considered fully by the Supreme Court was upheld, in the late 1890s. Utah had limited to eight hours a day the period that miners could work in underground mines except in an emergency. This law was challenged as denying both the worker and the employer their freedom of contract. In *Holden v. Hardy* (1898) the Court rejected the challenge and found the law a proper exercise of the police power by the state to protect its citizens' health by limiting the amount of time they spent in admittedly hazardous and unhealthy conditions.[122]

Bakery Workers: Lochner v. New York

Seven years after *Holden v. Hardy,* health considerations did not weigh so heavily when the Court considered and struck down New York's law limiting the hours that bakery employees might work. The Court found the law an infringement of the liberty of contract without due process of law. Justice Rufus Peckham wrote for the majority in *Lochner v. New York* (1905):

> Clean and wholesome bread does not depend upon whether the baker works but ten hours per day or only sixty hours a week. The limitation of the hours of labor does not come within the police power on that ground.
>
> It is a question of which of two powers or rights shall prevail—the power of the state to legislate or the right of the individual to liberty of person and freedom of contract....We think the limit of the police power has been reached and passed in this case. There is...no reasonable foundation for holding this to be necessary or appropriate as a health law to safeguard the public health....We think that there can be no fair doubt that the trade of a baker, in and of itself, is not an unhealthy one to that degree which would authorize the legislature to interfere with the right to labor, and with the right of free contract on the part of the individual, either as employer or employee.
>
> [If the Court upheld this law] no trade, no occupation, no mode of earning one's living, could

escape this all-pervading power, and the acts of the legislature in limiting the hours of labor in all employments would be valid, although such limitation might seriously cripple the ability of the laborer to support himself and his family. . . .

> Statutes of the nature of that under review, limiting the hours in which grown and intelligent men may labor to earn their living, are mere meddlesome interferences with the rights of the individual, and they are not saved from condemnation by the claim that they are passed in the exercise of the police power and upon the subject of the health of the individual whose rights are interfered with, unless there be some fair ground...to say that there is material danger to the public health, or to the health of the employees, if the hours of labor are not curtailed.[123]

Laundry Women: Muller v. Oregon

The vote in *Lochner* was 5-4, and the narrowness of that balance came into focus three years later, when the Court in *Muller v. Oregon* (1908) upheld Oregon's law setting a maximum ten-hour day for women working in laundries. Arguing this case for Oregon was Louis D. Brandeis, later to become one of the Court's most notable justices. In *Muller* Brandeis used what came to be called a "Brandeis brief," a brief heavily buttressed with sociological and statistical information intended to support the legal argument. The Court, in its opinion, paid a rare compliment to Brandeis by mentioning his brief and him by name. The information was apparently convincing. The Court upheld the law unanimously.[124]

Where the hazards of an occupation had distinguished *Hardy* from *Lochner,* sex apparently made the difference between *Lochner* and *Muller.* State regulation of working hours for women was seen as valid because women were thought to be physically less strong than men, and longer working hours were considered likely to impair their childbearing function. Ten years later, in 1917, the Court, 5-3, upheld a maximum hours law from Oregon establishing a ten-hour day as the maximum for all industrial workers. Justice Brandeis, counsel when these cases began, did not take part in the ruling. The Court made little effort to explain why it upheld this law, whereas it had struck down the New York law in *Lochner.* The opinion in *Bunting v. Oregon* (1917) indicated that the Court had given the benefit of the doubt to the law.

> It is enough for our decision if the legislation under review was passed in the exercise of an admitted power of government....There is a contention made that the law...is not either necessary or useful "for the preservation of the health of employees. . . ." The record contains no facts to support the contention.[125]

This ruling established the right of states to limit the hours of work for men and women in almost all occupations, free of challenge under the Due Process Clause, so long as the standard imposed had some clear relationship to the society's health and safety.

Wages of Women and Children

Lochner was not altogether dead, as it soon reappeared when the Court began striking down state and federal efforts to regulate wages. In *Adkins v. Children's Hospital* (1923) the Court invalidated, 5-3, a law enacted by Congress for the District of Columbia that set a minimum wage for women and children workers. Justice Brandeis did not participate, and the opinion was written by Justice George Sutherland, who had been named to the Court in 1922. Felix Frankfurter, at the time an attorney for the parties supporting the law, filed a long Brandeis brief demonstrating the unhappy effects of substandard wages on women. The majority found his statistics of little relevance to the validity of the law.

This was "simply and exclusively a price-fixing law," wrote Sutherland, "confined to adult women...who are legally as capable of contracting for themselves as men." A law could not prescribe the proper wage to preserve the health and moral character of a woman, he said. And it was lopsided, requiring an employer to pay a worker a certain amount regardless of whether the employer found the worker that valuable. "A statute which prescribes payment...solely with relation to circumstances apart from the contract of employment, the business affected by it and the work done under it," Sutherland concluded, "is so clearly the product of a naked, arbitrary exercise of power that it cannot be allowed to stand under the Constitution."[126] In dissent, Chief Justice William Howard Taft expressed his surprise at the revival of the doctrine of

freedom of contract, saying that he thought *Lochner* had been overruled after *Muller* and *Bunting*. Also in dissent, Justice Oliver Wendell Holmes Jr. wrote,

> This statute does not compel anybody to pay anything. It simply forbids employment at rates below those fixed as the minimum requirement of health and right living. It is safe to assume that women will not be employed at even the lowest wages allowed unless they earn them, or unless the employer's business can sustain the burden. In short, the law in its character and operation is like hundreds of so-called police laws that have been upheld.[127]

Holmes went on to say that he did not understand "the principle on which the power to fix a minimum for the wages of women can be denied by those who admit the power to fix a maximum for their hours of work....I perceive no difference in the kind or degree of interference with liberty...between one case and the other."[128]

The Court remained adamant. Fourteen years after *Adkins,* in a 5-4 vote it struck down a New York minimum wage law for women and children in *Morehead v. New York ex rel. Tipaldo* (1936). The four justices still serving who had formed the *Adkins* majority were joined by Justice Owen J. Roberts, who had been appointed to the Court after the earlier ruling. Writing for the majority, Justice Pierce Butler declared any minimum wage law a violation of due process: "[T]he state is without power by any form of legislation to prohibit, change or nullify contracts between employers and adult women workers as to the amount of wage to be paid."[129] The dissenters—Chief Justice Charles Evans Hughes and Justices Brandeis, Benjamin Cardozo, and Harlan Fiske Stone—viewed the matter as of broader concern to the community. Justice Stone wrote:

> We have had opportunity to perceive more clearly that a wage insufficient to support the worker does not visit its consequences upon him alone; that it may affect profoundly the entire economic structure of society and, in any case, that it casts on every tax payer, and on government itself, the burden of solving the problems of poverty, subsistence, health and morals of large numbers in the community. Because of their nature and extent, these are public problems. A generation ago they were for the individual to solve; today they are the burden of the nation.[130]

Within a year the Court reversed itself and over-ruled *Adkins*. In 1937, in the midst of the Court-packing fight, the Court, 5-4, upheld Washington state's law setting minimum wages for women and children workers. Elsie Parrish, a chambermaid, had sued the hotel for which she worked to recover the difference between her pay and the minimum wage, under the state law. The West Coast Hotel Company used *Adkins* as its defense. Justice Roberts, who had voted against the New York law, joined the dissenters from that case to form a majority upholding the Washington law in the decision in *West Coast Hotel Co. v. Parrish* (1937). Chief Justice Hughes wrote the opinion:

> What can be closer to the public interest than the health of women and their protection from unscrupulous and overreaching employers? And if the protection of women is a legitimate end of the exercise of state power, how can it be said that the requirement of the payment of a minimum wage fairly fixed in order to meet the very necessities of existence is not an admissible means to that end? ... The Legislature had the right to consider that its minimum wage requirements would be an important aid in carrying out its policy of protection. The adoption of similar requirements by many states evidences a deep-seated conviction both as to the presence of the evil and as to the means adapted to check it. Legislative response to that conviction cannot be regarded as arbitrary or capricious and that is all we have to decide. Even if the wisdom of the policy be regarded as debatable and its effects uncertain, still the Legislature is entitled to its judgment.[131]

Recent economic experience, wrote Hughes, required the Court to take a broader view of the purposes for which states might exercise their police power. The theory of the freedom of contract, upon which *Lochner* had been based, was defective when applied to situations where the contracting parties were clearly not of equal bargaining power.

> The exploitation of a class of workers who are in an unequal position with respect to bargaining power and are thus relatively defenseless against the denial of a living wage is not only detrimental to their health and well being but casts a direct burden for their support upon the community.

What these workers lose in wages the taxpayers are called upon to pay. The bare cost of living must be met.... The community is not bound to provide what is in effect a subsidy for unconscionable employers. The community may direct its law-making power to correct the abuse which springs from their selfish disregard of the public interest.[132]

Fair Labor Standards Act

Within a year, federal power had been extended the labor area, so recently opened to state regulation. Congress in 1938 approved the Fair Labor Standards Act, setting minimum wage and maximum hour standards for businesses using the facilities of interstate commerce and providing criminal penalties for violating those standards. Fred W. Darby, a lumber company president, was indicted for offenses under the law, and his case became a test of the constitutionality of the statute. In *United States v. Darby* (1941) the Court upheld the federal authority under the commerce power to impose wage and hour standards.[133] Congress later extended the protection of these standards through amendments to the act. In 1966 it included the employees of state hospitals, schools, and institutions. Two years later, in *Maryland v. Wirtz* (1968), the Court upheld this extension against challenge from the states that it encroached too far on their internal affairs.[134]

In 1974 Congress went even further and eliminated the traditional exemption of all state government employees from the minimum wage and overtime standards of the act. Two years later the Supreme Court overruled *Maryland v. Wirtz* and held the 1974 changes in the act unconstitutional. Held the Court, 5-4, in *National League of Cities v. Usery* (1976), "[B]oth the minimum wage and the maximum hour provisions will impermissibly interfere with the integral governmental functions" of the states.[135] The states' exemption was, however, short-lived, as in *Garcia v. San Antonio Metropolitan Transit Authority* (1985) the Court, again 5-4, overruled its 1976 holding and approved the application of federal minimum wage and maximum hour standards to employees of state and local governments.[136]

A TAX ON EXPORTS

The Supreme Court has had relatively few opportunities to elaborate on the constitutional application of the Export-Import Clause in regard to exports. By far, most of the rulings on this ban on state taxes have dealt with state efforts to tax imported goods. In 1860 the Court considered (and struck down) California's attempt to impose a stamp tax on bills of lading of gold to be taken out of the state. Writing for the Court, Chief Justice Roger B. Taney found little difference between this tax and the license law voided by the Court in *Brown v. Maryland* (1827), its first ruling on the clause.

"A bill of lading . . . is invariably associated with every cargo of merchandise exported to a foreign country, and consequently a duty upon that is, in substance and effect, a duty on the article exported," Taney wrote. "And if the law of California is constitutional, then every cargo of every description exported from the United States may be made to pay an export duty to the State, provided the tax is imposed in the form of a tax on the bill of lading, and this in direct opposition to the plain and express prohibition in the Constitution."[1]

In subsequent cases interpreting this clause with respect to exports, however, the Court has generally attempted to preserve the states' right to tax an item so long as it appears possible that the item will not actually leave the state. When it is clear, however, that the items are being shipped out of state, a state or local tax is doomed. In *Xerox Corp. v. County of Harris, Texas* (1982) the Court struck down a Texas law on items held in a customs-bonded warehouse prior to shipment abroad.[2]

---

1. *Almy v. California,* 24 How. (65 U.S.) 169 at 174 (1860); Brown v. Maryland, 12 Wheat. (25 U.S.) 419 (1827).

2. *Xerox Corp. v. County of Harris, Texas,* 459 U.S. 145 (1982).

THE TAXING OF COMMERCE

The Constitution imposes two limitations upon the state's power to raise revenue through taxes. The first is implicit in the Commerce Clause; the second is an explicit ban on state duties on imports or exports, or state-imposed tonnage duties, unless Congress should consent to such taxes. Most of the Court's interpretations of the taxing power of the states have been inextricably entwined with the Court's developing view of the Commerce Clause. Wrote Justice Felix Frankfurter in 1946,

> The power of the state to tax and the limitations upon that power imposed by the commerce clause have necessitated a long continuous process of judicial adjustment. The need for such adjustment is inherent in a federal government like ours, where the same transaction has aspects that may concern the interests and involve the authority of both the central government and the constituent states. . . . To attempt to harmonize all that has been said in the past would neither clarify what has gone before nor guide the future. Suffice it to say that especially in this field opinions must be read in the setting of the particular case and as the product of preoccupation with their special facts.[137]

This approach is less than satisfactory for many judges and legislators who attempt to gauge the proper reach of state taxes. "This case-by-case approach," noted Justice Byron R. White twenty years after Frankfurter wrote, "has left much 'room for controversy and confusion and little in the way of precise guides to the States in the exercise of their indispensable power of taxation.'" [138]

A Concurrent but Limited Power

There is a major difference between the commerce and the taxing powers in a constitutional sense: the taxing power may be exercised concurrently by the state and federal governments, and the commerce power may not be. In *Gibbons v. Ogden* (1824) Chief Justice John Marshall discussed the distinction:

> Although many of the powers formerly exercised by the states, are transferred to the government of the Union, yet the state governments remain, and constitute a most important part of our system. The power of taxation is indispensable to their existence, and is a power which, in its own nature, is capable of residing in, and being exercised by, different authorities at the same time. . . .

Congress is authorized to lay and collect taxes, etc., to pay the debts, and provide for the common defense and general welfare of the United States. This does not interfere with the power of the states to tax for the support of their own governments; nor is the exercise of that power by the states an exercise of any portion of the power that is granted to the United States. In imposing taxes for state purposes, they are not doing what Congress is empowered to do. Congress is not empowered to tax for those purposes which are within the exclusive province of the states. When, then, each government exercises the power of taxation, neither is exercising the power of the other.[139]

Even before Marshall wrote these words, the Court in *McCulloch v. Maryland* (1819)—its first major ruling affecting the states' power to tax—had made clear the limit that federal power placed upon that exercise of state sovereignty. The tax question in *McCulloch* involved the power of the state of Maryland to tax the Baltimore branch of the Bank of the United States. The tax was instituted by the state as an antibank measure, intended to curtail the issuance of bank notes by that institution. According to the Court, such a use of the state taxing power was a violation of the Constitution's provision that federal law is supreme over the states. Chief Justice Marshall explained:

[T]he Constitution and the laws made in pursuance thereof are supreme;…they control the constitution and laws of the respective states, and cannot be controlled by them. . . .

[T]he power to tax involves the power to destroy;…the power to destroy may defeat and render useless the power to create;…there is a plain repugnance, in conferring on one government a power to control the constitutional measures of another, which other, with respect to those very measures, is declared to be supreme.[140]

Marshall then described the consequences of allowing such a tax:

If the states may tax one instrument, employed by the government in the execution of its powers, they may tax any and every other instrument. They may tax the mail; they may tax the mint; they may tax patent rights; they may tax the papers of the custom-house; they may

tax judicial process; they may tax all the means employed by the government, to an excess which would defeat all the ends of government. This was not intended by the American people. They did not design to make their government dependent on the states.[141]

Limiting the sweep of the ruling, Marshall concluded:

This opinion does not deprive the states of any resources which they originally possessed. It does not extend to a tax paid by the real property of the bank, in common with other real property within the state, nor to a tax imposed on the interest which the citizens of Maryland may hold in this institution, in common with other property of the same description throughout the State. But this is a tax on the operations of the Bank, and is, consequently, a tax on the operation of an instrument employed by the government of the Union to carry its powers into execution. Such a tax must be unconstitutional.[142]

Taxing Imports

Within eight years of *McCulloch*, Maryland's use of the tax power was back before the Court. The state's attorney was Roger B. Taney, and the case was *Brown v. Maryland* (1827). The purpose of the constitutional ban on state taxes on imports and exports was to prevent discrimination against imports and against states within the interior of the country. State taxes could be used to make imported goods more expensive than similar domestic goods, and if coastal states were allowed to tax incoming goods passing on to other states, they could impose a considerable burden on the citizens of interior states.

Maryland law required persons who sold imported goods to purchase licenses. The law was challenged as violating the ban on import taxes and as interfering with the federal regulation of interstate and foreign commerce. The Court agreed with the challenge on both points. The license requirement was basically an indirect tax on imports. Chief Justice Marshall wrote,

The constitutional prohibition on the states to lay a duty on imports…may certainly come in conflict with their acknowledged power to tax persons and property within their territory. The power, and the restriction on it, though quite distinguishable when they do not approach each other, may yet, like the intervening colors between white and black, approach so nearly as to perplex the understanding. . . .

It is sufficient for the present to say, generally, that when the importer has so acted upon the thing imported that it has become incorporated and mixed up with the mass of property in the country, it has, perhaps, lost its distinctive character as an import, and has become subject to the taxing power of the state; but while remaining the property of the importer, in his warehouse, in the original form or package in which it was imported, a tax upon it is too plainly a duty on imports to escape the prohibition in the constitution. . . .

This indictment is against the importer, for selling a package of dry goods in the form in which it was imported, without a license. This state of things is changed if he sells them, or otherwise mixes them with the general property of the state, by breaking up his packages, and traveling with them as an itinerant peddler. In the first case, the tax intercepts the import, as an import, on its way to become incorporated with the general mass of property, and denies it the privilege of becoming so incorporated until it shall have contributed to the revenue of the state.[143]

With the ruling in *Brown v. Maryland,* wrote Felix Frankfurter more than a century later, Chief Justice Marshall "gave powerful practical application to the possibilities intimated in *Gibbons v. Ogden.* Imminent in the commerce clause were severe limitations upon the power of the states to tax as well as to regulate commerce."[144] The original package doctrine that Marshall first set out in this case would stand for decades as a valid limit on the exercise of state tax and police powers.

In *Brown v. Maryland* Marshall had concluded, "[W]e suppose the principles laid down in this case . . . apply equally to importations from a sister state," as well as to importation of goods from foreign countries.[145] Forty-two years later, auctioneer L. P. Woodruff cited this comment in his challenge to the sales tax that Mobile, Alabama, had placed on goods he brought into the state and sold, in their original package, at auction. Woodruff claimed that under *Brown v. Maryland* the tax was in violation of the Export-Import Clause.[146] Not so, held the

Supreme Court in 1869, dismissing Marshall's comment and limiting the prohibition on state import taxes to imports from foreign countries. Justice Samuel Miller, writing for the Court, explained the effect such a broad exemption from state taxes would have:

> The merchant of Chicago who buys his goods in New York and sells at wholesale in the original packages, may have his millions employed in trade for half a lifetime and escape all state, county, and city taxes: for all that he is worth is invested in goods which he claims to be protected as imports from New York. Neither the State nor the city which protects his life and property can make him contribute a dollar to support its government, improve its thoroughfares or educate its children.[147]

Two points were thus settled by the decision in *Woodruff v. Parham* (1869): the state power to tax goods imported from other states is not hindered by the Export-Import Clause, and once interstate transportation of those goods has ended, a state may tax them, even in their original package. So the protection of the original package (against state taxes) terminated earlier for goods from other states than for goods from other countries. The point was reaffirmed in the Court's decision in *Brown v. Houston* (1885), in which the Court held that Louisiana could tax coal from Pennsylvania even while it was on the barges in which it had entered the state.[148]

For two hundred years the Supreme Court steadfastly rejected all state efforts to tax imported foreign goods so long as those goods retained their character as imports. In 1872 the Court refused to allow a state to tax such goods, even just as property like any other within the state. Adolph Low of San Francisco, an importer, was assessed a state property tax on some $10,000 worth of French champagne he had imported and had stored in its original package, awaiting sale. The tax on the champagne was the same that fell upon all other personal and real property in the state, based upon its value. Low went before the Supreme Court arguing that this tax violated the ban of the Export-Import Clause. He won. The Court struck down the tax in *Low v. Austin* (1872).

Brown v. Maryland and the original package doctrine governed this case. Wrote Justice Stephen J. Field,

> In that case it was also held that the authority given to import, necessarily carried with it a right to sell the goods in the form and condition, that is, in the bale or package, in which they were imported; and that the exaction of a license tax for permission to sell in such case was not only invalid as being in conflict with the constitutional prohibition…but also as an interference with the power of Congress to regulate commerce with foreign nations.[149]

It made no difference that the tax did not fall directly upon imports as a class, but simply upon the whole category of citizen-owned property. The original package doctrine still prevented their taxation.

> The question is not as to the extent of the tax, or its equality with respect to taxes on other property, but as to the power of the State to levy any tax.…Imports, therefore, whilst retaining their distinctive character as such, must be treated as being without the jurisdiction of the taxing power of the State.[150]

The Court subsequently extended this principle even further, holding that a state could not tax imports brought into a state for the importer's own use.[151]

In 1976 *Low v. Austin* was overruled. The Court held that a state could assess a value-based property tax upon imported tires stored in a warehouse awaiting sale. *Low v. Austin* had been based upon a misinterpretation of *Brown v. Maryland* explained Justice William J. Brennan Jr. for the Court. Such a nondiscriminatory tax was not the type the Constitution or *Brown v. Maryland* prohibited:

> Such an exaction, unlike discriminatory state taxation against imported goods as imports, was not regarded as an impediment that severely hampered commerce or constituted a form of tribute by seaboard States to the disadvantage of the interior States. It is obvious that such nondiscriminatory property taxation can have no impact whatsoever on the Federal Government's exclusive regulation of foreign commerce. . . .
>
> Unlike imposts and duties, which are essentially taxes on the commercial privilege of bringing goods into a country, such property taxes are taxes by which a State apportions the cost of such services as police and fire protection among the beneficiaries according to their respective wealth; there is no reason why an importer should not bear his share of these costs along with his competitors handling only domestic goods. The Import-Export Clause clearly prohibits state taxation based on the foreign origin of the imported goods, but it cannot be read to accord imported goods preferential treatment that permits escape from uniform taxes imposed without regard to foreign origin for services which the State supplies.[152]

A decade later the Court reiterated this point in a North Carolina case involving local property taxes on imported tobacco, which was being aged in warehouses before it was made into cigarettes to be sold in the United States. The Court unanimously permitted the taxes, declaring that states may tax such imported goods so long as the tax is clearly not a duty and the goods are no longer "in transit" from their foreign point of origin.[153]

Commerce and Taxes

The classic description of the intricate and ever-shifting relationship between the national power to regulate interstate commerce to keep it flowing and the desire of the states to tax such commerce was delivered by Justice Tom C. Clark in *Northwestern States Portland Cement Co. v. Minnesota* (1959):

> Commerce between the States having grown up like Topsy, the Congress meanwhile not having undertaken to regulate taxation of it, and the States having understandably persisted in their efforts to get some return for the substantial benefits they have afforded it, there is little wonder that there has been no end of cases testing out state tax levies.
>
> The resulting judicial application of constitutional principles to specific state statutes leaves much room for controversy and confusion and little in the way of precise guides to the States in the exercise of their indispensable power of taxation. This Court alone has handed down some three hundred full-dress opinions.…[T]he decisions have been "not always clear…consistent or reconcilable.…" From the quagmire there emerge, however, some firm peaks of decision which remain unquestioned.
>
> [The Commerce Clause] requires that interstate commerce shall be free from any direct restrictions or impositions by the States [including any burdens

COINS, CURRENCY, AND CREDIT

The Constitution flatly forbids states to coin money, issue bills of credit, or make any changes in the legal tender. As Justice John McLean commented, "Here is an act inhibited in terms so precise that they cannot be mistaken. They are susceptible of but one construction."[1] In light of such clarity, it is not surprising that the Supreme Court has ruled on these prohibitions only a few times. Most of the rulings have dealt with the prohibition on state issuance of bills of credit.

In 1830 the Court ruled that the ban foreclosed a state from issuing loan certificates.[2] Seven years later, however, it found that the ban did not extend to preclude a state-chartered bank from issuing notes, even if the state owned all the bank's stock.[3] The leeway that this ruling appeared to afford the states in this area was, however, sharply curtailed shortly after the Civil War, when the Court held that federal power over the currency was broad enough to sanction the use of the taxing power of Congress to drive state bank notes out of circulation altogether.[4]

---

1. *Briscoe v. Bank of Kentucky,* 11 Pet. (36 U.S.) 257 at 318 (1837).

2. *Craig v. Missouri,* 4 Pet. (29 U.S.) 410 (1830).

3. *Briscoe v. Bank of Kentucky,* 11 Pet. (36 U.S.) 257 (1837).

4. *Veazie Bank v. Fenno,* 8 Wall. (75 U.S.) 533 (1869).

---

imposed by state taxes]. Nor may a State impose a tax which discriminates against interstate commerce either by providing a direct commercial advantage to local business…or by subjecting interstate commerce to the burden of "multiple taxation."[154]

The application of these principles to the questions raised by state taxes on commerce is best illustrated by three sets of cases: the railroad cases, the "privilege" cases, and the so-called "peddlers and drummers" cases of the late nineteenth century.

Railroad Cases

The railroad cases involve the effort of Pennsylvania to tax the Philadelphia & Reading Railroad. The government imposed a tonnage tax on freight that the railroad moved through the state, and it imposed a tax on the gross receipts of the company. The Supreme Court ruled in two cases, each challenging one of these taxes as in conflict with the Commerce Clause. It struck down the tonnage tax for being in conflict with the requirement that interstate commerce be unimpeded by the states. Writing for the Court, Justice William Strong declared,

It is of national importance that over that subject [transportation of people or products through a state or from one state to another] there should be but one regulating power, for if one State can directly tax persons or property passing through it, or tax them indirectly by levying a tax upon their transportation, every other may, and thus commercial intercourse between States remote from each other may be destroyed. The produce of Western States may thus be effectually excluded from Eastern markets, for though it might bear the imposition of a single tax, it would be crushed under the load of many. It was to guard against the possibility of such commercial embarrassments, no doubt, that the power of regulating commerce among other States was conferred upon the Federal Government.[155]

The Court, however, upheld Pennsylvania's tax on the gross receipts of the railroad even though some of those receipts obviously resulted from interstate commerce. Justice Strong wrote the opinion, starting from the proposition that

every tax upon personal property or upon occupations, business or franchises, affects more or less the subjects and the operations of commerce. Yet it is not everything that affects commerce that amounts to a regulation of it, within the meaning of the Constitution. We think it may safely be asserted that the States have authority to tax the estate, real and personal, of all their corporations, including carrying companies, precisely as they may tax similar property when belonging to natural persons, and to the same extent….A power to tax to this extent may be essential to the healthy existence of the state governments and the Federal Constitution ought not to be so construed as to impair, much less destroy, anything that is necessary to their efficient existence.

Strong then proceeded to apply a version of the original package doctrine to the issue:

> While it must be conceded that a tax upon interstate transportation is invalid, there seems to be no stronger reason for denying the power of a State to tax the fruits of such transportation after they have become intermingled with the general property of the carrier, than there is for denying her power to tax goods which have been imported, after their original packages have been broken, and after they have been mixed with the mass of personal property in the country.[156]

The Court ruled that a state could not tax goods still moving in interstate commerce but could tax them—even in their original package—once the interstate movement ended. How, then, does one define an interstate journey's beginning and end? The general principles developed by the Court hold that interstate commerce begins once an item is surrendered to a common carrier for transportation or otherwise begins its journey out of the state. The journey—and the protection of interstate commerce—ends when the item arrives at its destination, usually defined as in the possession of the person to whom it is sent. Temporary and unexpected interruptions in the journey do not terminate the protection of the Commerce Clause against state taxation, but a true break in the journey may allow a state to tax items in commerce.

Following the decision upholding Pennsylvania's gross receipts tax as applied to railroads, the Court dealt with a variety of state efforts to tax interstate corporations doing business within a state. The Court generally upheld net income and gross receipts taxes so long as they were fairly apportioned to reflect the share of the company's overall business done in the state and to accord with the services and protection provided by the state to the company.[157] In the 1980s and 1990s the Court steadily upheld against corporate challenges state taxes imposed on interstate and international corporations using the "worldwide unitary" method of taxation. The Court held that this method, when properly implemented, produced

a tax that violated neither the guarantee of due process nor the federal power to regulate interstate and foreign commerce.[158]

"Privilege" Cases

The privilege cases illustrate the Court's effort to apply the Commerce Clause requirement carefully but not too strictly to state taxation involving the question of state taxes on "the privilege of doing interstate business." In *Paul v. Virginia* (1869) the Court held that Virginia could impose conditions on its grant to an out-of-state insurance company of the right to do business in the state. Virginia's law required the company to obtain a license and to deposit security bonds of $30,000 to $50,000 with the state treasurer.[159] When Kentucky sought to enforce its law requiring out-of-state express companies to obtain a state license before carrying on business in the state, the United States Express Company protested that the requirement was an infringement of the federal power to regulate commerce. The Court decided against the state in *Crutcher v. Kentucky* (1891).

"To carry on interstate commerce is not a franchise or a privilege granted by the State," wrote Justice Joseph P. Bradley, "it is a right which every citizen of the United States is entitled to exercise under the Constitution and laws of the United States." A state could not use a license tax to exclude or burden corporations engaged in interstate commerce. Distinguishing the *Paul* decision, Bradley wrote, "The case is entirely different from that of foreign corporations seeking to do a business which does not belong to the regulating power of Congress." Insurance, the Court had held in *Paul v. Virginia* was not subject to that congressional power. *(See "Insurance," p. 403.)* The Court rejected any defense of the Kentucky law as an exercise of the police power: "[I]t does not follow that everything which the Legislature of a State may deem essential for the good order of society and the well being of its citizens can be set up against the exclusive power of Congress to regulate the operations of foreign and interstate commerce."[160]

For almost a century, with increasing confusion and diminishing effect, the Court adhered to this rule. As constitutional scholar Carl B. Swisher wrote,

The question whether state taxes bore so heavily upon interstate commerce as to be an unconstitutional burden arose perennially. If a generalization is to be made at all, it is perhaps to the effect that the principles involved became less clear with the passing years, and the decisions rested more obviously upon the beliefs of the Court as to what in each case would best serve the public welfare. The lines of the original-package doctrine…became increasingly blurred as decisions dealt with such matters as natural gas and electricity which only in a highly figurative sense could be thought of as in packages at all. The principle that state control began when the article shipped in interstate commerce came to rest in the state was likewise blurred because of the fact that so many of the items of interstate commerce could not be thought of as coming to rest. The absence of a clear line marking the taxing jurisdiction of the state resulted, not from any particular line of decisions of the Supreme Court, but from the nature of commerce itself and the nature of the federal system.[161]

By 1977 the Supreme Court realized that the prohibition on taxes on "the privilege of doing interstate business" had become little more than a formalism, "a trap for the unwary draftsman" who failed to choose other phrases for the state tax law. In that year the Court discarded its opposition to all taxes described in this way and adopted the practical approach already in evidence in most of its modern rulings on state tax. Rejecting the challenge of an interstate motor carrier to a Mississippi tax, Justice Harry A. Blackmun explained the Court's decision in *Complete Auto Transit Inc. v. Brady* (1977). Citing several recent state tax cases, he noted that they

> considered not the formal language of the tax statute, but rather the practical effect, and have sustained a tax against Commerce Clause challenge when the tax is applied to an activity with a substantial nexus with the taxing state, is fairly apportioned, does not discriminate against interstate commerce and is fairly related to the services provided by the State.
>
> [The modern Court] consistently has indicated that "interstate commerce may be made to pay its way," and has moved toward a standard of permissibility of state taxation based upon its actual effect rather than legal terminology.[162]

In this case, finding that the challenged tax resulted in no effect forbidden by the Commerce Clause, the Court upheld it. The full measure of this about-face by the Court was illustrated the following year, 1978, when the Court approved a Washington state tax on stevedoring virtually identical to one it had twice held an unconstitutional burden on interstate commerce.[163]

Business across Borders

The "peddlers and drummers" decisions of the late nineteenth century illustrate the intricate nature of the task of deciding when a state tax discriminates against interstate commerce and when it does not. Peddlers traveled through the country during the nineteenth century, carrying with them the goods they sold. Drummers, on the other hand, carried only samples, taking orders from their customers for future delivery. The distinction became significant when states tried to tax the peddlers and the drummers and were challenged in this effort as interfering with interstate commerce. The Court took up the issue in *Welton v. Missouri* (1876) and *Robbins v. Shelby County Taxing District* (1887).

M. M. Welton was a peddler in Missouri who sold sewing machines produced in another state. In 1876 the Supreme Court held that Missouri could not require Welton to obtain a license for his peddling because the law imposing that requirement affected only persons selling out-of-state goods and so discriminated against interstate commerce in violation of the Commerce Clause. The clause protects a commodity, "even after it has entered the State, from any burdens imposed by reason of its foreign origin," wrote Justice Stephen Field.[164] Four years later, however, the Court upheld Tennessee's requirement that all peddlers of sewing machines obtain licenses. That requirement applied to an agent of a Connecticut-based manufacturer. Justice Noah Swayne wrote for the Court:

> In all cases of this class, it is a test question whether there is any discrimination in favor of the State or of the citizens of the State which enacted the law. Wherever there is, such discrimination is fatal.…In the case before us, the statute…makes no such discrimination. It applies alike to sewing machines manufactured in the State and out of it. The exaction is not an unusual

or unreasonable one. The State, putting all such machines upon the same footing…had an unquestionable right to impose the burden.[165]

Seven years later, however, the Court held that the Commerce Clause forbade states to place any sort of license requirement or tax on drummers, who take orders in one state for future deliveries of goods from another state. These deliveries are interstate commerce, held the Court, and thus are not subject to state taxes. Sabine Robbins sold stationery by displaying samples and taking orders in Memphis, Tennessee. The stationery came from Ohio. Tennessee law required all such drummers to obtain a license, whether they were employed by in-state or out-of-state firms. Robbins failed to comply and was fined. He challenged his fine by arguing that the drummers' license was an improper interference with interstate commerce. The Supreme Court agreed. Writing for the majority in *Robbins v. Shelby County Taxing District* (1887), Justice Bradley held that "to tax the sale of such [out-of-state] goods, or the offer to sell them, before they are brought into the State…seems to us clearly a tax on interstate commerce itself." The fact that the license requirement applied also to the persons who sold in-state goods was irrelevant:

> Interstate commerce cannot be taxed at all, even though the same amount of tax should be laid on domestic commerce.…The negotiation of sales of goods which are in another State, for the purpose of introducing them into the State in which the negotiation is made, is interstate commerce.

This particular license tax discriminated against out-of-state businesses that had little alternative to this mode of selling, while in-state businesses could simply open stores in the state where they had their offices anyway. "This kind of taxation is usually imposed at the instance and solicitation of domestic dealers, as a means of protecting them from foreign competition," Bradley wrote. If this sort of tax were upheld, he concluded, "[T]he confusion into which the commerce of the country would be thrown…would be but a repetition of the disorder which prevailed under the Articles of Confederation."[166] The principle from *Robbins* was later extended to protect mail-order businesses from

state taxes, particularly the sales taxes increasingly adopted by states. Such taxes could affect only local sales, not those from out-of-state merchants.

In an effort to impose an equal tax burden on sales from out-of-state sources, states developed a "use tax"—a tax on the in-state use of an item acquired from an out-of-state seller. This tax was equivalent to the "sales tax" imposed on the in-state purchase of a similar item. The "use tax" was quickly challenged as in conflict with the Commerce Clause, but the Supreme Court found it nondiscriminatory and therefore permissible. Writing for the Court in *Henneford v. Silas Mason Co.* (1937), Justice Benjamin Cardozo explained that the tax was incurred after any interstate commerce had ceased, that the tax did not hamper commerce or discriminate against interstate commerce. "When the account is made up, the stranger from afar is subject to no greater burdens as a consequence of ownership than the dweller within the gates. The one pays upon one activity or incident, and the other upon another, but the sum is the same when the reckoning is closed."[167]

Subsequently, the Court held that a state imposing a use tax may require the out-of-state seller to collect it, so long as there is a sufficient connection between the state and the out-of-state seller to support imposition of this duty. The connection can be the fact that the seller has local agents in the taxing state, that a mail-order company has retail outlets in the taxing state, or even that a company that runs a mail-order business has offices within the taxing state that solicit advertising for a magazine also published by the mail-order company.[168]

The basic principle of *Welton* and *Robbins* survives as the effective guide for state taxation in this area. In 1977 the Court cited *Welton* when it struck down a New York tax that burdened stock transactions taking place on out-of-state stock exchanges, rather than the New York Stock Exchange or the New York–based American Stock Exchange. Writing for the Court, Justice Byron R. White noted that the consequence of the New York tax was that "the flow of securities sales is diverted from the most economically efficient channels and directed to New York. This diversion of interstate commerce and diminution of free competition in securities sales are wholly inconsistent with the free trade purpose of the Commerce Clause."[169]

Taxes on Mail Order Purchases and Real Estate

Fifteen years later, in *Quill Corp. v. North Dakota* (1992), the Court said states may not force out-of-state catalog companies to collect and remit sales taxes on purchases unless they have stores or a sales force within the state.[170] In support of North Dakota, the states said they were losing $3.2 billion in sales tax revenues per year on mail-order purchases. The case arose after North Dakota sought to require Quill Corp., a mail-order house with neither outlets nor sales representatives in North Dakota, to collect and pay taxes on goods purchased for use in the state. The Court left open the possibility that Congress could by law require catalog companies to collect and pay sales taxes to the states.

Many of the state tax cases the Court heard in the last quarter of the twentieth century sprang from states' new approaches to modern budget dilemmas. One important case of the era, however, grew out of citizens' concerns over escalating taxes. California voters in 1978 adopted Proposition 13, which fixed the property tax rate at 1 percent of the value and froze the value either at the 1975 level or the new purchase price. This approach allowed home owners to pay less in taxes, and over time, it created a sharp divide between longtime owners and new buyers. While the taxes of longtime owners remained the same, new buyers in the same neighborhood might be forced to pay as much as seventeen times more in taxes for a comparable house. A new owner in Los Angeles challenged the scheme as discriminatory and denying her the "equal protection of the laws."

But the Court has been wary of challenging economic discrimination, and it was unwilling to declare a state's real estate tax law as unconstitutional. By a vote of 8-1 in *Nordlinger v. Hahn* (1992), the justices said having lower taxes on longtime property owners rationally furthers legitimate state interests, notably in neighborhood preservation and stability. Further, the Court said, new home owners were on notice of how the tax law works, and they knew they would have to pay taxes based on the purchase price of the property.[171]

Writing for the Court, Harry A. Blackmun noted that the justices traditionally have given great deference to the democratic process of taxation. "Certainly, California's grand experiment appears to vest benefits in a broad, powerful, and entrenched segment of society, and, as the Court of Appeal surmised, ordinary democratic processes may be unlikely to prompt its reconsideration or repeal. Yet, many wise and well-intentioned laws suffer from the same malady. [The tax law] is not palpably arbitrary, and we must decline petitioner's request to upset the will of the people of California."[172]

Justice Stevens, the lone dissenter, said California was giving a "tremendous windfall" to its longtime residents. Moreover, it allowed them to pass on this benefit to their children if they bought their parents' house. The California law "establishes a privilege of a medieval character: Two families with equal needs and equal resources are treated differently solely because of their different heritage," Stevens said.[173]

Tax-Free Municipal Bonds

The Court also refused to knock down a state's traditional tax preference for its own municipal bonds. These bonds finance about two-thirds of the capital projects—schools, highways, and bridges, for example—undertaken by state or local governments, the Court noted. Taxpayers do not have to pay a federal tax on the income from these bonds, and in most states, they do not pay taxes on income from bonds issued within the state. Municipal bonds issued by other states are subject to taxes in Kentucky and most other states. A Kentucky couple, George and Catherine Davis, challenged this different tax treatment as unconstitutional. They won a state court ruling that held this tax scheme was a protectionist measure that discriminated against interstate commerce.

But in *Department of Revenue of Kentucky v. Davis* (2008) the Court reversed this ruling in a 7-2 decision and upheld the state's preferential tax treatment for its own bonds. States and local entities may favor their enterprises, including by encouraging residents to buy their bonds, said the Court. This "is a far cry from the private protectionism" that has been held to violate the Commerce Clause, Justice David Souter wrote.[174]

The State and the Individual

On its face, the Constitution imposes few restraints on how a state deals with an individual. In theory such protection was left to state constitutions and state bills of rights. Early in its history, the Supreme Court ruled that the guarantees of individual rights in the Constitution's first ten amendments, the Bill of Rights, did not apply directly to the states—a ruling the Court has yet to overturn. Although the Court addressed the issue of slavery in a variety of ways, it never did so as a human rights question. Slaves were property. Even after the addition of the Thirteenth, Fourteenth, and Fifteenth Amendments to the Constitution, the Supreme Court refused for decades to interpret them in a way that would provide protection of civil rights against state action. Citing the doctrine of reserved state powers, the Court held that most civil rights questions still remained within the purview of the states. Not until the twentieth century did the Court begin to use the Fourteenth Amendment's guarantees of due process and equal protection to apply the most fundamental guarantees of the Bill of Rights to state actions, and this revolution is still continuing.

THE CONSTITUTION

The Constitution forbids states or the federal government from passing bills of attainder or ex post facto laws. A bill of attainder, in English law, was an act of Parliament declaring a person guilty of treason, sentencing him to die, and confiscating his property. In American law, a bill of attainder has simply come to mean any measure that punishes an individual without a trial. An ex post facto law is one that operates retroactively to make an earlier action invalid, illegal, or criminal. Until the twentieth century, the prohibition on these two types of measures were the only explicit constitutional provisions interpreted by the Supreme Court as restraining state actions affecting the individual.

Evidence suggests that those who wrote the ban on ex post facto laws into the Constitution intended it to protect property as well as persons, to apply to civil as well as criminal laws, but the Supreme Court—in its first ruling on this portion of the Constitution—nullified such intent.[1] Rejecting the contention of a person named Calder that a state law nullifying his title to certain property was in conflict with this provision, the Court held that the ban on ex post facto laws applied only to criminal legislation. Writing for the Court, Justice Samuel Chase set out its views:

> I do not think it [the prohibition] was inserted to secure the citizen in his private rights, of either property or contracts...the restriction not to pass any ex post facto law, was to secure the person of the subject from injury, or punishment, in consequence of such law.
>
> I do not consider any law ex post facto, within the prohibition, that mollifies the rigor of the criminal law; but only those that create, or aggravate the crime; or increase the punishment; or change the rules of evidence, for the purpose of conviction.[2]

In later rulings on this language, the Court has held that it does not forbid a state from making retroactive changes in its trial procedure and rules of evidence. The Court has simply limited those changes that may be applied to the trials of persons who committed crimes before the change to those that work to the advantage of the defendant. In a pair of cases decided in 1898, the Court, for example, held that a state could alter the rules of evidence to allow the admission of additional evidence in cases already set for trial before the change—because that was simply a change in procedures—but that it could not reduce the size of a jury for the trial of crimes already committed—because it was easier to convince fewer jurors to convict.[3] In a 1977 ruling, the Supreme Court refused to use this clause to invalidate a death sentence imposed upon a man convicted of murder. He had argued that it should operate to nullify his sentence because the capital punishment law in operation at the time of the murders was subsequently declared unconstitutional and invalid, and he was sentenced under a new law passed after that Court decision. By a 6-3 vote the Court rejected his claim, holding that the change from the old law to the new one was simply procedural, and that in fact the new law worked more to the benefit of the defendant.[4] Also in 1977 the Court held that Congress had not violated this ban when it took the papers and tapes of the Nixon administration out of the custody of former president Richard Nixon and placed them under government control.[5]

The Ex Post Facto Clause continues, however, to limit the state's power to prosecute old crimes. In 2003 the Court struck down a California law that sought to revive sex crimes charges against persons who allegedly molested children decades ago. The law set a three-year time period for bringing charges of sexual abuse, but in 1993 the state legislature repealed the statute of limitations for sex crimes involving children. State prosecutors charged Marion Stogner with sexually molesting two of his children between 1955 and 1973. The Court, in a 5-4 decision, said that reviving a "long-dead prosecution" violated the Ex Post Facto Clause. "The government has refused to play by its own rules," wrote Justice Stephen G. Breyer in *Stogner v. California* (2003).[6]

The first broad application of the ban on bills of attainder, along with the ex post facto prohibition, came soon after the Civil War, when a number of states and Congress enacted laws requiring persons who wished to engage in a variety of activities to take "test oaths" to ensure their loyalty to the Union. In Missouri the test oath requirement was particularly severe. Before any person could vote, run for or hold office, practice law, teach, hold property in trust for a religious organization, or serve as a clergyman, he was required to take a sweeping oath that he had always been loyal to the United States and that he had never, by act or word, given any

aid or support to any enemy. The effect of the law was to exclude from those activities anyone who had even voiced sympathy with the Confederacy. John A. Cummings, a Catholic priest, refused to take the oath and was convicted and sentenced for acting as a priest in violation of the law. He challenged the requirement as a violation of the constitutional prohibitions on bills of attainder and ex post facto laws. In *Cummings v. Missouri* (1867) the Court agreed with his challenge on both points. In an opinion written by Justice Stephen J. Field, the Court declared,

> We admit…that among the rights reserved to the States is the right of each State to determine the qualifications for office, and the conditions upon which its citizens may exercise their various callings and pursuits within its jurisdiction.…But it by no means follows that, under the form of creating a qualification or attaching a condition, the States can, in effect, inflict a punishment for a past act which was not punishable at the time it was committed.[7]

The disabilities imposed by Missouri upon persons who did not take the oath certainly could be considered punishments, Field wrote. The state could not constitutionally pass a law that declared Cummings personally, or all clergymen, guilty of any crime, and, likewise, it could not pass a law *assuming* such guilt, Field continued:

> The Constitution deals with substance, not shadows. Its inhibition was leveled at the thing, not the name. It intended that the rights of the citizen would be secure against deprivation for past conduct by legislative enactment, under any form, however disguised.[8]

The Court also held the federal test oath invalid.[9] In subsequent rulings the Court relaxed somewhat its opposition to after-the-fact disqualifications of persons for certain actions. It has held that a state's police power—as applied to protect the public health—justified its forbidding a person convicted of a felony from resuming the practice of medicine, and it has upheld the right of a state to exclude convicted felons from holding certain labor union offices. The Court also has permitted states to require their public employees to take loyalty oaths so long as the oaths are narrowly drawn and carefully applied.[10]

The pre–Civil War Court, however, refused to apply any of the provisions of the Bill of Rights to state action. In paving its streets, the city of Baltimore disrupted the course of certain streams, which then dumped debris and gravel into the Baltimore harbor around the wharf owned by a man named John Barron. As a result, Barron's wharf became unusable, because the water around it had been made too shallow for vessels to approach to off-load. Barron sued the city, lost the case, and then appealed to the Supreme Court, arguing that the Fifth Amendment guarantee against the government's taking private property for public use without just compensation required the city to compensate him for his loss. The Court ruled against Barron. Writing for the Court, Chief Justice John Marshall stated, "These amendments contain no expression indicating an intention to apply them to the State governments. This Court cannot so apply them."[11]

THE CIVIL WAR AMENDMENTS

Few stranger chapters can be found in the history of the Court than the story of the way in which the justices, after the Civil War, read the Thirteenth, Fourteenth, and Fifteenth Amendments to the Constitution. The Court's interpretations were so narrow that they frustrated almost entirely the intentions of the people who drafted them and worked for their incorporation into the Constitution. The amendments' sponsors intended to extend federal protection to citizens against state action infringing the rights already protected by the Bill of Rights against federal action, but for decades the Court rejected this interpretation.

Servitude and Discrimination

"Neither slavery nor involuntary servitude, except as a punishment for crime whereof the party shall have been duly convicted, shall exist within the United States, or any place subject to their jurisdiction," reads the Thirteenth Amendment, abolishing slavery and authorizing Congress to pass legislation enforcing that

ban. Relying on this authority, the Reconstruction Congress enacted a national ban on discrimination against blacks at hotels and restaurants and on steamboats and the railroads. Several blacks brought lawsuits when they were turned away at theaters or hotels. The Court, in a devastating setback for the cause of civil rights, ruled unconstitutional the entire Civil Rights Act of 1875. Although it conceded that the Thirteenth Amendment empowered Congress to pass laws to abolish "all badges and incidents of slavery," the Court in the *Civil Rights Cases* (1883) refused to view racial discrimination as a "badge of slavery." Writing for the Court, Justice Joseph Bradley stated,

> Congress did not assume, under the authority given by the 13th Amendment, to adjust what may be called the social rights of men and races in the community; but only to declare and vindicate those fundamental rights which appertain to the essence of citizenship, and the enjoyment or deprivation of which constitutes the essential distinction between freedom and slavery.... It would be running the slavery argument into the ground, to make it apply to every act of discrimination which a person may see fit to make as to the guests he will entertain, or as to the people he will take into his coach or cab or car, or admit to his concert or theater, or deal with in other matters of intercourse or business.[12]

Early in the twentieth century the Court did cite the Thirteenth Amendment to strike down state peonage laws, which required a person who defaulted on a contract either to go to jail or to go to work for his creditor to "work off" his default.[13] The Court, however, has recognized a number of established exceptions to the "involuntary servitude" banned by the Thirteenth Amendment—among them work for the state on state roads, jury duty, and compulsory military service.[14]

Privileges and Immunities

"All persons born or naturalized in the United States, and subject to the jurisdiction thereof, are citizens of the United States and of the State wherein they reside," states the first section of the Fourteenth Amendment, overruling the Court's holding in *Scott v. Sandford* (1857) that

When Louisiana granted a twenty-five year monopoly to one slaughterhouse, every butcher in New Orleans was forced to use it. The butchers sued, basing their claim on the Fourteenth Amendment, which forbids states from passing laws that "abridge the privileges or immunities" of U.S. citizens. In the Slaughterhouse Cases (1873) the Supreme Court upheld the Louisiana law.

blacks were not citizens. The same section of the amendment, clearly directed against state action, also declares, "No State shall make or enforce any law which shall abridge the privileges or immunities of citizens of the United States; nor shall any State deprive any person of life, liberty, or property, without due process of law; nor deny to any person within its jurisdiction the equal protection of the laws." Adopted in 1868, this amendment contained four other sections, only one of which—giving Congress the authority to pass appropriate enforcing laws—is pertinent here. During congressional consideration of the Fourteenth Amendment, advocates of the measure in both chambers made clear their belief that it would extend federal protection for a broad range of basic rights, including those guaranteed by the Bill of Rights, to persons denied those rights by state action.[15]

Slaughterhouse Cases (1873)

Five years after the Fourteenth Amendment was ratified, the Supreme Court ruled that it did *not* give citizens the full protection of the Bill of Rights against actions by the states. Oddly enough, it was butchers,

not black men, bringing these landmark cases, known collectively as the *Slaughterhouse Cases*.[16] New Orleans butchers charged that the state of Louisiana had violated the Fourteenth Amendment by granting to one company the exclusive right to operate a slaughterhouse in the city. This monopoly, the butchers charged, deprived them of their right to carry on their business, a right included among the privileges and immunities guaranteed by the first section of the amendment. The monopoly was granted in 1869, and the case reached the Supreme Court the next year. It was argued in 1872 and then reargued in 1873. Representing the butchers was Alabaman and former justice John A. Campbell, who had left the Court when his state seceded from the Union. He placed the burden of his argument on the privileges and immunities section of the amendment, with reference also made to the due process and equal protection guarantees.

On April 14, 1873—eight years after the end of the Civil War—the Court issued its opinion in a 5-4 vote against the butchers. Justice Samuel F. Miller wrote the majority opinion. Chief Justice Salmon P. Chase and

Justices Bradley, Field, and Noah Swayne dissented. Miller wrote that the monopoly was granted by the state in the exercise of its police power, and it did not forbid the protesting butchers from practicing their trade; rather, it merely required that they do so at a particular slaughterhouse. By law, all other slaughterhouses in the area were to be closed.

Considering the citizenship section of the amendment, Miller made an important distinction: "It is quite clear, then, that there is a citizenship of the United States and a citizenship of a State, which are distinct from each other and which depend upon different characteristics or circumstances in the individual." Moving on to the next portion of the amendment, Miller continued,

> Of the privileges and immunities of the citizens of the United States, and of the privileges and immunities of the citizens of the State, and what they respectively are, we will presently consider; but we wish to state here that it is only the former which are placed by this clause under the protection of the Federal Constitution, and that the latter, whatever they may be, are not intended to have any additional protection by this paragraph of the Amendment.[17]

With the exception of the Constitution's language forbidding states to pass ex post facto laws, bills of attainder, and laws impairing the obligation of contract, Miller wrote,

> the entire domain of the privileges and immunities of citizens of the States lay within the constitutional and legislative power of the States, and without that of the Federal Government. Was it the purpose of the 14th Amendment...to transfer the security and protection of all the civil rights which we have mentioned, from the States to the Federal Government? And where it is declared that Congress shall have the power to enforce that article, was it intended to bring within the power of Congress the entire domain of civil rights heretofore belonging exclusively to the States?
>
> All this and more must follow, if the proposition of the plaintiffs [the butchers]...be sound.... [S]uch a construction...would constitute this Court a perpetual censor upon all legislation of the States, on the civil rights of their own citizens, with authority to nullify such as it did not approve as consistent with those rights, as they existed at the time of the adoption of this amendment. . . .

We are convinced that no such results were intended by the Congress which proposed these Amendments, nor by the Legislatures of the States, which ratified them.[18]

The butchers' challenge to the monopoly failed, for "the privileges and immunities relied on in the argument are those which belong to citizens of the States as such,...and are left to the state governments for security and protection, and not by this article placed under the special care of the Federal Government."[19] "The argument has not been much pressed in these cases that the defendants' charter deprives the plaintiffs of their property without due process of law, or that it denies to them the equal protection of the law," added Miller. He noted, however, that "under no construction of that provision that we have ever seen, or any that we deem admissible, can the restraint imposed by the State of Louisiana upon the exercise of their trade by the butchers of New Orleans be held to be a deprivation of property within the meaning of that provision."[20]

In dissent, Justice Field argued that the Fourteenth Amendment did extend protection to citizens against the deprivation of their common rights by state legislation:

> The fundamental rights, privileges and immunities which belong to him as a free man and a free citizen, now belong to him as a citizen of the United States, and are not dependent upon his citizenship of any State....They do not derive their existence from its legislation, and cannot be destroyed by its power.[21]

To hold the majority's view, confining this protection to the privileges and immunities specifically or implicitly set out as belonging to U.S. citizens, rendered this portion of the amendment "a vain and idle enactment, which accomplished nothing, and most unnecessarily excited Congress and the people on its passage. With privileges and immunities thus designated no State could ever have interfered by its laws, and no new constitutional provision was required to inhibit such interference.... But if the Amendment refers to the natural and inalienable rights which belong to all citizens, the inhibition has a profound significance and consequence."[22] Not surprisingly, the

Fourteenth Amendment so interpreted provided little protection for any of the disadvantaged groups—blacks, women, aliens, and criminal defendants—who sought its shelter during the next half-century.

Civil Rights Cases (1883)

In the *Slaughterhouse Cases* opinion, Justice Miller stated his doubts that "any action of a State not directed by way of discrimination against the negroes as a class, or on account of their race, will ever be held to come within the purview of this [equal protection] provision. It is so clearly a provision for that race and that emergency."[23] Yet, ten years later, in the *Civil Rights Cases* (1883), the Court so narrowly interpreted the amendment's protection for black citizens that even Miller's limited view of the Equal Protection Clause seemed too broad. During those years the Court struck down a number of the laws Congress had passed under the power granted by the Civil War Amendments to enforce those amendments. This narrowing process consisted of two elements: a limited category of federally protected rights and an insistence that the Fourteenth Amendment reached only state, not private, action.[24] In the *Civil Rights Cases* the Court struck down the Civil Rights Act of 1875 as beyond the power granted to Congress by the enforcing section of the Fourteenth Amendment. That act made it a crime to deny equal access and enjoyment of public accommodations to black persons. There were five such cases grouped under the rubric of the *Civil Rights Cases* and decided together by the Court.[25]

In *United States v. Stanley* and *United States v. Nichols,* the defendants were charged with refusing to allow blacks equal access to inns and hotels; in *United States v. Ryan* and *United States v. Singleton,* the defendants had refused to allow black people to sit in a certain part of theaters in San Francisco and New York; and *Robinson v. Memphis and Charleston Railroad Co.* resulted from a railroad conductor's refusal to allow a black woman to ride in the "ladies'" car on the train. The Court voted 8-1 to strike down the Civil Rights Act. Writing for the majority, Justice Bradley found the reason simple: The Fourteenth Amendment forbids state action, not "individual invasion of individual rights":

It does not invest Congress with power to legislate upon subjects which are within the domain of state legislation; but to provide modes of relief against state legislation or state action....It does not authorize Congress to create a code of municipal law for the regulation of private rights; but to provide modes of redress against the operation of state laws, and the action of state officers executive or judicial, when these are subversive of the fundamental rights specified in the Amendment.

Such legislation [as Congress is authorized to pass] cannot properly cover the whole domain of rights....That would be to establish a code of municipal law regulative of all private rights between man and man in society. It would be to make Congress take the place of the State Legislatures, and to supersede them....[T]he legislation which Congress is authorized to adopt in this behalf is not general legislation upon the rights of the citizen, but corrective legislation, that is, such as may be necessary and proper for counteracting such laws as the States may adopt or enforce....

In this connection it is proper to state that civil rights, such as are guarantied by the Constitution against state aggression, cannot be impaired by the wrongful acts of individuals, unsupported by state authority....The wrongful act of an individual, unsupported by any such authority, is simply a private wrong, or a crime of that individual, an invasion of the rights of the injured party, it is true, whether they affect his person, his property or his reputation; but if not sanctioned in some way by the State, or not done under state authority, his rights remain in full force and may presumably be vindicated by resort to the laws of the State for redress.[26]

In dissent, Justice John Marshall Harlan lamented,

Constitutional provisions, adopted in the interest of liberty, and for the purpose of securing, through national legislation, if need be, rights inhering in a state of freedom and belonging to American citizenship, have been so construed as to defeat the ends the people desired to accomplish, which they attempted to accomplish, and which they supposed they had accomplished by changes in their fundamental law.[27]

Harlan viewed Congress as authorized under the Thirteenth and Fourteenth Amendments to pass legislation barring private racial discrimination:

If, then, exemption from discrimination, in respect of civil rights, is a new constitutional right...and I do not see how this can now be questioned...why may not the Nation, by means of its own legislation of a primary direct character, guard, protect and enforce that right? It is a right and privilege which the nation conferred.[28]

Harlan's dissent had no effect on his colleagues. Thirteen years later he would again dissent alone, when the Court, in the infamous and since overruled *Plessy v. Ferguson* (1896), would hold state-imposed racial segregation no violation of the rights guaranteed to citizens by the Fourteenth Amendment. The majority found such segregation as on railway cars a proper and reasonable exercise of the state police power. Writing for the Court, Justice Henry B. Brown stated, "The object of the amendment was undoubtedly to enforce the absolute equality of the two races before the law, but in the nature of things, it could not have been intended to abolish distinctions based upon color, or to enforce social, as distinguished from political, equality." Brown rejected the "assumption that the enforced separation of the two races stamps the colored race with a badge of inferiority":

If this be so, it is not by reason of anything found in the act, but solely because the colored race chooses to put that construction upon it....The [plaintiff's] argument also assumes that social prejudices may be overcome by legislation, and that equal rights cannot be secured to the negro except by an enforced commingling of the two races. We cannot accept this proposition. If the two races are to meet on terms of social equality, it must be the result of natural affinities, a mutual appreciation of each other's merits and a voluntary consent of individuals.[29]

For sixty years *Plessy* would stand, allowing states to enforce "separate but equal" rules, despite the Fourteenth Amendment's command of equal protection. Not only did black citizens find little aid in the Court's view of the Fourteenth Amendment, but also the same plight afflicted women. In 1873 the Court refused to apply the Fourteenth Amendment's Privileges and Immunities Clause to require a state to license a woman to practice law in its courts.[30] Two years later it ruled in *Minor v. Happerset* (1875) that a state did not deny a woman

privileges and immunities guaranteed by the Fourteenth Amendment by refusing to allow her to vote.[31] Charles Warren comments that "it now became evident that the privileges and immunities clause of the Amendment, as construed by the Court, afforded slight protection to an individual and no protection to a corporation, affected by oppressive state legislation."[32]

Nor did the Fourteenth Amendment condemn state laws discriminating against aliens. In only one ruling during the late nineteenth century did the Court strike down any municipal ordinance or state law as denying aliens equal protection of the law.[33] The Fourteenth Amendment was equally useless to criminal defendants in state courts. In 1884 the Court refused to use the amendment's due process guarantee to require that a state, in prosecuting someone for a capital crime, first obtain a grand jury indictment.[34]

The Right to Vote

"The right of citizens of the United States to vote shall not be denied or abridged by the United States or by any State on account of race, color, or previous condition of servitude," declares the first section of the Fifteenth Amendment. The second section gives Congress the power to enforce that provision. Like the protections of the Fourteenth Amendment, this constitutional protection was also diminished during the post–Civil War years. The Supreme Court, in 1876, handed down a pair of decisions that effectively nullified the 1870 law Congress had passed to enforce the guarantee of the right to vote.

"Exemption from Discrimination"

Adhering closely to the wording of the amendment, the Court in *United States v. Reese* (1876) struck down the parts of the law that provided punishment for state election officials who refused to accept or count black votes or who otherwise obstructed citizens from voting. The Court held that the penalties covered a broader range of behavior than that proscribed by the amendment, and hence must fall. "The Fifteenth Amendment does not confer the right of suffrage upon anyone," wrote Chief Justice Morrison Waite for the Court. Continuing, he stated, the "Amendment has invested the citizens of the United States with a new constitutional right which is within the protecting power of Congress. That right is exemption from discrimination in the exercise of the elective franchise on account of race, color or previous condition of servitude." The law at issue was, however, too broad, covering actions outside the jurisdiction of Congress as well as those within. Therefore, it must be struck down: "Within its legitimate sphere, Congress is supreme and beyond the control of the courts; but if it steps outside of its constitutional limitation...the courts...must annul its encroachments upon the reserved power of the States and the people."[35]

The same day—March 27, 1876—the Court issued its opinion in *United States v. Cruikshank,* in which the 1870 act had been used to bring charges against several people for violent and fraudulent actions to keep blacks from exercising a number of constitutional rights— among them the right of assembly, the right to petition for redress of grievances, the right to bear arms, and the right to vote. Again, the Court held that these actions were outside federal jurisdiction, that the rights allegedly interfered with were not federally protected rights, and that Congress could not prescribe punishment for those who violated them. "The Government of the United States," wrote Chief Justice Waite,

> is one of delegated powers alone. Its authority is defined and limited by the Constitution. All powers not granted to it by that instrument are reserved to the States or the people. No rights can be acquired under the Constitution or laws of the United States, except such as the Government of the United States has the authority to grant or secure. All that cannot be so granted or secured are left under the protection of the States.

The Fourteenth Amendment, he continued, "adds nothing to the rights of one citizen as against another. It simply furnishes an additional guarantee against any encroachment by the States upon the fundamental rights which belong to every citizen as a member of society." Again, Waite made the point announced in *Reese:*

> The right to vote in the States comes from the States; but the right of exemption from the prohibited discrimination comes from the United States. The first

has not been granted or secured by the Constitution of the United States; but the last has been.

In this case there was no explicit charge that the fraud and violence that occurred had been intended to prevent blacks from voting on account of their race. "It does not appear," said Waite, "that it was their intent to interfere with any right granted or secured by the Constitution or laws of the United States." Although "[w]e may suspect that 'race' was the cause of the hostility;...it is not so averred."[36]

The Court did not, however, entirely undercut the force of the Fifteenth Amendment. In 1884 it upheld the convictions of several members of the Ku Klux Klan who had beaten up a black man to keep him from voting in federal elections. These convictions were obtained under the portions of the 1870 enforcement law that remained in effect after the Court's 1876 rulings in *Reese* and *Cruikshank.* "If this government is anything more than a mere aggregation of delegated agents of other States and governments, each of which is superior to the General Government, it must have the power to protect the elections on which its existence depends from violence and corruption," wrote Justice Miller for the Court in *Ex parte Yarbrough* (1884). In some circumstances, Miller continued, the Fifteenth Amendment did grant blacks the right to vote, "and Congress had the power to protect and enforce that right."[37]

Circumvention

Ex parte Yarbrough and federal enforcement power notwithstanding, the southern states adopted and used a number of devices that successfully kept most blacks from voting for about a century after the Civil War. Judicial action to outlaw these devices was belated. The first such device to fall was the grandfather clause, setting some literacy or other standard that prospective voters must meet unless they or their father or grandfather had been a registered voter in the years before adoption of the Fifteenth Amendment. In 1915 the Supreme Court struck down such a clause implemented by the state of Oklahoma, finding it a clear violation of the amendment. Oklahoma then required all persons who had not voted in the 1914 election to register within two weeks

After Joseph Lochner, the owner of a bakery located in Utica, New York, was convicted of violating a state maximum hour work law, he asked the Supreme Court to strike it down as violative of his constitutional rights. In *Lochner v. New York* (1905) the justices agreed. The majority found that the law impermissibly interfered with the right of employers to enter into contracts with their employees.

in order to become voters. In 1939 the Court held this requirement also in violation of the amendment.[38]

The "white primary" was used effectively to disenfranchise blacks until the Court in 1944 held the "white primary" impermissible as a violation of the equal protection guarantee and the Fifteenth Amendment.[39] In 1898 the Court had held that neither poll taxes nor a literacy test violated the amendment, and as recently as 1960 the Supreme Court upheld a North Carolina literacy requirement for voters.[40] In 1964 the adoption of the Twenty-fourth Amendment forbade the use of poll taxes in federal elections, and in 1966 the Supreme Court held a state's poll tax for state elections a denial of equal protection.[41] Four years later the Court upheld a 1970 act of Congress suspending all use of literacy tests. Such a ban was a proper implementation of the Fifteenth Amendment, held the Court.[42] Even before the Court moved into the general "political thicket" of reapportionment,

it in 1960 struck down the racial gerrymandering of electoral districts as a violation of the Fifteenth Amendment guarantee.[43]

DUE PROCESS GUARANTEE

It was doubly ironic that the first extended use of the Due Process Clause by the Supreme Court was to protect business against regulation by the state. This portion of the Fourteenth Amendment, which was enacted to protect individuals, was thereby turned into a shield for property. The provision first tested before the Court in an unsuccessful effort to claim its protection for the right to carry on business would, by the end of the nineteenth century, take the place of the Contract Clause as business's most effective weapon against state regulation. The first decision signaling this development appeared to be a defeat for propertied interests.

In *Allgeyer v. Louisiana* (1897) the Court held that due process protected a citizen's right to do business with out-of-state as well as in-state insurance companies. In writing the Court's opinion, Justice Rufus Peckham set out for the first time from the bench the theory that the liberty protected by the due process guarantee of the Fourteenth Amendment included the right to make contracts, free of state interference.

Liberty, wrote Peckham, includes "not only the right of the citizen to be free from the merely physical restraint of his person...but the term is deemed to embrace the right of the citizen to be free in the enjoyment of all his faculties; to be free to use them in all lawful ways; to live and work where he will; to earn his livelihood by any lawful calling; to pursue any livelihood or avocation, and for that purpose to enter into all contracts which may be proper, necessary and essential to his carrying out to a successful conclusion the purposes above mentioned."[44] Also in 1897 the Court held that due process required a state to compensate the owner of property taken for public use.[45] The following year the Court held that courts should review the railroad rates set by state commissions to ensure that they did not deprive the railroad company of due process by failing to provide a fair return on its investment.[46]

From these precedents, the Court had little philosophical distance to travel to its ruling in *Lochner v. New York* (1905) invalidating New York's maximum hours law for bakers as violating the freedom of contract and, therefore, due process. *Lochner* was the first in a long series of rulings in which the Court used this theory to strike down state efforts to set maximum hours or minimum wages for workers. *(See "Bakery Workers: Lochner v. New York," p. 415.)* This use of due process—to examine and test the constitutional validity of the substance of a law, not simply the procedures it provides—is called substantive due process. The effect of its use during the early twentieth century is described by one scholar as follows:

> From the standpoint of the development of the federal system, the rise of substantive due process meant two things: one, that a national agency—the Supreme Court—was to decide (in many instances) what the states could and could not do; it thus meant a diminution of state autonomy. Second, to the extent that the Court used substantive due process to frustrate state attempts to regulate business, there would be more pressure exerted by nonbusiness interests for the national government to act, thus accelerating the march to Washington and the accretion of power in the hands of federal officials.[47]

The conservative justices who espoused this use of substantive due process were "unwitting nationalists in the battle over the nature of the federal system."[48] The Court continued to employ this approach—and the theory of freedom of contract—until the New Deal was well under way.

The Quiet Revolution

The first crack in the Court's refusal to apply the Bill of Rights to protect individuals against state action came quietly and with little argument. In 1925 the Court was considering Benjamin Gitlow's argument that his right to due process of law—and his First Amendment freedom of expression—was violated by the state of New York. Gitlow, a member of the Socialist Party, was indicted for publishing and distributing allegedly subversive documents. The charges were based on New York's criminal anarchy law, which forbade the use of language or the distribution of publications advocating the forcible overthrow of organized government. Gitlow argued that this law also violated the due process guarantee because under it the state could punish someone for speaking his thoughts, without any evidence that concrete or substantive evil was likely to result from his words. His argument simply assumed that the "liberty" protected by the Fourteenth Amendment's Due Process Clause included the First Amendment guarantees of freedom of speech and of the press.

The Court upheld Gitlow's prosecution—finding the state law not in conflict with the due process guarantee—but in its opinion, written by conservative justice Edward Terry Sanford, the Court assumed that Gitlow was correct: the Fourteenth Amendment Due Process Clause *did* apply the First Amendment's protections to persons threatened by state action. "For present purposes," wrote Sanford, "we may and do assume that freedom of speech and of the press—which are protected by the 1st Amendment from

THE STATE AND PRIVACY

The constitutional right of personal privacy protects the individual from the interference of the state. This principle emerged as the basis for several Supreme Court decisions beginning in the 1960s, but the Court over the decades has struggled with its constitutional foundation. Nevertheless, a majority of the justices have accepted that right and because of it have struck down state laws prohibiting the use of contraceptives and criminalizing abortions, the possession of obscene material at home, and private, consensual sex between homosexual adults.

"We deal with a right of privacy older than the Bill of Rights," wrote Justice William O. Douglas when the Supreme Court struck down a Connecticut law forbidding the use—or counseling on the use—of contraceptives by anyone in the state.[1] Also suggested as the basis for this holding and this right were the due process guarantee of the Fourteenth Amendment, the "penumbra" of the privacy interests protected by the First, Third, Fourth, and Fifth Amendments, and the Ninth Amendment's statement that the enumeration of rights in the Constitution is not complete and exclusive and that other rights are "retained by the people."

In 1969 the Court held that a state could not forbid the possession of obscene material. The holding was based in part upon the fundamental First Amendment right "to receive information and ideas, regardless of their social worth," but also upon the "right to be free, except in very limited circumstances, from unwanted governmental intrusions into one's privacy." The state had no right to control the content of a person's thoughts, held the Court.[2]

In the most controversial of such rulings, the Court used the right of privacy as the basis for its holding that states could not stand in the way of a woman who decided early in a pregnancy to terminate it through an abortion. Writing the Court's opinion in *Roe v. Wade* (1973), Justice Harry A. Blackmun took note of the conflicting views on the foundation of the right and declared firmly: "This right of privacy, whether it be founded in the Fourteenth Amendment's concept of personal liberty and restrictions upon

state action, as we feel it is, or . . . in the Ninth Amendment's reservation of rights to the people, is broad enough to encompass a woman's decision whether or not to terminate her pregnancy."[3] The Court also recognized the right and interest of the state to regulate the factors or conditions governing the decision as pregnancy progressed toward the time at which a live child could be born and live outside the mother.

The issue of homosexual rights and privacy first came to the Court in 1986. Divided 5-4, the justices reversed a lower court's finding that the right of privacy protected private, consensual homosexual activity from being forbidden or punished by the state. Writing for the Court, Justice Byron R. White said that whatever constitutional right of privacy existed, and he—like Chief Justice William H. Rehnquist—was dubious that one did, it did not protect the right to engage in homosexual conduct.[4] The Court overruled this decision in 2003, holding that the privacy right shields gays and lesbians from being prosecuted for private sexual behavior. The 6-3 decision in *Lawrence v. Texas* (2003) voided the remaining thirteen state laws that made sodomy a crime. Justice Anthony M. Kennedy said the Court has recognized that "the most private human conduct, sexual behavior, and in the most private of places, the home" is off-limits to meddling by the government. When "two adults who, with full and mutual consent from each, engaged in sexual practices common to a homosexual lifestyle, [they] are entitled to respect for their private lives," he said. "It is a promise of the Constitution that there is a realm of personal liberty which the government may not enter."[5]

---

1. *Griswold v. Connecticut,* 381 U.S. 479 at 486 (1965).
2. *Stanley v. Georgia,* 394 U.S. 557 (1969).
3. *Roe v. Wade, Doe v. Bolton,* 410 U.S. 113 at 153 (1973).
4. *Bowers v. Hardwick,* 478 U.S. 186 (1986).
5. *Lawrence v. Texas,* 539 U.S. 558 (2003).

---

abridgment by Congress—are among the fundamental personal rights and 'liberties' protected by the due process clause of the 14th Amendment from impairment by the states."[49] The Court held, however, that the New York law did not violate those rights.

Gitlow v. New York opened the door to a gradual, case-by-case process during which the Court would use the due process guarantee of the Fourteenth Amendment to apply to the states those protections of

the Bill of Rights it found to be fundamental. Six years later, in *Stromberg v. California* (1931), the Court for the first time struck down a state law as violating freedom of speech.[50] The beneficiary of the ruling was Yetta Stromberg, a young woman who conducted a daily flag salute ceremony in a Young Communist League children's camp; the flags involved were those of the Soviet Union and the Communist Party. She was convicted of violating California's "red-flag" law, which forbade the display of a red flag for propaganda or protest purposes. The law denied Stromberg the freedom of political expression and discussion, wrote Chief Justice Charles Evans Hughes, finding it too broad to withstand challenge under the now-applicable First Amendment standards. In 1931 the Court invalidated, for the first time, a state law as infringing on freedom of the press. Struck down by the Court was a Minnesota law that allowed a newspaper or magazine publishing scandalous, malicious, defamatory, or obscene material to be "padlocked" as a nuisance by an injunction. If the newspaper were published despite the injunction, the publisher could be convicted of contempt of court. The padlocking would end only if the judge approving it was convinced that the publication would be unobjectionable in the future.[51]

In 1934 the Court held that freedom of religion was protected against state action by the due process guarantee. In the particular case decided, the Court held that although the guarantee applied, a state university did not abridge a student's freedom of religion by requiring him to take military drill.[52] Three years later freedom of assembly was granted the same protection when the Court overturned the conviction of a Communist Party member for conducting a party meeting.[53] In 1947 the Court made clear that not only the First Amendment freedoms but also the First Amendment guarantee against establishment of religion was protected by due process.[54] Again the Court held that this guarantee was not infringed upon by a school board policy of reimbursing parents for the costs of transporting their children to school, parochial as well as public. This was the first in a long and complicated series of rulings as the Court worked to determine what forms of state aid might be constitutionally provided to church-related schools.

The Court then expanded the reach of the First Amendment protection against state action to encompass the expression of ideas in handbills, meetings, and demonstrations and participation in patriotic programs. In 1938 the Court held that a city could not require everyone who wished to distribute any publication in the city—by hand or otherwise—to obtain written permission to do so. Overturning the conviction of a Jehovah's Witness for failing to obtain such permission, the

Court held the ordinance a violation of the freedom of the press, a freedom that included "every sort of publication which affords a vehicle of information and opinion."[55] In 1939 the justices held that a city could regulate but not absolutely deny the use of public parks, roads, and buildings to organizations wishing to use them for meetings and other forms of communication.[56]

Jehovah's Witnesses are taught that saluting a flag is contrary to the teachings of the Bible. The conflict between this teaching and the requirement of many public schools that children daily salute the U.S. flag came to the Court in the case of the *Minersville School District v. Gobitis* (1940). With its decision in this case, the Court appeared to halt its expansion of First Amendment protection against state action. By an 8-1 vote, the Court rejected the argument that the required flag salute abridged the freedom of religion guaranteed to the children of Jehovah's Witnesses.[57] Three years later—in the middle of World War II—the Court reversed itself. In *West Virginia Board of Education v. Barnette* (1943) the Court ruled that the state could not compel children to participate in a patriotic ceremony when to do so violated their religious beliefs. Justice Robert H. Jackson wrote for the Court:

> If there is any fixed star in our constitutional constellation, it is that no official…can prescribe what shall be orthodox in politics, nationalism, religion or other matters.…We think the action of the local authorities in compelling the flag salute and pledge transcends constitutional limitations on their power and invades the sphere of intellect and spirit which it is the purpose of the First Amendment…to reserve from all official control.[58]

Fair Criminal Procedures

After the Court began to extend First Amendment protections against state action, pressure began to build for a similar extension of other guarantees in the Bill of Rights, in particular those intended to protect persons charged with crimes.

Right to Counsel

The right first extended to persons charged with a crime was the right to counsel, guaranteed in federal cases by the Sixth Amendment. The case was that of the "Scottsboro Boys," nine black teenagers charged with raping two white women on a freight train passing through Alabama. Taken off the train and jailed in Scottsboro, the young men were never asked whether they wished to have the aid of lawyers. The first case came to trial without a defense attorney present, although lawyers eventually would act as defense counsel. The defendants were found guilty, but the Supreme Court reversed their convictions, holding in *Powell v. Alabama* (1932) that the denial of the right to the effective aid of legal counsel was, in the circumstances of this case, a denial of due process under the Fourteenth Amendment. Writing for the Court, Justice George Sutherland declared,

> [I]n a capital case, where the defendant is unable to employ counsel, and is incapable adequately of making his own defense because of ignorance, feeble-mindedness, illiteracy, or the like, it is the duty of the court, whether requested or not, to assign counsel for him as a necessary requisite of due process of law; and that duty is not discharged by an assignment at such a time or under such circumstances as to preclude the giving of effective aid in the preparation and trial of the case. To hold otherwise would be to ignore the fundamental postulate…"that there are certain immutable principles of justice which inhere in the very idea of free government which no member of the Union may disregard."[59]

Ten years later the Court limited the effect of this holding by ruling in *Betts v. Brady* (1942) that "[t]he due process clause of the Fourteenth Amendment does not incorporate, as such, the specific guarantees found in the Sixth Amendment although a denial by a state of rights or privileges specifically embodied in that…may…operate, in a given case, to deprive a litigant of due process of law."[60] The justices refused to require that the state must always furnish counsel to a defendant charged with a crime and unable to employ a lawyer. Thirty-one years after *Powell*, the Supreme Court overruled *Betts v. Brady* in *Gideon v. Wainwright* (1963), in which it held that the Sixth Amendment right to counsel was incorporated in the Due Process Clause and that every defendant in a state criminal trial, just as in a federal trial, was guaranteed representation by counsel whom he employed or who was appointed for him by the court.[61]

Judge and Jury

Early in the century the Court extended to state courts the requirement that a person tried for a crime be tried by an impartial judge. In 1927 the Court struck down an Ohio law that allowed a city's mayor to try bootleggers and to put half the fines assessed and collected into the city coffers. "It certainly violates the Fourteenth Amendment," wrote Chief Justice William Howard Taft, "and deprives a defendant in a criminal case of due process of law, to subject his liberty or property to the judgment of a court the judge of which has a direct, personal, substantial pecuniary interest in reaching a conclusion against him."[62] In a 1923 case the Court had ruled that five black men convicted in Arkansas of murdering a white man were denied due process because of the atmosphere in which their jury was selected and their trial conducted. If a jury was provided, the Court held, it must be fairly chosen. In another case arising out of the prosecution of the Scottsboro Boys, the Court reversed their convictions after a second trial. Due process had been denied them, the Court said, because blacks had been excluded from the juries that indicted and tried them. Subsequently, the Court ruled that indictments of blacks by grand juries from which blacks were excluded were invalid.[63]

In two decisions, in 1876 and 1900, the Court had held that the Fourteenth Amendment did not require states to provide jury trials to individuals accused of crimes, although the Sixth Amendment provided such a guarantee for those charged with federal crimes. In *Duncan v. Louisiana* (1968), the Court reversed those earlier rulings and extended the guarantee of trial by jury to state criminal defendants.[64] Earlier, in 1965, the Court had applied still another element of the fair trial guarantee to state courts—the right to confront witnesses against oneself.[65]

Fifth Amendment Protections

Few constitutional guarantees have generated as much controversy as the Fifth Amendment right not to be forced to incriminate oneself. One aspect of this right is the right to remain silent when accused and to refuse

CASES INCORPORATING PROVISIONS OF THE BILL OF RIGHTS INTO THE DUE PROCESS CLAUSE OF THE FOURTEENTH AMENDMENT

For more than a century after ratification of the Bill of Rights, the Supreme Court held that its protection of individual rights did not extend to persons threatened by state action. In the early twentieth century, however, the Court on a case-by-case basis began to federalize various of these protections. The justices did so by applying the due process guarantee of the Fourteenth Amendment to those rights deemed to be "fundamental." This process of selective incorporation unfolded over a number of years.

Constitutional Provision	Case
First Amendment	
Freedom of speech and press	*Gitlow v. New York* (1925)
Freedom of assembly	*DeJonge v. Oregon* (1937)
Freedom of petition	*Hague v. CIO* (1939)
Free exercise of religion	*Cantwell v. Connecticut* (1940)
Establishment of religion	*Everson v. Board of Education* (1947)
Fourth Amendment	
Unreasonable search and seizure	*Wolf v. Colorado* (1949)
Exclusionary rule	*Mapp v. Ohio* (1961)
Fifth Amendment	
Compensation for the taking of private property	*Chicago, Burlington and Quincy R. Co. v. Chicago* (1897)
Self-incrimination	*Malloy v. Hogan* (1964)
Double jeopardy	*Benton v. Maryland* (1969)
When jeopardy attaches	*Crist v. Bretz* (1978)
Sixth Amendment	
Public trial	*In re Oliver* (1948)
Due notice	*Cole v. Arkansas* (1948)
Right to counsel (felonies)	*Gideon v. Wainwright* (1963)
Confrontation and cross-examination of adverse witnesses	*Pointer v. Texas* (1965)
Speedy trial	*Klopfer v. North Carolina* (1967)
Compulsory process to obtain witnesses	*Washington v. Texas* (1967)
Jury trial	*Duncan v. Louisiana* (1968)
Right to counsel (misdemeanor when jail is possible)	*Argersinger v. Hamlin* (1972)
Eighth Amendment	
Cruel and unusual punishment	*Louisiana ex rel. Francis v. Resweber* (1947)
Ninth Amendment	
Privacy*	*Griswold v. Connecticut* (1965)

* The word *privacy* does not appear in the Ninth Amendment (or elsewhere in the Constitution). In *Griswold* several members of the Court viewed the Ninth Amendment as guaranteeing (and incorporating) that right.

NOTE: The Court has not incorporated the following provisions: Second Amendment right to keep and bear arms; Third Amendment right against quartering soldiers; Fifth Amendment right to a grand jury hearing; Seventh Amendment right to a jury in civil cases; and Eighth Amendment right against excessive bail and fines.

SOURCES: Lee Epstein and Thomas G. Walker, *Constitutional Law for a Changing America,* 6th ed. (Washington, D.C.: CQ Press, 2007).

to testify in one's own defense. In 1908 the Court held that this privilege was not protected in state proceedings by the due process guarantee. The Court declined to forbid a state judge to comment on a defendant's silence.[66] More than fifty years later, in *Malloy v. Hogan* (1964), the justices extended the Fifth Amendment protection to persons charged with state crimes. The following year the Court held it unfair for a judge or prosecutor to comment adversely during a trial upon a defendant's failure to testify in his or her own behalf.[67] As early as 1936 the Court had begun to use the Fifth Amendment to forbid the use of forced confessions in state trials. That year the Court reversed the murder convictions of three blacks because they were based in part upon confessions extracted from them through torture, a clear denial of due process.[68]

Malloy v. Hogan and *Gideon v. Wainwright* became the foundation for two of the Court's most criticized rulings of the 1960s. In *Escobedo v. Illinois* (1964) the Court ruled that a confession of murder could not be used against Danny Escobedo because it was obtained after intensive police interrogation during which the accused was denied his request to see a lawyer. The confession was obtained in clear violation of his constitutional right to counsel and could not properly be used against him, held the Court.[69] Two years later, with its decision in *Miranda v. Arizona* (1966), the Court kindled further controversy. Applying this "exclusionary rule" against illegally or unconstitutionally obtained evidence, the Court held that confessions could not be used as evidence if they were obtained from suspects interrogated by police without being advised of their rights to remain silent and to obtain legal counsel. In *Miranda* the Court required that police inform individuals who were held in custody of their right to remain silent, that anything they said could be used against them in court, and their right to have assistance of counsel before and during interrogation, even if they could not afford to hire an attorney themselves.[70] Law enforcement officials charged that such decisions made their tasks impossible. Congress considered acting to reverse the rulings, and the decisions were criticized repeatedly during the 1968 presidential campaign.

A less controversial portion of the Fifth Amendment protects people against being tried twice for the same action by the same sovereign. Because the U.S. system includes two systems of justice—one state and one national—everyone is subject to both criminal jurisdictions and may, without violating this guarantee, be tried by both for crimes arising from the same actions.[71] It was not until 1969 that the Court extended the guarantee against double jeopardy to protect defendants from being tried twice by a state for the same actions. Thirty-two years earlier the Court had held that this guarantee did not protect state defendants. In *Palko v. Connecticut* (1937) Justice Benjamin Cardozo explained why the Court viewed some of the guarantees of the Bill of Rights as applicable to the states while others were not. Certain rights, like the right to a jury trial, were valuable, he wrote, yet "they are not of the very essence of a scheme of ordered liberty. To abolish them is not to violate a 'principle of justice so rooted in the traditions and conscience of our people as to be ranked as fundamental.'" Other rights, which are applied to the states through the Fourteenth Amendment, are of such importance, wrote Cardozo, "that neither liberty nor justice would exist if they were sacrificed.…This is true, for illustration, of freedom of thought and speech."[72] In 1969 the Court overruled this holding to the extent that it restricted the double jeopardy guarantee to federal defendants. In *Benton v. Maryland* (1969) the Court held that the guarantee against double jeopardy in state courts was indeed fundamental to the U.S. system of justice.[73]

Unreasonable Search and Seizure

The Fourth Amendment protects citizens from searches and seizures that are unreasonable. In 1949 a Colorado abortionist challenged his state conviction because it was based on records seized from his office by officers acting without a warrant. He won a partial legal victory, but ultimately lost his case. The Supreme Court stated that the Fourth Amendment freedom from unreasonable searches was a necessary part of the concept of "ordered liberty"—to which Justice Cardozo had referred in *Palko*—and therefore was protected by the Fourteenth Amendment against state action.[74] It refused to say that this violation required the exclusion of the evidence.

As early as 1914 the Court had held that evidence obtained in searches violating the Fourth Amendment could not be used in federal courts.[75] In the 1949 state case, however, the Court did not forbid the use of evidence even if it was unconstitutionally obtained. A little more than a decade later, the Court reversed this stance and excluded illegally obtained evidence from use at state trials as well as federal ones. Justice Tom C. Clark explained the Court's opinion in *Mapp v. Ohio* (1961):

> The ignoble shortcut to conviction left open to the State [by the Court's failure to apply the exclusionary rule earlier] tends to destroy the entire system of constitutional restraints on which the liberties of the people rest. Having once recognized that the right to privacy embodied in the Fourth Amendment is enforceable against the States, and that the right to be secure against rude invasions of privacy by state officers is, therefore, constitutional in origin, we can no longer permit that right to remain an empty promise.[76]

The Fourth Amendment forbids only *unreasonable* searches and seizures. A long line of cases raises the question of what is *reasonable* in various circumstances. In 1963 the Court held that the same standards were to be used to judge the reasonableness of searches and seizures by state as well as federal officers.[77] Subsequently, the Court has upheld as reasonable "stop-and-frisk" searches by police, searches of the area within reach of a recently arrested suspect, and certain car searches—all without warrants.[78]

Cruel Punishment

The Eighth Amendment forbids cruel and unusual punishment. In a bizarre Louisiana case, Willie Francis, a convicted murderer, prepared for his death by electrocution, sat in the portable electric chair, heard the switch pulled—and nothing happened. The chair failed to function. Francis was then returned to his cell to await repair of the chair and a second "execution." In the meantime, he challenged this "sentence" as cruel and unusual punishment. The Supreme Court

assumed, but did not actually rule, that the Eighth Amendment applied to the states, but even if that standard applied, the justices found that it had not been violated in Francis's case.[79] In 1962 the Court directly applied this prohibition to the states, striking down a California law that made drug addiction a crime.[80]

During the 1970s the Court considered two sets of cases challenging the death penalty as cruel and unusual—and unconstitutional—punishment. In the first set, decided in 1972, the Court effectively invalidated all existing capital punishment laws by holding that the procedures they provided to guide judges and juries imposing the death sentence violated due process. The procedures left so much discretion to the judge or jury imposing the sentence, held the Court, that the result was a system under which receiving a death sentence was as arbitrary and irrational as being struck by lightning.[81] Four years later the Court held that death, in and of itself, was not an unconstitutionally cruel and unusual punishment for those convicted of first-degree murder, but it did strike down laws that made death the mandatory sentence for someone convicted of first-degree murder. The due process guarantee, the Court held, required individualized consideration of a crime and the criminal before such a final sentence could be imposed.[82]

The Court has found it difficult to resolve some state penalties as measured against the ban on cruel and unusual punishment. In 1980 it voted 5-4 to permit a state to impose a mandatory life sentence upon a man convicted of three relatively petty nonviolent crimes.[83] But in 1983 the Court, again 5-4, reversed its earlier holding. In *Solem v. Helm* the Court held that South Dakota had violated this ban by imposing a life sentence without parole on a man convicted on seven separate occasions of nonviolent felonies.[84]

Juvenile Rights

The Court also has extended certain of the guarantees of the Bill of Rights to juvenile court proceedings, including the right of a juvenile to be notified of charges against him, to have the aid of counsel, to confront witnesses against him, to be informed of his right to remain silent, and to be found guilty—or delinquent—beyond a reasonable doubt. The Court has refused, however, to extend the right to a jury trial to juvenile court proceedings, which by their nature are less formal than regular criminal court proceedings. To require a jury trial, the Court reasoned, would unnecessarily rigidify and formalize the operations of the juvenile courts. In one ruling concerning state power to deal with juveniles accused of crimes, the Court upheld a New York law permitting pretrial detention of juveniles when there is a high risk that they may commit serious crimes before trial.[85]

EQUAL PROTECTION GUARANTEE

For the first seventy years after it became a part of the Constitution, the Fourteenth Amendment's guarantee of equal protection of the laws seemed useless. Despite it, the Court steadfastly upheld the "separate but equal" segregation codes of the southern states, and in only one of the first ten cases brought under this provision, did a challenge to a state law succeed.[86] Not until 1938 did the Court begin reexamining segregation laws with an eye to the equality they were supposed to preserve, and not until the civil rights revolution of the 1950s and 1960s did the Equal Protection Clause take on the meaning its authors had intended.

Voting Rights

The right to vote—for which the Court had provided only narrow federal protection under the Fifteenth Amendment—was brought within the protection of the Fourteenth Amendment by a series of rulings culminating in the Court's famous "one person, one vote" edict of 1964.

White Primaries

Before the Court addressed directly the issue of malapportionment, it confronted one of the most effective discriminatory electoral devices—the white primary. In a campaign spending case decided in 1921, the Court appeared to limit federal regulation of elections to the final general election of an officer, excluding any regulation of primary contests.[87] With this understanding, many states in the South felt free to forbid

blacks to vote in Democratic primaries, which in most of the South were the actual election because of little or no Republican opposition to Democratic nominees.

The first time a white primary law came before the bench, in 1927, the Court struck it down as a clear violation of the equal protection guarantee.[88] Texas, the state involved in that case, next passed a law empowering the state's political parties to set qualifications for primary voters. The Democratic Party then exercised that power to exclude blacks from eligibility as primary voters. (The party established a private club to decide its candidate, and only whites could belong to the club.) In 1932 the Court held that law unconstitutional. Because the party had acted as the agent of the state, it held, the party's action fell under the Equal Protection Clause with which it clearly conflicted.[89] Persisting in its effort to keep black voters from participating in its electoral processes, the Texas Democratic Party then voted to confine party membership to whites. Without a connection to the state in this case, the Supreme Court upheld the exclusion in *Grovey v. Townsend* (1935).[90]

This form of discrimination did not survive for long. In 1941 the Court held that primary elections were, in many states, an integral part of the process of electing members of Congress. Therefore, Congress had the authority to regulate such primaries. Three years later, in *Smith v. Allwright* (1944), the Court reversed *Grovey*. It redefined state action to include political parties that followed state regulation of primary elections, thereby making the parties state agencies in that respect. Racial discrimination by political parties in primary voting came under the ban of the Fifteenth Amendment.[91]

Poll Taxes and Literacy Tests

In the late nineteenth century the Court had upheld the use of a poll tax and an "understanding," or literacy test, to screen out persons it considered too incompetent to vote. In 1964, after such devices had been abandoned by most states, the Twenty-fourth Amendment was added to the Constitution to prohibit the use of poll taxes to abridge the right to vote in federal elections. In 1966 the Court struck down poll tax requirements for state elections, finding them a violation of the equal protection guarantee.[92]

Voting Rights Act

The continuing success of many southern states in keeping black citizens from voting moved Congress during the 1950s and 1960s to enact progressively stronger civil rights laws authorizing federal action to counter such obstruction. By 1965, however, the lack of success of these new laws—coupled with the brutal response in the South to black demonstrations for equal rights—made it clear that Congress must act forcefully.

The result was the Voting Rights Act of 1965, which prohibited the use of any test or device as a qualification for voting in any state where less than half the voting age population was registered—or voted—at the time of the 1964 presidential election. That test applied the act to six southern states and a number of counties in other states. South Carolina, one of the affected states, immediately challenged the act as a violation of the Tenth Amendment, which reserves to the states any powers not delegated to the United States—in this case the power to set voter qualifications. A three-judge federal court agreed with the state, but the Supreme Court did not. The justices upheld the law as an appropriate exercise of congressional power to enforce the Fifteenth Amendment.[93]

Reapportionment Revolution

The most far-reaching extension of Supreme Court power into state affairs mandated under Chief Justice Earl Warren involved the Court's reapportionment rulings. In 1962 the Court ended years of abstention from the sensitive political issue of redistricting and reapportionment and agreed to assess the fairness of congressional and state legislative district lines. Only sixteen years earlier, in *Colegrove v. Green* (1946), the Court had refused to intervene in such matters, despite enormous disparity in population between state electoral districts. Justice Felix Frankfurter had explained:

> From the determination of such issues this Court has traditionally held aloof. It is hostile to a democratic system to involve the judiciary in the politics of the people....Courts ought not to enter this political thicket. The remedy for unfairness in districting is to

secure State legislatures that will apportion properly, or to invoke the ample powers of Congress.[94]

Less than twenty years later, however, the Court reversed that holding to rule that challenges to the fairness of the apportionment of state legislatures were, in fact, proper matters for the federal courts to resolve. In the landmark *Baker v. Carr* (1962) the Court directed a lower federal court to hear the challenge of certain Tennessee voters that the malapportionment of the state legislature denied them equal protection of laws under the Fourteenth Amendment. At that time the Tennessee legislature had not been reapportioned for more than sixty years, during which substantial shifts in population had occurred, chiefly from rural areas to urban areas. Writing for the Court, Justice William J. Brennan Jr. reviewed the history of the "political question" doctrine of judicial restraint. He concluded that the equal protection claim here did not require a decision of any truly political question and that the case was not removed from the purview of federal courts by the fact that it affected state government. "The right asserted is within the reach of judicial protection under the Fourteenth Amendment," he stated.[95]

One Person, One Vote

The following year the Court struck down Georgia's county system of electing state officials and set out the guidelines for the fair apportionment of legislative representation:

> Once the geographical unit for which a representative is to be chosen is designated, all who participate in the election are to have an equal vote—whatever their race, whatever their sex, whatever their occupation, whatever their income and wherever their home may be in that geographical unit. This is required by the Equal Protection Clause of the Fourteenth Amendment.[96]

Writing for the Court, Justice William O. Douglas concluded with the following statement:

> The conception of political equality from the Declaration of Independence, to Lincoln's Gettysburg Address, to the Fifteenth, Seventeenth, and Nineteenth

Amendments can mean only one thing—one person, one vote.[97]

The following year this standard was applied by the Court to require congressional redistricting and state legislative reapportionment.[98] Although in subsequent cases the Court set the strict rule of mathematical equality for newly drawn districts, it relaxed that standard in 1973 for state legislative districts, approving the creation of districts that were "as nearly of equal population as practicable" and allowing some legitimately based divergence from strict equality.[99]

Gerrymandering

The Court had no trouble concluding that drawing an electoral district along racial lines violated the Equal Protection Clause. In 1960 the Court in *Gomillion v. Lightfoot* unanimously struck down an effort by white officials to draw boundaries in Tuskegee, Alabama, so as to exclude black voters.[100] This decision led to additional rulings that protected blacks from having their voting power diluted through gerrymandering schemes. In 1993, however, the Court applied the same logic to rule that districts drawn to favor blacks were also unconstitutional. In *Shaw v. Reno* a five-justice majority set the stage for striking down oddly shaped districts that were drawn for the purpose of electing a black candidate.[101]

But the Court was unable to devise a formula for halting partisan gerrymandering, the practice of drawing district lines to favor one political party over the other. The one person, one vote rule set by the Court requires most states to redraw their electoral districts each decade to reflect the population changes shown by the census. When one party has control of the legislature, its leaders are inclined to draw the districts in a way that gives their party an edge in electing more of its candidates. One way to achieve this goal is to concentrate the voters who favor the opposite party into just a few districts. The results seem to defy the principle of equal treatment and the one person, one vote principle. In some elections, a party's deft use of gerrymandering allowed it to capture more than two-thirds of the congressional seats while winning only half of the votes statewide.

In the late 1980s the Court opened the door to challenging partisan gerrymanders as unconstitutional. In a case from Indiana, *Davis v. Bandemer* (1986), the Court responded to a challenge by the state's Democrats to a map of state legislative districts drawn by Republicans. For the first time the Court held that political gerrymanders were subject to review by the federal courts, even if they met the one person, one vote test.[102]

But these challenges ultimately proved fruitless. In all but a few states, politicians are charged with drawing the districts, and the justices concluded they could not determine when a line-drawing decision was so unfair as to be unconstitutional. In 2004 the Court in a 5-4 decision rejected a challenge to a Republican-drawn plan in Pennsylvania that helped GOP candidates win most of that state's congressional seats.[103] And in 2006 the Court rejected the Democrats' challenge to another GOP plan, this one from Texas.[104]

Housing, Schools, and Marriage

Even before the Court began to wield the Equal Protection Clause in behalf of voters, it had used it to strike down the racial segregation that had come to characterize so many parts of American life after the Civil War. As early as 1917 the Court made its first move against housing segregation. In that year it struck down a Louisville, Kentucky, residential segregation ordinance as an unconstitutional interference with the right of a property owner to sell his real estate to whomever he pleased.[105] What could not be accomplished legally by city action, however, could be achieved by private agreement, so "restrictive covenants" flourished through which a purchaser accepting a contract or title agreed not to sell the real estate to a black person. This maneuver was clearly a private action—and unreachable under the Fourteenth Amendment—according to the ruling in the *Civil Rights Cases*. Yet, in 1948 the Court effectively circumvented this "private action" limitation by holding that any state action to enforce such a covenant would violate the Fourteenth Amendment.[106] In subsequent rulings the Court held that state voters could not amend their constitution to restrict the efforts of state or local government to end racial discrimination nor could they require that all fair housing laws be approved by referendum. Where discrimination is not clearly based on race, however, the Court has hesitated to strike down such voter-approved requirements or to overturn local decisions concerning housing.[107]

Early in the twentieth century the Court had extended its tolerance of segregation, signaled by the "separate but equal" holding of *Plessy v. Ferguson* (1896), to schools, by upholding a Kentucky law forbidding colleges to teach whites and blacks at the same time and in the same place.[108] School segregation began to come under scrutiny by the Supreme Court in the 1930s, beginning at the graduate school level. In 1938 the Court held that a state providing graduate education in law to white students must, under the equal protection guarantee, offer substantially similar education to black state residents. The Court rejected the state's offer to pay a black student's tuition in an out-of-state law school. The state was obligated, held the Court in *Missouri ex rel. Gaines v. Canada* (1938) to provide equal protection within its own borders. Chief Justice Charles Evans Hughes wrote,

> That obligation is imposed by the Constitution upon the States severally as governmental entities,— each responsible for its own laws establishing the rights and duties of persons within its borders. It is an obligation the burden of which cannot be cast by one State upon another....That separate responsibility of each State within its own sphere is of the essence of statehood.[109]

This holding was reaffirmed in 1948, and in 1950 the Court struck down one state university's practice of making a black graduate student sit at a special seat and table in classrooms, the cafeteria, and the library.[110] Also in 1950 the Court ordered the University of Texas Law School to admit a qualified black student. The newly created "black" law school in the state did not provide equal opportunity for a legal education, held the Court. In *Sweatt v. Painter* (1950) the justices ruled that a qualified black student had a constitutional right to a state-provided legal education equal to that offered to qualified white students.[111] Then, four years later, the Court extended this principle to elementary and secondary education with the famous decisions known as

Brown v. Board of Education of Topeka (1954).[112] The separate but equal doctrine as applied to public schools was ruled a clear denial of equal protection of the laws. *Plessy v. Ferguson* was thereby overruled.

The southern states reacted belligerently to the *Brown* decision. The following year, in the second *Brown* decision, the Court required states to move with "all deliberate speed" to carry out the mandate to end public school segregation.[113] Implementation, however, was slow and painful, continuing for decades after the ruling. In a long line of follow-up rulings, the Court steadfastly rejected state and local efforts to obstruct or circumvent its requirements and made clear that it would sanction substantial changes in and costs to a school system as the price for carrying out the edict of *Brown*. Although *Brown*, decided upon an equal protection basis, dealt with states where segregated schools had been required by law, the Court did not hesitate to require an end to public school segregation in states that had not passed such laws.[114] In still another use of the Equal Protection Clause to end state discrimination, the Court in 1967 held that the Fourteenth Amendment guarantee was violated by a state law that prohibited persons of different races to marry.[115]

Rich and Poor

The Fourteenth Amendment provision that states may not deny a person equal protection of the laws could be read to forbid states from meting out any type of unequal treatment under law, but Reconstruction-era history makes clear that its sponsors sought to prevent blatant mistreatment of blacks. For that reason, the justices have wielded the Equal Protection Clause to forbid state discrimination based on race, but have been far more reluctant to strike down laws that discriminate against persons based on their economic status, including state programs that disproportionately affect the poor.

Funding for Education

A pivotal decision came in 1973, when the Court refused to strike down a Texas school funding system even though the schools in poor neighborhoods received only about half as much funding per student as those in more affluent communities. Texas, like most states, relies heavily on property taxes to support the public schools, which creates systematic inequalities. School reformers insisted that funding must be made more equal. At the same time, federal judges pressed for racial desegregation of the public schools based on earlier directives from the Supreme Court. Wary of the burden of policing school funding as well, the Court, in a 5-4 vote in *San Antonio School District v. Rodriquez* (1973), announced that it would not intervene in disputes over how public education is funded. "We are unwilling to assume for ourselves a level of wisdom superior to that of legislators, scholars and educational authorities in 50 states," said Justice Lewis F. Powell, himself a former school board president in Richmond, Virginia. "Education, of course, is not among the rights afforded explicit protection under our Federal Constitution," he said, nor is the Texas system of school funding "the product of purposeful discrimination against any group or class." Therefore, "fundamental reforms with respect to state taxation and education are matters reserved for the legislative process of the different states," Powell wrote.[116]

Fifteen years later, the Court reaffirmed its view that states need not guarantee absolute equality in the use of public schools. North Dakota allowed its schools to charge families a fee for the use of school buses, and a rural, low-income family said this cost made schooling prohibitively expensive. Paula Kadrmas brought a suit on behalf of her daughter Sarita on the grounds that, as the Court said, the "busing fee unconstitutionally places a greater obstacle to education in the path of the poor than it does in the path of wealthier families."[117] In a 5-4 decision in *Kadrmas v. Dickinson Public Schools* (1988) the Court reiterated that equal access to education is not a fundamental right.

Migration and Welfare

The Court has, however, voided state laws that discriminate against poor people who move into the state. In 1941 the Court struck down a depression-era law that made it a crime to bring "an indigent person" into California.[118] The petitioner, Fred Edwards, had picked up his wife's brother in Texas and brought him to their hometown of Marysville, California. The brother-in-law had $20 when the trip began, but the money was

spent by the time the two arrived in California. On that basis, Edwards was charged with violating California law. The law was struck down on the grounds it "imposes an unconstitutional burden upon interstate commerce." Justice Douglas, joined by two others, set out the view that "the right of free movement [within the nation] is a right of national citizenship" that cannot be taken away by a state.[119] The Court later used the same right-to-travel rationale to strike down state laws denying welfare benefits or medical care to poor persons new to the state.[120]

In the 1990s California lawmakers worried that the Golden State's generous welfare benefits acted as a "magnet" to draw poor persons, so they enacted a new two-tiered system. New residents for their first year in California would be paid the same level of welfare benefits as they would have received in the state they had left. The difference was substantial. A newcomer from Louisiana would receive $190 per month for a family of three, rather than $641 as a full-fledged Californian. The Court struck down the California law in 1999. "Citizens of the United States, whether rich or poor, have the right to choose to be citizens of the state where they reside. The States, however, do not have any right to select their citizens," said Justice John Paul Stevens for the 7-2 majority in *Saenz v. Roe* (1999).[121] His opinion was notable as the first in decades to rely on the largely ignored Privileges and Immunities Clause of the Fourteenth Amendment, which states, "No State shall make or enforce any law which shall abridge the privileges and immunities of citizens of the United States."

Shortly after ratification of the Fourteenth Amendment, the Court had sapped this clause of meaning by ruling that it referred only to particularly national privileges, such as traveling on the high seas. Stevens gave it new meaning: "What is at issue in this case," he said, "is the right of the newly arrived citizen to the same privileges and immunities enjoyed by other citizens of the same State." The two women who challenged the two-tiered system of welfare benefits were California residents, and, Stevens said, a state may not "discriminate among its own citizens on the basis of their prior residence."[122] In a brief aside, Stevens added that the welfare ruling did not undercut state laws that deny newcomers the lower in-state rates for college tuition. States may set new-resident rules for those who come to "acquire some readily portable benefit, such as a divorce or a college education," he said.[123] Most states forbid newcomers from obtaining in-state tuition rates for their public colleges until they have lived there for at least a year.

Court Fees

The Court has struck down measures that discriminate against the poor in several other areas. It has held that the equal protection guarantee forbids states to deny divorces to people too poor to pay the usual court fees. In the area of criminal law, states cannot require poor people to stay in prison to "work off" a fine they cannot pay while releasing others who can pay. The Court has ruled that a state must provide a lawyer for any person who is charged with an offense that could send him to prison but is too poor to pay for a lawyer. A poor defendant is also entitled to a free transcript of his trial when an official record of the proceeding is necessary for an appeal.[124] The Court has usually been unwilling to waive states' fees for indigent persons who bring a civil suit, but there was one exception to that rule in 1996, when a mother sought to appeal the loss of her children. The ex-husband of Melissa L. Brooks had custody of their two children, and after he remarried, he went to court in Mississippi to have his new wife adopt the children and to have the parental rights of their natural mother terminated. A judge granted the order, and when Brooks tried to appeal, the state court said she must first pay $2,352 in fees for transcripts. Brooks, working as a waitress and earning less than $3 an hour, said she could not afford the amount. Mississippi was one of the few states that refused to waive fees for the poor.

The Supreme Court took up her case and ruled that the state must waive its fees in cases so fundamental as one that would decide whether a mother could see her children again. "Parental termination decrees work a unique kind of deprivation," said Justice Ruth Bader Ginsburg for a 6-3 majority. They "involve the awesome authority of the State to destroy permanently all legal recognition of the parental relationship."[125]

The Rights of Aliens

The only successful equal protection challenge among the first cases brought to the Supreme Court in the decade after the Fourteenth Amendment was added to the Constitution involved the rights of aliens. Yick Wo, a Chinese resident of San Francisco, was denied the license necessary to run a laundry in the city, as were all other Chinese residents. Although the license requirement was superficially nondiscriminatory, it obviously was enforced in such a way as to deny equal protection. The Supreme Court struck it down in 1886. The Court, out of respect for a state's right to control property and resources within its territory, has, however, upheld state laws requiring that all persons working on its public works projects be citizens and denying to aliens ineligible to become citizens the right to acquire certain state land.[126]

The Court has never given a state carte blanche to discriminate against lawfully admitted aliens.[127] In 1915 the Court used the equal protection guarantee to void an Arizona law requiring that employers hire four citizens for every alien employed.[128] In 1948 the Court struck down a California law that denied aliens ineligible for citizenship the right to obtain the licenses necessary to earn a living as commercial fishermen. The guarantee of equal protection, stated the Court, meant that "all persons lawfully in this country shall abide 'in any state' on an equality of legal privileges with all citizens under nondiscriminatory law." A state cannot deny aliens the right to earn a living in the same way that citizens do.[129] Also in 1948 another California law fell before an equal protection challenge from aliens. That law—intended to prevent alien parents from buying land through their native-born children, that is, citizens—forbade ineligible aliens to pay for land being sold to a citizen.[130]

In the 1970s the Court further expanded the rights of aliens, in some instances allowing them to receive benefits provided by a state. The justices held that states could not deny resident aliens welfare benefits, the right to practice law in the state, or the right to be considered for state civil service jobs. In 1977 the Court held that a state could not exclude resident aliens from eligibility for state scholarships, but in the next two years it upheld

New York laws requiring state police officers and public school teachers to be citizens.[131] In another case, Texas, which had won the right to maintain a school funding system based on wildly unequal property taxes, lost its bid to deny free public schooling to the children of illegal immigrants. In *Plyler v. Doe* (1982) the Court ruled unconstitutional such state discrimination against the children of illegal immigrants. "Aliens, even aliens whose presence in this country is unlawful, have long been recognized as 'persons' guaranteed due process of law," wrote Justice Brennan for the 5-4 majority. He conceded that education is not a fundamental right, but "it can hardly be argued rationally that anyone benefits from the creation within our borders of a sub-class of illiterate persons."[132]

Women's Rights

Women as a class have been the least successful of the plaintiffs under the Equal Protection Clause. Efforts to use other portions of the Fourteenth Amendment to challenge state refusals to admit women to the practice of law or to register women to vote were rejected by the Court in the nineteenth century. In 1904 the Court not only rejected an equal protection challenge to a state law forbidding women to work in saloons, but went on to hold that a state could by law bar women from even entering such places.[133] As recently as 1948, the Court again upheld a state law forbidding women to work as barmaids, unless they were married to or the child of the bar owner.[134] In short, gender was considered a valid reason for state discrimination. In 1961 the Court upheld a Florida law that "exempted" women from jury duty on the basis of their function as "the center of home and family life."[135]

In 1971 the Court began to apply the equal protection test more strictly against state laws that discriminated simply on the basis of gender. In a case involving the appointment of an executor for a deceased child, the Court struck down an Idaho law that gave preference to male relatives over female relatives in selecting among equally qualified executors. "To give mandatory preference to members of either sex over members of the other, merely to accomplish the elimination of hearing on the merits, is to make the very kind of arbitrary legislative choice forbidden by the Equal Protection Clause," wrote Chief Justice Warren E. Burger for the Court.[136] Four years later, in 1975, the Court overruled its 1961 decision concerning women and jury duty, holding that state laws exempting women from jury duty violated the requirement that a jury be drawn from a fair cross-section of the community. Such a general exclusion of women from the group eligible for jury duty was not rational, held the Court.[137] Also in 1975 the Court overturned a Utah law that set different ages at which men and women were considered adults. In 1976 it struck down an Oklahoma law setting different drinking ages for men and women, and in 1977 an Alabama law which, by setting minimum height and weight requirements for prison guards, effectively denied such jobs to most women in the state.[138]

In the Court's important gender bias rulings of the last decades of the twentieth century, the justices did not adopt the stiff standard for testing sex discrimination by states that it used to judge race discrimination. States merely had to prove that laws discriminating on the basis of sex were reasonable and related to the achievement of important governmental goals. A law discriminating on the basis of race, however, would be held constitutional only if it was found necessary to serve a compelling state interest. Furthermore, the Court still allowed some vestiges of the view that women should be protected. In 1974, with Justice Douglas, a liberal, writing the opinion, the Court upheld a Florida law giving widows—but not widowers—a special property tax exemption.[139] Three years later, after striking down the height and weight requirements for prison guards in Alabama, the Court upheld a state regulation excluding women from certain prison guard jobs, saying that their sex made them vulnerable to attack in all-male prisons and therefore disqualified them for the job of preserving security there.[140] The Court also was reluctant to make states revise their disability insurance programs to include coverage for pregnant women unable to work for a time during or after pregnancy and childbirth. The decision to exclude women in this category from coverage of an otherwise comprehensive plan was upheld by the Court as rational in light of the state's fiscal objectives.[141]

In the late twentieth century this area of the law was still evolving. Justice Ginsburg, who as a lawyer had urged the Court to be more aggressive in its scrutiny of gender classifications, wrote in 1994, "[E]ven under the Court's equal protection jurisprudence, which requires 'an exceedingly persuasive justification,' it remains an open question whether 'classifications based upon gender are inherently suspect.'"[142] In 1996 Ginsburg was the author of a decision against the men-only admissions policy of the state-funded Virginia Military Institute. Although Ginsburg used "intermediate," rather than "strict," scrutiny—which was likely to win support from a majority of justices—she again emphasized that a state must show an "exceedingly persuasive justification" for any classification based on sex.[143]

This opinion did not hold that gender never can be considered when decisions are made by state or local governments, but it made clear that excluding women or girls from an opportunity available to men or boys can rarely, if ever, be justified. The success of the Court's effort to remove gender classifications from the law can be measured by what happened in the years afterward. Constitutional disputes over sexist state laws virtually disappeared from the Court's docket.

The State as Sovereign

During the twentieth century, power in government seemed to flow in one direction: toward Washington. The Great Depression and Franklin D. Roosevelt's New Deal put the federal government in the lead in reviving the economy and protecting workers and their families. World War II and the cold war thrust the United States into the role of world power. The civil rights movement in the South, stonewalled by segregationist state policies, carried its campaign for change to Washington. By the mid-1960s President Lyndon B. Johnson's Great Society programs had put the federal government in the forefront of funding schools and colleges and subsidizing medical care for the poor and the elderly. What then was left of the eighteenth-century vision that animated the Constitution's plan of government in which the states played the more central role in the daily lives of the people?

On many occasions and in several eras, the justices of the Supreme Court have stood in the path of on-rushing history and said "Stop," then proceeding to make decisions based on the Constitution's original vision of sovereign states standing on equal footing with a strong but limited federal government. "Federalism was our Nation's discovery. The Framers split the atom of sovereignty," Justice Anthony M. Kennedy wrote in 1995. "It was the genius of their idea that our citizens would have two political capacities, one state and one federal, each protected from incursion by the other."[1] The states are not "relegated to the role of mere provinces or political corporations, but retain the dignity, though not the full authority, of sovereignty."[2] Kennedy and his colleagues insisted that their shielding of the states from an all-powerful federal government was faithful to the words of James Madison, the leading author of the Constitution.

RESERVED STATE POWERS

The well-founded fear of the original thirteen states that a strong national government would limit their power and sovereignty was a major obstacle to ratification of the Constitution. Madison, writing in the *Federalist Papers,* attempted to calm such fears:

> The powers delegated by the proposed Constitution to the federal government are few and defined. Those which are to remain in the State governments are numerous and indefinite. The former will be exercised principally on external objects, as war, peace, negotiation, and foreign commerce; with which last the power of taxation will, for the most part, be connected. The powers reserved to the several States will extend to all the objects which, in the ordinary course of affairs, concern the lives, liberties, and properties of the people, and the internal order, improvement and prosperity of the State.[3]

To write this view into the Constitution, the first Congress approved the Tenth Amendment, which states, "The powers not delegated to the United States by the Constitution, nor prohibited by it to the States, are reserved to the States respectively, or to the people." In an action that would gain significance over the years, Congress, before approving this provision, rejected an amendment that would have inserted the word "expressly" before the word "delegated." Such an insertion, if approved, would have severely limited—or altogether prevented—any expansion of national power through the doctrine of implied powers. Until well into the twentieth century, the Tenth Amendment was wielded, with varying degrees of success, to curtail federal power, particularly federal power over the economy in areas claimed to be reserved for state regulation. The "reserved" subjects ranged from child labor to farm production.

ACTS VOIDED AS IMPINGING STATE POWERS

Of the 162 acts of Congress struck down by the Supreme Court during the past two hundred plus years, many were found invalid because Congress had reached too far into matters that were left to the states to regulate. The following, in reverse chronological order, are among the invalidated laws.

- *Board of Trustees of Univ. of Alabama v. Garrett,* 531 U.S. 356 (2001) – The Americans with Disabilities Act permits employees, including state workers, to sue if they are discriminated against because of disability.
- *Kimel v. Florida Board of Regents,* 528 U.S. 62 (2000) – The Age Discrimination in Employment Act permits employees, including state workers, to sue if they are discriminated against because of their age.
- *Printz v. United States,* 521 U.S. 898 (1997) – The Brady Handgun Control Act, which forbids gun purchases by felons, required state and local law enforcement officials to conduct background checks.
- *United States v. Lopez,* 514 U.S. 549 (1995) – The Gun-Free School Zones Act of 1990, which banned the possession of guns within 1,000 feet of local public schools.
- *New York v. United States,* 488 U.S. 1041 (1992) – The Low-Level Radioactive Waste Policy Amendments Act of 1985 insofar as it required a state that failed to provide for the disposal of radioactive waste generated within its borders to become the legal owner of the waste and assume liability for any injuries caused by it.
- *National League of Cities v. Usery,* 426 U.S. 833 (1976) – The Fair Labor Standards Act, as amended, to extend minimum wage and overtime provisions to employees of state and local governments.
- *Oregon v. Mitchell,* 400 U.S. 112 (1970) – The Voting Rights Act Amendments of 1970 insofar as they reduced to eighteen the voting age for state and local elections as well as federal elections; this change subsequently was made through the Twenty-sixth Amendment.
- *Ashton v. Cameron County District,* 298 U.S. 513 (1936) – The first Municipal Bankruptcy Act of the New Deal, which provided for the readjustment of municipal indebtedness; the Court later approved a revised version of this law.
- *Carter v. Carter Coal Company,* 298 U.S. 238 (1936) – The first Bituminous Coal Conservation Act to regulate the mining industry, a matter left until that time entirely to the states; the Court later approved a revised coal industry regulation law.
- *United States v. Butler,* 297 U.S. 1 (1936) – The New Deal's first Agricultural Adjustment Act regulating agricultural production, a matter previously left entirely to the states; the Court later approved a revised Agricultural Adjustment Act.
- *Hopkins Savings Assn. v. Cleary,* 296 U.S. 315 (1935) – The Home Owners' Loan Act of the New Deal insofar as it provided for the conversion of state building and loan associations into federal associations.
- *Washington v. Dawson & Co.,* 264 U.S. 219 (1924) – The Court struck down a second effort by Congress to delegate to states the power of setting maritime workers' rights and remedies in terms of workmen's compensation. See below, *Knickerbocker Ice Co. v. Stewart* (1920).

The first effort before the Court to use the Tenth Amendment to curtail federal power was a distinct failure. Maryland based its challenge to the Second Bank of the United States upon the argument that the Constitution did not grant Congress the power to create corporations and that the Tenth Amendment thereby reserved such power to the states. Maryland further argued that if Congress had the right to create the bank, the power of taxation reserved to the states—excluding taxes on imports and exports—gave the states the right to tax the bank. Speaking for the Court, Chief Justice John Marshall in *McCulloch v. Maryland* (1819) firmly rejected both prongs of the state's argument and the concept that the Tenth Amendment provided the states with an instrument to limit national power. "[T]he states have no power, by taxation or otherwise, to retard, impede, burden, or in any manner control the operations of the constitutional laws enacted by Congress to carry into execution the powers vested in the general government," Marshall wrote. The absence of the word *expressly* from the amendment left it up to the Court to decide if a particular power had been granted the national government, a decision to be made in light of its interpretation of the constitutional system as a whole.[4] Five years later, in *Gibbons v. Ogden* (1824), the New York steamboat case, Marshall felt it necessary in concluding his opinion to issue a further warning against a broad interpretation of the Tenth Amendment:

•*Bailey v. Drexel Furniture Co.,* 259 U.S. 20 (1922) – The Child Labor Tax Act of 1919, which sought to prohibit the employment of children under a certain age in manufacturing.

•*Hill v. Wallace,* 259 U.S. 44 (1922) – The Futures Trading Act, which taxed sales of grain for future delivery, a matter not deemed interstate commerce by the Court.

•*Newberry v. United States,* 256 U.S. 232 (1921) – The Federal Corrupt Practices Act insofar as it limited the spending of a senatorial candidate in a primary campaign; this ruling, limiting federal power over elections to the general elections alone, was later overruled.

•*Knickerbocker Ice Co. v. Stewart,* 253 U.S. 149 (1920) – Congress could not delegate to states the power of setting maritime workers' rights and remedies in terms of workmen's compensation; this delegation, held the Court, defeated the need (and the constitutional intention) of a uniform maritime law.

•*Hammer v. Dagenhart,* 247 U.S. 251 (1918) – The Child Labor Law of 1916, which sought to prohibit the employment of children under a certain age in manufacturing.

•*Coyle v. Smith,* 221 U.S. 559 (1911) – The Oklahoma Enabling Act, which conditioned the admission of Oklahoma to the Union in part on the requirement that its state capital should not be moved before 1913; such a decision was left to the discretion of other states, held the Court, and to impose that condition upon Oklahoma's admission to the Union placed it on an unequal footing with the other states.

•*Keller v. United States,* 213 U.S. 138 (1909) – The Immigration Act of 1907 insofar as it penalized the harboring of a prostitute who was an alien; the Court held that once aliens are admitted to the country, control over such matters passed to the states.

•*The Employers' Liability Cases,* 207 U.S. 463 (1908) – The Federal Employers' Liability Act, which regulated the liability of common carriers operating intrastate as well as interstate; the Court later upheld a similar law applying only to interstate carriers.

•*Civil Rights Cases,* 109 U.S. 3 (1883) – The Civil Rights Act of 1875 insofar as it penalized individuals who denied equal access to blacks seeking entry to public accommodations.

•*Trademark Cases,* 100 U.S. 82 (1879) – The original trademark law applying to trademarks for exclusive use within the United States, which, the Court found, applied to intrastate as well as interstate commerce.

•*Collector v. Day,* 11 Wall. (78 U.S.) 113 (1871) and *United States v. Baltimore & O. R. Co.,* 17 Wall. (84 U.S.) 322 (1873) – The Court held that the federal income tax law was void insofar as it applied to the salaries of state officials and that a city—as an agent of the state—was exempt from federal taxes on the interest paid on municipal bonds; the first ruling was later overturned by the Court.

•*United States v. DeWitt,* 9 Wall. (76 U.S.) 41 (1870) – The Internal Revenue Act of 1867 insofar as it banned the sale of illuminating oil within a state if it was flammable at too low a temperature; this was simply a police regulation, held the Court, and should be left to state officials.

Powerful and ingenious minds, taking as postulates, that the powers expressly granted to the government of the Union are to be contracted…into the narrowest possible compass, and that the original powers of the States are retained, if any possible construction will retain them, may…explain away the constitution…and leave it a magnificent structure indeed, to look at, but totally unfit for use.[5]

Dual Federalism

During the tenure of Marshall's successor, Chief Justice Roger B. Taney, Tenth Amendment arguments received a friendlier hearing, and the Court began to develop the concept of dual federalism. In this view, the respective domains of state and federal government are neatly defined: each government is sovereign and supreme within its own sphere, and the enumerated powers of the central government are limited by the reserved powers of the state. During a laissez-faire period, in the early part of the twentieth century, the Court used the Tenth Amendment to limit federal power, even while it used the concept of due process to limit state power to regulate property, thus creating a "twilight zone" within the economy where no effective regulation existed. During this time the Court wielded the Tenth Amendment to restrict the reach of federal antitrust laws, to nullify federal efforts to limit or prohibit child labor, and to strike down major New Deal programs intended to regulate agriculture, aid bankrupt cities, and restore order to the coal industry.[6]

In the child labor and agriculture cases, in particular, the Court essentially did what the first Congress had refused to do—insert the word *expressly* into the Tenth Amendment to qualify the enumerated powers of the federal government. Justice Owen J. Roberts wrote in 1936,

> From the accepted doctrine that the United States is a government of delegated powers, it follows that those not expressly granted or reasonably to be implied from such as are conferred, are reserved to the states or to the people. To forestall any suggestion to the contrary, the Tenth Amendment was adopted. The same proposition, otherwise stated, is that powers not granted are prohibited.[7]

Yet, the laissez-faire Court was not consistent in its application of the reserved powers doctrine. During the early part of the century, it rejected Tenth Amendment challenges to the exercise of the federal police power over lotteries, prostitution, colored oleo, and the repeal of Prohibition.[8] Its insistence on Tenth Amendment restrictions on national power in the 1930s provoked Roosevelt's "Court-packing" plan, and soon thereafter the dual federalism concept and the reserved powers doctrine both were discarded by the Court's majority. In 1937 the Court rebuffed a Tenth Amendment challenge to the Social Security Act as intruding upon the powers of the states. In its opinion, Justice Benjamin Cardozo acknowledged that changing economic and political facts made it necessary now for the national government to assume functions once considered the proper responsibility of state and local authority. The Court subsequently approved new versions of the agriculture, coal, and bankruptcy legislation that it had struck down just a few years earlier as intruding upon the reserved powers of the states.[9]

Cooperative Federalism

The Court formally interred the Tenth Amendment with its decision in *United States v. Darby Lumber Co.*

(1941) upholding the Fair Labor Standards Act, which, among other provisions, prohibited child labor. Finding the act constitutional as it extended federal regulation over working conditions in virtually all major sectors of the economy, Justice Harlan Fiske Stone wrote,

> Our conclusion is unaffected by the Tenth Amendment....The amendment states but a truism that all is retained which has not been surrendered. There is nothing in the history of its adoption to suggest that it was more than declaratory of the relationship between national and state governments as it had been established by the Constitution before the amendment or that its purpose was other than to allay fears that the new national government might seek to exercise powers not granted, and that the states might not be able to exercise fully their reserved powers....From the beginning and for many years the amendment has been construed as not depriving the national government of authority to resort to all means for the exercise of a granted power which are appropriate and plainly adapted to the permitted end.[10]

Dual federalism was replaced by cooperative federalism, as the Court abandoned attempts to neatly define the boundaries of state and federal power over matters of mutual interest. Instead, it began to sanction an overlapping system of complementary state and federal regulation. Domestic and international events quickly outstripped the cooperative ideal. The aftermath of World War II, the Korean conflict, and the cold war left the national government greatly enhanced in administrative capacity and with an expanded set of policy imperatives. President Harry S. Truman's executive order racially integrating the armed forces accelerated the pressure for national action on civil rights for blacks (particularly in the South), which eventually resulted in passage of the Civil Rights Act of 1964 and the Voting Rights Act of 1965. The expansion of federal programs under Johnson's Great Society further shifted power and authority over social policy to the national arena, touching off new debates about the proper scope of national versus state sovereignty. The tension between national and state sovereignty, best captured in the unfounded mandates imposed on the states by Congress, reached

No FOREIGN AFFAIRS!

The Constitution strictly forbids states from involving themselves in foreign affairs. States may not enter into treaties, alliances, and confederations; maintain troops or ships of war in peacetime or conclude any agreement or compact with a foreign power; or engage in war unless invaded or otherwise in imminent danger. The consent of Congress is required for states to tax imports, exports, or freight brought into their ports. The Constitution's provisions left relatively little need for interpretation in this arena by the Supreme Court.

One of the Court's first rulings made clear the supremacy of federal treaties over conflicting state laws.[1] And in 1920 the Court affirmed the power of a treaty to remove from state jurisdiction a subject, in this case migratory birds, normally left to its control.[2] *(See box, Fish But Not All Fowl, p. 470.)* In 1840 the Court held that the Constitution's ban on states making treaties denied a state the power even to return a fugitive to a foreign nation.[3]

One small crack in the Court's opposition to state laws involving matters of foreign import appeared shortly after World War I, when in 1920 the Court upheld state espionage laws as a proper exercise of state police power.[4] In 1956, however, the Court overturned that holding, ruling that the Smith Act of 1940, a national sedition law, had preempted all state power over espionage and sedition.[5]

The Court has also frowned upon state laws that are designed to show displeasure with a foreign country. In 2000 the justices struck down a Massachusetts law that barred state agencies from buying goods or services from companies that did business with Burma and its repressive military regime. In a unanimous opinion, the Court said Congress had authorized the president to impose economic sanctions on Burma, and states were not free to go further and impose additional sanctions of their own.[6]

---

1. *Ware v. Hylton, 3 Dall.* (3 U.S.) 199 (1796).

2. *Missouri v. Holland,* 252 U.S. 416 (1920).

3. *Holmes v. Jennison,* 14 Pet. (39 U.S.) 540 (1840).

4. *Gilbert v. Minnesota,* 254 U.S. 325 (1920).

5. *Pennsylvania v. Nelson,* 350 U.S. 497 (1956).

6. *Crosby v. National Foreign Trade Council,* 530 U.S. 363 (2000).

---

new heights in the 1990s. Under Chief Justice William H. Rehnquist's stewardship, the Court reinvigorated a federalism that shielded state sovereignty.

LIABILITY TO LAWSUITS

The states were stunned by the Supreme Court's first major ruling. In 1793 the Court held that a state could be hauled into federal court, without its consent, if it were sued by the citizens of another state. In response, Congress approved and the states ratified the Eleventh Amendment to overrule the decision in *Chisholm v. Georgia* (1793). The new amendment was in place by 1798.[11] *(See details of Chisholm v. Georgia, pp. 377–378.)* As added to the Constitution, the Eleventh Amendment denied federal jurisdiction over any "suit in law or equity" brought against a state by citizens of another state or of a foreign state. The amendment did not expressly forbid federal courts from taking jurisdiction over suits brought against a state by its own citizens, but the Supreme Court in 1890 held that the amendment did bar such suits. Later the Court also ruled that the amendment prohibited suits brought by a foreign nation against a state.[12] The amendment did not forbid suits against a state brought under the Constitution, an omission that became significant only in the twentieth century.[13]

States' Protection Narrowed

Over the years the Supreme Court has narrowed the protection that the Eleventh Amendment provides to the states. The first such ruling came in *Osborn v. Bank of the United States* (1824), in which the Court held that this immunity did not protect a state official who was acting under an unconstitutional state law or who was exceeding his properly granted authority.[14] Half a century later the bar imposed by the Eleventh Amendment appeared to deny any federal remedy to citizens holding bonds repudiated by the financially strained southern states. In frustration, some groups began to demand repeal of the Eleventh Amendment.[15] The Supreme Court, however, resolved the impasse. In *Poindexter v. Greenhow* (1885), a case involving the bond situation in Virginia, the Court ruled to allow suits against state officials who were carrying out an unconstitutional law or otherwise exceeding their proper authority.[16] In such circumstances, held the Court, the official acts as an individual and can be sued as such. The Eleventh Amendment did not bar such suits. In that and later rulings the Court has reasoned that the amendment was intended to forbid the use of the courts by citizens seeking to compel a state to take some affirmative action or to exercise its authority in some nonministerial and discretionary matter.

In subsequent cases the Court held that the Eleventh Amendment provides no protection for state officials who damage property or injure persons in deliberate and negligent disregard of state law or individual rights.[17] That point was reaffirmed in a 1974 case brought against state officials by the parents of children killed during an antiwar demonstration. The Court stated, "The Eleventh Amendment provides no shield for a state official confronted by a claim that he had deprived another of a federal right under color of state law."[18]

The Return of State Sovereignty

As noted above, in the 1990s the Rehnquist Court revived the doctrine of state sovereignty and held it up as a shield against federal lawsuits and a steady stream of regulatory commands from Washington. The justices did not rely on the Tenth Amendment alone, also pointing to the Eleventh Amendment, ratified in 1795, as giving the states a "sovereign immunity" from federal lawsuits. Sometimes they went further, arguing that the "structure" of the Constitution itself endorsed a states' rights approach, even when its words suggested otherwise. Equally important, the Court said it saw its duty as policing the boundaries between state and federal power. No longer would Congress be entrusted to police itself.

"As every school child learns, our Constitution establishes a system of dual sovereignty between the States and the Federal Government," wrote Justice Sandra Day O'Connor in 1991.[19] A former state legislator from Arizona, O'Connor became a leading voice on the Court calling for a revival of states' rights. In *Gregory v. Ashcroft* (1991) she spoke for the Court in ruling that Missouri can force its judges to retire at age seventy, despite a federal law that forbids age discrimination in employment. Judge Ellis Gregory, who was nearing seventy, claimed that the state's mandatory retirement rule violated federal antidiscrimination law and the Constitution's guarantee of equal protection of the laws. Missouri governor John Ashcroft, later a U.S. senator and attorney general of the United States, defended the state.

O'Connor said the states are free to run their own affairs in such basic matters as deciding who may serve in state government. "The authority of the people of the states to determine the qualifications of their most important government officials...is an authority that lies at the heart of representative government. It is a power reserved to the States under the Tenth Amendment and guaranteed them by that provision of the Constitution under which the United States 'guarantees to every State in this Union a Republican Form of Government.'"[20]

A year later, in 1992, the Court ruled that Congress may not force states and their legislatures to make difficult choices in solving a national problem. In this instance, the problem was disposing of low-level radioactive waste produced by hospitals and medical labs. In 1985 Congress had passed the Low-Level Radioactive Waste Policy Amendments, making the states responsible for disposing nonhazardous radioactive by-products generated within their borders. If a state did not designate a dump site, it would be required to "take title" to the material and be responsible for it. Several state governors went to federal court to challenge this law, and the Supreme Court ruled it unconstitutional in *New York v. United States* (1992). Justice O'Connor, speaking for the 6-3 majority, said Washington may not "commandeer" the services of a sovereign state for its purposes. "The federal government may not compel the States to enact or administer a federal regulatory program," she said.[21]

ANTITRUST IMMUNITY AND STATE ECONOMY

Recognizing that "the states are sovereign, save only as Congress may constitutionally subtract from their authority," the Supreme Court in 1943 held that the Sherman Antitrust Act of 1890 was not intended to prevent states from adopting policies or programs that restrained competition in some portion of the state's economy. The ruling came in *Parker v. Brown,* in which California's raisin marketing program—which clearly operated to limit competition among raisin growers—was challenged as in conflict with federal antitrust and agricultural laws. Chief Justice Harlan Fiske Stone explained the reasoning behind the Court's upholding the state's program and finding that states were immune from the federal antitrust law:

> We find nothing in the language of the Sherman Act or in its history which suggests that its purpose was to restrain a state or its officers or agents from activities directed by its legislature. In a dual system of government in which, under the Constitution, the states are sovereign, save only as Congress may constitutionally subtract from their authority, an unexpressed purpose to nullify a state's control over its officers and agents is not lightly to be attributed to Congress.
>
> The Sherman Act makes no mention of the state as such, and gives no hint that it was intended to restrain state action or official action directed by a state.... There is no suggestion of a purpose to restrain state action in the Act's legislative history. The sponsor of the bill which was ultimately enacted as the Sherman Act declared that it prevented only "business combinations."...
>
> True, a state does not give immunity to those who violated the Sherman Act by authorizing them to violate it, or by declaring that their action is lawful...and we have no question of the state...becoming a participant in a private agreement or combination by others for restraint of trade....Here the state command...is not rendered unlawful by the Sherman Act since...it must be taken to be a prohibition of individual and not state action....
>
> The state in adopting and enforcing the prorate program made no contract or agreement and entered into no conspiracy in restraint of trade or to establish monopoly but, as sovereign, imposed the restraint as an act of government which the Sherman Act did not undertake to prohibit.[1]

Thirty-five years later, in 1978, the Court held that this immunity did not extend to cities, unless their anticompetitive conduct was undertaken in carrying out state policy to replace competition with regulation or monopoly.[2]

1. *Parker v. Brown,* 317 U.S. 341 at 350–352 (1943).
2. *City of Lafayette, La. v. Louisiana Power & Light Co.,* 435 U.S. 389 (1978).

Suing the State in Federal Court

The most important twentieth-century opinion concerning the doctrine of state sovereign immunity is *Seminole Tribe v. Florida* (1996), which involved an unusual federal law intended to resolve squabbling over gambling on Indian lands in states that frowned upon wagering. The Indian Gaming Regulatory Act of 1988 required state officials to negotiate with tribal leaders and devise rules to govern gambling on reservations. Florida governor Lawton Chiles refused to negotiate with the Seminoles, who then went to federal court to obtain an order to force him to comply. In response, Chiles challenged the federal law as an affront to the state's sovereignty. Speaking for a 5-4 majority, Chief Justice Rehnquist agreed with the governor, stating that Congress had no authority to subject states to such legal claims. "Even when the Constitution vests in Congress complete law-making authority over a particular area, the Eleventh Amendment prevents congressional authorization of suits by private parties against unconsenting states," he wrote.[22]

Until this decision, it had been assumed that Congress could subject states and state agencies to private lawsuits if they violated federal law. During the twentieth century, Congress often had enforced laws against environmental pollution, workplace discrimination, copyright protection, and other matters by authorizing victims to sue violators for damages. For these purposes, lawmakers in Washington had relied on Article VI of the Constitution guaranteeing that federal law stands above all other law: "The laws of the United States...shall be the supreme Law of the Land, any Thing in the Constitution of the Laws of any State to the Contrary notwithstanding." In the Seminole case

STATE TERM LIMITS FOR FEDERAL OFFICEHOLDERS?

Skip Cook (*left*) and Tim Jacob of Arkansans for Governmental Reform spoke at a news conference concerning a 1992 ballot measure to limit the terms of the members of the Arkansas congressional delegation. Voters approved the measure, Amendment 73, in November 1992 by a 3–2 margin. Two years later, the Supreme Court struck down the Arkansas law in *U.S. Term Limits Inc. v. Thornton.*

Although debate over whether the terms of members of Congress should be limited is as old as the Constitution, the legal issue did not arrive at the Supreme Court until the mid-1990s. Between 1990 and 1995 a term limits movement erupted onto the national political scene, as supporters won ballot initiatives or gained term limit laws in twenty-three states. With opposition growing to business as usual in Washington, the slogan of the day became "throw the bums out."

But the term-limits movement suffered a major defeat in the Supreme Court. The case arose after voters in Arkansas approved a 1992 amendment to the state constitution that barred the state's congressional members from appearing on the ballot after a certain number of terms— three for representatives and two for senators. Arguing for term limits, state officials and national term limit activists contended that the nation's founders had envisioned a Congress of citizen legislators, but modern-day incumbency, with all its perquisites—including incomparable name recognition and the ability to raise large sums of money--had created lawmakers out of touch with the people.

Bobbie Hill, a former president of the state's League of Women Voters, challenged Arkansas's term limits law. Hill and other opponents of term limits cited Article I of the Constitution, which sets out only three qualifications for federal office: age, citizenship, and residency. No other qualifications could be imposed, opponents argued. If voters wanted to limit the tenure of their representatives, they could do so by voting them out of office. Advocates of term limits, however, also found support in Article I, specifically, in the clause giving states the power to regulate the "times, places and manner" of holding elections for members of Congress.

In *U.S. Term Limits Inc. v. Thornton* (1995) the Court rejected the state's term limits on a 5-4 vote. Justice John Paul Stevens wrote the

however, Rehnquist contended that the states had a sovereign immunity from suits that was "inherent" in the federal system. This immunity was confirmed, he said, by the Eleventh Amendment: "The Judicial Power of the United States shall not be construed to extend to any suit in law or equity, commenced or prosecuted against one of the United States by Citizens of another State, or Citizens or Subjects of any Foreign State."

No one had questioned the purpose of the Eleventh Amendment, which was designed to overrule the Supreme Court's decision in *Chisholm v. Georgia* (1793), a case that had begun as a dispute over Revolutionary War debts.[23] A South Carolina man had supplied materials to Georgia during the war and wanted to be repaid. Georgia refused. Later, Alexander Chisholm, the executor of the South Carolinian's estate, brought a suit in the Supreme Court seeking repayment because the Judiciary Act of 1789 had given the Court jurisdiction over suits brought against one state by citizens of another. (Though strange by today's standards, the plaintiff, Chisholm, was represented by attorney Edmund Randolph, who was also serving as the attorney general of the United States.) The justices, in a 4-1 vote, ruled for Chisholm, holding that Georgia must pay its debt. The decision sent a scare through the states, many of which feared that they soon would be sued by British creditors

opinion and was joined by Justices Anthony M. Kennedy, David H. Souter, Ruth Bader Ginsburg, and Stephen G. Breyer. Justice Clarence Thomas wrote the dissenting opinion, joined by Chief Justice William H. Rehnquist and Justices Sandra Day O'Connor and Antonin Scalia.

The people may choose whom they wish to govern them, said the Court. "Allowing individual States to adopt their own qualifications for congressional service would be inconsistent with the Framers' vision of a uniform National Legislature representing the people of the United States. If the qualifications set forth in the text of the Constitution are to be changed, that text must be amended," Justice Stevens wrote.[1] The Court relied on its ruling in *Powell v. McCormack* (1969) that even Congress lacked the power to add to or alter the qualifications of its members.[2] After Rep. Adam Clayton Powell, a veteran Democratic lawmaker from New York City, had won reelection in 1966 despite a conviction for criminal contempt and a record of misuse of public funds, the House of Representatives voted to "exclude" him. Powell sued. The Court ultimately agreed that the House action was illegal, ruling 8-1 that neither chamber of Congress can add to the qualifications for membership listed in the Constitution. According to Stevens, the fundamental ideas behind the decision in *Powell* were "that the opportunity to be elected was open to all" and "that sovereignty confers on the people the right to choose freely their representatives to the National Government."[3]

Directly addressing the question of state authority in this area, Stevens wrote, "[W]e conclude that the power to add qualifications is not within the 'original powers' of the States, and thus is not reserved to the States by the Tenth Amendment. Second, even if States possessed some original power in this area, we conclude that the Framers intended the Constitution to be the exclusive source of qualifications for members of Congress, and that the Framers thereby 'divested' States of any power to add qualifications."[4] Fearing that the diverse interests of the states would

undermine the national government, the framers tried to minimize the possibility of state interference with federal elections, the majority observed, noting that the framers unanimously had rejected a proposal to add term limits to the Constitution.

Concluding, Stevens wrote, "We are firmly convinced that allowing the several States to adopt term limits for congressional service would effect a fundamental change in the constitutional framework. Any such change must come not by legislation adopted either by Congress or by an individual State, but rather—as have other important changes in the electoral process—through the Amendment procedures set forth in Article V."[5]

In his dissent, Justice Thomas observed that he found it ironic that the majority "defends the right of the people of Arkansas to 'choose whom they please to govern them' by invalidating a provision that won nearly 60% of the votes cast in a direct election."[6] The dissenters assumed that states have such power over federal elections unless the Constitution explicitly states otherwise. Wrote Thomas, "I take it to be established that the people of Arkansas do enjoy 'reserved' powers over the selection of their representatives in Congress. Whatever one might think of the wisdom of this arrangement, we may not override the decision of the people of Arkansas unless something in the Federal Constitution deprives them of the power to enact such measures."[7]

---

1. *U.S. Term Limits Inc. v. Thornton,* 514 U.S. 779 at 783 (1995).

2. *Powell v. McCormack,* 395 U.S. 486 (1969).

3. *U.S. Term Limits Inc. v. Thornton,* 514 U.S. 779 at 794 (1995).

4. Id. at 800–801.

5. Id. at 837.

6. Id. at 845.

7. Id. at 865.

---

and American loyalists over lost property. In short order, Congress passed and the states ratified an amendment to shield them from such claims. By its very words, however, the amendment's shield did not extend to a state's own citizens. Nevertheless, according to Rehnquist's reading, the amendment confirms the understanding that "each state is a sovereign entity in our federal system, and that it is inherent in the nature of sovereignty not to be amenable to the suit of an individual without its consent."[24] As precedent, he pointed to an 1890 ruling that stopped a Louisiana man from suing the state in federal court for repayment on a bond. The case did not, however, involve a law passed by Congress.[25]

The opinion in *Seminole Tribe v. Florida* cast aside a fractured ruling from seven years earlier, when in *Pennsylvania v. Union Gas* (1989) the Court in a 5-4 vote upheld an environmental cleanup lawsuit against Pennsylvania, ruling that Congress had intended to authorize such suits as part of the Superfund program.[26] Rehnquist had dissented then, and in *Seminole Tribe* he announced *Union Gas* was overruled. What made the difference was the retirement of Justice Thurgood Marshall and his replacement with Justice Clarence Thomas, who sided with Rehnquist. The four dissenters remarked on the sweeping impact that the *Seminole Tribe* decision could have: "This case is about power—the power of the

Congress of the United States to create a private federal cause of action against a State, or its Governor, for the violation of a federal right," said Justice John Paul Stevens. He called the majority's ruling "a sharp break from the past" and "profoundly misguided." It "prevents Congress from providing a federal forum for a broad range of actions against the States, from those sounding in copyright and patent law, to those concerning bankruptcy, environmental law and the regulation of our vast national economy."[27]

State Agents and Background Checks for Gun Owners

In 1997 the Court took up a states' rights challenge to the Brady Handgun Violence Prevention Act, the 1993 federal measure that requires background checks on people who want to buy a handgun. Felons, fugitives, illegal aliens, and mental patients were among those who were barred from buying handguns. Although the law envisioned an instant background check to be run by the FBI, no such national system existed. In the interim, the act made state and local law enforcement personnel responsible for the checks. Jay Printz, the sheriff and coroner of Ravalli County, Montana, with the backing of the National Rifle Association, challenged the requirement that he conduct background checks. The Supreme Court agreed with him in 1997, ruling this provision unconstitutional under the Tenth Amendment. Justice Antonin Scalia, writing for the 5-4 majority in *Printz v. United States* (1997), said that rarely in U.S. history, except in wartime, had the federal government compelled state or local officials to carry out a task. Washington has frequently offered money to state agencies to undertake federal programs, but state officials remain free to say no.[28]

"The power of the Federal Government would be augmented immeasurably if it were able to impress into its service—and at no cost to itself—the police officers of the 50 States," Scalia wrote in *Printz*. "Laws conscripting state officers violate state sovereignty and are thus not in accord with the Constitution....The Federal Government may neither issue directives requiring the States to address particular problems, nor command the States' officers, or those of their political subdivisions, to administer or enforce a regulatory program," Scalia concluded.[29]

It is of note that his opinion referred to county sheriffs as state officers. In past decisions, the Court has drawn a distinction between municipal officials and state officers, ruling that only the latter are protected under the states' rights doctrine. In a concurring opinion, Justice Thomas raised the issue of the Second Amendment, pondering whether at some point the Court should consider whether Congress has the authority to restrict the sale of handguns. Wrote Thomas, "This Court has not had recent occasion to consider the nature of the substantive right safeguarded by the Second Amendment. If, however, the Second Amendment is read to confer a personal right to 'keep and bear arms,' a colorable argument exists that the Federal Government's regulatory scheme, at least as it pertains to the purely intrastate sale or possession of firearms, runs afoul of that Amendment's protections."[30]

In a dissenting opinion, later cast in a new light by subsequent events, Justice Stevens asserted that the ruling could create paralysis in a national emergency, including during a terrorist attack. "Matters such as the enlistment of air raid wardens, the administration of a military draft, the mass inoculation of children to forestall an epidemic, or perhaps the threat of an international terrorist, may require a national response before federal personnel can be made available to respond," he wrote. Moreover, the Court's opinion creates a perverse incentive for Washington to expand its reach. "In the name of States' rights the majority would have the Federal Government create vast national bureaucracies to implement its policies," he said.[31] Justices David H. Souter, Ruth Bader Ginsburg, and Stephen G. Breyer joined Stevens in dissent.

Probation Officers and Patents

The issue of state sovereignty figured in three major decisions handed down on the last day of the Court's term on June 23, 1999: *Alden v. Maine, Florida Prepaid Postsecondary Education Board v. College Savings Bank,* and *College Savings Bank v. Florida Prepaid.*[32] *Alden* concerned a technical matter of great practical importance. Most lawsuits are filed and decided in state courts. The Eleventh Amendment specifically limits the "Judicial Power of the United States," meaning the federal courts. The *Seminole Tribe* decision interpreted this amendment as stripping federal courts of the power to hear private suits against state agencies, but it did not resolve whether state courts could take up these claims. Article VI of the Constitution says federal law "shall be the supreme Law of the Land, and the Judges in every State shall be bound thereby." Undeterred, the Rehnquist Court ruled in *Alden* that states cannot be sued in their own courts for violating federal laws.

John Alden and a group of state probation officers had sued the state of Maine to recover overtime wages that had not been paid. The federal Fair Labor Standards Act required all employers, including state agencies, to pay minimum wages and extra pay for overtime. Nevertheless, the Court blocked Alden's suit. "The States' immunity from suit is a fundamental aspect of the sovereignty which the States enjoyed before the ratification of the Constitution and which they retain today," said Justice Kennedy for the 5-4 majority. "We hold that the States retain immunity from private suit in their own courts, an immunity beyond the congressional power to abrogate by Article I legislation."[33] Kennedy struggled to explain the source of the sovereign immunity in this case, because no one at the Constitutional Convention in Philadelphia bothered to speak up for this principle or to write it into the basic law. The Eleventh Amendment additionally could not be stretched to cover state courts. "The silence is most instructive," Kennedy said. "It suggests the sovereign's right to assert immunity from suit in its own courts was a principle so well established that no one conceived it would be altered by the new Constitution."[34]

The other two cases concerning state sovereignty involved property rights that Congress has the exclusive power to protect: patents and trademarks. Congress had enacted laws that gave the owners of patents and trademarks the right to sue those who stole their patents or infringed their trademarks. The potential violators included state agencies and state universities. The Fourteenth Amendment gives Congress the power to enforce laws against a state which "deprive[s] any person of…property without due process of law." The College Savings Bank of New Jersey devised a system

under which parents could pre-pay their child's college tuition, and it obtained a patent and a trademark for its system. The Florida Prepaid Postsecondary Expense Education Board, a state agency, essentially copied this system and advertised it as a good way for Floridians to save for college. The New Jersey bank sued for patent and trademark infringements, but in a pair of 5-4 decisions the Court threw out the claims, ruling that Florida's sovereign immunity shielded it from such suits. In *Florida Prepaid Postsecondary Education Board v. College Savings Bank,* Rehnquist noted that when Congress extended the Patent Remedy Act to states and state agencies in 1992, there were only a "handful of instances of state patent infringement," adding that this "scant support" for federal legislation was not enough to waive the state's shield of immunity.[35] Patent claims can be brought in state courts, he suggested. In dissent, Justice Stevens said the Patent Remedy Act "merely puts the States in the same position as all private users of the patent system.…Until this expansive and judicially crafted protection of States' rights runs its course, I shall continue" to dissent, Stevens said, speaking for Justices Souter, Ginsburg, and Breyer. The companion case, *College Savings Bank v. Florida Prepaid,* was nearly identical. The conservative majority, in an opinion by Justice Scalia, said states were shielded from being sued for violating trademarks. The liberal dissenters, speaking through Justice Breyer, said that when state agencies participate in business and commerce, they should abide by the same rules as all other participants.

The Rehnquist Court has also shielded states from being sued by state employees who allege that they were discriminated against because of age or a disability.[36]

In May 2002 the Court extended the states' shield of immunity in a dispute that arose in the harbor at Charleston, S.C.—where the Civil War began—and concerned a tiny and obscure federal agency. The case tested whether hearings held by such agencies are akin to hearings in a federal court. Many federal agencies enforce their laws in part by responding to private complaints alleging a violation of the law. Often, agency officials hold hearings to consider the facts and to listen to the competing parties. The Federal Maritime Commission (FMC) enforces a federal law that prohibits ports from discriminating in favor of some ships and against others.

The owners of the *Tropic Sea* cruise ship complained after it was denied a berth at Charleston, ostensibly because it offered gambling on board. Two Carnival Cruise ships that also offer gambling were permitted to dock in Charleston, they said. When the FMC sought to hold a hearing on the complaint lodged against the South Carolina State Ports Authority, the state agency refused to participate, citing state sovereign immunity. In a 5-4 vote, the state prevailed in the Supreme Court. It is "an affront to a State's dignity" to "allow a private party to haul a State in front of such an administrative tribunal," said Justice Thomas in *Federal Maritime Commission v. South Carolina State Ports Authority*. "As we have previously noted, the primary function of sovereign immunity is not to protect State treasuries but to afford the States the dignity and respect due sovereign entities."[37] In dissent, Justice Breyer said that he could not find in the Constitution this "hidden reservation" that shields state agencies from federal laws.[38] The 5-4 split over this issue appeared to be intractable. The majority, led by Chief Justice Rehnquist, felt that states' sovereignty trumped federal laws, no matter if the laws themselves were legitimate and constitutional. The four dissenters held that federal law trumped state law, even when it intruded on the core powers of the state.

Although the principle of state sovereignty has been firmly established, it does not always trump federal laws that regulate the states as employers. The justices have ruled that sovereign immunity shields the state from being sued by individuals. The federal government, however, may sue the state, and it may do so on behalf of a private party, asserted Justice Kennedy in *Alden v. Maine*. In such cases, Congress and federal agencies retain the authority to enforce the law if they are willing to pay the extra cost of government lawyers. Congress could also require states to waive their sovereign rights in exchange for obtaining federal funds.

Even Chief Justice Rehnquist agreed that states can be sued if they discriminate against persons based on their race or sex. The Fourteenth Amendment, through its wording and history, "quite clearly contemplates limitations of their [states] authority," Rehnquist wrote in *Fitzpatrick v. Bitzer,* upholding a sex discrimination lawsuit filed by state employees against a state agency. "No state shall…deny to any person within its jurisdiction the equal protection of the laws" means states may not discriminate against persons based on their race or gender, he said.[39] Relying on this principle, Rehnquist spoke for the Court in 2003 in upholding a Nevada state worker's lawsuit against his employer under the Family and Medical Leave Act (FMLA) of 1993. This federal measure gave employees a right to take up to twelve weeks of unpaid leave to care of a sick family member. William Hibbs, a Nevada welfare department employee, was fired in 1997 for his extended absence. He sued the state for violating his rights under the federal law.

To the surprise of many, Rehnquist agreed that the state could be sued in this instance because the federal law remedied a type of lingering sex bias. Women were seen as having the main duty of caring for sick children, and this in turn limited their work opportunities. At the same time, men were not given the same rights to take leave when they were needed at home. Although maternal leave was well established by the 1990s, paternal leave policies remained rare, he said. "The FMLA aims to protect the right to be free from gender-based discrimination in the workplace," Rehnquist wrote in *Nevada Dept. of Human Resources v. Hibbs* (2003).[40] Because the Fourteenth Amendment gives Congress the power to "enforce" federal civil rights, it has the power to enforce laws against sex discrimination through private suits against the states, he continued. The dissenters, Justices Kennedy, Scalia, and Thomas, described family leave as an "entitlement program" foisted on the states, not a remedy for discrimination. Nevertheless, the *Hibbs* ruling marked a clear limit to the succession of states' rights victories.

In *Hibbs* Rehnquist reiterated his view that "it falls to this Court, not Congress, to define the substance of constitutional guarantees."[41] The category of forbidden discriminations has so far been limited mostly to race and gender discrimination, rather than matters such as age, disability, or sexual orientation. States therefore may not be sued in federal court for such discrimination. The Court's decisions have also left it unclear just who or what is a state. The Court has had no difficulty agreeing that a state university or state hospital is the "state," and some opinions have suggested that county sheriffs or other county and regional offices are "state" agencies. In a few states, local school districts are considered state agencies, but the Supreme Court has yet to decide whether the doctrine of state sovereignty extends to them as well.

At times well-founded claims of state sovereignty have lost because they were trumped by superior claims of federal power. The court on a 5-4 vote struck down Arkansas's congressional term limits. Justice Kennedy, casting the pivotal vote with the liberal justices, said the qualifications for federal officeholders are a federal matter, not subject to differing rules set by the states.[42] Still, the Court maintained that it had a duty to maintain the "constitutional design" as a means of preserving liberty. "The constitutionally mandated balance of power between the States and the Federal Government was adopted by the Framers to ensure the protection of our fundamental liberties," said Justice Thomas. "By guarding against encroachments by the Federal government on fundamental aspects of state sovereignty, such as sovereign immunity, we strive to maintain the balance of power embodied in our Constitution and thus to reduce the risk of tyranny and abuse from either front."[43]

Halting State Action: Injunctions

State officials may be stopped from violating the Constitution or federal law through a court order, a century-old doctrine known as *Ex parte Young*. It is so-called after Minnesota attorney general Edward T. Young, who was sued in 1908 by the Northern Pacific Railroad for an allegedly unconstitutional limit on rail rates. Its significance outlived the age of the railroads: "The decision in *Ex parte Young* has long been recognized as a primary method…of ensuring state compliance with federal law," wrote constitutional law professor Erwin Chemerinsky.[44]

Under the Minnesota law challenged in *Young,* the officers and agents of the railroad faced up to five years in prison for violating the rate law. They could not risk violating the law first and then challenge its constitutionality in court. Instead, they persuaded a federal judge to issue an injunction barring enforcement of the law. Attorney General Young ignored the injunction and was held in contempt. He in turn appealed to the Supreme Court and asserted as a defense the Eleventh Amendment doctrine of state sovereignty. The Court rejected Young's defense in what scholars consider one of the most significant decisions in constitutional law. The ruling—a victory for business over government regulators—is a reflection of the times, but it also preserved the power of federal judges to uphold constitutional rights against violations by state officials. The Court's opinion drew a rather strained distinction between state officers and the state itself:

> The act to be enforced is alleged to be unconstitutional, and if it be so, the use of the name of the State to enforce an unconstitutional act to the injury of complainants is a proceeding without the authority of and one which does not affect the State in its sovereign or government capacity. It is simply an illegal act upon the part of a state official in attempting to use the name of the State to enforce a legislative enactment which is void because unconstitutional.[45]

Amid the civil rights conflicts of the 1960s, the Court appeared to broaden this exception to allow federal judges to halt state court proceedings when defendants claimed that the state laws under which they were charged violated their First Amendment freedom of expression. One such example was *Dombrowski v. Pfister* (1965), in which the Court held that such a threat existed and that it was a proper use of federal power to halt the enforcement of the challenged law until it was determined valid or invalid.[46]

Defendants prosecuted under state laws subject to this sort of First Amendment challenge took full advantage of the ruling, producing a wave of petitions to federal courts and a resulting flood of federal injunctions to halt enforcement. In 1971 the Court curtailed this trend. Justice Hugo L. Black wrote, "[T]he normal thing to do when federal courts are asked to enjoin pending proceedings in state courts is not to issue such injunctions."[47] Black explained that federal courts should abstain from interference in state business unless there was an immediate threat of irreparable injury resulting from continuation of the trial or enforcement of the law, unless the challenged law was flagrantly unconstitutional, or unless there had been official disregard of the law. According to Black, the policy of federal abstention was based upon "the notion of 'comity,'" which he defined as

> a proper respect for state functions, a recognition of the fact that the entire country is made up of a Union of separate state governments, and a continuance of the belief that the National Government will fare best if the States and their institutions are left free to perform their separate functions in their separate ways. This, perhaps for lack of a better and clearer way to describe it, is referred to by many as "Our Federalism." The concept does not mean blind deference to "States' Rights" any more than it means centralization of control over every important issue in our National Government and its courts. The Framers rejected both these courses. What the concept does represent is a system in which there is sensitivity to the legitimate interests of both State and National Governments, and in which the National Government, anxious though it may be to vindicate and protect federal rights and federal interests, always endeavors to do so in ways that will not unduly interfere with the legitimate activities of the States.[48]

These injunctions are intended to be temporary and a way to prevent constitutional violations. They do not result in damage verdicts against the states. Nevertheless, they came under attack in the Court in 1997 because they threatened the principle of state sovereign immunity. Justice Kennedy, joined by Chief Justice Rehnquist, said he would overrule *Ex parte Young* and give the states a new shield from federal court orders.[49] The 1908 decision was based on "an obvious fiction," he said. State officials were following state law, not exceeding it. Kennedy's opinion turned into a dissent, however, as the other seven justices voted to preserve the power of federal judges to enforce court orders against state officials.

POLITICAL POWERS

In no area of state affairs has the Supreme Court been more reluctant to intervene than in questions of state political power. This reluctance to involve itself in political questions was evident as early as the Court's decision in *Luther v. Borden* (1849).[50] That case arose under Article IV of the Constitution, which provides that "the United States shall guarantee to every State in this Union a Republican Form of Government." The dispute involved two competing groups claiming to be the legitimate government of the state of Rhode Island. The Court refused to resolve this "political question," holding that enforcement of the constitutional guarantee was a matter for Congress, not the courts. On the basis of this same "political question" doctrine, the Court in 1912 declined to decide whether Oregon—by adopting the direct legislative devices of the initiative and the referendum—had destroyed its republican form of government and thus its own lawful authority. The Court held that Congress, by seating the U.S. senators and House members from Oregon, had sanctioned these changes in the character of the state government.[51]

Electoral Districts

In Article I the Constitution states: "The Times, Places and Manner of holding Elections for Senators and Representatives, shall be prescribed in each State by the Legislature thereof," and it grants Congress some power to regulate these elections. Congress first exercised this authority in 1842, requiring states to divide themselves into districts for the election of House members. Subsequent laws also required that these districts be compact—that is, not gerrymandered. After a 1929 act omitted that requirement, however, the Court ruled in 1932 that without such statutory authority, it could not act to correct a state's gerrymandered districts.[52]

Until 1962 the Court held steadfastly to the position that malapportionment of legislative districts was a "political question," not for the courts to resolve. To leave this matter to the legislators elected from those very districts, however, was clearly to prevent any improvement in the situation. The Court eventually discarded the political question response with its decision in *Baker v. Carr* (1962). Using the Fourteenth Amendment's equal protection guarantee as the basis for intervention, the Court entered the "political thicket" and ordered states to draw new congressional and state legislative district lines to ensure the equality of votes cast within the state.[53] These rulings resulted in a long line of Supreme Court cases concerning implementation of the "one person, one vote" rule, and in 1973, while maintaining the standard of strict mathematical equality for congressional districts, the Court relaxed that standard slightly for state legislative districts. Some deviation might be justified, wrote Justice Rehnquist for the Court, citing a statement from an earlier reapportionment ruling: "So long as the divergences from a strict population standard are based on legitimate consideration incident to the effectuation of a rational state policy, some deviations from the equal population principle are constitutionally permissible with respect to the apportionment of seats" in the state legislature.[54]

That double standard—strict for congressional districts, lenient for state legislative districts—was illustrated vividly ten years later, when the Court issued two decisions concerning apportionment. In *Karcher v. Daggett* (1983) the Court, 5-4, struck down New Jersey's congressional redistricting plan because the state had not justified the less than 1 percent variation between the most populous and least populous districts.[55] That same day, by a very different 5-4 vote, the Court upheld Wyoming's requirement that each county have at least one representative in its state house, even though the result was an 89 percent population variance between the smallest county and the largest. The variance was permissible, the Court said, in light of the state's interest in making sure that each county has its own representative.[56]

State officials retain broad power to draw electoral districts for the state legislature and for Congress, so long as they do not realign voters based on their race. Some state leaders have used this authority for political advantage. They redrew districts with the aim of winning for their party the maximum numbers of seats in the legislature or in the House of Representatives. This so-called "partisan gerrymandering" was challenged before the Court as unconstitutional.

"Contemporary redistricting practices are subverting democracy," the Brennan Center, a liberal reform group, said in its brief to the Court in 2003 in *Vieth v. Jubelirer.*[57] Although in theory voters choose their political representatives, redistricting permits politicians to choose their voters, the group's lawyer argued. Aided by computerized voting rolls, state lawmakers can draw districts that virtually ensure their reelection and the reelection of their allies, the Brennan Center said.

But in the end, the Court could not agree on a formula for deciding these claims, and the challenges were rejected.[58] The cases highlighted the difference between politics and race. Government decisions are often made for political or partisan reasons. One party's members may vote for a proposal entirely because it is in line with their party's views. No one would claim these decisions are unconstitutional because they are politically motivated. But it is unconstitutional for the government or state officials to make decisions for racial motives. The Court had no trouble agreeing that racial gerrymandering was unconstitutional, but it could not agree that partisan gerrymandering was similarly unconstitutional.

In *Vieth v. Jubelirer* the Court in a 5-4 decision upheld Pennsylvania's districts and rejected a challenge from the state's Democrats. Republicans controlled the state legislature and the governor's office after the 2000 census, and they drew districts that gave the GOP a majority of the state's nineteen seats in Congress.[59] Justice Scalia, joined by Chief Justice Rehnquist and Justices O'Connor and Thomas, said that since colonial times, elected state officials have been drawing districts, and there were "no manageable standards" for deciding whether their maps were so political as to be unconstitutional. They called for overruling *Davis v. Bandemer* (1986), the decision that opened the door to legal challenges to partisan gerrymandering.[60] Justice Kennedy agreed to uphold Pennsylvania's districts, but he left the door open to future challenges to partisan gerrymandering.

Another challenge was looming. House Majority Leader Tom DeLay, a Texas Republican, had engineered a redrawing of his state's districts shortly after

Republicans took control of both houses of the Texas legislature in 2003. The Democrats cried foul, saying this "mid-decade redistricting based on purely partisan motives" violates the Constitution. But in *League of United Latin American Citizens v. Perry* (2006) the Court rejected the challenge and upheld DeLay's plan as constitutional. Justice Kennedy noted that the GOP's map was no less fair than the Democratic map it replaced. In 2002 Democrats won a 17 to 15 majority in the Texas delegation to the House of Representatives, even though Republicans won a 59 percent to 40 percent majority of the statewide vote. The districts were drawn when Democrats controlled the legislature. After the Republicans redrew the districts in 2003, Republicans won twenty-one of the state's thirty-two congressional seats in 2004. Statewide, Texans gave the Republicans a 58 percent to 41 percent majority.[61]

Although the Court upheld the Texas districts as a whole, Kennedy joined with the liberal justices to order a redrawing of one district because it diluted the voting power of the Latinos in the Rio Grande Valley, which, Kennedy said, violated a provision of the Voting Rights Act. In sharp dissent, Chief Justice John Roberts questioned the premise that the Texas map as a whole weakened the voting power of Latinos. "It is a sordid business, this divvying us up by race," Roberts wrote.[62]

Primaries and Voter Qualifications

Until 1941 the control of primary elections was left entirely to the states. This tradition was reinforced by the Supreme Court's ruling in *Newberry v. United States* (1921) that appeared to read the Constitution's references to "elections" to mean only the general election, not preliminary contests.[63] In 1941 that interpretation was overturned by the Court, which held that in states where primary elections were an integral part of the process of electing members of Congress, congressional power to regulate elections extended over them.[64] States have long been conceded the power to set qualifications for voters, but the national government—chiefly through the amending process—possesses the power to declare certain qualifications unreasonable. That power was

exercised in the Fifteenth, Nineteenth, Twenty-fourth, and Twenty-sixth Amendments, forbidding states to deny the right to vote because of race, sex, payment of franchise taxes, or age, so long as the prospective voter is at least eighteen years of age.

State challenges to these means of expanding the electorate were disposed of by the Court in 1922 with the dismissal of Tennessee's argument that its political autonomy had been destroyed by the Nineteenth Amendment, which added many new voters to its electorate without its consent.[65] In 1970 the Supreme Court ruled that Congress could lower the voting age for federal elections, but not for state and local ones. That ruling led to the approval and ratification of the Twenty-sixth Amendment, which lowered the voting age to eighteen for all elections. In that same decision, the Court upheld an act of Congress that restricted residence requirements to thirty days for presidential elections and forbade the use of literacy tests in all elections.[66]

The most comprehensive federal scheme of regulation for the conduct of elections by states was approved by Congress in the Voting Rights Act of 1965, legislation enacted in response to the continuing efforts of some parts of the South to deny qualified black residents the right to vote. The act authorized federal supervision of elections in those areas, forbade the affected states to use any literacy test or similar device to qualify voters, and required federal approval of any change in their voting laws, practices, or procedures. South Carolina and New York (affected because of a provision concerning tests for non-English-speaking voters) challenged the law as an invasion of the reserved rights of the states to set voter qualifications. The Supreme Court rejected this argument and upheld the law: "As against the reserved powers of the States, Congress may use any rational means to effectuate the constitutional prohibition of racial discrimination in voting."[67]

The Supreme Court in modern times also has struck down state election laws that made it unreasonably difficult for third parties to win a place on a ballot, required excessively high filing fees for candidates, set unreasonable primary registration requirements and long residency requirements for voters, or required political parties to hold "closed" primaries in which only one party could vote.[68] The Court's ruling on state power over elections in *U.S. Term Limits v. Thornton* (1995) became one of the best-known decisions of the 1990s. Entering the heated battle over term limits for members of Congress, the Court held that states could not deny incumbents access to the ballot in order to limit their tenure.

Voting Fraud and Photo Identification

In the first decade of the twenty-first century, Republicans and Democrats clashed in several states over the issue of alleged vote fraud and the need to check the identity of persons at polling places. Republicans contended that voting fraud was rampant, but they pointed mostly to evidence that the voting rolls were inflated. Included were the names of persons who were not eligible to vote, such as felons and noncitizens, or legal voters who had moved to a different residence. They said that before casting a ballot, prospective voters should be required to show a driver's license or other state-issued photo identification. Democrats said there was little or no evidence that persons were actually voting under assumed names. They also said a photo ID requirement would deter tens of thousands of low-income, minority, or elderly voters who do not drive a car.

In 2005 Indiana adopted a law requiring voters to show an approved ID card, but allowing elderly persons and those in nursing homes to vote by mail. Democrats and the American Civil Liberties Union sued and contended the requirement would burden the right to vote. The suit did not cite a single plaintiff who said he or she had been prevented from voting because of the ID requirement.

In *Crawford v. Marion County Election Board* (2008) the Court upheld the state in a 6-3 decision.[69] Justice Stevens said the ID law should be seen as a regulation of the electoral process, rather than as a denial of the fundamental right to vote. States require residents to register to vote, usually well in advance of election day, and this too may act to deter some persons from voting. But such regulations are not unconstitutional unless they are targeted at a class of voters, he said. In a footnote, he cited the trial judge's finding that about 99 percent of Indiana's voting-age population had a valid ID card.

"There is no question about the legitimacy or importance of the State's interest in counting only the votes of eligible voters. Moreover, the interest in orderly administration and accurate recordkeeping provides a sufficient justification for carefully identifying all voters participating in the election process. While the most effective method of preventing election fraud may well be debatable, the propriety of doing so is perfectly clear," Stevens wrote. But his opinion left open the possibility of a future suit that could, for example, allege that the ID requirement puts a heavy burden on certain elderly or disabled persons. Chief Justice Roberts and Justice Kennedy agreed with Stevens.

Justices Scalia, Thomas, and Samuel Alito said they would have gone further and closed the door to future lawsuits challenging the ID requirement. "That sort of detailed judicial supervision of the election process would flout the Constitution's express commitment of the task to the States," Scalia wrote. "It is for state legislatures to weigh the costs and benefits of possible changes to their election codes, and their judgment must prevail unless it imposes a severe and unjustified overall burden on the right to vote, or is intended to disadvantage a particular class."

Justices Souter, Ginsburg, and Breyer dissented. They said at least forty-three thousand Indiana voters did not have a valid ID card, and they would be required to go to the county seat to obtain one. They also said the state had no evidence that such persons were posing as others in order to sneak into a voting booth. The state "failed to justify the practical limitations placed on the right to vote, and the law imposes an unreasonable and irrelevant burden on voters who are poor and old," Souter wrote.

Campaign Spending and Fund Raising

State officials have broad power to draw electoral districts and to regulate the process of voting, but they may not limit how much state candidates spend in campaigning for office. The Court has said the First Amendment gives candidates a right to spend as much as they wish to run for office. It also prohibits the government from putting tight limits on how much contributors can give to candidates.

The ruling in *Buckley v. Valeo* (1976) established this two-part framework.[70] The Court struck down the spending limits for federal candidates, but it upheld limits on large contributions. The Court said that spending limits were a more serious restriction on a candidate's freedom of speech than were limits on the size of contributions he could receive. In 2000 the Court upheld a $1,000 limit on contributions for state candidates in Missouri.[71] In dissent, Justices Scalia, Thomas, and Kennedy said they were inclined to overrule *Buckley* and give candidates a free speech right to raise and spend as much as they chose. But Justice Stevens, in a concurring opinion, questioned the premise that campaign money deserves to be protected by the First Amendment. "Money is property; it is not speech," he wrote.[72]

In 1997 Vermont's lawmakers sought to rid their state's politics of the influence of big money. They adopted strict limits on spending and contributions for all candidate for state office. They wanted to restore the tradition of small-town democracy where office seekers spent their time meeting with voters, rather than raising money to pay for campaigns ads on radio and television. Under the new law, known as Act 64, candidates for governor could spend no more than $300,000 on their campaigns, and their contributions were limited to $400 per person. Candidates for the state senate were limited to spending $4,000, and contributions were limited to $300. The Republican National Committee and the American Civil Liberties Union challenged the law on free speech grounds, and the Court struck it down as unconstitutional in a 6-3 decision in 2006.[73] Justice Breyer said that spending limits for federal candidates were deemed unconstitutional in *Buckley,* and the same rule applies to state candidates. Further, Vermont had set the contribution limits too low, Breyer said, because they would prevent a little-known challenger from running an effective campaign. Chief Justice Roberts and Justice Alito joined with Breyer. Justices Scalia, Thomas, and Kennedy agreed on striking down the state law, although they would have gone further to challenge *Buckley.* The dissenters—Justices Souter, Stevens, and Ginsburg—said the state and its voters deserved more freedom to set reasonable limits on spending and fund raising in state campaigns.

THE TAXING POWER

Apart from the Commerce Clause, the Court has imposed three other limiting principles upon the state's power to raise money through taxes: (1) the tax must be imposed on persons or property or activities within its own jurisdiction; (2) the tax must be for public purposes; and (3) the tax cannot fall directly upon the federal government. A series of post–Civil War rulings established the first principle.[74] The second was settled by the Court's decision in *Loan Association v. Topeka* (1875), when the Court struck down a Kansas law authorizing a tax to pay for city bonds issued to assist a private bridge-building corporation. Writing for the Court, Justice Samuel Miller was candid in condemning such an action:

> To lay, with one hand, the power of the government on the property of the citizen, and with the other to bestow it upon favored individuals to aid private enterprises and build up private fortunes, is none the less a robbery because it is done under the forms of law and is called taxation.[75]

The third principle, set out emphatically by Chief Justice Marshall in *McCulloch v. Maryland* (1819), denies states the right to use taxes to hinder the operations of the federal government.[76] After determining that the states lacked the power to tax the Bank of the United States, the Court in 1829 issued the first in a series of rulings protecting government securities from state taxation. State taxes on federal stock, bonds, and even national bank shares, without congressional consent, impermissibly interfere with the federal power to borrow, a power expressly granted by the Constitution, held the Court.[77] In 1886 the Court for the first time ruled that a state may not tax federally owned real estate, a holding that has been expanded to include most federally owned property.[78]

Intergovernmental Immunity

In announcing the Court's decision in *McCulloch v. Maryland,* Chief Justice Marshall asserted that "the power to tax involves the power to destroy."[79] This statement became the basis for a long, involved series of rulings in which the Court—for a time—granted to federal and state governments and their officials immunity, each from taxation by the other. The first of these rulings came in *Dobbins v. Erie County* (1842), in which the Court held that a state could not tax the income of federal revenue officers without impermissibly interfering with federal functions.[80] Years later the Court granted a corresponding immunity to state officials with its ruling in *Collector v. Day* (1871), striking down a federal tax on the salary of a state judge.[81]

In 1895 the Court granted state and municipal bonds (and the interest they generated) immunity from federal taxation similar to that already enjoyed by national securities from state taxes. This was part of the Court's income tax ruling in *Pollock v. Farmers' Loan and Trust Co.*[82] Some limit on this immunity—for state governments—was recognized in 1905, when the Court held that only governmental functions of state governments were immune from federal taxes. Therefore, it upheld the imposition of federal taxes on the state-run liquor business in South Carolina.[83] Notwithstanding this decision, the Court continued to elaborate on the intergovernmental tax immunity question for three more decades. It struck down a federal tax on motorcycles that were to be sold to a city police department.[84] Also falling as impermissible were state taxes on income from federally granted copyrights and patents, on gasoline sold to the federal government, and on income from leases of public lands.[85] The end of this body of rulings was in sight even as some of these last decisions were announced late in the 1920s. In dissent from the gasoline tax case, Justice Oliver Wendell Holmes Jr. met Marshall's assertion head-on and declared: "The power to tax is not the power to destroy while this court sits."[86]

Diluted Immunity

Beginning with the reversal of the copyright royalties income case in 1932, the Court dropped its effort to preserve this immunity in such extended form. In *Helvering v. Gerhardt* (1938) and *Graves v. New York ex rel. O'Keefe* (1939) the Court overruled *Dobbins* and *Collector.*[87] The immunity granted to state officials in *Collector,* explained Justice Stone in the *Helvering* opinion, "was sustained only because it was one deemed necessary to protect the states from destruction by federal taxation of those governmental functions which they were exercising when the Constitution was adopted and which were essential to their continued existence." Such immunity is not justified "where the tax laid upon individuals affects the state only as the burden is passed on to it by the taxpayer."[88]

The remaining significant example of state immunity from federal taxes—the immunity granted the interest paid on municipal bonds—was erased, as a constitutional matter, by the Court in its 7-1 decision in *South Carolina v. Baker* (1988). The Court made clear that nothing in the Constitution limited federal power to tax state government. In *Garcia v. San Antonio Metropolitan Transit* (1985) the Court had said that the states could look to Congress to protect their interests, because the lawmakers represented their individual states. Repeating that reasoning, Justice William J. Brennan Jr. said that if the states were to be shielded from certain federal taxes, the immunity should be enacted by legislators, not by judges interpreting the Constitution.[89]

Federal immunity from state taxes protects the property, institutions, and activities of the federal government, but it no longer extends to persons merely doing business with the federal government, even if it means that state taxes are passed on as higher costs to the federal government.[90] Early in the Court's exposition of the Constitution's prohibition on state action impairing the obligation of contracts, the Court applied the Contract Clause to the state's power to grant and revoke exemptions from state taxes. Unless a reservation of the state's right to modify or nullify such a grant of exemption is included in the granting agreement, the Contract Clause forbids a state to rescind or modify such an exemption. The major impact of these holdings was simply to guarantee that states include reservation clauses in such grants.[91] *(See "Tax Exemptions," pp. 388–389.)*

FISH BUT NOT ALL FOWL

Under the police power, states have broad authority over fish and game and can prohibit, allow, or license hunting and fishing within their borders. In one of the more peculiar chapters in federal-state relations, the national government used the treaty power to take the subject of migratory birds out of state control. Spurred by conservationist concerns, Congress in 1913 enacted a law strictly regulating the killing of birds that migrated from state to state. Several federal courts held this law invalid, on the ground that it dealt with a subject Congress had no power to control.

Before a Supreme Court ruling was obtained on the matter, the U.S. government in 1916 signed a treaty with Canada providing for the protection of migratory birds. Using the treaty as a basis for action, Congress in 1918 enacted a new migratory bird protection law. The state of Missouri challenged the law as an invasion of the rights reserved to the states. The Court upheld the law on the basis that the treaty had removed the subject of migratory birds from state to federal jurisdiction.[1]

1. *Missouri v. Holland,* 252 U.S. 416 (1920).

THE POLICE POWER

The broadest of the powers reserved to the states is the police power—the authority of the state to govern its citizens, its land, and its resources and to restrict individual freedom to protect or promote the public good. Most of the Supreme Court's rulings on this power concern its impact on foreign or interstate commerce. *(See "The Police Power," pp. 393–394.)* Yet states exercise their police power in a multitude of ways that affect only matters within their borders. One use of the police power is illustrated by Louisiana's grant of a slaughterhouse monopoly, which was adjudicated in the *Slaughterhouse Cases* (1873). The Court upheld the monopoly against a constitutional challenge, finding it a proper exercise of the police power. Justice Miller acknowledged, for the Court, that this power "is, and must be from its very nature, incapable of any very exact definition or limitation. Upon it depends the security of social order, the life and health of the citizen, the comfort of an existence in a thickly populated community, the enjoyment of private and social life, and the beneficial use of property."[92] *(See "Slaughterhouse Cases," pp. 430–432.)*

In an earlier judicial description of the power, Justice Philip Barbour explained that under it a state had "the same undeniable and unlimited jurisdiction over all persons and things within its territorial limits, as any foreign nation, where...not...restrained by the Constitution."[93] The Court considers this internal use of the police power only when it is challenged as violating a constitutional right. When a state comes to the Court to defend its use of this power against such a challenge, the Court usually adopts a balancing approach, weighing the benefits the law provides against the constitutional cost. The Court in such decisions has recognized that the states have wide latitude to act to protect their natural resources from damage or diversion, to protect property values and the general quality of life in an area by the use of zoning requirements, and to protect the public health and morals through quarantine and health and even some censorship laws.

Environmental Protection

"It is a fair and reasonable demand on the part of a sovereign," wrote Justice Holmes in one of the first state environmental cases before the Court, "that the air over its territory should not be polluted on a great scale." Thus in 1907 the Court upheld Georgia's successful effort to win a court order directing a Tennessee copper company to stop the outpouring of sulphurous fumes that were destroying vegetation in the vicinity in both states.[94] The following year the Court upheld New Jersey's right to prohibit the diversion of water from its streams to New York, and in 1922 the justices, at the request of Wyoming, ordered Colorado to stop its diversion of the Laramie River.[95]

This police power of the state has its limits. In 1923 the Court refused to allow West Virginia to retain within the state and for its own use all the natural gas produced there. At the same time, however, the Court has approved state laws prohibiting the waste of its natural resources by companies exploiting them.[96] When Congress began enacting national environmental protection measures, the Court continued to uphold similar state laws. In 1973 the Court upheld Florida's water pollution law as complementary to federal legislation concerning oil spills in navigable waters. The Court reasoned that Congress had not preempted all state regulation of such matters and that the state could exercise its police power over maritime activities concurrently with the federal government. Five years later, however, the Court struck down Washington State's laws setting standards for the size and type of oil tankers permitted in Puget Sound, finding that they conflicted with federal law and the intent of Congress to set uniform national standards for such ships.[97] In the same vein the Court in 1990 said standards set by the Federal Energy Regulatory Commission for water flows in streams diverted by hydraulic power plants preempt tougher state regulations.[98] Two years later it ruled that states cannot impose licensing and training requirements on operators of hazardous waste sites that are stricter than the regulations under the Occupational Safety and Health Act.[99] In both cases the Court said federal law was clearly intended to preempt state regulation. *(See box, Supremacy, p. 380.)*

Occasionally, Congress's efforts to protect the environment have been curtailed to avoid impinging on state sovereignty. The Court in 1992 struck down part of a federal law intended to make states responsible for the low-level radioactive waste they generate. A principal section of that law made any state that failed to provide for the disposal of the waste generated within its borders the legal owner of the waste, liable for any injuries it might cause. Such a penalty, the Court held, violates the Tenth Amendment guarantee of state sovereignty by usurping states' legislative processes and compelling them to enforce a federal regulatory scheme.[100]

When the Environmental Protection Agency (EPA) in the George W. Bush administration refused to take action against global warming, twelve states, led by Massachusetts, went to court. They alleged that the EPA was required by the Clean Air Act to set tailpipe exhaust limits for cars and trucks for "any air pollutant…which may reasonably be anticipated to endanger public health or welfare." The act defined "welfare" to include "effects on weather…and climate." The states said that greenhouse gases, including carbon dioxide, were triggering a dangerous, and potentially catastrophic, rise in global temperatures. The administration lawyers, on behalf of the EPA, said the states did not have standing to sue. They also argued that carbon dioxide was not a true air pollutant and that the law called for the EPA administrator to use his best judgment on whether new emissions standards were needed.

In *Massachusetts v. Environmental Protection Agency* (2007) the Court ruled in favor of the states.[101] Environmentalists hailed the outcome, saying it repudiated the Bush administration's do-nothing approach to the climate crisis. The principal issue in the 5-4 decision was the question of standing. Could the states allege that they had suffered a "particularized injury" that gave them standing to sue the federal government? Justice Stevens relied heavily on Justice Holmes and the 1907 decision in the Tennessee copper case. There, he spoke of Georgia having "an independent interest…in all the earth and air within its domain."

"It is of considerable relevance that the party seeking review here is a sovereign state," Stevens wrote. "According to petitioners' unchallenged affidavits, global sea levels rose somewhere between 10 and 20 centimeters over the 20th century as a result of global warming. These rising seas have already begun to swallow Massachusetts' coastal land. Because the Commonwealth owns a substantial portion of the state's coastal property, it has alleged a particular injury in its capacity as a landowner."

Stevens went on to conclude that carbon dioxide was an "air pollutant" under the terms of the Clean Air Act, and he said the EPA must give a "reasoned justification" for its failure to set new emissions standards for vehicles. Justices Kennedy, Souter, Ginsburg, and Breyer agreed.

In dissent, Chief Justice Roberts insisted the states did not have standing. They did not present scientific evidence showing that global warming had caused an actual loss of coastal land. "It is pure conjecture," he said. And since climate change was a global phenomenon, he questioned whether a slight decline in carbon dioxide emissions in new American cars would have a global impact. The "desired emissions standards (for new motor vehicles) might reduce only a fraction of 4 percent of global emissions," he wrote. Standing is not a mere technicality, said the chief justice, but an issue of who decides. "This Court's standing jurisprudence simply recognizes that redress of grievances of the sort at issue here is the function of Congress and the Chief Executive, not the federal courts," he wrote. Justices Scalia, Thomas, and Alito joined his dissent.

Zoning and Property Rights

States and municipalities have long claimed broad powers to regulate the use of private property in the public interest. For example, no one wants to live next door to a garbage dump or a factory; the zoning power allows the government to keep garbage dumps and factories in industrial zones and away from residences by establishing regulations concerning the use of real property in certain areas. Repeated tests of this government power have come before the Supreme Court because the Constitution explicitly protects the rights of property owners. According to the Fourteenth Amendment, a state may not "deprive any person of life, liberty or property, without due process of law," and the Fifth Amendment states that "private property [shall not] be taken for public use without just compensation." Nevertheless, the Court generally has sided with state and local officials in ruling that zoning regulations do not deny property owners due process of law or "take" their property for public use.

In 1915 the Court upheld a Los Angeles ordinance that prohibited for health reasons brick making within city limits, even though the effect of the prohibition was to a put a brick maker out of business.[102] At times, a city's goal may be illegitimate. In 1917 the Court struck down a housing segregation ordinance in Louisville, Kentucky, that forbade blacks and whites to live in areas inhabited predominantly by members of the other race. This restriction, the Court held, interfered with the right of property, because it deprived a property owner of the right to sell to any qualified purchaser.[103] In 1922 the Court said for the first time that a government regulation of property had gone "too far" and resulted in an unconstitutional "taking" of private property. Usually, a "taking" meant the government had seized private property for its own purposes, such as to build a highway, an airport, or a military base. In these instances, the government would be obliged to compensate the property owner for the loss. Pennsylvania, however, had regulated coal mining, not to take the coal for its own use, but to protect homes and roads that might be damaged by the drilling of mines below them. It therefore passed a law prohibiting mining in areas where there was likely to be a harmful effect on houses.

The coal companies challenged this law as taking their private property, because in practical terms it meant that they had to leave the coal in the ground. In *Pennsylvania Coal v. Mahon* (1922) the Court agreed with the coal companies. Justice Holmes said that "while property can be regulated to a certain extent, if a regulation goes too far, it will be recognized as a taking." It was, he added, "a question of degree and therefore cannot be disposed of by general proposition."[104] Thereafter, Holmes's comment about land regulation that went "too far" was cited often by property rights advocates, but rarely was the Court persuaded that a mere regulation of property had the effect of taking it from its owners.

Zoning Upheld

Just four years later, in *Euclid v. Amber Realty* (1926), the justices handed down a landmark ruling upholding the zoning power of the government. The village of Euclid, Ohio, a suburb of Cleveland, had adopted a zoning plan that, among other things, prohibited businesses, hotels, and apartment houses from operating in certain residential neighborhoods. These limitations were challenged as a denial of the owner's right to the free use of his property. The Court heard the case argued twice. "Under the complex conditions of our day," Justice George Sutherland wrote for the 6-3 majority, new regulations can be imposed and upheld, even though had they been imposed a half-century earlier, they "probably would have been rejected as arbitrary."[105] Just as the advent of the automobile had demanded new traffic regulations, he said, the growth of cities and suburbs demanded new regulation of property and development. Sutherland continued:

> There is no serious difference of opinion in respect to the validity of laws and regulations fixing the height of buildings within reasonable limits, the character of materials and methods of construction, and the adjoining area to be left open, in order to minimize the danger of fire and collapse, the evils of overcrowding and the like, and excluding from residential sections offensive trades, industries and structures likely to cause nuisances.[106]

Although apartment houses are not "nuisances" in the normal sense of the law, they may bring with them the noise, traffic, and congestion that homeowners seek to avoid, he said. In this case, the city had decided that apartment houses created disadvantages for homeowners in an area, "interfering by their height and bulk with the free circulation of air and monopolizing the rays of the sun which otherwise would fall upon the smaller homes, and bringing…the disturbing noises incident to increased traffic and business…depriving children of the privilege of quiet and open spaces for play."[107] That value judgment would be allowed to stand. With this approach the Court consistently rebuffed challenges to zoning ordinances.

Clearing the Slums

In 1954 the Court upheld the use of the police power in a slum-clearance project intended to result in a more attractive community. Planning officials in the District of Columbia had decided to raze several blocks of a "blighted" area in the southwest quadrant of the city. A 1950 survey had found 64 percent of the dwellings there were "beyond repair," 58 percent had outdoor toilets, 60 percent had no baths, and 84 percent lacked central heating. Among the population of 5,012 persons, 97 percent were Negroes, according to the report. Once the land was condemned, the city planned to build streets,

schools, and other public facilities. It also planned to sell some land to developers, who pledged to build low-cost homes. But the executors for a deceased department store owner sued to save his business. They argued that the store was not blighted and that it was unconstitutional to take his property to sell it later to others. The suit invoked the Fifth Amendment, which says, "No person shall…be deprived of…property, without due process of law; nor shall private property be taken for public use without just compensation."

In *Berman v. Parker* (1954) the Court ruled unanimously that the city officials had broad power to act with the "public purpose" to seize and condemn homes and businesses to make way for redevelopment. Justice William O. Douglas said these projects should be evaluated based on the "need of the area as a whole," not on a "lot by lot, building by building" basis. "The experts concluded that, if the community were to be healthy, if it were not to revert again to a blighted or slum area, as though possessed of a congenital disease, the area must be planned as a whole."[108]

In another passage, he wrote:

> Miserable and disreputable housing conditions may do more than spread disease and crime and immorality. They may also suffocate the spirit by reducing the people who live there to the status of cattle. They may indeed make living an almost insufferable burden. They may also be an ugly sore, a blight on the community which robs it of charm, which makes it a place from which men turn. The misery of housing may despoil a community as an open sewer may ruin a river.[109]

Douglas's opinion in *Berman* put the Court's stamp of approval on the work of city planners. It voiced faith in their campaigns to eradicate the "disease" of substandard housing. It also cleared the way for urban renewal projects across the nation. Their impact was much disputed. Critics said these projects did more to "rob" cities of their life and "charm" than the neighborhoods they replaced.

Twenty years later Douglas again spoke for the Court as it upheld a zoning ordinance adopted by the village of Belle Terre, New York, which that restricted occupancy of its homes to single families, excluding groups of more than two unrelated persons:

The regimes of boarding houses, fraternity houses, and the like present urban problems. More people occupy a given space; more cars rather continuously pass by; more cars are parked; noise travels with crowds.

A quiet place where yards are wide, people few, and motor vehicles restricted are legitimate guidelines in a land use project addressed to family needs....The police power is not confined to elimination of filth, stench, and unhealthy places. It is ample to lay out zones where family values, youth values, and the blessings of quiet seclusion, and clean air make the area a sanctuary for people.[110]

The Court has, however, set some limits on the exercise of this police power. Just two years after the *Euclid* decision, the Court rejected a Seattle ordinance requiring the written consent of property owners in a neighborhood before a home for the aged could be built there. The justices found it unlikely that the home for the elderly could result in any injury, inconvenience, or annoyance to the community.[111] In 1977 the Court struck down a village ordinance that would deny a grandmother the right to live in the same household with her sons and grandsons. Writing for the 5-4 majority, Justice Lewis F. Powell Jr. declared that the challenged ordinance "slice[d] deeply into the family itself...select[ing] certain categories of relatives who may live together and declar[ing] that others may not....When a city undertakes such intrusive regulation of the family, neither *Belle Terre* nor *Euclid* governs; the usual judicial deference to the legislature is inappropriate."[112]

Seizing Houses

In 2005 the Court reaffirmed the broad power of city and state officials to condemn private property as a part of a redevelopment project. The public's reaction was immediate and vociferous. As a result, most states moved to put limits on the public power to seize houses and businesses for the purpose of spurring economic development.

Susette Kelo's case shone a stark light on the power of "eminent domain." The city of New London, Connecticut, was described as "economically distressed" after the navy closed its Undersea Warfare Center there. To revitalize its downtown and waterfront, a city agency planned to buy up 90 acres of land in hopes of attracting hotels, restaurants, stores, and urban townhouses. Pfizer, a pharmaceutical company, announced plans to build a research center there. City planners said the new development would bring jobs and more tax revenue to New London.

But Kelo and a few of her neighbors refused to sell their properties, even though the city offered to pay them more than the fair market value. Kelo's small pink Victorian-style house offered a view of Long Island Sound, and neither her home nor her neighborhood could be described as "blighted." She and her neighbors sued to block the seizure. A libertarian group, Institute for Justice, took up their case and argued it was unconstitutional for the government to seize private property to make way for private development. They relied on the Fifth Amendment's reference to "public use" and argued that private development is not a public use. In *Kelo v. New London* (2005) the Court in a 5-4 decision upheld the city's authority to seize the land and the homes.[113] Justice Stevens cited a long series of rulings "reflecting our longstanding policy of deference to legislative judgment in this field." In the nineteenth century land was seized by the government to build railroads and to flood fields with water that drove grist mills and factories. He also cited *Berman v. Parker* (1954), which upheld the razing of a D.C. neighborhood for the "public purpose" of revitalizing the area.

"Promoting economic development is a traditional and long accepted function of government," Stevens wrote. "Just as we decline to second-guess the city's considered judgments about the efficacy of its development plan, we also decline to second-guess the city's determinations as to what lands it needs to acquire in order to effectuate the project." It is not for courts or judges to decide what is a public purpose or which parcels of land are needed for the project to succeed, he said. Justices Kennedy, Souter, Ginsburg, and Breyer agreed.

In dissent, Justice O'Connor faulted the Court for abandoning a "long-held basic limitation on government power. Under the banner of economic development, all private property is now vulnerable to being taken and transferred to another private owner, so long as it might be upgraded," she wrote. "The specter of condemnation hangs over all property. Nothing is to prevent the State from replacing any Motel 6 with a Ritz-Carlton, any home with a shopping mall, or any farm with a factory."[114] Chief Justice Rehnquist and Justices Scalia and Thomas agreed. In separate dissent, Thomas said the Court had gone wrong by ignoring the language of the Constitution and relying on its own "misguided" precedents. "Something has gone seriously awry with this Court's interpretation of the Constitution. Though citizens are safe from the government in their homes, the homes themselves are not," Thomas wrote.[115] He and O'Connor said the victims of these redevelopment projects are most likely low-income, powerless persons. "Urban renewal projects have long been associated with the displacement of blacks," Thomas wrote. "In cities across the country, urban renewal came to be known as 'Negro removal,'" he said, quoting a critic of urban renewal.[116] Rehnquist, O'Connor and Scalia also joined his dissent.

Stevens stressed that states could revise their laws to limit such seizures. "Nothing in our opinion precludes any state from placing further restrictions on its exercise of the takings power," he wrote. In response to the ruling, most states considered legislation to forbid use of the "eminent domain" power to take houses or for the purpose of private development.

Historic Preservation

In 1978 the Court issued a major ruling that saved a historic landmark in New York City and helped to preserve historic and architectural landmarks across the nation. All fifty states and more than five hundred municipalities had enacted laws to preserve buildings, bridges, and other structures with historic or architectural significance. Some ordinances sought to preserve the character of a district, such as the French Quarter in New Orleans, while others focused on specific buildings that were judged to be of particular significance. For the buildings' owners, however, a high cost often came with the honor of possessing a building designated as a landmark. Regulations governing such property required that owners keep the old buildings in good repair and prevented them from making changes to the exterior without the approval of the state or local preservation board. In the late 1970s the Penn Central Railroad challenged New York City's Landmark Preservation Law after it was told that it could not sell the rights to build a fifty-five-story office tower above Grand Central Terminal. The eight-story beaux-arts terminal had stood at Park Avenue and 42nd Street in midtown Manhattan since 1913, but with the decline of the rail industry, Penn Central said it could not afford to preserve the station and lose out on the anticipated $3 million per year in extra revenue for renting the "air rights" above it.

New Yorkers and preservationists, including former first lady Jacqueline Kennedy Onassis, rallied to save Grand Central. In *Penn Central Transportation Co. v. New York City* (1978) the Court sided with the city and the preservationists, ruling that the special regulations governing landmarks do not go so far as to "take" private property for public use. Justice Brennan asserted that the city was not occupying the terminal for its use, but merely insisting on its preservation. Hundreds of other landmark buildings had similar restrictions, and taken together, these preservation activities benefited the entire city and its property owners, including the Penn Central Railroad. Speaking for the three dissenters, Justice Rehnquist said the cost of preserving the city's landmarks should be shared by all and not imposed on just a few property owners.[117]

Limits on "Taking" Private Property

After Rehnquist became chief justice in 1986, he led a revival of judicial protection for property rights. In a series of decisions, the Court ruled that the government had to justify special regulations preventing owners from enjoying the full use of their land. In 1987 the Court sided with the owner of a California beachfront home in ruling that the state could not force him to open his sandy beachfront to the public in exchange for a permit to enlarge his house. This is "not a valid regulation of land use, but an out-and-out plan of extortion," said Justice Scalia for the 5-4 majority in *Nollan v. California Coastal Commission* (1987). If the state "wants an easement across the Nollans' property, it must pay for it."[118]

Five years later, the Court ruled that state officials must pay compensation when they deny a property owner "all economically viable use of his land." David Lucas, a beachfront developer in South Carolina, bought two residential lots on the Isle of Palms near Charleston for $975,000. He intended to build two homes there, but shortly after his purchase, the state legislature passed the Beachfront Management Act, which prevented building on coastal land prone to erosion. The land owned by Lucas fell under this category, so he sued, contending that the state had taken his property without just compensation. The state supreme court disagreed, ruling that state officials had the power to prevent "harmful and noxious" uses of property. Overbuilding and erosion could ruin the state's precious beaches, the state judges said. In *Lucas v. South Carolina Coastal Council* (1992) the Court ruled that building a home is not a "noxious" use of land, and especially so where the land had been zoned for development, as in Lucas's case when he had purchased it. "When the owner of real property has been called upon to sacrifice all economically beneficial uses in the name of common good, that is, to leave his property economically idle, he has suffered a taking," said Justice Scalia for a 6-3 majority.[119]

In 1994 the Court came to the aid of the owner of a plumbing and electric supply store in Tigard, Oregon, who was told that she must allow a bike path to be built across her property in exchange for expanding her store. Florence Dolan's store sat near Fanno Creek, along which city officials wanted to build a "greenway" as a barrier against flooding. The bike path also might reduce traffic congestion, they said. Chief Justice Rehnquist said the city's rationales were unconvincing. "The city has never said why a public greenway, as opposed to a private one, was required in the interest of flood control," he wrote in *Dolan v. City of Tigard* (1994).[120] The chief justice noted that in cases involving the First Amendment, the Court had ruled that the government cannot force persons to give up their rights to free speech as a condition of participating in public programs; the same held for property rights. "We see no reason why the Takings Clause of the Fifth Amendment, as much a part of the Bill of Rights as the First Amendment or the Fourth Amendment, should be relegated to the status of a poor relation," Rehnquist wrote for the 5-4 majority.[121]

In this case, Dolan's enlarged store would not put a particular burden on the city by leading to a greater risk of flooding or increased traffic. Therefore, the city had exceeded its power by forcing her to give up part of her land in exchange for a building permit, he said. In the future, city and state officials must show a "rough proportionality" between the impact of a new development and their demands for exactions of property, Rehnquist said. This rule gave developers and landowners more clout in resisting the demands of government planners, though it did not mean that they would always win.

Indeed, the planners won a major victory in 2002, when the Court ruled that a temporary ban on development was not a taking. For thirty-two months between 1981 and 1984, the Tahoe Regional Planning Agency, a joint effort of California and Nevada, had prohibited all new construction on the hillsides surrounding Lake Tahoe. The clear blue waters of the mountain lake had been dulled by erosion, so planners said they needed time to formulate a new, go-slow approach to development. More than seven hundred owners of lots then filed a lawsuit contending that they had been denied all use of their land, just like David Lucas in South Carolina. The planning agency hired Washington lawyer John G. Roberts Jr. to represent it before the Court, and the future chief justice won a 6-3 decision. A delay in development, even a lengthy one, is not a taking, the Court ruled. "A regulation that affects only a portion of the parcel—whether limited by time, use or space—does not deprive the owner of all economically beneficial use," said Justice Stevens. If temporary delays were deemed to be takings, it "would transform government regulation into a luxury few governments could afford," he added.[122] Rehnquist dissented, along with Scalia and Thomas, arguing that although preserving Lake Tahoe makes sense, "the Constitution requires that the costs and burdens be borne by the public at large, not by a few targeted citizens."[123]

Zoning, Pornography, and Nude Dancing

The look of many urban downtowns changed dramatically in the 1970s and 1980s, thanks in large part to a pair of Court rulings that allowed city officials to zone out "adult" theaters, nightclubs, and bookstores. At the time, nearly every major city had a red-light district, where sex-related businesses tended to congregate. Their owners were shielded by the free speech protection of the First Amendment, so long as their entertainment was not judged to be obscene. The Court, in a divided opinion in 1976, upheld a Detroit ordinance that prohibited more than one adult business from operating on a city block or in a residential neighborhood. The five justices in the majority offered two rationales. Justice Stevens said sexually oriented expression was "low value" speech, not entitled to the same protections as discussion of politics and art. "Few of us would march our sons and daughters off to war to preserve the citizen's right to see 'Specified Sexual Activities' exhibited in the theaters of our choice," he wrote.[124] Others, including Justice Powell, said the restriction on adult businesses was justified because of their "secondary effects" on the neighborhood, such as leading to increasing crime, prostitution, and drug dealing.

In 1986 Justice Rehnquist spoke for a solid 7-2 majority, stating that city officials had broad power to force adult businesses out of downtown areas and into undesirable industrial zones. The city of Renton, Washington, near Seattle, had adopted an ordinance that prohibited an adult movie theater from operating within a thousand feet of a church, school, park, or residential area. The effect of the ordinance was to exclude such theaters from at least 95 percent of the property in the city. The theater's owners sued, arguing that the ordinance targeted them because of the content of their expression and deprived them of their right to do business. A lower court agreed, ruling that the ordinance violated the First Amendment. Rehnquist spoke for the Court in upholding the ordinance as a legitimate regulation of property

> The ordinance by its terms is designed to prevent crime, protect the city's retail trade, maintain property values, and generally protect and preserve the quality of the city's neighborhoods, commercial districts and the quality of urban life, not to suppress the expression of unpopular views.[125]

With this strengthened zoning power, New York City officials remade dark and seedy Times Square into a bright and popular nighttime entertainment district, and the same transformation took place on a smaller scale in cities across the nation.

The Court also gave states and cities the power to regulate what Rehnquist referred to as "bacchanalian revelries" that take place inside bars and nightclubs. In 1972 the Court upheld a California liquor control board regulation that prohibited sexual contact between dancers and patrons in bars and clubs that served alcohol. A lower court had determined that the regulation violated the freedom of expression protected by the First Amendment, but Rehnquist countered that the "broad sweep of the Twenty-first Amendment," which repealed Prohibition, gave state authorities the power to regulate the conditions for the sale alcohol.[126] The 6-3 decision marked one of the rare instances in which the Twenty-first Amendment was employed beyond the area of the state's power to sell beer, wine, and liquor.

In 1991 the Court went a step further by ruling that nude dancing can be prohibited under a state's laws against public indecency. A prosecutor in South Bend, Indiana, told the owners of the Kitty Kat Lounge that they could not offer the "totally nude dancing" that they had promised because state law forbids public nudity. Dancers must wear, at minimum, "pasties" and a "G-string," the prosecutor said. The theater's owner sued and won an appellate decision that nonobscene erotic dancing was protected by the First Amendment. In *Barnes v. Glen Theatre* (1991) the Court in a 5-4 decision upheld the state's power to regulate nude dancing, but the justices in the majority disagreed on the rationale. Chief Justice Rehnquist and Justices O'Connor and Kennedy contended that nude dancing is "expressive conduct within the outer perimeters of the First Amendment," but nevertheless may be prohibited under the state's authority to "protect societal order and morality." Rehnquist felt that "public indecency statutes such as the one before us reflect moral disapproval of people appearing in the nude among strangers in public places." The requirement that dancers wear pasties and G-strings is "narrowly tailored" to achieve the state's goal. Indeed, it is "the bare minimum necessary" to do so, he commented.[127]

Justice Scalia said he would uphold the state's requirement because it had nothing to do with free speech. The ban on public nudity "is a general law not specifically targeted at expressive conduct" and therefore "does not, in my view, implicate the First Amendment....The purpose of the Indiana statute...is to enforce the traditional moral belief that people should not expose their private parts indiscriminately," which is sufficient reason to uphold it, Scalia said.[128] Meanwhile, Justice Souter, in his first term, cast the deciding vote to uphold the ban because of the "pernicious secondary effects associated with nude dancing establishments," such as "higher incidence of prostitution and sexual assault in the vicinity of adult entertainment establishments."[129]

In *City of Erie v. Pap's A.M.* (2002) the Court reaffirmed that cities and states had the power to prohibit nude dancing, but once again the justices could not agree on the reasons why. Justice O'Connor spoke for the Court, with Chief Justice Rehnquist and Justices Kennedy and Breyer joining her, in upholding a city effort to forbid nude dancing as a crime control measure. The four of them asserted that a public indecency law that is not targeted at "expressive activity," but instead is "aimed at combating crime and other negative secondary effects caused by the presence of adult entertainment establishments," can stand, even if it restricts erotic dancing.[130] Justice Scalia, joined by Justice Thomas, again said the ban on such dancing had nothing to do with free expression and was justified by "the traditional power of government to foster good morals."[131] This time, Justice Souter dissented, expressing regret about his decision in the Indiana case and asserting that Erie's city officials had offered no evidence that nude dancing would bring crime to the area.

Public Health

The most drastic exercises of the police power upheld by the Court have involved protecting public health. In 1905 the Court rejected a man's challenge to the compulsory vaccination ordinance adopted by Cambridge, Massachusetts, to protect residents against smallpox. Justice John Marshall Harlan wrote the Court's opinion rejecting

the challenge to this requirement as depriving a citizen of his personal liberty without due process of law:

> Upon the principle of self-defense, of paramount necessity, a community has the right to protect itself against an epidemic of disease which threatens the safety of its members....[I]n every well-ordered society charged with the duty of conserving the safety of its members the rights of the individual in respect of his liberty may at times, under the pressure of great dangers be subject to such restraint...as the safety of the general public may demand.[132]

Twenty-two years later the Court applied this rationale to justify Virginia's decision, under state law, to sterilize Carrie Buck, a mentally slow woman with a "feeble-minded" mother and a "feeble-minded" child. The Court held that the sterilization was not a deprivation of rights without due process. Justice Holmes wrote,

> [T]he principle that sustains compulsory vaccination is broad enough to cover cutting the Fallopian tubes.
>
> We have seen more than once that the public welfare may call upon the best citizens for their lives. It would be strange if it could not call upon those who already sap the strength of the State for these lesser sacrifices...in order to prevent our being swamped with incompetence....Three generations of imbeciles are enough.[133]

Although this case has not been directly overruled, it was effectively nullified by the Court in 1942, when the justices struck down a similar Oklahoma law.[134]

Drugs and State Power to Regulate Doctors

The states' police powers have included the power to license physicians and to regulate the practice of medicine. In 2006 the Court rejected a move by the George W. Bush administration to punish physicians in Oregon who prescribed lethal doses of pain medication to patients who were terminally ill. Chief Justice Roberts had joined the Court just a few months before, and he dissented along with Justices Scalia and Thomas.[135]

In 1994 Oregon became the first state to legalize assisted suicide. Its voters approved a ballot measure known as the Death with Dignity Act, which authorized physicians to dispense or prescribe a lethal dose of medication at the request of a dying patient. In 1997 the Court in a case from Washington State ruled that the Constitution did not give persons a right to die or a right to assisted suicide, and its opinion said the development of this area of the law should be made by the people and their legislators, not judges.[136] With that implicit stamp of approval, Oregon put its new law into effect.

Sen. John Ashcroft, R-Mo., was among the social conservatives who opposed assisted suicide. He and several other lawmakers said prescribing drugs to hasten death was not a legitimate medical practice, and they urged the U.S. attorney general to declare that Oregon's doctors were violating the federal Controlled Substances Act. The law is enforced by the Drug Enforcement Administration, which comes under the authority of the Justice Department and the attorney general. But in 1998 Attorney General Janet Reno said the federal law did not give her the power "to displace the state as the primary regulators of the medical profession." Ashcroft and his allies tried but failed to win a majority in Congress to revise the statute.

In 2001 President Bush made Ashcroft the attorney general, and on November 9 Ashcroft issued an order saying that physicians who prescribed lethal medication would be in violation of federal drug control laws. Violators could lose their privilege to write prescriptions and could be prosecuted as drug criminals.

Oregon, joined by several physicians and patients, sued to block Ashcroft's order from taking effect. They won before a federal judge in Oregon and in the U.S. Court of Appeals for the Ninth Circuit. And in *Gonzales v. Oregon* the Court ruled Ashcroft had overstepped his power. The federal drug control law was intended to combat drug abuse and drug trafficking, Justice Kennedy said. It did not "delegate to a single Executive officer the power to effect a radical shift of authority from the states to the federal government to define general standards of medical practice in every locality."[137]

In dissent, Scalia said the Court should have deferred to Ashcroft's judgment on enforcing the law. This is especially true, he said, when "the judgment at issue had to do with the legitimacy of physician-assisted suicide, which ultimately rests, not on science or medicine, but on a naked value judgment."[138] Roberts cast his first significant dissent in the case, although he did not write separately.

THE JUDICIAL POWER

Federal judicial power clearly curtails the power of state courts. Most significant of these restraints is the Supreme Court's power to review the rulings of state courts on federal claims and questions. Initially granted by Congress in the Judiciary Act of 1789 and contested in the 1809 controversy with Gideon Olmstead, the power was upheld by the Court in *Martin v. Hunter's Lessee* (1816) and Cohens v. Virginia (1821). *(See "Judicial Review and the States," pp. 377–385.)* Once the power of the Supreme Court to have the last word on any federal question was made certain, however, the Court seemed quite willing, for decades, to leave large categories of litigation to the state courts. Until the mid-nineteenth century, almost all corporate and criminal litigation—as well as much admiralty litigation—was left to state courts. In 1810 the Court ruled that federal jurisdiction did not include cases brought by or against a corporation unless all the corporate stockholders lived in a state other than that of the opposing party. According to historian Charles Warren,

> As a result of this decision the reports of the Supreme Court and of the Circuit Courts during the first forty years thereafter reveal an almost complete absence of cases in which corporations (other than banking and insurance) were litigants; and the development of a body of corporation law by the Federal Courts was postponed to a late date in their history.[139]

Thirty-five years later the Court effectively reversed itself on this point, holding that a corporation was assumed to be a citizen of the state in which it was chartered. Therefore, any suit brought by or against a citizen of another state was properly within federal jurisdiction because of the diversity of citizenship.[140] In the same term that it decided *Martin v. Hunter's Lessee*, the Court ruled that federal courts lacked any criminal jurisdiction except that created by passage of federal laws declaring certain crimes to be federal.[141]

A CLASH OF COURTS: THE FEDERAL FUGITIVE SLAVE LAW

During the turbulent decade before the outbreak of the Civil War, the controversial Federal Fugitive Slave Act set off an extended tug-of-war between federal and state judicial power centering around one Sherman Booth, an abolitionist newspaper editor. In 1854 Booth, a resident of Milwaukee, Wisconsin, was arrested there and charged with violating the law by helping a fugitive slave escape from a deputy federal marshal. Because there was no federal prison in the area, Booth was confined after his arrest in a local jail.

From there he sought the aid of a state supreme court judge, who—like most people in Wisconsin—was not in sympathy with slavery or the federal law requiring the return of runaway slaves. The state judge issued a writ of habeas corpus to Stephen Ableman, the federal marshal holding Booth. He then declared the federal fugitive slave law unconstitutional and ordered Booth's release. Ableman complied, but after the order was upheld by the full state supreme court, he asked the U.S. Supreme Court to review the case *(Ableman v. Booth)*. Before the Court heard arguments, federal and state authorities clashed again. In 1855 Booth was indicted by a federal grand jury for violating the Federal Fugitive Slave Act. He was tried, convicted, and sentenced to spend one month in prison and to pay a $1,000 fine.

Three days after being sentenced, Booth again appealed to the Wisconsin courts for relief. The following day the court issued a writ of habeas corpus. It subsequently decided that Booth's imprisonment was illegal and ordered his release. He was set free, and the attorney general of the United States took the case to the Supreme Court *(United States v. Booth)*.

The Court did not resolve the matter until 1859, and when the decision came it was a vigorous assertion of national judicial supremacy. In writing the opinion, Chief Justice Roger B. Taney noted that it was the first time the state courts had tried to assert their supremacy over federal courts in cases arising under the Constitution and U.S. laws. That assertion was soundly rejected by a unanimous Court:

> It would seem to be hardly necessary to do more than to state the result to which these decisions of the state courts must inevitably lead. ... [N]o one will suppose that a government which has now lasted nearly seventy years, enforcing its laws by its own tribunals, and preserving the union of the States, could have lasted a single year, or fulfilled the high trusts committed to it, if the offenses against its laws could not have been punished without the consent of the State in which the culprit was found. ...
>
> [A]lthough the State of Wisconsin is sovereign within its territorial limits to certain extent, yet that sovereignty is limited and restricted by the Constitution of the United States. And the powers of the General Government, and of the State, although both exist and are exercised within the same territorial limits, are yet separate and distinct sovereignties, acting separately and independently of each other, within their respective spheres. And the sphere of action appropriated to the United States is as far beyond the reach of the judicial process issued by a state judge or a state court, as if the line of division was traced by landmarks and monuments visible to the eye.[1]

---

1. *Ableman v. Booth, United States v. Booth,* 21 How. (62 U.S.) 506 at 514–516 (1859).

As noted, until the mid-nineteenth century much of admiralty law was left to state courts, despite the Judiciary Act's explicit grant of admiralty jurisdiction to federal district courts. In 1825 the Supreme Court adopted a narrow definition of federal admiralty jurisdiction, limited to waters affected by the ebb and flow of the tides. This ruling left most of the nation's inland waterways under state control.[142] As steamboat and barge traffic increased, the Court reconsidered that definition and reversed it in 1851. Chief Justice Taney was frank about the impact of economic reality upon the Court's opinion: "[T]he conviction that this definition of admiralty powers was narrower than the Constitution contemplated, has been growing stronger every day with the growing commerce on the lakes and navigable rivers of the western States."[143] In *The Propeller Genesee Chief v. Fitzhugh* (1851) the Court ruled that federal admiralty courts had jurisdiction over all public, navigable waters upon which interstate or foreign commerce was carried. In 1866 the Court completed the removal of such matters from state courts, asserting exclusive federal jurisdiction over admiralty cases. States could still pass laws providing remedies in maritime accidents, but they could be enforced only in federal courts. This decision removed an "immense class of cases" from the state courts, reported Warren.[144]

Interference

Even after the establishment of the power of judicial review, questions steadily recurred concerning interference by state courts in federal matters and federal courts in state court matters. The Court ruled that state courts could not enjoin the judgment of a federal court or order a federal official to perform some duty by issuing a writ of mandamus; that states could not regulate the processes of federal courts; and that a state court's interpretation of state laws was not binding on federal courts.[145] The last holding was substantially modified in 1938, after almost a century. The Supreme Court held that in the absence of an applicable and controlling federal law or constitutional provision, federal courts should apply the appropriate state law to a situation before it.[146] The Court also has ruled that a federal court may not take property out of state court custody and that a state may not seize property attached by a federal court.[147]

Since the landmark ruling in *Ableman v. Booth* (1859) the Court has steadfastly denied to state courts the power to order federal officials to release a person they have in custody. *(See box, A Clash of Courts: The Fugitive Slave Law, p. 480.)* Federal courts, however, retain the power to issue a writ of habeas corpus to state officials ordering the release of a person held in custody in violation of his or her constitutional rights. The Judiciary Act of 1789 authorized federal courts to issue writs of habeas corpus as necessary "in the exercise of their respective jurisdictions," but that writ could be used only to order the release of federal, not state, prisoners until after the Civil War. In 1867 Congress expanded this power of habeas corpus to allow use of the writ to order the release of any person held "in violation of the Constitution or of any treaty or law of the United States."

The expansion of habeas corpus represented a new instrument for state prisoners who felt that their conviction had been obtained in a manner that violated their constitutional rights. The Supreme Court generally has required, however, that before a state prisoner uses this means of challenging a conviction in federal court that he exhaust all other avenues within the state court system. In the 1960s and 1970s the Supreme Court was divided over how strictly to apply this "exhaustion of remedies" requirement. In 1963 the Court held that a prisoner who missed the opportunity to raise federally based challenges to his conviction in state courts was not foreclosed by that failure from requesting a federal court to issue a writ of habeas corpus.[148] In subsequent years, however, the Court returned to its insistence on compliance with all state requirements before moving into the federal courts. In a 1977 ruling denying habeas corpus relief to a Florida prisoner who had failed to raise his constitutional claim at the proper time in state courts, Justice Rehnquist spoke of the need for ensuring that the state trial be the "'main event,' so to speak, rather than a tryout on the road for what will later be the determinative federal habeas hearing."[149] Later, in 1991, the Court said a prisoner could not file a habeas corpus petition in state court if he had failed to abide by state court procedural rules.[150]

State Constitutions and New Judicial Federalism

Cases come to the Supreme Court after a long journey through several lower courts, and sometimes the outcome reflects a mix of state and federal law. State courts are free to decide cases based on their state law or constitution—without being second-guessed by the U.S. Supreme Court. If, however, a state court's ruling also relies on the U.S. Constitution, that decision is subject to being reviewed by the Supreme Court. In 1983 the Court put state judges on notice that they must plainly set forth "an adequate and independent state ground" for their decisions if they wished to have them stand unchallenged. If "the state law ground is not clear from the face of the opinion, we will accept as the most reasonable explanation that the state court decided the case the way it did because it believed that federal law required it to do so," wrote Justice O'Connor in *Michigan v. Long* (1983).[151] "Both justice and judicial administration will be greatly improved" if state courts clearly say whether their decisions rely on state or federal law, she said.

Punitive Damages

"Punitive damages are a powerful weapon. Imposed wisely and with restraint, they have the potential to advance legitimate state interests. Imposed indiscriminately, however, they have a devastating potential for harm."[1] With those words in 1991, Justice Sandra Day O'Connor summarized the Court's growing concern over unlimited jury verdicts imposing punitive damages. In a civil suit, plaintiffs often seek money to compensate them for a loss or an injury, but sometimes the plaintiff's lawyer goes further and urges the jury to punish the defendant with an extra monetary penalty. Unlike a verdict for compensatory damages, the amount of punitive damages is not necessarily related to the defendant's loss. Indeed, plaintiffs' lawyers usually urge the jurors to look to the size and wealth of a corporate defendant when deciding on the proper punishment.

This system of punishment troubled most of the justices during the 1980s and 1990s even though they had a hard time agreeing on how the Constitution limits such state jury verdicts. They focused eventually on the Due Process Clause of the Fourteenth Amendment: "Although these awards serve the same purposes as criminal penalties, defendants subjected to punitive damages in civil cases have not been accorded the protections applicable in a criminal proceeding," wrote Justice Anthony M. Kennedy in 2003.[2] Without standards or limits, "punitive damages post an acute danger of arbitrary deprivation of property,"[3] he added. Nevertheless, the justices had several false starts before they agreed on how to limit punitive damages.

Previously, conservative leaders of the Court, including Chief Justice William H. Rehnquist and Justice Antonin Scalia, had faulted the liberal members for wielding the vague "Due Process" Clause to strike down state laws on contraceptives and abortion, and they were wary of doing the same to rein in state jury verdicts. They decided to wait instead for state legislatures to revise their laws. In 1989 business lawyers were disappointed when the Court upheld a Vermont jury's $6 million punitive verdict against an out-of-state trash hauler; the award was one hundred times greater than the damages to its local competitor.[4] On a 7-2 vote, the Court rejected the argument that this verdict was an "excessive fine" banned by the Eighth Amendment, which prohibits excessive punishment by the government, but not jury awards, the Court held. Two years later, the Court upheld an Alabama jury's $1 million punitive damage award against a California insurance company for failing to pay a medical claim of about $12,000. The Constitution does not set a "mathematical bright line" between acceptable and unacceptable jury awards, the 7-1 majority held.[5] In 1993 the Court upheld by a 6-3 vote a West Virginia jury's award of $10 million in punitive damages against a Texas corporation in a dispute over oil and gas drilling rights. The defendant, TXO Production Corp., argued that the award was grossly excessive when compared to the jury's award of $19,000 in compensatory damages.[6] Still waiting for the states to act, the Court's patience finally ran out.

In the case before the Court, David Long, a Michigan man, had challenged his conviction on drug charges for marijuana that was found in the trunk of his car. Officers had seen his car swerve and go off the road. Long contended the search of his trunk was illegal, and the Michigan Supreme Court agreed. In reversing that decision, O'Connor said the state court's ruling was based on an incorrect interpretation of the Court's past rulings on the Fourth Amendment. The Court therefore rejected Long's claim that his victory in the state courts was shielded from review in the Supreme Court. The rule set in *Michigan v. Long* has aided state as well as federal judges, wrote law professor Laurence Tribe. "Long advances interests that lie at the root of our federal system. It protects essentially federal interests by allowing the Court to maintain the supremacy and uniformity of federal law.... [It] also protects the autonomy of state law...and helps state judges by assuring them a firm basis for expounding their state constitutions, which may contain unexplored grounds for rights reaching beyond those contained in the federal Constitution."[152]

THE POWER TO GOVERN

Although the Supreme Court ruled firmly after the end of the Civil War that states have no power to secede from the Union, it left to the states a certain area of

In 1996 the Court for the first time invalidated a jury award as unconstitutionally excessive.[7] Ira Gore Jr., a Birmingham, Alabama, physician, had sued BMW of North America after discovering that his new black sedan had been partly repainted before it was sold. The car had been marred by acid rain as it was shipped from Germany to a U.S. distributor; BMW's policy was not to disclose repairs worth 3 percent or less of a car's retail price. A jury awarded Gore $4 million as punishment to BMW for fraud and breach of contract for failing to disclose the refinishing. A state court reduced the award to $2 million on appeal, still about five hundred times the amount of the actual damage to the car. The Court ruled 5-4 for BMW, holding that the Fourteenth Amendment's Due Process Clause prohibits awards that are "grossly out of proportion to the severity of the offense." "Elementary notions of fairness enshrined in our constitutional jurisprudence dictate that a person receive fair notice not only of the conduct that will subject him to punishment but also of the severity of the penalty that a state may impose," wrote Justice John Paul Stevens for the majority.[8] He set out three factors for determining whether an award breaches due process: the reprehensibility of the conduct; the harm suffered by the victim; and a comparison between the award and potential civil penalties authorized or imposed in comparable cases. Stevens was joined by Justices O'Connor, Kennedy, David H. Souter, and Stephen G. Breyer. Chief Justice Rehnquist and Justices Scalia, Clarence Thomas, and Ruth Bader Ginsburg dissented.

In 2003 the Court went further and warned state court judges that they must limit exorbitant jury verdicts that target wealthy, out-of-state companies. The 6-3 decision threw out a $145 million punitive damage award from Utah against an auto insurance firm for failing to settle a claim against one of its policyholders who caused a fatal accident. The policyholder, Curtis Campbell, sued State Farm, alleging that the company's failure to settle left him exposed to a ruinous verdict. Having heard testimony about State Farm's practices nationwide, the jury awarded Campbell $1 million for his emotional distress and $145 million in punitive damages.

"This case is neither close nor difficult," said Justice Kennedy. The 145 to 1 ratio should have set off alarms for Utah's judges. "Few awards exceeding a single-digit ratio between punitive and compensatory damages ... will satisfy due process," he said. Moreover, "the wealth of a defendant [such as State Farm] cannot justify an otherwise unconstitutional punitive damages award."[9] In dissent, Justices Scalia and Thomas repeated their view that the Due Process Clause does not limit state juries. Ginsburg separately defended the jury's decision, stating that "the numerical controls today's decision installs seem to me boldly out of order."[10]

---

1. *Pacific Mutual Life Insurance Co. v. Haslip,* 499 U.S. 1 at 42 (1991).

2. *State Farm Mut. Automobile Ins. Co. v. Campbell,* 538 U.S. 408 (2003).

3. Id.

4. *Browning-Ferris Industries of Vermont v. Kelco Disposal,* 492 U.S. 257 (1989).

5. *Pacific Mutual Life Insurance Co. v. Haslip,* 499 U.S. 1 (1991).

6. *TXO Production Corp. v. Alliance Resources,* 509 U.S. 43 (1993).

7. *BMW of North America v. Gore,* 517 U.S. 559 (1996).

8. Id.

9. *State Farm Mut. Automobile Ins. Co. v. Campbell,* 538 U.S. 408 (2003).

10. Id.

---

freedom concerning the conduct of their internal government.[153] In the nineteenth century the Court upheld the state's power to move a county seat or to reduce the pay of its officers. Both actions were challenged as violating the Contract Clause.[154] A twenty-year tug-of-war followed Congress's decision in the 1960s to extend federal minimum wage and overtime requirements to some state employees. The Court first upheld this action as proper, but later struck it down as undue federal interference in state business.[155] Justice Rehnquist wrote that the Constitution protected states from such federal interference with their traditional governmental functions, but after almost a decade of trying to sort those functions from "nontraditional" ones, in which Congress could interfere, the Court surrendered.[156] In 1985 it returned to its original position that it was proper for Congress to require state governments to pay their employees in line with federal minimum wage and overtime law.[157] The power of state and local governments to hire, fire, and retire individuals is constrained by the Constitution's guarantees of individual rights. In two decisions in the late twentieth century, the Court made that clear, applying the First Amendment to forbid states from basing decisions to hire, fire, and promote employees on party affiliation.[158]

Interstate Relations

Interstate relations, a matter given little thought by the average citizen, evoked great concern among the framers of the Constitution. The first effort to unite the former colonies into one nation—under the Articles of Confederation—had failed. As the framers labored at the Constitutional Convention in 1789, they were well aware of the situation that Charles Warren would later describe. The differences between the states were many, economically and socially, and "out of these differences arose materially hostile and discriminating state legislation....Pierce Butler of South Carolina said, in the Federal Convention, that he considered the interests of the Southern States and of the Eastern States 'to be as different as the interests of Russia and Turkey.'"[1] To facilitate smooth relationships between the newly linked states, the Constitution adopted some of the principles of international relations and converted them into provisions governing the relationships of the states.

FULL FAITH AND CREDIT

Article IV requires that each state give "full faith and credit" to the public acts of the other states, grant all citizens of all states certain privileges and immunities, and surrender a fugitive to the state where he is sought. Although the Constitution denies states the sovereign right to make treaties or alliances with foreign countries, it does recognize the potential usefulness of interstate agreements by providing, in Article I, that states could—with congressional consent—enter into compacts with each other. Congress is authorized by the Constitution to provide for the implementation of the full faith and credit provision, and it did so in laws passed in 1790 and 1804.

The meaning of the Full Faith and Credit Clause is simple. In civil cases, one state must treat the final judgment of the courts of another state as conclusive, settling the issues raised by the case. In 1813 the Supreme Court rejected the argument that the clause meant only that one state's judgment should be considered as important evidence when a second state's courts considered the same facts and the same question.[2] The judgment of one state, however, can be enforced or implemented in a second state only through that state's courts—where the second state, if opposed to the judgment, can usually block enforcement. Furthermore, the first state's judgment can be challenged in the second state with the claim that the first state court did not have jurisdiction over the matter decided or otherwise disregarded necessary technical points. Most modern Supreme Court cases arising under the Full Faith and Credit Clause involve questions of jurisdiction, especially called into play in cases when a divorce is granted to a temporary resident of a state. All states now, however, recognize divorces granted in other states.[3]

This requirement does not apply to criminal cases. One state does not enforce the criminal laws of another, chiefly because a person has the right to be tried for a crime in the place where the crime was committed, so the courts of other jurisdictions have no right to try him.[4] Edward S. Corwin wrote of the Full Faith and Credit Clause,

> There are few clauses of the Constitution, the literal possibilities of which have been so little developed. Congress has the power under the clause to decree the effect that the statutes of one State shall have in other States...power to enact standards whereby uniformity of State legislation may be secured as to almost any matter with which interstate recognition of private rights would be useful and valuable.[5]

PRIVILEGES AND IMMUNITIES

"The citizens of each state shall be entitled to all privileges and immunities of citizens in the several states," declares the Constitution in Article IV, section 2, leaving open the definition of "privileges and immunities." The primary purpose of this requirement, wrote Justice Samuel Miller a century after its adoption, was to require states to treat the citizens of other states in the same way as their own,

> to declare to the several States, that whatever those rights, as you grant or establish them to your own citizens, or as you limit or qualify, or impose restrictions on their exercise, the same, neither more nor less, shall be the measure of the rights of citizens of other states [when they are] within your jurisdiction.[6]

As to the definition of privileges and immunities, Miller referred to the case of *Corfield v. Coryell* (1823), which was decided by Justice Bushrod Washington, sitting as a circuit judge. Washington held that despite this clause, New Jersey could forbid out-of-state persons from gathering oysters in New Jersey. The privileges and immunities that New Jersey—and other states—were bound to grant all states' citizens were more general, such as the right to be protected by the government, the right to property, the right to travel through or live in a state other than the state of one's usual residence, and the right to bring lawsuits.[7]

In 1869 the Court held that the Privileges and Immunities Clause did not protect corporations from discriminatory treatment by states other than those where they were chartered. The Court has allowed states to distinguish in some areas between residents and nonresidents, upholding reasonable residency requirements and reasonably different nonresident license fees for people who wish to obtain fish and game licenses, business licenses, the right to practice a profession, to vote in state elections, or to run for state office.[8] The modern Court, however, has looked with increasing disfavor at state or city actions giving preference to local residents in the job market, whether it be in oil and gas development, public works, or the practice of law.[9] A state may not tax nonresidents (for example by imposing a commuter tax) if no comparable tax is imposed on its residents.[10] A state may not make medical services that are legal for its residents, such as abortions, illegal for nonresidents to obtain within its borders.[11] A state may not impose on goods brought from outside the state taxes higher than those on in-state purchases, even if the difference is small.[12]

Because states are not required to enforce each other's criminal laws, Article IV asserts that "[a] person charged in any state with treason, felony, or other crime, who shall flee from justice, and be found in another state, shall, on demand of the executive authority of the state from which he fled, be delivered up, to be removed to the state having jurisdiction of the crime." For more than a century, however, the Supreme Court effectively nullified this requirement. The Court in 1861 held that this clause imposed a moral obligation on the governor of Ohio to surrender a fugitive to Kentucky, where he had been indicted for helping a slave to escape. The Court, however, ruled that the federal government, whether through the courts or other means, could not compel the surrender of this fugitive. Such federal coercion of state officials would be unconstitutional, it held in *Kentucky v. Dennison* (1861).[13]

The resulting ineffectiveness of this clause has been somewhat offset by the enactment of a federal law making it a crime to flee from state to state to avoid prosecution and the adoption, by most states, of a uniform extradition act. In *Puerto Rico v. Branstad* (1987) the Court discarded *Kentucky v. Dennison,* declaring it "the product of another time." *Dennison,* it said, reflected a relationship between states and the federal government that "is fundamentally incompatible with more than a century of constitutional development." The Court held that federal courts could indeed act to compel the surrender of an extradited fugitive. In a declaration with meaning that rippled far beyond the subject of extradition, Justice Thurgood Marshall stated, "The fundamental premise of the holding in *Dennison*—'that the states and the Federal Government in all circumstances must be viewed as coequal sovereigns'—is not representative of the law today."[14]

THE COMPACT CLAUSE

Article I, section 10, declares that "no state shall, without the consent of Congress,...enter into any Agreement or Compact with another state." The Supreme Court, however, has never invalidated any compact on the basis that it lacked congressional approval. It adopted a relaxed approach to the congressional consent requirement, ruling in *Virginia v. Tennessee* (1893) that Congress, by its silence, had given its approval to a compact settling a boundary dispute between the two states. Justice Stephen J. Field interpreted the requirement of formal congressional consent to apply only to "the formation of any combination tending to the increase of political power in the States, which may encroach upon or impair the supremacy of the United States or interfere with their rightful management of particular subjects placed under their entire control."[15] Compacts that do not tend to increase the power of the states vis-á-vis that of the national government or otherwise infringe on national prerogatives are assumed—in the absence of congressional action to the contrary—to have the requisite consent.

Because New York and New Jersey resolved their long-standing dispute over New York harbor in the 1830s with a compact, ending their pending case before the Supreme Court, many states have found compacts useful means of resolving mutual problems, from boundaries to resource conservation to pollution control. In a 1978 ruling on the Compact Clause, the Court upheld—as valid without express congressional consent—the MultiState Tax Compact, in which more than a dozen states joined to improve their methods of taxing interstate corporations.[16] The Court had strengthened the usefulness of compacts when it ruled in 1951 that once a state has adopted a compact, and the approval of Congress is granted or assumed, the state cannot unilaterally withdraw from it.[17]

STATE DISPUTES AND FEDERAL JURISDICTION

When, despite the facilitating provisions of the Constitution, two states find themselves suing each other, it is the exclusive function of the Supreme Court to hear the case, as Article III specifically extends federal judicial power to controversies between two or more states. It would be decades, however, before the Court settled such a controversy on its merits. The first case between states—New York and Connecticut—arrived at the Court in 1799 but was dismissed before it was decided.[18] Thirty years later New Jersey brought to the Court its quarrel with New York over control of the port of New York. New York refused to acknowledge the Court's jurisdiction. Chief Justice John Marshall firmly rejected the state's claim of immunity from the Court's reach in such a matter, but the states then resolved their problems by compact, ending their case before the Court. The compact adopted was the ancestor of the agreement establishing the Port Authority of New York and New Jersey.[19]

In 1846—after *Rhode Island v. Massachusetts* had been before the bench for eight years—the Court settled its first boundary dispute between states. At issue were 150 square miles that both states claimed. Once again, before the Court could get to the merits of the dispute, it was obliged to assert its authority to decide such interstate matters, an authority disputed by Massachusetts. The Court reaffirmed its authority and then decided the case in favor of Massachusetts.[20] In another land dispute, Missouri and Iowa almost went to war over some 2,000 square miles of contested territory. Each state had called out its militia before the Supreme Court decided the case in favor of Iowa in 1850. With its decision in *Missouri v. Iowa* the Court placed the territory in a free state rather than a slave state, which was no small matter at the time.[21] The settlement of the dispute drew favorable notice in Congress, where a senator commented:

> In Europe armies run [boundary] lines and they run them with bayonets and cannon. They are marked with ruin and devastation. In our country, they are run by an order of the Court. They are run by an unarmed surveyor with his chain and his compass, and the monuments which he puts down are not monuments of devastation but peaceable ones.[22]

Only months before the onset of the Civil War, the Supreme Court's power over interstate matters was acknowledged by the submission to the Court of a boundary dispute between the states of Alabama and Georgia.[23] After the war, boundary disputes multiplied, with many involving changes in the courses of the rivers or channels that had marked an original boundary. By that period in history, the Court's authority to resolve such matters was so generally accepted that they came naturally to the justices for settlement. With this acceptance, the variety of interstate issues coming to the Court increased greatly.

The classic postwar interstate case was between Virginia and West Virginia. Upon becoming a state separate from Virginia, West Virginia had agreed to assume a certain portion of Virginia's state debt. Soon after the end of the war, Virginia opened negotiations with West Virginia for payment of the money, but West Virginia resisted. In 1906 Virginia brought the matter to the Supreme Court, which declared that it had jurisdiction over this sort of interstate dispute and that West Virginia—by 1915—owed Virginia some $12 million. West Virginia still refused to pay. Virginia then asked the Supreme Court to order the West Virginia legislature to impose a tax to raise the money to pay the debt. Realizing that if it granted this unprecedented request, it might well be met with resistance from West Virginia, the Court delayed. The justices scheduled arguments on the question of how they might enforce such an order. West Virginia finally agreed to pay the debt, without the necessity of an order from the Supreme Court, enacting a bond issue to retire the debt.[24] Earlier, the Court had held that South Dakota, which owned North Carolina bonds, not only could sue North Carolina to recover money due, but also could foreclose, if need be, on the security pledged to back the bonds.[25]

In water-related disputes that began with the one between New York and New Jersey in 1829, the Court has been quite willing to hear states argue their points, but hesitant to order one state to act or to cease acting without strong proof by the complaining state of the need for such a judicial decree. Early in the twentieth century, the Court heard Missouri argue, in defense of its citizens' health, that Illinois should be ordered to halt its diversion of sewage into the Mississippi River, because it was exposing the citizens of Missouri to the risk of typhoid. The Court did not issue such an order, holding that Missouri had not proved its case.[26] Similarly, the Court heard Kansas argue for an order halting Colorado's diversion of the Arkansas River, but it held in 1907 that Kansas had not presented sufficient evidence to support issuance of the order. Fifteen years later, in 1922, the Court granted Wyoming an injunction halting Colorado's diversion of the Laramie River.[27] Through the end of the twentieth century, disputes over water rights continued to be a staple of the Court's calendar. The justices often were called in to interpret water-use agreements, river boundaries, and flow allocations to states.

──────── ★ ────────

NOTES

INTRODUCTION (PP. 371–376)

1. *Texas v. White*, 7 Wall. (74 U.S.) 700 (1869).
2. *New York v. United States*, 505 U.S. 144 at 188 (1992).
3. *Cohens v. Virginia*, 6 Wheat. (19 U.S.) 264 at 382 (1821).
4. *Ableman v. Booth*, 21 How. (62 U.S.) 506 at 517 (1859).
5. Charles Warren, *The Supreme Court in United States History*, rev. ed., 2 vols. (Boston: Little, Brown, 1926), 1:5–6.
6. C. Herman Pritchett, *The American Constitution*, 3rd ed. (New York: McGraw Hill, 1977), 46.
7. Letter to William B. Giles, December 26, 1825, cited in Warren, *Supreme Court in United States History*, 1:620–621.
8. Warren, *Supreme Court in United States History*, 2:547–548.
9. Alpheus T. Mason, *The Supreme Court from Taft to Warren* (Baton Rouge: Louisiana State University Press, 1958), 167.
10. *Younger v. Harris*, 401 U.S. 37 at 44 (1971).
11. *National League of Cities v. Usery*, 426 U.S. 833 at 845 (1976).
12. *Garcia v. San Antonio Metropolitan Transit Authority*, 469 U.S. 528 (1985).
13. Id.
14. Sue Davis, *Justice Rehnquist and the Constitution* (Princeton, N.J.: Princeton University Press, 1989), 204.
15. *United States v. Lopez*, 514 U.S. 549 (1995).
16. Id.
17. *U.S. Term Limits v. Thornton*, 514 U.S. 779 (1995).
18. Id.

JUDICIAL REVIEW AND THE STATES (PP. 377–385)

1. Address to Harvard Law School Association of New York, February 15, 1913, in Oliver Wendell Holmes Jr., *Collected Legal Papers* (New York: Harcourt Brace, 1920), 295–296.
2. Charles Warren, *The Supreme Court in United States History*, rev. ed., 2 vols. (Boston: Little, Brown, 1926), 1:5.
3. *Chisholm v. Georgia*, 2 Dall. (2 U.S.) 419 (1793).
4. Id. at 473.
5. Id. at 478–479.

6. Warren, *Supreme Court in United States History,* 1:96.

7. Ibid., 99–101.

8. Ibid., 101.

9. Ibid., 102.

10. Ibid., 144.

11. Ibid., 145–146.

12. *Ware v. Hylton,* 3 Dall. (3 U.S.) 199 (1796).

13. Id. at 283.

14. *United States v. Judge Peters,* 5 Cr. (9 U.S.) 115 at 136 (1809).

15. Warren, *Supreme Court in United States History,* 1: 374–387; Charles G. Haines, *American Doctrine of Judicial Supremacy,* 2nd ed. (Berkeley: University of California Press, 1932), 290–292.

16. Warren, *Supreme Court in United States History,* 1:443.

17. Carl B. Swisher, *American Constitutional Development,* 2nd ed. (Cambridge, Mass.: Houghton Mifflin, 1954), 108.

18. *Hunter v. Fairfax's Devisee,* 3 Dall. (3 U.S.) 305 (1796).

19. *Fairfax's Devisee v. Hunter's Lessee,* 7 Cr. (11 U.S.) 602 (1813).

20. *Martin v. Hunter's Lessee,* 1 Wheat. (14 U.S.) 304 at 351 (1816).

21. Id. at 324–325.

22. Id. at 338.

23. Id. at 343–344.

24. Id. at 347–348. For additional details, see Warren, *Supreme Court in United States History,* 1:442–453.

25. *Cohens v. Virginia,* 6 Wheat. (19 U.S.) 264 at 413–415 (1821).

26. Id. at 385.

27. Id. at 387–388.

28. Warren, *Supreme Court in United States History,* 1:547–564.

29. Ibid., 729–779.

30. *Cherokee Nation v. Georgia,* 5 Pet. (30 U.S.) 1 at 20 (1831).

31. *Worcester v. Georgia,* 6 Pet. (31 U.S.) 515 (1832).

32. Warren, *Supreme Court in United States History,* 1:757, citing *Life and Letters of Joseph Story* (1851), 2:83, 86.

33. Ibid., 1:769, citing Massachusetts Historical Society Proceedings, 2nd series, XIV.

34. Warren, *Supreme Court in United States History,* 2:256–260.

35. Robert H. Jackson, *The Struggle for Judicial Supremacy* (New York: Knopf, 1941), 17.

THE STATES AND THE ECONOMY (PP. 386–426)

1. Thomas Reed Powell, *Vagaries and Varieties in Constitutional Interpretation* (New York: AMS Press, 1967), 85.

2. Felix Frankfurter, *The Commerce Clause under Marshall, Taney and Waite* (Chapel Hill: University of North Carolina Press, 1937), 66–67.

3. Ibid., 18–19.

4. Ibid., 27.

5. Powell, *Vagaries and Varieties,* 176.

6. Charles G. Haines, *American Doctrine of Judicial Supremacy,* 2nd ed. (Berkeley: University of California Press, 1932), 313–314.

7. *Fletcher v. Peck,* 6 Cr. 87 (10 U.S.) at 130, 131 (1810).

8. Id. at 134.

9. Id. at 135.

10. *New Jersey v. Wilson,* 7 Cr. (11 U.S.) 164 (1812).

11. *The Providence Bank v. Billings,* 4 Pet. (29 U.S.) 514 at 562 (1830).

12. Id. at 563.

13. *Piqua Branch of the State Bank of Ohio v. Knoop,* 16 How. (57 U.S.) 369 (1854).

14. Id. at 378, 380, 389.

15. *Dodge v. Woolsey,* 18 How. (59 U.S.) 331 at 360 (1856); see Charles Warren, *The Supreme Court in United States History,* rev. ed., 2 vols. (Boston: Little, Brown, 1926), 2:250–255.

16. *Dartmouth College v. Woodward,* 4 Wheat. (17 U.S.) 519 at 644 (1819).

17. Id.

18. Id. at 647–648.

19. Id. at 712.

20. Warren, *Supreme Court in United States History,* 1:491.

21. *Sturges v. Crowninshield,* 4 Wheat. (17 U.S.) 122 (1819).

22. *Ogden v. Saunders,* 12 Wheat. (25 U.S.) 213 (1827).

23. Id. at 270.

24. Id. at 339.

25. *Mason v. Haile,* 12 Wheat. (25 U.S.) 370 (1827).

26. *Sturges v. Crowninshield,* 4 Wheat. (17 U.S.) 122 at 201 (1819).

27. *Bronson v. Kinzie,* 1 How. (42 U.S.) 311 (1843).

28. *Kelo v. City of New London,* 545 U.S. 469 (2005).

29. *Charles River Bridge v. Warren Bridge,* 11 Pet. (36 U.S.) 420 at 546 (1837).

30. Id. at 547–550.

31. Id. at 552–553.

32. *West River Bridge Co. v. Dix,* 6 How. (47 U.S.) 530 at 531–532 (1848).

33. *Pennsylvania Hospital v. Philadelphia,* 245 U.S. 20 (1917).

34. *Stone v. Mississippi,* 101 U.S. 814 at 1079 (1880).

35. Library of Congress, *The Constitution of the United States of America: Analysis and Interpretation* (Washington, D.C.: U.S. Government Printing Office, 1964), 409–410.

36. *Allgeyer v. Louisiana,* 165 U.S. 578 (1897).

37. Library of Congress, *The Constitution,* 410.

38. *Home Building & Loan Association v. Blaisdell,* 290 U.S. 398 at 425–426 (1934).

39. Id. at 428.

40. Id. at 434–435.

41. Id. at 439–440.

42. *W. B. Worthen Co. v. Thomas,* 292 U.S. 426 (1934); *Worthen Co. v. Kavanaugh,* 295 U.S. 56 (1935).

43. Edward S. Corwin, *The Constitution and What It Means Today,* 14th ed. (Princeton, N.J.: Princeton University Press, 1978), 140.

44. *Allied Structural Steel Co. v. Spannaus,* 438 U.S. 234 at 241 (1978).

45. *United States Trust Co. v. New Jersey,* 431 U.S. 1 (1977).

46. James Madison, Alexander Hamilton, and John Jay, *The Federalist Papers,* ed. Clinton Rossiter (New York: New American Library, 1961), No. 7, 63; No. 22, 145.

47. Felix Frankfurter, "Some Observations on the Nature of the Judicial Process of Supreme Court Litigation," *Proceedings of the American Philosophical Society* 98 (1954): 233, reprinted in *The Supreme Court: Views from Inside,* ed. Alan F. Westin (New York: Norton, 1961), 39.

48. *United States v. Lopez,* 514 U.S. 549 (1995).

49. Warren, *Supreme Court in United States History,* 1:598.

50. *Gibbons v. Ogden,* 9 Wheat. (22 U.S.) 1 at 189–190 (1824).

51. Id. at 194, 196.

52. Id. at 210–211.

53. Frankfurter, *Commerce Clause,* 18–19.

54. Alfred H. Kelly and Winfred A. Harbison, *The American Constitution: Its Origins and Development,* 7th ed. (New York: Norton, 1991), 296.

55. Carl B. Swisher, *American Constitutional Development,* 2nd ed. (Cambridge, Mass.: Houghton Mifflin, 1954), 193.

56. Warren, *Supreme Court in United States History,* 2:627–628.

57. *Willson v. Blackbird Creek Marsh Co.,* 2 Pet. (27 U.S.) 245 at 251 (1829).

58. *Mayor of New York v. Miln,* 11 Pet. (36 U.S.) 102 (1837).

59. *Groves v. Slaughter,* 15 Pet. (40 U.S.) 449 (1841); see Swisher, *American Constitutional Development,* 198.

60. *Thurlow v. Massachusetts, Fletcher v. Rhode Island, Peirce v. New Hampshire,* 5 How. (46 U.S.) 504 (1847).

61. *Smith v. Turner, Norris v. Boston,* 7 How. (48 U.S.) 283 (1849).

62. Warren, *Supreme Court in United States History,* 2:178.

63. *Cooley v. Board of Wardens of the Port of Philadelphia,* 12 How. (53 U.S.) 299 at 318–320 (1852).

64. Powell, *Vagaries and Varieties,* 152.

65. *Pennsylvania v. Wheeling & Belmont Bridge Co.,* 13 How. (54 U.S.) 518 at 566 (1852).

66. Warren, *Supreme Court in United States History,* 2:236.

67. *Henderson v. Wickham, Commissioners of Immigration v. The North German Lloyd, Chy Lung v. Freeman,* 92 U.S. 259, 275 at 273 (1876).

68. Id. at 280.

69. *Chicago, Burlington & Quincy Railroad Co. v. Iowa,* 94 U.S. 155; *The Chicago, Milwaukee & St. Paul Railroad Co. v. Ackley,* 94 U.S. 179; *Peik v. Chicago & Northwestern Railway Co.,* 94 U.S. 164; *The Winona & St. Peter Railroad Co. v. Blake,* 94 U.S. 180; *Stone v. Wisconsin,* 94 U.S. 181; *Munn v. Illinois,* 94 U.S. 113 (1877).

70. *Peik v. Chicago & Northwestern Railway Co.,* 94 U.S. 164 at 178 (1877).

71. *Munn v. Illinois,* 94 U.S. 113 at 126 (1877).

72. *Budd v. New York,* 143 U.S. 517 (1892).

73. *Wabash, St. Louis & Pacific Railway Co. v. Illinois,* 118 U.S. 557 (1886).

74. Id. at 573.

75. Id. at 575.

76. Id. at 577.

77. *Paul v. Virginia,* 8 Wall. (75 U.S.) 168 (1869).

78. *United States v. Southeastern Underwriters Association,* 322 U.S. 533 at 553 (1944).

79. Id. at 544.

80. *Prudential Insurance Co. v. Benjamin, Robertson v. California,* 328 U.S. 408 (1946).

81. *Kidd v. Pearson,* 128 U.S. 1 at 20, 21, 22–23 (1888).

82. *United States v. E. C. Knight Co.,* 156 U.S. 1 at 11, 12, 13 (1895).

83. *Oliver Iron Mining Co. v. Lord,* 262 U.S. 172 (1923); *Champlin Refining Co. v. Corporation Commission,* 286 U.S. 210 (1932); *Utah Power & Light v. Pfost,* 286 U.S. 165 (1932).

84. *National Labor Relations Board v. Jones & Laughlin Steel Corp.,* 301 U.S. 1 (1937).

85. *Mulford v. Smith,* 307 U.S. 38 (1939).

86. *Wickard v. Filburn,* 317 U.S. 111 at 128 (1942).

87. *Parker v. Brown,* 317 U.S. 341 (1942).

88. *Hall v. DeCuir,* 95 U.S. 485 at 489, 490 (1878).

89. *Louisville, New Orleans & Texas Railway Company v. Mississippi,* 133 U.S. 587 (1890).

90. Id. at 594.

91. *Plessy v. Ferguson,* 163 U.S. 537 (1896).

92. *Morgan v. Virginia,* 328 U.S. 373 (1946).

93. *Gayle v. Browder,* 352 U.S. 903 (1956).

94. *Hammer v. Dagenhart,* 247 U.S. 251 at 272–274, 276–277 (1918).

95. Id. at 281.

96. *Bailey v. Drexel Furniture Co.,* 259 U.S. 20 at 38 (1922).

97. *United States v. Darby,* 312 U.S. 100 at 114, 115, 118 (1941).

98. Powell, *Vagaries and Varieties,* 85.

99. Ibid., 162–163.

100. *Gibbons v. Ogden,* 9 Wheat. (22 U.S.) 1 at 208, 203 (1824).

101. *Willson v. Blackbird Creek Marsh Co.,* 2 Pet. (27 U.S.) 245 (1829).

102. *Charles River Bridge v. Warren Bridge,* 11. Pet. (36 U.S.) 420 at 552 (1837).

103. *Mayor of New York v. Miln,* 11 Pet. (36 U.S.) 102 at 132–133 (1837).

104. Id. at 139, 142.

105. Alpheus T. Mason and William M. Beaney, *The Supreme Court in a Free Society* (Englewood Cliffs, N.J.: Prentice-Hall, 1959), 82.

106. *Bank of Augusta v. Earle,* 13 Pet. (38 U.S.) 519 (1839).

107. Frankfurter, *Commerce Clause,* 106; *Pensacola Telegraph Co. v. Western Union,* 96 U.S. 1 (1877).

108. *Smith v. Turner, Norris v. Boston,* 7 How. (48 U.S.) 283 at 408, 467 (1849).

109. *Edwards v. California,* 314 U.S. 160 (1941).

110. *Thurlow v. Massachusetts, Fletcher v. Rhode Island, Peirce v. New Hampshire,* 5 How. (46 U.S.) 504 at 589–590, 592 (1847).

111. *Bartemeyer v. Iowa,* 18 Wall. (85 U.S.) 129 (1874).

112. *Mugler v. Kansas,* 123 U.S. 623 at 691–692 (1887).

113. *Kidd v. Pearson,* 128 U.S. 1 (1888); *Bowman v. Chicago & Northwestern Railroad Co.,* 125 U.S. 465 (1888).

114. *Leisy v. Hardin,* 135 U.S. 100 (1890); *Brown v. Maryland,* 12 Wheat. (25 U.S.) 419 (1827).

115. *Leisy v. Hardin,* 135 U.S. 100 at 124–125 (1890).

116. *In re Rahrer,* 140 U.S. 545 (1891).

117. *Clark Distilling Co. v. Western Maryland Railway,* 242 U.S. 311 (1917).

118. *Collins v. Yosemite Park and Curry Co.,* 304 U.S. 518 (1938); *James & Co. v. Morgenthau,* 307 U.S. 171 (1939); *Duckworth v. Arkansas,* 314 U.S. 390 (1941); *Carter v. Virginia,* 321 U.S. 131 (1944).

119. *Munn v. Illinois,* 94 U.S. 113 at 125–126 (1877).

120. *Burns Baking Co. v. Bryan,* 264 U.S. 504 (1924); *Wolff Packing Co. v. Industrial Court,* 262 U.S. 522 (1923); *Tyson and Brother v. Banton,* 273 U.S. 418 (1927); *Ribnik v. McBride,* 277 U.S. 350 (1928); *Williams v. Standard Oil Co.,* 278 U.S. 235 (1929); *New State Ice Co. v. Liebmann,* 285 U.S. 262 (1932); *Cotting v. Kansas City Stock Yards Co.,* 183 U.S. 79 (1901); *Townsend v. Yeomans,* 301 U.S. 441 (1937); *German Alliance Ins. Co. v. Lewis,* 233 U.S. 389 (1914).

121. *Nebbia v. New York,* 291 U.S. 502 at 536–537, 539 (1934).

122. *Holden v. Hardy,* 169 U.S. 366 (1898).

123. *Lochner v. New York,* 198 U.S. 45 at 57–58, 59, 61 (1905).

124. *Muller v. Oregon,* 208 U.S. 412 (1908).

125. *Bunting v. Oregon,* 243 U.S. 426 at 438, 439 (1917).

126. *Adkins v. Children's Hospital,* 261 U.S. 525 at 554, 559 (1923).

127. Id. at 562.

128. Id. at 570, 569.

129. *Morehead v. New York ex rel. Tipaldo,* 298 U.S. 587 at 611 (1936).

130. Id. at 635.

131. *West Coast Hotel Co. v. Parrish,* 300 U.S. 379 at 398 (1937).

132. Id. at 399, 400.

133. *United States v. Darby,* 312 U.S. 100 (1941).

134. *Maryland v. Wirtz,* 392 U.S. 183 (1968).

135. *National League of Cities v. Usery,* 426 U.S. 833 at 851 (1976).

136. *Garcia v. San Antonio Metropolitan Transit Authority,* 469 U.S. 528 (1985).

137. *Freeman v. Hewit,* 329 U.S. 249 at 251 (1946).

138. *Boston Stock Exchange v. State Tax Commission,* 429 U.S. 318 at 329 (1977), quoting Justice Tom C. Clark in *Northwestern States Portland Cement Co. v. Minnesota,* 358 U.S. 450, 457 (1959).

139. *Gibbons v. Ogden,* 9 Wheat. (22 U.S.) 1 at 199 (1824).

140. *McCulloch v. Maryland,* 4 Wheat. (17 U.S.) 316 at 426, 431 (1819).

141. Id. at 432.

142. Id. at 436–437.

143. *Brown v. Maryland,* 12 Wheat. (25 U.S.) 419 at 441–442, 443 (1827).

144. Frankfurter, *Commerce Clause,* 149.

145. *Brown v. Maryland,* 12 Wheat. (25 U.S.) 419 at 449 (1827).

146. *Woodruff v. Parham,* 8 Wall. (75 U.S.) 123 (1869).

147. Id. at 137.

148. *Brown v. Houston,* 114 U.S. 622 (1885).

149. *Low v. Austin,* 13 Wall. (80 U.S.) 29 at 33 (1872).

150. Id. at 34–35.

151. *Hooven & Allison Co. v. Evatt,* 324 U.S. 652 (1945).

152. *Michelin Tire Corp. v. Wages,* 423 U.S. 276 at 286 (1976); see also *Limbach v. The Hooven & Allison Co.,* 466 U.S. 353 (1984).

153. *R. J. Reynolds v. Durham County,* N.C., 479 U.S. 130 (1986).

154. *Northwestern States Portland Cement Co. v. Minnesota,* 358 U.S. 450 at 457–458 (1959).

155. *State Freight Tax Case, Philadelphia & Reading RR v. Pennsylvania,* 15 Wall. (82 U.S.) 232 at 280 (1873).

156. *State Tax on Railroad Gross Receipts, Philadelphia & Reading Railroad Co. v. Pennsylvania,* 15 Wall. (82 U.S.) 284 at 293, 295 (1873).

157. *Coe v. Errol,* 116 U.S. 517 (1886); *General Oil v. Crain,* 209 U.S. 211 (1908); *Western Union Telegraph Co. v. Massachusetts,* 125 U.S. 530 (1888); *Hans Rees' Sons v. North Carolina,* 283 U.S. 123 (1931); *United States Glue Co. v. Oak Creek,* 247 U.S. 321 (1918); *Maine v. Grand Trunk Railway Co.,* 142 U.S. 217 (1891); *Wisconsin v. J. C. Penney Co.,* 311 U.S. 432 (1940); *General Motors Corp. v. Washington,* 377 U.S. 436 (1964); *Northwestern States Portland Cement Co. v. Minnesota,* 358 U.S. 450 (1959).

158. *Mobil v. Vermont,* 445 U.S. 425 (1980); *Exxon v. Wisconsin,* 447 U.S. 207 (1980); *ASARCO v. Idaho State Tax Commission,* 458 U.S. 307 (1982); *F. W. Woolworth Co. v. Taxation*

and Revenue Department of New Mexico, 458 U.S. 354 (1982); Container Corporation of America v. Franchise Tax Board, 463 U.S. 159 (1983); Shell Oil Co. v. Iowa Department of Revenue, U.S. (1989); Barclays Bank PLC v. Franchise Tax Board of California, 512 U.S. 298 (1994).

159. Paul v. Virginia, 8 Wall. (75 U.S.) 168 (1869).

160. Crutcher v. Kentucky, 141 U.S. 47 at 57, 59, 60 (1891).

161. Swisher, American Constitutional Development, 844.

162. Complete Auto Transit Inc. v. Brady, 430 U.S. 274 (1977).

163. Department of Revenue of the State of Washington v. Association of Washington Stevedoring Companies, 435 U.S. 734 (1978); Western and Southern Life Insurance Co. v. State Board of Equalization of California, 451 U.S. 648 (1981); D. H. Holmes Co. Ltd. v. McNamara, 486 U.S. 24 (1988); Goldberg v. Sweet, 488 U.S. 252 (1989).

164. Welton v. Missouri, 91 U.S. 275 at 282 (1876).

165. Howe Machine Co. v. Gage, 100 U.S. 676 at 679 (1880).

166. Robbins v. Shelby County Taxing District, 120 U.S. 489 at 497–499 (1887).

167. Henneford v. Silas Mason Co., 300 U.S. 577 at 584 (1937).

168. Felt & Tarrant Co. v. Gallagher, 306 U.S. 62 (1939); Nelson v. Sears, Roebuck & Co., 312 U.S. 359 (1941); Nelson v. Montgomery Ward & Co., 312 U.S. 373 (1941); Scripto v. Carson, 362 U.S. 207 (1960); National Geographic Society v. California Board of Equalization, 430 U.S. 551 (1977).

169. Boston Stock Exchange v. State Tax Commission, 429 U.S. 318 at 336 (1977); see also Maryland v. Louisiana, 452 U.S. 456 (1981); Commonwealth Edison v. Montana, 453 U.S. 609 (1981); Armco Inc. v. Hardesty, 467 U.S. 638 (1984); Bacchus Imports Ltd. v. Dias, 468 U.S. 263 (1984); Tyler Pipe Industries v. Washington State Department of Revenue, 483 U.S. 232 (1987); American Trucking Associations v. Scheiner, 483 U.S. 266 (1987); New Energy Company of Indiana v. Limbach, 486 U.S. 269 (1988).

170. Quill Corp. v. North Dakota, 504 U.S. 298 (1992).

171. Nordlinger v. Hahn, 505 U.S. 1 (1992).

172. Id.

173. Id.

174. Department of Revenue of Kentucky v. Davis, I 553 U.S. — (2008).

THE STATE AND THE INDIVIDUAL (PP. 427–450)

1. Some scholars view later rulings of the Marshall Court, which interpreted broadly the protection of the Contract Clause for property rights against legislative amendment or nullification, as an effort to reassert the protection for property lost through this narrow interpretation of the Ex Post Facto Clause. See Alpheus T. Mason and William M. Beaney, The Supreme Court in a Free Society (Englewood Cliffs, N.J.: Prentice-Hall, 1959), 197.

2. Calder v. Bull, 3 Dall. (3 U.S.) 386 at 390, 391 (1798).

3. Thompson v. Missouri, 171 U.S. 380 (1898); Thompson v. Utah, 170 U.S. 343 (1898).

4. Dobbert v. Florida, 432 U.S. 282 (1977).

5. Nixon v. Administrator of General Services, 433 U.S. 425 (1977).

6. Stogner v. California, 539 U.S. 607 (2003).

7. Cummings v. Missouri, 4 Wall. (71 U.S.) 277 at 319 (1867).

8. Id. at 325.

9. Ex parte Garland, 4 Wall. (71 U.S.) 333 (1867).

10. Hawker v. New York, 170 U.S. 189 (1898); DeVeau v. Braisted, 363 U.S. 144 (1960); Garner v. Board of Public Works, 341 U.S. 716 (1951); Cole v. Richardson, 405 U.S. 676 (1972); Elfbrandt v. Russell, 384 U.S. 11 (1966).

11. Barron v. Baltimore, 7 Pet. (32 U.S.) 243 at 250 (1833).

12. Civil Rights Cases, 109 U.S. 3 at 22, 24–25 (1883).

13. Bailey v. Alabama, 219 U.S. 219 (1911).

14. Butler v. Perry, 240 U.S. 328 (1916); Arver v. United States (Selective Service Draft Law Cases), 245 U.S. 366 (1918).

15. Carl B. Swisher, American Constitutional Development, 2nd ed. (Cambridge, Mass.: Houghton Mifflin, 1954), 330–333, citing Congressional Globe 36:1089–1090, 2542, 2765–2766, and Congressional Globe 44: appendix 84.

16. The Butchers' Benevolent Association of New Orleans v. The Crescent City Live-stock Landing and Slaughter-house Co., Esteben v. Louisiana (The Slaughterhouse Cases), 16 Wall. (83 U.S.) 36 (1873).

17. Id. at 74.

18. Id.

19. Id.

20. Id. at 77–78, 80–81.

21. Id.

22. Id. at 95–96.

23. Id. at 81.

24. United States v. Reese, 92 U.S. 214 (1876); United States v. Cruikshank, 92 U.S. 542 (1876); United States v. Harris, 106 U.S. 629 (1883).

25. United States v. Stanley, from Kansas; United States v. Ryan, from California; United States v. Nichols, from Missouri; United States v. Singleton, from New York; and Robinson v. Memphis and Charleston Railroad Co., from Tennessee.

26. The Civil Rights Cases, 109 U.S. 3 at 11, 13–14, 17 (1883).

27. Id. at 26.

28. Id. at 50.

29. Plessy v. Ferguson, 163 U.S. 537 at 544, 551 (1896).

30. Bradwell v. State [Illinois], 16 Wall. (83 U.S.) 130 (1873).

31. Minor v. Happerset, 21 Wall. (88 U.S.) 162 (1875).

32. Charles Warren, The Supreme Court in United States History, rev. ed., 2 vols. (Boston: Little, Brown, 1926), 2:567.

33. Yick Wo v. Hopkins, 118 U.S. 356 (1886).

34. Hurtado v. California, 110 U.S. 516 (1884).

35. *United States v. Reese*, 92 U.S. 214 at 217–218, 221 (1876).

36. *United States v. Cruikshank*, 92 U.S. 542 at 551, 554, 546 (1876).

37. *Ex parte Yarbrough*, 110 U.S. 651 at 657–658, 665 (1884).

38. *Guinn v. United States*, 238 U.S. 347 (1915); *Lane v. Wilson*, 307 U.S. 368 (1939).

39. *United States v. Classic*, 313 U.S. 299 (1941); *Smith v. Allwright*, 321 U.S. 649 (1944).

40. *Williams v. Mississippi*, 170 U.S. 213 (1898); *Lassiter v. Northampton County Board of Elections*, 360 U.S. 45 (1960).

41. *Harper v. Virginia State Board of Elections*, 383 U.S. 663 (1966).

42. *Oregon v. Mitchell*, *Texas v. Mitchell*, *United States v. Idaho*, *United States v. Arizona*, 400 U.S. 112 (1970).

43. *Gomillion v. Lightfoot*, 364 U.S. 339 (1960).

44. *Allgeyer v. Louisiana*, 165 U.S. 578 at 589 (1897).

45. *Chicago, Burlington & Quincy Railroad Co. v. Chicago*, 166 U.S. 226 (1897).

46. *Smyth v. Ames*, 169 U.S. 466 (1898).

47. Loren P. Beth, *The Development of the American Constitution, 1877–1917* (New York: Harper and Row, 1971), 67–68.

48. Ibid.

49. *Gitlow v. New York*, 268 U.S. 652 at 666 (1925).

50. *Stromberg v. California*, 283 U.S. 359 (1931).

51. *Near v. Minnesota*, 283 U.S. 697 (1931).

52. *Hamilton v. Board of Regents*, 293 U.S. 245 (1934).

53. *De Jonge v. Oregon*, 299 U.S. 353 (1937).

54. *Everson v. Board of Education*, 330 U.S. 1 (1947).

55. *Lovell v. Griffin*, 303 U.S. 444 (1938); *Cantwell v. Connecticut*, 310 U.S. 296 (1940).

56. *Hague v. CIO*, 307 U.S. 496 (1939).

57. *Minersville School District v. Gobitis*, 310 U.S. 586 (1940).

58. *West Virginia State Board of Education v. Barnette*, 319 U.S. 624 at 642 (1943).

59. *Powell v. Alabama*, 287 U.S. 45 at 71–72 (1932).

60. *Betts v. Brady*, 316 U.S. 455 at 461–462 (1942).

61. *Gideon v. Wainwright*, 372 U.S. 335 (1963).

62. *Tuney v. Ohio*, 273 U.S. 510 at 523 (1927).

63. *Moore v. Dempsey*, 261 U.S. 86 (1923); *Norris v. Alabama*, 294 U.S. 587 (1935); *Smith v. Texas*, 311 U.S. 128 (1940).

64. *Walker v. Sauvinet*, 92 U.S. 90 (1876); *Maxwell v. Dow*, 176 U.S. 581 (1900); *Duncan v. Louisiana*, 391 U.S. 145 (1968).

65. *Pointer v. Texas*, 380 U.S. 400 (1965).

66. *Twining v. New Jersey*, 211 U.S. 78 (1908).

67. *Malloy v. Hogan*, 378 U.S. 1 (1964); *Griffin v. California*, 380 U.S. 609 (1965).

68. *Brown v. Mississippi*, 297 U.S. 278 (1936).

69. *Escobedo v. Illinois*, 378 U.S. 478 (1964).

70. *Miranda v. Arizona*, 384 U.S. 436 (1966).

71. *United States v. Lanza*, 260 U.S. 377 (1922).

72. *Palko v. Connecticut*, 302 U.S. 319 at 325–326 (1937).

73. *Benton v. Maryland*, 395 U.S. 784 (1969).

74. *Wolf v. Colorado*, 338 U.S. 25 (1949).

75. *Weeks v. United States*, 232 U.S. 383 (1914).

76. *Mapp v. Ohio*, 367 U.S. 643 at 660 (1961).

77. *Ker v. California*, 374 U.S. 23 (1963).

78. *Terry v. Ohio*, 392 U.S. 1 (1968); *Chimel v. California*, 395 U.S. 752 (1969); *Schneckloth v. Bustamonte*, 412 U.S. 218 (1973); *Cady v. Dombrowski*, 413 U.S. 433 (1973); *Gustafson v. Florida, United States v. Robinson*, 414 U.S. 218 (1973); *Cardwell v. Lewis*, 417 U.S. 583 (1974); *South Dakota v. Opperman*, 428 U.S. 364 (1976).

79. *Louisiana ex. rel. Francis v. Resweber*, 329 U.S. 459 (1947).

80. *Robinson v. California*, 370 U.S. 660 (1962).

81. *Furman v. Georgia*, 408 U.S. 238 (1972).

82. *Gregg v. Georgia*, 428 U.S. 153 (1976); *Woodson v. North Carolina, Roberts v. Louisiana*, 428 U.S. 280, 325 (1976).

83. *Rummel v. Estelle*, 445 U.S. 263 (1980).

84. *Solem v. Helm*, 463 U.S. 277 (1983).

85. *In re Gault*, 387 U.S. 1 (1967). See also *Schall v. Martin, Abrams v. Martin*, 467 U.S. 253 (1984); *In re Winship*, 397 U.S. 358 (1970); *McKeiver v. Pennsylvania*, 403 U.S. 528 (1971).

86. *Yick Wo v. Hopkins*, 118 U.S. 356 (1886); Warren, *Supreme Court in United States History*, 2:596.

87. *Newberry v. United States*, 256 U.S. 232 (1921).

88. *Nixon v. Herndon*, 273 U.S. 536 (1927).

89. *Nixon v. Condon*, 286 U.S. 73 (1932).

90. *Grovey v. Townsend*, 295 U.S. 45 (1935).

91. *United States v. Classic*, 313 U.S. 45 (1941); *Smith v. Allwright*, 321 U.S. 649 (1944).

92. *Harper v. Virginia Board of Elections*, 383 U.S. 663 (1966).

93. *South Carolina v. Katzenbach*, 393 U.S. 301 (1966).

94. *Colegrove v. Green*, 328 U.S. 549 at 553–554, 556 (1946).

95. *Baker v. Carr*, 369 U.S. 186 at 237 (1962).

96. *Gray v. Sanders*, 372 U.S. 368 at 379 (1963).

97. Id. at 381.

98. *Reynolds v. Sims*, 377 U.S. 533 (1964); *Wesberry v. Sanders*, 376 U.S. 1 (1964).

99. *Kirkpatrick v. Preisler*, 394 U.S. 526 (1969); *Mahan v. Howell*, 410 U.S. 315 (1973).

100. *Gomillion v. Lightfoot*, 364 U.S. 339 (1960).

101. *Shaw v. Reno*, 509 U.S. 630 (1993).

102. *Davis v. Bandemer*, 478 U.S. 109 (1986).

103. *Vieth v. Jubelier*, 541 U.S. 267 (2004)

104. *League of United Latin American Citizens v. Perry*, 548 U.S. 399 (2006).

105. *Buchanan v. Warley*, 245 U.S. 601 (1917).

106. *Shelley v. Kraemer*, 334 U.S. 1 (1948).

107. *Reitman v. Mulkey*, 387 U.S. 369 (1967); *Hunter v. Erickson*, 393 U.S. 385 (1969); *James v. Valtierra*, 402 U.S. 137

(1971); *Village of Arlington Heights v. Metropolitan Housing Development Corp.,* 429 U.S. 252 (1977).

108. *Berea College v. Kentucky,* 211 U.S. 45 (1908).

109. *Missouri ex rel. Gaines v. Canada,* 305 U.S. 337 at 350 (1938).

110. *Sipuel v. University of Oklahoma,* 332 U.S. 631 (1948); *McLaurin v. Oklahoma State Regents,* 339 U.S. 637 (1950).

111. *Sweatt v. Painter,* 339 U.S. 629 (1950).

112. *Brown v. Board of Education of Topeka,* 347 U.S. 483 (1954).

113. *Brown v. Board of Education of Topeka (II),* 349 U.S. 294 (1955).

114. *Cooper v. Aaron,* 358 U.S. 1 (1958); *Griffin v. School Board,* 377 U.S. 218 (1964); *Green v. County School Board,* 391 U.S. 430 (1968); *Swann v. Charlotte-Mecklenburg Board of Education,* 402 U.S. 1 (1971); *Keyes v. Denver School District #1,* 413 U.S. 921 (1973).

115. *Loving v. Virginia,* 388 U.S. 1 (1967).

116. *San Antonio School District v. Rodriquez,* 411 U.S. 1 at 33, 55, 57 (1973).

117. *Kadrmas v. Dickinson Public Schools,* 487 U.S. 450 at 458 (1988).

118. *Edwards v. California,* 314 U.S. 160 (1941).

119. Id. at 178.

120. *Shapiro v. Thompson,* 394 U.S. 618 (1969), and *Memorial Hospital v. Maricopa County,* 415 U.S. 250 (1974).

121. *Saenz v. Roe,* 526 U.S. 489 at 510 (1999).

122. Id. at 502.

123. Id. at 505.

124. *Boddie v. Connecticut,* 401 U.S. 371 (1971); *Williams v. Illinois,* 399 U.S. 235 (1970); *Griffin v. Illinois,* 351 U.S. 12 (1955); *Argersinger v. Hamlin,* 407 U.S. 25 (1972).

125. *M.L.B. v. S.L.J.,* 519 U.S. 102 at 128 (1996).

126. *Yick Wo v. Hopkins,* 118 U.S. 356 (1886); *Heim v McCall,* 239 U.S. 175 (1915); *Crane v New York,* 239 U.S. 195 (1915).

127. *Heim v. McCall,* 239 U.S. 175 (1915); *Terrace v. Thompson,* 263 U.S. 197 (1923).

128. *Truax v. Raich,* 239 U.S. 33 (1915).

129. *Takahashi v. Fish & Game Commission,* 334 U.S. 410 (1948).

130. *Oyama v. California,* 332 U.S. 633 (1948).

131. *Graham v. Richardson,* 403 U.S. 365 (1971); *In re Griffiths,* 413 U.S. 717 (1973); *Sugarman v. Dougall,* 413 U.S. 634 (1973); *Nyquist v. Mauclet,* 422 U.S. 1 (1977); *Plyler v. Doe,* 457 U.S. 202 (1982); *Foley v. Connelie,* 435 U.S. 291 (1978); *Ambach v. Norwick,* 441 U.S. 68 (1979).

132. *Plyler v. Doe,* 457 U.S. 202 at 210, 230 (1982).

133. *Cronin v. Adams,* 192 U.S. 108 (1904).

134. *Goesaert v. Cleary,* 335 U.S. 465 (1948).

135. *Hoyt v. Florida,* 368 U.S. 57 (1961).

136. *Reed v. Reed,* 404 U.S. 71 (1971).

137. *Taylor v. Louisiana,* 419 U.S. 522 (1975).

138. *Stanton v. Stanton,* 421 U.S. 7 (1975); *Craig v. Boren,* 429 U.S. 190 (1976); *Dothard v. Rawlinson,* 433 U.S. 321 (1977).

139. *Kahn v. Shevin,* 416 U.S. 351 (1974).

140. *Dothard v. Rawlinson,* 433 U.S. 321 (1977).

141. *Geduldig v. Aiello,* 417 U.S. 484 (1974).

142. *Harris v. Forklift Systems Inc.,* 510 U.S. 17 (1994). Ginsburg is quoting from *Kirchberg v. Feenstra,* 450 U.S. 455, 461 (1982).

143. *United States v. Virginia,* 518 U.S. 515 (1996).

THE STATE AS SOVEREIGN (PP. 451–483)

1. *U.S. Term Limits v. Thornton,* 514 U.S. 779 at 838 (1995).

2. *Alden v. Maine,* 527 U.S. 706 at 715 (1997).

3. James Madison, Alexander Hamilton, and John Jay, *The Federalist Papers,* ed. Clinton Rossiter (New York: New American Library, 1961), No. 45, 292–293.

4. *McCulloch v. Maryland,* 4 Wheat. (17 U.S.) 316 at 436 (1819).

5. *Gibbons v. Ogden,* 9 Wheat. (21 U.S.) 1 at 222 (1824).

6. *United States v. E. C. Knight,* 156 U.S. 1 (1895); *Hammer v. Dagenhart,* 247 U.S. 251 (1918); *Bailey v. Drexel Furniture Co.,* 259 U.S. 20 (1922); *United States v. Butler,* 297 U.S. 1 (1936); *Ashton v. Cameron County,* 298 U.S. 513 (1936); *Carter v. Carter Coal Co.,* 298 U.S. 238 (1936).

7. *United States v. Butler,* 297 U.S. 1 at 68 (1936).

8. *Champion v. Ames,* 188 U.S. 321 (1903); *McCray v. United States,* 195 U.S. 27 (1904); *Rhode Island v. Palmer,* 253 U.S. 350 (1920); *Hoke v. United States,* 227 U.S. 308 (1913).

9. *Stewart Machine Co. v. Davis,* 301 U.S. 548 (1937); *Mulford v. Smith,* 307 U.S. 38 (1939); *Sunshine Anthracite Coal Co. v. Adkins,* 310 U.S. 381 (1940); *Chicot County Drainage District v. Baxter State Bank,* 308 U.S. 371 (1940).

10. *United States v. Darby Lumber Co.,* 312 U.S. 100 at 123–125 (1941).

11. *Chisholm v. Georgia,* 2 Dall. (2 U.S.) 419 (1793).

12. *Hans v. Louisiana,* 134 U.S. 1 (1890); *Monaco v. Mississippi,* 292 U.S. 313 (1934).

13. Thomas Reed Powell, *Vagaries and Varieties in Constitutional Interpretation* (New York: AMS Press, 1967), 19.

14. *Osborn v. Bank of the United States,* 9 Wheat. (22 U.S.) 738 (1824).

15. Charles Warren, *The Supreme Court in United States History,* rev. ed., 2 vols. (Boston: Little, Brown, 1926), 2:665.

16. *Poindexter v. Greenhow,* 114 U.S. 270 (1885).

17. *Johnson v. Lankford,* 245 U.S. 541 (1918).

18. *Scheuer v. Rhodes,* 416 U.S. 233 at 237 (1974).

19. *Gregory v. Ashcroft,* 501 U.S. 452 at 457 (1991).

20. Id. at 463.

21. *New York v. United States,* 505 U.S. 144 at 188 (1992).

22. *Seminole Tribe v. Florida,* 517 U.S. 44 at 72 (1996).

23. *Chisholm v. Georgia,* 2 Dall. (2 U.S.) 419 (1793).

24. Id. at 54.

25. *Hans v. Louisiana,* 134 U.S. 1 (1890).

26. *Pennsylvania v. Union Gas,* 491 U.S. 1 (1989).

27. *Seminole Tribe v. Florida,* 527 U.S. 44 at 76, 77 (1996).

28. *Printz v. United States,* 521 U.S. 898 (1997).

29. Id. at 922, 935.

30. Id. at 938–939.

31. Id. at 940, 970.

32. *Alden v. Maine,* 527 U.S. 706 (1999); *Florida Prepaid Postsecondary Education Board v. College Savings Bank,* 527 U.S. 627 (1999); *College Savings Bank v. Florida Prepaid,* 527 U.S. 666 (1999).

33. *Alden v. Maine,* 527 U.S. 706 at 736 (1999).

34. Id. at 741.

35. *Florida Prepaid Postsecondary Education Board v. College Savings Bank,* 527 U.S. 627 at 645 (1999).

36. Respectively, *Kimel v. Florida,* 528 U.S. 62 (2000) and *Alabama v. Garrett,* 531 U.S. 356 (2001).

37. *Federal Maritime Comm'n v. South Carolina Ports Authority,* 535 U.S. 743 (2002).

38. Id.

39. *Fitzpatrick v. Bitzer,* 427 U.S. 445 at 453 (1976).

40. *Nevada Dept. of Human Resources v. Hibbs,* 538 U.S. 721 (2003).

41. Id.

42. *U.S. Term Limits Inc. v. Thornton,* 514 U.S. 779 (1995).

43. *Federal Maritime Comm'n v. South Carolina Ports Authority,* 535 U.S. 743 (2002).

44. Erwin Chemerinsky, *Constitutional Law: Principles and Policies* (New York: Aspen Law and Business, 2002), 200.

45. *Ex parte Young,* 209 U.S. 123 at 159–160 (1908).

46. *Dombrowski v. Pfister,* 380 U.S. 479 (1965).

47. *Younger v. Harris,* 401 U.S. 37 at 45 (1971).

48. Id. at 44; *Pennzoil Co. v. Texaco Inc.,* 481 U.S. 1 (1987).

49. *Idaho v. Coeur d'Alene Tribe,* 521 U.S. 261 (1997).

50. *Luther v. Borden,* 7 How. (48 U.S.) 1 (1849).

51. *Pacific States Telephone & Telegraph Co. v. Oregon,* 223 U.S. 118 (1912).

52. *Wood v. Broom,* 287 U.S. 1 (1932).

53. *Colegrove v. Green,* 328 U.S. 549 (1946); *Baker v. Carr,* 369 U.S. 186 (1962); *Wesberry v. Sanders,* 376 U.S. 1 (1964); *Reynolds v. Sims,* 377 U.S. 533 (1964); *Davis v. Bandemer,* 478 U.S. 109 (1986).

54. *Mahan v. Howell,* 410 U.S. 315 (1973).

55. *Karcher v. Daggett,* 462 U.S. 725 (1983).

56. *Brown v. Thomson,* 462 U.S. 835 (1983).

57. *Vieth v. Jubelirer,* 541 U.S. 267 (2004).

58. Id.; *League of United Latin American Citizens v. Perry,* 548 U.S. 399 (2006).

59. *Vieth v. Jubelirer,* 541 U.S. 267 (2004).

60. *Davis v. Bandemer,* 478 U.S. 109 (1986).

61. *League of United Latin American Citizens v. Perry,* 548 U.S. 399 (2006).

62. Id.

63. *Newberry v. United States,* 256 U.S. 232 (1921).

64. *United States v. Classic,* 313 U.S. 299 (1941).

65. *Leser v. Garnett,* 258 U.S. 130 (1922).

66. *Oregon v. Mitchell, Texas v. Mitchell, United States v. Idaho, United States v. Arizona,* 400 U.S. 112 (1970).

67. *South Carolina v. Katzenbach,* 383 U.S. 301 at 324 (1966); *Katzenbach v. Morgan,* 384 U.S. 641 (1966).

68. *Williams v. Rhodes,* 393 U.S. 23 (1968); *Bullock v. Carter,* 405 U.S. 134 (1972); *Lubin v. Panish,* 415 U.S. 709 (1974); *Kusper v. Pontikes,* 414 U.S. 51 (1973); *Dunn v. Blumstein,* 405 U.S. 330 (1972); *Tashjian v. Republican Party of Connecticut,* 479 U.S. 208 (1986); *Munro v. Socialist Workers Party,* 479 U.S. 189 (1986).

69. *Crawford v. Marion County Election Board,* 553 U.S. — (2008).

70. *Buckley v. Valeo,* 424 U.S. 1 (1976).

71. *Nixon v. Shrink Missouri Government PAC,* 528 U.S. 377 (2000).

72. Id. at 398.

73. *Randall v. Sorrell,* 548 U.S. 230 (2006).

74. Warren, *Supreme Court in United States History,* 2:69.

75. *Loan Association v. Topeka,* 20 Wall. (87 U.S.) 655 (1875).

76. *McCulloch v. Maryland,* 4 Wheat. (17 U.S.) 316 (1819).

77. *Weston v. City Council of Charleston,* 2 Pet. (27 U.S.) 449 (1829); *Bank of Commerce v. New York,* 2 Bl. (67 U.S.) 620, 635 (1863); *Bank Tax Cases,* 2 Wall. (69 U.S.) 200 (1865).

78. *Van Brocklin v. Tennessee,* 117 U.S. 151 (1886).

79. *McCulloch v. Maryland,* 4 Wheat. (17 U.S.) 316 at 431 (1819).

80. *Dobbins v. Erie County,* 16 Pet. (41 U.S.) 435 (1842).

81. *Collector v. Day,* 11 Wall. (78 U.S.) 113 (1871).

82. *Pollock v. Farmers' Loan and Trust Co.,* 158 U.S. 601 (1895).

83. *South Carolina v. United States,* 199 U.S. 437 (1905).

84. *Indian Motorcycle Co. v. United States,* 283 U.S. 570 (1931).

85. *Long v. Rockwood,* 277 U.S. 142 (1928); *Panhandle Oil Co. v. Mississippi,* 277 U.S. 218 (1928); *Gillespie v. Oklahoma,* 257 U.S. 501 (1922).

86. *Panhandle Oil Co. v. Mississippi,* 277 U.S. 218 at 223 (1928).

87. *Fox Film Corp. v. Doyal,* 286 U.S. 123 (1932); *Helvering v. Gerhardt,* 304 U.S. 405 (1938); *Graves v. New York ex. rel. O'Keefe,* 306 U.S. 466 (1939).

88. *Helvering v. Gerhardt,* 304 U.S. 405 at 414, 419–420 (1938).

89. *South Carolina v. Baker*, 485 U.S. 505 (1988); *Garcia v. San Antonio Metropolitan Transit Authority*, 469 U.S. 528 (1985).

90. *United States v. Allegheny County*, 322 U.S. 174 (1944); *Alabama v. King & Boozer*, 314 U.S. 1 (1941). See also *United States v. New Mexico*, 455 U.S. 720 (1982); *Washington v. United States*, 460 U.S. 536 (1983); *Rockford Life Insurance Co. v. Illinois Department of Revenue*, 482 U.S. 182 (1987).

91. *New Jersey v. Wilson*, 7 Cr. (11 U.S.) 164 (1810); *The Providence Bank v. Billings*, 4 Pet. (29 U.S.) 514 (1830).

92. *The Butchers' Benevolent Association of New Orleans v. The Crescent City Livestock Landing and Slaughterhouse Co., Esteben v. Louisiana (The Slaughterhouse Cases)*, 16 Wall. (83 U.S.) 36 at 62 (1873).

93. *Mayor of New York v. Miln*, 11 Pet. (36 U.S.) 102 at 139 (1837).

94 *Georgia v. Tennessee Copper Co.*, 206 U.S. 230 at 238 (1907).

95. *Hudson Water Co. v. McCarter*, 209 U.S. 349 (1908); *Wyoming v. Colorado*, 259 U.S. 419 (1922).

96. *Pennsylvania v. West Virginia*, 262 U.S. 553 (1923); *Bandini Petroleum Co. v. Superior Court*, 284 U.S. 1 (1931); *Champlin Refining Co. v. Commission*, 286 U.S. 210 (1932).

97. *Askew v. American Waterways Operators Inc.*, 411 U.S. 325 (1973); *Ray v. Atlantic Richfield Co.*, 435 U.S. 151 (1978).

98. *California v. Federal Energy Regulatory Commission*, 495 U.S. 490 (1990).

99. *Gade v. National Solid Wastes Management Association*, 505 U.S. 88 (1992).

100. *New York v. United States*, 488 U.S. 1041 (1992).

101. *Massachusetts v. Environmental Protection Agency*, 549 U.S. —(2007).

102. *Hadacheck v. Los Angeles*, 239 U.S. 394 (1915).

103. *Buchanan v. Warley*, 245 U.S. 60 (1917).

104. *Pennsylvania Coal v. Mahon*, 260 U.S. 393 at 416 (1922).

105. *Euclid v. Amber Realty*, 272 U.S. 365 at 387 (1926).

106. Id. at 388.

107. Id. at 387, 388, 394.

108. *Berman v. Parker*, 348 U.S. 26 at 32 (1954).

109. Id. at 33.

110. *Village of Belle Terre v. Boraas*, 416 U.S. 1 at 9 (1974).

111. *Washington ex rel. Seattle Trust Co. v. Roberge*, 278 U.S. 116 (1928).

112. *Moore v. City of East Cleveland*, 431 U.S. 494 at 498–499 (1977).

113. *Kelo v. New London*, 545 U.S. 469 (2005).

114. Id. at 503.

115. Id. at 518.

116. Wendell E. Pritchett, "The Public Menace of Blight: Urban Renewal and the Private Uses of Eminent Domain," *Yale Law & Policy Review* 21, Issue 1 (2003): 47.

117. *Penn Central Transportation Co. v. New York City*, 438 U.S. 104 (1978).

118. *Nollan v. California Coastal Commission*, 483 U.S. 825 at 837, 842 (1987).

119. *Lucas v. South Carolina Coastal Council*, 505 U.S. 1003 at 1019 (1992).

120. *Dolan v. City of Tigard*, 512 U.S. 374 at 393 (1994).

121. Id. at 392.

122. *Tahoe-Sierra Preservation Council v. Tahoe Regional Planning Agency*, 535 U.S. 302 (2002).

123. Id. at 354.

124. *Young v. American Mini-Theaters*, 427 U.S. 50 at 70 (1976).

125. *Renton v. Playtime Theaters*, 475 U.S. 41 at 48 (1986).

126. *California v. LaRue*, 409 U.S. 109 (1972).

127. *Barnes v. Glen Theatre*, 501 U.S. 560 at 566, 568, 572 (1991).

128. Id. at 572, 575–576.

129. Id. at 586.

130. *City of Erie v. Pap's A.M.*, 529 U.S. 277 at 291 (2002).

134. Id. at 310.

132. *Jacobson v. Massachusetts*, 197 U.S. 11 at 27, 29 (1905).

133. *Buck v. Bell*, 274 U.S. 200 at 207 (1927).

134. *Skinner v. Oklahoma*, 316 U.S. 535 (1942).

135. *Gonzales v. Oregon*, 546 U.S. 243 (2006).

136. *Washington v. Glucksberg*, 521 U.S. 702 (1997).

137. *Gonzales v. Oregon*, 546 U.S. 243 at 275 (2006).

138. Id. at 296.

139. Warren, *Supreme Court in United States History*, 1:391.

140. *Bank of the United States v. Deveaux*, 5 Cr. (9 U.S.) 61 (1810); *Louisville Railroad v. Letson*, 2 How. (43 U.S.) 497 (1845).

141. *United States v. Hudson and Goodwin*, 7 Cr. (11 U.S.) 32 (1812); *United States v. Coolidge*, 1 Wheat. (14 U.S.) 415 (1816).

142. *The Thomas Jefferson*, 10 Wheat. (23 U.S.) 428 (1825).

143. *The Propeller Genesee Chief v. Fitzhugh*, 12 How. (53 U.S.) 443 at 451 (1851).

144. *The Moses Taylor, The Hine v. Trevor*, 4 Wall. (71 U.S.) 411, 555 (1866); Warren, *Supreme Court in United States History*, 2:415.

145. *McKim v. Voorhees*, 7 Cr. (11 U.S.) 279 (1812); *McClung v. Silliman*, 6 Wheat. (19 U.S.) 598 (1821); *Wayman v. Southand*, 10 Wheat. (23 U.S.) 1 (1825); *Swift v. Tyson*, 16 Pet. (41 U.S.) 1 (1842); *Martin v. Waddell's Lessee*, 16 Pet. (41 U.S.) 367 (1842).

146. *Erie Railroad Co. v. Tompkins*, 304 U.S. 64 (1938).

147. *Peck v. Jenness*, 7 How. (48 U.S.) 612 (1848); *Taylor v. Carryl*, 20 How. (61 U.S.) 583 (1858); *Freeman v. Howe*, 24 How. (65 U.S.) 450 (1861).

148. *Fay v. Noia*, 372 U.S. 391 (1963).

149. *Wainwright v. Sykes*, 433 U.S. 72 at 90 (1977).

150. *Coleman v. Thompson*, 501 U.S. 722 (1991).

151. *Michigan v. Long,* 463 U.S. 1032 at 1041 (1983).

152. Laurence H. Tribe, *American Constitutional Law* (New York: Foundation Press, 2000), 511–512.

153. *Texas v. White,* 7 Wall. (74 U.S.) 700 (1869).

154. *Newton v. Commissioners,* 100 U.S. 548 (1880); *Butler v. Pennsylvania,* 10 How. (51 U.S.) 402 (1851).

155. *Maryland v. Wirtz,* 392 U.S. 183 (1968); *National League of Cities v. Usery,* 426 U.S. 833 at 845, 851 (1976).

156. *National League of Cities v. Usery,* 426 U.S. 833 (1976).

157. *Garcia v. San Antonio Metropolitan Transit Authority,* 469 U.S. 528 (1985).

158. *Elrod v. Burns,* 427 U.S. 347 (1976); and *Rutan v. Republican Party of Illinois,* 497 U.S. 62 (1990). See also *O'Hare Truck Service v. Northlake,* 518 U.S. 712 (1996); *Board of County Commissioners, Wabaunsee County v. Umbehr,* 518 U.S. 668 (1996).

INTERSTATE RELATIONS (PP. 484–487)

1. Charles Warren, *The Supreme Court and Sovereign States* (Princeton, N.J.: Princeton University Press, 1924), 9.

2. *Mills v. Duryee,* 7 Cr. (11 U.S.) 481 (1813).

3. *Atherton v. Atherton,* 181 U.S. 155 (1901); *Haddock v. Haddock,* 201 U.S. 562 (1906); *Williams v. North Carolina,* 317 U.S. 387 (1942), and 325 U.S. 226 (1945); *Sherrer v. Sherrer,* 334 U.S. 343 (1948).

4. *Huntington v. Attrile,* 146 U.S. 657 (1892).

5. Edward S. Corwin, *The Constitution and What It Means Today,* 14th ed. (Princeton, N.J.: Princeton University Press, 1978), 166.

6. *Slaughterhouse Cases,* 16 Wall. (83 U.S.) 36 at 77 (1873).

7. *Corfield v. Coryell,* 6 F. Case 546, C.C.E.D. Pa. (1823).

8. *Paul v. Virginia,* 8 Wall. (75 U.S.) 168 (1869); *McCready v. Virginia,* 94 U.S. 391 (1877); *Toomer v. Witsell,* 334 U.S. 385 (1948); *LaTourette v. McMaster,* 248 U.S. 465 (1919); *Blake v. McClung,* 172 U.S. 239 (1898), and *Baldwin v. Montana Fish & Game Commission,* 436 U.S. 371 (1978).

9. Respectively, *Hicklin v. Orbeck,* 437 U.S. 518 (1978); *United Building and Construction Trades Council of Camden County v. Mayor and Council of City of Camden,* 465 U.S. 208 (1984); *Supreme Court of New Hampshire v. Piper,* 470 U.S. 274 (1985).

10. *Ward v. Maryland,* 12 Wall. (79 U.S.) 418 (1871); *Travis v. Yale and Towne Mfg. Co.,* 252 U.S. 60 (1920); *Austin v. New Hampshire,* 420 U.S. 656 (1975).

11. *Doe v. Bolton,* 410 U.S. 179 (1973).

12. *Associated Industries of Missouri v. Lohman,* 511 U.S. 641 (1994).

13. *Kentucky v. Dennison,* 24 How. (65 U.S.) 66 (1861).

14. *Puerto Rico v. Branstad,* 483 U.S. 219 (1987).

15. *Virginia v. Tennessee,* 148 U.S. 503 at 517–518 (1893).

16. *United States Steel Corp. v. MultiState Tax Commission,* 434 U.S. 452 (1978).

17. *West Virginia ex rel. Dyer v. Sims,* 341 U.S. 22 (1951).

18. Warren, *Supreme Court and Sovereign States,* 38–39.

19. *New Jersey v. New York,* 3 Pet. (28 U.S.) 461 (1830); also 5 Pet. (30 U.S.) 284 (1831); 6 Pet. (31 U.S.) 323 (1832).

20. *Rhode Island v. Massachusetts,* 4 How. (45 U.S.) 591 (1846).

21. *Missouri v. Iowa,* 7 How. (48 U.S.) 660 (1849), and 10 How. (51 U.S.) 1 (1850).

22. Charles Warren, *The Supreme Court in United States History,* rev. ed., 2 vols. (Boston: Little, Brown, 1926), 2:298.

23. *Alabama v. Georgia,* 23 How. (64 U.S.) 509 (1860).

24. *Virginia v. West Virginia,* 238 U.S. 202 (1915), 241 U.S. 531 (1916), and 246 U.S. 565 (1918).

25. *South Dakota v. North Carolina,* 192 U.S. 286 (1904).

26. *Missouri v. Illinois,* 180 U.S. 208 (1901).

27. *Kansas v. Colorado,* 206 U.S. 46 (1907); *Wyoming v. Colorado,* 259 U.S. 419 (1922).

chapter 5

Congressional Pressure

ONGRESS AND THE JUDICIARY are separate but interdependent branches of the federal government. The Supreme Court defines the limits of congressional authority under the terms of the Constitution; Congress confirms the Court's members, sets its jurisdiction, and pays its bills. Just as the Court has used its judicial review powers to influence the shape of federal legislation, so Congress has tried from time to time to use its powers over the Court to influence the outcome of particular rulings.

CONGRESSIONAL INFLUENCE

Congress can influence the Supreme Court in three general ways—through selection, confirmation, and impeachment of individual justices; through institutional and jurisdictional changes; and through direct reversal of the effects of specific Court decisions.

The Justices

Congress has limited influence over the president's choice of a Supreme Court nominee. There is no established procedure for Congress to advise the president on the choice of a nominee, although a majority in both houses at least twice has successfully petitioned the chief executive to nominate a particular person to a Court vacancy.

The Constitution does, however, require Senate confirmation of all Supreme Court nominees, and the Senate takes this responsibility seriously. Of the 150 nominations to the Court, 28 have failed to win confirmation. All but 6 of these rejections, most of them for partisan political reasons, occurred in the eighteenth and nineteenth centuries.

For a variety of reasons, Congress's power to impeach Supreme Court justices has been of little significance. Only one justice has been impeached—Samuel Chase in 1804—and he was acquitted by the Senate. Another justice, Abe Fortas, resigned in 1969 under threat of impeachment, but Justice William O. Douglas, accused a year later of committing similar improprieties, not only did not resign but also was cleared of all the charges. Through its appropriations process, Congress controls all of the money for the operation and maintenance of the federal judicial system, including the Supreme Court. It also sets the levels of the justices' salaries. Congress has never tried to pressure the Court by deliberately withholding operational funds. In 1964, however, after the Court handed down a series of controversial rulings, a majority in Congress voted to deny the justices as large a pay increase as other high-ranking federal employees received.

The Institution

Congress has been least successful in influencing the Court by making changes in the institution itself and in its procedures and functions. Only once has it stopped the Court from taking action by revoking its power to review a case while the case was pending. Proposals to limit the Court's jurisdiction so that it may not review federal legislation on specific subjects are offered whenever the Court issues a particularly controversial decision or series of rulings, but none of these proposals has been approved.

Congress has tried to influence the philosophical composition of the Court by changing its size. This ploy apparently worked once. In 1869, after the Court found a particular statute unconstitutional by a 4-3 vote, Congress increased the size of the Court by two members; the case was reconsidered, and the earlier decision was reversed by a 5-4 vote. Proposals to require unanimity or a two-thirds vote of the justices to declare federal statutes or state laws unconstitutional also have been made in Congress throughout the Court's history, but none has ever passed.

The Decisions

Congress has been far more adept at reversing specific Court decisions than at eliminating whole areas from Supreme Court review. Reversal may come about through legislation, if the Court's decision is based on statutory construction and interpretation, or through constitutional amendment, if the decision is an interpretation of a constitutional provision. The first constitutional amendment overturning a Supreme Court decision was the Eleventh, ratified in 1795; the first legislative reversal came in 1852.

Periods of Confrontation

There have been several major periods of confrontation between Congress and the Court. The first of these occurred in the early 1800s, when the national leadership passed from the Federalists to the Democratic-Republicans. The last confrontational period occurred in the mid-1950s and 1960s, when conservative members of Congress constantly challenged the liberal decisions on social issues handed down by the Warren Court.

In the 1800 elections, the Federalists lost Congress and the presidency to the Democratic-Republicans, and Thomas Jefferson was to replace President John Adams. To ensure that they would have some influence in the national government, the Federalists, in the final days of the Adams administration, passed legislation creating sixteen new circuit court judgeships and forty-two justice of the peace positions. The Federalists also stipulated that when the next vacancy occurred on the Court, it would go unfilled and the number of justices would be reduced by one. Adams quickly appointed Federalists to the new judgeships, but his midnight appointments came so late that some of the appointees never received their commissions. Their suit to force the Jefferson administration to honor the Adams appointments resulted in the famous *Marbury v. Madison* decision. *(See details of this case, pp. 79–83.)*

In 1802 the Democratic-Republicans repealed the new judgeships and raised the number of justices back to six. They also postponed the next Supreme Court term so that the Court would be unable to hear quickly an anticipated suit challenging the validity of the repeal. When the Court met again in 1803, it sustained the repeal. Still not satisfied, the Democratic-Republicans decided to attack the Federalists on the Supreme Court through impeachment, selecting as their first target Justice Samuel Chase, a man who had used his position on the bench to advance Federalist doctrine.

The House impeached Chase on a party-line vote, but the Democratic-Republicans did not hold together in the Senate, and he was acquitted. The House then passed a bill to authorize the president to remove a justice at the request of a majority of the House and Senate, but that effort also died in the Senate. After those two defeats, Democratic-Republicans ended their broadside attack on the Federalist judiciary, choosing instead to fill vacancies with individuals of their own persuasion as opportunities arose.

FEDERAL POWER VERSUS STATES' RIGHTS

In the 1820s and early 1830s controversial decisions expanded the powers of the national government at the expense of state sovereignty. This situation led Congress to try unsuccessfully to remove the Court's jurisdiction to hear cases challenging the validity of state laws. Repeal of this power would have prevented the

Court from reviewing the validity of any state law and would have resulted in conflict and confusion among the states. The proposals were, however, soundly defeated in the House in 1831.

Reconstruction

Congress had its greatest successes in curbing the Court during the post–Civil War Reconstruction era. In addition to reducing the number of justices, as vacancies occurred, from ten to seven to prevent President Andrew Johnson from making any appointments to the Court, Congress repealed the Court's jurisdiction to review certain denials of writs of habeas corpus. The repeal, which the Court ultimately sustained (but which Congress eventually reversed), prevented it from rendering an opinion in a pending case on the constitutionality of the congressional program of Reconstruction.

Once Johnson left office, Congress quickly raised the number of justices to nine. The additional seats proved critical to the Court's reversal of its decision that Congress could not make paper money a substitute currency for gold in the payment of debts.

Progressives

In the early 1920s Progressives in Congress tried to pressure the economically and socially conservative Court into rendering more liberal decisions, but these attempts were singularly unsuccessful. Indeed, few of their proposals won any consideration at all. Among the proposals were legislation to require two-thirds of the justices to concur in decisions declaring federal statutes unconstitutional and a measure to permit Congress to overrule a Court decision invalidating a federal law by repassing the statute with a two-thirds majority.

New Deal Crisis

Although an economically conservative Court clashed with Congress when it declared most of the early New Deal legislation invalid in the 1930s, the Court's real confrontation was with President Franklin D. Roosevelt, who sought to moderate the Court's conservatism by "packing" it with additional members. The plan was extremely unpopular; a majority in Congress opposed it and instead enacted legislation making retirement for elderly justices more financially attractive. Even though Roosevelt's plan to increase the size of the Court was defeated, at the cost of a serious rift in the Democratic Party, his goal of more economic power for the federal government was achieved.

In decisions reached before the Court-packing plan was unveiled but not announced, the Court indicated that it was adopting a broader view of federal economic regulatory powers. The Court reinforced its new stance by sustaining reenactment of much of the New Deal legislation it had previously found unconstitutional. Then, within months of enactment of the liberalized retirement bill, one of the conservative stalwarts on the Court announced his resignation. From that point on, Roosevelt was able to gradually make appointments that strengthened the liberal faction on the Court.

The Warren Court

During the fifteen years Earl Warren was chief justice (1954–1969), the Court consistently sustained individual and minority interests against what many citizens considered to be the best interests of the community. Warren began his career on the Court by writing the opinion declaring segregation in public schools unconstitutional. Under his guidance, the Court—often by narrow margins—sustained procedural rights for alleged wrongdoers and criminals, upheld the civil rights of blacks and other racial minorities, granted First Amendment protections to alleged subversives, narrowly defined what material was obscene and could therefore be banned, prohibited officially prescribed prayer and religious observances in public schools, and ordered state legislatures to reapportion on the basis of "one person, one vote."

Each of these decisions outraged some segment of the population. Complaints that the Court was too permissive and that its decisions would lead to the moral downfall of the country abounded, and billboards all across the country demanded Warren's impeachment.

Responding to their constituents and their own more conservative political and social philosophies, several groups in Congress tried to curb the Warren Court, but very few of these attempts were successful, and even fewer had any real effect on the Court. Efforts to cut back the Court's jurisdiction to review certain kinds of federal and state legislation failed, as did several attempts to reverse specific decisions by legislation or through constitutional amendment. Congress did succeed in reversing one decision relating to subversive activities and in modifying three decisions relating to criminal procedures in federal courts. The Court itself—under Warren and his successors, Warren E. Burger, William H. Rehnquist, and John G. Roberts Jr.—modified more of the disputed decisions than did Congress.

The Post-Warren Court

Although the Burger Court (1969–1986) was significantly more conservative than the Warren Court, a few of its decisions, including acceptance of forced busing as a method to achieve racial desegregation in public schools and its bar on state prohibition of abortions, elicited loud but ineffective calls from Congress for statutory reversal and jurisdictional curbs on the Court. In the 1980s, however, Congress succeeded in reversing two conservative decisions by the Court on questions of civil rights. In the area of voting rights, the Court had made challenges to discriminatory laws more difficult, but Congress amended the 1965 Voting Rights Act to contradict the ruling. A later Court decision that limited the impact of a sex discrimination ban, and affected similar language in other civil rights laws, was reversed by Congress, although the effort took several years to move through the legislative process. With Rehnquist as chief justice, the Court in 1989 cut back on the reach of federal laws against job discrimination. Another protracted legislative battle ensued, concluding in 1991 with passage of a broad-based reversal of several Court decisions.

In the second half of the 1990s, the Rehnquist Court struck down or limited a number of congressional measures that had been championed by liberal Democrats, including the Violence Against Women Act, the Brady Handgun Control Act, and the Americans with Disabilities Act. Senators Joseph Biden, D-Del., and Hillary Rodham Clinton, D-N.Y., spoke out against what they called "conservative judicial activism" by the Court. But Congress as a whole took no action seeking to reverse the decisions.

Republicans in Congress chafed at Court decisions that limited President George W. Bush's authority in the so-called war on terrorism. In *Hamdan v. Rumsfeld* (2006) the Court struck down Bush's rules for military commissions to try terrorists held at Guantánamo Bay, Cuba, on the grounds that these rules had not been written into law. Months later, Congress passed the Military Commissions Act to reverse the Court's decision and to give Bush the authority he needed. This victory proved to be short-lived, as the Court in *Boumediene v. Bush* (2008) struck down one provision of this law as unconstitutional because it barred prisoners from filing a writ of habeas corpus. In a 5-4 decision, the justices said prisoners can go to court to challenge the government's basis for holding them. And upon taking office, the Obama administration swiftly abandoned the use of military commission trials at Guantánamo.

For their part, Democrats in Congress objected when the Court made it harder for employees to sue over unequal pay. Writing for the 5-4 majority, Justice Alito said employees who sue must point to an unfair and discriminatory pay decision in the 180 days prior to the suit, citing the statute of limitation set in the law. This 2007 decision threw out a lower court verdict in favor of Lilly Ledbetter, an Alabama woman who learned she had been paid far less than men when she worked for Goodyear Tire Company. In 2009 the Democratic-led 111th Congress passed as its first measure the Lilly Ledbetter Fair Pay Act to reverse the Court's decision. The new law said each new paycheck could be considered an act of discrimination. The bill was signed into law by President Barack Obama.

Although Congress rarely has been successful—outside of reversing decisions through legislation—in directly pressuring the Court, it is impossible to measure how much, if any, indirect pressure is placed on the Court by consideration of Court-limiting proposals. Perhaps the overall impact of such congressional efforts has been not to weaken the Court's authority but to strengthen it. Each time Congress attempts to curb the Supreme Court and fails, the public perception is heightened that the Court as an institution is unassailable and that its decisions, except in extreme circumstances, are final.

Pressures on the Justices

Congress as an institution has little influence on the selection of nominees to the Supreme Court. Although the Constitution in Article II, section 2, stipulates that the president shall appoint Supreme Court justices by and with the advice and consent of the Senate, the advisory role usually occurs after the fact as the Senate considers confirmation.

SELECTION AND REJECTION

An individual senator or representative, particularly one who is personally close to the president, may wield some unofficial influence in the selection process. And because the Senate adheres to the custom of senatorial courtesy—a custom that reflects its reluctance to confirm a nominee who is repugnant to a senator of the nominee's home state—presidents do well to assure themselves in advance that their nominees will not be objectionable to the pertinent senators.

In at least two instances, a majority of the Senate and House successfully petitioned the president to nominate a specific individual. In 1862, 129 of 140 House members and all but four senators signed a petition urging President Abraham Lincoln to nominate Samuel F. Miller of Iowa to the vacancy created by the death of Justice Peter V. Daniel. The Senate confirmed Miller's nomination half an hour after receiving it.[1] After Justice Robert C. Grier announced his resignation in December 1869, members of Congress submitted a petition to President Ulysses S. Grant asking him to name former secretary of war Edwin M. Stanton to the seat. Already pending in the Senate was the nomination of Grant's attorney general, Ebenezer R. Hoar, to a second vacancy on the Court, but Hoar's nomination had run into some difficulty. Although Stanton was not Grant's first choice, the president acceded to the congressional request, thinking that the Stanton nomination might enhance Hoar's confirmation chances. Grant's strategy never bore fruit, however. Confirmed immediately upon nomination, Stanton died four days later of heart trouble. The Senate rejected Hoar in February 1870.[2]

Qualifications

Although the Constitution specifies qualifications that the president and members of Congress must meet, it sets no corresponding requirements for Supreme Court justices. Proposals to establish qualifications for the Court have been made throughout the nation's history, but few have received more than passing attention in Congress.

The most frequent recommendations are that justices be natural-born citizens, of a minimum age, and have a certain number of years of judicial experience. This last suggestion may grow into an informal requirement. Pressure from the legal community and the increasing complexity of the law have made experience on the bench an important consideration in the selection of nominees. Although the Senate does not play a significant role in the selection of justices, it plays a crucial one in the confirmation of Supreme Court nominees. Article II, section 2, of the Constitution provides that no nominee shall be seated unless confirmed by the Senate. Of the 148 individuals nominated to a seat on the Supreme Court, 29, nearly one-fifth, have failed to win confirmation. By contrast, the Senate has denied confirmation to only ten cabinet nominees.

Competence

Only two Supreme Court nominees have gone unconfirmed primarily on the grounds that they were not professionally qualified.[3] In 1873 President Grant nominated his attorney general, George H. Williams, to be chief justice. Williams had served as chief justice of the Oregon Territory, but his record was undistinguished.

When the Senate showed signs of balking at the nomination, Williams asked that his name be withdrawn.

Nearly one hundred years later President Richard Nixon's 1970 appointment of G. Harrold Carswell was rejected largely because of Carswell's mediocre juridical record. A second Nixon nominee, Clement F. Haynsworth Jr., although well qualified judicially, was rejected in part because he appeared insensitive to ethical improprieties and participated in cases where his financial interest might have involved him in conflicts of interest. Similar allegations of impropriety led to the resignation in 1969 of Justice Abe Fortas, nominated to the Court four years earlier by President Lyndon B. Johnson. (See "Fortas Resignation," pp. 510–511.)

Partisan Politics

By far, most Senate rejections of Supreme Court nominees have been grounded in political considerations. A primary factor in the rejection of fourteen nominees was the "lame-duck" status of the nominating president or the fact that the party in control of the Senate was confident that its presidential candidate would win the next election.

Both of these problems afflicted the Court nominations of President John Tyler, who has the dubious distinction of having more nominees rejected than any other president. Tyler had an opportunity to fill two vacancies, but only one of his six nominations was confirmed by the Senate. One nominee was rejected because his politics offended the party ruling the Senate. Two appointments were rejected because the Senate—anticipating correctly that Tyler, a Whig, would not be his party's candidate for election—wanted to hold the vacancies open. And two others, including one whom Tyler renominated, were rejected after the election of 1844, before the victor—Democrat James K. Polk—assumed office.

Ironically, Tyler made his only confirmed nomination during this period. As historian Charles Warren observed, Tyler's choice of Samuel Nelson "was so preeminently a wise one that the Senate at once confirmed it." [4] But the Senate's refusal to confirm any of Tyler's nominations to the second seat helped to create the longest vacancy in Supreme Court history. Other lame-duck presidents whose nominees were rejected include

John Quincy Adams, Millard Fillmore, James Buchanan, and Lyndon B. Johnson. (See "The 'Save-the-Seat' Syndrome," pp. 563–564.)

President Ronald Reagan was in the next to the last year of his eight-year stay at the White House when his nomination of Robert H. Bork was defeated by the Senate after one of the most vociferous confirmation battles in history. Bork's rejection stemmed largely from his often-articulated and well-known conservative views and the fact that he had been named to replace a "swing vote" on the Court, Justice Lewis F. Powell Jr. (Reagan's later selection of Douglas H. Ginsburg came to naught as well. Before his nomination was official, Ginsburg asked that his name be withdrawn because of the questions being raised about his possible conflicts of interest and his past drug use.[5] Reagan's third choice, Anthony M. Kennedy, was confirmed unanimously by the Senate in 1988.)

Several other nominations also were rejected because a majority of the Senate objected to specific political views or actions of the nominee. George Washington's nomination of John Rutledge for chief justice was refused because Rutledge had publicly attacked the Jay Treaty. Although it became apparent during the confirmation process that Rutledge suffered from occasional fits of insanity, "[t]he excited political situation was such that irrespective of Rutledge's mental condition his rejection by the Senate was certain," wrote Warren.[6]

Senate Whigs rejected future chief justice Roger B. Taney twice—first as Treasury secretary, forcing him to resign his recess appointment, and then as an associate justice because he had carried out President Andrew Jackson's orders to remove government deposits from the Bank of the United States.

James Madison's appointment of Alexander Wolcott failed in part because of his strict enforcement of the embargo and nonintercourse laws during his tenure as customs collector. James K. Polk's nomination of George W. Woodward did not succeed in part because Woodward held what were described as "native American sentiments" offensive to Irish Americans and other ethnic groups.

Jeremiah S. Black, a distinguished lawyer, had two strikes against him. He was a lame-duck appointment; President Buchanan nominated him a month before Abraham Lincoln was inaugurated. He also was

SUPREME COURT NOMINATIONS NOT CONFIRMED BY THE SENATE

Since the adoption of the U.S. Constitution in 1789, the Senate has rejected Supreme Court nominees twenty-eight times. One nominee, Edward King, twice failed to win Senate confirmation. A dozen have been rejected outright, and the remainder have been withdrawn or allowed to lapse when Senate rejection seemed imminent. Three were renominated later and confirmed. Following is the complete list of nominees failing to receive confirmation:

Nominee	President	Date of Nomination	Senate Action	Date of Senate Action
William Paterson	Washington	February 27, 1793	Withdrawn[1]	
John Rutledge[2]	Washington	July 1, 1795	Rejected (10–14)	December 15, 1795
Alexander Wolcott	Madison	February 4, 1811	Rejected (9–24)	February 13, 1811
John J. Crittenden	J. Q. Adams	December 17, 1828	Postponed	February 12, 1829
Roger Brooke Taney	Jackson	January 15, 1835	Postponed (24–21)[3]	March 3, 1835
John C. Spencer	Tyler	January 9, 1844	Rejected (21–26)	January 31, 1844
Reuben H. Walworth	Tyler	March 13, 1844	Withdrawn	
Edward King	Tyler	June 5, 1844	Postponed	June 15, 1844
Edward King	Tyler	December 4, 1844	Withdrawn	
John M. Read	Tyler	February 7, 1845	Not acted upon	
George W. Woodward	Polk	December 23, 1845	Rejected (20–29)	January 22, 1846
Edward A. Bradford	Fillmore	August 16, 1852	Not acted upon	
George E. Badger	Fillmore	January 10, 1853	Postponed	February 11, 1853
William C. Micou	Fillmore	February 24, 1853	Not acted upon	
Jeremiah S. Black	Buchanan	February 5, 1861	Rejected (25–26)	February 21, 1861
Henry Stanbery	A. Johnson	April 16, 1866	Not acted upon	
Ebenezer R. Hoar	Grant	December 15, 1869	Rejected (24–33)	February 3, 1870
George H. Williams[2]	Grant	December 1, 1873	Withdrawn	
Caleb Cushing[2]	Grant	January 9, 1874	Withdrawn	
Stanley Matthews	Hayes	January 26, 1881	Not acted upon[1]	
William B. Hornblower	Cleveland	September 19, 1893	Rejected (24–30)	January 15, 1894
Wheeler H. Peckham	Cleveland	January 22, 1894	Rejected (32–41)	February 16, 1894
John J. Parker	Hoover	March 21, 1930	Rejected (39–41)	May 7, 1930
Abe Fortas[2]	L. Johnson	June 26, 1968	Withdrawn	
Homer Thornberry	L. Johnson	June 26, 1968	Not acted upon	
Clement F. Haynsworth Jr.	Nixon	August 18, 1969	Rejected (45–55)	November 21, 1969
G. Harrold Carswell	Nixon	January 19, 1970	Rejected (45–51)	April 8, 1970
Robert H. Bork	Reagan	July 1, 1987	Rejected (42–58)	October 23, 1987
Harriet Ellan Miers	George W. Bush	October 3, 2005	Withdrawn	

SOURCE: Congressional Research Service, Library of Congress.

1. Later nominated and confirmed.

2. Nominated for chief justice.

3. Later nominated for chief justice and confirmed.

a northerner whose views on slavery were unacceptable to abolitionists. The Senate objected to Ebenezer Hoar for several reasons, two of which were that he had opposed the impeachment of President Andrew Johnson and had supported civil service reform. Rutherford B. Hayes's nomination of Stanley Matthews was initially rejected for political reasons and ethical considerations, but upon renomination he was confirmed.

In 1930 the American Federation of Labor (AFL) and the National Association for the Advancement of

Colored People (NAACP) mounted a successful lobbying campaign against confirmation of Herbert Hoover's appointee, John J. Parker. A well-qualified federal judge from North Carolina, Parker was accused of insensitivity to labor and racial problems. Civil rights activists might well have rued their success. Parker continued as a judge on the Fourth Circuit Court of Appeals where he handed down some of the earliest and most influential decisions in favor of rights for African Americans. The man elevated to the Supreme Court in his stead, Owen J. Roberts, was not so supportive on civil rights issues.

One nominee was denied the position of chief justice because the Senate could not decide what his political views were. In addition to being seventy-four years old at the time of his nomination in 1874, Caleb Cushing had been a Whig, a Tyler Whig, a Democrat, a Johnson Constitutional Conservative, and a Republican. Those shifting allegiances gained him so many political enemies that Senate opposition forced President Grant to withdraw the nomination.

Perhaps the most pointed political rejection of a nominee was the treatment of Henry Stanbery, President Andrew Johnson's attorney general. Stanbery was well liked, but the president was not. To deny Johnson any opportunity to make appointments to the Court, Radical Republicans in Congress engineered the passage of legislation that reduced the number of justices from ten to seven as vacancies occurred. The seat to which Stanbery had been appointed in 1865 was thereby abolished and his nomination was never considered. (See "Size of the Court," pp. 516–517.)

Senatorial Courtesy

A feud between a president and a senator prompted the only two rejections made solely on the grounds of senatorial courtesy. When Justice Samuel Blatchford died in 1893, President Grover Cleveland sought to replace him with another New Yorker. Sen. David B. Hill, D-N.Y., made several suggestions, but because he and Cleveland opposed each other on patronage matters, Cleveland ignored his recommendations and nominated New York attorney William B. Hornblower. Hill prevailed upon his colleagues, and the Senate rejected the nomination.

Undaunted, Cleveland next proposed another New Yorker, Wheeler Peckham. Again Hill objected, and again the Senate followed his wishes. To Hill's surprise, Cleveland abandoned his intention to nominate a New Yorker and instead selected Edward D. White of Louisiana, then serving as the Senate's Democratic majority leader. He was confirmed the same day he was nominated. In most instances, the Senate confirms sitting or former senators with little or no inquiry or opposition. One exception to that tradition was the rejection of North Carolina senator George E. Badger to fill the seat left vacant when Justice John McKinley died. President Fillmore, a Whig, named Badger, also a Whig, to the Court just three months before the inauguration of Democrat Franklin Pierce. Although it was highly irregular to reject one of its own members, the Democratic-controlled Senate wanted Pierce to fill the vacancy. As a result, Badger's nomination was postponed on February 11, 1853, by a one-vote margin, 26–25. Pierce took office the following month and nominated a fellow Democrat, John A. Campbell, who was confirmed.

CONTROVERSIAL CONFIRMATIONS

Perhaps because there has been some effort to submerge political considerations in favor of judicial experience when selecting and confirming Supreme Court nominees, fewer rejections have occurred in modern times. The Senate refused to confirm only five nominees as associate justices and one as chief justice in the twentieth century, compared with a total of twenty-two appointees rejected in the nineteenth century.

Six other twentieth-century nominations, however, faced stiff opposition—those of Louis D. Brandeis as associate justice in 1916, Harlan Fiske Stone as associate justice in 1925, Charles Evans Hughes as chief justice in 1930, Hugo L. Black as associate justice in 1937, William H. Rehnquist as chief justice in 1986, and Clarence Thomas as associate justice in 1991. To this list might be added Thurgood Marshall, the first black named to the Court. The Senate Judiciary Committee in 1961 and 1962 held up Marshall's confirmation as a judge of the Second Circuit Court of Appeals for a year before approving the nomination. In

The nomination of Louis D. Brandeis to the Supreme Court in January 1916 set off a four-month confirmation battle, in which conservative forces in industry and finance vigorously fought to keep Brandeis off the bench. President Woodrow Wilson and a host of progressive reform groups prevailed, and the Senate confirmed him by a wide margin.

1965 the same committee approved Marshall's appointment as solicitor general in less than a month. But when President Johnson named him to the Supreme Court in 1967, southern members of the Senate committee subjected Marshall to intense questioning about his opinions and judicial philosophy, after which Marshall was confirmed as an associate justice by a comfortable 69-11 vote.

Action on the Brandeis nomination a half-century earlier was delayed for months by the Senate Judiciary Committee as it pondered the nominee's "radical views." Although opposition to the nomination centered on Brandeis's liberal economic, political, and social posture, there is evidence that much of it was motivated by anti-Semitic prejudice.

At the time of his nomination, Stone was attorney general and was in the midst of prosecuting Burton K. Wheeler, a recently elected and influential Democratic senator from Montana, for oil land fraud. Wheeler was eventually acquitted of the charges, but with the aid of his home state colleague, Sen. Thomas J. Walsh, he fought Stone's nomination so vigorously on the Senate floor that it was recommitted for further investigation by the Judiciary Committee. Stone then personally appeared before the committee, something no previous Supreme Court nominee had done. Subjected to hostile questioning, Stone's performance was impressive, and the committee again recommended that he be confirmed. The full Senate concurred by a vote of 71-6.

Hughes's nomination as chief justice in 1930 was attacked primarily because the country was entering the Great Depression, and his views were considered too conservative for the times. Black encountered difficulties because he had once been a member of the Ku Klux Klan. Black repudiated his Klan involvement in a dramatic radio broadcast, and criticism waned.

Like the controversy over the nomination of Hughes as chief justice, the controversy that surrounded President Reagan's nomination of Justice Rehnquist as chief justice was in part a function of the point in time—and in the Court's history—at which it came. Reagan, who believed federal judges had become too activist and were interfering with civil rights and social policy that should be controlled by legislators, had made no secret of his desire to use his nominations to shape a more conservative Court. When he chose Rehnquist to succeed retiring chief justice Warren E. Burger, he moved the Court's most conservative member to its center chair. Rehnquist had been easily confirmed fifteen years earlier, but this time three months and five days of Senate debate passed before he won confirmation, 65–33. During that time, civil rights groups mounted an all-out effort to defeat his nomination as chief justice.[7]

The thirty-three votes cast against Rehnquist were the most ever cast against a Supreme Court nominee who won confirmation—until five years later when Clarence Thomas was nominated. Thomas, selected by President George H. W. Bush, was narrowly confirmed, 52-48, on October 15, 1991, after months

Clarence Thomas prepares to give testimony at a Senate Judiciary Committee hearing on his Supreme Court nomination, September 10, 1991. Thomas was narrowly confirmed, 52–48, after months of controversy.

of controversy over Thomas's conservative record and unprecedented last-minute hearings into a former Thomas employee's allegations of sexual harassment.

The harassment charges by Anita F. Hill, a law professor at the University of Oklahoma, had received only a cursory behind-the-scenes examination before the Senate Judiciary Committee deadlocked, 7-7, on the Thomas nomination on September 27. But the weekend before the full Senate's scheduled October 8 vote on the nomination, word of the allegations leaked out to reporters. Hill had submitted an affidavit to the Judiciary Committee outlining Thomas's unwelcome sexual advances to her when she worked with him in the early 1980s at the Department of Education and the Equal Employment Opportunity Commission.

The disclosure of the allegations—and the failure of the committee to investigate them thoroughly—touched off a storm of criticism and demands for more hearings.

The Judiciary Committee reopened its proceedings and took testimony from both Hill and Thomas, who denied the charges. The committee's awkward handling of the sexual harassment allegations, played out before a nation-wide television audience, and the lack of resolution of the charges prompted an outpouring of public anger and scorn against senators, particularly from women.

President George W. Bush, like his predecessor, Bill Clinton, hoped to avoid controversy by selecting well-regarded judges from the U.S. appeals courts for his Supreme Court nominees. Clinton chose Ruth Bader Ginsburg in 1993 and Stephen G. Breyer in 1994, and both won easy confirmation in a Democratic-controlled Senate with only a handful of "no" votes.

In 2005 Bush chose John G. Roberts Jr., followed shortly by Samuel A. Alito Jr. But, in between, Bush had a false start. On October 3 he selected Harriet Miers, his long-time lawyer from Texas, but after her name was officially submitted to the Senate, she withdrew because of outcries from Bush's conservative allies. Although Roberts and Alito were considered superbly qualified, each of them ran into opposition from the minority Democrats. Roberts won confirmation on a 78-22 vote, and Alito prevailed by a vote of 58 to 42. The vote count suggests that when the Senate is sharply divided along partisan lines, a president's nominee to the Supreme Court, even if well qualified, cannot count on support from the opposition party.

REMOVAL FROM OFFICE

The Constitution stipulates that Supreme Court justices, like all other federal judges, are appointed for life "during good behavior." A judge may die in office or retire, but the only method specified by the Constitution for forcible removal of a federal judge is through impeachment in the House and conviction by two-thirds of the Senate.

From time to time the other two branches of the federal government have thought to change the philosophical direction of the Supreme Court by proposing that justices serve a limited number of years. Thomas Jefferson wanted to limit the tenure of justices to six

The efforts of Rep. John Randolph (*right*) of Roanoke, Virginia, to prosecute Samuel Chase (*left*) in his 1805 impeachment trial before the Senate were no match for the defense, and Chase was acquitted. The House of Representatives had earlier voted to impeach Chase, a Federalist, for showing bias against Democratic-Republican defendants in circuit court trials.

years, with reappointment subject to approval of both the House and Senate. Such a scheme would have allowed the Democratic-Republican president and Congress to replace the Federalists on the Court with justices more in keeping with their political philosophy.

In 1957 Sen. James O. Eastland, D-Miss., and Rep. Thomas G. Abernethy, D-Miss., offered a constitutional amendment to limit terms of justices to four years and to require Senate approval of incumbent justices within six months of the ratification of the proposed amendment. This proposal showed the Mississippians' displeasure with some of the Warren Court's liberal rulings, including its decisions striking down state-imposed racial segregation.

None of the proposals to limit tenure has come close to passage. But proposals suggesting ways other than impeachment to remove judges who are physically or mentally incompetent or who conduct themselves unethically or improperly have received serious consideration. The Senate approved such a proposal in 1978, but the House took no action.

Impeachment

Article II, section 4, of the Constitution states that "all civil Officers of the United States, shall be removed from Office on Impeachment for, and conviction of, Treason, Bribery, or other high Crimes and Misdemeanors." The crimes of treason and bribery as grounds for impeachment have roused little debate, because treason is defined elsewhere in the Constitution and bribery is well defined in the criminal code. But throughout the nation's history there has been much debate about what the Constitution's authors meant by the phrase "high crimes and misdemeanors." Did they intend it to be read narrowly to mean that a judge could be removed from office only if he or she committed some indictable offense? Or did the framers intend that the phrase be construed broadly so that impeachment might be used as a political weapon?

The broad construction was the one held by the members of Congress who brought the only successful impeachment action against a Supreme Court justice. In 1804 Democratic-Republican members of the House of Representatives impeached Federalist justice Samuel Chase for misconduct. Their intent, if the Senate convicted Chase, was to then impeach other Federalist members of the Supreme Court, including the Democratic-Republicans' *bête noire,* Chief Justice John Marshall. But the Senate failed to convict Chase, Democratic-Republicans abandoned their plan, and Marshall's Federalist philosophy dominated the Court until his death in 1835.

Only two other justices have faced serious impeachment threats. Abe Fortas resigned from the Court in 1969 after the House threatened to begin an impeachment inquiry into his association with an industrialist convicted of securities irregularities. On two separate occasions the House investigated impeachment charges against William O. Douglas, first in 1953 because of his temporary stay of execution of two convicted spies, and again in 1970. The second attempt was spurred by conservative Republicans in part to retaliate for the Senate's rejection of two Nixon appointees, in part to reprimand the Court for issuing several decisions that conservatives disliked, and in part to punish Douglas for what they considered his inappropriate judicial and extrajudicial behavior. In neither instance did proceedings progress beyond the inquiry stage.

Chase Impeachment

The impeachment and trial of Justice Chase for partisan, harsh, and unfair judicial treatment while riding circuit had its roots in the Democratic-Republicans' desire to rid the federal judiciary of Federalist influence. When Jefferson was elected president and Democratic-Republicans gained control of Congress in 1800, the judiciary became the last Federalist stronghold in the national government.

Outgoing Federalist president John Adams sought to ensure continuation of his party's judicial influence by having Congress enact laws creating sixteen new circuit court judgeships and several dozen justice of the peace positions. He then filled these new posts with last-minute appointments, who quickly became known as "midnight judges."

In 1802 the Democratic-Republican Congress repealed the 1801 Judiciary Act creating the circuit court judgeships, and the Supreme Court upheld the repeal in 1803.[8] In the same year, Chief Justice Marshall, an ardent Federalist, announced the Court's unanimous decision in *Marbury v. Madison,* the case in which one of Adams's midnight appointees sued the Court to order the Jefferson administration to give him his commission. Marshall ruled that the Court did not have the constitutional authority to issue such an order, but in so doing he sharply rebuked President Jefferson and asserted for the Court the power to declare acts of Congress unconstitutional.[9] *(See "Marbury v. Madison," pp. 79–83.)* This decision convinced Democratic-Republicans that they should move against the Court. They had already used impeachment as a tool of intimidation, threatening to institute impeachment inquiries if the Court refused to approve repeal of the 1801 act or ruled against Jefferson in the *Marbury* case.

Other events were conspiring to make the idea of impeachment attractive. In January 1803 the Pennsylvania legislature had impeached and convicted a state judge of high crimes and misdemeanors, even though it was evident his only "crime" was being an active Federalist. In February, Jefferson sent to the House of Representatives documents complaining of the behavior of a U.S. district judge, John Pickering of New Hampshire. As one commentator described it, Pickering "was making a daily spectacle of himself on the bench because of intoxication aggravated by copious and blasphemous profanity."[10] The House responded immediately, passing on March 2 a resolution that impeached Pickering. He was later convicted and removed from office. Then, in May, Justice Chase provided the Democratic-Republicans with the excuse they needed to move against a member of the Supreme Court.

The Charges. An active patriot during the Revolutionary War, Chase was a signer of the Declaration of Independence and chief justice of Maryland before his appointment to the Supreme Court by President Washington in 1796. Chase's legal ability and integrity were unquestioned. But his personality made him unpopular with contemporaries; they found him arrogant, arbitrary, and guilty of using his position as a judge to advance his Federalist beliefs. As an associate justice, Chase openly approved passage of the despised Alien and Sedition Acts and actively campaigned for Adams's reelection in 1800. Although these activities aroused enmity, the greatest opprobrium fell on Chase for some of his judicial decisions.

Chase was severely condemned for his arbitrary and intemperate treatment of the sedition trial of James T. Callender, a Democratic-Republican printer indicted for writing during the 1800 presidential campaign, "Take your choice, then, between Adams, war and beggary, and Jefferson, peace and competency." Chase was apparently so rude to Callender's attorneys that they left the courtroom. Chase also was sharply criticized for his conduct of the trial of John Fries, the Pennsylvania farmer who had organized the Whiskey Rebellion against payment of the 1798 "war taxes" to the federal government. Although Fries and his men were armed, there was little violence during the uprising. Chase nevertheless insisted that the grand jury indict Fries for treason; he then found Fries guilty and sentenced him to death. To avoid public outrage, Adams later pardoned Fries.

On yet another occasion, Chase refused to discharge a Delaware grand jury that had ignored his hints that it should indict a Wilmington publisher Chase thought guilty of publishing seditious statements. Finally, in May 1803 Chase delivered what was described as a political harangue to a Baltimore grand jury in which he denounced the Democratic-Republican administration and its policies. Enraged at this extrajudicial behavior, Jefferson wrote on May 13 to Rep. Joseph R. Nicholson of Maryland:

> You must have heard of the extraordinary charge of Chace [sic] to the Grand Jury at Baltimore? Ought this seditious and official attack on the principles of our Constitution, and on the proceedings of a state, to go unpunished? and to whom so pointedly as yourself will the public look for the necessary measures? I ask these questions for your consideration, for myself it is better that I should not interfere.[11]

House Democratic-Republicans took Jefferson's broad hint. In January 1804, just as the Senate was beginning Judge Pickering's impeachment trial, Rep. John Randolph of Virginia introduced an impeachment resolution against Chase in the House. Randolph brought eight specific charges against Chase. Six of them dealt with his conduct of the Callender and Fries trials, the seventh with his conduct before the Delaware grand jury, and the eighth with his diatribe to the Baltimore grand jury.

Just an hour after the Senate voted on March 12 to remove Pickering from office, the full House voted to impeach Chase. The vote was 73 to 32, along strictly partisan lines.

Senate Trial. The Senate chamber was filled with spectators, including Chief Justice Marshall and the associate justices, as Chase's trial began on January 2, 1805. Vice President Aaron Burr, who had recently killed Alexander Hamilton in a duel, presided over the trial. John Randolph led the team of House managers who prosecuted Chase; Randolph's associates included Nicholson, George W. Campbell of Tennessee, Caesar Rodney of Delaware, and Peter Early of Georgia. Defending Chase was a battery of able lawyers, including a celebrated orator, Maryland attorney general Luther Martin, former representative Robert Goodloe Harper, Philip Barton Key, Joseph Hopkinson, and former U.S. attorney general Charles Lee.

Chase appeared before the Senate on the opening day of the trial to read a statement in which he maintained he had not engaged in impeachable conduct.

> To these articles . . . I say that I have committed no crime or misdemeanor . . . for which I am subject to impeachment according to the Constitution of the United States. I deny, with a few exceptions, the acts with which I am charged; I shall contend, that all acts admitted to have been done by me were legal, and I deny, in every instance, the improper intentions with which the acts charged are alleged to have been done, and in which their supposed criminality altogether consists.[12]

Chase asked for a delay in the trial so that he could prepare his defense and was granted a month. When the proceedings resumed in February, fifty-two witnesses, including Marshall, testified before the Senate. Marshall's principal biographer, Albert J. Beveridge, wrote that the chief justice's performance was marked by trepidation and that his responses were not favorable to Chase's cause. Marshall's demeanor may have been caused by his worry that should Chase be convicted, Marshall was sure to be the next target. In a letter to Chase dated January 23, 1804, Marshall even suggested that impeachment might be avoided by giving Congress the authority to reverse Court decisions that declared federal laws unconstitutional.[13] Once testimony was complete, the major debate centered on whether a justice must have committed an indictable crime to be impeached and convicted. Although Chase may have behaved in a highly questionable manner, he had not violated any federal law.

The House managers argued that offensive conduct was sufficient for impeachment. Representative Campbell contended:

> Impeachment, . . . according to the meaning of the Constitution, may fairly be considered a kind of inquest into the conduct of an officer [of the United States], merely as it regards his office; the manner in which he performs the duties thereof; and the effects that his conduct therein may have on society. It is more in the nature of a civil investigation than of a criminal prosecution.[14]

In Chase's behalf, attorney Hopkinson argued that

no judge can be impeached and removed from office for any act or offense for which he could not be indicted. . . . I maintain as a most important and indispensable principle, that no man should be criminally accused, no man can be criminally condemned, but for the violation of some known law by which he was bound to govern himself. Nothing is so necessary to justice and to safety as that the criminal code should be certain and known. Let the judge, as well as the citizen, precisely know the path he has to walk in, and what he may or may not do.[15]

On March 1, 1805, the Senate was ready to vote. Of the thirty-four members present, twenty-five were Democratic-Republicans, and nine were Federalists. Because twenty-three votes were needed for conviction, the Democratic-Republicans could carry the day if they voted together. But at least six Democratic-Republicans sided with the Federalists on each vote, and Chase was acquitted of all eight charges. On one charge the vote was unanimous in Chase's favor. The closest vote came on the complaint that triggered the impeachment—Chase's political harangue to the grand jury. Eighteen senators found Chase guilty; sixteen, not guilty.

Several factors accounted for Chase's acquittal. Manager Randolph's popularity in the House did not extend to the Senate. He may have reduced his influence further by boastfulness and by his extremely broad interpretation of the power of impeachment. There is also evidence that more moderate Democratic-Republicans were miffed at his opposition in the House to some of their legislative proposals. By all accounts, the case presented by the House managers was inept compared with that of Chase's defenders. Besides, Jefferson, having goaded the House into initiating impeachment, had taken no further part in the proceedings.

Randolph's response to the acquittal was immediate. He strode to the House floor and offered a constitutional amendment to provide for the removal of Supreme Court justices by the president at the request of a majority of both houses of Congress. The House approved the amendment by a 68-33 vote, but the proposal never emerged from the Senate.

The outcome of the trial meant that the Democratic-Republicans were forced to give up their plans for further impeachments and that Federalist judges on both the Supreme Court and inferior federal courts were secure for the first time since Jefferson's election. The exercise probably proved that impeachment and conviction could not succeed if the motivations were primarily partisan. But the episode did not resolve the fundamental constitutional question of whether only indictable offenses are impeachable. Some 165 years later, when members of Congress sought to impeach Justice Douglas primarily for political reasons, the leader of the movement raised the identical question when he argued that "an impeachable offense is whatever a majority of the House of Representatives considers it to be at a given moment in history."[16]

Fortas Resignation

In 1969 Justice Fortas became the first member of the Supreme Court to resign under threat of impeachment. Only eight months earlier the Senate had refused to act on President Johnson's proposal to elevate Fortas from associate justice to chief justice to replace retiring Earl Warren.

Fortas resigned on May 14, 1969, just ten days after an article about him was published in *Life* magazine. *Life* reported that in January 1966 Fortas had accepted a $20,000 check from a family foundation established by multimillionaire industrialist Louis E. Wolfson. Fortas had agreed to act as an adviser to the foundation, which worked to improve community relations and racial and religious cooperation. In September 1966 Wolfson was indicted (and later convicted) for selling unregistered securities. According to the article, Fortas had returned the $20,000 to Wolfson in December 1966 and severed his connection with the foundation.

The same day the *Life* article was published, Fortas issued a statement declaring that he did not feel the fee implied any inducement for him to try to influence Wolfson's case. But his statement did not reassure many members of Congress; they thought that Fortas had violated Canon 25 of the Canons of Judicial Ethics, prepared in 1922 for the American Bar Association by a committee headed by Chief Justice William Howard Taft. Canon 25 said that a "judge should avoid giving any ground for any reasonable suspicion that he is utilizing the power or prestige of his office to persuade or coerce others to patronize or contribute, either to the success of private business, or to charitable enterprises."

On May 11, Rep. H. R. Gross, R-Iowa, announced that he had prepared articles of impeachment against Fortas to present to the House within a "reasonable" time if the justice did not resign. The articles, Gross said, accused Fortas of malfeasance, misconduct, and impropriety. Calls for resignation began to come not only from the conservative Republicans and southern Democrats who had blocked his confirmation as chief justice, but also from liberal Democrats who had supported him in the earlier fight.

On May 13 Rep. Clark MacGregor, R-Minn., apparently with the blessing of the Nixon administration, proposed a preliminary inquiry into the affair by the House Judiciary Committee. The next day Fortas tendered his resignation to President Nixon, who promptly accepted it.

In a letter of explanation to Chief Justice Warren, Fortas maintained that he had done nothing wrong. But he said he feared that continued controversy over his association with the foundation would "adversely affect the work and position of the Court" and that his resignation "will enable the Court to proceed with its vital work free from extraneous stress."[17]

Douglas Impeachment Attempts

Twice during Justice Douglas's unprecedentedly long tenure on the Supreme Court bench (thirty-six years), the House initiated unsuccessful impeachment proceedings against him. Appointed to the Court in 1939, Douglas quickly became one of the most controversial justices in history. His staunchly liberal views, his outspoken opinions, and his several marriages, two to women considerably younger than he, made him the target of continuing criticism.

The first attempt to impeach Douglas stemmed from his temporary stay, on June 17, 1953, of the executions of convicted spies Julius and Ethel Rosenberg. One day later, Rep. W. M. "Don" Wheeler, D-Ga., introduced a resolution of impeachment, and the House Judiciary Committee immediately appointed a special subcommittee of inquiry. On June 19 the full Supreme Court overruled Douglas, setting aside the stay, and the Rosenbergs were executed. At the single subcommittee hearing, Wheeler was the only witness to testify, and on July 7 the full committee tabled the impeachment resolution.

The second attempt to impeach Douglas came on the heels of the resignation under threat of impeachment of Justice Fortas in 1969 and the Senate rejections in 1969 and 1970 of two Nixon nominees, Clement F. Haynsworth Jr. and G. Harrold Carswell, to fill the vacancy. On April 15, 1970, House minority leader Gerald R. Ford, R-Mich., made five major charges against Douglas in a floor speech. Douglas, Ford said, had engaged in "gross impropriety" when he did not disqualify himself from sitting on obscenity cases involving publisher Ralph Ginzburg. (In March 1969 one of Ginzburg's publications, *Evergreen Review,* had paid Douglas $350 for an article.) Ford also objected that an article by Douglas and photographs of nudes had appeared in an issue of the same publication.

The minority leader also charged that a book written by Douglas, *Points of Rebellion,* could be construed to advocate the violent overthrow of the existing

RETIREMENT

Congressional inaction on salary and benefits for the Supreme Court can exert pressure on the members of the Court. For example, for the first eighty years of the Court's existence Congress made no pension provisions for justices who wished to retire. As a result, several stayed on the Court until death even though they were physically and mentally incapable of performing their duties.

That situation was somewhat remedied by congressional passage on April 10, 1869, of an act that provided that any federal justice who reached seventy years of age and had ten years of service could resign and receive a pension equal to his salary at the time of resignation.

In 1936, when President Franklin D. Roosevelt announced a plan to rid the Court of aged conservatives who were blocking implementation of most of his economic recovery program, all members of the federal judiciary except Supreme Court justices were allowed to retire from regular service rather than resign. Judges who retired were still entitled to the salary of the office, including the increases in salary given to active judges.

Supreme Court justices, however, had to resign, and their pensions were subject to the same fluctuations as other retired government officials. When Justice Oliver Wendell Holmes Jr. was prevailed upon to resign in 1932, his pension was $10,000 a year—half his annual pay as a justice—because the Hoover administration, thinking to economize, set that amount as the maximum pension for former government employees.

Chief Justice Charles Evans Hughes thought later that two of the more conservative members of the Court would have joined Holmes and retired if Congress had not been so penurious. As it was, Justices Willis Van Devanter and George Sutherland remained on the Court, forming the nucleus of the conservative majority that struck down one New Deal law after another.

In response to Roosevelt's "Court-packing" proposal, which it opposed, Congress quickly approved the Supreme Court Retirement Act of 1937, which permitted justices aged seventy with ten years of service—or at age sixty-five with fifteen years of service—to retire at full salary rather than resign.

The statute quickly proved effective. Roosevelt signed it into law March 1, 1937, and on May 18 Justice Van Devanter announced his retirement.

SOURCES: William F. Swindler, *Court and Constitution in the Twentieth Century, The New Legality, 1932–1968* (Indianapolis: Bobbs-Merrill, 1970); Charles Fairman, *History of the Supreme Court of the United States*, vol. 6, *Reconstruction and Reunion, 1864–88, part 1* (New York: Macmillan, 1971); Leonard Baker, *Back to Back: The Duel between FDR and the Supreme Court* (New York: Macmillan, 1967).

---

political order and therefore violated the standard of good behavior.

The most serious charge against Douglas was that—in violation of federal law—he practiced law through his association with Albert Parvin and the Albert Parvin Foundation. Parvin was a multimillionaire industrialist who had an interest in a Las Vegas hotel and gambling casino; his foundation was established to promote international cooperation through education. There were allegations that the foundation received a substantial portion of its funding from gambling interests.

Ford charged that Douglas had assisted in the incorporation of the foundation and gave the institution legal advice in dealing with an Internal Revenue Service (IRS) investigation. Douglas maintained that he acted only as an adviser to the foundation, for which he received $12,000 a year plus travel expenses. He voluntarily ended his association with the foundation in May 1969.

Finally, Ford criticized Douglas's role as a consultant to the Center for the Study of Democratic Institutions at the same time the center was a recipient of Parvin Foundation funds. Ford urged creation of a special House committee to investigate these charges, but Rep. Andrew Jacobs Jr., D-Ind., a Douglas supporter, successfully offered an impeachment resolution to be referred to the House Judiciary Committee, where Douglas was likely to receive sympathetic treatment.

On April 21, 1970, the Judiciary Committee established a special five-member subcommittee to investigate Ford's charges. After months of hearings and deliberations, on December 3 the subcommittee voted 3-1, with one abstention, that it had found no grounds for impeachment.

In its formal report the subcommittee said that Douglas had not violated either judicial ethics or federal law when he failed to disqualify himself from the

Ginzburg obscenity cases or when he received payment from one of the Ginzburg publications for the article he had written. Nor was Douglas guilty of practicing law on behalf of the Parvin Foundation. Another attorney had assumed responsibility for incorporating the foundation, and it had retained outside tax counsel during the IRS investigation.

Douglas had done nothing unethical or illegal when he accepted payment from the foundation in return for his consulting services. The subcommittee said it considered other charges made against Douglas on the basis of his relationship to Parvin and the foundation but found them "difficult to analyze because of the extreme tenuousness of the circumstantial evidence." And the committee cleared Douglas of the charges related to his association with the Center for the Study of Democratic Institutions.

The subcommittee also found that Douglas had no control over publication by *Evergreen Review* of his writings; the arrangements had been made by Douglas's publisher without his knowledge. The charges that *Points of Rebellion* encouraged violence were based on a misinterpretation of the book, the subcommittee concluded.[18]

Douglas remained on the Court another five years, retiring in November 1975 after a stroke made it impossible for him to maintain his rigorous work schedule.

Other Means of Discipline

Is impeachment the only permissible method for removing a Supreme Court justice or other federal judge from office?

Because impeachment is so seldom used—only thirteen federal judges have been impeached, and of those, seven were convicted (but two impeached judges left office before the Senate could take up their cases)—it is widely viewed as an inadequate deterrent to misconduct on the bench. "[A]n impracticable thing—a mere scarecrow," Thomas Jefferson called it after the impeachment attempt against Justice Chase failed.

Furthermore, a judge may be impeached and convicted only for commission of treason, bribery, or high crimes and misdemeanors. But there has never been a conclusive answer to the question of what constitutes a high crime or misdemeanor. Can a judge be impeached for noncriminal but nevertheless improper judicial conduct? How can a judge who is physically or mentally unable to continue in office be removed?

These questions have prompted Congress to explore alternative methods for removal of judges. After Chase's acquittal in 1805, for example, Representative Randolph, the chief House prosecutor, rushed to the House floor and proposed a constitutional amendment that would permit the president to remove a justice at the request of a majority of both houses of Congress. The proposal was not approved.

Congress approved a modern alternative to impeachment in 1980 (Public Law 96-458). It gave the federal judiciary procedures for disciplining judges without going as far as impeaching them. The new law empowered the chief judge and the governing council of each judicial circuit to hear and investigate complaints against federal judges. The council could then certify that the judge was disabled; it could ask the judge to retire; it could suspend the judge temporarily. It could also refer cases to the Judicial Conference, which served as the review body for the council's disciplinary decisions and had the authority to send cases to the House of Representatives for possible impeachment.[19]

SALARIES

Article III, section 1, of the Constitution bars Congress from reducing the salaries of Supreme Court justices, but the legislature has absolute control over increases in wages and over appropriations for the operation of the Court itself. Only once—in 1964—has Congress deliberately exercised its power of the purse to show its displeasure with Court rulings.

In 1789 Congress set the initial salary of the associate justices at $3,500 per year. Traditionally, the chief justice has been paid more than the associate justices. John Jay earned $4,000 as the first chief justice; as of January 1, 2009, John Roberts earned a salary of $217,400 as chief justice.

Like most working people, the justices have not always been satisfied with the level of their compensation. At least one justice resigned from the Court partially because he was unable to support his family

Compensation Complaint

Supreme Court justices are very well paid compared with most American workers in the private or public sector. Compared with other prominent lawyers, however, they do not fare so well. The official salaries of the justices are only a fraction of those earned by the partners in well-established law firms.

At least one justice resigned from the Supreme Court because he found the salary too low. Justice Benjamin R. Curtis resigned on September 30, 1857, at the age of forty-eight. As an associate justice he earned $4,500 a year. An abolitionist, Curtis also was greatly disturbed by the Court's decision in the Dred Scott case in March 1857. Curtis wrote to his friend George Ticknor, a Boston historian and educator:

> Before [September] I shall have to come to a decision upon a matter of great moment to myself,—whether to continue to hold my present office. The expenses of living have so largely increased, that I do not find it practicable to live on my salary, even now; and, as my younger children will soon call for much increased expenses of education, I shall soon find it difficult to meet expenses by my entire income. Indeed I do not think I can do so without changing, in important particulars, my mode of life. Added to this, I cannot have a house in Washington, and I must either live apart from my family for four to six months every year while I go there, or subject them to a kind of migrant life in boarding-houses, neither congenial or useful. I had hoped it would prove otherwise, and looked forward to being able to have a house there for six months in a year. But what with the increase of luxury and the greatly enhanced prices there, I have now no hope of being able to do this. I can add something to my means by making books, but at the expense of all my vacations, when perhaps I ought not to labor hard. The constant labor of the summer has told on my health during the last two years. Such is the actual state of the case as respects my duty to my family. Then as regards the court and the public, I say to you in confidence, that I can not feel that confidence in the court, and that willingness to cooperate with them which are essential to the satisfactory discharge of my duties as a member of that body; and I do not expect its condition to be improved. On the other hand, I suppose there is a pretty large number of conservative people in the Northern, and some of the Southern States, who would esteem my retirement a public loss, and who would think that I had disappointed reasonable expectations in ceasing to hold the office; and particularly in my own circuit I believe my retirement would be felt to be a loss.... But I do not myself think it of great public importance that I should remain where I believe I can exercise little beneficial influence and I think all might abstain from blaming me when they remember that I have devoted six of the best years of my life to the public service.... I have no right to blame the public for not being willing to pay a larger salary; but they have no right to blame me for declining it on account of its inadequacy.

SOURCES: Benjamin R. Curtis, *The Life and Writings of Benjamin Robbins Curtis* (Boston: Little, Brown, 1879), 155; quoted by John R. Schmidhauser and Larry L. Berg, *The Supreme Court and Congress: Conflict and Interaction, 1945–1968* (New York: Free Press, 1972), 64–65.

in the manner he desired on his Court salary. *(See box, Compensation Complaint, p. 514.)*

During congressional debate in 1866 over reducing the size of the Court, Chief Justice Salmon P. Chase urged a three-seat reduction so that the salaries of the remaining justices might be raised. In a June 15, 1866, letter to Justice Samuel Miller, Chase wrote:

> It is very important—if it is important that adequate salaries should be paid to the Judges of the Supreme Court—that the number of Judges should be reduced proportionately as vacancies may occur, to seven. I think that the salaries of the highest Judicial Officers of the Nation ought not to be less than those of the highest Military Officers: and at least an approximation might be made if the number were not so large, and especially if by the reduction of the number the means of increase would ultimately be supplied.[20]

In 1866 the chief justice was paid $6,500 a year; associate justices, $6,000. Chase apparently wished an increase to $12,000 for himself and to $10,000 for his associates. Congress did reduce the size of the Court to seven as justices either died or retired, but it did not increase their salaries. The next pay raise occurred in 1871, when the salary of associate justices was increased to $8,000 and that of the chief justice to $8,500. *(See "Size of the Court," pp. 516–517.)*

In 1964 Congress considered legislation authorizing the first increases in pay since 1955 for top-level federal employees. The House approved a $7,500 increase for members of Congress and all federal judges, including Supreme Court justices. But when the bill reached the Senate, it, by a vote of 46 to 40, adopted an amendment to reduce the increase for the justices to $2,500. A compromise was struck in House-Senate conference, and the increase for the justices was set at $4,500—$3,000 less than the increase for other federal executives.

The amendment's chief sponsor, Sen. Gordon Allott, R-Colo., insisted that the reduced increase would establish a "semblance of equity" between justices and members of Congress. With the $7,500 increase, members of Congress would receive $30,000; with the $4,500 increase, associate justices would earn $39,500. But there was little doubt in anyone's mind that the amendment was approved out of congressional pique over several decisions handed down by the Warren Court on issues such as obscenity, school prayer, desegregation, and loyalty-security programs. The *American Bar Association Journal* published an editorial that said:

> The reason for this discriminating provision seems inescapably an effort on the part of Congress to punish members of our highest Court for performing their constitutional duty of deciding cases as they see

them. If indeed this was the purpose, it was unworthy of the principle of the division of powers of our government. But even worse it is an affront to the principle of the independence of the judiciary.[21]

Congress was not to be intimidated by such criticisms. In 1965 the House, after heated debate, rejected a measure that would have increased Supreme Court salaries by $3,000 retroactive to January 1, 1965. This bill would have provided the justices with the same increase awarded to members of Congress and other federal judges. The Supreme Court justices did not receive another raise until 1969.

The complaints over judicial salaries continued. In their year-end reports, Rehnquist and Roberts pointed out that Congress had failed to give judges and justices the same cost-of-living raise that went to other federal employees. In 2007 Roberts said judicial pay had declined 24 percent in constant dollars since 1969. But a year later, Congress failed to agree on a bill that would have given judges a substantial increase in salary. Even without a cost-of-living adjustment, the chief justice earned $217,400 in 2009, and the associate justices were paid $208,000.

Pressures on the Institution

Congress sometimes tries to influence the Supreme Court by enacting legislation that affects the Court as an institution rather than its individual members. To influence the outcome of certain decisions, Congress has changed the size of the Court, repealed its jurisdiction over certain kinds of cases, and even abolished a Court term.

But Congress has considered many more efforts to pressure the Court than it has approved. Proposals to require two-thirds of the Court to concur to declare an act of Congress or state statute unconstitutional have never been approved and seldom were even seriously considered. The major proposal for a change in the size of the Court—President Franklin D. Roosevelt's plan to add six new members—failed because a majority in Congress opposed it. And only once has Congress successfully removed a threat to its legislative policies by repealing the Court's jurisdiction; several other attempts have been defeated, most of them by large margins.

SIZE OF THE COURT

Congress has increased or reduced the number of justices on the Supreme Court seven times in the Court's 220-year history. Generally, laws decreasing the number of justices have been motivated by a desire to punish the president; increases have been aimed at influencing the philosophical balance of the Court itself.[1]

The Judiciary Act of 1789 set the number of Supreme Court seats at six. In the last days of John Adams's presidency, however, Congress reduced the number to five. Justice William Cushing was ill and not expected to live much longer, and the outgoing Federalists wanted to deny incoming Democratic-Republican president Thomas Jefferson an opportunity to name Cushing's replacement. The reduction in size never occurred. In 1802 the Democratic-Republican–controlled Congress repealed the 1801 law and restored the number of justices to six. (Cushing lived until 1810, and it was James Madison who named his successor.)

In 1807 Congress increased the number of justices by one, to seven, primarily because of the population growth in Kentucky, Tennessee, and Ohio. Justice Thomas Todd of Kentucky was the first justice to fill this new seat.

In 1837 Congress increased the Court by two, to nine, again because of the increasing population and expansion of the country into the West and Southwest. Presidents James Madison, James Monroe, and John Quincy Adams each had urged Congress to enlarge the Court so that the additional judges might ease some of the backlog of cases in the circuit courts, but Congress refused because it did not want the sitting president to name the justices.

The Judiciary Act of 1837 was passed on the last day of President Andrew Jackson's term. Jackson signed the bill and immediately named John Catron and William Smith to the seats. Both men were confirmed, but Smith then declined the appointment. The next increase, to ten justices, came in the midst of the Civil War. On the surface the increase was justified again by the westward expansion. The law created a tenth circuit comprising California and Oregon and later Nevada. But the additional seat meant that President Abraham Lincoln could appoint a justice who would help to ensure that the Court majority would decide issues in favor of the Union. Lincoln already had made three appointments in 1862, but his control of the Court was still not firm. The same day that the 1863 Judiciary Act went into effect, the Court upheld Lincoln's extraordinary exercise of his war powers by a slim 5-4 vote. To the new seat Lincoln appointed Californian Stephen J. Field, who supported the president on war issues. *(See "Prize Cases," pp. 263–265.)*

Congress was not so accommodating of Lincoln's successor, Andrew Johnson. When Justice Catron died in 1865, Johnson nominated Attorney General Henry

Stanbery, who was exceptionally well qualified for the position. The majority in Congress was, however, so opposed to Johnson's Reconstruction policies, and so fearful that his appointments to the Court might rule against Congress's Reconstruction programs, that it responded by reducing the number of seats on the Court from ten to seven. The vacancy to which Stanbery was nominated therefore no longer existed, and no action was taken on his appointment. The Court was reduced to eight members when Justice James M. Wayne died in July 1867.

No further vacancies occurred during Johnson's tenure. Little more than a month after President Ulysses S. Grant was inaugurated in March 1869, Congress passed another judiciary act raising the number of justices to nine. Because the Court had fallen to only eight in number, Grant had only one new seat to fill. But the resignation of Justice Robert C. Grier gave Grant two vacancies to fill during his first year in office. The president's first appointee was rejected; his second died just four days after confirmation. *(See details, p. 50.)*

Grant then nominated William Strong and Joseph P. Bradley just hours after the Court declared in *Hepburn v. Griswold* (1870) that the substitution of paper money for gold as legal tender for the payment of contracts entered into before 1862 was unconstitutional. Shortly after Strong and Bradley were confirmed in February and March, respectively, the Court voted to reconsider its decision in the legal tender case. Fifteen months after declaring "greenbacks" unconstitutional, the Court reversed itself, 5-4, and held that paper money was legal for the payment of all contracts. Because both of Grant's appointees voted in favor of reversal and because of the timing of their appointments, Grant was charged with "packing the Court," but these allegations have since been considered unwarranted. *(See "The 'Court-Packers,'" pp. 557–561; see Legal Tender Cases, pp. 158–160.)*

Congress has not changed the number of seats on the Supreme Court since 1869, although members of Congress frustrated by Court decisions have continued to propose such changes. The most serious of these proposals in the twentieth century came not from Congress but from the president. Franklin Roosevelt proposed in 1937 that the number of justices be raised to fifteen. Ostensibly to improve the efficiency of the Court, the increase was in reality designed to allow Roosevelt to appoint new justices who could be depended upon to support the constitutionality of his New Deal programs, several of which the Court had struck down.

The plan was unpopular with both the public and Congress and was not enacted, but much of the threat to the Court's independence was defused by the Court itself. Shortly after the proposal was made public, the Court upheld in quick succession a Washington State minimum wage law and the federal National Labor Relations Act. These rulings indicated that the Court was now willing to sanction broad federal regulation of private enterprise. *(See "The 'Court-Packers,'" pp. 557–561.)*

EXTRAORDINARY MAJORITY

Members of Congress occasionally have sought to restrain exercise of the Court's review powers by requiring that it find acts of Congress or state laws unconstitutional only if an extraordinary majority of the justices concurs in the decision. Most of these proposals have required that two-thirds of the justices concur; some of the more extreme proposals have urged that such decisions be unanimous.

The first proposal requiring an extraordinary majority to be considered seriously by Congress was offered in the 1820s after the Court ruled against the states in two controversial land claim suits.[2] Although the Court's vote was not announced, it was widely thought that because of absences and dissents the cases had been decided by a vote of less than a full majority of the Court.

At the behest of Kentucky, one of the states affected by the decisions, Sen. Richard M. Johnson, D-Ky., asked the Senate Judiciary Committee to consider increasing the number of justices to ten and requiring seven of them to agree in decisions rendering state laws invalid. The committee recommended against increasing the size of the Court, but it did report a bill to require five of the seven members to concur before the Court could nullify state laws. The full Senate voted to recommit this bill.

MORE IS LESS

In March 1838, at the end of the first term after the addition of two seats to the Supreme Court, Justice Joseph Story implied in a letter that the increased number had led to decreased efficiency:

> You may ask how the Judges got along together? We made very slow progress, and did less in the same time than I ever knew. The addition to our number has most sensibly affected our facility as well as rapidity of doing business. Many men of many minds require a great deal of discussion to compel them to come to definite results; and we found ourselves often involved in long and very tedious debates. I verily believe, if there were twelve Judges, we should do no business at all, or at least very little.

SOURCE: Charles Warren, *The Supreme Court in United States History*, rev. ed., 2 vols. (Boston: Little, Brown, 1926), 2:42.

Similar bills offered in both the House and Senate during the next few years also failed, but their consideration may have had the intended effect on the Court. In 1834 Chief Justice John Marshall announced that the Court would delay a decision in the case of *New York v. Miln*, saying, "The practice of this Court is not (except in cases of absolute necessity) to deliver any judgment in cases where constitutional questions are involved unless four [of the seven] judges concur in opinion, thus making the decision that of a majority of the whole Court." Five of the seven justices concurred in the judgment when the case was decided in 1837.[3] *(See details of New York v. Miln, pp. 408–409.)*

Other proposals would give Congress the final authority to determine the validity of its own legislation. One such proposal, offered by Sen. Robert M. La Follette, R-Wis., would have allowed Congress to reverse Supreme Court decisions holding federal legislation invalid by repassing it with a two-thirds majority vote. Like similar proposals, it died in committee.

TERMS

Congress has absolute power to set the terms of the Supreme Court. It once used this power to delay a particular decision by abolishing a term altogether.

In 1802 the Democratic-Republican–dominated Congress repealed the 1801 Judiciary Act. The statute, enacted by the Federalist lame-duck Congress, created several new federal judgeships. Outgoing president John Adams promptly filled the judgeships with Federalists, who in 1802 challenged the repeal. Concerned that the Supreme Court—which was composed completely of Federalists—would find the 1802 repeal unconstitutional, possibly on grounds that the Constitution forbids Congress to reduce judges' salaries, the Democratic-Republicans postponed the Court's next term.

During debate on the legislation, Rep. James A. Bayard, a Federalist from Delaware, opposed the delay, asking the House:

> Could a more dangerous precedent than this be established? May it not lead to the virtual abolition of a Court, the existence of which is guaranteed by the Constitution? If the functions of the Court can be extended by law for fourteen months, what time will arrest us before we arrive at ten or twenty years?[4]

When the Court convened fourteen months later, in February 1803, it upheld the repeal in *Stuart v. Laird* (1803). Since then Congress has not resorted to this method to restrain the Court.

REMOVAL OF JURISDICTION

Removal of the Supreme Court's authority to review certain categories of cases has been considered throughout U.S. history as one of the more serious threats to the independence of the Court. The Constitution authorizes Congress "to make exceptions" to the Court's appellate jurisdiction. Although this language probably was not intended as a political weapon, Congress has viewed it as such during three major confrontations with the Court.

An attempt to remove some of the Court's jurisdiction came in the 1820s and 1830s when Congress sought unsuccessfully to repeal Section 25 of the Judiciary Act of 1789. This section gave the Court power to review high state-court decisions upholding state laws challenged as in conflict with the federal Constitution, federal law, or treaties.

Only once has Congress repealed the Supreme Court's jurisdiction as a way of stopping the Court from issuing a decision. In 1868 Congress repealed the Court's power to review federal court denials of writs of habeas corpus. The repeal was specifically intended to prevent the Court from hearing a habeas corpus appeal that called into question the constitutionality of the Reconstruction Acts of 1867.

Since then Congress has considered legislation to repeal the Court's authority to review specific subjects, such as internal security programs, certain criminal procedures, local education problems such as desegregation and school prayer, and state laws forbidding abortions. Although the Court's decisions in all of these areas were controversial and generated an outpouring of opposition from the public and members of Congress, none of the jurisdictional repeal attempts was successful.

There has been much scholarly debate on whether the Constitution's authors intended to give Congress absolute control over the Court's authority to take appeals from lower-court decisions. Justice Felix Frankfurter was one constitutional expert who believed that Congress could "withdraw appellate jurisdiction once conferred" even if the withdrawal affected a pending case.[5] Justice William O. Douglas, on the other hand, thought it unlikely that the Court would uphold the constitutionality of repeal legislation.[6] Justice Owen J. Roberts in 1949 and the American Bar Association in 1950 sought to resolve the dilemma by recommending adoption of a constitutional amendment to make the Court and not Congress the determiner of the Court's appellate jurisdiction.

In his book analyzing Congress's failure to curb the Court during the mid- and late 1950s, constitutional historian C. Herman Pritchett makes the argument that the constitutional grant of authority to control the Court's appellate jurisdiction is now largely an anachronism, having been repealed in effect

> by the passage of time and by the recognition that exercise of such power would be in the truest sense subversive of the American tradition of an independent judiciary. Congress can no longer claim with good conscience the authority granted by Article III, Section 2, and every time proposals to exercise such authority are rejected . . . the Court's control over its appellate jurisdiction is correspondingly strengthened.[7]

The first congressional attempts to repeal the Supreme Court's jurisdiction were prompted by the Court's early decisions overturning state laws. Section 25 of the Judiciary Act of 1789 authorized the Supreme Court to review, and therefore declare invalid, decisions of the states' highest courts that upheld state laws challenged as conflicting with the federal Constitution, federal statutes, or treaties. With each successive ruling striking down a state law, opposition to Section 25 grew among proponents of states' rights. After the Supreme Court emphatically upheld its review power under Section 25 in the case of *Cohens v. Virginia (1821),* several states appealed to their congressional delegations to remove this review power from the Court.[8]

The first proposal along these lines was introduced in the Senate in 1821. Senator Johnson of Kentucky proposed a constitutional amendment to give the Senate appellate jurisdiction in cases raising a federal question where a state was a party. This suggestion, however, received little support, primarily because small states held the balance of power in the Senate and were considered likely to prefer a strong national government.

The next year, legislation to repeal the Court's Section 25 review power was introduced, but it received little attention then or in the next few years. However, the Court's rulings against state sovereignty in *Craig v. Missouri* (1830) and *Cherokee Nation v. Georgia* (1831), coupled with Georgia's outright defiance of the Court, generated a major clash over the proper balance of power between the states and the federal government.[9]

As part of that confrontation the House ordered its Judiciary Committee to report a measure repealing Section 25. The committee made its report on January 24, 1831, declaring that it was

> no more necessary to the harmonious action of the Federal and State governments, that the Federal court should have power to control the decisions of State courts by appeal, than that the Federal legislature should have power to control the legislation of the States, or the Federal Executive a State Executive.[10]

Repeal of Section 25 was viewed as a grave threat by members of the Court. Chief Justice John Marshall wrote that the "crisis of our Constitution is now upon us," and Justice Joseph Story lamented that "if the Twenty-Fifth Section is repealed, the Constitution is practically gone."[11]

In a letter written after the crisis had passed, former president James Madison commented on its seriousness:

> The jurisdiction claimed for the Federal Judiciary is truly the only defensive armor of the Federal Government, or rather for the Constitution and laws of the United States. Strip it of that armor, and the door is wide open for nullification, anarchy and convulsion.[12]

The measure was never fully debated in the House. Using parliamentary tactics, Court supporters were able to repulse the repeal movement by a wide margin. Moves to repeal the section were made in later years, but none came any closer to passage.

Although the Marshall Court feared the consequences of a successful repeal drive, a later Court resisted efforts to expand its Section 25 appellate jurisdiction. In the Act of February 5, 1867, Congress changed the wording of the section so that it could be interpreted to allow the Supreme Court to review all errors of law in high state-court decisions and not just those concerned with federal questions. It appeared that Congress might well have intended such an expansion to counter any obstruction to the federal judicial system from the recently rebellious states. Nevertheless, in *Murdock v. Memphis* (1875) the Court held that the 1867 law had not changed Section 25 in any way. Congress did not explicitly amend the section until 1914.[13] *(See "Appellate Jurisdiction," pp. 12–15.)*

THE McCARDLE CASE

Only once in the nation's history has Congress prevented the Supreme Court from deciding a pending case by repealing its appellate jurisdiction over the subject matter of the case. This extraordinary action was taken by a Congress dominated by Radical Republicans who wanted to prohibit the Court from reviewing the constitutionality of the Reconstruction Acts of 1867. The acts substituted military rule for civilian government in the ten southern states that initially refused to rejoin the Union. The acts also established procedures for those states to follow to gain readmittance and representation in the federal government.

The Supreme Court twice avoided ruling on the constitutionality of the Reconstruction Acts. In April 1867, just before the acts were scheduled to take effect, the state of Mississippi asked the Court for permission to seek an injunction to stop the president from implementing them. The Court unanimously rejected the request in *Mississippi v. Johnson* (1867), holding that the president's duties under the acts were political, and therefore the Court was without jurisdiction to order the injunction.[14]

In 1868 the Court dismissed a similar request by Georgia and Mississippi officials asking that the secretary of war and the commanders of the five military districts be stopped from enforcing the Reconstruction Acts. The Court again held that the suit raised political questions over which it had no jurisdiction.[15]

Reconstruction Attacked

It was not until November 1867, several months after military rule was established in the southern states, that the events that led to the confrontation between the Court and Congress began. Mississippian William H. McCardle, the editor of the *Vicksburg Times,* was not loath to express editorially his distaste for Reconstruction and his views that blacks should be excluded from participation in government and the Fourteenth Amendment should be left unratified.

His editorials continually attacked the imposition of military government in the South and the actions of the commanding generals. In one editorial he called the five district commanders "infamous, cowardly, and abandoned villains who should have their heads shaved, their ears cropped, their foreheads branded, and their precious persons lodged in a penitentiary."

In other columns the editor tried to rouse white Mississippians to oppose black political participation and promised to publish the names of the "sneaks" and "scoundrels" who ignored this advice.[16]

McCardle reserved his bitterest criticisms for Maj. Gen. Edward O. C. Ord, the commanding general of the Fourth Military District, which included Mississippi and Arkansas. Ord finally had McCardle arrested and held for trial by a military tribunal, charging him with disturbing the peace, inciting insurrection, slowing the pace of Reconstruction, and printing libelous statements.

The Tables Turned

A protection against illegal imprisonment, a writ of habeas corpus orders a person holding a prisoner to explain why the prisoner is being held. Seeking to protect blacks and federal officials in the South from harassment by white southerners, Congress in February 1867 enacted a statute expanding the Supreme Court's jurisdiction to review denials of writs of habeas corpus.

Prior to enactment of the 1867 law, the Supreme Court had no appellate jurisdiction over writs of habeas corpus. The 1867 statute permitted appeals from federal circuit courts to the Supreme Court in "all cases where any person may be restrained of his or her liberty in violation of the Constitution or of any treaty or law of the United States" and sought release through a writ of habeas corpus.

The statute was not intended to protect southern whites, but McCardle sought a writ of habeas corpus in a federal circuit court, charging that the Reconstruction Acts that allowed his arrest and trial by military tribunal were unconstitutional. When the circuit court denied the writ, he appealed directly to the Supreme Court.

Rumors abounded that the Court would use McCardle's case to declare the Reconstruction Acts unconstitutional. In *Ex parte Milligan* (1866) the Court had held unanimously that it was illegal for a military commission to try a civilian when civilian courts were available, and

five of the justices had gone so far as to say they did not think Congress had the power under any circumstances to authorize military trials of civilians where civilian courts were open.[17] Many observers interpreted this decision to indicate that the Court would not respond favorably to the military rule imposed in the South.

But the Radical Republicans could not risk having the Reconstruction Acts declared unconstitutional until after they had solidified their political power in the South and forced the southern states to ratify the Fourteenth Amendment as the price for readmittance to the Union. Therefore, when McCardle's attorney, Jeremiah S. Black, appealed to the Supreme Court in December 1867 to act quickly on the case, Republicans in the House moved just as quickly to stave off an adverse ruling. In January 1868 the House Judiciary Committee reported, and the House passed, a bill to require two-thirds of the justices to concur in opinions finding federal laws unconstitutional.

According to historian Charles Warren, this measure had little public support, and the Senate postponed action on it indefinitely.[18] Moreover, it was widely believed that the measure would have failed to accomplish its purpose; of the eight justices then on the Court, at least five were thought to believe the Reconstruction Acts invalid.

Meanwhile, the Supreme Court agreed to Black's request and set arguments for the first week in March. The government's attorney, Sen. Lyman Trumbull, R-Ill., sought to end the matter by moving for a dismissal of the case on the grounds that the Court did not have jurisdiction. But the justices denied the motion on February 17, 1868.

Arguments on the merits in *Ex parte McCardle* began on March 2, the same day the House approved the first of the articles of impeachment against President Andrew Johnson.[19] McCardle's attorneys included Black, who had been nominated as an associate justice of the Supreme Court by President James Buchanan in the last months of his term but was rejected by the Senate in 1861 largely because Senate Republicans wanted to hold the vacancy open for President Abraham Lincoln to fill. Another attorney for McCardle was David Dudley Field, brother of Justice Stephen J. Field, who was sitting on the case.

Because he considered the Reconstruction Acts unconstitutional, Attorney General Henry Stanbery refused to argue the government's position; his place was taken by Trumbull and the eminent attorney Matthew Hale Carpenter. By all accounts, the arguments by both sides were impressive.

Jurisdiction Repealed

Arguments concluded on March 9, 1868. On March 12 the Radical Republicans in Congress made their move. Pending in the House was an insignificant Senate-passed bill to expand the Supreme Court's appellate jurisdiction to cases concerning customs and revenue officers. James F. Wilson, R-Iowa, chairman of the House Judiciary Committee, offered an amendment to repeal the 1867 grant of appellate jurisdiction over habeas corpus writs and to prohibit the Court from acting on any appeals then pending. Democrats and moderate Republicans who might have opposed Wilson's measure apparently did not understand what was happening, and the amendment was passed without debate or objection. The bill as amended was then returned to the Senate, which approved it later in the same day by a 32-6 vote.

President Johnson waited as long as possible before vetoing the bill to see if the Supreme Court would defy Congress and decide the *McCardle* case before its jurisdiction was removed. Although the Court met in conference on March 21, it announced no decision on the case, taking note instead of the repeal bill and saying it would postpone a decision on the case until action on the legislation was concluded. Justices Field and Grier objected to the postponement. Field later wrote that the "judges had all formed their conclusions, and no excuse was urged that more time was wanted for examination."[20] Johnson vetoed the bill on March 25, declaring that the repeal "establishes a precedent which, if followed, may eventually sweep away every check on arbitrary and unconstitutional legislation."[21]

March 30 was the Court's next opinion day. When it became obvious that the justices would say nothing about the *McCardle* case, attorney Black asked that the effect of the repeal legislation on the case be argued formally before the Court. The Court agreed, but it also agreed to a postponement until the December 1868 term to give government attorneys time to prepare their arguments.

Justice Grier objected to this delay and read the following statement in open Court:

> This case was fully argued in the beginning of this month. It is a case which involves the liberty and rights, not only of the appellant, but of millions of our fellow citizens. The country and the parties had a right to expect that [the case] would receive the immediate and solemn attention of the Court. By the postponement of this case, we shall be subject ourselves, whether justly or unjustly, to the imputation that we have evaded the performance of a duty imposed on us by the Constitution, and waited for the Legislative interposition to supersede our action, and relieve us from responsibility. I am not willing to be a partaker of the eulogy or opprobrium that may follow. I can only say . . . I am ashamed that such opprobrium should be cast upon the Court, and that it cannot be refuted.[22]

Grier was not the only one to decry the Court's apparent submission to Congress. Gideon Welles, Lincoln's secretary of the navy and close ally, was a noted diarist, and he wrote that the "judges of the Supreme Court have caved in, fallen through, failed in the *McCardle* case."[23] Former justice Benjamin R. Curtis, who defended President Johnson at his impeachment trial, said, "Congress with the acquiescence of the country, has subdued the Supreme Court, as well as the President."[24] And Black in an April 1868 letter wrote that "the Court stood still to be ravished and did not even hallo while the thing was getting done."[25]

Final Submission, Aftermath

Final arguments in the *McCardle* case were anticlimactic. On April 12 the Court issued a unanimous decision upholding the repeal measure and dismissing the case for lack of jurisdiction. Chief Justice Salmon P. Chase wrote that the Constitution gave Congress authority to make exceptions to the Court's appellate jurisdiction and that Congress had expressly exercised that authority when it repealed the Court's right to review denials of writs of habeas corpus:

We are not at liberty to inquire into the motive of the legislature. We can only examine into its power under the Constitution, and the power to make exceptions to the appellate jurisdiction of this Court is given by express words. What, then, is the effect of the repealing act upon the case before us? We cannot doubt as to this. Without jurisdiction the Court cannot proceed at all in any cause. Jurisdiction is power to declare the law, and when it ceases to exist, the only function remaining to the Court is that of announcing the fact and dismissing the cause.[26]

Less than a month later Chase confirmed the belief that the Court would have declared at least part of the Reconstruction Acts unconstitutional. "I may say to you," he wrote to a district judge, "that had the merits of the *McCardle* Case been decided the Court would doubtless have held that his imprisonment for trial before a military commission was illegal."[27]

As it turned out, McCardle was never brought to trial. By the time the Supreme Court dismissed his case in 1869, Major General Ord was no longer the commanding officer in McCardle's military district. His replacement dropped the charges.

Historian Charles Fairman points out one major irony of the *McCardle* case. Had the Supreme Court defied Congress and issued a decision declaring the Reconstruction Acts invalid, it is possible that the Fourteenth Amendment to the Constitution would not have been ratified. One of the provisions of the Reconstruction Acts required the ten recalcitrant southern states to approve the amendment to gain reentry into the Union. Ratification of the amendment could occur only if some of the southern states approved it. As Fairman wrote, "One must believe that if Congress had failed to bring the weight of its authority to bear upon the ten States as then organized, there would have been no Fourteenth Amendment."[28]

Ex Parte Yerger

A McCardle-type confrontation between Congress and the Court about jurisdiction over habeas corpus granted the Court by the Judiciary Act of 1789 was narrowly avoided late in 1869. *Ex parte Yerger* concerned the imprisonment, conviction for murder, and sentencing

of another Mississippi newspaper editor by a military tribunal.[29] Edward M. Yerger applied to the Supreme Court for an original writ of habeas corpus, charging, like McCardle, that it was unconstitutional for military tribunals to try civilians for civilian crimes.

When the Court agreed to hear the case, a bill was introduced in the Senate to remove the Court's jurisdiction in cases involving the constitutionality of the Reconstruction Acts and over writs of habeas corpus until Reconstruction was completed. A second proposal would have prohibited Supreme Court review of any federal act.

Before the Senate could act, a compromise was struck between Yerger's lawyers and the attorney general. His case was removed to civilian court and his petition for the writ of habeas corpus withdrawn. No further congressional action was taken on the proposed jurisdictional limitations.

COURT JURISDICTION: MODERN REPEAL EFFORTS

The 1954 appointment of former California governor Earl Warren as chief justice of the United States initiated a period unique in the nation's history when the Court led other government institutions in protecting individual rights from majority discrimination. The first major ruling of the Warren Court struck down segregation in public schools, overturning sixty years of officially sanctioned racial discrimination.

These Warren Court decisions inspired a series of anti-Court efforts by members of Congress. Perhaps the most serious of these occurred in 1957 and 1958 when southerners opposed to desegregation allied with other conservative members of Congress who thought the Court's decisions protecting individuals alleged to have participated in communist activities threatened to undermine the nation's security. In addition to trying to reverse the individual decisions, the groups launched two major attacks on the Court's power to review certain classes of cases. But despite the conservative alliance and widespread opposition to the Court's decisions, Congress ultimately refused to adopt either proposal.

Jenner-Butler Bill

The broader of the two assaults on the jurisdiction of the Court during this uneasy period was initiated in the Senate by William E. Jenner, R-Ind.[30] His bill (S. 2646), introduced in July 1957, would have barred the Supreme Court from accepting appeals in five categories:

- Cases involving the powers of congressional investigating committees and contempt of Congress proceedings. This provision was aimed at *Watkins v. United States* (1957), in which the Court ruled that a witness before the House Un-American Activities Committee had not been guilty of contempt of Congress for refusing to answer certain questions, because the scope of the committee's inquiry had not been clearly defined by Congress and the committee had failed to show the pertinence of its question to its investigation.[31] *(See "Watkins v. United States," pp. 215–216.)*

- Cases involving federal laws and regulations governing hiring and firing of government employees on loyalty grounds. This provision was directed at the Court's ruling in *Cole v. Young* (1956), which held that loyalty-security procedures under the Summary Suspension Act of 1950 applied only to "sensitive" jobs and not to all federal employment.[32]

- Cases involving school regulations dealing with subversive activities by teachers. This provision was directed at the Court's jurisdiction to review cases like *Slochower v. Board of Higher Education of New York City* (1956), in which the Court ruled that New York City could not dismiss a city college professor from his job merely for refusing to cooperate with a congressional committee investigating subversive activities. Rather, it had to grant him all the procedural rights due under state and city laws regulating employment of teachers suspected of engaging in forbidden activities.[33]

- Cases involving state laws and regulations punishing subversive activities directed against the federal government. This provision was aimed at the Court's ruling in *Pennsylvania v. Nelson* (1956), in which it held that provisions of the Pennsylvania Sedition Act punishing subversive activities directed against the federal government were invalid because Congress had preempted this field of legislation when it passed the 1940 Smith Act.[34]

- Cases involving state regulations for admission to the bar, aimed at cases such as *Konigsberg v. State Bar of California* (1957), in which the Court ruled that an applicant could not be denied admission to a state bar solely because he refused to answer questions about past or present membership in the Communist Party.[35]

The "extreme liberal wing of the court" has "become a majority," said Senator Jenner on August 7, 1957, the opening day of hearings, "and we witness a court constantly changing the law, and even changing the meaning of the Constitution, in an apparent determination to make the law of the land what the court thinks it should be."[36]

But solving the problem by removing the Court's jurisdiction proved too strong a medicine for many witnesses, who perceived this threat to the independence of the judiciary as a graver danger to national security than that posed by communists. At the suggestion of Sen. John Marshall Butler, R-Md., Jenner's bill was substantially amended by the Senate Judiciary Committee. As reported in May 1958, only one section of the original Jenner proposal—the provision barring the Supreme Court from reviewing state bar admission rules—was retained. Instead of repealing the Court's jurisdiction to review the other categories of cases, the committee recommended language to overturn the particular offending decisions.

To nullify the *Nelson* decision, the reported bill provided that no past or future federal antisubversive laws should be construed by the courts as prohibiting enforcement of otherwise valid state laws punishing seditious activities directed at the state or federal government. To nullify the *Watkins* decision, the bill provided that each chamber of Congress would be the final judge of whether questions put to witnesses by investigating committees were pertinent to the authorized purpose of the committee's inquiry. The measure also provided that a person accused of contempt of Congress could not argue that the questions were not pertinent unless he had raised that objection at the time the questions were asked.

PRESSURE ON CONGRESS TO CURB THE COURT

In the middle of the 1957–1959 congressional effort to reverse Supreme Court decisions on internal security measures and to limit the Court's jurisdiction over such cases, Congress received outside pressure from two influential sources.

The first of these was the states' Conference of Chief Justices, which charged that recent Supreme Court decisions in some areas were significantly eroding the power of the states in the federal system. In a document entitled "Report of the Committee on Federal-State Relationships as Affected by Judicial Decisions," adopted on August 23, 1958, the chief justices contended that "the overall tendency of the Supreme Court over the last 25 years or more has been to press the extension of federal power and to press it rapidly" and that the Court "too often has tended to adopt the role of policy-maker without proper judicial restraint." In conclusion, the conference stated its "grave concern as to whether individual views of the members of the court as from time to time constituted, or of a majority

thereof, as to what is wise or desirable do not unconsciously override a more dispassionate consideration of what is or is not constitutionally warranted."

A second report, this one a set of resolutions urging Congress to "correct legislative defects in the field of internal security revealed by particular [Court] decisions," was adopted by the House of Delegates of the American Bar Association (ABA) on February 24, 1959. The ABA specifically opposed legislation to remove any Court jurisdiction, but it urged adoption of legislation to reverse the Court's rulings in *Cole v. Young* (1956), *Pennsylvania v. Nelson* (1956), *Yates v. United States* (1957), and *Watkins v. United States* (1957).

Because these reports coincided with the views of members of Congress opposed to the Court, they were cited frequently throughout the debate on the Jenner-Butler bill as expert testimony to buttress arguments to curb the Court.

The Butler amendment left the *Slochower* and *Cole* decisions standing. But it moved to overturn a Court ruling that the original Jenner bill had not touched. In *Yates v. United States* (1957), the Court ruled that the 1940 Smith Act did not prohibit "advocacy of forcible overthrow of the government as an abstract doctrine" but only as an incitement to action. The Court also held that the act's prohibition against organizing a group seeking to overthrow the government by force applied only to the original act of bringing the group into being and not to continued organizational activity such as recruitment of members.[37]

As reported, the compromise Jenner-Butler bill made all teaching and advocacy of forcible overthrow of the government a crime under the Smith Act. It also redefined the term "organize" to include both initial and continuing organizational activities.

The bill did not come to the Senate floor until August 20, 1958, one of the last days of the session. Senate majority leader Lyndon B. Johnson, D-Texas, apparently had hoped he could avoid bringing it up for

consideration altogether, but under pressure from southern colleagues and knowing that he had the votes to defeat it, he allowed it to be offered as an amendment to a minor House-passed bill (H.R. 6789) dealing with appeals from rulings of federal administrative agencies. After long supporting speeches by Jenner and Butler and rebuttals by Judiciary Committee opponents Thomas C. Hennings Jr., D Mo., and Alexander Wiley, R-Wis., Hennings offered a motion to table the Jenner-Butler bill. The motion was adopted, 49-41, and the bill was killed. Measures similar to individual parts of it were subsequently considered in the House and Senate, but none was enacted. (*See box, Domestic Security Rulings, p. 526.*)

Implied Preemption

The second attempt during this period to repeal Supreme Court jurisdiction was more limited in scope but came closer to passage. Under the preemption doctrine—based on Article IV, section 2, of the Constitution, which makes federal laws the "supreme law of the land"—courts have invalidated state laws for several reasons: because Congress

DOMESTIC SECURITY RULINGS: ONLY ONE REVERSED

Distressed by many of the Supreme Court's rulings in domestic security cases, Congress tried between 1957 and 1959 not only to remove the Court's jurisdiction to review such cases but also to reverse the rulings. Only one of these attempts--modifying the decision in *Jencks v. United States* (1957)—was successful. The rest failed, most of them in the Senate, where the two efforts to repeal jurisdiction also foundered.[1]

THE VICTORY

In June 1957 the Supreme Court reversed the conviction of labor leader Clinton E. Jencks, charged with perjury for swearing he was not a communist.[2] The five-justice majority held that reports filed by FBI-paid informants alleging Jencks's participation in Communist Party activities should have been made available to Jencks's defense attorneys when requested. The majority ruled that the prosecution either must turn over to the defense directly any portion of statements previously made by government witnesses that related to their trial testimony or drop the case.

Justice Tom C. Clark, a former U.S. attorney general, dissented, along with Justices Harold H. Burton and John Marshall Harlan. (Justice Charles E. Whittaker did not participate.) Clark said that unless Congress nullified the decision through new legislation, "those intelligence agencies of our government engaged in law enforcement may as well close up shop." He added that the decision would result in a "Roman holiday" for criminals to "rummage" through secret files.

Clark's dissent was seized upon by those in Congress opposed to the Court's decision. They also drew strength from the fact that the majority had not specified any right of the prosecution to withhold from the defense any irrelevant portions of testimony requested by the defense. As a result, lower courts were left to their own interpretations of the ruling, and the government was ordered in a number of subsequent trials to produce entire files in a case, regardless of relevancy. Several important

Labor union leader Clinton E. Jencks, appearing as himself in the blacklisted 1954 film *Salt of the Earth*, had his perjury conviction for swearing that he was not a communist reversed by the Court in *Jencks v United States* (1957). The negative public response to *Jencks* helped Congress impose the only modification of the Court's domestic security rulings during the tense 1957–1959 term.

prosecutions were dismissed because the government refused to produce the requested files.

At the behest of the White House, the Justice Department, and the Federal Bureau of Investigation, the House and Senate Judiciary Committees moved quickly to report bills to narrow the impact of the *Jencks* decision. The Senate passed its version by voice vote on August 26, 1957; the House passed its measure a day later with only seventeen dissenting votes. Both chambers agreed overwhelmingly on August 30 to a compromise version, and President Dwight D. Eisenhower signed the bill into law on September 2.[3]

stated an intention to preempt a given field of legislation, because a conflict emerged between the federal and state law, or because a court inferred an intention by Congress to preempt the field.

It was to prohibit this "preemption by implication" that H.R. 3, the most important of several antipreemption proposals, was offered. Its primary provision stated: "No act of Congress shall be construed as indicating an intent on the part of Congress to occupy the field in which such act operates, to the exclusion of all state laws on the same subject matter, unless such act contains an express provision to that effect or unless there is a direct and positive conflict between such act and a state law so that the two cannot be reconciled or consistently stand together."

H.R. 3 was introduced in the House in 1955 by Rules Committee chairman Howard W. Smith, D-Va., after the Pennsylvania Supreme Court held in 1954

Public Law 85-269 did not reverse *Jencks* but restricted it. After testimony by a government witness, a defendant in a criminal case could request relevant pretrial statements made by that witness if they were written and signed by the witness or if they were a transcription of oral statements made at the time. The statute authorized the trial judge to screen requested statements for relevance.

THE DEFEATS

Reversal of another Court decision came within a whisker of passage. In *Cole v. Young* (1956) the Court held that federal employee security procedures applied only to sensitive jobs and that government employees in nonsensitive jobs could not be summarily dismissed for suspected disloyalty.[4]

In August 1957 the Senate approved a bill (S. 1411) to permit government supervisors to transfer suspected security risks from sensitive to nonsensitive jobs instead of suspending them. In July 1958 the House approved an amended version of S. 1411 that extended federal employee security procedures to all government employees so that anyone suspected of subversive activities could be summarily dismissed.

The final compromise version was identical to the House amendment but limited to one year. The House passed it by voice vote, but the compromise was never taken up in the Senate and died at adjournment. In 1959 House and Senate committees held hearings on the issue; however, no further action was taken.[5]

YATES BILL

In 1958 and 1959 the House approved measures to reverse the portion of the Court ruling in *Yates v. United States* (1957) that defined the word *organize* to mean only the act of initially bringing together a group of people.[6] The legislation would have redefined the word to make it a crime

not only to bring into being a group seeking to overthrow the government by force but also to conduct continuing organizational activities. A similar provision was included in the Jenner-Butler bill killed in the Senate in 1958. The Senate took no action on the 1958 House-passed bill; in 1959 a Senate subcommittee approved the House bill, but the full Senate Judiciary Committee did not act on it.

PASSPORT CONTROL

After the Supreme Court held in *Kent v. Dulles* (1958) that Congress had not authorized the State Department to deny passports to American citizens affiliated with the Communist Party, the department proposed legislation to Congress to overturn the decision.[7] The House passed an amended version of the proposal by voice vote, but a threatened filibuster in the Senate blocked consideration there. The House passed similar legislation again in 1959. Although three Senate subcommittees held hearings on the issue, no bill was reported to the Senate floor.[8]

---

1. See C. Herman Pritchett, *Congress versus the Supreme Court, 1957–60*, reprinted. (New York: Da Capo Press, 1973); and Walter F. Murphy, *Congress and the Court: A Case Study in the American Political Process* (Chicago: University of Chicago Press, 1962).

2. *Jencks v. United States,* 353 U.S. 657 (1957).

3. *CQ Almanac 1957* (Washington, D.C.: Congressional Quarterly, 1958).

4. *Cole v. Young,* 351 U.S. 536 (1956).

5. See *CQ Almanac,* 1957, 1958, 1959, (Washington, D.C.: Congressional Quarterly, 1958, 1959, 1960).

6. *Yates v. United States, 354 U.S. 298 (1957); see also CQ Almanac,* 1958 and 1959.

7. *Kent v. Dulles,* 357 U.S. 116 (1958).

8. *CQ Almanac 1960* (Washington, D.C.: Congressional Quarterly, 1961).

that the 1940 Smith Act preempted provisions of state antisedition laws that punished persons found guilty of subversive activities directed against the federal government.

The ruling, when affirmed by the U.S. Supreme Court in *Pennsylvania v. Nelson* (1956), affected the antisubversive laws of forty-three states. Smith, who wrote the 1940 act affected by the ruling, said the Court decision was "the first intimation I have ever had

that Congress ever had the faintest notion of nullifying the concurrent jurisdiction of the respective sovereign states to pursue also their own prosecution for subversive activities."[38]

After his bill failed to pass, Smith reintroduced H.R. 3 in 1957. Spurred by opposition to the Supreme Court's ruling in *Nelson*, the House Judiciary Committee reported both a modified version of H.R. 3 and a bill that would overturn only the *Nelson* decision. The full House adopted H.R. 3 on July 17, 1958, by a 241-155 vote after merging it with the narrower bill.

Similar bills were reported to the full Senate. When one was called up for consideration on August 20, 1958, immediately after the Senate voted to table the Jenner-Butler bill, Sen. John L. McClellan, D-Ark., offered an amendment to substitute the House-passed version of H.R, 3 for the Senate bill. Over protests from the measure's supporters, Majority Leader Johnson won adjournment until the next day. Although it looked as though the McClellan amendment had enough votes for adoption, Johnson and other opponents of H.R. 3 lobbied hard throughout August 21. The lobbying paid off when a motion to recommit the bill to the Judiciary Committee was agreed to by a one-vote margin, 41-40.

Recommittal ended further consideration of H.R. 3 in the Eighty-fifth Congress. In 1959 the House again approved H.R. 3, although with diminished enthusiasm. Smith continued to introduce the measure for several more years, but it was never again considered by the full House or Senate.

The change in the congressional attitude on the preemption issue between 1958 and 1959 has been attributed to several factors, including an influx of "pro-Court" northern Democrats into the Senate after the 1958 elections, a series of rulings giving the states wider latitude over business matters, and Court affirmation that the states could prosecute subversive activities directed against them rather than the federal government.

★

Reversals of Rulings

Of all its methods of influencing the Supreme Court, Congress has had most success in reversing individual rulings through adoption of a constitutional amendment or passage of legislation.

Four of the twenty-seven amendments to the Constitution were adopted specifically to overrule the Supreme Court's interpretation of that document. The amendments reversed the Court's rulings on the ability of citizens of one state to bring suit against another state, on the application of the Bill of Rights to the states, on income taxes, and on the right of eighteen-year olds to vote.

It is difficult and time-consuming to amend the Constitution. Each chamber of Congress must approve the proposed amendment by a two-thirds vote, and it must then be ratified by three-fourths of all the states. Moreover, there is long-standing and deeply held sentiment that amendments to the Constitution should not be adopted every time there is a significant disagreement with a Supreme Court ruling. As a result, most proposals to amend the Constitution never emerge from Congress.

The more common way of reversing the Supreme Court is for Congress to repass an offending statute after modifying it to meet the Court's objections. In such cases the Court in its opinion will suggest rewording the legislation to achieve its original purpose. This kind of reversal through simple legislation is easily accomplished if the Court has interpreted a statute contrary to the construction intended by Congress. The House and Senate may then pass new legislation explicitly setting forth their intention.

Reversal is not so easily accomplished when the Court and Congress are at philosophical odds. For example, twice Congress passed legislation to end child labor, and twice the Supreme Court ruled that such legislation was not within Congress's powers to enact. That its interpretation was based on philosophical differences rather than purely constitutional considerations was evident when the Court reversed these two decisions several years later. In the mid-1930s it appeared that a similar confrontation would develop over New Deal legislation, but the Court retreated and upheld congressional authority to regulate economic matters, which eased the crisis.

In several instances Congress has passed reversal legislation that has had only a symbolic effect because Congress did not had comprehensive jurisdiction over the subject in question. In 1968, for example, Congress passed additions to an anticrime bill overturning several Court rulings on the admissibility into evidence of criminal confessions. The legislation affected only federal courts, which hear a very small fraction of all criminal cases; procedures for confessions in state courts were left untouched.

Whether such limited reversals have an indirect effect by warning the Court that it may be reaching politically unacceptable boundaries probably depends on a multitude of factors, including the nature of the issue involved, the strength of the congressional opposition, the position of the president, and public consensus.

CONSTITUTIONAL AMENDMENTS

Congress and the states have allied on four occasions to overturn Supreme Court decisions through constitutional amendments. Several other proposed amendments to nullify the Court's unpopular rulings have been offered, but have not been approved either by the requisite two-thirds majority of both the House and Senate or by three-fourths of the states.

States' Rights

The Eleventh Amendment, ratified in 1795, was the first amendment adopted to negate a Supreme Court decision; it is the only constitutional amendment that actually removed part of the jurisdiction of the federal courts. The other three overturned specific rulings of the Court.

Article III, section 2, of the Constitution gave the Supreme Court jurisdiction over cases arising between a state and citizens of another state or of a foreign country. During the writing of the Constitution, opponents of a strong central government opposed this grant, claiming that it would jeopardize the sovereignty of the individual states. But these fears were successfully allayed when proponents of the grant argued that it would permit suits only where the state was the plaintiff. As historian Charles Warren explained:

> The right of the Federal Judiciary to summon a State as defendant and to adjudicate its rights and liabilities had been the subject of deep apprehension and of active debate at the time of the adoption of the Constitution; but the existence of any such right had been disclaimed by many of the most eminent advocates of the new Federal Government, and it was largely owing to their successful dissipation of the fear of the existence of such Federal power that the Constitution was finally adopted.[1]

The Federalists' assurances, however, proved empty promises. The first case brought to the Supreme Court in the February 1791 term was a suit by Dutch bankers against the state of Maryland.[2] The case that would lead directly to adoption of the Eleventh Amendment was brought to the Court in the August 1792 term.

A South Carolinian named Chisholm, acting as executor for a British creditor, sued the state of Georgia for property confiscated from an Englishman. Chisholm had as his attorney Edmund Randolph, who, despite his position as the first U.S. attorney general, continued his private law practice.

The Court postponed arguments in *Chisholm v. Georgia* until February 1793. When the time came, Georgia officials refused to appear before the Court, claiming that the federal judiciary had no jurisdiction over the case. Randolph made his case in behalf of Chisholm, and when he was finished the justices asked if anyone would like to respond. No one did. The Court announced its decision on February 18, 1793, upholding the right of citizens of one state to sue in federal court another state for breach of contract.[3] *(See "Resistance: Chisholm v. Georgia," pp. 377–378.)*

The decision, according to Warren, "fell upon the country with a profound shock."[4] Anti-Federalists argued that the decision compromised the sovereignty of the states and made them nothing more than corporations. But the real fear was that the decision would lead to a proliferation of citizen suits against the states that would further jeopardize their already precarious financial plights. Warren wrote:

> In the crucial condition of the finance of most of the States at that time, only disaster was to be expected if suits could be successfully maintained by holders of State issues of paper and other credits, or by Loyalist refugees to recover property confiscated or sequestered by the States; and that this was not theoretical danger was shown by the immediate institution of such suits against the States in South Carolina, Georgia, Virginia and Massachusetts.[5]

The day after the *Chisholm* decision was announced, a resolution proposing a constitutional amendment to bar citizen suits against states was offered in the House. A similar resolution proposed in the Senate was tabled on February 25. That resolution was reintroduced in the Senate on January 2, 1794, and passed twelve days later by a 23 to 2 vote. The House approved it on March 4, 1794, by an 81 to 9 vote.

Three-fourths of the states approved the amendment in less than a year, but almost four years passed before its ratification was officially recognized. President John Adams sent a message to Congress on January 8, 1798, stating that three-fourths of the states having acted, the amendment "may now be deemed to be a part of the Constitution."

The Supreme Court acquiesced in the amendment in February 1798 when it dismissed the case of *Hollingsworth v. Virginia..* Shareholders of a company were suing for losses resulting from Virginia's nullification of the company's title to land in the state. The Court said that ratification of the Eleventh Amendment had removed its jurisdiction "in any case, past or future, in which a State was sued by citizens of another State, or by citizens or subjects of any foreign States."[6] In the 1990s the Rehnquist Court expanded the reach of this amendment and said it gave the states a "sovereign immunity" from some federal laws, even when the states were sued by their own citizens.

Citizenship and Civil Rights

After the surrender of the Confederacy in 1865, one of Congress's first actions was adoption of the Thirteenth Amendment abolishing slavery. The states ratified the amendment late in 1865, but expectations that it would compel the rebel states to protect the civil rights of former black slaves went unfulfilled. The South adopted black codes and continued its oppressive treatment of the former slaves.

Congress responded by enacting federal laws to give blacks some measure of protection, but because the constitutionality of one of the most important of these laws—the Civil Rights Act of 1866—was in doubt, the legislature looked to enactment of a constitutional amendment to force the South to give blacks their civil rights.

A specially created Joint Committee on Reconstruction drafted the Fourteenth Amendment in early 1866. Although the political attention of the day was focused on the amendment's second section, which unsuccessfully sought to ensure black voting rights, the first section of the amendment ultimately provided more protection to both blacks and whites.

As proposed by Rep. John A. Bingham, R-Ohio, this section gave Congress power to make laws "to secure to the citizens of each state all privileges and immunities of citizens in the several states, and to all persons in the several states equal protection in the rights of life, liberty and property."[7] Representative Bingham's intention was to undo the effect of the Supreme Court's ruling in the 1833 case of *Barron v. Baltimore,* which held that the first eight amendments to the Constitution protected individual rights only against infringement by the federal government and not by the states.[8]

As amended by the joint committee, passed by Congress, and ratified by the states, the first section did not give Congress a positive grant of power to guard against infringement by the states but simply prohibited the states from making any law that abridged the privileges and immunities of citizens of the United States; deprived any persons of life, liberty, or property without due process of the law; or denied anyone equal protection of the laws.

Although the record indicates that Bingham expected this amended version to have the same effect as his initial proposal, several rulings by the Supreme Court in the 1870s and 1880s so narrowly construed the language of the first section that it afforded little of its intended protection to any citizens. It was not until 1925 that the Court began to use the Fourteenth Amendment to secure the guarantees of the Bill of Rights against state action, and it was not until the middle of the twentieth century that the Court began to extend equal protection of the laws to blacks.

The first section of the Fourteenth Amendment overturned another Supreme Court ruling—the Dred Scott decision of 1857—which held that blacks were not and could never become U.S. citizens.[9] Adding a single sentence to the language already approved by the House, the Senate declared that all persons born or naturalized in the United States and subject to its jurisdiction are citizens of the United States. Although *Scott v. Sandford* was not mentioned during debate, it was clear that the Senate addition was intended to nullify that unfortunate Court ruling. *(See "Dred Scott," p. 180.)*

The debate shows that there was some opposition to the provision because it applied to Chinese and other ethnic groups that were discriminated against by the white majority. Nevertheless, it was approved by both the House and Senate and, upon ratification of the Fourteenth Amendment in 1868, became the only definition of citizenship to appear in the Constitution.

Income Taxes

When the Supreme Court struck down a federal income tax law in 1895 because the tax was not apportioned according to constitutional dictates, Chief Justice Melville W. Fuller invited Congress to overturn the Court's ruling. "If it be true that the Constitution should have been so framed that a tax of this kind could be laid, the instrument defines the way for its amendment," Fuller wrote in *Pollock v. Farmers' Loan and Trust Co.* (1895).[10]

Article I, section 9, clause 4, of the Constitution forbids Congress to levy any direct tax that is not apportioned by population. For the first one hundred years of the nation's life, the Court held that only per capita taxes and taxes on land were direct taxes. But in the 1895 income tax cases the Court held that taxes on income from real estate were also direct and must be levied proportionately among the states. *(See "The Income Tax Cases," pp. 144–147.)* The decisions were highly unpopular with both laborers and farmers who felt they were burdened with payment of disproportionately high amounts of indirect taxes, such as tariffs. With each election they returned to Congress more and more Democrats and progressive Republicans who favored enactment of an income tax. But nothing concrete happened until 1909. Then a two-year-long depression, which had depleted government revenues, and a Republican campaign promise to do something about the high tariffs made consideration of an income tax imperative.

When the Republicans' tariff bill was introduced, Democrats seized on it, offering an amendment almost identical to the income tax law that had been declared unconstitutional in 1895. Conservative Republicans opposed to the tax countered with a proposal for a constitutional amendment to permit an income tax without apportionment. For support they turned to President William Howard Taft, who favored an amendment over legislation. In a message to Congress he observed that simple reenactment of the income tax law would undoubtedly encounter "protracted litigation" before it could take effect. President Taft also suggested that congressional defiance of the Court's rulings would "not strengthen public confidence in the stability of judicial construction of the Constitution."[11]

Conservative Republicans banked on the hope that even if the amendment were approved by Congress, not enough state legislatures would ratify it. Democrats and progressive Republicans largely agreed with this analysis, but felt philosophically compelled to vote for the amendment anyway.

The amendment was submitted to the states in 1909. Contrary to all expectations, the requisite number of state legislatures ratified the amendment in less than four years, and it became part of the Constitution on February 25, 1913. *(See box, The "Income Tax" Amendment, p. 146.)*

The Right to Vote

Adoption of the fourth amendment to overturn a Supreme Court decision occurred with the apparent cooperation of the Court itself. As one of the amendments to the Voting Rights Act of 1965, Congress enacted in 1970 a provision lowering the voting age for federal, state, and local elections to eighteen years. President Richard Nixon objected to the provision even as he signed it into law in June 1970. He said he favored lowering the voting age but believed "along with most of the Nation's leading constitutional scholars—that Congress has no power to enact it by simple statute, but rather it requires a constitutional amendment."[12]

The Nixon administration quickly brought suit to test the validity of the legislative measure, and the Supreme Court cooperated by deciding the case just six months after the measure was signed into law. By a 5-4 vote, the Court ruled in December 1970 that Congress had the authority to lower the voting age for federal elections but not for state and local elections.[13]

This decision created immense administrative difficulties for the forty-seven states that did not allow eighteen-year-olds to vote. State election officials and legislators said the task of producing dual registration books, ballots, and voting machines could not be completed in time for the 1972 elections. Amendments to state constitutions changing voting age requirements would have been difficult, if not impossible, for some states to approve before 1972.

To assist the states, an amendment to the Constitution to lower the voting age to eighteen years in all elections was introduced in both houses of Congress in early 1971. The Senate approved the amendment unanimously on March 10, 1971. The House adopted it, 401-19, on March 23. The states also acted in record time, ratifying the amendment by July 1, 1971, just three months and seven days after it was submitted to them.

Child Labor Amendment

Although Congress adopted an amendment to overturn a pair of Supreme Court decisions on child labor, the amendment failed to win ratification by a sufficient number of states before the Supreme Court itself overruled its earlier decisions.

In 1916 Congress sought to discourage employment of children by enacting a law forbidding the shipment in interstate commerce of goods made by child laborers. The validity of the statute was challenged, and the Supreme Court declared it unconstitutional in *Hammer v. Dagenhart* (1918).[14] In passing the statute, the Court said, Congress was attempting to regulate not interstate commerce but labor, which was a matter reserved to the states for regulation under the Tenth Amendment. *(See "Child Labor," pp. 116–117.)*

Congress reacted to this ruling in February 1919 by passing a second child labor law that placed a tax of 10 percent on the net profits of any company employing children. But, in *Bailey v. Drexel Furniture Co.* (1922), the Court declared this statute unconstitutional as well, ruling that the tax was intended not to raise revenue but to penalize employers.[15] *(See "Child Labor," pp. 116–117.)*

Still unwilling to concede the fight to the Court, Congress in June 1924 submitted to the states a constitutional amendment that would give Congress authority to outlaw child labor. By 1938, however, only twenty-eight of the forty-eight states had ratified the amendment. In that year Congress again used its constitutional power to regulate interstate commerce and enacted a child labor law as part of the federal minimum wage statute. In 1941 the Supreme Court upheld the 1938 law in *United States v. Darby Lumber Co.,* specifically reversing its 1918 ruling in *Dagenhart.*[16] The effort to pass an amendment then faded. *(See details of Darby case, pp. 127–128.)*

Other Proposed Amendments

Other proposed constitutional amendments to invalidate Supreme Court decisions have failed to win congressional approval. The Court's controversial decisions on reapportionment, school prayer, school busing, abortion, and flag burning have prompted these efforts to amend the Constitution.

Reapportionment

A revolution in the apportionment of state legislatures was precipitated by the Supreme Court in 1962 when it held in *Baker v. Carr* that the judiciary could entertain suits challenging malapportionment. The decision overturned a line of legal precedent holding that the makeup of state legislatures was not a justiciable matter—rather, it was a political one—and that citizens had no standing to sue to effect a change.[17]

That decision did not generate much congressional opposition, but in 1964 the Court in *Reynolds v. Sims* applied its "one person, one vote" rule to state legislatures, holding that both chambers must be apportioned on a basis of substantial equality of population.[18] The decision struck not only at malapportioned state legislatures but also at those apportioned—sometimes under terms of the state constitution—on the basis of one state senator for each city, town, and county, regardless of population. The decision was opposed by many rural organizations and state legislators whose strength in the state legislatures was bound to be undermined by the ruling. They lost no time in making their views known to Congress, which responded quickly but ineffectively to the Court ruling. Within two months of the decision, the House passed a bill denying federal courts jurisdiction over state reapportionment, but it died at the end of the session when the Senate failed to act. In the Senate a six-week filibuster by liberals stymied an attempt by Senate minority leader Everett McKinley Dirksen, R-Ill., to require the Court to delay reapportionment orders until January 1966. Dirksen said such a delay would give Congress time to consider a constitutional amendment overturning the Court decision.

In 1965 and again in 1966 Dirksen tried to secure Senate passage of a constitutional amendment that would allow states to apportion one chamber of their legislatures on the basis of factors other than population. In both years, although a majority of the Senate approved the proposal, Dirksen's effort fell seven votes short of the two-thirds needed for approval of a constitutional amendment.

Discouraged by failure to win Senate approval, advocates of the constitutional amendment turned to the state legislatures themselves. By 1969 thirty-three states—one short of the two-thirds necessary—had submitted petitions to Congress calling for a constitutional convention to propose a reapportionment amendment. No further action has occurred.

Term Limits Amendment

The term limits movement exploded onto the national political scene in the early 1990s with repercussions in Congress and at the Supreme Court. Twenty-three states enacted laws limiting the time a senator or representative could represent the state in Congress. Proponents of these term limits contended that they offered an antidote for the gridlock and special interest politics ailing Washington. Opponents countered that term limits would deprive Congress of some of its most able and seasoned lawmakers.

The Supreme Court on May 22, 1995, put an end to state efforts to impose term limits. The Court in *U.S. Term Limits Inc. v. Thornton* said states have no constitutional role in determining the qualifications for serving in Congress.[1] *(See details of this case, p. 224.)* That left amending the Constitution as the only route for advocates of term limits.

Although the Republican-dominated Congress had touted term limits as part of its 1995 agenda, a proposed constitutional amendment stalled. The House of Representatives on March 29, 1995, rejected, 227-204, a proposed amendment to limit senators and House members to twelve years in office (two six-year terms for senators and six two-year terms for representatives). The vote fell short of the two-thirds majority required for adoption. Most Republicans supported the amendment, but the opposition of senior Republicans combined with Democrats' distaste for the proposal contributed to its defeat.[2] Afterward, the fervor for term limits quickly faded, as even the Republicans, who controlled Congress, lost enthusiasm for the idea of legislating themselves out of office.

---

1. *U.S. Term Limits v. Thornton*, 415 U.S. 779 (1995).
2. *CQ Almanac 1995* (Washington, D.C.: Congressional Quarterly, 1996), 1-35–1-36, 6-37.

School Prayer and School Busing

At about the same time it was causing havoc with the state legislatures, the Supreme Court created additional public controversy by ruling in 1962 and again in 1963 that the First Amendment's prohibition against establishment of religion barred officially prescribed or supported religious observances in public schools.[19] Although most major religious organizations were opposed to any constitutional amendments overriding these decisions, mail advocating them flooded into congressional offices. The House Judiciary Committee reluctantly held hearings on proposed amendments in 1964, but took no further action. In the Senate, Minority Leader Dirksen offered a proposed amendment in 1966, but the Senate failed by nine votes to approve it by the necessary two-thirds majority.

Little more happened on the proposals until 1971, when an intense two-year grassroots campaign succeeded in dislodging a school prayer amendment from the House Judiciary Committee. But this effort, too, was ultimately unsuccessful when the House failed to approve the amendment.

In the 1980s the support of the Reagan administration for a constitutional amendment permitting organized prayer in school revived efforts in Congress to win passage of such a proposal. In 1984 an amendment came to the Senate floor with administration backing. It failed, however, to win the necessary two-thirds approval; at 56–44, the vote was eleven short of the sixty-seven needed.

The next year, after the Court in *Wallace v. Jaffree* (1985) struck down Alabama's moment-of-silence law, the Senate Judiciary Committee approved an amendment to permit silent prayer in public schools, but the measure did not come to the floor.[20]

In 1979 congressional supporters of an amendment to ban school busing for desegregation purposes managed to bypass the House Judiciary Committee, but the amendment ultimately failed when the House on July 24 rejected it 216-209.

School prayer amendments were introduced intermittently in Congress through the 1980s and 1990s, and they became a priority for Republican lawmakers after they won majorities in both the House and Senate in the 1994 elections. No proposal to permit organized school prayer passed the floor of either chamber, however.

The Court's ruling in *Texas v. Johnson*, which held that flag burning was a form of political expression protected by the First Amendment, touched off a public and political outcry. Congress in1989 and 1990 considered a constitutional amendment that would have permitted it to outlaw flag desecration; the amendment was defeated in both the House and the Senate.

Abortion

Despite intense controversy over abortion, almost a decade passed after the Supreme Court's landmark decision in *Roe v. Wade* (1973) before a congressional committee approved a constitutional amendment nullifying the decision. The proposed language approved by the Senate Judiciary Committee in 1982 declared that the Constitution did not protect the right to have an abortion.

The full Senate did not vote on the amendment that year. When a similar amendment came to the Senate floor in 1983, it was rejected, 50-49, falling eighteen votes short of the two-thirds required to approve a constitutional amendment.

Flag Burning

In 1989 the Court touched off a public and political outcry with a 5-4 ruling that effectively invalidated existing state and federal laws against desecration of the U.S. flag. The decision in *Texas v. Johnson* (1989), which held that flag burning was a form of political expression protected by the First Amendment, brought swift demands from President George H. W. Bush for a constitutional amendment to reverse it.[21]

Yet despite an initial outpouring of protest and patriotic rhetoric, anger over the Court's ruling soon began to fade. Many people who had demanded reversal of the decision reconsidered their support for a constitutional amendment reversing it after Congress began debating the wisdom of amending the Bill of Rights. The Senate eventually voted in October 1989 on a proposed constitutional amendment to permit Congress to outlaw flag desecration, but the 51-48 vote was fifteen short of the required two-thirds of those present and voting.

A proposed amendment also failed in 1990. The furor over flag burning continued that year after the Court in *United States v. Eichman* invalidated a 1989 federal statute designed to protect the flag. The Court by 5-4 cited *Texas v. Johnson* in that opinion. The invalidated statute had been a second-best attempt by Congress to ban flag burning after the constitutional amendment plan failed in 1989. The 1990 case repeated the split from the 1989 case of *Texas v. Johnson*. Justice William J. Brennan Jr., writing again for the majority, said, "Although Congress cast the Flag Protection Act in somewhat broader terms than the Texas statute at issue in *Johnson,* the Act still suffers from the same fundamental flaw: it suppresses expression out of concern for its likely communicative impact."[22]

When the proposal for an amendment came to the House in June 1990, the House vote was 254-177, or thirty-four votes short of the two-thirds necessary for passage of an amendment. Within a week the Senate also defeated a resolution for such an amendment. The measure failed 58-42, nine votes short of the required two-thirds of senators present and voting.[23]

Gay Rights

In 2003, after the Court struck down a Texas law that singled out gays and lesbians for criminal prosecutions in *Lawrence v. Texas,* social conservatives feared the next step would be to give homosexuals a right to marry.[24] They rallied behind a constitutional amendment (H.J. Res. 56) that would define marriage as the union of a man and a woman. The House has failed to approve the amendment.

LEGISLATIVE REVERSALS

A speedier and frequently more successful method than the constitutional amendment for reversing Supreme Court decisions is congressional reversal or modification by legislative enactment. The Court generally acquiesces in such legislative overrides. Its opinions often actually suggest that Congress reenact the measure in question after tailoring it to remove the Court's objections to its validity.

The justices do not, however, always bow to congressional efforts to void Court decisions by legislation. After the Court declared the 1916 child labor law unconstitutional—it barred the shipment in interstate commerce of goods made by children—Congress passed a second measure that placed a prohibitively high tax on profits from such goods. The Court proceeded to declare this law invalid as well. Congress then approved a constitutional amendment forbidding child labor, but fewer than the necessary two-thirds of the states ratified it before the Supreme Court itself reversed its earlier holdings. (See "Child Labor," pp. 116–117, and "Wages and Hours," pp. 126–128.)

Early Examples

According to historian Charles Warren, Congress first reversed the Supreme Court by legislation in 1852. In *Pennsylvania v. Wheeling and Belmont Bridge Co.* (1852) the Court ruled that because a bridge built across the Ohio River obstructed interstate commerce and violated a congressionally sanctioned compact between Kentucky and Virginia, it must be either raised so that ships could pass under it or taken down.

Congress immediately passed a law reversing this decision by declaring that the bridge did not obstruct interstate commerce and requiring instead that ships be refitted so that they could pass under the bridge. In 1856 the Court sustained this legislative reversal.[25]

Congressional reversal by legislation occurred again after the Court held in 1890 that in the absence of congressional authorization, liquor in its original container imported into a state through interstate commerce was not subject to state prohibition laws. Accepting the Court's implicit invitation, Congress later in the year permitted the states to prohibit such shipments of liquor, and the Court upheld that statute in 1891.[26]

Another early example of legislative reversal of Supreme Court decisions concerns the Interstate Commerce Commission (ICC). Congress was able to modify the Court's rulings on the powers of the commission. In 1887 Congress created the ICC, the first federal regulatory agency, to provide uniform regulation of interstate railroad rates and to end unethical rebate and price-fixing practices. In 1894 the justices sustained the authority of Congress to create the agency. But in a series of cases decided over the next three years, the Court, which was dominated by men opposed to any government regulation impinging on the free development of business and industry, stripped the agency of all of its essential regulatory powers. The most damaging ruling held that the ICC had no rate-making powers and implied that Congress could not constitutionally delegate such powers to it.[27] The decisions led to a resumption of all the unsavory practices that prompted creation of the agency in the first place.

In the face of growing demands for reform from the public—and even from some of the railroad companies—Congress decided to confront the Court. In 1906 it enacted the Hepburn Act, which specifically authorized the ICC to adjust rates it judged to be unreasonable and unfair.

The Court upheld that grant of power in 1910. Changing Court personnel and shifting attitudes of sitting justices may explain the Court's new stance toward the ICC. Encouraged, Congress then gave the ICC authority to set original rates. Several railroads challenged this statute as an unconstitutional delegation of power, but the Court in 1914 said that contention was "without merit," thereby completely reversing its earlier decisions.[28] (See "Creation of the Interstate Commerce Commission," pp. 104–106.)

Civil Rights

In one area more than eighty years passed between a Supreme Court decision and its reversal by legislation. In 1883 the Court held unconstitutional the Civil Rights Act of 1875, which made it a misdemeanor for any individual to discriminate against another individual on account of race in the use of public accommodations, transportation, or public entertainment. The Court specifically ruled that Congress had exceeded its power under the Thirteenth and Fourteenth Amendments when it enacted the statute.[29]

Congress did not reverse the 1883 ruling until passage of the 1964 Civil Rights Act. In that statute Congress used its authority to regulate interstate commerce to bar racial discrimination in public accommodations that serve interstate travelers or that sell goods or provide entertainment, a substantial portion of which moves through interstate commerce. Six months after this statute was signed into law, the Court unanimously sustained its constitutionality.[30]

Unions and Antitrust

One particularly prolonged and hostile confrontation between the Court and Congress centered on whether labor unions were exempt from federal antitrust law. The 1894 statute making combinations in restraint of trade illegal was silent on the question of labor unions, and in 1908 the Court ruled that certain union practices, including the boycott, were illegal restraints of trade punishable under the antitrust law.[31]

That decision impelled Congress to add provisions to the Clayton Act of 1914 that specifically exempted labor unions pursuing lawful objectives from the reach of the antitrust law. The Clayton Act also stipulated that federal courts could not issue injunctions in any labor disputes unless necessary to prevent irreparable property damage.

Seven years later the Supreme Court subverted the intent of the Clayton Act. In a 1921 decision it interpreted the anti-injunction language of the act so narrowly that injunctions against striking workers became almost commonplace. The Court also held that, the Clayton Act notwithstanding, certain union practices illegally interfered with commerce and still fell afoul of the antitrust law.[32]

Congress made the next move, enacting the Norris-LaGuardia Act in 1932 to reverse the Court's 1921 decision and restore the vitality of the Clayton Act's provisions. A challenge to the 1932 statute did not reach the Court until 1938, a year after the majority conceded that Congress as part of its authority to

regulate interstate commerce had broad powers to regulate labor relations. Then, in a pair of cases, the Court upheld the constitutionality of the Norris-LaGuardia Act, ruling that Congress had clearly passed it to "obviate the results of the judicial construction" of the Clayton Act.[33]

New Deal Legislation

The New Deal period saw Congress overturn the Court on more important measures than in any other period in the country's history. At President Franklin D. Roosevelt's instigation, Congress in the 1930s enacted several statutes aimed at ending the Great Depression and restoring the nation's economic well-being. Of eight major statutes, the Supreme Court upheld only two—an act establishing the Tennessee Valley Authority and legislation abolishing gold clauses in public and private contracts.

At first frustrated by the economically conservative Court majority's unwillingness to sustain most of the New Deal programs and then encouraged by the Court's apparent economic liberalization in 1937, Congress revised five of the six laws the Court had declared invalid. The Court subsequently sustained all of the modified versions that were challenged. In lieu of the National Industrial Recovery Act, Congress enacted the National Labor Relations Act, which the Court also sustained.

The six original statutes, the cases striking them down, the revised laws, and the cases sustaining their validity were:

- National Industrial Recovery Act of 1933, struck down in *Panama Refining Co. v. Ryan* (1935) and *Schechter Poultry Co. v. United States* (1935), replaced by the National Labor Relations Act of 1935, upheld in *National Labor Relations Board v. Jones & Laughlin Steel Corp.* (1937).[34]

- Railroad Retirement Pension Act of 1934, struck down in *Railroad Retirement Board v. Alton* (1935), replaced by railroad retirement acts adopted in 1935, 1937, and 1938, which were never challenged before the Supreme Court.[35]

- Frazier-Lemke Farm Mortgage Act of 1934, struck down in *Louisville Joint Stock Land Bank v. Radford* (1935), modified by Frazier-Lemke Act of 1935, upheld in *Wright v. Vinton Branch* (1937).[36]

- Agricultural Adjustment Act of 1933, struck down in *United States v. Butler* (1936), modified in Agricultural Adjustment Act of 1937, upheld in *Mulford v. Smith* (1939).[37]

- Bituminous Coal Conservation Act of 1935, struck down by *Carter v. Carter Coal Co.* (1936), modified in Bituminous Coal Act of 1937, upheld in *Sunshine Anthracite Coal Co. v. Adkins* (1940).[38]

- Municipal Bankruptcy Act of 1934, struck down in *Ashton v. Cameron County District* (1936), modified in Municipal Bankruptcy Act of 1937, upheld in *United States v. Bekins* (1938).[39]

Insurance and Oil

Congress has used its power to reverse the Court to rid itself of regulatory functions it has not wanted. In 1944, for example, the Supreme Court issued a ruling that gave Congress control over insurance, a matter that traditionally had been regulated by the states, even though transactions were often conducted through interstate commerce.[40] Congress wanted no part of this new responsibility and in 1945 passed a law returning the authority to regulate insurance to the states. The Court upheld this delegation of control in 1946.[41]

Congress in one instance successfully overruled both the Court and a president. In *United States v. California* (1947) the Court ruled that the federal government, not the states, owned the three-mile strip of oil-rich submerged land adjacent to the ocean shores. Legislation to reverse this ruling was introduced in 1948, 1949, and 1950, but was not approved. After the Court reaffirmed its 1947 ruling in two 1950 cases affecting Louisiana and Texas, Congress in 1951 passed a law giving ownership of the tidelands to the states.[42] President Harry S. Truman, whose administration had brought the 1947 suit claiming federal ownership, vetoed it.

No attempt was made to override the veto, but the question of who was to control the submerged lands became a major campaign issue in the 1952 presidential elections, with Republicans promising to restore the lands and their oil deposits to the states. The Republicans won the election, and Congress in 1953 enacted the Submerged Lands Act ceding to the states the mineral rights to lands lying offshore between the low tide mark and the states' historic boundaries. The Supreme Court upheld this cession in 1954.[43]

Criminals and Confessions

Congress tried for decades to reverse some of the Supreme Court's decisions that seemed to enlarge the rights of criminal suspects and hamper law enforcement. Then, in 1968, rising crime rates, urban riots, and the assassinations of civil rights leader Martin Luther King Jr. and Democratic presidential candidate Robert F. Kennedy supplied the necessary impetus, and Congress, over the objection of President Lyndon B. Johnson, enacted legislation modifying the impact of these decisions. Most criminals, however, are prosecuted in state courts, and Congress has no jurisdiction to set their rules. Because this legislation affected only federal courts, its effect was largely symbolic.

The Mallory Decision

In 1943 the Court in *McNabb v. United States* ruled that a confession obtained by police during an "unnecessary delay" in a suspect's arraignment could not be used as evidence in federal court, even if the confession had been given voluntarily.[44]

In 1957 the Supreme Court sparked controversy when it reaffirmed the *McNabb* decision and overturned the rape conviction of Andrew Mallory.[45] Because police had not complied with the *McNabb* doctrine requiring prompt arraignment, the Court determined that Mallory had been detained illegally, and his confession was therefore inadmissible as evidence.

Reaction to the *Mallory* decision was immediate and widespread. The House in July 1958 passed "corrective" legislation by an overwhelming vote, 294-79. The House measure barred federal courts from disqualifying confessions otherwise admissible as evidence in criminal cases solely because of delay in arraigning the suspect. The Senate passed the bill, but it died before final passage.

The Miranda and Wade Decisions

In *Miranda v. Arizona* (1966) the Court expanded and formalized a new procedure for procuring confessions.

Under the so-called "Miranda rights" rule, confessions were inadmissible as evidence in state or federal criminal trials if the persons accused had not been informed of their right to remain silent, if they had not been warned that any statement they made might be used against them, and if they had not been informed of their right to have an attorney present during the police interrogation.[46]

The next year in *United States v. Wade* (1967) the Court held that identification of a defendant based solely on a police lineup staged when the defendant's attorney was not present was inadmissible.[47]

These two decisions angered the public, which pressured the president and Congress to reverse the Court. Congress in 1968

- modified the *Miranda* decision by making confessions admissible in evidence if voluntarily given;
- modified the *Mallory* decision to provide that a confession that is "voluntarily given" by a person in custody of law officers was not to be rejected as evidence solely because of delay in arraigning the defendant;
- modified the *Wade* decision to provide that the testimony of an eyewitness that he or she saw the accused commit the crime for which the accused was being tried was to be admissible in evidence in any federal criminal trial.

The bill, known as the Omnibus Crime Control Act of 1968, came to the House floor just hours after an assassin shot Robert Kennedy in a Los Angeles hotel kitchen. Although opponents of some Senate amendments moved to send the bill to a House-Senate conference where they hoped the provisions could be deleted, the House adopted the Senate bill unchanged. President Johnson signed the bill into law on June 19, 1968.

The congressional effort to reverse the *Miranda* decision proved, however, to be a failure. From the 1970s through the 1990s U.S. attorneys did not rely on the 1968 law to defend the use of confessions that were "voluntarily given." Most prosecutors believed—and judges held—that confessions could not be admitted as evidence unless the defendant had been warned of his or her rights, as required by *Miranda v Arizona*.

More than three decades after its enactment, the 1968 law was finally put to a test in the Court, thanks to Paul Cassell, a University of Utah law professor and a veteran of the Reagan administration's Justice Department. He had written critically of the refusal of federal prosecutors to invoke the 1968 law, and he intervened as a friend of the court in the case of a Virginia bank robber to argue that voluntary statements to FBI agents should be admitted as evidence. Cassell won a 2-1 decision from the U.S. court of appeals in Richmond, Va., but lost 7-2 in the Supreme Court.

In *Dickerson v. United States* (2000) Chief Justice William H. Rehnquist, long a critic of the *Miranda decision,* nevertheless described the 1966 decision as having set a "constitutional rule" that Congress "may not legislatively supersede."[48] Although the scope of the *Miranda* decision remained in some dispute, the ruling in *Dickerson* made clear that the Court, not Congress, would resolve the disputes.

In 2009 the Court further limited the impact of the 1968 law by ruling that even voluntary confessions should be rejected in federal cases if a crime suspect is held for more than six hours before coming before a magistrate. One provision of the 1968 law said a voluntary confession can be used as evidence if it occurs "within six hours" of an arrest. In *Corley v. United States* the Court in a 5-4 decision set aside the confession of a Philadelphia-area bank robber who was held and questioned by FBI agents for more than twenty-nine hours before he signed a written confession.[49]

Sex Discrimination, Environmental Issues

During the 1970s two congressional reversals of Supreme Court decisions concerned pregnant women and small fish. In 1978 Congress required employers to include benefits for pregnancy, childbirth, and related medical conditions in their health insurance and temporary disability plans. This measure overturned a 1976 Court ruling.[50] In another 1978 statute Congress modified the Endangered Species Act of 1973 to reverse the Court's 1978 ruling that a Tennessee Valley Authority dam could not be put into operation because it would destroy the only habitat of a tiny fish called the snail darter.[51] The modification authorized a special cabinet-level board to decide whether to allow operation of federally funded public works projects even if they threatened the existence of an endangered species.

Congress was less receptive to proposals to reverse the controversial Court decisions upholding abortion and forced school busings to overcome racial segregation. Unable to overturn the Court's 1973 decision forbidding states to deny abortions, Congress since 1975 has prohibited federal funds from being used to pay for abortions except under certain circumstances. The legislation, however, primarily affects poor women receiving Medicaid payments; privately funded abortions are not touched by the measures.

Since 1975 Congress also has approved language to prohibit the Department of Education from requiring busing of any student beyond the school closest to his home that offers the course of study sought by the student. The legislation had no effect on federal courts that order most busing to alleviate racial segregation in schools.

Voting Rights and Civil Rights

Concern about ensuring the right to vote and the right to fair treatment has brought about notable congressional reversals of Supreme Court rulings.

In 1980 the Court ruled in *Mobile v. Bolden* that those who wished to prove that an election law, practice, or procedure violated the Voting Rights Act of 1965 had to prove that it was intentionally discriminatory.[52] Effect alone—the fact that no blacks had won election in a particular jurisdiction, for example—was insufficient to prove a violation of the law.

When Congress amended the Voting Rights Act in 1982, it specifically included language declaring that a law or practice that resulted in discrimination could be held to violate the act, whether it was intended to discriminate or not.[53] The Reagan administration had opposed this change, preferring the "intent" test. The Court, however, acknowledged and implemented the will of Congress. When it applied the amended law for the first time, in 1986, it agreed that the effect of certain multimember electoral districts—those that elect

certain officials by means of at-large elections—was to dilute black votes in violation of the Voting Rights Act.[54]

In 1984 the Court was persuaded by the Reagan administration to give a narrow interpretation to language barring sex discrimination by schools that received federal aid. The language at issue, contained in Title IX of the 1972 education act amendments, forbade discrimination "under any education program or activity receiving federal financial assistance."

Since its enactment, the ban had been consistently interpreted to cover all programs and departments at any recipient school. But over the objections of fifty members of Congress, the Court in *Grove City College v. Bell* (1984) accepted the administration's view that the ban applied only to the specific part of the school receiving federal aid.[55]

Civil rights advocates were alarmed by the ruling, noting that the same language so narrowly construed in Title IX was also included in three other major civil rights laws—Title VI of the 1964 Civil Rights Act, barring discrimination by race, color, or national origin in all federally assisted programs; Section 504 of the Rehabilitation Act of 1973, barring discrimination against the disabled; and the 1975 Age Discrimination Act. They immediately began to urge Congress to overturn the *Grove City* decision.

The effort took four years; in early 1988 Congress cleared legislation that specified that if one part of an institution or entity received federal aid, the discrimination ban applied to the entire institution. President Reagan vetoed the bill, saying that it would vastly expand federal power over the decisions of private organizations and state and local governments. The veto was overridden 73-24 in the Senate and 292-133 in the House.[56]

When Congress passed the Civil Rights Act of 1991, it countered the effects of nine Supreme Court decisions restricting the reach and remedies of federal antidiscrimination law. Most of the Court decisions had been announced in 1989. They interpreted the law to put a greater burden on workers charging bias. The compromise bill strengthened antidiscrimination laws and provided new guarantees of money damages and reimbursement of court costs for aggrieved workers who prevailed in lawsuits. President George H. W. Bush had vetoed a 1990 version of the legislation after a battle with Democratic sponsors over whether the earlier version would induce employers to hire certain "quotas" of racial minorities and women to avoid lawsuits.[57]

Religious Exercise

With wide bipartisan support, Congress in 1993 reversed a controversial 1990 Court decision that made it easier for states or the federal government to pass general laws that incidentally restricted individual religious rights. The Court held in *Employment Division v. Smith* that states could impose laws that incidentally limited religious freedom as long as they served a valid state purpose and were not aimed at inhibiting religion.[58] Before that ruling, government regulations affecting religion had to meet a stricter legal standard of serving a "compelling" government interest and posing the least possible burden on religious freedom.

The *Smith* decision involved two Native Americans who were fired from jobs at a drug rehabilitation clinic for using the illegal hallucinogenic drug peyote during a religious ceremony. The state of Oregon refused to grant the men unemployment compensation benefits because they were fired for illegal behavior. The men sued, claiming the state's interest was not compelling enough to warrant infringement on their religious rights. But the Court ruled against them and effectively eliminated the compelling interest test for such free exercise cases.

Congress restored that "compelling interest" standard in 1993 when the Senate passed a bill 97-3 and the House approved the measure by voice vote. The government need not meet that standard to justify every law or action affecting a person's religious rights, stated the Religious Freedom Restoration Act, but only those that placed a "substantial burden" on their free exercise of religion.[59]

But the Court was determined to have the last word, and in *City of Boerne v. Flores* (1997) it struck down the Religious Freedom Restoration Act as unconstitutional. The 6-3 majority characterized Congress's action as an affront to the Court's authority to define

the substance of the Constitution—in this instance, the meaning of "free exercise" of religion in the First Amendment. Although Congress may "enforce" constitutional rights through "appropriate legislation," it "does not enforce a constitutional right by changing what the right is," said Justice Anthony M. Kennedy.[60]

The decisions in *City of Boerne* defining religious rights and *Dickerson* upholding *Miranda* rights made clear the Court would insist on determining the meaning of constitutional rights. Acts of Congress were another matter. When the Court narrowly interpreted voting rights in *Mobile* or the Title IX law in *Grove City College,* lawmakers in Congress moved quickly to correct what they saw as an error in interpretation by the Court. The justices, chastened, then applied the amended law.

The Court showed no deference, however, when lawmakers tried to revise a constitutional interpretation handed down by the justices. "Our national experience teaches that the Constitution is preserved best when each part of the government respects both the Constitution and the proper actions and determination of the other branches," wrote Justice Kennedy in *City of Boerne.* "When the Court has interpreted the Constitution, it has acted within the province of the Judicial Branch, which embraces the duty to say what the law is."[61]

War on Terror and Employer Sex Bias

Congress and the Court clashed when President George W. Bush was in the White House, but Republicans and Democrats took objection to quite different decisions.

In 2006 the justices said the president had overstepped his authority when he ordered military trials for accused terrorists at Guantánamo Bay, Cuba. The military commissions were patterned on models used by the U.S. military in Japan after World War II, but they were not specifically authorized by Congress. For that reason, in *Hamdan v. Bush* the Court ruled they were illegal.[62] Only months later, Congress under Republican control passed the Military Commissions Act (MCA) to reverse the *Hamdan* decision. The new

CONGRESS AND THE COURT'S WORKLOAD

For most of the Supreme Court's history, its members have complained that the workload is too heavy and that Congress should act to ease the burden. Only in 1988, the Court's 199th year, did the Court gain nearly complete control over which cases it chooses to hear. The first major complaint centered on the justices' circuit-riding duties. Congress removed them, but by then the number of appeals the Court was required by law to hear had swollen to almost unmanageable proportions. Congress gave the Court more discretion to choose the cases it reviews on the merits, but for decades several categories of cases required mandatory review. Although Congress in 1988 allowed the Court greater discretion over its docket, Congress continues intermittently to enact laws that require expedited judicial review by the high court.

CIRCUIT COURT DUTIES

In addition to establishing the size and jurisdiction of the Supreme Court, the Judiciary Act of 1789 required the justices to "ride circuit." Under the terms of the act, two justices sat with one district court judge at circuit courts in each of three circuits. In 1792 the six justices were required to attend a total of twenty-seven circuit courts a year and two sessions of the Supreme Court.

As the country expanded westward, circuit-riding duties grew more burdensome. One justice reported that he traveled ten thousand miles in 1838 to fulfill these responsibilities.[1] But Congress refused to do much more than tinker with the federal court system until 1891, when it established a separate system of circuit courts of appeals. Even then the appeals courts were composed of one justice and two circuit judges, although the

law allowed a district judge to sit instead of the justice. This exception soon became the rule, and in 1911 Congress finally relieved Supreme Court justices of all circuit court duties.

MANDATORY JURISDICTION

The Supreme Court's caseload began to increase dramatically after the Civil War. Factors involved in this increase included a rise in the number of diversity cases (cases involving citizens of different states), suits stemming from Reconstruction legislation, and congressional enlargement of the Court's jurisdiction.

In 1914 Congress began to ease this caseload by increasing the kinds of cases the Supreme Court could review at its own discretion by writ of certiorari. At about the same time, it began to cut back on the categories of cases that the Court was required to review. This shift from largely mandatory to primarily discretionary judicial review culminated in the Judiciary Act of 1925. The act increased the Court's jurisdiction and expanded the number of cases appealed to the Court, but it reduced considerably the percentage of cases the Court was required to review on the merits. In its 1923 term, 39 percent of the cases that were filed required review by the Court. In the 1930 term, that proportion had fallen to 15 percent.[2]

The solution was only temporary. By 1976 less than 10 percent of the petitions for review at the Supreme Court fell within its mandatory jurisdiction. These cases, however, made up slightly less than half of all cases argued and decided with full opinions that year.[3] In the 1970s Congress began to seriously consider recommendations that it abolish the

---

law restored Bush's authority, and the trials got underway.

The Court took up the issue again because one provision of the MCA stripped judges of the authority to hear writs of habeas corpus from the Guantánamo prisoners. In *Boumediene v. Bush,* (2008) the Court struck down this provision as unconstitutional.[63] The military commissions were suspended shortly after President Barack Obama took office in January 2009.

Democrats and women's rights advocates protested when the Court made it harder for employees to sue for unequal pay. The 5-4 decision in *Ledbetter v.*

Goodyear (2007) held that plaintiffs must point to a discriminatory pay decision within 180 days prior to their suit.[64] This statute of limitations was included in the Civil Rights Act of 1964. Led by Justice Ruth Bader Ginsburg, the dissenters said the decision ignores "the realities of the workplace," where most employees do not know how their salary compares to others who are doing the same work. President Bush said he would veto a bill overturning the Court's decision, but when Obama was elected president, Congress passed the Lilly Ledbetter Fair Pay Act to repeal the Court's decision. The new measure established that each paycheck could be considered an act of discrimination if an employee

remaining categories the Court was obliged to review. After almost a decade, Congress in 1988 gave the Court greater discretion to decide what cases to hear. It eliminated the Court's mandatory jurisdiction over direct appeals from decisions invalidating acts of Congress; appeals from courts of appeals finding state statutes unconstitutional; and final judgments of the highest state courts questioning the validity of a federal treaty or law.[4]

LEGISLATED BURDENS

Congress created much of the modern explosion in the federal court workload with legislation that places new burdens on federal courts. In addition, Congress's complex regulatory schemes are challenged by businesses and individuals nearly as soon as they are adopted. The Speedy Trial Act of 1974, for example, required that by 1980 all federal criminal defendants be tried within 180 days of their arrest.

To alleviate some of the crush of this work, Chief Justice Warren E. Burger urged Congress to include with the legislation a "court impact statement." If every committee reporting a measure that would affect the federal courts wrote such a statement, Burger said, Congress would be aware of those consequences and might more readily provide the system more resources with which to deal with the judicial impact of new laws.

Federal judges also contend that the workload could be relieved if Congress would make the difficult policy decisions in the course of enacting legislation, rather than passing them on to administrators to make under judicial supervision." The prevailing passion of Congress for judicial review is the central fact of life at the moment for federal judges at all levels of the system," wrote Judge Carl McGowan in 1976.[5] Chief Justice

William H. Rehnquist said in 1989 that the Court's ability to maintain a uniform body of federal law would be strained "beyond the breaking point" if Congress created any new federal causes of action.[6] Some justices have been similarly critical of complex legislation. For example, legislation in the areas of disability rights, telecommunications, and campaign finance reform immediately produced litigation in the federal courts.

Rehnquist and his colleagues solved the problem of Supreme Court's "crushing" workload by taking fewer cases. In 1986, when Rehnquist took over as chief justice, the Court was hearing and deciding about 150 cases per year. At the time of his death in 2005, the justices were hearing about half as many. Under his successor, John G. Roberts Jr., the Court has been deciding between 75 and 80 cases per term. The complaints about the "overworked" Court have long since faded.

---

1. Felix Frankfurter and James M. Landis, *The Business of the Supreme Court: A Study in the Federal Judicial System* (New York: Macmillan, 1928), 49.

2. Gerhard Casper and Richard A. Posner, *The Workload of the Supreme Court* (Chicago: American Bar Foundation, 1976), 20.

3. U.S. Senate, *The Supreme Court Jurisdiction Act of 1979*, S. Rept. 96-35 to Accompany S. 450, 96th Cong., 1st sess., 1979, 6.

4. *Congressional Quarterly Weekly Report*, June 11, 1988, 1596.

5. Quoted in Congressional Quarterly, "Judicial Workload: The Courtroom Explosion," in *The Supreme Court: Justice and the Law*, 2nd ed. (Washington, D.C.: Congressional Quarterly, 1977), 130.

6. *Congressional Quarterly Weekly Report*, June 3, 1989, 1324.

earned less because of her gender or race. It was the first bill signed into law by President Obama when he took office in 2009.

NOTES

PRESSURES ON THE JUSTICES (PP. 501–515)

1. Henry J. Abraham, *Justices and Presidents: A Political History of Appointments to the Supreme Court,* 3rd ed. (New York: Oxford University Press, 1992), 118–119.

2. Ibid., 118; see also Charles Warren, *The Supreme Court in United States History,* rev. ed., 2 vols. (Boston: Little, Brown, 1926), 2:501.

3. Sources for the information contained in this section on rejections came primarily from Abraham, *Justices and Presidents;* Warren, *Supreme Court in United States History;* and *Congress and the Nation,* (Washington, D.C.: Congressional Quarterly, 1965, 1969, 1973, 1977).

4. Warren, *Supreme Court in United States History,* 2:119.

5. *CQ Almanac 1987* (Washington, D.C.: Congressional Quarterly, 1988), 271–276.

6. Warren, *Supreme Court in United States History,* 1:137.

7. *CQ Almanac 1986* (Washington, D.C.: Congressional Quarterly, 1987), 67–72.

8. *Stuart v. Laird,* 1 Cr. (5 U.S.) 299 (1803).

9. *Marbury v. Madison,* 1 Cr. (5 U.S.) 137 (1803).

10. Irving Brant, *Impeachment: Trials and Errors* (New York: Knopf, 1972), 48.

11. Leonard Baker, *John Marshall: A Life in Law* (New York: Macmillan, 1974), 418.

12. Brant, *Impeachment,* 64.

13. Beveridge's account of Chase's impeachment is found in Albert J. Beveridge, *The Life of John Marshall,* 4 vols. (Cambridge, Mass.: Houghton Mifflin, Riverside Press, 1919), 3:157–222.

14. Brant, *Impeachment,* 65.

15. Ibid., 67–68.

16. House minority leader Gerald R. Ford's statement, quoted in Brant, *Impeachment,* 79–80.

17. For a summary of events leading to resignation, see *CQ Almanac 1969* (Washington, D.C.: Congressional Quarterly, 1970), 136–139.

18. For a summary of impeachment proceedings, see *CQ Almanac 1970* (Washington, D.C.: Congressional Quarterly, 1971), 1025–1027.

19. *Congress and the Nation,* vol. 5 (Washington, D.C.: Congressional Quarterly, 1981), 744–745.

20. Charles Fairman, *History of the Supreme Court of the United States,* vol. 6, *Reconstruction and Reunion, 1864–88, part 1* (New York: Macmillan, 1971), 163–164.

21. *American Bar Association Journal* (1964): 1151, quoted by John R. Schmidhauser and Larry L. Berg, *The Supreme Court and Congress: Conflict and Interaction, 1945–68* (New York: Free Press, 1972), 9.

PRESSURES ON THE INSTITUTION (PP. 516–528)

1. Sources for the information on changes in the size of the Court include Henry J. Abraham, *Justices and Presidents: A Political History of Appointments to the Supreme Court,* 3rd ed. (New York: Oxford University Press, 1992); and Charles Warren, *The Supreme Court in United States History,* rev. ed., 2 vols. (Boston: Little, Brown, 1926).

2. *Martin v. Hunter's Lessee,* 1 Wheat. (14 U.S.) 304 (1816); *Green v. Biddle,* 8 Wheat. (21 U.S.) 1 (1823).

3. Quoted by Walter F. Murphy in *Congress and the Court: A Case Study in the American Political Process* (Chicago: University of Chicago Press, 1962), 23.

4. Warren, *Supreme Court in United States History,* 1:223.

5. *National Mutual Insurance Co. v. Tidewater Transfer Co.,* 337 U.S. 582 at 655 (1949).

6. *Glidden Co. v. Zdanok,* 370 U.S. 530 (1962).

7. C. Herman Pritchett, *Congress versus the Supreme Court, 1957–60,* reprint ed. (New York: Da Capo Press, 1973), 122–123.

8. *Cohens v. Virginia,* 6 Wheat. (19 U.S.) 264 (1821); major sources for the information on attempts to repeal Section 25 are Warren, *Supreme Court in United States History,* and Murphy, *Congress and the Court.*

9. *Craig v. Missouri,* 4 Pet. (29 U.S.) 410 (1830); *Cherokee Nation v. Georgia,* 5 Pet. (30 U.S.) 1 (1831).

10. Murphy, *Congress and the Court,* 24.

11. Warren, *Supreme Court in United States History,* 1:727–740.

12. Ibid., 1:740.

13. *Murdock v. Memphis,* 20 Wall. (87 U.S.) 590 (1875).

14. *Mississippi v. Johnson,* 4 Wall. (71 U.S.) 475 (1867).

15. *Georgia v. Stanton,* 6 Wall. (73 U.S.) 50 (1868).

16. Charles Fairman, *History of the Supreme Court of the United States,* vol. 6, *Reconstruction and Reunion, 1864–88, part 1* (New York: Macmillan, 1971), 416, 420–421.

17. *Ex parte Milligan,* 4 Wall. (71) 2 (1866).

18. Warren, *Supreme Court in United States History,* 2:466–467.

19. *Ex parte McCardle,* 7 Wall.(74 U.S.) 506 (1869).

20. Julius J. Marke, *Vignettes of Legal History* (South Hackensack, N.J.: Fred B. Rothman, 1965), 157.

21. President Andrew Johnson's veto message to Congress, March 25, 1868, quoted by Ralph R. Martig, "Congress and the Appellate Jurisdiction of the Supreme Court," *Michigan Law Review* 34 (1936): 664.

22. Warren, *Supreme Court in United States History,* 2:482.

23. Ibid., 2:483.

24. Ibid.

25. Fairman, *Reconstruction and Reunion,* 478.

26. *Ex parte McCardle,* 7 Wall. (74 U.S.) 506 at 514–515 (1869).

27. Fairman, *Reconstruction and Reunion,* 494.

28. Ibid., 510.

29. *Ex parte Yerger,* 8 Wall. (U.S. 75) 85 (1869).

30. Major sources for the material included in this section are Murphy, *Congress and the Court;* Pritchett, *Congress versus the Supreme Court;* John R. Schmidhauser and Larry L. Berg, *The Supreme Court and Congress: Conflict and Interaction, 1945–1968* (New York: Free Press, 1972); *CQ Almanac,* 1956, 1957, 1958, 1959 (Washington, D.C.: Congressional Quarterly, 1957, 1958, 1959, 1960).

31. *Watkins v. United States,* 354 U.S. 178 (1957).

32. *Cole v. Young,* 351 U.S. 536 (1956).

33. *Slochower v. Board of Higher Education of New York City,* 350 U.S. 551 (1956).

34. *Pennsylvania v. Nelson,* 350 U.S. 497 (1956).

35. *Konigsberg v. State Bar of California,* 366 U.S. 252 (1957).

36. *CQ Almanac 1958,* 294.

37. *Yates v. United States,* 354 U.S. 298 (1957).

38. *CQ Almanac 1956,* 586.

REVERSALS OF RULINGS (PP. 529–543)

1. Charles Warren, *The Supreme Court in United States History,* rev. ed., 2 vols. (Boston: Little, Brown, 1926), 1:91.

2. *Vanstophorst v. Maryland.* No report of this case was made in the February 1791 term; see Warren, *Supreme Court in United States History,* 1:91.

3. *Chisholm v. Georgia,* 2 Dall. (2 U.S.) 419 (1793).

4. Warren, *Supreme Court in United States History,* 1:96.

5. Ibid., 99.

6. *Hollingsworth v. Virginia,* 3 Dall. (3 U.S.) 378 at 381 (1798).

7. Carl Brent Swisher, *American Constitutional Development,* 2nd ed. (Boston: Houghton Mifflin, 1974), 331.

8. *Barron v. Baltimore,* 7 Pet. (33 U.S.) 243 (1833).

9. *Scott v. Sandford,* 19 How. (60 U.S.) 393 (1857).

10. *Pollock v. Farmers' Loan and Trust Co.,* 158 U.S. 601 at 635 (1895).

11. Alfred H. Kelly and Winfred A. Harbison, *The American Constitution: Its Origins and Development,* 5th ed. (New York: Norton, 1976), 586.

12. Richard M. Nixon, *Public Papers of the Presidents of the United States, 1970* (Washington, D.C.: U.S. Government Printing Office, 1971), 521.

13. *Oregon v. Mitchell,* 400 U.S. 112 (1970).

14. *Hammer v. Dagenhart,* 247 U.S. 251 (1918).

15. *Bailey v. Drexel Furniture Co.,* 259 U.S. 20 (1922).

16. *United States v. Darby Lumber Co.,* 312 U.S. 100 (1941).

17. *Baker v. Carr,* 369 U.S. 186 (1962).

18. *Reynolds v. Sims,* 377 U.S. 533 (1964).

19. *Engel v. Vitale,* 370 U.S. 421 (1962); *School District of Abington Township v. Schempp,* 374 U.S. 203 (1963).

20. *Wallace v. Jaffree,* 472 U.S. 38 (1985).

21. *Texas v. Johnson,* 491 U.S. 397 (1989).

22. *United States v. Eichman,* 496 U.S. 310 (1990); see also *CQ Almanac 1989* (Washington, D.C.; Congressional Quarterly, 1990), 307–314.

23. *CQ Almanac 1990* (Washington, D.C.: Congressional Quarterly, 1991), 524–528.

24. *Lawrence v. Texas,* 539 U.S. 558 (2003).

25. *Pennsylvania v. Wheeling and Belmont Bridge Co.,* 13 How. (54 U.S.) 518 (1852); 18 How. (59 U.S.) 421 (1856).

26. *Leisy v. Hardin,* 135 U.S. 100 (1890); *In re Rahrer,* 140 U.S. 545 (1891).

27. *Interstate Commerce Commission v. Brimson,* 154 U.S. 447 (1894); *Interstate Commerce Commission v. Cincinnati, New Orleans & Texas Pacific Railway Co.,* 167 U.S. 479 (1897); *Interstate Commerce Commission v. Alabama-Midland Railway Co.,* 168 U.S. 144 (1897).

28. *Interstate Commerce Commission v. Chicago, Rock Island and Pacific Railway Co.,* 218 U.S. 88 (1910); *United States v. Atchison, Topeka and Santa Fe Railroad Co.,* 234 U.S. 476 at 486 (1914).

29. *Civil Rights Cases,* 109 U.S. 3 (1883).

30. *Heart of Atlanta Motel v. United States,* 379 U.S. 241 (1964).

31. *Loewe v. Lawlor (The Danbury Hatters Case),* 208 U.S. 274 (1908).

32. *Duplex Printing Press Co. v. Deering,* 254 U.S. 443 (1921).

33. *Lauf v. E. G. Shinner & Co.,* 303 U.S. 315 (1938); *New Negro Alliance v. Sanitary Grocery Co.,* 303 U.S. 552 (1938).

34. *Panama Refining Co. v. Ryan,* 293 U.S. 388 (1935); *Schechter Poultry Co. v. United States,* 295 U.S. 495 (1935); *National Labor Relations Board v. Jones & Laughlin Steel Corp.,* 301 U.S. 1 (1937).

35. *Railroad Retirement Board v. Alton,* 295 U.S. 330 (1935).

36. *Louisville Joint Stock Land Bank v. Radford,* 295 U.S. 555 (1935); *Wright v. Vinton Branch,* 300 U.S. 440 (1937).

37. *United States v. Butler,* 297 U.S. 1 (1936); *Mulford v. Smith,* 307 U.S. 38 (1939).

38. *Carter v. Carter Coal Co.,* 298 U.S. 238 (1936); *Sunshine Anthracite Coal Co. v. Adkins,* 310 U.S. 381 (1940).

39. *Ashton v. Cameron County District,* 298 U.S. 513 (1936); *United States v. Bekins,* 304 U.S. 27 (1938).

40. *United States v. South-Eastern Underwriters Assn.,* 322 U.S. 533 (1944).

41. *Prudential Insurance Co. v. Benjamin,* 328 U.S. 408 (1946).

42. *United States v. California,* 332 U.S. 19 (1947); *United States v. Louisiana,* 339 U.S. 699 (1950); *United States v. Texas,* 339 U.S. 707 (1950).

43. *Alabama v. Texas,* 347 U.S. 272 (1954); see also *United States v. Louisiana,* 363 U.S. 1 (1960).

44. *McNabb v. United States,* 318 U.S. 332 (1943).

45. *Mallory v. United States,* 354 U.S. 449 (1957); on Congress's reaction to the *Mallory* decision, see *CQ Almanac 1958,* and *CQ Almanac 1959* (Washington, D.C.: Congressional Quarterly, 1959, 1960).

46. *Miranda v. Arizona,* 384 U.S. 436 (1966).

47. *United States v. Wade,* 388 U.S. 218 (1967); on Congress's reaction to the *Miranda* and *Wade* decisions, see *CQ Almanac 1968* (Washington, D.C.: Congressional Quarterly, 1969), 226, 233.

48. *Dickerson v. United States,* 530 U.S. 428 (2000).

49. *Corley v. United States,* 556 U.S. —- (2009).

50. *General Electric Co. v. Gilbert,* 429 U.S. 125 (1976).

51. *Tennessee Valley Authority v. Hill,* 437 U.S. 153 (1978).

52. *Mobile v. Bolden,* 446 U.S. 55 (1980).

53. *CQ Almanac 1982* (Washington, D.C.: Congressional Quarterly, 1983), 373–377.

54. *Thornburg v. Gingles,* 478 U.S. 30 (1986).

55. *Grove City College v. Bell,* 465 U.S. 555 (1984).

56. *Congressional Quarterly Weekly Report,* March 26, 1988, 774–776.

57. *CQ Almanac 1991* (Washington, D.C.: Congressional Quarterly, 1992), 251–261.

58. *Employment Division v. Smith,* 494 U.S. 872 (1990).

59. *CQ Almanac 1993* (Washington, D.C.: Congressional Quarterly, 1994), 315.

60. *City of Boerne v. Flores,* 521 U.S. 507 at 519 (1997).

61. Id. at 535–536.

62. *Hamdan v. Rumsfeld,* 548 U.S. 557 (2006).

63. *Boumediene v. Bush,* 553 U.S. —- (2008).

64. *Ledbetter v. Goodyear,* 550 U.S. 618 (2007).

chapter 6

Presidential Pressure

THE MAJOR WAY a president exerts influence over the Supreme Court's work is through the power to select its members. And presidents throughout history have been well aware that the justices they select will shape public policy.

All presidents attempt to place on the Court justices—usually from their political party—whose views coincide with their own. But this effort has met with varying degrees of success. Presidents Thomas Jefferson, Andrew Jackson, Abraham Lincoln, Franklin D. Roosevelt, Richard Nixon, and Ronald Reagan were the most successful in influencing the Court's conduct through judicial appointments.

During presidential election campaigns, candidates also have attempted to influence the Court by criticizing the judiciary or earlier decisions by the Court. In at least seven campaigns (1800, 1860, 1896, 1924, 1936, 1968, and 1980), presidential candidates challenged the Court's effect on public policy.

Political scientist Robert G. Scigliano has described the intersecting relationship between the Court and the president:

> In their contemporary relationship, the Presidency has gained considerable influence over the Supreme Court.
>
> Yet the President cannot be said to dominate the Court. . . .
>
> Tension continues to exist between the two institutions. . . . A President cannot be sure that he is getting what he thinks he is getting in his appointments, a person may change his views after joining the Court, and the judicial obligation calls upon a justice to heed the Constitution and the laws, and not Presidential positions.[1]

A vacancy on the Supreme Court has occurred, on the average, about every two years. A president can expect to have at least one appointment per term.[2] At times, however, the Court has seemed to defy the actuarial tables, and its membership has remained stable for a much longer period, denying the incumbent president the opportunity to make an appointment to the Court. Jimmy Carter was the first full-term president denied the opportunity to name anyone to the Court; no vacancy occurred during his four years in the White House (1977–1981).

In contrast, President Nixon had an opportunity to appoint a new chief justice during his first year in office. Nixon then made three additional appointments to the Court during his first term. During his eight years as president, Reagan had several opportunities. He named three associate justices and a new chief justice to the Court. President Bill Clinton appointed the first Democrat to the Court in more than a quarter century when he named Ruth Bader Ginsburg in 1993. But neither that appointment nor Clinton's selection of Stephen G. Breyer in 1994 shifted the balance of the Court.

President George W. Bush made two appointments in his second term to replace two of Reagan's choices, Chief Justice William H. Rehnquist and Justice Sandra Day O'Connor. Bush chose John G. Roberts Jr.,

Thurgood Marshall is sworn in as solicitor general August 24, 1965. Two years later President Lyndon B. Johnson (shown here on Marshall's right) nominated Marshall as the first black justice of the Supreme Court.

a former clerk to Rehnquist, to succeed him as chief justice. And he chose another former Reagan administration lawyer, Samuel A. Alito Jr., to replace O'Connor.

QUALIFICATIONS

Presidents consider a variety of criteria in selecting justices. Among the most consistent are merit, friendship, geographic and religious balance, and ideology.

Almost all presidents have agreed that a Court nominee should have some legal training, but until the last half of the twentieth century, judicial experience was not considered particularly important. Many distinguished appointees—including eight chief justices—had no prior judicial experience.[3]

Franklin Roosevelt appointed six men who had no judicial experience: Chief Justice Harlan Fiske Stone and Justices Stanley F. Reed, Felix Frankfurter, William O. Douglas, James F. Byrnes, and Robert H. Jackson. Harry S. Truman appointed two men without judicial

experience: Harold H. Burton and Tom C. Clark. President Dwight D. Eisenhower, after appointing Earl Warren chief justice of the United States, insisted that all future nominees have judicial experience. (Warren had none.) But neither of President John F. Kennedy's two appointees, Arthur J. Goldberg and Byron R. White, had judicial experience. Nor did a Lyndon B. Johnson appointee, Abe Fortas, or two of Nixon's nominees, Rehnquist and Lewis F. Powell Jr.

Although prior judicial experience was not necessary to performing well as a Supreme Court justice, presidents increasingly looked to judges because they had a track record. In 1975 President Gerald R. Ford chose a highly regarded federal appeals court judge from Chicago, John Paul Stevens, for a Supreme Court seat— and a trend was set. For the next three decades, all of the successful nominees to the Court were judges on a U.S. court of appeals. Alito, a veteran of the U.S. Court of Appeals for the Third Circuit, completed the circle in 2006. When he replaced O'Connor, a former Arizona state judge, all the nine justices of the Supreme Court had been judges on the federal appellate court.

Merit

Almost every one of the 110 individuals who have served on the Court had some record of public service prior to their appointment. Many had held offices in the executive branch or had served as state or federal judges, senators, members of the House, governors, or law professors.[4]

High ethical standards, as well as experience in public life, are criteria presidents seek in a nominee. Louis D. Brandeis's nomination successfully weathered a challenge from charges that he had engaged in improper practices as an attorney. But the nominations of Clement F. Haynsworth Jr. and Fortas as chief justice failed to win approval by the Senate because of questions raised about possible conflicts of interest.

Friendship

Personal friendship has been the reason for several nominations to the Court. William Howard Taft's nomination of Horace H. Lurton, Woodrow Wilson's selection of Brandeis, Truman's choice of Burton, and Kennedy's nomination of White all had some basis in friendship.

President Johnson selected a reluctant Fortas for the bench in 1965 on the basis of personal friendship. And in 1968 Johnson unsuccessfully proposed an old Texas political associate, Homer Thornberry, to fill Fortas's seat. When Fortas's nomination as chief justice failed to win the Senate's approval, Thornberry's nomination died as well.

George W. Bush also failed in a brief bid to elevate his Texas friend and lawyer Harriet Miers to the Supreme Court. Bush proposed her to fill the seat left vacant by the retirement of Justice O'Connor, but Miers withdrew after her name was submitted to the Senate in the face of criticism from conservatives who questioned her qualifications.

Geographic Representation

Justices have come from thirty-one of the fifty states, and states have not been represented in any substantially equal appointment pattern. New York has been the home of sixteen justices. Among the other states that have been home to five or more justices are Kentucky, Massachusetts, Ohio, Pennsylvania, Tennessee, and Virginia.[5]

Early in the Court's history, geographic balance was a major consideration in the selection of nominees. Because the justices also functioned as circuit judges, conventional thinking was that each geographic area should have a spokesman on the Court. Until the Civil War, this kind of thinking resulted in a "New England" seat, a "Virginia" seat, a "New York" seat, and a "Pennsylvania" seat. With the nation's post–Civil War expansion and the end of the justices' circuit-riding duties, this tradition faded.

Religious Balance

The notion of sectarian religious representation stemmed from the fact that Americans are a pluralistic society and a politically group-conscious people. The idea of a "Roman Catholic" seat and a "Jewish" seat on the Court developed as a way of acknowledging the role of these religious minority groups in the nation. By the late twentieth century, however, the importance of a justice's religious affiliation declined.

Chief Justice Roger B. Taney was the first to hold the Catholic seat. Since Grover Cleveland appointed Edward D. White to that seat in 1894, it was held by Joseph McKenna, Pierce Butler, Frank Murphy, and William J. Brennan Jr. Truman's appointment of Tom Clark in 1949 after Murphy's death interrupted the tradition, but Eisenhower's appointment of Brennan in 1956 restored the notion of a "Catholic seat." The selection was regarded in part as an appeal to Catholic voters. But when President Reagan nominated Antonin Scalia and Anthony M. Kennedy in 1986 and 1987, respectively, their Catholicism was hardly an issue.

The Jewish seat, established in 1916 with Brandeis's appointment, was filled by Justices Frankfurter (1938), Goldberg (1963), and Fortas (1965). Benjamin N. Cardozo, also Jewish, served along with Brandeis. In 1969 President Nixon again broke the tradition by nominating three Protestants in succession to the seat Fortas vacated. President Clinton appointed two Jewish justices. The latter, Stephen Breyer, filled the seat once occupied by Fortas. Nixon appointee Harry A. Blackmun had held the Fortas seat in the intervening years.

In 2005 President George W. Bush named two Catholics to the Court: Roberts and Alito. Justice Clarence Thomas had also returned to the Catholic faith, so that when Alito was confirmed early in 2006, the Court for the first time had five justices—a majority—who were Catholics.

Subtler Influences

The special representational concerns of the Republican and Democratic Parties may govern, to some extent, the choice of nominees to the Court. African American and Jewish support of the Democratic Party enhances the likelihood that Democratic presidents will continue to consider those groups in making their selections.

In 1967 President Johnson nominated Thurgood Marshall as the first black justice of the Supreme Court. Marshall had been counsel for the National Association for the Advancement of Colored People (NAACP) and one of the attorneys responsible for successfully arguing the 1954 Court decision in *Brown v. Board of Education,* the school desegregation case. Marshall served as solicitor general of the United States prior to appointment to the Court. Johnson said as he nominated Marshall, "It is the right thing to do, the right time to do it, the right man and the right place."[6]

As the political power and professional participation of women grew in the mid-twentieth century, it became clear that it was time for a woman to sit on the Supreme Court. During the 1980 campaign, Reagan pledged he would appoint a woman to the Court, and within his first year in office he made good on that pledge. When Justice Potter Stewart retired in July 1981, Reagan named O'Connor as the first woman justice; she was easily confirmed in September.[7]

Scholar Henry J. Abraham soon after observed: "There is no doubt that there now exists a 'black seat' on the bench that is, in effect, far more secure than a 'Catholic seat' or a 'Jewish seat.' That is unquestionably also true of a 'woman's seat,' to all intents and purposes established with President Reagan's dramatic appointment of Judge Sandra Day O'Connor."[8]

Indeed, when Marshall retired in 1991, President George H. W. Bush appointed Clarence Thomas, an African American appeals court judge and former chairman of the Equal Employment Opportunity Commission. More possibilities opened for women, however, when President Clinton replaced the retiring White in 1993

with Ginsburg, an appeals court judge and former women's rights advocate. The second woman justice joined O'Connor, by then a veteran of twelve years on the Court.

Ideology has been a significant factor in several presidents' appointments to the high bench. Republican president Theodore Roosevelt considered naming Horace Lurton, a Democrat, to the Court. Roosevelt wrote to Sen. Henry Cabot Lodge, R-Mass., explaining that Lurton was "right" on all the important issues:

> The nominal politics of the man has nothing to do with his actions on the bench. His real politics are all important. . . . On every question that would come before the bench, he has so far shown himself to be in much closer touch with the policies in which you and I believe.[9]

Lodge agreed, but wondered why a Republican who held the same opinions could not be found. He suggested William H. Moody, the attorney general of Massachusetts, and Roosevelt appointed Moody in 1906. In 1909 Taft nominated Lurton to the Court. Taft, a Republican, like Roosevelt, thought Lurton was right for the job despite his Democratic Party affiliation.

More recently, the Reagan administration systematically screened the judicial philosophy of candidates for all federal courts. Reagan looked for judges and justices who would eschew the liberal "activism" of earlier decades, defined most notably by rulings establishing a constitutional right to abortion, prohibiting prayer in public schools, and expanding the rights of defendants in criminal cases. Reagan's choice of Rehnquist to be chief justice and Justice Scalia were applauded by conservatives because both had records of criticizing liberal activism from the bench. But when Reagan's choice of Judge Robert Bork was defeated in the Senate, he chose instead Anthony Kennedy, who penned one of the Court's most recent "activist" opinions, at least in the eyes of conservatives. *Lawrence v. Texas* (2003) struck down state antisodomy laws directed against the sexual privacy rights of homosexuals.[10]

George W. Bush's choices, Roberts and Alito, had served as young lawyers in the Reagan administration. Veterans of the Reagan era said both of them would be reliably conservative if they were chosen for the Supreme Court.

Party Loyalty

Presidents generally nominate members of their party to the Court. As noted, however, occasionally they nominate members of the opposition party.

Republican presidents have appointed nine Democratic justices to the Court, and Democratic presidents have named three Republicans. John Tyler, a Whig, appointed Democrat Samuel Nelson. Republican presidents Lincoln, Benjamin Harrison, Taft, Warren G. Harding, Herbert Hoover, Eisenhower, and Nixon appointed nominal Democrats to the Court.

Taft appointed Democrats Lurton, Edward White (promoted to chief justice), and Joseph R. Lamar. The other GOP presidents who successfully nominated Democrats were Lincoln (Stephen J. Field), Benjamin Harrison (Howell E. Jackson), Harding (Butler), Hoover (Cardozo), Eisenhower (Brennan), and Nixon (Powell).

Among Democratic presidents, Wilson appointed Brandeis; FDR appointed Stone as chief justice; and Truman appointed Burton, a Republican senator, to the Court.

OUTSIDE INFLUENCES

The appointment of a justice to the Supreme Court involves a complex pattern of personal and political transactions between the president and the individuals and groups seeking to influence that nomination.

Among the more important influence groups are the members of the president's administration, the legal community, and even the Court's sitting justices.

The Attorney General

Presidents normally seek the advice of their chief legal officer, the attorney general. In 1840 the attorney general assumed responsibility for judicial appointments, taking over the function from the secretary of state. Since that time the attorney general has become the president's liaison with the principal interest groups and individuals involved in the screening and selection of qualified candidates for appointment to the Court.

The attorney general has often played a prime role in Supreme Court selections. In 1975 Attorney General Edward H. Levi, a former dean of the University of Chicago Law School, recommended Chicago judge John Paul Stevens for the Court. President Ford agreed and chose Stevens to replace Justice Douglas. President Reagan's attorney general, Edwin Meese, recommended elevating Justice Rehnquist to be chief justice when Burger retired, and Scalia to fill Rehnquist's seat as an associate justice. Reagan followed both recommendations.

Since the 1980s the White House counsel's office has been an equally active player in judicial selection. In the George H. W. Bush and Clinton administrations, White House lawyers took the lead in the selection of Court nominees and in the promotion of the candidates with the Senate and public.[11] The same pattern was evident in the judicial selection process of George W. Bush's administration. Alberto R. Gonzales, the White House counsel, helped to screen Bush's nominees for the federal judiciary, and for a time he was mentioned as a possible Bush appointee to the Court.

The Senate's Role

The Senate's power to confirm or reject presidential nominees to the Court has resulted in the rejection of 28 of 148 nominations in the Court's history. In the nineteenth century the Senate rejected one-third of the nominees; in the twentieth century only six nominees were rejected. The Senate has rejected the presidents' choices because of the appointee's position on public issues, political characteristics, perceived lack of judicial qualifications, or opposition to the prevailing views on the Court.

In the tradition of senatorial courtesy, the Senate will not confirm a nominee opposed by the senators from the nominee's home state, at least if they are members of the president's political party. Application of senatorial courtesy accounted for several rejections of Supreme Court nominees in the nineteenth century, but that tradition has rarely been mentioned in connection with Supreme Court nominations in modern times. Instead, it is a more established practice with lower federal court nominations, especially to federal district courts.

In 1894 the Senate rejected President Cleveland's nominees, William B. Hornblower and Wheeler H. Peckham, both of New York. Sen. David B. Hill, D-N.Y., invoked senatorial courtesy to block the nominations in each instance because Cleveland had failed to consult with him about their selection. Cleveland then refused to name a third New Yorker and chose instead Edward White, D-La., the Democratic majority leader in the Senate.

Senatorial courtesy was a prominent factor in the rejection of Reuben H. Walworth of New York, the choice of President Tyler. And it was a factor in the negative vote the Senate gave to James K. Polk's nomination of Pennsylvanian George W. Woodward in 1846.[12]

Sometimes a Senate champion can make the difference for a Supreme Court nominee. When a seat came open in the summer of 1990, Sen. Warren Rudman, R-N.H., spoke up for Judge David Souter, a Rudman protégé and former New Hampshire attorney general. A few days later, President George H. W. Bush announced, to the surprise of many, that he had chosen the little-known New Hampshire judge for the Supreme Court.

A year later, when Justice Marshall retired, Sen. John Danforth, R-Mo., lobbied for the appointment of Judge Clarence Thomas. Two decades before, when Thomas graduated from Yale Law School but was unable to find a law firm position, Danforth recruited him to come to Missouri. Danforth was then Missouri's attorney general, and Thomas joined his staff. Danforth also encouraged Thomas to join the Reagan administration in 1981. Perhaps most important, Danforth played a crucial role within the Senate in shoring up support for Thomas when his nomination was in trouble.

Stephen Breyer probably owed his Supreme Court seat to Sen. Edward Kennedy, D-Mass. Breyer had worked on Kennedy's Senate staff, and in 1980 Kennedy helped Breyer become a judge on the U.S. Court of Appeals for the First Circuit. When Clinton became president, Kennedy made sure Breyer's name was at the top of the list of possible Supreme Court nominees.

The Justices' Role

For most of the Court's history, sitting justices rarely hesitated to voice their suggestions of especially qualified nominees for vacant seats. Some have offered negative advice. Justice Joseph P. Bradley prepared a report about those who would be qualified to succeed him and concluded that no candidate from his home state of New Jersey possessed the necessary qualifications for the post.

In the nineteenth century, justices often lobbied effectively with presidents to urge appointment of certain candidates. Justices John Catron and Benjamin R. Curtis, for example, urged President Franklin Pierce to nominate John A. Campbell to the Court. Their communications to Pierce included letters of support for Campbell from all their colleagues.[13] Other justices who successfully urged presidents to appoint certain individuals to the Court include Robert C. Grier for William Strong in 1870, Noah H. Swayne for Bradley in 1870, Morrison R. Waite for William B. Woods in 1880, Samuel F. Miller for David J. Brewer in 1889, and Henry B. Brown for Howell Jackson in 1893.[14]

In 1981 Chief Justice Burger suggested to President Reagan the judge who became the first woman justice. O'Connor also happened to be a classmate of Rehnquist at Stanford University Law School.[15]

Taft: Champion Influencer

William Howard Taft was the only president to become chief justice of the United States and to enjoy a unique double opportunity to influence the Court's personnel and work. Taft, the twenty-seventh president of the United States (1909–1913), served as chief justice from 1921 to 1930. During Harding's presidency (1921–1923), Taft either selected or approved three of the four men Harding appointed to the Court—George Sutherland, Pierce Butler, and Edward T. Sanford.

Taft also lobbied for his own appointment as chief justice. In 1920 the ex-president let it be known to the newly elected Harding that he wanted the job. Taft had named Edward White chief justice and, Taft told Harding, "many times in the past [White] had said he was holding the office for me and that he would give it back to a Republican administration."[16] On June 30, 1921, Harding appointed Taft chief justice.

Taft's most prodigious lobbying effort on presidential appointments resulted in Butler's appointment to the Court. Taft orchestrated a letter-writing campaign recommending him and played down the talents of other potential nominees. Taft dismissed the candidacy of Judge Cardozo of the New York Court of Appeals because, Taft wrote, Cardozo was "a Jew and a Democrat [and] a progressive judge." About Judge Learned Hand, another possible nominee, Taft warned that he "would almost certainly herd with Brandeis and be a dissenter."[17]

The chief justice sought and obtained endorsements for Butler from the Minnesota congressional delegation, members of the church hierarchy (Butler was a Catholic), and from local bar associations across the nation. Harding succumbed to the pressure and sent Butler's nomination to the Senate where, despite considerable opposition from Senate progressives, he won approval.

When Mahlon Pitney resigned from the Court in 1922, Taft heartily approved of Harding's choice of Sanford. Taft and Sanford had been acquaintances since Theodore Roosevelt's administration. Some observers felt that Sanford was so close to Taft that the chief justice had two votes on the bench. Their friendship and judicial affinity had a final coincidence: they died on the same day in 1930.[18]

Chief Justice Taft's influence over Harding's appointments to the Court gave that body a decidedly conservative majority during the 1920s—ending only with Franklin Roosevelt's appointments to the Court after 1937.

Hughes and Stone

Other chief justices have influentially advised presidents on Supreme Court appointments.

Charles Evans Hughes counseled three presidents on appointments. Herbert Hoover sought Hughes's advice in naming a replacement for Justice Holmes in 1931. The president particularly wanted to know Hughes's opinion of Cardozo, a fellow New Yorker.[19] In 1941 Hughes wanted President Franklin Roosevelt to name Justice Stone as his successor as chief justice. President Truman consulted Hughes in 1946 on his choice of a chief justice after Stone's death.[20]

Hoover also sought and obtained Stone's advice on filling Holmes's seat. Stone was so convinced of Cardozo's qualifications that he sent Hoover several memoranda recommending Cardozo in preference to alternate candidates. Stone tried to overcome Hoover's reservations about appointing another Jewish justice, even offering his own resignation from the Court to make room for Cardozo.[21]

Hoover appointed Cardozo on February 15, 1932; he was confirmed nine days later. Of the Cardozo nomination one author wrote:

The appointment and confirmation of Benjamin Cardozo . . . violated nearly all the "rules of the game." Judge Cardozo was a New Yorker, and there were already two judges from that state on the bench—Stone and Hughes. He was a nominal Democrat, and his "real" politics, highly tinged with liberalism, differed sharply from those of President Hoover. Moreover, he was a Jew and there was already one Jewish judge in the person of Louis Brandeis. Cardozo's selection is inexplicable except in terms of his pre-eminent position among American jurists and the overwhelming pressures on his behalf from leaders of the bench and bar throughout the land.[22]

American Bar Association

Through its standing committee on the federal judiciary, the American Bar Association (ABA) has participated in passing on the legal and intellectual qualifications of those selected for consideration as Supreme Court justices.

Established in 1945–1946, the committee began, with Brennan's nomination in 1956, to rate prospective justices as professionally qualified or unqualified. These ratings were used until Blackmun's appointment in 1970.

Blackmun was confirmed to a seat for which the Senate had rejected Haynsworth in 1969 and Carswell in 1970. The ABA committee had rated Haynsworth as "highly qualified" and Carswell as "qualified." Public criticism resulted in a change in the ABA rating system to three categories—"highly qualified," "not opposed," and "not qualified." Twenty years later, the ABA again revised its rating system to use the labels "well qualified," "qualified," and "not qualified."

After the embarrassment of the Haynsworth and Carswell rejections, Attorney General John N. Mitchell wrote the chairman of the committee in July 1970 to say that the Nixon administration would submit names of potential Supreme Court nominees to the ABA for preliminary screening prior to sending the president's choice to the Senate. But the agreement dissolved almost immediately when the names of prospective Nixon nominees to fill the next vacant seats reached the press while the ABA committee was studying their qualifications. The administration, suspecting a news leak in the committee, withdrew support of the practice.

Despite this rebuff, the ABA conducted its own investigation of the qualifications of nominees Powell and Rehnquist. The ABA approved both men—Powell unanimously as "one of the best lawyers available." Rehnquist received nine votes for a highly qualified rating, but three committee members said merely that they were "not opposed" to his appointment.

During the Reagan years, the ABA committee received harsh criticism from liberals and conservatives alike. President Reagan halted the practice of submitting a name to the committee before the nomination was made, sending it only after the nomination was official. The committee's approval of some controversial lower court nominations drew liberal criticism, while its split, 10-5, on Bork's Supreme Court nomination infuriated his supporters who felt that the division on the committee, once made public, made it respectable to oppose the nomination and contributed to its defeat.[23]

During the George H. W. Bush administration, the bar association continued to fend off charges from the Justice Department and some members of the Senate Judiciary Committee that its evaluation process was biased.

The Clinton White House sought the ABA's review of potential nominees. But in 2001, shortly after President George W. Bush took office, his White House counsel, Alberto Gonzales, said the administration would no longer give the ABA advance notice of its nominees for the courts. Gonzales said that although his office would be glad to receive advice from the ABA, the bar association did not deserve a special role in the nomination process.

Shortly after Barack Obama became president in 2009, White House lawyers announced they would return the ABA to its traditional role of evaluating potential nominees to the courts.

Politics and Appointments

Politics has always been a primary motivation in a president's selection of a Supreme Court nominee. It has also been a primary moving force in the process of senatorial confirmation. The oft-repeated disclaimer—that this process is, or should be, above politics—is simply not a true account.

In the early days of the Republic the Court was an open political battlefield between the competing interests of Federalists and Democratic-Republicans as each party sought to impose its ideology on the government of the new nation. George Washington, W. D. Coles wrote, "initiated the system of appointing political adherents only, to places on the Supreme Bench. That system has seldom been departed from."[1]

In modern times the political element has become less openly partisan and manipulative, with a few notable exceptions, as the Court has evolved into a more equal and autonomous branch of the federal system. The evolution of the Court into a relatively independent institution can be attributed in part to its growing stature under the weight of experience and tradition, and to the justices' sense of destiny and momentous undertaking as they assume their duties. In any event, service on the Court, however politically determined, began to engender a spirit of higher motive and unpredictable judgment that came to confound the political expectations of those who made it possible. Meanwhile, the rigid party-line ideology of the Senate became more amorphous, with liberal and conservative factions of each party uniting on common ideological ground in considering Court appointees.

In the beginning, however, the president's power to appoint Supreme Court justices was considered an out-and-out political opportunity and soon proved to be a political hornet's nest.

PRESIDENTIAL REASONING

On January 20, 1801, about two months before he left the White House and with little consultation and no fanfare, President John Adams appointed John Marshall chief justice of the United States. Adams wanted a loyal Federalist on the bench who would preserve the party's principles in the wake of Democratic-Republican Thomas Jefferson's election as president in 1800. Marshall was not Adams's first choice, however. He had appointed John Jay chief justice, but Jay declined the post because he dreaded circuit-riding duties and felt the fledgling Court lacked "energy, weight, and dignity."

The Senate exhibited little enthusiasm for Marshall—less because its members opposed him than because they preferred to see Justice William Paterson elevated to the post of chief justice. Yet Adams remained firm. The Federalist-dominated Senate realized that if they rejected Marshall, Adams might send them a "spite" nominee, or worse, and the post would be left vacant for Jefferson to fill.[2]

The Senate approved Marshall's nomination on January 27, 1801. No other single appointment affected the early Court or the young nation more profoundly. From the Court, Marshall championed the principles of federalism for thirty-four years. His dominance over the Court is indicated by the numbers. He wrote 519 of the 1,215 decisions handed down between 1801 and 1835, and 36 of the 62 decisions on major constitutional questions announced during his tenure.[3]

Unlike many of his successors, Adams was happy with his nominee. In 1826 he observed: "My gift of John Marshall to the people of the United States was the proudest act of my life. There is no act of my life on which I reflect with more pleasure."[4]

McLean and Taney

President Andrew Jackson's appointment of John McLean to the Supreme Court illustrates how easily Court nominees may break political promises to presidents.

McLean, a constant and persistent aspirant to high office, had been postmaster general under Presidents James Monroe and John Quincy Adams. In the tumultuous presidential election of 1828, McLean somehow maintained cordial ties with the forces of both Adams (a National-Republican) and Jackson (a Democratic-Republican). Jackson kept McLean on as postmaster general even though he did not trust him. He knew McLean was a popular figure in the West, and he did not wish to risk a political fight with McLean early in his administration.

In return for McLean's promise to abandon his presidential aspirations, Jackson nominated him to the vacant seat on the Supreme Court in 1829. McLean, however, failed to live up to his end of the bargain. While on the bench he was a serious contender for a presidential nomination three times, taking on the colors of a political chameleon. In 1832 Anti-Mason Party leaders tried to persuade him to become their nominee; they eventually settled on William Wirt of Maryland. In 1848 he was in the running for both the Whig and Free Soil Party nominations, but he was twice defeated. He suffered a similar fate in 1856, when he failed to win the Republican Party nomination. Unsuccessful in all four efforts, he served on the Court until his death in 1861.[5]

In contrast to the McLean selection was Jackson's appointment of Roger B. Taney as chief justice. With the resignation of Justice Gabriel Duval in January 1835, Jackson appointed Taney, his loyal supporter and Treasury secretary, to the vacant seat. Taney had demonstrated his loyalty by complying with Jackson's controversial order to remove government deposits from the Bank of the United States during the president's war against the bank.

The Senate countered the Taney nomination by postponing consideration on the last day of the 1835 session—effectively killing it. The same day, moreover, the Senate passed a bill abolishing the vacant seat. The House of Representatives refused to go along with that move.

Then, on July 6, 1835, Chief Justice Marshall died. Now Jackson had two seats to fill. Daniel Webster and Justice Joseph Story were mentioned as candidates for the chief justice's chair. Jackson also received suggestions that he promote John McLean.

In December Jackson nominated Philip P. Barbour of Virginia to fill the Duval seat and Taney to succeed Marshall as chief justice. After three months of debate the Senate confirmed both appointments in March 1836.

Taney presided as chief justice for twenty-eight years, earning a reputation as a great champion of states' rights. His best-known opinion, however, was an aberration in an otherwise notable judicial career. This 1857 ruling in the case of the slave Dred Scott said blacks could not be citizens of the United States. The decision hastened the onset of the Civil War and contributed to the Court's loss of public esteem during and after the conflict. (See "The Election of 1860," pp. 565–566.)

Salmon P. Chase

Chief Justice Taney died on October 12, 1864. In the midst of civil war, President Abraham Lincoln sought as a replacement for Taney a chief justice who would support him on matters of war policy and who could help close the widening breach in the Republican Party over Lincoln's conduct of the war.

Salmon Portland Chase was, from the outset, a serious candidate. Chase had been a governor and senator from Ohio and Lincoln's secretary of the Treasury. He was a talented public servant and seemed to hold the "right" opinions on the issues Lincoln considered important. But Chase was a political schemer, and he wanted desperately to be president. He had sought the Republican nomination in 1856 and in 1860, and even after becoming chief justice he vied for the 1868 presidential nomination of both parties.

Lincoln considered other political candidates for the post, including Justices James M. Wayne and Noah H. Swayne, Secretary of State William H. Seward, Secretary of War Edwin M. Stanton, and Montgomery Blair, Lincoln's former postmaster general. Blair was Lincoln's personal choice for chief justice. He was a distinguished public servant with roots in the original

Free Soil movement that became the Republican Party and a bitter foe of Chase.

But Lincoln appointed Chase—whom he did not trust—and not Blair—whom he trusted implicitly—because he believed that Chase commanded greater respect among Republicans and Unionists of all varieties and would help to unify the party and the nation. The Senate immediately confirmed the nomination in 1864.

Four months later Lincoln was assassinated. Chief Justice Chase found himself presiding over challenges both to the slain president's wartime policies and postwar plans for conciliation with the South, and to Congress's punitive Reconstruction legislation. By most accounts, Chase—notwithstanding his continuing political ambitions—acted with even-handed judicial restraint aimed at forestalling the Court's involvement in politics. His reluctance to preside at the trial for treason of Jefferson Davis, the president of the Confederacy, contributed to the eventual dismissal of charges against Davis; and his fair handling of the impeachment trial of Andrew Johnson is considered an important factor in Johnson's acquittal.

As chief justice, Chase joined the Court majority in *Ex parte Milligan* (1866), which limited the authority of military tribunals over civilians. In the *Slaughterhouse Cases* (1873) he dissented from the opinion allowing the maintenance of civil rights under state jurisdiction. *(See details of Ex parte Milligan, p. 266; on the Slaughterhouse Cases, see pp. 430–432.)*

Chase's main apostasy from Lincoln's doctrines came in the 1870 "legal tender" cases. Chase delivered the opinion that the act issuing Civil War currency without providing for redemption was unconstitutional—even though Chase had been Treasury secretary when the greenbacks were issued. He dissented when the decision was reversed in 1871.

THE "COURT-PACKERS"

The term *Court-packing* is usually associated with Franklin Roosevelt's blatant but unsuccessful bid in 1937 to reshape the Court into an instrument of his will. But the most successful, if unintentional, Court-packing ever accomplished by a president came in 1870 when Ulysses S. Grant appointed two associate justices who immediately played a role in a critical decision.

Grant and Legal Tender

In April 1869 Congress increased the size of the Court to nine, giving President Grant the opportunity to fill an extra seat. Then in December 1869 Justice Robert Grier resigned, and Grant had another vacancy to fill. Grant chose Edwin Stanton and Attorney General Ebenezer Hoar. Stanton was quickly confirmed but died suddenly, only four days after his confirmation. The Senate then rejected Hoar's nomination.

In February 1870 Grant nominated Joseph P. Bradley, a Republican railroad lawyer, and William Strong, a former Pennsylvania Supreme Court justice. Grant made the nominations even as the Court was announcing its 4-3 decision in *Hepburn v. Griswold*, declaring unconstitutional the Legal Tender Act of 1862, which had made greenbacks—paper money—legal tender for payment of debts.[6] Those supporting the gold standard for currency opposed the Court's ruling, arguing that it permitted debtors to pay off their debts in cheap currency.

Chief Justice Chase wrote the majority opinion, holding the law invalid insofar as it allowed the use of paper money to pay off debts contracted before its passage. Three Republican justices—Miller, Swayne, and Davis, all Lincoln appointees—dissented, arguing that a federal power with respect to money included the right to make paper money legal tender.

The Senate confirmed Bradley and Strong, and they took their seats in the spring of 1870, during which the Court agreed to hear arguments in a second legal tender case. A year later the Court, in *Knox v. Lee*, reversed *Hepburn v. Griswold*.[7] The vote was 5-4. Justices Bradley and Strong joined the three dissenters in *Hepburn* to form a majority in *Knox*.

Scholars later debated whether Grant intentionally packed the Court to get the legal tender ruling reversed. Charles Warren, historian of the Supreme Court, absolved Grant of the charge, saying that the president did not know in advance of the Court's ruling when he appointed Bradley and Strong and that, under any circumstances, Grant would have appointed men to the Court who agreed with his views on the money question.

APPOINTMENTS AND DISAPPOINTMENTS . . . PRESIDENTS AND JUDGES

Despite their best efforts to name individuals to the Court who share their views, presidents frequently have been disappointed. Their appointees failed to follow presidential political philosophy in their Court opinions. Donning the Court robe does seem to make a difference in the appointees' views. Justice Felix Frankfurter, when asked if appointment to the Court changed a person's views, allegedly retorted: "If he is any good, it does."[1]

Chief Justice Earl Warren, reflecting on sixteen years' service on the Court, said he did not see "how a man could be on the Court and not change his views substantially over a period of years for change you must if you are to do your duty on the Supreme Court."[2]

Historian Charles Warren wrote that "nothing is more striking in the history of the Court than the manner in which the hopes of those who expected a judge to follow the political views of the President appointing him are disappointed."[3]

JEFFERSON, MADISON, AND STORY

Presidents Thomas Jefferson and James Madison repeatedly registered their disappointment at the failure of those they appointed to the Court to resist the powerful and dominating influence of Chief Justice John Marshall. Madison failed to heed Jefferson's advice against appointing Joseph Story to the Court. Jefferson warned Madison that Story would side with Marshall on important legal questions—and Jefferson proved correct. Story not only joined Marshall in his interpretation of the Constitution but occasionally showed himself even more nationalistic than the chief justice.

ROOSEVELT AND HOLMES

Theodore Roosevelt named Oliver Wendell Holmes Jr. to the Court. Holmes then voted against the administration's antitrust efforts, most notably in the 1904 case of *Northern Securities v. United States*. Holmes's unexpected dissent left the government with a narrow 5-4 majority upholding the dissolution of the Northern Securities Company railroad conglomerate.

Following the decision, Roosevelt, referring to Holmes's defection, said that he "could carve out of a banana a Judge with more backbone than that!" Holmes reportedly smiled when told of the remark. Later, at a White House dinner, Holmes remarked to a labor leader and fellow guest: "What

you want is favor, not justice. But when I am on my job, I don't give a damn what you or Mr. Roosevelt want."[4]

Woodrow Wilson had reason to regret the appointment of James C. McReynolds to the bench when that justice proved to hold the opposite of Wilson's viewpoint on almost every question the administration argued before the Court.

COOLIDGE AND TRUMAN

Calvin Coolidge's sole appointee, Harlan F. Stone, sided within a year of his appointment with the liberal Holmes-Brandeis wing of the Court.

President Harry S. Truman noted that "packing the Supreme Court simply can't be done. I've tried and it won't work. Whenever you put a man on the Supreme Court he ceases to be your friend."[5]

And Truman should have known. In the important *Steel Seizure Case* (1952) the four Truman appointees divided 2-2 in the case that ruled the president's seizure of the steel mills unconstitutional. *(See details, p. 274.)*

EISENHOWER AND NIXON

President Dwight D. Eisenhower later suggested it was a mistake to appoint Earl Warren as chief justice. Warren's leadership commenced a judicial "revolution" that greatly disturbed the Republican president. But Warren's appointment made good political sense in 1953. Warren had delivered California delegates to Eisenhower at the Republican National Convention in 1952. Warren's removal from the California political scene, where he had proven an immensely popular three-term governor, placated conservative California Republican leaders, including Vice President Richard Nixon and Senate Majority Leader William F. Knowland, both of whom disliked Warren's progressive Republican views.

But Eisenhower reportedly regretted the liberalism of Warren and that of another of his appointees, Justice William J. Brennan Jr. Henry J. Abraham writes: "To Eisenhower, the new Warren represented all but a betrayal of older beliefs and understandings and his recognition of the chief justice's judicial independence, which he regarded as judicial legislating, was bitter and frustrating."[6]

President Richard Nixon had cause to regret some of the selections he made for the Court. Although the justices' views, on the whole, comported with the president's on "law and order" issues, some of the four appointees' opinions rejected Nixon's positions on abortion, aid to parochial schools, desegregation, and electronic surveillance. And in 1974 the Court, in an 8-0 opinion, handed down the decision in the tapes case that led to Nixon's resignation from office.[7] *(See "Nixon, Watergate, and the Court," pp. 349–355.)* Justice Lewis F. Powell Jr. proved to be moderate on the Court, while Harry A. Blackmun moved decidedly to the left. Although he was selected by Nixon as a law-and-order conservative, Blackmun renounced the death penalty as unconstitutional shortly before he retired in 1994.

REAGAN AND BUSH

Ronald Reagan made a concerted effort to make the Supreme Court more conservative, but like Nixon, he enjoyed mixed results. During his presidency, 1981–1989, Reagan appointed three reputed conservatives as associate justices (Sandra Day O'Connor, Antonin Scalia, and Anthony M. Kennedy) and elevated William H. Rehnquist to chief justice.

All told, these four appointments did move the Court to the right. The Court more narrowly interpreted the Constitution and federal statutes, reinvigorated federalism and state sovereignty, restricted appeals by prisoners sentenced to death, cut back use of affirmative action, and allowed greater government involvement with religion. But on the most symbolic constitutional issue of the era—abortion—two Reagan appointees, O'Connor and Kennedy, cast decisive votes in 1992 to affirm *Roe v. Wade*[8] President George H. W. Bush's first appointee, David H. Souter, would disappoint conservative partisans even more than had O'Connor and Kennedy. Not only did he vote with those two justices to uphold abortion rights, but by the mid-1990s, he was firmly ensconced in the Court's liberal wing on most controversial issues.

CLINTON AND G. W. BUSH

Bill Clinton chose for the Court two veteran appeals court judges who were reputed to be highly capable and moderately liberal, and Ruth Bader Ginsburg and Stephen G. Breyer lived up to their advance billing. Both supported abortion rights, affirmative action, and church-state separation, but neither was an outspoken liberal in the mold of William Brennan or Thurgood Marshall. Clinton did not get their votes in 1997 when he asked the Court to delay the Paula Jones sexual harassment suit until he left the White House. In *Clinton v. Jones* (1997) a unanimous Court said the president has no immunity to civil suits that arise from his private life.

George W. Bush followed the Clinton model in choosing two highly capable appeals court judges, albeit jurists with conservative leanings. John G. Roberts Jr. and Samuel A. Alito Jr. regularly joined with Justices Antonin Scalia and Clarence Thomas to form a reliable conservative bloc. When the Court rejected Bush's Guantánamo Bay prison policy in 2008, for example, Roberts and Alito dissented.

A DIFFERENT VIEW

In his book *God Save This Honorable Court,* Laurence H. Tribe argues against what he calls the "myth of the surprised president," contending that "for the most part, and especially in areas of particular and known concern to a President, Justices have been loyal to the ideals and perspectives of the men who have nominated them."[9]

Legal analyst Jeffrey Toobin also says the notion of a justice as turncoat has become outdated. Presidents and their lawyers have become ever more careful in selecting justices. "Souter's record pegged him as a moderate; Kennedy was nominated because the more conservative Robert Bork was rejected by the Senate," Toobin wrote in his book *The Nine.* "All of the subsequently appointed justices—Thomas, Ginsburg, Breyer, Roberts and Alito—have turned out precisely as might have been expected by the presidents who appointed them."[10]

1. Henry J. Abraham, *Justices and Presidents: A Political History of Appointments to the Supreme Court,* 3rd ed. (New York: Oxford University Press, 1992), 70.

2. Anthony Lewis, "A Talk with Warren on Crime, the Court, the Country," *New York Times Magazine,* October 19, 1969, 128–129.

3. Charles Warren, *The Supreme Court in United States History,* rev. ed., 2 vols. (Boston: Little, Brown, 1922, 1926), I:22.

4. Abraham, *Justices and Presidents,* 69.

5. Ibid., 70.

6. Ibid., 258, 266.

7. *United States v. Nixon,* 418 U.S. 683 (1974).

8. *Planned Parenthood of Southeastern Pennsylvania v. Casey,* 505 U.S. 833 (1992).

9. Laurence Tribe, *God Save This Honorable Court* (New York: Random House, 1985), 50.

10. Jeffrey Toobin, *The Nine: Inside the Secret World of the Supreme Court* (New York: Doubleday, 2007), 339.

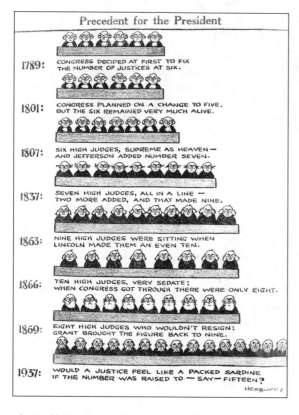

This Herblock cartoon lampoons President Franklin D. Roosevelt's proposal to enlarge the Supreme Court's membership.

But evidence not available when Warren wrote his history indicates that Grant did have prior knowledge of the outcome in *Hepburn*. Grant's secretary of the Treasury, George S. Boutwell, received word from Chief Justice Chase two weeks before the decision was announced what the decision would be. That information most likely was passed to Grant. Moreover, several years after the event, Grant said he had desired in his appointments of Strong and Bradley a Court decision that would sustain the constitutionality of legal tender. He got his wish.[8]

Roosevelt's Would-Be Court

The selection and confirmation of individual nominees to the Court have not been the only factors in the struggle between the president and Congress for a politically acceptable Court. From time to time both institutions have attempted to juggle the size of the Court's membership to achieve a judicial consensus more to their liking. Franklin Roosevelt's attempt to increase the Court's membership was the most transparent example yet of a president's political pressure on the Court—and it landed Roosevelt in his biggest political controversy up to that time.

In 1935 and 1936 the Court, in a series of 5-4 and 6-3 decisions, struck down every important measure of Roosevelt's New Deal program. The so-called "Four Horsemen"—Justices Willis Van Devanter, James C. McReynolds, George Sutherland, and Pierce Butler—were totally antagonistic to New Deal philosophy that called for government spending and work projects to help farmers, labor, and business survive the Great Depression. They were often joined by Chief Justice Charles Evans Hughes and Justice Owen J. Roberts to form an anti–New Deal majority. (See "New Deal and Old Court," pp. 343–345.)

Roosevelt won a stunning reelection victory in 1936 and on the strength of that popular mandate redoubled his efforts to prevent the "nine old men" on the Supreme Court from obstructing his legislative programs. But his "Court reform" bill—permitting a president to add a justice to the Supreme Court for every justice over seventy who refused to retire, up to a total of fifteen justices—was really a plan to pack the Court, and it offended some of FDR's ardent supporters in Congress and on the bench.

A confrontation was, however, averted. By the time the bill was unfavorably reported by the Senate Judiciary Committee, Roosevelt had begun to get greater cooperation from a Court suddenly more amenable to his legislation, and he had gained the opportunity to appoint new justices to recently vacated seats. The bill never reached the Senate floor, and the scheme was allowed to die.

The Court had signaled a more hospitable attitude toward the New Deal in three decisions in spring 1937 upholding major administration acts. And Van Devanter's retirement announcement came while the Judiciary Committee was considering the Court-packing bill. Van Devanter's retirement gave Roosevelt a chance to name his first appointee to the Court, and he chose a full-fledged New Dealer, Alabama senator Hugo L. Black—the first of nine appointments he would make before the end of 1943. As a result of Roosevelt's new appointments, the thrust and focus of the Court's decisions changed drastically in the next few years.

The retirement of Chief Justice Hughes in 1941 gave President Roosevelt an opportunity to name the person of his choice to that position. Eventually, he picked a Republican in the hope of increasing bipartisan political support for his administration in the face of World War II.

When Hughes, eighty years of age, announced on June 2, 1941, that he would be retiring on July 1, Roosevelt felt no urgency to move quickly to fill the post. The president had two candidates in mind: Justice Harlan Fiske Stone and Attorney General Robert H. Jackson. Roosevelt preferred Jackson, a New Deal loyalist. Hughes, on the other hand, felt Stone's record on the Court merited his elevation to chief justice.

Roosevelt also discussed the nomination with Justice Felix Frankfurter. When asked which of the two men he preferred, Frankfurter told the president:

> On personal grounds I'd prefer Bob [Jackson]. While I've known Stone longer and our relations are excellent and happy, I feel closer friendship with Bob. But from the national interest I am bound to say that there is no reason for preferring Bob to Stone—quite the contrary. Stone is senior and qualified professionally to be C. J. But for me the decisive consideration, considering the fact that Stone is qualified, is that Bob is of your personal and political family, as it were, while Stone is a Republican. . . . When war does come, the country should feel you are the Nation's . . . President, and not a partisan President. Few things would contribute as much to confidence in you as a national and not as a partisan president than for you to name a Republican, who has the profession's confidence, as chief justice.[9]

Roosevelt discussed the nomination with Jackson, who assured the president he agreed with Frankfurter's analysis. And Jackson personally delivered the news to Stone of his appointment as chief justice. Stone was confirmed in the Senate by a voice vote. The president later appointed Jackson to Stone's vacant justice seat.

ROUTES TO THE COURT

After Stone's death in 1946, President Harry Truman appointed Fred M. Vinson chief justice of the United States. Truman selected him because Vinson was an able administrator with broad experience in public service and he was a friend. Vinson had served with Truman in the Senate. When Truman became president, Vinson served as his Treasury secretary and ex officio adviser.

At the time of Stone's death the Court was seriously divided by personality clashes among the justices, especially the feud between Justices Jackson and Black, described by one of Black's biographers as "the bitterest internecine controversy in the court's history."[10] Among other things, the long-simmering antagonism involved Jackson's charges that Black was guilty of conflict of interest by participating in two decisions in 1944 and 1945.[11] Meanwhile, Black criticized Jackson's leave of absence from the Court in 1945 and 1946 to serve as U.S. prosecutor at the Nazi war crimes trial at Nuremberg, Germany—a trial Black called a "high-grade lynching party."[12]

Truman sought the advice of former chief justice Hughes and former associate justice Owen Roberts about the chief justice appointment. Both men urged Truman to appoint someone who could restore peace among the members of the Court, which apparently ruled out Jackson, believed by many, evidently including Jackson himself, to be next in line for the chief justiceship.[13] Truman nominated Vinson on June 7, 1946, and he was confirmed, uncontested, two weeks later amid a further volley of mutual public criticism between Jackson and Black.

In seven years as chief justice Vinson muted the clashes between members of the Court, but he did not restore harmony. There were proportionally more 5-4 opinions during the Vinson period than in any other era in the Court's history until the unprecedented division on the Rehnquist Court.[14] Vinson died in 1953, disappointed with the results of his term as chief justice.[15]

Creating a Vacancy

In 1965 President Lyndon Johnson persuaded Arthur Goldberg to leave the Court to create a vacancy to which Johnson could appoint his friend and trusted adviser Abe Fortas. Appealing to Goldberg's sense of duty and public service, Johnson urged him to resign from the Court so that he could serve as U.S. ambassador to the United Nations. Goldberg allowed himself to be persuaded, genuinely hoping that the UN forum would be the arena in which to negotiate an end to the war in Vietnam.

At the request of Lyndon B. Johnson, Arthur J. Goldberg (*above*) resigned from the Supreme Court in1965 to become the ambassador to the United Nations. Johnson persuaded his friend and adviser Abe Fortas to fill the vacancy. In the picture on the right, Fortas is subjected to a friendly dose of the well-known Johnson "treatment."

Goldberg, from a poor immigrant family background, had been general counsel for the nation's largest labor unions before becoming secretary of labor in the Kennedy administration. Both Chief Justice Earl Warren and Justice Frankfurter had approved of Goldberg's appointment in 1962 as Frankfurter's successor. But Goldberg was to serve only three years. President Johnson, fresh from an election victory, wanted to put his choice on the Court.

After coaxing Goldberg off the Court, Johnson had to persuade a reluctant Fortas to take the seat. Johnson invited Fortas to the White House on July 18, 1965, on the pretext of seeking his advice on another matter. The president then simply informed Fortas that he was going over to the East Wing of the White House to nominate him for the Supreme Court.

The prearranged session included Goldberg and his family. The resigning justice did not hide his disappointment at leaving the Court, saying, "I shall not, Mr. President, conceal the pain with which I leave the Court after three years of service. It has been the richest and most satisfying period of my career."[16]

Delaying a Vacancy

When Chief Justice Warren announced in 1968 his intention to retire, he gave President Johnson an opportunity to appoint his successor in the nation's highest judicial post. But Johnson had become a lame-duck president, declaring in March 1968 that he would not be a candidate for reelection. Nevertheless, Johnson took advantage of the Warren retirement announcement and nominated Justice Fortas as chief justice.

The Senate rejected Fortas. Republicans, hopeful of winning the White House in 1968, wanted to "save" the vacancy for the Republican president-to-be to fill. Fortas's continuing role as an unofficial adviser to the president on policy matters while on the Court and his acceptance of fees for a series of university seminars created enough doubts among enough senators to forestall confirmation in 1968. Fortas's nomination cleared the

Senate Judiciary Committee but ran into a filibuster on the floor. A motion to end the filibuster failed, and Fortas then asked President Johnson to withdraw his name from nomination.

Richard Nixon, the Republican candidate, won election as president soon thereafter, and in May 1969 he named his choice, Warren E. Burger, chief justice. By the time Burger was sworn in, Fortas had left the Court. In May 1969 *Life* magazine reported that Fortas in 1966 had accepted, and then returned, a large fee from the Louis E. Wolfson family foundation. Millionaire Wolfson later was sent to prison for illegal stock manipulations.[17] Rather than face a full-scale inquiry and possibly impeachment proceedings, Fortas resigned on May 15, 1969.

THE "SAVE-THE-SEAT" SYNDROME

The refusal of the Senate to confirm Fortas's nomination as chief justice was a modern example of the "save-the-seat" stratagem. During the nineteenth century the Senate denied confirmation to many late-term nominees to the Court simply because senators, for partisan reasons, wished to save the seat for the incoming president to fill and thereby place his stamp on the Court at the outset of his term. In early 1829, for example, the Senate refused to confirm lame-duck president John Quincy Adams's nomination of John J. Crittenden to the Court, which saved the vacancy for President Andrew Jackson to fill.

The unluckiest president for Court appointments was John Tyler. Five of his nominations failed to win Senate approval. Tyler, a Whig, was without a solid political base of his own after President William Henry Harrison died in office in 1841.

Tyler's first four nominees met Senate rejection after the president's policies collided with those advocated by Henry Clay's rival Whig Party supporters in the Senate. Tyler's fifth nominee—announced in February 1845 after Democrat James K. Polk won the 1844 presidential election—was a well-known Philadelphia lawyer, John M. Read, who had political ties with both the Whigs and Democrats. The Senate postponed consideration of the nomination made by the lame-duck Tyler and adjourned. President Polk therefore began

his term in office with an opportunity to fill Henry Baldwin's still-vacant seat. After rejecting Polk's first nominee, George W. Woodward, the Senate confirmed Robert Grier in August 1846.

After Franklin Pierce won the 1852 election, President Millard Fillmore, by then a lame duck, nominated Sen. George E. Badger of North Carolina to the Court. The Senate postponed action on the nomination—an unusual breach of a senatorial practice that usually grants immediate confirmation to a senator appointed to the Court. Fillmore, however, refused to accept defeat and named a prominent Louisiana lawyer, William C. Micou. But the Senate again refused to act, allowing Pierce to fill that vacancy at the outset of his administration.

In 1861, at the end of his presidential term, President James Buchanan, a Democrat, tried to fill the seat vacated by Peter V. Daniel. Buchanan found a worthy candidate in Pennsylvanian Jeremiah S. Black—a strong believer in the Union but not an abolitionist. Moreover, Black had been chief justice of the Pennsylvania Supreme Court and attorney general of the United States. But it was too late. In less than a month Lincoln would assume the presidency. Republicans in the Senate were not anxious to deny the first Republican president the opportunity to make the Court appointment. Black was denied confirmation, 25–26.

Rutherford B. Hayes, an avowed one-term president, nominated in late January 1881 his friend and former college classmate Stanley Matthews of Ohio to the seat made vacant by Noah Swayne's retirement. Matthews had a successful career as a public servant, but he was a political maverick. The major drawback to his candidacy, however, was that Matthews served as a prominent counsel to financier Jay Gould. The Senate Judiciary Committee refused to report the nomination for floor action, and it appeared Matthews's nomination was dead until Hayes's successor, James A. Garfield, renominated Matthews for the post in March 1881. He was confirmed by the narrowest of margins, 24–23.

William Howard Taft laid the groundwork for his own appointment as chief justice in 1921 when, as president in 1910, he chose the veteran justice Edward White for the post rather than Justice Hughes, the younger candidate. In April 1910 Taft had appointed

Hughes, age forty-eight, associate justice, filling the vacancy created by David J. Brewer's death. Taft had considered Hughes, who was recognized as presidential "timber" within Republican ranks, a threat to his own presidential nomination in 1908. At the time of Hughes's appointment Taft dangled before him the prospect of becoming chief justice when that vacancy occurred. Taft wrote to Hughes that he had no reservations about promoting an associate justice to chief justice. Then, in an equivocal addendum, Taft wrote:

> Don't misunderstand me as to the Chief Justice-ship. I mean if that office were now open, I should offer it to you and it is probable that if it were to become vacant during my term, I should promote you to it; but, of course, conditions change, so that it would not be right for me to say by way of promise what I would do in the future. Nor, on the other hand, would I have you think that your declination now would prevent my offering you the higher position, should conditions remain as they are.[18]

Hughes got the message and accepted, but conditions did change. In July 1910 Chief Justice Melville W. Fuller died, and in December 1910 Taft appointed Louisianan Edward White, age sixty-five, a Catholic, and a Democrat, to replace him. The public—not to mention Hughes—had expected Taft to name Hughes to the post. In 1916 Hughes resigned from the Court to run for the presidency.[19]

White had already served on the Court seventeen years when Taft named him chief justice. He was an able administrator whose views coincided with those of Taft. And because White was not a young man, the president counted on White's retirement, resignation, or death—preferably during a Republican administration—to create a vacancy in the Court's top spot, which Taft hoped to fill.

Taft did not conceal his ambitions. When he signed White's commission as chief justice he remarked aloud: "There is nothing I would have loved more than being Chief Justice of the United States. I cannot help seeing the irony in the fact that I, who desired that office so much, should now be signing the commission of another man."[20]

White died on May 19, 1921. After considerable lobbying by Taft in his own behalf, President Warren G. Harding appointed him chief justice. He served until 1930, when President Hoover appointed the man Taft had decided not to make chief justice—Charles Evans Hughes.

THE COURT AS A CAMPAIGN ISSUE

The Supreme Court—its personnel as well as its positions—has been a recurring issue in presidential campaigns since 1800. The candidates of both major parties, and those of some third parties, have found the Court's rulings on a variety of issues—from slavery to taxes to criminal procedure—all handy targets for election year rhetoric. Presidents Jefferson, Lincoln, Franklin Roosevelt, Nixon, and Reagan most successfully implemented their campaign criticism of the Court. Each of those presidents influenced the Court's decisions through his appointments and policies.

Thomas Jefferson

During the election of 1800, Jeffersonian Democratic-Republicans charged that the federal judiciary was a solid Federalist phalanx intent upon destroying republican liberties. Jeffersonians also criticized both Chief Justice John Jay and his successor in that post, Oliver Ellsworth, for accepting diplomatic assignments from Presidents Washington and Adams, respectively. Moreover, Jay had then negotiated the treaty that bore his name, a treaty reviled by all Jeffersonians as too pro-British. James T. Callender, the notorious Jeffersonian pamphleteer, wrote in his 1800 election campaign pamphlet, *The Prospect Before Us:* "Think of the gross and audacious prostitution of the federal bench by the successive selection of foreign ambassadors from that body."[21]

When Jefferson became president, he launched an attack on the judicial branch, encouraging Congress first to repeal the Judiciary Act of 1801 and then to impeach an associate justice, Samuel Chase, for his "crimes" of making political diatribes from the bench. The Jeffersonians succeeded in repealing the 1801 act but failed in their efforts to convict Chase. *(See "Chase Impeachment," pp. 508–510.)*

The Court's decision in *Scott v. Sandford* set the tenor of the 1860 presidential contest. The four presidential candidates of the battered national parties dance with members of their respective constituencies in this campaign cartoon. Clockwise from upper left are southern Democrat John C. Breckinridge, Republican Abraham Lincoln, Constitutional party candidate John Bell, and Democrat Stephen A. Douglas.

On the whole, Jefferson got what he wanted. The judges toned down their statements from the bench and the appointment of Jeffersonian Democratic-Republicans to all levels of the judiciary ended charges that the federal bench was a Federalist sanctuary. Nevertheless, all of Jefferson's Court appointees subsequently succumbed to the influence of Jefferson's Federalist archenemy, Chief Justice John Marshall.

The Election of 1860

The Court's decision in *Scott v. Sandford* (1857) permanently disrupted the fragile structure of political compromise and adjustment between North and South on the expansion of slavery into the territories beyond the Mississippi River.[22] The decision gave Abraham Lincoln an issue that carried him to the White House. The whole existence of the Republican Party rested on the twin pillars of free land and free men in the territories west of the Mississippi.

Republicans chose Lincoln as their standard-bearer in 1860—in large part because of his simple and eloquent refutation of the slavery expansion argument made by Sen. Stephen A. Douglas in the 1858 Illinois Senate race. Lincoln refused to compromise on the expansion question:

Now, I confess myself as belonging to the class in the country who contemplates slavery as a moral, social, and political evil, having due regard for its actual existence among us and the difficulties of getting rid of it in any satisfactory way, and to all constitutional obligations which have been thrown about it; but nevertheless, [I] desire a policy that looks to the prevention of it as a wrong, and looks hopefully to the time when as a wrong it may come to an end.[23]

The Dred Scott decision left antislavery advocates in a dilemma. If Congress could not act to halt the spread of slavery, then who could? The decision—and the Court—were primary campaign issues in 1860. Republicans argued that the Court's statements on the power of Congress were simply *dicta*—comments extraneous to resolution of the case itself and therefore not binding as constitutional law. They also argued that the Dred Scott ruling could be overturned by a future Court if Republicans gained control of both Congress and the White House and won the opportunity to appoint loyal Republicans to the Court. Several Republicans demanded that the Court be packed with Republicans should Lincoln win the election.

The Republican platform of 1860 sharply criticized the Dred Scott decision:

[T]he new dogma that the Constitution, of its own force, carries slavery into any or all of the territories of the United States, is a dangerous political heresy, at variance with the explicit provisions of that instrument itself, with contemporaneous exposition, and with legislative and judicial precedent; is revolutionary in its tendency, and subversive of the peace and harmony of the country.... [T]he normal condition of all territory of the United States is that of freedom.[24]

Lincoln won the election, but war, rather than his nominations to the Court, ultimately overruled the Dred Scott decision.

The Income Tax Issue

In 1895 the Court held the federal income tax unconstitutional in *Pollock v. Farmers' Loan and Trust Co.*[25] The decision angered progressives in Congress and other reformers who felt that it protected private vested rights and frustrated Congress's attempts to make the wealthy pay their fair share of taxes. Farmers and laborers considered the decision another victory of the rich and powerful. *(See "The Income Tax Cases," pp. 144–147.)*

The income tax ruling became an issue in the 1896 presidential campaign. The Democratic Party favored the income tax and decried such judicial "usurpation" of legislative power. Its candidate, William Jennings Bryan, championed the tax at the Democratic National Convention in Chicago in July 1896:

They criticize us for our criticism of the Supreme Court of the United States.... They say that we passed an unconstitutional law; we deny it. The income tax law was not unconstitutional when it was passed; it was not unconstitutional when it went before the Supreme Court for the first time; it did not become unconstitutional until one of the judges changed his mind, and we cannot be expected to know when a judge will change his mind. The income tax is just. It simply intends to put the burdens of government justly upon the backs of the people. I am in favor of an income tax. When I find a man who is not willing to share of the burdens of government which protects him, I find a man who is unworthy to enjoy the blessings of a government like ours.[26]

Bryan lost, and not until ratification of the Sixteenth Amendment in 1913 did Congress overturn the effect of the Court's 1895 decision.

La Follette on the Attack

In the 1924 presidential election Progressives made the Supreme Court's opposition to reform legislation a campaign issue. Sen. Robert M. La Follette, R-Wis., was the Progressive Party's candidate. He argued that the day had come

when the Federal judiciary must be made—to some extent at least—subject to the will of the people, or we must abandon the pretense that the people rule in this country.... We cannot live under a system of government where we are forced to amend the Constitution every time we want to pass a progressive law. The remedy must adequately cope with the disease, or there is no use applying it.[27]

La Follette's remedy was a single constitutional amendment that sharply curtailed the power of judicial review, denying any lower federal court authority to declare an act of Congress unconstitutional and providing that when the Supreme Court declared an act of Congress unconstitutional, Congress could override that decision by reenacting the law. The 1924 Progressive Party platform stated: "We favor submitting to the people, for their considerate judgment, a constitutional amendment providing that Congress may by enacting a statute make it effective over a judicial veto."[28]

But 1924 was not a year for reformers. Prosperity and "normalcy" were on the rise, and the nation voted to keep President Calvin Coolidge at the helm. The Court, Coolidge said in response to La Follette's criticism, was the chief defender of the American way of life—the chief obstacle preventing "breakdown [of] the guarantees of our fundamental law."[29]

"Fighting Bob" La Follette died in 1925. His constitutional amendment was never adopted.

The Election of 1968

In the presidential campaign of 1968, Richard Nixon made clear that if elected he intended to use his power of appointment to remake the Warren Court in the image of his own conservative value system. Nixon sharply criticized the Warren Court during a "law and order" campaign alleging that the Court's decisions on criminal procedure were "seriously hamstringing the peace forces in our society and strengthening the criminal forces."[30]

Once elected, Nixon nominated Warren Burger chief justice of the United States on May 21, 1969. Burger had a reputation as a hard-line "law and order" judge on the U.S. Court of Appeals for the District of Columbia Circuit.[31] He was quickly confirmed. Nixon's effort to name a second conservative ran into trouble, however. The difficulty came when he tried to fill the seat left vacant by Fortas's resignation on May 14, 1969.

During the campaign Nixon had said he would nominate to the Court a southerner who had a conservative judicial philosophy. In November 1969 the Senate rejected Nixon's first southern nominee, Judge Clement F. Haynsworth of the Fourth Circuit Court of Appeals, because of his participation in deciding cases in which, it was charged, he had a financial interest. Nixon then submitted the name of G. Harrold Carswell, another conservative southerner who was a judge of the Fifth Circuit Court of Appeals. Aware of

Carswell's record as a staunch segregationist and his lack of intellectual qualities, the Senate rejected his nomination. Nixon later filled the Fortas seat with Minnesotan Harry A. Blackmun, a conservative member of the Eighth Circuit Court of Appeals.

In 1971 the retirements of Hugo Black and John Marshall Harlan gave Nixon two more seats to fill on the Court. He named Lewis F. Powell Jr. to Black's seat. Powell was a distinguished Virginia lawyer who had criticized some of the Warren Court's civil liberties decisions. To Harlan's seat Nixon nominated William H. Rehnquist of Arizona, who was seen as both very conservative and brilliant, having graduated first in his Stanford law school class. Both men were confirmed in 1971.

By the end of 1971—his third year as president—Nixon had appointed four members of the Court. He had fulfilled his campaign pledges. The Court's rulings on criminal law reflected the conservative views of Burger and the new associate justices.

The Reagan Revolution

To win the White House in 1980, and again in 1984, Ronald Reagan said what the nation's most conservative voters wanted to hear: that he would work for the reversal of the Supreme Court's 1973 decision permitting abortion (*Roe v. Wade*) and its earlier rulings forbidding officially prescribed prayers in public schools (*Engel v. Vitale*, 1962; *Abington School District v. Schempp*, 1963).[32]

These decisions were just a few that Reagan hoped to persuade the Court to disavow. In addition, he wanted the Court to abandon the use of affirmative action, relax the Warren Court's rulings denying police and prosecutors the use of illegally obtained evidence, and lower the barrier separating church and state, particularly when the issue was state aid to parochial schools.

Like all presidents, Reagan had two ways to effect these changes in the Court—the power to appoint new members when vacancies occurred and the power to argue his point of view through the solicitor general. He used both to the maximum extent possible; in the end the former proved more effective than the latter.

Jimmy Carter had spent four years in the White House without any vacancy occurring on the Court;

ARGUING THE PRESIDENT'S CASE

When the White House wants the Supreme Court to take a certain position on an issue, it is the solicitor general, or one of the solicitor general's staff, who argues the administration's case to the Court. When the government is a party to a case, the solicitor general argues the government's side. When it is not a party, but nevertheless wishes to make its views known on the issue, the solicitor general files an amicus curiae—friend of the court—brief.

The government has been very successful in arguing cases before the Court. One study of the Court's opinions shows that the government won more than 60 percent of its cases in the eighteenth and nineteenth centuries. From 1953 through 1983 it won almost 70 percent of its cases.[1] Subsequent studies have found that success rate continuing.[2]

The government's record in cases where it filed as amicus curiae is even better. The position endorsed by the government prevailed in as many as 87 percent of the cases in some terms after World War II. For the terms between 1958 and 1967 the government's rate of success in such cases averaged 71 percent.[3]

In more recent terms, the solicitor general's office has participated in most of the cases heard before the Court and has been on the winning side most of the time. This is no surprise, as the solicitor general defends federal laws, federal agencies, and convictions won in the federal courts. It is the unusual case in which the Supreme Court rejects a federal law, the position of a federal agency, or a criminal conviction in the federal courts.

But these unusual cases do occur, and the solicitor general does not always win. Walter Dellinger, the acting solicitor general for President Bill Clinton, urged the Court in 1997 to rule that the president was shielded from responding to a sexual harassment suit while in the White House. The Court disagreed in a unanimous ruling.[4] During the George W. Bush administration, Solicitor General Theodore B. Olson urged the Court to rule that military prisoners held at Guantánamo Bay, Cuba, had no right to appeal their cases to federal judges. The Court disagreed, saying the right to habeas corpus extended to Guantánamo detainees.[5] And his successor, Solicitor General Paul Clement, argued that President Bush had the power as commander in chief to put Guantánamo prisoners on trial in "military commissions" that were established by Bush's military commanders. Once again, the Court disagreed and ruled the president had overstepped his authority.[6]

---

1. Lincoln Caplan, *The Tenth Justice: The Solicitor General and the Rule of Law* (New York: Knopf, 1987), 295.

2. Statistics compiled by Office of Solicitor General, 1996.

3. Robert G. Scigliano, *The Supreme Court and the Presidency* (New York: Free Press, 1971), 180.

4. *Clinton v. Jones,* 520 U.S. 681 (1997).

5. *Rasul v. Bush,* 542 U.S. 466 (2004).

6. *Hamdan v. Rumsfeld,* 548 U.S. 557 (2006).

Reagan had to wait only five months. Justice Potter Stewart retired in June 1981, and Reagan made good on another campaign pledge, naming the first woman justice of the U.S. Supreme Court. Reagan chose Judge Sandra Day O'Connor of the Arizona Court of Appeals. O'Connor quickly allied herself with Rehnquist, her Stanford Law School classmate, and the Court's other conservative members. She became an articulate voice for the conservative wing of the Court.

During Reagan's first term his solicitor general, Rex E. Lee, argued the administration's case for change in cases concerning criminal law, deregulation, affirmative action, and abortion, but with only limited success.

In the Court's October 1983 term the administration seemed to make some headway, winning favorable rulings on affirmative action, the exclusionary rule, and deregulation. But its success in those rulings was significantly diluted in the next two terms when the Court—in some cases with O'Connor's help—rejected the administration's position on school prayer, aid to parochial schools, and affirmative action.[33]

Then in the summer of 1986 Chief Justice Burger retired, giving Reagan the chance to name a new chief. Reagan selected Rehnquist, the Court's most conservative member, and to the seat Rehnquist vacated, he named Antonin Scalia, a highly respected conservative judge who was the first justice of Italian descent.

But even three Reagan justices were not enough to swing the Court firmly in a conservative direction. It took one more nomination, and Justice Powell provided the opportunity when he retired in 1987. Reagan's first choice, Robert H. Bork, was soundly defeated in the Senate. Opposition to Bork's nomination was led by civil rights groups who criticized his views, and it was intensified by awareness of the pivotal role the new justice would play in some of the Court's most controversial decisions.

In February 1988 Anthony Kennedy, Reagan's third choice to fill Powell's seat, was sworn in as the nation's 104th justice. The next term, Reagan's campaign for change finally bore fruit. In the October 1988 term the Supreme Court issued decisions limiting the use of affirmative action, and for the first time since *Roe v. Wade* it upheld a state law imposing significant restrictions on a woman's right to have an abortion.[34]

With Reagan's chosen successor, George H. W. Bush, in the White House, the goals of the Reagan revolution looked to be in sight. The Court's two most stalwart liberals, Justices William Brennan and Thurgood Marshall, retired in 1990 and 1991, respectively. But unlike the Reagan team, the Bush White House seemed less prepared. After a hurried weekend of internal debate, Bush chose David H. Souter, a little-known New Hampshire judge, to fill Brennan's seat. He was dubbed the "stealth nominee" because his views were unknown—even, it turned out, to his sponsors in the White House. A year later, Bush chose a young, black conservative, Clarence Thomas, to replace the Court's first black justice.

In 1992 the reconstituted Court surprised many, including Reagan's lawyers, when it upheld the right to abortion and held the line on the strict separation of church and state. A 5-4 ruling in a Pennsylvania case preserved the core of *Roe v. Wade*.[35] And a 5-4 ruling in a Rhode Island case prohibited public school officials from invoking God's name at a graduation ceremony.[36] The three Reagan-Bush appointees, O'Connor, Kennedy and Souter, voted with the majority.

Clinton and Bush Appointees

When Bill Clinton campaigned for the presidency in 1992, it had been a quarter century since a Democrat had chosen a Supreme Court justice. Since Lyndon Johnson selected Thurgood Marshall in 1967, all the subsequent nominees had been selected by Republicans. Clinton, a

Yale Law School graduate, also campaigned as a supporter of abortion rights and *Roe v. Wade*. Soon after he took office, Justice Byron White, the last remaining Democratic nominee, announced he planned to retire. For a time, Clinton aspired to nominate a prominent person with a public record outside the confines of the judiciary. He floated the idea of selecting New York governor Mario Cuomo (who said he was not interested), Senate Majority Leader George Mitchell, who was formerly a judge (he too said he was not interested), and Interior Secretary Bruce Babbitt, the former governor and attorney general of Arizona. Babbitt had strong opponents in the Senate. In the end, Clinton took a safer course and chose two well-regarded appellate judges. Ruth Bader Ginsburg replaced White in 1993, and Stephen G. Breyer replaced Justice Harry Blackmun in 1994.

Although Ginsburg and Breyer voted reliably on the liberal side of issues such as abortion, affirmative action, and the death penalty, they did not always go Clinton's way. In 1997 Clinton was facing a personal lawsuit that threatened to do great political damage to his presidency. He appealed to the Supreme Court and sought a "temporary immunity" from responding to Paula Jones's sexual harassment lawsuit until he left the White House. But Ginsburg and Breyer joined the unanimous ruling in *Clinton v. Jones,* which held the president has no immunity from civil suits that arise from his private life.[37]

When the 2000 presidential campaign got under way, Texas governor George W. Bush promised he would choose Supreme Court nominees in the mold of Justice Antonin Scalia and Clarence Thomas, the two most conservative justices. That pledge helped solidify his support among social conservatives. It was not until his second term that Bush had a chance to make good on his promise.

Bush was not a lawyer—and joked he was glad of it—and he did not have a personal friendship with either John G. Roberts Jr. or Samuel A. Alito Jr. Roberts had been a prominent lawyer in Washington, and Alito labored in near obscurity from a courthouse in Newark, New Jersey. But both were championed by the conservative activists and by lawyers in the White House counsel's office. They advised Bush that Roberts and Alito were smart, steady, and reliably conservative.

In spring 2005 the White House expected to nominate a successor to Chief Justice Rehnquist, who was battling thyroid cancer. Roberts, a former Rehnquist clerk, was high on the list to succeed him. But when the Court's term ended, Justice O'Connor announced she was retiring, not the chief justice. Thrown off stride, Bush's team pondered its prospects and took another look at several female candidates. But in mid-July the president announced he had chosen Roberts to replace O'Connor.

Roberts made a favorable impression when he met throughout the summer with senators, and his confirmation looked assured. On the Labor Day weekend, Rehnquist died. A few days later, Bush announced he was nominating Roberts to fill Rehnquist's seat as chief justice. By late September, Roberts had won confirmation by the Senate and was in the center seat when the new Court term opened in October.

Bush tried again to fill O'Connor's seat and turned to Harriet Miers, his Texas lawyer and White House counsel. Bush said he knew her well and trusted her judgment, but the nomination set off a rebellion on the right. Conservative pundits and activists said Miers was not qualified for the post because she had no record of writings or rulings on constitutional issues. She quietly withdrew her name after the White House could send it to the Senate. Bush then followed the advice of his staff and chose Alito, whose low-key, scholarly manner set off few sparks. Even so, Senate Democrats were unwilling to support another Bush nomination. The Republican majority ensured Alito would be confirmed, and he was on a 58 to 42 vote. When Alito took his seat early in 2006, Bush could take credit for having fulfilled his campaign promise to his conservative base.

———————— ★ ————————

NOTES

INTRODUCTION (PP. 547–554)

1. Robert G. Scigliano, *The Supreme Court and the Presidency* (New York: Free Press, 1971), 207–208.

2. Ibid., 86.

3. Henry J. Abraham, *Justices and Presidents: A Political History of Appointees to the Supreme Court*, 3rd ed. (New York: Oxford University Press, 1992), 56–59.

4. Ibid., Table 3, 62.

5. Ibid., Table 4, 62.

6. Ibid., 64.

7. Elder Witt, *A Different Justice: Reagan and the Supreme Court* (Washington, D.C.: Congressional Quarterly, 1986), chap. 3.

8. Abraham, *Justices and Presidents,* 64–65.

9. Henry Cabot Lodge, *Selections from the Correspondence of Theodore Roosevelt and Henry Cabot Lodge, 1884–1918,* 2 vols. (New York: Scribner's, 1925), 2:228, 230–231.

10. *Lawrence v. Texas,* 539 U.S. 558 (2003).

11. Daniel S. McHargue, "Appointments to the Supreme Court of the United States: The Factors that Have Affected Appointments, 1789–1932," Ph.D. diss., University of California at Los Angeles, 1949, 549; Sheldon Goldman, "Bush's Judicial Legacy: The Final Imprint," *Judicature* 76 (April-May 1993): 282–298, and "Judicial Selection under Clinton: A Midterm Examination," *Judicature* 78 (May-June 1995): 276–292.

12. Abraham, *Justices and Presidents,* 40–41.

13. Ibid., 29.

14. Ibid., 10.

15. Ibid., 8.

16. Alpheus T. Mason, *William Howard Taft: Chief Justice* (New York: Simon and Schuster, 1965), 76ff.

17. Ibid., 170–171.

18. Leon Friedman and Fred L. Israel, eds., *The Justices of the United States Supreme Court, 1789–1969,* 4 vols. (New York: Chelsea House, R. R. Bowker, 1969), 3:2209.

19. Abraham, *Justices and Presidents,* 31.

20. Ibid.

21. Alpheus T. Mason, *Harlan Fiske Stone: Pillar of the Law* (New York: Viking, 1956), 336.

22. Peter Odegaard, *American Politics,* 2nd ed. (New York: Harper and Bros., 1947), 172.

23. For details on the ABA role, see Herman Schwartz, *Packing the Courts: The Conservative Campaign to Rewrite the Constitution* (New York: Scribner's, 1988).

POLITICS AND APPOINTMENTS (PP. 555–570)

1. Quoted by Peter Odegaard in *American Politics,* 2nd ed. (New York: Harper and Bros., 1947), 169.

2. Charles Warren, *The Supreme Court in United States History,* rev. ed., 2 vols. (Boston: Little, Brown, 1926), 1:176–177.

3. Robert J. Steamer, *The Supreme Court in Crisis: A History of Conflict* (Amherst: University of Massachusetts Press, 1971), 35.

4. Warren, *Supreme Court in United States History,* 1:178.

5. Henry J. Abraham, *Justices and Presidents: A Political History of Appointees to the Supreme Court,* 3rd ed. (New York: Oxford University Press, 1992), 97.

6. *Hepburn v. Griswold,* 8 Wall. (75 U.S.) 603 (1870).

7. *Knox v. Lee,* 12 Wall. (79 U.S.) 457 (1871).

8. Warren, *Supreme Court in United States History,* 2:515–527; Sidney Ratner, "Was the Supreme Court Packed by President Grant?" *Political Science Quarterly* 50 (September 1935): 343–358.

9. Alpheus T. Mason, *Harlan Fiske Stone: Pillar of the Law* (New York: Viking, 1956), 566–567.

10. Gerald T. Dunne, *Hugo Black and the Judicial Revolution* (New York: Simon and Schuster, 1977), 225.

11. *Tennessee Coal, Iron and Railroad Co. v. Muscola Local 123,* 321 U.S. 590 (1944); *Jewell Ridge Coal Corp. v. Local 6167 U.M.W.,* 325 U.S. 161 (1945).

12. Dunne, *Hugo Black,* 241.

13. Ibid., 240–248.

14. Lee Epstein, Jeffrey A. Segal, Harold J. Spaeth, and Thomas G. Walker, *The Supreme Court Compendium: Data, Decisions, and Developments,* 4th ed. (Washington, D.C.: CQ Press, 2006), 224–225.

15. Abraham, *Justices and Presidents,* 245.

16. Ibid., 287.

17. Robert Shogan, *A Question of Judgment: The Fortas Case and the Struggle for the Supreme Court* (Indianapolis: Bobbs-Merrill, 1972), 233–236.

18. Merlo J. Pusey, *Charles Evans Hughes,* 2 vols. (New York: Macmillan, 1951), 1:271.

19. Henry F. Pringle, *The Life and Times of William Howard Taft* (New York: Farrar and Rinehart, 1939), 535.

20. Alpheus T. Mason, *William Howard Taft: Chief Justice* (New York: Simon and Schuster, 1965), 39.

21. Warren, *Supreme Court in United States History,* 1:167.

22. *Scott v. Sandford,* 19 How. (60 U.S.) 393 (1857).

23. Arthur M. Schlesinger Jr. and Fred L. Israel, eds., *History of American Presidential Elections, 1789–1968,* 4 vols. (New York: Chelsea House, 1971), 2:1110–1111.

24. Ibid., 1126.

25. *Pollock v. Farmers' Loan and Trust Co.,* 157 U.S. 429 (1895).

26. Schlesinger and Israel, *History of American Presidential Elections,* 2:1847.

27. William F. Swindler, *Court and Constitution in the Twentieth Century,* vol. 1, *The Old Legality 1889–1932* (Indianapolis: Bobbs-Merrill, 1969), 283–284.

28. Schlesinger and Israel, *History of American Presidential Elections,* 3:2520.

29. Alfred H. Kelly and Winfred A. Harbison, *The American Constitution: Its Origins and Development,* 7th ed. (New York: Norton, 1991).

30. Ibid., 981.

31. Stephen J. Wasby, *The Supreme Court in the Federal Judicial System* (New York: Holt, Rinehart, and Winston, 1978), 95.

32. *Roe v. Wade,* 410 U.S. 113 (1973); *Engel v. Vitale,* 370 U.S. 421 (1962); *Abington School District v. Schempp,* (374 U.S. 203 (1963).

33. Elder Witt, *A Different Justice: Reagan and the Supreme Court* (Washington, D.C.: Congressional Quarterly, 1986), chaps. 6 and 7.

34. *City of Richmond v. J. A. Croson Co.,* 488 U.S. 469 (1989); *Martin v. Wilks,* 490 U.S. 755 (1989); *Wards Cove Packing Co. v. Antonio,* 490 U.S. 642 (1989); *Webster v. Reproductive Health Services,* 492 U.S. 490 (1989).

35. *Planned Parenthood of Southeastern Pennsylvania v. Casey,* 505 U.S. 833 (1992).

36. *Lee v. Weisman,* 505 U.S. 577 (1992).

37. *Clinton v. Jones,* 520 U.S. 681 (1997).

CONTENTS

GLOSSARY OF LEGAL TERMS

Accessory. A person not present at the commission of a criminal offense who commands, advises, instigates, or conceals the offense.

Acquittal. Discharge of a person from a charge of guilt. A person is acquitted when a jury returns a verdict of not guilty; a person may also be acquitted when a judge determines that there is insufficient evidence to convict him or her or that a violation of due process precludes a fair trial.

Adjudicate. To decide by the exercise of judicial authority.

Affidavit. A voluntary, written statement of facts or charges affirmed under oath.

A fortiori. With stronger force or more reason (in drawing a conclusion).

Amicus curiae. A friend of the court; a person not a party to litigation who volunteers or is invited by the court to give his or her views on a case.

Appeal. To take a case to a higher court for review. In general, the losing party in a trial court may appeal once to an appellate court as a matter of right. If he or she loses in the appellate court, appeal to a higher court is within the discretion of the higher court. Most appeals to the U.S. Supreme Court are at the Court's discretion.

Appellant. The party that appeals a lower court decision to a higher court.

Appellee. One who has an interest in upholding the decision of a lower court and is compelled to respond when the case is appealed to a higher court by the appellant.

Arraignment. The formal process of charging a person with a crime, reading him or her the charge, asking whether he or she pleads guilty or not guilty, and entering his or her plea.

Attainder, Bill of. A legislative act pronouncing a particular individual guilty of a crime without trial or conviction and imposing a sentence upon him or her.

Bail. The security, usually money, given as assurance of a prisoner's due appearance at a designated time and place (as in court) in order to procure in the interim his or her release from jail.

Bailiff. A minor officer of a court usually serving as an usher or a messenger.

Brief. A document prepared by counsel to serve as the basis for an argument in court and setting out the facts of and the legal arguments in support of the case at hand.

Burden of proof. The need or duty of affirmatively proving a fact or facts in dispute.

Case Law. The law as defined by previously decided cases, distinct from statutes and other sources of law.

Cause. A civil or criminal case, suit, litigation, or action.

Certiorari, Writ of. An order issued by the Supreme Court, at its discretion, to order a lower court to prepare the record of a case and send it to the Court for review.

Civil law. Body of law dealing with the private rights of individuals, as distinguished from criminal law.

Class action. A lawsuit brought by one person or group on behalf of all persons similarly situated.

Code. A collection of laws arranged systematically.

Comity. Courtesy, respect; usually used in the legal sense to refer to the proper relationship between state and federal courts.

Common law. Collection of principles and rules of action, particularly from unwritten English law, that derive their authority from long-standing usage and custom or from courts recognizing and enforcing these customs; sometimes used synonymously with case law.

Consent decree. A court-sanctioned agreement settling a legal dispute and entered into by the consent of the parties.

Contempt. Civil contempt—the failure to comply with an order by the court to do something for the benefit of another party; criminal contempt—when a person willfully exhibits disrespect for the court or obstructs the administration of justice.

Conviction. Final judgment or sentence that the defendant is guilty as charged.

Criminal law. Branch of law that deals with the enforcement of laws and the punishment of persons who, by breaking laws, commit crimes.

Declaratory judgment. A court pronouncement declaring a legal right or interpretation but not ordering a specific action.

De facto. "In fact"; in reality.

Defendant. The party denying or defending itself in a civil action against charges brought by a plaintiff; the person indicted in a criminal action for commission of an offense.

De jure. "As a result of law"; as a result of official action.

Deposition. Oral testimony by a witness in preparation of a case. It is taken outside of court in response to written or oral questions and committed to in writing.

Dicta. See *Obiter dictum*.

Dismissal. Order disposing of a case without a trial.

Docket. See *Trial docket*.

Due process. Fair and regular procedure. The Fifth and Fourteenth Amendments guarantee persons that they will not be deprived of life, liberty, or property by the government until fair and usual procedures have been followed.

Error, Writ of. An order issued by an appeals court to a lower court requiring it to send to the appeals court the record of a case in which it has entered a final judgment and which the appeals court will now review for error.

Ex parte. "Only from one side" or "only on one side"; type of application to a court for some ruling or action on behalf of only one party.

Ex post facto. "After the fact." An ex post facto law makes an action a crime after it has already been committed or otherwise changes the legal consequences of some past action.

Ex rel. "Upon information from"; usually used to describe legal proceedings begun by an official in the name of the state, but at the instigation of and with information from a private individual interested in the matter.

Grand jury. Group of twelve to twenty-three persons impaneled to hear in closed sessions evidence presented by the state against persons accused of crime and to issue indictments when a majority of the jurors find probable cause to believe that the accused has committed a crime; called a "grand" jury because it comprises a greater number of persons than a "petit" jury.

Grand jury report. A public report released by a grand jury after an investigation into activities of public officials that fall short of criminal actions; often called "presentments."

Guilty. The word used by a defendant in entering a plea for having committed crime or other wrongdoing and by a jury in returning a verdict indicating that the defendant is legally responsible as charged.

Habeas corpus. "You have the body"; a writ issued to inquire whether a person is lawfully imprisoned or detained, demanding that the persons holding the prisoner justify his or her detention or release him or her. In current law, a habeas corpus appeal in a federal court allows a state prisoner to challenge his or her conviction or sentence as unconstitutional under federal law.

Immunity. A grant of exemption from prosecution in return for evidence or testimony.

In camera. "In chambers"; refers to court hearings in private, without spectators or jurors present.

In forma pauperis. "In the manner of a pauper"; without liability for court costs.

In personam. "Against the person"; done or directed against a particular person.

In re. "In the affair of" or "concerning"; title of judicial proceedings in which there are no adversaries, but the matter itself—for example, a bankrupt's estate—requires judicial action.

In rem. "Against a thing"; done or directed against the thing, not the person.

Indictment. A formal, written statement based on evidence presented by the prosecutor from a grand jury that has decided by a majority vote that sufficient evidence exists to charge one or more persons with specified offenses.

Information. A written set of accusations, similar to an indictment, but filed directly by a prosecutor (without the involvement of a grand jury).

Injunction. A court order prohibiting the person to whom it is directed from performing a particular act.

Interlocutory decree. A provisional decision of the court that temporarily settles an intervening matter before completion of a legal action.

Judgment. Official decision of a court based on the rights and claims of the parties to a case that was submitted for determination.

Jurisdiction. The power of a court to hear the case in question; exists when the proper parties are present and when the issue to be decided is among those authorized to be handled by the particular court.

Juries. See *Grand jury* and *Petit jury*.

Magistrate. A judicial officer having jurisdiction to try minor criminal cases and conduct preliminary examinations of persons charged with serious crimes.

Mandamus. "We command"; an order issued by a superior court directing a lower court or other authority to perform a particular act.

Moot. Unsettled, undecided. For example, a moot question is one that is no longer material; a moot case is one that has become hypothetical.

Motion. Written or oral application to a court or a judge to obtain a rule or an order.

Nolo contendere. "I will not contest it"; plea entered by a defendant, at the discretion of the judge, that has the same legal effect as a plea of guilty but may not be cited in other proceedings as an admission of guilt.

Obiter dictum. Statement by a judge or justice expressing an opinion and included with (but not essential to) an opinion resolving a case before the court. Dicta are not necessarily binding in future cases.

Parole. A conditional release from imprisonment by which a person who abides by the law and other restrictions that may be placed upon him or her is not required to serve the remainder of his or her sentence; failure to abide by the specified rules will result in being returned to prison.

Per curiam. "By the court"; an unsigned opinion of the court or an opinion written by the whole court.

Petit jury. A trial jury; originally a panel of twelve persons who tried to reach a unanimous verdict on questions of fact in criminal and civil proceedings. Since 1970 the Supreme Court has upheld the legality of state juries with fewer than twelve persons; called a "petit" jury because it comprises fewer persons than a "grand" jury.

Petitioner. One who files a petition with a court seeking action or relief, including a plaintiff or an appellant; also a person who files for other court action where charges are not necessarily made, for example, requesting an order requiring another person or party to produce documents. (The opposing party is called the respondent.) When a writ of certiorari is granted by the Supreme Court, the parties to the case are called petitioner and respondent, in contrast to the appellant and appellee terms used in an appeal.

Plaintiff. A party who brings a civil action or sues to obtain a remedy for injury to his or her rights. The party against whom action is brought is called the defendant.

Plea bargaining. Negotiations between prosecutor and defendant aimed at exchanging a plea of guilty from the defendant for concessions by the prosecutor, such as a reduction of charges or a request for leniency.

Pleas. See *Guilty* and *Nolo contendere*.

Presentment. See *Grand jury report*.

Prima facie. "At first sight"; referring to a fact or other evidence presumably sufficient to establish a defense or a claim unless otherwise contradicted.

Probation. Process under which a person convicted of an offense, usually a first offense, receives a suspended sentence and is given his or her freedom, usually under the guardianship of an appointed officer.

Quash. To overthrow, annul, or vacate; used in relation to actions taken involving subpoenas, indictments, and so on.

Recognizance. An obligation entered into before a court or magistrate requiring the performance of a specified act—usually to appear in court at a later date; is used as an alternative to bail for pretrial release.

Remand. To send back; act by which a higher court returns for further action a decision to the court from which it came.

Respondent. One who is compelled to answer the claims or questions posed in court by a petitioner. A defendant and an appellee may be called respondents, but the term also includes those parties who answer in court during actions where charges are not necessarily brought or where the Supreme Court has granted a writ of certiorari.

Seriatim. Separately; individually; one by one.

Stare Decisis. "Let the decision stand"; principle of adherence to settled cases; the doctrine that principles of law established in earlier judicial decisions should be accepted as authoritative in similar subsequent cases.

Statute. A written law enacted by a legislature. A collection of statutes for a particular governmental division is called a code.

Stay. To halt or suspend further judicial proceedings.

Subpoena. An order to present one's self before a grand jury, court, or legislative hearing.

Subpoena duces tecum. An order to produce specified documents or papers.

Tort. An injury or wrong to the person or property of another.

Transactional immunity. Status that protects a witness from prosecution for any offense mentioned in or related to his or her testimony, regardless of independent evidence against him or her.

Trial docket. A calendar prepared by the clerks of the court listing the cases set to be tried.

Use immunity. Status that protects a witness against the use of his or her own testimony against him or her for prosecution.

Vacate. To make void, annul, or rescind.

Writ. A written court order commanding the designated recipient to perform or not perform acts specified in the order.

SOURCES OF SUPREME COURT DECISIONS

PAPER SOURCES

The primary print source for Supreme Court decisions is *United States Reports*, the official record of Supreme Court decisions and opinions, published by the U.S. Government Printing Office. This source can be supplemented by *United States Law Week*, published by the Bureau of National Affairs; *Supreme Court Reporter*, published by West; and *United States Supreme Court Reports, Lawyers' Edition*, published by Lawyers Cooperative Publishing Company.

ONLINE SOURCES

The full text of recent Supreme Court opinions as well as decisions from the past are available on the Internet. The following four Web sites offer decisions and other Court information at no cost:

U.S. Supreme Court

www.supremecourtus.gov

The Supreme Court's Web site offers easy access to the Court's recent decisions as well as links to other sites that post opinions issued prior to 1990. It also has information on the Court's rules and procedures, current cases, transcripts of oral arguments, and a description and history of the building in which the Court sits.

Findlaw

www.findlaw.com/casecode/supreme.html

Findlaw features Court opinions dating back to 1893. These cases can be retrieved by name, by year, or by volume and page citations from *United States Reports*. The site also contains information on the Court's calendar and current cases, including key briefs of the opposing sides.

Cornell University Law School / Legal Information Institute

http://supct.law.cornell.edu

Cornell's easy-to-use cite offers Supreme Court opinions from 1990 to the present. The opinions can be accessed by topic, as well as by the name of a party, the date, or the official citation. The site features fifty historic Supreme Court decisions since World War II, including *Brown v. Board of Education* (1954), *Gideon v. Wainwright* (1963), *New York Times Co. v. Sullivan* (1964), and *Roe v. Wade* (1973). Links provide access to other Court opinions dating back to the 1890s.

Oyez: U.S. Supreme Court Media

www.oyez.org

Oyez, sponsored by Northwestern University, provides access to Supreme Court decisions in addition to multimedia presentations, including audio versions of past arguments before the Court, and previews of upcoming cases written for lay readers.

HOW TO READ A COURT CITATION

The official versions of Supreme Court decisions and opinions appear in *United States Reports*. Although there are several unofficial compilations of Court opinions—*United States Law Week, Supreme Court Reporter,* and *United States Supreme Court Reports, Lawyers' Edition*—the official record is the one generally cited. An unofficial version or the official slip opinion might be cited if a decision has not yet been officially reported.

A citation to a case includes, in order, the names of the parties to the case, the volume of *United States Reports* in which the decision appears, the page in the volume that the opinion begins on, the page from which any quoted material is taken, and the year the decision was made. For example, the citation *Colegrove v. Green,* 328 U.S. 549 at 553 (1946), indicates that the Supreme Court decision and opinion in the case of that Colegrove brought against Green can be found in volume 328 of *United States Reports* beginning on page 549. The specific quotation in question appears on page 553. The Court announced the decision in 1946.

Until 1875 the official reports of the Court were published under the names of the Court reporters. In these cases, the reporters' names, or abbreviated versions of them, appear in the citations. For example, the citation *Marbury v. Madison,* 1 Cranch 137 (1803), means that the opinion in the case that Marbury brought against Madison is found in the first volume of the reporter Cranch beginning on page 137. Of note, between 1875 and 1883, a Court reporter named William T. Otto compiled the decisions and opinions. His name appears on the volumes for those years along with the *United States Reports* volume number, but Otto is seldom cited. Some citations reference reporter and *United States Reports* volumes, as in the case of *Barron v. Baltimore,* 7 Pet. (32 U.S.) 243 (1833).

The titles of the volumes to 1875, the full names of the reporters, and the corresponding *United States Reports* volumes are as follows:

Reporter Volumes	Court Reporter	*United States Reports*
1–4 Dall.	Dallas	1–4 U.S.
1–9 Cranch or Cr.	Cranch	5–13 U.S.
1–12 Wheat.	Wheaton	14–25 U.S.
1–16 Pet.	Peters	26–41 U.S.
1–24 How.	Howard	42–65 U.S.
1–2 Black	Black	66–67 U.S.
1–23 Wall.	Wallace	68–90 U.S.

Constitution of the United States

The United States Constitution was written at a convention that Congress called on February 21, 1787, for the purpose of recommending amendments to the Articles of Confederation. Every state but Rhode Island sent delegates to Philadelphia, where the convention met that summer. The delegates decided to write an entirely new constitution, completing their labors on September 17. Nine states (the number the Constitution itself stipulated as sufficient) ratified by June 21, 1788.

The framers of the Constitution included only six paragraphs on the Supreme Court. Article III, section 1, created the Supreme Court and the federal system of courts. It provided that "[t]he judicial power of the United States, shall be vested in one supreme Court," and whatever inferior courts Congress "from time to time" saw fit to establish. Article III, section 2, delineated the types of cases and controversies that should be considered by a federal—rather than a state—court. But beyond this, the Constitution left many of the particulars of the Supreme Court and the federal court system for Congress to decide in later years in judiciary acts.

We the People of the United States, in Order to form a more perfect Union, establish Justice, insure domestic Tranquility, provide for the common defence, promote the general Welfare, and secure the Blessings of Liberty to ourselves and our Posterity, do ordain and establish this Constitution for the United States of America.

ARTICLE I

Section 1. All legislative Powers herein granted shall be vested in a Congress of the United States, which shall consist of a Senate and House of Representatives.

Section 2. The House of Representatives shall be composed of Members chosen every second Year by the People of the several States, and the Electors in each State shall have the Qualifications requisite for Electors of the most numerous Branch of the State Legislature.

No Person shall be a Representative who shall not have attained to the age of twenty five Years, and been seven Years a Citizen of the United States, and who shall not, when elected, be an Inhabitant of that State in which he shall be chosen.

[Representatives and direct Taxes shall be apportioned among the several States which may be included within this Union, according to their respective Numbers, which shall be determined by adding to the whole Number of free Persons, including those bound to Service for a Term of Years, and excluding Indians not taxed, three fifths of all other Persons.][1] The actual Enumeration shall be made within three Years after the first Meeting of the Congress of the United States, and within every subsequent Term of ten Years, in such Manner as they shall by Law direct. The Number of Representatives shall not exceed one for every thirty Thousand, but each State shall have at Least one Representative; and until such enumeration shall be made, the State of New Hampshire shall be entitled to chuse three, Massachusetts eight, Rhode-Island and Providence Plantations one, Connecticut five, New-York six, New Jersey four, Pennsylvania eight, Delaware one, Maryland six, Virginia ten, North Carolina five, South Carolina five, and Georgia three.

When vacancies happen in the Representation from any State, the Executive Authority thereof shall issue Writs of Election to fill such Vacancies.

The House of Representatives shall chuse their Speaker and other Officers; and shall have the sole Power of Impeachment.

Section 3. The Senate of the United States shall be composed of two Senators from each State, [chosen by the Legislature thereof,][2] for six Years; and each Senator shall have one Vote.

Immediately after they shall be assembled in Consequence of the first Election, they shall be divided as equally as may be into three Classes. The Seats of the Senators of the first Class shall be vacated at the Expiration of the second Year, of the second Class at the Expiration of the fourth Year, and of the third Class at the Expiration of the sixth Year, so that one third may be chosen every second Year; [and if Vacancies happen by Resignation, or otherwise, during the Recess of the Legislature of any State, the Executive thereof may make temporary Appointments until the next Meeting of the Legislature, which shall then fill such Vacancies.][3]

No Person shall be a Senator who shall not have attained to the Age of thirty Years, and been nine Years a Citizen of the United States, and who shall not, when elected, be an Inhabitant of that State for which he shall be chosen.

The Vice President of the United States shall be President of the Senate, but shall have no Vote, unless they be equally divided.

The Senate shall chuse their other Officers, and also a President pro tempore, in the Absence of the Vice President, or when he shall exercise the Office of President of the United States.

The Senate shall have the sole Power to try all Impeachments. When sitting for that Purpose, they shall be on Oath or Affirmation. When the President of the United States is tried, the Chief Justice shall preside: And no Person shall be convicted without the Concurrence of two thirds of the Members present.

Judgment in Cases of Impeachment shall not extend further than to removal from Office, and disqualification to hold and enjoy any Office of honor, Trust or Profit under the United States: but the Party convicted shall nevertheless be liable and subject to Indictment, Trial, Judgment and Punishment, according to Law.

Section 4. The Times, Places and Manner of holding Elections for Senators and Representatives, shall be prescribed in each State by the Legislature thereof; but the Congress may at any time by Law make or alter such Regulations, except as to the Places of chusing Senators.

The Congress shall assemble at least once in every Year, and such Meeting shall [be on the first Monday in December],[4] unless they shall by Law appoint a different Day.

Section 5. Each House shall be the Judge of the Elections, Returns and Qualifications of its own Members, and a Majority of each shall constitute a Quorum to do Business; but a smaller Number may adjourn from day to day, and may be authorized to compel the Attendance of absent Members, in such Manner, and under such Penalties as each House may provide.

Each House may determine the Rules of its Proceedings, punish its Members for disorderly Behaviour, and, with the Concurrence of two thirds, expel a Member.

Each House shall keep a Journal of its Proceedings, and from time to time publish the same, excepting such Parts as may in their Judgment require Secrecy; and the Yeas and Nays of the Members of either House on any question shall, at the Desire of one fifth of those Present, be entered on the Journal.

Neither House, during the Session of Congress, shall, without the Consent of the other, adjourn for more than three days, nor to any other Place than that in which the two Houses shall be sitting.

Section 6. The Senators and Representatives shall receive a Compensation for their Services, to be ascertained by Law, and paid out of the Treasury of the United States. They shall in all Cases, except Treason, Felony and Breach of the Peace, be privileged from Arrest during their Attendance at the Session of their respective Houses, and in going to and returning from the same; and for any Speech or Debate in either House, they shall not be questioned in any other Place.

No Senator or Representative shall, during the Time for which he was elected, be appointed to any civil Office under the Authority of the United States, which shall have been created, or the Emoluments whereof shall have been encreased during such time; and no Person holding any Office under the United States, shall be a Member of either House during his Continuance in Office.

Section 7. All Bills for raising Revenue shall originate in the House of Representatives; but the Senate may propose or concur with Amendments as on other Bills.

Every Bill which shall have passed the House of Representatives and the Senate, shall, before it become a Law, be presented to the President of the United States; If he approve he shall sign it, but if not he shall return it, with his Objections to that House in which it shall have originated, who shall enter the Objections at large on their Journal, and proceed to reconsider it. If after such Reconsideration two thirds of that House shall agree to pass the Bill, it shall be sent, together with the Objections, to the other House, by which it shall likewise be reconsidered, and if approved by two thirds of that House, it shall become a Law. But in all such Cases the Votes of both Houses shall be determined by yeas and Nays, and the Names of the Persons voting for and against the Bill shall be entered on the Journal of each House respectively. If any Bill shall not be returned by the President within ten Days (Sundays excepted) after it shall have been presented to him, the Same shall be a Law, in like Manner as if he had signed it, unless the Congress by their Adjournment prevent its Return, in which Case it shall not be a Law.

Every Order, Resolution, or Vote to which the Concurrence of the Senate and House of Representatives may be necessary (except on a question of Adjournment) shall be presented to the President of the United States; and before the Same shall take Effect, shall be approved by him, or being disapproved by him, shall be repassed by two thirds of the Senate and House of Representatives, according to the Rules and Limitations prescribed in the Case of a Bill.

Section 8. The Congress shall have Power To lay and collect Taxes, Duties, Imposts and Excises, to pay the Debts and provide for the common Defence and general Welfare of the United States; but all Duties, Imposts and Excises shall be uniform throughout the United States;

To borrow Money on the credit of the United States;

To regulate Commerce with foreign Nations, and among the several States, and with the Indian Tribes;

To establish an uniform Rule of Naturalization, and uniform Laws on the subject of Bankruptcies throughout the United States;

To coin Money, regulate the Value thereof, and of foreign Coin, and fix the Standard of Weights and Measures;

To provide for the Punishment of counterfeiting the Securities and current Coin of the United States;

To establish Post Offices and post Roads;

To promote the Progress of Science and useful Arts, by securing for limited Times to Authors and Inventors the exclusive Right to their respective Writings and Discoveries;

To constitute Tribunals inferior to the supreme Court;

To define and punish Piracies and Felonies committed on the high Seas, and Offences against the Law of Nations;

To declare War, grant Letters of Marque and Reprisal, and make Rules concerning Captures on Land and Water;

To raise and support Armies, but no Appropriation of Money to that Use shall be for a longer Term than two Years;

To provide and maintain a Navy;

To make Rules for the Government and Regulation of the land and naval Forces;

To provide for calling forth the Militia to execute the Laws of the Union, suppress Insurrections and repel Invasions;

To provide for organizing, arming, and disciplining, the Militia, and for governing such Part of them as may be employed in the Service of the United States, reserving to the States respectively, the Appointment of the Officers, and the Authority of training the Militia according to the discipline prescribed by Congress;

To exercise exclusive Legislation in all Cases whatsoever, over such District (not exceeding ten Miles square) as may, by Cession of particular States, and the Acceptance of Congress, become the Seat of the Government of the United States, and to exercise like Authority over all Places purchased by the Consent of the Legislature of the State in which the Same shall be, for the Erection of Forts, Magazines, Arsenals, dock-Yards, and other needful Buildings;—And

To make all Laws which shall be necessary and proper for carrying into Execution the foregoing Powers, and all other Powers vested by this Constitution in the Government of the United States, or in any Department or Officer thereof.

Section 9. The Migration or Importation of such Persons as any of the States now existing shall think proper to admit, shall not be prohibited by the Congress prior to the Year one thousand eight hundred and eight, but a Tax or duty may be imposed on such Importation, not exceeding ten dollars for each Person.

The Privilege of the Writ of Habeas Corpus shall not be suspended, unless when in Cases of Rebellion or Invasion the public Safety may require it.

No Bill of Attainder or ex post facto Law shall be passed.

No Capitation, or other direct, Tax shall be laid, unless in Proportion to the Census or Enumeration herein before directed to be taken.[5]

No Tax or Duty shall be laid on Articles exported from any State.

No Preference shall be given by any Regulation of Commerce or Revenue to the Ports of one State over those of another; nor shall Vessels bound to, or from, one State, be obliged to enter, clear, or pay Duties in another.

No Money shall be drawn from the Treasury, but in Consequence of Appropriations made by Law; and a regular Statement and Account of the Receipts and Expenditures of all public Money shall be published from time to time.

No Title of Nobility shall be granted by the United States: And no Person holding any Office of Profit or Trust under them, shall, without the Consent of the Congress, accept of any present, Emolument, Office, or Title, of any kind whatever, from any King, Prince, or foreign State.

Section 10. No State shall enter into any Treaty, Alliance, or Confederation; grant Letters of Marque and Reprisal; coin Money; emit Bills of Credit; make any

Thing but gold and silver Coin a Tender in Payment of Debts; pass any Bill of Attainder, ex post facto Law, or Law impairing the Obligation of Contracts, or grant any Title of Nobility.

No State shall, without the Consent of the Congress, lay any Imposts or Duties on Imports or Exports, except what may be absolutely necessary for executing it's inspection Laws: and the net Produce of all Duties and Imposts, laid by any State on Imports or Exports, shall be for the Use of the Treasury of the United States; and all such Laws shall be subject to the Revision and Controul of the Congress.

No State shall, without the Consent of Congress, lay any Duty of Tonnage, keep Troops, or Ships of War in time of Peace, enter into any Agreement or Compact with another State, or with a foreign Power, or engage in War, unless actually invaded, or in such imminent Danger as will not admit of delay.

ARTICLE II

Section 1. The executive Power shall be vested in a President of the United States of America. He shall hold his Office during the Term of four Years, and, together with the Vice President, chosen for the same Term, be elected, as follows

Each State shall appoint, in such Manner as the Legislature thereof may direct, a Number of Electors, equal to the whole Number of Senators and Representatives to which the State may be entitled in the Congress: but no Senator or Representative, or Person holding an Office of Trust or Profit under the United States, shall be appointed an Elector.

[The Electors shall meet in their respective States, and vote by Ballot for two Persons, of whom one at least shall not be an Inhabitant of the same State with themselves. And they shall make a List of all the Persons voted for, and of the Number of Votes for each; which List they shall sign and certify, and transmit sealed to the Seat of the Government of the United States, directed to the President of the Senate. The President of the Senate shall, in the Presence of the Senate and House of Representatives, open all the Certificates, and the Votes shall then be counted. The Person having the greatest Number of Votes shall be the President, if such Number be a Majority of the whole Number of Electors appointed; and if there be more than one who have such Majority, and have an equal Number of Votes, then the House of Representatives shall immediately chuse by Ballot one of them for President; and if no Person have a Majority, then from the five highest on the list the said House shall in like Manner chuse the President. But in chusing the President, the Votes shall be taken by States,

the Representation from each State having one Vote; A quorum for this Purpose shall consist of a Member or Members from two thirds of the States, and a Majority of all the States shall be necessary to a Choice. In every Case, after the Choice of the President, the Person having the greatest Number of Votes of the Electors shall be the Vice President. But if there should remain two or more who have equal Votes, the Senate shall chuse from them by Ballot the Vice President.][6]

The Congress may determine the Time of chusing the Electors, and the Day on which they shall give their Votes; which Day shall be the same throughout the United States.

No Person except a natural born Citizen, or a Citizen of the United States, at the time of the Adoption of this Constitution, shall be eligible to the Office of President; neither shall any Person be eligible to that Office who shall not have attained to the Age of thirty five Years, and been fourteen Years a Resident within the United States.

In Case of the Removal of the President from Office, or of his Death, Resignation, or Inability to discharge the Powers and Duties of the said Office,[7] the Same shall devolve on the Vice President, and the Congress may by Law provide for the Case of Removal, Death, Resignation or Inability, both of the President and Vice President, declaring what Officer shall then act as President, and such Officer shall act accordingly, until the Disability be removed, or a President shall be elected.

The President shall, at stated Times, receive for his Services, a Compensation, which shall neither be encreased nor diminished during the Period for which he shall have been elected, and he shall not receive within that Period any other Emolument from the United States, or any of them.

Before he enter on the Execution of his Office, he shall take the following Oath or Affirmation:—"I do solemnly swear (or affirm) that I will faithfully execute the Office of President of the United States, and will to the best of my Ability, preserve, protect and defend the Constitution of the United States."

Section 2. The President shall be Commander in Chief of the Army and Navy of the United States, and of the Militia of the several States, when called into the actual Service of the United States; he may require the Opinion, in writing, of the principal Officer in each of the executive Departments, upon any Subject relating to the Duties of their respective Offices, and he shall have Power to grant Reprieves and Pardons for Offences against the United States, except in Cases of Impeachment.

He shall have Power, by and with the Advice and Consent of the Senate, to make Treaties, provided two thirds of the Senators present concur; and he shall nominate, and by and with the Advice and Consent of the Senate, shall appoint Ambassadors, other public Ministers and Consuls, Judges of the supreme Court, and all other Officers of the United States, whose Appointments are not herein otherwise provided for, and which shall be established by Law: but the Congress may by Law vest the Appointment of such inferior Officers, as they think proper, in the President alone, in the Courts of Law, or in the Heads of Departments.

The President shall have Power to fill up all Vacancies that may happen during the Recess of the Senate, by granting Commissions which shall expire at the End of their next Session.

Section 3. He shall from time to time give to the Congress Information of the State of the Union, and recommend to their Consideration such Measures as he shall judge necessary and expedient; he may, on extraordinary Occasions, convene both Houses, or either of them, and in Case of Disagreement between them, with Respect to the Time of Adjournment, he may adjourn them to such Time as he shall think proper; he shall receive Ambassadors and other public Ministers; he shall take Care that the Laws be faithfully executed, and shall Commission all the Officers of the United States.

Section 4. The President, Vice President and all civil Officers of the United States, shall be removed from Office on Impeachment for, and Conviction of, Treason, Bribery, or other high Crimes and Misdemeanors.

ARTICLE III

Section 1. The judicial Power of the United States, shall be vested in one supreme Court, and in such inferior Courts as the Congress may from time to time ordain and establish. The Judges, both of the supreme and inferior Courts, shall hold their Offices during good Behaviour, and shall, at stated Times, receive for their Services, a Compensation, which shall not be diminished during their Continuance in Office.

Section 2. The judicial Power shall extend to all Cases, in Law and Equity, arising under this Constitution, the Laws of the United States, and Treaties made, or which shall be made, under their Authority; — to all Cases affecting Ambassadors, other public Ministers and Consuls; —to all Cases of admiralty and maritime Jurisdiction; —to Controversies to which the United States shall be a Party; —to Controversies between two or more States; —between a State and Citizens of another State;[8] —between Citizens of different States; —between Citizens of the same State claiming Lands under Grants of different States, and between a State, or the Citizens thereof, and foreign States, Citizens or Subjects.[9]

In all Cases affecting Ambassadors, other public Ministers and Consuls, and those in which a State shall be Party, the supreme Court shall have original Jurisdiction. In all the other Cases before mentioned, the supreme Court shall have appellate Jurisdiction, both as to Law and Fact, with such Exceptions, and under such Regulations as the Congress shall make.

The Trial of all Crimes, except in Cases of Impeachment, shall be by Jury; and such Trial shall be held in the State where the said Crimes shall have been committed; but when not committed within any State, the Trial shall be at such Place or Places as the Congress may by Law have directed.

Section 3. Treason against the United States, shall consist only in levying War against them, or in adhering to their Enemies, giving them Aid and Comfort. No Person shall be convicted of Treason unless on the Testimony of two Witnesses to the same overt Act, or on Confession in open Court.

The Congress shall have Power to declare the Punishment of Treason, but no Attainder of Treason shall work Corruption of Blood, or Forfeiture except during the Life of the Person attainted.

ARTICLE IV

Section 1. Full Faith and Credit shall be given in each State to the public Acts, Records, and judicial Proceedings of every other State. And the Congress may by general Laws prescribe the Manner in which such Acts, Records and Proceedings shall be proved, and the Effect thereof.

Section 2. The Citizens of each State shall be entitled to all Privileges and Immunities of Citizens in the several States.

A Person charged in any State with Treason, Felony, or other Crime, who shall flee from Justice, and be found in another State, shall on Demand of the executive Authority of the State from which he fled, be delivered up, to be removed to the State having Jurisdiction of the Crime.

[No Person held to Service or Labour in one State, under the Laws thereof, escaping into another, shall, in Consequence of any Law or Regulation therein, be discharged from such Service or Labour, but shall be delivered up on Claim of the Party to whom such Service or Labour may be due.]

Section 3. New States may be admitted by the Congress into this Union; but no new State shall be formed or erected within the Jurisdiction of any other State; nor any State be formed by the Junction of two or more States, or Parts of States, without the Consent of the Legislatures of the States concerned as well as of the Congress.

The Congress shall have Power to dispose of and make all needful Rules and Regulations respecting the Territory or other Property belonging to the United States; and nothing in this Constitution shall be so construed as to Prejudice any Claims of the United States, or of any particular State.

Section 4. The United States shall guarantee to every State in this Union a Republican Form of Government, and shall protect each of them against Invasion; and on Application of the Legislature, or of the Executive (when the Legislature cannot be convened) against domestic Violence.

ARTICLE V

The Congress, whenever two thirds of both Houses shall deem it necessary, shall propose Amendments to this Constitution, or, on the Application of the Legislatures of two thirds of the several States, shall call a Convention for proposing Amendments, which, in either Case, shall be valid to all Intents and Purposes, as Part of this Constitution, when ratified by the Legislatures of three fourths of the several States, or by Conventions in three fourths thereof, as the one or the other Mode of Ratification may be proposed by the Congress; Provided [that no Amendment which may be made prior to the Year One thousand eight hundred and eight shall in any Manner affect the first and fourth Clauses in the Ninth Section of the first Article; and][10] that no State, without its Consent, shall be deprived of its equal Suffrage in the Senate.

ARTICLE VI

All Debts contracted and Engagements entered into, before the Adoption of this Constitution, shall be as valid against the United States under this Constitution, as under the Confederation.

This Constitution, and the Laws of the United States which shall be made in Pursuance thereof; and all Treaties made, or which shall be made, under the Authority of the United States, shall be the supreme Law of the Land; and the Judges in every State shall be bound thereby, any Thing in the Constitution or Laws of any State to the Contrary notwithstanding.

The Senators and Representatives before mentioned, and the Members of the several State Legislatures, and all executive and judicial Officers, both of the United States and of the several States, shall be bound by Oath or Affirmation, to support this Constitution; but no religious Test shall ever be required as a Qualification to any Office or public Trust under the United States.

ARTICLE VII

The Ratification of the Conventions of nine States, shall be sufficient for the Establishment of this Constitution between the States so ratifying the Same.

Done in Convention by the Unanimous Consent of the States present the Seventeenth Day of September in the Year of our Lord one thousand seven hundred and Eighty seven and of the Independence of the United States of America the Twelfth. IN WITNESS whereof We have hereunto subscribed our Names,

George Washington,
President and deputy from Virginia.

New Hampshire:
John Langdon,
Nicholas Gilman.

Massachusetts:
Nathaniel Gorham,
Rufus King.

Connecticut:
William Samuel Johnson,
Roger Sherman.

New York:
Alexander Hamilton.

New Jersey:
William Livingston,
David Brearley,
William Paterson,
Jonathan Dayton.

Pennsylvania:
Benjamin Franklin,
Thomas Mifflin,
Robert Morris,
George Clymer,
Thomas FitzSimons,
Jared Ingersoll,
James Wilson,
Gouverneur Morris.

Delaware:
George Read,
Gunning Bedford Jr.,
John Dickinson,
Richard Bassett,
Jacob Broom.

Maryland:
James McHenry,
Daniel of St. Thomas Jenifer,
Daniel Carroll.

Virginia:
John Blair,
James Madison Jr.

North Carolina:.
William Blount,
Richard Dobbs Spaight,
Hugh Williamson.

South Carolina:
John Rutledge,
Charles Cotesworth
    Pinckney,
Charles Pinckney,
Pierce Butler.

Georgia:
William Few,
Abraham Baldwin

[The language of the original Constitution, not including the Amendments, was adopted by a convention of the states on September 17, 1787, and was subsequently ratified by the states on the following dates: Delaware, December 7, 1787; Pennsylvania, December 12, 1787; New Jersey, December 18, 1787; Georgia, January 2, 1788; Connecticut, January 9, 1788; Massachusetts, February 6,

1788; Maryland, April 28, 1788; South Carolina, May 23, 1788; New Hampshire, June 21, 1788.

Ratification was completed on June 21, 1788.

The Constitution subsequently was ratified by Virginia, June 25, 1788; New York, July 26, 1788; North Carolina, November 21, 1789; Rhode Island, May 29, 1790; and Vermont, January 10, 1791.]

AMENDMENTS

Amendment I

(First ten amendments ratified December 15, 1791.)

Congress shall make no law respecting an establishment of religion, or prohibiting the free exercise thereof; or abridging the freedom of speech, or of the press; or the right of the people peaceably to assemble, and to petition the Government for a redress of grievances.

Amendment II

A well regulated Militia, being necessary to the security of a free State, the right of the people to keep and bear Arms, shall not be infringed.

Amendment III

No Soldier shall, in time of peace be quartered in any house, without the consent of the Owner, nor in time of war, but in a manner to be prescribed by law.

Amendment IV

The right of the people to be secure in their persons, houses, papers, and effects, against unreasonable searches and seizures, shall not be violated, and no Warrants shall issue, but upon probable cause, supported by Oath or affirmation, and particularly describing the place to be searched, and the persons or things to be seized.

Amendment V

No person shall be held to answer for a capital, or otherwise infamous crime, unless on a presentment or indictment of a Grand Jury, except in cases arising in the land or naval forces, or in the Militia, when in actual service in time of War or public danger; nor shall any person be subject for the same offence to be twice put in jeopardy of life or limb; nor shall be compelled in any criminal case to be a witness against himself, nor be deprived of life, liberty, or property, without due process of law; nor shall private property be taken for public use, without just compensation.

Amendment VI

In all criminal prosecutions, the accused shall enjoy the right to a speedy and public trial, by an impartial jury of the State and district wherein the crime shall have been committed, which district shall have been previously ascertained by law, and to be informed of the nature and cause of the accusation; to be confronted with the witnesses against him; to have compulsory process for obtaining witnesses in his favor, and to have the Assistance of Counsel for his defence.

Amendment VII

In Suits at common law, where the value in controversy shall exceed twenty dollars, the right of trial by jury shall be preserved, and no fact tried by a jury, shall be otherwise re-examined in any Court of the United States, than according to the rules of the common law.

Amendment VIII

Excessive bail shall not be required, nor excessive fines imposed, nor cruel and unusual punishments inflicted.

Amendment IX

The enumeration in the Constitution, of certain rights, shall not be construed to deny or disparage others retained by the people.

Amendment X

The powers not delegated to the United States by the Constitution, nor prohibited by it to the States, are reserved to the States respectively, or to the people.

Amendment XI (Ratified February 7, 1795)

The Judicial power of the United States shall not be construed to extend to any suit in law or equity, commenced or prosecuted against one of the United States by Citizens of another State, or by Citizens or Subjects of any Foreign State.

Amendment XII (Ratified June 15, 1804)

The Electors shall meet in their respective states and vote by ballot for President and Vice-President, one of whom, at least, shall not be an inhabitant of the same state with themselves; they shall name in their ballots the person voted for as President, and in distinct ballots the person voted for as Vice-President, and they shall make distinct lists of all persons voted for as President, and of all persons voted for as Vice-President, and of the number of votes for each, which lists they shall sign and certify, and transmit sealed to the seat of the government of the

United States, directed to the President of the Senate; — The President of the Senate shall, in the presence of the Senate and House of Representatives, open all the certificates and the votes shall then be counted; — The person having the greatest number of votes for President, shall be the President, if such number be a majority of the whole number of Electors appointed; and if no person have such majority, then from the persons having the highest numbers not exceeding three on the list of those voted for as President, the House of Representatives shall choose immediately, by ballot, the President. But in choosing the President, the votes shall be taken by states, the representation from each state having one vote; a quorum for this purpose shall consist of a member or members from two-thirds of the states, and a majority of all the states shall be necessary to a choice. [And if the House of Representatives shall not choose a President whenever the right of choice shall devolve upon them, before the fourth day of March next following, then the Vice-President shall act as President, as in the case of the death or other constitutional disability of the President. —][11] The person having the greatest number of votes as Vice-President, shall be the Vice-President, if such number be a majority of the whole number of Electors appointed, and if no person have a majority, then from the two highest numbers on the list, the Senate shall choose the Vice-President; a quorum for the purpose shall consist of two-thirds of the whole number of Senators, and a majority of the whole number shall be necessary to a choice. But no person constitutionally ineligible to the office of President shall be eligible to that of Vice-President of the United States.

Amendment XIII (Ratified December 6, 1865)

Section 1. Neither slavery nor involuntary servitude, except as a punishment for crime whereof the party shall have been duly convicted, shall exist within the United States, or any place subject to their jurisdiction.

Section 2. Congress shall have power to enforce this article by appropriate legislation.

Amendment XIV (Ratified July 9, 1868)

Section 1. All persons born or naturalized in the United States, and subject to the jurisdiction thereof, are citizens of the United States and of the State wherein they reside. No State shall make or enforce any law which shall abridge the privileges or immunities of citizens of the United States; nor shall any State deprive any person of life, liberty, or property, without due process of law; nor deny to any person within its jurisdiction the equal protection of the laws.

Section 2. Representatives shall be apportioned among the several States according to their respective numbers, counting the whole number of persons in each State, excluding Indians not taxed. But when the right to vote at any election for the choice of electors for President and Vice President of the United States, Representatives in Congress, the Executive and Judicial officers of a State, or the members of the Legislature thereof, is denied to any of the male inhabitants of such State, being twenty-one years of age,[12] and citizens of the United States, or in any way abridged, except for participation in rebellion, or other crime, the basis of representation therein shall be reduced in the proportion which the number of such male citizens shall bear to the whole number of male citizens twenty-one years of age in such State.

Section 3. No person shall be a Senator or Representative in Congress, or elector of President and Vice President, or hold any office, civil or military, under the United States, or under any State, who, having previously taken an oath, as a member of Congress, or as an officer of the United States, or as a member of any State legislature, or as an executive or judicial officer of any State, to support the Constitution of the United States, shall have engaged in insurrection or rebellion against the same, or given aid or comfort to the enemies thereof. But Congress may by a vote of two-thirds of each House, remove such disability.

Section 4. The validity of the public debt of the United States, authorized by law, including debts incurred for payment of pensions and bounties for services in suppressing insurrection or rebellion, shall not be questioned. But neither the United States nor any State shall assume or pay any debt or obligation incurred in aid of insurrection or rebellion against the United States, or any claim for the loss or emancipation of any slave; but all such debts, obligations and claims shall be held illegal and void.

Section 5. The Congress shall have power to enforce, by appropriate legislation, the provisions of this article.

Amendment XV (Ratified February 3, 1870)

Section 1. The right of citizens of the United States to vote shall not be denied or abridged by the United States or by any State on account of race, color, or previous condition of servitude.

Section 2. The Congress shall have power to enforce this article by appropriate legislation.

Amendment XVI (Ratified February 3, 1913)

The Congress shall have power to lay and collect taxes on incomes, from whatever source derived, without apportionment among the several States, and without regard to any census or enumeration.

Amendment XVII (Ratified April 8, 1913)

The Senate of the United States shall be composed of two Senators from each State, elected by the people thereof, for six years; and each Senator shall have one vote. The electors in each State shall have the qualifications requisite for electors of the most numerous branch of the State legislatures.

When vacancies happen in the representation of any State in the Senate, the executive authority of such State shall issue writs of election to fill such vacancies: Provided, That the legislature of any State may empower the executive thereof to make temporary appointments until the people fill the vacancies by election as the legislature may direct.

This amendment shall not be so construed as to affect the election or term of any Senator chosen before it becomes valid as part of the Constitution.

Amendment XVIII (Ratified January 16, 1919)

Section 1. After one year from the ratification of this article the manufacture, sale, or transportation of intoxicating liquors within, the importation thereof into, or the exportation thereof from the United States and all territory subject to the jurisdiction thereof for beverage purposes is hereby prohibited.

Section 2. The Congress and the several States shall have concurrent power to enforce this article by appropriate legislation.

Section 3. This article shall be inoperative unless it shall have been ratified as an amendment to the Constitution by the legislatures of the several States, as provided in the Constitution, within seven years from the date of the submission hereof to the States by the Congress.][13]

Amendment XIX (Ratified August 18, 1920)

The right of citizens of the United States to vote shall not be denied or abridged by the United States or by any State on account of sex.

Congress shall have power to enforce this article by appropriate legislation.

Amendment XX (Ratified January 23, 1933)

Section 1. The terms of the President and Vice President shall end at noon on the 20th day of January, and the terms of Senators and Representatives at noon on the 3d day of January, of the years in which such terms would have ended if this article had not been ratified; and the terms of their successors shall then begin.

Section 2. The Congress shall assemble at least once in every year, and such meeting shall begin at noon on the 3d day of January, unless they shall by law appoint a different day.

Section 3.[14] If, at the time fixed for the beginning of the term of the President, the President elect shall have died, the Vice President elect shall become President. If a President shall not have been chosen before the time fixed for the beginning of his term, or if the President elect shall have failed to qualify, then the Vice President elect shall act as President until a President shall have qualified; and the Congress may by law provide for the case wherein neither a President elect nor a Vice President elect shall have qualified, declaring who shall then act as President, or the manner in which one who is to act shall be selected, and such person shall act accordingly until a President or Vice President shall have qualified.

Section 4. The Congress may by law provide for the case of the death of any of the persons from whom the House of Representatives may choose a President whenever the right of choice shall have devolved upon them, and for the case of the death of any of the persons from whom the Senate may choose a Vice President whenever the right of choice shall have devolved upon them.

Section 5. Sections 1 and 2 shall take effect on the 15th day of October following the ratification of this article.

Section 6. This article shall be inoperative unless it shall have been ratified as an amendment to the Constitution by the legislatures of three-fourths of the several States within seven years from the date of its submission.

Amendment XXI (Ratified December 5, 1933)

Section 1. The eighteenth article of amendment to the Constitution of the United States is hereby repealed.

Section 2. The transportation or importation into any State, Territory, or possession of the United States for delivery or use therein of intoxicating liquors, in violation of the laws thereof, is hereby prohibited.

Section 3. This article shall be inoperative unless it shall have been ratified as an amendment to the Constitution by conventions in the several States, as provided in the Constitution, within seven years from the date of the submission hereof to the States by the Congress.

Amendment XXII (Ratified February 27, 1951)

Section 1. No person shall be elected to the office of the President more than twice, and no person who has held the office of President, or acted as President, for more than two years of a term to which some other person was elected President shall be elected to the office of the President more than once. But this Article shall not apply to any person holding the office of President when this Article was proposed by the Congress, and shall not prevent any person who may be holding the office of President, or acting as President, during the term within which this Article becomes operative from holding the office of President or acting as President during the remainder of such term.

Section 2. This article shall be inoperative unless it shall have been ratified as an amendment to the Constitution by the legislatures of three-fourths of the several States within seven years from the date of its submission to the States by the Congress.

Amendment XXIII (Ratified March 29, 1961)

Section 1. The District constituting the seat of Government of the United States shall appoint in such manner as the Congress may direct:

A number of electors of President and Vice President equal to the whole number of Senators and Representatives in Congress to which the District would be entitled if it were a State, but in no event more than the least populous State; they shall be in addition to those appointed by the States, but they shall be considered, for the purposes of the election of President and Vice President, to be electors appointed by a State; and they shall meet in the District and perform such duties as provided by the twelfth article of amendment.

Section 2. The Congress shall have power to enforce this article by appropriate legislation.

Amendment XXIV (Ratified January 23, 1964)

Section 1. The right of citizens of the United States to vote in any primary or other election for President or Vice President, for electors for President or Vice President, or for Senator or Representative in Congress, shall not be denied or abridged by the United States or any State by reason of failure to pay any poll tax or other tax.

Section 2. The Congress shall have power to enforce this article by appropriate legislation.

Amendment XXV (Ratified February 10, 1967)

Section 1. In case of the removal of the President from office or of his death or resignation, the Vice President shall become President.

Section 2. Whenever there is a vacancy in the office of the Vice President, the President shall nominate a Vice President who shall take office upon confirmation by a majority vote of both Houses of Congress.

Section 3. Whenever the President transmits to the President pro tempore of the Senate and the Speaker of the House of Representatives his written declaration that he is unable to discharge the powers and duties of his office, and until he transmits to them a written declaration to the contrary, such powers and duties shall be discharged by the Vice President as Acting President.

Section 4. Whenever the Vice President and a majority of either the principal officers of the executive departments or of such other body as Congress may by law provide, transmit to the President pro tempore of the Senate and the Speaker of the House of Representatives their written declaration that the President is unable to discharge the powers and duties of his office, the Vice President shall immediately assume the powers and duties of the office as Acting President.

Thereafter, when the President transmits to the President pro tempore of the Senate and the Speaker of the House of Representatives his written declaration that no inability exists, he shall resume the powers and duties of his office unless the Vice President and a majority of either the principal officers of the executive departments or of such other body as Congress may by law provide, transmit within four days to the President pro tempore of the Senate and the Speaker of the House of Representatives their written declaration that the President is unable to discharge the powers and duties of his office. Thereupon Congress shall decide the issue, assembling within forty-eight hours for that purpose if not in session. If the Congress, within twenty-one days after receipt of the latter written declaration, or, if Congress is not in session, within twenty-one days after Congress is required to assemble, determines by two-thirds vote of both Houses that the President is unable to discharge the powers and duties of his office, the Vice President shall continue to discharge the same as Acting President; otherwise, the President shall resume the powers and duties of his office.

Amendment XXVI (Ratified July 1, 1971)

Section 1. The right of citizens of the United States, who are eighteen years of age or older, to vote shall not be denied or abridged by the United States or by any State on account of age.

Section 2. The Congress shall have power to enforce this article by appropriate legislation.

Amendment XXVII (Ratified May 7, 1992)

No law varying the compensation for the services of the Senators and Representatives shall take effect, until an election of Representatives shall have intervened.

Source: U.S. Congress, House, Committee on the Judiciary, The Constitution of the United States of America, as Amended, 100th Cong., 1st sess., 1987, H Doc 100–94.

Notes: 1. The part in brackets was changed by section 2 of the Fourteenth Amendment.

2. The part in brackets was changed by the first paragraph of the Seventeenth Amendment.

3. The part in brackets was changed by the second paragraph of the Seventeenth Amendment.

4. The part in brackets was changed by section 2 of the Twentieth Amendment.

5. The Sixteenth Amendment gave Congress the power to tax incomes.

6. The material in brackets was superseded by the Twelfth Amendment.

7. This provision was affected by the Twenty-fifth Amendment.

8. These clauses were affected by the Eleventh Amendment.

9. This paragraph was superseded by the Thirteenth Amendment.

10. Obsolete.

11. The part in brackets was superseded by section 3 of the Twentieth Amendment.

12. See the Nineteenth and Twenty-sixth Amendments.

13. This amendment was repealed by section 1 of the Twenty-first Amendment.

14. See the Twenty-fifth Amendment.

SELECTED BIBLIOGRAPHY

THE COURT'S ROLE IN SHAPING THE POWERS OF GOVERNMENT

Abraham, Henry J. *The Judicial Process.* 6th ed. New York: Oxford University Press, 1993.

Banks, Christopher P., and David M. O'Brien. *Courts and Judicial Policymaking.* Upper Saddle River, N.J.: Prentice Hall, 2008.

Beth, Loren P. *Politics, the Constitution and the Supreme Court.* Evanston, Ill.: Row, Peterson, 1962.

Bickel, Alexander M. *The Least Dangerous Branch.* 2nd ed. New Haven: Yale University Press, 1986.

Black, Charles L. Jr. *Perspectives in Constitutional Law.* Englewood Cliffs, N.J.: Prentice Hall, 1963.

Carp, Robert A., and Ronald Stidham. *The Federal Courts.* 4th ed. Washington, D.C.: CQ Press, 2001.

Carp, Robert A., Ronald Stidham, and Kenneth L. Manning. *Judicial Process in America.* 7th ed. Washington, D.C.: CQ Press, 2007.

Carr, Robert K. *The Supreme Court and Judicial Review.* New York: Farrar and Rinehart, 1942.

Corwin, Edward S. *The Constitution of the United States of America.* Washington, D.C.: U.S. Government Printing Office, 1953.

Early, Stephen T. *Constitutional Courts of the United States.* Totowa, N.J.: Littlefield, Adams, 1977.

Fisher, Louis. *American Constitutional Law: Separated Powers and Federalism.* 4th ed. Durham, N.C.: Carolina Academic Press, 2001.

Frankfurter, Felix. *The Commerce Clause under Marshall, Taney and Waite.* Chapel Hill: University of North Carolina Press, 1937.

Frankfurter, Felix, and James M. Landis. *The Business of the Supreme Court: A Study in the Federal Judicial System.* New York: Macmillan, 1928.

Freund, Paul A., and Stanley N. Katz, gen. eds. *History of the Supreme Court of the United States.* Vol. 1, *Antecedents and Beginnings to 1801,* by Julius Goebel Jr., 1971; Vol. 2, *Foundations of Power: John Marshall, 1801–1815,* by George L. Haskins and Herbert A. Johnson, 1981; Vols. 3 and 4, *The Marshall Court and Cultural Change, 1815–1835,* by G. Edward White, 1988; Vol. 5, *The Taney Period, 1836–1864,* by Carl B. Swisher, 1974; Vol. 6: *Reconstruction and Reunion, 1864–1888,* Part One, by Charles Fairman, 1971; Vol. 7, *Reconstruction and Reunion, 1864–1888,* Part Two, by Charles Fairman, 1987; Supplement to Vol. 7, *Five Justices and the Electoral Commission of 1877,* by Charles Fairman, 1988; Vol. 8, *Troubled Beginnings of the Modern State, 1888–1910,* by Owen M. Fiss, 1993; Vol. 9, *The Judiciary and Responsible Government, 1910–1921,* by Alexander M. Bickel and Benno C. Schmidt Jr., 1984. New York: Macmillan.

Graber, Mark A., and Michael Perhac, eds. *Marbury versus Madison: Documents and Commentary.* Washington, D.C.: CQ Press, 2002.

Haines, Charles G. *The American Doctrine of Judicial Supremacy.* 2nd ed. Berkeley: University of California Press, 1932.

Hart, Henry M. Jr., and Herbert Wechsler. *The Federal Courts and the Federal System.* 3rd ed. Westbury, N.Y.: Foundation Press, 1988.

Hughes, Charles Evans. *The Supreme Court of the United States: Its Foundation, Methods and Achievements: An Interpretation.* New York: Columbia University Press, 1928.

Ivers, Gregg. *American Constitutional Law: Power and Politics.* Vol. 1, *Constitutional Structure and Political Power.* Boston: Houghton Mifflin, 2001.

Library of Congress. Congressional Research Service. *The Constitution of the United States of America: Analysis and Interpretation.* Washington, D.C.: Government Printing Office, 1973; together with the 1976 Supplement. Washington, D.C.: U.S. Government Printing Office, 1982.

Madison, James, Alexander Hamilton, and John Jay. *The Federalist Papers.* Edited by Clinton Rossiter. New York: New American Library, 1961.

Mason, Alpheus T. *The Supreme Court from Taft to Burger.* 3rd ed. Baton Rouge: Louisiana State University Press, 1979.

Maveety, Nancy. *Queen's Court: Judicial Power in the Rehnquist Era.* Lawrence: University Press of Kansas, 2008.

McDowell, Gary L., and Eugene W. Hickok Jr. *Justice vs. Law: The Courts in America.* New York: Free Press, 1993.

Post, C. Gordon. *Supreme Court and Political Questions.* Baltimore: Johns Hopkins University Press, 1936; reprint ed. New York: Da Capo Press, 1969.

Powell, Thomas Reed. *Vagaries and Varieties in Constitutional Interpretation.* New York: Columbia University Press, 1956; reprint ed. New York: AMS Press, 1967.

Purcell, Edward A. Jr. *Originalism, Federalism, and the American Constitutional Enterprise: A Historical Inquiry.* New Haven: Yale University Press, 2007.

Scigliano, Robert, ed. *The Courts: A Reader in the Judicial Process.* Boston: Little, Brown, 1962.

Segal, Jeffrey A., Harold J. Spaeth, and Sara C. Benesh. *The Supreme Court in the American Legal System.* New York: Cambridge University Press, 2005.

Stern, Robert L., and Eugene Gressman. *Supreme Court Practice.* 7th ed. Washington, D.C.: Bureau of National Affairs, 1993.

Swisher, Carl B. *American Constitutional Development.* reprint ed. Westport, Conn.: Greenwood Press, 1978.

Warren, Charles. *The Supreme Court in United States History.* rev. ed., 2 vols. Boston: Little, Brown, 1926.

Westin, Alan F., ed. *The Supreme Court: Views from Inside.* New York: Norton, 1961.

Wolfe, Christopher, ed. *That Eminent Tribunal: Judicial Supremacy and the Constitution.* Princeton, N.J.: Princeton University Press, 2004.

THE COURT AND THE POWERS OF CONGRESS

Baxter, Maurice G. *The Steamboat Monopoly: Gibbons v. Ogden, 1824.* Borzoi Series in United States Constitutional History. New York: Knopf, Borzoi Books, 1972.

Beth, Loren P. *The Development of the American Constitution, 1877–1917.* New York: Harper and Row, 1971.

Black, Charles L. Jr. *Perspectives in Constitutional Law.* Englewood Cliffs, N.J.: Prentice Hall, 1963.

Carr, Robert K. *The Supreme Court and Judicial Review.* American Government in Action Series. New York: Farrar and Rinehart, 1942.

Claude, Richard. *The Supreme Court and the Electoral Process.* Baltimore: Johns Hopkins University Press, 1970.

Commager, Henry Steele, and Milton Cantor, eds. *Documents of American History.* 10th ed., 2 vols. Englewood Cliffs, N.J.: Prentice Hall, 1988.

Congressional Quarterly. *Guide to Congress.* 4th ed. Washington, D.C.: Congressional Quarterly, 1991; 5th ed., 1999.

Cortner, Richard C. *The Jones & Laughlin Case.* Borzoi Series in United States Constitutional History. New York: Knopf, Borzoi Books, 1970.

——. *The Iron Horse and the Constitution: Railroads and the Transformation of the Fourteenth Amendment.* Westport, Conn.: Greenwood Press, 1993.

Corwin, Edward S. *The Constitution and What It Means Today.* 14th ed. Revised by Harold W. Chase and Craig R. Ducat. Princeton, N.J.: Princeton University Press, 1978.

——. *The Doctrine of Judicial Review: Its Legal and Historical Basis and other Essays.* Princeton, N.J.: Princeton University Press, 1914; reprint ed., Gloucester, Mass.: Peter Smith, 1963.

Coyle, Dennis J. *Property Rights and the Constitution.* Albany: State University of New York Press, 1993.

Cushman, Robert E., and Robert F. Cushman. *Cases in Constitutional Law.* 4th ed. New York: Appleton-Century-Crofts, 1975.

Cushman, Robert F. *Leading Constitutional Decisions.* 15th ed. Englewood Cliffs, N.J.: Prentice Hall, 1977.

Dimock, Marshall E. *Congressional Investigating Committees.* Baltimore: Johns Hopkins University Press, 1929; reprint ed., New York: AMS Press, 1971.

Epstein, Lee, and Thomas G. Walker. *Constitutional Law for a Changing America: Institutional Powers and Constraints.* 6th ed. Washington, D.C.: CQ Press, 2007.

Fisher, Louis. *Constitutional Dialogues: Interpretation as Political Process.* Princeton, N.J.: Princeton University Press, 1988.

Frankfurter, Felix. *The Commerce Clause under Marshall, Taney and Waite.* Chapel Hill: University of North Carolina Press, 1937.

Freund, Paul A., and Stanley N. Katz, gen. eds. *History of the Supreme Court of the United States.* Vol. 1,

Antecedents and Beginnings to 1801, by Julius Goebel Jr., 1971; Vol. 2, *Foundations of Power: John Marshall, 1801–1815,* by George L. Haskins and Herbert A. Johnson, 1981; Vols. 3 and 4, *The Marshall Court and Cultural Change, 1815–1835,* by G. Edward White, 1988; Vol. 5, *The Taney Period, 1836–1864,* by Carl B. Swisher, 1974; Vol. 6, *Reconstruction and Reunion, 1864–1888,* Part One, by Charles Fairman, 1971; Vol. 7, *Reconstruction and Reunion, 1864–1888,* Part Two, by Charles Fairman, 1987; Supplement to Vol. 7, *Five Justices and the Electoral Commission of 1877,* by Charles Fairman, 1988; Vol. 8, *Troubled Beginnings of the Modern State, 1888–1910,* by Owen M. Fiss, 1993; Vol. 9, *The Judiciary and Responsible Government, 1910–1921,* by Alexander M. Bickel and Benno C. Schmidt Jr., 1984. New York: Macmillan.

Garraty, John A., ed. *Quarrels That Have Shaped the Constitution.* rev. ed. New York: Perennial Library, 1987.

Gillman, Howard. *The Constitution Besieged: The Rise and Demise of* Lochner *Era Police Powers Jurisprudence.* Baltimore: Johns Hopkins University Press, 1993.

Henkin, Louis. *Foreign Affairs and the Constitution.* New York: Norton, 1975.

Hughes, Charles Evans. *The Supreme Court of the United States: Its Foundations, Methods and Achievements, An Interpretation.* New York: Columbia University Press, 1928.

Jackson, Robert H. *The Struggle for Judicial Supremacy: A Study of a Crisis in American Power Politics.* New York: Random House, Vintage Books, 1941.

James, Leonard F. *The Supreme Court in American Life.* 2nd ed. Glenview, Ill.: Scott, Foresman, 1971.

Kauper, Paul G. *Constitutional Law: Cases and Materials.* 5th ed. Boston: Little, Brown, 1980.

Kelly, Alfred H., and Winfred A. Harbison. *The American Constitution: Its Origins and Development.* 7th ed., 2 vols. New York: Norton, 1991.

Kurland, Philip B. *Politics, the Constitution and the Warren Court.* Chicago: University of Chicago Press, 1970.

Kutler, Stanley I., ed. *The Supreme Court and the Constitution: Readings in American Constitutional History.* 3rd ed. New York: Norton, 1984.

Library of Congress. Congressional Research Service. *The Constitution of the United States of America: Analysis and Interpretation.* Washington, D.C.: Government Printing Office, 1973; together with the 1976 Supplement. Washington, D.C.: U.S. Government Printing Office, 1982.

Madison, James, Alexander Hamilton, John Jay. *The Federalist Papers.* Edited by Clinton Rossiter. New York: New American Library, 1961.

Mason, Alpheus T. *The Supreme Court from Taft to Burger* 3rd ed. Baton Rouge: Louisiana State University Press, 1979.

Mason, Alpheus T., and William M. Beaney. *The Supreme Court in a Free Society.* New York: Norton, 1968.

McCloskey, Robert G., with Sanford Levinson. *The Modern Supreme Court.* Chicago History of American Civilization Series. Chicago: University of Chicago Press, 1994.

Melone, Albert P. *Researching Constitutional Law.* 2nd ed. Liberty Heights, Ill.: Waveland Press, 2000.

Miller, Arthur Selwyn. *The Supreme Court and American Capitalism.* The Supreme Court in American Life Series. New York: Free Press, 1968.

Morgan, Donald G. *Congress and the Constitution: A Study of Responsibility.* Cambridge, Mass.: The Belknap Press of Harvard University Press, 1966.

Murphy, Walter F. *Congress and the Court: A Case Study in the American Political Process.* Chicago: University of Chicago Press, 1962.

O'Brien, David M. *Constitutional Law and Politics: Struggles for Power and Governmental Accountability.* 4th ed. New York: Norton, 2000.

Pfeffer, Leo. *This Honorable Court: A History of the United States Supreme Court.* Boston: Beacon Press, 1965.

Pollak, Louis H., ed. *The Constitution and the Supreme Court: A Documentary History.* 2 vols. Cleveland: World Publishing, 1966.

Pritchett, C. Herman. *Congress Versus the Supreme Court, 1957–1960.* Minneapolis: University of Minnesota Press, 1961.

———. *The American Constitution.* 3rd ed. New York: McGraw-Hill, 1977.

Ratner, Sidney. *American Taxation: Its History as a Social Force in Democracy.* New York: Norton, 1942.

Schmidhauser, John R., and Larry L. Berg. *The Supreme Court and Congress: Conflict and Interaction, 1945–1968.* The Supreme Court in American Life Series. New York: Free Press, 1972.

Schwartz, Bernard. *A History of the Supreme Court.* New York: Oxford University Press, 1993.

Swindler, William F. *Court and Constitution in the Twentieth Century: The Old Legality, 1889–1932.* Indianapolis: Bobbs-Merrill, 1969.

———. *Court and Constitution in the Twentieth Century: The New Legality, 1932–1968.* Indianapolis: Bobbs-Merrill, 1970.

Swisher, Carl B. *American Constitutional Development.* reprint ed. Westport, Conn.: Greenwood Press, 1978.

Tribe, Laurence H. *The Invisible Constitution.* New York: Oxford University Press, 2008.

Twiss, Benjamin R. *Lawyers and the Constitution: How Laissez-Faire Came to the Supreme Court.* Princeton, N.J.: Princeton University Press, 1942.

Waluchow, W. J. *A Common Law Theory of Judicial Review: The Living Tree.* New York: Cambridge University Press, 2007.

Warren, Charles. *The Supreme Court in United States History.* rev. ed., 2 vols. Boston: Little, Brown, 1926.

THE COURT AND THE POWERS OF THE PRESIDENCY

Abernethy, Thomas P. *The Burr Conspiracy.* New York: Oxford University Press, 1954.

Alsop, Joseph, and Turner Catledge. *The 168 Days.* New York: Da Capo Press, 1973.

Anderson, Frank M. "Contemporary Opinion of the Virginia and Kentucky Resolutions." *American Historical Review* 5: 45–63, 225–252.

Baker, Leonard. *Back to Back: The Duel Between FDR and the Supreme Court.* New York: Macmillan, 1967.

——. *John Marshall: A Life in Law.* New York: Collier Books, 1981.

Bassett, John S. *Life of Andrew Jackson.* 2 vols. Hamden, Conn.: Archon Books, 1967.

Bemis, Samuel F. *A Diplomatic History of the United States.* 5th ed. New York: Holt, Rinehart, and Winston, 1965.

Berger, Raoul. *Executive Privilege: A Constitutional Myth.* Cambridge: Harvard University Press, 1974.

Beveridge, Albert. *The Life of John Marshall.* 4 vols. Boston and New York: Houghton Mifflin, 1916–1919.

Binkley, Wilfred E. *The Powers of the President: Problems of American Democracy.* New York: Russell and Russell, 1973.

Burke, Joseph C. "The Cherokee Cases: A Study in Law, Politics and Morality." *Stanford Law Review* 21: 500–531.

Burns, James M. *Roosevelt: The Lion and the Fox.* New York: Harcourt Brace Jovanovich, 1960.

——. *Roosevelt: The Soldier of Freedom.* New York: Harcourt Brace Jovanovich, 1970.

Chapin, Bradley. *The American Law of Treason: Revolutionary and Early National Origins.* Seattle: University of Washington Press, 1964.

Commager, Henry Steele, and Milton Cantor, eds. *Documents of American History.* 10th ed., 2 vols. Englewood Cliffs, N.J.: Prentice Hall, 1988.

Congressional Quarterly. *Members of Congress since 1789.* 3rd ed. Washington, D.C.: Congressional Quarterly, 1985.

——. *Nixon, The Fifth Year of His Presidency.* Washington, D.C.: Congressional Quarterly, 1974.

——. *Watergate: Chronology of a Crisis.* Washington, D.C.: Congressional Quarterly, 1975.

Corwin, Edward S. *The Constitution and What It Means Today.* 14th ed. Revised by Harold W. Chase and Craig R. Ducat. Princeton, N.J.: Princeton University Press, 1978.

——. *The President: Offices and Powers.* 5th rev. ed. New York: New York University Press, 1984.

Cox, Archibald. *The Role of the Supreme Court in American Government.* New York: Oxford University Press, 1976.

CQ Press. *Congress and the Nation XI, 2001–2004.* Washington, D.C.: CQ Press, 2006.

——. *Guide to Congress.* 6th ed. Washington, D.C.: CQ Press, 2007.

——. *Guide to the Presidency.* 4th ed. Washington, D.C.: CQ Press, 2008.

——. *CQ Almanac 2007.* Online ed. Washington, D.C.: CQ Press, 2009.

Cunningham, Noble E., Jr. *The Jeffersonian Republicans: The Formation of Party Organization, 1789–1801.* Chapel Hill: University of North Carolina Press, 1957.

Cushman, Robert F. *Cases in Civil Liberties.* 6th ed. Englewood Cliffs, N.J.: Prentice Hall, 1984.

DeConde, Alexander. *The Quasi-War: The Politics and Diplomacy of the Undeclared War with France, 1797–1801.* New York: Scribner's, 1966.

Dewey, Donald O. *Marshall versus Jefferson: The Political Background of Marbury v. Madison.* New York: Knopf, 1970.

Dorson, Norman, and John H. F. Shattuck. "Executive Privilege, the Congress and the Court." *Ohio State Law Journal* 34: 1–40.

Doyle, Elisabeth Joan. "The Conduct of the War, 1861." In *Congress Investigates, 1792–1974.* Edited by Arthur M. Schlesinger Jr. and Roger Bruns. New York: Chelsea House, 1975.

Eisenhower, Dwight D. *Public Papers of the Presidents.* Washington, D.C.: U.S. Government Printing Office, 1950.

Ellis, Richard E. *The Jeffersonian Crisis: Courts and Politics in the Young Republic.* New York: Oxford University Press, 1971.

Ely, John Hart. *War and Responsibility: Constitutional Lessons of Vietnam and Its Aftermath.* Princeton, N.J.: Princeton University Press, 1993.

Farrand, Max, ed. *The Records of the Federal Convention of 1787.* rev. ed., 4 vols. New Haven, Conn.: Yale University Press, 1966.

Faulkner, Robert K. *The Jurisprudence of John Marshall.* Princeton, N.J.: Greenwood Press, 1980.

Fisher, Louis. *Constitutional Dialogues: Interpretation as Political Process.* Princeton, N.J.: Princeton University Press, 1988.

———. *Presidential War Power.* Lawrence: University of Kansas Press, 1995.

Fisher, Louis, and Neal Devins. *Political Dynamics of Constitutional Law.* St. Paul: West Publishing, 1992.

Ford, Paul L., ed. *The Writings of Thomas Jefferson.* 10 vols. New York: Putnam's, 1892–1899.

Freedman, Max, ann. *Roosevelt and Frankfurter: Their Correspondence, 1928–45.* Boston: Little, Brown, 1968.

Freund, Paul A., and Stanley N. Katz, gen. eds., *History of the Supreme Court of the United States.* Vol. 1, *Antecedents and Beginnings to 1801,* by Julius Goebel Jr., 1971; Vol. 2, *Foundations of Power: John Marshall, 1801–1815,* by George L. Haskins and Herbert A. Johnson, 1981; Vols. 3 and 4, *The Marshall Court and Cultural Change, 1815–1835,* by G. Edward White, 1988; Vol. 5, *The Taney Period, 1836–1864,* by Carl B. Swisher, 1974; Vol. 6: *Reconstruction and Reunion, 1864–1888,* Part One, by Charles Fairman, 1971; Vol. 7, *Reconstruction and Reunion, 1864–1888,* Part Two, by Charles Fairman, 1987; Supplement to Vol. 7, *Five Justices and the Electoral Commission of 1877,* by Charles Fairman, 1988; Vol. 8, *Troubled Beginnings of the Modern State, 1888–1910,* by Owen M. Fiss, 1993; Vol. 9, *The Judiciary and Responsible Government, 1910–1921,* by Alexander M. Bickel and Benno C. Schmidt Jr., 1984. New York: Macmillan.

Friedman, Leon, and Fred L. Israel, eds. *The Justices of the United States Supreme Court, 1789–1995, Their Lives and Major Opinions.* 5 vols. New York and London: Chelsea House, 1969–1995.

Garraty, John A., ed. *Quarrels That Have Shaped the Constitution.* rev. ed. New York: Perennial Library, 1987.

Hamilton, John C., ed. *The Works of Alexander Hamilton.* 7 vols. New York: John F. Trow, 1850–1851.

Henkin, Louis. *Foreign Affairs and the Constitution.* New York: Norton, 1975.

Ickes, Harold L. *The Secret Diary of Harold L. Ickes.* 3 vols. New York: Simon and Schuster, 1954.

Israel, Fred L., ed. *The State of the Union Messages of the Presidents, 1790–1966.* 13 vols. New York: Chelsea House, Robert Hector Publishers, 1966.

Jackson, Percival E. *Dissent in the Supreme Court: A Chronology.* Norman: University of Oklahoma Press, 1969.

Jackson, Robert H. *The Struggle for Judicial Supremacy.* New York: Random House, 1941.

Johnson, Lyndon B. *Public Papers of the Presidents, 1963–1964.* 2 vols. Washington, D.C.: U.S. Government Printing Office, 1965.

Kelly, Alfred H., and Winfred A. Harbison. *The American Constitution: Its Origins and Development.* 7th ed., 2 vols. New York: Norton, 1991.

Kennedy, John F. *Public Papers of the Presidents, 1962.* Washington, D.C.: U.S. Government Printing Office, 1963.

Key, V. O., Jr. *Politics, Parties and Pressure Groups.* 5th ed. New York: Crowell, 1964.

Koch, Adrienne. *Jefferson and Madison: The Great Collaboration.* Lanham, Md.: University Press of America, 1986.

Koenig, Louis. *The Chief Executive.* 5th. ed. San Diego: Harcourt Brace Jovanovich, 1986.

Kramer, Robert, and Herman Marcuse. "Executive Privilege: A Study of the Period 1953–1960." *George Washington Law Review* 29: 623–827.

Krislov, Samuel. *The Supreme Court in the Political Process.* New York: Macmillan, 1965.

Kurland, Philip B. *Politics, the Constitution and the Warren Court.* Chicago: University of Chicago Press, 1970.

Kutler, Stanley I. "*Ex Parte McCardle:* Judicial Impotency? The Supreme Court and Reconstruction Reconsidered." *American Historical Review* 72: 835–851.

Laski, Harold J. *The American Presidency: An Interpretation.* New Brunswick. N.J.: Transaction Books, 1980.

Lasser, William. *The Limits of Judicial Power: The Supreme Court in American Politics.* Chapel Hill: University of North Carolina Press, 1988.

Leopold, Richard W. *The Growth of American Foreign Policy.* New York: Knopf, 1962.

Leuchtenburg, William E. *Franklin D. Roosevelt and the New Deal: 1932–1940.* New York: Harper and Row, 1963.

———. *The Supreme Court Reborn: The Constitutional Revolution in the Age of Roosevelt.* New York: Oxford University Press, 1995.

Levy, Leonard. *Legacy of Suppression: Freedom of Speech and Press in Early American History.* New York: Harper and Row, 1963.

———. *Jefferson and Civil Liberties: The Darker Side.* New York: Quadrangle Books, 1973.

Library of Congress. Congressional Research Service. *The Constitution of the United States of America: Analysis and Interpretation.* Washington, D.C.: Government Printing Office, 1973; together with the 1976 Supplement. Washington, D.C.: U.S. Government Printing Office, 1982.

Library of Congress. "The Present Limits of Executive Privilege." A Study Prepared by the Government and General Research Division of the Library of Congress. *Congressional Record*. March 28, 1973. H. 2243–2264.

Lillich, Richard B. "The Chase Impeachment." *American Journal of Legal History* 4: 49–72.

Link, Arthur. *Wilson the Diplomatist: A Look at His Major Foreign Policies.* New York: New Viewpoints, 1974.

Link, Eugene P. *Democratic Republican Societies, 1790–1800.* New York: Columbia University Press, 1942.

Lofgren, Charles A. "*United States v. Curtiss-Wright*: An Historical Assessment." *Yale Law Journal* 83: 1–32.

Longaker, Richard P. "Andrew Jackson and the Judiciary." *Political Science Quarterly* 71: 341–364.

Madison, James, Alexander Hamilton, and John Jay. *The Federalist Papers.* Edited by Clinton Rossiter. New York: New American Library, 1961.

Mason, Alpheus T., and William M. Beaney. *The Supreme Court in a Free Society.* New York: Norton, 1968.

McClure, Wallace. *International Executive Agreements: Democratic Procedure under the Constitution of the United States.* New York: AMS Press, 1941.

Meeker, Leonard. "The Legality of United States' Participation in the Defense of Vietnam." United States Department of State, *Bulletin* 474 (1966).

Morgan, Donald G. *Congress and the Constitution.* Cambridge: Harvard University Press, 1966.

Morison, Samuel E., Henry S. Commager, and William E. Leuchtenberg. *The Growth of the American Republic.* 7th ed., 2 vols. New York: Oxford University Press, 1980.

Murphy, Paul L. *The Constitution in Crisis Times, 1918–1969.* New York: Harper and Row, 1972.

Neustadt, Richard E. *Presidential Power.* New York: Wiley, 1960.

Nicolay, John G., and John Hay, eds. *The Complete Works of Abraham Lincoln.* 12 vols. New York: Francis D. Tandy, 1905.

Patterson, James T. *Congressional Conservatism and the New Deal, 1933–1939.* Lexington: University of Kentucky Press, 1967.

Peltason, Jack W. *Corwin & Peltason's Understanding the Constitution.* 13th ed. Fort Worth: Harcourt Brace College Publishers, 1994.

Post, Gordon C. *The Supreme Court and Political Questions.* Baltimore: Johns Hopkins University Press, 1936.

Pritchett, C. Herman. *The Tennessee Valley Authority: A Study in Public Administration.* Chapel Hill: University of North Carolina Press, 1943.

———. *The American Constitution.* 3rd ed. New York: McGraw-Hill, 1977.

Pritchett, C. Herman, and Alan F. Westin. *The Third Branch of Government.* New York: Harcourt, Brace, and World, 1963.

Randall, James G. *Constitutional Problems under Lincoln.* rev. ed. Urbana: University of Illinois Press, 1951.

Reveley, W. Taylor, III. "Presidential War-Making: Constitutional Prerogative or Usurpation?" *Virginia Law Review* 55 (November 1969): 1243–1305.

Richardson, James D., ed. *Messages and Papers of the Presidents.* 10 vols. Washington, D.C.: Bureau of National Literature, 1904.

Rodell, Fred. *Nine Men: A Political History of the Supreme Court of the United States from 1790–1955.* New York: Random House, 1955.

Rosenman, Samuel I., comp. *The Public Papers and Addresses of Franklin D. Roosevelt.* 13 vols. New York: Russell and Russell, 1969.

Rossiter, Clinton. *The Supreme Court and the Commander in Chief.* expanded ed. Ithaca, N.Y.: Cornell University Press, 1976.

Rostow, Eugene V. "The Japanese American Cases: A Disaster." *Yale Law Journal* 54 (June 1945): 489–533.

Schlesinger, Arthur M., Jr. *The Imperial Presidency.* New York: Popular Library, 1973.

Schubert, Glendon A. *The Presidency in the Courts.* Minneapolis: University of Minnesota Press, 1957.

Smith, James M. *Freedom's Fetters: The Alien and Sedition Laws and American Civil Liberties.* Ithaca, N.Y.: Cornell University Press, 1956.

Stinchcombe, William. "The Diplomacy of the WXYZ Affair." *William and Mary Quarterly.* 3rd Series, 34: 590–617.

Surrency, Erwin C. "The Judiciary Act of 1801." *American Journal of Legal History* II: 53–65.

Sutherland, George. *Constitutional Power and World Affairs.* New York: Columbia University Press, 1919.

Swindler, William F. *Court and Constitution in the Twentieth Century* Indianapolis: Bobbs-Merrill, 1970.

———. *Court and Constitution in the Twentieth Century: The Old Legality, 1889–1932.* Indianapolis: Bobbs-Merrill, 1969.

Tribe, Laurence H. *God Save This Honorable Court.* New York: Random House, 1985.

Truman, Harry S. *Memoirs.* 2 vols. Garden City, N.Y.: Doubleday, 1956.

Turner, Kathryn. "Federalist Policy and the Judiciary Act of 1801." *William and Mary Quarterly* 22 (1965): 32.

U.S. Congress. *Debates and Proceedings, First Congress, First Session, March 3, 1789, to Eighteenth Congress, First Session, May 27, 1824. [Annals of Congress]* 42 vols. Washington, D.C.: Gales and Seaton, 1834–1856.

U.S. Congress. Senate. "A Decade of American Foreign Policy, Basic Documents, 1941–1949." Senate Document No. 123, 81st Cong., 1st sess., 1950, pt. 1.

U.S. Congress. Senate. Committee on the Judiciary. Subcommittee on the Separation of Powers. *Executive Privilege: The Withholding of Information by the Executive.* Hearings. 92nd Cong., 1st sess. Washington, D.C.: U.S. Government Printing Office, 1971.

U.S. Congress. Senate. *Hearings on S.J. Res. 1 and S.J. Res. 43 before a Subcommittee of the Senate Judiciary Committee.* 83rd Cong., 1st sess., 1953.

U.S. Congress. Senate. *Hearings on U.S. Commitments to Foreign Powers before the Senate Committee on Foreign Relations.* 90th Cong., 1st sess., 1967.

U.S. Department of State. "Authority of the President to Repel the Attack in Korea." *Bulletin* 23 (1950).

Warren, Charles. *The Supreme Court in United States History.* rev. ed., 2 vols. Boston: Little, Brown, 1926.

Whittington, Keith E. *Political Foundations of Judicial Supremacy: The Presidency, the Supreme Court, and Constitutional Leadership in U.S. History.* Princeton, N.J.: Princeton University Press, 2007.

Wiggins, J. Russell. "Government Operations and the Public's Right to Know." *Federal Bar Journal* 19: 62.

Wilson, Woodrow. *Congressional Government: A Study in American Politics.* Boston: Houghton, Mifflin, 1885.

——. *The State.* Boston: D. C. Heath, 1889.

——. *Constitutional Government in the United States.* New York: Columbia University Press, 1908.

Wolkinson, Herman. "Demand of Congressional Committees for Executive Papers." *Federal Bar Journal* 10 (April, July, October 1949): 103–150.

Wormuth, Francis D. "The Nixon Theory of the War Power: A Critique." *California Law Review* 60: 623–703.

Younger, Irving. "Congressional Investigations and Executive Secrecy: A Study in Separation of Powers." *University of Pittsburgh Law Review* 20: 755.

THE COURT AND THE STATES

Beth, Loren P. *The Development of the American Constitution: 1877–1917.* New York: Harper and Row, 1971.

Black, Charles L. Jr. *The People and the Court.* New York: Macmillan, 1960.

Carr, Robert K. *The Supreme Court and Judicial Review.* New York: Farrar and Rinehart, 1942.

Carson, Hampton L. *The Supreme Court of the United States: Its History.* Philadelphia: A. R. Keller, 1892.

Corwin, Edward S. *The Constitution and What It Means Today.* 14th ed. Revised by Harold W. Chase and Craig R. Ducat. Princeton, N.J.: Princeton University Press, 1978.

Frankfurter, Felix. *The Commerce Clause under Marshall, Taney and Waite.* Chapel Hill: University of North Carolina Press, 1937.

Ellis, Richard E. *Aggressive Nationalism: McCulloch v. Maryland and the Foundation of Federal Authority in the Young Republic.* New York: Oxford University Press, 2007.

Freund, Paul A. *The Supreme Court of the United States: Its Business, Purposes, and Performances.* Cleveland: Meridian Books, World Publishing Co., 1961.

Haines, Charles G. *The American Doctrine of Judicial Supremacy.* 2nd ed. Berkeley: University of California Press, 1932.

Jackson, Robert H. *The Struggle for Judicial Supremacy.* New York: Knopf, 1941.

Kelly, Alfred H., and Winfred A. Harbison. *The American Constitution: Its Origins and Development.* 7th ed., 2 vols. New York: Norton, 1991.

Kruman, Marc. *Between Authority and Liberty: State Constitution Making in Revolutionary America.* Chapel Hill: University of North Carolina Press, 1997.

Mason, Alpheus T. *The Supreme Court from Taft to Burger.* 3rd ed. Baton Rouge: Louisiana State University Press, 1979.

Mason, Alpheus T., and William M. Beaney. *The Supreme Court in a Free Society.* New York: Norton, 1968.

Powell, Thomas Reed. *Vagaries and Varieties in Constitutional Interpretation.* New York: Columbia University Press, 1956; reprint ed. New York: AMS Press, 1967.

Pritchett, C. Herman. *The American Constitution.* 3rd ed. New York: McGraw-Hill, 1977.

Swindler, William F. *Court and Constitution in the Twentieth Century.* 3 vols. Indianapolis: Bobbs-Merrill, 1969–1974.

Swisher, Carl B. *American Constitutional Development.* reprint ed. Westport, Conn.: Greenwood Press, 1978.

Warren, Charles. *The Supreme Court and Sovereign States.* Princeton, N.J.: Princeton University Press, 1924.

——. *The Supreme Court in United States History.* rev. ed., 2 vols. Boston: Little, Brown, 1926.

Westin, Alan F., ed. *The Supreme Court: Views from Inside.* New York: Norton, 1961.

CONGRESSIONAL PRESSURE

Abraham, Henry J. *Justices and Presidents: A Political History of Appointments to the Supreme Court.* 3rd ed. New York: Oxford University Press, 1992.

Baker, Leonard. *Back to Back: The Duel Between FDR and the Supreme Court.* New York: Macmillan, 1967.

———. *John Marshall: A Life in Law.* New York: Macmillan, 1974.

Beveridge, Albert J. *The Life of John Marshall.* 4 vols. Cambridge, Mass.: Houghton Mifflin, The Riverside Press, 1919.

Black, Charles L. Jr. *Perspectives in Constitutional Law.* Englewood Cliffs, N.J.: Prentice Hall, 1973.

Brant, Irving. *Impeachment: Trials and Errors.* New York: Knopf, 1972.

———. "Appellate Jurisdiction: Congressional Abuse of the Exceptions Clause." *Oregon Law Review* 53 (Fall 1973): 3.

Carter, Stephen L. *The Confirmation Mess: Cleaning Up the Federal Appointments Process.* New York: Basic Books, 1994.

Casper, Gerhard, and Richard A. Posner. *The Workload of the Supreme Court.* Chicago: American Bar Foundation, 1976.

Choper, J. H. "Supreme Court and the Political Branches: Democratic Theory and Practice." *University of Pennsylvania Law Review* 122 (April 1974): 810.

"Congress vs. Court: The Legislative Arsenal." *Villanova Law Review* 10 (Winter 1965): 347.

Curtis, Charles P. Jr. *Lions under the Throne.* Cambridge, Mass.: Houghton Mifflin, The Riverside Press, 1947.

Elliott, Shelden D. "Court Curbing Proposals in Congress." *Notre Dame Lawyer* 33 (August 1958): 597.

Fite, Katherine B., and Louis Baruch Rubinstein. "Curbing the Supreme Court—State Experiences and Federal Proposals." *Michigan Law Review* 35 (March 1937): 762.

Frankfurter, Felix, and James M. Landis. *The Business of the Supreme Court: A Study in the Federal Judicial System.* New York: Macmillan, 1928.

Freund, Paul A., and Stanley N. Katz, gen. eds. *History of the Supreme Court of the United States.* Vol. 1, *Antecedents and Beginnings to 1801,* by Julius Goebel Jr., 1971; Vol. 2, *Foundations of Power: John Marshall, 1801–1815,* by George L. Haskins and Herbert A. Johnson, 1981; Vols. 3 and 4, *The Marshall Court and Cultural Change, 1815–1835,* by G. Edward White, 1988; Vol. 5, *The Taney Period, 1836–1864,* by Carl B. Swisher, 1974; Vol. 6, *Reconstruction and Reunion, 1864–1888,* Part One, by Charles Fairman, 1971; Vol. 7, *Reconstruction and Reunion, 1864–1888,* Part Two, by Charles Fairman, 1987; Supplement to Vol. 7, *Five Justices and the Electoral Commission of 1877,* by Charles Fairman, 1988; Vol. 8, *Troubled Beginnings of the Modern State, 1888–1910,* by Owen M. Fiss, 1993; Vol. 9, *The Judiciary and Responsible Government, 1910–1921,* by Alexander M. Bickel and Benno C. Schmidt Jr., 1984. New York: Macmillan.

Gimpel, James G., and Robin M. Wolpert. "Rationalizing Support and Opposition to Supreme Court Nominees: The Role of Credentials." *Polity* 28 (1995): 67–82.

Hart, Henry M. Jr. "The Power of Congress to Limit the Jurisdiction of Federal Courts: An Exercise in Dialectic." *Harvard Law Review* 66 (June 1953): 1362.

Hughes, Charles Evans. *The Supreme Court of the United States; Its Foundations, Methods and Achievements, An Interpretation.* New York: Columbia University Press, 1928.

Ignagni, Joseph, and James Meernilo. "Explaining Congressional Attempts to Reverse Supreme Court Decisions." *Political Research Quarterly* 47 (1994): 353–371.

Jackson, Robert H. *The Struggle for Judicial Supremacy: A Study of a Crisis in American Power Politics.* New York: Random House, Vintage Books, 1941.

Kelly, Alfred H., and Winfred A. Harbison. *The American Constitution: Its Origins and Development.* 7th ed., 2 vols. New York: Norton, 1991.

Kurland, Philip B. *Politics, the Constitution and the Warren Court.* Chicago: University of Chicago Press, 1970.

Levinson, Sanford, ed. *Responding to Imperfection: The Theory and Practice of Constitutional Amendment.* Princeton, N.J.: Princeton University Press, 1995.

Marke, Julius J. *Vignettes of Legal History.* South Hackensack, N.J.: Fred B. Rothman, 1965.

Martig, Ralph R. "Congress and the Appellate Jurisdiction of the Supreme Court." *Michigan Law Review* 34 (March 1936): 650.

Murphy, Walter F. *Congress and the Court: A Case Study in the American Political Process.* Chicago: University of Chicago Press, 1962.

Nagel, Stuart S. "Court-Curbing Periods in American History." *Vanderbilt Law Review* 18 (June 1955): 925.

Posner, Richard A. *How Judges Think.* Cambridge: Harvard University Press, 2008.

Pritchett, C. Herman. *Congress Versus the Supreme Court, 1957–60.* Minneapolis: University of Minnesota Press, 1961; reprint ed. New York: Da Capo Press, 1973.

Ratner, Leonard G. "Congressional Power over the Appellate Jurisdiction of the Supreme Court." *University of Pennsylvania Law Review* 109 (December 1960): 157.

Ruckman, P. S. "The Supreme Court, Critical Nominations, and the Senate Confirmation Process." *Journal of Politics* 55 (1993): 793–805.

Schmidhauser, John R., and Larry L. Berg. *The Supreme Court and Congress: Conflict and Interaction, 1945–1968.* New York: Free Press, 1972.

Stumpf, Harry P. "Congressional Response to Supreme Court Rulings: The Interaction of Law and Politics." *Journal of Public Law* 14 (1965): 382.

Swindler, William F. *Court and Constitution in the Twentieth Century: The Old Legality, 1889–1932.* Indianapolis: Bobbs-Merrill, 1969.

——. *Court and Constitution in the Twentieth Century: The New Legality, 1932–1968.* Indianapolis: Bobbs-Merrill, 1970.

Swisher, Carl Brent. *American Constitutional Development.* 2nd ed. Cambridge, Mass.: Houghton Mifflin, Riverside Press, 1954.

Vose, Clement E. *Constitutional Change: Amendment Politics and Supreme Court Litigation Since 1900.* Lexington, Mass: D. C. Heath, Lexington Books, 1972.

Warren, Charles. *Congress, the Constitution and the Supreme Court.* Boston: Little, Brown, 1925.

——. "Legislative and Judicial Attacks on the Supreme Court of the United States." *American Law Review* 47 (January-February 1913): 4.

——. *The Supreme Court in United States History.* rev. ed., 2 vols. Boston: Little, Brown, 1926.

PRESIDENTIAL PRESSURE

Abraham, Henry J. *Justices and Presidents: A Political History of Appointments to the Supreme Court.* 3rd ed. New York: Oxford University Press, 1992.

Comiskey, Michael. *Seeking Justices: The Judging of Supreme Court Nominees.* Lawrence: University Press of Kansas, 2004.

Danielski, David J. *A Supreme Court Justice Is Appointed.* New York: Random House, 1964.

Dunne, Gerald T. *Hugo Black and the Judicial Revolution.* New York: Simon and Schuster, 1977.

Eisgruber, Christopher L. *The Next Justice: Repairing the Supreme Court Appointments Process.* Princeton, N.J.: Princeton University Press, 2007.

Kelly, Alfred H., and Winfred A. Harbison. *The American Constitution: Its Origins and Development.* 7th ed. New York: Norton, 1991.

Lasser, William. *The Limits of Judicial Power: The Supreme Court in American Politics.* Chapel Hill: University of North Carolina Press, 1988.

Leuchtenberg, William E. *The Supreme Court Reborn: The Constitutional Revolution in the Age of Roosevelt.* New York: Oxford University Press, 1995.

Mason, Alpheus T. *Harlan Fiske Stone: Pillar of the Law.* New York: Viking Press, 1956.

——. *William Howard Taft: Chief Justice.* New York: Simon and Schuster, 1965.

Massaro, John. *Supremely Political: The Role of Ideology and Presidential Management in Unsuccessful Supreme Court Nominations.* Albany: SUNY Press, 1990.

McHargue, Daniel S. "Appointments to the Supreme Court of the United States: The Factors that Have Affected Appointments, 1789–1932." Ph.D. diss., University of California at Los Angeles, 1949.

O'Brien, David M. *Storm Center: The Supreme Court in American Politics.* New York: Norton, 1986.

Odegaard, Peter. *American Politics.* 2nd ed. New York: Harper and Bros., 1947.

Pacelle, Richard L. Jr. *The Transformation of the Supreme Court's Agenda: From the New Deal to the Reagan Administration.* Boulder: Westview Press, 1991.

Perry, Barbara A. *A "Representative" Supreme Court? The Impact of Race, Religion, and Gender on Appointments.* Westport, Conn.: Greenwood Press, 1991.

Pringle, Henry F. *The Life and Times of William Howard Taft.* New York: Farrar and Rinehart, 1939.

Pusey, Merlo F. *Charles Evans Hughes.* 2 vols. New York: Macmillan, 1951.

Ratner, Sidney F. "Was the Supreme Court Packed by President Grant?" *Political Science Quarterly* 50 (September 1935): 343.

Schlesinger, Arthur M. Jr., and Fred L. Israel, eds. *History of American Presidential Elections.* 9 vols. New York: Chelsea House Publishers, 1985.

Schwartz, Herman. *Packing the Courts: The Conservatives' Campaign to Rewrite the Constitution.* New York: Scribner's, 1988.

Scigliano, Robert G. *The Supreme Court and the Presidency.* New York: Free Press, 1971.

Shogan, Robert. *A Question of Judgment: The Fortas Case and the Struggle for the Supreme Court.* Indianapolis: Bobbs-Merrill, 1972.

Steamer, Robert J. *The Supreme Court in Crisis: A History of Conflict.* Amherst: University of Massachusetts Press, 1971.

Swindler, William F. *Court and Constitution in the Twentieth Century.* 3 vols. Indianapolis: Bobbs-Merrill, 1969–1974.

Tribe, Laurence H. *God Save This Honorable Court.* New York: Random House, 1985.

Warren, Charles. *The Supreme Court in United States History.* rev. ed., 2 vols. Boston: Little, Brown, 1926.

Wasby, Stephen J. *The Supreme Court in the Federal Judicial System.* 4th ed. Chicago: Nelson-Hall, 1993.

Witt, Elder. *A Different Justice: Reagan and the Supreme Court.* Washington, D.C.: Congressional Quarterly, 1986.

★ ILLUSTRATION CREDITS AND ACKNOWLEDGMENTS

★ CASE INDEX